THE CTS NEW
SUNDAY MISSAL

PEOPLE'S EDITION

WITH THE NEW TRANSLATION OF THE MASS

Sunday Masses for the three-year cycle and Universal Solemnities
and the Solemnities of the National Calendars
of England and Wales, Ireland and Scotland.

Texts approved for use
in England and Wales, Scotland, and Ireland.

CATHOLIC TRUTH SOCIETY

Catholic Truth Society
40-46 Harleyford Road, London, SE11 5AY

First Published 2011

ISBN

Standard Edition (RM06): 978 1 86082 739 6
Burgundy Presentation Edition (RM10): 978 1 86082 757 0
White Presentation Edition (RM09): 978 1 86082 756 3

Concordat cum originali: Paul Moynihan

Imprimatur: ✠ Peter Smith, Archbishop of Southwark, 1 November 2011.

Acknowledgements:

The CTS is grateful for the help of the Association for Latin in the Liturgy in the preparation of this volume.

Extracts from scripture (excepting Psalm texts) from the Jerusalem Bible © 1966 Darton Longman and Todd and Doubleday & Company Inc.

The English translation of the Gospel Readings for the Palm Sunday Procession from the Catholic Edition of the Revised Standard Version of the Bible © 1965, 1966 by the Division of Christian Education of the National Council of the Churches of Christ in the United States of America. Used by permission. All rights reserved.

Psalm texts from the Grail Psalms © 1963 The Grail (England).

New English Translation 2010, granted recognitio by the Congregation for Divine Worship and the Discipline of the Sacraments, for the dioceses of the Bishops' Conferences of England and Wales (Prot. N. 915/06/L, 28 March 2010), and Scotland, (Prot. N. 1021/07/L, 23 June 2010), and Ireland (Prot. N. 516/05/L, 18 June 2010).

The English translation and chants of The Roman Missal © 2010, International Commission on English in the Liturgy Corporation. All rights reserved.

Latin text of Missale Romanum, Libreria Editrice Vaticana omnia sibi vindicat iura. Sine eiusdem licentia scripto data nemini liceat hunc Missale denuo imprimere aut in aliam linguam vertere © 2003, Libreria Editrice Vaticana.

Papal Magisterium used for introductions to feasts and seasons © Libreria Editrice Vaticana, Vatican City State.

Rite of Eucharistic Exposition and Benediction taken from *Holy Communion and Worship of the Eucharist Outside Mass* (The Roman Ritual) Vol. 1, Approved by the Bishops' Conference of England and Wales, Ireland and Scotland and confirmed by decreed of the Sacred Congregation for the Sacraments and Divine Worship 29th May 1976.

Rosary Meditations and material for Preparation for Mass and Thanksgiving after Mass taken from *Eucharistic Adoration* D667 first published CTS, 2004. Stations of the Cross taken from *Meditations on the Stations of the Cross* (D600) first published CTS, 1927. All illustrations from the 'Psautier d'Ingeburg de Danemark', c.1210 (vellum) by French School, (13th century) Musée Condé, Chantilly, France/ Giraudon/ The Bridgeman Art Library. Page 26: Ms 9/1695 fol.14v Tree of Jesse. Page 78: Ms 9/1695 fol.15v The Annunciation, Visitation and Nativity. Page 316: Ms 9/1695 fol.28 The Entombment of Christ and the Holy Women at the Tomb. Page 390: Ms 9/1695 fol.31 Christ and St Thomas and the Ascension. Page 404: Ms 9/1695 fol.32v. Pentecost.

TABLE OF CONTENTS

THE CHURCH'S TEACHING
ON THE EUCHARIST

THE CHURCH'S TEACHING
ON THE EUCHARIST

(Second Vatican Council, Sacrosanctum Concilium, §§ 5-8, 47-48)

God, "who desires all men to be saved and to come to the knowledge of the truth"[1], "in many and various ways spoke of old to our fathers by the prophets"[2], and, when the fullness of time had come, sent his Son, the Word made flesh, anointed by the Holy Spirit, to preach good news to the poor, to bind up the broken hearted[3], "the one physician at once both flesh and spirit"[4], the mediator between God and man[5]. His humanity, in the Word's oneness of Person, was the instrument by which our salvation was effected, and that is why we can say that in Christ "the perfect satisfaction required for our reconciliation has been already made, and on us has been bestowed the whole fullness of divine worship"[6].

This work - the redemption of mankind and the perfect glorification of God - was foretold by the mighty works of God wrought on behalf of the people of the Old Testament and effectively accomplished by the Lord Christ, above all in the Paschal Mystery of his blessed Passion, his Resurrection from the dead and his glorious Ascension. In this Paschal Mystery "dying, he has destroyed our death and by rising, restored our life"[7], for, from the side of Christ sleeping on the cross the wondrous sacrament of the whole Church came forth[8].

So then, as Christ was sent by the Father, even so did he send the apostles, filled with the Holy Spirit, to preach the gospel to the whole creation[9], and to proclaim that the Son of God, by his death and resurrection, had rescued us from the power of Satan[10] and from death, and transferred us to the Father's kingdom. At the same time, the work of salvation they

---

[1] 1 Tm 2:4
[2] Heb 1:1
[3] Cf. Is 61:1; Lk 4:18.
[4] St. Ignatius of Antioch, *To the Ephesians*, 7, 2.
[5] Cf. 1 Tm 2:5.
[6] *Sacramentarium Veronese* (ed. Mohlberg), n. 1265; cf. also n. 1241, 1248.
[7] Easter Preface of the Roman Missal.
[8] Prayer before the second lesson for Holy Saturday, as it was in the Roman Missal before the restoration of Holy Week.
[9] Cf. Mk 16:15.
[10] Cf. Ac 26:18.

were making known, this same work they were to put into effect, through the sacrifice and the sacraments round which, of course, all liturgical life revolves. For, in baptism men are grafted into Christ's Paschal Mystery - they die with him, they are buried with him, they are raised with him[11]. They receive the Spirit of adoption into sonship "in which we cry, 'Abba! Father!'"[12], and so become true worshippers, such as the Father seeks to worship him[13]. Likewise, each time they eat the Lord's Supper, they proclaim his death until he comes[14]. For this reason, on the day of Pentecost, the very day on which the Church appeared before the world, "those who received [Peter's] word were baptised". "And they devoted themselves to the apostles' teaching and fellowship, to the breaking of bread and the prayers ... praising God and having favour with all the people"[15]. From that day on, the Church has never failed to assemble together for the celebration of the paschal mystery, reading "in all the scriptures the things concerning [Christ]"[16], celebrating the Eucharist in which "are set forth the victory and triumph of his death"[17], and also giving thanks "to God for his inexpressible gift"[18] in Christ Jesus, in "praise of his glory"[19], through the power of the Holy Spirit. For the perfect and complete accomplishment of this great work Christ is ever present in his Church, more particularly in her liturgical acts. He is present in the sacrifice of the Mass, first of all in the person of the minister – "he now offers himself by the ministry of priests, who then offered himself on the cross"[20], - but chiefly under the Eucharistic species [of bread and wine]. He is present, by his active power, in the sacraments, for whenever anyone baptises, it is Christ himself who baptises[21]. He is present in his word, since it is he himself who speaks when the Holy Scriptures are read in the Church. Finally, he is present when the Church prays and sings, he who promised that "where two or three are gathered in my name, there am I in the midst of them"[22].

---

[11] Cf. Rm 6:4; Eph 2:6; Col 3:1; 2 Tm 2:11.
[12] Rm 8 :15
[13] Cf. Jn 4:23.
[14] Cf. 1 Co 11:26.
[15] Ac 2:41-47
[16] Lk 24:27
[17] Council of Trent, Session XIII, *Decree on the Holy Eucharist*, c.5.
[18] 2 Co 9:15
[19] Eph 1:12
[20] Council of Trent, Session XXII, *Doctrine on the Holy Sacrifice of the Mass*, c. 2.
[21] Cf. St. Augustine, *Tractatus in Ioannem*, VI, n. 7.
[22] Mt 18:20

In our liturgy here on earth, we receive a foretaste of and a share in the heavenly liturgy that is celebrated in the holy city Jerusalem towards which we journey as pilgrims and in which Christ is, seated at the right hand of God, a minister in the sanctuary and the true tabernacle[23]. With all the host of the army of heaven we join in singing to the Lord the hymn of glory. Reverencing the memory of the saints, we hope for some part and fellowship with them. We await the Saviour our Lord Jesus Christ until the day when he who is our life appears, and we too will appear with him in glory[24].

Our Saviour, at the Last Supper on the night on which he was betrayed, instituted the Eucharistic Sacrifice of his Body and Blood. He did this in order to perpetuate the sacrifice of the cross throughout the ages until he should come again, and, moreover, to entrust to the Church, his beloved Bride, a memorial of his death and resurrection: the sacrament of love, the sign of unity, the bond of charity[25], the paschal banquet in which Christ is eaten, our mind and soul are filled with grace, and a pledge of future glory is given to us[26].

The Church, therefore, earnestly desires that Christ's faithful, when present at this mystery of faith, should not be there as strangers or silent spectators. On the contrary, through a good understanding of the rites and prayers they should take part in the sacred action conscious of what they are doing, with devotion and full collaboration. They should be instructed by God's word and be nourished at the table of the Lord's Body. They should give thanks to God; by offering the Immaculate Victim, not only through the hands of the priest, but also with him, they should learn also to offer themselves; through Christ the Mediator[27], they should be drawn day by day into ever more perfect union with God and with each other, so that finally God may be all in all.

---

[23] Cf. Rv 21:2; Col. 3:1; Heb 8:2.
[24] Cf. Ph. 3:20; Col 3:4.
[25] Cf. St. Augustine, *Tractatus in Ioannem*, VI, n. 13.
[26] Roman Breviary, feast of Corpus Christi, Second Vespers, antiphon to the Magnificat.
[27] Cf. St. Cyril of Alexandria, *Commentary on the Gospel of John*, book XI, chap. XI-XII: *Migne, Patrologia Graeca*, 74, 557-564.

The Eucharistic Sacrifice

(Blessed Pope John Paul II, Ecclesia de Eucharistia, §§11-16)

"The Lord Jesus on the night he was betrayed"[28] instituted the Eucharistic Sacrifice of his body and his blood. The words of the Apostle Paul bring us back to the dramatic setting in which the Eucharist was born. The Eucharist is indelibly marked by the event of the Lord's passion and death, of which it is not only a reminder but the sacramental re-presentation. It is the sacrifice of the Cross perpetuated down the ages[29]. This truth is well expressed by the words with which the assembly in the Latin rite responds to the priest's proclamation of the "Mystery of Faith": *"We proclaim your death, O Lord"*.

The Church has received the Eucharist from Christ her Lord not as one gift – however precious – among so many others, but as *the gift par excellence*, for it is the gift of himself, of his person in his sacred humanity, as well as the gift of his saving work. Nor does it remain confined to the past, since "all that Christ is – all that he did and suffered for all men – participates in the divine eternity, and so transcends all times"[30].

When the Church celebrates the Eucharist, the memorial of her Lord's death and resurrection, this central event of salvation becomes really present and "the work of our redemption is carried out"[31]. This sacrifice is so decisive for the salvation of the human race that Jesus Christ offered it and returned to the Father only *after he had left us a means of sharing in it* as if we had been present there. Each member of the faithful can thus take part in it and inexhaustibly gain its fruits. This is the faith from which generations of Christians down the ages have lived. The Church's Magisterium has constantly reaffirmed this faith with joyful gratitude for its inestimable gift[32].

This aspect of the universal charity of the Eucharistic Sacrifice is based on the words of the Saviour himself. In instituting it, he did not merely say:

---

[28] 1 Co 11:23

[29] Cf. Second Vatican Ecumenical Council, Constitution *Sacrosanctum Concilium*, 47: "... our Saviour instituted the Eucharistic Sacrifice of his body and blood, in order to perpetuate the sacrifice of the Cross throughout time, until he should return".

[30] *Catechism of the Catholic Church*, 1085.

[31] Second Vatican Ecumenical Council, Dogmatic Constitution on the Church *Lumen Gentium*, 3.

[32] Cf. Paul VI, *Solemn Profession of Faith*, 30 June 1968, 24: AAS 60 (1968), 442; John Paul II, Apostolic Letter *Dominicae Cenae* (24 February 1980), 12: AAS 72 (1980), 142.

"This is my body", "this is my blood", but went on to add: "which is given for you", "which is poured out for you"[33]. Jesus did not simply state that what he was giving them to eat and drink was his body and his blood; he also expressed *its sacrificial meaning* and made sacramentally present his sacrifice which would soon be offered on the Cross for the salvation of all. "The Mass is at the same time, and inseparably, the sacrificial memorial in which the sacrifice of the Cross is perpetuated and the sacred banquet of communion with the Lord's body and blood"[34].

The Church constantly draws her life from the redeeming sacrifice; she approaches it not only through faith-filled remembrance, but also through a real contact, since *this sacrifice is made present ever anew*, sacramentally perpetuated, in every community which offers it at the hands of the consecrated minister. The Eucharist thus applies to men and women today the reconciliation won once for all by Christ for mankind in every age. "The sacrifice of Christ and the sacrifice of the Eucharist are *one single sacrifice*"[35]. Saint John Chrysostom put it well: "We always offer the same Lamb, not one today and another tomorrow, but always the same one. For this reason the sacrifice is always only one... Even now we offer that victim who was once offered and who will never be consumed"[36].

The Mass makes present the sacrifice of the Cross; it does not add to that sacrifice nor does it multiply it[37]. What is repeated is its *memorial* celebration, its "commemorative representation" (*memorialis demonstratio*),[38] which makes Christ's one, definitive redemptive sacrifice always present in time. The sacrificial nature of the Eucharistic mystery cannot therefore be understood as something separate, independent of the Cross or only indirectly referring to the sacrifice of Calvary.

By virtue of its close relationship to the sacrifice of Golgotha, the Eucharist is *a sacrifice in the strict sense*, and not only in a general way, as if it were simply a matter of Christ's offering himself to the faithful as their spiritual food. The gift of his love and obedience to the point of giving his life[39] is in the first place a gift to his Father. Certainly it is a gift given for our sake, and

---

[33] Lk 22:19-20
[34] *Catechism of the Catholic Church*, 1382.
[35] *Catechism of the Catholic Church*, 1367.
[36] *In Epistolam ad Hebraeos Homiliæ, Hom.* 17,3: PG 63, 131.
[37] Cf. Ecumenical Council of Trent, Session XXII, *Doctrina de ss. Missae Sacrificio*, Chapter 2: DS 1743: "It is one and the same victim here offering himself by the ministry of his priests, who then offered himself on the Cross; it is only the manner of offering that is different".
[38] Pius XII, Encyclical Letter *Mediator Dei* (20 November 1947): AAS 39 (1947), 548.
[39] cf. Jn 10:17-18

indeed that of all humanity[40], yet it is *first and foremost a gift to the Father*: "a sacrifice that the Father accepted, giving, in return for this total self-giving by his Son, who 'became obedient unto death'[41], his own paternal gift, that is to say the grant of new immortal life in the resurrection"[42].

In giving his sacrifice to the Church, Christ has also made his own the spiritual sacrifice of the Church, which is called to offer herself in union with the sacrifice of Christ. This is the teaching of the Second Vatican Council concerning all the faithful: "Taking part in the Eucharistic Sacrifice, which is the source and summit of the whole Christian life, they offer the divine victim to God, and offer themselves along with it".[43]

Christ's passover includes not only his passion and death, but also his resurrection. This is recalled by the assembly's acclamation following the consecration: *"We profess your resurrection"*. The Eucharistic Sacrifice makes present not only the mystery of the Saviour's passion and death, but also the mystery of the resurrection which crowned his sacrifice. It is as the living and risen One that Christ can become in the Eucharist the "bread of life"[44], the "living bread"[45]. Saint Ambrose reminded the newly-initiated that the Eucharist applies the event of the resurrection to their lives: "Today Christ is yours, yet each day he rises again for you"[46]. Saint Cyril of Alexandria also makes clear that sharing in the sacred mysteries "is a true confession and a remembrance that the Lord died and returned to life for us and on our behalf"[47].

The sacramental re-presentation of Christ's sacrifice, crowned by the resurrection, in the Mass involves a most special presence which – in the words of Paul VI – "is called 'real' not as a way of excluding all other types of presence as if they were 'not real', but because it is a presence in the fullest sense: a substantial presence whereby Christ, the God-Man, is wholly and entirely present"[48]. This sets forth once more the perennially valid teaching of the Council of Trent: "the consecration of the bread and wine effects the change of the whole substance of the bread into the substance of the body of Christ our Lord, and of the whole substance of the wine

---

[40] cf. Mt 26:28; Mk 14:24; Lk 22:20; Jn 10:15
[41] Ph 2:8
[42] John Paul II, Encyclical Letter *Redemptor Hominis* (15 March 1979), 20: AAS 71 (1979), 310.
[43] Dogmatic Constitution on the Church *Lumen Gentium*, 11.
[44] Jn 6:35, 48
[45] Jn 6:51
[46] *De Sacramentis*, V, 4, 26: CSEL 73, 70.
[47] *In Ioannis Evangelium*, XII, 20: PG 74, 726.
[48] Encyclical Letter *Mysterium Fidei* (3 September 1965): AAS 57 (1965), 764.

into the substance of his blood. And the holy Catholic Church has fittingly and properly called this change transubstantiation"[49]. Truly the Eucharist is a *mysterium fidei*, a mystery which surpasses our understanding and can only be received in faith, as is often brought out in the catechesis of the Church Fathers regarding this divine sacrament: "Do not see" – Saint Cyril of Jerusalem exhorts – "in the bread and wine merely natural elements, because the Lord has expressly said that they are his body and his blood: faith assures you of this, though your senses suggest otherwise"[50].

The saving efficacy of the sacrifice is fully realised when the Lord's body and blood are received in communion. The Eucharistic Sacrifice is intrinsically directed to the inward union of the faithful with Christ through communion; we receive the very One who offered himself for us, we receive his body which he gave up for us on the Cross and his blood which he "poured out for many for the forgiveness of sins"[51]. We are reminded of his words: "As the living Father sent me, and I live because of the Father, so he who eats me will live because of me"[52]. Jesus himself reassures us that this union, which he compares to that of the life of the Trinity, is truly realised. *The Eucharist is a true banquet,* in which Christ offers himself as our nourishment. When for the first time Jesus spoke of this food, his listeners were astonished and bewildered, which forced the Master to emphasise the objective truth of his words: "Truly, truly, I say to you, unless you eat the flesh of the Son of Man and drink his blood, you have no life within you"[53]. This is no metaphorical food: "My flesh is food indeed, and my blood is drink indeed"[54].

---

[49] Session XIII, *Decretum de ss. Eucharistia*, Chapter 4: DS 1642.
[50] *Mystagogical Catecheses*, IV, 6: SCh 126, 138.
[51] Mt 26:28
[52] Jn 6:57
[53] Jn 6:53
[54] Jn 6:55

The Blessed Trinity and the Eucharist; the New Covenant

(Pope Benedict XVI, Sacramentum Caritatis, §§7-11)

The bread come down from heaven

The first element of eucharistic faith is the mystery of God himself, trinitarian love. In Jesus's dialogue with Nicodemus, we find an illuminating expression in this regard: "God so loved the world that he gave his only Son, that whoever believes in him should not perish but have eternal life. For God sent the Son into the world, not to condemn the world, but that the world might be saved through him"[55]. These words show the deepest source of God's gift. In the Eucharist Jesus does not give us a "thing," but himself; he offers his own body and pours out his own blood. He thus gives us the totality of his life and reveals the ultimate origin of this love. He is the eternal Son, given to us by the Father. In the Gospel we hear how Jesus, after feeding the crowds by multiplying the loaves and fishes, says to those who had followed him to the synagogue of Capernaum: "My Father gives you the true bread from heaven; for the bread of God is he who comes down from heaven, and gives life to the world"[56], and even identifies himself, his own flesh and blood, with that bread: "I am the living bread which came down from heaven; if anyone eats of this bread, he will live forever; and the bread which I shall give for the life of the world is my flesh"[57]. Jesus thus shows that he is the bread of life which the eternal Father gives to mankind.

A free gift of the Blessed Trinity

The Eucharist reveals the loving plan that guides all of salvation history[58]. There the *Deus Trinitas*, who is essentially love[59], becomes fully a part of our human condition. In the bread and wine under whose appearances Christ gives himself to us in the paschal meal[60], God's whole life encounters us and is sacramentally shared with us. God is a perfect communion of love between Father, Son and Holy Spirit. At creation itself, man was called to have some share in God's breath of life[61]. But it is in Christ, dead and risen,

---

[55] Jn 3:16-17
[56] Jn 6:32-33
[57] Jn 6:51
[58] cf. Eph 1:10; 3:8- 11
[59] cf. 1 Jn 4:7-8
[60] cf. Lk 22:14-20; 1 Co 11:23-26
[61] cf. Gn 2:7

and in the outpouring of the Holy Spirit, given without measure[62], that we have become sharers of God's inmost life. Jesus Christ, who "through the eternal Spirit offered himself without blemish to God"[63], makes us, in the gift of the Eucharist, sharers in God's own life. This is an absolutely free gift, the superabundant fulfilment of God's promises. The Church receives, celebrates and adores this gift in faithful obedience. The "mystery of faith" is thus a mystery of trinitarian love, a mystery in which we are called by grace to participate. We too should therefore exclaim with Saint Augustine: "If you see love, you see the Trinity."[64]

The new and eternal covenant in the blood of the Lamb

The mission for which Jesus came among us was accomplished in the Paschal Mystery. On the Cross from which he draws all people to himself[65], just before "giving up the Spirit," he utters the words: "it is finished"[66]. In the mystery of Christ's obedience unto death, even death on a Cross[67], the new and eternal covenant was brought about. In his crucified flesh, God's freedom and our human freedom met definitively in an inviolable, eternally valid pact. Human sin was also redeemed once for all by God's Son[68]. As I have said elsewhere, "Christ's death on the Cross is the culmination of that turning of God against himself in which he gives himself in order to raise man up and save him. This is love in its most radical form."[69] In the Paschal Mystery, our deliverance from evil and death has taken place. In instituting the Eucharist, Jesus had spoken of the "new and eternal covenant" in the shedding of his blood[70]. This, the ultimate purpose of his mission, was clear from the very beginning of his public life. Indeed, when, on the banks of the Jordan, John the Baptist saw Jesus coming towards him, he cried out: "Behold, the Lamb of God, who takes away the sin of the world"[71]. It is significant that these same words are repeated at every celebration of Holy Mass, when the priest invites us to approach the altar: "Behold *the Lamb of God,* behold him who takes away the sins of the world. Blessed are those called to the supper

---

[62] cf. Jn 3:34
[63] Heb 9:14
[64] *De Trinitate*, VIII, 8, 12: CCL 50, 287.
[65] cf. Jn 12:32
[66] Jn 19:30
[67] cf. Ph 2:8
[68] cf. Heb 7:27; 1 Jn 2:2; 4:10
[69] Encyclical Letter *Deus Caritas Est* (25 December 2005), 12: AAS 98 (2006), 228.
[70] cf. Mt 26:28; Mk 14:24; Lk 22:20
[71] Jn 1:29

of the Lamb". Jesus is the *true* paschal lamb who freely gave himself in sacrifice for us, and thus brought about the new and eternal covenant. The Eucharist contains this radical newness, which is offered to us again at every celebration.

The institution of the Eucharist

This leads us to reflect on the institution of the Eucharist at the Last Supper. It took place within a ritual meal commemorating the foundational event of the people of Israel: their deliverance from slavery in Egypt. This ritual meal, which called for the sacrifice of lambs[72], was a remembrance of the past, but at the same time a prophetic remembrance, the proclamation of a deliverance yet to come. The people had come to realise that their earlier liberation was not definitive, for their history continued to be marked by slavery and sin. The remembrance of their ancient liberation thus expanded to the invocation and expectation of a yet more profound, radical, universal and definitive salvation. This is the context in which Jesus introduces the newness of his gift. In the prayer of praise, the *Berakah*, he does not simply thank the Father for the great events of past history, but also for his own "exaltation." In instituting the sacrament of the Eucharist, Jesus anticipates and makes present the sacrifice of the Cross and the victory of the resurrection. At the same time, he reveals that he himself is the *true* sacrificial lamb, destined in the Father's plan from the foundation of the world, as we read in the First Letter of Peter[73]. By placing his gift in this context, Jesus shows the salvific meaning of his death and resurrection, a mystery which renews history and the whole cosmos. The institution of the Eucharist demonstrates how Jesus's death, for all its violence and absurdity, became in him a supreme act of love and mankind's definitive deliverance from evil.

Figura transit in veritatem

Jesus thus brings his own radical *novum* to the ancient Hebrew sacrificial meal. For us Christians, that meal no longer need be repeated. As the Church Fathers rightly say, *figura transit in veritatem*: the foreshadowing has given way to the truth itself. The ancient rite has been brought to fulfilment and definitively surpassed by the loving gift of the incarnate Son of God. The food of truth, Christ sacrificed for our sake, *dat figuris*

---

[72] cf. Ex 12:1-28, 43-51
[73] cf. 1:18-20

terminum[74]. By his command to "do this in remembrance of me"[75], he asks us to respond to his gift and to make it sacramentally present. In these words the Lord expresses, as it were, his expectation that the Church, born of his sacrifice, will receive this gift, developing under the guidance of the Holy Spirit the liturgical form of the sacrament. The remembrance of his perfect gift consists not in the mere repetition of the Last Supper, but in the Eucharist itself, that is, in the radical newness of Christian worship. In this way, Jesus left us the task of entering into his "hour." "The Eucharist draws us into Jesus's act of self-oblation. More than just statically receiving the incarnate *Logos*, we enter into the very dynamic of his self-giving."[76] Jesus "draws us into himself."[77] The substantial conversion of bread and wine into his body and blood introduces within creation the principle of a radical change, a sort of "nuclear fission," to use an image familiar to us today, which penetrates to the heart of all being, a change meant to set off a process which transforms reality, a process leading ultimately to the transfiguration of the entire world, to the point where God will be all in all[78].

---

[74] Roman Breviary, *Hymn for the Office of Readings of the Solemnity of Corpus Christi*.
[75] Lk 22:19; 1 Co 11:25
[76] Benedict XVI, Encyclical Letter *Deus Caritas Est* (25 December 2005), 13: AAS 98 (2006), 228.
[77] Benedict XVI, Homily at Marienfeld Esplanade (21 August 2005): AAS 97 (2005), 891-892.
[78] cf. 1 Co 15:28

The Word of God and the Eucharist

(Pope Benedict XVI, Verbum Domini, §§ 52-56)

In discussing the importance of the liturgy for understanding the word of God, the Synod of Bishops highlighted the relationship between sacred Scripture and the working of the sacraments. There is great need for a deeper investigation of the relationship between word and sacrament in the Church's pastoral activity and in theological reflection[79]. Certainly "the liturgy of the word is a decisive element in the celebration of each one of the sacraments of the Church"[80]; in pastoral practice, however, the faithful are not always conscious of this connection, nor do they appreciate the unity between gesture and word. It is "the task of priests and deacons, above all when they administer the sacraments, to explain the unity between word and sacrament in the ministry of the Church"[81]. The relationship between word and sacramental gesture is the liturgical expression of God's activity in the history of salvation through the *performative character* of the word itself. In salvation history there is no separation between what God *says* and what he *does*. His word appears as alive and active[82], as the Hebrew term *dabar* itself makes clear. In the liturgical action too, we encounter his word which accomplishes what it says. By educating the People of God to discover the performative character of God's word in the liturgy, we will help them to recognise his activity in salvation history and in their individual lives.

What has been said in general about the relationship between the word and the sacraments takes on deeper meaning when we turn to the celebration of the Eucharist. The profound unity of word and Eucharist is grounded in the witness of Scripture[83], attested to by the Fathers of the Church,

---

[79] Cf. Benedict XVI, Post-Synodal Apostolic Exhortation *Sacramentum Caritatis* (22 February 2007), 44-45: AAS 99 (2007) 139-141.

[80] Pontifical Biblical Commission, *The Interpretation of the Bible in the Church* (15 April 1993) IV, C, 1: *Enchiridion Vaticanum* 13, No. 3123.

[81] Ibid., III, B, 3: *Enchiridion Vaticanum* 13, No. 3056.

[82] cf. Heb 4:12

[83] cf. Jn 6; Lk 24

and reaffirmed by the Second Vatican Council[84]. Here we think of Jesus's discourse on the bread of life in the synagogue of Capernaum[85], with its underlying comparison between Moses and Jesus, between the one who spoke face to face with God[86] and the one who makes God known[87]. Jesus's discourse on the bread speaks of the gift of God, which Moses obtained for his people with the manna in the desert, which is really the *Torah*, the life-giving word of God[88]. In his own person Jesus brings to fulfilment the ancient image: "The bread of God is that which comes down from heaven and gives life to the world" ... "I am the bread of life"[89]. Here "the law has become a person. When we encounter Jesus, we feed on the living God himself, so to speak; we truly eat 'the bread from heaven'"[90]. In the discourse at Capernaum, John's Prologue is brought to a deeper level. There God's *Logos* became flesh, but here this flesh becomes "*bread*" given for the life of the world[91], with an allusion to Jesus's self-gift in the mystery of the cross, confirmed by the words about his blood being given as *drink*[92]. The mystery of the Eucharist reveals the true manna, the true bread of heaven: it is God's *Logos* made flesh, who gave himself up for us in the Paschal Mystery.

Luke's account of the disciples on the way to Emmaus enables us to reflect further on this link between the hearing of the word and the breaking of the bread[93]. Jesus approached the disciples on the day after the Sabbath, listened as they spoke of their dashed hopes, and, joining them on their

---

[84] Cf. Second Vatican Ecumenical Council, Constitution on the Sacred Liturgy *Sacrosanctum Concilium*, 48, 51, 56; Dogmatic Constitution on Divine Revelation *Dei Verbum*, 21, 26; Decree on the Missionary Activity of the Church *Ad Gentes*, 6, 15; Decree on the Ministry and Life of Priests *Presbyterorum Ordinis*, 18; Decree on the Renewal of the Religious Life *Perfectae Caritatis*, 6. In the Church's great Tradition we find significant expressions such as "*Corpus Christi intelligitur etiam* [...] *Scriptura Dei*" ("God's Scripture is also understood as the Body of Christ"): Waltramus, *De Unitate Ecclesiae Conservanda*, 1, 14, ed. W. Schwenkenbecher, Hanoverae, 1883, p. 33; "The flesh of the Lord is true food and his blood true drink; this is the true good that is reserved for us in this present life, to nourish ourselves with his flesh and drink his blood, not only in the Eucharist but also in reading sacred Scripture. Indeed, true food and true drink is the word of God which we derive from the Scriptures": Saint Jerome, *Commentarius in Ecclesiasten*, III: PL 23, 1092A.
[85] cf. Jn 6:22-69
[86] cf. Ex 33:11
[87] cf. Jn 1:18
[88] cf. Ps 119; Pr 9:5
[89] Jn 6:33-35
[90] J. Ratzinger (Benedict XVI), *Jesus of Nazareth*, New York, 2007, 268.
[91] cf. Jn 6:51
[92] cf. Jn 6:53
[93] cf. Lk 24:13-35

journey, "interpreted to them in all the Scriptures the things concerning himself"[94]. The two disciples began to look at the Scriptures in a new way in the company of this traveller who seemed so surprisingly familiar with their lives. What had taken place in those days no longer appeared to them as failure, but as fulfilment and a new beginning. And yet, apparently not even these words were enough for the two disciples. The Gospel of Luke relates that "their eyes were opened and they recognised him"[95] only when Jesus took the bread, said the blessing, broke it and gave it to them, whereas earlier "their eyes were kept from recognising him"[96]. The presence of Jesus, first with his words and then with the act of breaking bread, made it possible for the disciples to recognise him. Now they were able to appreciate in a new way all that they had previously experienced with him: "Did not our hearts burn within us while he talked to us on the road, while he opened to us the Scriptures?"[97].

From these accounts it is clear that Scripture itself points us towards an appreciation of its own unbreakable bond with the Eucharist. "It can never be forgotten that the divine word, read and proclaimed by the Church, has as its one purpose the sacrifice of the new covenant and the banquet of grace, that is, the Eucharist"[98]. Word and Eucharist are so deeply bound together that we cannot understand one without the other: the word of God sacramentally takes flesh in the event of the Eucharist. The Eucharist opens us to an understanding of Scripture, just as Scripture for its part illumines and explains the mystery of the Eucharist. Unless we acknowledge the Lord's real presence in the Eucharist, our understanding of Scripture remains imperfect. For this reason "the Church has honoured the word of God and the Eucharistic mystery with the same reverence, although not with the same worship, and has always and everywhere insisted upon and sanctioned such honour. Moved by the example of her Founder, she has never ceased to celebrate his Paschal Mystery by coming together to read 'in all the Scriptures the things concerning him'[99] and to carry out the work of salvation through the celebration of the memorial of the Lord and through the sacraments"[100].

---

[94] 24:27
[95] 24:31
[96] 24:16
[97] 24:32
[98] *Ordo Lectionum Missæ*, 10.
[99] Lk 24:27
[100] Ibid.

The sacramentality of the word

Reflection on the performative character of the word of God in the sacramental action and a growing appreciation of the relationship between word and Eucharist lead to yet another significant theme which emerged during the synodal assembly, that of the *sacramentality* of the word. Here it may help to recall that Pope John Paul II had made reference to the "*sacramental* character of revelation" and in particular to "the sign of the Eucharist in which the indissoluble unity between the signifier and signified makes it possible to grasp the depths of the mystery"[101]. We come to see that at the heart of the sacramentality of the word of God is the mystery of the Incarnation itself: "the Word became flesh"[102], the reality of the revealed mystery is offered to us in the "flesh" of the Son. The Word of God can be perceived by faith through the "sign" of human words and actions. Faith acknowledges God's Word by accepting the words and actions by which he makes himself known to us. The sacramental character of revelation points in turn to the history of salvation, to the way that Word of God enters time and space, and speaks to men and women, who are called to accept his gift in faith.

The sacramentality of the word can thus be understood by analogy with the real presence of Christ under the appearances of the consecrated bread and wine[103]. By approaching the altar and partaking in the Eucharistic banquet we truly share in the body and blood of Christ. The proclamation of God's Word at the celebration entails an acknowledgment that Christ himself is present, that he speaks to us[104], and that he wishes to be heard. Saint Jerome speaks of the way we ought to approach both the Eucharist and the Word of God: "We are reading the sacred Scriptures. For me, the Gospel is the Body of Christ; for me, the holy Scriptures are his teaching. And when he says: *whoever does not eat my flesh and drink my blood*[105], even though these words can also be understood of the [Eucharistic] Mystery, Christ's body and blood are really the word of Scripture, God's teaching. When we approach the [Eucharistic] Mystery, if a crumb falls to the ground we are troubled. Yet when we are listening to the word of God, and God's Word and Christ's flesh and blood are being poured into our ears yet we

---

[101] Encyclical Letter *Fides et Ratio* (14 September 1998), 13: AAS 91 (1999), 16.
[102] Jn 1:14
[103] Cf. *Catechism of the Catholic Church*, 1373-1374.
[104] Cf. Second Vatican Council, Constitution on Sacred Liturgy *Sacrosanctum Concilium*, 7.
[105] Jn 6:53

pay no heed, what great peril should we not feel?"[106]. Christ, truly present under the species of bread and wine, is analogously present in the word proclaimed in the liturgy. A deeper understanding of the sacramentality of God's word can thus lead us to a more unified understanding of the mystery of revelation, which takes place through "deeds and words intimately connected"[107]; an appreciation of this can only benefit the spiritual life of the faithful and the Church's pastoral activity.

---

[106] *In Psalmum* 147: CCL 78, 337-338.
[107] Second Vatican Council, Dogmatic Constitution on Divine Revelation *Dei Verbum*, 2.

A.D.	Lectionary Cycles		Ash Wednesday	Easter	Ascension	Ascension in England & Wales and Ireland
	Dominical Letter	Sunday Cycle				
2010	c	C - A	17 February	4 April	13 May	16 May
2011	b	A - B	9 March	24 April	2 June	5 June
2012*	A g	B - C	22 February	8 April	17 May	20 May
2013	f	C - A	13 February	31 March	9 May	12 May
2014	e	A - B	5 March	20 April	29 May	1 June
2015	d	B - C	18 February	5 April	14 May	17 May
2016*	c b	C - A	10 February	27 March	5 May	8 May
2017	A	A - B	1 March	16 April	25 May	28 May
2018	g	B - C	14 February	1 April	10 May	13 May
2019	f	C - A	6 March	21 April	30 May	2 June
2020*	e d	A - B	26 February	12 April	21 May	24 May
2021	c	B - C	17 February	4 April	13 May	16 May
2022	b	C - A	2 March	17 April	26 May	29 May
2023	A	A - B	22 February	9 April	18 May	21 May
2024*	g f	B-C	14 February	31 March	9 May	12 May
2025	e	C-A	5 March	20 April	29 May	1 June
2026	d	A-B	18 February	5 April	14 May	17 May
2027	c	B-C	10 February	28 March	6 May	9 May
2028*	b A	C-A	1 March	16 April	25 May	28 May
2029	g	A-B	14 February	1 April	10 May	13 May
2030	f	B-C	6 March	21 April	30 May	2 June
2031	e	C-A	26 February	13 April	22 May	25 May
2032*	d c	A-B	11 February	28 March	6 May	9 May
2033	b	B-C	2 March	17 April	26 May	29 May
2034	A	C-A	22 February	9 April	18 May	21 May
2035	g	A-B	7 February	25 March	3 May	6 May
2036*	f e	B-C	27 February	13 April	22 May	25 May
2037	d	C-A	18 February	5 April	14 May	17 May
2038	c	A-B	10 March	25 April	3 June	6 June
2039	b	B-C	23 February	10 April	19 May	22 May

* Leap Years

PRINCIPAL CELEBRATIONS

| Pentecost | Ordinary Time | | | | First Sunday of Advent |
| | Before Lent | | After Easter Time | | |
	Up Until	Week	From	From Week	
23 May	16 February	6	24 May	8	28 November
12 June	8 March	9	13 June	11	27 November
27 May	21 February	7	28 May	8	2 December
19 May	12 February	5	20 May	7	1 December
8 June	4 March	8	9 June	10	30 November
24 May	17 February	6	25 May	8	29 November
15 May	9 February	5	16 May	7	27 November
4 June	28 February	8	5 June	9	3 December
20 May	13 February	6	21 May	7	2 December
9 June	5 March	8	10 June	10	1 December
31 May	25 February	7	1 June	9	29 November
23 May	16 February	6	24 June	8	28 November
5 June	1 March	8	6 June	10	27 November
28 May	21 February	7	29 May	8	3 December
19 May	13 February	6	20 May	7	1 December
8 June	4 March	8	9 June	10	30 November
24 May	17 February	6	25 May	8	29 November
16 May	9 February	5	17 May	7	28 November
4 June	29 February	8	5 June	9	3 December
20 May	13 February	6	21 May	7	2 December
9 June	5 March	8	10 June	10	1 December
1 June	25 February	7	2 June	9	30 November
16 May	10 February	5	17 May	7	28 November
5 June	1 March	8	6 June	10	27 November
28 May	21 February	7	29 May	8	3 December
13 May	6 February	5	14 May	6	2 December
1 June	26 February	7	2 June	9	30 November
24 May	17 February	6	25 May	8	29 November
13 June	9 March	9	14 June	11	28 November
29 May	22 February	7	30 May	9	27 November

PROPER OF TIME

ADVENT (YEAR A)

FIRST SUNDAY OF ADVENT

With the first Sunday of Advent a new liturgical year begins: the People of God begin again on the way to living the mystery of Christ in history. Christ is the same yesterday, today and for ever; history, instead, changes and requires constant evangelization; it needs to be renewed from within and the only true novelty is Christ: he is its fulfilment, the luminous future of humanity and of the world. Risen from the dead, Jesus is the Lord to whom God subjects all enemies, including death itself. Advent is therefore the propitious time to awaken in our hearts the expectation of he "who is and who was and who is to come" (Rv 1:8).

(Pope Benedict XVI)

Entrance Antiphon   Cf. Ps 24:1-3

To you, I lift up my soul,
O my God.
In you, I have trusted;
   let me not be put to shame.
Nor let my enemies exult over me;
and let none who hope in you
   be put to shame.

Ant. ad introitum

Ad te levavi animam meam,
Deus meus, in te confido,
   non erubescam.
Neque irrideant me inimici mei,
etenim universi qui te exspectant
   non confundentur.

The Gloria in excelsis (Glory to God in the highest) is not said.

Collect

Grant your faithful, we pray,
   almighty God,
the resolve to run forth
   to meet your Christ
with righteous deeds at his coming,
so that, gathered at his right hand,
they may be worthy to possess
   the heavenly Kingdom.
Through our Lord Jesus Christ,
   your Son,
who lives and reigns with you
   in the unity of the Holy Spirit,
one God, for ever and ever.

Collecta

Da, quæsumus, omnipotens Deus,
hanc tuis fidelibus voluntatem,
ut, Christo tuo venienti iustis
   operibus occurrentes,
eius dexteræ sociati, regnum
   mereantur possidere cæleste.
Per Dominum nostrum Iesum
   Christum Filium tuum,
qui tecum vivit et regnat in unitate
   Spiritus Sancti, Deus,
per omnia sæcula sæculorum.

FIRST READING

A reading from the prophet Isaiah   2:1-5

The Lord gathers all nations together into the eternal peace of God's kingdom.

The vision of Isaiah son of Amoz, concerning Judah and Jerusalem.

In the days to come
the mountain of the Temple of the Lord
shall tower above the mountains
and be lifted higher than the hills.
All the nations will stream to it,
peoples without number will come to it, and they will say:

> 'Come, let us go up to the mountain of the Lord,
> to the Temple of the God of Jacob
> that he may teach us his ways
> so that we may walk in his paths;
> since the Law will go out from Zion,
> and the oracle of the Lord from Jerusalem.'

He will wield authority over the nations
and adjudicate between many peoples;
these will hammer their swords into ploughshares,
their spears into sickles.
Nation will not lift sword against nation,
there will be no more training for war.

O House of Jacob, come,
let us walk in the light of the Lord.

The word of the Lord.

Responsorial Psalm   Ps 121:1-2,4-5,6-9. R. Cf. v.1

R. **I rejoiced when I heard them say:**
   'Let us go to God's house.'

I rejoiced when I heard them say:
'Let us go to God's house.'
And now our feet are standing
within your gates, O Jerusalem. R.

It is there that the tribes go up,
the tribes of the Lord.
For Israel's law it is
there to praise the Lord's name.

There were set the thrones of judgement
of the house of David. R.

For the peace of Jerusalem pray:
'Peace be to your homes!
May peace reign in your walls,
in your palaces, peace!' R.

For love of my brethren and friends
I say: 'Peace upon you!'
For love of the house of the Lord
I will ask for your good. R.

SECOND READING

A reading from the letter of St Paul to the Romans   13:11-14
Our salvation is near.

You know 'the time' has come: you must wake up now: our salvation is
even nearer than it was when we were converted. The night is almost over,
it will be daylight soon – let us give up all the things we prefer to do under
cover of the dark; let us arm ourselves and appear in the light. Let us live
decently as people do in the daytime: no drunken orgies, no promiscuity
or licentiousness, and no wrangling or jealousy. Let your armour be the
Lord Jesus Christ.

The word of the Lord.

Gospel Acclamation   Ps 84:8

R. **Alleluia, alleluia!**
Let us see, O Lord, your mercy
and give us your saving help.
R. **Alleluia!**

GOSPEL

A reading from the holy Gospel according to Matthew   24:37-44
Stay awake so that you may be ready.

Jesus said to his disciples: 'As it was in Noah's day, so will it be when the
Son of Man comes. For in those days before the Flood people were eating,
drinking, taking wives, taking husbands, right up to the day Noah went
into the ark, and they suspected nothing till the Flood came and swept all
away. It will be like this when the Son of Man comes. Then of two men in
the fields one is taken, one left; of two women at the millstone grinding,
one is taken, one left.

'So stay awake, because you do not know the day when your master is coming. You may be quite sure of this that if the householder had known at what time of the night the burglar would come, he would have stayed awake and would not have allowed anyone to break through the wall of his house. Therefore, you too must stand ready because the Son of Man is coming at an hour you do not expect.'

The Gospel of the Lord.

The Creed is said.

Prayer over the Offerings

Accept, we pray, O Lord,
    these offerings we make,
gathered from among your gifts
    to us,
and may what you grant us
    to celebrate devoutly here below,
gain for us the prize
    of eternal redemption.
Through Christ our Lord.

Preface I of Advent, pp.548-549.

Super oblata

Suscipe, quæsumus,
    Domine, munera
quæ de tuis offerimus
    collata beneficiis,
et, quod nostræ devotioni concedis
    effici temporali,
tuæ nobis fiat præmium
    redemptionis æternæ.
Per Christum Dominum nostrum.

Communion Antiphon Ps 84:13

The Lord will bestow his bounty,
and our earth shall yield its increase.

Ant. ad communionem

Dominus dabit benignitatem,
et terra nostra dabit fructum suum

Prayer after Communion

May these mysteries, O Lord,
in which we have participated,
profit us, we pray,
for even now, as we walk amid
    passing things,
you teach us by them to love
    the things of heaven
and hold fast to what endures.
Through Christ our Lord.

Post communionem

Prosint nobis, quæsumus, Domine,
    frequentata mysteria,
quibus nos,
    inter prætereuntia ambulantes,
iam nunc instituis amare cælestia
    et inhærere mansuris.
Per Christum Dominum nostrum.

A formula of Solemn Blessing, pp.642-643, may be used.

SECOND SUNDAY OF ADVENT (YEAR A)

The Gospel of this Second Sunday of Advent presents to us the figure of St John the Baptist, who, a famous prophecy of Isaiah says, withdrew to the desert of Judaea and, with his preaching, called the people to convert so as to be ready for the coming of the Messiah, now at hand. The Precursor of Jesus, situated between the Old Covenant and the New, is like a star that heralds the rising of the Sun, of Christ. In the Season of Advent we too are called to listen to God's voice, that cries out in the desert of the world through the Sacred Scriptures, especially when they are preached with the power of the Holy Spirit. Indeed, faith grows all the stronger the more it allows itself to be illumined by the divine word.

(Pope Benedict XVI)

Entrance Antiphon   Cf. Is 30:19,30

O PEOPLE of Sion, behold,
the Lord will come to save
the nations,
and the Lord will make the glory
of his voice heard
in the joy of your heart.

Ant. ad introitum

P OPULUS Sion, ecce Dominus
veniet ad salvandas gentes;
et auditam faciet Dominus gloriam
vocis suæ
in lætitia cordis vestri.

The Gloria in excelsis (Glory to God in the highest) is not said.

Collect

Almighty and merciful God,
may no earthly undertaking
hinder those
who set out in haste
to meet your Son,
but may our learning
of heavenly wisdom
gain us admittance to his company.
Who lives and reigns with you
in the unity of the Holy Spirit,
one God, for ever and ever.

Collecta

Omnipotens et misericors Deus,
in tui occursum Filii festinantes
nulla opera terreni actus impediant,
sed sapientiæ cælestis eruditio nos
faciat eius esse consortes.
Qui tecum vivit et regnat
in unitate Spiritus Sancti,
Deus, per omnia sæcula sæculorum.

FIRST READING

A reading from the prophet Isaiah   11:1-10

He judges the wretched with integrity.

A shoot springs from the stock of Jesse,
a scion thrusts from his roots:
on him the spirit of the Lord rests,
a spirit of wisdom and insight,
a spirit of counsel and power,
a spirit of knowledge and of the fear of the Lord.
(The fear of the Lord is his breath.)
He does not judge by appearances,
he gives no verdict on hearsay,
but judges the wretched with integrity,
and with equity gives a verdict for the poor of the land.
His word is a rod that strikes the ruthless,
his sentences bring death to the wicked.

Integrity is the loincloth round his waist,
faithfulness the belt about his hips.

The wolf lives with the lamb,
the panther lies down with the kid,
calf and lion cub feed together
with a little boy to lead them.
The cow and the bear make friends,
their young lie down together.
The lion eats straw like the ox.
The infant plays over the cobra's hole;
into the viper's lair
the young child puts his hand.
They do not hurt, no harm,
on all my holy mountain,
for the country is filled with the knowledge of the Lord
as the waters swell the sea.

That day, the root of Jesse
shall stand as a signal to the peoples.
It will be sought out by the nations
and its home will be glorious.

   The word of the Lord.

Responsorial Psalm   Ps 71:1-2,7-8,12-13,17. R. Cf. v.7

R. **In his days justice shall flourish**
   and peace till the moon fails.

O God, give your judgement to the king,
to a king's son your justice,
that he may judge your people in justice
and your poor in right judgement. R.

In his days justice shall flourish
and peace till the moon fails.
He shall rule from sea to sea,
from the Great River to earth's bounds. R.

For he shall save the poor when they cry
and the needy who are helpless.
He will have pity on the weak
and save the lives of the poor. R.

May his name be blessed for ever
and endure like the sun.
Every tribe shall be blessed in him,
all nations bless his name. R.

SECOND READING

A reading from the letter of St Paul to the Romans   15:4-9
Christ is the saviour of all men.

Everything that was written long ago in the scriptures was meant to teach
us something about hope from the examples scripture gives of how people
who did not give up were helped by God. And may he who helps us when
we refuse to give up, help you all to be tolerant with each other, following
the example of Christ Jesus, so that united in mind and voice you may give
glory to the God and Father of our Lord Jesus Christ.

It can only be to God's glory, then, for you to treat each other in the
same friendly way as Christ treated you. The reason Christ became the
servant of circumcised Jews was not only so that God could faithfully carry
out the promises made to the patriarchs, it was also to get the pagans to
give glory to God for his mercy, as scripture says in one place: For this I
shall praise you among the pagans and sing to your name.

The word of the Lord.

Gospel Acclamation   Lk 3:4,6

R. **Alleluia, alleluia!**
Prepare a way for the Lord, make his paths straight,
and all mankind shall see the salvation of God.
R. **Alleluia!**

GOSPEL

A reading from the holy Gospel according to Matthew   3:1-12
Repent, for the kingdom of heaven is close at hand.

In due course John the Baptist appeared; he preached in the wilderness
of Judaea and this was his message: 'Repent, for the kingdom of heaven is
close at hand.' This was the man the prophet Isaiah spoke of when he said:

> A voice cries in the wilderness:
> Prepare a way for the Lord,
> make his paths straight.

This man John wore a garment made of camel-hair with a leather belt
round his waist, and his food was locusts and wild honey. Then Jerusalem
and all Judaea and the whole Jordan district made their way to him, and as
they were baptised by him in the river Jordan they confessed their sins. But
when he saw a number of Pharisees and Sadducees coming for baptism he
said to them, 'Brood of vipers, who warned you to fly from the retribution
that is coming? But if you are repentant, produce the appropriate fruit,
and do not presume to tell yourselves, "We have Abraham for our father,"
because, I tell you, God can raise children for Abraham from these stones.
Even now the axe is laid to the roots of the trees, so that any tree which fails
to produce good fruit will be cut down and thrown on the fire. I baptise
you in water for repentance, but the one who follows me is more powerful
than I am, and I am not fit to carry his sandals; he will baptise you with
the Holy Spirit and fire. His winnowing-fan is in his hand; he will clear his
threshing-floor and gather his wheat into the barn; but the chaff he will
burn in a fire that will never go out.'

   The Gospel of the Lord.

The Creed is said.

Prayer over the Offerings

Be pleased, O Lord, with our
    humble prayers and offerings,
and, since we have no merits
    to plead our cause,
come, we pray, to our rescue
with the protection of your mercy.
Through Christ our Lord.

Preface I of Advent, pp.548-549.

Super oblata

Placare, Domine, quæsumus,
nostræ precibus humilitatis
    et hostiis,
et, ubi nulla suppetunt
    suffragia meritorum,
tuæ nobis indulgentiæ
    succurre præsidiis.
Per Christum Dominum nostrum.

Communion Antiphon Ba 5:5;4:36

Jerusalem, arise and stand upon
    the heights,
and behold the joy which comes
    to you from God.

Ant. ad communionem

Ierusalem, surge et sta in excelso,
et vide iucunditatem,
    quæ veniet tibi a Deo tuo.

Prayer after Communion

Replenished by the food
    of spiritual nourishment,
we humbly beseech you, O Lord,
that, through our partaking
    in this mystery,
you may teach us to judge wisely
    the things of earth
and hold firm to the things
    of heaven.
Through Christ our Lord.

Post communionem

Repleti cibo spiritalis alimoniæ,
supplices te, Domine, deprecamur,
ut, huius participatione mysterii,
doceas nos terrena
    sapienter perpendere,
et cælestibus inhærere.
Per Christum Dominum nostrum.

A formula of Solemn Blessing, pp.642-643, may be used.

THIRD SUNDAY OF ADVENT (YEAR A)

"Gaudete in Domino semper – Rejoice in the Lord always" (Ph 4:4). Holy Mass of the Third Sunday of Advent opens with these words of St Paul and is therefore called "Gaudete" Sunday. The Apostle urges Christians to rejoice because the Lord's coming, that is, his glorious return, is certain and will not be delayed. The Church makes this invitation her own while she prepares to celebrate Christmas and her gaze is focused ever more intently on Bethlehem. Indeed, we wait with hope, certain of Christ's second coming because we have experienced his first.

(Pope Benedict XVI)

Entrance Antiphon   Ph 4:4-5

REJOICE in the Lord always; again I say, rejoice. Indeed, the Lord is near.

Ant. ad introitum

GAUDETE in Domino semper: iterum dico, gaudete. Dominus enim prope est.

The Gloria in excelsis (Glory to God in the highest) is not said.

Collect

O God, who see how your people
faithfully await the feast
    of the Lord's Nativity,
enable us, we pray,
to attain the joys of so great
    a salvation
and to celebrate them always
with solemn worship
    and glad rejoicing.
Through our Lord Jesus Christ,
    your Son,
who lives and reigns with you
    in the unity of the Holy Spirit,
one God, for ever and ever.

Collecta

Deus, qui conspicis populum tuum
nativitatis dominicæ festivitatem
    fideliter exspectare,
præsta, quæsumus,
ut valeamus ad tantæ salutis
    gaudia pervenire,
et ea votis sollemnibus alacri
    semper lætitia celebrare.
Per Dominum nostrum
    Iesum Christum Filium tuum,
qui tecum vivit et regnat
    in unitate Spiritus Sancti,
Deus, per omnia sæcula sæculorum.

FIRST READING

A reading from the prophet Isaiah   35:1-6,10

God himself is coming to save you.

Let the wilderness and the dry-lands exult,
let the wasteland rejoice and bloom,

let it bring forth flowers like the jonquil,
let it rejoice and sing for joy.

The glory of Lebanon is bestowed on it,
the splendour of Carmel and Sharon;
they shall see the glory of the Lord,
the splendour of our God.

Strengthen all weary hands,
steady all trembling knees
and say to all faint hearts,
'Courage! Do not be afraid.

'Look, your God is coming,
vengeance is coming,
the retribution of God;
he is coming to save you.'

Then the eyes of the blind shall be opened,
the ears of the deaf unsealed,
then the lame shall leap like a deer
and the tongues of the dumb sing for joy,
for those the Lord has ransomed shall return.

They will come to Zion shouting for joy,
everlasting joy on their faces;
joy and gladness will go with them
and sorrow and lament be ended.

The word of the Lord.

Responsorial Psalm   Ps 145:6-10. R. Cf. Is 35:4

R. **Come, Lord, and save us.**
   or **Alleluia!**

   It is the Lord who keeps faith for ever,
   who is just to those who are oppressed.
   It is he who gives bread to the hungry,
   the Lord, who sets prisoners free. R.

   It is the Lord who gives sight to the blind,
   who raises up those who are bowed down,
   the Lord, who protects the stranger
   and upholds the widow and orphan. R.

It is the Lord who loves the just
but thwarts the path of the wicked.
The Lord will reign for ever,
Zion's God, from age to age. R.

R. **Come, Lord, and save us.**
  or **Alleluia!**

SECOND READING

A reading from the letter of St James   5:7-10
Do not lose heart, because the Lord's coming will be soon

Be patient, brothers, until the Lord's coming. Think of a farmer: how
patiently he waits for the precious fruit of the ground until it has had the
autumn rains and the spring rains! You too have to be patient; do not lose
heart, because the Lord's coming will be soon. Do not make complaints
against one another, brothers, so as not to be brought to judgement
yourselves; the Judge is already to be seen waiting at the gates. For your
example, brothers, in submitting with patience, take the prophets who
spoke in the name of the Lord.

  The word of the Lord.

Gospel Acclamation   Is 61:1 (Lk 4:18)

R. **Alleluia, alleluia!**
The Spirit of the Lord has been given to me.
He has sent me to bring good news to the poor.
R. **Alleluia!**

GOSPEL

A reading from the holy Gospel according to Matthew   11:2-11
Are you the one who is to come, or have we got to wait for someone else?

John in his prison had heard what Christ was doing and he sent his disciples
to ask him, 'Are you the one who is to come, or have we got to wait for
someone else?' Jesus answered, 'Go back and tell John what you hear and
see; the blind see again, and the lame walk, lepers are cleansed, and the
deaf hear, and the dead are raised to life and the Good News is proclaimed
to the poor; and happy is the man who does not lose faith in me.'

  As the messengers were leaving, Jesus began to talk to the people about
John: 'What did you go out into the wilderness to see? A reed swaying in

the breeze? No? Then what did you go out to see? A man wearing fine
clothes? Oh no, those who wear fine clothes are to be found in palaces.
Then what did you go out for? To see a prophet? Yes, I tell you, and much
more than a prophet: he is the one of whom scripture says: Look, I am
going to send my messenger before you; he will prepare your way before
you. I tell you solemnly, of all the children born of women, a greater than
John the Baptist has never been seen; yet the least in the kingdom of
heaven is greater than he is.'

The Gospel of the Lord.

The Creed is said.

Prayer over the Offerings

May the sacrifice of our worship,
    Lord, we pray,
be offered to you unceasingly,
to complete what was begun
    in sacred mystery
and powerfully accomplish for us
    your saving work.
Through Christ our Lord.

Preface I or II of Advent, pp.548-551.

Super oblata

Devotionis nostræ tibi,
    Domine, quæsumus,
hostia iugiter immoletur,
quæ et sacri peragat
    instituta mysterii
et salutare tuum nobis
    potenter operetur.
Per Christum Dominum nostrum.

Communion Antiphon   Cf. Is 35:4

Say to the faint of heart:
    Be strong and do not fear.
Behold, our God will come,
    and he will save us.

Ant. ad communionem

Dicite: Pusillanimes,
    confortamini et nolite timere:
ecce Deus noster veniet
    et salvabit nos.

Prayer after Communion

We implore your mercy, Lord,
that this divine sustenance may
    cleanse us of our faults
and prepare us for
    the coming feasts.
Through Christ our Lord.

Post communionem

Tuam, Domine,
    clementiam imploramus,
ut hæc divina subsidia,
    a vitiis expiatos,
ad festa ventura nos præparent.
Per Christum Dominum nostrum.

A formula of Solemn Blessing, pp.642-643, may be used.

FOURTH SUNDAY OF ADVENT (YEAR A)

On this Sunday the Gospel according to St Matthew recounts the birth of Jesus from St Joseph's viewpoint. He was betrothed to Mary who, "before they came together... was found to be with child of the Holy Spirit"... St Joseph is presented as "a just man", faithful to God's law and ready to do his will... Having given up the idea of divorcing Mary secretly, Joseph took her to himself because he then saw God's work in her with his own eyes. Although he had felt distressed, Joseph "did as the Angel of the Lord commanded him", certain that he was doing the right thing... the new man is outlined in him, who looks with trust and courage to the future. He does not follow his own plans but entrusts himself without reserve to the infinite mercy of the One who will fulfil the prophecies and open the time of salvation.

(Pope Benedict XVI)

Entrance Antiphon   Cf. Is 45:8

DROP down dew from above,
   you heavens,
and let the clouds rain down
      the Just One;
let the earth be opened
      and bring forth a Saviour.

Ant. ad introitum

RORATE, cæli, desuper,
   et nubes pluant iustum;
aperiatur terra
      et germinet Salvatorem.

The Gloria in excelsis (Glory to God in the highest) is not said.

Collect

Pour forth, we beseech you, O Lord,
your grace into our hearts,
that we, to whom the Incarnation
      of Christ your Son
was made known by the message
      of an Angel,
may by his Passion and Cross
be brought to the glory
      of his Resurrection.
Who lives and reigns with you
      in the unity of the Holy Spirit,
one God, for ever and ever.

Collecta

Gratiam tuam,
   quæsumus, Domine,
mentibus nostris infunde, ut qui,
      Angelo nuntiante,
Christi Filii tui
      incarnationem cognovimus,
per passionem eius et crucem
ad resurrectionis
      gloriam perducamur.
Per Dominum nostrum Iesum
      Christum Filium tuum,
qui tecum vivit et regnat
      in unitate Spiritus Sancti,
Deus, per omnia sæcula sæculorum.

FIRST READING

A reading from the prophet Isaiah 7:10-14

The maiden is with child.

The Lord spoke to Ahaz and said, 'Ask the Lord your God for a sign for yourself coming either from the depths of Sheol or from the heights above.' 'No,' Ahaz answered 'I will not put the Lord to the test.'

Then he said:

'Listen now, House of David:
are you not satisfied with trying the patience of men
without trying the patience of my God, too?
The Lord himself, therefore,
will give you a sign.
It is this: the maiden is with child
and will soon give birth to a son
whom she will call Emmanuel,
a name which means "God-is-with-us".'

The word of the Lord.

Responsorial Psalm Ps 23:1-6. R. Cf. vv.7,10

R. **Let the Lord enter!**
He is the king of glory.

The Lord's is the earth and its fullness,
the world and all its peoples.
It is he who set it on the seas;
on the waters he made it firm. R.

Who shall climb the mountain of the Lord?
Who shall stand in his holy place?
The man with clean hands and pure heart,
who desires not worthless things. R.

He shall receive blessings from the Lord
and reward from the God who saves him.
Such are the men who seek him,
seek the face of the God of Jacob. R.

SECOND READING

A reading from the letter of St Paul to the Romans   1:1-7
Jesus Christ, descendant of David, Son of God.

From Paul, a servant of Christ Jesus who has been called to be an apostle, and specially chosen to preach the Good News that God promised long ago through his prophets in the scriptures.

This news is about the Son of God who, according to the human nature he took, was a descendant of David: it is about Jesus Christ our Lord who, in the order of the spirit, the spirit of holiness that was in him, was proclaimed Son of God in all his power through his resurrection from the dead. Through him we received grace and our apostolic mission to preach the obedience of faith to all pagan nations in honour of his name. You are one of these nations, and by his call belong to Jesus Christ. To you all, then, who are God's beloved in Rome, called to be saints, may God our Father and the Lord Jesus Christ send grace and peace.

The word of the Lord.

Gospel Acclamation   Mt 1:23

R. **Alleluia, alleluia!**
The virgin will conceive and give birth to a son
and they will call him Emmanuel,
a name which means 'God-is-with-us'.
R. **Alleluia!**

GOSPEL

A reading from the holy Gospel according to Matthew   1:18-24
Jesus is born of Mary who was betrothed to Joseph, son of David.

This is how Jesus Christ came to be born. His mother Mary was betrothed to Joseph; but before they came to live together she was found to be with child through the Holy Spirit. Her husband Joseph, being a man of honour and wanting to spare her publicity, decided to divorce her informally. He had made up his mind to do this when the angel of the Lord appeared to him in a dream and said, 'Joseph son of David, do not be afraid to take Mary home as your wife, because she has conceived what is in her by the Holy Spirit. She will give birth to a son and you must name him Jesus, because he is the one who is to save his people from their sins.' Now all this took place to fulfil the words spoken by the Lord through the prophet:

The virgin will conceive and give birth to a son
and they will call him Emmanuel,
a name which means 'God-is-with-us'. When Joseph woke up he did what
the angel of the Lord had told him to do: he took his wife to his home.

The Gospel of the Lord.

The Creed is said.

Prayer over the Offerings

May the Holy Spirit, O Lord,
sanctify these gifts laid upon
    your altar,
just as he filled with his power the
    womb of the Blessed Virgin Mary.
Through Christ our Lord.

Preface II of Advent, pp.550-551.

Super oblata

Altari tuo, Domine,
    superposita munera
Spiritus ille sanctificet,
qui beatæ Mariæ viscera
    sua virtute replevit.
Per Christum Dominum nostrum.

Communion Antiphon   Is 7:14

Behold, a Virgin shall conceive
    and bear a son;
and his name will be
    called Emmanuel.

Ant. ad communionem

Ecce Virgo concipiet,
    et pariet filium;
et vocabitur nomen
    eius Emmanuel.

Prayer after Communion

Having received this pledge
    of eternal redemption,
we pray, almighty God,
that, as the feast day of our
    salvation draws ever nearer,
so we may press forward
    all the more eagerly
to the worthy celebration of the
    mystery of your Son's Nativity.
Who lives and reigns
    for ever and ever.

Post communionem

Sumpto pignore
    redemptionis æternæ,
quæsumus, omnipotens Deus,
ut quanto magis dies salutiferæ
    festivitatis accedit,
tanto devotius proficiamus
ad Filii tui digne nativitatis
    mysterium celebrandum.
Qui vivit et regnat
    in sæcula sæculorum.

A formula of Solemn Blessing, pp.642-643, may be used.

ADVENT (YEAR B)

FIRST SUNDAY OF ADVENT

In Advent, Christians relive a dual impulse of the spirit: on the one hand, they raise their eyes towards the final destination of their pilgrimage through history, which is the glorious return of the Lord Jesus; on the other, remembering with emotion his birth in Bethlehem, they kneel before the Crib. The hope of Christians is turned to the future but remains firmly rooted in an event of the past. In the fullness of time, the Son of God was born of the Virgin Mary: "Born of a woman, born under the law", as the Apostle Paul writes (Ga 4:4). We might say that Advent is the season in which Christians must rekindle in their hearts the hope that they will be able with God's help to renew the world.

(Pope Benedict XVI)

Entrance Antiphon Cf. Ps 24:1-3	Ant. ad introitum
To you, I lift up my soul, O my God. In you, I have trusted; let me not be put to shame. Nor let my enemies exult over me; and let none who hope in you be put to shame.	AD te levavi animam meam, Deus meus, in te confido, non erubescam. Neque irrideant me inimici mei, etenim universi qui te exspectant non confundentur.

The Gloria in excelsis (Glory to God in the highest) is not said.

Collect	Collecta
Grant your faithful, we pray, almighty God, the resolve to run forth to meet your Christ with righteous deeds at his coming, so that, gathered at his right hand, they may be worthy to possess the heavenly Kingdom. Through our Lord Jesus Christ, your Son, who lives and reigns with you in the unity of the Holy Spirit, one God, for ever and ever.	Da, quæsumus, omnipotens Deus, hanc tuis fidelibus voluntatem, ut, Christo tuo venienti iustis operibus occurrentes, eius dexteræ sociati, regnum mereantur possidere cæleste. Per Dominum nostrum Iesum Christum Filium tuum, qui tecum vivit et regnat in unitate Spiritus Sancti, Deus, per omnia sæcula sæculorum.

FIRST READING

A reading from the prophet Isaiah   63:16-17; 64:1,3-8

Oh, that you would tear the heavens open and come down.

You, Lord, yourself are our Father,
Our Redeemer is your ancient name.
Why, Lord, leave us to stray from your ways
and harden our hearts against fearing you?
Return, for the sake of your servants,
the tribes of your inheritance.
Oh, that you would tear the heavens open and come down
– at your Presence the mountains would melt.
No ear has heard,
no eye has seen
any god but you act like this
for those who trust him.
You guide those who act with integrity
and keep your ways in mind.
You were angry when we were sinners;
we had long been rebels against you.
We were all like men unclean,
all that integrity of ours like filthy clothing.
We have all withered like leaves
and our sins blew us away like the wind.
No one invoked your name
or roused himself to catch hold of you.
For you hid your face from us
and gave us up to the power of our sins.
And yet, Lord, you are our Father;
we the clay, you the potter,
we are all the work of your hand.

   The word of the Lord.

Responsorial Psalm   Ps 79:2-3,15-16,18-19. R. v.4

R. **God of hosts, bring us back;**
   let your face shine on us and we shall be saved.

   O shepherd of Israel, hear us,
   shine forth from your cherubim throne.
   O Lord, rouse up your might,
   O Lord, come to our help. R.

God of hosts, turn again, we implore,
look down from heaven and see.
Visit this vine and protect it,
the vine your right hand has planted. R.

May your hand be on the man you have chosen,
the man you have given your strength.
And we shall never forsake you again:
give us life that we may call upon your name. R.

R. **God of hosts, bring us back;**
let your face shine on us and we shall be saved.

SECOND READING

A reading from the first letter of St Paul to the Corinthians   1:3-9

We are waiting for our Lord Jesus Christ to be revealed.

May God our Father and the Lord Jesus Christ send you grace and peace.

I never stop thanking God for all the graces you have received through Jesus Christ. I thank him that you have been enriched in so many ways, especially in your teachers and preachers; the witness to Christ has indeed been strong among you so that you will not be without any of the gifts of the Spirit while you are waiting for our Lord Jesus Christ to be revealed; and he will keep you steady and without blame until the last day, the day of our Lord Jesus Christ, because God by calling you has joined you to his Son, Jesus Christ; and God is faithful.

The word of the Lord.

Gospel Acclamation   Ps 84:8

R. **Alleluia, alleluia!**
Let us see, O Lord, your mercy
and give us your saving help.
R. **Alleluia!**

GOSPEL

A reading from the holy Gospel according to Mark   13:33-37

Stay awake, because you do not know when the master of the house is coming.

Jesus said to his disciples: 'Be on your guard, stay awake, because you never know when the time will come. It is like a man travelling abroad: he has gone from home, and left his servants in charge, each with his own task; and he has told the doorkeeper to stay awake. So stay awake, because you do not know when the master of the house is coming, evening, midnight, cockcrow, dawn; if he comes unexpectedly, he must not find you asleep. And what I say to you I say to all: Stay awake!'

The Gospel of the Lord.

The Creed is said.

Prayer over the Offerings

Accept, we pray, O Lord,
     these offerings we make,
gathered from among your gifts to us,
and may what you grant us to
     celebrate devoutly here below,
gain for us the prize
     of eternal redemption.
Through Christ our Lord.

Preface I of Advent, pp.548-549.

Super oblata

Suscipe, quæsumus,
     Domine, munera
quæ de tuis offerimus
     collata beneficiis,
et, quod nostræ devotioni concedis
     effici temporali,
tuæ nobis fiat præmium
     redemptionis æternæ.
Per Christum Dominum nostrum.

Communion Antiphon   Ps 84:13

The Lord will bestow his bounty,
and our earth shall yield its increase.

Ant. ad communionem

Dominus dabit benignitatem,
et terra nostra dabit fructum suum.

Prayer after Communion

May these mysteries, O Lord,
in which we have participated,
profit us, we pray,
for even now,
     as we walk amid passing things,
you teach us by them to love
     the things of heaven
and hold fast to what endures.
Through Christ our Lord.

Post communionem

Prosint nobis, quæsumus, Domine,
     frequentata mysteria,
quibus nos,
     inter prætereuntia ambulantes,
iam nunc instituis amare cælestia
     et inhærere mansuris.
Per Christum Dominum nostrum.

A formula of Solemn Blessing, pp.642-643, may be used.

SECOND SUNDAY OF ADVENT (YEAR B)

A message full of hope resounds in the liturgy of Advent, inviting us to raise our gaze to the ultimate horizon but at the same time to recognise the signs of the God-with-us in the present. On this Second Sunday of Advent the Word of God acquires the moving tones of the so-called "Second Isaiah", who announced to the Israelites, tried by decades of bitter exile in Babylon, liberation at last: "Comfort, comfort my people". This is what the Lord wishes to do in Advent: to speak to the heart of his people and through it to the whole of humanity, to proclaim salvation.

(Pope Benedict XVI)

Entrance Antiphon Cf. Is 30:19,30	Ant. ad introitum
O PEOPLE of Sion, behold, the Lord will come to save the nations, and the Lord will make the glory of his voice heard in the joy of your heart.	P OPULUS Sion, ecce Dominus veniet ad salvandas gentes; et auditam faciet Dominus gloriam vocis suæ in lætitia cordis vestri.

The Gloria in excelsis (Glory to God in the highest) is not said.

Collect	Collecta
Almighty and merciful God, may no earthly undertaking hinder those who set out in haste to meet your Son, but may our learning of heavenly wisdom gain us admittance to his company. Who lives and reigns with you in the unity of the Holy Spirit, one God, for ever and ever.	Omnipotens et misericors Deus, in tui occursum Filii festinantes nulla opera terreni actus impediant, sed sapientiæ cælestis eruditio nos faciat eius esse consortes. Qui tecum vivit et regnat in unitate Spiritus Sancti, Deus, per omnia sæcula sæculorum.

FIRST READING

A reading from prophet Isaiah   40:1-5,9-11

Prepare a way for the Lord.

'Console my people, console them'
says your God.
'Speak to the heart of Jerusalem
and call to her
that her time of service is ended,
that her sin is atoned for,
that she has received from the hand of the Lord
double punishment for all her crimes.'

A voice cries, 'Prepare in the wilderness
a way for the Lord.
Make a straight highway for our God
across the desert.
Let every valley be filled in,
every mountain and hill be laid low,
let every cliff become a plain,
and the ridges a valley;
then the glory of the Lord shall be revealed
and all mankind shall see it;
for the mouth of the Lord has spoken.'

Go up on a high mountain,
joyful messenger to Zion.
Shout with a loud voice,
joyful messenger to Jerusalem.
Shout without fear,
say to the towns of Judah,
'Here is your God.'

Here is the Lord coming with power,
his arm subduing all things to him.
The prize of his victory is with him,
his trophies all go before him.
He is like a shepherd feeding his flock,
gathering lambs in his arms,
holding them against his breast
and leading to their rest the mother ewes.

The word of the Lord.

Responsorial Psalm   Ps 84:9-14. R. v.8

R. **Let us see, O Lord, your mercy
and give us your saving help.**

I will hear what the Lord God has to say,
a voice that speaks of peace,
peace for his people.
His help is near for those who fear him
and his glory will dwell in our land. R.

Mercy and faithfulness have met;
justice and peace have embraced.
Faithfulness shall spring from the earth
and justice look down from heaven. R.

The Lord will make us prosper
and our earth shall yield its fruit.
Justice shall march before him
and peace shall follow his steps. R.

SECOND READING

A reading from the second letter of St Peter   3:8-14
We are waiting for the new heavens and new earth.

There is one thing, my friends, that you must never forget: that with the
Lord, 'a day' can mean a thousand years, and a thousand years is like a
day. The Lord is not being slow to carry out his promises, as anybody else
might be called slow; but he is being patient with you all, wanting nobody
to be lost and everybody to be brought to change his ways. The Day of the
Lord will come like a thief, and then with a roar the sky will vanish, the
elements will catch fire and fall apart, the earth and all that it contains will
be burnt up.

   Since everything is coming to an end like this, you should be living
holy and saintly lives while you wait and long for the Day of God to come,
when the sky will dissolve in flames and the elements melt in the heat.
What we are waiting for is what he promised: the new heavens and new
earth, the place where righteousness will be at home. So then, my friends,
while you are waiting, do your best to live lives without spot or stain so
that he will find you at peace.

The word of the Lord.

Gospel Acclamation   Lk 3:4,6

R. **Alleluia, alleluia!**
Prepare a way for the Lord,
make his paths straight,
and all mankind shall see the salvation of God.
R. **Alleluia!**

GOSPEL

A reading from the holy Gospel according to Mark   1:1-8
Make his paths straight.

The beginning of the Good News about Jesus Christ, the Son of God. It is
written in the book of the prophet Isaiah:

Look, I am going to send my messenger before you;
he will prepare your way.
A voice cries in the wilderness:
Prepare a way for the Lord,
make his paths straight,

and so it was that John the Baptist appeared in the wilderness, proclaiming
a baptism of repentance for the forgiveness of sins. All Judaea and all the
people of Jerusalem made their way to him, and as they were baptised by him
in the river Jordan they confessed their sins. John wore a garment of camel-
skin, and he lived on locusts and wild honey. In the course of his preaching
he said, 'Someone is following me, someone who is more powerful than I
am, and I am not fit to kneel down and undo the strap of his sandals. I have
baptised you with water, but he will baptise you with the Holy Spirit.'

The Gospel of the Lord.

The Creed is said.

Prayer over the Offerings	Super oblata
Be pleased, O Lord, with our humble prayers and offerings, and, since we have no merits to plead our cause, come, we pray, to our rescue with the protection of your mercy. Through Christ our Lord.	Placare, Domine, quæsumus, nostræ precibus humilitatis et hostiis, et, ubi nulla suppetunt suffragia meritorum, tuæ nobis indulgentiæ succurre præsidiis. Per Christum Dominum nostrum.

Preface I of Advent, pp.548-549.

Communion Antiphon Ba 5:5;4:36	Ant. ad communionem
Jerusalem, arise and stand upon the heights, and behold the joy which comes to you from God.	Ierusalem, surge et sta in excelso, et vide iucunditatem, quæ veniet tibi a Deo tuo.
Prayer after Communion	Post communionem
Replenished by the food of spiritual nourishment, we humbly beseech you, O Lord, that, through our partaking in this mystery, you may teach us to judge wisely the things of earth and hold firm to the things of heaven. Through Christ our Lord.	Repleti cibo spiritalis alimoniæ, supplices te, Domine, deprecamur, ut, huius participatione mysterii, doceas nos terrena sapienter perpendere, et cælestibus inhærere. Per Christum Dominum nostrum.

A formula of Solemn Blessing, pp.642-643, may be used.

THIRD SUNDAY OF ADVENT (YEAR B)

What does "the Lord is at hand" mean? In what sense must we understand this "closeness" of God? The Church, illumined by the Holy Spirit, already at that time understood increasingly better that God's "closeness" is not a question of space and time but rather of love: love brings people together! This coming Christmas will remind us of this fundamental truth of our faith and in front of the manger we shall be able to savour Christian joy contemplating in the newborn Jesus the Face of God who made himself close to us out of love.

(Pope Benedict XVI)

Entrance Antiphon   Ph 4:4-5

REJOICE in the Lord always;
again I say, rejoice.
Indeed, the Lord is near.

Ant. ad introitum

GAUDETE in Domino semper:
iterum dico, gaudete.
Dominus enim prope est.

The Gloria in excelsis (Glory to God in the highest) is not said.

Collect

O God, who see how your people
faithfully await the feast
    of the Lord's Nativity,
enable us, we pray,
to attain the joys of so great
    a salvation
and to celebrate them always
with solemn worship
    and glad rejoicing.
Through our Lord Jesus Christ,
    your Son,
who lives and reigns with you
    in the unity of the Holy Spirit,
one God, for ever and ever.

Collecta

Deus, qui conspicis populum tuum
nativitatis dominicæ festivitatem
    fideliter exspectare,
præsta, quæsumus,
ut valeamus ad tantæ salutis
    gaudia pervenire,
et ea votis sollemnibus alacri
    semper lætitia celebrare.
Per Dominum nostrum
    Iesum Christum Filium tuum,
qui tecum vivit et regnat
    in unitate Spiritus Sancti,
Deus, per omnia sæcula sæculorum.

FIRST READING

A reading from the prophet Isaiah   61:1-2,10-11
I exult for joy in the Lord.

The spirit of the Lord has been given to me,
for the Lord has anointed me.

He has sent me to bring good news to the poor,
to bind up hearts that are broken;

to proclaim liberty to captives,
freedom to those in prison;
to proclaim a year of favour from the Lord.

'I exult for joy in the Lord,
my soul rejoices in my God,
for he has clothed me in the garments of salvation,
he has wrapped me in the cloak of integrity,
like a bridegroom wearing his wreath,
like a bride adorned in her jewels.

'For as the earth makes fresh things grow,
as a garden makes seeds spring up,
so will the Lord make both integrity and praise
spring up in the sight of the nations.'

   The word of the Lord.

Responsorial Psalm   Lk 1:46-50,53-54. R. Is 61:10

R. **My soul rejoices in my God.**

   My soul glorifies the Lord,
   my spirit rejoices in God, my Saviour.
   He looks on his servant in her nothingness;
   henceforth all ages will call me blessed. R.

   The Almighty works marvels for me.
   Holy his name!
   His mercy is from age to age,
   on those who fear him. R.

   He fills the starving with good things,
   sends the rich away empty.
   He protects Israel, his servant,
   remembering his mercy. R.

SECOND READING

A reading from the first letter of St Paul to the Thessalonians   5:16-24
May you all be kept safe, spirit, soul and body, for the coming of the Lord.

Be happy at all times; pray constantly; and for all things give thanks to
God, because this is what God expects you to do in Christ Jesus.

Never try to suppress the Spirit or treat the gift of prophecy with contempt; think before you do anything – hold on to what is good and avoid every form of evil.

May the God of peace make you perfect and holy; and may you all be kept safe and blameless, spirit, soul and body, for the coming of our Lord Jesus Christ. God has called you and he will not fail you.

The word of the Lord.

Gospel Acclamation   Is 61:1 (Lk 4:18)
R. **Alleluia, alleluia!**
The Spirit of the Lord has been given to me.
He has sent me to bring good news to the poor.
R. **Alleluia!**

GOSPEL

A reading from the holy Gospel according to John   1:6-8,19-28
There stands among you – unknown to you – the one who is coming after me.

A man came, sent by God.
His name was John.
He came as a witness,
as a witness to speak for the light,
so that everyone might believe through him.
He was not the light,
only a witness to speak for the light.

This is how John appeared as a witness. When the Jews sent priests and Levites from Jerusalem to ask him, 'Who are you?' he not only declared, but he declared quite openly, 'I am not the Christ.' 'Well then,' they asked 'are you Elijah?' 'I am not' he said. 'Are you the Prophet?' He answered, 'No.' So they said to him, 'Who are you? We must take back an answer to those who sent us. What have you to say about yourself?' So John said, 'I am, as Isaiah prophesied:

a voice that cries in the wilderness:
Make a straight way for the Lord.'

Now these men had been sent by the Pharisees, and they put this further question to him, 'Why are you baptising if you are not the Christ, and not Elijah, and not the prophet?' John replied, 'I baptise with water, but there stands among you – unknown to you – the one who is coming after me; and I am not fit to undo his sandal-strap.' This happened at Bethany, on the far side of the Jordan, where John was baptising.

The Gospel of the Lord.

The Creed is said.

Prayer over the Offerings

May the sacrifice of our worship,
    Lord, we pray,
be offered to you unceasingly,
to complete what was begun
    in sacred mystery
and powerfully accomplish for us
    your saving work.
Through Christ our Lord.

Preface I or II of Advent, pp.548-551.

Super oblata

Devotionis nostræ tibi,
    Domine, quæsumus,
hostia iugiter immoletur,
quæ et sacri peragat
    instituta mysterii
et salutare tuum nobis
    potenter operetur.
Per Christum Dominum nostrum.

Communion Antiphon   Cf. Is 35:4

Say to the faint of heart: Be strong
    and do not fear.
Behold, our God will come,
    and he will save us.

Ant. ad communionem

Dicite: Pusillanimes, confortamini
    et nolite timere:
ecce Deus noster veniet
    et salvabit nos.

Prayer after Communion

We implore your mercy, Lord,
that this divine sustenance may
    cleanse us of our faults
and prepare us for
    the coming feasts.
Through Christ our Lord.

Post communionem

Tuam, Domine,
    clementiam imploramus,
ut hæc divina subsidia,
    a vitiis expiatos,
ad festa ventura nos præparent.
Per Christum Dominum nostrum.

A formula of Solemn Blessing, pp.642-643, may be used.

FOURTH SUNDAY OF ADVENT (YEAR B)

The Gospel of this Fourth Sunday of Advent proposes to us the account of the Annunciation (Lk 1:26-38), the mystery to which we return every day in reciting the Angelus. *This prayer makes us relive the decisive moment at which God knocked at Mary's heart and, having received her "yes", began to take flesh, in her and from her. The Collect of today's Mass is the same as the one we recite at the end of the* Angelus. *With only a few days until the Feast of Christmas, we are invited to fix our gaze on the ineffable mystery that Mary treasured for nine months in her virginal womb: the mystery of God who is made man.*

(Pope Benedict XVI)

Entrance Antiphon   Cf. Is 45:8

DROP down dew from above,
you heavens,
and let the clouds rain down
    the Just One;
let the earth be opened
    and bring forth a Saviour.

Ant. ad introitum

RORATE, cæli, desuper,
et nubes pluant iustum;
aperiatur terra
    et germinet Salvatorem.

The Gloria in excelsis (Glory to God in the highest) is not said.

Collect

Pour forth, we beseech you, O Lord,
your grace into our hearts,
that we, to whom the Incarnation
    of Christ your Son
was made known by the message
    of an Angel,
may by his Passion and Cross
be brought to the glory
    of his Resurrection.
Who lives and reigns with you
    in the unity of the Holy Spirit,
one God, for ever and ever.

Collecta

Gratiam tuam,
    quæsumus, Domine,
mentibus nostris infunde,
    ut qui, Angelo nuntiante,
Christi Filii tui
    incarnationem cognovimus,
per passionem eius et crucem
ad resurrectionis
    gloriam perducamur.
Per Dominum nostrum Iesum
    Christum Filium tuum,
qui tecum vivit et regnat
    in unitate Spiritus Sancti,
Deus, per omnia sæcula sæculorum.

FIRST READING

A reading from the second book of Samuel   7:1-5,8-12,14,16

The kingdom of David will always stand secure before the Lord.

Once David had settled into his house and the Lord had given him rest from all the enemies surrounding him, the king said to the prophet Nathan, 'Look, I am living in a house of cedar while the ark of God dwells in a tent.' Nathan said to the king, 'Go and do all that is in your mind, for the Lord is with you.'

But that very night the word of the Lord came to Nathan:

'Go and tell my servant David, "Thus the Lord speaks: Are you the man to build me a house to dwell in? I took you from the pasture, from following the sheep, to be leader of my people Israel; I have been with you on all your expeditions; I have cut off all your enemies before you. I will give you fame as great as the fame of the greatest on earth. I will provide a place for my people Israel; I will plant them there and they shall dwell in that place and never be disturbed again; nor shall the wicked continue to oppress them as they did, in the days when I appointed judges over my people Israel; I will give them rest from all their enemies. The Lord will make you great; the Lord will make you a House. And when your days are ended and you are laid to rest with your ancestors, I will preserve the offspring of your body after you and make his sovereignty secure. I will be a father to him and he a son to me. Your House and your sovereignty will always stand secure before me and your throne be established for ever."'

The word of the Lord.

Responsorial Psalm   Ps 88:2-5,27,29. R. Cf. v.2

R. **I will sing for ever of your love, O Lord.**

> I will sing for ever of your love, O Lord;
> through all ages my mouth will proclaim your truth.
> Of this I am sure, that your love lasts for ever,
> that your truth is firmly established as the heavens. R.

> 'I have made a covenant with my chosen one;
> I have sworn to David my servant:
> I will establish your dynasty for ever
> and set up your throne through all ages.' R.

> He will say to me: 'You are my father,
> my God, the rock who saves me.'
> I will keep my love for him always;
> for him my covenant shall endure. R.

SECOND READING

A reading from the letter of St Paul to the Romans   16:25-27

The mystery, which was kept secret for endless ages, is now made clear.

Glory to him who is able to give you the strength to live according to the
Good News I preach, and in which I proclaim Jesus Christ, the revelation
of a mystery kept secret for endless ages, but now so clear that it must be
broadcast to pagans everywhere to bring them to the obedience of faith.
This is only what scripture has predicted, and it is all part of the way the
eternal God wants things to be. He alone is wisdom; give glory therefore to
him through Jesus Christ for ever and ever. Amen.

The word of the Lord.

Gospel Acclamation   Lk 1:38
R. **Alleluia, alleluia!**
I am the handmaid of the Lord:
let what you have said be done to me.
R. **Alleluia!**

GOSPEL

A reading from the holy Gospel according to Luke   1:26-38

Listen! You are to conceive and bear a son.

The angel Gabriel was sent by God to a town in Galilee called Nazareth,
to a virgin betrothed to a man named Joseph, of the house of David; and
the virgin's name was Mary. He went in and said to her, 'Rejoice, so highly
favoured! The Lord is with you.' She was deeply disturbed by these words
and asked herself what this greeting could mean, but the angel said to her,
'Mary, do not be afraid; you have won God's favour. Listen! You are to
conceive and bear a son, and you must name him Jesus. He will be great
and will be called Son of the Most High. The Lord God will give him the
throne of his ancestor David; he will rule over the House of Jacob for ever
and his reign will have no end.' Mary said to the angel, 'But how can this
come about, since I am a virgin?' 'The Holy Spirit will come upon you', the
angel answered, 'and the power of the Most High will cover you with its
shadow. And so the child will be holy and will be called Son of God. Know
this too: your kinswoman Elizabeth has, in her old age, conceived a son,
and she whom people called barren is now in her sixth month, for nothing
is impossible to God.' 'I am the handmaid of the Lord,' said Mary, 'let what
you have said be done to me.' And the angel left her.

The Gospel of the Lord.

The Creed is said.

Prayer over the Offerings

May the Holy Spirit, O Lord,
sanctify these gifts laid upon
    your altar,
just as he filled with his power the
    womb of the Blessed Virgin Mary.
Through Christ our Lord.

Preface II of Advent, pp.550-551.

Super oblata

Altari tuo, Domine,
    superposita munera
Spiritus ille sanctificet,
qui beatæ Mariæ viscera
    sua virtute replevit.
Per Christum Dominum nostrum.

Communion Antiphon   Is 7:14

Behold, a Virgin shall conceive
    and bear a son;
and his name will be called
    Emmanuel.

Ant. ad communionem

Ecce Virgo concipiet,
    et pariet filium;
et vocabitur nomen eius
    Emmanuel.

Prayer after Communion

Having received this pledge
    of eternal redemption,
we pray, almighty God,
that, as the feast day of our
    salvation draws ever nearer,
so we may press forward
    all the more eagerly
to the worthy celebration of the
    mystery of your Son's Nativity.
Who lives and reigns
    for ever and ever.

A formula of Solemn Blessing, pp.642-643, may be used.

Post communionem

Sumpto pignore
    redemptionis æternæ,
quæsumus, omnipotens Deus,
ut quanto magis dies salutiferæ
    festivitatis accedit,
tanto devotius proficiamus
ad Filii tui digne nativitatis
    mysterium celebrandum.
Qui vivit et regnat
    in sæcula sæculorum.

ADVENT (YEAR C)

FIRST SUNDAY OF ADVENT

In Advent, the liturgy frequently repeats and assures us, as if to overcome our natural diffidence, that God "comes": he comes to be with us in every situation of ours, he comes to dwell among us, to live with us and within us; he comes to fill the gaps that divide and separate us; he comes to reconcile us with him and with one another. He comes into human history to knock at the door of every man and every woman of good will, to bring to individuals, families and peoples the gifts of brotherhood, harmony and peace. This is why Advent is par excellence the season of hope in which believers in Christ are invited to remain in watchful and active waiting, nourished by prayer and by the effective commitment to love.
(Pope Benedict XVI)

Entrance Antiphon Cf. Ps 24:1-3	Ant. ad introitum

To you, I lift up my soul, O my God.
In you, I have trusted;
   let me not be put to shame.
Nor let my enemies exult over me;
and let none who hope in you
   be put to shame.
	Ad te levavi animam meam, Deus meus, in te confido,
	   non erubescam.
	Neque irrideant me inimici mei,
	etenim universi qui te exspectant
	   non confundentur.

The Gloria in excelsis (Glory to God in the highest) is not said.

Collect	Collecta

Grant your faithful, we pray,
   almighty God,
the resolve to run forth to meet
   your Christ
with righteous deeds at his coming,
so that, gathered at his right hand,
they may be worthy to possess
   the heavenly Kingdom.
Through our Lord Jesus Christ,
   your Son,
who lives and reigns with you
   in the unity of the Holy Spirit,
one God, for ever and ever.
	Da, quæsumus, omnipotens Deus,
	hanc tuis fidelibus voluntatem,
	ut, Christo tuo venienti iustis
	   operibus occurrentes,
	eius dexteræ sociati, regnum
	   mereantur possidere cæleste.
	Per Dominum nostrum Iesum
	   Christum Filium tuum,
	qui tecum vivit et regnat
	   in unitate Spiritus Sancti,
	Deus, per omnia sæcula sæculorum.

FIRST READING

A reading from the prophet Jeremiah   33:14-16

I will make a virtuous Branch grow for David.

See, the days are coming - it is the Lord who speaks - when I am going to fulfil the promise I made to the House of Israel and the House of Judah:

'In those days and at that time,
I will make a virtuous Branch grow for David,
who shall practise honesty and integrity in the land.
In those days Judah shall be saved
and Israel shall dwell in confidence.
And this is the name the city will be called:
The Lord-our-integrity.'

The word of the Lord.

Responsorial Psalm   Ps 24:4-5,8-9,10,14. R. v.1

R. **To you, O Lord, I lift up my soul.**

Lord, make me know your ways.
Lord, teach me your paths.
Make me walk in your truth, and teach me:
for you are God my saviour. R.

The Lord is good and upright.
He shows the path to those who stray,
he guides the humble in the right path;
he teaches his way to the poor. R.

His ways are faithfulness and love
for those who keep his covenant and will.
The Lord's friendship is for those who revere him;
to them he reveals his covenant. R.

SECOND READING

A reading from the first letter of St Paul to the Thessalonians   3:12-4:2

May the Lord confirm your hearts in holiness when Christ comes.

May the Lord be generous in increasing your love and make you love one another and the whole human race as much as we love you. And may he so confirm your hearts in holiness that you may be blameless in the sight of our God and Father when our Lord Jesus Christ comes with all his saints.

Finally, brothers, we urge you and appeal to you in the Lord Jesus to make more and more progress in the kind of life that you are meant to live: the life that God wants, as you learnt from us, and as you are already living it. You have not forgotten the instructions we gave you on the authority of the Lord Jesus.

The word of the Lord.

Gospel Acclamation   Ps 84:8

R. **Alleluia, alleluia!**
Let us see, O Lord, your mercy
and give us your saving help.
R. **Alleluia!**

GOSPEL

A reading from the holy Gospel according to Luke   21:25-28,34-36
Your liberation is near at hand.

Jesus said to his disciples: 'There will be signs in the sun and moon and stars; on earth nations in agony, bewildered by the clamour of the ocean and its waves; men dying of fear as they await what menaces the world, for the powers of heaven will be shaken. And then they will see the Son of Man coming in a cloud with power and great glory. When these things begin to take place, stand erect, hold your heads high, because your liberation is near at hand.

'Watch yourselves, or your hearts will be coarsened with debauchery and drunkenness and the cares of life, and that day will be sprung on you suddenly, like a trap. For it will come down on every living man on the face of the earth. Stay awake, praying at all times for the strength to survive all that is going to happen, and to stand with confidence before the Son of Man.'

The Gospel of the Lord

The Creed is said.

Prayer over the Offerings

Accept, we pray, O Lord,
   these offerings we make,
gathered from among
   your gifts to us,
and may what you grant us
   to celebrate devoutly here below,
gain for us the prize
   of eternal redemption.
Through Christ our Lord.

Preface I of Advent, pp.548-549.

Super oblata

Suscipe, quæsumus,
   Domine, munera,
quæ de tuis offerimus
   collata beneficiis,
et, quod nostræ devotioni concedis
   effici temporali,
tuæ nobis fiat præmium
   redemptionis æternæ.
Per Christum Dominum nostrum.

Communion Antiphon   Ps 84:13

The Lord will bestow his bounty,
and our earth shall yield its increase.

Ant. ad communionem

Dominus dabit benignitatem,
et terra nostra dabit fructum suum.

Prayer after Communion

May these mysteries, O Lord,
in which we have participated,
profit us, we pray,
for even now, as we walk amid
   passing things,
you teach us by them to love
   the things of heaven
and hold fast to what endures.
Through Christ our Lord.

A formula of Solemn Blessing, pp.642-643, may be used.

Post communionem

Prosint nobis, quæsumus, Domine,
   frequentata mysteria,
quibus nos,
   inter prætereuntia ambulantes,
iam nunc instituis amare cælestia
   et inhærere mansuris.
Per Christum Dominum nostrum.

SECOND SUNDAY OF ADVENT (YEAR C)

On this Sunday the Liturgy presents to us the Gospel passage in which St Luke prepares the scene on which Jesus is about to enter and begin his public ministry. The Evangelist focuses the spotlight on to John the Baptist, who was the Precursor of the Messiah, and with great precision outlines the space-time coordinates of his preaching. The Evangelist evidently wanted to warn those who read or hear about it that the Gospel is not a legend but the account of a true story, that Jesus of Nazareth is a historical figure who fits into that precise context. After this ample historical introduction, the subject becomes "the word of God", presented as a power that comes down from Heaven and settles upon John the Baptist.   *(Pope Benedict XVI)*

Entrance Antiphon   Cf. Is 30:19,30

O PEOPLE of Sion, behold,
    the Lord will come to save
the nations,
and the Lord will make the glory
    of his voice heard
in the joy of your heart.

Ant. ad introitum

P OPULUS Sion, ecce Dominus
    veniet ad salvandas gentes;
et auditam faciet Dominus gloriam
    vocis suæ
in lætitia cordis vestri.

The Gloria in excelsis (Glory to God in the highest) is not said.

Collect

Almighty and merciful God,
may no earthly undertaking
    hinder those
who set out in haste to meet
    your Son,
but may our learning
    of heavenly wisdom
gain us admittance to his company.
Who lives and reigns with you
    in the unity of the Holy Spirit,
one God, for ever and ever.

Collecta

Omnipotens et misericors Deus,
in tui occursum Filii festinantes
nulla opera terreni actus impediant,
sed sapientiæ cælestis eruditio nos
    faciat eius esse consortes.
Qui tecum vivit et regnat
    in unitate Spiritus Sancti,
Deus, per omnia sæcula sæculorum.

FIRST READING

A reading from the prophet Baruch   5:1-9

God means to show your splendour to every nation.

Jerusalem, take off your dress of sorrow and distress,
put on the beauty of the glory of God for ever,
wrap the cloak of the integrity of God around you,
put the diadem of the glory of the Eternal on your head:

since God means to show your splendour to every nation under heaven,
since the name God gives you for ever will be,
'Peace through integrity, and honour through devotedness.'
Arise, Jerusalem, stand on the heights
and turn your eyes to the east:
see your sons reassembled from west and east
at the command of the Holy One, jubilant that God has remembered them.
Though they left you on foot,
with enemies for an escort,
now God brings them back to you
like royal princes carried back in glory.
For God has decreed the flattening
of each high mountain, of the everlasting hills,
the filling of the valleys to make the ground level
so that Israel can walk in safety under the glory of God.
And the forests and every fragrant tree will provide shade
for Israel at the command of God;
for God will guide Israel in joy by the light of his glory
with his mercy and integrity for escort.

   The word of the Lord.

Responsial Psalm   Ps 125. R. v.3

R. **What marvels the Lord worked for us!**
  Indeed we were glad.

  When the Lord delivered Zion from bondage
  it seemed like a dream.
  Then was our mouth filled with laughter,
  on our lips there were songs. R.

  The heathens themselves said: 'What marvels
  the Lord worked for them!'
  What marvels the Lord worked for us!
  Indeed we were glad. R.

  Deliver us, O Lord, from our bondage
  as streams in dry land.
  Those who are sowing in tears
  will sing when they reap. R.

  They go out, they go out, full of tears
  carrying seed for the sowing:
  they come back, they come back, full of song,
  carrying their sheaves. R.

SECOND READING

A reading from the letter of St Paul to the Philippians   1:4-6,8-11
Be pure and blameless for the day of Christ.

Every time I pray for all of you, I pray with joy, remembering how you have helped to spread the Good News from the day you first heard it right up to the present. I am quite certain that the One who began this good work in you will see that it is finished when the Day of Christ Jesus comes. God knows how much I miss you all, loving you as Christ Jesus loves you. My prayer is that your love for each other may increase more and more and never stop improving your knowledge and deepening your perception so that you can always recognise what is best. This will help you to become pure and blameless, and prepare you for the Day of Christ, when you will reach the perfect goodness which Jesus Christ produces in us for the glory and praise of God.

The word of the Lord.

Gospel Acclamation   Lk 3:4,6

R. **Alleluia, alleluia!**
Prepare a way for the Lord,
make his paths straight,
and all mankind shall see the salvation of God.
R. **Alleluia!**

GOSPEL

A reading from the holy Gospel according to Luke   3:1-6
All mankind shall see the salvation of God.

In the fifteenth year of Tiberius Caesar's reign, when Pontius Pilate was governor of Judaea, Herod tetrarch of Galilee, his brother Philip tetrarch of the lands of Ituraea and Trachonitis, Lysanias tetrarch of Abilene, during the pontificate of Annas and Caiaphas, the word of God came to John son of Zechariah, in the wilderness. He went through the whole Jordan district proclaiming a baptism of repentance for the forgiveness of sins, as it is written in the book of sayings of the prophet Isaiah:

A voice cries in the wilderness:
Prepare a way for the Lord,
make his paths straight.
Every valley will be filled in,
every mountain and hill be laid low,
winding ways will be straightened
and rough roads made smooth.
And all mankind shall see the salvation of God.

The Gospel of the Lord.

The Creed is said.

Prayer over the Offerings

Be pleased, O Lord, with our
    humble prayers and offerings,
and, since we have no merits
    to plead our cause,
come, we pray, to our rescue
with the protection of your mercy.
Through Christ our Lord.

Preface I of Advent, pp.548-549.

Communion Antiphon Ba 5:5;4:36

Jerusalem, arise and stand upon
    the heights,
and behold the joy which comes
    to you from God.

Prayer after Communion

Replenished by the food
    of spiritual nourishment,
we humbly beseech you, O Lord,
that, through our partaking
    in this mystery,
you may teach us to judge wisely
    the things of earth
and hold firm to the things
    of heaven.
Through Christ our Lord.

A formula of Solemn Blessing, pp.642-643, may be used.

Super oblata

Placare, Domine, quæsumus,
nostræ precibus humilitatis et hostiis,
et, ubi nulla suppetunt
    suffragia meritorum,
tuæ nobis indulgentiæ
    succurre præsidiis.
Per Christum Dominum nostrum.

Ant. ad communionem

Ierusalem, surge et sta in excelso,
et vide iucunditatem,
    quæ veniet tibi a Deo tuo.

Post communionem

Repleti cibo spiritalis alimoniæ,
supplices te, Domine, deprecamur,
ut, huius participatione mysterii,
doceas nos terrena
    sapienter perpendere,
et cælestibus inhærere.
Per Christum Dominum nostrum.

THIRD SUNDAY OF ADVENT (YEAR C)

The first Reading of Mass is an invitation to joy. The Prophet Zephaniah at the end of the seventh century B.C. spoke to the city of Jerusalem and its people with these words: "Sing aloud, O daughter of Zion; shout, O Israel! Rejoice and exult with all your heart, O daughter of Jerusalem...! [T]he Lord your God is in your midst" As in the times of the Prophet Zephaniah, it is particularly to those being tested and to "life's wounded and orphans of joy" that God's Word is being addressed in a special way. To transform the world, God chose a humble young girl from a village in Galilee, Mary of Nazareth, and challenged her with this greeting: "Hail, full of grace, the Lord is with you". In these words lies the secret of an authentic Christmas. God repeats them to the Church, to each one of us: Rejoice, the Lord is close!

(Pope Benedict XVI)

Entrance Antiphon   Ph 4:4-5

REJOICE in the Lord always; again I say, rejoice. Indeed, the Lord is near.

Ant. ad introitum

GAUDETE in Domino semper: iterum dico, gaudete. Dominus enim prope est.

The Gloria in excelsis (Glory to God in the highest) is not said.

Collect

O God, who see how your people
faithfully await the feast
    of the Lord's Nativity,
enable us, we pray,
to attain the joys of so great
    a salvation
and to celebrate them always
with solemn worship
    and glad rejoicing.
Through our Lord Jesus Christ,
    your Son,
who lives and reigns with you
    in the unity of the Holy Spirit,
one God, for ever and ever.

Collecta

Deus, qui conspicis populum tuum
nativitatis dominicæ festivitatem
    fideliter exspectare,
præsta, quæsumus,
ut valeamus ad tantæ salutis
    gaudia pervenire,
et ea votis sollemnibus alacri
    semper lætitia celebrare.
Per Dominum nostrum Iesum
    Christum Filium tuum,
qui tecum vivit et regnat
    in unitate Spiritus Sancti,
Deus, per omnia sæcula sæculorum.

FIRST READING

A reading from the prophet Zephaniah   3:14-18

The Lord will dance with shouts of joy for you as on a day of festival.

Shout for joy, daughter of Zion,
Israel, shout aloud!
Rejoice, exult with all your heart,
daughter of Jerusalem!
The Lord has repealed your sentence;
he has driven your enemies away.
The Lord, the king of Israel, is in your midst;
you have no more evil to fear.
When that day comes, word will come to Jerusalem:
Zion, have no fear,
do not let your hands fall limp.
The Lord your God is in your midst,
a victorious warrior.
He will exult with joy over you,
he will renew you by his love;
he will dance with shouts of joy for you
as on a day of festival.

    The word of the Lord.

Responsorial Psalm   Is 12:2-6. R. v.6

R. **Sing and shout for joy**
   for great in your midst is the Holy One of Israel.

    Truly, God is my salvation,
    I trust, I shall not fear.
    For the Lord is my strength, my song,
    he became my saviour.
    With joy you will draw water
    from the wells of salvation. R.

    Give thanks to the Lord, give praise to his name!
    Make his mighty deeds known to the peoples!
    Declare the greatness of his name. R.

    Sing a psalm to the Lord
    for he has done glorious deeds,
    make them known to all the earth!
    People of Zion, sing and shout for joy
    for great in your midst is the Holy One of Israel. R.

SECOND READING

A reading from the letter of St Paul to the Philippians   4:4-7

The Lord is very near.

I want you to be happy, always happy in the Lord; I repeat, what I want is your happiness. Let your tolerance be evident to everyone: the Lord is very near. There is no need to worry; but if there is anything you need, pray for it, asking God for it with prayer and thanksgiving, and that peace of God, which is so much greater than we can understand, will guard your hearts and your thoughts, in Christ Jesus.

The word of the Lord.

Gospel Acclamation   Is 61:1 (Lk 4:18)

R. **Alleluia, alleluia!**
The spirit of the Lord has been given to me.
He has sent me to bring good news to the poor.
R. **Alleluia!**

GOSPEL

A reading from the holy Gospel according to Luke   3:10-18

What must we do?

When all the people asked John, 'What must we do?' he answered, 'If anyone has two tunics he must share with the man who has none, and the one with something to eat must do the same.' There were tax collectors too who came for baptism, and these said to him, 'Master what must we do?' He said to them, 'Exact no more than your rate.' Some soldiers asked him in their turn, 'What about us? What must we do?' He said to them, 'No intimidation! No extortion! Be content with your pay!'

A feeling of expectancy had grown among the people, who were beginning to think that John might be the Christ, so John declared before them all, 'I baptise you with water, but someone is coming, someone who is more powerful than I am, and I am not fit to undo the strap of his sandals; he will baptise you with the Holy Spirit and fire. His winnowing-fan is in his hand to clear his threshing-floor and to gather the wheat into his barn; but the chaff he will burn in a fire that will never go out.' As well as this, there were many other things he said to exhort the people and to announce the Good News to them.

The Gospel of the Lord.

The Creed is said.

Prayer over the Offerings

May the sacrifice of our worship,
   Lord, we pray,
be offered to you unceasingly,
to complete what was begun
   in sacred mystery
and powerfully accomplish
   for us your saving work.
Through Christ our Lord.

Preface I or II of Advent, pp.548-551.

Communion Antiphon Cf. Is 35:4

Say to the faint of heart:
   Be strong and do not fear.
Behold, our God will come,
   and he will save us.

Prayer after Communion

We implore your mercy, Lord,
that this divine sustenance
   may cleanse us of our faults
and prepare us for
   the coming feasts.
Through Christ our Lord.

A formula of Solemn Blessing, pp.642-643, may be used.

Super oblata

Devotionis nostræ tibi,
   Domine, quæsumus,
hostia iugiter immoletur,
quæ et sacri peragat
   instituta mysterii
et salutare tuum nobis
   potenter operetur.
Per Christum Dominum nostrum.

Ant. ad communionem

Dicite: Pusillanimes, confortamini
   et nolite timere:
ecce Deus noster veniet
   et salvabit nos.

Post communionem

Tuam, Domine,
   clementiam imploramus,
ut hæc divina subsidia,
   a vitiis expiatos,
ad festa ventura nos præparent.
Per Christum Dominum nostrum

FOURTH SUNDAY OF ADVENT (YEAR C)

With the Fourth Sunday of Advent, the Lord's Birth is at hand. With the words of the Prophet Micah, the Liturgy invites us to look at Bethlehem, the little town in Judea that witnessed the great event. Unfortunately, in our day, it does not represent an attained and stable peace, but rather a peace sought with effort and hope. Yet God is never resigned to this state of affairs, so that this year too, in Bethlehem and throughout the world, the mystery of Christmas will be renewed in the Church. Today, as in the times of Jesus, Christmas is not a fairy-tale for children but God's response to the drama of humanity in search of true peace.

(Pope Benedict XVI)

Entrance Antiphon   Cf. Is 45:8

DROP down dew from above,
   you heavens,
and let the clouds rain down
      the Just One;
let the earth be opened
      and bring forth a Saviour.

Ant. ad introitum

RORATE, cæli, desuper,
   et nubes pluant iustum;
aperiatur terra et
      germinet Salvatorem.

The Gloria in excelsis (Glory to God in the highest) is not said.

Collect

Pour forth, we beseech you, O Lord,
your grace into our hearts,
that we, to whom the Incarnation
   of Christ your Son
was made known by
   the message of an Angel,
may by his Passion and Cross
be brought to the glory
   of his Resurrection.
Who lives and reigns with you
   in the unity of the Holy Spirit,
one God, for ever and ever.

Collecta

Gratiam tuam,
   quæsumus, Domine,
mentibus nostris infunde,
   ut qui, Angelo nuntiante,
Christi Filii tui
   incarnationem cognovimus,
per passionem eius et crucem
ad resurrectionis
   gloriam perducamur.
Qui vivis et regnas cum Deo Patre
   in unitate Spiritus Sancti,
Deus, per omnia sæcula sæculorum.

FIRST READING

A reading from the prophet Micah   5:1-4

Out of you will be born the one who is to rule over Israel.

The Lord says this:

> You, Bethlehem Ephrathah,
> the least of the clans of Judah,
> out of you will be born for me
> the one who is to rule over Israel;
> his origin goes back to the distant past,
> to the days of old.
> The Lord is therefore going to abandon them
> till the time when she who is to give birth gives birth.
> Then the remnant of his brothers will come back
> to the sons of Israel.
> He will stand and feed his flock
> with the power of the Lord,
> with the majesty of the name of his God.
> They will live secure, for from then on he will extend his power
> to the ends of the land.
> He himself will be peace.

   The word of the Lord.

Responsorial Psalm   Ps 79:2-3,15-16,18-19. R. v.4

R. **God of hosts, bring us back;**
   let your face shine on us and we shall be saved.

> O shepherd of Israel, hear us,
> shine forth from your cherubim throne.
> O Lord, rouse up your might,
> O Lord, come to our help. R.

> God of hosts, turn again, we implore,
> look down from heaven and see.
> Visit this vine and protect it,
> the vine your right hand has planted. R.

> May your hand be on the man you have chosen,
> the man you have given your strength.
> And we shall never forsake you again:
> give us life that we may call upon your name. R.

SECOND READING

A reading from the letter to the Hebrews 10:5-10

Here I am! I am coming to obey your will.

This is what Christ said, on coming into the world:

> You who wanted no sacrifice or oblation,
> prepared a body for me.
> You took no pleasure in holocausts or sacrifices for sin;
> then I said,
> just as I was commanded in the scroll of the book,
> 'God, here I am! I am coming to obey your will.'

Notice that he says first: You did not want what the Law lays down as the things to be offered, that is: the sacrifices, the oblations, the holocausts and the sacrifices for sin, and you took no pleasure in them; and then he says: Here I am! I am coming to obey your will. He is abolishing the first sort to replace it with the second. And this will was for us to be made holy by the offering of his body made once and for all by Jesus Christ.

The word of the Lord.

Gospel Acclamation Lk 1:38

R. **Alleluia, alleluia!**
I am the handmaid of the Lord:
let what you have said be done to me.
R. **Alleluia!**

GOSPEL

A reading from the holy Gospel according to Luke 1:39-45

Why should I be honoured with a visit from the mother of my Lord?

Mary set out and went as quickly as she could to a town in the hill country of Judah. She went into Zechariah's house and greeted Elizabeth. Now as soon as Elizabeth heard Mary's greeting, the child leapt in her womb and Elizabeth was filled with the Holy Spirit. She gave a loud cry and said, 'Of all women you are the most blessed, and blessed is the fruit of your womb. Why should I be honoured with a visit from the mother of my Lord? For the moment your greeting reached my ears, the child in my womb leapt for joy. Yes, blessed is she who believed that the promise made her by the Lord would be fulfilled.'

The Gospel of the Lord.

The Creed is said.

Prayer over the Offerings | Super oblata

May the Holy Spirit, O Lord,
sanctify these gifts laid upon
    your altar,
just as he filled with his power the
    womb of the Blessed Virgin Mary.
Through Christ our Lord.

Altari tuo, Domine,
    superposita munera
Spiritus ille sanctificet,
qui beatæ Mariæ viscera
    sua virtute replevit.
Per Christum Dominum nostrum.

Preface II of Advent, pp.550-551.

Communion Antiphon   Is 7:14 | Ant. ad communionem

Behold, a Virgin shall conceive
    and bear a son;
and his name will be called
    Emmanuel.

Ecce Virgo concipiet,
    et pariet filium;
et vocabitur nomen eius
    Emmanuel.

Prayer after Communion | Post communionem

Having received this pledge
    of eternal redemption,
we pray, almighty God,
that, as the feast day of our
    salvation draws ever nearer,
so we may press forward
    all the more eagerly
to the worthy celebration of the
    mystery of your Son's Nativity.
Who lives and reigns
    for ever and ever.

Sumpto pignore
    redemptionis æternæ,
quæsumus, omnipotens Deus,
ut quanto magis dies salutiferæ
    festivitatis accedit,
tanto devotius proficiamus
ad Filii tui digne nativitatis
    mysterium celebrandum.
Qui vivit et regnat
    in sæcula sæculorum.

A formula of Solemn Blessing, pp.642-643, may be used.

CHRISTMAS TIME

CHRISTMAS TIME

25 December

THE NATIVITY OF THE LORD

(YEAR A,B,C)

The Gospel from Matthew proposes to us precisely the account of Jesus's birth. However, the Evangelist introduces it with a summary of his genealogy, which he sets at the beginning as a prologue. Here the full evidence of Mary's role in salvation history stands out: Mary's being is totally relative to Christ and in particular to his Incarnation. "Jacob the father of Joseph the husband of Mary, of whom Jesus was born, who is called Christ". The lack of continuity in the layout of the genealogy immediately meets the eye; we do not read "begot" but instead: "Mary, of whom Jesus was born who is called Christ". Precisely in this we perceive the beauty of the plan of God who, respecting the human being, makes him fertile from within, causing the most beautiful fruit of his creative and redeeming work to develop in the humble Virgin of Nazareth. Then the Evangelist brings on stage the figure of Joseph, his inner drama, his robust faith and his exemplary rectitude. Behind Joseph's thoughts and deliberations is his love for God and his firm determination to obey him. But how is it possible not to feel that Joseph's distress, hence his prayers and his decision, were motivated at the same time by esteem and love for his betrothed? God's beauty and that of Mary are inseparable in Joseph's heart; he knows that there can be no contradiction between them; he seeks the answer in God and finds it in the light of the Word and of the Holy Spirit: "The Virgin shall be with child and give birth to a son, and they shall call him Emmanuel (which means, God with us)".

(Pope Benedict XVI)

Solemnity

At the Vigil Mass

This Mass is used on the evening of 24 December, either before or after First Vespers (Evening Prayer I) of the Nativity.

Entrance Antiphon Cf. Ex 16:6-7	Ant. ad introitum
TODAY you will know that the Lord will come, and he will save us, and in the morning you will see his glory.	HODIE scietis, quia veniet Dominus, et salvabit nos, et mane videbitis gloriam eius.

The Gloria in excelsis (Glory to God in the highest) is said.

Collect	Collecta

O God, who gladden us year by year as we wait in hope
    for our redemption,
grant that, just as we joyfully welcome your Only Begotten Son
    as our Redeemer,
we may also merit to face
    him confidently
when he comes again as our Judge.
Who lives and reigns with you
    in the unity of the Holy Spirit,
one God, for ever and ever.
	Deus, qui nos redemptionis nostræ annua exspectatione lætificas,
	præsta, ut Unigenitum tuum,
	quem læti suscipimus Redemptorem,
	venientem quoque Iudicem securi
	    videre mereamur,
	Dominum nostrum,
	    Iesum Christum.
	Qui tecum vivit et regnat
	    in unitate Spiritus Sancti,
	Deus, per omnia sæcula sæculorum.

FIRST READING

A reading from the prophet Isaiah   62:1-5

The Lord takes delight in you.

About Zion I will not be silent,
about Jerusalem I will not grow weary,
until her integrity shines out like the dawn
and her salvation flames like a torch.
The nations then will see your integrity,
all the kings your glory,
and you will be called by a new name,
one which the mouth of the Lord will confer.
You are to be a crown of splendour in the hand of the Lord,
a princely diadem in the hand of your God;
no longer are you to be named 'Forsaken'
nor your land 'Abandoned',
but you shall be called 'My Delight'
and your land 'The Wedded';
for the Lord takes delight in you
and your land will have its wedding.
Like a young man marrying a virgin,
so will the one who built you wed you,
and as the bridegroom rejoices in his bride,
so will your God rejoice in you.

    The word of the Lord.

Responsorial Psalm   Ps 88:4-5,16-17,27,29. R. Cf. v.2

R. **I will sing for ever of your love, O Lord.**

'I have made a covenant with my chosen one;
I have sworn to David my servant:
I will establish your dynasty for ever
and set up your throne through all ages.' R.

Happy the people who acclaim such a king,
who walk, O Lord, in the light of your face,
who find their joy every day in your name,
who make your justice the source of their bliss. R.

'He will say to me: "You are my father,
my God, the rock who saves me."
I will keep my love for him always;
for him my covenant shall endure. R.

SECOND READING

A reading from the Acts of the Apostles   13:16-17,22-25

Paul's witness to Christ, the son of David.

When Paul reached Antioch in Pisidia, he stood up in the synagogue, held
up a hand for silence and began to speak:

'Men of Israel, and fearers of God, listen! The God of our nation Israel
chose our ancestors, and made our people great when they were living as
foreigners in Egypt; then by divine power he led them out.

'Then he made David their king, of whom he approved in these words,
"I have selected David son of Jesse, a man after my own heart, who will
carry out my whole purpose." To keep his promise, God has raised up for
Israel one of David's descendants, Jesus, as Saviour, whose coming was
heralded by John when he proclaimed a baptism of repentance for the
whole people of Israel. Before John ended his career he said, "I am not the
one you imagine me to be; that one is coming after me and I am not fit to
undo his sandal."'

The word of the Lord.

Gospel Acclamation

R. **Alleluia, alleluia!**
Tomorrow there will be an end to the sin of the world
and the saviour of the world will be our king.
R. **Alleluia!**

GOSPEL

A reading from the holy Gospel according to Matthew   1:1-25
The ancestry of Jesus Christ, the son of David.

A genealogy of Jesus Christ, the son of David, son of Abraham:

Abraham was the father of Isaac,
Isaac the father of Jacob,
Jacob the father of Judah and his brothers,
Judah the father of Perez and Zerah, Tamar being their mother,
Perez the father of Hezron,
Hezron the father of Ram,
Ram the father of Amminadab,
Amminadab the father of Nahshon,
Nahshon the father of Salmon,
Salmon was the father of Boaz, Rahab being his mother,
Boaz the father of Obed, Ruth being his mother,
Obed was the father of Jesse;
and Jesse was the father of King David.

David was the father of Solomon, whose mother had been Uriah's wife,
Solomon was the father of Rehoboam,
Rehoboam the father of Abijah,
Abijah the father of Asa,
Asa was the father of Jehoshaphat,
Jehoshaphat the father of Joram,
Joram the father of Azariah,
Azariah was the father of Jotham,
Jotham the father of Ahaz,
Ahaz the father of Hezekiah,
Hezekiah was the father of Manasseh,
Manasseh the father of Amon,
Amon the father of Josiah;
and Josiah was the father of Jechoniah and his brothers.
Then the deportation to Babylon took place.

After the deportation to Babylon:
Jechoniah was the father of Shealtiel,
Shealtiel the father of Zerubbabel,
Zerubbabel was the father of Abiud,
Abiud the father of Eliakim,
Eliakim the father of Azor,
Azor was the father of Zadok,
Zadok the father of Achim,

Achim the father of Eliud,
Eliud was the father of Eleazar,
Eleazar the father of Matthan,
Matthan the father of Jacob,
and Jacob was the father of Joseph the husband of Mary; of her was born
Jesus who is called Christ.

The sum of generations is therefore: fourteen from Abraham to David;
fourteen from David to the Babylonian deportation; and fourteen from
the Babylonian deportation to Christ.

[This is how Jesus Christ came to be born. His mother Mary was
betrothed to Joseph; but before they came to live together she was found
to be with child through the Holy Spirit. Her husband Joseph, being a
man of honour and wanting to spare her publicity, decided to divorce her
informally. He had made up his mind to do this when the angel of the Lord
appeared to him in a dream and said, 'Joseph son of David, do not be afraid
to take Mary home as your wife, because she has conceived what is in her by
the Holy Spirit. She will give birth to a son and you must name him Jesus,
because he is the one who is to save his people from their sins.' Now all this
took place to fulfil the words spoken by the Lord through the prophet:

The Virgin will conceive and give birth to a son
and they will call him Emmanuel,

a name which means 'God-is-with-us'. When Joseph woke up he did what
the angel of the Lord had told him to do: he took his wife to his home and,
though he had not had intercourse with her, she gave birth to a son; and
he named him Jesus.

The Gospel of the Lord.]

Shorter Form, verses 18-25. Read between [ ]

The Creed is said.
All kneel at the words **and by the Holy Spirit was incarnate**.

Prayer over the Offerings | Super oblata

As we look forward, O Lord,
to the coming festivities,
may we serve you
    all the more eagerly
for knowing that in them
you make manifest the beginnings
    of our redemption.
Through Christ our Lord.

Tanto nos, Domine, quæsumus,
promptiore servitio hæc præcurrere
    concede sollemnia,
quanto in his constare principium
nostræ redemptionis ostendis.
Per Christum Dominum nostrum.

Preface I, II or III of the Nativity of the Lord, pp.550-553.

Communion Antiphon Cf. Is 40:5	Ant. ad communionem
The glory of the Lord will be revealed, and all flesh will see the salvation of our God.	Revelabitur gloria Domini, et videbit omnis caro salutare Dei nostri.

Prayer after Communion	Post communionem
Grant, O Lord, we pray, that we may draw new vigour from celebrating the Nativity of your Only Begotten Son, by whose heavenly mystery we receive both food and drink. Who lives and reigns for ever and ever.	Da nobis, quæsumus, Domine, Unigeniti Filii tui recensita nativitate vegetari, cuius cælesti mysterio pascimur et potamur. Qui vivit et regnat in sæcula sæculorum.

A formula of Solemn Blessing, pp.642-645, may be used.

At the Mass during the Night

God's sign is simplicity. God's sign is the baby. God's sign is that he makes himself small for us. This is how he reigns. He does not come with power and outward splendour. He comes as a baby – defenceless and in need of our help. He does not want to overwhelm us with his strength. He takes away our fear of his greatness. He asks for our love: so he makes himself a child. He wants nothing other from us than our love, through which we spontaneously learn to enter into his feelings, his thoughts and his will – we learn to live with him and to practise with him that humility of renunciation that belongs to the very essence of love. God made himself small so that we could understand him, welcome him, and love him.

(Pope Benedict XVI)

On the Nativity of the Lord all Priests may celebrate or concelebrate three Masses, provided the Masses are celebrated at their proper times.

Entrance Antiphon Ps 2:7	Ant. ad introitum
THE Lord said to me: You are my Son. It is I who have begotten you this day.	DOMINUS dixit ad me: Filius meus es tu, ego hodie genui te.

Or:

Let us all rejoice in the Lord,
   for our Saviour has been born
   in the world.
Today true peace has come down
   to us from heaven.

Vel:

Gaudeamus omnes in Domino,
quia Salvator noster natus
   est in mundo.
Hodie nobis de cælo pax
   vera descendit.

The Gloria in excelsis (Glory to God in the highest) is said.

Collect

O God, who have made
   this most sacred night
radiant with the splendour
   of the true light,
grant, we pray, that we,
   who have known the mysteries
   of his light on earth,
may also delight in his gladness
   in heaven.
Who lives and reigns with you
   in the unity of the Holy Spirit,
one God, for ever and ever.

Collecta

Deus, qui hanc sacratissimam
   noctem
veri luminis fecisti
   illustratione clarescere,
da, quæsumus, ut, cuius in terra
   mysteria lucis agnovimus,
eius quoque gaudiis perfruamur
   in cælo.
Qui tecum vivit et regnat
   in unitate Spiritus Sancti,
Deus, per omnia sæcula sæculorum.

FIRST READING

A reading from the prophet Isaiah   9:1-7
A Son is given to us.

The people that walked in darkness
has seen a great light;
on those who live in a land of deep shadow
a light has shone.
You have made their gladness greater,
you have made their joy increase;
they rejoice in your presence
as men rejoice at harvest time,
as men are happy when they are dividing the spoils.
For the yoke that was weighing on him,
the bar across his shoulders,
the rod of his oppressor,
these you break as on the day of Midian.

For all the footgear of battle,
every cloak rolled in blood,
is burnt,
and consumed by fire.
For there is a child born for us,
a son given to us
and dominion is laid on his shoulders;
and this is the name they give him:
Wonder-Counsellor, Mighty-God,
Eternal-Father, Prince-of-Peace.
Wide is his dominion
in a peace that has no end,
for the throne of David
and for his royal power,
which he establishes and makes secure
in justice and integrity.
From this time onwards and for ever,
the jealous love of the Lord of hosts will do this.

   The word of the Lord.

Responsorial Psalm   Ps 95:1-3,11-13. R. Lk 2:11

R. **Today a saviour has been born to us;**
   he is Christ the Lord.

   O sing a new song to the Lord,
   sing to the Lord all the earth.
   O sing to the Lord, bless his name. R.

   Proclaim his help day by day,
   tell among the nations his glory
   and his wonders among all the peoples. R.

   Let the heavens rejoice and earth be glad,
   let the sea and all within it thunder praise,
   let the land and all it bears rejoice,
   all the trees of the wood shout for joy
   at the presence of the Lord for he comes,
   he comes to rule the earth. R.

   With justice he will rule the world,
   he will judge the peoples with his truth. R.

SECOND READING

A reading from the letter of St Paul to Titus   2:11-14

God's grace has been revealed to the whole human race.

God's grace has been revealed, and it has made salvation possible for the whole human race and taught us that what we have to do is to give up everything that does not lead to God, and all our worldly ambitions; we must be self-restrained and live good and religious lives here in this present world, while we are waiting in hope for the blessing which will come with the Appearing of the glory of our great God and saviour Christ Jesus. He sacrificed himself for us in order to set us free from all wickedness and to purify a people so that it could be his very own and would have no ambition except to do good.

The word of the Lord.

Gospel Acclamation   Lk 2:10-11

R. **Alleluia, alleluia!**
I bring you news of great joy:
today a saviour has been born to us, Christ the Lord.
R. **Alleluia!**

GOSPEL

A reading from the holy Gospel according to Luke   2:1-14

Today a saviour has been born to you.

Caesar Augustus issued a decree for a census of the whole world to be taken. This census – the first – took place while Quirinius was governor of Syria, and everyone went to his own town to be registered. So Joseph set out from the town of Nazareth in Galilee and travelled up to Judaea, to the town of David called Bethlehem, since he was of David's House and line, in order to be registered together with Mary, his betrothed, who was with child. While they were there the time came for her to have her child, and she gave birth to a son, her first-born. She wrapped him in swaddling clothes, and laid him in a manger because there was no room for them at the inn. In the countryside close by there were shepherds who lived in the fields and took it in turns to watch their flocks during the night. The angel of the Lord appeared to them and the glory of the Lord shone round them. They were terrified, but the angel said, 'Do not be afraid. Listen, I bring you news of great joy, a joy to be shared by the whole people. Today in the town of David a saviour has been born to you; he is Christ the Lord. And here is a sign for you: you will find a baby wrapped in swaddling clothes and lying in a manger.' And suddenly with the angel there was a great throng of the heavenly host, praising God and singing:

'Glory to God in the highest heaven,
    and peace to men who enjoy his favour'.

The Gospel of the Lord.

The Creed is said. All kneel at the words and by the Holy Spirit was incarnate.

Prayer over the Offerings | Super oblata

May the oblation of this day's feast
be pleasing to you, O Lord, we pray,
that through this most holy exchange
we may be found in the likeness
    of Christ,
in whom our nature is united to you.
Who lives and reigns
    for ever and ever.

Grata tibi sit, Domine, quæsumus,
hodiernæ festivitatis oblatio,
ut, per hæc sacrosancta commercia,
in illius inveniamur forma,
in quo tecum est nostra substantia.
Qui vivit et regnat
    in sæcula sæculorum.

Preface I, II or III of the Nativity of the Lord, pp.550-553.

Communion Antiphon   Jn 1:14 | Ant. ad communionem

The Word became flesh,
    and we have seen his glory.

Verbum caro factum est,
    et vidimus gloriam eius.

Prayer after Communion | Post communionem

Grant us, we pray, O Lord our God,
that we, who are gladdened
    by participation
in the feast of
    our Redeemer's Nativity,
may through an honourable way
    of life become worthy of union
    with him.
Who lives and reigns
    for ever and ever.

Da nobis, quæsumus,
    Domine Deus noster,
ut, qui nativitatem
    Redemptoris nostri
frequentare gaudemus,
dignis conversationibus
ad eius mereamur
    pervenire consortium.
Per Christum Dominum nostrum.

A formula of Solemn Blessing, pp.642-645, may be used.

At the Mass at Dawn

The shepherds, the simple souls, were the first to come to Jesus in the manger and to encounter the Redeemer of the world. The wise men from the East, representing those with social standing and fame, arrived much later. The shepherds lived nearby. They only needed to "come over", as we do when we go to visit our neighbours. The wise men, however, lived far away. They had to undertake a long and arduous journey in order to arrive in Bethlehem. And they needed guidance and direction. Today too there are simple and lowly souls who live very close to the Lord. They are, so to speak, his neighbours and they can easily go to see him. But most of us in the world today live far from Jesus Christ, the incarnate God who came to dwell amongst us. In all kinds of ways, God has to prod us and reach out to us again and again, so that we can manage to escape from the muddle of our thoughts and activities and discover the way that leads to him. But a path exists for all of us. The Lord provides everyone with tailor-made signals.

(Pope Benedict XVI)

Entrance Antiphon Cf. Is 9:1,5; Lk 1:33

TODAY a light will shine upon us,
for the Lord is born for us;
and he will be called Wondrous God,
Prince of peace, Father of future ages:
and his reign will be without end.

Ant. ad introitum

LUX fulgebit hodie super nos,
quia natus est nobis Dominus;
et vocabitur admirabilis, Deus,
    Princeps pacis,
Pater futuri sæculi:
    cuius regni non erit finis.

The Gloria in excelsis (Glory to God in the highest) is said.

Collect

Grant, we pray, almighty God,
that, as we are bathed in the new
    radiance of your incarnate Word,
the light of faith, which illumines
    our minds,
may also shine through in our deeds.
Through our Lord Jesus Christ,
    your Son,
who lives and reigns with you
    in the unity of the Holy Spirit,
one God, for ever and ever.

Collecta

Da, quæsumus, omnipotens Deus,
ut dum nova incarnati Verbi
    tui luce perfundimur,
hoc in nostro resplendeat opere,
quod per fidem fulget in mente.
Per Dominum nostrum Iesum
    Christum Filium tuum,
qui tecum vivit et regnat
    in unitate Spiritus Sancti,
Deus, per omnia sæcula sæculorum.

FIRST READING

A reading from the prophet Isaiah   62:11-12

Look, your saviour comes.

This the Lord proclaims
to the ends of the earth:

> Say to the daughter of Zion, 'Look,
> your saviour comes,
> the prize of his victory with him,
> his trophies before him.'
> They shall be called 'The Holy People',
> 'The Lord's Redeemed'.
> And you shall be called 'The-sought-after',
> 'City-not-forsaken'.

The word of the Lord.

Responsorial Psalm   Ps 96:1,6,11-12

R. **This day new light will shine upon the earth:**
   the Lord is born for us.

The Lord is king, let earth rejoice,
the many coastlands be glad.
The skies proclaim his justice;
all peoples see his glory. R.

Light shines forth for the just
and joy for the upright of heart.
Rejoice, you just, in the Lord;
give glory to his holy name. R.

SECOND READING

A reading from the letter of St Paul to Titus   3:4-7

It was for no reason except his own compassion that he saved us.

When the kindness and love of God our saviour for mankind were revealed,
it was not because he was concerned with any righteous actions we might
have done ourselves; it was for no reason except his own compassion that
he saved us, by means of the cleansing water of rebirth and by renewing
us with the Holy Spirit which he has so generously poured over us through
Jesus Christ our saviour. He did this so that we should be justified by his
grace, to become heirs looking forward to inheriting eternal life.

The word of the Lord.

Gospel Acclamation   Lk 2:14

R. **Alleluia, alleluia!**
Glory to God in the highest heaven,
and peace to men who enjoy his favour.
R. **Alleluia!**

GOSPEL

A reading from the holy Gospel according to Luke   2:15-20
The shepherds found Mary and Joseph and the baby.

Now when the angels had gone from them into heaven, the shepherds
said to one another, 'Let us go to Bethlehem and see this thing that has
happened which the Lord has made known to us.' So they hurried away
and found Mary and Joseph, and the baby lying in the manger. When
they saw the child they repeated what they had been told about him, and
everyone who heard it was astonished at what the shepherds had to say. As
for Mary, she treasured all these things and pondered them in her heart.
And the shepherds went back glorifying and praising God for all they had
heard and seen; it was exactly as they had been told.

The Gospel of the Lord.

The Creed is said. All kneel at the words and by the Holy Spirit was incarnate.

Prayer over the Offerings	Super oblata
May our offerings be worthy, we pray, O Lord, of the mysteries of the Nativity this day, that, just as Christ was born a man and also shone forth as God, so these earthly gifts may confer on us what is divine. Through Christ our Lord.	Munera nostra, quæsumus, Domine, nativitatis hodiernæ mysteriis apta proveniant, ut sicut homo genitus idem præfulsit et Deus, sic nobis hæc terrena substantia conferat quod divinum est. Per Christum Dominum nostrum.

Preface I, II or III of the Nativity of the Lord, pp.550-553.

Communion Antiphon Cf. Zc 9:9	Ant. ad communionem
Rejoice, O Daughter Sion; lift up praise, Daughter Jerusalem: Behold, your King will come, the Holy One and Saviour of the world.	Exsulta, filia Sion, lauda, filia Ierusalem: ecce Rex tuus veniet sanctus et salvator mundi.

Prayer after Communion	Post communionem

Grant us, Lord, as we honour
    with joyful devotion
the Nativity of your Son,
that we may come to know
    with fullness of faith
the hidden depths of this mystery
and to love them
    ever more and more.
Through Christ our Lord.
	Da nobis, Domine,
	    Filii tui nativitatem
	læta devotione colentibus,
	huius arcana mysterii
	    et plena fide cognoscere,
	et pleniore caritatis ardore diligere.
	Per Christum Dominum nostrum.

A formula of Solemn Blessing, pp.642-645, may be used.

At the Mass during the Day

Saint John, in his Gospel, went to the heart of the matter: "He came to his own home, and his own people received him not". This refers first and foremost to Bethlehem: the Son of David comes to his own city, but has to be born in a stable, because there is no room for him at the inn. Then it refers to Israel: the one who is sent comes among his own, but they do not want him. And truly, it refers to all mankind: he through whom the world was made, the primordial Creator-Word, enters into the world, but he is not listened to, he is not received. These words refer ultimately to us, to each individual and to society as a whole. Do we have time for our neighbour who is in need of a word from us, from me, or in need of my affection? Do we have time and space for God? Can he enter into our lives? Does he find room in us, or have we occupied all the available space in our thoughts, our actions, our lives for ourselves?

(Pope Benedict XVI)

Entrance Antiphon Cf. Is 9:5	Ant. ad introitum

A CHILD is born for us,
  and a son is given to us;
 his sceptre of power rests
    upon his shoulder,
and his name will be called
    Messenger of great counsel.
	P UER natus est nobis,
	  et filius datus est nobis,
	cuius imperium super
	    humerum eius,
	et vocabitur nomen eius magni
	    consilii Angelus.

The Gloria in excelsis (Glory to God in the highest) is said.

Collect	Collecta
O God, who wonderfully created the dignity of human nature and still more wonderfully restored it, grant, we pray, that we may share in the divinity of Christ, who humbled himself to share in our humanity. Who lives and reigns with you in the unity of the Holy Spirit, one God, for ever and ever.	Deus, qui humanæ substantiæ dignitatem et mirabiliter condidisti, et mirabilius reformasti, da, quæsumus, nobis eius divinitatis esse consortes, qui humanitatis nostræ fieri dignatus est particeps. Qui tecum vivit et regnat in unitate Spiritus Sancti, Deus, per omnia sæcula sæculorum.

FIRST READING

A reading from the prophet Isaiah   52:7-10

All the ends of the earth shall see the salvation of our God.

How beautiful on the mountains,
are the feet of one who brings good news,
who heralds peace, brings happiness,
proclaims salvation,
and tells Zion,
'Your God is king!'
Listen! Your watchmen raise their voices,
they shout for joy together,
for they see the Lord face to face,
as he returns to Zion.
Break into shouts of joy together,
you ruins of Jerusalem;
for the Lord is consoling his people,
redeeming Jerusalem.
The Lord bares his holy arm
in the sight of all the nations,
and all the ends of the earth shall see
the salvation of our God.

The word of the Lord.

Responsorial Psalm   Ps 97:1-6. R. v.3

R. **All the ends of the earth have seen the salvation of our God.**

Sing a new song to the Lord
for he has worked wonders.

His right hand and his holy arm
have brought salvation. R.

The Lord has made known his salvation;
has shown his justice to the nations.
He has remembered his truth and love
for the house of Israel. R.

All the ends of the earth have seen
the salvation of our God.
Shout to the Lord all the earth,
ring out your joy. R.

Sing psalms to the Lord with the harp,
with the sound of music.
With trumpets and the sound of the horn
acclaim the King, the Lord. R.

R. **All the ends of the earth have seen
the salvation of our God.**

SECOND READING

A reading from the letter to the Hebrews   1:1-6
God has spoken to us through his Son.

At various times in the past and in various different ways, God spoke to
our ancestors through the prophets; but in our own time, the last days, he
has spoken to us through his Son, the Son that he has appointed to inherit
everything and through whom he made everything there is. He is the
radiant light of God's glory and the perfect copy of his nature, sustaining
the universe by his powerful command; and now that he has destroyed the
defilement of sin, he has gone to take his place in heaven at the right hand
of divine Majesty. So he is now as far above the angels as the title which he
has inherited is higher than their own name.

   God has never said to any angel: You are my Son, today I have become
your father; or: I will be a father to him and he a son to me. Again, when
he brings the First-born into the world, he says: Let all the angels of God
worship him.

   The word of the Lord.

Gospel Acclamation.

R. **Alleluia, alleluia!**
A hallowed day has dawned upon us.
Come, you nations, worship the Lord,
for today a great light has shone down upon the earth.
R. **Alleluia!**

GOSPEL
A reading from the holy Gospel according to John   1:1-18
The Word was made flesh, and lived among us.

[In the beginning was the Word:
the Word was with God
and the Word was God.
He was with God in the beginning.
Through him all things came to be,
not one thing had its being but through him.
All that came to be had life in him
and that life was the light of men,
a light that shines in the dark,
a light that darkness could not overpower.]

A man came, sent by God.
His name was John.
He came as a witness,
as a witness to speak for the light,
so that everyone might believe through him.
He was not the light,
only a witness to speak for the light.

[The Word was the true light
that enlightens all men;
and he was coming into the world.
He was in the world
that had its being through him,
and the world did not know him.
He came to his own domain
and his own people did not accept him.
But to all who did accept him
he gave power to become children of God,
to all who believe in the name of him
who was born not out of human stock
or urge of the flesh
or will of man
but of God himself.
The Word was made flesh,
he lived among us,
and we saw his glory,
the glory that is his as the only Son of the Father,
full of grace and truth.]

John appears as his witness. He proclaims:
'This is the one of whom I said:
He who comes after me
ranks before me
because he existed before me.'

Indeed, from his fullness we have, all of us, received –
yes, grace in return for grace,
since, though the Law was given through Moses,
grace and truth have come through Jesus Christ.
No one has ever seen God,
it is the only Son, who is nearest to the Father's heart,
who has made him known.

| [The Gospel of the Lord.]

Shorter Form, verses 1-5,9-14. Read between []
The Creed is said. All kneel at the words and by the Holy Spirit was incarnate.

Prayer over the Offerings	Super oblata
Make acceptable, O Lord, our oblation on this solemn day, when you manifested the reconciliation that makes us wholly pleasing in your sight and inaugurated for us the fullness of divine worship. Through Christ our Lord.	Oblatio tibi sit, Domine, hodiernæ sollemnitatis accepta, qua et nostræ reconciliationis processit perfecta placatio, et divini cultus nobis est indita plenitudo. Per Christum Dominum nostrum.

Preface I, II or III of the Nativity of the Lord, pp.550-553.

Communion Antiphon Cf. Ps 97:3	Ant. ad communionem
All the ends of the earth have seen the salvation of our God.	Viderunt omnes fines terræ salutare Dei nostri.

Prayer after Communion	Post communionem
Grant, O merciful God, that, just as the Saviour of the world, born this day, is the author of divine generation for us, so he may be the giver even of immortality. Who lives and reigns for ever and ever.	Præsta, misericors Deus, ut natus hodie Salvator mundi, sicut divinæ nobis generationis est auctor, ita et immortalitatis sit ipse largitor. Qui vivit et regnat in sæcula sæculorum.

A formula of Solemn Blessing, pp.642-645, may be used.

The Sunday within the Octave of the Nativity of the Lord,
or, if there is no Sunday, 30 December.

THE HOLY FAMILY OF JESUS, MARY AND JOSEPH

*If we aspire to a deeper understanding of Jesus's life and mission, we must
draw close to the mystery of the Holy Family of Nazareth to observe and listen.
Today's liturgy offers us a providential opportunity to do so. For every believer,
and especially for Christian families, the humble dwelling place in Nazareth
is an authentic school of the Gospel. Here we admire, put into practice, the
divine plan to make the family an intimate community of life and love; here
we learn that every Christian family is called to be a small "domestic church"
that must shine with the Gospel virtues. Recollection and prayer, mutual
understanding and respect, personal discipline and community asceticism
and a spirit of sacrifice, work and solidarity are typical features that make the
family of Nazareth a model for every home.*

(Blessed Pope John Paul II)

(YEAR A)

Feast

Entrance Antiphon Lk 2:16	Ant. ad introitum
THE shepherds went in haste, and found Mary and Joseph and the Infant lying in a manger.	VENERUNT pastores festinantes, et invenerunt Mariam et Ioseph et Infantem positum in præsepio.

The Gloria in excelsis (Glory to God in the highest) is said.

Collect	Collecta
O God, who were pleased to give us the shining example of the Holy Family, graciously grant that we may imitate them in practising the virtues of family life and in the bonds of charity, and so, in the joy of your house, delight one day in eternal rewards. Through our Lord Jesus Christ, your Son, who lives and reigns with you in the unity of the Holy Spirit, one God, for ever and ever.	Deus, qui præclara nobis sanctæ Familiæ dignatus es exempla præbere, concede propitius, ut, domesticis virtutibus caritatisque vinculis illam sectantes, in lætitia domus tuæ præmiis fruamur æternis. Per Dominum nostrum Iesum Christum Filium tuum, qui tecum vivit et regnat in unitate Spiritus Sancti, Deus, per omnia sæcula sæculorum.

FIRST READING

A reading from the book of Ecclesiasticus   3:3-7,14-17

He who fears the Lord respects his parents.

The Lord honours the father in his children,
and upholds the rights of a mother over her sons.
Whoever respects his father is atoning for his sins,
he who honours his mother is like someone amassing a fortune.
Whoever respects his father will be happy with children of his own,
he shall be heard on the day when he prays.
Long life comes to him who honours his father,
he who sets his mother at ease is showing obedience to the Lord.
My son, support your father in his old age,
do not grieve him during his life.
Even if his mind should fail, show him sympathy,
do not despise him in your health and strength;
for kindness to a father shall not be forgotten
but will serve as reparation for your sins.

   The word of the Lord.

Responsorial Psalm   Ps 127:1-5. R. Cf. v.1

R. **O blessed are those who fear the Lord**
   and walk in his ways!

   O blessed are those who fear the Lord
   and walk in his ways!
   By the labour of your hands you shall eat.
   You will be happy and prosper. R.

   Your wife like a fruitful vine
   in the heart of your house;
   your children like shoots of the olive,
   around your table. R.

   Indeed thus shall be blessed
   the man who fears the Lord.
   May the Lord bless you from Zion
   all the days of your life. R.

SECOND READING .

A reading from the letter of St Paul to the Colossians   3:12-21

Family life in the Lord.

You are God's chosen race, his saints; he loves you, and you should be clothed in sincere compassion, in kindness and humility, gentleness and patience. Bear with one another; forgive each other as soon as a quarrel begins. The Lord has forgiven you; now you must do the same. Over all these clothes, to keep them together and complete them, put on love. And may the peace of Christ reign in your hearts, because it is for this that you were called together as parts of one body. Always be thankful.

Let the message of Christ, in all its richness, find a home with you. Teach each other, and advise each other, in all wisdom. With gratitude in your hearts sing psalms and hymns and inspired songs to God; and never say or do anything except in the name of the Lord Jesus, giving thanks to God the Father through him.

Wives, give way to your husbands, as you should in the Lord. Husbands, love your wives and treat them with gentleness. Children, be obedient to your parents always, because that is what will please the Lord. Parents, never drive your children to resentment or you will make them feel frustrated.

The word of the Lord.

Gospel Acclamation   Col 3:15,16

R. **Alleluia, alleluia!**
May the peace of Christ reign in your hearts;
let the message of Christ find a home with you.
R. **Alleluia!**

GOSPEL

A reading from the holy Gospel according to Matthew   2:13-15,19-23

Take the child and his mother and escape into Egypt.

After the wise men had left, the angel of the Lord appeared to Joseph in a dream and said, 'Get up, take the child and his mother with you, and escape into Egypt, and stay there until I tell you, because Herod intends to search for the child and do away with him.' So Joseph got up and, taking the child and his mother with him, left that night for Egypt, where he stayed until Herod was dead. This was to fulfil what the Lord had spoken through the prophet:

I called my son out of Egypt.

After Herod's death, the angel of the Lord appeared in a dream to Joseph in Egypt and said, 'Get up, take the child and his mother with you and go back to the land of Israel, for those who wanted to kill the child are dead.' So Joseph got up and, taking the child and his mother with him, went back to the land of Israel. But when he learnt that Archelaus had succeeded his father Herod as ruler of Judaea he was afraid to go there, and being warned in a dream he left for the region of Galilee. There he settled in a town called Nazareth. In this way the words spoken through the prophets were to be fulfilled:

He will be called a Nazarene.

The Gospel of the Lord.

When this feast is celebrated on Sunday, the Creed is said.

When this feast is not celebrated on Sunday, there is only one reading before the Gospel.

Prayer over the Offerings	Super oblata

We offer you, Lord,
    the sacrifice of conciliation,
humbly asking that,
through the intercession
    of the Virgin Mother of God
    and Saint Joseph,
you may establish our families firmly
    in your grace and your peace.
Through Christ our Lord.
	Hostiam tibi placationis offerimus,
	    Domine,
	suppliciter deprecantes,
	ut, Deiparæ Virginis beatique
	    Ioseph interveniente suffragio,
	familias nostras in tua gratia
	    firmiter et pace constituas.
	Per Christum Dominum nostrum.

Preface I, II or III of the Nativity of the Lord, pp.550-553.

Communion Antiphon Ba 3:38	Ant. ad communionem
Our God has appeared on the earth, and lived among us.	Deus noster in terris visus est, et cum hominibus conversatus est.

Prayer after Communion	Post communionem

Bring those you refresh
    with this heavenly Sacrament,
most merciful Father,
to imitate constantly the example
    of the Holy Family,
so that, after the trials of this world,
we may share their company for ever.
Through Christ our Lord.
	Quos cælestibus reficis sacramentis,
	fac, clementissime Pater,
	sanctæ Familiæ exempla
	    iugiter imitari,
	ut, post ærumnas sæculi,
	eius consortium
	    consequamur æternum.
	Per Christum Dominum nostrum.

THE HOLY FAMILY OF JESUS, MARY AND JOSEPH
(YEAR B)

Feast

Entrance Antiphon Lk 2:16	Ant. ad introitum
THE shepherds went in haste, and found Mary and Joseph and the Infant lying in a manger.	VENERUNT pastores festinantes, et invenerunt Mariam et Ioseph et Infantem positum in præsepio.

The Gloria in excelsis (Glory to God in the highest) is said.

Collect	Collecta
O God, who were pleased to give us the shining example of the Holy Family, graciously grant that we may imitate them in practising the virtues of family life and in the bonds of charity, and so, in the joy of your house, delight one day in eternal rewards. Through our Lord Jesus Christ, your Son, who lives and reigns with you in the unity of the Holy Spirit, one God, for ever and ever.	Deus, qui præclara nobis sanctæ Familiæ dignatus es exempla præbere, concede propitius, ut, domesticis virtutibus caritatisque vinculis illam sectantes, in lætitia domus tuæ præmiis fruamur æternis. Per Dominum nostrum Iesum Christum Filium tuum, qui tecum vivit et regnat in unitate Spiritus Sancti, Deus, per omnia sæcula sæculorum.

FIRST READING

A reading from the book of Genesis   15:1-6,21:1-3

Your heir shall be your own flesh and blood.

The word of the Lord was spoken to Abram in a vision, 'Have no fear, Abram, I am your shield; your reward will be very great.'

'My Lord,' Abram replied 'what do you intend to give me? I go childless...' Then Abram said, 'See, you have given me no descendants; some man of my household will be my heir.' And then this word of the Lord was spoken to him, 'He shall not be your heir; your heir shall be of your own flesh and blood.' Then taking him outside he said, 'Look up to heaven and count the stars if you can. Such will be your descendants' he told him. Abram put his faith in the Lord, who counted this as making him justified.

The Lord dealt kindly with Sarah as he had said, and did what he had promised her. So Sarah conceived and bore a son to Abraham in his old age, at the time God had promised. Abraham named the son born to him Isaac, the son to whom Sarah had given birth.

The word of the Lord.

Responsorial Psalm   Ps 104:1-6,8-9. R. vv.7-8

R. **He, the Lord, is our God.**
   He remembers his covenant for ever.

Give thanks to the Lord, tell his name,
make known his deeds among the peoples.
O sing to him, sing his praise;
tell all his wonderful works! R.

Be proud of his holy name,
let the hearts that seek the Lord rejoice.
Consider the Lord and his strength;
constantly seek his face. R.

Remember the wonders he has done,
his miracles, the judgements he spoke.
O children of Abraham, his servant,
O sons of the Jacob he chose. R.

He remembers his covenant for ever,
his promise for a thousand generations,
the covenant he made with Abraham,
the oath he swore to Isaac. R.

SECOND READING

A reading from the letter to the Hebrews   11:8,11-12,17-19
The faith of Abraham, Sarah and Isaac.

It was by faith that Abraham obeyed the call to set out for a country that was the inheritance given to him and his descendants, and that he set out without knowing where he was going.

It was equally by faith that Sarah, in spite of being past the age, was made able to conceive, because she believed that he who had made the promise would be faithful to it. Because of this, there came from one man, and one who was already as good as dead himself, more descendants than could be counted, as many as the stars of heaven or the grains of sand on the seashore.

It was by faith that Abraham, when put to the test, offered up Isaac. He offered to sacrifice his only son even though the promises had been made to him and he had been told: It is through Isaac that your name will be carried on. He was confident that God had the power even to raise the dead; and so, figuratively speaking, he was given back Isaac from the dead.

The word of the Lord.

Gospel Acclamation   Heb 1:1-2
R. **Alleluia, alleluia!**
At various times in the past
and in various different ways,
God spoke to our ancestors through the prophets;
but in our own time, the last days,
he has spoken to us through his Son.
R. **Alleluia!**

GOSPEL

A reading from the holy Gospel according to Luke   2:22-40
The child grew, filled with wisdom.

[When the day came for them to be purified as laid down by the Law of Moses, the parents of Jesus took him up to Jerusalem to present him to the Lord] – observing what stands written in the law of the Lord: Every first-born male must be consecrated to the Lord – and also to offer in sacrifice, in accordance with what is said in the Law of the Lord, a pair of turtledoves or two young pigeons. Now in Jerusalem there was a man named Simeon. He was an upright and devout man; he looked forward to Israel's comforting and the Holy Spirit rested on him. It had been revealed to him by the Holy Spirit that he would not see death until he had set eyes on the Christ of the Lord. Prompted by the Spirit he came to the Temple, and when the parents brought in the child Jesus to do for him what the Law required, he took him into his arms and blessed God; and he said:

'Now, Master, you can let your servant go in peace,
just as you promised;
because my eyes have seen the salvation
which you have prepared for all the nations to see,
a light to enlighten the pagans
and the glory of your people Israel.'

As the child's father and mother stood there wondering at the things that were being said about him, Simeon blessed them and said to Mary his mother, 'You see this child: he is destined for the fall and for the rising of many in Israel, destined to be a sign that is rejected – and a sword will pierce your own soul too – so that the secret thoughts of many may be laid bare.'

There was a prophetess also, Anna the daughter of Phanuel, of the tribe of Asher. She was well on in years. Her days of girlhood over, she had been married for seven years before becoming a widow. She was now eighty-four years old and never left the Temple, serving God night and day with fasting and prayer. She came by just at that moment and began to praise God; and she spoke of the child to all who looked forward to the deliverance of Jerusalem.

[When they had done everything the Law of the Lord required, they went back to Galilee, to their own town of Nazareth. Meanwhile the child grew to maturity, and he was filled with wisdom; and God's favour was with him.

The Gospel of the Lord.]

Shorter Form, verses 22,39-40. Read between [ ]
Alternatively the readings and psalm from Year A may be read along with the Gospel from Year B instead of those given.
When this feast is celebrated on Sunday, the Creed is said.
When this feast is not celebrated on Sunday, there is only one reading before the Gospel.

Prayer over the Offerings

We offer you, Lord,
the sacrifice of conciliation,
humbly asking that,
through the intercession of the Virgin
Mother of God and Saint Joseph,
you may establish our families firmly
in your grace and your peace.
Through Christ our Lord.

Super oblata

Hostiam tibi placationis offerimus,
Domine,
suppliciter deprecantes,
ut, Deiparæ Virginis beatique
Ioseph interveniente suffragio,
familias nostras in tua gratia
firmiter et pace constituas.
Per Christum Dominum nostrum.

Preface I, II or III of the Nativity of the Lord, pp.550-553.

Communion Antiphon   Ba 3:38

Our God has appeared on the earth,
and lived among us.

Ant. ad communionem

Deus noster in terris visus est,
et cum hominibus conversatus est.

Prayer after Communion

Bring those you refresh
with this heavenly Sacrament,
most merciful Father,
to imitate constantly the example
of the Holy Family,
so that, after the trials of this world,
we may share their company for ever.
Through Christ our Lord.

Post communionem

Quos cælestibus reficis sacramentis,
fac, clementissime Pater,
sanctæ Familiæ exempla
iugiter imitari,
ut, post ærumnas sæculi,
eius consortium
consequamur æternum.
Per Christum Dominum nostrum.

THE HOLY FAMILY OF JESUS, MARY AND JOSEPH
(YEAR C)

Feast

Entrance Antiphon Lk 2:16	Ant. ad introitum

THE shepherds went in haste,
and found Mary and Joseph
and the Infant lying in a manger.

VENERUNT pastores festinantes,
et invenerunt Mariam
et Ioseph et Infantem positum
in præsepio.

The Gloria in excelsis (Glory to God in the highest) is said.

Collect	Collecta

O God, who were pleased to give us
the shining example
  of the Holy Family,
graciously grant that we may
  imitate them
in practising the virtues of family life
  and in the bonds of charity,
and so, in the joy of your house,
delight one day in eternal rewards.
Through our Lord Jesus Christ,
  your Son,
who lives and reigns with you
  in the unity of the Holy Spirit,
one God, for ever and ever.

Deus, qui præclara nobis
  sanctæ Familiæ
dignatus es exempla præbere,
concede propitius,
ut, domesticis virtutibus caritatisque
  vinculis illam sectantes,
in lætitia domus tuæ præmiis
  fruamur æternis.
Per Dominum nostrum Iesum
  Christum Filium tuum,
qui tecum vivit et regnat
  in unitate Spiritus Sancti,
Deus, per omnia sæcula sæculorum.

FIRST READING

A reading from the first book of Samuel   1:20-22,24-28

Samuel is made over to the Lord for the whole of his life.

Hannah conceived and gave birth to a son, and called him Samuel 'since'
she said 'I asked the Lord for him.'

When a year had gone by, the husband Elkanah went up again with
all his family to offer the annual sacrifice to the Lord and to fulfil his vow.
Hannah, however, did not go up, having said to her husband, 'Not before
the child is weaned. Then I will bring him and present him before the Lord
and he shall stay there for ever.'

When she had weaned him, she took him up with her together with a three-year old bull, an ephah of flour and a skin of wine, and she brought him to the temple of the Lord at Shiloh; and the child was with them. They slaughtered the bull and the child's mother came to Eli. She said, 'If you please, my lord. As you live, my lord, I am the woman who stood here beside you, praying to the Lord. This is the child I prayed for, and the Lord granted me what I asked him. Now I make him over to the Lord for the whole of his life. He is made over to the Lord.'

There she left him, for the Lord.

The word of the Lord.

Responsorial Psalm
Ps 83:2-3,5-6,9-10. R. v.5

R. **They are happy who dwell in your house, O Lord.**

How lovely is your dwelling place,
Lord, God of hosts.
My soul is longing and yearning,
is yearning for the courts of the Lord.
My heart and my soul ring out their joy
to God, the living God. R.

They are happy, who dwell in your house,
for ever singing your praise.
They are happy, whose strength is in you;
they walk with ever growing strength. R.

O Lord, God of hosts, hear my prayer,
give ear, O God of Jacob.
Turn your eyes, O God, our shield,
look on the face of your anointed. R.

SECOND READING

A reading from the first letter of St John
3:1-2,21-24

We are called God's children, and that is what we are.

Think of the love that the Father has lavished on us,
by letting us be called God's children;
and that is what we are.
Because the world refused to acknowledge him,
therefore it does not acknowledge us.
My dear people, we are already the children of God
but what we are to be in the future has not yet been revealed,

all we know is, that when it is revealed
we shall be like him
because we shall see him as he really is.

My dear people,
if we cannot be condemned by our own conscience,
we need not be afraid in God's presence,
and whatever we ask him,
we shall receive,
because we keep his commandments
and live the kind of life that he wants.
His commandments are these:
that we believe in the name of his Son Jesus Christ
and that we love one another
as he told us to.
Whoever keeps his commandments
lives in God and God lives in him.
We know that he lives in us
by the Spirit that he has given us.

The word of the Lord.

Gospel Acclamation   Cf. Ac 16:14
R. **Alleluia, alleluia!**
Open our heart, O Lord,
to accept the words of your Son.
R. **Alleluia!**

GOSPEL

A reading from the holy Gospel according to Luke   2:41-52
Jesus is found by his parents sitting among the doctors.

Every year the parents of Jesus used to go to Jerusalem for the feast of the
Passover. When he was twelve years old, they went up for the feast as usual.
When they were on their way home after the feast, the boy Jesus stayed
behind in Jerusalem without his parents knowing it. They assumed he was
with the caravan, and it was only after a day's journey that they went to
look for him among their relations and acquaintances. When they failed
to find him they went back to Jerusalem looking for him everywhere.

Three days later, they found him in the Temple, sitting among the
doctors, listening to them, and asking them questions; and all those who
heard him were astounded at his intelligence and his replies. They were

overcome when they saw him, and his mother said to him, 'My child, why have you done this to us? See how worried your father and I have been, looking for you.' 'Why were you looking for me?' he replied. 'Did you not know that I must be busy with my Father's affairs?' But they did not understand what he meant.

He then went down with them and came to Nazareth and lived under their authority. His mother stored up all these things in her heart. And Jesus increased in wisdom, in stature, and in favour with God and men.

The Gospel of the Lord.

Alternatively the readings and psalm from Year A may be read along with the Gospel from Year C instead of those given.

When this feast is celebrated on Sunday, the Creed is said.

When this feast is not celebrated on Sunday, there is only one reading before the Gospel.

Prayer over the Offerings

We offer you, Lord,
    the sacrifice of conciliation,
humbly asking that,
through the intercession of the Virgin
    Mother of God and Saint Joseph,
you may establish our families firmly
    in your grace and your peace.
Through Christ our Lord.

Super oblata

Hostiam tibi placationis offerimus,
    Domine,
suppliciter deprecantes,
ut, Deiparæ Virginis beatique
    Ioseph interveniente suffragio,
familias nostras in tua gratia
    firmiter et pace constituas.
Per Christum Dominum nostrum.

Preface I, II or III of the Nativity of the Lord, pp.550-553.

Communion Antiphon   Ba 3:38

Our God has appeared on the earth,
    and lived among us.

Ant. ad communionem

Deus noster in terris visus est,
et cum hominibus conversatus est.

Prayer after Communion

Bring those you refresh
    with this heavenly Sacrament,
most merciful Father,
to imitate constantly the example
    of the Holy Family,
so that, after the trials of this world,
we may share their company for ever.
Through Christ our Lord.

Post communionem

Quos cælestibus reficis sacramentis,
fac, clementissime Pater,
sanctæ Familiæ exempla
    iugiter imitari,
ut, post ærumnas sæculi,
eius consortium
    consequamur æternum.
Per Christum Dominum nostrum.

1 January

The Octave Day of the Nativity of the Lord

SOLEMNITY OF MARY, THE HOLY MOTHER OF GOD

(YEAR A,B,C)

The Octave of Christmas ends on the first day of the new year, which is dedicated to the Blessed Virgin, venerated as the Mother of God. The Gospel reminds us that she "kept all these things, pondering them in her heart" (Lk 2:19). So she did in Bethlehem, on Golgotha at the foot of the cross, and on the day of Pentecost, when the Holy Spirit descended in the Upper Room. And so she does today too. The Mother of God and of human beings keeps in her heart all of humanity's problems, great and difficult, and meditates upon them. The Alma Redemptoris Mater walks with us and guides us with motherly tenderness towards the future. Thus she helps humanity cross all the "thresholds" of the years, the centuries, the millenniums, by sustaining their hope in the One who is the Lord of history.

(Blessed Pope John Paul II)

Entrance Antiphon

HAIL, Holy Mother, who gave birth to the King who rules heaven and earth for ever.

Ant. ad introitum

SALVE, sancta Parens, enixa puerpera Regem, qui cælum terramque regit in sæcula sæculorum.

Or: Cf. Is 9:1,5; Lk 1:33

Today a light will shine upon us,
    for the Lord is born for us;
and he will be called Wondrous God,
Prince of peace, Father of future ages:
and his reign will be without end.

Vel:

Lux fulgebit hodie super nos,
quia natus est nobis Dominus;
et vocabitur admirabilis, Deus,
    Princeps pacis,
Pater futuri sæculi:
    cuius regni non erit finis.

The Gloria in excelsis (Glory to God in the highest) is said.

Collect

O God, who through the fruitful
    virginity of Blessed Mary
bestowed on the human race
the grace of eternal salvation,
grant, we pray,
that we may experience
    the intercession of her,
through whom we were
    found worthy
to receive the author of life,
our Lord Jesus Christ, your Son.
Who lives and reigns with you
    in the unity of the Holy Spirit,
one God, for ever and ever.

Collecta

Deus, qui salutis æternæ,
beatæ Mariæ virginitate fecunda,
humano generi præmia præstitisti,
    tribue, quæsumus,
ut ipsam pro nobis
    intercedere sentiamus,
per quam meruimus
    auctorem vitæ suscipere,
Dominum nostrum Iesum Christum,
    Filium tuum.
Qui tecum vivit et regnat
    in unitate Spiritus Sancti,
Deus, per omnia sæcula sæculorum.

FIRST READING

A reading from the book of Numbers   6:22-27

They are to call down my name on the sons of Israel, and I will bless them.

The Lord spoke to Moses and said, 'Say this to Aaron and his sons: "This is
how you are to bless the sons of Israel. You shall say to them:

　　May the Lord bless you and keep you.
　　May the Lord let his face shine on you and be gracious to you.
　　May the Lord uncover his face to you and bring you peace."

This is how they are to call down my name on the sons of Israel, and I will
bless them.'

　　The word of the Lord.

Responsorial Psalm   Ps 66:2-3,5,6,8. R. v.2

R. **O God, be gracious and bless us.**

　　God, be gracious and bless us
　　and let your face shed its light upon us.
　　So will your ways be known upon earth
　　and all nations learn your saving help. R.

　　Let the nations be glad and exult
　　for you rule the world with justice.
　　With fairness you rule the peoples,
　　you guide the nations on earth. R.

Let the peoples praise you, O God;
let all the peoples praise you.
May God still give us his blessing
till the ends of the earth revere him. R.

SECOND READING

A reading from the letter of St Paul to the Galatians   4:4-7

God sent his Son, born of a woman.

When the appointed time came, God sent his Son, born of a woman, born a subject of the Law, to redeem the subjects of the Law and to enable us to be adopted as sons. The proof that you are sons is that God has sent the Spirit of his Son into our hearts: the Spirit that cries, 'Abba, Father', and it is this that makes you a son, you are not a slave any more; and if God has made you son, then he has made you heir.

The word of the Lord.

Gospel Acclamation   Heb 1:1-2

R. **Alleluia, alleluia!**
At various times in the past
and in various different ways,
God spoke to our ancestors through the prophets;
but in our own time, the last days,
he has spoken to us through his Son.
R. **Alleluia!**

GOSPEL

A reading from the holy Gospel according to Luke   2:16-21

They found Mary and Joseph and the baby ... When the eighth day came, they gave him the name Jesus.

The shepherds hurried away to Bethlehem and found Mary and Joseph, and the baby lying in the manger. When they saw the child they repeated what they had been told about him, and everyone who heard it was astonished at what the shepherds had to say. As for Mary, she treasured all these things and pondered them in her heart. And the shepherds went back glorifying and praising God for all they had heard and seen; it was exactly as they had been told.

When the eighth day came and the child was to be circumcised, they gave him the name Jesus, the name the angel had given him before his conception.

The Gospel of the Lord.

The Creed is said.

Prayer over the Offerings

O God, who in your kindness begin
    all good things
and bring them to fulfilment,
grant to us, who find joy
    in the Solemnity of the holy
    Mother of God,
that, just as we glory in the
    beginnings of your grace,
so one day we may rejoice
    in its completion.
Through Christ our Lord.

Super oblata

Deus, qui bona cuncta inchoas
    benignus et perficis,
da nobis, de sollemnitate sanctæ
    Dei Genetricis lætantibus,
sicut de initiis tuæ gratiæ gloriamur,
ita de perfectione gaudere.
Per Christum Dominum nostrum.

Preface: The Motherhood
of the Blessed Virgin Mary.

It is truly right and just,
    our duty and our salvation,
always and everywhere to give
    you thanks,
Lord, holy Father,
    almighty and eternal God,
and to praise, bless,
    and glorify your name
on the Solemnity of the Motherhood
of the Blessed ever-Virgin Mary.

For by the overshadowing
    of the Holy Spirit
she conceived your
    Only Begotten Son,
and without losing the glory
    of virginity,
brought forth into the world
    the eternal Light,
Jesus Christ our Lord.

Præfatio: De Maternitate
beatæ Mariæ Virginis.

Vere dignum et iustum est,
    æquum et salutare,
nos tibi semper
    et ubique gratias agere:
Domine, sancte Pater,
    omnipotens æterne Deus:

Et te in Maternitate
beatæ Mariæ semper Virginis
    collaudare,
benedicere et prædicare.

Quæ et Unigenitum tuum Sancti
    Spiritus obumbratione concepit,
et, virginitatis gloria permanente,
lumen æternum mundo effudit,
Iesum Christum Dominum nostrum.

Through him the Angels praise
  your majesty,
Dominions adore and Powers
  tremble before you.
Heaven and the Virtues of heaven
  and the blessed Seraphim
worship together with exultation.
May our voices, we pray,
  join with theirs
in humble praise, as we acclaim:

Holy, Holy, Holy Lord God of hosts...

Per quem maiestatem
  laudant Angeli,
adorant Dominationes,
  tremunt Potestates.
Cæli cælorumque Virtutes,
  ac beata Seraphim,
socia exsultatione concelebrant.
Cum quibis et nostras voces ut
  admitti iubeas, deprecamur,
supplici confessione dicentes:

Sanctus, Sanctus, Sanctus. . .

Communion Antiphon   Heb 13:8

Jesus Christ is the same yesterday,
  today, and for ever.

Ant. ad communionem

Iesus Christus heri et hodie,
  ipse et in sæcula.

Prayer after Communion

We have received this heavenly
  Sacrament with joy, O Lord:
grant, we pray,
that it may lead us to eternal life,
for we rejoice to proclaim
  the blessed ever-Virgin Mary
Mother of your Son
  and Mother of the Church.
Through Christ our Lord.

Post communionem

Sumpsimus, Domine,
  læti sacramenta cælestia:
præsta, quæsumus,
ut ad vitam nobis
  proficiant sempiternam,
qui beatam semper Virginem Mariam
Filii tui Genetricem
  et Ecclesiæ Matrem
profiteri gloriamur.
Per Christum Dominum nostrum.

A formula of Solemn Blessing, pp.654-655, may be used.

SECOND SUNDAY AFTER THE NATIVITY

(YEAR A,B,C)

Our hope is in God, not in the sense of a generic religiosity or a fatalism cloaked in faith. We trust in God who revealed completely and definitively in Jesus Christ his desire to be with human beings, to share in our history, to guide us all to his Kingdom of love and life. And this great hope enlivens and at times corrects our human hopes. Three extraordinarily rich biblical Readings speak to us today of this revelation: chapter 24 of the Book of Ecclesiasticus, the opening hymn of St Paul's Letter to the Ephesians and the Prologue of John's Gospel. These texts affirm that God is not only the Creator of the universe, an aspect common to other religions too, but that he is the Father who "chose us in him before the foundation of the world.... He destined us in love to be his sons through Jesus Christ", and that for this reason he even, inconceivably, went so far as to make himself man: "the Word became flesh and dwelled among us".

(Pope Benedict XVI)

Entrance Antiphon Ws 18:14-15	Ant. ad introitum

WHEN a profound silence covered all things
and night was in the middle
    of its course,
your all-powerful Word, O Lord,
bounded from heaven's royal throne.

DUM medium silentium tenerent omnia,
et nox in suo cursu medium
    iter haberet,
omnipotens sermo tuus, Domine,
de cælis a regalibus sedibus venit.

The Gloria in excelsis (Glory to God in the highest) is said.

Collect	Collecta

Almighty ever-living God,
splendour of faithful souls,
graciously be pleased to fill
    the world with your glory,
and show yourself to all peoples
    by the radiance of your light.
Through our Lord Jesus Christ,
    your Son,
who lives and reigns with you
    in the unity of the Holy Spirit,
one God, for ever and ever.

Omnipotens sempiterne Deus,
    fidelium splendor animarum,
dignare mundum gloria tua
    implere benignus,
et cunctis populis appare
    per tui luminis claritatem.
Per Dominum nostrum Iesum
    Christum Filium tuum,
qui tecum vivit et regnat
    in unitate Spiritus Sancti,
Deus, per omnia sæcula sæculorum.

FIRST READING

A reading from the book of Ecclesiasticus   24:1-2,8-12

The wisdom of God has pitched her tent among the chosen people.

Wisdom speaks her own praises,
in the midst of her people she glories in herself.
She opens her mouth in the assembly of the Most High,
she glories in herself in the presence of the Mighty One;

'Then the creator of all things instructed me,
and he who created me fixed a place for my tent.
He said, "Pitch your tent in Jacob,
make Israel your inheritance."
From eternity, in the beginning, he created me,
and for eternity I shall remain.
I ministered before him in the holy tabernacle,
and thus was I established on Zion.
In the beloved city he has given me rest,
and in Jerusalem I wield my authority.
I have taken root in a privileged people
in the Lord's property, in his inheritance.'

The word of the Lord.

Responsorial Psalm   Ps 147:12-15,19-20. R. Jn 1:14

R. **The Word was made flesh,**
   and lived among us.
   Or: **Alleluia!**

O praise the Lord, Jerusalem!
Zion, praise your God!
He has strengthened the bars of your gates,
he has blessed the children within you. R.

He established peace on your borders,
he feeds you with finest wheat.
He sends out his word to the earth
and swiftly runs his command. R.

He makes his word known to Jacob,
to Israel his laws and decrees.
He has not dealt thus with other nations;
he has not taught them his decrees. R.

SECOND READING

A reading from the letter of St Paul to the Ephesians   1:3-6,15-18

He determined that we should become his adopted sons through Jesus.

Blessed be God the Father of our Lord Jesus Christ, who has blessed us
with all the spiritual blessings of heaven in Christ. Before the world was
made, he chose us, chose us in Christ, to be holy and spotless, and to live
through love in his presence, determining that we should become his
adopted sons, through Jesus Christ, for his own kind purposes, to make us
praise the glory of his grace, his free gift to us in the Beloved.

That will explain why I, having once heard about your faith in the Lord
Jesus, and the love that you show towards all the saints, have never failed
to remember you in my prayers and to thank God for you. May the God of
our Lord Jesus Christ, the Father of glory, give you a spirit of wisdom and
perception of what is revealed, to bring you to full knowledge of him. May
he enlighten the eyes of your mind so that you can see what hope his call
holds for you, what rich glories he has promised the saints will inherit.

The word of the Lord.

Gospel Acclamation   Cf. 1 Tm 3:16

R. **Alleluia, alleluia!**
Glory be to you, O Christ, proclaimed to the pagans;
Glory be to you, O Christ, believed in by the world.
R. **Alleluia!**

GOSPEL

A reading from the holy Gospel according to John   1:1-18

The Word was made flesh, and lived among us.

[In the beginning was the Word:
the Word was with God
and the Word was God.
He was with God in the beginning.
Through him all things came to be,
not one thing had its being but through him.
All that came to be had life in him
and that life was the light of men,
a light that shines in the dark,
a light that darkness could not overpower.]

A man came, sent by God.
His name was John.
He came as a witness,

as a witness to speak for the light,
so that everyone might believe through him.
He was not the light,
only a witness to speak for the light.

[The Word was the true light
that enlightens all men;
and he was coming into the world.
He was in the world
that had its being through him,
and the world did not know him.
He came to his own domain
and his own people did not accept him.
But to all who did accept him
he gave power to become children of God,
to all who believe in the name of him
who was born not out of human stock
or urge of the flesh
or will of man
but of God himself.
The Word was made flesh,
he lived among us,
and we saw his glory,
the glory that is his as the only Son of the Father,
full of grace and truth.]

John appears as his witness. He proclaims:
'This is the one of whom I said:
He who comes after me
ranks before me
because he existed before me.'

Indeed, from his fullness we have, all of us, received –
yes, grace in return for grace,
since though the Law was given through Moses,
grace and truth have come through Jesus Christ.
No one has ever seen God;
it is the only Son, who is nearest to the Father's heart,
who has made him known.

  [The Gospel of the Lord.]

Shorter Form, verses 1-5,9-14. Read between [ ]

The Creed is said.

Prayer over the Offerings

Sanctify, O Lord,
   the offerings we make
on the Nativity of your
   Only Begotten Son,
for by it you show us the way of truth
and promise the life
   of the heavenly Kingdom.
Through Christ our Lord.

Super oblata

Oblata, Domine, munera Unigeniti
   tui nativitate sanctifica,
qua nobis et via ostenditur veritatis,
et regni cælestis vita promittitur.
Per Christum Dominum nostrum.

Preface I, II or III of the Nativity of the Lord, pp.550-553.

Communion Antiphon Cf. Jn 1:12

To all who would accept him,
he gave the power to become
   children of God.

Ant. ad communionem

Omnibus qui receperunt eum,
dedit eis potestatem filios Dei fieri.

Prayer after Communion

Lord our God, we humbly ask you,
that, through the working
   of this mystery,
our offences may be cleansed
and our just desires fulfilled.
Through Christ our Lord.

Post communionem

Domine Deus noster,
   suppliciter te rogamus,
ut, huius operatione mysterii,
vitia nostra purgentur,
   et iusta desideria compleantur.
Per Christum Dominum nostrum.

A formula of Solemn Blessing, pp.642-645, may be used.

THE EPIPHANY OF THE LORD

(YEAR A,B,C)

Men and women of every generation need on their pilgrim journey to be directed: what star can we therefore follow? After coming to rest "over the place where the child was", the purpose of the star that guided the Magi ended, but its spiritual light is always present in the Word of the Gospel, which is still able today to guide every person to Jesus. This same Word, which is none other than the reflection of Christ, true man and true God, is authoritatively echoed by the Church for every well-disposed heart. The Church too, therefore, carries out the mission of the star for humanity. But something of the sort could be said of each Christian, called to illuminate the path of the brethren by word and example of life.

(Pope Benedict XVI)

Solemnity

Where the Solemnity of the Epiphany is not to be observed as a Holyday of Obligation, it is assigned to the Sunday occurring between 2 and 8 January as its proper day.

At the Vigil Mass

This Mass is used on the evening of the day before the Solemnity, either before or after First Vespers (Evening Prayer I) of the Epiphany.

Entrance Antiphon Cf. Ba 5:5	Ant. ad introitum
ARISE, Jerusalem, and look to the East and see your children gathered from the rising to the setting of the sun.	SURGE, Ierusalem, et circumspice ad orientem et vide congregatos filios tuos a solis ortu usque ad occasum.

The Gloria in excelsis (Glory to God in the highest) is said.

Collect	Collecta

May the splendour of your majesty,
   O Lord, we pray,
shed its light upon our hearts,
that we may pass through
   the shadows of this world
	Corda nostra, quæsumus, Domine,
	tuæ maiestatis splendor illustret,
	quo per mundi huius tenebras
	   transire valeamus,
	et perveniamus ad patriam

and reach the brightness
of our eternal home.
Through our Lord Jesus Christ,
your Son,
who lives and reigns with you
in the unity of the Holy Spirit,
one God, for ever and ever.

claritatis æternæ.
Per Dominum nostrum Iesum
Christum Filium tuum,
qui tecum vivit et regnat
in unitate Spiritus Sancti,
Deus, per omnia sæcula sæculorum.

FIRST READING

A reading from the prophet Isaiah   60:1-6

Above you the glory of the Lord appears.

Arise, shine out Jerusalem, for your light has come,
the glory of the Lord is rising on you,
though night still covers the earth
and darkness the peoples.

Above you the Lord now rises
and above you his glory appears.
The nations come to your light
and kings to your dawning brightness.

Lift up your eyes and look around:
all are assembling and coming towards you,
your sons from far away
and daughters being tenderly carried.

At this sight you will glow radiant,
your heart throbbing and full;
since the riches of the sea will flow to you;
the wealth of the nations come to you;

camels in throngs will cover you,
and dromedaries of Midian and Ephah;
everyone in Sheba will come,
bringing gold and incense
and singing the praise of the Lord.

The word of the Lord.

Responsorial Psalm   Ps 71:1-2,7-8,10-13. R. Cf. v.11

R. **All nations shall fall prostrate before you, O Lord.**

O God, give your judgement to the king,
to a king's son your justice,
that he may judge your people in justice
and your poor in right judgement. R.

In his days justice shall flourish
and peace till the moon fails.
He shall rule from sea to sea,
from the Great River to earth's bounds. R.

The Kings of Tarshish and the sea coasts
shall pay him tribute.
The kings of Sheba and Seba
shall bring him gifts.
Before him all kings shall fall prostrate,
all nations shall serve him. R.

For he shall save the poor when they cry
and the needy who are helpless.
He will have pity on the weak
and save the lives of the poor. R.

SECOND READING

A reading from the letter of St Paul to the Ephesians   3:2-3,5-6

It has now been revealed that pagans share the same inheritance.

You have probably heard how I have been entrusted by God with the grace he meant for you, and that it was by a revelation that I was given the knowledge of the mystery. This mystery that has now been revealed through the Spirit to his holy apostles and prophets was unknown to any men in past generations; it means that pagans now share the same inheritance, that they are parts of the same body, and that the same promise has been made to them, in Christ Jesus, through the gospel.

The word of the Lord.

Gospel Acclamation   Mt 2:2

R. **Alleluia, alleluia!**
We saw his star as it rose
and have come to do the Lord homage.
R. **Alleluia!**

GOSPEL

A reading from the holy Gospel according to Matthew   2:1-12

We saw his star and have come to do the king homage.

After Jesus had been born at Bethlehem in Judaea during the reign of King Herod, some wise men came to Jerusalem from the east. 'Where is the infant king of the Jews?' they asked. 'We saw his star as it rose and have come to do him homage.' When King Herod heard this he was perturbed, and so was the whole of Jerusalem. He called together all the chief priests and the scribes of the people, and enquired of them where the Christ was to be born. 'At Bethlehem in Judaea,' they told him 'for this is what the prophet wrote:

And you, Bethlehem, in the land of Judah
you are by no means least among the leaders of Judah,
for out of you will come a leader
who will shepherd my people Israel.'

Then Herod summoned the wise men to see him privately. He asked them the exact date on which the star had appeared, and sent them on to Bethlehem. 'Go and find out all about the child,' he said 'and when you have found him, let me know, so that I too may go and do him homage.' Having listened to what the king had to say, they set out. And there in front of them was the star they had seen rising; it went forward and halted over the place where the child was. The sight of the star filled them with delight, and going into the house they saw the child with his mother Mary, and falling to their knees they did him homage. Then, opening their treasures, they offered him gifts of gold and frankincense and myrrh. But they were warned in a dream not to go back to Herod, and returned to their own country by a different way.

     The Gospel of the Lord.

The Creed is said.

Prayer over the Offerings	Super oblata
Accept we pray, O Lord, our offerings, in honour of the appearing of your Only Begotten Son and the first fruits of the nations, that to you praise may be rendered and eternal salvation be ours. Through Christ our Lord.	Suscipe, quæsumus, Domine, munera nostra pro apparitione Unigeniti Filii tui et primitiis gentium dicata, ut et tibi celebretur laudatio et nobis fiat æterna salvatio. Per Christum Dominum nostrum.

Preface of the Epiphany of the Lord, pp.554-555.

Communion Antiphon Cf. Rv 21:23	Ant. ad communionem
The brightness of God illumined the holy city Jerusalem, and the nations will walk by its light.	Claritas Dei illuminavit civitatem sanctam Ierusalem et ambulabant gentes in lumine eius.

Prayer after Communion	Post communionem
Renewed by sacred nourishment, we implore your mercy, O Lord, that the star of your justice may shine always bright in our minds and that our true treasure may ever consist in our confession of you. Through Christ our Lord.	Sacra alimonia renovati, tuam, Domine, misericordiam deprecamur, ut semper in mentibus nostris tuæ appareat stella iustitiæ et noster in tua sit confessione thesaurus. Per Christum Dominum nostrum.

A formula of Solemn Blessing, pp.644-645, may be used.

At the Mass during the Day

Entrance Antiphon Cf.Ml 3:1;1Ch 29:12	Ant. ad introitum
BEHOLD, the Lord, the Mighty One, has come; and kingship is in his grasp, and power and dominion.	ECCE advenit Dominator Dominus; et regnum in manu eius et potestas et imperium.

The Gloria in excelsis (Glory to God in the highest) is said.

Collect	Collecta
O God, who on this day revealed your Only Begotten Son to the nations by the guidance of a star, grant in your mercy that we, who know you already by faith, may be brought to behold the beauty of your sublime glory. Through our Lord Jesus Christ, your Son, who lives and reigns with you in the unity of the Holy Spirit, one God, for ever and ever.	Deus, qui hodierna die Unigenitum tuum gentibus stella duce revelasti, concede propitius, ut qui iam te ex fide cognovimus, usque ad contemplandam speciem tuæ celsitudinis perducamur. Per Dominum nostrum Iesum Christum Filium tuum, qui tecum vivit et regnat in unitate Spiritus Sancti, Deus, per omnia sæcula sæculorum.

FIRST READING

A reading from the prophet Isaiah   60:1-6

Above you the glory of the Lord appears.

Arise, shine out Jerusalem, for your light has come,
the glory of the Lord is rising on you,
though night still covers the earth
and darkness the peoples.
Above you the Lord now rises
and above you his glory appears.
The nations come to your light
and kings to your dawning brightness.

Lift up your eyes and look around:
all are assembling and coming towards you,
your sons from far away
and daughters being tenderly carried.

At this sight you will glow radiant,
your heart throbbing and full;
since the riches of the sea will flow to you;
the wealth of the nations come to you;

camels in throngs will cover you,
and dromedaries of Midian and Ephah;
everyone in Sheba will come,
bringing gold and incense
and singing the praise of the Lord.

    The word of the Lord.

Responsorial Psalm   Ps 71:1-2,7-8,10-13. R. Cf. v.11

R. **All nations shall fall prostrate before you, O Lord.**

    O God, give your judgement to the king,
    to a king's son your justice,
    that he may judge your people in justice
    and your poor in right judgement. R.

    In his days justice shall flourish
    and peace till the moon fails.
    He shall rule from sea to sea,
    from the Great River to earth's bounds. R.

The Kings of Tarshish and the sea coasts
shall pay him tribute.
The kings of Sheba and Seba
shall bring him gifts.
Before him all kings shall fall prostrate,
all nations shall serve him. R.

For he shall save the poor when they cry
and the needy who are helpless.
He will have pity on the weak
and save the lives of the poor. R.

SECOND READING

A reading from the letter of St Paul to the Ephesians   3:2-3,5-6

It has now been revealed that pagans share the same inheritance.

You have probably heard how I have been entrusted by God with the
grace he meant for you, and that it was by a revelation that I was given
the knowledge of the mystery. This mystery that has now been revealed
through the Spirit to his holy apostles and prophets was unknown to
any men in past generations; it means that pagans now share the same
inheritance, that they are parts of the same body, and that the same
promise has been made to them, in Christ Jesus, through the gospel.

The word of the Lord.

Gospel Acclamation   Mt 2:2
R. **Alleluia, alleluia!**
We saw his star as it rose
and have come to do the Lord homage.
R. **Alleluia!**

GOSPEL

A reading from the holy Gospel according to Matthew   2:1-12

We saw his star and have come to do the king homage.

After Jesus had been born at Bethlehem in Judaea during the reign of King
Herod, some wise men came to Jerusalem from the east. 'Where is the infant
king of the Jews?' they asked. 'We saw his star as it rose and have come to
do him homage.' When King Herod heard this he was perturbed, and so
was the whole of Jerusalem. He called together all the chief priests and the
scribes of the people, and enquired of them where the Christ was to be born.

'At Bethlehem in Judaea,' they told him 'for this is what the prophet wrote:

> And you, Bethlehem, in the land of Judah
> you are by no means least among the leaders of Judah,
> for out of you will come a leader
> who will shepherd my people Israel.'

Then Herod summoned the wise men to see him privately. He asked them the exact date on which the star had appeared, and sent them on to Bethlehem. 'Go and find out all about the child,' he said 'and when you have found him, let me know, so that I too may go and do him homage.' Having listened to what the king had to say, they set out. And there in front of them was the star they had seen rising; it went forward and halted over the place where the child was. The sight of the star filled them with delight, and going into the house they saw the child with his mother Mary, and falling to their knees they did him homage. Then, opening their treasures, they offered him gifts of gold and frankincense and myrrh. But they were warned in a dream not to go back to Herod, and returned to their own country by a different way.

The Gospel of the Lord.

Where it is the practice, if appropriate, the moveable Feasts of the current year may be proclaimed after the Gospel.

The Creed is said.

Prayer over the Offerings

Look with favour, Lord, we pray,
on these gifts of your Church,
in which are offered now not gold
　　or frankincense or myrrh,
but he who by them is proclaimed,
sacrificed and received, Jesus Christ.
Who lives and reigns
　　for ever and ever.

Super oblata

Ecclesiæ tuæ, quæsumus, Domine,
　　dona propitius intuere,
quibus non iam aurum,
　　thus et myrrha profertur,
sed quod eisdem muneribus
declaratur, immolatur et sumitur,
　　Iesus Christus.
Qui vivit et regnat
　　in sæcula sæculorum.

Preface of the Epiphany of the Lord, pp.554-555.

Communion Antiphon Cf. Mt 2:2	Ant. ad communionem
We have seen his star in the East, and have come with gifts to adore the Lord.	Vidimus stellam eius in Oriente, et venimus cum muneribus adorare Dominum.

Prayer after Communion	Post communionem
Go before us with heavenly light, O Lord, always and everywhere, that we may perceive with clear sight and revere with true affection the mystery in which you have willed us to participate. Through Christ our Lord.	Cælesti lumine, quæsumus, Domine, semper et ubique nos præveni, ut mysterium, cuius nos participes esse voluisti, et puro cernamus intuitu, et digno percipiamus affectu. Per Christum Dominum nostrum.

A formula of Solemn Blessing, pp.644-645, may be used.

THE BAPTISM OF THE LORD

(YEAR A)

Feast

Where the Solemnity of the Epiphany is transferred to Sunday, if this Sunday occurs on 7 or 8 January, the Feast of the Baptism of the Lord is celebrated on the following Monday. There is only one reading before the Gospel and the Creed is omitted.

Entrance Antiphon Cf. Mt 3:16-17

AFTER the Lord was baptised,
the heavens were opened,
and the Spirit descended upon him
    like a dove,
and the voice
    of the Father thundered:
This is my beloved Son,
    with whom I am well pleased.

Ant. ad introitum

BAPTIZATO Domino,
aperti sunt cæli,
et sicut columba super eum
    Spiritus mansit,
et vox Patris intonuit:
Hic est Filius meus dilectus,
in quo mihi bene complacui.

The Gloria in excelsis (Glory to God in the highest) is said.

Collect

Almighty ever-living God,
who, when Christ had been
    baptised in the River Jordan
and as the Holy Spirit descended
    upon him,
solemnly declared him
    your beloved Son,
grant that your children by adoption,
reborn of water and the Holy Spirit,
may always be well pleasing to you.
Through our Lord Jesus Christ,
    your Son,
who lives and reigns with you
    in the unity of the Holy Spirit,
one God, for ever and ever.

Collecta

Omnipotens sempiterne Deus,
qui Christum,
    in Iordane flumine baptizatum,
Spiritu Sancto super
    eum descendente,
dilectum Filium tuum
    sollemniter declarasti,
concede filiis adoptionis tuæ,
ex aqua et Spiritu Sancto renatis,
ut in beneplacito tuo
    iugiter perseverent.
Per Dominum nostrum
    Iesum Christum Filium tuum,
qui tecum vivit et regnat
    in unitate Spiritus Sancti,
Deus, per omnia sæcula sæculorum.

Or:

O God, whose Only Begotten Son
has appeared in our very flesh,
grant, we pray, that we may be
    inwardly transformed
through him whom we recognise
    as outwardly like ourselves.
Who lives and reigns with you in
    the unity of the Holy Spirit,
one God, for ever and ever.

Vel:

Deus, cuius Unigenitus in substantia
    nostræ carnis apparuit,
præsta, quæsumus,
ut per eum, quem similem
    nobis foris agnovimus,
intus reformari mereamur.
Qui tecum vivit et regnat
    in unitate Spiritus Sancti,
Deus, per omnia sæcula sæculorum.

FIRST READING

A reading from the prophet Isaiah   42:1-4,6-7

Here is my servant in whom my soul delights.

Thus says the Lord:

Here is my servant whom I uphold,
    my chosen one in whom my soul delights.
I have endowed him with my spirit
    that he may bring true justice to the nations.

He does not cry out or shout aloud,
    or make his voice heard in the streets.
He does not break the crushed reed,
    nor quench the wavering flame.

Faithfully he brings true justice;
    he will neither waver, nor be crushed
until true justice is established on earth,
    for the islands are awaiting his law.

I, the Lord, have called you to serve the cause of right;
    I have taken you by the hand and formed you;
    I have appointed you as covenant of the people and light of the nations,

to open the eyes of the blind
to free captives from prison,
    and those who live in darkness from the dungeon.

The word of the Lord.

Responsorial Psalm   Ps 28:1-4,9-10. R. v.11

R. **The Lord will bless his people with peace.**

O give the Lord you sons of God,
give the Lord glory and power;
give the Lord the glory of his name.
Adore the Lord in his holy court. R.

The Lord's voice resounding on the waters,
the Lord on the immensity of waters;
the voice of the Lord, full of power,
the voice of the Lord, full of splendour. R.

The God of glory thunders.
In his temple they all cry: 'Glory!'
The Lord sat enthroned over the flood;
the Lord sits as king for ever. R.

SECOND READING

A reading from Acts of the Apostles   10:34-38
God had anointed him with the Holy Spirit.

Peter addressed Cornelius and his household: 'The truth I have now come
to realise' he said 'is that God does not have favourites, but that anybody of
any nationality who fears God and does what is right is acceptable to him.

'It is true, God sent his word to the people of Israel, and it was to them
that the good news of peace was brought by Jesus Christ-but Jesus Christ
is Lord of all men. You must have heard about the recent happenings in
Judaea; about Jesus of Nazareth and how he began in Galilee, after John
had been preaching baptism. God had anointed him with the Holy Spirit
and with power, and because God was with him, Jesus went about doing
good and curing all who had fallen into the power of the devil.'

The word of the Lord.

Gospel Acclamation   Cf. Mk 9:7

R. **Alleluia, alleluia!**
The heavens opened and the Father's voice resounded:
'This is my Son, the Beloved. Listen to him.'
R. **Alleluia!**

GOSPEL

A reading from the holy Gospel according to Matthew   3:13-17
As soon as Jesus was baptised he saw the Spirit of God coming down on him.

Jesus came from Galilee to the Jordan to be baptised by John. John tried
to dissuade him. 'It is I who need baptism from you' he said 'and yet you

come to me!' But Jesus replied, 'Leave it like this for the time being; it is fitting that we should, in this way, do all that righteousness demands.' At this, John gave in to him.

As soon as Jesus was baptised he came up from the water, and suddenly the heavens opened and he saw the Spirit of God descending like a dove and coming down on him. And a voice spoke from heaven, 'This is my Son, the Beloved; my favour rests on him.'

The Gospel of the Lord.

When this feast is celebrated on Sunday, the Creed is said.

Prayer over the Offerings

Accept, O Lord, the offerings
we have brought to honour the
    revealing of your beloved Son,
so that the oblation of your faithful
may be transformed into the
    sacrifice of him
who willed in his compassion
to wash away the sins of the world.
Who lives and reigns
    for ever and ever.

Super oblata

Suscipe munera, Domine,
in dilecti Filii tui revelatione delata,
ut fidelium tuorum oblatio in eius
    sacrificium transeat,
qui mundi voluit peccata
    miseratus abluere.
Qui vivit et regnat in
    sæcula sæculorum.

Preface: The Baptism of the Lord.

It is truly right and just,
    our duty and our salvation,
always and everywhere
    to give you thanks,
Lord, holy Father,
    almighty and eternal God.

For in the waters of the Jordan
you revealed with signs
    and wonders a new Baptism,
so that through the voice
    that came down from heaven
we might come to believe in your
    Word dwelling among us,

Præfatio: De Baptismate Domini.

Vere dignum et iustum est,
    æquum et salutare,
nos tibi semper et ubique
    gratias agere:
Domine, sancte Pater,
    omnipotens æterne Deus:

Qui miris signasti mysteriis novum
    in Iordane lavacrum,
ut, per vocem de cælo delapsam,
habitare Verbum tuum inter
    homines crederetur;

and by the Spirit's descending
    in the likeness of a dove
we might know that Christ
    your Servant
has been anointed with the oil
    of gladness
and sent to bring the good news
    to the poor.

And so, with the Powers of heaven,
we worship you constantly on earth,
and before your majesty
without end we acclaim:

Holy, Holy, Holy Lord God of hosts...

et, per Spiritum in columbæ
    specie descendentem,
Christus Servus tuus oleo
    perungi lætitiæ
ac mitti ad evangelizandum
    pauperibus nosceretur.

Et ideo cum cælorum virtutibus
in terris te iugiter celebramus,
maiestati tuæ sine fine clamantes:

Sanctus, Sanctus, Sanctus. . .

Communion Antiphon Jn 1:32,34

Behold the One of whom John said:
I have seen and testified that
    this is the Son of God.

Ant. ad communionem

Ecce de quo dicebat Ioannes:
Ego vidi et testimonium perhibui,
    quia hic est Filius Dei.

Prayer after Communion

Nourished with these sacred gifts,
we humbly entreat your mercy,
    O Lord,
that, faithfully listening to your
    Only Begotten Son,
we may be your children in name
    and in truth.
Through Christ our Lord.

Post communionem

Sacro munere satiati,
clementiam tuam, Domine,
    suppliciter exoramus,
ut, Unigenitum tuum
    fideliter audientes,
filii tui vere nominemur et simus.
Per Christum Dominum nostrum.

THE BAPTISM OF THE LORD

(YEAR B)

Feast

Where the Solemnity of the Epiphany is transferred to Sunday, if this Sunday occurs on 7 or 8 January, the Feast of the Baptism of the Lord is celebrated on the following Monday. There is only one reading before the Gospel and the Creed is omitted.

Entrance Antiphon Cf. Mt 3:16-17	Ant. ad introitum
AFTER the Lord was baptised, the heavens were opened, and the Spirit descended upon him like a dove, and the voice of the Father thundered: This is my beloved Son, with whom I am well pleased.	BAPTIZATO Domino, aperti sunt cæli, et sicut columba super eum Spiritus mansit, et vox Patris intonuit: Hic est Filius meus dilectus, in quo mihi bene complacui.

The Gloria in excelsis (Glory to God in the highest) is said.

Collect	Collecta
Almighty ever-living God, who, when Christ had been baptised in the River Jordan and as the Holy Spirit descended upon him, solemnly declared him your beloved Son, grant that your children by adoption, reborn of water and the Holy Spirit, may always be well pleasing to you. Through our Lord Jesus Christ, your Son, who lives and reigns with you in the unity of the Holy Spirit, one God, for ever and ever.	Omnipotens sempiterne Deus, qui Christum, in Iordane flumine baptizatum, Spiritu Sancto super eum descendente, dilectum Filium tuum sollemniter declarasti, concede filiis adoptionis tuæ, ex aqua et Spiritu Sancto renatis, ut in beneplacito tuo iugiter perseverent. Per Dominum nostrum Iesum Christum Filium tuum, qui tecum vivit et regnat in unitate Spiritus Sancti, Deus, per omnia sæcula sæculorum.

Or:

O God, whose Only Begotten Son
has appeared in our very flesh,
grant, we pray, that we may
    be inwardly transformed
through him whom we recognise
    as outwardly like ourselves.
Who lives and reigns with you in
    the unity of the Holy Spirit,
one God, for ever and ever.

Vel:

Deus, cuius Unigenitus in
    substantia nostræ
    carnis apparuit,
præsta, quæsumus,
ut per eum, quem similem nobis
    foris agnovimus,
intus reformari mereamur.
Qui tecum vivit et regnat
    in unitate Spiritus Sancti,
Deus, per omnia sæcula sæculorum.

FIRST READING

A reading from the prophet Isaiah   55:1-11

Come to the water. Listen and your soul will live.

Oh, come to the water all you who are thirsty;
though you have no money, come!
Buy corn without money, and eat,
and, at no cost, wine and milk.
Why spend money on what is not bread,
your wages on what fails to satisfy?
Listen, listen to me, and you will have good things to eat
and rich food to enjoy.
Pay attention, come to me;
listen, and your soul will live.

With you I will make an everlasting covenant
out of the favours promised to David.
See, I have made of you a witness to the peoples,
a leader and a master of the nations.
See, you will summon a nation you never knew,
those unknown will come hurrying to you,
for the sake of the Lord your God,
of the Holy One of Israel who will glorify you.

Seek the Lord while he is still to be found,
call to him while he is still near.
Let the wicked man abandon his way,
the evil man his thoughts.

Let him turn back to the Lord who will take pity on him,
to our God who is rich in forgiving;
for my thoughts are not your thoughts,
my ways not your ways – it is the Lord who speaks.
Yes, the heavens are as high above earth
as my ways are above your ways,
my thoughts above your thoughts.

Yes, as the rain and the snow come down from the heavens and do not
return without watering the earth, making it yield and giving growth to
provide seed for the sower and bread for the eating, so the word that goes
from my mouth does not return to me empty, without carrying out my
will and succeeding in what it was sent to do.

The word of the Lord.

Responsorial Psalm   Is 12:2-6 R. v.3

R. **With joy you will draw water
from the wells of salvation.**

Truly, God is my salvation,
I trust, I shall not fear.
For the Lord is my strength, my song,
he became my saviour.
With joy you will draw water
from the wells of salvation. R.

Give thanks to the Lord, give praise to his name!
Make his mighty deeds known to the peoples!
Declare the greatness of his name. R.

Sing a psalm to the Lord
for he has done glorious deeds,
make them known to all the earth!
People of Zion, sing and shout for joy
for great in your midst is the Holy One of Israel. R.

SECOND READING

A reading from the first letter of St John   5:1-9

The Spirit and water and blood.

Whoever believes that Jesus is the Christ
has been begotten by God;
and whoever loves the Father that begot him
loves the child whom he begets.

We can be sure that we love God's children
if we love God himself and do what he has commanded us;
this is what loving God is –
keeping his commandments;
and his commandments are not difficult,
because anyone who has been begotten by God
has already overcome the world;
this is the victory over the world –
our faith.
Who can overcome the world?
Only the man who believes that Jesus is the Son of God:
Jesus Christ who came by water and blood,
not with water only,
but with water and blood;
with the Spirit as another witness –
since the Spirit is the truth –
so that there are three witnesses,
the Spirit, the water and the blood,
and all three of them agree.
We accept the testimony of human witnesses,
but God's testimony is much greater,
and this is God's testimony,
given as evidence for his Son.

   The word of the Lord.

Gospel Acclamation   cf. Jn 1:29

R. **Alleluia, alleluia!**
John saw Jesus coming towards him, and said:
This is the Lamb of God who takes away the sin of the world.
R. **Alleluia!**

GOSPEL

A reading from the holy Gospel according to Mark   1:7-11
You are my Son, the Beloved; my favour rests on you.

In the course of his preaching John the Baptist said, 'Someone is following
me, someone who is more powerful than I am, and I am not fit to kneel
down and undo the strap of his sandals. I have baptised you with water,
but he will baptise you with the Holy Spirit.'

   It was at this time that Jesus came from Nazareth in Galilee and was baptised in the Jordan by John. No sooner had he come up out of the water than he saw the heavens torn apart and the Spirit, like a dove, descending on him. And a voice came from heaven, 'You are my Son, the Beloved; my favour rests on you.'

The Gospel of the Lord.

Alternatively the readings and psalm of Year A may be read instead with the Gospel of Year B.

When this feast is celebrated on Sunday, the Creed is said.

Prayer over the Offerings

Accept, O Lord, the offerings
we have brought to honour
    the revealing of your
    beloved Son,
so that the oblation of your faithful
may be transformed into
    the sacrifice of him
who willed in his compassion
to wash away the sins of the world.
Who lives and reigns
    for ever and ever.

Super oblata

Suscipe munera, Domine,
in dilecti Filii tui revelatione delata,
ut fidelium tuorum oblatio
    in eius sacrificium transeat,
qui mundi voluit peccata
    miseratus abluere.
Qui vivit et regnat
    in sæcula sæculorum.

Preface: The Baptism of the Lord pp.131-132.

Communion Antiphon Jn 1:32,34

Behold the One of whom
    John said:
I have seen and testified that
    this is the Son of God.

Ant. ad communionem

Ecce de quo dicebat Ioannes:
Ego vidi et testimonium perhibui,
    quia hic est Filius Dei.

Prayer after Communion

Nourished with these sacred gifts,
we humbly entreat your mercy,
    O Lord,
that, faithfully listening to your
    Only Begotten Son,
we may be your children in
    name and in truth.
Through Christ our Lord.

Post communionem

Sacro munere satiati,
clementiam tuam, Domine,
    suppliciter exoramus,
ut, Unigenitum tuum
    fideliter audientes,
filii tui vere nominemur et simus.
Per Christum Dominum nostrum.

THE BAPTISM OF THE LORD

(YEAR C)

Feast

Where the Solemnity of the Epiphany is transferred to Sunday, if this Sunday occurs on 7 or 8 January, the Feast of the Baptism of the Lord is celebrated on the following Monday. There is only one reading before the Gospel and the Creed is omitted.

Entrance Antiphon Cf. Mt 3:16-17	Ant. ad introitum

AFTER the Lord was baptised,
the heavens were opened,
and the Spirit descended upon him
   like a dove,
and the voice of the
   Father thundered:
This is my beloved Son,
   with whom I am well pleased.

BAPTIZATO Domino,
aperti sunt cæli,
et sicut columba super eum
   Spiritus mansit,
et vox Patris intonuit:
Hic est Filius meus dilectus,
in quo mihi bene complacui.

The Gloria in excelsis (Glory to God in the highest) is said.

Collect	Collecta

Almighty ever-living God,
who, when Christ had been
   baptised in the River Jordan
and as the Holy Spirit descended
   upon him,
solemnly declared him your
   beloved Son,
grant that your children
   by adoption,
reborn of water and the Holy Spirit,
may always be well pleasing to you.
Through our Lord Jesus Christ,
   your Son,
who lives and reigns with you in
   the unity of the Holy Spirit,
one God, for ever and ever.

Omnipotens sempiterne Deus,
qui Christum, in Iordane
   flumine baptizatum,
Spiritu Sancto super eum
   descendente,
dilectum Filium tuum
   sollemniter declarasti,
concede filiis adoptionis tuæ,
ex aqua et Spiritu Sancto renatis,
ut in beneplacito tuo
   iugiter perseverent.
Per Dominum nostrum
   Iesum Christum Filium tuum,
qui tecum vivit et regnat
   in unitate Spiritus Sancti,
Deus, per omnia sæcula sæculorum.

Or:

O God, whose Only Begotten Son has appeared in our very flesh, grant, we pray, that we may be inwardly transformed through him whom we recognise as outwardly like ourselves. Who lives and reigns with you in the unity of the Holy Spirit, one God, for ever and ever.	Vel: Deus, cuius Unigenitus in substantia nostræ carnis apparuit, præsta, quæsumus, ut per eum, quem similem nobis foris agnovimus, intus reformari mereamur. Qui tecum vivit et regnat in unitate Spiritus Sancti, Deus, per omnia sæcula sæculorum.

FIRST READING

A reading from the prophet Isaiah   40:1-5.9-11

The glory of the Lord shall be revealed and all mankind shall see it.

'Console my people, console them'
says your God.
'Speak to the heart of Jerusalem
and call to her
that her time of service is ended,
that her sin is atoned for,
that she has received from the hand of the Lord
double punishment for all her crimes.'

A voice cries, 'prepare in the wilderness
a way for the Lord.
Make a straight highway for our God
across the desert.
Let every valley be filled in,
every mountain and hill be laid low,
let every cliff become a plain,
and the ridges a valley;
then the glory of the Lord shall be revealed
and all mankind shall see it;
for the mouth of the Lord has spoken.'

Go up on a high mountain,
joyful messenger to Zion.
Shout with a loud voice,
joyful messenger to Jerusalem.
Shout without fear,
say to the towns of Judah,
'Here is your God.'

Here is the Lord coming with power,
his arm subduing all things to him.
The prize of his victory is with him,
his trophies all go before him.
He is like a shepherd feeding his flock,
gathering lambs in his arms,
holding them against his breast
and leading to their rest the mother ewes.

    The word of the Lord.

Responsorial Psalm   Ps 103:1-2,3-4,24-25,27-30. R. v.1

R. **Bless the Lord, my soul!**
   Lord God, how great you are.

   Lord God, how great you are,
   clothed in majesty and glory,
   wrapped in light as in a robe!
   You stretch out the heavens like a tent. R.

   Above the rains you build your dwelling.
   You make the clouds your chariot,
   you walk on the wings of the wind,
   you make the winds your messengers
   and flashing fire your servants. R.

   How many are your works, O Lord!
   In wisdom you have made them all.
   The earth is full of your riches.
   There is the sea, vast and wide,
   with its moving swarms past counting
   living things great and small. R.

   All of these look to you
   to give them their food in due season.
   You give it, they gather it up:
   you open your hand, they have their fill. R.

   You take back your spirit, they die,
   returning to the dust from which they came.
   You send forth your spirit, they are created;
   and you renew the face of the earth. R.

SECOND READING

A reading from the letter of St Paul to Titus 2:11-14, 3:4-7

He saved us by the cleansing water of rebirth and by renewing us with the Holy Spirit.

God's grace has been revealed, and it has made salvation possible for the whole human race and taught us that what we have to do is to give up everything that does not lead to God, and all our worldly ambitions; we must be self-restrained and live good and religious lives here in this present world, while we are waiting in hope for the blessing which will come with the Appearing of the glory of our great God and saviour Christ Jesus. He sacrificed himself for us in order to set us free from all wickedness and to purify a people so that it could be his very own and would have no ambition except to do good.

When the kindness and love of God our saviour for mankind were revealed, it was not because he was concerned with any righteous actions we might have done ourselves; it was for no reason except his own compassion that he saved us, by means of the cleansing water of rebirth and by renewing us with the Holy Spirit which he has so generously poured over us through Jesus Christ our saviour. He did this so that we should be justified by his grace, to become heirs looking forward to inheriting eternal life.

The word of the Lord.

Gospel Acclamation Cf. Lk 3:13

R. **Alleluia, alleluia!**
Someone is coming, said John, someone greater than I.
He will baptise you with the Holy Spirit and with fire.
R. **Alleluia!**

GOSPEL

A reading from the holy Gospel according to Luke 3:15-16,21-22

While Jesus after his own baptism was at prayer, heaven opened.

A feeling of expectancy had grown among the people, who were beginning to think that John might be the Christ, so John declared before them all, 'I baptise you with water, but someone is coming, someone who is more powerful than I am and I am not fit to undo the strap of his sandals; he will baptise you with the Holy Spirit and fire.'

Now when all the people had been baptised and while Jesus after his own baptism was at prayer, heaven opened and the Holy Spirit descended on him in bodily shape, like a dove. And a voice came from heaven, 'You are my Son, the Beloved; my favour rests on you.'

The Gospel of the Lord.

Alternatively the readings and psalm of Year A may be read instead with the Gospel of Year C.

When this feast is celebrated on Sunday, the Creed is said.

Prayer over the Offerings

Accept, O Lord, the offerings
we have brought to honour the
    revealing of your beloved Son,
so that the oblation of your faithful
may be transformed into the
    sacrifice of him
who willed in his compassion
to wash away the sins of the world.
Who lives and reigns
    for ever and ever.

Super oblata

Suscipe munera, Domine,
in dilecti Filii tui revelatione delata,
ut fidelium tuorum oblatio
    in eius sacrificium transeat,
qui mundi voluit peccata
    miseratus abluere.
Qui vivit et regnat
    in sæcula sæculorum.

Preface: The Baptism of the Lord pp.131-132.

Communion Antiphon Jn 1:32,34

Behold the One of whom
    John said:
I have seen and testified that this is
    the Son of God.

Ant. ad communionem

Ecce de quo dicebat Ioannes:
Ego vidi et testimonium perhibui,
    quia hic est Filius Dei.

Prayer after Communion

Nourished with these sacred gifts,
we humbly entreat your mercy,
    O Lord,
that, faithfully listening to your
    Only Begotten Son,
we may be your children
    in name and in truth.
Through Christ our Lord.

Post communionem

Sacro munere satiati,
clementiam tuam, Domine,
    suppliciter exoramus,
ut, Unigenitum tuum
    fideliter audientes,
filii tui vere nominemur et simus.
Per Christum Dominum nostrum.

ASH WEDNESDAY (YEAR A,B,C)

In the course of today's Mass, ashes are blessed and distributed. These are made from the olive branches or branches of other trees that were blessed the previous year.

Introductory Rites and Liturgy of the Word

Entrance Antiphon Ws 11:24,25,27

YOU are merciful to all, O Lord,
and despise nothing that you
have made.
You overlook people's sins,
to bring them to repentance,
and you spare them,
for you are the Lord our God.

Ant. ad introitum

MISERERIS omnium, Domine,
et nihil odisti eorum
quæ fecisti,
dissimulans peccata hominum
propter pænitentiam
et parcens illis,
quia tu es Dominus Deus noster.

The Penitential Act is omitted, and the Distribution of Ashes takes its place.

Collect

Grant, O Lord, that we may begin
with holy fasting
this campaign of Christian service,
so that, as we take up battle
against spiritual evils,
we may be armed with weapons
of self-restraint.
Through our Lord Jesus Christ,
your Son,
who lives and reigns with you
in the unity of the Holy Spirit,
one God, for ever and ever.

Collecta

Concede nobis, Domine,
præsidia militiæ christianæ sanctis
inchoare ieiuniis,
ut, contra spiritales
nequitias pugnaturi,
continentiæ muniamur auxiliis.
Per Dominum nostrum
Iesum Christum Filium tuum,
qui tecum vivit et regnat
in unitate Spiritus Sancti,
Deus, per omnia sæcula sæculorum.

FIRST READING

A reading from the prophet Joel   2:12-18
Let your hearts be broken, not your garments torn.

'Now, now – it is the Lord who speaks –
come back to me with all your heart,
fasting, weeping, mourning.'

Let your hearts be broken not your garments torn,
turn to the Lord your God again,
for he is all tenderness and compassion,
slow to anger, rich in graciousness,
and ready to relent.
Who knows if he will not turn again, will not relent,
will not leave a blessing as he passes,
oblation and libation
for the Lord your God?
Sound the trumpet in Zion!
Order a fast,
proclaim a solemn assembly,
call the people together,
summon the community,
assemble the elders,
gather the children,
even the infants at the breast.
Let the bridegroom leave his bedroom
and the bride her alcove.
Between vestibule and altar let the priests,
the ministers of the Lord, lament.
Let them say,
'Spare your people, Lord!
Do not make your heritage a thing of shame,
a byword for the nations.
Why should it be said among the nations,
"Where is their God?"'
Then the Lord, jealous on behalf of his land,
took pity on his people.

   The word of the Lord.

Responsorial Psalm   Ps 50:3-6,12-14,17. R. v.3

R. **Have mercy on us, O Lord, for we have sinned.**

   Have mercy on me, God, in your kindness.
   In your compassion blot out my offence.
   O wash me more and more from my guilt
   and cleanse me from my sin. R.

My offences truly I know them;
my sin is always before me.
Against you, you alone, have I sinned:
what is evil in your sight I have done. R.

A pure heart create for me, O God,
put a steadfast spirit within me.
Do not cast me away from your presence,
nor deprive me of your holy spirit. R.

Give me again the joy of your help;
with a spirit of fervour sustain me.
O Lord, open my lips
and my mouth shall declare your praise. R.

SECOND READING

A reading from the second letter of St Paul to the Corinthians   5:20-6:2

Be reconciled to God ... now is the favourable time.

We are ambassadors for Christ; it is as though God were appealing through us, and the appeal that we make in Christ's name is: be reconciled to God. For our sake God made the sinless one into sin, so that in him we might become the goodness of God. As his fellow workers, we beg you once again not to neglect the grace of God that you have received. For he says: At the favourable time, I have listened to you, on the day of salvation I came to your help. Well, now is the favourable time; this is the day of salvation.

The word of the Lord.

Gospel Acclamation   Ps 50:12,14

R. **Praise to you, O Christ, king of eternal glory!**
A pure heart create for me, O God,
and give me again the joy of your help.
R. **Praise to you, O Christ, king of eternal glory!**

Or: Cf. Ps 94:8
R. **Praise to you, O Christ, king of eternal glory!**
Harden not your hearts today,
but listen to the voice of the Lord.
R. **Praise to you, O Christ, king of eternal glory!**

GOSPEL

A reading from holy Gospel according to Matthew   6:1-6,16-18

Your Father, who sees all that is done in secret, will reward you.

Jesus said to his disciples:

'Be careful not to parade your good deeds before men to attract their notice; by doing this you will lose all reward from your Father in heaven. So when you give alms, do not have it trumpeted before you; this is what the hypocrites do in the synagogues and in the streets to win men's admiration. I tell you solemnly, they have had their reward. But when you give alms, your left hand must not know what your right is doing; your almsgiving must be secret, and your Father who sees all that is done in secret will reward you.

'And when you pray, do not imitate the hypocrites: they love to say their prayers standing up in the synagogues and at the street corners for people to see them. I tell you solemnly, they have had their reward. But when you pray go to your private room and, when you have shut your door, pray to your Father who is in that secret place, and your Father who sees all that is done in secret will reward you.

'When you fast do not put on a gloomy look as the hypocrites do: they pull long faces to let men know they are fasting. I tell you solemnly, they have had their reward. But when you fast, put oil on your head and wash your face, so that no one will know you are fasting except your Father who sees all that is done in secret; and your Father who sees all that is done in secret will reward you.'

The Gospel of the Lord.

Blessing and Distribution of Ashes

After the Homily, the Priest, standing with hands joined, says:

Dear brethren (brothers and sisters), let us humbly ask God our Father that he be pleased to bless with the abundance of his grace these ashes, which we will put on our heads in penitence.	Deum Patrem, fratres carissimi, suppliciter deprecemur, ut hos cineres, quos pænitentiæ causa capitibus nostris imponimus, ubertate gratiæ suæ benedicere dignetur.

After a brief prayer in silence, and, with hands extended, he continues:

O God, who are moved
    by acts of humility
and respond with forgiveness
    to works of penance,
lend your merciful ear to our prayers
and in your kindness pour out
    the grace of your ✠ blessing
on your servants who are marked
    with these ashes,
that, as they follow
    the Lenten observances,
they may be worthy to come
    with minds made pure
to celebrate the Paschal Mystery
    of your Son.
Who lives and reigns
    for ever and ever.

R. Amen.

Deus, qui humiliatione flecteris
    et satisfactione placaris,
aurem tuæ pietatis precibus
    nostris inclina,
et super famulos tuos,
horum cinerum aspersione contactos,
gratiam tuæ benedictionis ✠
    effunde propitius,
ut, quadragesimalem
    observantiam prosequentes,
ad Filii tui paschale
    mysterium celebrandum
purificatis mentibus
    pervenire mereantur.
Per Christum Dominum nostrum.

R. Amen.

Or:

O God, who desire not
    the death of sinners,
but their conversion,
mercifully hear our prayers
and in your kindness be pleased
    to bless ✠ these ashes,
which we intend to receive
    upon our heads,
that we, who acknowledge
    we are but ashes
and shall return to dust,
may, through a steadfast
    observance of Lent,
gain pardon for sins
    and newness of life
after the likeness of your Risen Son.
Who lives and reigns
    for ever and ever.

R. Amen.

Vel:

Deus, qui non mortem
    sed conversionem
desideras peccatorum,
preces nostras clementer exaudi,
et hos cineres,
quos capitibus nostris
    imponi decernimus,
benedicere ✠ pro tua pietate dignare,
ut qui nos cinerem esse
et in pulverem
    reversuros cognoscimus,
quadragesimalis exercitationis studio,
peccatorum veniam
et novitatem vitæ,
ad imaginem Filii tui resurgentis,
    consequi valeamus.
Qui vivit et regnat
    in sæcula sæculorum.

R. Amen.

He sprinkles the ashes with holy water, without saying anything.

Then the Priest places ashes on the head of all those present who come to him, and says to each one:

Repent, and believe in the Gospel.	Pænitemini, et credite Evangelio.
Or:	Vel:

Remember that you are dust,
    and to dust you shall return.
	Memento, homo, quia pulvis es,
	    et in pulverem reverteris.

Meanwhile, the following are sung:

Antiphon 1	Antiphona 1

Let us change our garments
    to sackcloth and ashes,
let us fast and weep before the Lord,
that our God, rich in mercy,
    might forgive us our sins.
	Immutemur habitu,
	    in cinere et cilicio,
	ieiunemus,
	    et ploremus ante Dominum,
	quia multum misericors est
	dimittere peccata nostra
	    Deus noster.

Antiphon 2 Cf. Jl 2:17; Est 4:17	Antiphona 2

Let the priests,
    the ministers of the Lord,
stand between the porch and
    the altar and weep and cry out:
Spare, O Lord, spare your people;
do not close the mouths of those
    who sing your praise, O Lord.
	Inter vestibulum et altare
	plorabunt sacerdotes
	    ministri Domini,
	et dicent: Parce, Domine,
	    parce populo tuo,
	et ne claudas ora canentium te,
	    Domine.

Antiphon 3 Ps 50:3	Antiphona 3
Blot out my transgressions, O Lord.	Dele, Domine, iniquitatem meam.

This may be repeated after each verse of Psalm 50

| (Have mercy on me, O God). | Miserere mei, Deus. |

Responsory Cf. Ba 3:2; Ps 78:9	Responsorium
R. Let us correct our faults which we have committed in ignorance, let us not be taken unawares by the day of our death, looking in vain for leisure to repent. * Hear us, O Lord, and show us your mercy, for we have sinned against you.	R. Emendemus in melius, quæ ignoranter peccavimus, ne subito præoccupati die mortis quæramus spatium pænitentiæ, et invenire non possimus. *Attende, Domine, et miserere, quia peccavimus tibi.
V. Help us, O God our Saviour; for the sake of your name, O Lord, set us free. * Hear us, O Lord. . .	V. Adiuva nos, Deus salutaris noster, et propter honorem nominis tui, Domine, libera nos. *Attende, Domine. . .

Another appropriate chant may also be sung.

After the distribution of ashes, the Priest washes his hands and proceeds to the Universal Prayer, and continues the Mass in the usual way.

The Creed is not said.

The Liturgy of the Eucharist

Prayer over the Offerings	Super oblata

As we solemnly offer
the annual sacrifice for
   the beginning of Lent,
we entreat you, O Lord,
that, through works of penance
   and charity,
we may turn away from
   harmful pleasures
and, cleansed from our sins,
   may become worthy
to celebrate devoutly the Passion
   of your Son.
Who lives and reigns
   for ever and ever.
	Sacrificium quadragesimalis initii
	   sollemniter immolamus,
	te, Domine, deprecantes,
	ut per pænitentiæ
	   caritatisque labores
	a noxiis voluptatibus temperemus,
	et, a peccatis mundati,
	ad celebrandam Filii tui passionem
	mereamur esse devoti.
	Qui vivit et regnet
	   in sæcula sæculorum.

Preface III or IV of Lent, pp.556-557.

Communion Antiphon Cf. Ps 1:2-3 | Ant. ad communionem

He who ponders the law
of the Lord day and night
will yield fruit in due season.

Qui meditabitur in lege
Domini die ac nocte,
dabit fructum suum in tempore suo.

Prayer after Communion | Post communionem

May the Sacrament we have
received sustain us, O Lord,
that our Lenten fast may
be pleasing to you
and be for us a healing remedy.
Through Christ our Lord.

Percepta nobis, Domine,
præbeant sacramenta subsidium,
ut tibi grata sint nostra ieiunia,
et nobis proficiant ad medelam.
Per Christum Dominum nostrum.

For the dismissal, the Priest stands facing the people and, extending his hands over
them, says this prayer:

Prayer over the People | Oratio super populum

Pour out a spirit of compunction,
O God,
on those who bow before
your majesty,
and by your mercy may they
merit the rewards you promise
to those who do penance.
Through Christ our Lord.

Super inclinantes se tuæ maiestati,
Deus,
spiritum compunctionis
propitius effunde,
et præmia pænitentibus repromissa
misericorditer consequi mereantur.
Per Christum Dominum nostrum.

The blessing and distribution of ashes may also take place outside Mass. In this
case, the rite is preceded by a Liturgy of the Word, with the Entrance Antiphon, the
Collect, and the readings with their chants as at Mass. Then there follow the Homily
and the blessing and distribution of ashes. The rite is concluded with the Universal
Prayer, the Blessing, and the Dismissal of the Faithful.

FIRST SUNDAY OF LENT (YEAR A)

What does "entering Lent" mean? It means we enter a season of special commitment in the spiritual battle to oppose the evil present in the world, in each one of us and around us. It means not off-loading the problem of evil onto others, onto society or onto God but rather recognising one's own responsibility and assuming it with awareness. In this regard Jesus's invitation to each one of us Christians to take up our "cross" and follow him with humility and trust is particularly pressing. Although the "cross" may be heavy it is not synonymous with misfortune, with disgrace, to be avoided on all accounts; rather it is an opportunity to follow Jesus and thereby to acquire strength in the fight against sin and evil.

(Pope Benedict XVI)

Entrance Antiphon Cf. Ps 90:15-16

WHEN he calls on me,
I will answer him;
I will deliver him
and give him glory,
I will grant him length of days.

Ant. ad introitum

INVOCABIT me,
et ego exaudiam eum;
eripiam eum, et glorificabo eum,
longitudine dierum
adimplebo eum.

The Gloria in excelsis (Glory to God in the highest) is not said.

Collect

Grant, almighty God,
through the yearly observances
of holy Lent,
that we may grow in understanding
of the riches hidden in Christ
and by worthy conduct pursue
their effects.
Through our Lord Jesus Christ,
your Son,
who lives and reigns with you
in the unity of the Holy Spirit,
one God, for ever and ever.

Collecta

Concede nobis, omnipotens Deus,
ut, per annua quadragesimalis
exercitia sacramenti,
et ad intellegendum Christi
proficiamus arcanum,
et effectus eius digna
conversatione sectemur.
Per Dominum nostrum Iesum
Christum Filium tuum,
qui tecum vivit et regnat
in unitate Spiritus Sancti,
Deus, per omnia sæcula sæculorum.

FIRST READING

A reading from the book of Genesis   2:7-9; 3:1-7

The creation and sin of our first parents.

The Lord God fashioned man of dust from the soil. Then he breathed into his nostrils a breath of life, and thus man became a living being.

The Lord God planted a garden in Eden which is in the east, and there he put the man he had fashioned. The Lord God caused to spring up from the soil every kind of tree, enticing to look at and good to eat, with the tree of life and the tree of the knowledge of good and evil in the middle of the garden.

The serpent was the most subtle of all the wild beasts that the Lord God had made. It asked the woman, 'Did God really say you were not to eat from any of the trees in the garden?' The woman answered the serpent, 'We may eat the fruit of the trees in the garden. But of the fruit of the tree in the middle of the garden God said, "You must not eat it, nor touch it, under pain of death."' Then the serpent said to the woman, 'No! You will not die! God knows in fact that on the day you eat it your eyes will be opened and you will be like gods, knowing good and evil.' The woman saw that the tree was good to eat and pleasing to the eye, and that it was desirable for the knowledge that it could give. So she took some of its fruit and ate it. She gave some also to her husband who was with her, and he ate it. Then the eyes of both of them were opened and they realised that they were naked. So they sewed fig-leaves together to make themselves loin-cloths.

The word of the Lord.

Responsorial Psalm   Ps 50:3-6,12-14,17. R. Cf. v.3

R. **Have mercy on us, O Lord, for we have sinned.**

Have mercy on me, God, in your kindness.
In your compassion blot out my offence.
O wash me more and more from my guilt
and cleanse me from my sin. R.

My offences truly I know them;
my sin is always before me.
Against you, you alone, have I sinned;
what is evil in your sight I have done. R.

A pure heart create for me, O God,
put a steadfast spirit within me.
Do not cast me away from your presence,
nor deprive me of your holy spirit. R.

Give me again the joy of your help;
with a spirit of fervour sustain me.
O Lord, open my lips
and my mouth shall declare your praise. R.

SECOND READING

A reading from the letter of St Paul to the Romans   5:12-19

However great the number of sins committed, grace was even greater.

[Sin entered the world through one man, and through sin death, and thus
death has spread through the whole human race because everyone has
sinned.] Sin existed in the world long before the Law was given. There was
no law and so no one could be accused of the sin of 'law-breaking', yet
death reigned over all from Adam to Moses, even though their sin, unlike
that of Adam, was not a matter of breaking a law.

Adam prefigured the One to come, but the gift itself considerably
outweighed the fall. If it is certain that through one man's fall so many
died, it is even more certain that divine grace, coming through the one
man, Jesus Christ, came to so many as an abundant free gift. The results
of the gift also outweigh the results of one man's sin: for after one single
fall came judgement with a verdict of condemnation, now after many falls
comes grace with its verdict of acquittal. [If it is certain that death reigned
over everyone as the consequence of one man's fall, it is even more certain
that one man, Jesus Christ, will cause everyone to reign in life who receives
the free gift that he does not deserve, of being made righteous. Again, as
one man's fall brought condemnation on everyone, so the good act of
one man brings everyone life and makes them justified. As by one man's
disobedience many were made sinners, so by one man's obedience many
will be made righteous.

The word of the Lord.]

Shorter Form, verses 12,17-19. Read between [ ]

Gospel Acclamation   Mt 4:4

R. **Praise to you, O Christ, king of eternal glory!**
Man does not live on bread alone
but on every word that comes from the mouth of God.
R. **Praise to you, O Christ, king of eternal glory!**

GOSPEL

A reading from the holy Gospel according to Matthew   4:1-11
Jesus fasts for forty days and is tempted.

Jesus was led by the Spirit out into the wilderness to be tempted by the devil. He fasted for forty days and forty nights, after which he was very hungry, and the tempter came and said to him, 'If you are the Son of God, tell these stones to turn into loaves.' But he replied, 'Scripture says:

Man does not live on bread alone
but on every word that comes from the mouth of God.'

The devil then took him to the holy city and made him stand on the parapet of the Temple. 'If you are the Son of God' he said 'throw yourself down; for scripture says:

He will put you in his angels' charge,
and they will support you on their hands
in case you hurt your foot against a stone.'

Jesus said to him, 'Scripture also says:

You must not put the Lord your God to the test.'

Next, taking him to a very high mountain, the devil showed him all the kingdoms of the world and their splendour. 'I will give you all these' he said, 'if you fall at my feet and worship me.' Then Jesus replied, 'Be off, Satan! For scripture says:

You must worship the Lord your God,
and serve him alone.'

Then the devil left him, and angels appeared and looked after him.

The Gospel of the Lord.

The Creed is said.

Prayer over the Offerings	Super oblata
Give us the right dispositions, O Lord, we pray, to make these offerings, for with them we celebrate the beginning of this venerable and sacred time. Through Christ our Lord.	Fac nos, quæsumus, Domine, his muneribus offerendis convenienter aptari, quibus ipsius venerabilis sacramenti celebramus exordium. Per Christum Dominum nostrum.

Preface: The Temptation of the Lord. | Praefatio: De tentatione Domini.

It is truly right and just,
  our duty and our salvation,
always and everywhere
  to give you thanks,
Lord, holy Father,
  almighty and eternal God,
through Christ our Lord.

By abstaining forty long days
  from earthly food,
he consecrated through his fast
the pattern of our Lenten observance
and, by overturning all the snares
  of the ancient serpent,
taught us to cast out the leaven
  of malice,
so that, celebrating worthily
  the Paschal Mystery,
we might pass over at last
  to the eternal paschal feast.

And so, with the company
  of Angels and Saints,
we sing the hymn of your praise,
as without end we acclaim:

Holy, Holy, Holy Lord God of hosts...

Vere dignum et iustum est,
  aequum et salutare,
nos tibi semper et ubique
  gratias agere:
Domine, sancte Pater, omnipotens
  aeterne Deus:
per Christum Dominum nostrum:

Qui quadraginta diebus,
terrenis abstinens alimentis,
formam huius observantiae
  ieiunio dedicavit,
et, omnes evertens antiqui
  serpentis insidias,
fermentum malitiae nos
  docuit superare,
ut, paschale mysterium dignis
  mentibus celebrantes,
ad pascha demum
  perpetuum transeamus.

Et ideo, cum Angelorum
  atque Sanctorum turba,
hymnum laudis tibi canimus,
  sine fine dicentes:

Sanctus, Sanctus, Sanctus. . .

Communion Antiphon   Mt 4:4 | Ant. ad communionem

One does not live by bread alone,
but by every word that comes forth
  from the mouth of God.

Non in solo pane vivit homo,
sed in omni verbo quod procedit
  de ore Dei.

Or: Cf. Ps 90:4 | Vel:

The Lord will conceal you
  with his pinions,
and under his wings you will trust.

Scapulis suis obumbrabit
  tibi Dominus,
et sub pennis eius sperabis.

Prayer after Communion

Renewed now with heavenly bread,
by which faith is nourished,
    hope increased,
and charity strengthened,
we pray, O Lord,
that we may learn to hunger
    for Christ,
the true and living Bread,
and strive to live by every word
which proceeds from your mouth.
Through Christ our Lord.

Prayer over the People

May bountiful blessing, O Lord,
    we pray,
come down upon your people,
that hope may grow in tribulation,
virtue be strengthened in temptation,
and eternal redemption be assured.
Through Christ our Lord.

Post communionem

Cælesti pane refecti,
quo fides alitur, spes provehitur
    et caritas roboratur,
quæsumus, Domine,
ut ipsum, qui est panis vivus
    et verus, esurire discamus,
et in omni verbo,
    quod procedit de ore tuo,
vivere valeamus.
Per Christum Dominum nostrum.

Oratio super populum

Super populum tuum,
    Domine, quæsumus,
benedictio copiosa descendat,
ut spes in tribulatione succrescat,
virtus in tentatione firmetur,
æterna redemptio tribuatur.
Per Christum Dominum nostrum.

SECOND SUNDAY OF LENT (YEAR A)

Today, the Second Sunday of Lent, as we continue on the penitential journey, the liturgy invites us, after presenting the Gospel of Jesus's temptations in the desert last week, to reflect on the extraordinary event of the Transfiguration on the mountain. Considered together, these episodes anticipate the Paschal Mystery: Jesus' struggle with the tempter preludes the great final duel of the Passion, while the light of his transfigured Body anticipates the glory of the Resurrection. This is the crucial point: the Transfiguration is an anticipation of the Resurrection, but this presupposes death. Jesus expresses his glory to the Apostles so that they may have the strength to face the scandal of the Cross and understand that it is necessary to pass through many tribulations in order to reach the Kingdom of God.

(Pope Benedict XVI)

Entrance Antiphon Cf. Ps 26:8-9	Ant. ad introitum

OF you my heart has spoken:
   Seek his face.
It is your face, O Lord, that I seek;
   hide not your face from me.

TIBI dixit cor meum quæsivi
   vultum tuum,
vultum tuum, Domine, requiram.
Ne avertas faciem tuam a me.

Or: Cf. Ps 24:6,2,22   **Vel:**

Remember your compassion,
   O Lord,
and your merciful love,
   for they are from of old.
Let not our enemies exult over us.
Redeem us, O God of Israel,
   from all our distress.

Reminiscere miserationum tuarum,
   Domine,
et misericordiæ tuæ,
   quæ a sæculo sunt.
Ne umquam dominentur nobis
   inimici nostri;
libera nos, Deus Israel,
   ex omnibus angustiis nostris.

The Gloria in excelsis (Glory to God in the highest) is not said.

Collect   **Collecta**

O God, who have commanded us
to listen to your beloved Son,
be pleased, we pray,
to nourish us inwardly by your word,
that, with spiritual sight made pure,
we may rejoice to behold your glory.

Deus, qui nobis dilectum Filium
   tuum audire præcepisti,
verbo tuo interius nos
   pascere digneris,
ut, spiritali purificato intuitu,
gloriæ tuæ lætemur aspectu.

| Through our Lord Jesus Christ, your Son, who lives and reigns with you in the unity of the Holy Spirit, one God, for ever and ever. | Per Dominum nostrum Iesum Christum Filium tuum, qui tecum vivit et regnat in unitate Spiritus Sancti, Deus, per omnia sæcula sæculorum. |

Through our Lord Jesus Christ,
 your Son,
who lives and reigns with you
 in the unity of the Holy Spirit,
one God, for ever and ever.

Per Dominum nostrum Iesum
 Christum Filium tuum,
qui tecum vivit et regnat
 in unitate Spiritus Sancti,
Deus, per omnia sæcula sæculorum.

FIRST READING

A reading from the book of Genesis   12:1-4

The call of Abraham, the father the People of God.

The Lord said to Abram, 'Leave your country, your family and your father's house, for the land I will show you. I will make you a great nation; I will bless you and make your name so famous that it will be used as a blessing.

> 'I will bless those who bless you:
> I will curse those who slight you.
> All the tribes of the earth
> shall bless themselves by you.'

So Abram went as the Lord told him.

The word of the Lord.

Responsorial Psalm   Ps 32:4-5,18-20,22. R. v.22

R. **May your love be upon us, O Lord,**
 as we place all our hope in you.

> The word of the Lord is faithful
> and all his works to be trusted.
> The Lord loves justice and right
> and fills the earth with his love. R.

> The Lord looks on those who revere him,
> on those who hope in his love,
> to rescue their souls from death,
> to keep them alive in famine. R.

> Our soul is waiting for the Lord.
> The Lord is our help and our shield.
> May your love be upon us, O Lord,
> as we place all our hope in you. R.

SECOND READING

A reading from the second letter of St Paul to Timothy   1:8-10

God calls and enlightens us.

With me, bear the hardships for the sake of the Good News, relying on the power of God who has saved us and called us to be holy - not because of anything we ourselves have done but for his own purpose and by his own grace. This grace had already been granted to us, in Christ Jesus, before the beginning of time, but it has only been revealed by the Appearing of our saviour Christ Jesus. He abolished death, and he has proclaimed life and immortality through the Good News.

The word of the Lord.

Gospel Acclamation   Mt 17:5

R. **Glory and praise to you, O Christ!**
From the bright cloud the Father's voice was heard:
'This is my Son, the Beloved. Listen to him.'
R. **Glory and praise to you, O Christ!**

GOSPEL

A reading from the holy Gospel according to Matthew   17:1-9

His face shone like the sun.

Jesus took with him Peter and James and his brother John and led them up a high mountain where they could be alone. There in their presence he was transfigured; his face shone like the sun and his clothes became as white as the light. Suddenly Moses and Elijah appeared to them; they were talking with him. Then Peter spoke to Jesus. 'Lord,' he said 'it is wonderful for us to be here; if you wish, I will make three tents here, one for you, one for Moses and one for Elijah.' He was still speaking when suddenly a bright cloud covered them with shadow, and from the cloud there came a voice which said, 'This is my Son, the Beloved; he enjoys my favour. Listen to him.' When they heard this, the disciples fell on their faces, overcome with fear. But Jesus came up and touched them. 'Stand up,' he said 'do not be afraid.' And when they raised their eyes they saw no one but only Jesus.

As they came down from the mountain Jesus gave them this order. 'Tell no one about the vision until the Son of Man has risen from the dead.'

The Gospel of the Lord.

The Creed is said.

Prayer over the Offerings

May this sacrifice, O Lord, we pray,
cleanse us of our faults
and sanctify your faithful
    in body and mind
for the celebration
    of the paschal festivities.
Through Christ our Lord.

Super oblata

Hæc hostia, Domine, quæsumus,
    emundet nostra delicta,
et ad celebranda festa paschalia
fidelium tuorum corpora
    mentesque sanctificet.
Per Christum Dominum nostrum.

Preface: The Transfiguration
of the Lord.

It is truly right and just,
    our duty and our salvation,
always and everywhere
    to give you thanks,
Lord, holy Father,
    almighty and eternal God,
through Christ our Lord.

For after he had told the disciples
    of his coming Death,
on the holy mountain
    he manifested to them his glory,
to show, even by the testimony
    of the law and the prophets,
that the Passion leads to the glory
    of the Resurrection.

And so, with the Powers of heaven,
we worship you constantly on earth,
and before your majesty
without end we acclaim:

Holy, Holy, Holy Lord God of hosts...

Praefatio: De transfiguratione Domini.

Vere dignum et iustum est,
    aequum et salutare,
nos tibi semper et ubique
    gratias agere:
Domine, sancte Pater,
    omnipotens aeterne Deus:
per Christum Dominum nostrum:

Qui, propria morte
    praenuntiata discipulis,
in monte sancto suam eis
    aperuit claritatem,
ut per passionem, etiam lege
    prophetisque testantibus,
ad gloriam resurrectionis
    perveniri constaret.

Et ideo, cum caelorum Virtutibus,
in terris te iugiter celebramus,
maiestati tuae sine fine clamantes:

Sanctus, Sanctus, Sanctus. . .

Communion Antiphon   Mt 17:5

This is my beloved Son,
    with whom I am well pleased;
listen to him.

Ant. ad communionem

Hic est Filius meus dilectus,
in quo mihi bene complacui;
ipsum audite.

Prayer after Communion

As we receive these
  glorious mysteries,
we make thanksgiving to you,
  O Lord,
for allowing us while still on earth
to be partakers even now
  of the things of heaven.
Through Christ our Lord.

Post communionem

Percipientes, Domine,
  gloriosa mysteria,
gratias tibi referre satagimus,
quod, in terra positos,
iam cælestium præstas
  esse participes.
Per Christum Dominum nostrum.

Prayer over the People

Bless your faithful, we pray, O Lord,
with a blessing that endures for ever,
and keep them faithful
to the Gospel of your
  Only Begotten Son,
so that they may always desire
  and at last attain
that glory whose beauty he showed
  in his own Body,
to the amazement of his Apostles.
Through Christ our Lord.

Oratio super populum

Benedic, Domine, fideles tuos
  benedictione perpetua,
et fac eos Unigeniti tui Evangelio
  sic adhærere,
ut ad illam gloriam, cuius in se
  speciem Apostolis ostendit,
et suspirare iugiter et feliciter
  valeant pervenire.
Per Christum Dominum nostrum.

THIRD SUNDAY OF LENT (YEAR A)

This year, on this Third Sunday of Lent, the liturgy again presents one of the most beautiful and profound passages of the Bible: the dialogue between Jesus and the Samaritan woman. The Samaritan woman represents the existential dissatisfaction of one who does not find what he seeks. She had "five husbands" and now she lives with another man; her going to and from the well to draw water expresses a repetitive and resigned life. However, everything changes for her that day, thanks to the conversation with the Lord Jesus. Like the Samaritan woman, let us also open our hearts to listen trustingly to God's Word in order to encounter Jesus who reveals his love to us and tells us: "I who speak to you am he", the Messiah, your Saviour.

(Pope Benedict XVI)

Entrance Antiphon Cf. Ps 24:15-16

MY eyes are always on the Lord,
    for he rescues my feet
from the snare.
Turn to me and have mercy on me,
for I am alone and poor.

Or: Cf. Ezk 36:23-26

When I prove my holiness
among you,

I will gather you from all
    the foreign lands;
and I will pour clean water upon you
and cleanse you from all
    your impurities,
and I will give you a new spirit,
    says the Lord.

Ant. ad introitum

OCULI mei semper
    ad Dominum,
quia ipse evellet de laqueo
    pedes meos.
Respice in me et miserere mei,
quoniam unicus et pauper sum ego.

Vel:

Cum sanctificatus fuero in vobis,
congregabo vos de universis terris;
et effundam super vos
    aquam mundam,
et mundabimini ab omnibus
    inquinamentis vestris,
et dabo vobis spiritum novum,
    dicit Dominus.

The Gloria in excelsis (Glory to God in the highest) is not said.

Collect

O God, author of every mercy
    and of all goodness,
who in fasting, prayer and almsgiving
have shown us a remedy for sin,
look graciously on this confession
    of our lowliness,
that we, who are bowed down
    by our conscience,
may always be lifted up
    by your mercy.
Through our Lord Jesus Christ,
    your Son,
who lives and reigns with you
    in the unity of the Holy Spirit,
one God, for ever and ever.

Collecta

Deus, omnium misericordiarum
    et totius bonitatis auctor,
qui peccatorum remedia in ieiuniis,
orationibus et eleemosynis
    demonstrasti,
hanc humilitatis nostræ
    confessionem propitius intuere,
ut, qui inclinamur conscientia nostra,
tua semper misericordia sublevemur.
Per Dominum nostrum Iesum
    Christum Filium tuum,
qui tecum vivit et regnat
    in unitate Spiritus Sancti,
Deus, per omnia sæcula sæculorum.

FIRST READING

A reading from the book of Exodus   17:3-7

Give us water to drink.

Tormented by thirst, the people complained against Moses. 'Why did you bring us out of Egypt?' they said. 'Was it so that I should die of thirst, my children too, and my cattle?' Moses appealed to the Lord. 'How am I to deal with this people?' he said. 'A little more and they will stone me!' The Lord said to Moses, 'Take with you some of the elders of Israel and move on to the forefront of the people; take in your hand the staff with which you struck the river, and go. I shall be standing before you there on the rock, at Horeb. You must strike the rock, and water will flow from it for the people to drink.' This is what Moses did, in the sight of the elders of Israel. The place was named Massah and Meribah because of the grumbling of the sons of Israel and because they put the Lord to the test by saying, 'Is the Lord with us, or not?'

The word of the Lord.

Responsorial Psalm   Ps 94:1-2,6-9. R. v.8

R. **O that today you would listen to his voice:**
    'Harden not your hearts.'

    Come, ring out our joy to the Lord;
    hail the rock who saves us.
    Let us come before him, giving thanks,
    with songs let us hail the Lord. R.

Come in; let us bow and bend low;
let us kneel before the God who made us
for he is our God and we
the people who belong to his pasture,
the flock that is led by his hand. R.

O that today you would listen to his voice!
'Harden not your hearts as at Meribah,
as on that day at Massah in the desert
when your fathers put me to the test;
when they tried me, though they saw my work.' R.

R. **O that today you would listen to his voice:
'Harden not your hearts.'**

SECOND READING

A reading from the letter of St Paul to the Romans   5:1-2,5-8

The love of God has been poured into our hearts by the Holy Spirit which has been given us.

Through our Lord Jesus Christ by faith we are judged righteous and at peace with God, since it is by faith and through Jesus that we have entered this state of grace in which we can boast about looking forward to God's glory. This hope is not deceptive, because the love of God has been poured into our hearts by the Holy Spirit which has been given us. We were still helpless when at his appointed moment Christ died for sinful men. It is not easy to die even for a good man – though of course for someone really worthy, a man might be prepared to die – but what proves that God loves us is that Christ died for us while we were still sinners.

The word of the Lord.

Gospel Acclamation   Cf. Jn 4:42,15

R. **Glory to you, O Christ, you are the Word of God!**
Lord, you are really the saviour of the world;
give me the living water, so that I may never get thirsty.
R. **Glory to you, O Christ, you are the Word of God!**

GOSPEL

A reading from the holy Gospel according to John   4:5-42

A spring of water welling up to eternal life.

[Jesus came to the Samaritan town called Sychar, near the land that Jacob gave to his son Joseph. Jacob's well is there and Jesus, tired by the journey, sat straight down by the well. It was about the sixth hour. When a Samaritan woman came to draw water, Jesus said to her, 'Give me a drink.'

His disciples had gone into the town to buy food. The Samaritan woman said to him, 'What? You are a Jew and you ask me, a Samaritan for a drink?' – Jews in fact, do not associate with Samaritans. Jesus replied:

> 'If you only knew what God is offering
> and who it is that is saying to you:
> Give me a drink,
> you would have been the one to ask,
> and he would have given you living water.'

'You have no bucket, sir,' she answered, 'and the well is deep: how could you get this living water? Are you a greater man than our father Jacob who gave us this well and drank from it himself with his sons and his cattle?' Jesus replied:

> 'Whoever drinks this water
> will get thirsty again;
> but anyone who drinks the water that I shall give
> will never be thirsty again:
> the water that I shall give
> will turn into a spring inside him, welling up to eternal life.'

'Sir,' said the woman, 'give me some of that water, so that I may never get thirsty and never have to come here again to draw water.'] 'Go and call your husband' said Jesus to her 'and come back here.' The woman answered, 'I have no husband.' He said to her, 'You are right to say, "I have no husband"; for although you have had five, the one you have now is not your husband. You spoke the truth there.' ['I see you are a prophet, sir' said the woman. 'Our fathers worshipped on this mountain, while you say that Jerusalem is the place where one ought to worship.' Jesus said:

> 'Believe me, woman, the hour is coming
> when you will worship the Father
> neither on this mountain nor in Jerusalem.
> You worship what you do not know;
> we worship what we do know;
> for salvation comes from the Jews.
> But the hour will come – in fact it is here already –
> when true worshippers will worship the Father in spirit and truth:
> that is the kind of worshipper
> the Father wants.
> God is spirit,
> and those who worship
> must worship in spirit and truth.'

The woman said to him, 'I know that Messiah – that is, Christ – is coming; and when he comes he will tell us everything.' 'I who am speaking to you,' said Jesus 'I am he.']

At this point his disciples returned, and were surprised to find him speaking to a woman, though none of them asked, 'What do you want from her?' or, 'Why are you talking to her?' The woman put down her water jar and hurried back to the town to tell the people, 'Come and see a man who has told me everything I ever did; I wonder if he is the Christ?' This brought people out of the town and they started walking towards him.

Meanwhile, the disciples were urging him, 'Rabbi, do have something to eat'; but he said, 'I have food to eat that you do not know about.' So the disciples asked one another, 'Has someone been bringing him food?' But Jesus said:

'My food
is to do the will of the one who sent me,
and to complete his work.
Have you not got a saying:
Four months and then the harvest?
Well, I tell you:
Look around you, look at the fields;
already they are white, ready for harvest!
Already the reaper is being paid his wages,
already he is bringing in the grain for eternal life,
and thus sower and reaper rejoice together.
For here the proverb holds good:
one sows, another reaps;
I sent you to reap
a harvest you had not worked for.
Others worked for it;
and you have come into the rewards of their trouble.'

[Many Samaritans of that town had believed in him on the strength of the woman's testimony when she said, 'He told me all I have ever done,' so, when the Samaritans came up to him, they begged him to stay with them. He stayed for two days, and when he spoke to them many more came to believe; and they said to the woman, 'Now we no longer believe because of what you told us; we have heard him ourselves and we know that he really is the saviour of the world.'

The Gospel of the Lord.]

Shorter Form, verses 5-15,19-26,39-42. Read between [ ]
The Creed is said.

Prayer over the Offerings

Be pleased, O Lord,
    with these sacrificial offerings,
and grant that we who beseech
    pardon for our own sins,
may take care to forgive
    our neighbour.
Through Christ our Lord.

Preface: The Samaritan Woman.

It is truly right and just,
    our duty and our salvation,
always and everywhere
    to give you thanks,
Lord, holy Father,
    almighty and eternal God,
through Christ our Lord.

For when he asked the Samaritan
    woman for water to drink,
he had already created
    the gift of faith within her
and so ardently did he thirst
    for her faith,
that he kindled in her the fire
    of divine love.
And so we, too, give you thanks
and with the Angels
praise your mighty deeds,
    as we acclaim:

Holy, Holy, Holy Lord God of hosts...

Communion Antiphon Jn 4:13-14

For anyone who drinks it,
    says the Lord,
the water I shall give will become
    in him
a spring welling up to eternal life.

Super oblata

His sacrificiis, Domine,
    concede placatus,
ut, qui propriis oramus
    absolvi delictis,
fraterna dimittere studeamus.
Per Christum Dominum nostrum.

Praefatio: De Samaritana.

Vere dignum et iustum est,
    aequum et salutare,
nos tibi semper et ubique
    gratias agere:
Domine, sancte Pater,
    omnipotens aeterne Deus:
per Christum Dominum nostrum:

Qui, dum aquae sibi petiit potum
    a Samaritana praeberi,
iam in ea fidei donum ipse creaverat,
et ita eius fidem sitire dignatus est,
ut ignem in illa divini
    amoris accenderet.

Unde et nos tibi gratias agimus,
et tuas virtutes cum Angelis
    praedicamus, dicentes:

Sanctus, Sanctus, Sanctus. . .

Ant. ad communionem

Qui biberit aquam, quam ego dabo
    ei, dicit Dominus,
fiet in eo fons aquæ salientis
    in vitam æternam.

Prayer after Communion

As we receive the pledge
of things yet hidden in heaven
and are nourished while still
    on earth
with the Bread that comes
    from on high,
we humbly entreat you, O Lord,
that what is being brought about
    in us in mystery
may come to true completion.
Through Christ our Lord.

Post communionem

Sumentes pignus cælestis arcani,
et in terra positi iam superno
    pane satiati,
te, Domine, supplices deprecamur,
ut, quod in nobis mysterio geritur,
    opere impleatur.
Per Christum Dominum nostrum.

Prayer over the People

Direct, O Lord, we pray,
    the hearts of your faithful,
and in your kindness grant
    your servants this grace:
that, abiding in the love of you
    and their neighbour,
they may fulfil the whole
    of your commands.
Through Christ our Lord.

Oratio super populum

Rege, Domine, quæsumus,
    tuorum corda fidelium,
et servis tuis hanc gratiam
    largire propitius,
ut in tui et proximi
    dilectione manentes
plenitudinem mandatorum
    tuorum adimpleant.
Per Christum Dominum nostrum.

FOURTH SUNDAY OF LENT (YEAR A)

On these Sundays in Lent the liturgy takes us on a true and proper baptismal route through the texts of John's Gospel: last Sunday, Jesus promised the gift of "living water" to the Samaritan woman; today, by healing the man born blind, he reveals himself as "the light of the world"; next Sunday, in raising his friend Lazarus, he will present himself as "the resurrection and the life". Water, light and life are symbols of Baptism, the Sacrament that "immerses" believers in the mystery of the death and Resurrection of Christ, liberating them from the slavery of sin and giving them eternal life.

(Pope Benedict XVI)

Entrance Antiphon Cf. Is 66:10-11

REJOICE, Jerusalem,
and all who love her.
Be joyful, all who were
    in mourning;
exult and be satisfied at her
    consoling breast.

Ant. ad introitum

LÆTARE, Ierusalem,
et conventum facite,
    omnes qui diligitis eam;
gaudete cum lætitia,
    qui in tristitia fuistis,
ut exsultetis, et satiemini ab
    uberibus consolationis vestræ.

The Gloria in excelsis (Glory to God in the highest) is not said.

Collect

O God, who through your Word
reconcile the human race
    to yourself in a wonderful way,
grant, we pray,
that with prompt devotion
    and eager faith
the Christian people may hasten
toward the solemn celebrations
    to come.
Through our Lord Jesus Christ,
    your Son,
who lives and reigns with you
    in the unity of the Holy Spirit,
one God, for ever and ever.

Collecta

Deus, qui per Verbum tuum
humani generis reconciliationem
    mirabiliter operaris,
præsta, quæsumus,
    ut populus christianus
prompta devotione et alacri fide
ad ventura sollemnia valeat festinare.
Per Dominum nostrum Iesum
    Christum Filium tuum,
qui tecum vivit et regnat
    in unitate Spiritus Sancti,
Deus, per omnia sæcula sæculorum.

FIRST READING

A reading from the first book of Samuel   16:1,6-7,10-13

David is anointed king of Israel.

The Lord said to Samuel, 'Fill your horn with oil and go. I am sending you to Jesse of Bethlehem, for I have chosen myself a king among his sons.' When Samuel arrived, he caught sight of Eliab and thought, 'Surely the Lord's anointed one stands there before him,' but the Lord said to Samuel, 'Take no notice of his appearance or his height for I have rejected him; God does not see as man sees; man looks at appearances but the Lord looks at the heart.' Jesse presented his seven sons to Samuel, but Samuel said to Jesse, 'The Lord has not chosen these.' He then asked Jesse, 'Are these all the sons you have?' He answered, 'There is still one left, the youngest; he is out looking after the sheep.' Then Samuel said to Jesse, 'Send for him; we will not sit down to eat until he comes.' Jesse had him sent for, a boy of fresh complexion, with fine eyes and pleasant bearing. The Lord said, 'Come, anoint him, for this is the one.' At this, Samuel took the horn of oil and anointed him where he stood with his brothers; and the spirit of the Lord seized on David and stayed with him from that day on.

The word of the Lord.

Responsorial Psalm   Ps 22. R. v.1

R. **The Lord is my shepherd;**
   there is nothing I shall want.

The Lord is my shepherd;
there is nothing I shall want.
Fresh and green are the pastures
where he gives me repose.
Near restful waters he leads me,
to revive my drooping spirit. R.

He guides me along the right path;
he is true to his name.
If I should walk in the valley of darkness
no evil would I fear.
You are there with your crook and your staff;
with these you give me comfort. R.

You have prepared a banquet for me
in the sight of my foes.
My head you have anointed with oil;
my cup is overflowing. R.

Surely goodness and kindness shall follow me
all the days of my life.
In the Lord's own house shall I dwell
for ever and ever. R.

SECOND READING

A reading from the letter of St Paul to the Ephesians   5:8-14

Rise from the dead and Christ will shine on you.

You were darkness once, but now you are light in the Lord; be like children
of light, for the effects of the light are seen in complete goodness and right
living and truth. Try to discover what the Lord wants of you, having nothing
to do with the futile works of darkness but exposing them by contrast.
The things which are done in secret are things that people are ashamed
even to speak of; but anything exposed by the light will be illuminated and
anything illuminated turns into light. That is why it is said:

Wake up from your sleep,
rise from the dead,
and Christ will shine on you.

The word of the Lord.

Gospel Acclamation   Jn 8:12

R. **Glory to you, O Christ, you are the Word of God!**
I am the light of the world, says the Lord;
anyone who follows me will have the light of life.
R. **Glory to you, O Christ, you are the Word of God!**

GOSPEL

A reading from the holy Gospel according to John   9:1-41

The blind man went off and washed himself, and came away with his sight restored.

| [As Jesus went along, he saw a man who had been blind from birth.] His
disciples asked him, 'Rabbi, who sinned, this man or his parents, for him to
have been born blind?' 'Neither he nor his parents sinned,' Jesus answered
'he was born blind so that the works of God might be displayed in him.

'As long as the day lasts
I must carry out the work of the one who sent me;
the night will soon be here when no one can work.
As long as I am in the world
I am the light of the world.'

Having said this, [he spat on the ground, made a paste with the spittle, put this over the eyes of the blind man and said to him, 'Go and wash in the Pool of Siloam' (a name that means 'sent'). So the blind man went off and washed himself, and came away with his sight restored.

His neighbours and people who earlier had seen him begging said, 'Isn't this the man who used to sit and beg?' Some said, 'Yes, it is the same one.' Others said, 'No, he only looks like him.' The man himself said, 'I am the man.'] So they said to him, 'Then how do your eyes come to be open?' 'The man called Jesus' he answered 'made a paste, daubed my eyes with it and said to me, "Go and wash at Siloam"; so I went, and when I washed I could see.' They asked, 'Where is he?' 'I don't know' he answered.

[They brought the man who had been blind to the Pharisees. It had been a sabbath day when Jesus made the paste and opened the man's eyes, so when the Pharisees asked him how he had come to see, he said, 'He put a paste on my eyes, and I washed, and I can see.' Then some of the Pharisees said, 'This man cannot be from God: he does not keep the sabbath.' Others said, 'How could a sinner produce signs like this?' And there was disagreement among them. So they spoke to the blind man again, 'What have you to say about him yourself, now that he has opened your eyes?' 'He is a prophet' replied the man.]

However, the Jews would not believe that the man had been blind and had gained his sight, without first sending for his parents and asking them, 'Is this man really your son who you say was born blind? If so, how is it that he is now able to see?' His parents answered, 'We know he is our son and we know he was born blind, but we don't know how it is that he can see now, or who opened his eyes. He is old enough: let him speak for himself.' His parents spoke like this out of fear of the Jews, who had already agreed to expel from the synagogue anyone who should acknowledge Jesus as the Christ. This was why his parents said, 'He is old enough; ask him.'

So the Jews again sent for the man and said to him, 'Give glory to God! For our part, we know that this man is a sinner.' The man answered, 'I don't know if he is a sinner; I only know that I was blind and now I can see.' They said to him, 'What did he do to you? How did he open your eyes?' He replied, 'I have told you once and you wouldn't listen. Why do you want to hear it all again? Do you want to become his disciples too?' At this they hurled abuse at him: 'You can be his disciple,' they said 'we are disciples of Moses: we know that God spoke to Moses, but as for this man, we don't know where he comes from.' The man replied, 'Now here is an astonishing thing! He has opened my eyes and you don't know where he comes from! We know that God doesn't listen to sinners, but God does listen to men who are devout and do his will. Ever since the world began it is unheard of for anyone to open the eyes of a man who was born blind; if this man were not from God, he couldn't do a thing.' ['Are you trying to teach us,' they replied 'and you a sinner through and through, since you were born!' And they drove him away.

Jesus heard they had driven him away, and when he found him he said to him, 'Do you believe in the Son of Man?' 'Sir,' the man replied 'tell me who he is so that I may believe in him.' Jesus said, 'You are looking at him; he is speaking to you.' The man said, 'Lord, I believe', and worshipped him.]

Jesus said:

'It is for judgement
that I have come into this world,
so that those without sight may see
and those with sight turn blind.'

Hearing this, some Pharisees who were present said to him, 'We are not blind, surely?' Jesus replied:

'Blind? If you were,
you would not be guilty,
but since you say, "We see",
your guilt remains.'

| [The Gospel of the Lord.]

Shorter Form, verses 1,6-9,13-17,34-38. Read between [ ]

The Creed is said.

Prayer over the Offerings

We place before you with joy
    these offerings,
which bring eternal remedy, O Lord,
praying that we may both faithfully
    revere them
and present them to you, as is fitting,
for the salvation of all the world.
Through Christ our Lord.

Preface: The Man Born Blind.

It is truly right and just,
    our duty and our salvation,
always and everywhere
    to give you thanks,
Lord, holy Father,
    almighty and eternal God,
through Christ our Lord.

By the mystery of the Incarnation,
he has led the human race
    that walked in darkness
into the radiance of the faith
and has brought those born
    in slavery to ancient sin
through the waters of regeneration
to make them your adopted children.

Therefore, all creatures
    of heaven and earth
sing a new song in adoration,
and we, with all the host of Angels,
cry out, and without end acclaim:

Holy, Holy, Holy Lord God of hosts...

Super oblata

Remedii sempiterni munera,
    Domine,
lætantes offerimus,
    suppliciter exorantes,
ut eadem nos et fideliter venerari,
et pro salute mundi congruenter
    exhibere perficias.
Per Christum Dominum nostrum.

Praefatio: De caeco nato.

Vere dignum et iustum est,
    aequum et salutare,
nos tibi semper et ubique
    gratias agere:
Domine, sancte Pater,
    omnipotens aeterne Deus:
per Christum Dominum nostrum:

Qui genus humanum,
    in tenebris ambulans,
ad fidei claritatem
per mysterium incarnationis adduxit,
et, qui servi peccati
    veteris nascebantur,
per lavacrum regenerationis
in filios adoptionis assumpsit.

Propter quod caelestia tibi
    atque terrestria
canticum novum
    concinunt adorando,
et nos cum omni exercitu Angelorum
proclamamus, sine fine dicentes:

Sanctus, Sanctus, Sanctus. . .

Communion Antiphon Cf. Jn 9:11,38

The Lord anointed my eyes:
    I went, I washed,
I saw and I believed in God.

Ant. ad communionem

Dominus linivit oculos meos:
et abii, et lavi, et vidi, et credidi Deo.

Prayer after Communion

O God, who enlighten everyone
   who comes into this world,
illuminate our hearts, we pray,
with the splendour of your grace,
that we may always ponder
what is worthy and pleasing
   to your majesty
and love you in all sincerity.
Through Christ our Lord.

Prayer over the People

Look upon those who call to you,
   O Lord,
and sustain the weak;
give life by your unfailing light
to those who walk in the shadow
   of death,
and bring those rescued by your
   mercy from every evil
to reach the highest good.
Through Christ our Lord.

Post communionem

Deus, qui illuminas
   omnem hominem
venientem in hunc mundum,
illumina, quæsumus, corda nostra
   gratiæ tuæ splendore,
ut digna ac placita maiestati tuæ
   cogitare semper,
et te sincere diligere valeamus.
Per Christum Dominum nostrum.

Oratio super populum

Tuere, Domine, supplices tuos,
   sustenta fragiles,
et inter tenebras mortalium
   ambulantes
tua semper luce vivifica,
atque a malis omnibus
   clementer ereptos,
ad summa bona pervenire concede.
Per Christum Dominum nostrum.

FIFTH SUNDAY OF LENT (YEAR A)

There are only two weeks to go until Easter and the Bible Readings of this Sunday all speak about resurrection. It is not yet that of Jesus, which bursts in as an absolute innovation, but our own resurrection, to which we aspire and which Christ himself gave to us, in rising from the dead. Indeed, death represents a wall as it were, which prevents us from seeing beyond it; yet our hearts reach out beyond this wall and even though we cannot understand what it conceals, we nevertheless think about it and imagine it, expressing with symbols our desire for eternity. Christ pulls down the wall of death and in him dwells all the fullness of God, who is life, eternal life.

(Pope Benedict XVI)

Entrance Antiphon   Cf. Ps 42:1-2

GIVE me justice, O God,
and plead my cause against
a nation that is faithless.
From the deceitful and cunning
rescue me,
for you, O God, are my strength.

Ant. ad introitum

IUDICA me, Deus,
et discerne causam meam
de gente non sancta;
ab homine iniquo et doloso eripe me,
quia tu es Deus meus
et fortitudo mea.

The Gloria in excelsis (Glory to God in the highest) is not said.

Collect

By your help, we beseech you,
Lord our God,
may we walk eagerly
in that same charity
with which, out of love for the world,
your Son handed himself
over to death.
Through our Lord Jesus Christ,
your Son,
who lives and reigns with you
in the unity of the Holy Spirit,
one God, for ever and ever.

Collecta

Quæsumus, Domine Deus noster,
ut in illa caritate
qua Filius tuus diligens mundum
morti se tradidit,
inveniamur ipsi, te opitulante,
alacriter ambulantes.
Per Dominum nostrum Iesum
Christum Filium tuum,
qui tecum vivit et regnat
in unitate Spiritus Sancti,
Deus, per omnia sæcula sæculorum.

FIRST READING

A reading from the prophet Ezekiel   37:12-14

I shall put my spirit in you, and you will live.

The Lord says this: I am now going to open your graves; I mean to raise you from your graves, my people, and lead you back to the soil of Israel. And you will know that I am the Lord, when I open your graves and raise you from your graves, my people. And I shall put my spirit in you, and you will live, and I shall resettle you on your own soil; and you will know that I, the Lord, have said and done this – it is the Lord who speaks.

The word of the Lord.

Responsial Psalm   Ps 129. R. v.7

R. **With the Lord there is mercy
and fullness of redemption.**

Out of the depths I cry to you, O Lord,
Lord, hear my voice!
O let your ears be attentive
to the voice of my pleading. R.

If you, O Lord, should mark our guilt,
Lord, who would survive?
But with you is found forgiveness:
for this we revere you. R.

My soul is waiting for the Lord,
I count on his word.
My soul is longing for the Lord
more than watchman for daybreak.
(Let the watchman count on daybreak
and Israel on the Lord.) R.

Because with the Lord there is mercy
and fullness of redemption,
Israel indeed he will redeem
from all its iniquity. R.

SECOND READING

A reading from the letter of St Paul to the Romans   8:8-11
The Spirit of him who raised Jesus from the dead is living in you.

People who are interested only in unspiritual things can never be pleasing to God. Your interests, however, are not in the unspiritual, but in the spiritual, since the Spirit of God has made his home in you. In fact, unless you possessed the Spirit of Christ you would not belong to him. Though your body may be dead it is because of sin, but if Christ is in you then your spirit is life itself because you have been justified; and if the Spirit of him who raised Jesus from the dead is living in you, then he who raised Jesus from the dead will give life to your own mortal bodies through his Spirit living in you.

The word of the Lord.

Gospel Acclamation   Jn 11:25-26

R. **Glory and praise to you, O Christ!**
I am the resurrection and the life, says the Lord:
whoever believes in me will never die.
R. **Glory and praise to you, O Christ!**

GOSPEL

A reading from the holy Gospel according to John   11:1-45
I am the resurrection and the life.

There was a man named Lazarus who lived in the village of Bethany with the
two sisters, Mary and Martha, and he was ill. It was the same Mary, the sister
of the sick man Lazarus, who anointed the Lord with ointment and wiped his
feet with her hair. [The sisters sent this message to Jesus, 'Lord, the man you
love is ill.' On receiving the message, Jesus said, 'This sickness will end not
in death but in God's glory, and through it the Son of God will be glorified.'

Jesus loved Martha and her sister and Lazarus, yet when he heard that
Lazarus was ill he stayed where he was for two more days before saying to
the disciples, 'Let us go to Judaea.'] The disciples said, 'Rabbi, it is not long
since the Jews wanted to stone you; are you going back again?' Jesus replied:

'Are there not twelve hours in the day?
A man can walk in the daytime without stumbling
because he has the light of this world to see by;
but if he walks at night he stumbles,
because there is no light to guide him.'

He said that and then added, 'Our friend Lazarus is resting, I am going
to wake him.' The disciples said to him, 'Lord, if he is able to rest he is sure
to get better.' The phrase Jesus used referred to the death of Lazarus, but
they thought that by 'rest' he meant 'sleep', so Jesus put it plainly, 'Lazarus
is dead; and for your sake I am glad I was not there because now you will
believe. But let us go to him.' Then Thomas – known as the Twin – said to
the other disciples, 'Let us go too, and die with him.'

[On arriving, Jesus found that Lazarus had been in the tomb for four
days already.] Bethany is only about two miles from Jerusalem, and many
Jews had come to Martha and Mary to sympathise with them over their
brother. [When Martha heard that Jesus had come she went to meet him.
Mary remained sitting in the house. Martha said to Jesus, 'If you had
been here, my brother would not have died, but I know that, even now,
whatever you ask of God, he will grant you.' 'Your brother' said Jesus to her
'will rise again.' Martha said, 'I know he will rise again at the resurrection
on the last day.' Jesus said:

'I am the resurrection and the life.
If anyone believes in me, even though he dies he will live,
and whoever lives and believes in me
will never die.
Do you believe this?'
'Yes Lord,' she said 'I believe that you are the Christ, the Son of God, the
one who was to come into this world.]

   When she had said this, she went and called her sister Mary, saying in
a low voice, 'The Master is here and wants to see you.' Hearing this, Mary
got up quickly and went to him. Jesus had not yet come into the village; he
was still at the place where Martha had met him. When the Jews who were
in the house sympathising with Mary saw her get up so quickly and go out,
they followed her, thinking that she was going to the tomb to weep there.

   Mary went to Jesus, and as soon as she saw him she threw herself at his
feet, saying, 'Lord, if you had been here, my brother would not have died.'
At the sight of her tears, and those of the Jews who followed her, [Jesus said
in great distress, with a sigh that came straight from the heart, 'Where have
you put him?' They said, 'Lord, come and see.' Jesus wept; and the Jews
said, 'See how much he loved him!' But there were some who remarked, 'He
opened the eyes of the blind man, could he not have prevented this man's
death?' Still sighing, Jesus reached the tomb: it was a cave with a stone to
close the opening. Jesus said, 'Take the stone away.' Martha said to him,
'Lord, by now he will smell; this is the fourth day.' Jesus replied, 'Have I not
told you that if you believe you will see the glory of God?' So they took away
the stone. Then Jesus lifted up his eyes and said:

'Father, I thank you for hearing my prayer.
I knew indeed that you always hear me,
but I speak
for the sake of all these who stand round me,
so that they may believe it was you who sent me.'

   When he had said this, he cried in a loud voice, 'Lazarus, here! Come
out!' The dead man came out, his feet and hands bound with bands of stuff
and a cloth round his face. Jesus said to them, 'Unbind him, let him go free.'

   Many of the Jews who had come to visit Mary and had seen what he did
believed in him.

   The Gospel of the Lord.]

Shorter Form, verses 3-7,17,20-27,33-45. Read between [ ]
The Creed is said.

Prayer over the Offerings

Hear us, almighty God,
and, having instilled in your servants
the teachings of the Christian faith,
graciously purify them
by the working of this sacrifice.
Through Christ our Lord.

Preface: Lazarus.

It is truly right and just,
    our duty and our salvation,
always and everywhere
    to give you thanks,
Lord, holy Father,
    almighty and eternal God,
through Christ our Lord.

For as true man he wept
    for Lazarus his friend
and as eternal God raised him
    from the tomb,
just as, taking pity on
    the human race,
he leads us by sacred mysteries
    to new life.

Through him the host
    of Angels adores your majesty
and rejoices in your presence
    for ever.
May our voices, we pray,
    join with theirs
in one chorus of exultant praise,
    as we acclaim:

Holy, Holy, Holy Lord God of hosts...

Communion Antiphon Cf. Jn 11:26

Everyone who lives and believes
    in me
will not die for ever, says the Lord.

Super oblata

Exaudi nos, omnipotens Deus,
et famulos tuos, quos fidei christianæ
    eruditionibus imbuisti,
huius sacrificii tribuas
    operatione mundari.
Per Christum Dominum nostrum.

Praefatio: De Lazaro.

Vere dignum et iustum est,
    aequum et salutare,
nos tibi semper
    et ubique gratias agere:
Domine, sancte Pater,
    omnipotens aeterne Deus:
per Christum Dominum nostrum:

Ipse enim verus homo Lazarum
    flevit amicum,
et Deus aeternus
    e tumulo suscitavit,
qui, humani generis miseratus,
ad novam vitam sacris
    mysteriis nos adducit.

Per quem maiestatem tuam adorat
    exercitus Angelorum,
ante conspectum tuum
    in aeternitate laetantium.
Cum quibus et nostras voces
    ut admitti iubeas, deprecamur,
socia exsultatione dicentes:

Sanctus, Sanctus, Sanctus. . .

Ant. ad communionem

Omnis qui vivit et credit in me,
non morietur in æternum,
    dicit Dominus.

Prayer after Communion

We pray, almighty God,
that we may always be counted
    among the members of Christ,
in whose Body and Blood
    we have communion.
Who lives and reigns
    for ever and ever.

Prayer over the People

Bless, O Lord, your people,
who long for the gift of your mercy,
and grant that what,
    at your prompting, they desire
they may receive
    by your generous gift.
Through Christ our Lord.

Post communionem

Quæsumus, omnipotens Deus,
ut inter eius membra
    semper numeremur,
cuius Corpori communicamus
    et Sanguini.
Qui vivit et regnat
    in sæcula sæculorum.

Oratio super populum

Benedic, Domine, plebem tuam,
quæ munus tuæ
    miserationis exspectat,
et concede, ut, quod,
    te inspirante, desiderat,
te largiente percipiat.
Per Christum Dominum nostrum.

LENT (YEAR B)

ASH WEDNESDAY

FIRST SUNDAY OF LENT (YEAR B)

Following their Teacher and Lord, Christians also enter the Lenten desert in spirit in order to face with him the "fight against the spirit of evil". The image of the desert is a very eloquent metaphor of the human condition. The Book of Exodus recounts the experience of the People of Israel who, after leaving Egypt, wandered through the desert of Sinai for forty years before they reached the Promised Land. During that long journey, the Jews experienced the full force and persistence of the tempter, who urged them to lose trust in the Lord and to turn back; but at the same time, thanks to Moses's mediation, they learned to listen to God's voice calling them to become his holy People. In meditating on this biblical passage, we understand that to live life to the full in freedom we must overcome the test that this freedom entails, that is, temptation.

(Pope Benedict XVI)

Entrance Antiphon Cf. Ps 90:15-16

WHEN he calls on me,
I will answer him;
I will deliver him and give him glory,
I will grant him length of days.

The Gloria in excelsis (Glory to God in the highest) is not said.

Collect

Grant, almighty God,
through the yearly observances
    of holy Lent,
that we may grow in understanding
of the riches hidden in Christ
and by worthy conduct pursue
    their effects.
Through our Lord Jesus Christ,
    your Son,
who lives and reigns with you
    in the unity of the Holy Spirit,
one God, for ever and ever.

Ant. ad introitum

INVOCABIT me,
et ego exaudiam eum;
eripiam eum, et glorificabo eum,
longitudine dierum adimplebo eum.

Collecta

Concede nobis, omnipotens Deus,
ut, per annua quadragesimalis
    exercitia sacramenti,
et ad intellegendum Christi
    proficiamus arcanum,
et effectus eius digna
    conversatione sectemur.
Per Dominum nostrum Iesum
    Christum Filium tuum,
qui tecum vivit et regnat
    in unitate Spiritus Sancti,
Deus, per omnia sæcula sæculorum.

FIRST READING

A reading from the book of Genesis 9:8-15

God's covenant with Noah after he had saved him from the waters of the flood.

God spoke to Noah and his sons, 'See, I establish my Covenant with you, and with your descendants after you; also with every living creature to be found with you, birds, cattle and every wild beast with you: everything that came out of the ark, everything that lives on the earth. I establish my Covenant with you: no thing of flesh shall be swept away again by the waters of the flood. There shall be no flood to destroy the earth again.'

God said, 'Here is the sign of the Covenant I make between myself and you and every living creature with you for all generations: I set my bow in the clouds and it shall be a sign of the Covenant between me and the earth. When I gather the clouds over the earth and the bow appears in the clouds, I will recall the Covenant between myself and you and every living creature of every kind. And so the waters shall never again become a flood to destroy all things of flesh.'

The word of the Lord.

Responsional Psalm Ps 24:4-9. R. Cf. v.10

R. **Your ways, Lord, are faithfulness and love**
for those who keep your covenant.

Lord, make me know your ways.
Lord, teach me your paths.
Make me walk in your truth, and teach me:
for you are God my saviour. R.

Remember your mercy, Lord
and the love you have shown from of old.
In your love remember me,
because of your goodness, O Lord. R.

The Lord is good and upright.
He shows the path to those who stray,
he guides the humble in the right path;
he teaches his way to the poor. R.

SECOND READING

A reading from the first letter of St Peter 3:18-22

That water is a type of the baptism which saves you now.

Christ himself, innocent though he was, died once for sins, died for the guilty, to lead us to God. In the body he was put to death, in the spirit he was raised to life, and, in the spirit, he went to preach to the spirits in prison. Now it was long ago, when Noah was still building that ark which saved only a small group of eight people 'by water', and when God was still waiting patiently, that these spirits refused to believe. That water is a type of the baptism which saves you now, and which is not the washing off of physical dirt but a pledge made to God from a good conscience, through the resurrection of Jesus Christ, who has entered heaven and is at God's right hand, now that he has made the angels and Dominations and Powers his subjects.

The word of the Lord.

Gospel Acclamation   Mt 4:4

R. **Praise to you, O Christ, king of eternal glory!**
Man does not live on bread alone,
but on every word that comes from the mouth of God.
R. **Praise to you, O Christ, king of eternal glory!**

GOSPEL

A reading from the holy Gospel according to Mark   1:12-15
Jesus was tempted by Satan, and the angels looked after him.

The Spirit drove Jesus out into the wilderness and he remained there for forty days, and was tempted by Satan. He was with the wild beasts, and the angels looked after him.

After John had been arrested, Jesus went into Galilee. There he proclaimed the Good News from God. 'The time has come' he said 'and the kingdom of God is close at hand. Repent, and believe the Good News.'

The Gospel of the Lord.

The Creed is said.

Prayer over the Offerings
Give us the right dispositions,
    O Lord, we pray,
to make these offerings,
for with them we celebrate
    the beginning
of this venerable and sacred time.
Through Christ our Lord.

Super oblata
Fac nos, quæsumus, Domine,
his muneribus offerendis
    convenienter aptari,
quibus ipsius venerabilis sacramenti
    celebramus exordium.
Per Christum Dominum nostrum.

Preface: The Temptation of the Lord, p.155.

Communion Antiphon   Mt 4:4

One does not live by bread alone,
but by every word that comes forth
　　from the mouth of God.

Or: Cf. Ps 90:4

The Lord will conceal you
　　with his pinions,
and under his wings you will trust.

Prayer after Communion

Renewed now with heavenly bread,
by which faith is nourished,
　　hope increased,
and charity strengthened,
we pray, O Lord,
that we may learn to hunger
　　for Christ,
the true and living Bread,
and strive to live by every word
which proceeds from your mouth.
Through Christ our Lord.

Prayer over the People

May bountiful blessing,
　　O Lord, we pray,
come down upon your people,
that hope may grow in tribulation,
virtue be strengthened in temptation,
and eternal redemption be assured.
Through Christ our Lord.

Ant. ad communionem

Non in solo pane vivit homo,
sed in omni verbo quod procedit
　　de ore Dei.

Vel:

Scapulis suis obumbrabit
　　tibi Dominus,
et sub pennis eius sperabis.

Post communionem

Cælesti pane refecti,
quo fides alitur, spes provehitur
　　et caritas roboratur,
quæsumus, Domine,
ut ipsum, qui est panis vivus
　　et verus, esurire discamus,
et in omni verbo,
　　quod procedit de ore tuo,
vivere valeamus.
Per Christum Dominum nostrum.

Oratio super populum

Super populum tuum,
　　Domine, quæsumus,
benedictio copiosa descendat,
ut spes in tribulatione succrescat,
virtus in tentatione firmetur,
æterna redemptio tribuatur.
Per Christum Dominum nostrum.

SECOND SUNDAY OF LENT (YEAR B)

When one has the grace to live a strong experience of God, it is as if one is living an experience similar to that of the disciples during the Transfiguration: a momentary foretaste of what will constitute the happiness of Paradise. No one, however, is permitted to live "on Tabor" while on earth. Indeed, human existence is a journey of faith and as such, moves ahead more in shadows than in full light, and is no stranger to moments of obscurity and also of complete darkness. While we are on this earth, our relationship with God takes place more by listening than by seeing . . . And so, this is the gift and duty for each one of us during the season of Lent: to listen to Christ, like Mary. To listen to him in his Word, contained in Sacred Scripture. To listen to him in the events of our lives, seeking to decipher in them the messages of Providence. Finally, to listen to him in our brothers and sisters, especially in the lowly and the poor, for whom Jesus himself demands our concrete love.

(Pope Benedict XVI)

Entrance Antiphon   Cf. Ps 26:8-9

OF you my heart has spoken:
    Seek his face.
It is your face, O Lord, that I seek;
hide not your face from me.

Or: Cf. Ps 24:6,2,22

Remember your compassion,
    O Lord,
and your merciful love,
    for they are from of old.
Let not our enemies exult over us.
Redeem us, O God of Israel,
    from all our distress.

Ant. ad introitum

TIBI dixit cor meum quæsivi
    vultum tuum,
vultum tuum, Domine, requiram.
Ne avertas faciem tuam a me.

Vel:

Reminiscere miserationum tuarum,
    Domine,
et misericordiæ tuæ,
    quæ a sæculo sunt.
Ne umquam dominentur nobis
    inimici nostri;
libera nos, Deus Israel, ex omnibus
    angustiis nostris.

The Gloria in excelsis (Glory to God in the highest) is not said.

Collect	Collecta

O God, who have commanded us
to listen to your beloved Son,
be pleased, we pray,
to nourish us inwardly by your word,
that, with spiritual sight made pure,
we may rejoice to behold your glory.
Through our Lord Jesus Christ,
   your Son,
who lives and reigns with you
   in the unity of the Holy Spirit,
one God, for ever and ever.
	Deus, qui nobis dilectum Filium
	   tuum audire præcepisti,
	verbo tuo interius
	   nos pascere digneris,
	ut, spiritali purificato intuitu,
	gloriæ tuæ lætemur aspectu.
	Per Dominum nostrum Iesum
	   Christum Filium tuum,
	qui tecum vivit et regnat
	   in unitate Spiritus Sancti,
	Deus, per omnia sæcula sæculorum.

FIRST READING

A reading from the book of Genesis   22:1-2,9-13,15-18

The sacrifice of Abraham, our father in faith.

God put Abraham to the test. 'Abraham, Abraham' he called. 'Here I am' he replied. 'Take your son,' God said 'your only child Isaac, whom you love, and go to the land of Moriah. There you shall offer him as a burnt offering, on a mountain I will point out to you.'

When they arrived at the place God had pointed out to him, Abraham built an altar there, and arranged the wood. Then he stretched out his hand and seized the knife to kill his son.

But the angel of the Lord called to him from heaven. 'Abraham, Abraham' he said. 'I am here' he replied. 'Do not raise your hand against the boy' the angel said. 'Do not harm him, for now I know you fear God. You have not refused me your son, your only son.' Then looking up, Abraham saw a ram caught by its horns in a bush. Abraham took the ram and offered it as a burnt-offering in place of his son.

The angel of the Lord called Abraham a second time from heaven. 'I swear by my own self – it is the Lord who speaks – because you have done this, because you have not refused me your son, your only son, I will shower blessings on you, I will make your descendants as many as the stars of heaven and the grains of sand on the seashore. Your descendants shall gain possession of the gates of their enemies. All the nations of the earth shall bless themselves by your descendants, as a reward for your obedience.'

The word of the Lord.

Responsorial Psalm   Ps 115:10,15-19. R. Ps 114:9

R. **I will walk in the presence of the Lord**
   in the land of the living.

I trusted, even when I said:
'I am sorely afflicted.'
O precious in the eyes of the Lord
is the death of his faithful. R.

Your servant, Lord, your servant am I;
you have loosened my bonds.
A thanksgiving sacrifice I make:
I will call on the Lord's name. R.

My vows to the Lord I will fulfil
before all his people,
in the courts of the house of the Lord,
in your midst, O Jerusalem. R.

SECOND READING
A reading from the letter of St Paul to the Romans   8:31-34
God did not spare his own Son.

With God on our side who can be against us? Since God did not spare his
own Son, but gave him up to benefit us all, we may be certain, after such
a gift, that he will not refuse anything he can give. Could anyone accuse
those that God has chosen? When God acquits, could anyone condemn?
Could Christ Jesus? No! He not only died for us – he rose from the dead,
and there at God's right hand he stands and pleads for us.

The word of the Lord.

Gospel Acclamation   Mt 17:5
R. **Glory and praise to you, O Christ!**
From the bright cloud the Father's voice was heard:
'This is my Son, the Beloved. Listen to him.'
R. **Glory and praise to you, O Christ!**

GOSPEL
A reading from the holy Gospel according to Mark   9:2-10
This is my Son, the Beloved.

Jesus took with him Peter and James and John and led them up a high
mountain where they could be alone by themselves. There in their
presence he was transfigured: his clothes became dazzlingly white, whiter

than any earthly bleacher could make them. Elijah appeared to them with Moses; and they were talking with Jesus. Then Peter spoke to Jesus: 'Rabbi,' he said 'it is wonderful for us to be here; so let us make three tents, one for you, one for Moses and one for Elijah.' He did not know what to say; they were so frightened. And a cloud came, covering them in shadow; and there came a voice from the cloud, 'This is my Son, the Beloved. Listen to him.' Then suddenly, when they looked round, they saw no one with them any more but only Jesus.

As they came down the mountain he warned them to tell no one what they had seen, until after the Son of Man had risen from the dead. They observed the warning faithfully, though among themselves they discussed what 'rising from the dead' could mean.

The Gospel of the Lord.

The Creed is said.

Prayer over the Offerings	Super oblata
May this sacrifice, O Lord, we pray, cleanse us of our faults and sanctify your faithful in body and mind for the celebration of the paschal festivities. Through Christ our Lord.	Hæc hostia, Domine, quæsumus, emundet nostra delicta, et ad celebranda festa paschalia fidelium tuorum corpora mentesque sanctificet. Per Christum Dominum nostrum.

Preface: The Transfiguration of the Lord, p.160.

Communion Antiphon　Mt 17:5	Ant. ad communionem
This is my beloved Son, with whom I am well pleased; listen to him.	Hic est Filius meus dilectus, in quo mihi bene complacui; ipsum audite.

Prayer after Communion	Post communionem
As we receive these glorious mysteries, we make thanksgiving to you, O Lord, for allowing us while still on earth to be partakers even now of the things of heaven. Through Christ our Lord.	Percipientes, Domine, gloriosa mysteria, gratias tibi referre satagimus, quod, in terra positos, iam cælestium præstas esse participes. Per Christum Dominum nostrum.

Prayer over the People

Bless your faithful, we pray, O Lord,
with a blessing that endures for ever,
and keep them faithful
to the Gospel of your
    Only Begotten Son,
so that they may always desire
    and at last attain
that glory whose beauty he showed
    in his own Body,
to the amazement of his Apostles.
Through Christ our Lord.

Oratio super populum

Benedic, Domine, fideles tuos
    benedictione perpetua,
et fac eos Unigeniti tui Evangelio
    sic adhærere,
ut ad illam gloriam, cuius in se
    speciem Apostolis ostendit,
et suspirare iugiter et feliciter
    valeant pervenire.
Per Christum Dominum nostrum.

THIRD SUNDAY OF LENT (YEAR B)

The words of the Apostle Paul, which today the liturgy proposes for our meditation, resound in my mind: "We preach Christ crucified: a stumbling block to Jews and folly to Gentiles, but to those who are called, both Jews and Greeks, Christ [is] the power of God and the wisdom of God". I have nothing to propose or give to those whom I shall meet except Christ and the Good News of his Cross, a mystery of supreme love, of divine love that overcomes all human resistance and even makes forgiveness and love for one's enemies possible. This is the grace of the Gospel that is capable of transforming the world. The Church, therefore, does not pursue economic, social or political objectives; the Church proclaims Christ, certain that the Gospel can move the hearts of all and transform them, thereby renewing people and societies from within.

(Pope Benedict XVI)

Entrance Antiphon Cf. Ps 24:15-16

MY eyes are always on the Lord,
for he rescues my feet
   from the snare.
Turn to me and have mercy on me,
for I am alone and poor.

Ant. ad introitum

OCULI mei semper
ad Dominum,
quia ipse evellet de laqueo
   pedes meos.
Respice in me et miserere mei,
quoniam unicus et pauper sum ego.

Or: Cf. Ezk 36:23-26

When I prove my holiness
   among you,
I will gather you from all
   the foreign lands;
and I will pour clean water upon you
and cleanse you from
   all your impurities,
and I will give you a new spirit,
   says the Lord.

Vel:

Cum sanctificatus fuero in vobis,
congregabo vos
   de universis terris;
et effundam super vos
   aquam mundam,
et mundabimini ab omnibus
   inquinamentis vestris,
et dabo vobis spiritum novum,
   dicit Dominus.

The Gloria in excelsis (Glory to God in the highest) is not said.

Collect	Collecta
O God, author of every mercy and of all goodness,	Deus, omnium misericordiarum et totius bonitatis auctor,
who in fasting, prayer and almsgiving have shown us a remedy for sin,	qui peccatorum remedia in ieiuniis, orationibus et eleemosynis demonstrasti,
look graciously on this confession of our lowliness,	hanc humilitatis nostræ confessionem propitius intuere,
that we, who are bowed down by our conscience,	ut, qui inclinamur conscientia nostra,
may always be lifted up by your mercy.	tua semper misericordia sublevemur.
Through our Lord Jesus Christ, your Son,	Per Dominum nostrum Iesum Christum Filium tuum,
who lives and reigns with you in the unity of the Holy Spirit,	qui tecum vivit et regnat in unitate Spiritus Sancti,
one God, for ever and ever.	Deus, per omnia sæcula sæculorum.

The readings for Year A may be used as alternative readings. See pp.163-166. If this is done, the Preface (p.167) and Communion Antiphon (p.167) as in Year A are also used.

FIRST READING

A reading from the book of Exodus   20:1-17

The Law was given through Moses.

[God spoke all these words. He said, 'I am the Lord your God who brought you out of the land of Egypt, out of the house of slavery.

'You shall have no gods except me.]

'You shall not make yourself a carved image or any likeness of anything in heaven or on earth beneath or in the waters under the earth; you shall not bow down to them or serve them. For I, the Lord your God, am a jealous God and I punish the father's fault in the sons, the grandsons, and the great-grandsons of those who hate me; but I show kindness to thousands of those who love me and keep my commandments.

['You shall not utter the name of the Lord your God to misuse it, for the Lord will not leave unpunished the man who utters his name to misuse it.]

'Remember the sabbath day and keep it holy. For six days you shall labour and do all your work, but the seventh day is a sabbath for the Lord your God. You shall do no work that day, neither you nor your son nor your daughter nor your servants, men or women, nor your animals nor the stranger who lives with you. For in six days the Lord made the heavens and the earth and the sea and all that these hold, but on the seventh day he rested; that is why the Lord has blessed the sabbath day and made it sacred.

[‘Honour your father and your mother so that you may have a long life in the land that the Lord your God has given to you.

‘You shall not kill.

‘You shall not commit adultery.

‘You shall not steal.

‘You shall not bear false witness against your neighbour.

‘You shall not covet your neighbour’s house. You shall not covet your neighbour’s wife, or his servant, man or woman, or his ox, or his donkey, or anything that is his.’

The word of the Lord.]

Shorter Form, verses 1-3,7-8,12-17. Read between [ ]

Responsorial Psalm   Ps 18:8-11. R. Jn 6:68

R. **You, Lord, have the message of eternal life.**

The law of the Lord is perfect,
it revives the soul.
The rule of the Lord is to be trusted,
it gives wisdom to the simple. R.

The precepts of the Lord are right,
they gladden the heart.
The command of the Lord is clear,
it gives light to the eyes. R.

The fear of the Lord is holy,
abiding for ever.
The decrees of the Lord are truth
and all of them just. R.

They are more to be desired than gold,
than the purest of gold
and sweeter are they than honey,
than honey from the comb. R.

SECOND READING

A reading from the first letter of St Paul to the Corinthians 1:22-25

Here we are preaching a crucified Christ, an obstacle to men, but to those who are called, the wisdom of God.

While the Jews demand miracles and the Greeks look for wisdom, here are we preaching a crucified Christ; to the Jews an obstacle that they cannot get over, to the pagans madness, but to those who have been called, whether they are Jews or Greeks, a Christ who is the power and the wisdom of God. For God's foolishness is wiser than human wisdom, and God's weakness is stronger than human strength.

The word of the Lord.

Gospel Acclamation Jn 11:25,26

R. **Praise to you, O Christ, king of eternal glory!**
I am the resurrection and the life, says the Lord,
whoever believes in me will never die.
R. **Praise to you, O Christ, king of eternal glory!**

Or: Jn 3:16

R. **Praise to you, O Christ, king of eternal glory!**
God loved the world so much that he gave his only Son;
everyone who believes in him has eternal life.
R. **Praise to you, O Christ, king of eternal glory!**

GOSPEL

A reading from the holy Gospel according to John 2:13-25

Destroy this sanctuary, and in three days I will raise it up.

Just before the Jewish Passover Jesus went up to Jerusalem, and in the Temple he found people selling cattle and sheep and pigeons, and the money changers sitting at their counters there. Making a whip out of some cord, he drove them all out of the Temple, cattle and sheep as well, scattered the money changers' coins, knocked their tables over and said to the pigeon-sellers, 'Take all this out of here and stop turning my Father's house into a market.' Then his disciples remembered the words of scripture: Zeal for your house will devour me. The Jews intervened and said, 'What sign can you show us to justify what you have done?' Jesus answered, 'Destroy this sanctuary, and in three days I will raise it up.' The

Jews replied, 'It has taken forty-six years to build this sanctuary: are you going to raise it up in three days?' But he was speaking of the sanctuary that was his body, and when Jesus rose from the dead, his disciples remembered that he had said this, and they believed the scripture and the words he had said.

During his stay in Jerusalem for the Passover many believed in his name when they saw the signs that he gave, but Jesus knew them all and did not trust himself to them; he never needed evidence about any man; he could tell what a man had in him.

The Gospel of the Lord.

The Creed is said.

Prayer over the Offerings	Super oblata

Be pleased, O Lord,
    with these sacrificial offerings,
and grant that we who beseech
    pardon for our own sins,
may take care to forgive
    our neighbour.
Through Christ our Lord.
	His sacrificiis, Domine,
	    concede placatus,
	ut, qui propriis oramus
	    absolvi delictis,
	fraterna dimittere studeamus.
	Per Christum Dominum nostrum.

Preface I or II of Lent, pp.554-557.

Communion Antiphon Cf. Ps 83:4-5	Ant. ad communionem

The sparrow finds a home,
and the swallow a nest for her young:
by your altars, O Lord of hosts,
    my King and my God.
Blessed are they who dwell
    in your house,
for ever singing your praise.
	Passer invenit sibi domum,
	et turtur nidum,
	    ubi reponat pullos suos:
	altaria tua, Domine virtutum,
	    Rex meus, et Deus meus!
	Beati qui habitant in domo tua,
	in sæculum sæculi laudabunt te.

Prayer after Communion

As we receive the pledge
of things yet hidden in heaven
and are nourished while still on earth
with the Bread that comes
    from on high,
we humbly entreat you, O Lord,
that what is being brought about
    in us in mystery
may come to true completion.
Through Christ our Lord.

Prayer over the People

Direct, O Lord, we pray,
    the hearts of your faithful,
and in your kindness grant
    your servants this grace:
that, abiding in the love of you
    and their neighbour,
they may fulfil the whole
    of your commands.
Through Christ our Lord.

Post communionem

Sumentes pignus cælestis arcani,
et in terra positi iam superno
    pane satiati,
te, Domine, supplices deprecamur,
ut, quod in nobis mysterio geritur,
    opere impleatur.
Per Christum Dominum nostrum.

Oratio super populum

Rege, Domine, quæsumus,
    tuorum corda fidelium,
et servis tuis hanc gratiam
    largire propitius,
ut in tui et proximi
    dilectione manentes
plenitudinem mandatorum
    tuorum adimpleant.
Per Christum Dominum nostrum.

FOURTH SUNDAY OF LENT (YEAR B)

*Today, the Fourth Sunday of Lent, the Gospel reminds us that God "so loved
the world that he gave his only Son, so that everyone who believes in him might
not perish but might have eternal life" (Jn 3:16). We hear this comforting
proclamation at a time when painful armed confrontation threatens the hope
of humanity for a better future. Jesus affirmed "God so loved the world". So
then, the Father's love reaches every human being who lives in the world. How
can one not see the obligation that springs from such an initiative of God?
Conscious of such great love, the human being can only open himself to an
attitude of fraternal welcome towards his fellow human beings.*

(Pope Benedict XVI)

Entrance Antiphon   Cf. Is 66:10-11

REJOICE, Jerusalem,
and all who love her.
Be joyful, all who were in mourning;
exult and be satisfied at her
   consoling breast.

Ant. ad introitum

LÆTARE, Ierusalem,
et conventum facite,
   omnes qui diligitis eam;
gaudete cum lætitia,
   qui in tristitia fuistis,
ut exsultetis, et satiemini ab
   uberibus consolationis vestræ.

The Gloria in excelsis (Glory to God in the highest) is not said.

Collect

O God, who through your Word
reconcile the human race
   to yourself in a wonderful way,
grant, we pray,
that with prompt devotion
   and eager faith
the Christian people may hasten
toward the solemn celebrations
   to come.
Through our Lord Jesus Christ,
   your Son,
who lives and reigns with you
   in the unity of the Holy Spirit,
one God, for ever and ever.

Collecta

Deus, qui per Verbum tuum
humani generis reconciliationem
   mirabiliter operaris,
præsta, quæsumus,
   ut populus christianus
prompta devotione et alacri fide
ad ventura sollemnia
   valeat festinare.
Per Dominum nostrum Iesum
   Christum Filium tuum,
qui tecum vivit et regnat
   in unitate Spiritus Sancti,
Deus, per omnia sæcula sæculorum.

The readings for Year A may be used as alternative readings. See pp.170-173. If this is
done, the Preface (p.174) and Communion Antiphon (p.174) as in Year A are also used.

FIRST READING

A reading from the second book of Chronicles   36:14-16,19-23

The wrath and mercy of God are revealed in the exile and in the release of his people.

All the heads of the priesthood, and the people too, added infidelity to infidelity, copying all the shameful practices of the nations and defiling the Temple that the Lord had consecrated for himself in Jerusalem. The Lord, the God of their ancestors, tirelessly sent them messenger after messenger, since he wished to spare his people and his house. But they ridiculed the messengers of God, they despised his words, they laughed at his prophets, until at last the wrath of the Lord rose so high against his people that there was no further remedy.

Their enemies burned down the Temple of God, demolished the walls of Jerusalem, set fire to all its palaces, and destroyed everything of value in it. The survivors were deported by Nebuchadnezzar to Babylon; they were to serve him and his sons until the kingdom of Persia came to power. This is how the word of the Lord was fulfilled that he spoke through Jeremiah, 'Until this land has enjoyed its sabbath rest, until seventy years have gone by, it will keep sabbath throughout the days of its desolation.'

And in the first year of Cyrus king of Persia, to fulfil the word of the Lord that was spoken through Jeremiah, the Lord roused the spirit of Cyrus king of Persia to issue a proclamation and to have it publicly displayed throughout his kingdom: 'Thus speaks Cyrus king of Persia, "The Lord, the God of heaven, has given me all the kingdoms of the earth; he has ordered me to build him a Temple in Jerusalem, in Judah. Whoever there is among you of all his people, may his God be with him! Let him go up."'

The word of the Lord.

Responsorial Psalm   Ps 136:1-6. R. v.6

R. **O let my tongue**
   cleave to my mouth
   if I remember you not!

By the rivers of Babylon
there we sat and wept,
remembering Zion;
on the poplars that grew there
we hung up our harps. R.

For it was there that they asked us,
our captors, for songs,
our oppressors, for joy.
'Sing to us,' they said,
'one of Zion's songs.' R.

O how could we sing
the song of the Lord
on alien soil?
If I forget you, Jerusalem,
let my right hand wither! R.

O let my tongue
cleave to my mouth
if I remember you not,
if I prize not Jerusalem
above all my joys! R.

SECOND READING

A reading from the letter of St Paul to the Ephesians   2:4-10
You who were dead through your sins have been saved through grace.

God loved us with so much love that he was generous with his mercy:
when we were dead through our sins, he brought us to life with Christ – it
is through grace that you have been saved – and raised us up with him and
gave us a place with him in heaven, in Christ Jesus.

   This was to show for all ages to come, through his goodness towards us
in Christ Jesus, how infinitely rich he is in grace. Because it is by grace that
you have been saved, through faith; not by anything of your own, but by
a gift from God; not by anything that you have done, so that nobody can
claim the credit. We are God's work of art, created in Christ Jesus to live the
good life as from the beginning he had meant us to live it.

   The word of the Lord.

Gospel Acclamation   Jn 3:16
R. **Glory and praise to you, O Christ!**
God loved the world so much that he gave his only Son;
everyone who believes in him has eternal life.
R. **Glory and praise to you, O Christ!**

GOSPEL

A reading from the holy Gospel according to John   3:14-21
God sent his Son so that through him the world might be saved.

Jesus said to Nicodemus:
   'The Son of Man must be lifted up
   as Moses lifted up the serpent in the desert,
   so that everyone who believes may have eternal life in him.

Yes, God loved the world so much
that he gave his only Son,
so that everyone who believes in him may not be lost
but may have eternal life.
For God sent his Son into the world
not to condemn the world,
but so that through him the world might be saved.
No one who believes in him will be condemned;
but whoever refuses to believe is condemned already,
because he has refused to believe
in the name of God's only Son.
On these grounds is sentence pronounced:
that though the light has come into the world
men have shown they prefer
darkness to the light
because their deeds were evil.
And indeed, everybody who does wrong
hates the light and avoids it,
for fear his actions should be exposed;
but the man who lives by the truth
comes out into the light,
so that it may be plainly seen that what he does is done in God.'

The Gospel of the Lord.

The Creed is said.

Prayer over the Offerings

We place before you with joy
  these offerings,
which bring eternal remedy, O Lord,
praying that we may both faithfully
  revere them
and present them to you, as is fitting,
for the salvation of all the world.
Through Christ our Lord.

Preface I or II of Lent, pp.554-557.

Super oblata

Remedii sempiterni munera,
  Domine,
lætantes offerimus,
  suppliciter exorantes,
ut eadem nos et fideliter venerari,
et pro salute mundi congruenter
  exhibere perficias.
Per Christum Dominum nostrum.

Communion Antiphon Cf. Ps 121:3-4

Jerusalem is built as a city bonded
    as one together.
It is there that the tribes go up,
    the tribes of the Lord,
to praise the name of the Lord.

Ant. ad communionem

Ierusalem, quæ ædificatur ut civitas,
cuius participatio eius in idipsum.
Illuc enim ascenderunt tribus,
    tribus Domini,
ad confitendum nomini tuo,
    Domine.

Prayer after Communion

O God, who enlighten everyone
    who comes into this world,
illuminate our hearts, we pray,
with the splendour of your grace,
that we may always ponder
what is worthy and pleasing
    to your majesty
and love you in all sincerity.
Through Christ our Lord.

Post communionem

Deus, qui illuminas
    omnem hominem
venientem in hunc mundum,
illumina, quæsumus, corda nostra
    gratiæ tuæ splendore,
ut digna ac placita maiestati tuæ
    cogitare semper,
et te sincere diligere valeamus.
Per Christum Dominum nostrum.

Prayer over the People

Look upon those who call to you,
    O Lord,
and sustain the weak;
give life by your unfailing light
to those who walk in the shadow
    of death,
and bring those rescued by your
    mercy from every evil
to reach the highest good.
Through Christ our Lord.

Oratio super populum

Tuere, Domine, supplices tuos,
    sustenta fragiles,
et inter tenebras mortalium
    ambulantes
tua semper luce vivifica,
atque a malis omnibus
    clementer ereptos,
ad summa bona pervenire concede.
Per Christum Dominum nostrum.

FIFTH SUNDAY OF LENT (YEAR B)

In the imminence of his Passion Jesus declared: "Unless a grain of wheat falls into the earth and dies, it remains alone; but if it dies, it bears much fruit" (Jn 12:24). Now is no longer the time for words and discourses; indeed the crucial hour has come for which the Son of God came into the world and although his soul is troubled, he makes himself available to fulfil the Father's will to the end. And this is the will of God: to give eternal life to us who have lost it. However, in order for this to be brought about Jesus dies, like a grain of wheat that God the Father has sown in the world. Indeed, only in this way can a new humanity germinate and grow, free from the dominion of sin and able to live in brotherhood, as sons and daughters of the one Father who is in Heaven.

(Pope Benedict XVI)

Entrance Antiphon   Cf. Ps 42:1-2

GIVE me justice, O God,
　　and plead my cause against
　　a nation that is faithless.
From the deceitful and cunning
　　rescue me,
for you, O God, are my strength.

Ant. ad introitum

IUDICA me, Deus,
　　et discerne causam meam
　　de gente non sancta;
ab homine iniquo et doloso eripe me,
quia tu es Deus meus
　　et fortitudo mea.

The Gloria in excelsis (Glory to God in the highest) is not said.

Collect

By your help, we beseech you,
　　Lord our God,
may we walk eagerly
　　in that same charity
with which, out of love for the world,
your Son handed himself
　　over to death.
Through our Lord Jesus Christ,
　　your Son,
who lives and reigns with you
　　in the unity of the Holy Spirit,
one God, for ever and ever.

Collecta

Quæsumus, Domine Deus noster,
　　ut in illa caritate
qua Filius tuus diligens mundum
　　morti se tradidit,
inveniamur ipsi, te opitulante,
　　alacriter ambulantes.
Per Dominum nostrum Iesum
　　Christum Filium tuum,
qui tecum vivit et regnat
　　in unitate Spiritus Sancti,
Deus, per omnia sæcula sæculorum.

The readings for Year A may be used as alternative readings. See pp.176-179. If this is done, the Preface (p.180) and Communion Antiphon (p.180) as in Year A are also used.

FIRST READING

A reading from the prophet Jeremiah   31:31-34

I will make a new covenant and never call their sin to mind.

See, the days are coming – it is the Lord who speaks – when I will make a
new covenant with the House of Israel and the House of Judah, but not a
covenant like the one I made with their ancestors on the day I took them by
the hand to bring them out of the land of Egypt. They broke that covenant
of mine, so I had to show them who was master. It is the Lord who speaks.
No, this is the covenant I will make with the House of Israel when those
days arrive – it is the Lord who speaks. Deep within them I will plant my
Law, writing it on their hearts. Then I will be their God and they shall be
my people. There will be no further need for neighbour to try to teach
neighbour, or brother to say to brother, 'Learn to know the Lord!' No, they
will all know me, the least no less than the greatest – it is the Lord who
speaks – since I will forgive their iniquity and never call their sin to mind.

   The word of the Lord.

Responsorial Psalm   Ps 50:3-4,12-15. R. v.12

R. **A pure heart create for me, O God.**

   Have mercy on me, God, in your kindness.
   In your compassion blot out my offence.
   O wash me more and more from my guilt
   and cleanse me from my sin. R.

   A pure heart create for me, O God,
   put a steadfast spirit within me.
   Do not cast me away from your presence,
   nor deprive me of your holy spirit. R.

   Give me again the joy of your help;
   with a spirit of fervour sustain me,
   that I may teach transgressors your ways
   and sinners may return to you. R.

SECOND READING

A reading from the letter to the Hebrews   5:7-9

He learnt to obey and became for all the source of eternal salvation.

During his life on earth, Christ offered up prayer and entreaty, aloud and
in silent tears, to the one who had the power to save him out of death, and
he submitted so humbly that his prayer was heard. Although he was Son,
he learnt to obey through suffering; but having been made perfect, he
became for all who obey him the source of eternal salvation.

   The word of the Lord.

Gospel Acclamation   Jn 12:26

R. **Glory to you, O Christ, you are the Word of God!**
If a man serves me, says the Lord, he must follow me;
wherever I am, my servant will be there too.
R. **Glory to you, O Christ, you are the Word of God!**

GOSPEL

A reading from the holy Gospel according to John   12:20-30
If a grain of wheat falls on the ground and dies, it yields a rich harvest.

Among those who went up to worship at the festival were some Greeks.
These approached Philip, who came from Bethsaida in Galilee, and put this
request to him, 'Sir, we should like to see Jesus.' Philip went to tell Andrew,
and Andrew and Philip together went to tell Jesus. Jesus replied to them:
    'Now the hour has come
    for the Son of Man to be glorified.
    I tell you, most solemnly,
    unless a wheat grain falls on the ground and dies,
    it remains only a single grain;
    but if it dies,
    it yields a rich harvest.
    Anyone who loves his life loses it;
    anyone who hates his life in this world
    will keep it for the eternal life.
    If a man serves me, he must follow me,
    wherever I am, my servant will be there too.
    If anyone serves me, my Father will honour him.
    Now my soul is troubled.
    What shall I say:
    Father, save me from this hour?
    But it was for this very reason that I have come to this hour.
    Father, glorify your name!'
    A voice came from heaven, 'I have glorified it, and I will glorify it again.'
People standing by, who heard this, said it was a clap of thunder; others
said, 'It was an angel speaking to him.' Jesus answered, 'It was not for my
sake that this voice came, but for yours.
    'Now sentence is being passed on this world;
    now the prince of this world is to be overthrown.

And when I am lifted up from the earth,
I shall draw all men to myself.'
By these words he indicated the kind of death he would die.
The Gospel of the Lord.

The Creed is said.

Prayer over the Offerings	Super oblata
Hear us, almighty God,	Exaudi nos, omnipotens Deus,
and, having instilled in your servants	et famulos tuos, quos fidei
the teachings of the Christian faith,	christianæ eruditionibus imbuisti,
graciously purify them	huius sacrificii tribuas
by the working of this sacrifice.	operatione mundari.
Through Christ our Lord.	Per Christum Dominum nostrum.

Preface I or II of Lent, pp.554-557.

Communion Antiphon Jn 12:24	Ant. ad communionem
Amen, Amen I say to you:	Amen, amen dico vobis:
Unless a grain of wheat	Nisi granum frumenti
falls to the ground and dies,	cadens in terram mortuum fuerit,
it remains a single grain.	ipsum solum manet;
But if it dies, it bears much fruit.	si autem mortuum fuerit,
	multum fructum affert.

Prayer after Communion	Post communionem
We pray, almighty God,	Quæsumus, omnipotens Deus,
that we may always be counted	ut inter eius membra
among the members of Christ,	semper numeremur,
in whose Body and Blood	cuius Corpori communicamus
we have communion.	et Sanguini.
Who lives and reigns	Qui vivit et regnat
for ever and ever.	in sæcula sæculorum.

Prayer over the People	Oratio super populum
Bless, O Lord, your people,	Benedic, Domine, plebem tuam,
who long for the gift of your mercy,	quæ munus tuæ
and grant that what,	miserationis exspectat,
at your prompting, they desire	et concede, ut, quod,
they may receive	te inspirante, desiderat,
by your generous gift.	te largiente percipiat.
Through Christ our Lord.	Per Christum Dominum nostrum.

LENT (YEAR C)

ASH WEDNESDAY

See above, p.143.

FIRST SUNDAY OF LENT (YEAR C)

St Luke recounts that after receiving Baptism from John, "Jesus, full of the Holy Spirit, returned from the Jordan, and was led by the Spirit for forty days in the wilderness, tempted by the devil" (Lk 4:1). There is a clear insistence on the fact that the temptations were not just an incident on the way, but rather the consequence of Jesus's decision to carry out the mission entrusted to him by the Father: to live, to the very end, his reality as the beloved Son who trusts totally in him. Christ came into the world to set us free from sin and from the ambiguous fascination of planning our life while leaving God out. He did not do so with loud proclamations but rather by fighting the tempter himself, until the Cross. This example applies to everyone: the world is improved by starting with oneself, changing, with God's grace, everything in one's life that is not going well.

(Pope Benedict XVI)

Entrance Antiphon Cf. Ps 90:15-16	Ant. ad introitum
WHEN he calls on me, I will answer him; I will deliver him and give him glory, I will grant him length of days.	INVOCABIT me, et ego exaudiam eum; eripiam eum, et glorificabo eum, longitudine dierum adimplebo eum.

The Gloria in excelsis (Glory to God in the highest) is not said.

Collect	Collecta
Grant, almighty God, through the yearly observances of holy Lent, that we may grow in understanding of the riches hidden in Christ and by worthy conduct pursue their effects. Through our Lord Jesus Christ, your Son, who lives and reigns with you in the unity of the Holy Spirit, one God, for ever and ever.	Concede nobis, omnipotens Deus, ut, per annua quadragesimalis exercitia sacramenti, et ad intellegendum Christi proficiamus arcanum, et effectus eius digna conversatione sectemur. Per Dominum nostrum Iesum Christum Filium tuum, qui tecum vivit et regnat in unitate Spiritus Sancti, Deus, per omnia sæcula sæculorum.

FIRST READING

A reading from the book of Deuteronomy   26:4-10

The creed of the chosen people.

Moses said to the people: 'The priest shall take the pannier from your hand and lay it before the altar of the Lord your God. Then, in the sight of the Lord your God, you must make this pronouncement:

"My father was a wandering Aramaean. He went down into Egypt to find refuge there, few in numbers; but there he became a nation, great, mighty, and strong. The Egyptians ill-treated us, they gave us no peace and inflicted harsh slavery on us. But we called on the Lord, the God of our fathers. The Lord heard our voice and saw our misery, our toil and our oppression; and the Lord brought us out of Egypt with mighty hand and outstretched arm, with great terror, and with signs and wonders. He brought us here and gave us this land, a land where milk and honey flow. Here then I bring the first-fruits of the produce of the soil that you, Lord, have given me." You must then lay them before the Lord your God, and bow down in the sight of the Lord your God.'

The word of the Lord.

Responsorial Psalm   Ps 90:1-2,10-15. R. v.15

R. **Be with me, O Lord, in my distress.**

He who dwells in the shelter of the Most High
and abides in the shade of the Almighty
says to the Lord: 'My refuge
my stronghold, my God in whom I trust!' R.

Upon you no evil shall fall,
no plague approach where you dwell.
For you has he commanded his angels,
to keep you in all your ways. R.

They shall bear you upon their hands
lest you strike your foot against a stone.
On the lion and the viper you will tread
and trample the young lion and the dragon. R.

His love he set on me, so I will rescue him;
protect him for he knows my name.
When he calls I shall answer: 'I am with you.'
I will save him in distress and give him glory. R.

SECOND READING

A reading from the letter of St Paul to the Romans   10:8-13

The creed of the Christian.

Scripture says: The word, that is the faith we proclaim, is very near to you, it is on your lips and in your heart. If your lips confess that Jesus is Lord and if you believe in your heart that God raised him from the dead, then you will be saved. By believing from the heart you are made righteous; by confessing with your lips you are saved. When scripture says: those who believe in him will have no cause for shame, it makes no distinction between Jew and Greek: all belong to the same Lord who is rich enough, however many ask his help, for everyone who calls on the name of the Lord will be saved.

The word of the Lord.

Gospel Acclamation   Mt 4:4

R. **Praise to you, O Christ, king of eternal glory!**
Man does not live on bread alone,
but on every word that comes from the mouth of God.
R. **Praise to you, O Christ, king of eternal glory!**

GOSPEL

A reading from the holy Gospel according to Luke   4:1-13

Jesus was led by the Spirit through the wilderness and was tempted there.

Filled with the Holy Spirit, Jesus left the Jordan and was led by the Spirit through the wilderness being tempted there by the devil for forty days. During that time he ate nothing and at the end he was hungry. Then the devil said to him, 'If you are the Son of God, tell this stone to turn into a loaf.' But Jesus replied 'Scripture says: Man does not live on bread alone.'

Then leading him to a height, the devil showed him in a moment of time all the kingdoms of the world and said to him, 'I will give you all this power and the glory of these kingdoms, for it has been committed to me and I give it to anyone I choose. Worship me, then, and it shall all be yours.' But Jesus answered him, 'Scripture says:

You must worship the Lord your God,
and serve him alone.'

Then he led him to Jerusalem and made him stand on the parapet of the Temple. 'If you are the Son of God,' he said to him 'throw yourself down from here, for scripture says:

He will put his angels in charge of you
to guard you,

and again:

They will hold you up on their hands
in case you hurt your foot against a stone.'

But Jesus answered him, 'It has been said:

You must not put the Lord your God to the test.'

Having exhausted all these ways of tempting him, the devil left him, to return at the appointed time.

The Gospel of the Lord.

The Creed is said.

Prayer over the Offerings	Super oblata

Give us the right dispositions,
    O Lord, we pray,
to make these offerings,
for with them we celebrate
    the beginning
of this venerable and sacred time.
Through Christ our Lord.
	Fac nos, quæsumus, Domine,
	his muneribus offerendis
	    convenienter aptari,
	quibus ipsius venerabilis
	    sacramenti celebramus
	    exordium.
	Per Christum Dominum nostrum.

Preface: The Temptation of the Lord, p.155.

Communion Antiphon Mt 4:4	Ant. ad communionem

One does not live by bread alone,
but by every word that comes forth
    from the mouth of God.
	Non in solo pane vivit homo,
	sed in omni verbo quod procedit
	    de ore Dei.

Or: Cf. Ps 90:4	Vel:

The Lord will conceal you
    with his pinions,
and under his wings you will trust.
	Scapulis suis obumbrabit
	    tibi Dominus,
	et sub pennis eius sperabis.

Prayer after Communion

Renewed now with heavenly bread,
by which faith is nourished,
    hope increased,
and charity strengthened,
we pray, O Lord,
that we may learn to hunger
    for Christ,
the true and living Bread,
and strive to live by every word
which proceeds from your mouth.
Through Christ our Lord.

Prayer over the People

May bountiful blessing,
    O Lord, we pray,
come down upon your people,
that hope may grow in tribulation,
virtue be strengthened
    in temptation,
and eternal redemption be assured.
Through Christ our Lord.

Post communionem

Cælesti pane refecti,
quo fides alitur, spes provehitur
    et caritas roboratur,
quæsumus, Domine,
ut ipsum, qui est panis vivus
    et verus, esurire discamus,
et in omni verbo,
    quod procedit de ore tuo,
vivere valeamus.
Per Christum Dominum nostrum.

Oratio super populum

Super populum tuum,
    Domine, quæsumus,
benedictio copiosa descendat,
ut spes in tribulatione succrescat,
virtus in tentatione firmetur,
æterna redemptio tribuatur.
Per Christum Dominum nostrum.

SECOND SUNDAY OF LENT (YEAR C)

Another detail proper to St Luke's narrative deserves emphasis: the mention of the topic of Jesus' conversation with Moses and Elijah, who appeared beside him when he was transfigured. As the Evangelist tells us, they "talked with him ... and spoke of his departure" (in Greek, éxodos), "which he was to accomplish at Jerusalem" (9:31). Therefore, Jesus listens to the Law and the Prophets who spoke to him about his death and Resurrection. In his intimate dialogue with the Father, he did not depart from history, he did not flee the mission for which he came into the world, although he knew that to attain glory he would have to pass through the Cross. On the contrary, Christ enters more deeply into this mission, adhering with all his being to the Father's will; he shows us that true prayer consists precisely in uniting our will with that of God. For a Christian, therefore, to pray is not to evade reality and the responsibilities it brings, but rather, fully to assume them, trusting in the faithful and inexhaustible love of the Lord.

(Pope Benedict XVI)

Entrance Antiphon   Cf. Ps 26:8-9

OF you my heart has spoken:
   Seek his face.
It is your face, O Lord, that I seek;
   hide not your face from me.

Or: Cf. Ps 24:6,2,22

Remember your compassion,
   O Lord,
and your merciful love,
   for they are from of old.
Let not our enemies exult over us.
Redeem us, O God of Israel,
   from all our distress.

Ant. ad introitum

TIBI dixit cor meum quæsivi
   vultum tuum,
vultum tuum, Domine, requiram.
Ne avertas faciem tuam a me.

Vel:

Reminiscere miserationum tuarum,
   Domine,
et misericordiæ tuæ,
   quæ a sæculo sunt.
Ne umquam dominentur nobis
   inimici nostri;
libera nos, Deus Israel, ex omnibus
   angustiis nostris.

The Gloria in excelsis (Glory to God in the highest) is not said.

Collect	Collecta
O God, who have commanded us to listen to your beloved Son, be pleased, we pray, to nourish us inwardly by your word, that, with spiritual sight made pure, we may rejoice to behold your glory. Through our Lord Jesus Christ, your Son, who lives and reigns with you in the unity of the Holy Spirit, one God, for ever and ever.	Deus, qui nobis dilectum Filium tuum audire præcepisti, verbo tuo interius nos pascere digneris, ut, spiritali purificato intuitu, gloriæ tuæ lætemur aspectu. Per Dominum nostrum Iesum Christum Filium tuum, qui tecum vivit et regnat in unitate Spiritus Sancti, Deus, per omnia sæcula sæculorum.

FIRST READING

A reading from the book of Genesis   15:5-12,17-18

God enters into a Covenant with Abraham, the man of faith.

Taking Abram outside the Lord said, 'Look up to heaven and count the stars if you can. Such will be your descendants' he told him. Abram put his faith in the Lord, who counted this as making him justified.

'I am the Lord' he said to him 'who brought you out of Ur of the Chaldaeans to make you heir to this land.' 'My Lord, the Lord' Abram replied 'how am I to know that I shall inherit it?' He said to him, 'Get me a three-year-old heifer, a three-year-old goat, a three-year-old ram, a turtledove and a young pigeon.' He brought him all these, cut them in half and put half on one side and half facing it on the other; but the birds he did not cut in half. Birds of prey came down on the carcasses but Abram drove them off.

Now as the sun was setting Abram fell into a deep sleep, and terror seized him. When the sun had set and darkness had fallen, there appeared a smoking furnace and a firebrand that went between the halves. That day the Lord made a Covenant with Abram in these terms:

'To your descendants I give this land,
from the wadi of Egypt to the Great River.'

The word of the Lord.

Responsorial Psalm   Ps 26:1,7-9,13-14. R. v.1

R. **The Lord is my light and my help.**

The Lord is my light and my help;
whom shall I fear?
The Lord is the stronghold of my life;
before whom shall I shrink? R.

O Lord, hear my voice when I call;
have mercy and answer.
Of you my heart has spoken:
'Seek his face.' R.

It is your face, O Lord, that I seek;
hide not your face.
Dismiss not your servant in anger;
you have been my help. R.

I am sure I shall see the Lord's goodness
in the land of the living.
Hope in him, hold firm and take heart.
Hope in the Lord! R.

SECOND READING

A reading from the letter of St Paul to the Philippians   3:17-4:1

Christ will transfigure our bodies into copies of his glorious body.

My brothers, be united in following my rule of life. Take as your models
everybody who is already doing this and study them as you used to study us.
I have told you often, and I repeat it today with tears, there are many who
are behaving as the enemies of the cross of Christ. They are destined to be
lost. They make foods into their god and they are proudest of something
they ought to think shameful; the things they think important are earthly
things. [For us, our homeland is in heaven, and from heaven comes the
saviour we are waiting for, the Lord Jesus Christ, and he will transfigure
these wretched bodies of ours into copies of his glorious body. He will do
that by the same power with which he can subdue the whole universe.

So then, my brothers and dear friends, do not give way but remain
faithful in the Lord. I miss you very much, dear friends; you are my joy and
my crown.

The word of the Lord.]

Shorter Form, 3:20-4:1. Read between [ ]

Gospel Acclamation   Mt 17:5

R. **Glory and praise to you, O Christ!**
From the bright cloud the Father's voice was heard:
'This is my Son, the Beloved. Listen to him.'
R. **Glory and praise to you, O Christ!**

GOSPEL

A reading from the holy Gospel according to Luke   9:28-36
As Jesus prayed, the aspect of his face was changed.

Jesus took with him Peter and John and James and went up the mountain
to pray. As he prayed, the aspect of his face was changed and his clothing
became brilliant as lightning. Suddenly there were two men there talking
to him; they were Moses and Elijah appearing in glory, and they were
speaking of his passing which he was to accomplish in Jerusalem. Peter
and his companions were heavy with sleep, but they kept awake and saw
his glory and the two men standing with him. As these were leaving him,
Peter said to Jesus, 'Master, it is wonderful for us to be here; so let us make
three tents, one for you, one for Moses and one for Elijah.' – He did not
know what he was saying. As he spoke, a cloud came and covered them
with shadow; and when they went into the cloud the disciples were afraid.
And a voice came from the cloud saying, 'This is my Son, the Chosen One.
Listen to him.' And after the voice had spoken, Jesus was found alone. The
disciples kept silence and, at that time, told no one what they had seen.

The Gospel of the Lord.

The Creed is said.

Prayer over the Offerings	Super oblata
May this sacrifice, O Lord, we pray, cleanse us of our faults and sanctify your faithful in body and mind for the celebration of the paschal festivities. Through Christ our Lord.	Hæc hostia, Domine, quæsumus, emundet nostra delicta, et ad celebranda festa paschalia fidelium tuorum corpora mentesque sanctificet. Per Christum Dominum nostrum.

Preface: The Transfiguration of the Lord, p.160.

Communion Antiphon   Mt 17:5

This is my beloved Son,
    with whom I am well pleased;
listen to him.

Ant. ad communionem

Hic est Filius meus dilectus,
in quo mihi bene complacui;
ipsum audite.

Prayer after Communion

As we receive these glorious mysteries,
we make thanksgiving to you,
    O Lord,
for allowing us while still on earth
to be partakers even now
    of the things of heaven.
Through Christ our Lord.

Post communionem

Percipientes, Domine,
    gloriosa mysteria,
gratias tibi referre satagimus,
quod, in terra positos,
iam cælestium præstas
    esse participes.
Per Christum Dominum nostrum.

Prayer over the People

Bless your faithful, we pray, O Lord,
with a blessing that endures for ever,
and keep them faithful
to the Gospel of your
    Only Begotten Son,
so that they may always desire
    and at last attain
that glory whose beauty he showed
    in his own Body,
to the amazement of his Apostles.
Through Christ our Lord.

Oratio super populum

Benedic, Domine, fideles tuos
    benedictione perpetua,
et fac eos Unigeniti tui Evangelio
    sic adhærere,
ut ad illam gloriam, cuius in se
    speciem Apostolis ostendit,
et suspirare iugiter et feliciter
    valeant pervenire.
Per Christum Dominum nostrum.

THIRD SUNDAY OF LENT (YEAR C)

In today's Gospel passage, Jesus is questioned on certain distressing events. In the face of the easy conclusion of considering evil as an effect of divine punishment, Jesus restores the true image of God who is good and cannot desire evil. Jesus asks us to interpret these events differently, putting them in the perspective of conversion: misfortunes, sorrowful events must not awaken curiosity in us or the quest for presumed sins; instead they must be opportunities for reflection, in order to overcome the illusion of being able to live without God, and to reinforce, with the Lord's help, the commitment to change our way of life.

(Pope Benedict XVI)

Entrance Antiphon   Cf. Ps 24:15-16

MY eyes are always on the Lord, for he rescues my feet from the snare. Turn to me and have mercy on me, for I am alone and poor.

Or: Cf. Ezk 36:23-26

When I prove my holiness among you, I will gather you from all the foreign lands; and I will pour clean water upon you and cleanse you from all your impurities, and I will give you a new spirit, says the Lord.

Ant. ad introitum

OCULI mei semper ad Dominum, quia ipse evellet de laqueo pedes meos. Respice in me et miserere mei, quoniam unicus et pauper sum ego.

Vel:

Cum sanctificatus fuero in vobis, congregabo vos de universis terris; et effundam super vos aquam mundam, et mundabimini ab omnibus inquinamentis vestris, et dabo vobis spiritum novum, dicit Dominus.

The Gloria in excelsis (Glory to God in the highest) is not said.

Collect	Collecta

O God, author of every mercy
    and of all goodness,
who in fasting, prayer and almsgiving
have shown us a remedy for sin,
look graciously on this confession
    of our lowliness,
that we, who are bowed down
    by our conscience,
may always be lifted up
    by your mercy.
Through our Lord Jesus Christ,
    your Son,
who lives and reigns with you
    in the unity of the Holy Spirit,
one God, for ever and ever.
	Deus, omnium misericordiarum
	    et totius bonitatis auctor,
	qui peccatorum remedia in ieiuniis,
	orationibus et eleemosynis
	    demonstrasti,
	hanc humilitatis nostræ
	    confessionem propitius intuere,
	ut, qui inclinamur
	    conscientia nostra,
	tua semper misericordia sublevemur.
	Per Dominum nostrum Iesum
	    Christum Filium tuum,
	qui tecum vivit et regnat
	    in unitate Spiritus Sancti,
	Deus, per omnia sæcula sæculorum.

The readings for Year A may be used as alternative readings. See pp.163-166. If this is done, the Preface (p.167) and Communion Antiphon (p.167) as in Year A are also used.

FIRST READING

A reading from the book of Exodus   3:1-8,13-15

I Am has sent me to you.

Moses was looking after the flock of Jethro, his father-in-law, priest of Midian. He led his flock to the far side of the wilderness and came to Horeb, the mountain of God. There the angel of the Lord appeared to him in the shape of a flame of fire, coming from the middle of a bush. Moses looked; there was the bush blazing but it was not being burnt up. 'I must go and look at this strange sight,' Moses said 'and see why the bush is not burnt.' Now the Lord saw him go forward to look, and God called to him from the middle of the bush. 'Moses, Moses!' he said. 'Here I am' he answered. 'Come no nearer' he said. 'Take off your shoes, for the place on which you stand is holy ground. I am the God of your father,' he said 'the God of Abraham, the God of Isaac and the God of Jacob.' At this Moses covered his face, afraid to look at God.

  And the Lord said, 'I have seen the miserable state of my people in Egypt. I have heard their appeal to be free of their slave-drivers. Yes, I am well aware of their sufferings. I mean to deliver them out of the hands of the Egyptians and bring them up out of that land to a land rich and broad, a land where milk and honey flow.'

Then Moses said to God, 'I am to go, then, to the sons of Israel and say to them, "The God of your fathers has sent me to you". But if they ask me what his name is, what am I to tell them?' And God said to Moses, 'I Am who I Am. This' he added 'is what you must say to the sons of Israel: "The Lord, the God of your fathers, the God of Abraham, the God of Isaac, and the God of Jacob, has sent me to you." This is my name for all time; by this name I shall be invoked for all generations to come.'

The word of the Lord

Responsorial Psalm   Ps 102:1-4,6-8,11. R. v.8

R. **The Lord is compassion and love.**

My soul, give thanks to the Lord,
all my being, bless his holy name.
My soul give thanks to the Lord
and never forget all his blessings. R.

It is he who forgives all your guilt,
who heals every one of your ills,
who redeems your life from the grave,
who crowns you with love and compassion. R.

The Lord does deeds of justice,
gives judgement for all who are oppressed.
He made known his ways to Moses
and his deeds to Israel's sons. R.

The Lord is compassion and love,
slow to anger and rich in mercy.
For as the heavens are high above the earth
so strong is his love for those who fear him. R.

SECOND READING

A reading from the first letter of St Paul to the Corinthians   10:1-6,10-12
The life of the people under Moses in the desert was written down to be a lesson for us.

I want to remind you, brothers, how our fathers were all guided by a cloud above them and how they all passed through the sea. They were all baptised into Moses in this cloud and in this sea; all ate the same spiritual food and all drank the same spiritual drink since they all drank from the spiritual rock that followed them as they went, and that rock was Christ. In spite of this, most of them failed to please God and their corpses littered the desert.

These things all happened as warnings for us, not to have the wicked lusts for forbidden things that they had. You must never complain: some of them did, and they were killed by the Destroyer.

All this happened to them as a warning, and it was written down to be a lesson for us who are living at the end of the age. The man who thinks he is safe must be careful that he does not fall.

The word of the Lord.

Gospel Acclamation   Mt 4:17
R. **Glory to you, O Christ, you are the Word of God!**
Repent, says the Lord,
for the kingdom of heaven is close at hand.
R. **Glory to you, O Christ, you are the Word of God!**

GOSPEL

A reading from the holy Gospel according to Luke   13:1-9
Unless you repent you will all perish as they did.

Some people arrived and told Jesus about the Galileans whose blood Pilate had mingled with that of their sacrifices. At this he said to them, 'Do you suppose these Galileans who suffered like that were greater sinners than any other Galileans? They were not, I tell you. No; but unless you repent you will all perish as they did. Or those eighteen on whom the tower at Siloam fell and killed them? Do you suppose that they were more guilty than all the other people living in Jerusalem? They were not, I tell you. No; but unless you repent you will all perish as they did.'

He told this parable: 'A man had a fig tree planted in his vineyard, and he came looking for fruit on it but found none. He said to the man who looked after the vineyard, "Look here, for three years now I have been coming to look for fruit on this fig tree and finding none. Cut it down: why should it be taking up the ground?" "Sir," the man replied "leave it one more year and give me time to dig round it and manure it: it may bear fruit next year; if not, then you can cut it down."'

The Gospel of the Lord.

The Creed is said.

Prayer over the Offerings

Be pleased, O Lord,
   with these sacrificial offerings,
and grant that we who beseech
   pardon for our own sins,
may take care to forgive
   our neighbour.
Through Christ our Lord.

Preface I or II of Lent, pp.554-557.

Communion Antiphon   Cf. Ps 83:4-5

The sparrow finds a home,
and the swallow a nest for her young:
by your altars, O Lord of hosts,
   my King and my God.
Blessed are they who dwell
   in your house,
for ever singing your praise.

Prayer after Communion

As we receive the pledge
of things yet hidden in heaven
and are nourished while still on earth
with the Bread that comes
   from on high,
we humbly entreat you, O Lord,
that what is being brought about
   in us in mystery
may come to true completion.
Through Christ our Lord.

Prayer over the People

Direct, O Lord, we pray,
   the hearts of your faithful,
and in your kindness grant
   your servants this grace:
that, abiding in the love of you
   and their neighbour,
they may fulfil the whole
   of your commands.
Through Christ our Lord.

Super oblata

His sacrificiis, Domine,
   concede placatus,
ut, qui propriis oramus
   absolvi delictis,
fraterna dimittere studeamus.
Per Christum Dominum nostrum.

Ant. ad communionem

Passer invenit sibi domum,
et turtur nidum,
   ubi reponat pullos suos:
altaria tua, Domine virtutum,
   Rex meus, et Deus meus!
Beati qui habitant in domo tua,
in sæculum sæculi laudabunt te.

Post communionem

Sumentes pignus cælestis arcani,
et in terra positi iam superno
   pane satiati,
te, Domine, supplices deprecamur,
ut, quod in nobis mysterio geritur,
   opere impleatur.
Per Christum Dominum nostrum.

Oratio super populum

Rege, Domine, quæsumus,
   tuorum corda fidelium,
et servis tuis hanc gratiam
   largire propitius,
ut in tui et proximi
   dilectione manentes
plenitudinem mandatorum
   tuorum adimpleant.
Per Christum Dominum nostrum.

FOURTH SUNDAY OF LENT (YEAR C)

On this Fourth Sunday of Lent, the Gospel of the father and the two sons better known as the Parable of the "Prodigal Son" (Lk 15:11-32) is proclaimed. This passage of St Luke constitutes one of the peaks of spirituality and literature of all time. After Jesus has told us of the merciful Father, things are no longer as they were before. We now know God; he is our Father who out of love created us to be free and endowed us with a conscience, who suffers when we get lost and rejoices when we return. The two sons represent two immature ways of relating to God: rebellion and childish obedience. Both these forms are surmounted through the experience of mercy. Only by experiencing forgiveness, by recognizing one is loved with a freely given love, a love greater than our wretchedness but also than our own merit, do we at last enter into a truly filial and free relationship with God.

(Pope Benedict XVI)

Entrance Antiphon Cf. Is 66:10-11

REJOICE, Jerusalem,
and all who love her.
Be joyful, all who were in mourning;
exult and be satisfied at her
    consoling breast.

Ant. ad introitum

LÆTARE, Ierusalem,
et conventum facite,
    omnes qui diligitis eam;
gaudete cum lætitia,
    qui in tristitia fuistis,
ut exsultetis, et satiemini ab
    uberibus consolationis vestræ.

The Gloria in excelsis (Glory to God in the highest) is not said.

Collect

O God, who through your Word
reconcile the human race
    to yourself in a wonderful way,
grant, we pray,
that with prompt devotion
    and eager faith
the Christian people may hasten
toward the solemn celebrations
    to come.
Through our Lord Jesus Christ,
    your Son,
who lives and reigns with you
    in the unity of the Holy Spirit,
one God, for ever and ever.

Collecta

Deus, qui per Verbum tuum
humani generis reconciliationem
    mirabiliter operaris,
præsta, quæsumus,
    ut populus christianus
prompta devotione et alacri fide
ad ventura sollemnia
    valeat festinare.
Per Dominum nostrum Iesum
    Christum Filium tuum,
qui tecum vivit et regnat
    in unitate Spiritus Sancti,
Deus, per omnia sæcula sæculorum.

The readings for Year A may be used as alternative readings. See pp.170-173. If this is done, the Preface (p.174) and Communion Antiphon (p.174) as in Year A are also used.

FIRST READING

A reading from the book of Joshua   5:9-12

The People of God keep the Passover on their entry into the promised land.

The Lord said to Joshua, 'Today I have taken the shame of Egypt away from you.'

The Israelites pitched their camp at Gilgal and kept the Passover there on the fourteenth day of the month, at evening in the plain of Jericho. On the morrow of the Passover they tasted the produce of that country, unleavened bread and roasted ears of corn, that same day. From that time, from their first eating of the produce of that country, the manna stopped falling. And having manna no longer, the Israelites fed from that year onwards on what the land of Canaan yielded.

The word of the Lord.

Responsorial Psalm   Ps 33:2-7. R. v.9

R. **Taste and see that the Lord is good.**

I will bless the Lord at all times,
his praise always on my lips;
in the Lord my soul shall make its boast.
The humble shall hear and be glad. R.

Glorify the Lord with me.
Together let us praise his name.
I sought the Lord and he answered me;
from all my terrors he set me free. R.

Look towards him and be radiant;
let your faces not be abashed.
This poor man called; the Lord heard him
and rescued him from all his distress. R.

SECOND READING

A reading from the second letter of St Paul to the Corinthians   5:17-21

God reconciled us to himself through Christ.

For anyone who is in Christ, there is a new creation; the old creation has gone, and now the new one is here. It is all God's work. It was God who reconciled us to himself through Christ and gave us the work of handing on this reconciliation. In other words, God in Christ was reconciling the world to himself, not holding men's faults against them, and he has entrusted to us the news that they are reconciled. So we are ambassadors for Christ; it is as though God were appealing through us, and the appeal that we make in Christ's name is: be reconciled to God. For our sake God made the sinless one into sin, so that in him we might become the goodness of God.

The word of the Lord.

Gospel Acclamation   Lk 15:18

R. **Praise and honour to you, Lord Jesus!**
I will leave this place and go to my father and say:
'Father, I have sinned against heaven and against you.'
R. **Praise and honour to you, Lord Jesus!**

GOSPEL

A reading from the holy Gospel according to Luke   15:1-3,11-32
Your brother here was dead and has come to life.

The tax collectors and the sinners were all seeking the company of Jesus to hear what he had to say, and the Pharisees and the scribes complained. 'This man' they said 'welcomes sinners and eats with them.' So he spoke this parable to them:

'A man had two sons. The younger said to his father, "Father, let me have the share of the estate that would come to me." So the father divided the property between them. A few days later, the younger son got together everything he had and left for a distant country where he squandered his money on a life of debauchery.

'When he had spent it all, that country experienced a severe famine, and now he began to feel the pinch, so he hired himself out to one of the local inhabitants who put him on his farm to feed the pigs. And he would willingly have filled his belly with the husks the pigs were eating but no one offered him anything. Then he came to his senses and said, "How many of my father's paid servants have more food than they want, and here am I dying of hunger! I will leave this place and go to my father and say: Father, I have sinned against heaven and against you; I no longer deserve to be called your son; treat me as one of your paid servants." So he left the place and went back to his father.

'While he was still a long way off, his father saw him and was moved with pity. He ran to the boy, clasped him in his arms and kissed him tenderly. Then his son said, "Father, I have sinned against heaven and against you. I no longer deserve to be called your son." But the father said to his servants, "Quick! Bring out the best robe and put it on him; put a ring on his finger and sandals on his feet. Bring the calf we have been fattening, and kill it; we are going to have a feast, a celebration, because this son of mine was dead and has come back to life; he was lost and is found." And they began to celebrate.

'Now the elder son was out in the fields, and on his way back, as he drew near the house, he could hear music and dancing. Calling one of the servants he asked what it was all about. "Your brother has come" replied the servant "and your father has killed the calf we had fattened because he has got him back safe and sound." He was angry then and refused to go in, and his father came out to plead with him; but he answered his father, "Look, all these years I have slaved for you and never once disobeyed your orders, yet you never offered me so much as a kid for me to celebrate with my friends. But, for this son of yours, when he comes back after swallowing up your property – he and his women – you kill the calf we had been fattening."

'The father said, "My son, you are with me always and all I have is yours. But it is only right we should celebrate and rejoice, because your brother here was dead and has come to life; he was lost and is found."'

The Gospel of the Lord.

The Creed is said.

Prayer over the Offerings	Super oblata

We place before you
   with joy these offerings,
which bring eternal remedy, O Lord,
praying that we may both faithfully
   revere them
and present them to you, as is fitting,
for the salvation of all the world.
Through Christ our Lord.
	Remedii sempiterni munera,
	   Domine,
	lætantes offerimus,
	   suppliciter exorantes,
	ut eadem nos et fideliter venerari,
	et pro salute mundi congruenter
	   exhibere perficias.
	Per Christum Dominum nostrum.

Preface I or II of Lent, pp.554-557.

Communion Antiphon   Lk 15:32

You must rejoice, my son,
for your brother was dead
   and has come to life;
he was lost and is found.

Prayer after Communion

O God, who enlighten everyone
   who comes into this world,
illuminate our hearts, we pray,
with the splendour of your grace,
that we may always ponder
what is worthy and pleasing
   to your majesty
and love you in all sincerity.
Through Christ our Lord.

Prayer over the People

Look upon those who call to you,
   O Lord,
and sustain the weak;
give life by your unfailing light
to those who walk in the shadow
   of death,
and bring those rescued
   by your mercy from every evil
to reach the highest good.
Through Christ our Lord.

Ant. ad communionem

Oportet te, fili, gaudere,
quia frater tuus mortuus fuerat,
   et revixit;
perierat, et inventus est.

Post communionem

Deus, qui illuminas
   omnem hominem
venientem in hunc mundum,
illumina, quæsumus, corda nostra
   gratiæ tuæ splendore,
ut digna ac placita maiestati tuæ
   cogitare semper,
et te sincere diligere valeamus.
Per Christum Dominum nostrum.

Oratio super populum

Tuere, Domine, supplices tuos,
   sustenta fragiles,
et inter tenebras
   mortalium ambulantes
tua semper luce vivifica,
atque a malis omnibus
   clementer ereptos,
ad summa bona pervenire concede.
Per Christum Dominum nostrum.

FIFTH SUNDAY OF LENT (YEAR C)

We have reached the Fifth Sunday of Lent in which the liturgy this year presents to us the Gospel episode of Jesus who saves an adulterous woman condemned to death. St John the Evangelist highlights one detail: while his accusers are insistently interrogating him, Jesus bends down and starts writing with his finger on the ground. St Augustine notes that this gesture portrays Christ as the divine legislator: in fact, God wrote the law with his finger on tablets of stone. Thus Jesus is the Legislator, he is Justice in person. And what is his sentence? "Let him who is without sin among you be the first to throw a stone at her." These words are full of the disarming power of truth that pulls down the wall of hypocrisy and opens consciences to a greater justice, that of love, in which consists the fulfilment of every precept.

(Pope Benedict XVI)

Entrance Antiphon   Cf. Ps 42:1-2

GIVE me justice, O God,
and plead my cause against
a nation that is faithless.
From the deceitful and cunning
rescue me,
for you, O God, are my strength.

Ant. ad introitum

IUDICA me, Deus,
et discerne causam meam
de gente non sancta;
ab homine iniquo et doloso eripe me,
quia tu es Deus meus
et fortitudo mea.

The Gloria in excelsis (Glory to God in the highest) is not said.

Collect

By your help, we beseech you,
Lord our God,
may we walk eagerly
in that same charity
with which, out of love for the world,
your Son handed himself
over to death.
Through our Lord Jesus Christ,
your Son,
who lives and reigns with you
in the unity of the Holy Spirit,
one God, for ever and ever.

Collecta

Quæsumus, Domine Deus noster,
ut in illa caritate
qua Filius tuus diligens mundum
morti se tradidit,
inveniamur ipsi, te opitulante,
alacriter ambulantes.
Per Dominum nostrum Iesum
Christum Filium tuum,
qui tecum vivit et regnat
in unitate Spiritus Sancti,
Deus, per omnia sæcula sæculorum.

The readings for Year A may be used as alternative readings. See pp.176-179. If this is done, the Preface (p.180) and Communion Antiphon (p.180) as in Year A are also used.

FIRST READING

A reading from the prophet Isaiah   43:16-21

See, I am doing a new deed, and I will give my chosen people drink.

Thus says the Lord,
who made a way through the sea,
a path in the great waters;
who put chariots and horse in the field
and a powerful army,
which lay there never to rise again,
snuffed out, put out like a wick:

No need to recall the past,
no need to think about what was done before.
See, I am doing a new deed,
even now it comes to light; can you not see it?
Yes, I am making a road in the wilderness,
paths in the wilds.

The wild beasts will honour me,
jackals and ostriches,
because I am putting water in the wilderness
(rivers in the wild)
to give my chosen people drink.
The people I have formed for myself
will sing my praises.

The word of the Lord.

Responsorial Psalm   Ps 125. R. v.3

R. **What marvels the Lord worked for us!
Indeed we were glad.**

When the Lord delivered Zion from bondage,
it seemed like a dream.
Then was our mouth filled with laughter,
on our lips there were songs. R.

The heathens themselves said: 'What marvels
the Lord worked for them!'

What marvels the Lord worked for us!
Indeed we were glad. R.

Deliver us, O Lord, from our bondage
as streams in dry land.
Those who are sowing in tears
will sing when they reap. R.

They go out, they go out, full of tears,
carrying seed for the sowing:
they come back, they come back, full of song,
carrying their sheaves. R.

R. **What marvels the Lord worked for us!
Indeed we were glad.**

SECOND READING

A reading from the letter of St Paul to the Philippians   3:8-14

Reproducing the pattern of his death, I have accepted the loss of everything for Christ.

I believe nothing can happen that will outweigh the supreme advantage of knowing Christ Jesus my Lord. For him I have accepted the loss of everything, and I look on everything as so much rubbish if only I can have Christ and be given a place in him. I am no longer trying for perfection by my own efforts, the perfection that comes from the Law, but I want only the perfection that comes through faith in Christ, and is from God and based on faith. All I want is to know Christ and the power of his resurrection and to share his sufferings by reproducing the pattern of his death. That is the way I can hope to take my place in the resurrection of the dead. Not that I have become perfect yet: I have not yet won, but I am still running, trying to capture the prize for which Christ Jesus captured me. I can assure you my brothers, I am far from thinking that I have already won. All I can say is that I forget the past and I strain ahead for what is still to come; I am racing for the finish, for the prize to which God calls us upwards to receive in Christ Jesus.

The word of the Lord.

Gospel Acclamation   Cf. Am 5:14

R. **Praise to you, O Christ, king of eternal glory!**
Seek good and not evil so that you may live,
and that the Lord God of hosts may really be with you.
R. **Praise to you, O Christ, king of eternal glory!**

Or: Jl 2:12-13

R. **Praise to you, O Christ, king of eternal glory!**
Now, now – it is the Lord who speaks –
come back to me with all your heart,
for I am all tenderness and compassion.
R. **Praise to you, O Christ, king of eternal glory!**

GOSPEL

A reading from the holy Gospel according to John   8:1-11
If there is one of you who has not sinned, let him be the first to throw a stone at her.

Jesus went to the Mount of Olives. At daybreak he appeared in the Temple again; and as all the people came to him, he sat down and began to teach them.

The scribes and Pharisees brought a woman along who had been caught committing adultery; and making her stand there in full view of everybody, they said to Jesus, 'Master, this woman was caught in the very act of committing adultery, and Moses has ordered us in the Law to condemn women like this to death by stoning. What have you to say?' They asked him this as a test, looking for something to use against him. But Jesus bent down and started writing on the ground with his finger. As they persisted with their question, he looked up and said, 'If there is one of you who has not sinned, let him be the first to throw a stone at her.' Then he bent down and wrote on the ground again. When they heard this they went away one by one, beginning with the eldest, until Jesus was left alone with the woman, who remained standing there. He looked up and said, 'Woman, where are they? Has no one condemned you?' 'No one, sir,' she replied. 'Neither do I condemn you,' said Jesus 'go away, and don't sin any more.'

The Gospel of the Lord.

The Creed is said.

Prayer over the Offerings

Hear us, almighty God,
and, having instilled in your servants
the teachings of the Christian faith,
graciously purify them
by the working of this sacrifice.
Through Christ our Lord.

Preface I or II of Lent, pp.554-557.

Communion Antiphon   Jn 8:10-11

Has no one condemned you,
    woman?
No one, Lord.
Neither shall I condemn you.
From now on, sin no more.

Prayer after Communion

We pray, almighty God,
that we may always be counted
    among the members of Christ,
in whose Body and Blood
    we have communion.
Who lives and reigns
    for ever and ever.

Prayer over the People

Bless, O Lord, your people,
who long for the gift of your mercy,
and grant that what,
    at your prompting, they desire
they may receive by your
    generous gift.
Through Christ our Lord.

Super oblata

Exaudi nos, omnipotens Deus,
et famulos tuos, quos fidei
    christianæ eruditionibus
    imbuisti,
huius sacrificii tribuas
    operatione mundari.
Per Christum Dominum nostrum.

Ant. ad communionem

Nemo te condemnavit, mulier?
    Nemo, Domine.
Nec ego te condemnabo:
    iam amplius noli peccare.

Post communionem

Quæsumus, omnipotens Deus,
ut inter eius membra
    semper numeremur,
cuius Corpori communicamus
    et Sanguini.
Qui vivit et regnat
    in sæcula sæculorum.

Oratio super populum

Benedic, Domine, plebem tuam,
quæ munus tuæ
    miserationis exspectat,
et concede, ut, quod,
    te inspirante, desiderat,
te largiente percipiat.
Per Christum Dominum nostrum.

HOLY WEEK

HOLY WEEK

PALM SUNDAY OF THE PASSION OF THE LORD
(YEAR A,B,C)

It is a moving experience each year on Palm Sunday as we go up the mountain with Jesus, towards the Temple, accompanying him on his ascent. But what are we really doing when we join this procession as part of the throng which went up with Jesus to Jerusalem and hailed him as King of Israel? Does it have anything to do with the reality of our life and our world? To answer this, we must first be clear about what Jesus himself wished to do and actually did. He was journeying towards the Temple in the Holy City, towards that place which for Israel ensured in a particular way God's closeness to his people. The ultimate goal of his pilgrimage was the heights of God himself; to those heights he wanted to lift every human being. Our procession today is meant, then, to be an image of something deeper, to reflect the fact that, together with Jesus, we are setting out on pilgrimage along the high road that leads to the living God.

(Pope Benedict XVI)

On this day the Church recalls the entrance of Christ the Lord into Jerusalem to accomplish his Paschal Mystery. Accordingly, the memorial of this entrance of the Lord takes place at all Masses, by means of the Procession or the Solemn Entrance before the principal Mass or the Simple Entrance before other Masses. The Solemn Entrance, but not the Procession, may be repeated before other Masses that are usually celebrated with a large gathering of people.

It is desirable that, where neither the Procession nor the Solemn Entrance can take place, there be a sacred celebration of the Word of God on the messianic entrance and on the Passion of the Lord, either on Saturday evening or on Sunday at a convenient time.

The Commemoration of the Lord's Entrance into Jerusalem

First Form: The Procession

At an appropriate hour, a gathering takes place at a smaller church or other suitable place other than inside the church to which the procession will go. The faithful hold branches in their hands.

Wearing the red sacred vestments as for Mass, the Priest and the Deacon, accompanied by other ministers, approach the place where the people are gathered. Instead of the chasuble, the Priest may wear a cope, which he leaves aside when the procession is over, and puts on a chasuble.

Meanwhile, the following antiphon or another appropriate chant is sung.

Ant.	Mt 21:9	Ant.
Hosanna to the Son of David;		Hosanna filio David:
blessed is he who comes		benedictus qui venit
in the name of the Lord,		in nomine Domini.
the King of Israel.		Rex Israel:
Hosanna in the highest.		Hosanna in excelsis.

After this, the Priest and people sign themselves, while the Priest says: In the name of the Father, and of the Son, and of the Holy Spirit. Then he greets the people in the usual way. A brief address is given, in which the faithful are invited to participate actively and consciously in the celebration of this day, in these or similar words:

Dear brethren (brothers and sisters),	Fratres carissimi,
since the beginning of Lent until now	postquam iam ab initio
we have prepared our hearts	Quadragesimæ corda nostra
by penance and charitable works.	pænitentia et operibus
Today we gather together to herald	caritatis præparavimus,
with the whole Church	hodierna die congregamur,
the beginning of the celebration	ut cum tota Ecclesia præludamus
of our Lord's Paschal Mystery,	paschale Domini nostri mysterium,
that is to say, of his Passion	eius nempe passionem
and Resurrection.	atque resurrectionem,
For it was to accomplish this mystery	ad quod implendum
that he entered his own city	ipse ingressus est civitatem
of Jerusalem.	suam Ierusalem.
Therefore, with all faith	Quare cum omni fide et devotione
and devotion,	memoriam agentes
let us commemorate	huius salutiferi ingressus,
the Lord's entry into the city	sequamur Dominum,
for our salvation,	ut, per gratiam consortes
following in his footsteps,	effecti crucis,
so that, being made by his grace	partem habeamus resurrectionis
partakers of the Cross,	et vitæ.
we may have a share also in his	
Resurrection and in his life.	

After the address, the Priest says one of the following prayers with hands extended.

Let us pray.	Oremus.

Almighty ever-living God,
sanctify ✠ these branches
    with your blessing,
that we, who follow Christ the King
    in exultation,
may reach the eternal Jerusalem
    through him.
Who lives and reigns
    for ever and ever.
R. Amen.
	Omnipotens sempiterne Deus,
	hos palmites tua
	    benedictione ✠ sanctifica,
	ut nos, qui Christum Regem
	    exsultando prosequimur,
	per ipsum valeamus ad æternam
	    Ierusalem pervenire.
	Qui vivit et regnat
	    in sæcula sæculorum.
	R. Amen.

Or:	Vel:

Increase the faith of those who
    place their hope in you, O God,
and graciously hear the prayers
    of those who call on you,
that we, who today hold high
    these branches
to hail Christ in his triumph,
may bear fruit for you by good
    works accomplished in him.
Who lives and reigns
    for ever and ever.
R. Amen.
	Auge fidem in te sperantium, Deus,
	et supplicum preces
	    clementer exaudi,
	ut, qui hodie Christo triumphanti
	    palmites exhibemus,
	in ipso fructus tibi bonorum
	    operum afferamus.
	Qui vivit et regnat
	    in sæcula sæculorum.
	R. Amen.

He sprinkles the branches with holy water without saying anything.

Then a Deacon or, if there is no Deacon, a Priest, proclaims in the usual way the Gospel concerning the Lord's entrance according to one of the four Gospels. If appropriate, incense may be used.

YEAR A

A reading from the holy Gospel according to Matthew   21:1-11

'Blessed is he who comes in the name of the Lord.'

When they drew near to Jerusalem
and came to Bethphage, to the Mount of Olives,
Jesus sent two disciples, saying to them,
'Go into the village opposite you,
and immediately you will find an ass tied,
and a colt with her; untie them and bring them to me.

If any one says anything to you, you shall say,
"The Lord has need of them,"
and he will send them immediately.'
This took place to fulfil
what was spoken by the prophet, saying,

> 'Tell the daughter of Sion,
> Behold, your king is coming to you,
> humble, and mounted on an ass,
> and on a colt, the foal of an ass.'

The disciples went and did as Jesus had directed them;
they brought the ass and the colt,
and put their garments on them, and he sat thereon.
Most of the crowd spread their garments on the road,
and others cut branches from the trees
and spread them on the road.
And the crowds that went before him
and that followed him shouted,
'Hosanna to the Son of David!
Blessed is he who comes in the name of the Lord!
Hosanna in the highest!'
And when he entered Jerusalem,
all the city was stirred, saying, 'Who is this?'
And the crowds said,
'This is the prophet Jesus from Nazareth of Galilee.'

   The Gospel of the Lord.

YEAR B

A reading from the holy Gospel according to Mark   11:1-10
Blessings on him who comes in the name of the Lord.

When they drew near to Jerusalem,
to Bethphage and Bethany, at the Mount of Olives,
Jesus sent two of his disciples, and said to them,
'Go into the village opposite you,
and immediately as you enter it
you will find a colt tied, on which no one has ever sat;
untie it and bring it.
If any one says to you,
"Why are you doing this?" say,

"The Lord has need of it
and will send it back here immediately.""
And they went away,
and found a colt tied at the door out in the open street;
and they untied it.
And those who stood there said to them,
'What are you doing, untying the colt?'
And they told them what Jesus had said;
and they let them go.
And they brought the colt to Jesus,
and threw their garments on it;
and he sat upon it.
And many spread their garments on the road,
and others spread leafy branches
which they had cut from the fields.
And those who went before
and those who followed cried out,
'Hosanna!
Blessed is he who comes in the name of the Lord!
Blessed is the kingdom of our father David that is coming!
Hosanna in the highest!'

   The Gospel of the Lord.

ALTERNATIVE GOSPEL FOR YEAR B

A reading from the holy Gospel according to John   12:12-16
Blessings on him who comes in the name of the Lord.

A great crowd who had come to the feast
heard that Jesus was coming to Jerusalem.
So they took branches of palm trees
and went out to meet him, crying,
'Hosanna!
Blessed is he who comes in the name of the Lord,
even the king of Israel!'
And Jesus found a young ass and sat upon it; as is written,
    'Fear not, daughter of Sion;
    behold, your king is coming,
    sitting on an ass's colt!'

His disciples did not understand this at first;
but when Jesus was glorified,
then they remembered that this had been written of him
and had been done to him.

The Gospel of the Lord.

YEAR C

A reading from the holy Gospel according to Luke   19:28-40

Blessings on him who comes in the name of the Lord.

Jesus went on ahead, going up to Jerusalem.
When he drew near to Bethphage and Bethany,
at the mount that is called Olivet,
he sent two disciples,
saying, 'Go into the village opposite,
where on entering you will find a colt tied,
on which no one has ever yet sat;
untie it and bring it here.
If any one asks you,
"Why are you untying it?"
you shall say this,
"The Lord has need of it."'
So those who were sent
went away and found it as he had told them.
And as they were untying the colt,
its owners said to them,
'Why are you untying the colt?'
And they said,
'The Lord has need of it.'
And they brought it to Jesus,
and throwing their garments on the colt
they set Jesus upon it.
And as he rode along,
they spread their garments on the road.
As he was drawing near,
at the descent of the Mount of Olives,
the whole multitude of the disciples
began to rejoice and praise God with a loud voice
for all the mighty works that they had seen,

saying,
'Blessed is the King who comes in the name of the Lord!
Peace in heaven and glory in the highest!'
And some of the Pharisees in the multitude said to him,
'Teacher, rebuke your disciples.'
He answered,
'I tell you, if these were silent,
the very stones would cry out.'

The Gospel of the Lord.

After the Gospel, a brief homily may be given. Then, to begin the Procession, an invitation may be given by a Priest or a Deacon or a lay minister, in these or similar words:

Dear brethren (brothers and sisters), like the crowds who acclaimed Jesus in Jerusalem, let us go forth in peace.	Imitemur, fratres carissimi, turbas acclamantes Iesum, et procedamus in pace.
Or:	Vel:
Let us go forth in peace.	Procedamus in pace.
In this latter case, all respond:	
In the name of Christ. Amen.	In nomine Christi. Amen.

The Procession to the church where Mass will be celebrated then sets off in the usual way. If incense is used, the thurifer goes first, carrying a thurible with burning incense, then an acolyte or another minister, carrying a cross decorated with palm branches according to local custom, between two ministers with lighted candles. Then follow the Deacon carrying the Book of the Gospels, the Priest with the ministers, and, after them, all the faithful carrying branches.

As the Procession moves forward, the following or other suitable chants in honour of Christ the King are sung by the choir and people.

Antiphon 1	Antiphona 1
The children of the Hebrews, carrying olive branches, went to meet the Lord, crying out and saying: Hosanna in the highest.	Pueri Hebræorum, portantes ramos olivarum, obviaverunt Domino, clamantes et dicentes: Hosanna in excelsis.

If appropriate, this antiphon is repeated between the strophes of the following Psalm.

PSALM 23

The Lord's is the earth
    and its fullness,*
the world, and those who dwell in it.
It is he who set it on the seas;*
on the rivers he made it firm. Ant.

Who shall climb the mountain
    of the Lord?*
The clean of hands and pure of heart,
whose soul is not set on vain things,†
who has not sworn
    deceitful words.* Ant.

Blessings from the Lord
    shall he receive,*
and right reward from the God
    who saves him.
Such are the people who seek him,*
who seek the face of the God
    of Jacob. Ant.

O gates, lift high your heads,†
grow higher, ancient doors.*
Let him enter, the king of glory!
Who is this king of glory?*
The Lord, the mighty, the valiant;
the Lord, the valiant in war. Ant.

O gates, lift high your heads;†
grow higher, ancient doors.*
Let him enter, the king of glory!
Who is this king of glory?*
He, the Lord of hosts,
he is the king of glory. Ant.

Domini est terra et plenitudo eius,*
orbis terrarum et qui habitant in eo.
Quia ipse super maria fundavit eum*
et super flumina firmavit eum. Ant.

Quis ascendet in montem Domini,*
aut quis stabit in loco sancto eius?
Innocens manibus et mundo corde,†
qui non levavit ad vana
    animam suam,*
nec iuravit in dolum. Ant.

Hic accipiet benedictionem
    a Domino*
et iustificationem a Deo salutari suo.
Hæc est generatio
    quærentium eum,*
quærentium faciem Dei Iacob. Ant.

Attollite, portæ, capita vestra,†
et elevamini, portæ æternales,*
et introibit rex gloriæ.
Quis est iste rex gloriæ?*
Dominus fortis et potens,
Dominus potens in prœlio. Ant.

Attollite, portæ, capita vestra, †
et elevamini, portæ æternales,*
et introibit rex gloriæ.
Quis est iste rex gloriæ?*
Dominus virtutum ipse est rex
    gloriæ. Ant.

Antiphon 2

The children of the Hebrews spread
    their garments on the road,
crying out and saying:
    Hosanna to the Son of David;
blessed is he who comes
    in the name of the Lord.

Antiphona 2

Pueri Hebræorum vestimenta
    prosternebant in via,
et clamabant dicentes:
    Hosanna filio David;
benedictus, qui venit
    in nomine Domini.

If appropriate, this antiphon is repeated between the strophes of the following Psalm.

PSALM 46

All peoples, clap your hands.*
Cry to God with shouts of joy!
For the Lord, the Most high,
    is awesome,*
the great king over all the earth. Ant.

He humbles peoples under us*
and nations under our feet.
Our heritage he chose for us,*
the pride of Jacob whom he loves.
God goes up with shouts of joy.*
The Lord goes up
    with trumpet blast. Ant.

Sing praise for God; sing praise!*
Sing praise to our king; sing praise!
God is king of all earth.*
Sing praise with all your skill. Ant.

God reigns over the nations.*
God sits upon his holy throne.
The princes of the peoples
    are assembled
with the people of the God
    of Abraham.†
The rulers of the earth belong
    to God,*
who is greatly exalted. Ant.

Omnes gentes, plaudite manibus,*
iubilate Deo in voce exsultationis,
quoniam Dominus Altissimus,
    terribilis,*
rex magnus super omnem terram.
    Ant.

Subiecit populos nobis,*
et gentes sub pedibus nostris.
Elegit nobis hereditatem nostram,*
gloriam Iacob, quem dilexit.
Ascendit Deus in iubilo,*
et Dominus in voce tubæ. Ant.

Psallite Deo, psallite;*
psallite regi nostro, psallite.
Quoniam rex omnis terræ Deus,*
psallite sapienter. Ant.

Regnavit Deus super gentes,*
Deus sedet super sedem
    sanctam suam.
Principes populorum congregati sunt
cum populo Dei Abraham,†
quoniam Dei sunt scuta terræ:*
vehementer elevatus est. Ant.

Hymn to Christ the King

Chorus:

Glory and honour and praise be to
    you, Christ, King and Redeemer,
to whom young children cried out
    loving Hosannas with joy.
All repeat: Glory and honour. . .

Chorus:

Israel's King are you, King David's
    magnificent offspring;
you are the ruler who come blest
    in the name of the Lord.
All repeat: Glory and honour. . .

Hymnus ad Christum Regem

Gloria, laus et honor tibi sit,
    rex Christe redemptor,
cui puerile decus prompsit
    Hosanna pium.
Omnes repetunt: Gloria, laus. . .

Israel es tu rex, Davidis
    et inclita proles,
nomine qui in Domini,
    rex benedicte, venis.
Omnes repetunt: Gloria, laus. . .

Chorus:

Heavenly hosts on high unite
  in singing your praises;
men and women on earth
  and all creation join in.
All repeat: Glory and honour. . .

Chorus:

Bearing branches of palm, Hebrews
  came crowding to greet you;
see how with prayers and hymns
  we come to pay you our vows.
All repeat: Glory and honour. . .

Chorus:

They offered gifts of praise to you,
  so near to your Passion;
see how we sing this song now
  to you reigning on high.
All repeat: Glory and honour. . .

Chorus:

Those you were pleased to accept;
  now accept our gifts of devotion,
good and merciful King,
  lover of all that is good.
All repeat: Glory and honour. . .

Cœtus in excelsis te laudat
  cælicus omnis,
et mortalis homo,
  et cuncta creata simul.
Omnes repetunt: Gloria, laus. . .

Plebs Hebræa tibi cum palmis
  obvia venit;
cum prece, voto,
  hymnis adsumus ecce tibi.
Omnes repetunt: Gloria, laus. . .

Hi tibi passuro solvebant
  munia laudis;
nos tibi regnanti
  pangimus ecce melos.
Omnes repetunt: Gloria, laus. . .

Hi placuere tibi,
  placeat devotio nostra:
rex bone, rex clemens,
  cui bona cuncta placent.
Omnes repetunt: Gloria, laus. . .

As the procession enters the church, there is sung the following responsory or another chant, which should speak of the Lord's entrance.

R. As the Lord entered the holy city,
the children of the Hebrews
proclaimed the resurrection of life.
*Waving their branches of palm,
  they cried:
Hosanna in the Highest.

V. When the people heard that
  Jesus was coming to Jerusalem,
  they went out to meet him.

*Waving their branches. . .

R. Ingrediente Domino
  in sanctam civitatem,
Hebræorum pueri, resurrectionem
  vitæ pronuntiantes,
*Cum ramis palmarum:
Hosanna, clamabant, in excelsis.

V. Cum audisset populus, quod
  Iesus veniret Hierosolymam,
  exierunt obviam ei.

*Cum ramis. . .

When the Priest arrives at the altar, he venerates it and, if appropriate, incenses it. Then he goes to the chair, where he puts aside the cope, if he has worn one, and puts on the chasuble. Omitting the other Introductory Rites of the Mass and, if appropriate, the Kyrie (Lord, have mercy), he says the Collect of the Mass, and then continues the Mass in the usual way.

Second Form: The Solemn Entrance

When a procession outside the church cannot take place, the entrance of the Lord is celebrated inside the church by means of a Solemn Entrance before the principal Mass.

Holding branches in their hands, the faithful gather either outside, in front of the church door, or inside the church itself. The Priest and ministers and a representative group of the faithful go to a suitable place in the church outside the sanctuary, where at least the greater part of the faithful can see the rite.

While the Priest approaches the appointed place, the antiphon Hosanna or another appropriate chant is sung. Then the blessing of branches and the proclamation of the Gospel of the Lord's entrance into Jerusalem take place. After the Gospel, the Priest processes solemnly with the ministers and the representative group of the faithful through the church to the sanctuary, while the responsory As the Lord entered or another appropriate chant is sung.

Arriving at the altar, the Priest venerates it. He then goes to the chair and, omitting the Introductory Rites of the Mass and, if appropriate, the Kyrie (Lord, have mercy), he says the Collect of the Mass, and then continues the Mass in the usual way.

Third Form: The Simple Entrance

At all other Masses of this Sunday at which the Solemn Entrance is not held, the memorial of the Lord's entrance into Jerusalem takes place by means of a Simple Entrance.

While the Priest proceeds to the altar, the Entrance Antiphon with its Psalm or another chant on the same theme is sung. Arriving at the altar, the Priest venerates it and goes to the chair. After the Sign of the Cross, he greets the people and continues the Mass in the usual way.

At other Masses, in which singing at the entrance cannot take place, the Priest, as soon as he has arrived at the altar and venerated it, greets the people, reads the Entrance Antiphon, and continues the Mass in the usual way.

Entrance Antiphon Cf. Jn 12:1,12-13; Ps 23:9-10 | Ant. ad introitum

SIX days before the Passover,
when the Lord came into
 the city of Jerusalem,
the children ran to meet him;
in their hands they carried
 palm branches
and with a loud voice cried out:

*Hosanna in the highest!
Blessed are you, who have come
 in your abundant mercy!

O gates, lift high your heads;
grow higher, ancient doors.
Let him enter, the king of glory!
Who is this king of glory?
He, the Lord of hosts,
 he is the king of glory.

*Hosanna in the highest!
Blessed are you, who have come
 in your abundant mercy!

ANTE sex dies sollemnis Paschæ,
quando venit Dominus
 in civitatem Ierusalem,
occurrerunt ei pueri:
et in manibus portabant
 ramos palmarum
et clamabant voce magna, dicentes:

*Hosanna in excelsis:
Benedictus, qui venisti
 in multitudine misericordiæ tuæ.

Attollite, portæ, capita vestra,
et elevamini, portæ æternales,
et introibit rex gloriæ.
Quis est iste rex gloriæ?
Dominus virtutum ipse est
 rex gloriæ.

*Hosanna in excelsis:
Benedictus, qui venisti
 in multitudine misericordiæ tuæ.

At the Mass

After the Procession or Solemn Entrance the Priest begins the Mass with the Collect.

Collect | Collecta

Almighty ever-living God,
who as an example of humility
 for the human race to follow
caused our Saviour to take flesh
 and submit to the Cross,
graciously grant that we may heed
 his lesson of patient suffering
and so merit a share
 in his Resurrection.
Who lives and reigns with you
 in the unity of the Holy Spirit,
one God, for ever and ever.

Omnipotens sempiterne Deus,
qui humano generi, ad imitandum
 humilitatis exemplum,
Salvatorem nostrum carnem sumere,
et crucem subire fecisti,
concede propitius,
ut et patientiæ ipsius
 habere documenta
et resurrectionis consortia mereamur.
Qui tecum vivit et regnat
 in unitate Spiritus Sancti,
Deus, per omnia sæcula sæculorum.

FIRST READING

A reading from the prophet Isaiah   50:4-7

I did not cover my face against insult - I know I shall not be shamed.

The Lord has given me
a disciple's tongue.
So that I may know how to reply to the wearied
he provides me with speech.
Each morning he wakes me to hear,
to listen like a disciple.
The Lord has opened my ear.
For my part, I made no resistance,
neither did I turn away.
I offered my back to those who struck me,
my cheeks to those who tore at my beard;
I did not cover my face
against insult and spittle.
The Lord comes to my help,
so that I am untouched by the insults.
So, too, I set my face like flint,
I know I shall not be shamed.

   The word of the Lord.

Responsorial Psalm   Ps 21:8-9,17-20,23-24. R. v.2

R. **My God, my God, why have you forsaken me?**

   All who see me deride me.
   They curl their lips, they toss their heads.
   'He trusted in the Lord, let him save him;
   let him release him if this is his friend.' R.

   Many dogs have surrounded me,
   a band of the wicked beset me.
   They tear holes in my hands and my feet.
   I can count every one of my bones. R.

   They divide my clothing among them.
   They cast lots for my robe.
   O Lord, do not leave me alone,
   my strength, make haste to help me! R.

I will tell of your name to my brethren
and praise you where they are assembled.
'You who fear the Lord give him praise;
all sons of Jacob, give him glory.
Revere him, Israel's sons.' R.

SECOND READING

A reading from the letter of St Paul to the Philippians   2:6-11
He humbled himself, but God raised him high.

His state was divine,
yet Christ Jesus did not cling
to his equality with God
but emptied himself
to assume the condition of a slave,
and became as men are;
and being as all men are,
he was humbler yet,
even to accepting death,
death on a cross.
But God raised him high
and gave him the name
which is above all other names
so that all beings
in the heavens, on earth and in the underworld,
should bend the knee at the name of Jesus
and that every tongue should acclaim
Jesus Christ as Lord,
to the glory of God the Father.

The word of the Lord.

Gospel Acclamation   Ph 2:8-9

R. **Praise to you, O Christ, king of eternal glory.**
Christ was humbler yet,
even to accepting death, death on a cross.
But God raised him high
and gave him the name which is above all names.
R. **Praise to you, O Christ, king of eternal glory.**

The narrative of the Lord's Passion is read without candles and without incense, with no greeting or signing of the book. It is read by a Deacon or, if there is no Deacon, by a Priest. It may also be read by readers, with the part of Christ, if possible, reserved to a Priest.

Deacons, but not others, ask for the blessing of the Priest before singing the Passion, as at other times before the Gospel.

GOSPEL

YEAR A

The passion of our Lord Jesus Christ according to Matthew 26:14-27:66

The symbols in the following passion narrative represent:

N Narrator   J Jesus   O Other single speaker

C Crowd, or more than one speaker

N   One of the Twelve, the man called Judas Iscariot, went to the chief priests and said:

O   What are you prepared to give me if I hand him over to you?

N   They paid him thirty silver pieces, and from that moment he looked for an opportunity to betray him.

     Now on the first day of Unleavened Bread the disciples came to Jesus to say,

C   Where do you want us to make the preparations for you to eat the Passover?

N   He replied:

J   Go to so-and-so in the city and say to him, 'The Master says: My time is near. It is at your house that I am keeping Passover with my disciples.'

N   The disciples did what Jesus told them and prepared the Passover. When the evening came he was at table with the twelve disciples. And while they were eating he said:

J   I tell you solemnly, one of you is about to betray me.

N   They were greatly distressed and started asking him in turn,

C   Not I, Lord, surely?

N   He answered:

J   Someone who has dipped his hand into the dish with me, will betray me. The Son of Man is going to his fate, as the scriptures say he will, but alas for that man by whom the Son of Man is betrayed! Better for that man if he had never been born!

N   Judas, who was to betray him, asked in his turn,

O   Not I, Rabbi, surely?

N   Jesus answered:

J   They are your own words.

N   Now as they were eating, Jesus took some bread, and when he had said the blessing he broke it and gave it to the disciples and said:

J   Take it and eat; this is my body.

N   Then he took a cup, and when he had returned thanks he gave it to them saying:

J   Drink all of you from this, for this is my blood, the blood of the covenant, which is to be poured out for many for the forgiveness of sins. From now on, I tell you, I shall not drink wine until the day I drink the new wine with you in the kingdom of my Father.

N   After psalms had been sung they left for the Mount of Olives. Then Jesus said to them,

J   You will all lose faith in me this night, for the scripture says: I shall strike the shepherd and the sheep of the flock will be scattered. But after my resurrection I shall go before you to Galilee.

N   At this, Peter said:

O   Though all lose faith in you, I will never lose faith.

N   Jesus answered him,

J   I tell you solemnly, this very night, before the cock crows, you will have disowned me three times.

N   Peter said to him,

O   Even if I have to die with you, I will never disown you.

N   And all the disciples said the same.

     Then Jesus came with them to a small estate called Gethsemane; and he said to his disciples,

J   Stay here while I go over there to pray.

N   He took Peter and the two sons of Zebedee with him. And sadness came over him, and great distress. Then he said to them:

J   My soul is sorrowful to the point of death. Wait here and keep awake with me.

N   And going on a little further he fell on his face and prayed:

J   My Father, if it is possible let this cup pass me by. Nevertheless, let it be as you, not I, would have it.

N   He came back to the disciples and found them sleeping, and he said to Peter:

J   So you had not the strength to keep awake with me one hour? You should be awake, and praying not to be put to the test. The spirit is willing, but the flesh is weak.

N   Again, a second time, he went away and prayed:

J   My Father, if this cup cannot pass by without my drinking it, your will be done!

N   And he came again back and found them sleeping, their eyes were so heavy. Leaving them there, he went away again and prayed for the third time, repeating the same words. Then he came back to the disciples and said to them,

J   You can sleep on now and take your rest. Now the hour has come when the Son of Man is to be betrayed into the hands of sinners. Get up! Let us go! My betrayer is already close at hand.

N   He was still speaking when Judas, one of the Twelve, appeared, and with him a large number of men armed with swords and clubs, sent by the chief priests and elders of the people Now the traitor had arranged a sign with them. He had said:

O   'The one I kiss, he is the man. Take him in charge.'

N   So he went straight up to Jesus and said:

O   Greetings, Rabbi,

N   and kissed him. Jesus said to him,

J   My friend, do what you are here for.

N   Then they came forward, seized Jesus and took him in charge. At that, one of the followers of Jesus grasped his sword and drew it; he struck out at the high priest's servant and cut off his ear. Jesus then said:

J   Put your sword back, for all who draw the sword will die by the sword. Or do you think that I cannot appeal to my Father who would promptly send more than twelve legions of angels to my defence? But then, how would the scriptures be fulfilled that say this is the way it must be?

N   It was at this time that Jesus said to the crowds:

J   Am I a brigand, that you had to set out to capture me with swords and clubs? I sat teaching in the Temple day after day and you never laid hands on me.

N   Now all this happened to fulfil the prophecies in scripture. Then all the disciples deserted him and ran away.

The men who had arrested Jesus led him off to Caiaphas the high priest, where the scribes and the elders were assembled. Peter followed him at a distance, and when he reached the high priest's palace, he went in and sat down with the attendants to see what the end would be.

The chief priests and the whole Sanhedrin were looking for evidence against Jesus, however false, on which they might pass the death-sentence. But they could not find any, though several lying witnesses came forward. Eventually two stepped forward and made a statement,

O   This man said: 'I have power to destroy the Temple of God and in three days build it up.'

N   The high priest then stood up and said to him:

O   Have you no answer to that? What is this evidence these men are bringing against you?

N   But Jesus was silent. And the high priest said to him:

O   I put you on oath by the living God to tell us if you are the Christ, the Son of God.

N   Jesus answered:

J   The words are your own. Moreover, I tell you that from this time onward you will see the Son of Man seated at the right hand of the Power and coming on the clouds of heaven.

N   At this, the high priest tore his clothes and said:

O   He has blasphemed. What need of witnesses have we now? There! You have just heard the blasphemy. What is your opinion?

N   They answered:

C   He deserves to die

N   Then they spat in his face and hit him with their fists; others said as they struck him:

C   Play the prophet, Christ! Who hit you then?

N   Meanwhile Peter was sitting outside in the courtyard, and a servant-girl came up to him and said:

O   You too were with Jesus the Galilean.

N   But he denied it in front of them all, saying:

O   I do not know what you are talking about.

N   When he went out to the gateway another servant-girl saw him and said to the people there:

O   This man was with Jesus the Nazarene.

N   And again, with an oath, he denied it,

O   I do not know the man.

N   A little later the bystanders came up and said to Peter:

C   You are one of them for sure! Why, your accent gives you away.

N   Then he started calling down curses on himself and swearing:

O   I do not know the man.

N   At that moment the cock crew, and Peter remembered what Jesus had said, 'Before the cock crows you will have disowned me three times.'

And he went outside and wept bitterly.

When morning came, all the chief priests and the elders of the people met in council to bring about the death of Jesus. They had him bound, and led him away to hand him over to Pilate, the governor. When he found that Jesus had been condemned, Judas his betrayer was filled with remorse and took the thirty pieces of silver back to the chief priests and elders, saying:

O I have sinned. I have betrayed innocent blood.

N They replied:

C What is that to us? That is your concern.

N And flinging down the silver pieces in the sanctuary he made off, and went and hanged himself. The chief priests picked up the silver pieces and said:

C It is against the Law to put this into the treasury; it is blood money.

N So they discussed the matter and bought the potter's field with it as a graveyard for foreigners, and this is why the field is called the Field of Blood today. The words of the prophet Jeremiah were then fulfilled: And they took the thirty silver pieces, the sum at which the precious One was priced by children of Israel, and they gave them for the potter's field, just as the Lord directed me.

[Jesus, then, was brought before the governor, and the governor put to him this question:

O Are you the king of the Jews?

N Jesus replied:

J It is you who say it.

N But when he was accused by the chief priests and the elders he refused to answer at all. Pilate then said to him:

O Do you not hear how many charges they have brought against you?

N But to the governor's complete amazement, he offered no reply to any of the charges.

At festival time it was the governor's practice to release a prisoner for the people, anyone they chose. Now there was at that time a notorious prisoner whose name was Barabbas. So when the crowd gathered, Pilate said to them,

O Which do you want me to release for you: Barabbas or Jesus who is called Christ?

N For Pilate knew it was out of jealousy that they had handed him over. Now as he was seated in the chair of judgement, his wife sent him a message,

O   Have nothing to do with that man; I have been upset all day by a dream I had about him.

N   The chief priests and the elders, however, had persuaded the crowd to demand the release of Barabbas and the execution of Jesus. So when the governor spoke and asked them:

O   Which of the two do you want me to release for you?

N   They said:

C   Barabbas.

N   Pilate said to them:

O   What am I to do with Jesus who is called Christ?

N   They all said:

C   Let him be crucified!

N   Pilate asked:

O   Why? What harm has he done?

N   But they shouted all the louder,

C   Let him be crucified!

N   Then Pilate saw that he was making no impression, that in fact a riot was imminent. So he took some water, washed his hands in front of the crowd and said:

O   I am innocent of this man's blood. It is your concern.

N   And the people, to a man, shouted back:

C   His blood be on us and on our children!

N   Then he released Barabbas for them. He ordered Jesus to be first scourged and then handed over to be crucified.

The governor's soldiers took Jesus with them into the Praetorium and collected the whole cohort round him. Then they stripped him and made him wear a scarlet cloak, and having twisted some thorns into a crown they put this on his head and placed a reed in his right hand. To make fun of him they knelt to him saying:

C   Hail, king of the Jews!

N   And they spat on him and took the reed and struck him on the head with it. And when they had finished making fun of him, they took off the cloak and dressed him in his own clothes and led him away to crucify him.

On their way out, they came across a man from Cyrene, Simon by name, and enlisted him to carry his cross. When they had reach a place called Golgotha, that is, the place of the skull, they gave him wine to drink. When they had finished crucifying him they shared out his clothing by casting lots, and then sat down and stayed there keeping guard over him. Above his head was placed the charge against him; it read: 'This is Jesus, the King of the Jews.' At the same time two robbers were crucified with him, one on the right and one on the left.

The passers-by jeered at him; they shook their heads and said:

C So you would destroy the Temple and rebuild it in three days! Then save yourself! If you are God's son, come down from the cross!

N The chief priests with the scribes and elders mocked him in the same way, saying:

C He saved others; he cannot save himself. He is the King of Israel; let him come down from the cross now, and we will believe in him. He put his trust in God; now let God rescue him if he wants him. For he did say, 'I am the son of God.'

N Even the robbers who were crucified with him taunted him in the same way.

From the sixth hour there was darkness over all the land until the ninth hour. And about the ninth hour, Jesus cried out in a loud voice:

J Eli, Eli, lama sabachthani?

N That is: 'My God, my God, why have you deserted me?' When some of those who stood there heard this, they said:

C The man is calling on Elijah,

N and one of them quickly ran to get a sponge which he dipped in vinegar and, putting it on a reed, gave it him to drink. The rest of them said:

C Wait! See if Elijah will come to save him.

N But Jesus, again crying out in a loud voice, yielded up his spirit.

All kneel and pause a moment.

N At that, the veil of the Temple was torn in two from top to bottom; the earth quaked; the rocks were split; the tombs opened and the bodies of many holy men rose from the dead, and these, after his resurrection, came out of the tombs, entered the Holy City and appeared to a number of people.

Meanwhile the centurion, together with the others guarding Jesus, had seen the earthquake and all that was taking place, and they were terrified and said:

C In truth this was a son of God.]

N And many women were there, watching from a distance, the same women who had followed Jesus from Galilee and looked after him. Among them were Mary of Magdala, Mary the mother of James and

Joseph, and the mother of Zebedee's sons.

When it was evening, there came a rich man of Arimathaea called Joseph, who had himself become a disciple of Jesus. This man went to Pilate and asked for the body of Jesus. Pilate thereupon ordered it to be handed over. So Joseph took the body, wrapped it in a clean shroud and put it in his own new tomb which he had hewn out of the rock. He then rolled a large stone across the entrance of the tomb and went away. Now Mary of Magdala and the other Mary were there, sitting opposite the sepulchre.

Next day, that is, when Preparation Day was over, the chief priests and the Pharisees went in a body to Pilate and said to him,

C Your Excellency, we recall that this impostor said, while he was still alive, 'After three days I shall rise again.' Therefore give the order to have the sepulchre kept secure until the third day, for fear his disciples come and steal him away and tell the people, 'He has risen from the dead.' This last piece of fraud would be worse than what went before.

N Pilate said to them:

O You may have your guards. Go and make all as secure as you know how.

N So they went and made the sepulchre secure, putting seals on the stone and mounting a guard.

| [The Gospel of the Lord.]

Shorter Form, verses 27:11-54. Read between [ ]

YEAR B

The symbols in the following passion narrative represent:

N Narrator   J Jesus   O Other single speaker
C Crowd, or more than one speaker

The passion of our Lord Jesus Christ according to Mark   14:1-15:47

N It was two days before the Passover and the feast of Unleavened Bread, and the chief priests and scribes were looking for a way to arrest Jesus by some trick and have him put to death. For they said,

C It must not be during the festivities, or there will be a disturbance among the people.

N Jesus was at Bethany in the house of Simon the leper; he was at dinner when a woman came in with an alabaster jar of very costly ointment, pure nard. She broke the jar and poured the ointment on his head. Some who were there said to one another indignantly,

C   Why this waste of ointment? Ointment like this could have been sold for over three hundred denarii and the money given to the poor;

N   and they were angry with her. But Jesus said,

J   Leave her alone. Why are you upsetting her? What she has done for me is one of the good works. You have the poor with you always and you can be kind to them whenever you wish but you will not always have me. She has done what was in her power to do; she has anointed my body beforehand for its burial. I tell you solemnly, wherever throughout all the world the Good News is proclaimed, what she has done will be told also, in remembrance of her.

N   Judas Iscariot, one of the Twelve, approached the chief priests with an offer to hand Jesus over to them. They were delighted to hear it, and promised to give him money; and he looked for a way of betraying him when the opportunity should occur.

On the first day of Unleavened Bread, when the Passover lamb was sacrificed, his disciples said to him,

C   Where do you want us to go and make the preparations for you to eat the Passover?

N   So he sent two of his disciples, saying to them,

J   Go into the city and you will meet a man carrying a pitcher of water. Follow him, and say to the owner of the house which he enters, 'The Master says: Where is my dining room in which I can eat the Passover with my disciples?' He will show you a large upper room furnished with couches, all prepared. Make the preparations for us there.

N   The disciples set out and went to the city and found everything as he had told them, and prepared the Passover.

When evening came he arrived with the Twelve. And while they were at table eating, Jesus said,

J   I tell you solemnly, one of you is about to betray me, one of you eating with me.

N   They were distressed and asked him, one after another,

O   Not I, surely?

N   He said to them,

J   It is one of the Twelve, one who is dipping into the same dish with me. Yes, the Son of Man is going to his fate, as the scriptures say he will, but alas for that man by whom the Son of Man is betrayed! Better for that man if he had never been born!

N   And as they were eating he took some bread, and when he had said the blessing he broke it and gave it to them, saying,

J   Take it; this is my body.

N   Then he took a cup, and when he had returned thanks he gave it to them, and all drank from it, and he said to them,

J   This is my blood, the blood of the covenant, which is to be poured out for many. I tell you solemnly, I shall not drink any more wine until the day I drink the new wine in the kingdom of God.

N   After psalms had been sung they left for the Mount of Olives. And Jesus said to them,

J   You will all lose faith, for the scripture says, 'I shall strike the shepherd and the sheep will be scattered.' However after my resurrection I shall go before you to Galilee.

N   Peter said,

O   Even if all lose faith, I will not.

N   And Jesus said to him,

J   I tell you solemnly, this day, this very night, before the cock crows twice, you will have disowned me three times.

N   But he repeated still more earnestly,

O   If I have to die with you, I will never disown you.

N   And they all said the same.

     They came to a small estate called Gethsemane, and Jesus said to his disciples,

J   Stay here while I pray.

N   Then he took Peter and James and John with him. And a sudden fear came over him, and great distress. And he said to them,

J   My soul is sorrowful to the point of death. Wait here, and keep awake.

N   And going on a little further he threw himself on the ground and prayed that, if it were possible, this hour might pass him by. He said,

J   Abba (Father)! Everything is possible for you. Take this cup away from me. But let it be as you, not I, would have it.

N   He came back and found them sleeping, and he said to Peter,

J   Simon, are you asleep? Had you not the strength to keep awake one hour? You should be awake, and praying not to be put to the test. The spirit is willing but the flesh is weak.

N   Again he went away and prayed, saying the same words. And once more he came back and found them sleeping, their eyes were so heavy; and they could find no answer for him. He came back a third time and said to them,

J   You can sleep on now and take your rest. It is all over. The hour has come. Now the Son of Man is to be betrayed into the hands of sinners. Get up! Let us go! My betrayer is close at hand already.

N   Even while he was still speaking, Judas, one of the Twelve, came up with a number of men armed with swords and clubs, sent by the chief priests and the scribes and the elders. Now the traitor had arranged a signal with them. He had said,

O   The one I kiss, he is the man. Take him in charge, and see he is well guarded when you lead him away.'

N   So when the traitor came, he went straight up to Jesus and said,

O   Rabbi!

N   and kissed him. The others seized him and took him in charge. Then one of the bystanders drew his sword and struck out at the high priest's servant, and cut off his ear.

    Then Jesus spoke,

J   Am I a brigand that you had to set out to capture me with swords and clubs? I was among you teaching in the Temple day after day and you never laid hands on me. But this is to fulfil the scriptures.

N   And they all deserted him and ran away. A young man who followed him had nothing on but a linen cloth. They caught hold of him, but he left the cloth in their hands and ran away naked.

    They led Jesus off to the high priest; and all the chief priests and the elders and the scribes assembled there. Peter had followed him at a distance, right into the high priest's palace, and was sitting with the attendants warming himself at the fire.

    The chief priests and the whole Sanhedrin were looking for evidence against Jesus on which they might pass the death-sentence. But they could not find any. Several, indeed, brought false evidence against him, but their evidence was conflicting. Some stood up and submitted this false evidence against him,

C   We heard him say, 'I am going to destroy this Temple made by human hands, and in three days build another, not made by human hands.'

N   But even on this point their evidence was conflicting. The high priest then stood up before the whole assembly and put this question to Jesus,

O   Have you no answer to that? What is this evidence these men are bringing against you?

N   But he was silent and made no answer at all. The high priest put a second question to him,

O   Are you the Christ the Son of the Blessed One?

N   Jesus said,

J   I am, and you will see the Son of Man seated at the right hand of the Power and coming with the clouds of heaven.

N   The high priest tore his robes, and said,

O   What need of witnesses have we now? You heard the blasphemy. What is your finding?

N   And they all gave their verdict: he deserved to die.
    Some of them started spitting at him and, blindfolding him, began hitting him with their fists and shouting,

C   Play the prophet!

N   And the attendants rained blows on him.
    While Peter was down below in the courtyard, one of the high-priest's servant-girls came up. She saw Peter warming himself there, stared at him and said,

O   You too were with Jesus, the man from Nazareth.

N   But he denied it, saying,

O   I do not know, I do not understand what you are talking about.

N   And he went out into the forecourt. The servant-girl saw him and again started telling the bystanders,

O   This fellow is one of them.

N   But he again denied it. A little later the bystanders themselves said to Peter,

C   You are one of them for sure! Why, you are a Galilean.

N   But he started calling down curses on himself and swearing,

O   I do not know the man you speak of.

N   At that moment the cock crew for the second time, and Peter recalled how Jesus had said to him, 'Before the cock crows twice, you will have disowned me three times.' And he burst into tears.

    [First thing in the morning, the chief priest together with the elders and scribes, in short the whole Sanhedrin, had their plan ready. They had Jesus bound and took him away and handed him over to Pilate.
    Pilate questioned him,

O   Are you the king of the Jews?

N   He answered,

J   It is you who say it.

N   And the chief priests brought many accusations against him. Pilate questioned him again,

O   Have you no reply at all? See how many accusations they are bringing against you!

N   But to Pilate's amazement, Jesus made no further reply.
    At festival time Pilate used to release a prisoner for them, anyone they asked for. Now a man called Barabbas was then in prison with the rioters who had committed murder during the uprising. When the

N crowd went up and began to ask Pilate the customary favour, Pilate answered them,

O Do you want me to release for you the king of the Jews?

N For he realised it was out of jealousy that the chief priests had handed Jesus over. The chief priests, however, had incited the crowd to demand that he should release Barabbas for them instead. Then Pilate spoke again.

O But in that case, what am I to do with the man you call king of the Jews?

N They shouted back.

C Crucify him!

N Pilate asked them,

O Why? What harm has he done?

N But they shouted all the louder,

C Crucify him!

N So Pilate, anxious to placate the crowd, released Barabbas for them and, having ordered Jesus to be scourged, handed him over to be crucified.

    The soldiers led him away to the inner part of the palace, that is, the Praetorium, and called the whole cohort together. They dressed him up in purple, twisted some thorns into a crown and put it on him. And they began saluting him,

C Hail, king of the Jews!

N They struck his head with a reed and spat on him; and they went down on their knees to do him homage. And when they had finished making fun of him, they took off the purple and dressed him in his own clothes.

    They led him out to crucify him. They enlisted a passer-by, Simon of Cyrene, father of Alexander and Rufus, who was coming in from the country, to carry his cross. They brought Jesus to the place called Golgotha, which means the place of the skull.

    They offered him wine mixed with myrrh, but he refused it. Then they crucified him, and shared out his clothing, casting lots to decide what each should get. It was the third hour when they crucified him. The inscription giving the charge against him read: 'The King of the Jews.' And they crucified two robbers with him, one on his right and one on his left.

    The passers-by jeered at him; they shook their heads and said,

C Aha! So you would destroy the Temple and rebuild it in three days! Then save yourself: come down from the cross!

N The chief priests and the scribes mocked him among themselves in the

N   same way. They said,

C   He saved others, he cannot save himself. Let the Christ, the king of Israel, come down from the cross now, for us to see it and believe.

N   Even those who were crucified with him taunted him.

When the sixth hour came there was darkness over the whole land until the ninth hour. And at the ninth hour Jesus cried out in a loud voice,

J   Eloi, Eloi, lama sabachthani?

N   This means 'My God, my God, why have you deserted me?' When some of those who stood by heard this, they said,

C   Listen, he is calling on Elijah.

N   Someone ran and soaked a sponge in vinegar and, putting it on a reed, gave it him to drink, saying,

O   Wait and see if Elijah will come to take him down.

N   But Jesus gave a loud cry and breathed his last.

All kneel and pause a moment.

N   And the veil of the Temple was torn in two from top to bottom. The centurion, who was standing in front of him, had seen how he had died, and he said,

O   In truth this man was a son of God.]

N   There were some women watching from a distance. Among them were Mary of Magdala, Mary who was the mother of James the younger, and Joset, and Salome. These used to follow him and look after him when he was in Galilee. And there were many other women there who had come up to Jerusalem with him.

It was now evening, and since it was Preparation Day (that is the vigil of the sabbath), there came Joseph of Arimathaea, a prominent member of the Council, who himself lived in the hope of seeing the kingdom of God, and he boldly went to Pilate and asked for the body of Jesus. Pilate, astonished that he should have died so soon, summoned the centurion and enquired if he was already dead. Having been assured of this by the centurion, he granted the corpse to Joseph who brought a shroud, took Jesus down from the cross, wrapped him in the shroud and laid him in a tomb which had been hewn out of the rock. He then rolled a stone against the entrance to the tomb. Mary of Magdala and Mary the mother of Joset were watching and took note of where he was laid.

| [The Gospel of the Lord.]

Shorter Form, verses 15:1-39. Read between [ ]

YEAR C

The passion of our Lord Jesus Christ according to Luke   22:14-23:56

N   When the hour came Jesus took his place at table, and the apostles with him. And he said to them,

J   I have longed to eat this Passover with you before I suffer; because, I tell you, I shall not eat it again until it is fulfilled in the kingdom of God.

N   Then, taking a cup, he gave thanks and said,

J   Take this and share it among you, because from now on, I tell you, I shall not drink wine until the kingdom of God comes.

N   Then he took some bread, and when he had given thanks, broke it and gave it to them, saying,

J   This is my body which will be given for you; do this as a memorial of me.

N   He did the same with the cup after supper, and said,

J   This cup is the new covenant in my blood which will be poured out for you.

    And yet, here with me on the table is the hand of the man who betrays me. The Son of Man does indeed go to his fate even as it has been decreed, but alas for that man by whom he is betrayed!

N   And they began to ask one another which of them it could be who was to do this thing.

    A dispute arose also between them about which should be reckoned the greatest, but he said to them,

J   Among pagans it is the kings who lord it over them, and those who have authority over them are given the title Benefactor. This must not happen with you. No; the greatest among you must behave as if he were the youngest, the leader as if he were the one who serves. For who is the greater: the one at table or the one who serves? The one at table, surely? Yet here I am among you as one who serves!

    You are the men who have stood by me faithfully in my trials; and now I confer a kingdom on you, just as my Father conferred one on me: you will eat and drink at my table in my kingdom, and you will sit on thrones to judge the twelve tribes of Israel.

    Simon, Simon! Satan, you must know, has got his wish to sift you all like wheat; but I have prayed for you, Simon, that your faith may not fail, and once you have recovered, you in your turn must strengthen your brothers.

N   He answered,

O   Lord, I would be ready to go to prison with you, and to death.

N Jesus replied,

J I tell you, Peter, by the time the cock crows today you will have denied three times that you know me.

N He said to them,

J When I sent you out without purse or haversack or sandals, were you short of anything?

N They answered,

C No.

N He said to them,

J But now if you have a purse, take it: if you have a haversack, do the same; if you have no sword, sell your cloak and buy one, because I tell you these words of scripture have to be fulfilled in me: He let himself be taken for a criminal. Yes, what scripture says about me is even now reaching its fulfilment.

N They said,

C Lord, there are two swords here now.

N He said to them,

J That is enough!

N He then left the upper room to make his way as usual to the Mount of Olives, with the disciples following. When they reached the place he said to them,

J Pray not to be put to the test.

N Then he withdrew from them, about a stone's throw away, and knelt down and prayed, saying,

J Father, if you are willing, take this cup away from me. Nevertheless, let your will be done, not mine.

N Then an angel appeared to him coming from heaven to give him strength. In his anguish he prayed even more earnestly and his sweat fell to the ground like great drops of blood.

   When he rose from prayer he went to the disciples and found them sleeping for sheer grief. He said to them,

J Why are you asleep? Get up and pray not to be put to the test.

N He was still speaking when a number of men appeared, and at the head of them the man called Judas, one of the Twelve, who went up to Jesus to kiss him. Jesus said,

J Judas, are you betraying the Son of Man with a kiss?

N His followers, seeing what was happening, said,

C Lord, shall we use our swords?

N   And one of them struck out at the high priest's servant, and cut off his right ear. But at this Jesus spoke,

J   Leave off! That will do!

N   And touching the man's ear he healed him.

Then Jesus spoke to the chief priests and captains of the Temple guard and elders who had come for him. He said,

J   Am I a brigand that you had to set out with swords and clubs? When I was among you in the Temple day after day you never moved to lay hands on me. But this is your hour; this is the reign of darkness.

N   They seized him then and led him away, and they took him to the high priest's house. Peter followed at a distance. They had lit a fire in the middle of the courtyard and Peter sat down among them, and as he was sitting there by the blaze a servant-girl saw him, peered at him and said,

O   This person was with him too.

N   But he denied it, saying,

O   Woman, I do not know him.

N   Shortly afterwards, someone else saw him and said,

O   You are another of them.

N   But Peter replied,

O   I am not, my friend.

N   About an hour later, another man insisted, saying,

O   This fellow was certainly with him. Why, he is a Galilean.

N   Peter said,

O   My friend, I do not know what you are talking about.

N   At that instant, while he was still speaking, the cock crew, and the Lord turned and looked straight at Peter, and Peter remembered what the Lord had said to him, 'Before the cock crows today, you will have disowned me three times.' And he went outside and wept bitterly.

Meanwhile the men who guarded Jesus were mocking and beating him. They blindfolded him and questioned him, saying,

C   Play the prophet. Who hit you then?

N   And they continued heaping insults on him.

When day broke there was a meeting of the elders of the people, attended by the chief priests and scribes. He was brought before their council, and they said to him,

C   If you are the Christ, tell us.

N   He replied,

J   If I tell you, you will not believe me, and if I question you, you will not answer. But from now on, the Son of Man will be seated at the right hand of the Power of God.

N Then they all said,

C So you are the Son of God then?

N He answered,

J It is you who say I am.

N They said,

C What need of witnesses have we now? We have heard it for ourselves from his own lips.

N [The whole assembly then rose, and they brought him before Pilate. They began their accusation by saying,

C We found this man inciting our people to revolt, opposing payment of the tribute to Caesar, and claiming to be Christ, a king.

N Pilate put to him this question,

O Are you the king of the Jews?

N He replied,

J It is you who say it.

N Pilate then said to the chief priests and the crowd,

O I find no case against this man.

N But they persisted,

C He is inflaming the people with his teaching all over Judaea; it has come all the way from Galilee, where he started, down to here.

N When Pilate heard this, he asked if the man were a Galilean; and finding that he came under Herod's jurisdiction he passed him over to Herod who was also in Jerusalem at that time.

Herod was delighted to see Jesus; he had heard about him and had been wanting for a long time to set eyes on him; moreover, he was hoping to see some miracle worked by him. So he questioned him at some length; but without getting any reply. Meanwhile the chief priests and the scribes were there, violently pressing their accusations. Then Herod, together with his guards, treated him with contempt and made fun of him; he put a rich cloak on him and sent him back to Pilate. And though Herod and Pilate had been enemies before, they were reconciled that same day.

Pilate then summoned the chief priests and the leading men and the people. He said,

O You brought this man before me as a political agitator. Now I have gone into the matter myself in your presence and found no case against the man in respect of all the charges you bring against him. Nor has Herod either, since he has sent him back to us. As you can see, the man has done nothing that deserves death, so I shall have him flogged and then let him go.

N But as one man they howled,

C Away with him! Give us Barabbas!

N This man had been thrown into prison for causing a riot in the city and for murder.

Pilate was anxious to set Jesus free and addressed them again, but they shouted back,

C Crucify him! Crucify him!

N And for the third time he spoke to them,

O Why? What harm has this man done? I have found no case against him that deserves death, so I shall have him punished and let him go.

N But they kept on shouting at the top of their voices, demanding that he should be crucified, and their shouts were growing louder.

Pilate then gave his verdict: their demand was to be granted. He released the man they asked for, who had been imprisoned for rioting and murder, and handed Jesus over to them to deal with as they pleased.

As they were leading him away they seized on a man, Simon from Cyrene, who was coming in from the country, and made him shoulder the cross and carry it behind Jesus. Large numbers of people followed him, and of women too who mourned and lamented for him. But Jesus turned to them and said,

J Daughters of Jerusalem, do not weep for me; weep rather for yourselves and for your children. For the days will surely come when people will say, 'Happy are those who are barren, the wombs that have never borne, the breasts that have never suckled!' Then they will begin to say to the mountains, 'Fall on us!'; to the hills, 'Cover us!' For if men use the green wood like this, what will happen when it is dry?

N Now with him they were also leading out two other criminals to be executed.

When they reached the place called The Skull, they crucified him there and the criminals also, one on the right, the other on the left. Jesus said,

J Father, forgive them; they do not know what they are doing.

N Then they cast lots to share out his clothing. The people stayed there watching him. As for the leaders, they jeered at him, saying,

C He saved others; let him save himself if he is the Christ of God, the Chosen One.

N The soldiers mocked him too, and when they approached to offer him vinegar they said,

C   If you are the king of the Jews, save yourself.

N   Above him there was an inscription: 'This is the King of the Jews.'
      One of the criminals hanging there abused him, saying,

O   Are you not the Christ? Save yourself and us as well.

N   But the other spoke up and rebuked him,

O   Have you no fear of God at all? You got the same sentence as he did,
    but in our case we deserved it: we are paying for what we did. But this
    man has done nothing wrong. Jesus, remember me when you come
    into your kingdom.

N   He replied,

J   Indeed, I promise you, today you will be with me in paradise.

N   It was now about the sixth hour and, with the sun eclipsed, a darkness
    came over the whole land until the ninth hour. The veil of the Temple
    was torn right down the middle; and when Jesus had cried out in a
    loud voice, he said,

J   Father, into your hands I commit my spirit.

N   With these words he breathed his last.

All kneel and pause a moment.

      When the centurion saw what had taken place, he gave praise to
    God and said,

O   This was a great and good man.

N   And when all the people who had gathered for the spectacle saw what
    had happened, they went home beating their breasts.

      All his friends stood at a distance; so also did the women who had
    accompanied him from Galilee, and they saw all this happen.]

      Then a member of the council arrived, an upright and virtuous man
    named Joseph. He had not consented to what the others had planned
    and carried out. He came from Arimathaea, a Jewish town, and he lived
    in the hope of seeing the kingdom of God. This man went to Pilate and
    asked for the body of Jesus. He then took it down, wrapped it in a shroud
    and put him in a tomb which was hewn in stone in which no one had
    yet been laid. It was Preparation Day and the sabbath was imminent.

      Meanwhile the women who had come from Galilee with Jesus were
    following behind. They took note of the tomb and of the position of
    the body.

      Then they returned and prepared spices and ointments. And on the
    sabbath day they rested, as the law required.

| [The Gospel of the Lord.]

Shorter Form, verses 23:1-49. Read between [ ]

After the narrative of the Passion, a brief homily should take place, if appropriate. A period of silence may also be observed.

The Creed is said, and the Universal Prayer takes place.

Prayer over the Offerings

Through the Passion of your Only
    Begotten Son, O Lord,
may our reconciliation with you
    be near at hand,
so that, though we do not merit it
    by our own deeds,
yet by this sacrifice made once
    for all,
we may feel already the effects
    of your mercy.
Through Christ our Lord.

Super oblata

Per Unigeniti tui passionem
placatio tua nobis, Domine,
    sit propinqua,
quam, etsi nostris operibus
    non meremur,
interveniente sacrificio singulari,
tua percipiamus
    miseratione præventi.
Per Christum Dominum nostrum.

Preface: The Passion of the Lord.

It is truly right and just,
    our duty and our salvation,
always and everywhere to give
    you thanks,
Lord, holy Father, almighty
    and eternal God,
through Christ our Lord.

For, though innocent, he suffered
    willingly for sinners
and accepted unjust condemnation
    to save the guilty.
His Death has washed away our sins,
and his Resurrection has purchased
    our justification.

And so, with all the Angels,
we praise you, as in joyful
    celebration we acclaim:

Holy, Holy, Holy Lord God of hosts...

Præfatio: De dominica Passione.

Vere dignum et iustum est,
    æquum et salutare,
nos tibi semper et ubique
    gratias agere:
Domine, sancte Pater, omnipotens
    æterne Deus:
per Christum Dominum nostrum.

Qui pati pro impiis dignatus
    est innocens,
et pro sceleratis
    indebite condemnari.
Cuius mors delicta nostra detersit,
et iustificationem nobis
    resurrectio comparavit.

Unde et nos cum omnibus Angelis
    te laudamus,
iucunda celebratione clamantes:

Sanctus, Sanctus, Sanctus. . .

Communion Antiphon   Mt 26:42

Father, if this chalice cannot pass
   without my drinking it,
your will be done.

Prayer after Communion

Nourished with these sacred gifts,
we humbly beseech you, O Lord,
that, just as through the death
   of your Son
you have brought us to hope
   for what we believe,
so by his Resurrection
you may lead us to where you call.
Through Christ our Lord.

Prayer over the People

Look, we pray, O Lord,
   on this your family,
for whom our Lord Jesus Christ
did not hesitate to be delivered
   into the hands of the wicked
and submit to the agony
   of the Cross.
Who lives and reigns
   for ever and ever.

Ant. ad communionem

Pater, si non potest
   hic calix transire,
nisi bibam illum, fiat voluntas tua.

Post communionem

Sacro munere satiati,
supplices te, Domine, deprecamur,
ut, qui fecisti nos
morte Filii tui sperare
   quod credimus,
facias nos, eodem resurgente,
pervenire quo tendimus.
Per Christum Dominum nostrum.

Oratio super populum

Respice, quæsumus, Domine,
   super hanc familiam tuam,
pro qua Dominus noster
   Iesus Christus
non dubitavit manibus
   tradi nocentium,
et crucis subire tormentum.
Qui vivit et regnat
   in sæcula sæculorum.

THURSDAY OF HOLY WEEK

The Chrism Mass

The blessing of the Oil of the Sick and of the Oil of Catechumens and the consecration of the Chrism are carried out by the Bishop, according to the Rite described in the Roman Pontifical, usually on this day, at a proper Mass to be celebrated during the morning.

If, however, it is very difficult for the clergy and the people to gather with the Bishop on this day, the Chrism Mass may be anticipated on another day, but near to Easter.

This Mass, which the Bishop concelebrates with his presbyterate, should be, as it were, a manifestation of the Priests' communion with their Bishop. Accordingly it is desirable that all the Priests participate in it, insofar as is possible, and during it receive Communion even under both kinds. To signify the unity of the presbyterate of the diocese, the Priests who concelebrate with the Bishop should be from different regions of the diocese.

In accord with traditional practice, the blessing of the Oil of the Sick takes place before the end of the Eucharistic Prayer, but the blessing of the Oil of Catechumens and the consecration of the Chrism take place after Communion. Nevertheless, for pastoral reasons, it is permitted for the entire rite of blessing to take place after the Liturgy of the Word.

Entrance Antiphon Rv 1:6	Ant. ad introitum
JESUS Christ has made us into a kingdom, priests for his God and Father. To him be glory and power for ever and ever. Amen.	JESUS Christus fecit nos regnum et sacerdotes Deo et Patri suo: ipsi gloria et imperium in sæcula sæculorum. Amen.

The Gloria in excelsis (Glory to God in the highest) is said.

Collect	Collecta
O God, who anointed your Only Begotten Son with the Holy Spirit and made him Christ and Lord, graciously grant that, being made sharers in his consecration, we may bear witness to your Redemption in the world. Through our Lord Jesus Christ, your Son,	Deus, qui Unigenitum Filium tuum unxisti Spiritu Sancto Christumque Dominum constituisti, concede propitius, ut, eiusdem consecrationis participes effecti, testes Redemptionis inveniamur in mundo. Per Dominum nostrum Iesum Christum Filium tuum,

who lives and reigns with you
    in the unity of the Holy Spirit,
one God, for ever and ever.

qui tecum vivit et regnat
    in unitate Spiritus Sancti,
Deus, per omnia sæcula sæculorum.

FIRST READING

A reading from the prophet Isaiah   61:1-3,6,8-9

The Lord has anointed me and has sent me to bring Good News to the poor, to give them the oil of gladness.

The spirit of the Lord has been given to me,
for the Lord has anointed me.
He has sent me to bring good news to the poor,
to bind up hearts that are broken;

to proclaim liberty to captives,
freedom to those in prison;
to proclaim a year of favour from the Lord,
a day of vengeance for our God;

to comfort all those who mourn and to give them
for ashes a garland;
for mourning robe the oil of gladness,
for despondency, praise.

But you, you will be named 'priests of the Lord',
they will call you 'ministers of our God'.
I reward them faithfully
and make an everlasting covenant with them.

Their race will be famous throughout the nations,
their descendants throughout the peoples.
All who see them will admit
that they are a race whom the Lord has blessed.

    The word of the Lord.

Responsorial Psalm   Ps 88:21-22,25,27. R. v.2

R. **I will sing for ever of your love, O Lord.**

    I have found David my servant
    and with my holy oil anointed him.
    My hand shall always be with him
    and my arm shall make him strong. R.

    My truth and my love shall be with him;
    by my name his might shall be exalted.

He will say to me: 'You are my father,
my God, the rock who saves me.' R.

R. **I will sing for ever of your love, O Lord.**

SECOND READING
A reading from the book of the Apocalypse   1:5-8
He made us a line of kings, priests to serve his God and Father.

Grace and peace to you from Jesus Christ, the faithful witness, the First-
born from the dead, the Ruler of the kings of the earth. He loves us and has
washed away our sins with his blood, and made us a line of kings, priests
to serve his God and Father; to him, then, be glory and power for ever and
ever. Amen. It is he who is coming on the clouds; everyone will see him,
even those who pierced him, and all the races of the earth will mourn over
him. This is the truth. Amen. 'I am the Alpha and the Omega' says the Lord
God, who is, who was, and who is to come, the Almighty.

    The word of the Lord

Gospel Acclamation   Is 61:1 (Lk 4:18)

R. **Praise to you, O Christ, King of eternal glory!**
The spirit of the Lord has been given to me;
he sent me to bring the good news to the poor.
R. **Praise to you, O Christ, King of eternal glory!**

GOSPEL
A reading from the holy Gospel according to Luke   4:16-21
The spirit of the Lord has been given to me, for he has anointed me.

Jesus came to Nazara, where he had been brought up, and went into the
synagogue on the sabbath day as he usually did. He stood up to read, and
they handed him the scroll of the prophet Isaiah. Unrolling the scroll he
found the place where it is written:

    The spirit of the Lord has been given to me,
    for he has anointed me.
    He has sent me to bring the good news to the poor,
    to proclaim liberty to captives
    and to the blind new sight,
    to set the downtrodden free,
    to proclaim the Lord's year of favour.

    He then rolled up the scroll, gave it back to the assistant and sat down.
And all eyes in the synagogue were fixed on him. Then he began to speak
to them, 'This text is being fulfilled today even as you listen.'

    The Gospel of the Lord.

After the reading of the Gospel, the Bishop preaches the Homily in which, taking his starting point from the text of the readings proclaimed in the Liturgy of the Word, he speaks to the people and to his Priests about priestly anointing, urging the Priests to be faithful in their office and calling on them to renew publicly their priestly promises.

Renewal of Priestly Promises

After the homily the bishop speaks to the priests in these or similar words:

Beloved sons,
on the anniversary of that day
when Christ our Lord conferred
   his priesthood
on his Apostles and on us,
are you resolved to renew,
in the presence of your Bishop
   and God's holy people,
the promises you once made?

Priests, all together, respond: I am.

Are you resolved to be more united
   with the Lord Jesus
and more closely conformed to him,
denying yourselves and confirming
   those promises
about sacred duties towards
   Christ's Church
which, prompted by love of him,
you willingly and joyfully pledged
on the day of your
   priestly ordination?

Priests: I am.

Are you resolved to be faithful
   stewards of the mysteries of God
in the Holy Eucharist and the other
   liturgical rites
and to discharge faithfully
   the sacred office of teaching,
following Christ the Head
   and Shepherd,
not seeking any gain,
but moved only by zeal for souls?

Priests: I am.

Filii carissimi,
   annua redeunte memoria diei,
qua Christus Dominus sacerdotium
   suum cum Apostolis
   nobisque communicavit,
vultis olim factas promissiones
   coram Episcopo vestro
et populo sancto Dei renovare?

Presbyteri: Volo.

Vultis Domino Iesu arctius
   coniungi et conformari,
vobismetipsis abrenuntiantes atque
   promissa confirmantes sacrorum
   officiorum,
quæ, Christi amore inducti, erga
   eius Ecclesiam,
sacerdotalis vestræ ordinationis die,
   cum gaudio suscepistis?

Presbyteri: Volo.

Vultis fideles esse dispensatores
   mysteriorum Dei
per sanctam Eucharistiam
   ceterasque liturgicas actiones,
   atque sacrum docendi munus,
Christum Caput atque
   Pastorem sectando,
fideliter implere,
non bonorum cupidi,
sed animarum zelo tantum inducti?

Presbyteri: Volo.

Then the bishop addresses the people:

As for you, dearest sons
    and daughters,
pray for your Priests,
that the Lord may pour out his gifts
    abundantly upon them,
and keep them faithful as ministers
    of Christ, the High Priest,
so that they may lead you to him,
who is the source of salvation.

People: **Christ, hear us.**
Christ, graciously hear us.

And pray also for me,
that I may be faithful
    to the apostolic office
entrusted to me in my lowliness
and that in your midst I may be
    made day by day
a living and more perfect image
    of Christ,
the Priest, the Good Shepherd,
the Teacher and the Servant of all.

People: **Christ, hear us.**
Christ, graciously hear us.

May the Lord keep us all
    in his charity
and lead all of us,
shepherds and flock,
to eternal life.

All: Amen.

Vos autem, filii dilectissimi,
pro presbyteris vestris orate,
ut Dominus super eos bona sua
    abundanter effundat,
quatenus fideles ministri Christi,
    Summi Sacerdotis,
vos ad eum perducant,
qui fons est salutis.

Populus: **Christe, audi nos.**
Christe, exaudi nos.

Et pro me etiam orate:
ut fidelis sim muneri apostolico
    humilitati meæ commisso,
et inter vos efficiar viva
    et perfectior in dies imago
    Christi Sacerdotis,
Boni Pastoris,
Magistri et omnium Servi.

Populus: **Christe, audi nos.**
Christe, exaudi nos.

Dominus nos omnes
    in sua caritate custodiat,
et ipse nos universos,
pastores et oves,
    ad vitam perducat æternam.

Omnes: Amen.

The Creed is not said.

Prayer over the Offerings

May the power of this sacrifice,
   O Lord, we pray,
mercifully wipe away what is old in us
and increase in us grace
   of salvation and newness of life.
Through Christ our Lord.

Preface: The Priesthood of Christ
and the Ministry of Priests

It is truly right and just,
   our duty and our salvation,
always and everywhere
   to give you thanks,
Lord, holy Father,
   almighty and eternal God.

For by the anointing
   of the Holy Spirit
you made your Only Begotten Son
High Priest of the new
   and eternal covenant,
and by your wondrous design
   were pleased to decree
that his one Priesthood should
   continue in the Church.

For Christ not only adorns
   with a royal priesthood
the people he has made his own,
but with a brother's kindness
   he also chooses men
to become sharers
   in his sacred ministry
through the laying on of hands.

They are to renew in his name
the sacrifice of human redemption,
to set before your children
   the paschal banquet,
to lead your holy people in charity,
to nourish them with the word

Super oblata

Huius sacrificii potentia,
Domine, quæsumus,
et vetustatem nostram
   clementer abstergat,
et novitatem nobis augeat et salutem.
Per Christum Dominum nostrum.

Præfatio: De sacerdotio Christi
et de ministerio sacerdotum.

Vere dignum et iustum est,
   æquum et salutare,
nos tibi semper et ubique
   gratias agere:
Domine, sancte Pater,
   omnipotens æterne Deus:

Qui Unigenitum tuum
   Sancti Spiritus unctione
novi et æterni testamenti
   constituisti Pontificem,
et ineffabili dignatus es
   dispositione sancire,
ut unicum eius sacerdotium in
   Ecclesia servaretur.

Ipse enim non solum
   regali sacerdotio
populum acquisitionis exornat,
sed etiam fraterna homines
   eligit bonitate,
ut sacri sui ministerii fiant
   manuum impositione participes.

Qui sacrificium renovent,
   eius nomine,
redemptionis humanæ,
tuis apparantes filiis
   paschale convivium,
et plebem tuam sanctam
   caritate præveniant,
verbo nutriant, reficiant sacramentis.

and strengthen them
   with the Sacraments.

As they give up their lives for you
and for the salvation of their
   brothers and sisters,
they strive to be conformed
   to the image of Christ himself
and offer you a constant witness
   of faith and love.

And so, Lord,
   with all the Angels and Saints,
we, too, give you thanks,
   as in exultation we acclaim:

Holy, Holy, Holy Lord God of hosts...

Qui, vitam pro te fratrumque
   salute tradentes,
ad ipsius Christi nitantur
   imaginem conformari,
et constantes tibi fidem
   amoremque testentur.

Unde et nos, Domine, cum Angelis
   et Sanctis universis
tibi confitemur,
   in exsultatione dicentes:

Sanctus, Sanctus, Sanctus. . .

Communion Antiphon   Ps 88:2

I will sing for ever of your mercies,
   O Lord;
through all ages my mouth will
   proclaim your fidelity.

Ant. ad communionem

Misericordias Domini
   in æternum cantabo;
in generationem et generationem
annuntiabo veritatem tuam
   in ore meo.

Prayer after Communion

We beseech you, almighty God,
that those you renew by
   your Sacraments
may merit to become the
   pleasing fragrance of Christ.
Who lives and reigns
   for ever and ever.

Post communionem

Supplices te rogamus,
   omnipotens Deus,
ut, quos tuis reficis sacramentis,
Christi bonus odor
   effici mereantur.
Qui vivit et regnat in
   sæcula sæculorum.

The reception of the Holy Oils may take place in individual parishes either before
the celebration of the Evening Mass of the Lord's Supper or at another time that
seems more appropriate.

THE SACRED PASCHAL TRIDUUM

(YEAR A,B,C)

In the Sacred Triduum, the Church solemnly celebrates the greatest mysteries of our redemption, keeping by means of special celebrations the memorial of her Lord, crucified, buried, and risen.

The Paschal Fast should also be kept sacred. It is to be celebrated everywhere on the Friday of the Lord's Passion and, where appropriate, prolonged also through Holy Saturday as a way of coming, with spirit uplifted, to the joys of the Lord's Resurrection.

For a fitting celebration of the Sacred Triduum, a sufficient number of lay ministers is required, who must be carefully instructed as to what they are to do.

The singing of the people, the ministers, and the Priest Celebrant has a special importance in the celebrations of these days, for when texts are sung, they have their proper impact.

Pastors should, therefore, not fail to explain to the Christian faithful, as best they can, the meaning and order of the celebrations and to prepare them for active and fruitful participation.

The celebrations of the Sacred Triduum are to be carried out in cathedral and parochial churches and only in those churches in which they can be performed with dignity, that is, with a good attendance of the faithful, an appropriate number of ministers, and the means to sing at least some of the parts.

Consequently, it is desirable that small communities, associations, and special groups of various kinds join together in these churches to carry out the sacred celebrations in a more noble manner.

THURSDAY OF THE LORD'S SUPPER

(MAUNDY THURSDAY)

If we listen attentively to the Gospel, we can discern two different dimensions in the event of the washing of the feet. The cleansing that Jesus offers his disciples is first and foremost simply his action - the gift of purity, of the "capacity for God" that is offered to them. But the gift then becomes a model, the duty to do the same for one another. The gift and example overall, which we find in the passage on the washing of the feet, is a characteristic of the nature of Christianity in general. Christianity is not a type of moralism, simply a system of ethics. It does not originate in our action, our moral capacity. Christianity is first and foremost a gift: God gives himself to us – he does not give something, but himself. And this does not only happen at the beginning, at the moment of our conversion. He constantly remains the One who gives. He continually offers us his gifts. He always precedes us. This is why the central act of Christian being is the Eucharist: gratitude for having been gratified, joy for the new life that he gives us.

(Pope Benedict XVI)

In accordance with a most ancient tradition of the Church, on this day all Masses without the people are forbidden.

At the Evening Mass

The Mass of the Lord's Supper is celebrated in the evening, at a convenient time, with the full participation of the whole local community and with all the Priests and ministers exercising their office.

All Priests may concelebrate even if they have already concelebrated the Chrism Mass on this day, or if they have to celebrate another Mass for the good of the Christian faithful.

Where a pastoral reason requires it, the local Ordinary may permit another Mass to be celebrated in churches and oratories in the evening and, in case of genuine necessity, even in the morning, but only for the faithful who are in no way able to participate in the evening Mass. Care should, nevertheless, be taken that celebrations of this sort do not take place for the advantage of private persons or special small groups, and do not prejudice the evening Mass.

Holy Communion may only be distributed to the faithful during Mass; but it may be brought to the sick at any hour of the day.

The altar may be decorated with flowers with a moderation that accords with the character of this day. The tabernacle should be entirely empty; but a sufficient amount of bread should be consecrated in this Mass for the Communion of the clergy and the people on this and the following day.

Entrance Antiphon   Cf. Ga 6:14

WE should glory in the Cross of our Lord Jesus Christ, in whom is our salvation, life and resurrection, through whom we are saved and delivered.

Ant. ad introitum

NOS autem gloriari oportet in cruce Domini nostri Iesu Christi, in quo est salus, vita et resurrectio nostra, per quem salvati et liberati sumus.

The Gloria in excelsis (Glory to God in the highest) is said. While the hymn is being sung, bells are rung, and when it is finished, they remain silent until the Gloria in excelsis of the Easter Vigil, unless, if appropriate, the Diocesan Bishop has decided otherwise. Likewise, during this same period, the organ and other musical instruments may be used only so as to support the singing.

Collect

O God, who have called us
   to participate
in this most sacred Supper,
in which your Only Begotten Son,
when about to hand himself over
   to death,
entrusted to the Church a sacrifice
   new for all eternity,
the banquet of his love,
grant, we pray,
that we may draw from so great
   a mystery,
the fullness of charity and of life.
Through our Lord Jesus Christ,
   your Son,
who lives and reigns with you
   in the unity of the Holy Spirit,
one God, for ever and ever.

Collecta

Sacratissimam, Deus,
   frequentantibus Cenam,
in qua Unigenitus tuus,
   morti se traditurus,
novum in sæcula sacrificium
dilectionisque suæ convivium
   Ecclesiæ commendavit,
da nobis, quæsumus,
   ut ex tanto mysterio
plenitudinem caritatis hauriamus
   et vitæ.
Per Dominum nostrum Iesum
   Christum Filium tuum,
qui tecum vivit et regnat
   in unitate Spiritus Sancti,
Deus, per omnia sæcula sæculorum.

FIRST READING

A reading from the book of Exodus   12:1-8,11-14

Instructions concerning the Passover meal.

The Lord said to Moses and Aaron in the land of Egypt, 'This month is to be the first of all the others for you, the first month of your year. Speak to the whole community of Israel and say, "On the tenth day of this month each man must take an animal from the flock, one for each family: one animal for each household. If the household is too small to eat the animal, a man must join with his neighbour, the nearest to his house, as the number of persons requires. You must take into account what each can eat in deciding the number for the animal. It must be an animal without blemish, a male one year old; you may take it from either sheep or goats. You must keep it till the fourteenth day of the month when the whole assembly of the community of Israel shall slaughter it between the two evenings. Some of the blood must then be taken and put on the two doorposts and the lintel of the houses where it is eaten. That night, the flesh is to be eaten, roasted over the fire; it must be eaten with unleavened bread and bitter herbs. You shall eat it like this: with a girdle round your waist, sandals on your feet, a staff in your hand. You shall eat it hastily; it is a passover in honour of the

Lord. That night, I will go through the land of Egypt and strike down all the first-born in the land of Egypt, man and beast alike, and I shall deal out punishment to all the gods of Egypt, I am the Lord. The blood shall serve to mark the houses that you live in. When I see the blood I will pass over you and you shall escape the destroying plague when I strike the land of Egypt. This day is to be a day of remembrance for you, and you must celebrate it as a feast in the Lord's honour. For all generations you are to declare it a day of festival, for ever.'"

The word of the Lord.

Responsorial Psalm   Ps 115:12-13,15-18. R. Cf. 1 Co 10:16

R. **The blessing-cup that we bless**
   is a communion with the blood of Christ.

How can I repay the Lord
for his goodness to me?
The cup of salvation I will raise;
I will call on the Lord's name. R.

O precious in the eyes of the Lord
is the death of his faithful.
Your servant, Lord, your servant am I;
you have loosened my bonds. R.

A thanksgiving sacrifice I make:
I will call on the Lord's name.
My vows to the Lord I will fulfil
before all his people. R.

SECOND READING
A reading from the first letter of St Paul to the Corinthians   11:23-26
Every time you eat this bread and drink this cup, you are proclaiming the death of the Lord.

This is what I received from the Lord, and in turn passed on to you: that on the same night that he was betrayed, the Lord Jesus took some bread, and thanked God for it and broke it, and he said, 'This is my body, which is for you; do this as a memorial of me.' In the same way he took the cup after supper, and said,'This cup is the new covenant in my blood. Whenever you drink it, do this as a memorial of me.' Until the Lord comes, therefore, every time you eat this bread and drink this cup, you are proclaiming his death.

The word of the Lord.

Gospel Acclamation   Jn 13:34

R. **Praise and honour to you, Lord Jesus!**
I give you a new commandment:
love one another just as I have loved you, says the Lord.
R. **Praise and honour to you, Lord Jesus!**

GOSPEL

A reading from the holy Gospel according to John   13:1-15

Now he showed how perfect his love was.

It was before the festival of the Passover, and Jesus knew that the hour had
come for him to pass from this world to the Father. He had always loved those
who were his in the world, but now he showed how perfect his love was.

They were at supper, and the devil had already put it into the mind of
Judas Iscariot son of Simon, to betray him. Jesus knew that the Father had
put everything into his hands, and that he had come from God and was
returning to God, and he got up from table, removed his outer garment
and, taking a towel, wrapped it round his waist; he then poured water into
a basin and began to wash the disciples' feet and to wipe them with the
towel he was wearing.

He came to Simon Peter, who said to him, 'Lord, are you going to wash
my feet?' Jesus answered, 'At the moment you do not know what I am
doing, but later you will understand.' 'Never!' said Peter 'You shall never
wash my feet.' Jesus replied, 'If I do not wash you, you can have nothing in
common with me.' 'Then, Lord,' said Simon Peter 'not only my feet, but
my hands and my head as well!' Jesus said, 'No one who has taken a bath
needs washing, he is clean all over. You too are clean, though not all of you
are.' He knew who was going to betray him, that was why he said, 'though
not all of you are.'

When he had washed their feet and put on his clothes again he went
back to the table. 'Do you understand' he said 'what I have done to you?
You call me Master and Lord, and rightly; so I am. If I, then, the Lord and
Master, have washed your feet, you should wash each other's feet. I have
given you an example so that you may copy what I have done to you.'

The Gospel of the Lord.

After the proclamation of the Gospel, the Priest gives a homily in which light is
shed on the principal mysteries that are commemorated in this Mass, namely, the
institution of the Holy Eucharist and of the priestly Order, and the commandment
of the Lord concerning fraternal charity.

The Washing of Feet

After the Homily, where a pastoral reason suggests it, the Washing of Feet follows. The men who have been chosen are led by the ministers to seats prepared in a suitable place. Then the Priest (removing his chasuble if necessary) goes to each one, and, with the help of the ministers, pours water over each one's feet and then dries them.

Meanwhile some of the following antiphons or other appropriate chants are sung.

Antiphon 1 Cf. Jn 13:4,5,15	**Antiphona 1**
After the Lord had risen from supper, he poured water into a basin and began to wash the feet of his disciples: he left them this example.	Postquam surrexit Dominus a cena, misit aquam in pelvim, et cœpit lavare pedes discipulorum: hoc exemplum reliquit eis.
Antiphon 2 Cf. Jn 13:12,13,15	**Antiphona 2**
The Lord Jesus, after eating supper with his disciples, washed their feet and said to them: Do you know what I, your Lord and Master, have done for you? I have given you an example, that you should do likewise.	Dominus Iesus, postquam cenavit cum discipulis suis, lavit pedes eorum, et ait illis: 'Scitis quid fecerim vobis ego, Dominus et Magister? Exemplum dedi vobis, ut et vos ita faciatis.'
Antiphon 3 Jn 13:6,7,8	**Antiphona 3**
Lord, are you to wash my feet? Jesus said to him in answer: If I do not wash your feet, you will have no share with me.	Domine, tu mihi lavas pedes? Respondit Iesus et dixit ei: Se non lavero tibi pedes, non habebis partem mecum.
V. So he came to Simon Peter and Peter said to him: – Lord, are you to wash my feet?. . .	V. Venit ergo ad Simonem Petrum, et dixit ei Petrus: – Domine, tu mihi lavas pedes?. . .
V. What I am doing, you do not know for now, but later you will come to know. – Lord, are you to wash my feet?. . .	V. Quod ego facio, tu nescis modo: scies autem postea. – Domine, tu mihi lavas pedes?. . .
Antiphon 4 Cf. Jn 13:14	**Antiphona 4**
If I, your Lord and Master, have washed your feet, how much more should you wash each other's feet?	Si ego, Dominus et Magister vester, lavi vobis pedes: quanto magis debetis alter alterius lavare pedes?

Antiphon 5 Jn 13:35	Antiphona 5
This is how all will know that you are my disciples: if you have love for one another.	In hoc cognoscent omnes, quia discipuli mei estis, si dilectionem habueritis ad invicem.
V. Jesus said to his disciples: – This is how all will know. . .	V. Dixit Iesus discipulis suis. – In hoc cognoscent omnes. . .
Antiphon 6 Jn 13:34	Antiphona 6
I give you a new commandment, that you love one another as I have loved you, says the Lord.	Mandatum novum do vobis, ut diligatis invicem, sicut dilexi vos, dicit Dominus.
Antiphon 7 1 Co 13:13	Antiphona 7
Let faith, hope and charity, these three, remain among you, but the greatest of these is charity.	Maneant in vobis fides, spes, caritas, tria hæc: maior autem horum est caritas.
V. Now faith, hope and charity, these three, remain; but the greatest of these is charity. – Let faith, hope and charity. . .	V. Nunc autem manent fides, spes, caritas, tria hæc: maior horum est caritas. – Maneant in vobis fides. . .

After the Washing of Feet, the Priest washes and dries his hands, puts the chasuble back on, and returns to the chair, and from there he directs the Universal Prayer.

The Creed is not said.

The Liturgy of the Eucharist

At the beginning of the Liturgy of the Eucharist, there may be a procession of the faithful in which gifts for the poor may be presented with the bread and wine.

Meanwhile the following, or another appropriate chant, is sung.

Ant. Where true charity is dwelling, God is present there.	Ant. Ubi caritas est vera, Deus ibi est.
V. By the love of Christ we have been brought together:	V. Congregavit nos in unum Christi amor.
V. let us find in him our gladness and our pleasure;	V. Exsultemus et in ipso iucundemur.
V. may we love him and revere him, God the living,	V. Timeamus et amemus Deum vivum.
V. and in love respect each other with sincere hearts.	V. Et ex corde diligamus nos sincero

Ant. Where true charity is dwelling,
    God is present there.

V. So when we as one are gathered
    all together,

V. let us strive to keep our minds
    free of division;

V. may there be an end to malice,
    strife and quarrels,

V. and let Christ our God
    be dwelling here among us.

Ant. Where true charity is dwelling,
    God is present there.

V. May your face thus be our vision,
    bright in glory,

V. Christ our God, with all
    the blessed Saints in heaven:

V. such delight is pure and faultless,
    joy unbounded,

V. which endures through
    countless ages
    world without end. Amen.

Ant. Ubi caritas est vera,
    Deus ibi est.

V. Simul ergo cum in
    unum congregamur:

V. Ne nos mente dividamur,
    caveamus.

V. Cessent iurgia maligna,
    cessent lites.

V. Et in medio nostri sit
    Christus Deus.

Ant. Ubi caritas est vera,
    Deus ibi est.

V. Simul quoque cum beatis
    videamus

V. Glorianter vultum tuum,
    Christe Deus:

V. Gaudium, quod est immensum
    atque probum,

V. Sæcula per infinita sæculorum.
    Amen.

Prayer over the Offerings

Grant us, O Lord, we pray,
that we may participate worthily
    in these mysteries,
for whenever the memorial
    of this sacrifice is celebrated
the work of our redemption
    is accomplished.
Through Christ our Lord.

Super oblata

Concede nobis,
    quæsumus, Domine,
hæc digne frequentare mysteria,
quia, quoties huius hostiæ
    commemoratio celebratur,
opus nostræ redemptionis exercetur.
Per Christum Dominum nostrum.

Preface I of the Most Holy Eucharist, pp.574-575.
If the Roman Canon is said, the following special forms are used.

Celebrating the most sacred day
on which our Lord Jesus Christ
was handed over for our sake,
and in communion with those
    whose memory we venerate,
especially the glorious
    ever-Virgin Mary,

Communicantes, et diem
    sacratissimum celebrantes,
quo Dominus noster Iesus Christus
pro nobis est traditus,
sed et memoriam venerantes,
in primis gloriosæ semper
    Virginis Mariæ,

Mother of our God and Lord,
    Jesus Christ,
and blessed Joseph, her Spouse,
your blessed Apostles and Martyrs,
Peter and Paul, Andrew,
(James, John,
Thomas, James, Philip,
Bartholomew, Matthew,
Simon and Jude;
Linus, Cletus, Clement, Sixtus,
Cornelius, Cyprian,
Lawrence, Chrysogonus,
John and Paul,
Cosmas and Damian)
and all your Saints;
we ask that through their merits
    and prayers,
in all things we may be defended
by your protecting help.
(Through Christ our Lord. Amen.)

Therefore, Lord, we pray:
graciously accept this oblation of
    our service,
that of your whole family,
which we make to you
as we observe the day
on which our Lord Jesus Christ
handed on the mysteries
    of his Body and Blood
for his disciples to celebrate;
order our days in your peace,
and command that we be delivered
    from eternal damnation
and counted among the flock of
    those you have chosen.
(Through Christ our Lord. Amen.)

Genetricis eiusdem Dei et Domini
    nostri Iesu Christi:
sed et beati Ioseph,
    eiusdem Virginis Sponsi,
et beatorum Apostolorum ac
    Martyrum tuorum,
Petri et Pauli, Andreæ,
(Iacobi, Ioannis,
Thomæ, Iacobi, Philippi,
Bartholomæi, Matthæi,
Simonis et Thaddæi:
Lini, Cleti, Clementis, Xysti,
Cornelii, Cypriani,
Laurentii, Chrysogoni,
Ioannis et Pauli,
Cosmæ et Damiani)
et omnium Sanctorum tuorum;
quorum meritis precibusque
    concedas,
ut in omnibus protectionis tuæ
    muniamur auxilio.
(Per Christum Dominum nostrum.
    Amen.)

Hanc igitur oblationem
    servitutis nostræ,
sed et cunctæ familiæ tuæ,
quam tibi offerimus ob diem,
in qua Dominus noster Iesus Christus
tradidit discipulis suis
Corporis et Sanguinis
    sui mysteria celebranda,
quæsumus, Domine,
    ut placatus accipias:
diesque nostros in tua pace disponas,
atque ab æterna damnatione
    nos eripi
et in electorum tuorum iubeas
    grege numerari.
(Per Christum Dominum nostrum.
    Amen.)

Be pleased, O God, we pray,
to bless, acknowledge,
and approve this offering
    in every respect;
make it spiritual and acceptable,
so that it may become for us
the Body and Blood of your most
    beloved Son,
our Lord Jesus Christ.

On the day before he was to suffer
for our salvation and the salvation
    of all,
that is today,
he took bread in his holy
    and venerable hands,
and with eyes raised to heaven
to you, O God, his almighty Father,
giving you thanks,
    he said the blessing,
broke the bread
and gave it to his disciples, saying:

TAKE THIS, ALL OF YOU,
    AND EAT OF IT,
FOR THIS IS MY BODY,
WHICH WILL BE GIVEN UP FOR YOU.

Quam oblationem tu, Deus,
    in omnibus, quæsumus,
benedictam, adscriptam, ratam,
rationabilem, acceptabilemque
    facere digneris:
ut nobis Corpus et Sanguis fiat
    dilectissimi Filii tui,
Domini nostri Iesu Christi.

Qui, pridie quam pro nostra
omniumque salute pateretur,
hoc est hodie,
accepit panem in sanctus ac
    venerabiles manus suas,
et elevatis oculis in cælum
ad te Deum Patrem suum
    omnipotentem,
tibi gratias agens benedixit,
fregit, deditque discipulis suis, dicens:

ACCIPITE ET MANDUCATE
    EX HOC OMNES:
HOC EST ENIM CORPUS MEUM,
QUOD PRO VOBIS TRADETUR.

Then follows the remainder of the Roman Canon as usual (see p.596) and the Communion Rite, p.630.

At an appropriate moment during Communion, the Priest entrusts the Eucharist from the table of the altar to Deacons or acolytes or other extraordinary ministers, so that afterwards it may be brought to the sick who are to receive Holy Communion at home.

Communion Antiphon 1 Co 11:24-25
This is the Body that will be given
    up for you;
this is the Chalice of the new
    covenant in my Blood,
    says the Lord;
do this, whenever you receive it,
    in memory of me.

Ant. ad communionem
Hoc Corpus, quod pro
    vobis tradetur:
hic calix novi testamenti
    est in meo Sanguine,
dicit Dominus;
hoc facite, quotiescumque sumitis,
in meam commemorationem.

After the distribution of Communion, the ciborium with hosts for Communion on the following day is left on the altar. The Priest, standing at the chair, says the Prayer after Communion.

Prayer after Communion	Post communionem
Grant, almighty God,	Concede nobis, omnipotens Deus,
that, just as we are renewed	ut, sicut Cena Filii tui
by the Supper of your Son	reficimur temporali,
in this present age,	ita satiari mereamur æterna.
so we may enjoy his banquet	Per Christum Dominum nostrum.
for all eternity.	
Who lives and reigns	
for ever and ever.	

The Transfer of the Most Blessed Sacrament

After the Prayer after Communion, the Priest puts incense in the thurible while standing, blesses it and then, kneeling, incenses the Blessed Sacrament three times. Then, having put on a white humeral veil, he rises, takes the ciborium, and covers it with the ends of the veil.

A procession is formed in which the Blessed Sacrament, accompanied by torches and incense, is carried through the church to a place of repose prepared in a part of the church or in a chapel suitably decorated. A lay minister with a cross, standing between two other ministers with lighted candles leads off. Others carrying lighted candles follow. Before the Priest carrying the Blessed Sacrament comes the thurifer with a smoking thurible. Meanwhile, the hymn Pange, lingua (exclusive of the last two stanzas) or another eucharistic chant is sung.

When the procession reaches the place of repose, the Priest, with the help of the Deacon if necessary, places the ciborium in the tabernacle, the door of which remains open. Then he puts incense in the thurible and, kneeling, incenses the Blessed Sacrament, while Tantum ergo Sacramentum or another eucharistic chant is sung. Then the Deacon or the Priest himself places the Sacrament in the tabernacle and closes the door.

After a period of adoration in silence, the Priest and ministers genuflect and return to the sacristy.

At an appropriate time, the altar is stripped and, if possible, the crosses are removed from the church. It is expedient that any crosses which remain in the church be veiled.

Vespers (Evening Prayer) is not celebrated by those who have attended the Mass of the Lord's Supper.

The faithful are invited to continue adoration before the Blessed Sacrament for a suitable length of time during the night, according to local circumstances, but after midnight the adoration should take place without solemnity.

If the celebration of the Passion of the Lord on the following Friday does not take place in the same church, the Mass is concluded in the usual way and the Blessed Sacrament is placed in the tabernacle.

FRIDAY OF THE PASSION OF THE LORD
(GOOD FRIDAY)

(YEAR A,B,C)

The liturgy applies to Jesus's descent into the night of death the words of Psalm 23[24]: "Lift up your heads, O gates; be lifted up, O ancient doors!" The gates of death are closed, no one can return from there. There is no key for those iron doors. But Christ has the key. His Cross opens wide the gates of death, the stern doors. They are barred no longer. His Cross, his radical love, is the key that opens them. The love of the One who, though God, became man in order to die – this love has the power to open those doors. This love is stronger than death.

(Pope Benedict XVI)

On this and the following day, by a most ancient tradition, the Church does not celebrate the Sacraments at all, except for Penance and the Anointing of the Sick.

On this day, Holy Communion is distributed to the faithful only within the celebration of the Lord's Passion; but it may be brought at any hour of the day to the sick who cannot participate in this celebration.

The altar should be completely bare: without a cross, without candles and without cloths.

The Celebration of the Passion of the Lord

On the afternoon of this day, about three o'clock (unless a later hour is chosen for a pastoral reason), there takes place the celebration of the Lord's Passion consisting of three parts, namely, the Liturgy of the Word, the Adoration of the Cross, and Holy Communion.

The Priest and the Deacon, if a Deacon is present, wearing red vestments as for Mass, go to the altar in silence and, after making a reverence to the altar, prostrate themselves or, if appropriate, kneel and pray in silence for a while. All others kneel.

Then the Priest, with the ministers, goes to the chair where, facing the people, who are standing, he says, with hands extended, one of the following prayers, omitting the invitation Let us pray.

Prayer

Remember your mercies, O Lord,
and with your eternal protection
    sanctify your servants,
for whom Christ your Son,
by the shedding of his Blood,
established the Paschal Mystery.
Who lives and reigns
    for ever and ever.
R. Amen.

Or:

O God, who by the Passion
    of Christ your Son, our Lord,
abolished the death inherited
    from ancient sin
by every succeeding generation,
grant that just as,
    being conformed to him,
we have borne by the law of nature
the image of the man of earth,
so by the sanctification of grace
we may bear the image of the Man
    of heaven.
Through Christ our Lord.
R. Amen.

Oratio

Reminiscere miserationum
    tuarum, Domine,
et famulos tuos æterna
    protectione sanctifica,
pro quibus Christus, Filius tuus,
per suum cruorem instituit
    paschale mysterium.
Qui vivit et regnat
    in sæcula sæculorum.
R. Amen.

Vel:

Deus, qui peccati veteris
    hereditariam mortem,
in qua posteritatis genus
    omne successerat,
Christi Filii tui, Domini nostri,
    passione solvisti,
da, ut conformes eidem facti,
sicut imaginem terreni hominis
naturæ necessitate portavimus,
ita imaginem cælestis
gratiæ sanctificatione portemus.
Per Christum Dominum nostrum.
R. Amen.

FIRST PART:

The Liturgy of the Word

FIRST READING

A reading from the prophet Isaiah   52:13-53:12
He was pierced through our faults.

See, my servant will prosper,
he shall be lifted up, exalted, rise to great heights.
As the crowds were appalled on seeing him
 – so disfigured did he look

that he seemed no longer human –
so will the crowds be astonished at him,
and kings stand speechless before him;
for they shall see something never told
and witness something never heard before:
'Who could believe what we have heard,
and to whom has the power of the Lord been revealed?'

Like a sapling he grew up in front of us,
like a root in arid ground.
Without beauty, without majesty (we saw him),
no looks to attract our eyes;
a thing despised and rejected by men,
a man of sorrows and familiar with suffering,
a man to make people screen their faces;
he was despised and we took no account of him.

And yet ours were the sufferings he bore,
ours the sorrows he carried.
But we, we thought of him as someone punished,
struck by God, and brought low.
Yet he was pierced through for our faults,
crushed for our sins.
On him lies a punishment that brings us peace,
and through his wounds we are healed.

We had all gone astray like sheep,
each taking his own way,
and the Lord burdened him
with the sins of all of us.
Harshly dealt with, he bore it humbly,
he never opened his mouth,
like a lamb that is led to the slaughter-house,
like a sheep that is dumb before its shearers
never opening its mouth.

By force and by law he was taken;
would anyone plead his cause?
Yes, he was torn away from the land of the living;
for our faults struck down in death.
They gave him a grave with the wicked,
a tomb with the rich,
though he had done no wrong
and there had been no perjury in his mouth.

The Lord has been pleased to crush him with suffering.
If he offers his life in atonement,
he shall see his heirs, he shall have a long life
and through him what the Lord wishes will be done.
His soul's anguish over
he shall see the light and be content.
By his sufferings shall my servant justify many,
taking their faults on himself.

Hence I will grant whole hordes for his tribute,
he shall divide the spoil with the mighty,
for surrendering himself to death
and letting himself be taken for a sinner,
while he was bearing the faults of many
and praying all the time for sinners.

The word of the Lord.

Responsorial Psalm   Ps 30:2,6,12-13,15-17,25. R. Lk 23:46

R. **Father, into your hands I commend my spirit.**

In you, O Lord, I take refuge.
Let me never be put to shame.
In your justice, set me free.
Into your hands I commend my spirit.
It is you who will redeem me, Lord. R.

In the face of all my foes
I am a reproach,
an object of scorn to my neighbours
and of fear to my friends. R.

Those who see me in the street
run far away from me.
I am like a dead man, forgotten in men's hearts,
like a thing thrown away. R.

But as for me, I trust in you, Lord,
I say: 'You are my God.'
My life is in your hands, deliver me
from the hands of those who hate me. R.

Let your face shine on your servant.
Save me in your love.
Be strong, let your heart take courage,
all who hope in the Lord. R.

SECOND READING

A reading from the letter to the Hebrews   4:14-16; 5:7-9

He learnt to obey through suffering and became for all who obey him the source of eternal salvation.

Since in Jesus, the Son of God, we have the supreme high priest who has gone through to the highest heaven, we must never let go of the faith that we have professed. For it is not as if we had a high priest who was incapable of feeling our weaknesses with us; but we have one who has been tempted in every way that we are, though he is without sin. Let us be confident, then, in approaching the throne of grace, that we shall have mercy from him and find grace when we are in need of help.

During his life on earth, he offered up prayer and entreaty, aloud and in silent tears, to the one who had the power to save him out of death, and he submitted so humbly that his prayer was heard. Although he was Son, he learnt to obey through suffering; but having been made perfect, he became for all who obey him the source of eternal salvation.

The word of the Lord.

Gospel Acclamation   Ph 2:8-9

R. **Glory and praise to you, O Christ!**
Christ was humbler yet,
even accepting death, death on a cross.
But God raised him high
and gave him the name which is above all names.
R. **Glory and praise to you, O Christ!**

GOSPEL

The symbols in the following passion narrative represent:

N Narrator   J Jesus   O Other single speaker
C Crowd, or more than one speaker

The passion of our Lord Jesus Christ according to John   18:1-19:42

N   Jesus left with his disciples and crossed the Kedron valley. There was a garden there, and he went into it with his disciples. Judas the traitor knew the place well, since Jesus had often met his disciples there, and he brought the cohort to this place together with a detachment of guards sent by the chief priests and the Pharisees, all with lanterns and torches and weapons. Knowing everything that was going to happen to him, Jesus then came forward and said,

J Who are you looking for?

N They answered,

C Jesus the Nazarene.

N He said,

J I am he.

N Now Judas the traitor was standing among them. When Jesus said, 'I am he', they moved back and fell to the ground. He asked them a second time,

J Who are you looking for?

N They said,

C Jesus the Nazarene.

N Jesus replied,

J I have told you that I am he. If I am the one you are looking for, let these others go.

N This was to fulfil the words he has spoken: 'Not one of those you gave me have I lost.'

    Simon Peter, who carried a sword, drew it and wounded the high priest's servant, cutting off his right ear. The servant's name was Malchus. Jesus said to Peter,

J Put your sword back in its scabbard; am I not to drink the cup that the Father has given me?

N The cohort and its captain and the Jewish guards seized Jesus and bound him. They took him first to Annas, because Annas was the father-in-law of Caiaphas, who was high priest that year. It was Caiaphas who had suggested to the Jews, 'It is better for one man to die for the people.'

    Simon Peter, with another disciple, followed Jesus. This disciple, who was known to the high priest, went with Jesus into the high priest's palace, but Peter stayed outside the door. So the other disciple, the one known to the high priest, went out, spoke to the woman who was keeping the door and brought Peter in. The maid on duty at the door said to Peter,

O Aren't you another of that man's disciples?

N He answered,

O I am not.

N Now it was cold, and the servants and guards had lit a charcoal fire and were standing there warming themselves; so Peter stood there too, warming himself with the others.

    The high priest questioned Jesus about his disciples and his teaching. Jesus answered,

J   I have spoken openly for all the world to hear; I have always taught in the synagogue and in the Temple where all the Jews meet together: I have said nothing in secret. But why ask me? Ask my hearers what I taught: they know what I said.

N   At these words, one of the guards standing by gave Jesus a slap in the face, saying,

O   Is that the way to answer the high priest?

N   Jesus replied,

J   If there is something wrong in what I said, point it out; but if there is no offence in it, why do you strike me?

N   Then Annas sent him, still bound, to Caiaphas, the high priest. As Simon Peter stood there warming himself, someone said to him,

O   Aren't you another of his disciples?

N   He denied it saying,

O   I am not.

N   One of the high priest's servants, a relation of the man whose ear Peter had cut off, said,

O   Didn't I see you in the garden with him?

N   Again Peter denied it, and at once a cock crew.

      They then led Jesus from the house of Caiaphas to the Praetorium. It was now morning. They did not go into the Praetorium themselves or they would be defiled and unable to eat the passover. So Pilate came outside to them and said,

O   What charge do you bring against this man?

N   They replied,

C   If he were not a criminal, we should not be handing him over to you.

N   Pilate said,

O   Take him yourselves, and try him by your own Law.

N   The Jews answered,

C   We are not allowed to put a man to death.

N   This was to fulfil the words Jesus had spoken indicating the way he was going to die.

      So Pilate went back into the Praetorium and called Jesus to him, and asked,

O   Are you the king of Jews?

N   Jesus replied,

J   Do you ask this of your own accord, or have others spoken to you about me?

N   Pilate answered,

O   Am I a Jew? It is your own people and the chief priests who have handed you over to me: what have you done?

N   Jesus replied,

J   Mine is not a kingdom of this world; if my kingdom were of this world, my men would have fought to prevent me being surrendered to the Jews. But my kingdom is not of this kind.

N   Pilate said,

O   So you are the king then?

N   Jesus answered,

J   It is you who say it. Yes, I am a king. I was born for this; I came into the world for this; to bear witness to the truth, and all who are on the side of truth listen to my voice.

N   Pilate said,

O   Truth? What is that?

N   And with that he went out again to the Jews and said,

O   I find no case against him. But according to a custom of yours I should release one prisoner at the Passover; would you like me, then, to release the king of Jews?

N   At this they shouted:

C   Not this man, but Barabbas.

N   Barabbas was a brigand.

      Pilate then had Jesus taken away and scourged; and after this, the soldiers twisted some thorns into a crown and put it on his head, and dressed him in a purple robe. They kept coming up to him and saying,

C   Hail, king of the Jews!

N   and they slapped him in the face.

      Pilate came outside again and said to them,

O   Look, I am going to bring him out to you to let you see that I find no case.

N   Jesus then came out wearing the crown of thorns and the purple robe. Pilate said,

O   Here is the man.

N   When they saw him the chief priests and the guards shouted,

C   Crucify him! Crucify him!

N   Pilate said,

O   Take him yourselves and crucify him: I can find no case against him

N   The Jews replied,

C   We have a Law, and according to the Law he ought to die, because he has claimed to be the son of God.

N   When Pilate heard them say this his fears increased. Re-entering the

Praetorium, he said to Jesus,

O   Where do you come from?

N   But Jesus made no answer. Pilate then said to him,

O   Are you refusing to speak to me? Surely you know I have power to release you and I have power to crucify you?

N   Jesus replied,

J   You would have no power over me if it had not been given you from above; that is why the one who handed me over to you has the greater guilt.

N   From that moment Pilate was anxious to set him free, but the Jews shouted,

C   If you set him free you are no friend of Caesar's; anyone who makes himself king is defying Caesar.

N   Hearing these words, Pilate had Jesus brought out, and seated himself on the chair of judgement at a place called the Pavement, in Hebrew Gabbatha. It was Passover Preparation Day, about the sixth hour. Pilate said to the Jews,

O   Here is your king.

N   They said,

C   Take him away, take him away. Crucify him!

N   Pilate said,

O   Do you want me to crucify your king?

N   The chief priests answered,

C   We have no king except Caesar.

N   So in the end Pilate handed him over to them to be crucified.

They then took charge of Jesus, and carrying his own cross he went out of the city to the place of the skull, or, as it was called in Hebrew, Golgotha, where they crucified him with two others, one on either side with Jesus in the middle. Pilate wrote out a notice and had it fixed to the cross; it ran: 'Jesus the Nazarene, King of the Jews.' This notice was read by many of the Jews, because the place where Jesus was crucified was not far from the city, and the writing was in Hebrew, Latin and Greek. So the Jewish chief priests said to Pilate,

C   You should not write 'King of the Jews', but 'This man said: I am King of the Jews'.

N   Pilate answered,

O   What I have written, I have written.

N   When the soldiers had finished crucifying Jesus they took his clothing and divided it into four shares, one for each soldier. His undergarment was seamless, woven in one piece from neck to hem; so they said to one another,

C   Instead of tearing it, let's throw dice to decide who is to have it.

N   In this way the words of scripture were fulfilled:

> They shared out my clothing among them.
> They cast lots for my clothes.

This is exactly what the soldiers did.

Near the cross of Jesus stood his mother and his mother's sister, Mary the wife of Clopas, and Mary of Magdala. Seeing his mother and the disciple he loved standing near her, Jesus said to his mother,

J   Woman, this is your son.

N   Then to the disciple he said,

J   This is your mother.

N   And from that moment the disciple made a place for her in his home.

After this, Jesus knew that everything had now been completed, and to fulfil the scripture perfectly he said:

J   I am thirsty.

N   A jar full of vinegar stood there, so putting a sponge soaked in vinegar on a hyssop stick they held it up to his mouth. After Jesus had taken the vinegar he said,

J   It is accomplished;

N   and bowing his head he gave up the spirit.

All kneel and pause a moment.

N   It was Preparation Day, and to prevent the bodies remaining on the cross during the sabbath – since that sabbath was a day of special solemnity – the Jews asked Pilate to have the legs broken and the bodies taken away. Consequently the soldiers came and broke the legs of the first man who had been crucified with him and then of the other. When they came to Jesus, they found that he was already dead, and so instead of breaking his legs one of the soldiers pierced his side with a lance; and immediately there came out blood and water. This is the evidence of one who saw it – trustworthy evidence, and he knows he speaks the truth – and he gives it so that you may believe as well. Because all this happened to fulfil the words of scripture:

> Not one bone of his will be broken,

and again, in another place scripture says:

> They will look on the one whom they have pierced.

After this, Joseph of Arimathaea, who was a disciple of Jesus – though a secret one because he was afraid of the Jews – asked Pilate to let him remove the body of Jesus. Pilate gave permission, so they came and took it away. Nicodemus came as well – the same one who had first come to Jesus at night – time – and he brought a mixture of myrrh and aloes, weighing about a hundred pounds. They took the body of Jesus and wrapped it with the spices in linen cloths, following the Jewish burial custom. At the place where he had been crucified there was a garden, and in the garden a new tomb in which no one had yet been buried. Since it was the Jewish Day of Preparation and the tomb was near at hand, they laid Jesus there.

The Gospel of the Lord.

After the reading of the Lord's Passion, the Priest gives a brief homily and, at its end, the faithful may be invited to spend a short time in prayer.

The Solemn Intercessions

The Liturgy of the Word concludes with the Solemn Intercessions, which take place in this way: the Deacon, if a Deacon is present, or if he is not, a lay minister, stands at the ambo, and sings or says the invitation in which the intention is expressed. Then all pray in silence for a while, and afterwards the Priest, standing at the chair or, if appropriate, at the altar, with hands extended, sings or says the prayer.

The faithful may remain either kneeling or standing throughout the entire period of the prayers.

Before the Priest's prayer, in accord with tradition, it is permissible to use the Deacon's invitations Let us kneel – Let us stand, (Flectamus genua – Levate), with all kneeling for silent prayer.

The Conferences of Bishops may provide other invitations to introduce the prayer of the Priest.

In a situation of grave public need, the Diocesan Bishop may permit or order the addition of a special intention.

The prayer is sung in the simple tone or, if the invitations Let us kneel – Let us stand (Flectamus genua – Levate) are used, in the solemn tone.

I. For Holy Church	I. Pro sancta Ecclesia

Let us pray, dearly beloved,
    for the holy Church of God,
that our God and Lord be pleased
    to give her peace,
to guard her and to unite her
    throughout the whole world
and grant that, leading our life
    in tranquillity and quiet,
we may glorify God
    the Father almighty.
	Oremus, dilectissimi nobis,
	    pro Ecclesia sancta Dei,
	ut eam Deus et Dominus noster
	pacificare, adunare
	    et custodire dignetur
	toto orbe terrarum,
	detque nobis, quietam et tranquillam
	    vitam degentibus,
	glorificare Deum
	    Patrem omnipotentem.

Prayer in silence. Then the Priest says:

Almighty ever-living God,
who in Christ revealed your glory
   to all the nations,
watch over the works of your mercy,
that your Church, spread
   throughout all the world,
may persevere with steadfast faith
   in confessing your name.
Through Christ our Lord.
R. Amen.

Omnipotens sempiterne Deus,
qui gloriam tuam omnibus
   in Christo gentibus revelasti:
custodi opera misericordiæ tuæ,
ut Ecclesia tua, toto orbe diffusa,
stabili fide in confessione
   tui nominis perseveret.
Per Christum Dominum nostrum.
R. Amen.

II. For the Pope

Let us pray also for our most
   Holy Father Pope N.,
that our God and Lord,
who chose him for the
   Order of Bishops,
may keep him safe and unharmed
   for the Lord's holy Church,
to govern the holy People of God.

II. Pro Papa

Oremus et pro beatissimo
   Papa nostro N.,
ut Deus et Dominus noster,
qui elegit eum
   in ordine episcopatus,
salvum atque incolumem custodiat
   Ecclesiæ suæ sanctæ,
ad regendum populum
   sanctum Dei.

Prayer in silence. Then the Priest says:

Almighty ever-living God,
by whose decree all things
   are founded,
look with favour on our prayers
and in your kindness protect
   the Pope chosen for us,
that, under him,
   the Christian people,
governed by you their maker,
may grow in merit by reason
   of their faith.
Through Christ our Lord.
R. Amen.

Omnipotens sempiterne Deus,
cuius iudicio universa fundantur,
respice propitius ad preces nostras,
et electum nobis Antistitem
   tua pietate conserva,
ut christiana plebs,
   quæ te gubernatur auctore,
sub ipso Pontifice,
   fidei suæ meritis augeatur.
Per Christum Dominum nostrum.
R. Amen.

III. For all orders and degrees of the faithful

Let us pray also for our Bishop N.,
for all Bishops, Priests,
   and Deacons of the Church
and for the whole
   of the faithful people.

Prayer in silence. Then the Priest says:

Almighty ever-living God,
by whose Spirit the whole body
   of the Church
is sanctified and governed,
hear our humble prayer
   for your ministers,
that, by the gift of your grace,
all may serve you faithfully.
Through Christ our Lord.
R. Amen.

III. Pro omnibus ordinibus gradibusque fidelium

Oremus et pro Episcopo nostro N.,
pro omnibus Episcopis, presbyteris,
   diaconis Ecclesiæ,
et universa plebe fidelium.

Omnipotens sempiterne Deus,
cuius Spiritu totum corpus Ecclesiæ
sanctificatur et regitur,
exaudi nos pro ministris
   tuis supplicantes,
ut, gratiæ tuæ munere, ab omnibus
   tibi fideliter serviatur.
Per Christum Dominum nostrum.
R. Amen.

IV. For catechumens

Let us pray also
   for (our) catechumens,
that our God and Lord
may open wide the ears
   of their inmost hearts
and unlock the gates of his mercy,
that, having received forgiveness
   of all their sins
through the waters of rebirth,
they, too, may be one with Christ
   Jesus our Lord.

Prayer in silence. Then the Priest says:

Almighty ever-living God,
who make your Church ever
   fruitful with new offspring,
increase the faith and understanding
   of (our) catechumens,
that, reborn in the font of Baptism,

IV. Pro catechumenis

Oremus et pro
   catechumenis (nostris),
ut Deus et Dominus noster
adaperiat aures
   præcordiorum ipsorum
ianuamque misericordiæ,
ut, per lavacrum regenerationis
accepta remissione
   omnium peccatorum,
et ipsi inveniantur in Christo Iesu
   Domino nostro.

Omnipotens sempiterne Deus,
qui Ecclesiam tuam nova semper
   prole fecundas,
auge fidem et intellectum
   catechumenis (nostris),
ut, renati fonte baptismatis,

they may be added to the number
of your adopted children.
Through Christ our Lord.
R. Amen.

adoptionis tuæ filiis aggregentur.
Per Christum Dominum nostrum.
R. Amen.

V. For the unity of Christians

Let us pray also for all our brothers
and sisters who believe in Christ,
that our God and Lord may
be pleased,
as they live the truth,
to gather them together and keep
them in his one Church.

Prayer in silence. Then the Priest says:

Almighty ever-living God,
who gather what is scattered
and keep together what you
have gathered,
look kindly on the flock of your Son,
that those whom one Baptism
has consecrated
may be joined together by integrity
of faith
and united in the bond of charity.
Through Christ our Lord.
R. Amen.

V. Pro unitate Christianorum

Oremus et pro universis fratribus
in Christum credentibus,
ut Deus et Dominus noster eos,
veritatem facientes,
in una Ecclesia sua congregare
et custodire dignetur.

Omnipotens sempiterne Deus,
qui dispersa congregas
et congregata conservas,
ad gregem Filii tui placatus intende,
ut, quos unum baptisma sacravit,
eos et fidei iungat integritas
et vinculum societ caritatis.
Per Christum Dominum nostrum.
R. Amen.

VI. For the Jewish people

Let us pray also for the Jewish people,
to whom the Lord our God
spoke first,
that he may grant them to advance
in love of his name
and in faithfulness to his covenant.

Prayer in silence. Then the Priest says:

Almighty ever-living God,
who bestowed your promises on
Abraham and his descendants,

VI. Pro Iudæis

Oremus et pro Iudæis,
ut, ad quos prius locutus est
Dominus Deus noster,
eis tribuat in sui nominis amore
et in sui fœderis fidelitate proficere.

Omnipotens sempiterne Deus,
qui promissiones tuas Abrahæ
eiusque semini contulisti,

graciously hear the prayers
   of your Church,
that the people you first made
   your own
may attain the fullness
   of redemption.
Through Christ our Lord.
R. Amen.

Ecclesiæ tuæ preces
   clementer exaudi,
ut populus acquisitionis prioris
ad redemptionis mereatur
   plenitudinem pervenire.
Per Christum Dominum nostrum.
R. Amen.

VII. For those who do not believe in Christ

Let us pray also for those who
   do not believe in Christ,
that, enlightened by the Holy Spirit,
they, too, may enter on the way
   of salvation.

VII. Pro iis qui Christum non credunt

Oremus et pro iis qui in Christum
   non credunt,
ut, luce Sancti Spiritus illustrati,
viam salutis et ipsi valeant introire.

Prayer in silence. Then the Priest says:

Almighty ever-living God,
grant to those who do not
   confess Christ
that, by walking before you
   with a sincere heart,
they may find the truth,
and that we ourselves, being
   constant in mutual love
and striving to understand more
   fully the mystery of your life,
may be made more perfect witnesses
   to your love in the world.
Through Christ our Lord.
R. Amen.

Omnipotens sempiterne Deus,
fac ut qui Christum
   non confitentur,
coram te sincero corde ambulantes,
   inveniant veritatem,
nosque, mutuo proficientes
   semper amore
et ad tuæ vitæ mysterium plenius
   percipiendum sollicitos,
perfectiores effice tuæ testes
   caritatis in mundo.
Per Christum Dominum nostrum.
R. Amen.

VIII. For those who do not believe in God

Let us pray also for those who
   do not acknowledge God,
that, following what is right
   in sincerity of heart,
they may find the way
   to God himself.

VIII. Pro iis qui in Deum non credunt

Oremus et pro iis qui Deum
   non agnoscunt,
ut, quæ recta sunt sincero
   corde sectantes,
ad ipsum Deum
   pervenire mereantur.

Prayer in silence. Then the Priest says:

Almighty ever-living God,
who created all people
to seek you always by desiring you
and, by finding you, come to rest,
grant, we pray,
that, despite every harmful obstacle,
all may recognise the signs
    of your fatherly love
and the witness of the good works
done by those who believe in you,
and so in gladness confess you,
the one true God and Father
    of our human race.
Through Christ our Lord.
R. Amen.

Omnipotens sempiterne Deus,
qui cunctos homines condidisti,
ut te semper desiderando quærerent
et inveniendo quiescerent,
præsta, quæsumus,
ut inter noxia quæque obstacula
omnes, tuæ signa pietatis
et in te credentium testimonium
bonorum operum percipientes,
te solum verum Deum nostrique
    generis Patrem
gaudeant confiteri.
Per Christum Dominum nostrum.
R. Amen.

IX. For those in public office

Let us pray also for those
    in public office,
that our God and Lord
may direct their minds and hearts
    according to his will
for the true peace and freedom of all.

Prayer in silence. Then the Priest says:

Almighty ever-living God,
in whose hand lies every
    human heart
and the rights of peoples,
look with favour, we pray,
on those who govern
    with authority over us,
that throughout the whole world,
the prosperity of peoples,
the assurance of peace,
and freedom of religion
may through your gift
    be made secure.
Through Christ our Lord.
R. Amen.

IX. Pro rempublicam moderantibus

Oremus et pro omnibus
    rempublicam moderantibus,
ut Deus et Dominus noster
mentes et corda eorum secundum
    voluntatem suam dirigat
ad veram omnium pacem
    et libertatem.

Omnipotens sempiterne Deus,
in cuius manu sunt hominum
    corda et iura populorum,
respice benignus ad eos,
    qui nos in potestate moderantur,
ut ubique terrarum populorum
    prosperitas,
pacis securitas et religionis libertas,
te largiente, consistant.
Per Christum Dominum nostrum.
R. Amen.

X. For those in tribulation

Let us pray, dearly beloved,
to God the Father almighty,
that he may cleanse the world
   of all errors,
banish disease, drive out hunger,
unlock prisons, loosen fetters,
granting to travellers safety,
   to pilgrims return,
health to the sick,
   and salvation to the dying.

X. Pro tribulatis

Oremus, dilectissimi nobis,
   Deum Patrem omnipotentem,
ut cunctis mundum
   purget erroribus,
morbos auferat, famem depellat,
aperiat carceres, vincula solvat,
viatoribus securitatem,
   peregrinantibus reditum,
infirmantibus sanitatem
atque morientibus
   salutem indulgeat.

Prayer in silence. Then the Priest says:

Almighty ever-living God,
comfort of mourners,
   strength of all who toil,
may the prayers of those who cry out
   in any tribulation
come before you,
that all may rejoice,
because in their hour of need
your mercy was at hand.
Through Christ our Lord.
R. Amen.

Omnipotens sempiterne Deus,
mæstorum consolatio,
   laborantium fortitudo,
perveniant ad te preces
de quacumque
   tribulatione clamantium,
ut omnes sibi in necessitatibus suis
misericordiam tuam
   gaudeant affuisse.
Per Christum Dominum nostrum.
R. Amen.

SECOND PART:

THE ADORATION OF THE HOLY CROSS

After the Solemn Intercessions, the solemn Adoration of the Holy Cross takes place. Of the two forms of the showing of the Cross presented here, the more appropriate one, according to pastoral needs, should be chosen.

The Showing of the Holy Cross

First Form

The Deacon accompanied by ministers, or another suitable minister, goes to the sacristy, from which, in procession, accompanied by two ministers with lighted candles, he carries the Cross, covered with a violet veil, through the church to the middle of the sanctuary.

The Priest, standing before the altar and facing the people, receives the Cross, uncovers a little of its upper part and elevates it while beginning the Ecce lignum

Crucis (Behold the wood of the Cross). He is assisted in singing by the Deacon or, if need be, by the choir. All respond, Come, let us adore. At the end of the singing, all kneel and for a brief moment adore in silence, while the Priest stands and holds the Cross raised.

Behold the wood of the Cross, on which hung the salvation of the world. R. Come, let us adore.	Ecce lignum Crucis, in quo salus mundi pependit. R. Venite, adoremus.

Then the Priest uncovers the right arm of the Cross and again, raising up the Cross, begins, Behold the wood of the Cross and everything takes place as above.

Finally, he uncovers the Cross entirely and, raising it up, he begins the invitation Behold the wood of the Cross a third time and everything takes place like the first time.

Second Form

The Priest or the Deacon accompanied by ministers, or another suitable minister, goes to the door of the church, where he receives the unveiled Cross, and the ministers take lighted candles; then the procession sets off through the church to the sanctuary. Near the door, in the middle of the church, and before the entrance of the sanctuary, the one who carries the Cross elevates it, singing, Behold the wood of the Cross, to which all respond, Come, let us adore. After each response all kneel and for a brief moment adore in silence, as above.

The Adoration of the Holy Cross

Then, accompanied by two ministers with lighted candles, the Priest or the Deacon carries the Cross to the entrance of the sanctuary or to another suitable place and there puts it down or hands it over to the ministers to hold. Candles are placed on the right and left sides of the Cross.

For the Adoration of the Cross, first the Priest Celebrant alone approaches, with the chasuble and his shoes removed, if appropriate. Then the clergy, the lay ministers, and the faithful approach, moving as if in procession, and showing reverence to the Cross by a simple genuflection or by some other sign appropriate to the usage of the region, for example, by kissing the Cross.

Only one Cross should be offered for adoration. If, because of the large number of people, it is not possible for all to approach individually, the Priest, after some of the clergy and faithful have adored, takes the Cross and, standing in the middle before the altar, invites the people in a few words to adore the Holy Cross and afterwards holds the Cross elevated higher for a brief time, for the faithful to adore it in silence.

While the adoration of the Holy Cross is taking place, the antiphon Crucem tuam adoramus (We adore your Cross, O Lord), the Reproaches, the hymn Crux fidelis (Faithful Cross) or other suitable chants are sung, during which all who have already adored the Cross remain seated.

Chants to be Sung
during the Adoration of the Holy Cross

Ant. We adore your Cross, O Lord, we praise and glorify your holy Resurrection, for behold, because of the wood of a tree joy has come to the whole world.	Ant. Crucem tuam adoramus, Domine, et sanctam resurrectionem tuam laudamus et glorificamus: ecce enim propter lignum venit gaudium in universo mundo.

Cf. Ps 66:2

May God have mercy on us and bless us; may he let his face shed its light upon us and have mercy on us.	Deus misereatur nostri, et benedicat nobis: illuminet vultum suum super nos, et misereatur nostri.

And the antiphon is repeated:

We adore. . .	Crucem tuam. . .

THE REPROACHES

Parts assigned to one of the two choirs separately are indicated by the numbers 1 (first choir) and 2 (second choir); parts sung by both choirs together are marked: 1 and 2. Some of the verses may also be sung by two cantors.

1 and 2 My people, what have I done to you? Or how have I grieved you? Answer me!	1 et 2 Popule meus, quid feci tibi? Aut in quo contristavi te? Responde mihi!
1 Because I led you out of the land of Egypt, you have prepared a Cross for your Saviour.	1 Quia eduxi te de terra Ægypti: parasti Crucem Salvatori tuo.

1 Hagios o Theos,	1 Hagios o Theos.
2 Holy is God,	2 Sanctus Deus.
1 Hagios Ischyros,	1 Hagios Ischyros.
2 Holy and Mighty,	2 Sanctus Fortis.
1 Hagios Athanatos, eleison himas.	1 Hagios Athanatos, eleison himas.
2 Holy and Immortal One, have mercy on us.	2 Sanctus Immortalis, miserere nobis.

1 and 2 Because I led you out
through the desert forty years
and fed you with manna and
brought you into a land of plenty,
you have prepared a Cross
for your Saviour.

1   Hagios o Theos,
2   Holy is God,
1   Hagios Ischyros,
2   Holy and Mighty,
1   Hagios Athanatos, eleison himas.
2   Holy and Immortal One,
have mercy on us.

1 and 2 What more should I have
done for you and have not done?
Indeed, I planted you as my most
beautiful chosen vine
and you have turned very bitter
for me,
for in my thirst you gave me
vinegar to drink
and with a lance you pierced your
Saviour's side.

1   Hagios o Theos,
2   Holy is God,
1   Hagios Ischyros,
2   Holy and Mighty,
1   Hagios Athanatos,
eleison himas.
2   Holy and Immortal One, have
mercy on us.

1 et 2 Quia eduxi te per desertum
quadraginta annis,
et manna cibavi te,
et introduxi te in terram
satis bonam:
parasti Crucem Salvatori tuo.

1   Hagios o Theos.
2   Sanctus Deus.
1   Hagios Ischyros.
2   Sanctus Fortis.
1   Hagios Athanatos, eleison himas.
2   Sanctus Immortalis,
miserere nobis.

1 et 2 Quid ultra debui facere tibi,
et non feci?
Ego quidem plantavi te
vineam electam
meam speciosissimam:
et tu facta es mihi nimis amara:
aceto namque sitim meam potasti,
et lancea perforasti latus
Salvatori tuo.

1   Hagios o Theos.
2   Sanctus Deus.
1   Hagios Ischyros.
2   Sanctus Fortis.
1   Hagios Athanatos,
eleison himas.
2   Sanctus Immortalis,
miserere nobis.

II

Cantors:
I scourged Egypt for your sake
with its firstborn sons,
and you scourged me and handed
me over.

Cantores:
Ego propter te flagellavi Ægyptum
cum primogenitis suis:
et tu me flagellatum tradidisti.

1 and 2 repeat:
My people, what have I done to you?
Or how have I grieved you?
Answer me!

Cantors:
I led you out from Egypt as Pharaoh
    lay sunk in the Red Sea,
and you handed me over
    to the chief priests.

1 and 2 repeat:
My people. . .

Cantors:
I opened up the sea before you,
and you opened my side with a lance.

1 and 2 repeat:
My people. . .

Cantors:
I went before you in a pillar of cloud,
and you led me into Pilate's palace.

1 and 2 repeat:
My people. . .

Cantors:
I fed you with manna in the desert,
and on me you rained blows
    and lashes.

1 and 2 repeat:
My people. . .

Cantors:
I gave you saving water
    from the rock to drink,
and for drink you gave me gall
    and vinegar.

1 and 2 repeat:
My people. . .

---

1 et 2 repetunt:
Popule meus, quid feci tibi?
Aut in quo contristavi te?
Responde mihi!

Cantores:
Ego eduxi te de Ægypto,
demerso Pharaone in Mare Rubrum:
et tu me tradidisti
    principibus sacerdotum.

1 et 2 repetunt:
Popule meus. . .

Cantores:
Ego ante te aperui mare:
et tu aperuisti lancea latus meum.

1 et 2 repetunt:
Popule meus. . .

Cantores:
Ego ante te præivi in columna nubis:
et tu me duxisti ad prætorium Pilati.

1 et 2 repetunt:
Popule meus. . .

Cantores:
Ego te pavi manna per desertum:
et tu me cecidisti alapis et flagellis.

1 et 2 repetunt:
Popule meus. . .

Cantores:
Ego te potavi aqua salutis de petra:
et tu me potasti felle et aceto.

1 et 2 repetunt:
Popule meus. . .

Cantors:

I struck down for you the kings
    of the Canaanites,
and you struck my head with a reed.

1 and 2 repeat:
My people. . .

Cantors:

I put in your hand a royal sceptre,
and you put on my head
    a crown of thorns.

1 and 2 repeat:
My people. . .

Cantors:

I exalted you with great power,
and you hung me on the scaffold
    of the Cross.

1 and 2 repeat:
My people. . .

Cantores:

Ego propter te Chananæorum
    reges percussi:
et tu percussisti arundine
    caput meum.

1 et 2 repetunt:
Popule meus. . .

Cantores:

Ego dedi tibi sceptrum regale:
et tu dedisti capiti meo spineam
    coronam.

1 et 2 repetunt:
Popule meus. . .

Cantores:

Ego te exaltavi magna virtute:
et tu me suspendisti
    in patibulo Crucis.

1 et 2 repetunt:
Popule meus. . .

HYMN

All:

Faithful Cross the Saints rely on,
Noble tree beyond compare!
Never was there such a scion,
Never leaf or flower so rare.
Sweet the timber, sweet the iron,
Sweet the burden that they bear!

Cantors:

Sing, my tongue, in exultation
Of our banner and device!
Make a solemn proclamation
Of a triumph and its price:
How the Saviour of creation
Conquered by his sacrifice!

Omnes:

Crux fidelis, inter omnes
    arbor una nobilis,
Nulla talem silva profert,
    flore, fronde, germine!
Dulce lignum dulci clavo
    dulce pondus sustinens!

Cantores:

Pange, lingua, gloriosi
    prœlium certaminis,
Et super crucis tropæo
    dic triumphum nobilem,
Qualiter Redemptor orbis
    immolatus vicerit.

All:
Faithful Cross the Saints rely on,
Noble tree beyond compare!
Never was there such a scion,
Never leaf or flower so rare.

Cantors:
For, when Adam first offended,
Eating that forbidden fruit,
Not all hopes of glory ended
With the serpent at the root:
Broken nature would be mended
By a second tree and shoot.

All:
Sweet the timber, sweet the iron,
Sweet the burden that they bear!

Cantors:
Thus the tempter was outwitted
By a wisdom deeper still:
Remedy and ailment fitted,
Means to cure and means to kill;
That the world might be acquitted,
Christ would do his Father's will.

All:
Faithful Cross the Saints rely on,
Noble tree beyond compare!
Never was there such a scion,
Never leaf or flower so rare.

Cantors:
So the Father, out of pity
For our self-inflicted doom,
Sent him from the heavenly city
When the holy time had come:
He, the Son and the Almighty,
Took our flesh in Mary's womb.

All:
Sweet the timber, sweet the iron,
Sweet the burden that they bear!

Omnes:
Crux fidelis, inter omnes
    arbor una nobilis,
Nulla talem silva profert,
    flore, fronde, germine!

Cantores:
De parentis protoplasti
    fraude factor condolens,
Quando pomi noxialis
    morte morsu corruit,
Ipse lignum tunc notavit,
    damna ligni ut solveret.

Omnes:
Dulce lignum dulci clavo
    dulce pondus sustinens!

Cantores:
Hoc opus nostræ salutis
    ordo depoposcerat,
Multiformis perditoris
    arte ut artem falleret,
Et medelam ferret inde,
    hostis unde læserat.

Omnes:
Crux fidelis, inter omnes
    arbor una nobilis,
Nulla talem silva profert,
    flore, fronde, germine!

Cantores:
Quando venit ergo sacri
    plenitudo temporis,
Missus est ab arce Patris
    Natus, orbis conditor,
Atque ventre virginali
    carne factus prodiit.

Omnes:
Dulce lignum dulci clavo
    dulce pondus sustinens!

Cantors:

Hear a tiny baby crying,
Founder of the seas and strands;
See his virgin Mother tying
Cloth around his feet and hands;
Find him in a manger lying
Tightly wrapped in swaddling-bands!

All:

Faithful Cross the Saints rely on,
Noble tree beyond compare!
Never was there such a scion,
Never leaf or flower so rare.

Cantors:

So he came, the long-expected,
Not in glory, not to reign;
Only born to be rejected,
Choosing hunger, toil and pain,
Till the scaffold was erected
And the Paschal Lamb was slain.

All:

Sweet the timber, sweet the iron,
Sweet the burden that they bear!

Cantors:

No disgrace was too abhorrent:
Nailed and mocked and
    parched he died;
Blood and water, double warrant,
Issue from his wounded side,
Washing in a mighty torrent
Earth and stars and oceantide.

All:

Faithful Cross the Saints rely on,
Noble tree beyond compare!
Never was there such a scion,
Never leaf or flower so rare.

Cantores:

Vagit infans inter arta
    conditus præsepia,
Membra pannis involuta
    Virgo Mater alligat,
Et manus pedesque et crura
    stricta cingit fascia.

Omnes:

Crux fidelis, inter omnes
    arbor una nobilis,
Nulla talem silva profert,
    flore, fronde, germine!

Cantores:

Lustra sex qui iam peracta,
    tempus implens corporis,
se volente, natus ad hoc,
    passioni deditus,
agnus in crucis levatur
    immolandus stipite.

Omnes:

Dulce lignum dulci clavo
    dulce pondus sustinens!

Cantores:

En acetum, fel, arundo,
    sputa, clavi, lancea;
Mite corpus perforatur,
    sanguis unde profluit;
Terra, pontus, astra, mundus
    quo lavantur flumine!

Omnes:

Crux fidelis, inter omnes
    arbor una nobilis,
Nulla talem silva profert,
    flore, fronde, germine!

Cantors:

Lofty timber,
   smooth your roughness,
Flex your boughs for blossoming;
Let your fibres lose their toughness,
Gently let your tendrils cling;
Lay aside your native gruffness,
Clasp the body of your King!

All:

Sweet the timber, sweet the iron,
Sweet the burden that they bear!

Cantors:

Noblest tree of all created,
Richly jewelled and embossed:
Post by Lamb's blood consecrated;
Spar that saves the tempest-tossed;
Scaffold-beam which, elevated,
Carries what the world has cost!

All:

Faithful Cross the Saints rely on,
Noble tree beyond compare!
Never was there such a scion,
Never leaf or flower so rare.

Cantores:

Flecte ramos, arbor alta,
   tensa laxa viscera,
Et rigor lentescat ille,
   quem dedit nativitas,
Ut superni membra Regis
   miti tendas stipite.

Omnes:

Dulce lignum dulci clavo
   dulce pondus sustinens!

Cantores:

Sola digna tu fuisti
   ferre sæcli pretium
Atque portum præparare
   nauta mundo naufrago,
Quem sacer cruor perunxit
   fusus Agni corpore.

Omnes:

Crux fidelis, inter omnes
   arbor una nobilis,
Nulla talem silva profert,
   flore, fronde, germine!

The following conclusion is never to be omitted:

All:

Wisdom, power, and adoration
To the blessed Trinity
For redemption and salvation
Through the Paschal Mystery,
Now, in every generation,
And for all eternity. Amen.

Omnes:

Æqua Patri Filioque,
   inclito Paraclito,
Sempiterna sit beatæ
   Trinitati gloria;
cuius alma nos redemit
   atque servat gratia. Amen.

In accordance with local circumstances or popular traditions and if it is pastorally appropriate, the Stabat Mater may be sung, as found in the Graduale Romanum, or another suitable chant in memory of the compassion of the Blessed Virgin Mary.

When the adoration has been concluded, the Cross is carried by the Deacon or a minister to its place at the altar. Lighted candles are placed around or on the altar or near the Cross.

THIRD PART:

Holy Communion

A cloth is spread on the altar, and a corporal and the Missal put in place. Meanwhile the Deacon or, if there is no Deacon, the Priest himself, putting on a humeral veil, brings the Blessed Sacrament back from the place of repose to the altar by a shorter route, while all stand in silence. Two ministers with lighted candles accompany the Blessed Sacrament and place their candlesticks around or upon the altar.

When the Deacon, if a Deacon is present, has placed the Blessed Sacrament upon the altar and uncovered the ciborium, the Priest goes to the altar and genuflects.

Then the Priest, with hands joined, says aloud:

At the Saviour's command and formed by divine teaching, we dare to say:	Præceptis salutaribus moniti, et divina institutione formati, audemus dicere:

The Priest, with hands extended says, and all present continue:

Our Father, who art in heaven, hallowed be thy name; thy kingdom come, thy will be done on earth as it is in heaven. Give us this day our daily bread, and forgive us our trespasses, as we forgive those who trespass against us; and lead us not into temptation, but deliver us from evil.	Pater noster, qui es in cælis: sanctificetur nomen tuum; adveniat regnum tuum; fiat voluntas tua, sicut in cælo, et in terra. Panem nostrum cotidianum da nobis hodie; et dimitte nobis debita nostra, sicut et nos dimittimus debitoribus nostris; et ne nos inducas in tentationem; sed libera nos a malo.

Text with music, pp.630-631.

With hands extended, the Priest continues alone:

Deliver us, Lord, we pray, from every evil, graciously grant peace in our days, that, by the help of your mercy, we may be always free from sin and safe from all distress, as we await the blessed hope and the coming of our Saviour, Jesus Christ.	Libera nos, quæsumus, Domine, ab omnibus malis, da propitius pacem in diebus nostris, ut, ope misericordiæ tuæ adiuti, et a peccato simus semper liberi et ab omni perturbatione securi: exspectantes beatam spem et adventum Salvatoris nostri Iesu Christi.

He joins his hands.

The people conclude the prayer, acclaiming:

For the kingdom, the power and the glory are yours now and for ever.	Quia tuum est regnum, et potestas, et gloria in sæcula.

Text with music, pp.632-633.

Then the Priest, with hands joined, says quietly:

May the receiving of your Body and Blood, Lord Jesus Christ, not bring me to judgement and condemnation, but through your loving mercy be for me protection in mind and body and a healing remedy.	Perceptio Corporis tui, Domine Iesu Christe, non mihi proveniat in iudicium et condemnationem: sed pro tua pietate prosit mihi ad tutamentum mentis et corporis, et ad medelam percipiendam.

The Priest then genuflects, takes a particle, and, holding it slightly raised over the ciborium, while facing the people, says aloud:

Behold the Lamb of God, behold him who takes away the sins of the world. Blessed are those called to the supper of the Lamb.	Ecce Agnus Dei, ecce qui tollit peccata mundi. Beati qui ad cenam Agni vocati sunt.

And together with the people he adds once:

Lord, I am not worthy that you should enter under my roof, but only say the word and my soul shall be healed.	Domine, non sum dignus, ut intres sub tectum meum, sed tantum dic verbo, et sanabitur anima mea.

And facing the altar, he reverently consumes the Body of Christ, saying quietly:

May the Body of Christ keep me safe for eternal life.	Corpus Christi custodiat me in vitam æternam.

He then proceeds to distribute Communion to the faithful. During Communion, Psalm 21 or another appropriate chant may be sung.

When the distribution of Communion has been completed, the ciborium is taken by the Deacon or another suitable minister to a place prepared outside the church or, if circumstances so require, it is placed in the tabernacle.

Then the Priest says: Let us pray, and, after a period of sacred silence, if circumstances so suggest, has been observed, he says the Prayer after Communion.

Almighty ever-living God,
who have restored us to life
by the blessed Death
     and Resurrection of your Christ,
preserve in us the work
     of your mercy,
that, by partaking of this mystery,
we may have a life unceasingly
     devoted to you.
Through Christ our Lord.
R. **Amen.**

Omnipotens sempiterne Deus,
qui nos Christi tui beata morte
     et resurrectione reparasti,
conserva in nobis opus
     misericordiæ tuæ,
ut huius mysterii participatione
perpetua devotione vivamus.
Per Christum Dominum nostrum.
R. Amen.

For the Dismissal the Deacon or, if there is no Deacon, the Priest himself, may say the invitation Bow down for the blessing.

Then the Priest, standing facing the people and extending his hands over them, says this Prayer over the People:

May abundant blessing, O Lord,
     we pray,
descend upon your people,
who have honoured the Death
     of your Son
in the hope of their resurrection:
may pardon come,
comfort be given,
holy faith increase,
and everlasting redemption
     be made secure.
Through Christ our Lord.
R. **Amen.**

Super populum tuum,
     quæsumus, Domine,
qui mortem Filii tui in spe suæ
     resurrectionis recoluit,
benedictio copiosa descendat,
indulgentia veniat,
     consolatio tribuatur,
fides sancta succrescat,
     redemptio sempiterna firmetur.
Per Christum Dominum nostrum.
R. Amen.

And all, after genuflecting to the Cross, depart in silence.

After the celebration, the altar is stripped, but the Cross remains on the altar with two or four candlesticks.

Vespers (Evening Prayer) is not celebrated by those who have been present at the solemn afternoon liturgical celebration.

HOLY SATURDAY

On Holy Saturday the Church waits at the Lord's tomb in prayer and fasting, meditating on his Passion and Death and on his Descent into Hell, and awaiting his Resurrection.

The Church abstains from the Sacrifice of the Mass, with the sacred table left bare, until after the solemn Vigil, that is, the anticipation by night of the Resurrection, when the time comes for paschal joys, the abundance of which overflows to occupy fifty days.

Holy Communion may only be given on this day as Viaticum.

EASTER TIME

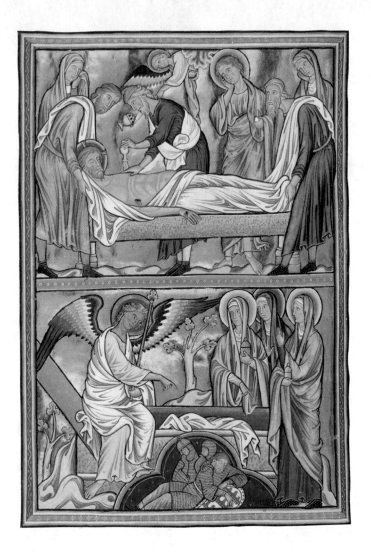

EASTER SUNDAY OF THE RESURRECTION OF THE LORD

THE EASTER VIGIL IN THE HOLY NIGHT

During the Easter Vigil, the Church reads the account of creation as a prophecy. In the resurrection, we see the most sublime fulfilment of what this text describes as the beginning of all things. God says once again: "Let there be light!" The resurrection of Jesus is an eruption of light. Death is conquered, the tomb is thrown open. The Risen One himself is Light, the Light of the world. With the resurrection, the Lord's day enters the nights of history. Beginning with the resurrection, God's light spreads throughout the world and throughout history. Day dawns. This Light alone – Jesus Christ – is the true light, something more than the physical phenomenon of light. He is pure Light: God himself, who causes a new creation to be born in the midst of the old, transforming chaos into cosmos.

(Pope Benedict XVI)

By most ancient tradition, this is the night of keeping vigil for the Lord (Ex 12:42), in which, following the Gospel admonition (Lk 12:35-37), the faithful, carrying lighted lamps in their hands, should be like those looking for the Lord when he returns, so that at his coming he may find them awake and have them sit at his table.

Of this night's Vigil, which is the greatest and most noble of all solemnities, there is to be only one celebration in each church. It is arranged, moreover, in such a way that after the Lucernarium and Easter Proclamation (which constitutes the first part of this Vigil), Holy Church meditates on the wonders the Lord God has done for his people from the beginning, trusting in his word and promise (the second part, that is, the Liturgy of the Word) until, as day approaches, with new members reborn in Baptism (the third part), the Church is called to the table the Lord has prepared for his people, the memorial of his Death and Resurrection until he comes again (the fourth part).

The entire celebration of the Easter Vigil must take place during the night, so that it begins after nightfall and ends before daybreak on the Sunday.

The Mass of the Vigil, even if it is celebrated before midnight, is a paschal Mass of the Sunday of the Resurrection.

Anyone who participates in the Mass of the night may receive Communion again at Mass during the day. A Priest who celebrates or concelebrates the Mass of the night may again celebrate or concelebrate Mass during the day.

The Easter Vigil takes the place of the Office of Readings.

The Priest is usually assisted by a Deacon. If, however, there is no Deacon, the duties of his Order, except those indicated below, are assumed by the Priest Celebrant or by a concelebrant.

The Priest and Deacon vest as at Mass, in white vestments.

Candles should be prepared for all who participate in the Vigil. The lights of the church are extinguished.

FIRST PART:

THE SOLEMN BEGINNING OF THE VIGIL OR LUCERNARIUM

The Blessing of the Fire and Preparation of the Candle

A blazing fire is prepared in a suitable place outside the church. When the people are gathered there, the Priest approaches with the ministers, one of whom carries the paschal candle. The processional cross and candles are not carried.

Where, however, a fire cannot be lit outside the church, the rite is carried out as below.

The Priest and faithful sign themselves while the Priest says: In the name of the Father, and of the Son, and of the Holy Spirit, and then he greets the assembled people in the usual way and briefly instructs them about the night vigil in these or similar words:

Dear brethren (brothers and sisters), on this most sacred night, in which our Lord Jesus Christ passed over from death to life, the Church calls upon her sons and daughters, scattered throughout the world, to come together to watch and pray. If we keep the memorial of the Lord's paschal solemnity in this way, listening to his word and celebrating his mysteries, then we shall have the sure hope of sharing his triumph over death and living with him in God.

Fratres carissimi, hac sacratissima nocte, in qua Dominus noster Iesus Christus de morte transivit ad vitam, Ecclesia invitat filios dispersos per orbem terrarum, ut ad vigilandum et orandum conveniant. Si ita memoriam egerimus Paschatis Domini, audientes verbum et celebrantes mysteria eius, spem habebimus participandi triumphum eius de morte et vivendi cum ipso in Deo.

Then the Priest blesses the fire, saying with hands extended:

Let us pray.	Oremus.

O God, who through your Son	Deus, qui per Filium tuum
bestowed upon the faithful the fire	claritatis tuæ ignem
of your glory,	fidelibus contulisti,
sanctify ✠ this new fire, we pray,	novum hunc ignem ✠ sanctifica,
and grant that,	et concede nobis,
by these paschal celebrations,	ita per hæc festa paschalia
we may be so inflamed	cælestibus desideriis inflammari,
with heavenly desires,	ut ad perpetuæ claritatis
that with minds made pure	puris mentibus valeamus
we may attain festivities	festa pertingere.
of unending splendour.	Per Christum Dominum nostrum.
Through Christ our Lord.	R. Amen.
R. Amen.	

After the blessing of the new fire, one of the ministers brings the paschal candle to the Priest, who cuts a cross into the candle with a stylus. Then he makes the Greek letter Alpha above the cross, the letter Omega below, and the four numerals of the current year between the arms of the cross, saying meanwhile:

1. Christ yesterday and today	1. Christus heri et hodie
2. the Beginning and the End	2. Principium et Finis
3. the Alpha	3. Alpha
4. and the Omega	4. et Omega
5. All time belongs to him	5. Ipsius sunt tempora
6. and all the ages	6. et sæcula
7. To him be glory and power	7. Ipsi gloria et imperium
8. through every age and for ever.	8. per universa æternitatis sæcula.
Amen	Amen

When the cutting of the cross and of the other signs has been completed, the Priest may insert five grains of incense into the candle in the form of a cross, meanwhile saying:

1. By his holy	1. Per sua sancta vulnera
2. and glorious wounds,	2. gloriosa
3. may Christ the Lord	3. custodiat
4. guard us	4. et conservet nos
5. and protect us. Amen.	5. Christus Dominus. Amen.

Where, because of difficulties that may occur, a fire is not lit, the blessing of fire is adapted to the circumstances. When the people are gathered in the church as on other occasions, the Priest comes to the door of the church, along with the ministers carrying the paschal candle. The people, insofar as is possible, turn to face the Priest.

The greeting and address take place as above; then the fire is blessed and the candle is prepared, as above.

The Priest lights the paschal candle from the new fire, saying:

May the light of Christ rising in glory dispel the darkness of our hearts and minds.	Lumen Christi gloriose resurgentis dissipet tenebras cordis et mentis.

As regards the preceding elements, Conferences of Bishops may also establish other forms more adapted to the culture of the different peoples.

Procession

When the candle has been lit, one of the ministers takes burning coals from the fire and places them in the thurible, and the Priest puts incense into it in the usual way. The Deacon or, if there is no Deacon, another suitable minister, takes the paschal candle and a procession forms. The thurifer with the smoking thurible precedes the Deacon or other minister who carries the paschal candle. After them follows the Priest with the ministers and the people, all holding in their hands unlit candles.

At the door of the church the Deacon, standing and raising up the candle, sings:

The Light of Christ.	Lumen Christi.

And all reply:

Thanks be to God.	Deo gratias.

The Priest lights his candle from the flame of the paschal candle.

Then the Deacon moves forward to the middle of the church and, standing and raising up the candle, sings a second time:

The Light of Christ.	Lumen Christi.

And all reply:

Thanks be to God.	Deo gratias.

All light their candles from the flame of the paschal candle and continue in procession.

When the Deacon arrives before the altar, he stands facing the people, raises up the candle and sings a third time:

The Light of Christ.	Lumen Christi.

And all reply:

Thanks be to God.	Deo gratias.

Then the Deacon places the paschal candle on a large candlestand prepared next to the ambo or in the middle of the sanctuary.

And lights are lit throughout the church, except for the altar candles.

The Easter Proclamation (Exsultet)

Arriving at the altar, the Priest goes to his chair, gives his candle to a minister, puts incense into the thurible and blesses the incense as at the Gospel at Mass. The Deacon goes to the Priest and saying, **Your blessing, Father**, asks for and receives a blessing from the Priest, who says in a low voice:

May the Lord be in your heart and on your lips,	Dominus sit in corde tuo et in labiis tuis,
that you may proclaim his paschal praise worthily and well,	ut digne et competenter annunties suum paschale præconium:
in the name of the Father and of the Son, ✠ and of the Holy Spirit.	in nomine Patris, et Filii, ✠ et Spiritus Sancti.
The Deacon replies: **Amen.**	Amen.

This blessing is omitted if the Proclamation is made by someone who is not a Deacon.

The Deacon, after incensing the book and the candle, proclaims the Easter Proclamation (Exsultet) at the ambo or at a lectern, with all standing and holding lighted candles in their hands.

The Easter Proclamation may be made, in the absence of a Deacon, by the Priest himself or by another concelebrating Priest. If, however, because of necessity, a lay cantor sings the Proclamation, the words Therefore, dearest friends up to the end of the invitation are omitted, along with the greeting The Lord be with you.

The Proclamation may also be sung in the shorter form p.325.

Longer Form of the Easter Proclamation

Exult, let them exult, the hosts of heaven,	Exsultet iam angelica turba cælorum:
exult, let Angel ministers of God exult,	exsultent divina mysteria:
let the trumpet of salvation sound aloud our mighty King's triumph!	et pro tanti Regis victoria tuba insonet salutaris.
Be glad, let earth be glad, as glory floods her,	Gaudeat et tellus tantis irradiata fulgoribus:
ablaze with light from her eternal King,	et, æterni Regis splendore illustrata,
let all corners of the earth be glad, knowing an end to gloom and darkness.	totius orbis se sentiat amisisse caliginem.

Rejoice, let Mother Church
   also rejoice,
arrayed with the lightning
   of his glory,
let this holy building shake with joy,
filled with the mighty voices
   of the peoples.

(Therefore, dearest friends,
standing in the awesome glory
   of this holy light,
invoke with me, I ask you,
the mercy of God almighty,
that he, who has been pleased
   to number me,
though unworthy, among the Levites,
may pour into me his light
   unshadowed,
that I may sing this candle's
   perfect praises.)

(V. The Lord be with you.
R. And with your spirit.)
V. Lift up your hearts.
R. We lift them up to the Lord.
V. Let us give thanks to the Lord
   our God.
R. It is right and just.
It is truly right and just,
with ardent love of mind and heart
and with devoted service of our voice,
to acclaim our God invisible,
   the almighty Father,
and Jesus Christ, our Lord, his Son,
   his Only Begotten.

Who for our sake paid Adam's debt
   to the eternal Father,
and, pouring out his own dear Blood,
wiped clean the record of our
   ancient sinfulness.

Lætetur et mater Ecclesia,
tanti luminis adornata fulgoribus:
et magnis populorum vocibus hæc
   aula resultet.

(Quapropter astantes vos,
   fratres carissimi,
ad tam miram huius sancti
   luminis claritatem,
una mecum, quæso,
Dei omnipotentis
   misericordiam invocate.
Ut, qui me non meis meritis
intra Levitarum numerum dignatus
   est aggregare,
luminis sui claritatem infundens,
cerei huius laudem
   implere perficiat.)

(V. Dominus vobiscum.
R. Et cum spiritu tuo.)
V. Sursum corda.
R. Habemus ad Dominum.
V. Gratias agamus Domino
   Deo nostro.
R. Dignum et iustum est.
Vere dignum et iustum est,
invisibilem Deum
   Patrem omnipotentem
Filiumque eius Unigenitum,
Dominum nostrum
   Iesum Christum,
toto cordis ac mentis affectu
   et vocis ministerio personare.

Qui pro nobis æterno Patri Adæ
   debitum solvit,
et veteris piaculi cautionem
   pio cruore detersit.

These then are the feasts of Passover,
in which is slain the Lamb,
the one true Lamb,
whose Blood anoints the doorposts
of believers.

This is the night,
when once you led our forebears,
Israel's children,
from slavery in Egypt
and made them pass dry-shod
through the Red Sea.

This is the night
that with a pillar of fire
banished the darkness of sin.

This is the night
that even now, throughout the world,
sets Christian believers apart
from worldly vices
and from the gloom of sin,
leading them to grace
and joining them to his holy ones.

This is the night,
when Christ broke the prison-bars
of death
and rose victorious
from the underworld.

Our birth would have been no gain,
had we not been redeemed.
O wonder of your humble care for us!
O love, O charity beyond all telling,
to ransom a slave you gave away
your Son!

O truly necessary sin of Adam,
destroyed completely by the Death
of Christ!

Hæc sunt enim festa paschalia,
in quibus verus ille Agnus occiditur,
cuius sanguine postes
fidelium consecrantur.

Hæc nox est,
in qua primum patres nostros,
filios Israel eductos de Ægypto,
Mare Rubrum sicco vestigio
transire fecisti.

Hæc igitur nox est,
quæ peccatorum tenebras columnæ
illuminatione purgavit.

Hæc nox est,
quæ hodie per universum mundum
in Christo credentes,
a vitiis sæculi et caligine
peccatorum segregatos,
reddit gratiæ, sociat sanctitati.

Hæc nox est,
in qua, destructis vinculis mortis,
Christus ab inferis victor ascendit.

Nihil enim nobis nasci profuit,
nisi redimi profuisset.
O mira circa nos tuæ pietatis
dignatio!
O inæstimablilis dilectio caritatis:
ut servum redimeres,
Filium tradidisti!

O certe necessarium
Adæ peccatum,
quod Christi morte deletum est!

O happy fault
that earned so great,
    so glorious a Redeemer!

O truly blessed night,
worthy alone to know the time
    and hour
when Christ rose
    from the underworld!

This is the night
of which it is written:
The night shall be as bright as day,
dazzling is the night for me,
and full of gladness.

The sanctifying power of this night
dispels wickedness,
    washes faults away,
restores innocence to the fallen,
    and joy to mourners,
drives out hatred, fosters concord,
    and brings down the mighty.

On this, your night of grace,
    O holy Father,
accept this candle, a solemn offering,
the work of bees and of your
    servants' hands,
an evening sacrifice of praise,
this gift from your most holy Church.

But now we know the praises
    of this pillar,
which glowing fire ignites
    for God's honour,
a fire into many flames divided,
yet never dimmed by sharing
    of its light,
for it is fed by melting wax,
drawn out by mother bees
to build a torch so precious.

O felix culpa,
quæ talem ac tantum meruit
    habere Redemptorem!

O vere beata nox,
quæ sola meruit scire tempus
    et horam,
in qua Christus ab inferis resurrexit!

Hæc nox est, de qua scriptum est:
Et nox sicut dies illuminabitur:
et nox illuminatio mea
    in deliciis meis.

Huius igitur sanctificatio noctis
    fugat scelera, culpas lavat:
et reddit innocentiam lapsis
    et mæstis lætitiam.
Fugat odia, concordiam parat
    et curvat imperia.

In huius igitur noctis gratia,
suscipe, sancte Pater, laudis huius
    sacrificium vespertinum,
quod tibi in hac cerei
    oblatione sollemni,
per ministrorum manus
de operibus apum,
    sacrosancta reddit Ecclesia.

Sed iam columnæ huius
    præconia novimus,
quam in honorem Dei rutilans
    ignis accendit.
Qui, licet sit divisus in partes,
mutuati tamen luminis detrimenta
    non novit.
Alitur enim liquantibus ceris,
quas in substantiam pretiosæ
    huius lampadis
apis mater eduxit.

O truly blessed night,
when things of heaven are wed
    to those of earth,
and divine to the human.

Therefore, O Lord,
we pray you that this candle,
hallowed to the honour of
    your name,
may persevere undimmed,
to overcome the darkness
    of this night.
Receive it as a pleasing fragrance,
and let it mingle with
    the lights of heaven.
May this flame be found still burning
by the Morning Star:
the one Morning Star who never sets,
Christ your Son,
who, coming back
    from death's domain,
has shed his peaceful light
    on humanity,
and lives and reigns
    for ever and ever.
R. Amen.

O vere beata nox,
in qua terrenis cælestia,
    humanis divina iunguntur!

Oramus ergo te, Domine,
ut cereus iste in honorem tui
    nominis consecratus,
ad noctis huius
    caliginem destruendam,
indeficiens perseveret.

Et in odorem suavitatis acceptus,
supernis luminaribus misceatur.
Flammas eius lucifer
    matutinus inveniat:

Ille, inquam, lucifer,
    qui nescit occasum:
Christus Filius tuus,
qui, regressus ab inferis, humano
    generi serenus illuxit,
et vivit et regnat
    in sæcula sæculorum.
R. Amen.

Shorter Form of the Easter Proclamation

Exult, let them exult,
    the hosts of heaven,
exult, let Angel ministers
    of God exult,
let the trumpet of salvation
sound aloud our mighty
    King's triumph!

Be glad, let earth be glad, as glory
    floods her,
ablaze with light from her
    eternal King,
let all corners of the earth be glad,
knowing an end to gloom
    and darkness.

Exsultet iam angelica
    turba cælorum:
exsultent divina mysteria:
et pro tanti Regis victoria tuba
    insonet salutaris.

Gaudeat et tellus tantis
    irradiata fulgoribus:
et, æterni Regis splendore illustrata,
totius orbis se sentiat
    amisisse caliginem.

Rejoice, let Mother Church
also rejoice,
arrayed with the lightning
of his glory,
let this holy building shake with joy,
filled with the mighty voices
of the peoples.

(V. The Lord be with you.
R. And with your spirit.)
V. Lift up your hearts.
R. We lift them up to the Lord.
V. Let us give thanks to the Lord
our God.
R. It is right and just.

It is truly right and just,
with ardent love of mind and heart
and with devoted service of our voice,
to acclaim our God invisible,
the almighty Father,
and Jesus Christ, our Lord, his Son,
his Only Begotten.

Who for our sake paid Adam's debt
to the eternal Father,
and, pouring out his own dear Blood,
wiped clean the record
of our ancient sinfulness.

These then are the feasts of Passover,
in which is slain the Lamb,
the one true Lamb,
whose Blood anoints the doorposts
of believers.

This is the night,
when once you led our forebears,
Israel's children,
from slavery in Egypt
and made them pass dry-shod
through the Red Sea.

Lætetur et mater Ecclesia,
tanti luminis adornata fulgoribus:
et magnis populorum vocibus hæc
aula resultet.

(V. Dominus vobiscum.
R. Et cum spiritu tuo.)
V. Sursum corda.
R. Habemus ad Dominum.
V. Gratias agamus Domino
Deo nostro.
R. Dignum et iustum est.

Vere dignum et iustum est,
invisibilem Deum
Patrem omnipotentem
Filiumque eius Unigenitum,
Dominum nostrum
Iesum Christum,
toto cordis ac mentis affectu
et vocis ministerio personare.

Qui pro nobis æterno Patri Adæ
debitum solvit,
et veteris piaculi cautionem pio
cruore detersit.

Hæc sunt enim festa paschalia,
in quibus verus ille
Agnus occiditur,
cuius sanguine postes
fidelium consecrantur.

Hæc nox est,
in qua primum patres nostros,
filios Israel
eductos de Ægypto,
Mare Rubrum sicco vestigio
transire fecisti.

This is the night
that with a pillar of fire
banished the darkness of sin.

This is the night
that even now, throughout the world,
sets Christian believers apart
      from worldly vices
and from the gloom of sin,
leading them to grace
and joining them to his holy ones.

This is the night,
when Christ broke the prison-bars
      of death
and rose victorious
      from the underworld.

O wonder of your humble care for us!
O love, O charity beyond all telling,
to ransom a slave you gave away
      your Son!

O truly necessary sin of Adam,
destroyed completely by the Death
      of Christ!

O happy fault
that earned so great,
      so glorious a Redeemer!

The sanctifying power of this night
dispels wickedness,
      washes faults away,
restores innocence to the fallen,
      and joy to mourners.

O truly blessed night,
when things of heaven are wed
      to those of earth,
and divine to the human.

On this, your night of grace,
      O holy Father,
accept this candle, a solemn offering,
the work of bees and of your

Hæc igitur nox est,
quæ peccatorum tenebras columnæ
      illuminatione purgavit.

Hæc nox est,
quæ hodie per universum mundum
      in Christo credentes,
a vitiis sæculi et caligine
peccatorum segregatos,
reddit gratiæ, sociat sanctitati.

Hæc nox est,
in qua, destructis vinculis mortis,
Christus ab inferis victor ascendit.

O mira circa nos tuæ
      pietatis dignatio!
O inæstimablilis dilectio caritatis:
ut servum redimeres,
      Filium tradidisti!

O certe necessarium Adæ peccatum,
quod Christi morte deletum est!

O felix culpa,
quæ talem ac tantum meruit
      habere Redemptorem!

Huius igitur sanctificatio noctis
      fugat scelera, culpas lavat:
et reddit innocentiam lapsis
      et mæstis lætitiam.

O vere beata nox,
in qua terrenis cælestia,
      humanis divina iunguntur!

In huius igitur noctis gratia,
suscipe, sancte Pater, laudis huius
      sacrificium vespertinum,
quod tibi in hac cerei

servants' hands,
an evening sacrifice of praise,
this gift from your most
    holy Church.

Therefore, O Lord,
we pray you that this candle,
hallowed to the honour
    of your name,
may persevere undimmed,
to overcome the darkness
    of this night.
Receive it as a pleasing fragrance,
and let it mingle with the lights
    of heaven.
May this flame be found
    still burning
by the Morning Star:
the one Morning Star who never sets,
Christ your Son,
who, coming back from
    death's domain,
has shed his peaceful light
    on humanity,
and lives and reigns
    for ever and ever.
℟. Amen.

oblatione sollemni,
per ministrorum manus
de operibus apum,
    sacrosancta reddit Ecclesia.

Oramus ergo te, Domine,
ut cereus iste in honorem tui
    nominis consecratus,
ad noctis huius
    caliginem destruendam,
indeficiens perseveret.
Et in odorem suavitatis acceptus,
supernis luminaribus misceatur.
Flammas eius lucifer
    matutinus inveniat:
Ille, inquam, lucifer,
    qui nescit occasum:
Christus Filius tuus,
qui, regressus ab inferis,
    humano generi serenus illuxit,
et vivit et regnat
    in sæcula sæculorum.
℟. Amen.

SECOND PART:
The Liturgy of the Word

In this Vigil, the mother of all Vigils, nine readings are provided, namely seven from the Old Testament and two from the New (the Epistle and Gospel), all of which should be read whenever this can be done, so that the character of the Vigil, which demands an extended period of time, may be preserved.

Nevertheless, where more serious pastoral circumstances demand it, the number of readings from the Old Testament may be reduced, always bearing in mind that the reading of the Word of God is a fundamental part of this Easter Vigil. At least three readings should be read from the Old Testament, both from the Law and from the Prophets, and their respective Responsorial Psalms should be sung. Never, moreover, should the reading of chapter 14 of Exodus with its canticle be omitted.

After setting aside their candles, all sit. Before the readings begin, the Priest instructs the people in these or similar words:

Dear brethren (brothers and sisters), now that we have begun our solemn Vigil, let us listen with quiet hearts to the Word of God. Let us meditate on how God in times past saved his people and in these, the last days, has sent us his Son as our Redeemer. Let us pray that our God may complete this paschal work of salvation by the fullness of redemption.	Vigiliam sollemniter ingressi, fratres carissimi, quieto corde nunc verbum Dei audiamus. Meditemur, quomodo Deus populum suum elapsis temporibus salvum fecerit, et novissime nobis Filium suum miserit Redemptorem. Oremus, ut Deus noster hoc paschale salvationis opus ad plenam redemptionem perficiat.

Then the readings follow. A reader goes to the ambo and proclaims the reading. Afterwards a psalmist or a cantor sings or says the Psalm with the people making the response. Then all rise, the Priest says, Let us pray and, after all have prayed for a while in silence, he says the prayer corresponding to the reading. In place of the Responsorial Psalm a period of sacred silence may be observed, in which case the pause after Let us pray is omitted.

FIRST READING

A reading from the book of Genesis   1:1-2:2

God saw all he made, and indeed it was very good.

[In the beginning God created the heavens and the earth.] Now the earth was a formless void, there was darkness over the deep, and God's spirit hovered over the water.

God said, 'Let there be light,' and there was light. God saw that light was good, and God divided light from darkness. God called light 'day', and darkness he called 'night'. Evening came and morning came: the first day.

God said, 'Let there be a vault in the waters to divide the waters in two.' And so it was. God made the vault, and it divided the waters above the vault from the waters under the vault. God called the vault 'heaven'. Evening came and morning came: the second day.

God said, 'Let the waters under heaven come together into a single mass, and let dry land appear.' And so it was. God called the dry land 'earth' and the mass of waters 'seas', and God saw that it was good.

God said, 'Let the earth produce vegetation: seed-bearing plants, and fruit trees bearing fruit with their seed inside, on the earth.' And so it was.

The earth produced vegetation: plants bearing seed in their several kinds, and trees bearing fruit with their seed inside in their several kinds. God saw that it was good. Evening came and morning came: the third day.

God said, 'Let there be lights in the vault of heaven to divide day from night, and let them indicate festivals, days and years. Let them be lights in the vault of heaven to shine on the earth.' And so it was. God made the two great lights: the greater light to govern the day, the smaller light to govern the night, and the stars. God set them in the vault of heaven to shine on the earth, to govern the day and the night and to divide light from darkness. God saw that it was good. Evening came and morning came: the fourth day.

God said, 'Let the waters teem with living creatures, and let birds fly above the earth within the vault of heaven.' And so it was. God created great sea-serpents and every kind of living creature with which the waters teem, and every kind of winged creature. God saw that it was good. God blessed them, saying, 'Be fruitful, multiply, and fill the waters of the seas, and let the birds multiply upon the earth.' Evening came and morning came: the fifth day.

God said, 'Let the earth produce every kind of living creature: cattle, reptiles, and every kind of wild beast.' And so it was. God made every kind of wild beast, every kind of cattle, and every kind of land reptile. God saw that it was good.

[God said, 'Let us make man in our own image, in the likeness of ourselves, and let them be masters of the fish of the sea, the birds of heaven, the cattle, all the wild beasts and all the reptiles that crawl upon the earth.'

God created man in the image of himself,
in the image of God he created him,
male and female he created them.

God blessed them, saying to them, 'Be fruitful, multiply, fill the earth and conquer it. Be masters of the fish of the sea, the birds of heaven and all living animals on the earth.' God said, 'See, I give you all the seed-bearing plants that are upon the whole earth, and all the trees with seed-bearing fruit; this shall be your food. To all wild beasts, all birds of heaven and all living reptiles on the earth I give all the foliage of plants for food.' And so it was. God saw all he had made, and indeed it was very good. Evening came and morning came: the sixth day.

Thus heaven and earth were completed with all their array. On the seventh day God completed the work he had been doing. He rested on the seventh day after all the work he had been doing.

The word of the Lord.]

Shorter Form, verses 1, 26-31. Read between [ ]

Responsorial Psalm   Ps 103:1-2,5-6,10,12-14,24,35. R. Cf. v.30

R. **Send forth your spirit, O Lord,**
and renew the face of the earth.
   Bless the Lord, my soul!
   Lord God, how great you are,
   clothed in majesty and glory,
   wrapped in light as in a robe! R.

   You founded the earth on its base,
   to stand firm from age to age.
   You wrapped it with the ocean like a cloak:
   the waters stood higher than the mountains. R.

   You make springs gush forth in the valleys:
   they flow in between the hills.
   On their banks dwell the birds of heaven;
   from the branches they sing their song. R.

   From your dwelling you water the hills;
   earth drinks its fill of your gift.
   You make the grass grow for the cattle
   and the plants to serve man's needs. R.

   How many are your works, O Lord!
   In wisdom you have made them all.
   The earth is full of your riches.
   Bless the Lord, my soul! R.

Alternative Psalm   Ps 32:4-7,12-13,20,22. R. v.5

R. **The Lord fills the earth with his love.**

   The word of the Lord is faithful
   and all his works to be trusted.
   The Lord loves justice and right
   and fills the earth with his love. R.

   By his word the heavens were made,
   by the breath of his mouth all the stars.
   He collects the waves of the ocean;
   he stores up the depths of the sea. R.

   They are happy, whose God is the Lord,
   the people he has chosen as his own.
   From the heavens the Lord looks forth,
   he sees all the children of men. R.

Our soul is waiting for the Lord.
The Lord is our help and our shield.
May your love be upon us, O Lord,
as we place all our hope in you. R.

R. **The Lord fills the earth with his love.**

Prayer

Let us pray.

Almighty ever-living God,
who are wonderful in the ordering
of all your works,
may those you have
redeemed understand
that there exists nothing
more marvellous
than the world's creation
in the beginning
except that, at the end of the ages,
Christ our Passover
has been sacrificed.
Who lives and reigns
for ever and ever.
R. Amen.

Or, On the creation of man:

O God, who wonderfully created
human nature
and still more wonderfully
redeemed it,
grant us, we pray,
to set our minds against
the enticements of sin,
that we may merit to attain
eternal joys.
Through Christ our Lord.
R. Amen.

Oremus.

Omnipotens sempiterne Deus,
qui es in omnium operum tuorum
dispensatione mirabilis,
intellegant redempti tui,
non fuisse excellentius,
quod initio factus est mundus,
quam quod in fine sæculorum
Pascha nostrum immolatus
est Christus.
Qui vivit et regnat
in sæcula sæculorum.
R. Amen.

Deus, qui mirabiliter creasti hominem
et mirabilius redemisti,
da nobis, quæsumus,
contra oblectamenta peccati mentis
ratione persistere,
ut mereamur ad æterna
gaudia pervenire.
Per Christum Dominum nostrum.
R. Amen.

SECOND READING

A reading from the book of Genesis   22:1-18

The sacrifice of Abraham, our father in faith.

[God put Abraham to the test. 'Abraham, Abraham,' he called. 'Here I am'
he replied. 'Take your son,' God said 'your only child Isaac, whom you

love, and go to the land of Moriah. There you shall offer him as a burnt offering, on a mountain I will point out to you.']

Rising early next morning Abraham saddled his ass and took with him two of his servants and his son Isaac. He chopped wood for the burnt offering and started on his journey to the place God had pointed out to him. On the third day Abraham looked up and saw the place in the distance. Then Abraham said to his servants, 'Stay here with the donkey. The boy and I will go over there; we will worship and come back to you.'

Abraham took the wood for the burnt offering, loaded it on Isaac, and carried in his own hands the fire and the knife. Then the two of them set out together. Isaac spoke to his father Abraham, 'Father' he said. 'Yes, my son' he replied. 'Look,' he said 'here are the fire and the wood, but where is the lamb for the burnt offering?' Abraham answered, 'My son, God himself will provide the lamb for the burnt offering.' Then the two of them went on together.

[When they arrived at the place God had pointed out to him, Abraham built an altar there, and arranged the wood. Then he bound his son Isaac and put him on the altar on top of the wood. Abraham stretched out his hand and seized the knife to kill his son.

But the angel of the Lord called to him from heaven. 'Abraham, Abraham' he said. 'I am here' he replied. 'Do not raise your hand against the boy' the angel said. 'Do not harm him, for now I know you fear God. You have not refused me your son, your only son.' Then looking up, Abraham saw a ram caught by its horns in a bush. Abraham took the ram and offered it as a burnt-offering in place of his son.] Abraham called this place 'The Lord provides', and hence the saying today: On the mountain the Lord provides.

[The angel of the Lord called Abraham a second time from heaven. 'I swear by my own self – it is the Lord who speaks – because you have done this, because you have not refused me your son, your only son, I will shower blessings on you, I will make your descendants as many as the stars of heaven and the grains of sand on the seashore. Your descendants shall gain possession of the gates of their enemies. All the nations of the earth shall bless themselves by your descendants, as a reward for your obedience.

The word of the Lord.]

Shorter Form, verses 1-2,9-13,15-18. Read between [ ]

Responsorial Psalm   Ps 15:5,8-11, R. v.1

R. **Preserve me, God, I take refuge in you.**

O Lord, it is you who are my portion and cup;
it is you yourself who are my prize.
I keep the Lord ever in my sight:
since he is at my right hand, I shall stand firm. R.

And so my heart rejoices, my soul is glad;
even my body shall rest in safety.
For you will not leave my soul among the dead,
nor let your beloved know decay. R.

You will show me the path of life,
the fullness of joy in your presence,
at your right hand happiness for ever. R.

Prayer

Let us pray.

O God, supreme Father
    of the faithful,
who increase the children
    of your promise
by pouring out the grace
    of adoption
throughout the whole world
and who through the Paschal Mystery
make your servant Abraham father
    of nations,
as once you swore,
grant, we pray,
that your peoples may enter worthily
into the grace to which you call them.
Through Christ our Lord.
R. Amen.

Oremus.

Deus, Pater summe fidelium,
qui promissionis tuæ filios diffusa
    adoptionis gratia
in toto terrarum orbe multiplicas,
et per paschale sacramentum
Abraham puerum tuum
universarum, sicut iurasti,
    gentium efficis patrem,
da populis tuis digne ad gratiam
    tuæ vocationis intrare.
Per Christum Dominum nostrum.
R. Amen.

The following reading must always be read.

THIRD READING

A reading from book of Exodus   14:15-15:1

The sons of Israel went on dry ground right into the sea.

The Lord said to Moses, 'Why do you cry to me so? Tell the sons of Israel to march on. For yourself, raise your staff and stretch out your hand over the sea and part it for the sons of Israel to walk through the sea on dry ground. I for my part will make the heart of the Egyptians so stubborn that they will follow them. So shall I win myself glory at the expense of Pharaoh, of all his army, his chariots, his horsemen. And when I have won glory for myself, at the expense of Pharaoh and his chariots and his army, the Egyptians will learn that I am the Lord.'

Then the angel of the Lord, who marched at the front of the army of Israel, changed station and moved to their rear. The pillar of cloud changed station from the front to the rear of them, and remained there. It came between the camp of the Egyptians and the camp of Israel. The cloud was dark, and the night passed without the armies drawing any closer the whole night long. Moses stretched out his hand over the sea. The Lord drove back the sea with a strong easterly wind all night, and he made dry land of the sea. The waters parted and the sons of Israel went on dry ground right into the sea, walls of water to right and to left of them. The Egyptians gave chase: after them they went, right into the sea, all Pharaoh's horses, his chariots, and his horsemen. In the morning watch, the Lord looked down on the army of the Egyptians from the pillar of fire and of cloud, and threw the army into confusion. He so clogged their chariot wheels that they could scarcely make headway. 'Let us flee from the Israelites,' the Egyptians cried 'the Lord is fighting for them against the Egyptians!' 'Stretch out your hand over the sea,' the Lord said to Moses 'that the waters may flow back on the Egyptians and their chariots and their horsemen.' Moses stretched out his hand over the sea and, as day broke, the sea returned to its bed. The fleeing Egyptians marched right into it, and the Lord overthrew the Egyptians in the very middle of the sea. The returning waters overwhelmed the chariots and the horsemen of Pharaoh's whole army, which had followed the Israelites into the sea; not a single one of them was left. But the sons of Israel had marched through the sea on dry ground, walls of water to right and to left of them. That day, the Lord rescued Israel from the Egyptians, and Israel saw the Egyptians lying dead on the shore. Israel witnessed the great act that the Lord had performed against the Egyptians, and the people venerated the Lord; they put their faith in the Lord and in Moses, his servant.

It was then that Moses and the sons of Israel sang this song in honour of the Lord:

The choir takes up the Responsorial Psalm immediately.

Responsorial Psalm   Ex 15:1-6,17-18. R. v.1

R. **I will sing to the Lord, glorious his triumph!**

I will sing to the Lord, glorious his triumph!
Horse and rider he has thrown into the sea!
The Lord is my strength, my song, my salvation.
This is my God and I extol him,
my father's God and I give him praise. R.

The Lord is a warrior! The Lord is his name.
The chariots of Pharaoh he hurled into the sea,
the flower of his army is drowned in the sea.
The deeps hide them; they sank like a stone. R.

Your right hand, Lord, glorious in its power,
your right hand, Lord, has shattered the enemy.
In the greatness of your glory you crushed the foe. R.

You will lead your people and plant them on your mountain,
the place, O Lord, where you have made your home,
the sanctuary, Lord, which your hands have made.
The Lord will reign for ever and ever. R.

Prayer

Let us pray.

O God, whose ancient wonders
remain undimmed in splendour
    even in our day,
for what you once bestowed
    on a single people,
freeing them from
    Pharaoh's persecution
by the power of your right hand
now you bring about as the salvation
    of the nations
through the waters of rebirth,
grant, we pray,
    that the whole world
may become children of Abraham
and inherit the dignity
    of Israel's birthright.
Through Christ our Lord.
R. Amen.

Oremus.

Deus, cuius antiqua miracula
etiam nostris temporibus
    coruscare sentimus,
dum, quod uni populo
a persecutione Pharaonis liberando
dexteræ tuæ potentia contulisti,
id in salutem gentium
per aquam regenerationis operaris,
præsta, ut in Abrahæ filios
et in Israeliticam dignitatem
totius mundi transeat plenitudo.
Per Christum Dominum nostrum.
R. Amen.

Or:

O God, who by the light
    of the New Testament
have unlocked the meaning
of wonders worked in former times,
so that the Red Sea prefigures
    the sacred font
and the nation delivered from slavery
foreshadows the Christian people,
grant, we pray, that all nations,
obtaining the privilege of Israel
    by merit of faith,
may be reborn by partaking
    of your Spirit.
Through Christ our Lord.
R. Amen.

Vel:

Deus, qui primis temporibus
impleta miracula novi testamenti
    luce reserasti,
ut et Mare Rubrum forma sacri
    fontis exsisteret,
et plebs a servitute liberata
christiani populi
    sacramenta præferret,
da, ut omnes gentes,
Israelis privilegium merito
    fidei consecutæ,
Spiritus tui participatione
    regenerentur.
Per Christum Dominum nostrum.
R. Amen.

FOURTH READING

A reading from the prophet Isaiah   54:5-14

With everlasting love the Lord your redeemer has taken pity on you.

Now your creator will be your husband,
his name, the Lord of hosts;
your redeemer will be the Holy One of Israel,
he is called the God of the whole earth.
Yes, like a forsaken wife, distressed in spirit,
the Lord calls you back.
Does a man cast off the wife of his youth?
says your God.

I did forsake you for a brief moment,
but with great love will I take you back.
In excess of anger, for a moment
I hid my face from you.
But with everlasting love I have taken pity on you,
says the Lord, your redeemer.

I am now as I was in the days of Noah
when I swore that Noah's waters
should never flood the world again.
So now I swear concerning my anger with you
and the threats I made against you;

for the mountains may depart,

the hills be shaken,
but my love for you will never leave you;
and my covenant of peace with you will never be shaken,
says the Lord who takes pity on you.

Unhappy creature, storm-tossed, disconsolate,
see, I will set your stones on carbuncles
and your foundations on sapphires.
I will make rubies your battlements,
your gates crystal,
and your entire wall precious stones.
Your sons will all be taught by the Lord.
The prosperity of your sons will be great.
You will be founded on integrity;
remote from oppression, you will have nothing to fear;
remote from terror, it will not approach you.

The word of the Lord.

Responsial Psalm   Ps 29:2,4-6,11-13. R. v.2

R. **I will praise you, Lord, you have rescued me.**

I will praise you, Lord, you have rescued me
and have not let my enemies rejoice over me.
O Lord, you have raised my soul from the dead,
restored me to life from those who sink into the grave. R.

Sing psalms to the Lord, you who love him,
give thanks to his holy name.
His anger lasts but a moment; his favour through life.
At night there are tears, but joy comes with dawn. R.

The Lord listened and had pity.
The Lord came to my help.
For me you have changed my mourning into dancing,
O Lord my God, I will thank you for ever. R.

Prayer

Let us pray.	Oremus.
Almighty ever-living God,	Omnipotens sempiterne Deus,
surpass, for the honour of your name,	multiplica in honorem nominis tui
what you pledged to the Patriarchs	quod patrum fidei spopondisti,
by reason of their faith,	et promissionis filios sacra
and through sacred adoption increase	adoptione dilata,
the children of your promise,	ut, quod priores sancti non

so that what the Saints of old never
  doubted would come to pass
your Church may now see in great
  part fulfilled.
Through Christ our Lord. R. Amen.

dubitaverunt futurum,
Ecclesia tua magna ex parte iam
  cognoscat impletum.
Per Christum Dominum nostrum.
R. Amen.

Alternatively, other prayers may be used from among those which follow the
readings that have been omitted.

FIFTH READING

A reading from the prophet Isaiah   55:1-11
Come to me and your soul will live, and I will make an everlasting covenant with you.

Thus says the Lord:
    Oh, come to the water all you who are thirsty;
    though you have no money, come!
    Buy corn without money, and eat,
    and, at no cost, wine and milk.
    Why spend money on what is not bread,
    your wages on what fails to satisfy?
    Listen, listen to me, and you will have good things to eat
    and rich food to enjoy.
    Pay attention, come to me;
    and your soul will live.

    With you I will make an everlasting covenant
    out of the favours promised to David.
    See, I have made of you a witness to the peoples,
    a leader and a master of the nations.
    See, you will summon a nation you never knew,
    those unknown will come hurrying to you,
    for the sake of the Lord your God,
    of the Holy One of Israel who will glorify you.

    Seek the Lord while he is still to be found,
    call to him while he is still near.
    Let the wicked man abandon his way,
    the evil man his thoughts.
    Let him turn back to the Lord who will take pity on him,
    to our God who is rich in forgiving;
    for my thoughts are not your thoughts,
    my ways not your ways – it is the Lord who speaks.
    Yes, the heavens are as high above earth
    as my ways are above your ways,
    my thoughts above your thoughts.

Yes, as the rain and the snow come down from the heavens and do not return without watering the earth, making it yield and giving growth to provide seed for the sower and bread for the eating, so the word that goes from my mouth does not return to me empty, without carrying out my will and succeeding in what it was sent to do.

The word of the Lord.

Responsorial Psalm   Is 12:2-6. R. v.3

R. **With joy you will draw water from the wells of salvation.**

Truly God is my salvation,
I trust, I shall not fear.
For the Lord is my strength, my song,
he became my saviour.
With joy you will draw water
from the wells of salvation. R.

Give thanks to the Lord, give praise to his name!
Make his mighty deeds known to the peoples,
declare the greatness of his name. R.

Sing a psalm to the Lord
for he has done glorious deeds,
make them known to all the earth!
People of Zion, sing and shout for joy
for great in your midst is the Holy One of Israel. R.

Prayer

Let us pray.

Almighty ever-living God,
sole hope of the world,
who by the preaching
    of your Prophets
unveiled the mysteries
    of this present age,
graciously increase the longing
    of your people,
for only at the prompting
    of your grace
do the faithful progress in any
    kind of virtue.
Through Christ our Lord.
R. Amen.

Oremus.

Omnipotens sempiterne Deus,
spes unica mundi,
qui prophetarum tuorum præconio
præsentium temporum
    declarasti mysteria,
auge populi tui vota placatus,
quia in nullo fidelium nisi ex tua
    inspiratione proveniunt
quarumlibet incrementa virtutum.
Per Christum Dominum nostrum.
R. Amen.

SIXTH READING

A reading from the prophet Baruch   3:9-15,32-4:4

In the radiance of the Lord make your way to light.

Listen, Israel, to commands that bring life;
hear, and learn what knowledge means.
Why, Israel, why are you in the country of your enemies,
growing older and older in an alien land,
sharing defilement with the dead,
reckoned with those who go to Sheol?
Because you have forsaken the fountain of wisdom.
Had you walked in the way of God,
you would have lived in peace for ever.
Learn where knowledge is, where strength,
where understanding, and so learn
where length of days is, where life,
where the light of the eyes and where peace.
But who has found out where she lives,
who has entered her treasure house?

But the One who knows all knows her,
he has grasped her with his own intellect,
he has set the earth firm for ever
and filled it with four-footed beasts,
he sends the light – and it goes,
he recalls it – and trembling it obeys;
the stars shine joyfully at their set times:
when he calls them, they answer, 'Here we are';
they gladly shine for their creator.
It is he who is our God,
no other can compare with him.
He has grasped the whole way of knowledge,
and confided it to his servant Jacob,
to Israel his well-beloved;
so causing her to appear on earth
and move among men.

This is the book of the commandments of God,
the Law that stands for ever;
those who keep her live,
those who desert her die.
Turn back, Jacob, seize her,
in her radiance make your way to light:

do not yield your glory to another,
your privilege to a people not your own.
Israel, blessed are we:
what pleases God has been revealed to us.

   The word of the Lord.

Responsorial Psalm   Ps 18:8-11. R. Jn 6:69

R. **You have the message of eternal life, O Lord.**

   The law of the Lord is perfect,
   it revives the soul.
   The rule of the Lord is to be trusted,
   it gives wisdom to the simple. R.

   The precepts of the Lord are right,
   they gladden the heart.
   The command of the Lord is clear,
   it gives light to the eyes. R.

   The fear of the Lord is holy,
   abiding for ever.
   The decrees of the Lord are truth
   and all of them just. R.

   They are more to be desired than gold,
   than the purest of gold
   and sweeter are they than honey,
   than honey from the comb. R.

Prayer

Let us pray.

O God, who constantly increase
   your Church
by your call to the nations,
graciously grant
to those you wash clean
   in the waters of Baptism
the assurance of your
   unfailing protection.
Through Christ our Lord.
R. Amen.

Oremus.

Deus, qui Ecclesiam tuam
semper gentium
   vocatione multiplicas,
concede propitius,
ut, quos aqua baptismatis abluis,
continua protectione tuearis.
Per Christum Dominum nostrum.
R. Amen.

SEVENTH READING

A reading from the prophet Ezekiel   36:16-28

I shall pour clean water over you, and I shall give you a new heart.

The word of the Lord was addressed to me as follows: 'Son of man, the members of the House of Israel used to live in their own land, but they defiled it by their conduct and actions. I then discharged my fury at them because of the blood they shed in their land and the idols with which they defiled it. I scattered them among the nations and dispersed them in foreign countries. I sentenced them as their conduct and actions deserved. And now they have profaned my holy name among the nations where they have gone, so that people say of them, "These are the people of the Lord; they have been exiled from his land." But I have been concerned about my holy name, which the House of Israel has profaned among the nations where they have gone. And so, say to the House of Israel, "The Lord says this: I am not doing this for your sake, House of Israel, but for the sake of my holy name, which you have profaned among the nations where you have gone. I mean to display the holiness of my great name, which has been profaned among the nations, which you have profaned among them. And the nations will learn that I am the Lord – it is the Lord who speaks – when I display my holiness for your sake before their eyes. Then I am going to take you from among the nations and gather you together from all the foreign countries, and bring you home to your own land. I shall pour clean water over you and you will be cleansed; I shall cleanse you of all your defilement and all your idols. I shall give you a new heart, and put a new spirit in you; I shall remove the heart of stone from your bodies and give you a heart of flesh instead. I shall put my spirit in you, and make you keep my laws and sincerely respect my observances. You will live in the land which I gave your ancestors. You shall be my people and I will be your God."'

The word of the Lord.

Responsorial Psalm   Pss 41:3,5; 42:3,4. R. Ps 41:1

R. **Like the deer that yearns for running streams,**
   so my soul is yearning for you, my God.

   My soul is thirsting for God.
   the God of my life;
   when can I enter and see
   the face of God? R.

These things I will remember
as I pour out my soul:
how I would lead the rejoicing crowd
into the house of God,
amid cries of gladness and thanksgiving,
the throng wild with joy. R.

O send forth your light and your truth;
let these be my guide.
Let them bring me to your holy mountain
to the place where you dwell. R.

And I will come to the altar of God,
the God of my joy.
My redeemer, I will thank you on the harp,
O God, my God. R.

R. **Like the deer that yearns for running streams,
so my soul is yearning for you, my God.**

If a Baptism takes place the Responsorial Psalm which follows the Fifth Reading, see p.340 is used, or Psalm 50 as follows.

Responsorial Psalm   Ps 50:12-15,18,19. R. v.12

R. **A pure heart create for me, O God.**

A pure heart create for me, O God,
put a steadfast spirit within me.
Do not cast me away from your presence,
nor deprive me of your holy spirit. R.

Give me again the joy of your help;
with a spirit of fervour sustain me,
that I may teach transgressors your ways
and sinners may return to you. R.

For in sacrifice you take no delight,
burnt offering from me you would refuse,
my sacrifice, a contrite spirit.
A humbled, contrite heart you will not spurn. R.

Prayer

Let us pray.	Oremus.
O God of unchanging power and eternal light, look with favour on the wondrous mystery of the whole Church	Deus, incommutabilis virtus et lumen æternum, respice propitius ad totius Ecclesiæ mirabile sacramentum,

and serenely accomplish the work
of human salvation,
which you planned from all eternity;
may the whole world know and see
that what was cast down is raised up,
what had become old is made new,
and all things are restored
   to integrity through Christ,
just as by him they came into being.
Who lives and reigns
   for ever and ever.
R. Amen.

Or:

O God, who by the pages
   of both Testaments
instruct and prepare us to celebrate
   the Paschal Mystery,
grant that we may comprehend
   your mercy,
so that the gifts we receive
   from you this night
may confirm our hope of the gifts
   to come.
Through Christ our Lord.
R. Amen.

et opus salutis humanæ
perpetuæ dispositionis effectu
tranquillius operare;
totusque mundus experiatur
   et videat
deiecta erigi, inveterata renovari
et per ipsum Christum redire
   omnia in integrum,
a quo sumpsere principium.
Qui vivit et regnat
   in sæcula sæculorum.
R. Amen.

Vel:

Deus, qui nos ad celebrandum
   paschale sacramentum
utriusque Testamenti
   paginis instruis,
da nobis intellegere
   misericordiam tuam,
ut ex perceptione
   præsentium munerum
firma sit exspectatio futurorum.
Per Christum Dominum nostrum.
R. Amen.

After the last reading from the Old Testament with its Responsorial Psalm and its prayer, the altar candles are lit, and the Priest intones the hymn Gloria in excelsis Deo (Glory to God in the highest), which is taken up by all, while bells are rung, according to local custom.

The complete musical setting of the Latin text is found in the Graduale Romanum. When the hymn is concluded, the Priest says the Collect in the usual way.

Collect

Let us pray.

O God, who make this most sacred
   night radiant
with the glory
   of the Lord's Resurrection,
stir up in your Church a spirit
   of adoption,

Collecta

Oremus.

Deus, qui hanc
   sacratissimam noctem
gloria dominicæ
   resurrectionis illustras,
excita in Ecclesia tua
   adoptionis spiritum,

so that, renewed in body and mind,	ut, corpore et mente renovati,
we may render you undivided service.	puram tibi exhibeamus servitutem.
Through our Lord Jesus Christ,	Per Dominum nostrum Iesum
your Son,	Christum Filium tuum,
who lives and reigns with you	qui tecum vivit et regnat
in the unity of the Holy Spirit,	in unitate Spiritus Sancti,
one God, for ever and ever.	Deus, per omnia sæcula sæculorum.

FIRST READING

A reading from the letter of St Paul to the Romans   6:3-11

Christ, having been raised from the dead, will never die again.

When we were baptised in Christ Jesus we were baptised in his death; in other words, when we were baptised we went into the tomb with him and joined him in death, so that as Christ was raised from the dead by the Father's glory, we too might live a new life.

If in union with Christ we have imitated his death, we shall also imitate him in his resurrection. We must realise that our former selves have been crucified with him to destroy this sinful body and to free us from the slavery of sin. When a man dies, of course, he has finished with sin.

But we believe that having died with Christ we shall return to life with him: Christ, as we know, having been raised from the dead will never die again. Death has no power over him any more. When he died, he died, once for all, to sin, so his life now is life with God; and in that way, you too must consider yourselves to be dead to sin but alive for God in Christ Jesus.

The word of the Lord.

After the Epistle has been read, all rise, then the Priest solemnly intones the Alleluia three times, raising his voice by a step each time, with all repeating it. If necessary, the psalmist intones the Alleluia.

Responsorial Psalm   Ps 117:1-2,16-17,22-23

R. **Alleluia, alleluia, alleluia!**
   Give thanks to the Lord for he is good,
   for his love has no end.
   Let the sons of Israel say:
   'His love has no end.' R.

   The Lord's right hand has triumphed;
   his right hand raised me.
   I shall not die, I shall live
   and recount his deeds. R.

The stone which the builders rejected
has become the corner stone.
This is the work of the Lord,
a marvel in our eyes. R.

The Priest, in the usual way, puts incense in the thurible and blesses the Deacon. At the Gospel lights are not carried, but only incense.

GOSPEL

YEAR A

A reading from the holy Gospel according to Matthew   28:1-10
He has risen from the dead and now he is going before you into Galilee.

After the sabbath, and towards dawn on the first day of the week, Mary of Magdala and the other Mary went to visit the sepulchre. And all at once there was a violent earthquake, for the angel of the Lord, descending from heaven, came and rolled away the stone and sat on it. His face was like lightning, his robe white as snow. The guards were so shaken, so frightened of him, that they were like dead men. But the angel spoke; and he said to the women, 'There is no need for you to be afraid. I know you are looking for Jesus, who was crucified. He is not here, for he has risen, as he said he would. Come and see the place where he lay, then go quickly and tell his disciples, "He has risen from the dead and now he is going before you to Galilee; it is there you will see him." Now I have told you.' Filled with awe and great joy, the women came quickly away from the tomb and ran to tell the disciples.

And there, coming to meet them, was Jesus. 'Greetings' he said. And the women came up to him and, falling down before him, clasped his feet. Then Jesus said to them, 'Do not be afraid; go and tell my brothers that they must leave for Galilee; they will see me there.'

The Gospel of the Lord.

YEAR B

A reading from the holy Gospel according to Mark   16:1-7
Jesus of Nazareth, who was crucified, has risen.

When the sabbath was over, Mary of Magdala, Mary the mother of James, and Salome, bought spices with which to go and anoint him. And very early in the morning on the first day of the week they went to the tomb, just as the sun was rising.

They had been saying to one another, 'Who will roll away the stone for us from the entrance to the tomb?' But when they looked they could see that the stone – which was very big – had already been rolled back. On entering the tomb they saw a young man in a white robe seated on the right-hand side, and they were struck with amazement. But he said to them, 'There is no need for alarm. You are looking for Jesus of Nazareth, who was crucified: he has risen, he is not here. See, here is the place where they laid him. But you must go and tell his disciples and Peter, "He is going before you to Galilee; it is there you will see him, just as he told you."'

The Gospel of the Lord.

YEAR C

A reading from the holy Gospel according to Luke   24:1-12
Why look among the dead for someone who is alive?

On the first day of week, at the first sign of dawn, the women went to the tomb with the spices they had prepared. They found that the stone had been rolled away from the tomb, but on entering discovered that the body of the Lord Jesus was not there. As they stood there not knowing what to think, two men in brilliant clothes suddenly appeared at their side. Terrified, the women lowered their eyes. But the two men said to them, 'Why look among the dead for someone who is alive? He is not here; he has risen. Remember what he told you when he was still in Galilee: that the Son of Man had to be handed over into the power of sinful men and be crucified, and rise again on the third day?' And they remembered his words.

When the women returned from the tomb they told all this to the Eleven and to all the others. The women were Mary of Magdala, Joanna, and Mary the mother of James. The other women with them also told the apostles, but this story of theirs seemed pure nonsense, and they did not believe them.

Peter, however, went running to the tomb. He bent down and saw the binding cloths, but nothing else; he then went back home, amazed at what had happened.

The Gospel of the Lord.

After the Gospel, the Homily, even if brief, is not to be omitted.

THIRD PART:

Baptismal Liturgy

After the Homily the Baptismal Liturgy begins. The Priest goes with the ministers to the baptismal font, if this can be seen by the faithful. Otherwise a vessel with water is placed in the sanctuary.

Catechumens, if there are any, are called forward and presented by their godparents in front of the assembled Church or, if they are small children, are carried by their parents and godparents.

Then, if there is to be a procession to the baptistery or to the font, it forms immediately. A minister with the paschal candle leads off, and those to be baptised follow him with their godparents, then the ministers, the Deacon, and the Priest. During the procession, the Litany is sung. When the Litany is completed, the Priest gives the address.

If, however, the Baptismal Liturgy takes place in the sanctuary, the Priest immediately makes an introductory statement in these or similar words.

If there are candidates to be baptised:

Dearly beloved,	Precibus nostris, carissimi,
with one heart and one soul,	fratrum nostrorum beatam spem
let us by our prayers	unanimes adiuvemus,
come to the aid of these our brothers	ut Pater omnipotens ad fontem
and sisters in their blessed hope,	regenerationis euntes
so that, as they approach the font	omni misericordiæ suæ
of rebirth,	auxilio prosequatur.
the almighty Father may bestow	
on them	
all his merciful help.	

If the font is to be blessed, but no one is to be baptised:

Dearly beloved,	Dei Patris omnipotentis gratiam,
let us humbly invoke upon	carissimi,
this font	super hunc fontem
the grace of God the almighty Father,	supplices invocemus,
that those who from it are born anew	ut qui ex eo renascentur
may be numbered among the	adoptionis filiis in
children of adoption in Christ.	Christo aggregentur.

The Litany

The Litany is sung by two cantors, with all standing (because it is Easter Time) and responding.

If, however, there is to be a procession of some length to the baptistery, the Litany is sung during the procession; in this case, those to be baptised are called forward before the procession begins, and the procession takes place led by the paschal candle, followed by the catechumens with their godparents, then the ministers, the Deacon, and the Priest. The address should occur before the Blessing of Water.

If no one is to be baptised and the font is not to be blessed, the Litany is omitted, and the Blessing of Water takes place at once.

In the Litany the names of some Saints may be added, especially the Titular Saint of the church and the Patron Saints of the place and of those to be baptised.

Lord, have mercy.			Kyrie, eleison.	
	Lord, have mercy.			Kyrie, eleison.
Christ, have mercy.			Christe, eleison.	
	Christ, have mercy.			Christe, eleison.
Lord, have mercy.			Kyrie, eleison.	
	Lord have mercy.			Kyrie, eleison.
Holy Mary,			Sancta Maria,	
Mother of God,	pray for us.		Mater Dei,	ora pro nobis.
Saint Michael,	pray for us.		Sancte Michael,	ora pro nobis.
Holy Angels of God,	pray for us.		Sancti Angeli Dei,	orate pro nobis.
Saint John the Baptist,	pray for us.		Sancte Ioannes Baptista,	ora pro nobis.
Saint Joseph,	pray for us.		Sancte Ioseph,	ora pro nobis.
Saint Peter and Saint Paul,	pray for us.		Sancti Petre et Paule,	orate pro nobis.
Saint Andrew,	pray for us.		Sancte Andrea,	ora pro nobis.
Saint John,	pray for us.		Sancte Ioannes,	ora pro nobis.
Saint Mary Magdalene,	pray for us.		Sancta Maria Magdalena,	ora pro nobis.
Saint Stephen,	pray for us.		Sancte Stephane,	ora pro nobis.
Saint Ignatius of Antioch,	pray for us.		Sancte Ignati Antiochene,	ora pro nobis.
Saint Lawrence,	pray for us.		Sancte Laurenti,	ora pro nobis.
Saint Perpetua and Saint Felicity,	pray for us.		Sanctæ Perpetua et Felicitas,	orate pro nobis.
Saint Agnes,	pray for us.		Sancta Agnes,	ora pro nobis.
Saint Gregory,	pray for us.		Sancte Gregori,	ora pro nobis.
Saint Augustine,	pray for us.		Sancte Augustine,	ora pro nobis.

Saint Athanasius,	pray for us.	Sancte Athanasi,	ora pro nobis.
Saint Basil,	pray for us.	Sancte Basili,	ora pro nobis.
Saint Martin,	pray for us.	Sancte Martine,	ora pro nobis.
Saint Benedict,	pray for us.	Sancte Benedicte,	ora pro nobis.

Saint Francis and
    Saint Dominic,   pray for us.

Saint Francis Xavier,   pray for us.

Saint John Vianney,   pray for us.

Saint Catherine
    of Siena,   pray for us.

Saint Teresa of Jesus,   pray for us.

All holy men and women,
    Saints of God,   pray for us.

Lord, be merciful
    Lord, deliver us, we pray.

From all evil,
    Lord, deliver us, we pray.

From every sin,
    Lord, deliver us, we pray.

From everlasting death,
    Lord, deliver us, we pray.

By your Incarnation,
    Lord, deliver us, we pray.

By your Death and Resurrection,
    Lord, deliver us, we pray.

By the out-pouring of the Holy
    Spirit,   Lord, deliver us, we pray.

Be merciful to us sinners,
    Lord we ask you to hear our prayer.

If there are candidates to be baptised

Bring these chosen ones to new birth
    through the grace of Baptism,
    Lord, we ask you, hear our prayer.

Sancti Francisce
    et Dominice,   orate pro nobis.

Sancte Francisce
    (Xavier),   ora pro nobis.

Sancte Ioannes
    Maria (Vianney),   ora pro nobis.

Sancta Catharina
    (Senensis),   ora pro nobis.

Sancta Teresia a Iesu, ora pro nobis.

Omnes Sancti
    et Sanctæ Dei,   orate pro nobis.

Propitius esto,   libera nos, Domine.

Ab omni malo, libera nos, Domine.

Ab omni peccato,
             libera nos, Domine.

A morte perpetua,
             libera nos, Domine.

Per incarnationem tuam,
             libera nos, Domine.

Per mortem et
    resurrectionem tuam,
             libera nos, Domine.

Per effusionem Spiritus Sancti,
             libera nos, Domine.

Peccatores,   te rogamus, audi nos.

Ut hos electos per gratiam
    Baptismi regenerare digneris
            te rogamus, audi nos.

If there is no one to be baptised:

Make this font holy by your grace
    for the new birth of your children,
Lord, we ask you, hear our prayer.
	Ut hunc fontem,
	    regenerandis tibi filiis,
	    gratia tua sanctificare digneris
	        te rogamus, audi nos.

Jesus, Son of the Living God,
    Lord, we ask you, hear our prayer.
	Iesu, Fili Dei vivi,
	        te rogamus, audi nos.

Christ, hear us.   Christ, hear us.
Christ, graciously hear us.
    Christ graciously hear us.
	Christe, audi nos. Christe, audi nos.
	Christe, exaudi nos.
	    Christe, exaudi nos.

If there are candidates to be baptised, the Priest, with hands extended, says the following prayer:

Almighty ever-living God,
be present by the mysteries of your
    great love
and send forth the spirit of adoption
to create the new peoples
brought to birth for you in the font
    of Baptism,
so that what is to be carried out
    by our humble service
may be brought to fulfilment
    by your mighty power.
Through Christ our Lord.
R. Amen.
	Omnipotens sempiterne Deus,
	adesto magnæ pietatis
	    tuæ sacramentis,
	et ad recreandos novos populos,
	quos tibi fons baptismatis parturit,
	spiritum adoptionis emitte,
	ut, quod nostræ humilitatis
	    gerendum est ministerio,
	virtutis tuæ impleatur effectu.
	Per Christum Dominum nostrum.
	R. Amen.

Blessing of Baptismal Water

The Priest then blesses the baptismal water, saying the following prayer with hands extended:

O God, who by invisible power
accomplish a wondrous effect
through sacramental signs
and who in many ways have
    prepared water, your creation,
to show forth the grace of Baptism;
	Deus, qui invisibili potentia
	per sacramentorum signa
	    mirabilem operaris effectum,
	et creaturam aquæ multis
	    modis præparasti,
	ut baptismi gratiam demonstraret;

O God, whose Spirit
in the first moments
    of the world's creation
hovered over the waters,
so that the very substance of water
would even then take to itself
    the power to sanctify;

O God, who by the outpouring
    of the flood
foreshadowed regeneration,
so that from the mystery of one
    and the same element of water
would come an end to vice
    and a beginning of virtue;

O God, who caused the children
    of Abraham
to pass dry-shod through the Red Sea,
so that the chosen people,
set free from slavery to Pharaoh,
would prefigure the people
    of the baptised;

O God, whose Son,
baptised by John in the waters
    of the Jordan,
was anointed with the Holy Spirit,
and, as he hung upon the Cross,
gave forth water from his side
    along with blood,
and after his Resurrection,
    commanded his disciples:
'Go forth, teach all nations,
    baptising them
in the name of the Father and of the
    Son and of the Holy Spirit',
look now, we pray, upon the face
    of your Church
and graciously unseal for her
    the fountain of Baptism.

Deus, cuius Spiritus
super aquas inter ipsa mundi
    primordia ferebatur,
ut iam tunc virtutem sanctificandi
aquarum natura conciperet;

Deus, qui regenerationis speciem
in ipsa diluvii effusione signasti,
ut unius eiusdemque
    elementi mysterio
et finis esset vitiis et origo virtutum;

Deus, qui Abrahæ filios
per Mare Rubrum sicco vestigio
    transire fecisti,
ut plebs, a Pharaonis
    servitute liberata,
populum baptizatorum
    præfiguraret;

Deus, cuius Filius, in aqua Iordanis
    a Ioanne baptizatus,
Sancto Spiritu est inunctus,
et, in cruce pendens,
una cum sanguine aquam de latere
    suo produxit,
ac, post resurrectionem suam,
    discipulis iussit:

'Ite, docete omnes gentes,
    baptizantes eos
in nomine Patris et Filii
    et Spiritus Sancti':
respice in faciem Ecclesiæ tuæ,
eique dignare fontem
    baptismatis aperire.

May this water receive
    by the Holy Spirit
the grace of your Only Begotten Son,
so that human nature,
    created in your image,
and washed clean through
    the Sacrament of Baptism
from all the squalor of the life of old,
may be found worthy to rise
    to the life of newborn children
through water and the Holy Spirit.
	Sumat hæc aqua Unigeniti tui
	    gratiam de Spiritu Sancto,
	ut homo, ad imaginem
	    tuam conditus,
	sacramento baptismatis
	a cunctis squaloribus
	    vetustatis ablutus,
	in novam infantiam
	ex aqua et Spiritu Sancto
	    resurgere mereatur.

And, if appropriate, lowering the paschal candle into the water either once or three times, he continues:

May the power of the Holy Spirit, O Lord, we pray, come down through your Son into the fullness of this font,	Descendat, quæsumus, Domine, in hanc plenitudinem fontis per Filium tuum virtus Spiritus Sancti,

and, holding the candle in the water, he continues:

so that all who have been buried
    with Christ
by Baptism into death
may rise again to life with him.
Who lives and reigns with you
    in the unity of the Holy Spirit,
one God, for ever and ever.
R. **Amen.**
	ut omnes, cum Christo consepulti
	per baptismum in mortem,
	ad vitam cum ipso resurgant.
	Qui tecum vivit et regnat
	    in unitate Spiritus Sancti,
	Deus, per omnia sæcula sæculorum.
	R. **Amen.**

Then the candle is lifted out of the water, as the people acclaim:

Springs of water, bless the Lord;
praise and exalt him above all
    for ever.
	Benedicite, fontes, Domino,
	laudate et superexaltate eum
	    in sæcula.

After the blessing of baptismal water and the acclamation of the people, the Priest, standing, puts the prescribed questions to the adults and the parents or godparents of the children, as is set out in the respective Rites of the Roman Ritual, in order for them to make the required renunciation.

If the anointing of the adults with the Oil of Catechumens has not taken place beforehand, as part of the immediately preparatory rites, it occurs at this moment.

Then the Priest questions the adults individually about the faith and, if there are children to be baptised, he requests the triple profession of faith from all the parents and godparents together, as is indicated in the respective Rites.

Where many are to be baptised on this night, it is possible to arrange the rite so that, immediately after the response of those to be baptised and of the godparents and the parents, the Celebrant asks for and receives the renewal of baptismal promises of all present.

When the interrogation is concluded, the Priest baptises the adult elect and the children.

After the Baptism, the Priest anoints the infants with chrism. A white garment is given to each, whether adults or children. Then the Priest or Deacon receives the paschal candle from the hand of the minister, and the candles of the newly baptised are lighted. For infants the rite of Ephphetha is omitted.

Afterwards, unless the baptismal washing and the other explanatory rites have occurred in the sanctuary, a procession returns to the sanctuary, formed as before, with the newly baptised or the godparents or parents carrying lighted candles. During this procession, the baptismal canticle Vidi aquam (I saw water) or another appropriate chant is sung.

If adults have been baptised, the Bishop or, in his absence, the Priest who has conferred Baptism, should at once administer the Sacrament of Confirmation to them in the sanctuary, as is indicated in the Roman Pontifical or Roman Ritual.

The Blessing of Water

If no one present is to be baptised and the font is not to be blessed, the Priest introduces the faithful to the blessing of water, saying:

Dear brothers and sisters,
let us humbly beseech the Lord
    our God
to bless this water he has created,
which will be sprinkled upon us
as a memorial of our Baptism.
May he graciously renew us,
that we may remain faithful
    to the Spirit
whom we have received.
	Dominum Deum nostrum,
	    fratres carissimi,
	suppliciter exoremus,
	ut hanc creaturam aquæ
	    benedicere dignetur,
	super nos aspergendam in nostri
	    memoriam baptismi.
	Ipse autem nos adiuvare dignetur,
	ut Spiritui, quem accepimus,
	    fideles maneamus.

And after a brief pause in silence, he proclaims the following prayer, with hands extended:

Lord our God,
in your mercy be present
   to your people
who keep vigil on this most
   sacred night,
and, for us who recall the wondrous
   work of our creation
and the still greater work
   of our redemption,
graciously bless this water.
For you created water to make
   the fields fruitful
and to refresh and cleanse our bodies.
You also made water the instrument
   of your mercy:
for through water you freed
   your people from slavery
and quenched their thirst
   in the desert;
through water the Prophets
   proclaimed the new covenant
you were to enter upon
   with the human race;
and last of all,
through water, which Christ made
   holy in the Jordan,
you have renewed our
   corrupted nature
in the bath of regeneration.
Therefore, may this water be for us
a memorial of the Baptism
   we have received,
and grant that we may share
in the gladness of our brothers
   and sisters,
who at Easter have received
   their Baptism.
Through Christ our Lord.
R. Amen.

Domine Deus noster,
populo tuo hac nocte
   sacratissima vigilanti
adesto propitius;
et nobis, mirabile nostræ
   creationis opus,
sed et redemptionis nostræ
   mirabilius, memorantibus,
hanc aquam benedicere tu dignare.

Ipsam enim tu fecisti,
ut et arva fecunditate donaret,
et levamen corporibus nostris
   munditiamque præberet.

Aquam etiam tuæ ministram
   misericordiæ condidisti;
nam per ipsam solvisti tui
   populi servitutem
illiusque sitim in deserto sedasti;
per ipsam novum fœdus
   nuntiaverunt prophetæ,
quod eras cum hominibus initurus;
per ipsam denique, quam Christus
   in Iordane sacravit,
corruptam naturæ
   nostræ substantiam
in regenerationis lavacro renovasti.

Sit igitur hæc aqua nobis suscepti
   baptismatis memoria,
et cum fratribus nostris,
   qui sunt in Paschate baptizati,
gaudia nos tribuas sociare.
Per Christum Dominum nostrum.
R. Amen.

The Renewal of Baptismal Promises

When the Rite of Baptism (and Confirmation) has been completed or, if this has not taken place, after the blessing of water, all stand, holding lighted candles in their hands, and renew the promise of baptismal faith, unless this has already been done together with those to be baptised.

The Priest addresses the faithful in these or similar words:

Dear brethren (brothers and sisters), through the Paschal Mystery we have been buried with Christ in Baptism, so that we may walk with him in newness of life. And so, now that our Lenten observance is concluded, let us renew the promises of Holy Baptism, by which we once renounced Satan and his works and promised to serve God in the holy Catholic Church. And so I ask you:

Priest: Do you renounce Satan?
All: I do.

Priest: And all his works?
All: I do.

Priest: And all his empty show?
All: I do.

Or:

Priest: Do you renounce sin, so as to live in the freedom of the children of God?
All: I do.

Priest: Do you renounce the lure of evil, so that sin may have no mastery over you?
All: I do.

Per paschale mysterium, fratres carissimi, in baptismo consepulti sumus cum Christo, ut cum eo in novitate vitæ ambulemus. Quapropter, quadragesimali observatione absoluta, sancti baptismatis promissiones renovemus, quibus olim Satanæ et operibus eius abrenuntiavimus, et Deo in sancta Ecclesia catholica servire promisimus. Quapropter:

Sacerdos: Abrenutiatis Satanæ?
Omnes: Abrenuntio.

Sacerdos: Et omnibus operibus eius?
Omnes: Abrenuntio.

Sacerdos: Et omnibus pompis eius?
Omnes: Abrenuntio.

Vel:

Sacerdos: Abrenuntiatis peccato, ut in libertate filiorum Dei vivatis?
Omnes: Abrenuntio.

Sacerdos: Abrenuntiatis seductionibus iniquitatis, ne pecccatum vobis dominetur?
Omnes: Abrenuntio.

Priest: Do you renounce Satan,
the author and prince of sin?
All:　I do.

Sacerdos:　Abrenuntiatis Satanæ,
qui est auctor et princeps peccati?
Omnes:　Abrenuntio.

If the situation warrants, this second formula may be adapted by Conferences of Bishops according to local needs.

Then the Priest continues:

Priest:　　Do you believe in God,
the Father almighty,
Creator of heaven and earth?
All:　I do.

Sacerdos:　Creditis in Deum Patrem
omnipotentem,
creatorem cæli et terræ?
Omnes:　Credo.

Priest: Do you believe in Jesus
Christ, his only Son, our Lord,
who was born of the Virgin Mary,
suffered death and was buried,
rose again from the dead
and is seated at the right hand
of the Father?
All:　I do.

Sacerdos:　Creditis in Iesum
Christum, Filium eius unicum,
Dominum nostrum,
natum ex Maria Virgine,
passum et sepultum,
qui a mortuis resurrexit
et sedet ad dexteram Patris?
Omnes:　Credo.

Priest: Do you believe
in the Holy Spirit,
the holy Catholic Church,
the communion of saints,
the forgiveness of sins,
the resurrection of the body,
and life everlasting?
All:　I do.

Sacerdos:　Creditis in Spiritum
Sanctum,
sanctam Ecclesiam catholicam,
sanctorum communionem,
remissionem peccatorum,
carnis resurrectionem et
vitam æternam?
Omnes:　Credo.

And the Priest concludes:

And may almighty God, the Father
of our Lord Jesus Christ,
who has given us new birth by water
and the Holy Spirit
and bestowed on us forgiveness
of our sins,
keep us by his grace,
in Christ Jesus our Lord,
for eternal life.
All: Amen.

Et Deus omnipotens, Pater Domini
nostri Iesu Christi,
qui nos regeneravit ex aqua
et Spiritu Sancto,
quique nobis dedit
remissionem peccatorum,
ipse nos custodiat gratia sua,
in Christo Iesu Domino nostro,
in vitam æternam.
Omnes: Amen.

The Priest sprinkles the people with the blessed water, while all sing:

Antiphon

I saw water flowing
    from the Temple,
from its right-hand side, alleluia;
and all to whom this water
    came were saved
and shall say: Alleluia, alleluia.
	Vidi aquam egredientem
	    de templo,
	a latere dextro, alleluia;
	et omnes, ad quos pervenit aqua
	    ista, salvi facti sunt
	et dicent: Alleluia, alleluia.

Another chant that is baptismal in character may also be sung.

Meanwhile the newly baptised are led to their place among the faithful.

If the blessing of baptismal water has not taken place in the baptistery, the Deacon and the ministers reverently carry the vessel of water to the font.

If the blessing of the font has not occurred, the blessed water is put aside in an appropriate place.

After the sprinkling, the Priest returns to the chair where, omitting the Creed, he directs the Universal Prayer, in which the newly baptised participate for the first time.

FOURTH PART:
The Liturgy of the Eucharist

The Priest goes to the altar and begins the Liturgy of the Eucharist in the usual way.

It is desirable that the bread and wine be brought forward by the newly baptised or, if they are children, by their parents or godparents.

Prayer over the Offerings	Super oblata

Accept, we ask, O Lord,
the prayers of your people
with the sacrificial offerings,
that what has begun
    in the paschal mysteries
may, by the working of your power,
bring us to the healing of eternity.
Through Christ our Lord.
	Suscipe, quæsumus, Domine,
	    preces populi tui
	cum oblationibus hostiarum,
	ut, paschalibus initiata mysteriis,
	ad æternitatis nobis medelam,
	    te operante, proficiant.
	Per Christum Dominum nostrum.

Preface I of Easter: The Paschal Mystery (. . .on this night above all. . .), pp.558-561.

In the Eucharistic Prayer, a commemoration is made of the baptised and their godparents in accord with the formulas which are found in the Roman Missal and Roman Ritual for each of the Eucharistic Prayers.

Before the Ecce Agnus Dei (Behold the Lamb of God), the Priest may briefly address the newly baptised about receiving their first Communion and about the excellence of this great mystery, which is the climax of Initiation and the centre of the whole of Christian life.

It is desirable that the newly baptised receive Holy Communion under both kinds, together with their godfathers, godmothers, and Catholic parents and spouses, as well as their lay catechists. It is even appropriate that, with the consent of the Diocesan Bishop, where the occasion suggests this, all the faithful be admitted to Holy Communion under both kinds.

Communion Antiphon 1 Co 5:7-8
Christ our Passover
    has been sacrificed;
therefore let us keep the feast
with the unleavened bread
    of purity and truth, alleluia.
Psalm 117 may appropriately be sung.

Ant. ad communionem
Pascha nostrum immolatus
    est Christus;
itaque epulemur in azymis
    sinceritatis et veritatis, alleluia.

Prayer after Communion
Pour out on us, O Lord,
    the Spirit of your love,
and in your kindness make those
    you have nourished
by this paschal Sacrament
one in mind and heart.
Through Christ our Lord.

Post communionem
Spiritum nobis, Domine,
    tuæ caritatis infunde,
ut, quos sacramentis
    paschalibus satiasti,
tua facias pietate concordes.
Per Christum Dominum nostrum.

Solemn Blessing
May almighty God bless you
through today's Easter Solemnity
and, in his compassion,
defend you from every assault of sin.
R. Amen.

Benedictio sollemnis
Benedicat vos omnipotens Deus,
hodierna interveniente
    sollemnitate paschali,
et ab omni miseratus defendat
    incursione peccati.
R. Amen.

And may he, who restores you
    to eternal life
in the Resurrection
    of his Only Begotten,
endow you with the prize
    of immortality.
R. Amen.

Et qui ad æternam vitam
in Unigeniti sui resurrectione
    vos reparat,
vos præmiis
    immortalitatis adimpleat.
R. Amen.

Now that the days of the Lord's
    Passion have drawn to a close,
may you who celebrate
    the gladness of the Paschal Feast
come with Christ's help,
    and exulting in spirit,
to those feasts that are celebrated
    in eternal joy.
R. Amen.

Et qui, expletis passionis
    dominicæ diebus,
paschalis festi gaudia celebratis,
ad ea festa, quæ lætitiis
    peraguntur æternis,
ipso opitulante, exsultantibus
animis veniatis.
R. Amen.

And may the blessing
of almighty God,
the Father, and the Son,
✠ and the Holy Spirit,
come down on you and remain
with you for ever.
R. Amen.

Et benedictio Dei omnipotentis,
Patris, et Filii, ✠ et Spiritus Sancti,
descendat super vos
et maneat semper.
R. Amen.

The final blessing formula from the Rite of Baptism of Adults or of Children may also be used, according to circumstances.

To dismiss the people the Deacon or, if there is no Deacon, the Priest himself sings or says:

Go forth, the Mass is ended,
alleluia, alleluia.

Ite, missa est, alleluia, alleluia.

Or:

Vel:

Go in peace, alleluia, alleluia.

Ite in pace, alleluia, alleluia

All reply:

Omnes respondent:

Thanks be to God, alleluia, alleluia.

Deo gratias, alleluia, alleluia.

This practice is observed throughout the Octave of Easter.

The paschal candle is lit in all the more solemn liturgical celebrations of this period.

At the Mass during the Day

We know that Christ has truly risen from the dead. Yes, indeed! This is the fundamental core of our profession of faith; this is the cry of victory that unites us all today. And if Jesus is risen, and is therefore alive, who will ever be able to separate us from him? Who will ever be able to deprive us of the love of him who has conquered hatred and overcome death? The Easter proclamation spreads throughout the world with the joyful song of the Alleluia. Let us sing it with our lips, and let us sing it above all with our hearts and our lives, with a manner of life that is "unleavened", that is to say, simple, humble, and fruitful in good works. The Risen One goes before us and he accompanies us along the paths of the world. He is our hope, He is the true peace of the world.

(Pope Benedict XVI)

Entrance Antiphon Cf. Ps 138:18,5-6

I HAVE risen, and I am with you still, alleluia.
You have laid your hand upon me, alleluia.
Too wonderful for me, this knowledge, alleluia, alleluia.

Or: Lk 24:34; Cf. Rv 1:6

The Lord is truly risen, alleluia.
To him be glory and power
for all the ages of eternity, alleluia, alleluia.

Ant. ad introitum

RESURREXI, et adhuc tecum sum, alleluia:
posuisti super me manum tuam, alleluia:
mirabilis facta est scientia tua, alleluia, alleluia.

Vel:

Surrexit Dominus vere, alleluia.
Ipsi gloria et imperium
per universa æternitatis sæcula, alleluia, alleluia.

The Gloria in excelsis (Glory to God in the highest) is said.

Collect

O God, who on this day,
through your Only Begotten Son,
have conquered death
and unlocked for us the path
to eternity,
grant, we pray, that we who keep
the solemnity of the
Lord's Resurrection
may, through the renewal brought
by your Spirit,
rise up in the light of life.

Collecta

Deus, qui hodierna die,
per Unigenitum tuum,
æternitatis nobis aditum,
devicta morte, reserasti,
da nobis, quæsumus,
ut, qui resurrectionis dominicæ
sollemnia colimus,
per innovationem tui Spiritus
in lumine vitæ resurgamus.
Per Dominum nostrum Iesum
Christum Filium tuum,

Through our Lord Jesus Christ,
    your Son,
who lives and reigns with you
    in the unity of the Holy Spirit,
one God, for ever and ever.

qui tecum vivit et regnat
    in unitate Spiritus Sancti,
Deus, per omnia sæcula sæculorum.

FIRST READING

A reading from the Acts of the Apostles   10:34,37-43

We have eaten and drunk with him after his resurrection.

Peter addressed Cornelius and his household: 'You must have heard about the recent happenings in Judaea; about Jesus of Nazareth and how he began in Galilee, after John had been preaching baptism. God had anointed him with the Holy Spirit and with power, and because God was with him, Jesus went about doing good and curing all who had fallen into the power of the devil. Now I, and those with me, can witness to everything he did throughout the countryside of Judaea and in Jerusalem itself: and also to the fact that they killed him by hanging him on a tree, yet three days afterwards God raised him to life and allowed him to be seen, not by the whole people but only by certain witnesses God had chosen beforehand. Now we are those witnesses – we have eaten and drunk with him after his resurrection from the dead – and he has ordered us to proclaim this to his people and to tell them that God has appointed him to judge everyone, alive or dead. It is to him that all the prophets bear this witness: that all who believe in Jesus will have their sins forgiven through his name.'

The word of the Lord.

Responsorial Psalm   Ps 117:1-2,16-17,22-23. R. v. 24

R. **This day was made by the Lord;**
    we rejoice and are glad.
    Or: **Alleluia, alleluia, alleluia!**

Give thanks to the Lord for he is good,
for his love has no end.
Let the sons of Israel say:
'His love has no end.' R.

The Lord's right hand has triumphed;
his right hand raised me.
I shall not die, I shall live
and recount his deeds. R.

The stone which the builders rejected
has become the corner stone.
This is the work of the Lord,
a marvel in our eyes. R.

SECOND READING

A reading from the letter of St Paul to the Colossians   3:1-4

You must look for the things that are in heaven, where Christ is.

Since you have been brought back to true life with Christ, you must look for the things that are in heaven, where Christ is, sitting at God's right hand. Let your thoughts be on heavenly things, not on the things that are on the earth, because you have died, and now the life you have is hidden with Christ in God. But when Christ is revealed – and he is your life – you too will be revealed in all your glory with him.

The word of the Lord.

ALTERNATIVE SECOND READING

A reading from the first letter of St Paul to the Corinthians   5:6-8

Get rid of the old yeast, and make yourselves into a completely new batch of bread.

You must know how even a small amount of yeast is enough to leaven all the dough, so get rid of all the old yeast, and make yourselves into a completely new batch of bread, unleavened as you are meant to be. Christ, our Passover, has been sacrificed; let us celebrate the feast, by getting rid of all the old yeast of evil and wickedness, having only the unleavened bread of sincerity and truth.

The word of the Lord.

The sequence is said or sung on this day. On the weekdays of the Octave of Easter, its use is optional.

SEQUENCE

Christians, to the Paschal Victim
    offer sacrifice and praise.
The sheep are ransomed
    by the Lamb;
and Christ, the undefiled,
hath sinners to his Father reconciled.
	Victimæ paschali laudes
	    immolent Christiani.
	Agnus redemit oves:
	    Christus innocens Patri
	    reconciliavit peccatores.

Death with life contended:
    combat strangely ended!
Life's own Champion, slain,
    yet lives to reign.
	Mors et vita duello
	    conflixere mirando:
	    dux vitæ mortuus regnat vivus.

Tell us, Mary:
    say what thou didst see
    upon the way.
	Dic nobis, Maria,
	    quid vidisti in via?

The tomb the Living did enclose;	Sepulcrum Christi viventis,
I saw Christ's glory as he rose!	gloriam vidi resurgentis.
The angels there attesting;	Angelicos testes,
shroud with grave-clothes resting.	sudarium et vestes.
Christ, my hope, has risen:	Surrexit Christus spes mea:
he goes before you into Galilee.	præcedet vos in Galilæam.
That Christ is truly risen	Scimus Christum surrexisse
from the dead we know.	a mortuis vere:
Victorious king, thy mercy show!	tu nobis, victor Rex, miserere.

Gospel Acclamation   1 Co 5:7-8

R. **Alleluia, alleluia!**
Christ, our passover, has been sacrificed;
let us celebrate the feast then, in the Lord.
R. **Alleluia!**

GOSPEL
A reading from the holy Gospel according to John   20:1-9
He must rise from the dead.

It was very early on the first day of the week and still dark, when Mary of Magdala came to the tomb. She saw that the stone had been moved away from the tomb and came running to Simon Peter and the other disciple, the one Jesus loved. 'They have taken the Lord out of the tomb' she said 'and we don't know where they have put him.'

So Peter set out with the other disciple to go to the tomb. They ran together, but the other disciple, running faster than Peter, reached the tomb first; he bent down and saw the linen cloths lying on the ground, but did not go in. Simon Peter who was following now came up, went right into the tomb, saw the linen cloths on the ground, and also the cloth that had been over his head; this was not with the linen cloths but rolled up in a place by itself. Then the other disciple who had reached the tomb first also went in; he saw and he believed. Till this moment they had failed to understand the teaching of scripture, that he must rise from the dead.

The Gospel of the Lord.

As an alternative, the Gospel of the Mass of Easter Night may be read pp.347-348.
At an evening Mass, Luke 24:13-35 may be used as an alternative pp.375-376.

The Creed is said. However, in Easter Sunday Masses which are celebrated with a congregation, the rite of the renewal of baptismal promises may take place after the homily, according to the text used at the Easter Vigil (pp.357-359). In that case the Creed is omitted.

Prayer over the Offerings	Super oblata
Exultant with paschal gladness, O Lord,	Sacrificia, Domine, paschalibus gaudiis
we offer the sacrifice	exsultantes offerimus,
by which your Church	quibus Ecclesia tua
is wondrously reborn and nourished.	mirabiliter renascitur et nutritur.
Through Christ our Lord.	Per Christum Dominum nostrum.

Preface I of Easter, The Paschal Mystery, pp.558-561.

When the Roman Canon is used, the proper forms of the Communicantes (In communion with those) and Hanc igitur (Therefore, Lord, we pray) are said.

Communion Antiphon 1 Co 5:7-8	Ant. ad communionem
Christ our Passover has been sacrificed, alleluia;	Pascha nostrum immolatus est Christus, alleluia;
therefore let us keep the feast with the unleavened bread	itaque epulemur in azymis sinceritatis
of purity and truth, alleluia, alleluia.	et veritatis, alleluia, alleluia.

Prayer after Communion	Post communionem
Look upon your Church, O God, with unfailing love and favour,	Perpetuo, Deus, Ecclesiam tuam pio favore tuere,
so that, renewed by the paschal mysteries,	ut, paschalibus renovata mysteriis,
she may come to the glory of the resurrection.	ad resurrectionis perveniat claritatem.
Through Christ our Lord.	Per Christum Dominum nostrum.

To impart the blessing at the end of Mass, the Priest may appropriately use the formula of Solemn Blessing for the Mass of the Easter Vigil, pp.360-361.

For the dismissal of the people, the following is sung or said:

Go forth, the Mass is ended, alleluia, alleluia.	Ite, missa est, alleluia, alleluia.
Or:	Vel:
Go in peace, alleluia, alleluia.	Ite in pace, alleluia, alleluia
R. Thanks be to God, alleluia, alleluia.	R. Deo gratias, alleluia, alleluia.

SECOND SUNDAY OF EASTER
(YEAR A)

(or of Divine Mercy)

"Peace be with you!" This is how Jesus greets his Apostles in the Gospel for this Sunday, that closes the Octave of Easter. Peace is the gift of God. The Creator himself has written the law of respect for life on the human heart: "If anyone sheds the blood of a man, by man shall his blood be shed; for in the image of God has he made man", is said in Genesis (9:6). When the merciless logic of arms prevails everywhere, only God can redirect hearts to thoughts of peace. Only he can give the energies that are necessary to be freed from hatred and the thirst for revenge and to undertake the process of negotiation for an agreement and for peace. The liturgy today invites us to see in Divine Mercy the source of that authentic peace that the risen Christ offers us. The wounds of the risen and glorious Lord are the permanent sign of God's merciful love for humanity. From them flows a spiritual light that enlightens consciences and pours into hearts comfort and hope.

(Blessed Pope John Paul II)

Entrance Antiphon 1 P 2:2	Ant. ad introitum

LIKE newborn infants,
  you must long for the pure,
spiritual milk,
that in him you may grow
  to salvation, alleluia.

QUASI modo geniti infantes,
  rationabile, sine dolo
  lac concupiscite,
ut in eo crescatis in salutem,
  alleluia.

Or: 4 Esdr 2:36-37	Vel:

Receive the joy of your glory,
  giving thanks to God,
who has called you into
  the heavenly kingdom, alleluia.

Accipite iucunditatem gloriæ vestræ,
gratias agentes Deo,
qui vos ad cælestia regna vocavit,
  alleluia.

The Gloria in excelsis (Glory to God in the highest) is said.

Collect

God of everlasting mercy,
who, in the very recurrence
    of the paschal feast
kindle the faith of the people you
    have made your own,
increase, we pray, the grace you
    have bestowed,
that all may grasp
    and rightly understand
in what font they have been washed,
by whose Spirit they have
    been reborn,
by whose Blood they have
    been redeemed.
Through our Lord Jesus Christ,
    your Son,
who lives and reigns with you
    in the unity of the Holy Spirit,
one God, for ever and ever.

Collecta

Deus misericordiæ sempiternæ,
qui in ipso paschalis festi recursu
fidem sacratæ tibi plebis accendis,
auge gratiam quam dedisti,
ut digna omnes
    intellegentia comprehendant,
quo lavacro abluti,
    quo Spiritu regenerati,
quo sanguine sunt redempti.
Per Dominum nostrum Iesum
    Christum Filium tuum,
qui tecum vivit et regnat
    in unitate Spiritus Sancti,
Deus, per omnia sæcula sæculorum.

FIRST READING

A reading from the Acts of the Apostles   2:42-47

The faithful all lived together and owned everything in common.

The whole community remained faithful to the teaching of the apostles, to the brotherhood, to the breaking of bread and to the prayers.

The many miracles and signs worked through the apostles made a deep impression on everyone.

The faithful all lived together and owned everything in common; they sold their goods and possessions and shared out the proceeds among themselves according to what each one needed.

They went as a body to the Temple every day but met in their houses for the breaking of bread; they shared their food gladly and generously; they praised God and were looked up to by everyone. Day by day the Lord added to their community those destined to be saved.

The word of the Lord.

Responsorial Psalm   Ps 117:2-4,13-15,22-24. R. v.1

R. **Give thanks to the Lord for he is good,**
    for his love has no end.
    Or: **Alleluia, alleluia, alleluia!**

Let the sons of Israel say:
'His love has no end.'
Let the sons of Aaron say:
'His love has no end.'
Let those who fear the Lord say:
'His love has no end.' R.

I was thrust, thrust down and falling
but the Lord was my helper.
The Lord is my strength and my song;
he was my saviour.
There are shouts of joy and victory
in the tents of the just. R.

The stone which the builders rejected
has become the corner stone.
This is the work of the Lord
a marvel in our eyes.
This day was made by the Lord;
we rejoice and are glad. R.

SECOND READING

A reading from the first letter of St Peter   1:3-9

In his great mercy he has given us a new birth as his sons by raising Jesus from the dead.

Blessed be God the Father of our Lord Jesus Christ, who in his great mercy has given us a new birth as his sons, by raising Jesus Christ from the dead, so that we have a sure hope and the promise of an inheritance that can never be spoilt or soiled and never fade away, because it is being kept for you in the heavens. Through your faith, God's power will guard you until the salvation which had been prepared is revealed at the end of time. This is a cause of great joy for you, even though you may for a short time have to bear being plagued by all sorts of trials; so that, when Jesus Christ is revealed, your faith will have been tested and proved like gold – only it is more precious than gold, which is corruptible even though it bears testing by fire – and then you will have praise and glory and honour. You did not see him, yet you love him; and still without seeing him, you are already filled with a joy so glorious that it cannot be described, because you believe; and you are sure of the end to which your faith looks forward, that is, the salvation of your souls.

The word of the Lord.

Easter Sequence can be sung here, see pp.364-365.

Gospel Acclamation   Jn 20:29

R. **Alleluia, alleluia!**
Jesus said: 'You believe because you can see me.
Happy are those who have not seen and yet believe.'
R. **Alleluia!**

GOSPEL

A reading from the holy Gospel according to John   20:19-31

Eight days later, Jesus came.

In the evening of that same day, the first day of the week, the doors were closed in the room where the disciples were, for fear of the Jews. Jesus came and stood among them. He said to them, 'Peace be with you,' and showed them his hands and his side. The disciples were filled with joy when they saw the Lord, and he said to them again,

'Peace be with you.
As the Father sent me,
so am I sending you.'

After saying this he breathed on them and said:

'Receive the Holy Spirit.
For those whose sins you forgive,
they are forgiven;
for those whose sins you retain,
they are retained.'

Thomas, called the Twin, who was one of the Twelve, was not with them when Jesus came. When the disciples said, 'We have seen the Lord,' he answered, 'Unless I see the holes that the nails made in his hands and can put my finger into the holes they made, and unless I can put my hand into his side, I refuse to believe.' Eight days later the disciples were in the house again and Thomas was with them. The doors were closed, but Jesus came in and stood among them. 'Peace be with you,' he said. Then he spoke to Thomas, 'Put your finger here; look, here are my hands. Give me your hand; put it into my side. Doubt no longer but believe.' Thomas replied, 'My Lord and my God!'

Jesus said to him:

'You believe because you can see me.

Happy are those who have not seen and yet believe.'

There were many other signs that Jesus worked and the disciples saw, but they are not recorded in this book. These are recorded so that you may believe that Jesus is the Christ, the Son of God, and that believing this you may have life through his name.

The Gospel of the Lord.

The Creed is said.

Prayer over the Offerings
Accept, O Lord, we pray,
the oblations of your people
(and of those you have brought
    to new birth),
that, renewed by confession of your
    name and by Baptism,
they may attain unending happiness.
Through Christ our Lord.

Super oblata
Suscipe, quæsumus, Domine,
    plebis tuæ
(et tuorum renatorum) oblationes,
ut, confessione tui nominis
    et baptismate renovati,
sempiternam beatitudinem
    consequantur.
Per Christum Dominum nostrum.

Preface I of Easter: The Paschal Mystery (. . .on this day above all. . .), pp.558-561. When the Roman Canon is used, the proper forms of the Communicantes (In communion with those) and Hanc igitur (Therefore, Lord, we pray) are said.

Communion Antiphon Cf. Jn 20:27
Bring your hand and feel the place
    of the nails,
and do not be unbelieving
    but believing, alleluia.

Ant. ad communionem
Mitte manum tuam, et cognosce
    loca clavorum,
et noli esse incredulus, sed fidelis,
    alleluia.

Prayer after Communion
Grant, we pray, almighty God,
that our reception of this paschal
    Sacrament
may have a continuing effect
in our minds and hearts.
Through Christ our Lord.

Post communionem
Concede, quæsumus,
    omnipotens Deus,
ut paschalis perceptio sacramenti
continua in nostris
    mentibus perseveret.
Per Christum Dominum nostrum.

A formula of Solemn Blessing, pp.360-361, may be used.

For the dismissal of the people, the following is sung or said: Go forth, the Mass is ended, alleluia, alleluia. Or: Go in peace, alleluia, alleluia. The people respond: Thanks be to God, alleluia, alleluia.

THIRD SUNDAY OF EASTER (YEAR A)

The Gospel of this Sunday – the Third of Easter – is the famous account of the disciples of Emmaus. The locality of Emmaus has not been identified with certainty. There are various hypotheses and this one is not without an evocativeness of its own for it allows us to think that Emmaus actually represents every place: the road that leads there is the road every Christian, every person, takes. The Risen Jesus makes himself our travelling companion as we go on our way, to rekindle the warmth of faith and hope in our hearts and to break the bread of eternal life.

(Pope Benedict XVI)

Entrance Antiphon   Cf. Ps 65:1-2

CRY out with joy to God,
all the earth;
O sing to the glory of his name.
O render him glorious praise,
    alleluia.

Ant. ad introitum

IUBILATE Deo, omnis terra,
psalmum dicite nomini eius,
date gloriam laudi eius, alleluia.

The Gloria in excelsis (Glory to God in the highest) is said.

Collect

May your people exult for ever,
    O God,
in renewed youthfulness of spirit,
so that, rejoicing now in the restored
    glory of our adoption,
we may look forward
    in confident hope
to the rejoicing of the day
    of resurrection.
Through our Lord Jesus Christ,
    your Son,
who lives and reigns with you
    in the unity of the Holy Spirit,
one God, for ever and ever.

Collecta

Semper exsultet populus tuus, Deus,
renovata animæ iuventute,
ut, qui nunc lætatur in adoptionis
    se gloriam restitutum,
resurrectionis diem spe certæ
    gratulationis exspectet.
Per Dominum nostrum Iesum
    Christum Filium tuum,
qui tecum vivit et regnat
    in unitate Spiritus Sancti,
Deus, per omnia sæcula sæculorum.

FIRST READING

A reading from the Acts of the Apostles   2:14,22-33

It was impossible for him to be held in the power of Hades.

On the day of Pentecost Peter stood up with the Eleven and addressed the crowd in a loud voice: 'Men of Israel, listen to what I am going to say: Jesus the Nazarene was a man commended to you by God by the miracles and portents and signs that God worked through him when he was among you, as you all know. This man, who was put into your power by the deliberate intention and foreknowledge of God, you took and had crucified by men outside the Law. You killed him, but God raised him to life, freeing him from the pangs of Hades; for it was impossible for him to be held in its power since, as David says of him:

> I saw the Lord before me always,
> for with him at my right hand nothing can shake me.
> So my heart was glad
> and my tongue cried out with joy;
> my body, too, will rest in the hope
> that you will not abandon my soul to Hades
> nor allow your holy one to experience corruption.
> You have made known the way of life to me,
> you will fill me with gladness through your presence.

'Brothers, no one can deny that the patriarch David himself is dead and buried: his tomb is still with us. But since he was a prophet, and knew that God had sworn him an oath to make one of his descendants succeed him on the throne, what he foresaw and spoke about was the resurrection of the Christ: he is the one who was not abandoned to Hades, and whose body did not experience corruption. God raised this man Jesus to life, and all of us are witnesses to that. Now raised to the heights by God's right hand, he has received from the Father the Holy Spirit, who was promised, and what you see and hear is the outpouring of that Spirit.'

The word of the Lord.

Responsorial Psalm   Ps 15:1-2,5,7-11. R. v.11

R. **Show us, Lord, the path of life.**
Or: **Alleluia!**

> Preserve me, God, I take refuge in you.
> I say to the Lord: 'You are my God.

O Lord, it is you who are my portion and cup;
it is you yourself who are my prize.' R.

I will bless the Lord who gives me counsel,
who even at night directs my heart.
I keep the Lord ever in my sight:
since he is at my right hand, I shall stand firm. R.

And so my heart rejoices, my soul is glad;
even my body shall rest in safety.
For you will not leave my soul among the dead,
nor let your beloved know decay. R.

You will show me the path of life,
the fullness of joy in your presence,
at your right hand happiness for ever. R.

R. **Show us, Lord, the path of life.**
Or: **Alleluia!**

SECOND READING

A reading from the first letter of St Peter   1:17-21

*Your ransom was paid in the precious blood of a lamb without spot or stain,
namely, Christ.*

If you are acknowledging as your Father one who has no favourites and
judges everyone according to what he has done, you must be scrupulously
careful as long as you are living away from your home. Remember, the
ransom that was paid to free you from the useless way of life your ancestors
handed down was not paid in anything corruptible, neither in silver nor
gold, but in the precious blood of a lamb without spot or stain, namely
Christ; who though known since before the world was made, has been
revealed only in our time, the end of the ages, for your sake. Through him
you now have faith in God, who raised him from the dead and gave him
glory for that very reason – so that you would have faith and hope in God.

The word of the Lord.

Gospel Acclamation   Cf. Lk 24:32

R. **Alleluia, alleluia!**
Lord Jesus, explain the scriptures to us.
Make our hearts burn within us as you talk to us.
R. **Alleluia!**

GOSPEL

A reading from the holy Gospel according to Luke   24:13-35

They recognised him at the breaking of bread.

Two of the disciples of Jesus were on their way to a village called Emmaus, seven miles from Jerusalem, and they were talking together about all that had happened. Now as they talked this over, Jesus himself came up and walked by their side; but something prevented them from recognising him. He said to them, 'What matters are you discussing as you walk along?' They stopped short, their faces downcast.

Then one of them, called Cleopas, answered him, 'You must be the only person staying in Jerusalem who does not know the things that have been happening there these last few days.' 'What things?' he asked. 'All about Jesus of Nazareth' they answered 'who proved he was a great prophet by the things he said and did in the sight of God and of the whole people; and how our chief priests and our leaders handed him over to be sentenced to death, and had him crucified. Our own hope had been that he would be the one to set Israel free. And this is not all: two whole days have gone by since it all happened; and some women from our group have astounded us: they went to the tomb in the early morning, and when they did not find the body, they came back to tell us they had seen a vision of angels who declared he was alive. Some of our friends went to the tomb and found everything exactly as the women had reported, but of him they saw nothing.'

Then he said to them, 'You foolish men! So slow to believe the full message of the prophets! Was it not ordained that the Christ should suffer and so enter into his glory?' Then, starting with Moses and going through all the prophets, he explained to them the passages throughout the scriptures that were about himself.

When they drew near to the village to which they were going, he made as if to go on; but they pressed him to stay with them. 'It is nearly evening' they said 'and the day is almost over.' So he went in to stay with them. Now while he was with them at table, he took the bread and said the blessing; then he broke it and handed it to them. And their eyes were opened and they recognised him; but he had vanished from their sight. Then they said to each other, 'Did not our hearts burn within us as he talked to us on the road and explained the scriptures to us?'

They set out that instant and returned to Jerusalem. There they found the Eleven assembled together with their companions, who said to them, 'Yes, it is true. The Lord has risen and has appeared to Simon.' Then they told their story of what had happened on the road and how they had recognised him at the breaking of bread.

The Gospel of the Lord.

The Creed is said.

Prayer over the Offerings

Receive, O Lord, we pray,
   these offerings of your
      exultant Church,
and, as you have given her cause
      for such great gladness,
grant also that the gifts we bring
may bear fruit in perpetual happiness.
Through Christ our Lord.

Preface of Easter, pp.558-563.

Super oblata

Suscipe munera, Domine,
   quæsumus, exsultantis Ecclesiæ,
et cui causam tanti gaudii præstitisti,
perpetuæ fructum concede lætitiæ.
Per Christum Dominum nostrum.

Communion Antiphon   Lk 24:35

The disciples recognised
   the Lord Jesus
in the breaking of the bread, alleluia.

Ant. ad communionem

Cognoverunt discipuli
   Dominum Iesum
in fractione panis, alleluia.

Prayer after Communion

Look with kindness upon
   your people, O Lord,
and grant, we pray,
that those you were pleased
   to renew by eternal mysteries
may attain in their flesh
the incorruptible glory
   of the resurrection.
Through Christ our Lord.

Post communionem

Populum tuum, quæsumus,
   Domine, intuere benignus,
et, quem æternis dignatus
   es renovare mysteriis,
ad incorruptibilem glorificandæ
   carnis resurrectionem
pervenire concede.
Per Christum Dominum nostrum.

A formula of Solemn Blessing, pp.646-649, may be used.

FOURTH SUNDAY OF EASTER (YEAR A)

The Liturgy of the Fourth Sunday of Easter presents to us one of the most beautiful images that has portrayed the Lord Jesus since the earliest centuries of the Church: the Good Shepherd. The flock's attitude to the Good Shepherd, Christ, is presented by the Evangelist with two specific verbs: "to listen" and "to follow". These terms suggest the fundamental characteristics of those who live out the following of the Lord. First of all by listening to his word, from which faith is born and by which it is nurtured. Only those who are attentive to the Lord's voice can assess in their own conscience the right decisions for acting in accordance with God. Thus the following of Jesus derives from listening: we act as disciples only after hearing and inwardly accepting the Master's teachings in order to put them into practice every day. On this Sunday, therefore, it comes naturally to remember to God the pastors of the Church and those who are training to become pastors.

(Pope Benedict XVI)

Entrance Antiphon   Cf. Ps 32:5-6

THE merciful love of the Lord
fills the earth;
by the word of the Lord
the heavens were made, alleluia.

Ant. ad introitum

MISERICORDIA Domini plena
est terra;
verbo Domini cæli firmati sunt,
alleluia.

The Gloria in excelsis (Glory to God in the highest) is said.

Collect

Almighty ever-living God,
lead us to a share in the joys
of heaven,
so that the humble flock may reach
where the brave Shepherd
has gone before.
Who lives and reigns with you
in the unity of the Holy Spirit,
one God, for ever and ever.

Collecta

Omnipotens sempiterne Deus,
deduc nos ad societatem
cælestium gaudiorum,
ut eo perveniat humilitas gregis,
quo processit fortitudo pastoris.
Per Dominum nostrum Iesum
Christum Filium tuum,
qui tecum vivit et regnat
in unitate Spiritus Sancti,
Deus, per omnia sæcula sæculorum.

FIRST READING

A reading from the Acts of the Apostles   2:14,36-41
God has made him both Lord and Christ.

On the day of Pentecost Peter stood up with the Eleven and addressed the crowd with a loud voice: 'The whole House of Israel can be certain that God has made this Jesus whom you crucified both Lord and Christ.'

Hearing this, they were cut to the heart and said to Peter and the apostles, 'What must we do, brothers?' 'You must repent,' Peter answered 'and every one of you must be baptised in the name of Jesus Christ for the forgiveness of your sins, and you will receive the gift of the Holy Spirit. The promise that was made is for you and your children, and for all those who are far away, for all those whom the Lord our God will call to himself.' He spoke to them for a long time using many arguments, and he urged them, 'Save yourselves from this perverse generation.' They were convinced by his arguments, and they accepted what he said and were baptised. That very day about three thousand were added to their number.

The word of the Lord.

Responsorial Psalm   Ps 22:1-6. R. v.1

R. **The Lord is my shepherd;**
   there is nothing I shall want.
   Or: **Alleluia!**

The Lord is my shepherd;
there is nothing I shall want.
Fresh and green are the pastures
where he gives me repose.
Near restful waters he leads me,
to revive my drooping spirit. R.

He guides me along the right path;
he is true to his name.
If I should walk in the valley of darkness
no evil would I fear.
You are there with your crook and your staff;
with these you give me comfort. R.

You have prepared a banquet for me
in the sight of my foes.
My head you have anointed with oil;
my cup is overflowing. R.

Surely goodness and kindness shall follow me
all the days of my life.
In the Lord's own house shall I dwell
for ever and ever. R.

SECOND READING

A reading from the first letter of St Peter 2:20-25

You have come back to the shepherd of your souls.

The merit, in the sight of God, is in bearing punishment patiently when you are punished after doing your duty.

This, in fact, is what you were called to do, because Christ suffered for you and left an example for you to follow the way he took. He had not done anything wrong, and there had been no perjury in his mouth. He was insulted and did not retaliate with insults; when he was tortured he made no threats but he put his trust in the righteous judge. He was bearing our faults in his own body on the cross, so that we might die to our faults and live for holiness; through his wounds you have been healed. You had gone astray like sheep but now you have come back to the shepherd and guardian of your souls.

The word of the Lord.

Gospel Acclamation Jn 10:14

R. **Alleluia, alleluia!**
I am the good shepherd, says the Lord;
I know my own sheep and my own know me.
R. **Alleluia!**

GOSPEL

A reading from the holy Gospel according to John 10:1-10

I am the gate of the sheepfold.

Jesus said: 'I tell you most solemnly, anyone who does not enter the sheepfold through the gate, but gets in some other way is a thief and a brigand. The one who enters through the gate is the shepherd of the flock; the gatekeeper lets him in, the sheep hear his voice, one by one he calls his own sheep and leads them out. When he has brought out his flock, he goes ahead of them, and the sheep follow because they know his voice. They never follow a stranger but run away from him: they do not recognise the voice of strangers.'

Jesus told them this parable but they failed to understand what he meant by telling it to them.

So Jesus spoke to them again:

'I tell you most solemnly,
I am the gate of the sheepfold.
All others who have come
are thieves and brigands;

but the sheep took no notice of them.
I am the gate.
Anyone who enters through me will be safe:
he will go freely in and out
and be sure of finding pasture.
The thief comes
only to steal and kill and destroy.
I have come so that they may have life
and have it to the full.'

The Gospel of the Lord.

The Creed is said.

Prayer over the Offerings

Grant, we pray, O Lord,
that we may always find delight
   in these paschal mysteries,
so that the renewal constantly
   at work within us
may be the cause of our unending joy.
Through Christ our Lord.

Preface of Easter, pp.558-563.

Super oblata

Concede, quæsumus, Domine,
semper nos per hæc mysteria
   paschalia gratulari,
ut continua nostræ
   reparationis operatio
perpetuæ nobis fiat causa lætitiæ.
Per Christum Dominum nostrum.

Communion Antiphon

The Good Shepherd has risen,
who laid down his life for his sheep
and willingly died for his flock,
   alleluia.

Ant. ad communionem

Surrexit Pastor bonus, qui animam
   suam posuit pro ovibus suis,
et pro grege suo mori dignatus est,
   alleluia.

Prayer after Communion

Look upon your flock,
   kind Shepherd,
and be pleased to settle
   in eternal pastures
the sheep you have redeemed
by the Precious Blood of your Son.
Who lives and reigns
   for ever and ever.

Post communionem

Gregem tuum, Pastor bone,
   placatus intende,
et oves, quas pretioso Filii
   tui sanguine redemisti,
in æternis pascuis collocare digneris.
Per Christum Dominum nostrum.

A formula of Solemn Blessing, pp.646-649, may be used.

FIFTH SUNDAY OF EASTER (YEAR A)

The Gospel of this Sunday, the Fifth of Easter, proposes a twofold commandment of faith: to believe in God and to believe in Jesus. In fact, the Lord said to his disciples: "Believe in God, believe also in me" (Jn 14:1). They are not two separate acts but one single act of faith, full adherence to salvation wrought by God the Father through his Only-begotten Son. The New Testament puts an end to the Father's invisibility. God has shown his face, as Jesus's answer to the Apostle Philip confirms: "He who has seen me has seen the Father" (Jn 14:9). With his Incarnation, death and Resurrection, the Son of God has freed us from the slavery of sin to give us the freedom of the children of God and he has shown us the face of God, which is love: God can be seen, he is visible in Christ.

(Pope Benedict XVI)

Entrance Antiphon   Cf. Ps 97:1-2

O SING a new song to the Lord,
for he has worked wonders;
in the sight of the nations
he has shown his deliverance,
    alleluia.

Ant. ad introitum

C ANTATE Domino
canticum novum,
quia mirabilia fecit Dominus;
ante conspectum gentium revelavit
    iustitiam suam, alleluia.

The Gloria in excelsis (Glory to God in the highest) is said.

Collect

Almighty ever-living God,
constantly accomplish the Paschal
    Mystery within us,
that those you were pleased
    to make new in Holy Baptism
may, under your protective care,
    bear much fruit
and come to the joys of life eternal.
Through our Lord Jesus Christ,
    your Son,
who lives and reigns with you
    in the unity of the Holy Spirit,
one God, for ever and ever.

Collecta

Omnipotens sempiterne Deus,
semper in nobis paschale
    perfice sacramentum,
ut, quos sacro baptismate dignatus
    es renovare,
sub tuæ protectionis auxilio multos
    fructus afferant,
et ad æternæ vitæ gaudia
    pervenire concedas.
Per Dominum nostrum Iesum
    Christum Filium tuum,
qui tecum vivit et regnat
    in unitate Spiritus Sancti,
Deus, per omnia sæcula sæculorum.

FIRST READING

A reading from the Acts of the Apostles   6:1-7
They elected seven men full of the Holy Spirit.

About this time, when the number of disciples was increasing, the Hellenists made a complaint against the Hebrews: in the daily distribution their own widows were being overlooked. So the Twelve called a full meeting of the disciples and addressed them, 'It would not be right for us to neglect the word of God so as to give out food; you, brothers, must select from among yourselves seven men of good reputation, filled with the Spirit and with wisdom; we will hand over this duty to them, and continue to devote ourselves to prayer and to the service of the word.' The whole assembly approved of this proposal and elected Stephen, a man full of faith and of the Holy Spirit, together with Philip, Prochorus, Nicanor, Timon, Parmenas, and Nicolaus of Antioch, a convert to Judaism. They presented these to the apostles, who prayed and laid their hands on them.

The word of the Lord continued to spread: the number of disciples in Jerusalem was greatly increased, and a large group of priests made their submission to the faith.

The word of the Lord.

Responsorial Psalm   Ps 32:1-2,4-5,18-19. R. v.22

R. **May your love be upon us, O Lord,**
    as we place all our hope in you.
    Or: **Alleluia!**

Ring out your joy to the Lord, O you just;
for praise is fitting for loyal hearts.
Give thanks to the Lord upon the harp,
with a ten-stringed lute sing him songs. R.

For the word of the Lord is faithful
and all his works to be trusted.
The Lord loves justice and right
and fills the earth with his love. R.

The Lord looks on those who revere him,
on those who hope in his love,
to rescue their souls from death,
to keep them alive in famine. R.

SECOND READING

A reading from the first letter of St Peter   2:4-9

But you are a chosen race, a royal priesthood.

The Lord is the living stone, rejected by men but chosen by God and precious to him; set yourselves close to him so that you too, the holy priesthood that offers the spiritual sacrifices which Jesus Christ has made acceptable to God, may be living stones making a spiritual house. As scripture says: See how I lay in Zion a precious cornerstone that I have chosen and the man who rests his trust on it will not be disappointed. That means that for you who are believers, it is precious; but for unbelievers, the stone rejected by the builders has proved to be the keystone, a stone to stumble over, a rock to bring men down. They stumble over it because they do not believe in the word; it was the fate in store for them.

But you are a chosen race, a royal priesthood, a consecrated nation, a people set apart to sing the praises of God who called you out of the darkness into his wonderful light.

The word of the Lord.

Gospel Acclamation   Jn 14:6
R. **Alleluia, alleluia!**
Jesus said: 'I am the Way, the Truth, and the Life.
No one can come to the Father except through me.'
R. **Alleluia!**

GOSPEL

A reading from the holy Gospel according to John   14:1-12
I am the Way, the Truth and the Life.

Jesus said to his disciples:

'Do not let your hearts be troubled.
Trust in God still, and trust in me.
There are many rooms in my Father's house;
if there were not, I should have told you.
I am going now to prepare a place for you,
and after I have gone and prepared you a place,
I shall return to take you with me;
so that where I am
you may be too.
You know the way to the place where I am going.'

Thomas said, 'Lord, we do not know where you are going, so how can we know the way?' Jesus said:

'I am the Way, the Truth and the Life.
No one can come to the Father except through me.
If you know me, you know my Father too.
From this moment you know him and have seen him.'

Philip said, 'Lord, let us see the Father and then we shall be satisfied.' 'Have I been with you all this time, Philip,' said Jesus to him 'and you still do not know me?

'To have seen me is to have seen the Father,
so how can you say, "Let us see the Father"?
Do you not believe
that I am in the Father and the Father is in me?

The words I say to you I do not speak as from myself:
it is the Father, living in me, who is doing this work.
You must believe me when I say
that I am in the Father and the Father is in me;
believe it on the evidence of this work, if for no other reason.

'I tell you most solemnly,
whoever believes in me
will perform the same works as I do myself,
he will perform even greater works,
because I am going to the Father.'

The Gospel of the Lord.

The Creed is said.

Prayer over the Offerings

O God, who by the wonderful
   exchange effected in this sacrifice
have made us partakers of the one
   supreme Godhead,
grant, we pray,
that, as we have come to know
   your truth,
we may make it ours by a worthy
   way of life.
Through Christ our Lord.

Preface of Easter, pp.558-563.

Super oblata

Deus, qui nos, per huius sacrificii
   veneranda commercia,
unius summæque divinitatis
   participes effecisti,
præsta, quæsumus,
ut, sicut tuam cognovimus veritatem,
sic eam dignis moribus assequamur.
Per Christum Dominum nostrum.

Communion Antiphon Cf. Jn 15:1,5

I am the true vine and you
   are the branches, says the Lord.
Whoever remains in me, and I in
   him, bears fruit in plenty, alleluia.

Ant. ad communionem

Ego sum vitis vera et vos palmites,
   dicit Dominus;
qui manet in me et ego in eo,
hic fert fructum multum, alleluia.

Prayer after Communion

Graciously be present to your
   people, we pray, O Lord,
and lead those you have imbued
   with heavenly mysteries
to pass from former ways
   to newness of life.
Through Christ our Lord.

Post communionem

Populo tuo, quæsumus, Domine,
   adesto propitius,
et, quem mysteriis
   cælestibus imbuisti,
fac ad novitatem vitæ
   de vetustate transire.
Per Christum Dominum nostrum.

A formula of Solemn Blessing, pp.646-649, may be used.

SIXTH SUNDAY OF EASTER (YEAR A)

The book of the Acts of the Apostles states that after a first violent persecution, the Christian community of Jerusalem, except for the Apostles, spread to the surrounding areas. Philip, one of the deacons, arrived in a city of Samaria. There he preached the Risen Christ, and his proclamation was supported by numerous healings, so that the outcome of the episode was very positive: "there was much joy in that city" (Ac 8:8). We are repeatedly impressed in a profound way by this expression, which in essence communicates a sense of hope, as if saying: It is possible! It is possible for humanity to know true joy, because wherever the Gospel comes, life flourishes, just as arid ground, irrigated by rain, immediately turns back to green.

(Pope Benedict XVI)

Entrance Antiphon   Cf. Is 48:20

PROCLAIM a joyful sound
and let it be heard;
proclaim to the ends of the earth:
The Lord has freed his people,
   alleluia.

Ant. ad introitum

VOCEM iucunditatis annuntiate,
   et audiatur,
annuntiate usque ad extremum terræ:
liberavit Dominus populum suum,
   alleluia.

The Gloria in excelsis (Glory to God in the highest) is said.

Collect

Grant, almighty God,
that we may celebrate with heartfelt
   devotion these days of joy,
which we keep in honour
   of the risen Lord,
and that what we relive
   in remembrance
we may always hold to in what we do.
Through our Lord Jesus Christ,
   your Son,
who lives and reigns with you
   in the unity of the Holy Spirit,
one God, for ever and ever.

Collecta

Fac nos, omnipotens Deus,
   hos lætitiæ dies,
quos in honorem Domini
   resurgentis exsequimur,
affectu sedulo celebrare,
ut quod recordatione percurrimus
semper in opere teneamus.
Per Dominum nostrum Iesum
   Christum Filium tuum,
qui tecum vivit et regnat
   in unitate Spiritus Sancti,
Deus, per omnia sæcula sæculorum.

FIRST READING

A reading from the Acts of the Apostles   8:5-8,14-17

They laid hands on them, and they received the Holy Spirit.

Philip went to a Samaritan town and proclaimed the Christ to them. The people united in welcoming the message Philip preached, either because they had heard of the miracles he worked or because they saw them for themselves. There were, for example, unclean spirits that came shrieking out of many who were possessed, and several paralytics and cripples were cured. As a result there was great rejoicing in that town.

When the apostles in Jerusalem heard that Samaria had accepted the word of God, they sent Peter and John to them, and they went down there, and prayed for the Samaritans to receive the Holy Spirit, for as yet he had not come down on any of them: they had only been baptised in the name of the Lord Jesus. Then they laid hands on them, and they received the Holy Spirit.

The word of the Lord.

Responsorial Psalm   Ps 65:1-7,16,20. R. v.1

R. **Cry out with joy to God all the earth.**
    Or: **Alleluia!**

Cry out with joy to God all the earth,
O sing to the glory of his name.
O render him glorious praise.
Say to God: 'How tremendous your deeds! R.

'Before you all the earth shall bow;
shall sing to you, sing to your name!'
Come and see the works of God,
tremendous his deeds among men. R.

He turned the sea into dry land,
they passed through the river dry-shod.
Let our joy then be in him;
he rules for ever by his might. R.

Come and hear, all who fear God.
I will tell what he did for my soul:
Blessed be God who did not reject my prayer
nor withhold his love from me. R.

SECOND READING

A reading from the first letter of St Peter   3:15-18

In the body he was put to death, in the spirit he was raised to life.

Reverence the Lord Christ in your hearts, and always have your answer ready
for people who ask you the reason for the hope that you all have. But give
it with courtesy and respect and with a clear conscience, so that those who
slander you when you are living a good life in Christ may be proved wrong
in the accusations that they bring. And if it is the will of God that you should
suffer, it is better to suffer for doing right than for doing wrong.

Why, Christ himself, innocent though he was, had died once for sins,
died for the guilty, to lead us to God. In the body he was put to death, in
the spirit he was raised to life.

The word of the Lord.

Gospel Acclamation   Jn 14:23

R. **Alleluia, alleluia!**
Jesus said: 'If anyone loves me he will keep my word,
and my Father will love him, and we shall come to him.'
R. **Alleluia.**

GOSPEL

A reading from the holy Gospel according to John   14:15-21

I shall ask the Father, and he will give you another Advocate.

Jesus said to his disciples:

'If you love me you will keep my commandments.
I shall ask the Father,
and he will give you another Advocate
to be with you for ever,
that Spirit of truth
whom the world can never receive
since it neither sees nor knows him,
but you know him,
because he is with you, he is in you.
I will not leave you orphans;
I will come back to you.
In a short time the world will no longer see me;
but you will see me,
because I live and you will live.
On that day
you will understand that I am in my Father

and you in me and I in you.
Anybody who receives my commandments and keeps them
will be one who loves me;
and anybody who loves me will be loved by my Father,
and I shall love him and show myself to him.'

The Gospel of the Lord.

The Creed is said.

Prayer over the Offerings

May our prayers rise up to you,
    O Lord,
together with the sacrificial offerings,
so that, purified by
    your graciousness,
we may be conformed to the
    mysteries of your mighty love.
Through Christ our Lord.

Preface of Easter, pp.558-563.

Super oblata

Ascendant ad te, Domine,
    preces nostræ
cum oblationibus hostiarum,
ut, tua dignatione mundati,
sacramentis magnæ
    pietatis aptemur.
Per Christum Dominum nostrum.

Communion Antiphon Jn 14:15-16

If you love me, keep my
    commandments, says the Lord,
and I will ask the Father and he will
    send you another Paraclete,
to abide with you for ever, alleluia.

Ant. ad communionem

Si diligitis me, mandata mea
    servate, dicit Dominus.
Et ego rogabo Patrem,
    et alium Paraclitum dabit vobis,
ut maneat vobiscum in æternum,
    alleluia.

Prayer after Communion

Almighty ever-living God,
who restore us to eternal life
    in the Resurrection of Christ,
increase in us, we pray, the fruits
    of this paschal Sacrament
and pour into our hearts
    the strength of this saving food.
Through Christ our Lord.

Post communionem

Omnipotens sempiterne Deus,
qui ad æternam vitam in Christi
    resurrectione nos reparas,
fructus in nobis paschalis
    multiplica sacramenti,
et fortitudinem cibi salutaris nostris
    infunde pectoribus.
Per Christum Dominum nostrum.

A formula of Solemn Blessing, pp.646-649, may be used.

THE ASCENSION OF THE LORD

THE ASCENSION OF THE LORD (YEAR A)

Solemnity

Where the Solemnity of the Ascension is not to be observed as a Holyday of Obligation, it is assigned to the Seventh Sunday of Easter as its proper day.

What does the Feast of the Ascension of the Lord mean for us? It does not mean that the Lord has departed to some place far from people and from the world. Christ's Ascension is not a journey into space toward the most remote stars; for basically, the planets, like the earth, are also made of physical elements. Christ's Ascension means that he no longer belongs to the world of corruption and death that conditions our life. It means that he belongs entirely to God. He, the Eternal Son, led our human existence into God's presence, taking with him flesh and blood in a transfigured form. The human being finds room in God; through Christ, the human being was introduced into the very life of God. And since God embraces and sustains the entire cosmos, the Ascension of the Lord means that Christ has not departed from us, but that he is now, thanks to his being with the Father, close to each one of us for ever. Each one of us can be on intimate terms with him; each can call upon him. The Lord is always within hearing. We can inwardly draw away from him. We can live turning our backs on him. But he always waits for us and is always close to us.

(Pope Benedict XVI)

At the Vigil Mass

This Mass is used on the evening of the day before the Solemnity, either before or after First Vespers (Evening Prayer I) of the Ascension.

When the Ascension is celebrated on the Seventh Sunday of Easter, the Second Reading and Gospel assigned to the Seventh Sunday may be read on the Sixth Sunday.

Entrance Antiphon Ps 67:33,35	Ant. ad introitum
YOU kingdoms of the earth, sing to God; praise the Lord, who ascends above the highest heavens; his majesty and might are in the skies, alleluia.	REGNA terræ cantate Deo, psallite Domino, qui ascendit super cælum cæli; magnificentia et virtus eius in nubibus, alleluia.

The Gloria in excelsis (Glory to God in the highest) is said.

Collect

O God, whose Son today ascended
   to the heavens
as the Apostles looked on,
grant, we pray, that, in accordance
   with his promise,
we may be worthy for him to live
   with us always on earth,
and we with him in heaven.
Who lives and reigns with you
   in the unity of the Holy Spirit,
one God, for ever and ever.

Collecta

Deus, cuius Filius hodie in cælos,
Apostolis astantibus, ascendit,
concede nobis, quæsumus,
ut secundum eius promissionem
et ille nobiscum semper in terris
et nos cum eo in cælo
   vivere mereamur.
Qui tecum vivit et regnat
   in unitate Spiritus Sancti,
Deus, per omnia sæcula sæculorum.

FIRST READING

A reading from the Acts of the Apostles   1:1-11

He was lifted up while they looked on.

In my earlier work, Theophilus, I dealt with everything Jesus had done and taught from the beginning until the day he gave his instructions to the apostles he had chosen through the Holy Spirit, and was taken up to heaven. He had shown himself alive to them after his Passion by many demonstrations: for forty days he had continued to appear to them and tell them about the kingdom of God. When he had been at table with them, he had told them not to leave Jerusalem, but to wait there for what the Father had promised. 'It is' he had said 'what you have heard me speak about: John baptised with water but you, not many days from now, will be baptised with the Holy Spirit.'

Now having met together, they asked him, 'Lord, has the time come? Are you going to restore the kingdom to Israel?' He replied, 'It is not for you to know times or dates that the Father has decided by his own authority, but you will receive power when the Holy Spirit comes on you, and then you will be my witnesses not only in Jerusalem but throughout Judaea and Samaria, and indeed to the ends of the earth.'

As he said this he was lifted up while they looked on, and a cloud took him from their sight. They were still staring into the sky when suddenly two men in white were standing near them and they said, 'Why are you men from Galilee standing here looking into the sky? Jesus who has been taken up from you into heaven, this same Jesus will come back in the same way as you have seen him go there.'

The word of the Lord.

Responsorial Psalm   Ps 46:2-3,6-9. R. v.6

R. **God goes up with shouts of joy;**
   the Lord goes up with trumpet blast.
   Or: **Alleluia!**

All peoples, clap your hands,
cry to God with shouts of joy!
For the Lord, the Most High, we must fear,
great king over all the earth. R.

God goes up with shouts of joy;
the Lord goes up with trumpet blast.
Sing praise for God, sing praise,
sing praise to our king, sing praise. R.

God is king of all the earth.
Sing praise with all your skill.
God is king over the nations;
God reigns on his holy throne. R.

SECOND READING

A reading from the letter of St Paul to the Ephesians   1:17-23
He made him sit at his right hand in heaven.

May the God of our Lord Jesus Christ, the Father of glory, give you a spirit of
wisdom and perception of what is revealed, to bring you to full knowledge
of him. May he enlighten the eyes of your mind so that you can see what
hope his call holds for you, what rich glories he has promised the saints
will inherit and how infinitely great is the power that he has exercised for
us believers. This you can tell from the strength of his power at work in
Christ, when he used it to raise him from the dead and to make him sit at
his right hand, in heaven, far above every Sovereignty, Authority, Power, or
Domination, or any other name that can be named, not only in this age,
but also in the age to come. He has put all things under his feet, and made
him as the ruler of everything, the head of the Church; which is his body,
the fullness of him who fills the whole creation.

The word of the Lord.

Gospel Acclamation   Mt 28:19,20

R. **Alleluia, alleluia!**
Go, make disciples of all the nations;
I am with you always; yes, to the end of time.
R. **Alleluia!**

GOSPEL

A reading from the holy Gospel according to Matthew   28:16-20

All authority in heaven and earth has been given to me.

The eleven disciples set out for Galilee, to the mountain where Jesus had arranged to meet them. When they saw him they fell down before him, though some hesitated. Jesus came up and spoke to them. He said, 'All authority in heaven and on earth has been given to me. Go, therefore, make disciples of all the nations; baptise them in the name of the Father and of the Son and of the Holy Spirit, and teach them to observe all the commands I gave you. And know that I am with you always; yes, to the end of time.'

The Gospel of the Lord.

The Creed is said.

Prayer over the Offerings

O God, whose Only Begotten Son,
  our High Priest,
is seated ever-living at your right
  hand to intercede for us,
grant that we may approach with
  confidence the throne of grace
and there obtain your mercy.
Through Christ our Lord.

Super oblata

Deus, cuius Unigenitus,
  Pontifex noster,
semper vivens sedet
  ad dexteram tuam
ad interpellandum pro nobis,
concede nos adire cum fiducia ad
  thronum gratiæ,
ut misericordiam tuam consequamur.
Per Christum Dominum nostrum.

Preface I or II of the Ascension of the Lord, pp.564-565.

When the Roman Canon is used, the proper form of the Communicantes (In communion with those) is said.

Communion Antiphon Cf. Heb 10:12

Christ, offering a single sacrifice
  for sins,
is seated for ever at God's right hand,
  alleluia.

Ant. ad communionem

Christus, unam pro peccatis
  offerens hostiam,
in sempiternum sedet in dextera Dei,
  alleluia.

Prayer after Communion

May the gifts we have received
  from your altar, Lord,
kindle in our hearts a longing
  for the heavenly homeland
and cause us to press forward,
  following in the
  Saviour's footsteps,
to the place where for our sake he

Post communionem

Quæ ex altari tuo, Domine,
  dona percepimus,
accendant in cordibus nostris
  cælestis patriæ desiderium,
et quo præcursor pro nobis
  introivit Salvator,
faciant nos, eius vestigia

entered before us.
Who lives and reigns
    for ever and ever.

sectantes, contendere.
Qui vivit et regnat
    in sæcula sæculorum.

A formula of Solemn Blessing, pp.648-649, may be used.

At the Mass during the Day

Entrance Antiphon   Ac 1:11

MEN of Galilee, why gaze
    in wonder at the heavens?
This Jesus whom you saw ascending
    into heaven
will return as you saw him go,
    alleluia.

Ant. ad introitum

VIRI Galilæi, quid admiramini
    aspicientes in cælum?
Quemadmodum vidistis eum
    ascendentem in cælum,
    ita veniet, alleluia.

The Gloria in excelsis (Glory to God in the highest) is said.

Collect
Gladden us with holy joys,
    almighty God,
and make us rejoice with
    devout thanksgiving,
for the Ascension of Christ your Son
is our exaltation,
and, where the Head has gone
    before in glory,
the Body is called to follow in hope.
Through our Lord Jesus Christ,
    your Son,
who lives and reigns with you
    in the unity of the Holy Spirit,
one God, for ever and ever.
Or:
Grant, we pray, almighty God,
that we, who believe that your Only
    Begotten Son, our Redeemer,
ascended this day to the heavens,
may in spirit dwell already
    in heavenly realms.
Who lives and reigns with you
    in the unity of the Holy Spirit,
one God, for ever and ever.

Collecta
Fac nos, omnipotens Deus,
    sanctis exsultare gaudiis,
et pia gratiarum actione lætari,
quia Christi Filii tui ascensio
    est nostra provectio,
et quo processit gloria capitis,
    eo spes vocatur et corporis.
Per Dominum nostrum Iesum
    Christum Filium tuum,
qui tecum vivit et regnat
    in unitate Spiritus Sancti,
Deus, per omnia sæcula sæculorum.

Vel:
Concede, quæsumus,
    omnipotens Deus,
ut, qui hodierna die
Unigenitum tuum
    Redemptorem nostrum
ad cælos ascendisse credimus,
ipsi quoque mente in
    cælestibus habitemus.
Qui tecum vivit et regnat
    in unitate Spiritus Sancti,
Deus, per omnia sæcula sæculorum.

FIRST READING

A reading from the Acts of the Apostles   1:1-11

He was lifted up while they looked on.

In my earlier work, Theophilus, I dealt with everything Jesus had done and taught from the beginning until the day he gave his instructions to the apostles he had chosen through the Holy Spirit, and was taken up to heaven. He had shown himself alive to them after his Passion by many demonstrations: for forty days he had continued to appear to them and tell them about the kingdom of God. When he had been at table with them, he had told them not to leave Jerusalem, but to wait there for what the Father had promised. 'It is' he had said 'what you have heard me speak about: John baptised with water but you, not many days from now, will be baptised with the Holy Spirit.'

Now having met together, they asked him, 'Lord, has the time come? Are you going to restore the kingdom to Israel?' He replied, 'It is not for you to know times or dates that the Father has decided by his own authority, but you will receive power when the Holy Spirit comes on you, and then you will be my witnesses not only in Jerusalem but throughout Judaea and Samaria, and indeed to the ends of the earth.'

As he said this he was lifted up while they looked on, and a cloud took him from their sight. They were still staring into the sky when suddenly two men in white were standing near them and they said, 'Why are you men from Galilee standing here looking into the sky? Jesus who has been taken up from you into heaven, this same Jesus will come back in the same way as you have seen him go there.'

The word of the Lord.

Responsorial Psalm   Ps 46:2-3,6-9. R. v.6

R. **God goes up with shouts of joy;**
   the Lord goes up with trumpet blast.
   Or: **Alleluia!**

All peoples, clap your hands,
cry to God with shouts of joy!
For the Lord, the Most High, we must fear,
great king over all the earth. R.

God goes up with shouts of joy;
the Lord goes up with trumpet blast.
Sing praise for God, sing praise,
sing praise to our king, sing praise. R.

God is king of all the earth.
Sing praise with all your skill.
God is king over the nations;
God reigns on his holy throne. R.

SECOND READING

A reading from the letter of St Paul to the Ephesians   1:17-23
He made him sit at his right hand in heaven.

May the God of our Lord Jesus Christ, the Father of glory, give you a spirit of wisdom and perception of what is revealed, to bring you to full knowledge of him. May he enlighten the eyes of your mind so that you can see what hope his call holds for you, what rich glories he has promised the saints will inherit and how infinitely great is the power that he has exercised for us believers. This you can tell from the strength of his power at work in Christ, when he used it to raise him from the dead and to make him sit at his right hand, in heaven, far above every Sovereignty, Authority, Power, or Domination, or any other name that can be named, not only in this age, but also in the age to come. He has put all things under his feet, and made him as the ruler of everything, the head of the Church; which is his body, the fullness of him who fills the whole creation.

The word of the Lord.

Gospel Acclamation   Mt 28:19.20
R. **Alleluia, alleluia!**
Go, make disciples of all the nations;
I am with you always; yes, to the end of time.
R. **Alleluia!**

GOSPEL

A reading from the holy Gospel according to Matthew   28:16-20
All authority in heaven and earth has been given to me.

The eleven disciples set out for Galilee, to the mountain where Jesus had arranged to meet them. When they saw him they fell down before him, though some hesitated. Jesus came up and spoke to them. He said, 'All authority in heaven and on earth has been given to me. Go, therefore, make disciples of all the nations; baptise them in the name of the Father and of the Son and of the Holy Spirit, and teach them to observe all the commands I gave you. And know that I am with you always; yes, to the end of time.'

The Gospel of the Lord.

The Creed is said.

Prayer over the Offerings

We offer sacrifice now
   in supplication, O Lord,
to honour the wondrous Ascension
   of your Son:
grant, we pray,
that through this most holy exchange
we, too, may rise up
   to the heavenly realms.
Through Christ our Lord.

Super oblata

Sacrificium, Domine,
   pro Filii tui supplices
venerabili nunc
   ascensione deferimus:
præsta, quæsumus,
   ut his commerciis sacrosanctis
ad cælestia consurgamus.
Per Christum Dominum nostrum.

Preface I or II of the Ascension of the Lord, pp.564-565.

When the Roman Canon is used, the proper form of the Communicantes (In communion with those) is said.

Communion Antiphon   Mt 28:20

Behold, I am with you always,
even to the end of the age, alleluia.

Ant. ad communionem

Ecce ego vobiscum sum
   omnibus diebus,
usque ad consummationem sæculi,
   alleluia.

Prayer after Communion

Almighty ever-living God,
who allow those on earth
   to celebrate divine mysteries,
grant, we pray,
that Christian hope may draw
   us onward
to where our nature is united
   with you.
Through Christ our Lord.

Post communionem

Omnipotens sempiterne Deus,
qui in terra constitutos divina
   tractare concedis,
præsta, quæsumus,
ut illuc tendat christianæ
   devotionis affectus,
quo tecum est nostra substantia.
Per Christum Dominum nostrum.

A formula of Solemn Blessing, pp.648-649, may be used.

SEVENTH SUNDAY OF EASTER (YEAR A)

In his farewell discourses to the disciples, Jesus stressed the importance of his "return to the Father", the culmination of his whole mission: indeed, he came into the world to bring man back to God, not on the ideal level - like a philosopher or a master of wisdom – but really, like a shepherd who wants to lead his sheep back to the fold. It was for our sake that he came down from Heaven and for our sake that he ascended to it, after making himself in all things like men, humbling himself even to death on a cross and after having touched the abyss of the greatest distance from God. For this very reason the Father was pleased with him and "highly exalted" him (Ph 2:9), restoring to him the fullness of his glory, but now with our humanity. God in man – man in God: this is even now a reality, not a theoretical truth.

(Pope Benedict XVI)

Entrance Antiphon　　Cf. Ps 26:7-9	Ant. ad introitum
O LORD, hear my voice, 　　for I have called to you; of you my heart has spoken: 　Seek his face; hide not your face from me, alleluia.	E XAUDI, Domine, vocem meam, 　qua clamavi ad te. Tibi dixit cor meum, 　quæsivi vultum tuum, vultum tuum requiram; ne avertas faciem tuam a me, alleluia.

The Gloria in excelsis (Glory to God in the highest) is said.

Collect	Collecta
Graciously hear our supplications, 　O Lord, so that we, who believe that 　the Saviour of the human race is with you in your glory, may experience, as he promised, until the end of the world, his abiding presence among us. Who lives and reigns with you 　in the unity of the Holy Spirit, one God, for ever and ever.	Supplicationibus nostris, Domine, 　adesto propitius, ut, sicut humani generis Salvatorem tecum in tua credimus maiestate, ita eum usque ad 　consummationem sæculi manere nobiscum, sicut ipse promisit, sentiamus. Qui tecum vivit et regnat 　in unitate Spiritus Sancti, Deus, per omnia sæcula sæculorum.

FIRST READING

A reading from the Acts of the Apostles 1:12-14

All joined in continuous prayer.

After Jesus was taken up into heaven, the apostles went back from the Mount of Olives, as it is called, to Jerusalem, a short distance away, no more than a sabbath walk; and when they reached the city they went to the upper room where they were staying; there were Peter and John, James and Andrew, Philip and Thomas, Bartholomew and Matthew, James son of Alphaeus and Simon the Zealot, and Jude son of James. All these joined in continuous prayer, together with several women, including Mary the mother of Jesus, and with his brothers.

The word of the Lord.

Responsorial Psalm Ps 26:1,4,7-8. R. v.13

R. **I am sure I shall see the Lord's goodness
in the land of the living.**
Or: **Alleluia!**

The Lord is my light and my help;
whom shall I fear?
The Lord is the stronghold of my life;
before whom shall I shrink? R.

There is one thing I ask of the Lord,
for this I long,
to live in the house of the Lord,
all the days of my life,
to savour the sweetness of the Lord,
to behold his temple. R.

O Lord, hear my voice when I call;
have mercy and answer.
Of you my heart has spoken;
'Seek his face.' R.

SECOND READING

A reading from the first letter of St Peter 4:13-16

It is a blessing for you when they insult you for bearing the name of Christ.

If you can have some share in the sufferings of Christ, be glad, because you will enjoy a much greater gladness when his glory is revealed. It is a blessing for you when they insult you for bearing the name of Christ, because it means that you have the Spirit of glory, the Spirit of God resting on you. None of you should ever deserve to suffer for being a murderer, a thief, a criminal or an informer; but if anyone of you should suffer for being a Christian, then he is not to be ashamed of it; he should thank God that he has been called one.

The word of the Lord.

Gospel Acclamation   Cf. Jn 14:18

R. **Alleluia, alleluia!**
I will not leave you orphans, says the Lord;
I will come back to you, and your hearts will be full of joy.
R. **Alleluia!**

GOSPEL

A reading from the holy Gospel according to John   17:1-11
Father, glorify your Son.

Jesus raised his eyes to heaven and said:
    'Father, the hour has come:
    glorify your Son
    so that your Son may glorify you;
    and, through the power over all mankind that you have given him,
    let him give eternal life to all those you have entrusted to him.
    And eternal life is this:
    to know you,
    the only true God,
    and Jesus Christ whom you have sent.
    I have glorified you on earth
    and finished the work
    that you gave me to do.
    Now, Father, it is time for you to glorify me
    with that glory I had with you
    before ever the world was.
    I have made your name known
    to the men you took from the world to give me.
    They were yours and you gave them to me,
    and they have kept your word.
    Now at last they know
    that all you have given me comes indeed from you;
    for I have given them
    the teaching you gave to me,
    and they have truly accepted this, that I came from you,
    and have believed that it was you who sent me.

I pray for them;
I am not praying for the world
but for those you have given me,
because they belong to you:
all I have is yours
and all you have is mine,
and in them I am glorified.
I am not in the world any longer,
but they are in the world,
and I am coming to you.'

The Gospel of the Lord.

The Creed is said.

Prayer over the Offerings

Accept, O Lord, the prayers
   of your faithful
with the sacrificial offerings,
that through these acts
   of devotedness
we may pass over to the glory
   of heaven.
Through Christ our Lord.

Super oblata

Suscipe, Domine, fidelium preces
cum oblationibus hostiarum,
ut, per hæc piæ devotionis officia,
ad cælestem gloriam transeamus.
Per Christum Dominum nostrum.

Preface of Easter, or of the Ascension, pp.558-565.

Communion Antiphon   Jn 17:22

Father, I pray that they may be one
as we also are one, alleluia.

Ant. ad communionem

Rogo, Pater, ut sint unum,
sicut et nos unum sumus, alleluia.

Prayer after Communion

Hear us, O God our Saviour,
and grant us confidence,
that through these sacred mysteries
there will be accomplished
   in the body of the whole Church
what has already come to pass
   in Christ her Head.
Who lives and reigns
   for ever and ever.

Post communionem

Exaudi nos, Deus, salutaris noster,
ut per hæc sacrosancta mysteria
in totius Ecclesiæ confidamus
   corpore faciendum,
quod eius præcessit in capite.
Per Christum Dominum nostrum.

A formula of Solemn Blessing, pp.646-649, may be used.

PENTECOST SUNDAY

PENTECOST SUNDAY

(YEAR A,B,C)

The Holy Spirit is first and foremost a Creator Spirit, hence Pentecost is also a feast of creation. For us Christians, the world is the fruit of an act of love by God who has made all things and in which he rejoices because it is "good", it is "very good", as the creation narrative tells us (cf. Gn 1:1-31). Consequently God is not totally Other, unnameable and obscure. God reveals himself, he has a face. God is reason, God is will, God is love, God is beauty. Faith in the Creator Spirit and faith in the Spirit whom the Risen Christ gave to the Apostles and gives to each one of us are therefore inseparably united. The Gospel passage offers us a marvellous image to clarify the connection between Jesus, the Holy Spirit and the Father: the Holy Spirit is portrayed as the breath of the Risen Jesus Christ. Here the Evangelist John takes up an image of the creation narrative, where it says that God breathed into the nostrils of man the breath of life (cf. Gn 2:7). The breath of God is life. Now, the Lord breathes into our soul the new breath of life, the Holy Spirit, his most intimate essence, and in this way welcomes us into God's family. With Baptism and Confirmation this gift was given to us specifically, and with the sacraments of the Eucharist and Penance it is continuously repeated: the Lord breathes a breath of life into our soul.

(Pope Benedict XVI)

Solemnity

At the Vigil Mass
EXTENDED FORM

This Vigil Mass may be celebrated on the Saturday evening, either before or after First Vespers (Evening Prayer I) of Pentecost Sunday.

In churches where the Vigil Mass is celebrated in an extended form, this may be done as follows.

a) If First Vespers (Evening Prayer I) celebrated in choir or in common immediately precede Mass, the celebration may begin either from the introductory verse and the hymn (Veni, creator Spiritus) or else from the singing of the Entrance Antiphon with the procession and greeting of the Priest; in either case the Penitential Act is omitted (Cf. General Instruction of the Liturgy of the Hours, nos. 94 and 96).

Then the Psalmody prescribed for Vespers follows, up to but not including the Short Reading.

After the Psalmody, omitting the Penitential Act, and if appropriate, the Kyrie (Lord, have mercy), the Priest says the prayer Grant, we pray, almighty God, that the splendour, as at the Vigil Mass.

b) If Mass is begun in the usual way, after the Kyrie (Lord, have mercy), the Priest says the prayer Grant, we pray, almighty God, that the splendour, as at the Vigil Mass.

Then the Priest may address the people in these or similar words:

Dear brethren (brothers and sisters), we have now begun our
Pentecost Vigil,
after the example of the Apostles and disciples
who with Mary, the Mother of Jesus, persevered in prayer,
awaiting the Spirit promised by the Lord;
like them, let us, too, listen with quiet hearts to the Word of God.
Let us meditate on how many great deeds
God in times past did for his people and let us pray that the Holy Spirit,
whom the Father sent as the first fruits for those who believe,
may bring to perfection his work in the world.

Vigiliam Pentecostes ingressi,
fratres carissimi, ad exemplum
Apostolorum et discipulorum qui,
cum Maria, Matre Iesu,
instabant in oratione,
exspectantes Spiritum a Domino promissum, quieto corde nunc verbum Dei audiamus.
Meditemur quanta fecit Deus populo suo et oremus,
ut Spiritus Sanctus
quem Pater misit
primitias credentibus,
opus suum
in mundo perficiat.

Then follow the readings proposed as options in the Lectionary. A reader goes to the ambo and proclaims the reading. Afterwards a psalmist or a cantor sings or says the Psalm with the people making the response. Then all rise, the Priest says, Let us pray and, after all have prayed for a while in silence, he says the prayer corresponding to the reading. In place of the Responsorial Psalm a period of sacred silence may be observed, in which case the pause after Let us pray is omitted.

FIRST READING

A reading from the book of Genesis   11:1-9

It was named Babel because there the language of the whole earth was confused.

Throughout the earth men spoke the same language, with the same vocabulary. Now as they moved eastwards they found a plain in the land of Shinar where they settled. They said to one another, 'Come, let us make bricks and bake them in the fire.' – For stone they used bricks, and for mortar they used bitumen. – 'Come,' they said 'let us build ourselves a town and a tower with its top reaching heaven. Let us make a name for ourselves, so that we may not be scattered about the whole earth.'

Now the Lord came down to see the town and the tower that the sons of man had built. 'So they are all a single people with a single language!'

said the Lord. 'This is but the start of their undertakings! There will be nothing too hard for them to do. Come, let us go down and confuse their language on the spot so that they can no longer understand one another.' The Lord scattered them thence over the whole face of the earth, and they stopped building the town. It was named Babel therefore, because there the Lord confused the language of the whole earth. It was from there that the Lord scattered them over the whole face of the earth.

The word of the Lord.

Responsorial Psalm   Ps 32:10-11,12-13,14-15 R. v.12b

R. **Happy the people the Lord has chosen as his own.**

He frustrates the designs of the nations,
he defeats the plans of the peoples.
His own designs shall stand for ever,
the plans of his heart from age to age. R.

They are happy, whose God is the Lord,
the people he has chosen as his own.
From the heavens the Lord looks forth,
he sees all the children of men. R.

From the place where he dwells he gazes
on all the dwellers on the earth,
he who shapes the hearts of them all
and considers all their deeds. R.

Prayer

Let us pray.
Grant, we pray, almighty God,
that your Church may always
    remain that holy people,
formed as one by the unity
    of Father, Son and Holy Spirit,
which manifests to the world
the Sacrament of your holiness
    and unity
and leads it to the perfection
    of your charity.
Through Christ our Lord.
R. Amen.

Oremus.
Concede, qucesumus,
    omnipotens Deus,
ut Ecclesia tua semper ea plebs
    sancta permaneat
de unitate Patris et Filii
    et Spiritus Sancti adunata,
quce tuce sanctitatis
    et unitatis sacramentum
mundo manifestet
et ipsum ad perfectionem
    tuce conducat caritatis.
Per Christum Dominum nostrum.
R. Amen.

SECOND READING

A reading from the book of Exodus   19:3-8,16-20

The Lord came down on the mountain of Sinai before all the people.

Moses went up to God, and the Lord called to him from the mountain, saying, 'Say this to the House of Jacob, declare this to the sons of Israel, "You yourselves have seen what I did with the Egyptians, how I carried you on eagle's wings and brought you to myself. From this you know that now, if you obey my voice and hold fast to my covenant, you of all the nations shall be my very own, for all the earth is mine. I will count you a kingdom of priests, a consecrated nation." Those are the words you are to speak to the sons of Israel.' So Moses went and summoned the elders of the people, putting before them all that the Lord had bidden him. Then all the people answered as one, 'All that the Lord has said, we will do.'

Now at daybreak on the third day there were peals of thunder on the mountain and lightning flashes, a dense cloud, and a loud trumpet blast, and inside the camp all the people trembled. Then Moses led the people out of the camp to meet God; and they stood at the bottom of the mountain. The mountain of Sinai was entirely wrapped in smoke, because the Lord had descended on it in the form of fire. Like smoke from a furnace the smoke went up, and the whole mountain shook violently. Louder and louder grew the sound of the trumpet. Moses spoke, and God answered him with peals of thunder. The Lord came down on the mountain of Sinai, on the mountain top, and the Lord called Moses to the top of the mountain.

The word of the Lord.

Responsorial Psalm   Dn 3:52,53,54,55,56. R. v.52b

R. **To you glory and praise for evermore.**

> You are blest, Lord God of our fathers. R.
> Blest your glorious holy name. R.
> You are blest in the temple of your glory. R.
> You are blest on the throne of your kingdom. R.
> You are blest who gaze into the depths. R.
> You are blest in the firmament of heaven. R.

Or   Ps 18:8,9,10,11. R. Jn v.6:68c

R. **You have the message of eternal life, O Lord.**

> The law of the Lord is perfect,
> it revives the soul.
> The rule of the Lord is to be trusted,
> it gives wisdom to the simple. R.

The precepts of the Lord are right,
they gladden the heart.
The command of the Lord is clear,
it gives light to the eyes. R.

The fear of the Lord is holy,
abiding for ever.
The decrees of the Lord are truth
and all of them just. R.

They are more to be desired than gold,
than the purest of gold
and sweeter are they than honey,
than honey from the comb. R.

Prayer

Let us pray.
O God, who in fire and lightning
gave the ancient Law to Moses
on Mount Sinai
and on this day manifested
the new covenant
in the fire of the Spirit,
grant, we pray,
that we may always be aflame
with that same Spirit
whom you wondrously poured out
on your Apostles,
and that the new Israel,
gathered from every people,
may receive with rejoicing
the eternal commandment
of your love.
Through Christ our Lord.
R. Amen.

Oremus.
Deus, qui in fulgure ignis
in monte Sinai
legem antiquam Moysi dedisti
et fœdus novum in igne Spiritus
hoc die manifestasti,
presta, quæsumus,
ut ilio iugiter Spiritu ferveamus,
quem Apostolis tuis
ineffabiliter infudisti,
et novus Israel,
ex omni populo congregatus,
mandatum æternum tui amoris
lætanter accipiat.
Per Christum Dominum nostrum.
R. Amen.

THIRD READING

A reading from the prophet Ezekiel   37:1-14

Dry bones, I am going to make the breath enter you, and you will live.

The hand of the Lord was laid on me, and he carried me away by the
spirit of the Lord and set me down in the middle of a valley, a valley full

of bones. He made me walk up and down among them. There were vast quantities of these bones on the ground the whole length of the valley; and they were quite dried up. He said to me, 'Son of man, can these bones live?' I said, 'You know, Lord.' He said, 'Prophesy over these bones. Say, "Dry bones, hear the word of the Lord. The Lord says this to these bones: I am now going to make the breath enter you, and you will live. I shall put sinews on you, I shall make flesh grow on you, I shall cover you with skin and give you breath, and you will live, and you will learn that I am the Lord."' I prophesied as I had been ordered. While I was prophesying, there was a noise, a sound of clattering; and the bones joined together. I looked, and saw that they were covered with sinews; flesh was growing on them and skin was covering them, but there was no breath in them. He said to me, 'Prophesy to the breath; prophesy, son of man. Say to the breath, "The Lord says this: Come from the four winds, breath; breathe on these dead; let them live!"' I prophesied as he had ordered me, and the breath entered them; they came to life again and stood up on their feet, a great, an immense army.

Then he said, 'Son of man, these bones are the whole House of Israel. They keep saying, "Our bones are dried up, our hope has gone; we are as good as dead." So prophesy. Say to them, "The Lord says this: I am now going to open your graves; I mean to raise you from your graves, my people, and lead you back to the soil of Israel. And you will know that I am the Lord, when I open your graves and raise you from your graves, my people. And I shall put my spirit in you, and you will live, and I shall resettle you on your own soil; and you will know that I, the Lord have said and done this – it is the Lord who speaks."'

The word of the Lord.

Responsorial Psalm   Ps 106:2-3,4-5,6–7,8–9. R. v.1

R. **O give thanks to the Lord, for he is good;**
　　for his love has no end.
　　Or: **Alleluia!**

Let them say this, the Lord's redeemed,
whom he redeemed from the hand of the foe
and gathered from far-off lands,
from east and west, north and south. R.

Some wandered in the desert, in the wilderness,
finding no way to a city they could dwell in.
Hungry they were and thirsty;
their soul was fainting within them. R.

Then they cried to the Lord in their need
and he rescued them from their distress
and he led them along the right way,
to reach a city they could dwell in. R.

Let them thank the Lord for his love,
for the wonders he does for men.
For he satisfies the thirsty soul;
he fills the hungry with good things. R.

Prayer

Let us pray.	Oremus.
Lord, God of power,	Domine, Deus virtutum,
who restore what has fallen	qui coliapsa reparas
and preserve what you have restored,	et reparata conservas,
increase, we pray, the peoples	auge populos in tui nominis
to be renewed by the sanctification	sanctificatione renovandos,
of your name,	ut omnes, qui sacro
that all who are washed clean	Baptismate diluuntur,
by holy Baptism	tua semper inspiratione dirigantur.
may always be directed	Per Christum Dominum nostrum.
by your prompting.	R. Amen.
Through Christ our Lord.	
R. Amen.	
Or:	Vel:
O God, who have brought us	Deus, qui nos verbo vitæ regenerasti,
to rebirth by the word of life,	effunde super nos
pour out upon us your Holy Spirit,	Spiritum Sanctum tuum,
that, walking in oneness of faith,	ut, in unitate fidei ambulantes,
we may attain in our flesh	ad incorruptibilem glorificandæ
the incorruptible glory	carnis resurrectionem
of the resurrection.	pervenlre mereamur.
Through Christ our Lord.	Per Christum Dominum nostrum.
R. Amen.	R. Amen.
Or:	Vel:
May your people exult for ever,	Semper exsultet populus
O God,	tuus, Deus,
in renewed youthfulness of spirit,	Spiritu Sancto tuo renovata
so that, rejoicing now in the restored	animce iuventute,
glory of our adoption,	ut, qui nunc lætatur in adoptionis
we may look forward	se gloriam restitutum,

in confident hope
to the rejoicing of the day
    of resurrection.
Through Christ our Lord.
R. Amen.

resurrectionis diem spe certæ
    gratulationis exspectet.
Per Christum Dominum nostrum.
R. Amen.

FOURTH READING

A reading from the prophet Joel   3:1-5
I will pour out my spirit on all people.

Thus says the Lord:

'I will pour out my spirit on all mankind.
Your sons and daughters shall prophesy,
your old men shall dream dreams,
and your young men see visions.
Even on the slaves, men and women,
will I pour out my spirit in those days.
I will display portents in heaven and on earth,
blood and fire and columns of smoke.'

The sun will be turned into darkness,
and the moon into blood,
before the day of the Lord dawns,
that great and terrible day.
All who call on the name of the Lord will be saved,
for on Mount Zion there will be some who have escaped,
as the Lord has said,
and in Jerusalem some survivors whom the Lord will call.

The word of the Lord.

Responsorial Psalm   Ps 103:1-2a,24,35c,27–28,29bc-30. R. v.30

R. **Send forth your Spirit, O Lord,**
and renew the face of the earth.

Or: **Alleluia!**

Bless the Lord, my soul!
Lord God, how great you are,
clothed in majesty and glory,
wrapped in light as in a robe! R.

How many are your works, O Lord!
In wisdom you have made them all.
The earth is full of your riches.
Bless the Lord, my soul. R.

All of these look to you
to give them their food in due season.
You give it, they gather it up:
you open your hand, they have their fill. R.

You take back your spirit, they die,
returning to the dust from which they came.
You send forth your spirit, they are created;
and you renew the face of the earth. R.

Prayer

Let us pray.	Oremus.
Fulfil for us your gracious promise,	Promissionem tuam,
O Lord, we pray,	quæsumus, Domine,
so that by his coming	super nos propitiatus adimple,
the Holy Spirit may make us	ut Spiritus Sanctus adveniens
witnesses before the world	nos coram mundo testes efficiat
to the Gospel of our Lord Jesus Christ.	Evangelii Domini nostri
Who lives and reigns	Iesu Christi.
for ever and ever.	Qui tecum vivit et regnat
R. Amen.	in sæcula sæculorum.
	R. Amen.

Then the Priest intones the hymn Gloria in excelsis Deo (Glory to God in the highest).

When the hymn is concluded, the Priest says the Collect in the usual way: Almighty ever-living God, who willed, as here below (p.414).

Then the reader proclaims the reading from the Apostle (Rm 8:22-27) pp.415-416, and Mass continues in the usual way.

If Vespers (Evening Prayer) are joined to Mass, after Communion with the Communion Antiphon (On the last day), the Magnificat is sung, with its Vespers antiphon (Veni, Sancte Spiritus); then the Prayer after Communion is said and the rest follows as usual.

At the Vigil Mass

SIMPLE FORM

This Mass is used on the Saturday evening, either before or after First Vespers (Evening Prayer I) of Pentecost Sunday.

Entrance Antiphon Rm 5:5; Cf. 8:11	Ant. ad introitum
THE love of God has been poured into our hearts through the Spirit of God dwelling within us, alleluia.	CARITAS Dei diffusa est in cordibus nostris per inhabitantem Spiritum eius in nobis, alleluia.

The Gloria in excelsis (Glory to God in the highest) is said.

Collect	Collecta
Almighty ever-living God, who willed the Paschal Mystery to be encompassed as a sign in fifty days, grant that from out of the scattered nations the confusion of many tongues may be gathered by heavenly grace into one great confession of your name. Through our Lord Jesus Christ, your Son, who lives and reigns with you in the unity of the Holy Spirit, one God, for ever and ever.	Omnipotens sempiterne Deus, qui paschale sacramentum quinquaginta dierum voluisti mysterio contineri, præsta, ut, gentium facta dispersione, divisiones linguarum ad unam confessionem tui nominis cælesti munere congregentur. Per Dominum nostrum Iesum Christum Filium tuum, qui tecum vivit et regnat in unitate Spiritus Sancti, Deus, per omnia sæcula sæculorum.
Or:	Vel:
Grant, we pray, almighty God, that the splendour of your glory may shine forth upon us and that, by the bright rays of the Holy Spirit, the light of your light may confirm the hearts of those born again by your grace.	Præsta, quæsumus, omnipotens Deus, ut claritatis tuæ super nos splendor effulgeat, et lux tuæ lucis corda eorum, qui per tuam gratiam sunt renati, Sancti Spiritus illustratione confirmet.

| Through our Lord Jesus Christ,
    your Son,
who lives and reigns with you
    in the unity of the Holy Spirit,
one God, for ever and ever. | Per Dominum nostrum Iesum
    Christum Filium tuum,
qui tecum vivit et regnat
    in unitate Spiritus Sancti,
Deus, per omnia sæcula sæculorum. |

FIRST READING

There is a choice of four texts for the First Reading: Either Genesis 11:1-9 (On Babel), p.000; or Exodus 19:3-8,16-20 (On God's descent on Mount Sinai), p.000; or Ezekiel 37:1-14 (On the dry bones and God's spirit), p.000; or Joel 3:1-5 (On the outpouring of the Spirit), p.000.

Responsorial Psalm   Ps 103:1-2,24,27-30,35. R. Cf. v.30

R. **Send forth your spirit, O Lord,**
    and renew the face of the earth.
    Or: **Alleluia!**

Bless the Lord, my soul!
Lord God, how great you are,
clothed in majesty and glory,
wrapped in light as in a robe! R.

How many are your works, O Lord!
In wisdom you have made them all.
The earth is full of your riches.
Bless the Lord, my soul. R.

All of these look to you
to give them their food in due season.
You give it, they gather it up:
you open your hand, they have their fill. R.

You take back your spirit, they die,
returning to the dust from which they came.
You send forth your spirit, they are created;
and you renew the face of the earth. R.

SECOND READING

A reading from the letter of St Paul to the Romans   8:22-27

The Spirit himself expresses our plea in a way that could never be put into words.

From the beginning till now the entire creation, as we know, has been groaning in one great act of giving birth; and not only creation, but all of us who possess the first-fruits of the Spirit, we too groan inwardly as we wait for our bodies to be set free. For we must be content to hope that we shall be saved – our salvation is not in sight, we should not have to be hoping for it if it were – but, as I say, we must hope to be saved since we are not saved yet – it is something we must wait for with patience.

The Spirit too comes to help us in our weakness. For when we cannot choose words in order to pray properly, the Spirit himself expresses our plea in a way that could never be put into words, and God who knows everything in our hearts knows perfectly well what he means, and that the pleas of the saints expressed by the Spirit are according to the mind of God.

The word of the Lord.

Gospel Acclamation
R. **Alleluia, alleluia!**
Come, Holy Spirit, fill the hearts of your faithful
and kindle in them the fire of your love.
R. **Alleluia!**

GOSPEL

A reading from the holy Gospel according to John   7:37-39

From his breast shall flow fountains of living water.

On the last day and greatest day of the festival, Jesus stood there and cried out:

'If any man is thirsty, let him come to me!
Let the man come and drink who believes in me!'

As scripture says: From his breast shall flow fountains of living water.

He was speaking of the Spirit which those who believed in him were to receive; for there was no Spirit as yet because Jesus had not yet been glorified.

The Gospel of the Lord.

The Creed is said.

Prayer over the Offerings	Super oblata
Pour out upon these gifts the blessing of your Spirit, we pray, O Lord, so that through them your Church may be imbued with such love that the truth of your saving mystery may shine forth for the whole world. Through Christ our Lord.	Præsentia munera, quæsumus, Domine, Spiritus tui benedictione perfunde, ut per ipsa Ecclesiæ tuæ ea dilectio tribuatur, per quam salutaris mysterii toto mundo veritas enitescat. Per Christum Dominum nostrum.

Preface of Pentecost as in the following Mass, p.422.

When the Roman Canon is used, the proper form of the Communicantes (In communion with those) is said.

Communion Antiphon Jn 7:37	Ant. ad communionem

On the last day of the festival,
    Jesus stood and cried out:
If anyone is thirsty, let him come
    to me and drink, alleluia.
	Ultimo festivitatis die, stabat Iesus
	    et clamabat dicens:
	Si quis sitit, veniat ad me et bibat,
	    alleluia.

Prayer after Communion	Post communionem

May these gifts we have consumed
benefit us, O Lord,
that we may always be aflame
    with the same Spirit,
whom you wondrously poured out
    on your Apostles.
Through Christ our Lord.
	Hæc nobis, Domine,
	    munera sumpta proficiant,
	ut illo iugiter Spiritu ferveamus,
	quem Apostolis tuis
	    ineffabiliter infudisti.
	Per Christum Dominum nostrum.

A formula of Solemn Blessing, pp.648-649, may be used.

To dismiss the people the Deacon or, if there is no Deacon, the Priest himself sings or says:

Go forth, the Mass is ended, alleluia, alleluia.	Ite, missa est, alleluia, alleluia.
Or:	Vel:
Go in peace, alleluia, alleluia.	Ite in pace, alleluia, alleluia.
And the people reply:	Omnes respondent:
Thanks be to God, alleluia, alleluia.	R. Deo gratias, alleluia, alleluia.

At the Mass during the Day

(YEAR A)

Entrance Antiphon Ws 1:7	Ant. ad introitum

THE Spirit of the Lord has filled
    the whole world
and that which contains all things
understands what is said, alleluia.
	SPIRITUS Domini replevit
	    orbem terrarum,
	et hoc quod continet omnia
	scientiam habet vocis, alleluia.

Or: Rm 5:5; Cf. 8:11	Vel:

The love of God has been poured
    into our hearts
through the Spirit of God dwelling
    within us, alleluia.
	Caritas Dei diffusa est in cordibus
	    nostris
	per inhabitantem Spiritum eius
	    in nobis, alleluia.

The Gloria in excelsis (Glory to God in the highest) is said.

Collect	Collecta
O God, who by the mystery of today's great feast	Deus, qui sacramento festivitatis hodiernæ
sanctify your whole Church in every people and nation,	universam Ecclesiam tuam in omni gente et natione sanctificas,
pour out, we pray, the gifts of the Holy Spirit	in totam mundi latitudinem Spiritus Sancti dona defunde,
across the face of the earth and, with the divine grace that was at work	et, quod inter ipsa evangelicæ prædicationis exordia operata est divina dignatio,
when the Gospel was first proclaimed, fill now once more the hearts of believers.	nunc quoque per credentium corda perfunde.
Through our Lord Jesus Christ, your Son,	Per Dominum nostrum Iesum Christum Filium tuum,
who lives and reigns with you in the unity of the Holy Spirit,	qui tecum vivit et regnat in unitate Spiritus Sancti,
one God, for ever and ever.	Deus, per omnia sæcula sæculorum.

FIRST READING

A reading from the Acts of the Apostles   2:1-11

They were all filled with the Holy Spirit and began to speak.

When Pentecost day came round, the apostles had all met in one room, when suddenly they heard what sounded like a powerful wind from heaven, the noise of which filled the entire house in which they were sitting; and something appeared to them that seemed like tongues of fire; these separated and came to rest on the head of each of them. They were all filled with the Holy Spirit, and began to speak foreign languages as the Spirit gave them the gift of speech.

Now there were devout men living in Jerusalem from every nation under heaven, and at this sound they all assembled, each one bewildered to hear these men speaking his own language. They were amazed and astonished. 'Surely' they said 'all these men speaking are Galileans? How does it happen that each of us hears them in his own native language? Parthians, Medes and Elamites; people from Mesopotamia, Judaea and Cappadocia, Pontus and Asia, Phrygia and Pamphylia, Egypt and the parts of Libya round Cyrene; as well as visitors from Rome – Jews and proselytes alike – Cretans and Arabs; we hear them preaching in our own language about the marvels of God.'

The word of the Lord.

Responsorial Psalm   Ps 103:1,24,29-31,34. R. Cf. v.30

R. **Send forth your Spirit, O Lord,**
   and renew the face of the earth.
   Or: **Alleluia!**

Bless the Lord, my soul!
Lord God, how great you are.
How many are your works, O Lord!
The earth is full of your riches. R.

You take back your spirit, they die,
returning to the dust from which they came.
You send forth your spirit, they are created;
and you renew the face of the earth. R.

May the glory of the Lord last for ever!
May the Lord rejoice in his works!
May my thoughts be pleasing to him.
I find my joy in the Lord. R.

SECOND READING

A reading from the first letter of St Paul to the Corinthians   12:3-7,12-13

In the one Spirit we were all baptised.

No one can say, 'Jesus is Lord' unless he is under the influence of the
Holy Spirit.

There is a variety of gifts but always the same Spirit; there are all sorts
of service to be done, but always to the same Lord; working in all sorts of
different ways in different people, it is the same God who is working in all
of them. The particular way in which the Spirit is given to each person is
for a good purpose.

Just as a human body, though it is made up of many parts, is a single
unit because all these parts, though many, make one body, so it is with
Christ. In the one Spirit we were all baptised, Jews as well as Greeks, slaves
as well as citizens, and one Spirit was given to us all to drink.

The word of the Lord.

SEQUENCE

The sequence may be said or sung.

Holy Spirit, Lord of light,
From the clear celestial height
Thy pure beaming radiance give.

Come, thou Father of the poor,
Come with treasures which endure;
Come, thou light of all that live!

Thou, of all consolers best,
Thou, the soul's delightful guest,
Dost refreshing peace bestow.

Thou in toil art comfort sweet;
Pleasant coolness in the heat;
Solace in the midst of woe.

Light immortal, light divine,
Visit thou these hearts of thine,
And our inmost being fill:

If thou take thy grace away,
Nothing pure in man will stay;
All his good is turned to ill.

Heal our wounds,
    our strength renew;
On our dryness pour thy dew;
Wash the stains of guilt away.

Bend the stubborn heart and will;
Melt the frozen, warm the chill;
Guide the steps that go astray.

Thou, on us who evermore
Thee confess and thee adore,
thy sevenfold gifts descend:

Give us comfort when we die,
Give us life with thee on high;
Give us joys that never end.

Veni, Sancte Spiritus,
    et emitte cælitus
lucis tuæ radium.

Veni, pater pauperum,
    veni, dator munerum,
veni, lumen cordium.

Consolator optime,
    dulcis hospes animæ,
dulce refrigerium.

In labore requies,
    in æstu temperies,
in fletu solacium.

O lux beatissima,
    reple cordis intima
tuorum fidelium.

Sine tuo numine,
nihil est in homine,
nihi est innoxium.

Lava quod est sordidum,
riga quod est aridum,
sana quod est saucium.

Flecte quod est rigidum,
fove quod est frigidum,
rege quod est devium.

Da tuis fidelibus,
    in te confidentibus,
sacrum septenarium.

Da virtutis meritum
    da salutis exitum,
da perenne gaudium.

Gospel Acclamation

R. **Alleluia, alleluia!**
Come, Holy Spirit, fill the hearts of your faithful
and kindle in them the fire of your love.
R. **Alleluia!**

GOSPEL

A reading from the holy Gospel according to John   20:19-23

As the Father sent me, so am I sending you: receive the Holy Spirit.

In the evening of the first day of the week, the doors were closed in the room where the disciples were, for fear of the Jews. Jesus came and stood among them. He said to them, 'Peace be with you,' and showed them his hands and his side. The disciples were filled with joy when they saw the Lord, and he said to them again, 'Peace be with you.

'As the Father sent me,
so am I sending you.'

After saying this he breathed on them and said:

'Receive the Holy Spirit.
For those whose sins you forgive,
they are forgiven;
for those whose sins you retain,
they are retained.'

The Gospel of the Lord.

The Creed is said.

Prayer over the Offerings	Super oblata
Grant, we pray, O Lord,	Præsta, quæsumus, Domine,
that, as promised by your Son,	ut, secundum promissionem Filii tui,
the Holy Spirit may reveal to us more abundantly	Spiritus Sanctus huius nobis sacrificii
the hidden mystery of this sacrifice	copiosius revelet arcanum,
and graciously lead us into all truth.	et omnem propitius reseret veritatem.
Through Christ our Lord.	Per Christum Dominum nostrum.

Preface: The Mystery of Pentecost.

It is truly right and just,
  our duty and our salvation,
always and everywhere
  to give you thanks,
Lord, holy Father,
  almighty and eternal God.

For, bringing your Paschal Mystery
  to completion,
you bestowed the Holy Spirit today
on those you made
  your adopted children
by uniting them to your Only
  Begotten Son.
This same Spirit,
  as the Church came to birth,
opened to all peoples
  the knowledge of God
and brought together the many
  languages of the earth
in profession of the one faith.

Therefore, overcome with paschal joy,
every land, every people exults
  in your praise
and even the heavenly Powers,
  with the angelic hosts,
sing together the unending hymn
  of your glory,
as they acclaim:

Holy, Holy, Holy Lord God of hosts...

Præfatio: De mysterio Pentecostes.

Vere dignum et iustum est,
  æquum et salutare,
nos tibi semper et ubique
  gratias agere:
Domine, sancte Pater,
  omnipotens æterne Deus.

Tu enim, sacramentum
  paschale consummans,
quibus, per Unigeniti tui consortium,
filios adoptionis esse tribuisti,
hodie Spiritum Sanctum es largitus;
qui, principio nascentis Ecclesiæ,
et cunctis gentibus scientiam
  indidit deitatis,
et linguarum diversitatem in unius
  fidei confessione sociavit.

Quapropter, profusis
  paschalibus gaudiis,
totus in orbe terrarum
  mundus exsultat.
Sed et supernæ virtutes atque
  angelicæ potestates
hymnum gloriæ tuæ concinunt,
  sine fine dicentes:

Sanctus, Sanctus, Sanctus. . .

When the Roman Canon is used, the proper form of the Communicantes (In communion with those) is said.

Communion Antiphon Ac 2:4,11

They were all filled
  with the Holy Spirit
and spoke of the marvels of God,
  alleluia.

Ant. ad communionem

Repleti sunt omnes Spiritu Sancto,
loquentes magnalia Dei, alleluia.

Prayer after Communion

O God, who bestow heavenly gifts upon your Church,
safeguard, we pray, the grace you have given,
that the gift of the Holy Spirit poured out upon her
may retain all its force
and that this spiritual food
may gain her abundance of eternal redemption.
Through Christ our Lord.

Post communionem

Deus, qui Ecclesiæ tuæ cælestia dona largiris,
custodi gratiam quam dedisti,
ut Spiritus Sancti vigeat semper munus infusum,
et ad æternæ redemptionis augmentum
spiritalis esca proficiat.
Per Christum Dominum nostrum.

A formula of Solemn Blessing, pp.648-649, may be used.
To dismiss the people the Deacon or, if there is no Deacon, the Priest himself sings or says:

Go forth, the Mass is ended, alleluia, alleluia.

Ite, missa est, alleluia, alleluia.

Or:

Go in peace, alleluia, aleluia.

Vel:

Ite in pace, alleluia, alleluia.

And the people reply:

Thanks be to God, alleluia, alleluia.

Omnes respondent:

Deo gratias, alleluia, alleluia.

With Easter Time now concluded, the paschal candle is extinguished. It is desirable to keep the paschal candle in the baptistery with due honour so that it is lit at the celebration of Baptism and the candles of those baptised are lit from it.

SECOND SUNDAY OF EASTER
(YEAR B)
(or of Divine Mercy)

Humanity must let itself be touched and pervaded by the Spirit given to it by the risen Christ. It is the Spirit who heals the wounds of the heart, pulls down the barriers that separate us from God and divide us from one another, and at the same time, restores the joy of the Father's love and of fraternal unity. It is important then that we accept the whole message that comes to us from the word of God on this Second Sunday of Easter, which from now on throughout the Church will be called "Divine Mercy Sunday". Christ has taught us that "man not only receives and experiences the mercy of God, but is also called 'to practise mercy' towards others: "Blessed are the merciful, for they shall obtain mercy" (Mt 5:7).

(Blessed Pope John Paul II)

Entrance Antiphon 1 P 2:2	Ant. ad introitum

LIKE newborn infants,
you must long for the pure,
spiritual milk,
that in him you may grow
to salvation, alleluia.

QUASI modo geniti infantes,
rationabile, sine dolo
lac concupiscite,
ut in eo crescatis in salutem,
alleluia.

Or: 4 Esdr 2:36-37	Vel:

Receive the joy of your glory,
giving thanks to God,
who has called you into the heavenly
kingdom, alleluia.

Accipite iucunditatem gloriæ vestræ,
gratias agentes Deo,
qui vos ad cælestia regna vocavit,
alleluia.

The Gloria in excelsis (Glory to God in the highest) is said.

Collect	Collecta

God of everlasting mercy,
who, in the very recurrence
of the paschal feast
kindle the faith of the people you
have made your own,
increase, we pray, the grace you
have bestowed,
that all may grasp
and rightly understand

Deus misericordiæ sempiternæ,
qui in ipso paschalis festi recursu
fidem sacratæ tibi plebis accendis,
auge gratiam quam dedisti,
ut digna omnes intellegentia
comprehendant,
quo lavacro abluti,
quo Spiritu regenerati,
quo sanguine sunt redempti.

in what font they have been washed,
by whose Spirit they have
    been reborn,
by whose Blood they have
    been redeemed.
Through our Lord Jesus Christ,
    your Son,
who lives and reigns with you
    in the unity of the Holy Spirit,
one God, for ever and ever.

Per Dominum nostrum Iesum
    Christum Filium tuum,
qui tecum vivit et regnat
    in unitate Spiritus Sancti,
Deus, per omnia sæcula sæculorum.

FIRST READING

A reading from the Acts of the Apostles   4:32-35
United, heart and soul.

The whole group of believers was united, heart and soul; no one claimed
for his own use anything that he had, as everything they owned was held
in common.

   The apostles continued to testify to the resurrection of the Lord Jesus
with great power, and they were all given great respect.

   None of their members was ever in want, as all those who owned land
or houses would sell them, and bring the money from them, to present it to
the apostles; it was then distributed to any members who might be in need.

   The word of the Lord.

Responsorial Psalm   Ps 117:2-4,15-18,22-24. R. v.1

R. **Give thanks to the Lord for he is good,**
    for his love has no end.
    Or: **Alleluia, alleluia, alleluia!**

Let the sons of Israel say:
'His love has no end.'
Let the sons of Aaron say:
'His love has no end.'
Let those who fear the Lord say:
'His love has no end.' R.

The Lord's right hand has triumphed;
his right hand raised me up.
I shall not die, I shall live
and recount his deeds.
I was punished, I was punished by the Lord,
but not doomed to die. R.

The stone which the builders rejected
has become the corner stone.
This is the work of the Lord
a marvel in our eyes.
This day was made by the Lord;
we rejoice and are glad. R.

R. **Give thanks to the Lord for he is good,**
for his love has no end.
Or: **Alleluia, alleluia, alleluia!**

SECOND READING

A reading from the first letter of St John   5:1-6

Anyone who has been begotten by God has already overcome the world.

Whoever believes that Jesus is the Christ
has been begotten by God;
and whoever loves the Father that begot him
loves the child whom he begets.
We can be sure that we love God's children
if we love God himself and do what he has commanded us;
this is what loving God is –
keeping his commandments;
and his commandments are not difficult,
because anyone who has been begotten by God
has already overcome the world;
this is the victory over the world –
our faith.
Who can overcome the world?
Only the man who believes that Jesus is the Son of God:
Jesus Christ who came by water and blood,
not with water only,
but with water and blood;
with the Spirit as another witness –
since the Spirit is the truth.

The word of the Lord.

Easter Sequence can be sung here, see pp.364-365.

Gospel Acclamation   Jn 20:29

R. **Alleluia, alleluia!**
Jesus said: 'You believe because you can see me.
Happy are those who have not seen and yet believe.'
R. **Alleluia!**

GOSPEL

A reading from the holy Gospel according to John   20:19-31

Eight days later, Jesus came.

In the evening of that same day, the first day of the week, the doors were closed in the room where the disciples were, for fear of the Jews. Jesus came and stood among them. He said to them 'Peace be with you,' and showed them his hands and his side. The disciples were filled with joy when they saw the Lord, and he said to them again, 'Peace be with you.

'As the Father sent me,
so am I sending you.'

After saying this he breathed on them and said:

'Receive the Holy Spirit.
For those whose sins you forgive,
they are forgiven;
for those whose sins you retain,
they are retained.'

Thomas, called the Twin, who was one of the Twelve, was not with them when Jesus came. When the disciples said, 'We have seen the Lord,' he answered, 'Unless I see the holes that the nails made in his hands and can put my finger into the holes they made, and unless I can put my hand into his side, I refuse to believe.' Eight days later the disciples were in the house again and Thomas was with them. The doors were closed, but Jesus came in and stood among them. 'Peace be with you,' he said. Then he spoke to Thomas, 'Put your finger here; look, here are my hands. Give me your hand; put it into my side. Doubt no longer but believe.' Thomas replied, 'My Lord and my God!' Jesus said to him:

'You believe because you can see me.
Happy are those who have not seen and yet believe.'

There were many other signs that Jesus worked and the disciples saw, but they are not recorded in this book. These are recorded so that you may believe that Jesus is the Christ, the Son of God, and that believing this you may have life through his name.

The Gospel of the Lord.

The Creed is said.

Prayer over the Offerings	Super oblata
Accept, O Lord, we pray,	Suscipe, quæsumus, Domine,
the oblations of your people	plebis tuæ
(and of those you have brought	(et tuorum renatorum) oblationes,
to new birth),	ut, confessione tui nominis et
that, renewed by confession of your	baptismate renovati,
name and by Baptism,	sempiternam beatitudinem
they may attain unending happiness.	consequantur.
Through Christ our Lord.	Per Christum Dominum nostrum.

Preface I of Easter (. . .on this day above all. . .), pp.558-561

When the Roman Canon is used, the proper forms of Communicantes (In communion with those) and Hanc igitur (Therefore, Lord, we pray) are said.

Communion Antiphon Cf. Jn 20:27	Ant. ad communionem
Bring your hand and feel the place	Mitte manum tuam, et cognosce
of the nails,	loca clavorum,
and do not be unbelieving	et noli esse incredulus, sed fidelis,
but believing, alleluia.	alleluia.

Prayer after Communion	Post communionem
Grant, we pray, almighty God,	Concede, quæsumus,
that our reception of this paschal	omnipotens Deus,
Sacrament	ut paschalis perceptio sacramenti
may have a continuing effect	continua in nostris
in our minds and hearts.	mentibus perseveret.
Through Christ our Lord.	Per Christum Dominum nostrum.

A formula of Solemn Blessing, pp.360-361, may be used.

For the dismissal of the people, there is sung or said: Go forth, the Mass is ended, alleluia, alleluia. Or: Go in peace, alleluia, alleluia. The people respond: Thanks be to God, alleluia, alleluia.

THIRD SUNDAY OF EASTER (YEAR B)

The Resurrection of Christ is central to Christianity. It is a fundamental truth to be reasserted vigorously in every epoch, since to deny it, as has been, and continues to be attempted, or to transform it into a purely spiritual event, is to thwart our very faith. St Paul states: "If Christ has not been raised, then our preaching is in vain and your faith is in vain" (1 Co 15:14). In the days that followed the Lord's Resurrection, the Apostles stayed together, comforted by Mary's presence, and after the Ascension they persevered with her in prayerful expectation of Pentecost. Our Lady was a mother and teacher to them, a role that she continues to play for Christians of all times.

(Pope Benedict XVI)

Entrance Antiphon   Cf. Ps 65:1-2

CRY out with joy to God,
all the earth;
O sing to the glory of his name.
O render him glorious praise,
     alleluia.

Ant. ad introitum

IUBILATE Deo, omnis terra,
psalmum dicite nomini eius,
date gloriam laudi eius, alleluia.

The Gloria in excelsis (Glory to God in the highest) is said.

Collect

May your people exult for ever,
     O God,
in renewed youthfulness of spirit,
so that, rejoicing now in the restored
     glory of our adoption,
we may look forward
     in confident hope
to the rejoicing of the day
     of resurrection.
Through our Lord Jesus Christ,
     your Son,
who lives and reigns with you
     in the unity of the Holy Spirit,
one God, for ever and ever.

Collecta

Semper exsultet populus
     tuus, Deus,
renovata animæ iuventute,
ut, qui nunc lætatur in adoptionis
     se gloriam restitutum,
resurrectionis diem spe certæ
     gratulationis exspectet.
Per Dominum nostrum Iesum
     Christum Filium tuum,
qui tecum vivit et regnat
     in unitate Spiritus Sancti,
Deus, per omnia sæcula sæculorum.

FIRST READING

A reading from the Acts of the Apostles   3:13-15,17-19

You killed the prince of life. God, however, raised him from the dead.

Peter said to the people: 'You are Israelites, and it is the God of Abraham, Isaac and Jacob, the God of our ancestors, who has glorified his servant Jesus, the same Jesus you handed over and then disowned in the presence of Pilate, after Pilate had decided to release him. It was you who accused the Holy One, the Just One, you who demanded the reprieve of a murderer while you killed the prince of life. God, however, raised him from the dead, and to that fact we are the witnesses.

'Now I know, brothers, that neither you nor your leaders had any idea what you were really doing; this was the way God carried out what he had foretold, when he said through all his prophets that his Christ would suffer. Now you must repent and turn to God, so that your sins may be wiped out.'

The word of the Lord.

Responsorial Psalm   Ps 4:2,4,7,9. R. v.7

R. **Lift up the light of your face on us, O Lord.**
   Or: **Alleluia!**

   When I call, answer me, O God of justice;
   from anguish you released me, have mercy and hear me! R.

   It is the Lord who grants favours to those whom he loves;
   the Lord hears me whenever I call him. R.

   'What can bring us happiness?' many say.
   Lift up the light of your face on us, O Lord. R.

   I will lie down in peace and sleep comes at once,
   for you alone, Lord, make me dwell in safety. R.

SECOND READING

A reading from the first letter of St John   2:1-5

He is the sacrifice that takes our sins away, and not only ours, but the whole world's.

I am writing this, my children,
to stop you sinning;
but if anyone should sin,
we have our advocate with the Father,
Jesus Christ, who is just;
he is the sacrifice that takes our sins away,
and not only ours,

but the whole world's.
We can be sure that we know God
only by keeping his commandments.
Anyone who says, 'I know him',
and does not keep his commandments,
is a liar,
refusing to admit the truth.
But when anyone does obey what he has said,
God's love comes to perfection in him.

The word of the Lord.

Gospel Acclamation   Cf. Lk 24:32
R. **Alleluia, alleluia!**
Lord Jesus, explain the scriptures to us.
Make our hearts burn within us as you talk to us.
R. **Alleluia!**

GOSPEL

A reading from the holy Gospel according to Luke   24:35-48

So you see how it is written that the Christ would suffer and on the third day rise from the dead.

The disciples told their story of what had happened on the road and how they had recognised Jesus at the breaking of bread.

They were still talking about this when Jesus himself stood among them and said to them, 'Peace be with you!' In a state of alarm and fright, they thought they were seeing a ghost. But he said, 'Why are you so agitated, and why are these doubts rising in your hearts? Look at my hands and feet; yes, it is I indeed. Touch me and see for yourselves; a ghost has no flesh and bones as you can see I have.' And as he said this he showed them his hands and feet. Their joy was so great that they could not believe it, and they stood there dumbfounded; so he said to them, 'Have you anything here to eat?' And they offered him a piece of grilled fish, which he took and ate before their eyes.

Then he told them, 'This is what I meant when I said, while I was still with you, that everything written about me in the Law of Moses, in the Prophets and in the Psalms, has to be fulfilled.' He then opened their minds to understand the scriptures, and he said to them, 'So you see how it is written that the Christ would suffer and on the third day rise from the dead, and that, in his name, repentance for the forgiveness of sins would be preached to all the nations, beginning from Jerusalem. You are witnesses to this.'

The Gospel of the Lord.

The Creed is said.

Prayer over the Offerings

Receive, O Lord, we pray,
  these offerings of your
      exultant Church,
and, as you have given her cause
      for such great gladness,
grant also that the gifts we bring
may bear fruit
      in perpetual happiness.
Through Christ our Lord.

Super oblata

Suscipe munera, Domine,
      quæsumus, exsultantis Ecclesiæ,
et cui causam tanti
      gaudii præstitisti,
perpetuæ fructum concede lætitiæ.
Per Christum Dominum nostrum.

Preface of Easter, pp.558-563.

Communion Antiphon   Lk 24:35

The disciples recognised
      the Lord Jesus
in the breaking of the bread,
      alleluia.

Ant. ad communionem

Cognoverunt discipuli
      Dominum Iesum
in fractione panis, alleluia.

Optional for Year B: Lk 24:46-47

The Christ had to suffer and on
      the third day rise from the dead;
in his name repentance
      and remission of sins
must be preached to all the nations,
      alleluia.

Ad libitum pro anno B

Oportebat Christum pati,
      et resurgere a mortuis tertia die,
et prædicari in nomine
      eius pænitentiam,
et remissionem peccatorum
      in omnes gentes, alleluia.

Prayer after Communion

Look with kindness upon your
      people, O Lord,
and grant, we pray,
that those you were pleased
      to renew by eternal mysteries
may attain in their flesh
the incorruptible glory
      of the resurrection.
Through Christ our Lord.

Post communionem

Populum tuum, quæsumus,
      Domine, intuere benignus,
et, quem æternis dignatus
      es renovare mysteriis,
ad incorruptibilem glorificandæ
      carnis resurrectionem
pervenire concede.
Per Christum Dominum nostrum.

A formula of Solemn Blessing, pp.646-649, may be used.

FOURTH SUNDAY OF EASTER (YEAR B)

"I am the good shepherd. The good shepherd lays down his life for the sheep".
How can we fail to see in these words an implicit reference to the mystery of the
Lord's Death and Resurrection? "I lay down my life that I may take it again. No
one takes it from me, but I lay it down of my own accord, and I have power to
take it up again" (Jn 10:17-18). Christ freely offered himself on the Cross and rose
by virtue of his own divine power. Therefore the allegory of the good shepherd
has a strongly paschal character and for this reason the Church proposes it for
our reflection during this Easter season. Christ's pastoral mission is a universal
mission, which is not limited to the sons and daughters of Israel, but, by virtue
of his sacrifice on the Cross, embraces all men and all peoples.

(Blessed Pope John Paul II)

Entrance Antiphon   Cf. Ps 32:5-6

THE merciful love of the Lord
fills the earth;
by the word of the Lord the heavens
were made, alleluia.

Ant. ad introitum

MISERICORDIA Domini plena
est terra;
verbo Domini cæli firmati sunt,
alleluia

The Gloria in excelsis (Glory to God in the highest) is said.

Collect

Almighty ever-living God,
lead us to a share in the joys
of heaven,
so that the humble flock may reach
where the brave Shepherd
has gone before.
Who lives and reigns with you
in the unity of the Holy Spirit,
one God, for ever and ever.

Collecta

Omnipotens sempiterne Deus,
deduc nos ad societatem
cælestium gaudiorum,
ut eo perveniat humilitas gregis,
quo processit fortitudo pastoris.
Per Dominum nostrum
Iesum Christum Filium tuum,
qui tecum vivit et regnat
in unitate Spiritus Sancti,
Deus, per omnia sæcula sæculorum.

FIRST READING

A reading from the Acts of the Apostles   4:8-12

This is the only name by which we can be saved.

Filled with the Holy Spirit, Peter said: 'Rulers of the people, and elders! If you
are questioning us today about an act of kindness to a cripple, and asking us
how he was healed, then I am glad to tell you all, and would indeed be glad

to tell the whole people of Israel, that it was by the name of Jesus Christ the Nazarene, the one you crucified, whom God raised from the dead, by this name and by no other that this man is able to stand up perfectly healthy, here in your presence, today. This is the stone rejected by you the builders, but which has proved to be the keystone. For of all the names in the world given to men, this is the only one by which we can be saved.'

The word of the Lord.

Responsorial Psalm   Ps 117:1,8-9,21-23,26,28-29. R. v.22

R. **The stone which the builders rejected**
   has become the corner stone.
   Or: **Alleluia!**

Give thanks to the Lord for he is good,
for his love has no end.
It is better to take refuge in the Lord
than to trust in men:
it is better to take refuge in the Lord
than to trust in princes. R.

I will thank you for you have given answer
and you are my saviour.
The stone which the builders rejected
has become the corner stone.
This is the work of the Lord,
a marvel in our eyes. R.

Blessed in the name of the Lord
is he who comes.
We bless you from the house of the Lord;
I will thank you for you have given answer
and you are my saviour.
Give thanks to the Lord for he is good;
for his love has no end. R.

SECOND READING

A reading from the first letter of St John   3:1-2
We shall see God as he really is.

Think of the love that the Father has lavished on us,
by letting us be called God's children;
and that is what we are.

Because the world refused to acknowledge him,
therefore it does not acknowledge us.
My dear people, we are already the children of God
but what we are to be in the future has not yet been revealed;
all we know is, that when it is revealed
we shall be like him
because we shall see him as he really is.

The word of the Lord.

Gospel Acclamation   Jn 10:14

R. **Alleluia, alleluia!**
I am the good shepherd, says the Lord;
I know my own sheep and my own know me.
R. **Alleluia!**

GOSPEL

A reading from the holy Gospel according to John   10:11-18
The good shepherd is one who lays down his life for his sheep.

Jesus said:

'I am the good shepherd:
the good shepherd is one who lays down his life for his sheep.
The hired man, since he is not the shepherd
and the sheep do not belong to him,
abandons the sheep and runs away
as soon as he sees a wolf coming,
and then the wolf attacks and scatters the sheep;
this is because he is only a hired man
and has no concern for the sheep.
I am the good shepherd;
I know my own
and my own know me,
just as the Father knows me
and I know the Father;
and I lay down my life for my sheep.
And there are other sheep I have
that are not of this fold,
and these I have to lead as well.
They too will listen to my voice,
and there will be only one flock,
and one shepherd.

The Father loves me,
because I lay down my life
in order to take it up again.
No one takes it from me;
I lay it down of my own free will,
and as it is in my power to lay it down,
so it is in my power to take it up again;
and this is the command I have been given by my Father.'

The Gospel of the Lord.

The Creed is said.

Prayer over the Offerings
Grant, we pray, O Lord,
that we may always find delight
    in these paschal mysteries,
so that the renewal constantly
    at work within us
may be the cause of our
    unending joy.
Through Christ our Lord.

Preface of Easter, pp.558-563.

Super oblata
Concede, quæsumus, Domine,
semper nos per hæc mysteria
    paschalia gratulari,
ut continua nostræ
    reparationis operatio
perpetuæ nobis fiat causa lætitiæ.
Per Christum Dominum nostrum.

Communion Antiphon
The Good Shepherd has risen,
who laid down his life for his sheep
and willingly died for his flock,
    alleluia.

Ant. ad communionem
Surrexit Pastor bonus,
qui animam suam posuit pro
    ovibus suis,
et pro grege suo mori dignatus est,
    alleluia.

Prayer after Communion
Look upon your flock,
    kind Shepherd,
and be pleased to settle
    in eternal pastures
the sheep you have redeemed
by the Precious Blood of your Son.
Who lives and reigns
    for ever and ever.

Post communionem
Gregem tuum, Pastor bone,
    placatus intende,
et oves, quas pretioso Filii tui
    sanguine redemisti,
in æternis pascuis collocare digneris.
Per Christum Dominum nostrum.

A formula of Solemn Blessing, pp.646-649, may be used.

FIFTH SUNDAY OF EASTER (YEAR B)

On this Fifth Sunday of Easter, the liturgy presents us with the Gospel passage of John in which Jesus, speaking to the disciples at the Last Supper, exhorts them to remain united to him like the branches to the vine. It is a truly meaningful parable as it expresses with great effectiveness that Christian life is a mystery of communion with Jesus: "Whoever remains in me", says the Lord, "will bear much fruit, because without me you can do nothing" (Jn 15:5). The secret of spiritual fruitfulness is union with God, union that is realised especially in the Eucharist, also rightly called "Communion".

(Pope Benedict XVI)

Entrance Antiphon   Cf. Ps 97:1-2

O SING a new song to the Lord,
for he has worked wonders;
in the sight of the nations
he has shown his deliverance,
    alleluia.

Ant. ad introitum

CANTATE Domino
canticum novum,
quia mirabilia fecit Dominus;
ante conspectum gentium revelavit
    iustitiam suam, alleluia.

The Gloria in excelsis (Glory to God in the highest) is said.

Collect

Almighty ever-living God,
constantly accomplish the Paschal
    Mystery within us,
that those you were pleased
    to make new in Holy Baptism
may, under your protective care,
    bear much fruit
and come to the joys of life eternal.
Through our Lord Jesus Christ,
    your Son,
who lives and reigns with you
    in the unity of the Holy Spirit,
one God, for ever and ever.

Collecta

Omnipotens sempiterne Deus,
semper in nobis paschale
perfice sacramentum,
ut, quos sacro baptismate dignatus
    es renovare,
sub tuæ protectionis auxilio multos
    fructus afferant,
et ad æternæ vitæ gaudia
pervenire concedas.
Per Dominum nostrum Iesum
    Christum Filium tuum,
qui tecum vivit et regnat
    in unitate Spiritus Sancti,
Deus, per omnia sæcula sæculorum.

FIRST READING

A reading from the Acts of the Apostles   9:26-31

Barnabas explained how the Lord had appeared to Saul on his journey.

When Saul got to Jerusalem he tried to join the disciples, but they were
all afraid of him: they could not believe he was really a disciple. Barnabas,
however, took charge of him, introduced him to the apostles, and explained
how the Lord had appeared to Saul and spoken to him on his journey, and
how he had preached boldly at Damascus in the name of Jesus. Saul now
started to go round with them in Jerusalem, preaching fearlessly in the
name of the Lord. But after he had spoken to the Hellenists, and argued
with them, they became determined to kill him. When the brothers knew,
they took him to Caesarea, and sent him off from there to Tarsus.

The churches throughout Judaea, Galilee and Samaria were now left
in peace, building themselves up, living in the fear of the Lord, and filled
with the consolation of the Holy Spirit.

The word of the Lord.

Responsorial Pslam   Ps 21:26-28,30-32. R. v.26

R. **You, Lord, are my praise in the great assembly.**
    Or: **Alleluia!**

My vows I will pay before those who fear him.
The poor shall eat and shall have their fill.
They shall praise the Lord, those who seek him.
May their hearts live for ever and ever! R.

All the earth shall remember and return to the Lord,
all families of the nations worship before him.
They shall worship him, all the mighty of the earth;
before him shall bow all who go down to the dust. R.

And my soul shall live for him, my children serve him.
They shall tell of the Lord to generations yet to come,
declare his faithfulness to peoples yet unborn:
'These things the Lord has done.' R.

SECOND READING

A reading from the first letter of St John   3:18-24

His commandments are these: that we believe in his Son and that we love one another.

My children,
our love is not to be just words or mere talk,
but something real and active;
only by this can we be certain
that we are the children of the truth
and be able to quieten our conscience in his presence,
whatever accusations it may raise against us,
because God is greater than our conscience and he knows everything.
My dear people,
if we cannot be condemned by our own conscience,
we need not be afraid in God's presence,
and whatever we ask him,
we shall receive,
because we keep his commandments
and live the kind of life that he wants.
His commandments are these:
that we believe in the name of his Son Jesus Christ
and that we love one another
as he told us to.
Whoever keeps his commandments
lives in God and God lives in him.
We know that he lives in us
by the Spirit that he has given us.

   The word of the Lord.

Gospel Acclamation   Jn 15:4,5

R. **Alleluia, alleluia!**
Make your home in me, as I make mine in you.
Whoever remains in me bears fruit in plenty.
R. **Alleluia!**

GOSPEL

A reading from the holy Gospel according to John   15:1-8

Whoever remains in me, with me in him, bears fruit in plenty.

Jesus said to his disciples:

   'I am the true vine,
   and my Father is the vinedresser.

Every branch in me that bears no fruit
he cuts away,
and every branch that does bear fruit he prunes
to make it bear even more.
You are pruned already,
by means of the word that I have spoken to you.
Make your home in me, as I make mine in you.
As a branch cannot bear fruit all by itself,
but must remain part of the vine,
neither can you unless you remain in me.
I am the vine,
you are the branches.
Whoever remains in me, with me in him,
bears fruit in plenty;
for cut off from me you can do nothing.
Anyone who does not remain in me
is like a branch that has been thrown away
– he withers;
these branches are collected and thrown on the fire,
and they are burnt.
If you remain in me
and my words remain in you,
you may ask what you will
and you shall get it.
It is to the glory of my Father that you should bear much fruit,
and then you will be my disciples.'

The Gospel of the Lord.

The Creed is said.

Prayer over the Offerings

O God, who by the wonderful
  exchange effected in this sacrifice
have made us partakers of the one
  supreme Godhead,
grant, we pray,
that, as we have come to know
  your truth,
we may make it ours by a worthy
  way of life.
Through Christ our Lord.

Super oblata

Deus, qui nos, per huius sacrificii
  veneranda commercia,
unius summæque divinitatis
  participes effecisti,
præsta, quæsumus,
ut, sicut tuam
  cognovimus veritatem,
sic eam dignis
  moribus assequamur.
Per Christum Dominum nostrum.

Preface of Easter, pp.558-563.

Communion Antiphon Cf. Jn 15:1,5	Ant. ad communionem
I am the true vine and you are the branches, says the Lord. Whoever remains in me, and I in him, bears fruit in plenty, alleluia.	Ego sum vitis vera et vos palmites, dicit Dominus; qui manet in me et ego in eo, hic fert fructum multum, alleluia.

Prayer after Communion	Post communionem
Graciously be present to your people, we pray, O Lord, and lead those you have imbued with heavenly mysteries to pass from former ways to newness of life. Through Christ our Lord.	Populo tuo, quæsumus, Domine, adesto propitius, et, quem mysteriis cælestibus imbuisti, fac ad novitatem vitæ de vetustate transire. Per Christum Dominum nostrum.

A formula of Solemn Blessing, pp.646-649, may be used.

SIXTH SUNDAY OF EASTER (YEAR B)

The history of salvation begins with the choice of a man, Abraham, and a people, Israel, but its scope is universal, the salvation of all peoples. The history of salvation has always been marked by this interweaving of particularity and universality. We see this connection clearly in today's First Reading: on seeing in Cornelius's home the faith of the Gentiles and their desire for God, St Peter says: "Truly I perceive that God shows no partiality, but in every nation any one who fears him and does what is right is acceptable to him". Learning to fear God and practise justice thus opens the world to the Kingdom of God: this is the most profound purpose of all interreligious dialogue.

(Pope Benedict XVI)

Entrance Antiphon Cf. Is 48:20	Ant. ad introitum
PROCLAIM a joyful sound and let it be heard; proclaim to the ends of the earth: The Lord has freed his people, alleluia.	VOCEM iucunditatis annuntiate, et audiatur, annuntiate usque ad extremum terræ: liberavit Dominus populum suum, alleluia.

The Gloria in excelsis (Glory to God in the highest) is said.

Collect

Grant, almighty God,
that we may celebrate with heartfelt
   devotion these days of joy,
which we keep in honour
   of the risen Lord,
and that what we relive
   in remembrance
we may always hold to in what we do.
Through our Lord Jesus Christ,
   your Son,
who lives and reigns with you
   in the unity of the Holy Spirit,
one God, for ever and ever.

Collecta

Fac nos, omnipotens Deus,
   hos lætitiæ dies,
quos in honorem Domini
   resurgentis exsequimur,
affectu sedulo celebrare,
ut quod recordatione percurrimus
semper in opere teneamus.
Per Dominum nostrum Iesum
   Christum Filium tuum,
qui tecum vivit et regnat
   in unitate Spiritus Sancti,
Deus, per omnia sæcula sæculorum.

FIRST READING

A reading from the Acts of the Apostles   10:25-26,34-35,44-48

The Holy Spirit has been poured out on the pagans too.

As Peter reached the house Cornelius went out to meet him, knelt at his feet and prostrated himself. But Peter helped him up. 'Stand up,' he said 'I am only a man after all!'

Then Peter addressed them: 'The truth I have now come to realise' he said 'is that God does not have favourites, but that anybody of any nationality who fears God and does what is right is acceptable to him.'

While Peter was still speaking the Holy Spirit came down on all the listeners. Jewish believers who had accompanied Peter were all astonished that the gift of the Holy Spirit should be poured out on the pagans too, since they could hear them speaking strange languages and proclaiming the greatness of God. Peter himself then said, 'Could anyone refuse the water of baptism to these people, now they have received the Holy Spirit just as much as we have?' He then gave orders for them to be baptised in the name of Jesus Christ. Afterwards they begged him to stay on for some days.

The word of the Lord.

Responsorial Psalm   Ps 97:1-4. R. Cf. v.2

R. **The Lord has shown his salvation to the nations.**
   Or: **Alleluia!**

   Sing a new song to the Lord
   for he has worked wonders.

His right hand and his holy arm
have brought salvation. R.

The Lord has made known his salvation;
has shown his justice to the nations.
He has remembered his truth and love
for the house of Israel. R.

All the ends of the earth have seen
the salvation of our God.
Shout to the Lord all the earth,
ring out your joy. R.

When the Ascension is celebrated on the Seventh Sunday of Easter, the Second
Reading and Gospel assigned to the Seventh Sunday, may be read on the Sixth
Sunday.

SECOND READING

A reading from the first letter of St John   4:7-10
God is love.

My dear people,
let us love one another
since love comes from God
and everyone who loves is begotten by God and knows God.
Anyone who fails to love can never have known God,
because God is love.
God's love for us was revealed
when God sent into the world his only Son
so that we could have life through him;
this is the love I mean:
not our love for God,
but God's love for us when he sent his Son
to be the sacrifice that takes our sins away.

The word of the Lord.

Gospel Acclamation   Jn 14:23

R. **Alleluia, alleluia!**
Jesus said: 'If anyone loves me he will keep my word,
and my Father will love him, and we shall come to him.'
R. **Alleluia!**

GOSPEL

A reading from the holy Gospel according to John   15:9-17

A man can have no greater love than to lay down his life for his friends.

Jesus said to his disciples:

> 'As the Father has loved me,
> so I have loved you.
> Remain in my love.
> If you keep my commandments
> you will remain in my love,
> just as I have kept my Father's commandments
> and remain in his love.
> I have told you this
> so that my own joy may be in you
> and your joy be complete.
> This is my commandment:
> love one another,
> as I have loved you.
> A man can have no greater love
> than to lay down his life for his friends.
> You are my friends,
> if you do what I command you.
> I shall not call you servants any more,
> because a servant does not know
> his master's business;
> I call you friends,
> because I have made known to you
> everything I have learnt from my Father.
> You did not choose me,
> no, I chose you;
> and I commissioned you
> to go out and to bear fruit,
> fruit that will last;
> and then the Father will give you
> anything you ask him in my name.
> What I command you
> is to love one another.'

The Gospel of the Lord.

The Creed is said.

Prayer over the Offerings

May our prayers rise up to you,
    O Lord,
together with the sacrificial offerings,
so that, purified by your graciousness,
we may be conformed to
    the mysteries of your mighty love.
Through Christ our Lord.

Preface of Easter, pp.558-563.

Super oblata

Ascendant ad te, Domine,
    preces nostræ
cum oblationibus hostiarum,
ut, tua dignatione mundati,
sacramentis magnæ
    pietatis aptemur.
Per Christum Dominum nostrum.

Communion Antiphon Jn 14:15-16

If you love me, keep my
    commandments, says the Lord,
and I will ask the Father and he will
    send you another Paraclete,
to abide with you for ever, alleluia.

Ant. ad communionem

Si diligitis me, mandata mea
    servate, dicit Dominus.
Et ego rogabo Patrem, et alium
    Paraclitum dabit vobis,
ut maneat vobiscum in æternum,
    alleluia.

Prayer after Communion

Almighty ever-living God,
who restore us to eternal life
    in the Resurrection of Christ,
increase in us, we pray, the fruits
    of this paschal Sacrament
and pour into our hearts
    the strength of this saving food.
Through Christ our Lord.

Post communionem

Omnipotens sempiterne Deus,
qui ad æternam vitam in Christi
    resurrectione nos reparas,
fructus in nobis paschalis
    multiplica sacramenti,
et fortitudinem cibi salutaris nostris
    infunde pectoribus.
Per Christum Dominum nostrum.

A formula of Solemn Blessing, pp.646-649, may be used.

THE ASCENSION OF THE LORD (YEAR B)

Solemnity

This Mass is used on the evening of the day before the Solemnity, either before or after First Vespers (Evening Prayer I) of the Ascension.

Today we hear once again this question from the Acts of the Apostles. This time it is directed to all of us: "Why do you stand looking up to heaven?" We have read that, just as the Apostles were asking the Risen Lord about the restoration of Israel's earthly kingdom, "He was lifted up and a cloud took him out of their sight." And "they looked up to heaven as he went". They looked up to heaven because they looked to Jesus Christ, the Crucified and Risen One, raised up on high. We do not know whether at that precise moment they realised that a magnificent, infinite horizon was opening up before their eyes: the ultimate goal of our earthly pilgrimage. Perhaps they only realised this at Pentecost, in the light of the Holy Spirit. But for us, at a distance of two thousand years, the meaning of that event is quite clear. Here on earth, we are called to look up to heaven, to turn our minds and hearts to the inexpressible mystery of God. We are called to look towards this divine reality, to which we have been directed from our creation. For there we find life's ultimate meaning. Where the Solemnity of the Ascension is not to be observed as a Holyday of Obligation, it is assigned to the Seventh Sunday of Easter as its proper day.

(Pope Benedict XVI)

At the Vigil Mass

Entrance Antiphon Ps 67:33,35	Ant. ad introitum
YOU kingdoms of the earth, sing to God; praise the Lord, who ascends above the highest heavens; his majesty and might are in the skies, alleluia.	REGNA terræ cantate Deo, psallite Domino, qui ascendit super cælum cæli; magnificentia et virtus eius in nubibus, alleluia.

The Gloria in excelsis (Glory to God in the highest) is said.

Collect

O God, whose Son today ascended
   to the heavens
as the Apostles looked on,
grant, we pray, that, in accordance
   with his promise,
we may be worthy for him to live
   with us always on earth,
and we with him in heaven.
Who lives and reigns with you
   in the unity of the Holy Spirit,
one God, for ever and ever.

Collecta

Deus, cuius Filius hodie in cælos,
Apostolis astantibus, ascendit,
concede nobis, quæsumus,
ut secundum eius promissionem
et ille nobiscum semper in terris
et nos cum eo in cælo
   vivere mereamur.
Qui tecum vivit et regnat
   in unitate Spiritus Sanci, Deus,
per omnia sæcula sæculorum.

FIRST READING

A reading from the Acts of the Apostles   1:1-11

He was lifted up while they looked on.

In my earlier work, Theophilus, I dealt with everything Jesus had done and taught from the beginning until the day he gave his instructions to the apostles he had chosen through the Holy Spirit, and was taken up to heaven. He had shown himself alive to them after his Passion by many demonstrations: for forty days he had continued to appear to them and tell them about the kingdom of God. When he had been at table with them, he had told them not to leave Jerusalem, but to wait there for what the Father had promised. 'It is', he had said, 'what you have heard me speak about: John baptised with water but you, not many days from now, will be baptised with the Holy Spirit.'

Now having met together, they asked him, 'Lord, has the time come? Are you going to restore the kingdom to Israel?' He replied, 'It is not for you to know times or dates that the Father has decided by his own authority, but you will receive power when the Holy Spirit comes on you, and then you will be my witnesses not only in Jerusalem but throughout Judaea and Samaria, and indeed to the ends of the earth.'

As he said this he was lifted up while they looked on, and a cloud took him from their sight. They were still staring into the sky when suddenly two men in white were standing near them and they said, 'Why are you men from Galilee standing here looking into the sky? Jesus who has been taken up from you into heaven, this same Jesus will come back in the same way as you have seen him go there.'

The word of the Lord.

Responsorial Psalm   Ps 46:2-3,6-9. R. v.6

R. **God goes up with shouts of joy;**
   the Lord goes up with trumpet blast.
   Or: **Alleluia!**

All peoples, clap your hands,
cry to God with shouts of joy!
For the Lord, the Most High, we must fear,
great king over all the earth. R.

God goes up with shouts of joy;
the Lord goes up with trumpet blast.
Sing praise for God, sing praise,
sing praise to our king, sing praise. R.

God is king of all the earth.
Sing praise with all your skill.
God is king over the nations;
God reigns on his holy throne. R.

SECOND READING

The reading of Year A, Ep 1:17-23, p.393, may be used in place of the following.

A reading from the letter of St Paul to the Ephesians   4:1-13

Fully mature with the fullness of Christ.

[I, the prisoner in the Lord, implore you therefore to lead a life worthy of
your vocation. Bear with one another charitably, in complete selflessness,
gentleness and patience. Do all you can to preserve the unity of the Spirit
by the peace that binds you together. There is one Body, one Spirit, just
as you were all called into one and the same hope when you were called.
There is one Lord, one faith, one baptism, and one God who is Father of
all, over all, through all and within all.

Each one of us, however, has been given his own share of grace, given
as Christ allotted it.] It was said that he would:

When he ascended to the height, he captured prisoners,
he gave gifts to men.

When it says, 'he ascended', what can it mean if not that he descended
right down to the lower regions of the earth? [The one who rose higher
than all the heavens to fill all things is none other than the one who
descended. And to some, his gift was that they should be apostles; to some,
prophets; to some, evangelists; to some, pastors and teachers; so that the
saints together make a unity in the work of service, building up the body
of Christ. In this way we are all to come to unity in our faith and in our

knowledge of the Son of God, until we become the perfect Man, fully mature with the fullness of Christ himself.

The word of the Lord.]

Shorter Form, verses 1-7,11-13. Read between [ ]

Gospel Acclamation   Mt 28:19,20

R. **Alleluia, alleluia!**
Go, make disciples of all nations;
I am with you always; yes, to the end of time.
R. **Alleluia!**

GOSPEL

A reading from the holy Gospel according to Mark   16:15-20
He was taken up into heaven: there at the right hand of God he took his place.

Jesus showed himself to the Eleven, and said to them, 'Go out to the whole world; proclaim the Good News to all creation. He who believes and is baptised will be saved; he who does not believe will be condemned. These are the signs that will be associated with believers: in my name they will cast out devils; they will have the gift of tongues; they will pick up snakes in their hands, and be unharmed should they drink deadly poison; they will lay their hands on the sick, who will recover.'

And so the Lord Jesus, after he had spoken to them, was taken up into heaven: there at the right hand of God he took his place, while they, going out, preached everywhere, the Lord working with them and confirming the word by the signs that accompanied it.

The Gospel of the Lord.

The Creed is said.

Prayer over the Offerings	Super oblata
O God, whose Only Begotten Son, our High Priest,	Deus, cuius Unigenitus, Pontifex noster,
is seated ever-living at your right hand to intercede for us,	semper vivens sedet ad dexteram tuam
grant that we may approach with confidence the throne of grace	ad interpellandum pro nobis, concede nos adire cum fiducia
and there obtain your mercy.	ad thronum gratiæ,
Through Christ our Lord.	ut misericordiam tuam consequamur.
	Per Christum Dominum nostrum.

Preface I or II of the Ascension of the Lord, pp.564-565.
When the Roman Canon is used, the proper form of the Communicantes (In communion with those) is said.

Communion Antiphon Cf. Heb 10:12

Christ, offering a single sacrifice
for sins,
is seated for ever at God's right hand,
alleluia.

Prayer after Communion

May the gifts we have received
from your altar, Lord,
kindle in our hearts a longing
for the heavenly homeland
and cause us to press forward,
following in
the Saviour's footsteps,
to the place where for our sake
he entered before us.
Who lives and reigns
for ever and ever.

Ant. ad communionem

Christus, unam pro peccatis
offerens hostiam,
in sempiternum sedet in dextera Dei,
alleluia.

Post communionem

Quæ ex altari tuo, Domine,
dona percepimus,
accendant in cordibus nostris
cælestis patriæ desiderium,
et quo præcursor pro nobis
introivit Salvator,
faciant nos, eius vestigia sectantes,
contendere.
Qui vivit et regnat
in sæcula sæculorum.

A formula of Solemn Blessing, pp.648-649, may be used.

At the Mass during the Day

Entrance Antiphon Ac 1:11

MEN of Galilee, why gaze
in wonder at the heavens?
This Jesus whom you saw
ascending into heaven
will return as you saw him go,
alleluia.

Ant. ad introitum

VIRI Galilæi, quid admiramini
aspicientes in cælum?
Quemadmodum vidistis eum
ascendentem in cælum,
ita veniet, alleluia.

The Gloria in excelsis (Glory to God in the highest) is said.

Collect

Gladden us with holy joys,
almighty God,
and make us rejoice with devout
thanksgiving,
for the Ascension of Christ your Son
is our exaltation,
and, where the Head has gone
before in glory,
the Body is called to follow in hope.

Collecta

Fac nos, omnipotens Deus,
sanctis exsultare gaudiis,
et pia gratiarum actione lætari,
quia Christi Filii tui ascensio
est nostra provectio,
et quo processit gloria capitis,
eo spes vocatur et corporis.

Through our Lord Jesus Christ,
    your Son,
who lives and reigns with you
    in the unity of the Holy Spirit,
one God, for ever and ever.

Or:

Grant, we pray, almighty God,
that we, who believe that your Only
    Begotten Son, our Redeemer,
ascended this day to the heavens,
may in spirit dwell already
    in heavenly realms.
Who lives and reigns with you
    in the unity of the Holy Spirit,
one God, for ever and ever.

Per Dominum nostrum Iesum
    Christum Filium tuum,
qui tecum vivit et regnat
    in unitate Spiritus Sancti,
Deus, per omnia sæcula sæculorum.

Vel:

Concede, quæsumus,
    omnipotens Deus,
ut, qui hodierna die
Unigenitum tuum
    Redemptorem nostrum
ad cælos ascendisse credimus,
ipsi quoque mente
    in cælestibus habitemus.
Qui tecum vivit et regnat
    in unitate Spiritus Sancti,
Deus, per omnia sæcula sæculorum.

FIRST READING

A reading from the Acts of the Apostles   1:1-11

He was lifted up while they looked on.

In my earlier work, Theophilus, I dealt with everything Jesus had done and taught from the beginning until the day he gave his instructions to the apostles he had chosen through the Holy Spirit, and was taken up to heaven. He had shown himself alive to them after his Passion by many demonstrations: for forty days he had continued to appear to them and tell them about the kingdom of God. When he had been at table with them, he had told them not to leave Jerusalem, but to wait there for what the Father had promised. 'It is' he had said 'what you have heard me speak about: John baptised with water but you, not many days from now, will be baptised with the Holy Spirit.'

Now having met together, they asked him, 'Lord, has the time come? Are you going to restore the kingdom to Israel?' He replied, 'It is not for you to know times or dates that the Father has decided by his own authority, but you will receive power when the Holy Spirit comes on you, and then you will be my witnesses not only in Jerusalem but throughout Judaea and Samaria, and indeed to the ends of the earth.'

As he said this he was lifted up while they looked on, and a cloud took him from their sight. They were still staring into the sky when suddenly two men in white were standing near them and they said, 'Why are you men from Galilee standing here looking into the sky? Jesus who has been taken up from you into heaven, this same Jesus will come back in the same way as you have seen him go there.'

The word of the Lord.

Responsorial Psalm   Ps 46:2-3,6-9. R. v.6

R. **God goes up with shouts of joy**
   the Lord goes up with trumpet blast.
   Or: **Alleluia!**

All peoples, clap your hands,
cry to God with shouts of joy!
For the Lord, the Most High, we must fear,
great king over all the earth. R.

God goes up with shouts of joy;
the Lord goes up with trumpet blast.
Sing praise for God, sing praise,
sing praise to our king, sing praise. R.

God is king of all the earth.
Sing praise with all your skill.
God is king over the nations;
God reigns on his holy throne. R.

The Second Reading from Year A, p.393, may be used in place of the following.

SECOND READING

A reading from the letter of St Paul to the Ephesians   4:1-13
Fully mature with the fullness of Christ.

[I, the prisoner in the Lord, implore you therefore to lead a life worthy of your vocation. Bear with one another charitably, in complete selflessness, gentleness and patience. Do all you can to preserve the unity of the Spirit by the peace that binds you together. There is one Body, one Spirit, just as you were all called into one and the same hope when you were called. There is one Lord, one faith, one baptism, and one God who is Father of all, over all, through all and within all.

Each one of us, however, has been given his own share of grace, given as Christ allotted it.] It was said that he would:

When he ascended to the height, he captured prisoners,
he gave gifts to men.

When it says, 'he ascended', what can it mean if not that he descended right down to the lower regions of the earth? [The one who rose higher than all the heavens to fill all things is none other than the one who descended. And to some, his gift was that they should be apostles; to some, prophets; to some, evangelists; to some, pastors and teachers; so that the saints together make a unity in the work of service, building up the body of Christ. In this way we are all to come to unity in our faith and in our knowledge of the Son of God, until we become the perfect Man, fully mature with the fullness of Christ himself.

The word of the Lord.]

Shorter Form, verses 1-7,11-13. Read between [ ]

Gospel Acclamation   Mt 28:19,20

R. **Alleluia, alleluia!**
Go, make disciples of all nations;
I am with you always; yes, to the end of time.
R. **Alleluia!**

GOSPEL

A reading from the holy Gospel according to Mark   16:15-20

He was taken up into heaven: there at the right hand of God he took his place.

Jesus showed himself to the Eleven, and said to them, 'Go out to the whole world; proclaim the Good News to all creation. He who believes and is baptised will be saved; he who does not believe will be condemned. These are the signs that will be associated with believers: in my name they will cast out devils; they will have the gift of tongues; they will pick up snakes in their hands, and be unharmed should they drink deadly poison; they will lay their hands on the sick, who will recover.'

And so the Lord Jesus, after he had spoken to them, was taken up into heaven: there at the right hand of God he took his place, while they, going out, preached everywhere, the Lord working with them and confirming the word by the signs that accompanied it.

The Gospel of the Lord.

The Creed is said.

Prayer over the Offerings	Super oblata

We offer sacrifice now
    in supplication, O Lord,
to honour the wondrous Ascension
    of your Son:
grant, we pray,
that through this most holy exchange
we, too, may rise up
    to the heavenly realms.
Through Christ our Lord.
	Sacrificium, Domine,
	    pro Filii tui supplices
	venerabili nunc
	    ascensione deferimus:
	præsta, quæsumus, ut his
	    commerciis sacrosanctis
	ad cælestia consurgamus.
	Per Christum Dominum nostrum.

Preface I or II of the Ascension of the Lord, pp.564-565.

When the Roman Canon is used, the proper form of the Communicantes (In communion with those) is said.

Communion Antiphon Mt 28:20	Ant. ad communionem

Behold, I am with you always,
even to the end of the age, alleluia.
	Ecce ego vobiscum sum
	    omnibus diebus,
	usque ad consummationem sæculi,
	    alleluia.

Prayer after Communion	Post communionem

Almighty ever-living God,
who allow those on earth
    to celebrate divine mysteries,
grant, we pray,
that Christian hope may draw
    us onward
to where our nature is united
    with you.
Through Christ our Lord.
	Omnipotens sempiterne Deus,
	qui in terra constitutos divina
	    tractare concedis,
	præsta, quæsumus,
	ut illuc tendat christianæ
	    devotionis affectus,
	quo tecum est nostra substantia.
	Per Christum Dominum nostrum.

A formula of Solemn Blessing, pp.648-649, may be used.

SEVENTH SUNDAY OF EASTER (YEAR B)

In his Gospel, Saint John, more fully than the other three evangelists, reports in his own distinctive way the farewell discourses of Jesus; they appear as his testament and a synthesis of the core of his message. Twice in the course of the priestly prayer Jesus speaks of revealing God's name. Jesus thus means to say that he is bringing to fulfilment what began with the burning bush; that in him God, who had made himself known to Moses, now reveals himself fully. And that in doing so he brings about reconciliation; that the love with which God loves his Son in the mystery of the Trinity now draws men and women into this divine circle of love. To give one's name means to enter into relationship with another. The revelation of the divine name, then, means that God, infinite and self-subsistent, enters into the network of human relationships; that he comes out of himself, so to speak, and becomes one of us, present among us and for us.

(Pope Benedict XVI)

Entrance Antiphon   Cf. Ps 26:7-9

O LORD, hear my voice,
   for I have called to you;
of you my heart has spoken:
   Seek his face;
hide not your face from me,
   alleluia.

Ant. ad introitum

E XAUDI, Domine, vocem meam,
   qua clamavi ad te.
Tibi dixit cor meum,
   quæsivi vultum tuum,
vultum tuum requiram;
ne avertas faciem tuam a me,
   alleluia.

The Gloria in excelsis (Glory to God in the highest) is said.

Collect

Graciously hear our supplications,
   O Lord,
so that we, who believe that
   the Saviour of the human race
is with you in your glory,
may experience, as he promised,
until the end of the world,
his abiding presence among us.
Who lives and reigns with you
   in the unity of the Holy Spirit,
one God, for ever and ever.

Collecta

Supplicationibus nostris, Domine,
   adesto propitius,
ut, sicut humani generis Salvatorem
tecum in tua credimus maiestate,
ita eum usque ad
   consummationem sæculi
manere nobiscum,
sicut ipse promisit, sentiamus.
Qui tecum vivit et regnat
   in unitate Spiritus Sancti,
Deus, per omnia sæcula sæculorum.

FIRST READING

A reading from the Acts of the Apostles   1:15-17,20-26

We must choose one of these to be a witness to his resurrection with us.

One day Peter stood up to speak to the brothers – there were about a hundred and twenty persons in the congregation: 'Brothers, the passage of scripture had to be fulfilled in which the Holy Spirit, speaking through David, foretells the fate of Judas, who offered himself as a guide to the men who arrested Jesus – after having been one of our number and actually sharing this ministry of ours.

'In the Book of Psalms it says:

Let someone else take his office.

'We must therefore choose someone who has been with us the whole time that the Lord Jesus was travelling around with us, someone who was with us right from the time when John was baptising until the day when he was taken up from us – and he can act with us as a witness to his resurrection.'

Having nominated two candidates, Joseph known as Barsabbas, whose surname was Justus, and Matthias, they prayed, 'Lord, you can read everyone's heart; show us therefore which of these two you have chosen to take over this ministry and apostolate, which Judas abandoned to go to his proper place.' They then drew lots for them, and as the lot fell to Matthias, he was listed as one of the twelve apostles.

The word of the Lord.

Responsorial Psalm   Ps 102:1-2,11-12,19-20. R. v.19

R. **The Lord has set his sway in heaven.**
   Or: **Alleluia!**

   My soul, give thanks to the Lord;
   all my being, bless his holy name.
   My soul, give thanks to the Lord
   and never forget all his blessings. R.

   For as the heavens are high above the earth
   so strong is his love for those who fear him.
   As far as the east is from the west
   so far does he remove our sins. R.

   The Lord has set his sway in heaven
   and his kingdom is ruling over all.
   Give thanks to the Lord, all his angels,
   mighty in power, fulfilling his word. R.

SECOND READING

A reading from the first letter of St John   4:11-16

Anyone who lives in love lives in God, and God lives in him.

My dear people,
since God has loved us so much,
we too should love one another.
No one has ever seen God;
but as long as we love one another
God will live in us
and his love will be complete in us.
We can know that we are living in him
and he is living in us
because he lets us share his Spirit.
We ourselves saw and we testify
that the Father sent his Son
as saviour of the world.
If anyone acknowledges that Jesus is the Son of God,
God lives in him, and he in God.
We ourselves have known and put our faith in
God's love towards ourselves.
God is love
and anyone who lives in love lives in God,
and God lives in him.

The word of the Lord.

Gospel Acclamation   Cf. Jn 14:18

R. **Alleluia, alleluia!**
I will not leave you orphans, says the Lord;
I will come back to you, and your hearts will be full of joy.
R. **Alleluia!**

GOSPEL

A reading from the holy Gospel according to John   17:11-19

That they may be one like us!

Jesus raised his eyes to heaven and said:

'Holy Father,
keep those you have given me true to your name,
so that they may be one like us.
While I was with them,
I kept those you had given me true to your name.

I have watched over them and not one is lost
except the one who chose to be lost,
and this was to fulfil the scriptures.
But now I am coming to you
and while still in the world I say these things
to share my joy with them to the full.
I passed your word on to them,
and the world hated them,
because they belong to the world
no more than I belong to the world.
I am not asking you to remove them from the world,
but to protect them from the evil one.
They do not belong to the world
any more than I belong to the world.
Consecrate them in the truth,
your word is truth.
As you sent me into the world,
I have sent them into the world,
and for their sake I consecrate myself
so that they too may be consecrated in truth.'

The Gospel of the Lord.

The Creed is said.

Prayer over the Offerings

Accept, O Lord, the prayers
   of your faithful
with the sacrificial offerings,
that through these acts
   of devotedness
we may pass over to the glory
   of heaven.
Through Christ our Lord.

Super oblata

Suscipe, Domine, fidelium preces
cum oblationibus hostiarum,
ut, per hæc piæ devotionis officia,
ad cælestem gloriam transeamus.
Per Christum Dominum nostrum.

Preface of Easter, or of the Ascension, pp.558-565.

Communion Antiphon   Jn 17:22

Father, I pray that they may be one
as we also are one, alleluia.

Ant. ad communionem

Rogo, Pater, ut sint unum,
sicut et nos unum sumus, alleluia.

Prayer after Communion	Post communionem
Hear us, O God our Saviour,	Exaudi nos, Deus, salutaris noster,
and grant us confidence,	ut per hæc sacrosancta mysteria
that through these sacred mysteries	in totius Ecclesiæ confidamus
there will be accomplished	corpore faciendum,
in the body of the whole Church	quod eius præcessit in capite.
what has already come to pass	Per Christum Dominum nostrum.
in Christ her Head.	
Who lives and reigns	
for ever and ever.	

A formula of Solemn Blessing, pp.646-649, may be used.

PENTECOST SUNDAY (YEAR B)

The Holy Spirit overcomes fear. We know that the disciples sought shelter in the Upper Room after the arrest of their Lord and that they had remained isolated for fear of suffering the same fate. After Jesus' Resurrection their fear was not suddenly dispelled. But here at Pentecost, when the Holy Spirit rested upon them, those men emerged fearless and began to proclaim the Good News of the Crucified and Risen Christ to all. They were not afraid because they felt they were in the hands of the strongest One. Yes, dear brothers and sisters, wherever the Spirit of God enters he puts fear to flight; he makes us know and feel that we are in the hands of an Omnipotence of love: something happens, his infinite love does not abandon us. It is demonstrated by the very existence of the Church which, despite the limitations and sins of men and women, continues to cross the ocean of history, blown by the breath of God and enlivened by his purifying fire.

(Pope Benedict XVI)

For the Vigil Mass, see pp.405-417.

At the Mass during the Day

Entrance Antiphon	Ws 1:7	Ant. ad introitum

THE Spirit of the Lord has filled the whole world
and that which contains all things
understands what is said, alleluia.

SPIRITUS Domini replevit orbem terrarum,
et hoc quod continet omnia
scientiam habet vocis, alleluia.

Or: Rm 5:5; Cf. 8:11   Vel:

The love of God has been poured
    into our hearts
through the Spirit of God dwelling
    within us, alleluia.

Caritas Dei diffusa est in
    cordibus nostris
per inhabitantem Spiritum eius in
    nobis, alleluia.

The Gloria in excelsis (Glory to God in the highest) is said.

Collect

O God, who by the mystery
    of today's great feast
sanctify your whole Church
    in every people and nation,
pour out, we pray, the gifts
    of the Holy Spirit

Collecta

Deus, qui sacramento
    festivitatis hodiernæ
universam Ecclesiam tuam
in omni gente et
    natione sanctificas,
in totam mundi latitudinem

across the face of the earth
and, with the divine grace that
    was at work
when the Gospel was first proclaimed,
fill now once more the hearts
    of believers.
Through our Lord Jesus Christ,
    your Son,
who lives and reigns with you
    in the unity of the Holy Spirit,
one God, for ever and ever.

Spiritus Sancti dona defunde,
et, quod inter ipsa evangelicæ
    prædicationis exordia
operata est divina dignatio,
nunc quoque per credentium corda
    perfunde.
Per Dominum nostrum Iesum
    Christum Filium tuum,
qui tecum vivit et regnat
    in unitate Spiritus Sancti,
Deus, per omnia sæcula sæculorum.

FIRST READING

A reading from the Acts of the Apostles   2:1-11

They were all filled with the Holy Spirit and began to speak.

When Pentecost day came round, the apostles had all met in one room, when suddenly they heard what sounded like a powerful wind from heaven, the noise of which filled the entire house in which they were sitting; and something appeared to them that seemed like tongues of fire; these separated and came to rest on the head of each of them. They were all filled with the Holy Spirit, and began to speak foreign languages as the Spirit gave them the gift of speech.

Now there were devout men living in Jerusalem from every nation under heaven, and at this sound they all assembled, each one bewildered to hear these men speaking his own language. They were amazed and astonished. 'Surely' they said 'all these men speaking are Galileans? How does it happen that each of us hears them in his own native language? Parthians, Medes and Elamites; people from Mesopotamia, Judaea and Cappadocia, Pontus and Asia, Phrygia and Pamphylia, Egypt and the parts of Libya round Cyrene; as well as visitors from Rome – Jews and proselytes alike – Cretans and Arabs; we hear them preaching in our own language about the marvels of God.'

The word of the Lord.

Responsorial Psalm   Ps 103:1,24,29-31,34. R. Cf. v.30

R. **Send forth your Spirit, O Lord,**
    and renew the face of the earth.
    Or: **Alleluia!**

    Bless the Lord, my soul!
    Lord God, how great you are.
    How many are your works, O Lord!
    The earth is full of your riches. R.

You take back your spirit, they die,
returning to the dust from which they came.
You send forth your spirit, they are created;
and you renew the face of the earth. R.

May the glory of the Lord last for ever!
May the Lord rejoice in his works!
May my thoughts be pleasing to him.
I find my joy in the Lord. R.

R. **Send forth your Spirit, O Lord,**
   and renew the face of the earth.
   Or: **Alleluia!**

The Second Reading and the Gospel may be taken from Year A, see pp.419-421.
Alternatively, the Second Reading and the Gospel given below may be used.

SECOND READING

A reading from the letter of St Paul to the Galatians   5:16-25
The fruit of the Spirit.

If you are guided by the Spirit you will be in no danger of yielding to self-
indulgence, since self-indulgence is the opposite of the Spirit, the Spirit
is totally against such a thing, and it is precisely because the two are so
opposed that you do not always carry out your good intentions. If you
are led by the Spirit, no law can touch you. When self-indulgence is at
work the results are obvious: fornication, gross indecency and sexual
irresponsibility; idolatry and sorcery; feuds and wrangling, jealousy, bad
temper and quarrels; disagreements, factions, envy; drunkenness, orgies
and similar things. I warn you now, as I warned you before: those who
behave like this will not inherit the kingdom of God. What the Spirit
brings is very different: love, joy, peace, patience, kindness, goodness,
trustfulness, gentleness and self-control. There can be no law against
things like that, of course. You cannot belong to Christ Jesus unless you
crucify all self-indulgent passions and desire.

Since the Spirit is our life, let us be directed by the Spirit.

The word of the Lord.

For the sequence, see p.420. This may be said or sung.

Gospel Acclamation

R. **Alleluia, alleluia!**
Come, Holy Spirit, fill the hearts of your faithful
and kindle in them the fire of your love.
R. **Alleluia!**

GOSPEL

A reading from the holy Gospel according to John   15:26-27; 16:12-15
The Spirit of truth will lead you to the complete truth.

Jesus said to his disciples:
  'When the Advocate comes,
  whom I shall send to you from the Father,
  the Spirit of truth who issues from the Father,
  he will be my witness.
  And you too will be witnesses,
  because you have been with me from the outset.

  I still have many things to say to you
  but they would be too much for you now.
  But when the Spirit of truth comes
  he will lead you to the complete truth,
  since he will not be speaking as from himself
  but will say only what he has learnt,
  and he will tell you of the things to come.
  He will glorify me,
  since all he tells you
  will be taken from what is mine.
  Everything the Father has is mine;
  that is why I said:
  All he tells you
  will be taken from what is mine.'

  The Gospel of the Lord.

The Creed is said.

Prayer over the Offerings	Super oblata
Grant, we pray, O Lord,	Præsta, quæsumus, Domine,
that, as promised by your Son,	ut, secundum promissionem
the Holy Spirit may reveal to us	Filii tui,
more abundantly	Spiritus Sanctus huius
the hidden mystery of this sacrifice	nobis sacrificii
and graciously lead us into all truth.	copiosius revelet arcanum,
Through Christ our Lord.	et omnem propitius reseret veritatem.
	Per Christum Dominum nostrum.

Preface: The Mystery of Pentecost, p.422.

Communion Antiphon   Ac 2:4,11

They were all filled with
    the Holy Spirit
and spoke of the marvels of God,
    alleluia.

Prayer after Communion

O God, who bestow heavenly gifts
    upon your Church,
safeguard, we pray, the grace you
    have given,
that the gift of the Holy Spirit
    poured out upon her
may retain all its force
and that this spiritual food
may gain her abundance
    of eternal redemption.
Through Christ our Lord.

Ant. ad communionem

Repleti sunt omnes Spiritu Sancto,
loquentes magnalia Dei, alleluia.

Post communionem

Deus, qui Ecclesiæ tuæ cælestia
    dona largiris,
custodi gratiam quam dedisti,
ut Spiritus Sancti vigeat semper
    munus infusum,
et ad æternæ
    redemptionis augmentum
spiritalis esca proficiat.
Per Christum Dominum nostrum.

A formula of Solemn Blessing, pp.648-651, may be used.

To dismiss the people the Deacon or, if there is no Deacon, the Priest himself sings
or says:

Go forth, the Mass is ended,
    alleluia, alleluia.

Ite, missa est,
    alleluia, alleluia.

Or:

Go in peace, alleluia, aleluia.

Vel:

Ite in pace, alleluia, alleluia.

And the people reply:

Thanks be to God, alleluia, alleluia.

Omnes respondent:

Deo gratias, alleluia, alleluia.

With Easter Time now concluded, the paschal candle is extinguished. It is desirable
to keep the paschal candle in the baptistery with due honour so that it is lit at the
celebration of Baptism and the candles of those baptised are lit from it.

SECOND SUNDAY OF EASTER
(YEAR C)
(or of Divine Mercy)

"Fear not, I am the first and the last, and the living one; I died, and behold I am alive for evermore". We hear these comforting words in the Second Reading taken from the Book of Revelation. They invite us to turn our gaze to Christ, to experience his reassuring presence. To each person, whatever his condition, even if it were the most complicated and dramatic, the Risen One repeats: "Fear not!"; I died on the Cross but now "I am alive for evermore"; "I am the first and the last, and the living one".

(Blessed Pope John Paul II)

Entrance Antiphon 1 P 2:2	Ant. ad introitum

LIKE newborn infants,
  you must long for the pure,
spiritual milk,
that in him you may grow
  to salvation, alleluia.

QUASI modo geniti infantes,
  rationabile, sine dolo
  lac concupiscite,
ut in eo crescatis in salutem,
  alleluia.

Or: 4 Esdr 2:36-37	Vel:

Receive the joy of your glory,
  giving thanks to God,
who has called you into the heavenly
  kingdom, alleluia.

Accipite iucunditatem gloriæ vestræ,
gratias agentes Deo,
qui vos ad cælestia regna vocavit,
  alleluia.

The Gloria in excelsis (Glory to God in the highest) is said.

Collect	Collecta

God of everlasting mercy,
who, in the very recurrence
  of the paschal feast
kindle the faith of the people you
  have made your own,
increase, we pray, the grace you
  have bestowed,

Deus misericordiæ sempiternæ,
qui in ipso paschalis festi recursu
fidem sacratæ tibi plebis accendis,
auge gratiam quam dedisti,
ut digna omnes intellegentia
  comprehendant,
quo lavacro abluti, quo

that all may grasp
  and rightly understand
in what font they have been washed,
by whose Spirit they have
  been reborn,
by whose Blood they have
  been redeemed.
Through our Lord Jesus Christ,
  your Son,
who lives and reigns with you
  in the unity of the Holy Spirit,
one God, for ever and ever.

Spiritu regenerati,
quo sanguine sunt redempti.
Per Dominum nostrum Iesum
  Christum Filium tuum,
qui tecum vivit et regnat
  in unitate Spiritus Sancti,
Deus, per omnia sæcula sæculorum.

FIRST READING

A reading from the Acts of the Apostles   5:12-16

The numbers of men and women who came to believe in the Lord increased steadily.

The faithful all used to meet by common consent in the Portico of Solomon. No one else even dared to join them, but the people were loud in their praise and the numbers of men and women who came to believe in the Lord increased steadily. So many signs and wonders were worked among the people at the hands of the apostles that the sick were even taken out into the streets and laid on beds and sleeping-mats in the hope that at least the shadow of Peter might fall across some of them as he went past. People even came crowding in from the towns round about Jerusalem, bringing with them their sick and those tormented by unclean spirits, and all of them were cured.

The word of the Lord.

Responsorial Psalm   Ps 117:2-4,22-27. R. v.1

R. **Give thanks to the Lord for he is good,
   for his love has no end.**
   Or: **Alleluia, alleluia, alleluia!**

Let the sons of Israel say:
'His love has no end.'
Let the sons of Aaron say:
'His love has no end.'
Let those who fear the Lord say:
'His love has no end.' R.

The stone which the builders rejected
has become the corner stone.
This is the work of the Lord
a marvel in our eyes.
This day was made by the Lord;
we rejoice and are glad. R.

O Lord, grant us salvation;
O Lord, grant success.
Blessed in the name of the Lord
is he who comes.
We bless you from the house of the Lord;
the Lord God is our light. R.

SECOND READING

A reading from the book of the Apocalypse   1:9-13,17-19
I was dead and now I am to live for ever and ever.

My name is John, and through our union in Jesus I am your brother and share your sufferings, your kingdom, and all you endure. I was on the island of Patmos for having preached God's word and witnessed for Jesus; it was the Lord's day and the Spirit possessed me, and I heard a voice behind me, shouting like a trumpet, 'Write down all that you see in a book.' I turned round to see who had spoken to me, and when I turned I saw seven golden lamp-stands and, surrounded by them, a figure like a Son of man, dressed in a long robe tied at the waist with a golden girdle.

When I saw him, I fell in a dead faint at his feet, but he touched me with his right hand and said, 'Do not be afraid; it is I, the First and the Last; I am the Living One. I was dead and now I am to live for ever and ever, and I hold the keys of death and of the underworld. Now write down all that you see of present happenings and things that are still to come.'

The word of the Lord.

Easter Sequence can be sung here, see pp.364-365.

Gospel Acclamation   Jn 20:29

R. **Alleluia, alleluia!**
Jesus said: 'You believe because you can see me.
Happy are those who have not seen and yet believe.'
R. **Alleluia!**

GOSPEL

A reading from the holy Gospel according to John   20:19-31

Eight days later, Jesus came.

In the evening of that same day, the first day of the week, the doors were closed in the room where the disciples were, for fear of the Jews. Jesus came and stood among them. He said to them, 'Peace be with you,' and showed them his hands and his side. The disciples were filled with joy when they saw the Lord, and he said to them again, 'Peace be with you.

> 'As the Father sent me,
> so am I sending you.'
> After saying this he breathed on them and said:
> 'Receive the Holy Spirit.
> For those whose sins you forgive,
> they are forgiven;
> for those whose sins you retain,
> they are retained.'

Thomas, called the Twin, who was one of the Twelve, was not with them when Jesus came. When the disciples said, 'We have seen the Lord,' he answered, 'Unless I see the holes that the nails made in his hands and can put my finger into the holes they made, and unless I can put my hand into his side, I refuse to believe.' Eight days later the disciples were in the house again and Thomas was with them. The doors were closed, but Jesus came in and stood among them. 'Peace be with you,' he said. Then he spoke to Thomas, 'Put your finger here; look, here are my hands. Give me your hand; put it into my side. Doubt no longer but believe.' Thomas replied, 'My Lord and my God!'

> Jesus said to him:
> 'You believe because you can see me.
> Happy are those who have not seen and yet believe.'

There were many other signs that Jesus worked and the disciples saw, but they are not recorded in this book. These are recorded so that you may believe that Jesus is the Christ, the Son of God, and that believing this you may have life through his name.

The Gospel of the Lord.

The Creed is said.

Prayer over the Offerings	Super oblata
Accept, O Lord, we pray, the oblations of your people (and of those you have brought to new birth), that, renewed by confession of your name and by Baptism, they may attain unending happiness. Through Christ our Lord.	Suscipe, quæsumus, Domine, plebis tuæ (et tuorum renatorum) oblationes, ut, confessione tui nominis et baptismate renovati, sempiternam beatitudinem consequantur. Per Christum Dominum nostrum.

Preface I of Easter (. . .on this day above all. . .), pp.558-561.

When the Roman Canon is used, the proper forms of Communicantes (In communion with those) and Hanc igitur (Therefore, Lord, we pray) are said.

Communion Antiphon Cf. Jn 20:27	Ant. ad communionem
Bring your hand and feel the place of the nails, and do not be unbelieving but believing, alleluia.	Mitte manum tuam, et cognosce loca clavorum, et noli esse incredulus, sed fidelis, alleluia.

Prayer after Communion	Post communionem
Grant, we pray, almighty God, that our reception of this paschal Sacrament may have a continuing effect in our minds and hearts. Through Christ our Lord.	Concede, quæsumus, omnipotens Deus, ut paschalis perceptio sacramenti continua in nostris mentibus perseveret. Per Christum Dominum nostrum.

A formula of Solemn Blessing, p.360, may be used.

For the dismissal of the people, the following is sung or said: Go forth, the Mass is ended, alleluia, alleluia. Or: Go in peace, alleluia, alleluia. The people respond: Thanks be to God, alleluia, alleluia.

THIRD SUNDAY OF EASTER (YEAR C)

*"It is the Lord!" (Jn 21:7). This exclamation of the Apostle John emphasises
the intense emotion experienced by the disciples on recognizing the risen Jesus,
who appeared to them for the third time on the shore of the Sea of Tiberias.
After a long night of loneliness and toil, the dawn arrives and his appearance
radically changes everything: the darkness is overcome by light, the fruitless
work becomes an easy and abundant catch of fish, the feeling of tiredness
and loneliness is transformed into joy and peace. Since then, these same
sentiments enliven the Church. If at a superficial level it sometimes seems
that the darkness of evil and the toil of everyday life have the upper hand, the
Church knows with certainty that the light of Easter now shines eternally on
those who follow Christ. The great message of the Resurrection fills the hearts
of the faithful with inner joy and renewed hope.*

(Blessed Pope John Paul II)

Entrance Antiphon   Cf. Ps 65:1-2

CRY out with joy to God,
all the earth;
O sing to the glory of his name.
O render him glorious praise,
    alleluia.

Ant. ad introitum

IUBILATE Deo, omnis terra,
psalmum dicite nomini eius,
date gloriam laudi eius, alleluia.

The Gloria in excelsis (Glory to God in the highest) is said.

Collect

May your people exult for ever,
    O God,
in renewed youthfulness of spirit,
so that, rejoicing now in the restored
    glory of our adoption,
we may look forward
    in confident hope
to the rejoicing of the day
    of resurrection.
Through our Lord Jesus Christ,
    your Son,
who lives and reigns with you
    in the unity of the Holy Spirit,
one God, for ever and ever.

Collecta

Semper exsultet populus tuus, Deus,
renovata animæ iuventute,
ut, qui nunc lætatur in adoptionis
    se gloriam restitutum,
resurrectionis diem spe certæ
    gratulationis exspectet.
Per Dominum nostrum Iesum
    Christum Filium tuum,
qui tecum vivit et regnat
    in unitate Spiritus Sancti,
Deus, per omnia sæcula sæculorum.

FIRST READING

A reading from the Acts of the Apostles 5:27-32,40-41

We are witnesses of all this, we and the Holy Spirit.

The high priest demanded an explanation of the apostles. 'We gave you a formal warning' he said 'not to preach in this name, and what have you done? You have filled Jerusalem with your teaching, and seem determined to fix the guilt of this man's death on us.' In reply Peter and the apostles said, 'Obedience to God comes before obedience to men; it was the God of our ancestors who raised up Jesus, but it was you who had him executed by hanging on a tree. By his own right hand God has now raised him up to be leader and saviour, to give repentance and forgiveness of sins through him to Israel. We are witnesses to all this, we and the Holy Spirit whom God has given to those who obey him.' They warned the apostles not to speak in the name of Jesus and released them. And so they left the presence of the Sanhedrin glad to have had the honour of suffering humiliation for the sake of the name.

The word of the Lord.

Responsorial Psalm Ps 29:2,4-6,11-13. R. v.2

R. **I will praise you, Lord,**
   you have rescued me.
   Or: **Alleluia!**

I will praise you, Lord, you have rescued me
and have not let my enemies rejoice over me.
O Lord, you have raised my soul from the dead,
restored me to life from those who sink into the grave. R.

Sing psalms to the Lord, you who love him,
give thanks to his holy name.
His anger lasts but a moment; his favour through life.
At night there are tears, but joy comes with dawn. R.

The Lord listened and had pity.
The Lord came to my help.
For me you have changed my mourning into dancing;
O Lord my God, I will thank you for ever. R.

SECOND READING

A reading from the book of the Apocalypse   5:11-14

The Lamb that was sacrificed is worthy to be given riches and power.

In my vision, I, John, heard the sound of an immense number of angels gathered round the throne and the animals and the elders; there were ten thousand times ten thousand of them and thousands upon thousands, shouting, 'The Lamb that was sacrificed is worthy to be given power, riches, wisdom, strength, honour, glory and blessing.' Then I heard all the living things in creation – everything that lives in the air, and on the ground, and under the ground, and in the sea, crying, 'To the One who is sitting on the throne and to the Lamb, be all praise, honour, glory and power, for ever and ever.' And the four animals said, 'Amen'; and the elders prostrated themselves to worship.

The word of the Lord.

Gospel Acclamation   Cf. Lk 24:32

R. **Alleluia, alleluia!**
Lord Jesus, explain the scriptures to us.
Make our hearts burn within us as you talk to us.
R. **Alleluia!**

Or:

R. **Alleluia, alleluia!**
Christ has risen: he who created all things,
and has granted his mercy to men.
R. **Alleluia!**

GOSPEL

A reading from the holy Gospel according to John   21:1-19

Jesus stepped forward, took the bread and gave it to them, and the same with the fish.

[Jesus showed himself again to the disciples. It was by the Sea of Tiberias, and it happened like this: Simon Peter, Thomas called the Twin, Nathanael from Cana in Galilee, the sons of Zebedee and two more of his disciples were together. Simon Peter said, 'I'm going fishing.' They replied, 'We'll come with you.' They went out and got into the boat but caught nothing that night.

It was light by now and there stood Jesus on the shore, though the disciples did not realise that it was Jesus. Jesus called out, 'Have you caught anything, friends?' And when they answered, 'No,' he said, 'Throw the net

THIRD SUNDAY OF EASTER (YEAR C)

out to starboard and you'll find something.' So they dropped the net, and there were so many fish that they could not haul it in. The disciple Jesus loved said to Peter, 'It is the Lord.' At these words 'It is the Lord', Simon Peter, who had practically nothing on, wrapped his cloak round him and jumped into the water. The other disciples came on in the boat, towing the net and the fish; they were only about a hundred yards from land.

As soon as they came ashore they saw that there was some bread there, and a charcoal fire with fish cooking on it. Jesus said, 'Bring some of the fish you have just caught.' Simon Peter went aboard and dragged the net to the shore, full of big fish, one hundred and fifty-three of them; and in spite of there being so many the net was not broken. Jesus said to them, 'Come and have breakfast.' None of the disciples was bold enough to ask, 'Who are you?'; they knew quite well it was the Lord. Jesus then stepped forward, took the bread and gave it to them, and the same with the fish. This was the third time that Jesus showed himself to the disciples after rising from the dead.]

After the meal Jesus said to Simon Peter, 'Simon son of John, do you love me more than these others do?' He answered 'Yes Lord, you know I love you.' Jesus said to him, 'Feed my lambs.' A second time, he said to him, 'Simon son of John, do you love me?' He replied, 'Yes, Lord, you know I love you.' Jesus said to him, 'Look after my sheep.' Then he said to him a third time, 'Simon son of John, do you love me?' Peter was upset that he asked him the third time, 'Do you love me?' and said, 'Lord, you know everything; you know I love you.' Jesus said to him, 'Feed my sheep.

> 'I tell you most solemnly,
> when you were young
> you put on your own belt
> and walked where you liked;
> but when you grow old
> you will stretch out your hands,
> and somebody else will put a belt round you
> and take you where you would rather not go.'

In these words he indicated the kind of death by which Peter would give glory to God. After this he said, 'Follow me.'

[The Gospel of the Lord.]

Shorter Form, verses 1-14. Read between [ ]

The Creed is said.

Prayer over the Offerings

Receive, O Lord, we pray,
these offerings of your
    exultant Church,
and, as you have given her cause
    for such great gladness,
grant also that the gifts we bring
may bear fruit in perpetual happiness.
Through Christ our Lord.

Preface of Easter, pp.558-563.

Communion Antiphon   Lk 24:35

The disciples recognised
    the Lord Jesus
in the breaking of the bread,
    alleluia.

Optional for Year C: Cf. Jn 21:12-13

Jesus said to his disciples:
    Come and eat.
And he took bread and gave it
    to them, alleluia.

Prayer after Communion

Look with kindness upon your
    people, O Lord,
and grant, we pray,
that those you were pleased
    to renew by eternal mysteries
may attain in their flesh
the incorruptible glory
    of the resurrection.
Through Christ our Lord.

A formula of Solemn Blessing, pp.646-649, may be used.

Super oblata

Suscipe munera, Domine,
    quæsumus, exsultantis Ecclesiæ,
et cui causam tanti gaudii præstitisti,
perpetuæ fructum concede lætitiæ.
Per Christum Dominum nostrum.

Ant. ad communionem

Cognoverunt discipuli
    Dominum Iesum
in fractione panis, alleluia.

Ad libitum pro anno C

Dixit Iesus discipulis suis:
    Venite, prandete.
Et accepit panem, et dedit eis,
    alleluia.

Post communionem

Populum tuum, quæsumus,
    Domine, intuere benignus,
et, quem æternis dignatus
    es renovare mysteriis,
ad incorruptibilem glorificandæ
    carnis resurrectionem
pervenire concede.
Per Christum Dominum nostrum.

FOURTH SUNDAY OF EASTER (YEAR C)

In presenting the mystery of the Church in our time, the Second Vatican Council gave priority to the category of "communion". In this perspective, the rich variety of gifts and ministries acquires great importance for the People of God. All the baptised are called to contribute to the work of salvation. In the Church, however, there are some vocations which are dedicated especially to the service of communion. The person primarily responsible for Catholic communion is the Pope, Successor of Peter and Bishop of Rome; with him, the Bishops, successors of the Apostles, are custodians and teachers of unity, assisted by the priests. But consecrated persons and all the faithful are also at the service of communion. At the heart of Church communion is the Eucharist: the different vocations draw from this supreme Sacrament the spiritual power to build constantly, in charity, the one ecclesial Body.

(Pope Benedict XVI)

Entrance Antiphon   Cf. Ps 32:5-6

THE merciful love of the Lord
  fills the earth;
by the word of the Lord the
  heavens were made, alleluia.

Ant. ad introitum

MISERICORDIA Domini plena
  est terra;
verbo Domini cæli firmati sunt,
  alleluia

The Gloria in excelsis (Glory to God in the highest) is said.

Collect

Almighty ever-living God,
lead us to a share in the joys
  of heaven,
so that the humble flock may reach
where the brave Shepherd
  has gone before.
Who lives and reigns with you
  in the unity of the Holy Spirit,
one God, for ever and ever.

Collecta

Omnipotens sempiterne Deus,
deduc nos ad societatem
  cælestium gaudiorum,
ut eo perveniat humilitas gregis,
quo processit fortitudo pastoris.
Per Dominum nostrum Iesum
  Christum Filium tuum,
qui tecum vivit et regnat
  in unitate Spiritus Sancti,
Deus, per omnia sæcula sæculorum.

FIRST READING

A reading from the Acts of the Apostles   13:14,43-52

We must turn to the pagans.

Paul and Barnabas carried on from Perga till they reached Antioch in
Pisidia. Here they went to synagogue on the Sabbath and took their seats.

When the meeting broke up, many Jews and devout converts joined
Paul and Barnabas, and in their talks with them Paul and Barnabas urged
them to remain faithful to the grace God had given them.

The next sabbath almost the whole town assembled to hear the word
of God. When they saw the crowds, the Jews, prompted by jealousy,
used blasphemies and contradicted everything Paul said. Then Paul and
Barnabas spoke out boldly. 'We had to proclaim the word of God to you
first, but since you have rejected it, since you do not think yourselves
worthy of eternal life, we must turn to the pagans. For this is what the
Lord commanded us to do when he said:

I have made you a light for the nations,
so that my salvation may reach the ends of the earth.'

It made the pagans very happy to hear this and they thanked the Lord
for his message; all who were destined for eternal life became believers.
Thus the word of the Lord spread through the whole countryside.

But the Jews worked upon some of the devout women of the upper
classes and the leading men of the city and persuaded them to turn against
Paul and Barnabas and expel them from their territory. So they shook the
dust from their feet in defiance and went off to Iconium; but the disciples
were filled with joy and the Holy Spirit.

The word of the Lord.

Responsorial Psalm   Ps 99:1-3,5. R. v.3

R. **We are his people, the sheep of his flock.**
   Or: **Alleluia!**

Cry out with joy to the Lord, all the earth.
Serve the Lord with gladness.
Come before him, singing for joy. R.

Know that he, the Lord, is God.
He made us, we belong to him,
we are his people, the sheep of his flock. R.

Indeed, how good is the Lord,
eternal his merciful love.
He is faithful from age to age. R.

SECOND READING

A reading from the book of the Apocalypse   7:9,14-17

The Lamb will be their shepherd and will lead them to springs of living water.

I, John, saw a huge number, impossible to count, of people from every nation, race, tribe and language; they were standing in front of the throne and in front of the Lamb, dressed in white robes and holding palms in their hands. One of the elders said to me, 'These are the people who have been through the great persecution, and because they have washed their robes white again in the blood of the Lamb, they now stand in front of God's throne and serve him day and night in his sanctuary; and the One who sits on the throne will spread his tent over them. They will never hunger or thirst again; neither the sun nor scorching wind will ever plague them, because the Lamb who is at the throne will be their shepherd and will lead them to springs of living water; and God will wipe away all tears from their eyes.'

The word of the Lord.

Gospel Acclamation   Jn 10:14

R. **Alleluia, alleluia!**
I am the good shepherd, says the Lord;
I know my own sheep and my own know me.
R. **Alleluia!**

GOSPEL

A reading from the holy Gospel according to John   10:27-30

I give eternal life to the sheep that belong to me.

Jesus said:

'The sheep that belong to me listen to my voice;
I know them and they follow me.
I give them eternal life;
they will never be lost
and no one will ever steal them from me.
The Father who gave them to me is greater than anyone,
and no one can steal from the Father.
The Father and I are one.'

The Gospel of the Lord.

The Creed is said.

Prayer over the Offerings

Grant, we pray, O Lord,
that we may always find delight
    in these paschal mysteries,
so that the renewal constantly
    at work within us
may be the cause of our
    unending joy.
Through Christ our Lord.

Preface of Easter, pp.558-563.

Super oblata

Concede, quæsumus, Domine,
semper nos per hæc mysteria
    paschalia gratulari,
ut continua nostræ
    reparationis operatio
perpetuæ nobis fiat causa lætitiæ.
Per Christum Dominum nostrum.

Communion Antiphon

The Good Shepherd has risen,
who laid down his life for his sheep
and willingly died for his flock,
    alleluia.

Ant. ad communionem

Surrexit Pastor bonus,
qui animam suam posuit pro
    ovibus suis,
et pro grege suo mori dignatus est,
    alleluia.

Prayer after Communion

Look upon your flock,
    kind Shepherd,
and be pleased to settle
    in eternal pastures
the sheep you have redeemed
by the Precious Blood of your Son.
Who lives and reigns
    for ever and ever.

Post communionem

Gregem tuum, Pastor bone,
    placatus intende,
et oves, quas pretioso Filii tui
    sanguine redemisti,
in æternis pascuis collocare digneris.
Per Christum Dominum nostrum.

A formula of Solemn Blessing, pp.646-649, may be used.

FIFTH SUNDAY OF EASTER (YEAR C)

"I, John, saw the holy city, new Jerusalem, coming down out of heaven from God". The splendid vision of the heavenly Jerusalem, which today's Liturgy of the Word presents to us again, closes the Book of Revelation and the whole series of sacred books which comprise the Bible. With this magnificent description of the City of God, the author of Revelation indicates the definitive defeat of evil and the achievement of perfect communion between God and men. From the beginning, the history of salvation aims at this goal. Before the community of believers, who are also called to proclaim the Gospel and to witness to their own faith in Christ amid various trials, the supreme goal shines forth: the heavenly Jerusalem! We are all advancing towards that goal, where the saints and martyrs have preceded us down the centuries. On our earthly pilgrimage, these brethren of ours, who have passed victoriously through "great tribulations", serve as an example, incentive and encouragement to us.

(Blessed Pope John Paul II)

Entrance Antiphon   Cf. Ps 97:1-2

O SING a new song to the Lord,
for he has worked wonders;
in the sight of the nations
he has shown his deliverance,
    alleluia.

Ant. ad introitum

C ANTATE Domino
canticum novum,
quia mirabilia fecit Dominus;
ante conspectum gentium revelavit
    iustitiam suam, alleluia.

The Gloria in excelsis (Glory to God in the highest) is said.

Collect

Almighty ever-living God,
constantly accomplish the Paschal
    Mystery within us,
that those you were pleased
    to make new in Holy Baptism
may, under your protective care,
    bear much fruit
and come to the joys of life eternal.
Through our Lord Jesus Christ,
    your Son,
who lives and reigns with you
    in the unity of the Holy Spirit,
one God, for ever and ever.

Collecta

Omnipotens sempiterne Deus,
semper in nobis paschale
    perfice sacramentum,
ut, quos sacro baptismate dignatus
    es renovare,
sub tuæ protectionis auxilio multos
    fructus afferant,
et ad æternæ vitæ gaudia
    pervenire concedas.
Per Dominum nostrum Iesum
    Christum Filium tuum,
qui tecum vivit et regnat
    in unitate Spiritus Sancti,
Deus, per omnia sæcula sæculorum.

FIRST READING

A reading from the Acts of the Apostles   14:21-27

They gave an account to the church of all that God had done with them.

Paul and Barnabas went back through Lystra and Iconium to Antioch. They put fresh heart into the disciples, encouraging them to persevere in the faith. 'We all have to experience many hardships' they said 'before we enter the kingdom of God.' In each of these churches they appointed elders, and with prayer and fasting they commended them to the Lord in whom they had come to believe.

They passed through Pisidia and reached Pamphylia. Then after proclaiming the word at Perga they went down to Attalia and from there sailed for Antioch, where they had originally been commended to the grace of God for the work they had now completed.

On their arrival they assembled the church and gave an account of all that God had done with them, and how he had opened the door of faith to the pagans.

The word of the Lord.

Responsorial Psalm   Ps 144:8-13. R. Cf. v.1

R. **I will bless your name for ever, O God my King.**
Or: **Alleluia!**

The Lord is kind and full of compassion,
slow to anger, abounding in love.
How good is the Lord to all,
compassionate to all his creatures. R.

All your creatures shall thank you, O Lord,
and your friends shall repeat their blessing.
They shall speak of the glory of your reign
and declare your might, O God,
to make known to men your mighty deeds
and the glorious splendour of your reign. R.

Yours is an everlasting kingdom;
your rule lasts from age to age. R.

SECOND READING

A reading from the book of the Apocalypse   21:1-5

God will wipe away all tears from their eyes.

I, John, saw a new heaven and a new earth; the first heaven and the first earth had disappeared now, and there was no longer any sea. I saw the holy city, and the new Jerusalem, coming down from God out of heaven, as beautiful as a bride all dressed for her husband. Then I heard a loud voice call from the throne, 'You see this city? Here God lives among men. He will make his home among them; they shall be his people, and he will be their God; his name is God-with-them. He will wipe away all tears from their eyes; there will be no more death, and no more mourning or sadness. The world of the past has gone.'

Then the One sitting on the throne spoke: 'Now I am making the whole of creation new.'

The word of the Lord.

Gospel Acclamation   Jn 13:34
R. **Alleluia, alleluia!**
Jesus said: 'I give you a new commandment:
love one another, just as I have loved you.'
R. **Alleluia!**

GOSPEL

A reading from the holy Gospel according to John   13:31-35

I give you a new commandment: love one another.

When Judas had gone Jesus said:
'Now has the Son of Man been glorified,
and in him God has been glorified.
If God has been glorified in him,
God will in turn glorify him in himself,
and will glorify him very soon.
My little children,
I shall not be with you much longer.
I give you a new commandment:
love one another;
just as I have loved you,
you also must love one another.
By this love you have for one another,
everyone will know that you are my disciples.'

The Gospel of the Lord.

The Creed is said.

Prayer over the Offerings	Super oblata
O God, who by the wonderful exchange effected in this sacrifice have made us partakers of the one supreme Godhead, grant, we pray, that, as we have come to know your truth, we may make it ours by a worthy way of life. Through Christ our Lord.	Deus, qui nos, per huius sacrificii veneranda commercia, unius summæque divinitatis participes effecisti, præsta, quæsumus, ut, sicut tuam cognovimus veritatem, sic eam dignis moribus assequamur. Per Christum Dominum nostrum.

Preface of Easter, pp.558-563.

Communion Antiphon Cf. Jn 15:1,5	Ant. ad communionem
I am the true vine and you are the branches, says the Lord. Whoever remains in me, and I in him, bears fruit in plenty, alleluia.	Ego sum vitis vera et vos palmites, dicit Dominus; qui manet in me et ego in eo, hic fert fructum multum, alleluia.

Prayer after Communion	Post communionem
Graciously be present to your people, we pray, O Lord, and lead those you have imbued with heavenly mysteries to pass from former ways to newness of life. Through Christ our Lord.	Populo tuo, quæsumus, Domine, adesto propitius, et, quem mysteriis cælestibus imbuisti, fac ad novitatem vitæ de vetustate transire. Per Christum Dominum nostrum.

A formula of Solemn Blessing, pp.646-649, may be used.

SIXTH SUNDAY OF EASTER (YEAR C)

This Sunday's Gospel, taken from Chapter Fourteen of the Gospel according to St John, gives us an implicit spiritual portrait of the Virgin Mary when Jesus says: "Whoever loves me will keep my word, and my Father will love him, and we will come to him and make our home with him". These words are addressed to the disciples but can be applied to a maximum degree precisely to the One who was the first and perfect disciple of Jesus. Mary, in fact, observed first and fully the words of her Son, showing that she loved him not only as a mother, but first of all as a humble and obedient handmaid. For this reason God the Father loved her and the Most Holy Trinity made its dwelling place in her.

(Pope Benedict XVI)

Entrance Antiphon   Cf. Is 48:20

PROCLAIM a joyful sound
and let it be heard;
proclaim to the ends of the earth:
The Lord has freed his people,
    alleluia.

Ant. ad introitum

VOCEM iucunditatis
annuntiate, et audiatur,
annuntiate usque ad
    extremum terræ:
liberavit Dominus populum suum,
    alleluia.

The Gloria in excelsis (Glory to God in the highest) is said.

Collect

Grant, almighty God,
that we may celebrate with heartfelt
    devotion these days of joy,
which we keep in honour
    of the risen Lord,
and that what we relive
    in remembrance
we may always hold to in what we do.
Through our Lord Jesus Christ,
    your Son,
who lives and reigns with you in
    the unity of the Holy Spirit,
one God, for ever and ever.

Collecta

Fac nos, omnipotens Deus,
    hos lætitiæ dies,
quos in honorem Domini
    resurgentis exsequimur,
affectu sedulo celebrare,
ut quod recordatione percurrimus
semper in opere teneamus.
Per Dominum nostrum Iesum
    Christum Filium tuum,
qui tecum vivit et regnat
    in unitate Spiritus Sancti,
Deus, per omnia sæcula sæculorum.

FIRST READING

A reading from the Acts of the Apostles   15:1-2,22-29

It has been decided by the Holy Spirit and by ourselves not to saddle you with any burden beyond these essentials.

Some men came down from Judaea and taught the brothers, 'Unless you have yourselves circumcised in the tradition of Moses you cannot be saved.' This led to disagreement, and after Paul and Barnabas had had a long argument with these men it was arranged that Paul and Barnabas and others of the church should go up to Jerusalem and discuss the problem with the apostles and elders.

Then the apostles and elders decided to choose delegates to send to Antioch with Paul and Barnabas; the whole church concurred with this. They chose Judas known as Barsabbas and Silas, both leading men in the brotherhood, and gave them this letter to take with them:

'The apostles and elders, your brothers, send greetings to the brothers of pagan birth in Antioch, Syria and Cilicia. We hear that some of our members have disturbed you with their demands and have unsettled your minds. They acted without any authority from us, and so we have decided unanimously to elect delegates and to send them to you with Barnabas and Paul, men we highly respect who have dedicated their lives to the name of our Lord Jesus Christ. Accordingly we are sending you Judas and Silas, who will confirm by word of mouth what we have written in this letter. It has been decided by the Holy Spirit and by ourselves not to saddle you with any burden beyond these essentials: you are to abstain from food sacrificed to idols, from blood, from the meat of strangled animals and from fornication. Avoid these, and you will do what is right. Farewell.'

The word of the Lord.

Responsorial Psalm   Ps 66:2-3,5-6,8. R. v.4

R. **Let the peoples praise you, O God;**
   let all the peoples praise you.
   Or: **Alleluia!**

   O God, be gracious and bless us
   and let your face shed its light upon us.
   So will your ways be known upon earth
   and all nations learn your saving help. R.

Let the nations be glad and exult
for you rule the world with justice.
With fairness you rule the peoples,
you guide the nations on earth. R.

Let the peoples praise you, O God;
let all the peoples praise you.
May God still give us his blessing
till the ends of the earth revere him. R.

When the Ascension is celebrated on the Seventh Sunday of Easter, the Second
Reading and Gospel assigned to the Seventh Sunday may be read on the Sixth
Sunday.

SECOND READING

A reading from the book of the Apocalypse   21:10-14,22-23

He showed me the holy city coming down out of heaven.

In the spirit, the angel took me to the top of an enormous high mountain
and showed me Jerusalem, the holy city, coming down from God out of
heaven. It had all the radiant glory of God and glittered like some precious
jewel of crystal-clear diamond. The walls of it were of a great height, and
had twelve gates; at each of the twelve gates there was an angel, and over the
gates were written the names of the twelve tribes of Israel; on the east there
were three gates, on the north three gates, on the south three gates, and on
the west three gates. The city walls stood on twelve foundation stones, each
one of which bore the name of one of the twelve apostles of the Lamb.

I saw that there was no temple in the city since the Lord God Almighty
and the Lamb were themselves the temple, and the city did not need the
sun or the moon for light, since it was lit by the radiant glory of God and
the Lamb was a lighted torch for it.

The word of the Lord.

Gospel Acclamation   Jn 14:23

R. **Alleluia, alleluia!**
Jesus said: 'If anyone loves me he will keep my word,
and my Father will love him, and we shall come to him.'
R. **Alleluia!**

GOSPEL

A reading from the holy Gospel according to John   14:23-29

The Holy Spirit will remind you of all I have said to you.

Jesus said to his disciples:

'If anyone loves me he will keep my word,
and my Father will love him,
and we shall come to him
and make our home with him.
Those who do not love me do not keep my words.
And my word is not my own:
it is the word of the one who sent me.
I have said these things to you
while still with you;
but the Advocate, the Holy Spirit,
whom the Father will send in my name,
will teach you everything
and remind you of all I have said to you.
Peace I bequeath to you,
my own peace I give you,
a peace the world cannot give, this is my gift to you.
Do not let your hearts be troubled or afraid.
You heard me say:
I am going away, and shall return.
If you loved me you would have been glad to know that I am going to
    the Father,
for the Father is greater than I.
I have told you this now before it happens,
so that when it does happen you may believe.'

The Gospel of the Lord.

The Creed is said.

Prayer over the Offerings	Super oblata

May our prayers rise up to you,
    O Lord,
together with the sacrificial offerings,
so that, purified by your graciousness,
we may be conformed to the
    mysteries of your mighty love.
Through Christ our Lord.
	Ascendant ad te, Domine,
	    preces nostræ
	cum oblationibus hostiarum,
	ut, tua dignatione mundati,
	sacramentis magnæ
	    pietatis aptemur.
	Per Christum Dominum nostrum.

Preface of Easter, pp.558-563.

Communion Antiphon Jn 14:15-16

If you love me, keep my
    commandments, says the Lord,
and I will ask the Father and he will
    send you another Paraclete,
to abide with you for ever, alleluia.

Prayer after Communion

Almighty ever-living God,
who restore us to eternal life
    in the Resurrection of Christ,
increase in us, we pray, the fruits
    of this paschal Sacrament
and pour into our hearts
    the strength of this saving food.
Through Christ our Lord.

Ant. ad communionem

Si diligitis me, mandata mea
    servate, dicit Dominus.
Et ego rogabo Patrem, et alium
    Paraclitum dabit vobis,
ut maneat vobiscum in æternum,
    alleluia.

Post communionem

Omnipotens sempiterne Deus,
qui ad æternam vitam in Christi
    resurrectione nos reparas,
fructus in nobis paschalis
    multiplica sacramenti,
et fortitudinem cibi salutaris nostris
    infunde pectoribus.
Per Christum Dominum nostrum.

A formula of Solemn Blessing, pp.646-649, may be used.

THE ASCENSION OF THE LORD (YEAR C)

Solemnity

Where the Solemnity of the Ascension is not to be observed as a Holyday of Obligation, it is assigned to the Seventh Sunday of Easter as its proper day.

St Bernard of Clairvaux explains that Jesus' Ascension into Heaven is accomplished in three steps: "The first is the glory of the Resurrection; the second is the power to judge; and the third is sitting at the right hand of the Father" (Sermo de Ascensione Domini 60, 2). Such an event is preceded by the blessing of the disciples, whom he prepares to receive the gift of the Holy Spirit, in order that salvation is proclaimed everywhere. Jesus himself says to them: "You are witnesses of these things. And behold, I send the promise of my Father upon you". The Lord draws the gaze of the Apostles, our gaze toward Heaven to show how to travel the road of good during earthly life. Nevertheless, he remains within the framework of human history, he is near to each of us and guides our Christian journey: he is the companion of the those persecuted for the faith, he is in the heart of those who are marginalised, he is present in those whom the right to life is denied. We can hear, see and touch our Lord Jesus in the Church, especially through the word and the sacraments.

(Pope Benedict XVI)

At the Vigil Mass

This Mass is used on the evening of the day before the Solemnity, either before or after First Vespers (Evening Prayer I) of the Ascension.

Entrance Antiphon Ps 67:33,35	Ant. ad introitum
YOU kingdoms of the earth, sing to God; praise the Lord, who ascends above the highest heavens; his majesty and might are in the skies, alleluia.	REGNA terræ cantate Deo, psallite Domino, qui ascendit super cælum cæli; magnificentia et virtus eius in nubibus, alleluia.

The Gloria in excelsis (Glory to God in the highest) is said.

Collect	Collecta
O God, whose Son today ascended to the heavens as the Apostles looked on, grant, we pray, that, in accordance with his promise,	Deus, cuius Filius hodie in cælos, Apostolis astantibus, ascendit, concede nobis, quæsumus, ut secundum eius promissionem et ille nobiscum semper in terris

| we may be worthy for him to live with us always on earth, and we with him in heaven. Who lives and reigns with you in the unity of the Holy Spirit, one God, for ever and ever. | et nos cum eo in cælo vivere mereamur. Qui tecum vivit et regnat in unitate Spiritus Sancti, Deus, per omnia sæcula sæculorum. |

FIRST READING

A reading from the Acts of the Apostles   1:1-11

He was lifted up while they looked on.

In my earlier work, Theophilus, I dealt with everything Jesus had done and taught from the beginning until the day he gave his instructions to the apostles he had chosen through the Holy Spirit, and was taken up to heaven. He had shown himself alive to them after his Passion by many demonstrations: for forty days he had continued to appear to them and tell them about the kingdom of God. When he had been at table with them, he had told them not to leave Jerusalem, but to wait there for what the Father had promised. 'It is', he had said, 'what you have heard me speak about: John baptised with water but you, not many days from now, will be baptised with the Holy Spirit.'

Now having met together, they asked him, 'Lord, has the time come? Are you going to restore the kingdom to Israel?' He replied, 'It is not for you to know times or dates that the Father has decided by his own authority, but you will receive power when the Holy Spirit comes on you, and then you will be my witnesses not only in Jerusalem but throughout Judaea and Samaria, and indeed to the ends of the earth.'

As he said this he was lifted up while they looked on, and a cloud took him from their sight. They were still staring into the sky when suddenly two men in white were standing near them and they said, 'Why are you men from Galilee standing here looking into the sky? Jesus who has been taken up from you into heaven, this same Jesus will come back in the same way as you have seen him go there.'

The word of the Lord.

Responsorial Psalm   Ps 46:2-3,6-7,8-9. R. v.6

R. **God goes up with shouts of joy**
   the Lord goes up with trumpet blast.
   Or: **Alleluia!**

   All peoples, clap your hands,
   cry to God with shouts of joy!

For the Lord, the Most High, we must fear,
great king over all the earth. R.

God goes up with shouts of joy;
the Lord goes up with trumpet blast.
Sing praise for God, sing praise,
sing praise to our king, sing praise. R.

God is king of all the earth.
Sing praise with all your skill.
God is king over the nations;
God reigns on his holy throne. R.

R. **God goes up with shouts of joy**
the Lord goes up with trumpet blast.
Or: **Alleluia!**

The Second Reading from Year A, p.393, may be used in place of the following.

SECOND READING

A reading from the letter to the Hebrews   9:24-28,10:19-23
Christ entered into heaven itself.

It is not as though Christ had entered a man-made sanctuary which was
only modelled on the real one; but it was heaven itself, so that he could
appear in the actual presence of God on our behalf. And he does not have to
offer himself again and again, like the high priest going into the sanctuary
year after year with the blood that is not his own, or else he would have
had to suffer over and over again since the world began. Instead of that,
he has made his appearance once and for all, now at the end of the last
age, to do away with sin by sacrificing himself. Since men only die once,
and after that comes judgement, so Christ, too, offers himself only once
to take the faults of many on himself, and when he appears a second time,
it will not be to deal with sin but to reward with salvation those who are
waiting for him.

In other words, brothers, through the blood of Jesus we have the right
to enter the sanctuary, by a new way which he had opened for us, a living
opening through the curtain, that is to say, his body. And we have the
supreme high priest over all the house of God. So as we go in, let us be
sincere in heart and filled with faith, our minds sprinkled and free from
any trace of bad conscience and our bodies washed with pure water. Let us
keep firm in the hope we profess, because the one who made the promise
is faithful.

The word of the Lord.

Gospel Acclamation   Mt 28:19,20

R. **Alleluia, alleluia!**
Go, make disciples of all nations;
I am with you always; yes, to the end of time.
R. **Alleluia!**

GOSPEL

A reading from the holy Gospel according to Luke   24:46-53

As he blessed them he was carried up to heaven.

Jesus said to his disciples: 'You see how it is written that the Christ would suffer and on the third day rise from the dead, and that, in his name, repentance for the forgiveness of sins would be preached to all the nations, beginning from Jerusalem. You are witnesses to this.

'And now I am sending down to you what the Father has promised. Stay in the city then, until you are clothed with the power from on high.' Then he took them out as far as the outskirts of Bethany, and lifting up his hands he blessed them. Now as he blessed them, he withdrew from them and was carried up to heaven. They worshipped him and then went back to Jerusalem full of joy; and they were continually in the Temple praising God.

The Gospel of the Lord.

The Creed is said.

Prayer over the Offerings	Super oblata
O God, whose Only Begotten Son, our High Priest,	Deus, cuius Unigenitus, Pontifex noster,
is seated ever-living at your right hand to intercede for us,	semper vivens sedet ad dexteram tuam
grant that we may approach with confidence the throne of grace	ad interpellandum pro nobis, concede nos adire cum fiducia ad thronum gratiæ,
and there obtain your mercy.	ut misericordiam tuam consequamur.
Through Christ our Lord.	Per Christum Dominum nostrum.

Preface I or II of the Ascension of the Lord, pp.564-565.

When the Roman Canon is used, the proper form of the Communicantes (In communion with those) is said.

Communion Antiphon Cf. Heb 10:12	Ant. ad communionem
Christ, offering a single sacrifice for sins, is seated for ever at God's right hand, alleluia.	Christus, unam pro peccatis offerens hostiam, in sempiternum sedet in dextera Dei, alleluia.

Prayer after Communion	Post communionem
May the gifts we have received from your altar, Lord, kindle in our hearts a longing for the heavenly homeland and cause us to press forward, following in the Saviour's footsteps, to the place where for our sake he entered before us. Who lives and reigns for ever and ever.	Quæ ex altari tuo, Domine, dona percepimus, accendant in cordibus nostris cælestis patriæ desiderium, et quo præcursor pro nobis introivit Salvator, faciant nos, eius vestigia sectantes, contendere. Qui vivit et regnat in sæcula sæculorum.

A formula of Solemn Blessing, pp.648-649, may be used.

At the Mass during the Day

Entrance Antiphon   Ac 1:11

MEN of Galilee, why gaze
in wonder at the heavens?
This Jesus whom you saw
  ascending into heaven
will return as you saw him go,
  alleluia.

Ant. ad introitum

VIRI Galilæi, quid admiramini
aspicientes in cælum?
Quemadmodum vidistis eum
  ascendentem in cælum,
  ita veniet, alleluia.

The Gloria in excelsis (Glory to God in the highest) is said.

Collect

Gladden us with holy joys,
  almighty God,
and make us rejoice with devout
  thanksgiving,
for the Ascension of Christ your Son
is our exaltation,
and, where the Head has gone
  before in glory,
the Body is called to follow in hope.
Through our Lord Jesus Christ,
  your Son,
who lives and reigns with you
  in the unity of the Holy Spirit,
one God, for ever and ever.

Collecta

Fac nos, omnipotens Deus, sanctis
  exsultare gaudiis,
et pia gratiarum actione lætari,
quia Christi Filii tui ascensio est
  nostra provectio,
et quo processit gloria capitis, eo
  spes vocatur et corporis.
Per Dominum nostrum Iesum
  Christum Filium tuum,
qui tecum vivit et regnat
  in unitate Spiritus Sancti,
Deus, per omnia sæcula sæculorum.

Or:

Grant, we pray, almighty God,
that we, who believe that your Only
  Begotten Son, our Redeemer,
ascended this day to the heavens,
may in spirit dwell already
  in heavenly realms.
Who lives and reigns with you
  in the unity of the Holy Spirit,
one God, for ever and ever.

Vel:

Concede, quæsumus,
  omnipotens Deus,
ut, qui hodierna die
Unigenitum tuum
  Redemptorem nostrum
ad cælos ascendisse credimus,
ipsi quoque mente
  in cælestibus habitemus.
tecum vivit et regnat
  in unitate Spiritus Sancti,
Deus, per omnia sæcula sæculorum.

FIRST READING

A reading from the Acts of the Apostles   1:1-11

He was lifted up while they looked on.

In my earlier work, Theophilus, I dealt with everything Jesus had done and taught from the beginning until the day he gave his instructions to the apostles he had chosen through the Holy Spirit, and was taken up to heaven. He had shown himself alive to them after his Passion by many demonstrations: for forty days he had continued to appear to them and tell them about the kingdom of God. When he had been at table with them, he had told them not to leave Jerusalem, but to wait there for what the Father had promised. 'It is', he had said, 'what you have heard me speak about: John baptised with water but you, not many days from now, will be baptised with the Holy Spirit.'

Now having met together, they asked him, 'Lord, has the time come? Are you going to restore the kingdom to Israel?' He replied, 'It is not for you to know times or dates that the Father has decided by his own authority, but you will receive power when the Holy Spirit comes on you, and then you will be my witnesses not only in Jerusalem but throughout Judaea and Samaria, and indeed to the ends of the earth.'

As he said this he was lifted up while they looked on, and a cloud took him from their sight. They were still staring into the sky when suddenly two men in white were standing near them and they said, 'Why are you men from Galilee standing here looking into the sky? Jesus who has been taken up from you into heaven, this same Jesus will come back in the same way as you have seen him go there.'

The word of the Lord.

Responsorial Psalm   Ps 46:2-3,6-7,8-9. R. v.6

R. **God goes up with shouts of joy**
   the Lord goes up with trumpet blast.
   Or: **Alleluia!**

   All peoples, clap your hands,
   cry to God with shouts of joy!
   For the Lord, the Most High, we must fear,
   great king over all the earth. R.

God goes up with shouts of joy;
the Lord goes up with trumpet blast.
Sing praise for God, sing praise,
sing praise to our king, sing praise. R.

God is king of all the earth.
Sing praise with all your skill.
God is king over the nations;
God reigns on his holy throne. R.

The reading of Year A, Ep 1:17-23, p.393, may be used in place of the following.

SECOND READING

A reading from the letter to the Hebrews   9:24-28,10:19-23

Christ entered into heaven itself.

It is not as though Christ had entered a man-made sanctuary which was only modelled on the real one; but it was heaven itself, so that he could appear in the actual presence of God on our behalf. And he does not have to offer himself again and again, like the high priest going into the sanctuary year after year with the blood that is not his own, or else he would have had to suffer over and over again since the world began. Instead of that, he has made his appearance once and for all, now at the end of the last age, to do away with sin by sacrificing himself. Since men only die once, and after that comes judgement, so Christ, too, offers himself only once to take the faults of many on himself, and when he appears a second time, it will not be to deal with sin but to reward with salvation those who are waiting for him.

In other words, brothers, through the blood of Jesus we have the right to enter the sanctuary, by a new way which he had opened for us, a living opening through the curtain, that is to say, his body. And we have the supreme high priest over all the house of God. So as we go in, let us be sincere in heart and filled with faith, our minds sprinkled and free from any trace of bad conscience and our bodies washed with pure water. Let us keep firm in the hope we profess, because the one who made the promise is faithful.

The word of the Lord.

Gospel Acclamation   Mt 28:19,20

R. **Alleluia, alleluia!**
Go, make disciples of all nations;
I am with you always; yes, to the end of time.
R. **Alleluia!**

GOSPEL

A reading from the holy Gospel according to Luke   24:46-53

As he blessed them he was carried up to heaven.

Jesus said to his disciples: 'You see how it is written that the Christ would suffer and on the third day rise from the dead, and that, in his name, repentance for the forgiveness of sins would be preached to all the nations, beginning from Jerusalem. You are witnesses to this.

'And now I am sending down to you what the Father has promised. Stay in the city then, until you are clothed with the power from on high.' Then he took them out as far as the outskirts of Bethany, and lifting up his hands he blessed them. Now as he blessed them, he withdrew from them and was carried up to heaven. They worshipped him and then went back to Jerusalem full of joy; and they were continually in the Temple praising God.

The Gospel of the Lord.

The Creed is said.

Prayer over the Offerings	Super oblata

We offer sacrifice now
    in supplication, O Lord,
to honour the wondrous Ascension
    of your Son:
grant, we pray,
that through this most holy exchange
we, too, may rise up to
    the heavenly realms.
Through Christ our Lord.
	Sacrificium, Domine,
	    pro Filii tui supplices
	venerabili nunc
	    ascensione deferimus:
	præsta, quæsumus,
	    ut his commerciis sacrosanctis
	ad cælestia consurgamus.
	Per Christum Dominum nostrum.

Preface I or II of the Ascension of the Lord, pp.564-565.

When the Roman Canon is used, the proper form of the Communicantes (In communion with those) is said.

Communion Antiphon Mt 28:20	Ant. ad communionem
Behold, I am with you always,	Ecce ego vobiscum sum
even to the end of the age, alleluia.	omnibus diebus,
	usque ad consummationem sæculi,
	alleluia.
Prayer after Communion	Post communionem
Almighty ever-living God,	Omnipotens sempiterne Deus,
who allow those on earth	qui in terra constitutos divina
to celebrate divine mysteries,	tractare concedis,
grant, we pray,	præsta, quæsumus,
that Christian hope may draw	ut illuc tendat christianæ
us onward	devotionis affectus,
to where our nature is united	quo tecum est nostra substantia.
with you.	Per Christum Dominum nostrum.
Through Christ our Lord.	

A formula of Solemn Blessing, pp.648-649, may be used.

SEVENTH SUNDAY OF EASTER (YEAR C)

From Luke, and especially from John, we know that Jesus, during the Last Supper, also prayed to the Father – prayers which also contain a plea to his disciples of that time and of all times. Here I would simply like to take one of these which, as John tells us, Jesus repeated four times in his Priestly Prayer. How deeply it must have concerned him! It remains his constant prayer to the Father on our behalf: the prayer for unity. Jesus explicitly states that this prayer is not meant simply for the disciples then present, but for all who would believe in him. He prays that all may be one "as you, Father, are in me and I am in you, so that the world may believe". Christian unity can exist only if Christians are deeply united to him, to Jesus.

(Pope Benedict XVI)

Entrance Antiphon   Cf. Ps 26:7-9

O LORD, hear my voice,
  for I have called to you;
of you my heart has spoken:
  Seek his face;
hide not your face from me,
  alleluia.

Ant. ad introitum

EXAUDI, Domine, vocem meam,
  qua clamavi ad te.
Tibi dixit cor meum,
  quæsivi vultum tuum,
vultum tuum requiram;
ne avertas faciem tuam a me,
  alleluia.

The Gloria in excelsis (Glory to God in the highest) is said.

Collect

Graciously hear our supplications,
  O Lord,
so that we, who believe that
  the Saviour of the human race
is with you in your glory,
may experience, as he promised,
until the end of the world,
his abiding presence among us.
Who lives and reigns with you
  in the unity of the Holy Spirit,
one God, for ever and ever.

Collecta

Supplicationibus nostris, Domine,
  adesto propitius,
ut, sicut humani generis Salvatorem
tecum in tua credimus maiestate,
ita eum usque
  ad consummationem sæculi
manere nobiscum,
sicut ipse promisit, sentiamus.
Qui tecum vivit et regnat
  in unitate Spiritus Sancti,
Deus, per omnia sæcula sæculorum.

FIRST READING

A reading from the Acts of the Apostles   7:55-60
I can see the Son of Man standing at the right hand of God.

Stephen, filled with the Holy Spirit, gazed into heaven and saw the glory of God, and Jesus standing at God's right hand. 'I can see heaven thrown open' he said 'and the Son of Man standing at the right hand of God.' At this all the members of the council shouted out and stopped their ears with their hands; then they all rushed at him, sent him out of the city and stoned him. The witnesses put down their clothes at the feet of a young man called Saul. As they were stoning him, Stephen said in invocation, 'Lord Jesus, receive my spirit.' Then he knelt down and said aloud, 'Lord, do not hold this sin against them'; and with these words he fell asleep.

The word of the Lord.

Responsorial Psalm   Ps 96:1-2,6-7,9. R. vv.1-9

R. **The Lord is king, most high above all the earth.**
   Or: **Alleluia!**

The Lord is king, let earth rejoice,
the many coastlands be glad.
His throne is justice and right. R.

The skies proclaim his justice;
all peoples see his glory.
All you spirits, worship him. R.

For you indeed are the Lord
most high above all the earth
exalted far above all spirits. R.

SECOND READING

A reading from the book of the Apocalypse   22:12-14,16-17,20
Come, Lord Jesus.

I, John, heard a voice speaking to me: 'Very soon now, I shall be with you again, bringing the reward to be given to every man according to what he deserves. I am the Alpha and the Omega, the First and the Last, the Beginning and the End. Happy are those who will have washed their robes clean, so that they will have the right to feed on the tree of life and can come through the gates into the city.'

I, Jesus, have sent my angel to make these revelations to you for the sake of the churches. I am of David's line, the root of David and the bright star of the morning.

The Spirit and the Bride say, 'Come.' Let everyone who listens answer, 'Come.' Then let all who are thirsty come; all who want it may have the water of life, and have it free.

The one who guarantees these revelations repeats his promise: I shall indeed be with you soon. Amen; come, Lord Jesus.

The word of the Lord.

Gospel Acclamation   Cf. Jn 14:18

R. **Alleluia, alleluia!**
I will not leave you orphans, says the Lord;
I will come back to you, and your hearts will be full of joy.
R. **Alleluia!**

GOSPEL

A reading from the holy Gospel according to John   17:20-26

May they be completely one.

Jesus raised his eyes to heaven and said:
    'Holy Father,
    I pray not only for these,
    but for those also
    who through their words will believe in me.
    May they all be one.
    Father, may they be one in us
    as you are in me and I am in you,
    so that the world may believe it was you who sent me.
    I have given them the glory you gave to me,
    that they may be one as we are one.
    With me in them and you in me,
    may they be so completely one
    that the world will realise that it was you who sent me
    and that I have loved them as much as you love me.
    Father,
    I want those you have given me
    to be with me where I am,
    so that they may always see the glory
    you have given me
    because you loved me
    before the foundation of the world.
    Father, Righteous One,

the world has not known you,
but I have known you,
and these have known
that you have sent me.
I have made your name known to them
and will continue to make it known,
so that the love with which you loved me may be in them,
and so that I may be in them.'

The Gospel of the Lord.

The Creed is said.

Prayer over the Offerings

Accept, O Lord, the prayers
   of your faithful
with the sacrificial offerings,
that through these acts
   of devotedness
we may pass over to the glory
   of heaven.
Through Christ our Lord.

Super oblata

Suscipe, Domine, fidelium preces
cum oblationibus hostiarum,
ut, per hæc piæ devotionis officia,
ad cælestem gloriam transeamus.
Per Christum Dominum nostrum.

Preface of Easter, or of the Ascension, pp.558-565.

Communion Antiphon   Jn 17:22

Father, I pray that they may be one
as we also are one, alleluia.

Ant. ad communionem

Rogo, Pater, ut sint unum,
sicut et nos unum sumus, alleluia.

Prayer after Communion

Hear us, O God our Saviour,
and grant us confidence,
that through these sacred mysteries
there will be accomplished
   in the body of the whole Church
what has already come to pass
   in Christ her Head.
Who lives and reigns
   for ever and ever.

Post communionem

Exaudi nos, Deus, salutaris noster,
ut per hæc sacrosancta mysteria
in totius Ecclesiæ confidamus
   corpore faciendum,
quod eius præcessit in capite.
Per Christum Dominum nostrum.

A formula of Solemn Blessing, pp.646-649, may be used.

PENTECOST SUNDAY (YEAR C)

In the solemn celebration of Pentecost we are invited to profess our faith in the presence and in the action of the Holy Spirit and to invoke his outpouring upon us, upon the Church and upon the whole world. With special intensity, let us make our own the Church's invocation: Veni, Sancte Spiritus! It is such a simple and spontaneous invocation, yet also extraordinarily profound, which came first of all from the heart of Christ. The Spirit is indeed the gift that Jesus asked and continues to ask of his Father for his friends; the first and principal gift that he obtained for us through his Resurrection and Ascension into heaven.

Today's Gospel passage, which has the Last Supper as its context, speaks to us of this prayer of Christ. The Lord Jesus said to his disciples: "If you love me, you will keep my commandments. And I will pray the Father, and he will give you another Counsellor, to be with you for ever". Here the praying heart of Jesus is revealed to us, his filial and fraternal heart. This prayer reaches its apex and its fulfilment on the Cross, where Christ's invocation is one with the total gift that he makes of himself, and thus his prayer becomes, so to speak, the very seal of his self-gift out of love of the Father and humanity.

(Pope Benedict XVI)

For the Vigil Mass, see pp.403-413.

At the Mass during the Day

Entrance Antiphon Ws 1:7	Ant. ad introitum

THE Spirit of the Lord has filled the whole world
and that which contains all things
understands what is said, alleluia.

SPIRITUS Domini replevit orbem terrarum,
et hoc quod continet omnia
scientiam habet vocis, alleluia.

Or: Rm 5:5; Cf. 8:11

Vel:

The love of God has been poured
   into our hearts
through the Spirit of God dwelling
   within us, alleluia.

Caritas Dei diffusa
   est in cordibus nostris
per inhabitantem Spiritum eius
   in nobis, alleluia.

The Gloria in excelsis (Glory to God in the highest) is said.

Collect

O God, who by the mystery
    of today's great feast
sanctify your whole Church
    in every people and nation,
pour out, we pray, the gifts
    of the Holy Spirit
across the face of the earth
and, with the divine grace that
    was at work
when the Gospel
    was first proclaimed,
fill now once more the hearts
    of believers.
Through our Lord Jesus Christ,
    your Son,
who lives and reigns with you
    in the unity of the Holy Spirit,
one God, for ever and ever.

Collecta

Deus, qui sacramento
    festivitatis hodiernæ
universam Ecclesiam tuam
in omni gente et natione sanctificas,
in totam mundi latitudinem
    Spiritus Sancti dona defunde,
et, quod inter ipsa evangelicæ
    prædicationis exordia
operata est divina dignatio,
nunc quoque per credentium
    corda perfunde.
Per Dominum nostrum Iesum
    Christum Filium tuum,
qui tecum vivit et regnat
    in unitate Spiritus Sancti,
Deus, per omnia sæcula sæculorum.

FIRST READING

A reading from the Acts of the Apostles   2:1-11

They were all filled with the Holy Spirit and began to speak.

When Pentecost day came round, the apostles had all met in one room, when suddenly they heard what sounded like a powerful wind from heaven, the noise of which filled the entire house in which they were sitting; and something appeared to them that seemed like tongues of fire; these separated and came to rest on the head of each of them. They were all filled with the Holy Spirit, and began to speak foreign languages as the Spirit gave them the gift of speech.

Now there were devout men living in Jerusalem from every nation under heaven, and at this sound they all assembled, each one bewildered to hear these men speaking his own language. They were amazed and astonished. 'Surely' they said 'all these men speaking are Galileans? How does it happen that each of us hears them in his own native language? Parthians, Medes and Elamites; people from Mesopotamia, Judaea and Cappadocia, Pontus and Asia, Phrygia and Pamphylia, Egypt and the parts of Libya round Cyrene; as well as visitors from Rome – Jews and proselytes alike – Cretans and Arabs; we hear them preaching in our own language about the marvels of God.'

The word of the Lord.

Responsorial Psalm   Ps 103:1,24,29-31,34. R. Cf. v.30

R. **Send forth your Spirit, O Lord,**
   and renew the face of the earth.
   Or: **Alleluia!**

Bless the Lord, my soul!
Lord God, how great you are.
How many are your works, O Lord!
The earth is full of your riches. R.

You take back your spirit, they die,
returning to the dust from which they came.
You send forth your spirit, they are created;
and you renew the face of the earth. R.

May the glory of the Lord last for ever!
May the Lord rejoice in his works!
May my thoughts be pleasing to him.
I find my joy in the Lord. R.

The Second Reading and the Gospel may be taken from Year A, see pp.419-421.
Alternatively, the Second Reading and the Gospel given below may be used.

SECOND READING

A reading from the letter of St Paul to the Romans   8:8-17
Everyone moved by the Spirit is a son of God.

People who are interested only in unspiritual things can never be pleasing to
God. Your interests, however, are not in the unspiritual, but in the spiritual,
since the Spirit of God has made his home in you. In fact, unless you
possessed the Spirit of Christ you would not belong to him. Though your
body may be dead it is because of sin, but if Christ is in you then your spirit
is life itself because you have been justified; and if the Spirit of him who
raised Jesus from the dead is living in you, then he who raised Jesus from the
dead will give life to your own mortal bodies through his Spirit living in you.

So then, my brothers, there is no necessity for us to obey our unspiritual
selves or to live unspiritual lives. If you do live in that way, you are doomed to
die; but if by the Spirit you put an end to the misdeeds of the body you will live.

Everyone moved by the Spirit is a son of God. The spirit you received
is not the spirit of slaves bringing fear into your lives again; it is the spirit
of sons, and it makes us cry out, 'Abba, Father!' The Spirit himself and
our spirit bear united witness that we are children of God. And if we are
children we are heirs as well: heirs of God and coheirs with Christ, sharing
his sufferings so as to share his glory.

The word of the Lord.

For the sequence, see p.420. This may be said or sung.

Gospel Acclamation

R. **Alleluia, alleluia!**
Come, Holy Spirit, fill the hearts of your faithful
and kindle in them the fire of your love.
R. **Alleluia!**

GOSPEL

A reading from the holy Gospel according to John 14:15-16,23-26

The Holy Spirit will teach you everything.

Jesus said to his disciples:
    'If you love me you will keep my commandments.
    I shall ask the Father,
    and he will give you another Advocate
    to be with you for ever.

    'If anyone loves me he will keep my word,
    and my Father will love him,
    and we shall come to him
    and make our home with him.
    Those who do not love me do not keep my words.
    And my word is not my own;
    it is the word of the one who sent me.
    I have said these things to you
    while still with you;
    but the Advocate, the Holy Spirit,
    whom the Father will send in my name,
    will teach you everything
    and remind you of all I have said to you.'

The Gospel of the Lord.

The Creed is said.

Prayer over the Offerings	Super oblata
Grant, we pray, O Lord,	Præsta, quæsumus, Domine,
that, as promised by your Son,	ut, secundum promissionem
the Holy Spirit may reveal to us	Filii tui,
more abundantly	Spiritus Sanctus huius nobis sacrificii
the hidden mystery of this sacrifice	copiosius revelet arcanum,
and graciously lead us into all truth.	et omnem propitius reseret veritatem.
Through Christ our Lord.	Per Christum Dominum nostrum.

Preface: The Mystery of Pentecost, p.422.

Communion Antiphon   Ac 2:4,11

They were all filled
    with the Holy Spirit
and spoke of the marvels of God,
    alleluia.

Prayer after Communion

O God, who bestow heavenly gifts
    upon your Church,
safeguard, we pray, the grace you
    have given,
that the gift of the Holy Spirit
    poured out upon her
may retain all its force
and that this spiritual food
may gain her abundance
    of eternal redemption.
Through Christ our Lord.

Ant. ad communionem

Repleti sunt omnes Spiritu Sancto,
loquentes magnalia Dei, alleluia.

Post communionem

Deus, qui Ecclesiæ tuæ cælestia
    dona largiris,
custodi gratiam quam dedisti,
ut Spiritus Sancti vigeat semper
    munus infusum,
et ad æternæ
    redemptionis augmentum
spiritalis esca proficiat.
Per Christum Dominum nostrum.

A formula of Solemn Blessing, pp.648-651, may be used.
To dismiss the people the Deacon or, if there is no Deacon, the Priest himself sings
or says:

Go forth, the Mass is ended,
    alleluia, alleluia.

Or:
Go in peace, alleluia, aleluia.

And the people reply:
Thanks be to God, alleluia, alleluia.

Ite, missa est,
    alleluia, alleluia.

Vel:
Ite in pace, alleluia, alleluia.

Omnes respondent:
Deo gratias, alleluia, alleluia.

With Easter Time now concluded, the paschal candle is extinguished. It is desirable
to keep the paschal candle in the baptistery with due honour so that it is lit at the
celebration of Baptism and the candles of those baptised are lit from it.

PRAYERS

PREPARATION FOR MASS

PREPARATION FOR MASS

Prayer of Saint Ambrose

I draw near, loving Lord Jesus Christ,
to the table of your most
delightful banquet
in fear and trembling,
a sinner, presuming not
upon my own merits,
but trusting rather in your
goodness and mercy.
I have a heart and body
defiled by my many offences,
a mind and tongue
over which I have kept
no good watch.
Therefore, O loving God,
O awesome Majesty,
I turn in my misery,
caught in snares,
to you the fountain of mercy,
hastening to you for healing,
flying to you for protection;
and while I do not look forward
to having you as Judge,
I long to have you as Saviour.
To you, O Lord,
I display my wounds,
to you I uncover my shame.
I am aware of my many and
great sins,
for which I fear,
but I hope in your mercies,
which are without number.
Look upon me, then,
with eyes of mercy,
Lord Jesus Christ, eternal King,
God and Man, crucified for mankind.

Oratio S. Ambrosii

Ad mensam dulcissimi convivii tui,
    pie Domine Iesu Christe,
ego peccator de propriis meis
    meritis nihil præsumens,
sed de tua confidens misericordia
    et bonitate,
accedere vereor et contremisco.
Nam cor et corpus habeo multis
    criminibus maculatum,
mentem et linguam non
    caute custoditam.

Ergo, o pia Deitas,
    o tremenda maiestas,
ego miser,
    inter angustias deprehensus,
ad te fontem misericordiæ recurro,
ad te festino sanandus,
sub tuam protectionem fugio;
et, quem Iudicem sustinere nequeo,
Salvatorem habere suspiro.

Tibi, Domine, plagas meas ostendo,
tibi verecundiam meam detego.
Scio peccata mea multa
    et magna, pro quibus timeo:
spero in misericordias tuas,
    quarum non est numerus.

Respice ergo in me oculis
    misericordiæ tuæ,
Domine Iesu Christe, Rex æterne,
    Deus et homo,
crucifixus propter hominem.

Listen to me,
as I place my hope in you,
have pity on me, full of miseries
and sins,
you, who will never cease
to let the fountain of
compassion flow.
Hail, O Saving Victim,
offered for me and
for the whole human race
on the wood of the Cross.
Hail, O noble and precious Blood,
flowing from the wounds
of Jesus Christ, my crucified Lord,
and washing away the sins
of all the world.
Remember, Lord, your creature,
whom you redeemed
by your Blood.
I am repentant of my sins,
I desire to put right
what I have done.
Take from me, therefore, most
merciful Father,
all my iniquities and sins,
so that, purified in mind and body,
I may worthily taste
the Holy of Holies.
And grant that this sacred foretaste
of your Body and Blood
which I, though unworthy,
intend to receive,
may be the remission of my sins,
the perfect cleansing of my faults,
the banishment of
shameful thoughts,
and the rebirth of right sentiments;

Exaudi me sperantem in te:
miserere mei pleni miseriis
et peccatis,
tu qui fontem miserationis
numquam manare cessabis.

Salve, salutaris victima,
pro me et omni humano genere
in patibulo Crucis oblata.

Salve, nobilis et pretiose Sanguis,
de vulneribus crucifixi Domini mei
Iesu Christi profluens,
et peccata totius mundi abluens.

Recordare, Domine, creaturæ tuæ,
quam tuo Sanguine redemisti.

Pænitet me peccasse,
cupio emendare quod feci.

Aufer ergo a me,
clementissime Pater,
omnes iniquitates et peccata mea,
ut, purificatus mente et corpore,
digne degustare merear
Sancta sanctorum.

Et concede, ut hæc sancta
prælibatio Corporis
et Sanguinis tui,
quam ego indignus
sumere intendo,
sit peccatorum meorum remissio,
sit delictorum perfecta purgatio,
sit turpium cogitationum effugatio
ac bonorum sensuum regeneratio,

and may it encourage
a wholesome and
    effective performance
of deeds pleasing to you
and be a most firm defence
    of body and soul
against the snares of my enemies.
Amen.

Prayer of Saint Thomas Aquinas

Almighty eternal God,
behold, I come to the Sacrament
of your Only Begotten Son,
our Lord Jesus Christ,
as one sick to the physician of life,
as one unclean to
    the fountain of mercy,
as one blind to the light
    of eternal brightness,
as one poor and needy to
    the Lord of heaven and earth.
I ask, therefore, for the abundance
    of your immense generosity,
that you may graciously cure
    my sickness,
wash away my defilement,
give light to my blindness,
enrich my poverty,
clothe my nakedness,
so that I may receive
    the bread of Angels,
the King of kings and Lord of lords,
with such reverence and humility,
such contrition and devotion,
such purity and faith,
such purpose and intention
as are conducive to the salvation of
    my soul.

operumque tibi placentium
    salubris efficacia,
animæ quoque et corporis
contra inimicorum meorum
    insidias firmissima tuitio.

Amen.

Oratio S. Thomæ Aquinatis

Omnipotens sempiterne Deus,
ecce accedo ad sacramentum
    Unigeniti Filii tui,
Domini nostri Iesu Christi,
accedo tamquam infirmus
    ad medicum vitæ
immundus ad
    fontem misericordiæ,
cæcus ad lumen claritatis æternæ,
pauper et egenus ad
    Dominum cæli et terræ.
Rogo ergo immensæ largitatis
    tuæ abundantiam,
quatenus meam curare
    digneris infirmitatem,
lavare fœditatem,
    illuminare cæcitatem,
ditare paupertatem,
    vestire nuditatem,
ut panem Angelorum,
    Regem regum
    et Dominum dominantium,
tanta suscipiam reverentia
    et humilitate,
tanta contritione et devotione,
    tanta puritate et fide,
tali proposito et intentione,
sicut expedit saluti animæ meæ.

Grant, I pray, that I may receive
not only the Sacrament
    of the Lord's Body and Blood,
but also the reality and power
    of that Sacrament.
O most gentle God,
grant that I may so receive
the Body of your Only Begotten
    Son our Lord Jesus Christ,
which he took from
    the Virgin Mary,
that I may be made worthy
    to be incorporated into his
    Mystical Body
and to be counted among
    its members.
O most loving Father,
grant that I may at last gaze for ever
upon the unveiled face
    of your beloved Son,
whom I, a wayfarer,
propose to receive now veiled
    under these species:
Who lives and reigns with you for
    ever and ever.
Amen.

Da mihi, quæso,
    dominici Corporis et Sanguinis
non solum suscipere sacramentum,
sed etiam rem
    et virtutem sacramenti.
O mitissime Deus,
da mihi Corpus Unigeniti Filii tui,
    Domini nostri Iesu Christi,
quod traxit de Virgine Maria,
    sic suscipere,
ut corpori suo mystico
    merear incorporari
et inter eius membra connumerari.

O amantissime Pater,
    concede mihi dilectum
    Filium tuum,
quem nunc velatum
    in via suscipere propono,
revelata tandem facie
    perpetuo contemplari:
Qui tecum vivit et regnat
in sæcula sæculorum.
Amen.

PRAYER BEFORE MASS

O God, to whom every heart is open, every desire known and from whom no secrets are hidden; purify the thoughts of our hearts by the inspiration of your Holy Spirit, that we may perfectly love you, and worthily praise your holy name. Amen.

Before Holy Communion

Prayer for Help

O God, help me to make a good Communion. Mary, my dearest mother, pray to Jesus for me. My dear Angel Guardian, lead me to the Altar of God.

Act of Faith

O God, because you have said it, I believe that I shall receive the Sacred Body of Jesus Christ to eat, and his Precious Blood to drink. My God, I believe this with all my heart.

Act of Humility

My God, I confess that I am a poor sinner; I am not worthy to receive the Body and Blood of Jesus, on account of my sins. Lord, I am not worthy to receive you under my roof; but only say the word, and my soul will be healed.

Act of Sorrow

My God, I detest all the sins of my life. I am sorry for them, because they have offended you, my God, you who are so good. I resolve never to commit sin any more. My good God, pity me, have mercy on me, forgive me.

Act of Adoration

O Jesus, great God, present on the Altar, I bow down before you. I adore you.

Act of Love and Desire

Jesus, I love you. I desire with all my heart to receive you. Jesus, come into my poor soul, and give me your Flesh to eat and your Blood to drink.

Give me your whole Self, Body, Blood, Soul and Divinity, that I may live for ever with you.

PENITENTIAL PRAYERS

SACRAMENT OF RECONCILIATION

Remember that the sacrament is above all an act of God's love. It is a personal moment to be lived in a relationship of love with God. It is not routine, nor an ordeal to be gone through, but is very much part of the personal renewal which takes place in each person. You are invited, in the light of God's love, to recognise the sinfulness of your life, to have true sorrow for your sins, and a firm intention to avoid them in future.

Essential elements of a good confession

To make a good confession, we should:

1. Pray first, asking God to help us.

2. Make a sincere examination of conscience to see how we have sinned since our last confession.

3. Confess our sins simply, with humility and honesty.

4. Make our act of contrition with heartfelt sorrow and a "firm purpose of amendment", being determined that we will avoid the occasions of sin.

5. Devoutly carry out the penance prescribed and pray in thanksgiving for God's overflowing love and mercy.

Prayer before Confession

Almighty and merciful God,
you have brought me here in the name of your Son
to receive your mercy and grace in my time of need.
Open my eyes to see the evil I have done.
Touch my heart and convert me to yourself.
Where sin has separated me from you,
may your love unite me to you again:
where sin has brought weakness,
may your power heal and strengthen;
where sin has brought death,
may your Spirit raise to new life.
Give me a new heart to love you,
so that my life may reflect the image of your Son.
May the world see the glory
of Christ revealed in your Church,
and come to know that he is the one whom
you have sent, Jesus Christ, your Son, our Lord. Amen.

The Confiteor

I confess to almighty God	Confiteor Deo omnipotenti
and to you my brothers and sisters,	et vobis, fratres,
that I have greatly sinned,	quia peccavi nimis
in my thoughts and in my words,	cogitatione, verbo,
in what I have done,	opere et omissione:
and in what I have failed to do,	mea culpa, mea culpa,
through my fault,	mea maxima culpa.
through my fault,	Ideo precor beatam Mariam
through my most grievous fault;	semper Virginem,
therefore I ask blessed Mary,	omnes Angelos et Sanctos
ever-virgin,	et vos, fratres, orare pro me
all the Angels and Saints,	ad Dominum Deum nostrum.
and you, my brothers and sisters,	
to pray for me to the Lord our God.	

An Act of Contrition

O my God, I am sorry and beg pardon for all my sins, and detest them above all things, because they deserve your dreadful punishments, because they have crucified my loving Saviour Jesus Christ, and, most of all, because they offend your infinite goodness; and I firmly resolve, by the help of your grace, never to offend you again, and carefully to avoid the occasions of sin.

Examination of Conscience

Careful preparation is vital in order to make the most of this encounter with our loving heavenly Father. Find some time to be alone and quiet to reflect on your life, your relationship with God and others. An examination of conscience provides us with what we are going to say in the confessional. Without time given to such examination our confession is in danger of being incomplete. There are many ways: one is to use a gospel passage, especially one of the many healing miracles or occasions of forgiveness (eg Lk 15:11-32; Jn 4:5-42; Mt 18:21-35; Lk 18:9-14). Imagine you are the person being healed or forgiven by Jesus. Read the scripture passage, imagine you are in the scene, and listen to the words of Jesus. He speaks to you! What do you say? Alternatively, Jesus summed up and extended the Ten Commandments by his two great commandments (Mk 12:28-42): love God and your neighbour.

Mortal sin is sin whose object is a grave matter and which is also committed with full knowledge and deliberate consent (*Catechism* 1857). We must confess all mortal sins. We are not obliged to confess all venial sins.

We commit venial sin when, in a less serious matter, we do not observe the standard prescribed by the moral law, or when we disobey the moral law in a grave matter, but without full knowledge or without complete consent (*Catechism* 1862). Confession of venial sins is an act of devotion. We need not be unduly anxious to confess them all, but may rather choose to focus on areas of our life that are most in need of God's grace.

The following examination of conscience can help us to measure our lives by the objective standard of Christ's teaching. We may also consider more generally how we may have failed in our lives to live fully as disciples of Christ.

Sins against God

Have I rejected my faith, refused to find out more about it?

Have I forgotten my daily prayers or said them badly?

Have I experimented with the occult or put my trust in fortune tellers or horoscopes?

Have I blasphemed against God or used bad language?

Have I shown disrespect for holy things, places or people?

Have I missed Mass on Sundays or Holydays through my own fault?

Have I let myself be distracted at Mass or distracted others?

Have I received Holy Communion in a state of mortal sin?

Have I received Holy Communion without proper reverence, care or thanksgiving?

Sins against myself and others

Have I been impatient, angry or jealous?

Have I brooded over injuries or refused to forgive?

Have I taken part in or encouraged abortion, the destruction of human embryos, euthanasia or any other means of taking human life?

Have I been verbally or physically violent to others?

Have I been racist in my thoughts, words or deeds?

Have I hurt anyone by speaking badly about them?

Have I betrayed confidences without good cause or revealed things simply to hurt others?

Have I judged others rashly?

Have I been drunk or used illegal drugs?

Have I driven dangerously or inconsiderately?

Have I spoken in an obscene way?

Have I looked at obscene pictures, films or books?

Have I been involved in any impure behaviour on my own or with someone else?

Have I been vain, proud, selfish or self-seeking?

Have I told lies to excuse myself, to hurt others or to make myself look more important?

Have I stolen anything?

Have I failed to contribute to the support of the Church in proportion to
    my means?

Have I been disobedient, rude or insolent to those in authority over me?

Have I been harsh, overbearing or sarcastic to those under my authority?

Have I cheated my employers or employees?

Have I misused or damaged the property of others?

Have I set my heart greedily on possessing things?

Have I given scandal or bad example?

Have I been lazy at my work, study or domestic duties?

Have I been jealous of others – of their looks, their popularity,
    their good work?

Have I encouraged others to do wrong in any way?

For spouses

Have I neglected to foster the warmth of my love and affection
    for my spouse?

Have I prolonged disagreements through resentment or failing to
    apologise when I have been in the wrong?

Have I mistreated my spouse verbally, emotionally or physically?

Have I used artificial means of birth control?

Have I been unfaithful to my spouse in any way?

For parents

Have I neglected to teach my children to pray?

Have I neglected the religious education of my children?

Have I failed to bring my children to Sunday Mass?

Have I argued with my spouse in front of my children?

Have I failed to exercise vigilance over what my children read, see on
    television or on the internet?

Have I been harsh or overbearing to my children?

Have I neglected my children's welfare in any way?

For young people

Have I been disobedient to my parents?

Have I been unhelpful at home?

Have I failed to try to understand my parents and talk with them?

Have I upset the peace of my home for selfish reasons?

Have I lost control when I have been angry?

Have I sulked or been sarcastic instead of asking for help?

Have I failed to work properly at school?
Have I treated teachers or other adults with disrespect?
Have I played unfairly at games or sports?
Have I taken part in fights?

Rite of Reconciliation

Reception

The priest welcomes the penitent warmly. The penitent and priest begin by making the sign of the cross, while saying:

In the name of the Father,
    and of the Son,
    and of the Holy Spirit.
Amen.
	In nomine Patris, et Filii,
	    et Spiritus Sancti.
	
	Amen.

The priest invites you to trust in God. The response is Amen. You may indicate your state of life, and anything else which may help the priest as confessor.

The Word of God

The priest may invite you to reflect on a passage from Holy Scripture, speaking of God's mercy and call to conversion.

Reconciliation

Then you can speak in your own words or you can say: Bless me Father for I have sinned. My last confession was . . . ago (say roughly how long) and these are my sins.

Now tell your sins simply in your own words. When you have finished, let the priest know. You can use these words if you wish: I am sorry for all these sins and for any that I cannot now remember.

Listen carefully to the advice of the priest and ask the Holy Spirit to help him to say what is best to help you to grow in the Christian life. You can ask him questions if you want. The priest may propose an Act of Penance, which should serve not only to make up for the past but also to help begin a new life and provide an antidote to weakness. It may take the form of prayer, self-denial, and especially of service to one's neighbour and works of mercy.

Then the priest invites you to say a prayer of sorrow (an Act of Contrition), such as:

O my God,
because you are so good,
I am very sorry that I have sinned against you,
and by the help of your grace
I will not sin again.

Wait while the priest says the prayer of "Absolution" (where Christ forgives you all your sins).

God, the Father of mercies,	Deus, Pater misericordiarum,
through the death and resurrection of his Son	qui per mortem et resurrectionem Filii sui
has reconciled the world to himself	mundum sibi reconciliavit
and sent the Holy Spirit among us	et Spiritum Sanctum effudit
for the forgiveness of sins;	in remissionem peccatorum,
through the ministry of the Church	per ministerium Ecclesiæ
may God give you pardon and peace,	indulgentiam tibi tribuat et pacem.
and I absolve you from your sins	et ego te absolvo a peccatis tuis
in the name of the Father,	in nomine Patris, et Filii,
and of the Son,	et Spiritus Sancti.
and of the Holy Spirit.	R. Amen.
R. Amen.	

After the Rite of Reconciliation

Take some time in the quiet of the Church to reflect on the grace of the sacrament and to thank God for his mercy and forgiveness. Here is a prayer of thanksgiving:

Father, in your love you have brought me from evil to good and from misery to happiness.

Through your blessings give me the courage of perseverance. Amen.

THE ORDER OF MASS

ORDO MISSÆ CUM POPULO

THE INTRODUCTORY RITES

Before Mass begins, the people gather in a spirit of recollection, preparing for their participation in the Mass.

All stand during the entrance procession.

SIGN OF THE CROSS

After the Entrance Chant, the Priest and the faithful sign themselves with the Sign of the Cross:

Priest: In nómine Patris, et Fílii, et Spíritus Sancti.

A-men.

Response: **Amen.**

GREETING

The Priest greets the people, with one of the following:

1. **Pr.** Grátia Dómini nostri Iesu Christi,
   et cáritas Dei,
   et communicátio Sancti Spíritus
   sit cum ómnibus vobis.

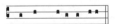

Et cum spí-ri-tu tu-o.

    R. **Et cum spíritu tuo.**

2. **Pr.** Grátia vobis et pax a Deo Patre nostro
   et Dómino Iesu Christo.
       R. **Et cum spíritu tuo.**

3. **Pr.** Dóminus vobíscum.
       R. **Et cum spíritu tuo.**

The Priest, or a Deacon, or another minister, may very briefly introduce the faithful to the Mass of the day.

THE ORDER OF MASS WITH A CONGREGATION

THE INTRODUCTORY RITES

Before Mass begins, the people gather in a spirit of recollection, preparing for their participation in the Mass.

All stand during the entrance procession.

SIGN OF THE CROSS

After the Entrance Chant, the Priest and the faithful sign themselves with the Sign of the Cross:

Priest: In the name of the Father, and of the Son, and of the Holy Spirit.

A-men.

Response: Amen.

GREETING

The Priest greets the people, with one of the following:

1. **Pr.** The grace of our Lord Jesus Christ,
   and the love of God,
   and the communion of the Holy Spirit
   be with you all.

And with your spir-it.

    R. And with your spirit.

2. **Pr.** Grace to you and peace from God our Father
   and the Lord Jesus Christ.
   R. And with your spirit.

3. **Pr.** The Lord be with you.
   R. And with your spirit.

The Priest, or a Deacon, or another minister, may very briefly introduce the faithful to the Mass of the day.

PENITENTIAL ACT*

There are three forms of the Penitential Act which may be chosen from as appropriate.
Each Penitential Act begins with the invitation to the faithful by the Priest:

Pr. Fratres, agnoscámus peccáta nostra,
    ut apti simus ad sacra mystéria celebránda.

A brief pause for silence follows.

Then one of the following forms is used:

---

1. Confíteor Deo omnipoténti et vobis, fratres,
quia peccávi nimis
cogitatióne, verbo, ópere et omissióne:

(and, striking their breast, they say:)
mea culpa, mea culpa, mea máxima culpa.
Ideo precor beátam Mariám semper Vírginem,
omnes Angelos et Sanctos,
et vos, fratres, oráre pro me
ad Dóminum Deum nostrum.

---

2.   Pr. Miserére nostri, Dómine.

Qui- a peccá- vi- mus ti- bi.

R.   Quia peccávimus tibi.

Pr. Osténde nobis, Dómine, misericórdiam tuam.

Et sa- lu- tá- re tu- um da no- bis.

R.   Et salutáre tuum da nobis.

---

* From time to time on Sundays, especially in Easter Time, instead of the customary Penitential Act,
the blessing and sprinkling of water may take place (as in pp.530-531) as a reminder of Baptism.

PENITENTIAL ACT*

There are three forms of the Penitential Act which may be chosen from as appropriate. Each Penitential Act begins with the invitation to the faithful by the Priest:

Pr. Brethren (brothers and sisters),
      let us acknowledge our sins,
    and so prepare ourselves to celebrate the sacred mysteries.

A brief pause for silence follows.

Then one of the following forms is used:

**1. I confess to almighty God
and to you, my brothers and sisters,
that I have greatly sinned,
in my thoughts and in my words,
in what I have done and in what I have failed to do,**

(and, striking their breast, they say:)

**through my fault, through my fault,
through my most grievous fault;
therefore I ask blessed Mary ever-Virgin,
all the Angels and Saints,
and you, my brothers and sisters,
to pray for me to the Lord our God.**

---

2. **Pr.** Have mercy on us, O Lord.

For we have sinned a-gainst you.

   R. **For we have sinned against you.**

   Pr. Show us, O Lord, your mercy.

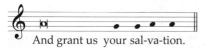

And grant us your sal-va-tion.

   R. **And grant us your salvation.**

---

* From time to time on Sundays, especially in Easter Time, instead of the customary Penitential Act, the blessing and sprinkling of water may take place (as in pp.530-531) as a reminder of Baptism.

Invocations naming the gracious works of the Lord may be made, as in the example below:

3. Pr. Qui missus es sanáre contrítos corde:
   Kýrie, eléison.

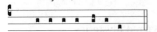

Ký- ri- e, e- lé- i- son.

R. Kýrie, eléison.

Pr. Qui peccatóres vocáre venísti:
   Christe, eléison.

Chri- ste, e- lé- i- son.

R. Christe, eléison.

Pr. Qui ad déxteram Patris sedes, ad interpellándum pro nobis:
   Kýrie, eléison.

Ký- ri- e, e- lé- i- son.

R. Kýrie, eléison.

The absolution by the Priest follows:

Pr. Miscreátur nostri omnípotens Deus
   et, dimíssis peccátis nostris,
   perdúcat nos ad vitam ætérnam.

A-men.

R. Amen.

The Kýrie, eléison (Lord, have mercy) invocations follow, unless they have just occurred.

Pr. Kýrie, eléison.

y-ri-e, e-lé- i-son.

Invocations naming the gracious works of the Lord may be made, as in the example below:

3. Pr. You were sent to heal the contrite of heart:
Lord, have mercy. Or: Kýrie, eléison.

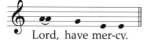
Or: repeat music/words from Latin, p.524.

Lord, have mer-cy.

R. Lord, have mercy.

Pr. You came to call sinners:
Christ, have mercy. Or: Christe, eléison.

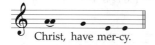
Or: repeat music/words from Latin, p.524.

Christ, have mer-cy.

R. Christ, have mercy.

Pr. You are seated at the right hand of the Father to intercede for us:
Lord, have mercy. Or: Kýrie, eléison.

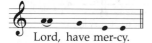
Or: repeat music/words from Latin, p.524.

Lord, have mer-cy.

R. Lord, have mercy.

The absolution by the Priest follows:
Pr. May almighty God have mercy on us,
forgive us our sins,
and bring us to everlasting life.

A-men.

R. Amen.

The Kýrie, eléison (Lord, have mercy) invocations follow, unless they have just occurred.

Pr. Lord, have mercy.

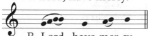
R. Lord, have mer-cy.

Pr. Christe, eléison.

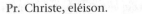

R.   Chris-te, e-lé-i-son.

Pr. Kýrie eléison.

R.   Ky-ri-e, e-lé-i-son. Vel: R.   Ky-ri-e, e-lé-i-son.

THE GLORIA

On Sundays (outside of Advent and Lent), Solemnities and Feast Days, this hymn is either sung or said:

G ló-ri-a in ex-cél-sis De- o.   Et in ter-ra pax ho-mí-ni-bus   bo-næ

vol-un-tá-tis. Lau-dá- mus te.   Be-ne-dí-ci-mus te   Ado-rá-

mus te. Glo-ri-fi-cámus te.   Grá-ti- as á-gi-mus ti-bi   prop-ter

mag-nam gló-ri-am tu-am. Dó-mi-ne De- us, Rex cæ-léstis,   De-us

Pa-ter om-ní-po-tens. Dómi-ne Fí-li uni-gé-ni-te,   Ie-su Christe.

Dómi-ne De-us, Agnus De-i,   Fí-li-us Pa-tris, Qui tollis peccáta

Pr. Christ, have mercy.

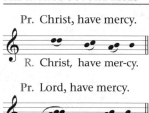

R. Christ, have mer-cy.

Pr. Lord, have mercy.

R. Lord, have mer-cy.

THE GLORIA

On Sundays (outside of Advent and Lent), Solemnities and Feast Days, this hymn is
either sung or said:

Glo-ry to God in the high-est,

and on earth peace to peo-ple of good will.

We praise you, we bless you, we a-dore you, we glo-ri-fy you,

we give you thanks for your great glo-ry,

Lord God, heav-en-ly King, O God, al-might-y Fa-ther.

Lord Je-sus Christ, On-ly Be-got-ten Son,

Lord God, Lamb of God, Son of the Fa-ther,

you take a-way the sins of the world, have mer-cy on us;

mun- di, mi-se-ré- re nobis. Qui tollis peccáta mundi, súscipe de-

pre-ca-ti-ó-nem no- stram. Qui sedes ad déxteram Patris, mi-seré-

re nobis. Quóni-am tu solus Sanctus. Tu solus Dó-mi-nus Tu so-

lus Al-tíssimus, Ie-su Christe. Cum Sancto Spí-ri-tu, in gló-ri-a

De- i Pa- tris. A- men.

**Glória in excélsis Deo
et in terra pax homínibus bonæ voluntátis.**

**Laudámus te,
benedícimus te,
adorámus te,
glorificámus te,
grátias ágimus tibi propter magnam glóriam tuam,
Dómine Deus, Rex cæléstis,
Deus Pater omnípotens.**

**Dómine Fili Unigénite, Iesu Christe,
Dómine Deus, Agnus Dei, Fílius Patris,
qui tollis peccáta mundi, miserére nobis;
qui tollis peccáta mundi, súscipe deprecatiónem nostram.
Qui sedes ad déxteram Patris, miserére nobis.
Quóniam tu solus Sanctus, tu solus Dóminus, tu solus Altíssimus,
Iesu Christe, cum Sancto Spíritu: in glória Dei Patris.
Amen.**

When this hymn is concluded, the Priest, says: **Pr. Orémus.**

And all pray in silence. Then the Priest says the Collect prayer, which ends:

R. Amen.

you take a-way the sins of the world, re-ceive our prayer;

you are seat-ed at the right hand of the Fa-ther, have mer-cy on us.

For you a-lone are the Ho-ly One, you a-lone are the Lord,

you a-lone are the Most High, Je-sus Christ, with the Ho-ly Spir-it,

in the glo-ry of God the Fa - ther. A - men.

**Glory to God in the highest,
and on earth peace to people of good will.
We praise you,
we bless you,
we adore you,
we glorify you,
we give you thanks for your great glory,
Lord God, heavenly King,
O God, almighty Father.**

**Lord Jesus Christ, Only Begotten Son,
Lord God, Lamb of God, Son of the Father,
you take away the sins of the world, have mercy on us;
you take away the sins of the world, receive our prayer;
you are seated at the right hand of the Father,
have mercy on us.**

**For you alone are the Holy One,
you alone are the Lord,
you alone are the Most High,
Jesus Christ,
with the Holy Spirit,
in the glory of God the Father.
Amen.**

When this hymn is concluded, the Priest, says: **Pr. Let us pray.**
And all pray in silence. Then the Priest says the Collect prayer, which ends: **R. Amen.**

RITE FOR THE BLESSING AND SPRINKLING OF WATER

If this rite is celebrated during Mass, it takes the place of the usual Penitential Act at the beginning of Mass. After the greeting, the Priest calls upon the people to pray in these or similar words:

Dear brethren (brothers and sisters),
let us humbly beseech the Lord our God
to bless this water he has created,
which will be sprinkled on us
as a memorial of our Baptism.
May he help us by his grace
to remain faithful to the Spirit we have received.

Almighty ever-living God,
who willed that through water,
the fountain of life and the source of purification,
even souls should be cleansed
and receive the gift of eternal life;
be pleased, we pray, to ✠ bless this water,
by which we seek protection on this your day, O Lord.
Renew the living spring of your grace within us
and grant that by this water we may be defended
from all ills of spirit and body,
and so approach you with hearts made clean
and worthily receive your salvation.
Through Christ our Lord.
R. Amen.

Or:

Almighty Lord and God,
who are the source and origin of all life,
whether of body or soul,
we ask you to ✠ bless this water,
which we use in confidence
to implore forgiveness for our sins
and to obtain the protection of your grace
against all illness and every snare of the enemy.
Grant, O Lord, in your mercy,
that living waters may always spring up for our salvation,
and so may we approach you with a pure heart
and avoid all danger to body and soul.
Through Christ our Lord.
R. Amen.

Or, during Easter Time:

Lord our God,
in your mercy be present to your people's prayers,
and, for us who recall the wondrous work of our creation
and the still greater work of our redemption,
graciously ✠ bless this water.
For you created water to make the fields fruitful
and to refresh and cleanse our bodies.
You also made water the instrument of your mercy:
for through water you freed your people from slavery
and quenched their thirst in the desert;
through water the Prophets proclaimed the new covenant
you were to enter upon with the human race;
and last of all,
through water, which Christ made holy in the Jordan,
you have renewed our corrupted nature
in the bath of regeneration.
Therefore, may this water be for us
a memorial of the Baptism we have received,
and grant that we may share
in the gladness of our brothers and sisters
who at Easter have received their Baptism.
Through Christ our Lord.
R. Amen.

Where the circumstances of the place or the custom of the people suggest that the mixing of salt be preserved in the blessing of water, the Priest may bless salt, saying:

We humbly ask you, almighty God:
be pleased in your faithful love to bless ✠ this salt
you have created,
for it was you who commanded the prophet Elisha
to cast salt into water,
that impure water might be purified.
Grant, O Lord, we pray,
that, wherever this mixture of salt and water is sprinkled,
every attack of the enemy may be repulsed
and your Holy Spirit may be present
to keep us safe at all times.
Through Christ our Lord.
R. Amen.

THE LITURGY OF THE WORD

By hearing the word proclaimed in worship, the faithful again enter into the unending dialogue between God and the covenant people.

FIRST READING

The reader goes to the ambo and proclaims the First Reading, while all sit and listen. The reader ends:

Verbum Dómini.

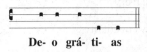

De- o grá- ti- as

R. **Deo grátias.**

It is appropriate to have a brief time of quiet between readings as those present take the word of God to heart.

PSALM

The psalmist or cantor sings or says the Psalm, with the people making the response.

SECOND READING

On Sundays and certain other days there is a second reading. The reader ends:

Verbum Dómini.

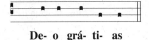

De- o grá- ti- as

R. **Deo grátias.**

GOSPEL

The assembly stands for the Gospel Acclamation. Except during Lent the Acclamation is:

R. **Allelúia!**

During Lent the following forms may be used or another similar phrase:

R. **Laus tibi, Christe, Rex ætérnæ glóriæ!** Or:

R. **Laus et honor tibi, Dómine Iesu!** Or:

R. **Glória et laus tibi, Christe!** Or:

R. **Glória tibi, Christe, Verbo Dei!**

THE LITURGY OF THE WORD

By hearing the word proclaimed in worship, the faithful again enter into the unending dialogue between God and the covenant people.

FIRST READING

The reader goes to the ambo and proclaims the First Reading, while all sit and listen. The reader ends:

The word of the Lord.

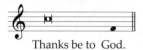

Thanks be to God.

R. **Thanks be to God.**

It is appropriate to have a brief time of quiet between readings as those present take the word of God to heart.

PSALM

The psalmist or cantor sings or says the Psalm, with the people making the response.

SECOND READING

On Sundays and certain other days there is a second reading. The reader ends:

The word of the Lord.

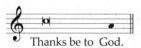

Thanks be to God.

R. **Thanks be to God.**

GOSPEL

The assembly stands for the Gospel Acclamation. Except during Lent the Acclamation is:

R. **Alleluia!**

During Lent the following forms may be used or another similar phrase:

R. **Praise to you, O Christ, king of eternal glory!** Or:

R. **Praise and honour to you, Lord Jesus!** Or:

R. **Glory and praise to you, O Christ!** Or:

R. **Glory to you, O Christ, you are the Word of God!**

At the ambo the Deacon, or the Priest says:

Pr. Dóminus vobíscum.

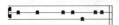

Et cum spíritu tuo.

R. **Et cum spíritu tuo.**

Pr. Léctio sancti Evangélii secúndum **N.**

He makes the Sign of the Cross on the book and, together with the people, on his forehead, lips, and breast.

Glória tibi Dómine.

R. **Glória tibi, Dómine.**

At the end of the Gospel:

Pr. Verbum Dómini.

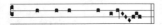

Laus ti-bi, Christe.

R. **Laus tibi, Christe.**

THE HOMILY

Then follows the Homily, which is preached by a Priest or Deacon on all Sundays and Holydays of Obligation. After a brief silence all stand.

THE CREED

On Sundays and Solemnities, the Profession of Faith will follow. Especially during Lent and Easter Time, the Apostles' Creed may be used.

THE NICENO-CONSTANTINOPOLITAN CREED

Credo in unum De- um, Patrem omni-poténtem factó-rem cæli et terræ, vi-sibili-um óm-nium et invi-si-bí- lium. Et in unum Dó-

At the ambo the Deacon, or the Priest says:

Pr. The Lord be with you.

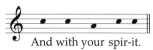

And with your spir-it.

R. And with your spirit.

Pr. A reading from the holy Gospel according to N.

He makes the Sign of the Cross on the book and, together with the people, on his forehead, lips, and breast.

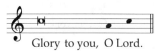

Glory to you, O Lord.

R. Glory to you, O Lord.

At the end of the Gospel:

Pr. The Gospel of the Lord.

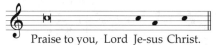

Praise to you, Lord Je-sus Christ.

R. Praise to you, Lord Jesus Christ.

THE HOMILY

Then follows the Homily, which is preached by a Priest or Deacon on all Sundays and Holydays of Obligation. After a brief silence all stand.

THE CREED

On Sundays and Solemnities, the Profession of Faith will follow. Especially during Lent and Easter Time, the Apostles' Creed may be used.

THE NICENO-CONSTANTINOPOLITAN CREED

I be-lieve in one God, the Fa-ther al-might-y, mak-er of heav-en and earth, of all things vis - i-ble and in-vis- i-ble.

minum Iesum Christum, Fí-lium De-i uni-gé-ni-tum. Et ex Pa-

tre na- tum ante ómni-a sæ- cu-la. De-um de De-o, lumen de

lumine, De-um verum de De-o vero. Géni-tum, non fac-tum, con-

substanti-á-lem Patri: per quem ómni-a facta sunt. Qui propter nos

At the words

homines et propter nostram sa-lútem descéndit de cæ-lis.   Et in-

that follow, up to and including **et homo factus est,** all bow.

carná-tus est de Spí-ri-tu Sancto   ex Ma-rí-a Vírgi-ne, et homo

factus est. Cru-ci-fí- xus é-ti-am pro nobis sub Pónti-o Pi-lá-to,

passus et sepúl- tus est. Et resurré-xit térti-a di-e, secúndum Scrip-

turas, Et ascéndit in cæ- lum, sedet ad déxteram Patris. Et í-terum

I be-lieve in one Lord Je-sus Christ, the Only Be-got-ten Son

of God, born of the Father be-fore all a-ges. God from God,

Light from Light, true God from true God, be-got-ten, not made,

con-sub-stan-tial with the Fa-ther; through him all things were

made. For us men and for our sal-va-tion he came down from

At the words that follow, up to and including **and became man,** all bow.

heav-en, and by the Ho-ly Spir-it was in-car-nate of the Vir-gin

Mar-y, and be-came man.

For our sake he was cru-ci-fied un-der Pon-tius Pi-late, he

suffered death and was bur-ied, and rose a-gain on the third day

in accordance with the Scrip-tures. He as-cend-ed in-to heav-en

ventúrus est cum gló-ri-a,   iudicá-re vivos et mórtu-os, cu-ius reg-

ni non e-rit fi-nis.   Et in Spí-ri-tum Sanctum, Dóminum   et vi-vi-

fi-cántem: qui ex Patre Fi-li-óque pro-cédit.   Qui cum Patre et Fí-

li-o   simul adorá-tur   et conglo-ri-ficá-tur: qui locú-tus est per

prophé-tas.   Et unam, sanctam, cathó-li-cam et apostó-li-cam Ec-

clé-si-am. Confí-te-or unum baptísma   in remissi - ónem pec-ca

tó-rum. Et exspécto resurrecti-ó-nem mortu-ó-rum.   Et vi-tam ven-

túri sæ-cu-li.   A-   men

and is seated at the right hand of the Fa-ther. He will come a-gain in glo-ry to judge the living and the dead and his kingdom will have no end.

I be-lieve in the Ho-ly Spir-it, the Lord, the giv-er of life, who pro-ceeds from the Father and the Son, who with the Fa-ther and the Son is adored and glo-ri-fied, who has spoken through the proph-ets. I be-lieve in one, ho-ly, ca-tho-lic and a-pos-tol-ic Church. I con-fess one Bap-tism for the for-give-ness of sins and I look for-ward to the res-ur-rec-tion of the dead and the life of the world to come. A - men.

Credo in unum Deum,
Patrem omnipoténtem,
factórem cæli et terræ,
visibílium ómnium et invisibílium.

Et in unum Dóminum Iesum Christum,
Fílium Dei Unigénitum,
et ex Patre natum ante ómnia sǽcula.
Deum de Deo, lumen de lúmine,
    Deum verum de Deo vero,
génitum, non factum, consubstantiálem Patri:
per quem ómnia facta sunt.
Qui propter nos hómines et propter nostram salútem
descéndit de cælis.

(all bow)

Et incarnátus est de Spíritu Sancto
ex María Vírgine, et homo factus est.

Crucifíxus étiam pro nobis sub Póntio Piláto;
passus et sepúltus est,
et resurréxit tértia die, secúndum Scriptúras,
et ascéndit in cælum, sedet ad déxteram Patris.

Et íterum ventúrus est cum glória,
    iudicáre vivos et mórtuos,
cuius regni non erit finis.
Et in Spíritum Sanctum, Dóminum et vivificántem:
qui ex Patre Filióque procédit.
Qui cum Patre et Fílio simul adorátur et conglorificátur:
qui locútus est per prophétas.

Et unam, sanctam, cathólicam et apostólicam Ecclésiam.
Confíteor unum baptísma in remissiónem peccatórum.
Et exspécto resurrectiónem mortuórum,
et vitam ventúri sǽculi. Amen.

I believe in one God,
the Father almighty,
maker of heaven and earth,
of all things visible and invisible.

I believe in one Lord Jesus Christ,
the Only Begotten Son of God,
born of the Father before all ages.
God from God, Light from Light,
true God from true God,
begotten, not made, consubstantial with the Father;
through him all things were made.
For us men and for our salvation
he came down from heaven,

(all bow)

and by the Holy Spirit was incarnate of the Virgin Mary,
and became man.

For our sake he was crucified under Pontius Pilate,
he suffered death and was buried,
and rose again on the third day
in accordance with the Scriptures.
He ascended into heaven
and is seated at the right hand of the Father.
He will come again in glory
to judge the living and the dead
and his kingdom will have no end.

I believe in the Holy Spirit, the Lord, the giver of life,
who proceeds from the Father and the Son,
who with the Father and the Son is adored and glorified,
who has spoken through the prophets.

I believe in one, holy, catholic and apostolic Church.
I confess one Baptism for the forgiveness of sins
and I look forward to the resurrection of the dead
and the life of the world to come. Amen.

THE APOSTLES' CREED

Credo in Deum, Patrem omnipoténtem,
Creatórem cæli et terræ,
et in Iesum Christum, Fílium eius únicum,
Dóminum nostrum,

at the words that follow up to and including Maria Virgine, all bow.

qui concéptus est de Spíritu Sancto,
natus ex María Vírgine,
passus sub Póntio Piláto,
crucifíxus, mórtuus, et sepúltus,
descéndit ad ínferos,
tértia die resurréxit a mórtuis,
ascéndit ad cælos,
sedet ad déxteram Dei Patris omnipoténtis,
inde ventúrus est iudicáre vivos et mórtuos.

Credo in Spíritum Sanctum,
sanctam Ecclésiam cathólicam,
Sanctórum communiónem,
remissiónem peccatórum,
carnis resurrectiónem,
vitam ætérnam. Amen.

THE PRAYER OF THE FAITHFUL (BIDDING PRAYERS)

Intentions will normally be for the Church; for the world; for those in particular need; and for the local community. After each there is time for silent prayer, followed by the next intention, or concluded with a sung phrase such as Christe audi nos, or Christe exaudi nos, or by a responsory such as:

R.   **Præsta, ætérne omnípotens Deus.** Or:
R.   **Te rogámus audi nos.** Or:
R.   **Kýrie, eléison.**

The Priest concludes the Prayer with a collect.

THE APOSTLES' CREED

**I believe in God,
the Father almighty
Creator of heaven and earth,
and in Jesus Christ, his only Son, our Lord,**

at the words that follow up to and including the Virgin Mary, all bow.

**who was conceived by the Holy Spirit,
born of the Virgin Mary,
suffered under Pontius Pilate,
was crucified, died and was buried;
he descended into hell;
on the third day he rose again from the dead;
he ascended into heaven,
and is seated at the right hand of God
the Father almighty;
from there he will come to judge the living and the dead.**

**I believe in the Holy Spirit,
the holy catholic Church,
the communion of saints,
the forgiveness of sins,
the resurrection of the body,
and life everlasting. Amen.**

THE PRAYER OF THE FAITHFUL (BIDDING PRAYERS)

Intentions will normally be for the Church; for the world; for those in particular need; and for the local community. After each there is time for silent prayer, followed by the next intention, or concluded with a sung phrase such as Christ, hear us, or Christ graciously hear us, or by a responsory such as:

Let us pray to the Lord.
R. **Grant this, almighty God.** Or:
R. **Lord, have mercy.** Or:
R. **Kýrie, eléison.**

The Priest concludes the Prayer with a collect.

THE LITURGY OF THE EUCHARIST

For Catholics, the Eucharist is the source and summit of the whole Christian life.

After the Liturgy of the Word, the people sit and the Offertory Chant begins. The faithful express their participation by making an offering, bringing forward bread and wine for the celebration of the Eucharist and perhaps other gifts to relieve the needs of the Church and of the poor.

PREPARATORY PRAYERS

Standing at the altar, the Priest takes the paten with the bread and holds it slightly raised above the altar with both hands, saying:

Pr. Benedíctus es, Dómine, Deus univérsi,
    quia de tua largitáte accépimus panem,
    quem tibi offérimus,
    fructum terræ et óperis mánuum hóminum:
    ex quo nobis fiet panis vitæ.

R. **Benedíctus Deus in sǽcula.**

The Priest then takes the chalice and holds it slightly raised above the altar with both hands, saying:

Pr. Benedíctus es, Dómine, Deus univérsi,
    quia de tua largitáte accépimus vinum,
    quod tibi offérimus,
    fructum vitis et óperis mánuum hóminum,
    ex quo nobis fiet potus spiritális.

R. **Benedíctus Deus in sǽcula.**

The Priest completes additional personal preparatory rites, and the people rise as he says:

Pr. Oráte, fratres:
    ut meum ac vestrum sacrifícium
    acceptábile fiat apud Deum Patrem omnipoténtem.

R. **Suscípiat Dóminus sacrifícium de mánibus tuis**
   ad laudem et glóriam nóminis sui,
   ad utilitátem quoque nostram
   totiúsque Ecclésiæ suæ sanctæ.

PRAYER OVER THE OFFERINGS

The Priest says the Prayer over the Offerings, at the end of which the people acclaim:

R. **Amen.**

THE LITURGY OF THE EUCHARIST

For Catholics, the Eucharist is the source and summit of the whole Christian life.

After the Liturgy of the Word, the people sit and the Offertory Chant begins. The faithful express their participation by making an offering, bringing forward bread and wine for the celebration of the Eucharist and perhaps other gifts to relieve the needs of the Church and of the poor.

PREPARATORY PRAYERS

Standing at the altar, the Priest takes the paten with the bread and holds it slightly raised above the altar with both hands, saying:

Pr. Blessed are you, Lord God of all creation,
for through your goodness we have received
the bread we offer you:
fruit of the earth and work of human hands,
it will become for us the bread of life.

R. **Blessed be God for ever.**

The Priest then takes the chalice and holds it slightly raised above the altar with both hands, saying:

Pr. Blessed are you, Lord God of all creation,
for through your goodness we have received
the wine we offer you:
fruit of the vine and work of human hands,
it will become our spiritual drink.

R. **Blessed be God for ever.**

The Priest completes additional personal preparatory rites, and the people rise as he says:

Pr. Pray, brethren (brothers and sisters),
that my sacrifice and yours
may be acceptable to God,
the almighty Father.

R. **May the Lord accept the sacrifice at your hands**
for the praise and glory of his name,
for our good
and the good of all his holy Church.

PRAYER OVER THE OFFERINGS

The Priest says the Prayer over the Offerings, at the end of which the people acclaim:

R. **Amen.**

THE EUCHARISTIC PRAYER

Extending his hands, the Priest says:

Pr. Dóminus vobíscum.

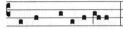

Et cum spí-ri-tu tu-o.

R. Et cum spíritu tuo.

Pr. Sursum corda.

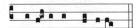

Habémus ad Dóminum.

R. Habémus ad Dóminum.

Pr. Grátias agámus Dómino Deo nostro.

Dignum et iustum est.

R. Dignum et iustum est.

The Priest continues with the Preface appropriate to the Season or Feast at the end of which all sing or say:

Sanc-tus, * Sanc-tus, Sanc-tus Dó-mi-nus De-us Sá-ba-oth. Ple-ni sunt cæ-li et ter-ra gló-ri-a tu-a. Ho-sán-na in ex-cél-sis. Be-ne-díc-tus qui ve-nit in nómine Dómini. Ho-sán-na in excél-sis.

THE EUCHARISTIC PRAYER

Extending his hands, the Priest says:

Pr. The Lord be with you.

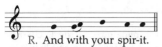

R. And with your spir-it.

R. **And with your spirit.**

Pr. Lift up your hearts.

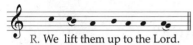

R. We lift them up to the Lord.

R. **We lift them up to the Lord.**

Pr. Let us give thanks to the Lord our God.

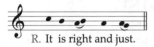

R. It is right and just.

R. **It is right and just.**

The Priest continues with the Preface appropriate to the Season or Feast at the end of which all sing or say:

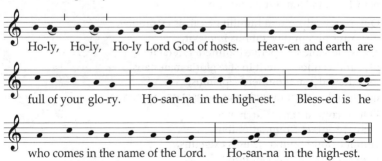

Ho-ly, Ho-ly, Ho-ly Lord God of hosts. Heav-en and earth are full of your glo-ry. Ho-san-na in the high-est. Bless-ed is he who comes in the name of the Lord. Ho-san-na in the high-est.

Sanctus, Sanctus, Sanctus Dóminus Deus Sábaoth.
Pleni sunt cæli et terra glória tua.
Hosánna in excélsis.
Benedíctus qui venit in nómine Dómini.
Hosánna in excélsis.

After the Sanctus the congregation kneels for the remainder of the Eucharistic Prayer. (Texts for the four principal Eucharistic Prayers follow: Eucharistic Prayer I at p.591, II at p.602, III at p.610, IV at p.620.)

PREFACES

ADVENT

PRÆFATIO I DE ADVENTU

De duobus adventibus Christi

In Missis de tempore a prima dominica Adventus usque ad diem 16 decembris

Vere dignum et iustum est, æquum et salutare,
nos tibi semper et ubique gratias agere:
Domine, sancte Pater, omnipotens æterne Deus:
per Christum Dominum nostrum.

Qui, primo adventu in humilitate carnis assumptæ,
dispositionis antiquæ munus implevit,
nobisque salutis perpetuæ tramitem reseravit:
ut, cum secundo venerit in suæ gloria maiestatis,
manifesto demum munere capiamus,
quod vigilantes nunc audemus exspectare promissum.

Et ideo cum Angelis et Archangelis,
cum Thronis et Dominationibus,
cumque omni militia cælestis exercitus,
hymnum gloriæ tuæ canimus,
sine fine dicentes:

Sanctus, Sanctus, Sanctus Dominus Deus Sabaoth. . .

Holy, Holy, Holy Lord God of hosts.
Heaven and earth are full of your glory.
Hosanna in the highest.
Blessed is he who comes in the name of the Lord.
Hosanna in the highest.

After the Sanctus the congregation kneels for the remainder of the Eucharistic Prayer. (Texts for the four principal Eucharistic Prayers follow: Eucharistic Prayer I at p.592, II at p.603, III at p.611, IV at p.621.)

PREFACES

ADVENT

PREFACE I OF ADVENT

The two comings of Christ

From the First Sunday of Advent until 16 December

It is truly right and just, our duty and our salvation,
always and everywhere to give you thanks,
Lord, holy Father, almighty and eternal God,
through Christ our Lord.

For he assumed at his first coming
the lowliness of human flesh,
and so fulfilled the design you formed long ago,
and opened for us the way to eternal salvation,
that, when he comes again in glory and majesty
and all is at last made manifest,
we who watch for that day
may inherit the great promise
in which now we dare to hope.

And so, with Angels and Archangels,
with Thrones and Dominions,
and with all the hosts and Powers of heaven,
we sing the hymn of your glory,
as without end we acclaim:

Holy, Holy, Holy Lord God of hosts. . .

PRÆFATIO II DE ADVENTU

De duplici exspectatione Christi

17 decembris-24 decembris

Vere dignum et iustum est, æquum et salutare,
nos tibi semper et ubique gratias agere:
Domine, sancte Pater, omnipotens æterne Deus:
per Christum Dominum nostrum.

Quem prædixerunt cunctorum præconia prophetarum,
Virgo Mater ineffabili dilectione sustinuit,
Ioannes cecinit affuturum et adesse monstravit.
Qui suæ nativitatis mysterium
tribuit nos prævenire gaudentes,
ut et in oratione pervigiles
et in suis inveniat laudibus exsultantes.

Et ideo cum Angelis et Archangelis,
cum Thronis et Dominationibus,
cumque omni militia cælestis exercitus,
hymnum gloriæ tuæ canimus,
sine fine dicentes:
Sanctus, Sanctus, Sanctus Dominus Deus Sabaoth. . .

CHRISTMAS

PRÆFATIO I DE NATIVITATE DOMINI

De Christo luce

Vere dignum et iustum est, æquum et salutare,
nos tibi semper et ubique gratias agere:
Domine, sancte Pater, omnipotens æterne Deus:

Quia per incarnati Verbi mysterium
nova mentis nostræ oculis lux tuæ claritatis infulsit:
ut, dum visibiliter Deum cognoscimus,
per hunc in invisibilium amorem rapiamur.

Et ideo cum Angelis et Archangelis,
cum Thronis et Dominationibus,
cumque omni militia cælestis exercitus,
hymnum gloriæ tuæ canimus, sine fine dicentes:
Sanctus, Sanctus, Sanctus Dominus Deus Sabaoth. . .

PREFACE II OF ADVENT

The twofold expectation of Christ

17 December-24 December

It is truly right and just, our duty and our salvation,
always and everywhere to give you thanks,
Lord, holy Father, almighty and eternal God,
through Christ our Lord.

For all the oracles of the prophets foretold him,
the Virgin Mother longed for him
with love beyond all telling,
John the Baptist sang of his coming
and proclaimed his presence when he came.

It is by his gift that already we rejoice
at the mystery of his Nativity,
so that he may find us watchful in prayer
and exultant in his praise.

And so, with Angels and Archangels,
with Thrones and Dominions,
and with all the hosts and Powers of heaven,
we sing the hymn of your glory,
as without end we acclaim:

Holy, Holy, Holy Lord God of hosts. . .

CHRISTMAS

PREFACE I OF THE NATIVITY OF THE LORD

Christ the Light

It is truly right and just, our duty and our salvation,
always and everywhere to give you thanks,
Lord, holy Father, almighty and eternal God.

For in the mystery of the Word made flesh
a new light of your glory has shone upon the eyes of our mind,
so that, as we recognise in him God made visible,
we may be caught up through him in love of things invisible.

And so, with Angels and Archangels,
with Thrones and Dominions,
and with all the hosts and Powers of heaven,
we sing the hymn of your glory,
as without end we acclaim:

Holy, Holy, Holy Lord God of hosts. . .

PRÆFATIO II DE NATIVITATE DOMINI

De restauratione universa in Incarnatione

Vere dignum et iustum est, æquum et salutare,
nos tibi semper et ubique gratias agere:
Domine, sancte Pater, omnipotens æterne Deus:
per Christum Dominum nostrum.

Qui, in huius venerandi festivitate mysterii,
invisibilis in suis, visibilis in nostris apparuit,
et ante tempora genitus esse cœpit in tempore;
ut, in se erigens cuncta deiecta,
in integrum restitueret universa,
et hominem perditum ad cælestia regna revocaret.

Unde et nos, cum omnibus Angelis te laudamus,
iucunda celebratione clamantes:

Sanctus, Sanctus, Sanctus Dominus Deus Sabaoth. . .

PRÆFATIO III DE NATIVITATE DOMINI

De commercio in Incarnatione Verbi

Vere dignum et iustum est, æquum et salutare,
nos tibi semper et ubique gratias agere:
Domine, sancte Pater, omnipotens æterne Deus:
per Christum Dominum nostrum.

Per quem hodie commercium nostræ reparationis effulsit,
quia, dum nostra fragilitas a tuo Verbo suscipitur,
humana mortalitas non solum
in perpetuum transit honorem,
sed nos quoque, mirando consortio, reddit æternos.

Et ideo, choris angelicis sociati,
te laudamus in gaudio confitentes:

Sanctus, Sanctus, Sanctus Dominus Deus Sabaoth. . .

PREFACE II OF THE NATIVITY OF THE LORD

The restoration of all things in the Incarnation

It is truly right and just, our duty and our salvation,
always and everywhere to give you thanks,
Lord, holy Father, almighty and eternal God,
through Christ our Lord.

For on the feast of this awe-filled mystery,
though invisible in his own divine nature,
he has appeared visibly in ours;
and begotten before all ages,
he has begun to exist in time;
so that, raising up in himself all that was cast down,
he might restore unity to all creation
and call straying humanity back to the heavenly Kingdom.

And so, with all the Angels, we praise you,
as in joyful celebration we acclaim:

Holy, Holy, Holy Lord God of hosts. . .

PREFACE III OF THE NATIVITY OF THE LORD

The exchange in the Incarnation of the Word

It is truly right and just, our duty and our salvation,
always and everywhere to give you thanks,
Lord, holy Father, almighty and eternal God,
through Christ our Lord.

For through him the holy exchange that restores our life
has shone forth today in splendour:
when our frailty is assumed by your Word
not only does human mortality receive unending honour
but by this wondrous union we, too, are made eternal.

And so, in company with the choirs of Angels,
we praise you, and with joy we proclaim:

Holy, Holy, Holy Lord God of hosts. . .

PRÆFATIO DE EPIPHANIA DOMINI
De Christo lumine gentium

Vere dignum et iustum est, æquum et salutare,
nos tibi semper et ubique gratias agere:
Domine, sancte Pater, omnipotens æterne Deus:

Quia ipsum in Christo salutis nostræ mysterium
hodie ad lumen gentium revelasti,
et, cum in substantia nostræ mortalitatis apparuit,
nova nos immortalitatis eius gloria reparasti.

Et ideo cum Angelis et Archangelis,
cum Thronis et Dominationibus,
cumque omni militia cælestis exercitus,
hymnum gloriæ tuæ canimus,
sine fine dicentes:

Sanctus, Sanctus, Sanctus Dominus Deus Sabaoth. . .

LENT
PRÆFATIO I DE QUADRAGESIMA
De spiritali significatione Quadregesimæ

Vere dignum et iustum est, æquum et salutare,
nos tibi semper et ubique gratias agere:
Domine, sancte Pater, omnipotens æterne Deus:
per Christum Dominum nostrum.

Quia fidelibus tuis dignanter concedis
quotannis paschalia sacramenta
in gaudio purificatis mentibus exspectare:
ut, pietatis officia et opera caritatis propensius exsequentes,
frequentatione mysteriorum, quibus renati sunt,
ad gratiæ filiorum plenitudinem perducantur.

Et ideo cum Angelis et Archangelis,
cum Thronis et Dominationibus,
cumque omni militia cælestis exercitus,
hymnum gloriæ tuæ canimus,
sine fine dicentes:

Sanctus, Sanctus, Sanctus Dominus Deus Sabaoth. . .

PREFACE OF THE EPIPHANY OF THE LORD
Christ the light of the nations

It is truly right and just, our duty and our salvation,
always and everywhere to give you thanks,
Lord, holy Father, almighty and eternal God.

For today you have revealed the mystery
of our salvation in Christ
as a light for the nations,
and, when he appeared in our mortal nature,
you made us new by the glory of his immortal nature.

And so, with Angels and Archangels,
with Thrones and Dominions,
and with all the hosts and Powers of heaven,
we sing the hymn of your glory,
as without end we acclaim:

Holy, Holy, Holy Lord God of hosts. . .

LENT
PREFACE I OF LENT
The spiritual meaning of Lent

It is truly right and just, our duty and our salvation,
always and everywhere to give you thanks,
Lord, holy Father, almighty and eternal God,
through Christ our Lord.

For by your gracious gift each year
your faithful await the sacred paschal feasts
with the joy of minds made pure,
so that, more eagerly intent on prayer
and on the works of charity,
and participating in the mysteries
by which they have been reborn,
they may be led to the fullness of grace
that you bestow on your sons and daughters.

And so, with Angels and Archangels,
with Thrones and Dominions,
and with all the hosts and Powers of heaven,
we sing the hymn of your glory,
as without end we acclaim:

Holy, Holy, Holy Lord God of hosts. . .

PRÆFATIO II DE QUADRAGESIMA

De spiritali pænitentia

Vere dignum et iustum est, æquum et salutare,
nos tibi semper et ubique gratias agere:
Domine, sancte Pater, omnipotens æterne Deus:

Qui filiis tuis ad reparandam mentium puritatem,
tempus præcipuum salubriter statuisti,
quo, mente ab inordinatis affectibus expedita,
sic incumberent transituris
ut rebus potius perpetuis inhærerent.

Et ideo, cum Sanctis et Angelis universis,
te collaudamus, sine fine dicentes:
Sanctus, Sanctus, Sanctus Dominus Deus Sabaoth. . .

PRÆFATIO III DE QUADRAGESIMA

De fructibus abstinentiæ

Vere dignum et iustum est, æquum et salutare,
nos tibi semper et ubique gratias agere:
Domine, sancte Pater, omnipotens æterne Deus:

Qui nos per abstinentiam tibi gratias referre voluisti,
ut ipsa et nos peccatores ab insolentia mitigaret,
et, egentium proficiens alimento,
imitatores tuæ benignitatis efficeret.

Et ideo, cum innumeris Angelis,
una te magnificamus laudis voce dicentes:

Sanctus, Sanctus, Sanctus Dominus Deus Sabaoth. . .

PRÆFATIO IV DE QUADRAGESIMA

De fructibus ieiunii

Vere dignum et iustum est, æquum et salutare,
nos tibi semper et ubique gratias agere:
Domine, sancte Pater, omnipotens æterne Deus:

Qui corporali ieiunio vitia comprimis, mentem elevas,
virtutem largiris et præmia:
per Christum Dominum nostrum.

PREFACE II OF LENT

Spiritual penance

It is truly right and just, our duty and our salvation,
always and everywhere to give you thanks,
Lord, holy Father, almighty and eternal God.

For you have given your children a sacred time
for the renewing and purifying of their hearts,
that, freed from disordered affections,
they may so deal with the things of this passing world
as to hold rather to the things that eternally endure.

And so, with all the Angels and Saints,
we praise you, as without end we acclaim:

Holy, Holy, Holy Lord God of hosts. . .

PREFACE III OF LENT

The fruits of abstinence

It is truly right and just, our duty and our salvation,
always and everywhere to give you thanks,
Lord, holy Father, almighty and eternal God.

For you will that our self-denial should give you thanks,
humble our sinful pride,
contribute to the feeding of the poor,
and so help us imitate you in your kindness.

And so we glorify you with countless Angels,
as with one voice of praise we acclaim:

Holy, Holy, Holy Lord God of hosts. . .

PREFACE IV OF LENT

The fruits of fasting

It is truly right and just, our duty and our salvation,
always and everywhere to give you thanks,
Lord, holy Father, almighty and eternal God.

For through bodily fasting you restrain our faults,
raise up our minds,
and bestow both virtue and its rewards,
through Christ our Lord.

Per quem maiestatem tuam laudant Angeli,
adorant Dominationes, tremunt Potestates.
Cæli cælorumque Virtutes, ac beata Seraphim,
socia exsultatione concelebrant.

Cum quibus et nostras voces ut admitti iubeas, deprecamur,
supplici confessione dicentes:

Sanctus, Sanctus, Sanctus Dominus Deus Sabaoth. . .

PRÆFATIO I DE PASSIONE DOMINI
De virtute Crucis

Vere dignum et iustum est, æquum et salutare,
nos tibi semper et ubique gratias agere:
Domine, sancte Pater, omnipotens æterne Deus:

Quia per Filii tui salutiferam passionem
sensum confitendæ tuæ maiestatis totus mundus accepit,
dum ineffabili crucis potentia
iudicium mundi et potestas emicat Crucifixi.

Unde et nos, Domine, cum Angelis et Sanctis universis,
tibi confitemur, in exsultatione dicentes:

Sanctus, Sanctus, Sanctus Dominus Deus Sabaoth. . .

EASTER

PRÆFATIO PASCHALIS I
De mysterio paschali

Vere dignum et iustum est, æquum et salutare:
Te quidem, Domine, omni tempore confiteri,
sed in hac potissimum nocte (die) gloriosius prædicare,
(sed in hoc potissimum gloriosius prædicare,)
cum Pascha nostrum immolatus est Christus.

Ipse enim verus est Agnus
qui abstulit peccata mundi.
Qui mortem nostram moriendo destruxit,
et vitam resurgendo reparavit.

Quapropter, profusis paschalibus gaudiis,
totus in orbe terrarum mundus exsultat.

Through him the Angels praise your majesty,
Dominions adore and Powers tremble before you.
Heaven and the Virtues of heaven and the blessed Seraphim
worship together with exultation.
May our voices, we pray, join with theirs
in humble praise, as we acclaim:

Holy, Holy, Holy Lord God of hosts. . .

PREFACE I OF THE PASSION OF THE LORD

The power of the Cross

It is truly right and just, our duty and our salvation,
always and everywhere to give you thanks,
Lord, holy Father, almighty and eternal God.

For through the saving Passion of your Son
the whole world has received a heart
to confess the infinite power of your majesty,
since by the wondrous power of the Cross
your judgement on the world is now revealed
and the authority of Christ crucified.

And so, Lord, with all the Angels and Saints,
we, too, give you thanks, as in exultation we acclaim:

Holy, Holy, Holy Lord God of hosts. . .

EASTER

PREFACE I OF EASTER

The Paschal Mystery

It is truly right and just, our duty and our salvation,
at all times to acclaim you, O Lord,
but (on this night / on this day / in this time) above all
to laud you yet more gloriously,
when Christ our Passover has been sacrificed.

For he is the true Lamb
who has taken away the sins of the world;
by dying he has destroyed our death,
and by rising, restored our life.

Therefore, overcome with paschal joy,
every land, every people exults in your praise

Sed et supernæ virtutes atque angelicæ potestates
hymnum gloriæ tuæ concinunt, sine fine dicentes:

Sanctus, Sanctus, Sanctus Dominus Deus Sabaoth. . .

PRÆFATIO PASCHALIS II

De vita nova in Christo

Vere dignum et iustum est, æquum et salutare:
Te quidem, Domine, omni tempore confiteri,
sed in hoc potissimum gloriosius prædicare,
cum Pascha nostrum immolatus est Christus.

Per quem in æternam vitam filii lucis oriuntur,
et regni cælestis atria fidelibus reserantur.
Quia mors nostra est eius morte redempta,
et in eius resurrectione vita omnium resurrexit.

Quapropter, profusis paschalibus gaudiis,
totus in orbe terrarum mundus exsultat.
Sed et supernæ virtutes atque angelicæ potestates
hymnum gloriæ tuæ concinunt, sine fine dicentes:

Sanctus, Sanctus, Sanctus Dominus Deus Sabaoth. . .

PRÆFATIO PASCHALIS III

De Christo vivente et semper interpellante pro nobis

Vere dignum et iustum est, æquum et salutare:
Te quidem, Domine, omni tempore confiteri,
sed in hoc potissimum gloriosius prædicare,
cum Pascha nostrum immolatus est Christus.

Qui se pro nobis offerre non desinit,
nosque apud te perenni advocatione defendit;
qui immolatus iam non moritur,
sed semper vivit occisus.

Quapropter, profusis paschalibus gaudiis,
totus in orbe terrarum mundus exsultat.
Sed et supernæ virtutes atque angelicæ potestates
hymnum gloriæ tuæ concinunt, sine fine dicentes:

Sanctus, Sanctus, Sanctus Dominus Deus Sabaoth. . .

and even the heavenly Powers, with the angelic hosts,
sing together the unending hymn of your glory,
as they acclaim:

Holy, Holy, Holy Lord God of hosts. . .

PREFACE II OF EASTER

New life in Christ

It is truly right and just, our duty and our salvation,
at all times to acclaim you, O Lord,
but in this time above all to laud you yet more gloriously,
when Christ our Passover has been sacrificed.

Through him the children of light rise to eternal life
and the halls of the heavenly Kingdom
are thrown open to the faithful;
for his Death is our ransom from death,
and in his rising the life of all has risen.

Therefore, overcome with paschal joy,
every land, every people exults in your praise
and even the heavenly Powers, with the angelic hosts,
sing together the unending hymn of your glory,
as they acclaim:

Holy, Holy, Holy Lord God of hosts. . .

PREFACE III OF EASTER

Christ living and always interceding for us

It is truly right and just, our duty and our salvation,
at all times to acclaim you, O Lord,
but in this time above all to laud you yet more gloriously,
when Christ our Passover has been sacrificed.

He never ceases to offer himself for us
but defends us and ever pleads our cause before you:
he is the sacrificial Victim who dies no more,
the Lamb, once slain, who lives for ever.

Therefore, overcome with paschal joy,
every land, every people exults in your praise
and even the heavenly Powers, with the angelic hosts,
sing together the unending hymn of your glory,
as they acclaim:

Holy, Holy, Holy Lord God of hosts. . .

PRÆFATIO PASCHALIS IV

De restauratione universi per mysterium paschale

Vere dignum et iustum est, æquum et salutare:
Te quidem, Domine, omni tempore confiteri,
sed in hoc potissimum gloriosius prædicare,
cum Pascha nostrum immolatus est Christus.

Quia, vetustate destructa, renovantur universa deiecta,
et vitæ nobis in Christo reparatur integritas.

Quapropter, profusis paschalibus gaudiis,
totus in orbe terrarum mundus exsultat.
Sed et supernæ virtutes atque angelicæ potestates
hymnum gloriæ tuæ concinunt, sine fine dicentes:

Sanctus, Sanctus, Sanctus Dominus Deus Sabaoth. . .

PRÆFATIO PASCHALIS V

De Christo sacerdote et victima

Vere dignum et iustum est, æquum et salutare:
Te quidem, Domine, omni tempore confiteri,
sed in hoc potissimum gloriosius prædicare,
cum Pascha nostrum immolatus est Christus.

Qui, oblatione corporis sui,
antiqua sacrificia in crucis veritate perfecit,
et, seipsum tibi pro nostra salute commendans,
idem sacerdos, altare et agnus exhibuit.

Quapropter, profusis paschalibus gaudiis,
totus in orbe terrarum mundus exsultat.
Sed et supernæ virtutes atque angelicæ potestates
hymnum gloriæ tuæ concinunt, sine fine dicentes:

Sanctus, Sanctus, Sanctus Dominus Deus Sabaoth. . .

PREFACE IV OF EASTER

The restoration of the universe through the Paschal Mystery

It is truly right and just, our duty and our salvation,
at all times to acclaim you, O Lord,
but in this time above all to laud you yet more gloriously,
when Christ our Passover has been sacrificed.

For, with the old order destroyed,
a universe cast down is renewed,
and integrity of life is restored to us in Christ.

Therefore, overcome with paschal joy,
every land, every people exults in your praise
and even the heavenly Powers, with the angelic hosts,
sing together the unending hymn of your glory,
as they acclaim:

Holy, Holy, Holy Lord God of hosts. . .

PREFACE V OF EASTER

Christ, Priest and Victim

It is truly right and just, our duty and our salvation,
at all times to acclaim you, O Lord,
but in this time above all to laud you yet more gloriously,
when Christ our Passover has been sacrificed.

By the oblation of his Body,
he brought the sacrifices of old to fulfilment
in the reality of the Cross
and, by commending himself to you for our salvation,
showed himself the Priest, the Altar, and the Lamb of sacrifice.

Therefore, overcome with paschal joy,
every land, every people exults in your praise
and even the heavenly Powers, with the angelic hosts,
sing together the unending hymn of your glory,
as they acclaim:

Holy, Holy, Holy Lord God of hosts. . .

PRÆFATIO I DE ASCENSIONE DOMINI

De mysterio Ascensionis

Vere dignum et iustum est, æquum et salutare,
nos tibi semper et ubique gratias agere:
Domine, sancte Pater, omnipotens æterne Deus:

Quia Dominus Iesus, Rex gloriæ,
peccati triumphator et mortis,
mirantibus Angelis, ascendit (hodie) summa cælorum,
Mediator Dei et hominum,
Iudex mundi Dominusque virtutum;
non ut a nostra humilitate discederet,
sed ut illuc confideremus, sua membra, nos subsequi
quo ipse, caput nostrum principiumque, præcessit.

Quapropter, profusis paschalibus gaudiis,
totus in orbe terrarum mundus exsultat.
Sed et supernæ virtutes atque angelicæ potestates
hymnum gloriæ tuæ concinunt, sine fine dicentes:

Sanctus, Sanctus, Sanctus Dominus Deus Sabaoth. . .

PRÆFATIO II DE ASCENSIONE DOMINI

De mysterio Ascensionis

Vere dignum et iustum est, æquum et salutare,
nos tibi semper et ubique gratias agere:
Domine, sancte Pater, omnipotens æterne Deus:
per Christum Dominum nostrum.

Qui post resurrectionem suam
omnibus discipulis suis manifestus apparuit,
et ipsis cernentibus est elevatus in cælum,
ut nos divinitatis suæ tribueret esse participes.

Quapropter, profusis paschalibus gaudiis,
totus in orbe terrarum mundus exsultat.
Sed et supernæ virtutes atque angelicæ potestates
hymnum gloriæ tuæ concinunt, sine fine dicentes:

Sanctus, Sanctus, Sanctus Dominus Deus Sabaoth. . .

PREFACE I OF THE ASCENSION OF THE LORD

The mystery of the Ascension

It is truly right and just, our duty and our salvation,
always and everywhere to give you thanks,
Lord, holy Father, almighty and eternal God.

For the Lord Jesus, the King of glory,
conqueror of sin and death,
ascended (today) to the highest heavens,
as the Angels gazed in wonder.

Mediator between God and man,
judge of the world and Lord of hosts,
he ascended, not to distance himself from our lowly state
but that we, his members, might be confident of following
where he, our Head and Founder, has gone before.

Therefore, overcome with paschal joy,
every land, every people exults in your praise
and even the heavenly Powers, with the angelic hosts,
sing together the unending hymn of your glory,
as they acclaim:

Holy, Holy, Holy Lord God of hosts. . .

PREFACE II OF THE ASCENSION OF THE LORD

The mystery of the Ascension

It is truly right and just, our duty and our salvation,
always and everywhere to give you thanks,
Lord, holy Father, almighty and eternal God,
through Christ our Lord.

For after his Resurrection
he plainly appeared to all his disciples
and was taken up to heaven in their sight,
that he might make us sharers in his divinity.

Therefore, overcome with paschal joy,
every land, every people exults in your praise
and even the heavenly Powers, with the angelic hosts,
sing together the unending hymn of your glory,
as they acclaim:

Holy, Holy, Holy Lord God of hosts. . .

PRÆFATIO I DE DOMINICIS « PER ANNUM »

De mysterio paschali et de populo Dei

Vere dignum et iustum est, æquum et salutare,
nos tibi semper et ubique gratias agere:
Domine, sancte Pater, omnipotens æterne Deus:
per Christum Dominum nostrum.

Cuius hoc mirificum fuit opus per paschale mysterium,
ut de peccato et mortis iugo ad hanc gloriam vocaremur,
qua nunc genus electum, regale sacerdotium,
gens sancta et acquisitionis populus diceremur,
et tuas annuntiaremus ubique virtutes,
qui nos de tenebris ad tuum admirabile lumen vocasti.

Et ideo cum Angelis et Archangelis,
cum Thronis et Dominationibus,
cumque omni militia cælestis exercitus,
hymnum gloriæ tuæ canimus,
sine fine dicentes:

Sanctus, Sanctus, Sanctus Dominus Deus Sabaoth. . .

PRÆFATIO II DE DOMINICIS « PER ANNUM »

De mysterio salutis

Vere dignum et iustum est, æquum et salutare,
nos tibi semper et ubique gratias agere:
Domine, sancte Pater, omnipotens æterne Deus:
per Christum Dominum nostrum.

Qui, humanis miseratus erroribus,
de Virgine nasci dignatus est.
Qui, crucem passus, a perpetua morte nos liberavit
et, a mortuis resurgens, vitam nobis donavit æternam.

Et ideo cum Angelis et Archangelis,
cum Thronis et Dominationibus,
cumque omni militia cælestis exercitus,
hymnum gloriæ tuæ canimus,
sine fine dicentes:

Sanctus, Sanctus, Sanctus Dominus Deus Sabaoth. . .

PREFACE I OF THE SUNDAYS IN ORDINARY TIME

The Paschal Mystery and the People of God

It is truly right and just, our duty and our salvation,
always and everywhere to give you thanks,
Lord, holy Father, almighty and eternal God,
through Christ our Lord.

For through his Paschal Mystery,
he accomplished the marvellous deed,
by which he has freed us from the yoke of sin and death,
summoning us to the glory of being now called
a chosen race, a royal priesthood,
a holy nation, a people for your own possession,
to proclaim everywhere your mighty works,
for you have called us out of darkness
into your own wonderful light.

And so, with Angels and Archangels,
with Thrones and Dominions,
and with all the hosts and Powers of heaven,
we sing the hymn of your glory,
as without end we acclaim:

Holy, Holy, Holy Lord God of hosts. . .

PREFACE II OF THE SUNDAYS IN ORDINARY TIME

The mystery of salvation

It is truly right and just, our duty and our salvation,
always and everywhere to give you thanks,
Lord, holy Father, almighty and eternal God,
through Christ our Lord.

For out of compassion for the waywardness that is ours,
he humbled himself and was born of the Virgin;
by the passion of the Cross he freed us from unending death,
and by rising from the dead he gave us life eternal.

And so, with Angels and Archangels,
with Thrones and Dominions,
and with all the hosts and Powers of heaven,
we sing the hymn of your glory,
as without end we acclaim:

Holy, Holy, Holy Lord God of hosts. . .

PRÆFATIO III DE DOMINICIS « PER ANNUM »

De salvatione hominis per hominem

Vere dignum et iustum est, æquum et salutare,
nos tibi semper et ubique gratias agere:
Domine, sancte Pater, omnipotens æterne Deus:

Ad cuius immensam gloriam pertinere cognoscimus
ut mortalibus tua deitate succurreres;
sed et nobis provideres de ipsa
mortalitate nostra remedium,
et perditos quosque unde perierant, inde salvares,
per Christum Dominum nostrum.

Per quem maiestatem tuam adorat exercitus Angelorum,
ante conspectum tuum in æternitate lætantium.

Cum quibus et nostras voces ut admitti iubeas, deprecamur,
socia exsultatione dicentes:

Sanctus, Sanctus, Sanctus Dominus Deus Sabaoth. . .

PRÆFATIO IV DE DOMINICIS « PER ANNUM »

De historia salutis

Vere dignum et iustum est, æquum et salutare,
nos tibi semper et ubique gratias agere:
Domine, sancte Pater, omnipotens æterne Deus:
per Christum Dominum nostrum.

Ipse enim nascendo vetustatem hominum renovavit,
patiendo delevit nostra peccata,
æternæ vitæ aditum præstitit a mortuis resurgendo,
ad te Patrem ascendendo cælestes ianuas reseravit.

Et ideo, cum Angelorum atque Sanctorum turba,
hymnum laudis tibi canimus, sine fine dicentes:

Sanctus, Sanctus, Sanctus Dominus Deus Sabaoth. . .

PREFACE III OF THE SUNDAYS IN ORDINARY TIME

The salvation of man by a man

It is truly right and just, our duty and our salvation,
always and everywhere to give you thanks,
Lord, holy Father, almighty and eternal God.

For we know it belongs to your boundless glory,
that you came to the aid of mortal beings with your divinity
and even fashioned for us a remedy out of mortality itself,
that the cause of our downfall
might become the means of our salvation,
through Christ our Lord.

Through him the host of Angels adores your majesty
and rejoices in your presence for ever.
May our voices, we pray, join with theirs
in one chorus of exultant praise, as we acclaim:

Holy, Holy, Holy Lord God of hosts. . .

PREFACE IV OF THE SUNDAYS IN ORDINARY TIME

The history of salvation

It is truly right and just, our duty and our salvation,
always and everywhere to give you thanks,
Lord, holy Father, almighty and eternal God,
through Christ our Lord.

For by his birth he brought renewal
to humanity's fallen state,
and by his suffering cancelled out our sins;
by his rising from the dead
he has opened the way to eternal life,
and by ascending to you, O Father,
he has unlocked the gates of heaven.

And so, with the company of Angels and Saints,
we sing the hymn of your praise,
as without end we acclaim:

Holy, Holy, Holy Lord God of hosts. . .

PRÆFATIO V DE DOMINICIS « PER ANNUM »

De creatione

Vere dignum et iustum est, æquum et salutare,
nos tibi semper et ubique gratias agere:
Domine, sancte Pater, omnipotens æterne Deus:

Qui omnia mundi elementa fecisti,
et vices disposuisti temporum variari;
hominem vero formasti ad imaginem tuam,
et rerum ei subiecisti universa miracula,
ut vicario munere dominaretur omnibus quæ creasti,
et in operum tuorum magnalibus iugiter te laudaret,
per Christum Dominum nostrum.

Unde et nos cum omnibus Angelis te laudamus,
iucunda celebratione clamantes:

Sanctus, Sanctus, Sanctus Dominus Deus Sabaoth. . .

PRÆFATIO VI DE DOMINICIS « PER ANNUM »

De pignore æterni Paschatis

Vere dignum et iustum est, æquum et salutare,
nos tibi semper et ubique gratias agere:
Domine, sancte Pater, omnipotens æterne Deus:

In quo vivimus, movemur et sumus,
atque in hoc corpore constituti
non solum pietatis tuæ cotidianos experimur effectus,
sed æternitatis etiam pignora iam tenemus.
Primitias enim Spiritus habentes,
per quem suscitasti Iesum a mortuis,
paschale mysterium speramus nobis esse perpetuum.

Unde et nos cum omnibus Angelis te laudamus,
iucunda celebratione clamantes:

Sanctus, Sanctus, Sanctus Dominus Deus Sabaoth. . .

PREFACE V OF THE SUNDAYS IN ORDINARY TIME

Creation

It is truly right and just, our duty and our salvation,
always and everywhere to give you thanks,
Lord, holy Father, almighty and eternal God.

For you laid the foundations of the world
and have arranged the changing of times and seasons;
you formed man in your own image
and set humanity over the whole world in all its wonder,
to rule in your name over all you have made
and for ever praise you in your mighty works,
through Christ our Lord.

And so, with all the Angels, we praise you,
as in joyful celebration we acclaim:

Holy, Holy, Holy Lord God of hosts. . .

PREFACE VI OF THE SUNDAYS IN ORDINARY TIME

The pledge of the eternal Passover

It is truly right and just, our duty and our salvation,
always and everywhere to give you thanks,
Lord, holy Father, almighty and eternal God.

For in you we live and move and have our being,
and while in this body
we not only experience the daily effects of your care,
but even now possess the pledge of life eternal.

For, having received the first fruits of the Spirit,
through whom you raised up Jesus from the dead,
we hope for an everlasting share in the Paschal Mystery.

And so, with all the Angels, we praise you,
as in joyful celebration we acclaim:

Holy, Holy, Holy Lord God of hosts. . .

PRÆFATIO VII DE DOMINICIS « PER ANNUM »

De salute per obœdientiam Christi

Vere dignum et iustum est, æquum et salutare,
nos tibi semper et ubique gratias agere:
Domine, sancte Pater, omnipotens æterne Deus:

Quia sic mundum misericorditer dilexisti,
ut ipsum nobis mitteres Redemptorem,
quem absque peccato
in nostra voluisti similitudine conversari,
ut amares in nobis quod diligebas in Filio,
cuius obœdientia sumus ad tua dona reparati,
quæ per inobœdientiam amiseramus peccando.

Unde et nos, Domine, cum Angelis et Sanctis universis
tibi confitemur, in exsultatione dicentes:

Sanctus, Sanctus, Sanctus Dominus Deus Sabaoth. . .

PRÆFATIO VIII DE DOMINICIS « PER ANNUM »

De Ecclesia adunata ex unitate Trinitatis

Vere dignum et iustum est, æquum et salutare,
nos tibi semper et ubique gratias agere:
Domine, sancte Pater, omnipotens æterne Deus:

Quia filios, quos longe peccati crimen abstulerat,
per sanguinem Filii tui Spiritusque virtute,
in unum ad te denuo congregare voluisti:
ut plebs, de unitate Trinitatis adunata,
in tuæ laudem sapientiæ multiformis
Christi corpus templumque Spiritus nosceretur Ecclesia.

Et ideo, choris angelicis sociati,
te laudamus in gaudio confitentes:

Sanctus, Sanctus, Sanctus Dominus Deus Sabaoth. . .

PREFACE VII OF THE SUNDAYS IN ORDINARY TIME

Salvation through the obedience of Christ

It is truly right and just, our duty and our salvation,
always and everywhere to give you thanks,
Lord, holy Father, almighty and eternal God.

For you so loved the world
that in your mercy you sent us the Redeemer,
to live like us in all things but sin,
so that you might love in us what you loved in your Son,
by whose obedience we have been restored to those gifts of yours
that, by sinning, we had lost in disobedience.

And so, Lord, with all the Angels and Saints,
we, too, give you thanks, as in exultation we acclaim:

Holy, Holy, Holy Lord God of hosts. . .

PREFACE VIII OF THE SUNDAYS IN ORDINARY TIME

The Church united by the unity of the Trinity

It is truly right and just, our duty and our salvation,
always and everywhere to give you thanks,
Lord, holy Father, almighty and eternal God.

For, when your children were scattered afar by sin,
through the Blood of your Son and the power of the Spirit,
you gathered them again to yourself,
that a people, formed as one by the unity of the Trinity,
made the body of Christ and the temple of the Holy Spirit,
might, to the praise of your manifold wisdom,
be manifest as the Church.

And so, in company with the choirs of Angels,
we praise you, and with joy we proclaim:

Holy, Holy, Holy Lord God of hosts. . .

PRÆFATIO I DE SS.MA EUCHARISTIA

De sacrificio et de sacramento Christi

Vere dignum et iustum est, æquum et salutare,
nos tibi semper et ubique gratias agere:
Domine, sancte Pater, omnipotens æterne Deus:
per Christum Dominum nostrum.

Qui, verus æternusque Sacerdos,
formam sacrificii perennis instituens,
hostiam tibi se primus obtulit salutarem,
et nos, in sui memoriam, præcepit offerre.
Cuius carnem pro nobis immolatam
dum sumimus, roboramur,
et fusum pro nobis sanguinem dum potamus, abluimur.

Et ideo cum Angelis et Archangelis,
cum Thronis et Dominationibus,
cumque omni militia cælestis exercitus,
hymnum gloriæ tuæ canimus,
sine fine dicentes:

Sanctus, Sanctus, Sanctus Dominus Deus Sabaoth. . .

PRÆFATIO II DE SS.MA EUCHARISTIA

De fructibus Sanctissimæ Eucharistiæ

Vere dignum et iustum est, æquum et salutare,
nos tibi semper et ubique gratias agere:
Domine, sancte Pater, omnipotens æterne Deus:
per Christum Dominum nostrum.

Qui cum Apostolis suis in novissima cena convescens,
salutiferam crucis memoriam prosecuturus in sæcula,
Agnum sine macula se tibi obtulit,
perfectæ laudis munus acceptum.

Quo venerabili mysterio fideles tuos alendo sanctificas,
ut humanum genus, quod continet unus orbis,
una fides illuminet, caritas una coniungat.

Ad mensam igitur accedimus tam mirabilis sacramenti,
ut, gratiæ tuæ suavitate perfusi,
ad cælestis formæ imaginem transeamus.

PREFACE I OF THE MOST HOLY EUCHARIST

The Sacrifice and the Sacrament of Christ

It is truly right and just, our duty and our salvation,
always and everywhere to give you thanks,
Lord, holy Father, almighty and eternal God,
through Christ our Lord.

For he is the true and eternal Priest,
who instituted the pattern of an everlasting sacrifice,
and was the first to offer himself as the saving Victim,
commanding us to make this offering as his memorial.
As we eat his flesh that was sacrificed for us,
we are made strong,
and, as we drink his Blood that was poured out for us,
we are washed clean.

And so, with Angels and Archangels,
with Thrones and Dominions,
and with all the hosts and Powers of heaven,
we sing the hymn of your glory,
as without end we acclaim:

Holy, Holy, Holy Lord God of hosts. . .

PREFACE II OF THE MOST HOLY EUCHARIST

The fruits of the Most Holy Eucharist

It is truly right and just, our duty and our salvation,
always and everywhere to give you thanks,
Lord, holy Father, almighty and eternal God,
through Christ our Lord.

For at the Last Supper with his Apostles,
establishing for the ages to come the saving memorial of the Cross,
he offered himself to you as the unblemished Lamb,
the acceptable gift of perfect praise.

Nourishing your faithful by this sacred mystery,
you make them holy, so that the human race,
bounded by one world,
may be enlightened by one faith
and united by one bond of charity.

And so, we approach the table of this wondrous Sacrament,
so that, bathed in the sweetness of your grace,
we may pass over to the heavenly realities here foreshadowed.

Propter quod cælestia tibi atque terrestria
canticum novum concinunt adorando,
et nos cum omni exercitu Angelorum proclamamus,
sine fine dicentes:

Sanctus, Sanctus, Sanctus Dominus Deus Sabaoth. . .

PRÆFATIO I DE APOSTOLIS

De Apostolis pastoribus populi Dei

Vere dignum et iustum est, æquum et salutare,
nos tibi semper et ubique gratias agere:
Domine, sancte Pater, omnipotens æterne Deus:

Qui gregem tuum, Pastor æterne, non deseris,
sed per beatos Apostolos continua protectione custodis,
ut iisdem rectoribus gubernetur,
quos Filii tui vicarios eidem contulisti præesse pastores.

Et ideo cum Angelis et Archangelis,
cum Thronis et Dominationibus,
cumque omni militia cælestis exercitus,
hymnum gloriæ tuæ canimus,
sine fine dicentes:

Sanctus, Sanctus, Sanctus Dominus Deus Sabaoth. . .

PRÆFATIO II DE APOSTOLIS

De apostolico fundamento et testimonio

Vere dignum et iustum est, æquum et salutare,
nos tibi semper et ubique gratias agere:
Domine, sancte Pater, omnipotens æterne Deus:
per Christum Dominum nostrum.

Quoniam Ecclesiam tuam
in apostolicis tribuisti consistere fundamentis,
ut signum sanctitatis tuæ in terris maneret ipsa perpetuum,
et cælestia præberet cunctis hominibus documenta.

Quapropter nunc et usque in sæculum
cum omni militia Angelorum
devota tibi mente concinimus,
clamantes atque dicentes:

Sanctus, Sanctus, Sanctus Dominus Deus Sabaoth. . .

Therefore, all creatures of heaven and earth
sing a new song in adoration,
and we, with all the host of Angels,
cry out, and without end we acclaim:

Holy, Holy, Holy Lord God of hosts. . .

PREFACE I OF APOSTLES

The Apostles, shepherds of God's people

It is truly right and just, our duty and our salvation,
always and everywhere to give you thanks,
Lord, holy Father, almighty and eternal God.

For you, eternal Shepherd, do not desert your flock,
but through the blessed Apostles
watch over it and protect it always,
so that it may be governed
by those you have appointed shepherds
to lead it in the name of your Son.

And so, with Angels and Archangels,
with Thrones and Dominions,
and with all the hosts and Powers of heaven,
we sing the hymn of your glory,
as without end we acclaim:

Holy, Holy, Holy Lord God of hosts. . .

PREFACE II OF APOSTLES

The apostolic foundation and witness

It is truly right and just, our duty and our salvation,
always and everywhere to give you thanks,
Lord, holy Father, almighty and eternal God,
through Christ our Lord.

For you have built your Church
to stand firm on apostolic foundations,
to be a lasting sign of your holiness on earth
and offer all humanity your heavenly teaching.

Therefore, now and for ages unending,
with all the host of Angels,
we sing to you with all our hearts,
crying out as we acclaim:

Holy, Holy, Holy Lord God of hosts. . .

PRÆFATIO I DE SANCTIS
De gloria Sanctorum

Vere dignum et iustum est, æquum et salutare,
nos tibi semper et ubique gratias agere:
Domine, sancte Pater, omnipotens æterne Deus:

Qui in Sanctorum concilio celebraris,
et eorum coronando merita tua dona coronas.
Qui nobis eorum conversatione largiris exemplum,
et communione consortium, et intercessione subsidium;
ut, tantis testibus confirmati,
ad propositum certamen curramus invicti
et immarcescibilem cum eis coronam gloriæ consequamur,
per Christum Dominum nostrum.

Et ideo cum Angelis et Archangelis,
cumque multiplici congregatione Sanctorum,
hymnum laudis tibi canimus, sine fine dicentes:

Sanctus, Sanctus, Sanctus Dominus Deus Sabaoth. . .

PRÆFATIO II DE SANCTIS
De actione Sanctorum

Vere dignum et iustum est, æquum et salutare,
nos tibi semper et ubique gratias agere:
Domine, sancte Pater, omnipotens æterne Deus:
per Christum Dominum nostrum.
Tu enim Sanctorum tuorum confessione mirabili
Ecclesiam tuam nova semper virtute fecundas,
nobisque certissima præbes tuæ dilectionis indicia.
Sed etiam, ad mysteria salutis implenda,
et ipsorum insigni incitamur exemplo
et pia intercessione perpetuo commendamur.

Unde et nos, Domine, cum Angelis et Sanctis universis
tibi confitemur, in exsultatione dicentes:

Sanctus, Sanctus, Sanctus Dominus Deus Sabaoth. . .

PREFACE I OF SAINTS
The glory of the Saints

It is truly right and just, our duty and our salvation,
always and everywhere to give you thanks,
Lord, holy Father, almighty and eternal God.

For you are praised in the company of your Saints
and, in crowning their merits, you crown your own gifts.
By their way of life you offer us an example,
by communion with them you give us companionship,
by their intercession, sure support,
so that, encouraged by so great a cloud of witnesses,
we may run as victors in the race before us
and win with them the imperishable crown of glory,
through Christ our Lord.

And so, with the Angels and Archangels,
and with the great multitude of the Saints,
we sing the hymn of your praise,
as without end we acclaim:

Holy, Holy, Holy Lord God of hosts. . .

PREFACE II OF SAINTS
The action of the Saints

It is truly right and just, our duty and our salvation,
always and everywhere to give you thanks,
Lord, holy Father, almighty and eternal God,
through Christ our Lord.

For in the marvellous confession of your Saints,
you make your Church fruitful with strength ever new
and offer us sure signs of your love.
And that your saving mysteries may be fulfilled,
their great example lends us courage,
their fervent prayers sustain us in all we do.

And so, Lord, with all the Angels and Saints,
we, too, give you thanks, as in exultation we acclaim:

Holy, Holy, Holy Lord God of hosts. . .

PRÆFATIO I DE SANCTIS MARTYRIBUS
De signo et exemplo martyrii

Vere dignum et iustum est, æquum et salutare,
nos tibi semper et ubique gratias agere:
Domine, sancte Pater, omnipotens æterne Deus:

Quoniam beati martyris N. pro confessione nominis tui,
ad imitationem Christi,
sanguis effusus tua mirabilia manifestat,
quibus perficis in fragilitate virtutem,
et vires infirmas ad testimonium roboras,
per Christum Dominum nostrum.

Et ideo, cum cælorum Virtutibus,
in terris te iugiter celebramus,
maiestati tuæ sine fine clamantes:

Sanctus, Sanctus, Sanctus Dominus Deus Sabaoth. . .

PRÆFATIO II DE SANCTIS MARTYRIBUS
De mirabilibus Dei in martyrum victoria

Vere dignum et iustum est, æquum et salutare,
nos tibi semper et ubique gratias agere:
Domine, sancte Pater, omnipotens æterne Deus:

Quoniam tu magnificaris in tuorum laude Sanctorum,
et quidquid ad eorum pertinet passionem,
tuæ sunt opera miranda potentiæ:
qui huius fidei tribuis clementer ardorem,
qui suggeris perseverantiæ firmitatem,
qui largiris in agone victoriam,
per Christum Dominum nostrum.

Propter quod cælestia tibi atque terrestria
canticum novum concinunt adorando,
et nos cum omni exercitu Angelorum
proclamamus, sine fine dicentes:
Sanctus, Sanctus, Sanctus Dominus Deus Sabaoth. . .

PREFACE I OF HOLY MARTYRS

The sign and example of martyrdom

It is truly right and just, our duty and our salvation,
always and everywhere to give you thanks,
Lord, holy Father, almighty and eternal God.

For the blood of your blessed Martyr N.,
poured out like Christ's to glorify your name,
shows forth your marvellous works,
by which in our weakness you perfect your power
and on the feeble bestow strength to bear you witness,
through Christ our Lord.

And so, with the Powers of heaven,
we worship you constantly on earth,
and before your majesty
without end we acclaim:

Holy, Holy, Holy Lord God of hosts. . .

PREFACE II OF HOLY MARTYRS

The wonders of God in the victory of the Martyrs

It is truly right and just, our duty and our salvation,
always and everywhere to give you thanks,
Lord, holy Father, almighty and eternal God.

For you are glorified when your Saints are praised;
their very sufferings are but wonders of your might:
in your mercy you give ardour to their faith,
to their endurance you grant firm resolve,
and in their struggle the victory is yours,
through Christ our Lord.

Therefore, all creatures of heaven and earth
sing a new song in adoration,
and we, with all the host of Angels,
cry out, and without end we acclaim:

Holy, Holy, Holy Lord God of hosts. . .

PRÆFATIO DE SANCTIS PASTORIBUS

De præsentia sanctorum Pastorum in Ecclesia

Vere dignum et iustum est, æquum et salutare,
nos tibi semper et ubique gratias agere:
Domine, sancte Pater, omnipotens æterne Deus:
per Christum Dominum nostrum.

Quia sic tribuis Ecclesiam tuam sancti N. festivitate gaudere,
ut eam exemplo piæ conversationis corrobores,
verbo prædicationis erudias,
grataque tibi supplicatione tuearis.

Et ideo, cum Angelorum atque Sanctorum turba,
hymnum laudis tibi canimus, sine fine dicentes:

Sanctus, Sanctus, Sanctus Dominus Deus Sabaoth. . .

PRÆFATIO DE SANCTIS VIRGINIBUS ET RELIGIOSIS

De signo vitæ Deo consecratæ

Vere dignum et iustum est, æquum et salutare,
nos tibi semper et ubique gratias agere:
Domine, sancte Pater, omnipotens æterne Deus:

In Sanctis enim, qui Christo se dedicaverunt
propter regnum cælorum,
tuam decet providentiam celebrare mirabilem,
qua humanam substantiam
et ad primæ originis revocas sanctitatem,
et perducis ad experienda dona,
quæ in novo sæculo sunt habenda.

Et ideo, cum Sanctis et Angelis universis,
te collaudamus, sine fine dicentes:

Sanctus, Sanctus, Sanctus Dominus Deus Sabaoth. . .

PREFACE OF HOLY PASTORS

The presence of holy Pastors in the Church

It is truly right and just, our duty and our salvation,
always and everywhere to give you thanks,
Lord, holy Father, almighty and eternal God,
through Christ our Lord.

For, as on the festival of Saint N. you bid your Church rejoice,
so, too, you strengthen her by the example of his holy life,
teach her by his words of preaching,
and keep her safe in answer to his prayers.

And so, with the company of Angels and Saints,
we sing the hymn of your praise,
as without end we acclaim:

Holy, Holy, Holy Lord God of hosts. . .

PREFACE OF HOLY VIRGINS AND RELIGIOUS

The sign of a life consecrated to God

It is truly right and just, our duty and our salvation,
always and everywhere to give you thanks,
Lord, holy Father, almighty and eternal God.

For in the Saints who consecrated themselves to Christ
for the sake of the Kingdom of Heaven,
it is right to celebrate the wonders of your providence,
by which you call human nature back to its original holiness
and bring it to experience on this earth
the gifts you promise in the new world to come.

And so, with all the Angels and Saints,
we praise you, as without end we acclaim:

Holy, Holy, Holy Lord God of hosts. . .

PRÆFATIO I DE DEFUNCTIS

De spe resurrectionis in Christo

Vere dignum et iustum est, æquum et salutare,
nos tibi semper et ubique gratias agere:
Domine, sancte Pater, omnipotens æterne Deus:
per Christum Dominum nostrum.

In quo nobis spes beatæ resurrectionis effulsit,
ut, quos contristat certa moriendi condicio,
eosdem consoletur futuræ immortalitatis promissio.
Tuis enim fidelibus, Domine, vita mutatur, non tollitur,
et, dissoluta terrestris huius incolatus domo,
æterna in cælis habitatio comparatur.

Et ideo cum Angelis et Archangelis,
cum Thronis et Dominationibus,
cumque omni militia cælestis exercitus,
hymnum gloriæ tuæ canimus,
sine fine dicentes:

Sanctus, Sanctus, Sanctus Dominus Deus Sabaoth. . .

PRÆFATIO II DE DEFUNCTIS

Christus mortuus est pro vita nostra

Vere dignum et iustum est, æquum et salutare,
nos tibi semper et ubique gratias agere:
Domine, sancte Pater, omnipotens æterne Deus:
per Christum Dominum nostrum.

Ipse enim mortem unus accepit,
ne omnes nos moreremur;
immo unus mori dignatus est,
ut omnes tibi perpetuo viveremus.

Et ideo, choris angelicis sociati,
te laudamus in gaudio confitentes:

Sanctus, Sanctus, Sanctus Dominus Deus Sabaoth. . .

PREFACE I FOR THE DEAD
The hope of resurrection in Christ

It is truly right and just, our duty and our salvation,
always and everywhere to give you thanks,
Lord, holy Father, almighty and eternal God,
through Christ our Lord.

In him the hope of blessed resurrection has dawned,
that those saddened by the certainty of dying
might be consoled by the promise of immortality to come.
Indeed for your faithful, Lord,
life is changed not ended,
and, when this earthly dwelling turns to dust,
an eternal dwelling is made ready for them in heaven.

And so, with Angels and Archangels,
with Thrones and Dominions,
and with all the hosts and Powers of heaven,
we sing the hymn of your glory,
as without end we acclaim:

Holy, Holy, Holy Lord God of hosts. . .

PREFACE II FOR THE DEAD
Christ died so that we might live

It is truly right and just, our duty and our salvation,
always and everywhere to give you thanks,
Lord, holy Father, almighty and eternal God,
through Christ our Lord.

For as one alone he accepted death,
so that we might all escape from dying;
as one man he chose to die,
so that in your sight we all might live for ever.

And so, in company with the choirs of Angels,
we praise you, and with joy we proclaim:

Holy, Holy, Holy Lord God of hosts. . .

PRÆFATIO III DE DEFUNCTIS

Christus, salus et vita

Vere dignum et iustum est, æquum et salutare,
nos tibi semper et ubique gratias agere:
Domine, sancte Pater, omnipotens æterne Deus:
per Christum Dominum nostrum:

Qui est salus mundi, vita hominum, resurrectio mortuorum.

Per quem maiestatem tuam adorat exercitus Angelorum,
ante conspectum tuum in æternitate lætantium.
Cum quibus et nostras voces ut admitti iubeas, deprecamur,
socia exsultatione dicentes:

Sanctus, Sanctus, Sanctus Dominus Deus Sabaoth. . .

PRÆFATIO IV DE DEFUNCTIS

De vita terrena ad gloriam cælestem

Vere dignum et iustum est, æquum et salutare,
nos tibi semper et ubique gratias agere:
Domine, sancte Pater, omnipotens æterne Deus:

Cuius imperio nascimur, cuius arbitrio regimur,
cuius præcepto in terra, de qua sumpti sumus,
peccati lege absolvimur.
Et, qui per mortem Filii tui redempti sumus,
ad ipsius resurrectionis gloriam
tuo nutu excitamur.

Et ideo, cum Angelorum atque Sanctorum turba,
hymnum laudis tibi canimus, sine fine dicentes:

Sanctus, Sanctus, Sanctus Dominus Deus Sabaoth. . .

PREFACE III FOR THE DEAD

Christ, the salvation and the life

It is truly right and just, our duty and our salvation,
always and everywhere to give you thanks,
Lord, holy Father, almighty and eternal God,
through Christ our Lord.

For he is the salvation of the world,
the life of the human race,
the resurrection of the dead.

Through him the host of Angels adores your majesty
and rejoices in your presence for ever.
May our voices, we pray, join with theirs
in one chorus of exultant praise, as we acclaim:

Holy, Holy, Holy Lord God of hosts. . .

PREFACE IV FOR THE DEAD

From earthly life to heavenly glory

It is truly right and just, our duty and our salvation,
always and everywhere to give you thanks,
Lord, holy Father, almighty and eternal God.

For it is at your summons that we come to birth,
by your will that we are governed,
and at your command that we return,
on account of sin,
to that earth from which we came.

And when you give the sign,
we who have been redeemed by the Death of your Son,
shall be raised up to the glory of his Resurrection.

And so, with the company of Angels and Saints,
we sing the hymn of your praise,
as without end we acclaim:

Holy, Holy, Holy Lord God of hosts. . .

PRÆFATIO V DE DEFUNCTIS

De resurrectione nostra per victoriam Christi

Vere dignum et iustum est, æquum et salutare,
nos tibi semper et ubique gratias agere:
Domine, sancte Pater, omnipotens æterne Deus:

Quia, etsi nostri est meriti quod perimus,
tuæ tamen est pietatis et gratiæ
quod, pro peccato morte consumpti,
per Christi victoriam redempti,
cum ipso revocamur ad vitam.

Et ideo, cum cælorum Virtutibus,
in terris te iugiter celebramus,
maiestati tuæ sine fine clamantes:

Sanctus, Sanctus, Sanctus Dominus Deus Sabaoth. . .

PREFACE V FOR THE DEAD

Our resurrection through the victory of Christ

It is truly right and just, our duty and our salvation,
always and everywhere to give you thanks,
Lord, holy Father, almighty and eternal God.

For even though by our own fault we perish,
yet by your compassion and your grace,
when seized by death according to our sins,
we are redeemed through Christ's great victory,
and with him called back into life.

And so, with the Powers of heaven,
we worship you constantly on earth,
and before your majesty
without end we acclaim:

Holy, Holy, Holy Lord God of hosts. . .

EUCHARISTIC PRAYER I
(THE ROMAN CANON)

Pr. Te ígitur, clementíssime Pater,
per Iesum Christum, Fílium tuum,
Dóminum nostrum,
súpplices rogámus ac pétimus,
uti accépta hábeas
et benedícas ✠ hæc dona, hæc múnera,
hæc sancta sacrifícia illibáta,
in primis, quæ tibi offérimus
pro Ecclésia tua sancta cathólica:
quam pacificáre, custodíre, adunáre
et régere dignéris toto orbe terrárum:
una cum fámulo tuo Papa nostro N.
et Antístite nostro N*.
et ómnibus orthodóxis atque cathólicæ
et apostólicæ fídei cultóribus.

Commemoration of the Living.

Meménto, Dómine,
famulórum famularúmque tuárum N. et N.
et ómnium circumstántium,
quorum tibi fides cógnita est et nota devótio,
pro quibus tibi offérimus:
vel qui tibi ófferunt hoc sacrifícium laudis,
pro se suísque ómnibus:
pro redemptióne animárum suárum,
pro spe salútis et incolumitátis suæ:
tibíque reddunt vota sua
ætérno Deo, vivo et vero.

Within the Action

Communicántes,
et memóriam venerántes,
in primis gloriósæ semper Vírginis Maríæ,
Genetrícis Dei et Dómini nostri Iesu Christi:
† sed et béati Ioseph, eiúsdem Vírginis Sponsi,
et beatórum Apostolórum ac Mártyrum tuórum,
Petri et Pauli, Andréæ,
(Iacóbi, Ioánnis,
Thomæ, Iacóbi, Philíppi,

---

*Mention may be made here of the Coadjutor Bishop or Auxiliary Bishops.

EUCHARISTIC PRAYER I

(THE ROMAN CANON)

Pr. To you, therefore, most merciful Father,
we make humble prayer and petition
through Jesus Christ, your Son, our Lord:
that you accept
and bless ✠ these gifts, these offerings,
these holy and unblemished sacrifices,
which we offer you firstly
for your holy catholic Church.
Be pleased to grant her peace,
to guard, unite and govern her
throughout the whole world,
together with your servant N. our Pope
and N. our Bishop,*
and all those who, holding to the truth,
hand on the catholic and apostolic faith.

Commemoration of the Living.
Remember, Lord, your servants N. and N.
and all gathered here,
whose faith and devotion are known to you.
For them, we offer you this sacrifice of praise
or they offer it for themselves
and all who are dear to them:
for the redemption of their souls,
in hope of health and well-being,
and paying their homage to you,
the eternal God, living and true.

Within the Action
In communion with those whose memory we venerate,
especially the glorious ever-Virgin Mary,
Mother of our God and Lord, Jesus Christ,
† and blessed Joseph, her Spouse,
your blessed Apostles and Martyrs,
Peter and Paul, Andrew,
(James, John,
Thomas, James, Philip,

---

*Mention may be made here of the Coadjutor Bishop or Auxiliary Bishops.

Bartholomǽi, Matthǽi,
Simónis et Thaddǽi:
Lini, Cleti, Cleméntis, Xysti,
Cornélii, Cypriáni,
Lauréntii, Chrysógoni,
Ioánnis et Pauli,
Cosmæ et Damiáni)
et ómnium Sanctórum tuórum;
quorum méritis precibúsque concédas,
ut in ómnibus protectiónis tuæ muniámur auxílio.
(Per Christum Dóminum nostrum. Amen.)

PROPER FORMS OF THE COMMUNICANTES

On the Nativity of the Lord and throughout the Octave

Communicántes,
et (noctem sacratíssimam) diem sacratíssimum celebrántes,
(qua) quo beátæ Maríæ intemeráta virgínitas
huic mundo édidit Salvatórem:
sed et memóriam venerántes,
in primis eiúsdem gloriósæ semper Vírginis Maríæ,
Genetrícis eiúsdem Dei et Dómini nostri Iesu Christi: †

On the Epiphany of the Lord

Communicántes,
et diem sacratíssimum celebrántes,
quo Unigénitus tuus, in tua tecum glória coætérnus,
in veritáte carnis nostræ visibíliter corporális appáruit:
sed et memóriam venerántes,
in primis gloriósæ semper Vírginis Maríæ,
Genetrícis eiúsdem Dei et Dómini nostri Iesu Christi: †

From the Mass of the Easter Vigil until the Second Sunday of Easter

Communicántes,
et (noctem sacratíssimam) diem sacratíssimum celebrántes
Resurrectiónis Dómini nostri Iesu Christi secúndum carnem:
sed et memóriam venerántes,
in primis gloriósæ semper Vírginis Maríæ,
Genetrícis eiúsdem Dei et Dómini nostri Iesu Christi: †

Bartholomew, Matthew,
Simon and Jude;
Linus, Cletus, Clement, Sixtus,
Cornelius, Cyprian,
Lawrence, Chrysogonus,
John and Paul,
Cosmas and Damian)
and all your Saints;
we ask that through their merits and prayers,
in all things we may be defended
by your protecting help.
(Through Christ our Lord. Amen.)

PROPER FORMS OF THE COMMUNICANTES

On the Nativity of the Lord and throughout the Octave

Celebrating the most sacred night (day)
on which blessed Mary the immaculate Virgin
brought forth the Saviour for this world,
and in communion with those whose memory we venerate,
especially the glorious ever-Virgin Mary,
Mother of our God and Lord, Jesus Christ, †

On the Epiphany of the Lord

Celebrating the most sacred day
on which your Only Begotten Son,
eternal with you in your glory,
appeared in a human body, truly sharing our flesh,
and in communion with those whose memory we venerate,
especially the glorious ever-Virgin Mary,
Mother of our God and Lord, Jesus Christ, †

From the Mass of the Easter Vigil until the Second Sunday of Easter

Celebrating the most sacred night (day)
of the Resurrection of our Lord Jesus Christ in the flesh,
and in communion with those whose memory we venerate,
especially the glorious ever-Virgin Mary,
Mother of our God and Lord, Jesus Christ, †

On the Ascension of the Lord

> Communicántes,
> et diem sacratíssimum celebrántes,
> quo Dóminus noster, Unigénitus Fílius tuus,
> unítam sibi fragilitátis nostræ substántiam
> in glóriæ tuæ déxtera collocávit:
> sed et memóriam venerántes,
> in primis gloriósæ semper Vírginis Maríæ,
> Genetrícis eiúsdem Dei et Dómini nostri Iesu Christi: †

On Pentecost Sunday

> Communicántes,
> et diem sacratíssimum Pentecóstes celebrántes,
> quo Spíritus Sanctus
> Apóstolis in ígneis linguis appáruit:
> sed et memóriam venerántes,
> in primis gloriósæ semper Vírginis Maríæ,
> Genetrícis Dei et Dómini nostri Iesu Christi: †

Hanc ígitur oblatiónem servitútis nostræ,
sed et cunctæ famíliæ tuæ,
quǽsumus, Dómine, ut placátus accípias:
diésque nostros in tua pace dispónas,
atque ab ætérna damnatióne nos éripi
et in electórum tuórum iúbeas grege numerári.
(Per Christum Dóminum nostrum. Amen.)

From the Mass of the Easter Vigil until the Second Sunday of Easter

> Hanc ígitur oblatiónem servitútis nostræ,
> sed et cunctæ famíliæ tuæ,
> quam tibi offérimus
> pro his quoque, quos regeneráre dignátus es ex aqua et Spíritu Sancto,
> tríbuens eis remissiónem ómnium peccatórum,
> quǽsumus, Dómine, ut placátus accípias:
> diésque nostros in tua pace dispónas,
> atque ab ætérna damnatióne nos éripi
> et in electórum tuórum iúbeas grege numerári.
> (Per Christum Dóminum nostrum. Amen.)

On the Ascension of the Lord

> Celebrating the most sacred day
> on which your Only Begotten Son, our Lord,
> placed at the right hand of your glory
> our weak human nature,
> which he had united to himself,
> and in communion with those whose memory we venerate,
> especially the glorious ever-Virgin Mary,
> Mother of our God and Lord, Jesus Christ, †

On Pentecost Sunday

> Celebrating the most sacred day of Pentecost,
> on which the Holy Spirit
> appeared to the Apostles in tongues of fire,
> and in communion with those whose memory we venerate,
> especially the glorious ever-Virgin Mary,
> Mother of our God and Lord, Jesus Christ, †

Therefore, Lord, we pray:
graciously accept this oblation of our service,
that of your whole family;
order our days in your peace,
and command that we be delivered from eternal damnation
and counted among the flock of those you have chosen.
(Through Christ Our Lord. Amen.)

From the Mass of the Easter Vigil until the Second Sunday of Easter

> Therefore, Lord, we pray:
> graciously accept this oblation of our service,
> that of your whole family,
> which we make to you
> also for those to whom you have been pleased to give
> the new birth of water and the Holy Spirit,
> granting them forgiveness of all their sins;
> order our days in your peace,
> and command that we be delivered from eternal damnation
> and counted among the flock of those you have chosen.
> (Through Christ our Lord. Amen.)

Quam oblatiónem tu, Deus, in ómnibus, quǽsumus,
benedíctam, adscríptam, ratam,
rationábilem, acceptabilémque fácere dignéris:
ut nobis Corpus et Sanguis fiat dilectíssimi Fílii tui,
Dómini nostri Iesu Christi.

Qui, prídie quam paterétur,
accépit panem in sanctas ac venerábiles manus suas,
et elevátis óculis in cælum
ad te Deum Patrem suum omnipoténtem,
tibi grátias agens benedíxit,
fregit,
dedítque discípulis suis, dicens:

Accípite et manducáte ex hoc omnes:
hoc est enim Corpus meum,
quod pro vobis tradétur.

Símili modo, postquam cenátum est,
accípiens et hunc præclárum cálicem
in sanctas ac venerábiles manus suas,
item tibi grátias agens benedíxit,
dedítque discípulis suis dicens:

Accípite et bíbite ex eo omnes:
hic est enim calix Sánguinis mei
novi et ætérni testaménti,
qui pro vobis et pro multis effundétur
in remissiónem peccatórum.
Hoc fácite in meam commemoratiónem.

Be pleased, O God, we pray,
to bless, acknowledge,
and approve this offering in every respect;
make it spiritual and acceptable,
so that it may become for us
the Body and Blood of your most beloved Son,
our Lord Jesus Christ.

On the day before he was to suffer,
he took bread in his holy and venerable hands,
and with eyes raised to heaven
to you, O God, his almighty Father,
giving you thanks, he said the blessing,
broke the bread
and gave it to his disciples, saying:

TAKE THIS, ALL OF YOU, AND EAT OF IT,
FOR THIS IS MY BODY,
WHICH WILL BE GIVEN UP FOR YOU.

In a similar way, when supper was ended,
he took this precious chalice
in his holy and venerable hands,
and once more giving you thanks, he said the blessing
and gave the chalice to his disciples, saying:

TAKE THIS, ALL OF YOU, AND DRINK FROM IT,
FOR THIS IS THE CHALICE OF MY BLOOD,
THE BLOOD OF THE NEW AND ETERNAL COVENANT,
WHICH WILL BE POURED OUT FOR YOU AND FOR MANY
FOR THE FORGIVENESS OF SINS.

DO THIS IN MEMORY OF ME.

Pr. Mystérium fídei.

The people continue, acclaiming one of the following:

Mortem tu-am annunti-ámus, Dómi-ne,   et tu-am resurrecti-ó-

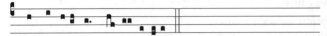

nem confi-témur, do-nec vé-ni-as.

1. **Mortem tuam annuntiámus, Dómine,**
et tuam resurrectiónem confitémur, donec vénias.

Quoti-escúmque manducámus panem hunc   et cálicem bíbimus,

mortem tu-am annunti-ámus, Dómine, donec vé- ni-as.

2. **Quotiescúmque manducámus panem hunc**
et cálicem bíbimus,
mortem tuam annuntiámus, Dómine, donec vénias.

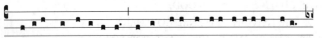

Salvátor mundi, salva nos, qui per crucem et resurrecti-ónem tu-am

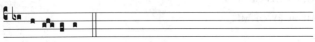

li-be-rá- sti nos.

3. **Salvátor mundi, salva nos,**
qui per crucem et resurrectiónem tuam liberásti nos.

Pr. The mystery of faith.

The people continue, acclaiming one of the following:

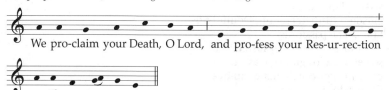

We pro-claim your Death, O Lord, and pro-fess your Res-ur-rec-tion un-til you come a-gain.

1. **We proclaim your Death, O Lord,
and profess your Resurrection
until you come again.**

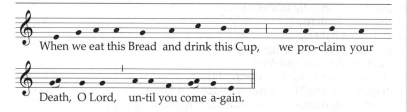

When we eat this Bread and drink this Cup, we pro-claim your Death, O Lord, un-til you come a-gain.

2. **When we eat this Bread and drink this Cup,
we proclaim your Death, O Lord,
until you come again.**

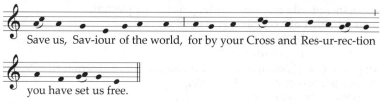

Save us, Sav-iour of the world, for by your Cross and Res-ur-rec-tion you have set us free.

3. **Save us, Saviour of the world,
for by your Cross and Resurrection
you have set us free.**

Only in Ireland: 4. **My Lord and my God.**

Pr. Unde et mémores, Dómine,
nos servi tui,
sed et plebs tua sancta,
eiúsdem Christi, Fílii tui, Dómini nostri,
tam beátæ passiónis,
necnon et ab ínferis resurrectiónis,
sed et in cælos gloriósæ ascensiónis:
offérimus præcláræ maiestáti tuæ
de tuis donis ac datis
hóstiam puram,
hóstiam sanctam,
hóstiam immaculátam,
Panem sanctum vitæ ætérnæ
et Cálicem salútis perpétuæ.

Supra quæ propítio ac seréno vultu
respícere dignéris:
et accépta habére,
sícuti accépta habére dignátus es
múnera púeri tui iusti Abel,
et sacrifícium Patriárchæ nostri Abrahæ,
et quod tibi óbtulit summus sacérdos tuus Melchísedech,
sanctum sacrifícium, immaculátam hóstiam.

Súpplices te rogámus, omnípotens Deus:
iube hæc perférri per manus sancti Angeli tui
in sublíme altáre tuum,
in conspéctu divínæ maiestátis tuæ;
ut, quotquot ex hac altáris participatióne
sacrosánctum Fílii tui Corpus et Sánguinem sumpsérimus,
omni benedictióne cælésti et grátia repleámur
(Per Christum Dóminum nostrum. Amen.)

Commemoration of the Dead.

Meménto étiam, Dómine, famulórum famularúmque tuárum N. et N.,
qui nos præcessérunt cum signo fídei,
et dórmiunt in somno pacis.
Ipsis, Dómine, et ómnibus in Christo quiescéntibus,
locum refrigérii, lucis et pacis,
ut indúlgeas, deprecámur.
(Per Christum Dóminum nostrum. Amen.)

Nobis quoque peccatóribus fámulis tuis,
de multitúdine miseratiónum tuárum sperántibus,

Pr. Therefore, O Lord,
as we celebrate the memorial of the blessed Passion,
the Resurrection from the dead,
and the glorious Ascension into heaven
of Christ, your Son, our Lord,
we, your servants and your holy people,
offer to your glorious majesty
from the gifts that you have given us,
this pure victim,
this holy victim,
this spotless victim,
the holy Bread of eternal life
and the Chalice of everlasting salvation.

Be pleased to look upon these offerings
with a serene and kindly countenance,
and to accept them,
as once you were pleased to accept
the gifts of your servant Abel the just,
the sacrifice of Abraham, our father in faith,
and the offering of your high priest Melchizedek,
a holy sacrifice, a spotless victim.

In humble prayer we ask you, almighty God:
command that these gifts be borne
by the hands of your holy Angel
to your altar on high
in the sight of your divine majesty,
so that all of us, who through this participation at the altar
receive the most holy Body and Blood of your Son,
may be filled with every grace and heavenly blessing.
(Through Christ our Lord. Amen.)

Commemoration of the Dead.
Remember also, Lord, your servants N. and N.,
who have gone before us with the sign of faith
and rest in the sleep of peace.
Grant them, O Lord, we pray,
and all who sleep in Christ,
a place of refreshment, light and peace.
(Through Christ our Lord. Amen.)

To us, also, your servants, who, though sinners,
hope in your abundant mercies,

partem áliquam et societátem donáre dignéris
cum tuis sanctis Apóstolis et Martýribus:
cum Ioánne, Stéphano,
Matthía, Bárnaba,
(Ignátio, Alexándro,
Marcellíno, Petro,
Felicitáte, Perpétua,
Agatha, Lúcia,
Agnéte, Cæcília, Anastásia)
et ómnibus Sanctis tuis:
intra quorum nos consórtium,
non æstimátor mériti,
sed véniæ, quæsumus, largítor admítte.
Per Christum Dóminum nostrum.

Per quem hæc ómnia, Dómine,
semper bona creas, sanctíficas, vivíficas, benedícis,
et præstas nobis.

Pr. Per ipsum, et cum ipso, et in ipso,
est tibi Deo Patri omnipoténti,
in unitáte Spíritus Sancti,
omnis honor et glória
per ómnia sǽcula sæculórum.

A-men.
R. **Amen.**

Then follows the Communion Rite, p.630.

EUCHARISTIC PRAYER II

Pr. Dóminus vóbiscum.
R. **Et cum spíritu tuo.**
Pr. Sursum corda.
R. **Habémus ad Dóminum.**
Pr. Grátias agámus Dómino Deo nostro.
R. **Dignum et iustum est.**
Pr. Vere dignum et iustum est, æquum et salutáre, nos tibi, sancte Pater,

graciously grant some share
and fellowship with your holy Apostles and Martyrs:
with John the Baptist, Stephen,
Matthias, Barnabas,
(Ignatius, Alexander,
Marcellinus, Peter,
Felicity, Perpetua,
Agatha, Lucy,
Agnes, Cecilia, Anastasia)
and all your Saints;
admit us, we beseech you,
into their company,
not weighing our merits,
but granting us your pardon,
through Christ our Lord.

Through whom
you continue to make all these good things, O Lord;
you sanctify them, fill them with life,
bless them, and bestow them upon us.

Pr. Through him, and with him, and in him,
O God, almighty Father,
in the unity of the Holy Spirit,
all glory and honour is yours,
for ever and ever.

A-men.

R. **Amen.**

Then follows the Communion Rite, p.631.

EUCHARISTIC PRAYER II

Pr. The Lord be with you.
R. **And with your spirit.**
Pr. Lift up your hearts.
R. **We lift them up to the Lord.**
Pr. Let us give thanks to the Lord our God.
R. **It is right and just.**
Pr. It is truly right and just, our duty and our salvation,

semper et ubíque grátias ágere
per Fílium dilectiónis tuæ Iesum Christum,
Verbum tuum per quod cuncta fecísti:
quem misísti nobis Salvatórem et Redemptórem,
incarnátum de Spíritu Sancto et ex Vírgine natum.

Qui voluntátem tuam adímplens
et pópulum tibi sanctum acquírens
exténdit manus cum paterétur,
ut mortem sólveret et resurrectiónem manifestáret.

Et ídeo cum Angelis et ómnibus Sanctis
glóriam tuam prædicámus, una voce dicéntes:

The people sing or say aloud the Sanctus.

Sanc-tus, * Sanc-tus, Sanc-tus Dó-mi-nus De-us Sá-ba-oth. Ple-ni
sunt cæ-li et ter-ra gló-ri-a tu-a. Ho-sán-na in ex-cél-sis. Be-ne-díc-
tus qui ve-nit in nómine Dómini. Ho-sán-na in excél-sis.

Sanctus, Sanctus, Sanctus Dóminus Deus Sábaoth.
Pleni sunt cæli et terra glória tua.
Hosánna in excélsis.
Benedíctus qui venit in nómine Dómini.
Hosánna in excélsis.

Pr. Vere Sanctus es, Dómine, fons omnis sanctitátis.
Hæc ergo dona, quǽsumus,
Spíritus tui rore sanctífica,
ut nobis Corpus et ✠ Sanguis fiant
Dómini nostri Iesu Christi.

always and everywhere to give you thanks, Father most holy,
through your beloved Son, Jesus Christ,
your Word through whom you made all things,
whom you sent as our Saviour and Redeemer,
incarnate by the Holy Spirit and born of the Virgin.

Fulfilling your will and gaining for you a holy people,
he stretched out his hands as he endured his Passion,
so as to break the bonds of death and manifest the resurrection.

And so, with the Angels and all the Saints
we declare your glory,
as with one voice we acclaim:

The people sing or say aloud the Sanctus.

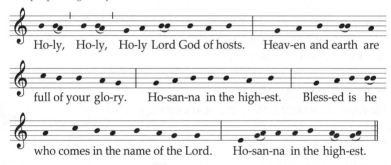

Ho-ly, Ho-ly, Ho-ly Lord God of hosts. Heav-en and earth are
full of your glo-ry. Ho-san-na in the high-est. Bless-ed is he
who comes in the name of the Lord. Ho-san-na in the high-est.

Holy, Holy, Holy Lord God of hosts.
Heaven and earth are full of your glory.
Hosanna in the highest.
Blessed is he who comes in the name of the Lord.
Hosanna in the highest.

Pr. You are indeed Holy, O Lord,
the fount of all holiness.
Make holy, therefore, these gifts, we pray,
by sending down your Spirit upon them like the dewfall,
so that they may become for us
the Body and ✠ Blood of our Lord Jesus Christ.

Qui cum Passióni voluntárie traderétur,
accépit panem et grátias agens fregit,
dedítque discípulis suis, dicens:

Accípite et manducáte ex hoc omnes:
hoc est enim Corpus meum,
quod pro vobis tradétur.

Símili modo, postquam cenátum est,
accípiens et cálicem,
íterum grátias agens dedit discípulis suis, dicens:

Accípite et bíbite ex eo omnes:
hic est enim calix Sánguinis mei
novi et ætérni testaménti,
qui pro vobis et pro multis effundétur
in remissiónem peccatórum.
Hoc fácite in meam commemoratiónem.

Pr. Mystérium fídei.

The people continue, acclaiming one of the following:

Mortem tu-am annunti-ámus, Dómi-ne,   et tu-am resurrecti-ó-

nem confi-témur, do-nec vé-ni-as.

1. **Mortem tuam annuntiámus, Dómine,
et tuam resurrectiónem confitémur, donec vénias.**

At the time he was betrayed
and entered willingly into his Passion,
he took bread and, giving thanks, broke it,
and gave it to his disciples, saying:

Take this, all of you, and eat of it,
for this is my Body,
which will be given up for you.

In a similar way, when supper was ended,
he took the chalice
and, once more giving thanks,
he gave it to his disciples, saying:

Take this, all of you, and drink from it,
for this is the chalice of my Blood,
the Blood of the new and eternal covenant,
which will be poured out for you and for many
for the forgiveness of sins.
Do this in memory of me.

Pr. The mystery of faith.

The people continue, acclaiming one of the following:

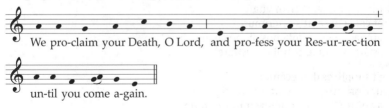

We pro-claim your Death, O Lord, and pro-fess your Res-ur-rec-tion un-til you come a-gain.

1. We proclaim your Death, O Lord,
and profess your Resurrection
until you come again.

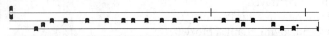

Quoti-escúmque manducámus panem hunc   et cálicem bíbimus,

mortem tu-am annunti-ámus, Dómine, donec vé- ni-as.

2. **Quotiescúmque manducámus panem hunc**
et cálicem bíbimus,
mortem tuam annuntiámus, Dómine, donec vénias.

Salvátor mundi, salva nos, qui per crucem et resurrecti-ónem tu-am

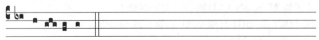

li-be-rá- sti nos.

3. **Salvátor mundi, salva nos,**
qui per crucem et resurrectiónem tuam liberásti nos.

Pr. Mémores ígitur mortis et resurrectiónis eius,
tibi, Dómine, panem vitæ
et cálicem salútis offérimus,
grátias agéntes quia nos dignos habuísti
astáre coram te et tibi ministráre.

Et súpplices deprecámur
ut Córporis et Sánguinis Christi partícipes
a Spíritu Sancto congregémur in unum.

Recordáre, Dómine, Ecclésiæ tuæ toto orbe diffúsæ,
ut eam in caritáte perfícias
una cum Papa nostro N. et Epíscopo nostro N.*
et univérso clero.

---

*Mention may be made here of the Coadjutor Bishop or Auxiliary Bishops.

When we eat this Bread and drink this Cup, we pro-claim your Death, O Lord, un-til you come a-gain.

**2. When we eat this Bread and drink this Cup,
we proclaim your Death, O Lord,
until you come again.**

Save us, Sav-iour of the world, for by your Cross and Res-ur-rec-tion you have set us free.

**3. Save us, Saviour of the world,
for by your Cross and Resurrection
you have set us free.**

Only in Ireland: **4. My Lord and my God.**

Pr. Therefore, as we celebrate
the memorial of his Death and Resurrection,
we offer you, Lord,
the Bread of life and the Chalice of salvation,
giving thanks that you have held us worthy
to be in your presence and minister to you.

Humbly we pray
that, partaking of the Body and Blood of Christ,
we may be gathered into one by the Holy Spirit.

Remember, Lord, your Church,
spread throughout the world,
and bring her to the fullness of charity,
together with **N.** our Pope and **N.** our Bishop[*]
and all the clergy.

[*] Mention may be made here of the Coadjutor Bishop or Auxiliary Bishops.

In Masses for the Dead, the following may be added:
Meménto fámuli tui (fámulæ tuæ) N.,
quem (quam) (hódie) ad te ex hoc mundo vocásti.
Concéde, ut, qui (quæ) complantátus (complantáta) fuit
     similitúdini mortis Fílii tui,
simul fiat et resurrectiónis ipsíus.

Meménto étiam fratrum nostrórum,
qui in spe resurrectiónis dormiérunt,
omniúmque in tua miseratióne defunctórum,
et eos in lumen vultus tui admítte.
Omnium nostrum, quǽsumus, miserére,
ut cum beáta Dei Genetríce Vírgine María,
     beáto Ioseph, eius Sponso, beátis Apostólis et ómnibus Sanctis,
qui tibi a sǽculo placuérunt,
ætérnæ vitæ mereámur esse consórtes,
et te laudémus et glorificémus
per Fílium tuum Iesum Christum.

Per ipsum, et cum ipso, et in ipso,
est tibi Deo Patri omnipoténti,
in unitáte Spíritus Sancti,
omnis honor et glória
per ómnia sǽcula sæculórum.

A-men.
R. **Amen.**

Then follows the Communion Rite, p.630.

EUCHARISTIC PRAYER III

Pr. Vere Sanctus es, Dómine,
et mérito te laudat omnis a te cóndita creatúra,
quia per Fílium tuum,
Dóminum nostrum Iesum Christum,
Spíritus Sancti operánte virtúte,
vivíficas et sanctíficas univérsa,
et pópulum tibi congregáre non désinis,

In Masses for the Dead, the following may be added:
Remember your servant N.,
whom you have called (today)
from this world to yourself.
Grant that he (she) who was united with your Son in a death like his,
may also be one with him in his Resurrection.

Remember also our brothers and sisters
who have fallen asleep in the hope of the resurrection,
and all who have died in your mercy:
welcome them into the light of your face.
Have mercy on us all, we pray,
that with the Blessed Virgin Mary, Mother of God,
   with blessed Joseph, her Spouse, with the blessed Apostles,
and all the Saints who have pleased you throughout the ages,
we may merit to be coheirs to eternal life,
and may praise and glorify you
through your Son, Jesus Christ.

Through him, and with him, and in him,
O God, almighty Father,
in the unity of the Holy Spirit,
all glory and honour is yours,
for ever and ever.

A-men.

R. **Amen.**

Then follows the Communion Rite, p.631.

EUCHARISTIC PRAYER III

Pr. You are indeed Holy, O Lord,
and all you have created
rightly gives you praise,
for through your Son our Lord Jesus Christ,
by the power and working of the Holy Spirit,
you give life to all things and make them holy,
and you never cease to gather a people to yourself,

ut a solis ortu usque ad occásum
oblátio munda offerátur nómini tuo.

Súpplices ergo te, Dómine, deprecámur,
ut hæc múnera, quæ tibi sacránda detúlimus,
eódem Spíritu sanctificáre dignéris,
ut Corpus et ✠ Sanguis fiant
Fílii tui Dómini nostri Iesu Christi,
cuius mandáto hæc mystéria celebrámus.

Ipse enim in qua nocte tradebátur
accépit panem
et tibi grátias agens benedíxit,
fregit, dedítque discípulis suis, dicens:

Accípite et manducáte ex hoc omnes:
hoc est enim Corpus meum,
quod pro vobis tradétur.

Símili modo, postquam cenátum est,
accípiens cálicem,
et tibi grátias agens benedíxit,
dedítque discípulis suis, dicens:

Accípite et bíbite ex eo omnes:
hic est enim calix Sánguinis mei
novi et ætérni testaménti,
qui pro vobis et pro multis effundétur
in remissiónem peccatórum.

Hoc fácite in meam commemoratiónem.

so that from the rising of the sun to its setting
a pure sacrifice may be offered to your name.

Therefore, O Lord, we humbly implore you:
by the same Spirit graciously make holy
these gifts we have brought to you for consecration,
that they may become the Body and ✠ Blood
of your Son our Lord Jesus Christ,
at whose command we celebrate these mysteries.

For on the night he was betrayed
he himself took bread,
and, giving you thanks, he said the blessing,
broke the bread and gave it to his disciples, saying:

TAKE THIS, ALL OF YOU, AND EAT OF IT,
FOR THIS IS MY BODY,
WHICH WILL BE GIVEN UP FOR YOU.

In a similar way, when supper was ended,
he took the chalice,
and, giving you thanks, he said the blessing,
and gave the chalice to his disciples, saying:

TAKE THIS, ALL OF YOU, AND DRINK FROM IT,
FOR THIS IS THE CHALICE OF MY BLOOD,
THE BLOOD OF THE NEW AND ETERNAL COVENANT,
WHICH WILL BE POURED OUT FOR YOU AND FOR MANY
FOR THE FORGIVENESS OF SINS.

DO THIS IN MEMORY OF ME.

Pr. Mystérium fídei.

The people continue, acclaiming one of the following:

Mortem tu-am annunti-ámus, Dómi-ne,   et tu-am resurrecti-ó-

nem confi-témur, do-nec vé-ni-as.

1. **Mortem tuam annuntiámus, Dómine,**
et tuam resurrectiónem confitémur, donec vénias.

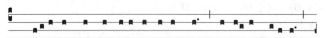

Quoti-escúmque manducámus panem hunc   et cálicem bíbimus,

mortem tu-am annunti-ámus, Dómine, donec vé- ni-as.

2. **Quotiescúmque manducámus panem hunc**
et cálicem bíbimus,
mortem tuam annuntiámus, Dómine, donec vénias.

Salvátor mundi, salva nos, qui per crucem et resurrecti-ónem tu-am

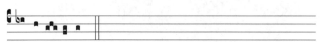

li-be-rá- sti nos.

3. **Salvátor mundi, salva nos,**
qui per crucem et resurrectiónem tuam liberásti nos.

Pr. The mystery of faith.

The people continue, acclaiming one of the following:

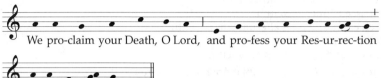

We pro-claim your Death, O Lord, and pro-fess your Res-ur-rec-tion un-til you come a-gain.

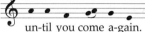

1. **We proclaim your Death, O Lord,**
and profess your Resurrection
until you come again.

When we eat this Bread and drink this Cup, we pro-claim your Death, O Lord, un-til you come a-gain.

2. **When we eat this Bread and drink this Cup,**
we proclaim your Death, O Lord,
until you come again.

Save us, Sav-iour of the world, for by your Cross and Res-ur-rec-tion you have set us free.

3. **Save us, Saviour of the world,**
for by your Cross and Resurrection
you have set us free.

Only in Ireland: 4. **My Lord and my God.**

Pr. Mémores ígitur, Dómine,
eiúsdem Fílii tui salutíferæ passiónis
necnon mirábilis resurrectiónis
et ascensiónis in cælum,
sed et præstolántes álterum eius advéntum,
offérimus tibi, grátias reIeréntes,
hoc sacrifícium vivum et sanctum.

Réspice, quǽsumus, in oblatiónem Ecclésiæ tuæ
et, agnóscens Hóstiam,
cuius voluísti immolatióne placári,
concéde, ut qui Córpore et Sánguine Fílii tui refícimur,
Spíritu eius Sancto repléti,
unum corpus et unus spíritus inveniámur in Christo.

Ipse nos tibi perfíciat munus ætérnum,
ut cum eléctis tuis hereditátem cónsequi valeámus,
in primis cum beátissima Vírgine, Dei Genetríce, María,
cum beáto Ioseph, eius Sponso,
cum beátis Apóstolis tuis et gloriósis Martýribus
(cum Sancto N.: the saint of the day or Patron Saint)
et ómnibus Sanctis,
quorum intercessióne
perpétuo apud te confídimus adiuvári.

Hæc Hóstia nostræ reconciliatiónis profíciat,
quǽsumus, Dómine,
ad totíus mundi pacem atque salútem.
Ecclésiam tuam, peregrinántem in terra,
in fide et caritáte firmáre dignéris
cum fámulo tuo Papa nostro N. et Epíscopo nostro N.*,
cum episcopáli órdine et univérso clero
et omni pópulo acquisitiónis tuæ.

Votis huius famíliæ, quam tibi astáre voluísti,
adésto propítius.
Omnes fílios tuos ubíque dispérsos
tibi, clemens Pater, miserátus coniúnge.

† Fratres nostros defúnctos
et omnes qui, tibi placéntes, ex hoc sǽculo transiérunt,

---

* Mention may be made here of the Coadjutor Bishop or Auxiliary Bishops.

Pr. Therefore, O Lord, as we celebrate the memorial
of the saving Passion of your Son,
his wondrous Resurrection
and Ascension into heaven,
and as we look forward to his second coming,
we offer you in thanksgiving
this holy and living sacrifice.

Look, we pray, upon the oblation of your Church
and, recognising the sacrificial Victim by whose death
you willed to reconcile us to yourself,
grant that we, who are nourished
by the Body and Blood of your Son
and filled with his Holy Spirit,
may become one body, one spirit in Christ.

May he make of us an eternal offering to you,
so that we may obtain an inheritance with your elect,
especially with the most Blessed Virgin Mary, Mother of God,
with blessed Joseph, her Spouse,
with your blessed Apostles and glorious Martyrs
(with Saint N.: the Saint of the day or Patron Saint)
and with all the Saints,
on whose constant intercession in your presence
we rely for unfailing help.

May this Sacrifice of our reconciliation,
we pray, O Lord,
advance the peace and salvation of all the world.
Be pleased to confirm in faith and charity
your pilgrim Church on earth,
with your servant N. our Pope and N. our Bishop*,
the Order of Bishops, all the clergy,
and the entire people you have gained for your own.

Listen graciously to the prayers of this family,
whom you have summoned before you:
in your compassion, O merciful Father,
gather to yourself all your children
scattered throughout the world.

† To our departed brothers and sisters
and to all who were pleasing to you

---

*Mention may be made here of the Coadjutor Bishop or Auxiliary Bishops.

in regnum tuum benígnus admítte,
ubi fore sperámus,
ut simul glória tua perénniter satiémur,
per Christum Dóminum nostrum,
per quem mundo bona cuncta largíris. †

Per ipsum, et cum ipso, et in ipso,
est tibi Deo Patri omnipoténti,
in unitáte Spíritus Sancti,
omnis honor et glória
per ómnia sǽcula sæculórum.

A-men.
R. **Amen.**

Then follows the Communion Rite, p.630.

When this Eucharistic Prayer is used in Masses for the Dead, the following may be said:
† Meménto fámuli tui (fámulæ tuæ) N.,
quem (quam) (hódie) ad te ex hoc mundo vocásti.
Concéde, ut, qui (quæ) complantátus (complantáta)
    fuit símilitudini mortis Fílii tui,
simul fiat et resurrectiónis ipsíus,
quando mórtuos suscitábit in carne de terra
et corpus humilitátis nostræ
configurábit córpori claritátis suæ.
Sed et fratres nostros defúnctos,
et omnes qui, tibi placéntes, ex hoc sǽculo transiérunt,
in regnum tuum benígnus admítte,
ubi fore sperámus,
ut simul glória tua perénniter satiémur,
quando omnem lácrimam abstérges ab óculis nostris,
quia te, sícuti es, Deum nostrum vidéntes,
tibi símiles érimus cuncta per sǽcula,
et te sine fine laudábimus,
per Christum Dóminum nostrum,
per quem mundo bona cuncta largíris. †

at their passing from this life,
give kind admittance to your kingdom.
There we hope to enjoy for ever the fullness of your glory
through Christ our Lord,
through whom you bestow on the world all that is good. †

Through him, and with him, and in him,
O God, almighty Father,
in the unity of the Holy Spirit,
all glory and honour is yours,
for ever and ever.

A-men.

R. **Amen.**

Then follows the Communion Rite, p.631.

When this Eucharistic Prayer is used in Masses for the Dead, the following may be said:
† Remember your servant N.
whom you have called (today)
from this world to yourself.
Grant that he (she) who was united with your Son in a death like his,
may also be one with him in his Resurrection,
when from the earth
he will raise up in the flesh those who have died,
and transform our lowly body
after the pattern of his own glorious body.
To our departed brothers and sisters, too,
and to all who were pleasing to you
at their passing from this life,
give kind admittance to your kingdom.
There we hope to enjoy for ever the fullness of your glory,
when you wipe away every tear from our eyes.
For seeing you, our God, as you are,
we shall be like you for all the ages
and praise you without end,
through Christ our Lord,
through whom you bestow on the world all that is good. †

EUCHARISTIC PRAYER IV

Pr. Dóminus vóbiscum.

R. Et cum spíritu tuo.

Pr. Sursum corda.

R. Habémus ad Dóminum.

Pr. Grátias agámus Dómino Deo nostro.

R. Dignum et iustum est.

Pr. Vere dignum est tibi grátias ágere,
vere iustum est te glorificáre, Pater sancte,
quia unus es Deus vivus et verus,
qui es ante sǽcula et pérmanes in ætérnum,
inaccessíbilem lucem inhábitans;
sed et qui unus bonus atque fons vitæ cuncta fecísti,
ut creatúras tuas benedictiónibus adimpléres
multásque lætificáres tui lúminis claritáte.

Et ídeo coram te innúmeræ astant turbæ Angelórum,
qui die ac nocte sérviunt tibi
et, vultus tui glóriam contemplántes,
te incessánter gloríficant.

Cum quibus et nos et, per nostram vocem,
omnis quæ sub cælo est creatúra
nomen tuum in exsultatióne confitémur, canéntes:

The people sing or say aloud the Sanctus.

S anc-tus, * Sanc-tus, Sanc-tus Dó-mi-nus De-us Sá-ba-oth. Ple-ni

sunt cæ-li et ter-ra gló-ri-a tu-a. Ho-sán-na in ex-cél-sis. Be-ne-díc-

tus qui ve-nit in nómine Dómini. Ho-sán-na in excél-sis.

EUCHARISTIC PRAYER IV

Pr. The Lord be with you.

R. **And with your spirit.**

Pr. Lift up your hearts.

R. **We lift them up to the Lord.**

Pr. Let us give thanks to the Lord our God.

R. **It is right and just.**

Pr. It is truly right to give you thanks,
truly just to give you glory, Father most holy,
for you are the one God living and true,
existing before all ages and abiding for all eternity,
dwelling in unapproachable light;
yet you, who alone are good, the source of life,
have made all that is,
so that you might fill your creatures with blessings
and bring joy to many of them by the glory of your light.

And so, in your presence are countless hosts of Angels,
who serve you day and night
and, gazing upon the glory of your face,
glorify you without ceasing.

With them we, too, confess your name in exultation,
giving voice to every creature under heaven,
as we acclaim:

The people sing or say aloud the Sanctus.

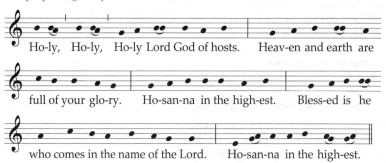

Ho-ly, Ho-ly, Ho-ly Lord God of hosts. Heav-en and earth are full of your glo-ry. Ho-san-na in the high-est. Bless-ed is he who comes in the name of the Lord. Ho-san-na in the high-est.

Sanctus, Sanctus, Sanctus Dóminus Deus Sábaoth.
Pleni sunt cæli et terra glória tua.
Hosánna in excélsis.
Benedíctus qui venit in nómine Dómini.
Hosánna in excélsis.

Pr. Confitémur tibi, Pater sancte,
quia magnus es et ómnia ópera tua
in sapiéntia et caritáte fecísti.
Hóminem ad tuam imáginem condidísti,
eíque commisísti mundi curam univérsi,
ut, tibi soli Creatóri sérviens,
creatúris ómnibus imperáret.
Et cum amicítiam tuam, non obœdiens, amisísset,
non eum dereliquísti in mortis império.
Omnibus enim misericórditer subvenísti,
ut te quæréntes invenírent.
Sed et fœdera plúries homínibus obtulísti
eósque per prophétas erudísti in exspectatióne salútis.

Et sic, Pater sancte, mundum dilexísti,
ut, compléta plenitúdine témporum,
Unigénitum tuum nobis mítteres Salvatórem.
Qui, incarnátus de Spíritu Sancto
et natus ex María Vírgine,
in nostra condiciónis forma est conversátus
per ómnia absque peccáto;
salútem evangelizávit paupéribus,
redemptiónem captívis,
mæstis corde lætítiam.
Ut tuam vero dispensatiónem impléret,
in mortem trádidit semetípsum
ac, resúrgens a mórtuis,
mortem destrúxit vitámque renovávit.

Et, ut non ámplius nobismetípsis viverémus,
sed sibi qui pro nobis mórtuus est atque surréxit,
a te, Pater, misit Spíritum Sanctum
primítias credéntibus,

Holy, Holy, Holy Lord God of hosts.
Heaven and earth are full of your glory.
Hosanna in the highest.
Blessed is he who comes in the name of the Lord.
Hosanna in the highest.

Pr. We give you praise, Father most holy,
for you are great
and you have fashioned all your works
in wisdom and in love.
You formed man in your own image
and entrusted the whole world to his care,
so that in serving you alone, the Creator,
he might have dominion over all creatures.
And when through disobedience he had lost your friendship,
you did not abandon him to the domain of death.
For you came in mercy to the aid of all,
so that those who seek might find you.
Time and again you offered them covenants
and through the prophets
taught them to look forward to salvation.

And you so loved the world, Father most holy,
that in the fullness of time
you sent your Only Begotten Son to be our Saviour.
Made incarnate by the Holy Spirit
and born of the Virgin Mary,
he shared our human nature
in all things but sin.
To the poor he proclaimed the good news of salvation,
to prisoners, freedom,
and to the sorrowful of heart, joy.
To accomplish your plan,
he gave himself up to death,
and, rising from the dead,
he destroyed death and restored life.

And that we might live no longer for ourselves
but for him who died and rose again for us,
he sent the Holy Spirit from you, Father,

qui, opus suum in mundo perfíciens,
omnem sanctificatiónem compléret.

Quǽsumus ígitur, Dómine,
ut idem Spíritus Sanctus
hæc múnera sanctificáre dignétur,
ut Corpus et ✠ Sanguis fiant
Dómini nostri Iesu Christi
ad hoc magnum mystérium celebrándum,
quod ipse nobis relíquit in fœdus ætérnum.

Ipse enim, cum hora venísset
ut glorificarétur a te, Pater sancte,
ac dilexísset suos qui erant in mundo,
in finem diléxit eos:
et cenántibus illis
accépit panem, benedíxit ac fregit,
dedítque discípulis suis, dicens:

Accípite et manducáte ex hoc omnes:
hoc est enim Corpus meum,
quod pro vobis tradétur.

Símili modo
accípiens cálicem, ex genímine vitis replétum,
grátias egit, dedítque discípulis suis, dicens:

Accípite et bíbite ex eo omnes:
hic est enim calix Sánguinis mei
novi et ætérni testaménti,
qui pro vobis et pro multis effundétur
in remissiónem peccatórum.
Hoc fácite in meam commemoratiónem.

Pr. Mystérium fídei.

The people continue, acclaiming one of the following:

as the first fruits for those who believe,
so that, bringing to perfection his work in the world,
he might sanctify creation to the full.

Therefore, O Lord, we pray:
may this same Holy Spirit
graciously sanctify these offerings,
that they may become
the Body and ✠ Blood of our Lord Jesus Christ
for the celebration of this great mystery,
which he himself left us
as an eternal covenant.

For when the hour had come
for him to be glorified by you, Father most holy,
having loved his own who were in the world,
he loved them to the end:
and while they were at supper,
he took bread, blessed and broke it,
and gave it to his disciples, saying:

Take this, all of you, and eat of it,
for this is my Body,
which will be given up for you.

In a similar way,
taking the chalice filled with the fruit of the vine,
he gave thanks,
and gave the chalice to his disciples, saying:

Take this, all of you, and drink from it,
for this is the chalice of my Blood,
the Blood of the new and eternal covenant,
which will be poured out for you and for many
for the forgiveness of sins.

Do this in memory of me.

Pr. The mystery of faith.

The people continue, acclaiming one of the following:

Mortem tu-am annunti-ámus, Dómi-ne,   et tu-am resurrecti-ó-

nem confi-témur, do-nec vé-ni-as.

**1. Mortem tuam annuntiámus, Dómine,
et tuam resurrectiónem confitémur, donec vénias.**

Quoti-escúmque manducámus panem hunc   et cálicem bíbimus,

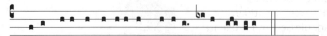

mortem tu-am annunti-ámus, Dómine, donec vé- ni-as.

**2. Quotiescúmque manducámus panem hunc
et cálicem bíbimus,
mortem tuam annuntiámus, Dómine, donec vénias.**

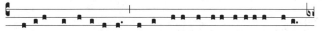

Salvátor mundi, salva nos, qui per crucem et resurrecti-ónem tu-am

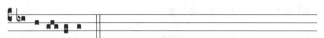

li-be-rá- sti nos.

**3. Salvátor mundi, salva nos,
qui per crucem et resurrectiónem tuam liberásti nos.**

Pr. Unde et nos, Dómine, redemptiónis nostræ memoriále nunc celebrántes,
mortem Christi
eiúsque descénsum ad ínferos recólimus,
eius resurrectiónem
et ascensiónem ad tuam déxteram profitémur,

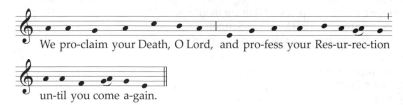

We pro-claim your Death, O Lord, and pro-fess your Res-ur-rec-tion un-til you come a-gain.

**1. We proclaim your Death, O Lord,
and profess your Resurrection
until you come again.**

When we eat this Bread and drink this Cup, we pro-claim your Death, O Lord, un-til you come a-gain.

**2. When we eat this Bread and drink this Cup,
we proclaim your Death, O Lord,
until you come again.**

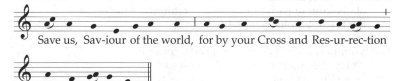

Save us, Sav-iour of the world, for by your Cross and Res-ur-rec-tion you have set us free.

**3. Save us, Saviour of the world,
for by your Cross and Resurrection
you have set us free.**

Only in Ireland: **4. My Lord and my God.**

Pr. Therefore, O Lord,
as we now celebrate the memorial of our redemption,
we remember Christ's Death
and his descent to the realm of the dead,
we proclaim his Resurrection
and his Ascension to your right hand,

et, exspectántes ipsíus advéntum in glória,
offérimus tibi eius Corpus et Sánguinem,
sacrifícium tibi acceptábile et toti mundo salutáre.

Réspice, Dómine, in Hóstiam,
quam Ecclésiæ tuæ ipse parásti,
et concéde benígnus ómnibus
qui ex hoc uno pane participábunt et cálice,
ut, in unum corpus a Sancto Spíritu congregáti,
in Christo hóstia viva perficiántur,
ad laudem glóriæ tuæ.

Nunc ergo, Dómine, ómnium recordáre,
pro quibus tibi hanc oblatiónem offérimus:
in primis fámuli tui, Papæ nostri N.,
Epíscopi nostri N.*, et Episcopórum órdinis univérsi,
sed et totíus cleri, et offeréntium,
et circumstántium,
et cuncti pópuli tui,
et ómnium, qui te quærunt corde sincéro.

Meménto étiam illórum,
    qui obiérunt in pace Christi tui, et ómnium defunctórum,
quorum fidem tu solus cognovísti.

Nobis ómnibus, fíliis tuis, clemens Pater, concéde,
ut cæléstem hereditátem cónsequi valeámus
cum beáta Vírgine, Dei Genetríce, María,
cum beáto Ioseph, eius Sponso,
cum Apóstolis et Sanctis tuis
in regno tuo, ubi cum univérsa creatúra,
a corruptióne peccáti et mortis liberáta,
te glorificémus per Christum Dóminum nostrum,
per quem mundo bona cuncta largíris.

Per ipsum, et cum ipso, et in ipso,
est tibi Deo Patri omnipoténti,
in unitáte Spíritus Sancti,
omnis honor et glória
per ómnia sǽcula sæculórum.

---

* Mention may be made here of the Coadjutor Bishop or Auxiliary Bishops.

and, as we await his coming in glory,
we offer you his Body and Blood,
the sacrifice acceptable to you
which brings salvation to the whole world.

Look, O Lord, upon the Sacrifice
which you yourself have provided for your Church,
and grant in your loving kindness
to all who partake of this one Bread and one Chalice
that, gathered into one body by the Holy Spirit,
they may truly become a living sacrifice in Christ
to the praise of your glory.

Therefore, Lord, remember now
all for whom we offer this sacrifice:
especially your servant N. our Pope,
N. our Bishop,* and the whole Order of Bishops,
all the clergy,
those who take part in this offering,
    those gathered here before you, your entire people,
and all who seek you with a sincere heart.

Remember also
those who have died in the peace of your Christ
and all the dead,
whose faith you alone have known.

To all of us, your children,
grant, O merciful Father,
that we may enter into a heavenly inheritance
with the Blessed Virgin Mary, Mother of God,
with blessed Joseph, her Spouse,
and with your Apostles and Saints in your kingdom.
There, with the whole of creation,
freed from the corruption of sin and death,
may we glorify you through Christ our Lord,
through whom you bestow on the world all that is good.

Through him, and with him, and in him,
O God, almighty Father,
in the unity of the Holy Spirit,
all glory and honour is yours,
for ever and ever.

---

* Mention may be made here of the Coadjutor Bishop or Auxiliary Bishops.

A-men.

R. Amen.

Then follows the Communion Rite.

THE COMMUNION RITE

The eating and drinking together of the Lord's Body and Blood in a Paschal meal is the culmination of the Eucharist

THE LORD'S PRAYER

After the chalice and paten have been set down, the congregation stands and the Priest says:

Pr. Præcéptis salutáribus móniti,
et divína institutióne formáti,
audémus dícere:

Together with the people, he continues:

P a-ter noster, qui es in cæ-lis: sancti-fi-cé-tur nomen tu-um; advéni-at

regnum tu-um; fi-at volúntas tu-a, sic-ut in cæ-lo, et in terra. Pa-

nem nostrum coti-di-ánum da nobis hódi-e; et dimítte nobis débi-

ta nostra, sicut et nos dimíttimus de-bi-tó-ribus nostris; et ne nos

indúcas in tenta-ti-ó-nem; sed líbera nos a ma-lo.

A-men.

R. **Amen.**

Then follows the Communion Rite.

THE COMMUNION RITE

The eating and drinking together of the Lord's Body and Blood in a Paschal meal is the culmination of the Eucharist

THE LORD'S PRAYER

After the chalice and paten have been set down, the congregation stands and the Priest says:

Pr. At the Saviour's command
and formed by divine teaching,
we dare to say:

Together with the people, he continues:

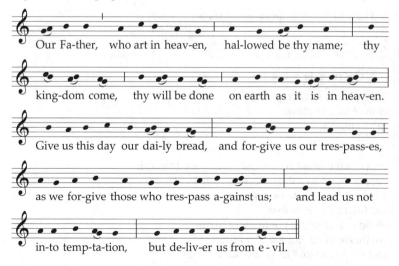

Our Fa-ther, who art in heav-en, hal-lowed be thy name; thy king-dom come, thy will be done on earth as it is in heav-en. Give us this day our dai-ly bread, and for-give us our tres-pass-es, as we for-give those who tres-pass a-gainst us; and lead us not in-to temp-ta-tion, but de-liv-er us from e-vil.

R. **Pater noster, qui es in cælis:**
sanctificétur nomen tuum;
advéniat regnum tuum;
fiat volúntas tua, sicut in cælo, et in terra.
Panem nostrum cotidiánum da nobis hódie;
et dimítte nobis debíta nostra,
sicut et nos dimíttimus debitóribus nostris;
et ne nos indúcas in tentatiónem;
sed líbera nos a malo.

Pr. Líbera nos, quǽsumus, Dómine, ab ómnibus malis,
da propítius pacem in diébus nostris,
ut, ope misericórdiæ tuæ adiúti,
et a peccáto simus semper líberi
et ab omni perturbatióne secúri:
exspectántes beátam spem
et advéntum Salvatóris nostri Iesu Christi.

Qui-a tu-um est regnum, et po-téstas,

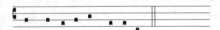

et gló- ri- a in saecu-la.

R. **Quia tuum est regnum,**
et potéstas, et glória
in sǽcula.

THE PEACE

Pr. Dómine Iesu Christe, qui dixísti Apostólis tuis:
Pacem relínquo vobis, pacem meam do vobis:
ne respícias peccáta nostra,
sed fidem Ecclésiæ tuæ;
eámque secúndum voluntátem tuam
pacificáre et coadunáre dignéris.
Qui vivis et regnas in sǽcula sæculórum.

R. **Amen.**

R. **Our Father, who art in heaven,**
hallowed be thy name;
thy kingdom come,
thy will be done
on earth as it is in heaven.
Give us this day our daily bread,
and forgive us our trespasses,
as we forgive those who trespass against us;
and lead us not into temptation,
but deliver us from evil.

Pr. Deliver us, Lord, we pray, from every evil,
graciously grant peace in our days,
that, by the help of your mercy,
we may be always free from sin
and safe from all distress,
as we await the blessed hope
and the coming of our Saviour, Jesus Christ.

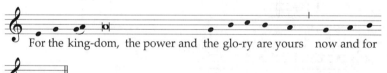

For the king-dom, the power and the glo-ry are yours   now and for ev-er.

R. **For the kingdom,**
the power and the glory are yours
now and for ever.

THE PEACE

Pr. Lord Jesus Christ,
who said to your Apostles:
Peace I leave you, my peace I give you;
look not on our sins,
but on the faith of your Church,
and graciously grant her peace and unity
in accordance with your will.
Who live and reign for ever and ever.
R. **Amen.**

Pr. Pax Dómini sit semper vobíscum.

Et cum spí-ri- tu tu- o.

R. Et cum spíritu tuo.

Then, if appropriate, the Deacon, or the Priest, adds:

Pr. Offérte vobis pacem.

And all offer one another the customary sign of peace.

BREAKING OF THE BREAD

Then the Priest takes the host, breaks it over the paten, and places a small piece in the chalice. Meanwhile the following is sung or said:

Ag-nus De-i, * qui tol-lis pec-cá-ta mundi:

mi-se-ré-re no-bis.

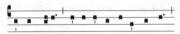

Ag-nus De-i, * qui tol-lis pec-cá-ta mundi:

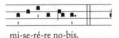

mi-se-ré-re no-bis.

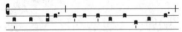

Ag-nus De-i, * qui tol-lis pec-cá-ta mun-di:

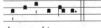

do-na no-bis pa-cem.

Pr. The peace of the Lord be with you always.

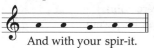
And with your spir-it.

R. And with your spirit.

Then, if appropriate, the Deacon, or the Priest, adds:

Pr. Let us offer each other the sign of peace.

And all offer one another the customary sign of peace.

BREAKING OF THE BREAD

Then the Priest takes the host, breaks it over the paten, and places a small piece in the chalice. Meanwhile the following is sung or said:

Lamb of God, you take a-way the sins of the world,

have mer-cy on us.

Lamb of God, you take a-way the sins of the world,

have mer-cy on us.

Lamb of God, you take a-way the sins of the world,

grant us peace.

The invocation may even be repeated several times if the fraction is prolonged. Only the final time, however, is grant us peace said.

Agnus Dei, qui tollis peccáta mundi: miserére nobis.
Agnus Dei, qui tollis peccáta mundi: miserére nobis.
Agnus Dei, qui tollis peccáta mundi: dona nobis pacem.

Then the Priest, with hands joined, says quietly:

Domine Iesu Christe, Fili Dei vivi,
qui ex voluntate Patris,
cooperante Spiritu Sancto,
per mortem tuam mundum vivificasti:
libera me per hoc sacrosanctum Corpus et Sanguinem tuum
ab omnibus iniquitatibus meis et universis malis:
et fac me tuis semper inhærere mandatis,
et a te numquam separari permittas.

Or:

Perceptio Corporis et Sanguinis tui, Domine Iesu Christe,
non mihi proveniat in iudicium et condemnationem:
sed pro tua pietate prosit mihi
ad tutamentum mentis et corporis,
et ad medelam percipiendam.

INVITATION TO COMMUNION

All kneel. The Priest genuflects, takes the host and, holding it slightly raised above the paten or above the chalice says aloud:

Pr. Ecce Agnus Dei, ecce qui tollit peccáta mundi.
      Beáti qui ad cenam Agni vocáti sunt.

R. **Dómine, non sum dignus, ut intres sub tectum meum,**
      sed tantum dic verbo, et sanábitur ánima mea.

While the Priest is receiving the Body of Christ, the Communion Chant begins.

COMMUNION PROCESSION

After the priest has reverently consumed the Body and Blood of Christ he takes the paten or ciborium and approaches the communicants.

The Priest raises the host slightly and shows it to each of the communicants, saying:

Pr. Corpus Christi.

R. **Amen.**

Lamb of God, you take away the sins of the world, have mercy on us.
Lamb of God, you take away the sins of the world, have mercy on us.
Lamb of God, you take away the sins of the world, grant us peace.

Then the Priest, with hands joined, says quietly:

Lord Jesus Christ, Son of the living God,
who, by the will of the Father
and the work of the Holy Spirit,
through your Death gave life to the world,
free me by this, your most holy Body and Blood,
from all my sins and from every evil;
keep me always faithful to your commandments,
and never let me be parted from you.

Or:

May the receiving of your Body and Blood,
Lord Jesus Christ,
not bring me to judgement and condemnation,
but through your loving mercy
be for me protection in mind and body
and a healing remedy.

INVITATION TO COMMUNION

All kneel. The Priest genuflects, takes the host and, holding it slightly raised above the paten or above the chalice says aloud:

Pr. Behold the Lamb of God,
    behold him who takes away the sins of the world.
    Blessed are those called to the supper of the Lamb.

R. **Lord, I am not worthy**
   that you should enter under my roof,
   but only say the word
   and my soul shall be healed.

While the Priest is receiving the Body of Christ, the Communion Chant begins.

COMMUNION PROCESSION

After the priest has reverently consumed the Body and Blood of Christ he takes the paten or ciborium and approaches the communicants.

The Priest raises the host slightly and shows it to each of the communicants, saying:

Pr. The Body of Christ.
R. **Amen.**

When Communion is ministered from the chalice:

Pr. Sanguis Christi.

R. Amen.

After the distribution of Communion, if appropriate, a sacred silence may be observed for a while, or a psalm or other canticle of praise or a hymn may be sung.

PRAYER AFTER COMMUNION

Then, the Priest says:

Pr. Orémus.

All stand and pray in silence for a while, unless silence has just been observed. Then the Priest says the Prayer after Communion, at the end of which the people acclaim:

R. Amen.

THE CONCLUDING RITES

The Mass closes, sending the people forth to put what they have celebrated into effect in their daily lives.

Any brief announcements follow here. Then the dismissal takes place.

Pr. Dóminus vóbiscum.

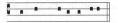

Et cum spí-ri-tu tu-o.

R. Et cum spíritu tuo.

The Priest blesses the people, saying:

Pr. Benedícat vos omnípotens Deus,
Pater, et Fílius, ✠ et Spíritus Sanctus.

A-men.

R. Amen.

When Communion is ministered from the chalice:

Pr. The Blood of Christ.

R. Amen.

After the distribution of Communion, if appropriate, a sacred silence may be observed for a while, or a psalm or other canticle of praise or a hymn may be sung.

PRAYER AFTER COMMUNION

Then, the Priest says:

Pr. Let us pray.

All stand and pray in silence for a while, unless silence has just been observed. Then the Priest says the Prayer after Communion, at the end of which the people acclaim:

R. Amen.

THE CONCLUDING RITES

The Mass closes, sending the people forth to put what they have celebrated into effect in their daily lives.

Any brief announcements follow here. Then the dismissal takes place.

Pr. The Lord be with you.

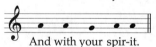

And with your spir-it.

R. And with your spirit.

The Priest blesses the people, saying:

Pr. May almighty God bless you,
    the Father, and the Son, ✠ and the Holy Spirit.

A-men.

R. Amen.

Then the Deacon, or the Priest himself says the Dismissal:

Pr. Ite, missa est.

Or:

Pr. Ite, ad Evangélium Dómini annuntiándum.

Or:

Pr. Ite in pace, glorificándo vita vestra Dóminum.

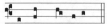

De- o grá- ti-as.

R. Deo grátias.

Or:

Pr. Ite in pace.

De- o grá- ti- as.

R. Deo grátias.

Then the Priest venerates the altar as at the beginning. After making a profound bow with the ministers, he withdraws.

Then the Deacon, or the Priest himself says the Dismissal:

Pr. Go forth, the Mass is ended.

Or:

Pr. Go and announce the Gospel of the Lord.

Or:

Pr. Go in peace, glorifying the Lord by your life.

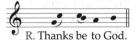

R. Thanks be to God.

R. **Thanks be to God.**

Or:

Pr. Go in peace.

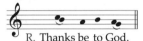

R. Thanks be to God.

R. **Thanks be to God.**

Then the Priest venerates the altar as at the beginning. After making a profound bow with the ministers, he withdraws.

SOLEMN BLESSINGS

The following blessings may be used, at the discretion of the Priest, at the end of the celebration of Mass, or of a Liturgy of the Word, or of the Office, or of the Sacraments.

The Deacon or, in his absence, the Priest himself, says the invitation: *Inclinate vos ad benedictionem.* Then the Priest, with hands extended over the people, says the blessing, with all responding: Amen.

I. For Celebrations in the Different Liturgical Times

1. In Adventu

Omnipotens et misericors Deus, cuius Unigeniti adventum
et præteritum creditis, et futurum exspectatis,
eiusdem adventus vos illustratione sanctificet
et sua benedictione locupletet.
R. Amen.

In præsentis vitæ stadio reddat vos in fide stabiles,
spe gaudentes, et in caritate efficaces.
R. Amen.

Ut, qui de adventu Redemptoris nostri
secundum carnem devota mente lætamini,
in secundo, cum in maiestate sua venerit,
præmiis æternæ vitæ ditemini.
R. Amen.

Et benedictio Dei omnipotentis,
Patris, et Filii, ✠ et Spiritus Sancti,
descendat super vos et maneat semper.
R. Amen.

2. In Nativitate Domini

Deus infinitæ bonitatis,
qui incarnatione Filii sui mundi tenebras effugavit,
et eius gloriosa nativitate
hanc noctem (diem) sacratissimam irradiavit,
effuget a vobis tenebras vitiorum,
et irradiet corda vestra luce virtutum.
R. Amen.

Quique eius salutiferæ nativitatis gaudium magnum
pastoribus ab Angelo voluit nuntiari,
ipse mentes vestras suo gaudio impleat,
et vos Evangelii sui nuntios efficiat.
R. Amen.

SOLEMN BLESSINGS

The following blessings may be used, at the discretion of the Priest, at the end of the celebration of Mass, or of a Liturgy of the Word, or of the Office, or of the Sacraments.

The Deacon or, in his absence, the Priest himself, says the invitation: Bow down for the blessing. Then the Priest, with hands extended over the people, says the blessing, with all responding: Amen.

I. For Celebrations in the Different Liturgical Times

1. Advent

May the almighty and merciful God,
by whose grace you have placed your faith
in the First Coming of his Only Begotten Son
and yearn for his coming again,
sanctify you by the radiance of Christ's Advent
and enrich you with his blessing.
R. Amen.

As you run the race of this present life,
may he make you firm in faith,
joyful in hope and active in charity.
R. Amen.

So that, rejoicing now with devotion
at the Redeemer's coming in the flesh,
you may be endowed with the rich reward of eternal life
when he comes again in majesty.
R. Amen.

And may the blessing of almighty God,
the Father, and the Son, ✠ and the Holy Spirit,
come down on you and remain with you for ever.
R. Amen.

2. The Nativity of the Lord

May the God of infinite goodness,
who by the Incarnation of his Son has driven darkness from the world
and by that glorious Birth has illumined this most holy night (day),
drive far from you the darkness of vice
and illumine your hearts with the light of virtue.
R. Amen.

May God, who willed that the great joy
of his Son's saving Birth
be announced to shepherds by the Angel,
fill your minds with the gladness he gives
and make you heralds of his Gospel.
R. Amen.

Et, qui per eius incarnationem terrena cælestibus sociavit,
dono vos suæ pacis et bonæ repleat voluntatis,
et vos faciat Ecclesiæ consortes esse cælestis.
R. Amen.

Et benedictio Dei omnipotentis,
Patris, et Filii, ✠ et Spiritus Sancti,
descendat super vos et maneat semper.
R. Amen.

3. Initio anni

Deus, fons et origo totius benedictionis,
gratiam vobis concedat,
benedictionis suæ largitatem infundat,
atque per totum annum vos salvos et incolumes protegat.
R. Amen.

Custodiat fidei vobis integritatem,
tribuat spei longanimitatem,
perseverantem usque ad finem
cum sancta patientia caritatem.
R. Amen.

Dies et actus vestros in sua pace disponat,
preces hic et ubique exaudiat,
et ad vitam æternam feliciter vos perducat.
R. Amen.

Et benedictio Dei omnipotentis,
Patris, et Filii, ✠ et Spiritus Sancti,
descendat super vos et maneat semper.
R. Amen.

4. In Epiphania Domini

Deus, qui vos de tenebris vocavit in admirabile lumen suum,
suam vobis benedictionem benignus infundat,
et corda vestra fide, spe et caritate stabiliat.
R. Amen.

Et quia Christum sequimini confidenter,
qui hodie mundo apparuit lux relucens in tenebris,
faciat et vos lucem esse fratribus vestris.
R. Amen.

And may God, who by the Incarnation
brought together the earthly and heavenly realm,
fill you with the gift of his peace and favour
and make you sharers with the Church in heaven.
R. Amen.

And may the blessing of almighty God,
the Father, and the Son, ✠ and the Holy Spirit,
come down on you and remain with you for ever.
R. Amen.

3. The Beginning of the Year

May God, the source and origin of all blessing,
grant you grace,
pour out his blessing in abundance,
and keep you safe from harm throughout the year.
R. Amen.

May he give you integrity in the faith,
endurance in hope,
and perseverance in charity
with holy patience to the end.
R. Amen.

May he order your days and your deeds in his peace,
grant your prayers in this and in every place,
and lead you happily to eternal life.
R. Amen.

And may the blessing of almighty God,
the Father, and the Son, ✠ and the Holy Spirit,
come down on you and remain with you for ever.
R. Amen.

4. The Epiphany of the Lord

May God, who has called you
out of darkness into his wonderful light,
pour out in kindness his blessing upon you
and make your hearts firm
in faith, hope and charity.
R. Amen.

And since in all confidence you follow Christ,
who today appeared in the world
as a light shining in darkness,
may God make you, too,
a light for your brothers and sisters.
R. Amen.

Quatenus, peregrinatione peracta,
perveniatis ad eum, quem magi stella prævia quæsierunt,
et gaudio magno, lucem de luce,
Christum Dominum invenerunt.
R. Amen.

Et benedictio Dei omnipotentis,
Patris, et Filii, ✠ et Spiritus Sancti,
descendat super vos et maneat semper.
R. Amen.

5. De Passione Domini

Deus, Pater misericordiarum, qui Unigeniti sui passione
tribuit vobis caritatis exemplum,
præstet ut, per servitium Dei et hominum,
percipiatis suæ benedictionis ineffabile donum.
R. Amen.

Ut ab eo sempiternæ vitæ munus obtineatis,
per cuius temporalem mortem, æternam vos evadere creditis.
R. Amen.

Quatenus, cuius humilitatis sequimini documenta,
eius resurrectionis possideatis consortia.
R. Amen.

Et benedictio Dei omnipotentis,
Patris, et Filii, ✠ et Spiritus Sancti,
descendat super vos et maneat semper.
R. Amen.

6. Tempore paschali

Deus, qui per resurrectionem Unigeniti sui
dignatus est vobis bonum redemptionis
adoptionisque conferre,
sua benedictione vos tribuat congaudere.
R. Amen.

And so when your pilgrimage is ended,
may you come to him
whom the Magi sought as they followed the star
and whom they found with great joy, the Light from Light,
who is Christ the Lord.
R. Amen.

And may the blessing of almighty God,
the Father, and the Son, ✠ and the Holy Spirit,
come down on you and remain with you for ever.
R. Amen.

5. The Passion of the Lord

May God, the Father of mercies,
who has given you an example of love
in the Passion of his Only Begotten Son,
grant that, by serving God and your neighbour,
you may lay hold of the wondrous gift of his blessing.
R. Amen.

So that you may receive the reward of everlasting life from him,
through whose earthly Death
you believe that you escape eternal death.
R. Amen.

And by following the example of his self-abasement,
may you possess a share in his Resurrection.
R. Amen.

And may the blessing of almighty God,
the Father, and the Son, ✠ and the Holy Spirit,
come down on you and remain with you for ever.
R. Amen.

6. Easter Time

May God, who by the Resurrection of his Only Begotten Son
was pleased to confer on you
the gift of redemption and of adoption,
give you gladness by his blessing.
R. Amen.

Et quo redimente percepistis donum perpetuæ libertatis,
eo largiente hereditatis æternæ consortes effici valeatis.
R. Amen.

Et cui resurrexistis in baptismate iam credendo,
adiungi mereamini in patria cælesti nunc recte vivendo.
R. Amen.

Et benedictio Dei omnipotentis,
Patris, et Filii, ✠ et Spiritus Sancti,
descendat super vos et maneat semper.
R. Amen.

7. In Ascensione Domini
Benedicat vos omnipotens Deus,
cuius Unigenitus hodierna die cælorum alta penetravit,
et vobis, ubi est ipse, ascendendi aditum reservavit.
R. Amen.

Concedat ut, sicut Christus post resurrectionem suam
visus est discipulis manifestus,
ita vobis in iudicium veniens
appareat pro æternitate placatus.
R. Amen.

Et qui eum consedere Patri in sua creditis maiestate,
ipsum usque in finem sæculi vobiscum permanere
secundum eius promissionem læti valeatis experire.
R. Amen.

Et benedictio Dei omnipotentis,
Patris, et Filii, ✠ et Spiritus Sancti,
descendat super vos et maneat semper.
R. Amen.

8. De Spiritu Sancto
Deus, Pater luminum, qui discipulorum mentes
Spiritus Paracliti infusione dignatus est illustrare,
sua vos faciat benedictione gaudere,
et perpetuo donis eiusdem Spiritus abundare.
R. Amen.

May he, by whose redeeming work
you have received the gift of everlasting freedom,
make you heirs to an eternal inheritance.
R. Amen.

And may you, who have already risen with Christ
in Baptism through faith,
by living in a right manner on this earth,
be united with him in the homeland of heaven.
R. Amen.

And may the blessing of almighty God,
the Father, and the Son, ✠ and the Holy Spirit,
come down on you and remain with you for ever.
R. Amen.

7. The Ascension of the Lord

May almighty God bless you,
for on this very day his Only Begotten Son
pierced the heights of heaven
and unlocked for you the way
to ascend to where he is.
R. Amen.

May he grant that,
as Christ after his Resurrection
was seen plainly by his disciples,
so when he comes as Judge
he may show himself merciful to you for all eternity.
R. Amen.

And may you, who believe he is seated
with the Father in his majesty,
know with joy the fulfilment of his promise
to stay with you until the end of time.
R. Amen.

And may the blessing of almighty God,
the Father, and the Son, ✠ and the Holy Spirit,
come down on you and remain with you for ever.
R. Amen.

8. The Holy Spirit

May God, the Father of lights,
who was pleased to enlighten the disciples' minds
by the outpouring of the Spirit, the Paraclete,
grant you gladness by his blessing
and make you always abound with the gifts of the same Spirit.
R. Amen.

Ignis ille, qui super discipulos mirandus apparuit,
corda vestra ab omni malo potenter expurget,
et sui luminis infusione perlustret.
R. Amen.

Quique dignatus est in unius fidei confessione
diversitatem adunare linguarum,
in eadem fide perseverare vos faciat,
et per illam a spe ad speciem pervenire concedat.
R. Amen.

Et benedictio Dei omnipotentis,
Patris, et Filii, ✠ et Spiritus Sancti,
descendat super vos et maneat semper.
R. Amen.

9. Per annum, I
Benedicat vobis Dominus, et custodiat vos.
R. Amen.

Illuminet faciem suam super vos, et misereatur vestri.
R. Amen.

Convertat vultum suum ad vos, et donet vobis suam pacem.
R. Amen.

Et benedictio Dei omnipotentis,
Patris, et Filii, ✠ et Spiritus Sancti,
descendat super vos et maneat semper.
R. Amen.

10. Per annum, II
Pax Dei, quæ exsuperat omnem sensum,
custodiat corda vestra et intellegentias vestras
in scientia et caritate Dei,
et Filii sui, Domini nostri Iesu Christi.
R. Amen.

Et benedictio Dei omnipotentis,
Patris, et Filii, ✠ et Spiritus Sancti,
descendat super vos et maneat semper.
R. Amen.

11. Per annum, III
Omnipotens Deus sua vos clementia benedicat,
et sensum in vobis sapientiæ salutaris infundat.
R. Amen.

May the wondrous flame that appeared above the disciples,
powerfully cleanse your hearts from every evil
and pervade them with its purifying light.
R. Amen.

And may God, who has been pleased to unite many tongues
in the profession of one faith,
give you perseverance in that same faith
and, by believing, may you journey from hope to clear vision.
R. Amen.

And may the blessing of almighty God,
the Father, and the Son, ✠ and the Holy Spirit,
come down on you and remain with you for ever.
R. Amen.

9. Ordinary Time I

May the Lord bless you and keep you.
R. Amen.

May he let his face shine upon you
and show you his mercy.
R. Amen.

May he turn his countenance towards you
and give you his peace.
R. Amen.

And may the blessing of almighty God,
the Father, and the Son, ✠ and the Holy Spirit,
come down on you and remain with you for ever.
R. Amen.

10. Ordinary Time II

May the peace of God,
which surpasses all understanding,
keep your hearts and minds
in the knowledge and love of God,
and of his Son, our Lord Jesus Christ.
R. Amen.

And may the blessing of almighty God,
the Father, and the Son, ✠ and the Holy Spirit,
come down on you and remain with you for ever.
R. Amen.

11. Ordinary Time III

May almighty God bless you in his kindness
and pour out saving wisdom upon you.
R. Amen.

Fidei documentis vos semper enutriat,
et in sanctis operibus, ut perseveretis, efficiat.
R. Amen.

Gressus vestros ad se convertat,
et viam vobis pacis et caritatis ostendat.
R. Amen.

Et benedictio Dei omnipotentis,
Patris, et Filii, ✠ et Spiritus Sancti,
descendat super vos et maneat semper.
R. Amen.

12. Per annum, IV
Deus totius consolationis dies vestros in sua pace disponat,
et suæ vobis benedictionis dona concedat.
R. Amen.

Ab omni semper perturbatione vos liberet,
et corda vestra in suo amore confirmet.
R. Amen.

Quatenus donis spei, fidei et caritatis divites,
et præsentem vitam transigatis in opere efficaces,
et possitis ad æternam pervenire felices.
R. Amen.

Et benedictio Dei omnipotentis,
Patris, et Filii, ✠ et Spiritus Sancti,
descendat super vos et maneat semper.
R. Amen.

13. Per annum, V
Omnipotens Deus universa a vobis adversa semper excludat,
et suæ super vos benedictionis dona propitiatus infundat.
R. Amen.

Corda vestra efficiat divinis intenta eloquiis,
ut repleri possint gaudiis sempiternis.
R. Amen.

Quatenus, quæ bona et recta intellegentes,
viam mandatorum Dei inveniamini semper currentes,
et civium supernorum efficiamini coheredes.
R. Amen.

Et benedictio Dei omnipotentis,
Patris, et Filii, ✠ et Spiritus Sancti,
descendat super vos et maneat semper.
R. Amen.

May he nourish you always with the teachings of the faith
and make you persevere in holy deeds.
R. Amen.

May he turn your steps towards himself
and show you the path of charity and peace.
R. Amen.

And may the blessing of almighty God,
the Father, and the Son, ✠ and the Holy Spirit,
come down on you and remain with you for ever.
R. Amen.

12. Ordinary Time IV

May the God of all consolation order your days in his peace
and grant you the gifts of his blessing.
R. Amen.

May he free you always from every distress
and confirm your hearts in his love.
R. Amen.

So that on this life's journey
you may be effective in good works,
rich in the gifts of hope, faith and charity,
and may come happily to eternal life.
R. Amen.

And may the blessing of almighty God,
the Father, and the Son, ✠ and the Holy Spirit,
come down on you and remain with you for ever.
R. Amen.

13. Ordinary Time V

May almighty God always keep every adversity far from you
and in his kindness pour out upon you the gifts of his blessing.
R. Amen.

May God keep your hearts attentive to his words,
that they may be filled with everlasting gladness.
R. Amen.

And so, may you always understand what is good and right,
and be found ever hastening along
in the path of God's commands,
made coheirs with the citizens of heaven.
R. Amen.

And may the blessing of almighty God,
the Father, and the Son, ✠ and the Holy Spirit,
come down on you and remain with you for ever.
R. Amen.

14. Per annum, VI

Benedicat vos Deus omni benedictione cælesti,
sanctosque vos et puros
in conspectu suo semper efficiat;
divitias gloriæ suæ in vos abundanter effundat,
verbis veritatis instruat, Evangelio salutis erudiat,
et caritate fraterna semper locupletet.
Per Christum Dominum nostrum.
R. Amen.

Et benedictio Dei omnipotentis,
Patris, et Filii, ✠ et Spiritus Sancti,
descendat super vos et maneat semper.
R. Amen.

II. For Celebrations of the Saints

15. De beata Maria Virgine

Deus, qui per beatæ Mariæ Virginis partum
genus humanum sua voluit benignitate redimere,
sua vos dignetur benedictione ditare.
R. Amen.

Eiusque semper et ubique patrocinia sentiatis,
per quam auctorem vitæ suscipere meruistis.
R. Amen.

Et qui hodierna die devotis mentibus convenistis,
spiritalium gaudiorum cælestiumque præmiorum
vobiscum munera reportetis.
R. Amen.

Et benedictio Dei omnipotentis,
Patris, et Filii, ✠ et Spiritus Sancti,
descendat super vos et maneat semper.
R. Amen.

16. De sanctis Petro et Paulo

Benedicat vos omnipotens Deus,
qui in beati Petri confessione vos saluberrima stabilivit,
et per eam in Ecclesiæ soliditate fidei fundavit.
R. Amen.

Et quos beati Pauli instruxit indefessa prædicatione,
suo semper exemplo doceat Christo fratres lucrifacere.
R. Amen.

14. Ordinary Time VI

May God bless you with every heavenly blessing,
make you always holy and pure in his sight,
pour out in abundance upon you the riches of his glory,
and teach you with the words of truth;
may he instruct you in the Gospel of salvation,
and ever endow you with fraternal charity.
Through Christ our Lord.
R. Amen.

And may the blessing of almighty God,
the Father, and the Son, ✠ and the Holy Spirit,
come down on you and remain with you for ever.
R. Amen.

II. For Celebrations of the Saints

15. The Blessed Virgin Mary

May God, who through the childbearing of the Blessed Virgin Mary
willed in his great kindness to redeem the human race,
be pleased to enrich you with his blessing.
R. Amen.

May you know always and everywhere
the protection of her,
through whom you have been found worthy to receive
the author of life.
R. Amen.

May you, who have devoutly gathered on this day,
carry away with you the gifts of spiritual joys and heavenly rewards.
R. Amen.

And may the blessing of almighty God,
the Father, and the Son, ✠ and the Holy Spirit,
come down on you and remain with you for ever.
R. Amen.

16. Saints Peter and Paul, Apostles

May almighty God bless you,
for he has made you steadfast in Saint Peter's saving confession
and through it has set you on the solid rock of the Church's faith.
R. Amen.

And having instructed you
by the tireless preaching of Saint Paul,
may God teach you constantly by his example
to win brothers and sisters for Christ.
R. Amen.

Ut Petrus clave, Paulus verbo,
ope intercessionis uterque
in illam patriam nos certent inducere,
ad quam meruerunt illi, alter cruce, alter gladio,
feliciter pervenire.
R. Amen.

Et benedictio Dei omnipotentis,
Patris, et Filii, ✠ et Spiritus Sancti,
descendat super vos et maneat semper.
R. Amen.

17. De Apostolis

Deus, qui vos in apostolicis tribuit consistere fundamentis,
benedicere vobis dignetur
beatorum Apostolorum N. et N. (beati Apostoli N.)
meritis intercedentibus gloriosis.
R. Amen.

Et apostolicis præsidiis vos pro cunctis faciat testes veritatis,
qui vos eorum munerari documentis voluit et exemplis.
R. Amen.

Ut eorum intercessione
ad æternæ patriæ hereditatem pervenire possitis,
per quorum doctrinam fidei firmitatem possidetis.
R. Amen.

Et benedictio Dei omnipotentis,
Patris, et Filii, ✠ et Spiritus Sancti,
descendat super vos et maneat semper.
R. Amen.

18. De omnibus Sanctis

Deus, gloria et exsultatio Sanctorum,
benedicat vos benedictione perpetua,
qui vobis tribuit eximiis suffragiis roborari.
R. Amen.

Eorum intercessione a præsentibus malis liberati,
et exemplis sanctæ conversationis instructi,
in servitio Dei fratrumque inveniamini semper intenti.
R. Amen.

So that by the keys of St Peter and the words of St Paul,
and by the support of their intercession,
God may bring us happily to that homeland
that Peter attained on a cross
and Paul by the blade of a sword.
R. Amen.

And may the blessing of almighty God,
the Father, and the Son, ✠ and the Holy Spirit,
come down on you and remain with you for ever.
R. Amen.

17. The Apostles

May God, who has granted you
to stand firm on apostolic foundations,
graciously bless you through the glorious merits
of the holy Apostles N. and N. (the holy Apostle N.).
R. Amen.

And may he, who endowed you
with the teaching and example of the Apostles,
make you, under their protection,
witnesses to the truth before all.
R. Amen.

So that through the intercession of the Apostles,
you may inherit the eternal homeland,
for by their teaching you possess firmness of faith.
R. Amen.

And may the blessing of almighty God,
the Father, and the Son, ✠ and the Holy Spirit,
come down on you and remain with you for ever.
R. Amen.

18. All Saints

May God, the glory and joy of the Saints,
who has caused you to be strengthened
by means of their outstanding prayers,
bless you with unending blessings.
R. Amen.

Freed through their intercession from present ills
and formed by the example of their holy way of life,
may you be ever devoted
to serving God and your neighbour.
R. Amen.

Quatenus cum iis omnibus
valeatis illius patriæ vos gaudia possidere,
in qua filios suos supernis coniungi civibus
in pace perpetua sancta lætatur Ecclesia.
R. Amen.

Et benedictio Dei omnipotentis,
Patris, et Filii, ✠ et Spiritus Sancti,
descendat super vos et maneat semper.
R. Amen.

III. Other Blessings

19. In dedicatione ecclesiæ

Deus, Dominus cæli et terræ,
qui vos hodie ad huius domus dedicationem adunavit,
ipse vos cælesti benedictione faciat abundare.
R. Amen.

Concedatque vobis fieri templum suum
et habitaculum Spiritus Sancti,
qui omnes filios dispersos voluit in Filio suo congregari.
R. Amen.

Quatenus feliciter emundati,
habitatorem Deum in vobismetipsis possitis habere,
et æternæ beatitudinis hereditatem
cum omnibus Sanctis possidere.
R. Amen.

Et benedictio Dei omnipotentis,
Patris, et Filii, ✠ et Spiritus Sancti,
descendat super vos et maneat semper.
R. Amen.

20. In celebrationibus pro defunctis

Benedicat vos Deus totius consolationis,
qui hominem ineffabili bonitate creavit,
et in resurrectione Unigeniti sui
spem credentibus resurgendi concessit.
R. Amen.

Nobis, qui vivimus, veniam tribuat pro peccatis,
et omnibus defunctis locum concedat lucis et pacis.
R. Amen.

So that, together with all,
you may possess the joys of the homeland,
where Holy Church rejoices
that her children are admitted in perpetual peace
to the company of the citizens of heaven.
R. Amen.

And may the blessing of almighty God,
the Father, and the Son, ✠ and the Holy Spirit,
come down on you and remain with you for ever.
R. Amen.

III. Other Blessings

19. For the Dedication of a Church

May God, the Lord of heaven and earth,
who has gathered you today for the dedication of this church,
make you abound in heavenly blessings.
R. Amen.

And may he, who has willed that all his scattered children
should be gathered together in his Son,
grant that you may become his temple
and the dwelling place of the Holy Spirit.
R. Amen.

And so, when you are thoroughly cleansed,
may God dwell within you
and grant you to possess with all the Saints
the inheritance of eternal happiness.
R. Amen.

And may the blessing of almighty God,
the Father, and the Son, ✠ and the Holy Spirit,
come down on you and remain with you for ever.
R. Amen.

20. In Celebrations for the Dead

May the God of all consolation bless you,
for in his unfathomable goodness he created the human race,
and in the Resurrection of his Only Begotten Son
he has given believers the hope of rising again.
R. Amen.

To us who are alive, may God grant pardon for our sins,
and to all the dead, a place of light and peace.
R. Amen.

Ut omnes cum Christo sine fine feliciter vivamus,
quem resurrexisse a mortuis veraciter credimus.
R. Amen.
Et benedictio Dei omnipotentis,
Patris, et Filii, ✠ et Spiritus Sancti,
descendat super vos et maneat semper.
R. Amen.

PRAYERS OVER THE PEOPLE

The following prayers may be used, at the discretion of the Priest, at the end of the
celebration of Mass, or of a Liturgy of the Word, or of the Office, or of the Sacraments.

The Deacon or, in his absence, the Priest himself, says the invitation: Bow down
for the blessing. Then the Priest, with hands outstretched over the people, says the
prayer, with all responding: **Amen**.

After the prayer, the Priest always adds: **And may the blessing of almighty God, the
Father, and the Son, ✠ and the Holy Spirit, come down on you and remain with you
for ever. R. Amen.**

1. Esto, Domine, propitius plebi tuæ,
   et temporali consolatione non deseras,
   quam vis ad æterna contendere.
   Per Christum Dominum nostrum.

2. Da, quæsumus, Domine, populis christianis,
   et quæ profitentur agnoscere,
   et cæleste munus diligere, quod frequentant.
   Per Christum Dominum nostrum.

3. Plebs tua, Domine, quæsumus,
   benedictionis sanctæ munus accipiat,
   per quod et noxia quæque declinet,
   et optata reperiat.
   Per Christum Dominum nostrum.

4. Populum tuum, Domine, quæsumus,
   ad te toto corde converte,
   quia, quos defendis etiam delinquentes,
   maiore pietate tueris sincera mente devotos.
   Per Christum Dominum nostrum.

So may we all live happily for ever with Christ,
whom we believe truly rose from the dead.
R. Amen.

And may the blessing of almighty God,
the Father, and the Son, ✠ and the Holy Spirit,
come down on you and remain with you for ever.
R. Amen.

PRAYERS OVER THE PEOPLE

The following prayers may be used, at the discretion of the Priest, at the end of the
celebration of Mass, or of a Liturgy of the Word, or of the Office, or of the Sacraments.

The Deacon or, in his absence, the Priest himself, says the invitation: Bow down
for the blessing. Then the Priest, with hands outstretched over the people, says the
prayer, with all responding: Amen.

After the prayer, the Priest always adds: And may the blessing of almighty God, the
Father, and the Son, ✠ and the Holy Spirit, come down on you and remain with you
for ever. R. Amen.

1. Be gracious to your people, O Lord,
    and do not withhold consolation on earth
    from those you call to strive for heaven.
    Through Christ our Lord.

2. Grant, O Lord, we pray,
    that the Christian people
    may understand the truths they profess
    and love the heavenly liturgy
    in which they participate.
    Through Christ our Lord.

3. May your people receive your holy blessing,
    O Lord, we pray,
    and, by that gift,
    spurn all that would harm them
    and obtain what they desire.
    Through Christ our Lord.

4. Turn your people to you with all their heart,
    O Lord, we pray,
    for you protect even those who go astray,
    but when they serve you with undivided heart,
    you sustain them with still greater care.
    Through Christ our Lord.

5. Familiam tuam, quæsumus, Domine, propitiatus illustra,
   ut, beneplacitis inhærendo,
   cuncta quæ bona sunt mereatur exercere.
   Per Christum Dominum nostrum.

6. Largire, quæsumus, Domine,
   fidelibus tuis indulgentiam placatus et pacem,
   ut pariter ab omnibus mundentur offensis,
   et secura tibi mente deserviant.
   Per Christum Dominum nostrum.

7. Subiectum tibi populum, quæsumus, Domine,
   propitiatio cælestis amplificet,
   et tuis semper faciat servire mandatis.
   Per Christum Dominum nostrum.

8. Propitiare populo tuo,
   Deus, ut, ab omni malo liberatus,
   et toto tibi corde deserviat,
   et sub tua semper protectione consistat.
   Per Christum Dominum nostrum.

9. Familia tua, Deus,
   et de celebratis mysteriis
   suæ redemptionis iugiter collætetur,
   et eius dona perseveranter acquirat.
   Per Christum Dominum nostrum.

10. Domine Deus, de abundantia misericordiarum tuarum
    famulos præsta locupletes, præsta securos,
    ut, confirmati benedictionibus tuis,
    in omni gratiarum actione semper abundent,
    teque perpetua exsultatione benedicant.
    Per Christum Dominum nostrum.

11. Familiam tuam, quæsumus, Domine,
    continua pietate custodi,
    ut a cunctis adversitatibus,
    te protegente, sit libera,
    et in bonis actibus tuo nomini sit devota.
    Per Christum Dominum nostrum.

12. Fideles tuos, quæsumus, Domine,
    corpore pariter et mente purifica,

5. Graciously enlighten your family, O Lord, we pray,
   that by holding fast to what is pleasing to you,
   they may be worthy to accomplish all that is good.
   Through Christ our Lord.

6. Bestow pardon and peace, O Lord, we pray,
   upon your faithful,
   that they may be cleansed from every offence
   and serve you with untroubled hearts.
   Through Christ our Lord.

7. May your heavenly favour, O Lord, we pray,
   increase in number the people subject to you
   and make them always obedient to your commands.
   Through Christ our Lord.

8. Be propitious to your people, O God,
   that, freed from every evil,
   they may serve you with all their heart
   and ever stand firm under your protection.
   Through Christ our Lord.

9. May your family always rejoice together, O God,
   over the mysteries of redemption they have celebrated,
   and grant its members the perseverance
   to attain the effects that flow from them.
   Through Christ our Lord.

10. Lord God, from the abundance of your mercies
    provide for your servants and ensure their safety,
    so that, strengthened by your blessings,
    they may at all times abound in thanksgiving
    and bless you with unending exultation.
    Through Christ our Lord.

11. Keep your family, we pray, O Lord,
    in your constant care,
    so that, under your protection,
    they may be free from all troubles
    and by good works show dedication to your name.
    Through Christ our Lord.

12. Purify your faithful, both in body and in mind,
    O Lord, we pray,

ut, tua inspiratione compuncti,
noxias delectationes vitare prævaleant,
atque tua semper suavitate pascantur.
Per Christum Dominum nostrum.

13. Adsit, Domine,
fidelibus tuis sacræ benedictionis effectus,
qui mentes omnium spiritali vegetatione disponat,
ut ad opera sua exercenda
virtute caritatis tuæ roborentur.
Per Christum Dominum nostrum.

14. Auxilium tuum, Domine,
nomine tuo subdita poscunt corda fidelium,
ut quia sine te nihil possunt
implere quod iustum est,
tua misericordia largiente,
et quæ recta sunt apprehendant
et omnia sibi profutura percipiant.
Per Christum Dominum nostrum.

15. Succurre, Domine, quæsumus, populo fideli deprecanti
et opem tribue benignus fragilitati humanæ,
ut sincera tibi mente devotus
et præsentis vitæ remediis gaudeat et futuræ.
Per Christum Dominum nostrum.

16. Respice, Domine, propitius familiam tuam
et perpetuam largire misericordiam supplicanti;
ut sine qua nihil potest tui dignum prorsus efficere,
per eam salutaria tua præcepta mereatur implere.
Per Christum Dominum nostrum.

17. Gratiam cælestem, Domine, super fideles tuos multiplica:
quorum laudent te ora, laudet anima, laudet et vita,
et quia tui muneris est quod sumus,
tuum sit omne quod vivemus.
Per Christum Dominum nostrum.

so that, feeling the compunction you inspire,
they may be able to avoid harmful pleasures
and ever feed upon your delights.
Through Christ our Lord.

13. May the effects of your sacred blessing, O Lord,
make themselves felt among your faithful,
to prepare with spiritual sustenance the minds of all,
that they may be strengthened by the power of your love
to carry out works of charity.
Through Christ our Lord.

14. The hearts of your faithful submitted to your name,
entreat your help, O Lord,
and since without you they can do nothing that is just,
grant by your abundant mercy
that they may both know what is right
and receive all that they need for their good.
Through Christ our Lord.

15. Hasten to the aid of your faithful people
who call upon you, O Lord, we pray,
and graciously give strength in their human weakness,
so that, being dedicated to you in complete sincerity,
they may find gladness in your remedies
both now and in the life to come.
Through Christ our Lord.

16. Look with favour on your family, O Lord,
and bestow your endless mercy on those who seek it:
and just as without your mercy,
they can do nothing truly worthy of you,
so through it,
may they merit to obey your saving commands.
Through Christ our Lord.

17. Bestow increase of heavenly grace
on your faithful, O Lord;
may they praise you with their lips,
with their souls, with their lives;
and since it is by your gift that we exist,
may our whole lives be yours.
Through Christ our Lord.

18. Populum tuum, Domine, quæsumus,
    cælestibus instrue disciplinis,
    ut, omnia vitando quæ mala sunt
    et bona cuncta sectando,
    non indignationem tuam,
    sed iugiter misericordiam consequatur.
    Per Christum Dominum nostrum.

19. Adesto, Domine, supplicibus tuis,
    et spem suam in tua misericordia collocantes
    tuere propitius,
    ut in sancta conversatione fideles permaneant
    et, consequentes sufficientiam temporalem,
    promissionis tuæ perficiantur heredes in æternum.
    Per Christum Dominum nostrum.

20. Tuæ largire pietatis gratiam, Domine,
    populo tuo supplicanti
    ut qui te factore conditus,
    te est reparatus auctore,
    te iugiter operante salvetur.
    Per Christum Dominum nostrum.

21. Proficiat, quæsumus, Domine,
    fidelibus populus tuæ pietatis instinctu
    et, salubri compunctione motus,
    gratanter quæ præcipis exsequatur,
    ut quæ promittis accipiat.
    Per Christum Dominum nostrum.

22. Moveat pietatem tuam, quæsumus, Domine,
    fragilitas plebis tibi devotæ
    et misericordiam tuam supplicatio fidelis obtineat,
    ut quod meritis non præsumit,
    indulgentiæ tuæ largitate percipiat.
    Per Christum Dominum nostrum.

23. Ad defensionem filiorum, Domine, quæsumus,
    dexteram tuæ maiestatis extende
    et paternæ voluntati obœdientes
    perpetua pietatis tuæ protectione muniantur.
    Per Christum Dominum nostrum.

18. Direct your people, O Lord, we pray,
    with heavenly instruction,
    that by avoiding every evil
    and pursuing all that is good,
    they may earn not your anger
    but your unending mercy.
    Through Christ our Lord.

19. Be near to those who call on you, O Lord,
    and graciously grant your protection
    to all who place their hope in your mercy,
    that they may remain faithful in holiness of life
    and, having enough for their needs in this world,
    they may be made full heirs of your promise for eternity.
    Through Christ our Lord.

20. Bestow the grace of your kindness
    upon your supplicant people, O Lord,
    that, formed by you, their creator,
    and restored by you, their sustainer,
    through your constant action they may be saved.
    Through Christ our Lord.

21. May your faithful people, O Lord, we pray,
    always respond to the promptings of your love
    and, moved by wholesome compunction,
    may they do gladly what you command,
    so as to receive the things you promise.
    Through Christ our Lord.

22. May the weakness of your devoted people
    stir your compassion, O Lord, we pray,
    and let their faithful pleading win your mercy,
    that what they do not presume upon by their merits
    they may receive by your generous pardon.
    Through Christ our Lord.

23. In defence of your children, O Lord, we pray,
    stretch forth the right hand of your majesty,
    so that, obeying your fatherly will,
    they may have the unfailing protection
    of your fatherly care.
    Through Christ our Lord.

24. Respice, Domine, familiæ tuæ preces
et opem tribue suppliciter imploranti,
ut congruis subsidiis roboratus
in confessione tui nominis perseveret.
Per Christum Dominum nostrum.

25. Conserva, Domine, quæsumus, familiam tuam
et misericordiarum tuarum
propitius ubertatem concede,
ut cælestibus eruditionibus multiplicetur et donis.
Per Christum Dominum nostrum.

26. Lætetur, Domine, quæsumus,
populus fidelis dextera tua sublevatus
et christiana conversatione proficiens,
et præsentibus gaudeat bonis et futuris.
Per Christum Dominum nostrum.

On Feasts of Saints

27. Exsultet, Domine, populus christianus
de magnorum Filii tui glorificatione membrorum.
et in quorum est celebritate tibi devotus,
partem acquirat in eorum sorte perpetua,
atque de tua gloria semper congaudeat.
Per Christum Dominum nostrum.

28. Plebis tuæ, quæsumus, Domine,
ad te semper corda converte,
et quam tantis facis patrociniis adiuvari,
perpetuis non desinas gubernare præsidiis.
Per Christum Dominum nostrum.

24. Look, O Lord, on the prayers of your family,
    and grant them the assistance they humbly implore,
    so that, strengthened by the help they need,
    they may persevere in confessing your name.
    Through Christ our Lord.

25. Keep your family safe, O Lord, we pray,
    and grant them the abundance of your mercies,
    that they may find growth
    through the teachings and the gifts of heaven.
    Through Christ our Lord.

26. May your faithful people rejoice, we pray, O Lord,
    to be upheld up by your right hand,
    and, progressing in the Christian life,
    may they delight in good things
    both now and in the time to come.
    Through Christ our Lord.

On Feasts of Saints

27. May the Christian people exult, O Lord,
    at the glorification of the illustrious members
    of your Son's Body,
    and may they gain a share in the eternal lot
    of the Saints on whose feast day
    they reaffirm their devotion to you,
    rejoicing with them for ever in your glory.
    Through Christ our Lord.

28. Turn the hearts of your people
    always to you, O Lord, we pray,
    and, as you give them the help
    of such great patrons as these,
    grant also the unfailing help of your protection.
    Through Christ our Lord.

PRAYERS

Thanksgiving after Mass

THANKSGIVING AFTER MASS

Prayer of Saint Thomas Aquinas

I give you thanks,
Lord, holy Father,
    almighty and eternal God,
who have been pleased
    to nourish me,
a sinner and your
    unworthy servant,
with the precious Body and Blood
of your Son, our Lord Jesus Christ:
this through no merits of mine,
but due solely to
    the graciousness of your mercy.

And I pray that this
    Holy Communion
may not be for me an offence
    to be punished,
but a saving plea for forgiveness.
May it be for me the armour of faith,
and the shield of good will.
May it cancel my faults,
destroy concupiscence
    and carnal passion,
increase charity and patience,
    humility and obedience
and all the virtues,
may it be a firm defence against
    the snares of all my enemies,
both visible and invisible,
the complete calming of
    my impulses,
both of the flesh and of the spirit,
a firm adherence to you,
    the one true God,
and the joyful completion of my
    life's course.

Oratio S. Thomas Aquinatis

Gratias tibi ago, Domine,
sancte Pater,
    omnipotens æterne Deus,
qui me peccatorem,
    indignum famulum tuum,
nullis meis meritis, sed sola
    dignatione misericordiæ tuæ
satiare dignatus es pretioso Corpore
    et Sanguine Filii tui,
Domini nostri Iesu Christi.

Et precor,
    ut hæc sancta communio
non sit mihi reatus ad pœnam,
sed intercessio salutaris ad veniam.
Sit mihi armatura fidei,
    et scutum bonæ voluntatis.
Sit vitiorum meorum evacuatio,
concupiscentiæ
    et libidinis exterminatio,
caritatis et patientiæ,
    humilitatis et obœdientiæ,
omniumque virtutum
    augmentatio:
contra insidias
    inimicorum omnium
tam visibilium quam invisibilium,
    firma defensio:
motuum meorum, tam carnalium
    quam spiritalium,
perfecta quietatio:
in te uno ac vero Deo
    firma adhæsio,
atque finis mei felix consummatio.

And I beseech you to lead me,
    a sinner,
to that banquet beyond all telling,
where with your Son and the
    Holy Spirit
you are the true light of
    your Saints,
fullness of satisfied desire,
    eternal gladness,
consummate delight and
    perfect happiness.
Through Christ our Lord.
Amen.

Et precor te,
    ut ad illud ineffabile convivium
me peccatorem perducere digneris,
ubi tu, cum Filio tuo et
    Spiritu Sancto,
Sanctis tuis es lux vera,
    satietas plena,
gaudium sempiternum,
iucunditas consummata et
    felicitas perfecta.
Per Christum Dominum nostrum.
Amen.

Prayer to the Most Holy Redeemer

Aspirationes ad Ss.mum Redemptorem

Soul of Christ, sanctify me.
Body of Christ, save me.
Blood of Christ, embolden me.
Water from the side of Christ,
    wash me.
Passion of Christ, strengthen me.
O good Jesus, hear me.
Within your wounds hide me.
Never permit me to be parted
    from you.
From the evil Enemy defend me.
At the hour of my death call me
and bid me come to you,
that with your Saints
    I may praise you
for age upon age.
Amen.

Anima Christi, sanctifica me.
Corpus Christi, salva me.
Sanguis Christi, inebria me.
Aqua lateris Christi, lava me.

Passio Christi, conforta me.
O bone Iesu, exaudi me.
Intra tua vulnera absconde me.
Ne permittas me separari a te.

Ab hoste maligno defende me.
In hora mortis meæ voca me.
Et iube me venire ad te,
ut cum Sanctis tuis laudem te
in sæcula sæculorum.

Amen.

Prayer of Self-Offering

Oblatio sui

Receive, Lord, my entire freedom.
Accept the whole of my memory,
my intellect and my will.

Suscipe, Domine,
    universam meam libertatem.
Accipe memoriam, intellectum
    atque voluntatem omnem.

Whatever I have or possess,
it was you who gave it to me;
I restore it to you in full,
and I surrender it completely
to the guidance of your will.
Give me only love of you
together with your grace,
and I am rich enough
and ask for nothing more.
Amen.

Quidquid habeo vel possideo,
    mihi largitus es:
id tibi totum restituo,
ac tuæ prorsus voluntati
    trado gubernandum.
Amorem tui solum cum gratia tua
    mihi dones,
et dives sum satis, nec aliud
    quidquam ultra posco.
Amen.

Prayer to Our Lord Jesus Christ Crucified

Oratio ad Dominum nostrum Iesum Christum Crucifixum

Behold, O good and loving Jesus,
that I cast myself on my knees
    before you
and, with the greatest fervour
    of spirit,
I pray and beseech you to instill
    into my heart
ardent sentiments of faith,
    hope and charity,
with true repentance for my sins
and a most firm purpose
    of amendment.
With deep affection and sorrow
I ponder intimately
and contemplate in my mind
    your five wounds,
having before my eyes what
    the prophet David
had already put in your mouth
    about yourself, O good Jesus:
They have pierced my hands and
    my feet;
they have numbered all my bones
    (Ps 21:17-18).

En ego, o bone et dulcissime Iesu,
ante conspectum tuum genibus
    me provolvo,
ac maximo animi ardore te oro
    atque obtestor,
ut meum in cor vividos fidei,
    spei et caritatis sensus,
atque veram peccatorum
    meorum pœnitentiam,
eaque emendandi firmissimam
    voluntatem velis imprimere;

dum magno animi affectu et dolore
tua quinque vulnera mecum
    ipse considero
ac mente contemplor,
illud præ oculis habens,
quod iam in ore ponebat tuo David
    propheta de te, o bone Iesu:

Foderunt manus meas
    et pedes meos:
dinumeraverunt omnia ossa mea
    (Ps 21:17-18).

The Universal Prayer Attributed to Pope Clement XI

I believe, O Lord,
   but may I believe more firmly;
I hope,
   but may I hope more securely;
I love,
   but may I love more ardently;
I sorrow,
   but may I sorrow more deeply.

I adore you as my first beginning;
I long for you as my last end;
I praise you as my
   constant benefactor;
I invoke you as my
   gracious protector.

By your wisdom direct me,
by your righteousness restrain me,
by your indulgence console me,
by your power protect me.

I offer you, Lord, my thoughts to
   be directed to you,
my words, to be about you,
my deeds, to respect your will,
my trials, to be endured for you.

I will whatever you will,
I will it because you will it,
I will it in the way you will it,
I will it for as long as you will it.

Lord, enlighten my understanding,
   I pray:
arouse my will,
cleanse my heart,
sanctify my soul.

Oratio universalis sub nomine Clementis Pp. XI vulgata

Credo, Domine,
   sed credam firmius;
spero, sed sperem securius;
amo, sed amem ardentius;
doleo, sed doleam vehementius.

Adoro te ut primum principium;
desidero ut finem ultimum;
laudo ut benefactorem perpetuum;
invoco ut defensorem propitium.

Tua me sapientia dirige,
iustitia contine,
clementia solare,
potentia protege.

Offero tibi, Domine, cogitanda,
   ut sint ad te;
dicenda, ut sint de te;
facienda, ut sint secundum te;
ferenda, ut sint propter te.

Volo quidquid vis,
volo quia vis,
volo quomodo vis,
volo quamdiu vis.

Oro, Domine:
   intellectum illumines,
voluntatem inflammes,
cor emundes,
animam sanctifices.

May I weep for past sins,
repel future temptations,
correct evil inclinations,
nurture appropriate virtues.

Give me, good God,
love for you, hatred for myself,
zeal for my neighbour,
contempt for the world.

May I strive to obey superiors,
to help those dependent on me,
to have care for my friends,
forgiveness for my enemies.

May I conquer sensuality
    by austerity,
avarice by generosity,
anger by gentleness,
lukewarmness by fervour.

Render me prudent in planning,
steadfast in dangers,
patient in adversity,
humble in prosperity.

Make me, O Lord, attentive at prayer,
moderate at meals,
diligent in work,
steadfast in intent.

May I be careful to maintain
    interior innocence,
outward modesty,
exemplary behaviour,
a regular life.

May I be always watchful in
    subduing nature,
in nourishing grace,
in observing your law,
in winning salvation.

Defleam præteritas iniquitates,
repellam futuras tentationes,
corrigam vitiosas propensiones,
excolam idoneas virtutes.

Tribue mihi, bone Deus,
amorem tui, odium mei,
zelum proximi,
contemptum mundi.

Studeam superioribus obœdire,
inferioribus subvenire,
amicis consulere,
inimicis parcere.

Vincam voluptatem austeritate,
avaritiam largitate,
iracundiam lenitate,
tepiditatem fervore.

Redde me prudentem in consiliis,
constantem in periculis,
patientem in adversis,
humilem in prosperis.

Fac, Domine,
    ut sim in oratione attentus,
in epulis sobrius,
in munere sedulus,
in proposito firmus.

Curem habere innocentiam
    interiorem,
modestiam exteriorem,
conversationem exemplarem,
vitam regularem.

Assidue invigilem naturæ
    domandæ,
gratiæ fovendæ,
legi servandæ,
saluti promerendæ.

May I learn from you
how precarious are earthly things,
how great divine things,
how fleeting is time,
how lasting things eternal.

Grant that I may prepare for death,
fear judgement,
flee hell,
gain paradise.
Through Christ our Lord.
Amen.

Prayers to the Blessed Virgin Mary

O Mary, Virgin and
    Mother most holy,
behold, I have received your
    most dear Son,
whom you conceived in
    your immaculate womb,
brought forth, nursed and
    embraced most tenderly.
Behold him at whose sight
you used to rejoice and be filled
    with all delight;
him whom, humbly and lovingly,
once again I present
and offer him to you
to be clasped in your arms,
to be loved by your heart,
and to be offered up to
    the Most Holy Trinity
as the supreme worship of adoration,
for your own honour and glory
and for my needs and for those of
    the whole world.
I ask you therefore,
    most loving Mother:

Discam a te quam tenue quod
    terrenum,
quam grande quod divinum,
quam breve quod temporaneum,
quam durabile quod æternum.

Da, ut mortem præveniam,
iudicium pertimeam,
infernum effugiam,
paradisum obtineam.
Per Christum Dominum nostrum.
Amen.

Orationes ad B. Mariam Virginem

O Maria, Virgo
    et Mater sanctissima,
ecce suscepi dilectissimum
    Filium tuum,
quem immaculato utero
    tuo concepisti,
genuisti, lactasti atque suavissimis
    amplexibus strinxisti.
Ecce, cuius aspectu lætabaris
    et omnibus deliciis replebaris,
illum ipsum tibi humiliter
    et amanter repræsento et offero,

tuis bracchiis constringendum,
    tuo corde amandum,

sanctissimæque Trinitati in
    supremum latriæ cultum,
pro tui ipsius honore et gloria
et pro meis totiusque mundi
    necessitatibus, offerendum.
Rogo ergo te, piissima Mater,

entreat for me the forgiveness
of all my sins
and, in abundant measure,
the grace
of serving him in the future
more faithfully,
and at the last, final grace,
so that with you I may praise him
for all the ages of ages.
Amen.

Hail, Mary, full of grace, the Lord is
with thee;
blessed art thou amongst women,
and blessed is the fruit of thy
womb, Jesus.
Holy Mary, Mother of God,
pray for us sinners
now and at the hour of our death.
Amen.

impetra mihi veniam omnium
peccatorum meorum,
uberemque gratiam ipsi deinceps
fidelius serviendi,
ac denique gratiam finalem,
ut eum tecum laudare possim
per omnia sæcula sæculorum.

Amen.

Ave Maria, gratia plena, Dominus
tecum;
benedicta tu in mulieribus,
et benedictus fructus ventris tui,
Iesus.
Sancta Maria, Mater Dei,
ora pro nobis peccatoribus
nunc et in hora mortis nostræ.
Amen.

AFTER HOLY COMMUNION

Act of Faith

O Jesus, I believe that I have received your Flesh to eat and your Blood to drink, because you have said it, and your word is true. All that I have and all that I am are your gift and now you have given me yourself.

Act of Adoration

O Jesus, my God, my Creator, I adore you, because from your hands I came and with you I am to be happy for ever.

Act of Humility

O Jesus, I am not worthy to receive you, and yet you have come to me that my poor heart may learn of you to be meek and humble.

Act of Love

Jesus, I love you; I love you with all my heart. You know that I love you, and wish to love you daily more and more.

Act of Thanksgiving

My good Jesus, I thank you with all my heart. How good, how kind you are to me. Blessed be Jesus in the most holy Sacrament of the Altar.

Act of Offering

O Jesus, receive my poor offering.
Jesus, you have given yourself to me,
and now let me give myself to you:
I give you my body, that I may be chaste and pure.
I give you my soul, that I may be free from sin.
I give you my heart, that I may always love you.
I give you my every breath that I shall breathe,
and especially my last.
I give you myself in life and in death,
that I may be yours for ever and ever.

For Yourself

O Jesus, wash away my sins with your Precious Blood.

O Jesus, the struggle against temptation is not yet finished. My Jesus, when temptation comes near me, make me strong against it. In the moment of temptation may I always say: "My Jesus, mercy! Mary, help!"

O Jesus, may I lead a good life; may I die a happy death. May I receive you before I die. May I say when I am dying: "Jesus, Mary and Joseph, I give you my heart and my soul".

Listen now for a moment to Jesus Christ; perhaps he has something to say to you. Answer Jesus in your heart, and tell him all your troubles. Then say:

For Perseverance

Jesus, I am going away for a time, but, I trust, not without you. You are with me by your grace. I resolve never to leave you by mortal sin. Although I am so weak I have such hope in you. Give me grace to persevere. Amen.

IF I CAN'T GET TO MASS

Spiritual Communion

Spiritual Communion is the heartfelt desire to receive Our Lord, even when we are unable because of the distance or for some other reason. This desire to receive him through spiritual Communion is an act of love which prolongs our thanksgiving even when we are not in the Eucharistic presence of Our Lord. The wish to live constantly in his presence can be fuelled by acts of love and desire to be united with him and is a means of drawing more deeply from the life of the Holy Spirit dwelling within our souls in the state of grace. 'The effects of a sacrament can be received by desire. Although in such a case the sacrament is not received physically . . . nevertheless the actual reception of the sacrament itself brings with it fuller effect than receiving it through desire alone' (St Thomas Aquinas). The writings of the saints reveal many formulae for making a spiritual Communion:

Acts of Spiritual Communion

My Jesus, I believe that You are truly present in the Most Holy Sacrament. I love You above all things, and I desire to receive You into my soul. Since I cannot at this moment receive You sacramentally, come at least spiritually into my heart. I embrace You as being already there and unite myself wholly to You. Never permit me to be separated from You. Amen.

(St Alphonsus Liguori)

I wish, my Lord, to receive You with the purity, humility and devotion with which your Most Holy Mother received You, with the spirit and fervour of the saints. Come, Lord Jesus.

Give me, good Lord, a longing to be with You ... give me warmth, delight and quickness in thinking upon You. And give me Your grace to long for Your holy sacraments, and specially to rejoice in the presence of Your very blessed Body, Sweet Saviour Christ, in the Holy Sacrament of the altar.

(St Thomas More)

OTHER PRAYERS OF THANKSGIVING

Canticle of the Three Children
(Dn 3:57-88; 56)

Ant. Let us sing the hymn of the
three children,* which these
holy ones sang of old in the fiery
furnace, giving praise to the Lord.
(E.T. Alleluia).

1. Bless the Lord,
   all you works of the Lord;
   praise and exalt him above
   all forever.
2. Heavens, bless the Lord;
   angels of the Lord,
   bless the Lord.
3. All you waters that are above the
   heavens, bless the Lord,
   let all the powers bless the Lord.
4. Sun and moon, bless the Lord;
   stars of heaven, bless the Lord.
5. Every shower and dew,
   bless the Lord;
   all you winds, bless the Lord.
6. Fire and heat,
   bless the Lord;
   cold and heat,
   bless the Lord.
7. Dews and hoar frosts,
   bless the Lord;
   frost and cold,
   bless the Lord.
8. Ice and snow,
   bless the Lord;
   nights and days,
   bless the Lord.

Canticum Trium Puerorum

Ant. Trium puerorum*cantemus
hymnum, quem cantabant sancti
in camino ignis,
    benedicentes Dominum.
(T.P. Alleluia).

1. Benedicite, omnia opera
   Domini, Domino,*
   laudate et superexaltate
   eum in sæcula.
2. Benedicite, cæli, Domino,*
   benedicite,
   angeli Domini, Domino.
3. Benedicite, aquæ omnes
   quæ super cælos sunt Domino,*
   benedicat omnis virtus Domino.
4. Benedicite, sol et luna, Domino,*
   benedicite, stellæ cæli, Domino.
5. Benedicite,
   omnis imber et ros, Domino,*
   benedicite, omnes venti, Domino.
6. Benedicite,
   ignis et æstus, Domino,*
   benedicite,
   frigus et æstus, Domino.
7. Benedicite,
   rores et pruina, Domino,*
   benedicite,
   gelu et frigus, Domino.
8. Benedicite,
   glacies et nives, Domino,*
   benedicite,
   noctes et dies, Domino.

9. Light and darkness,
   bless the Lord;
   lightnings and clouds,
   bless the Lord.

10. Let the earth bless the Lord;
    let it praise and exalt him
    above all forever.

11. Mountains and hills
    bless the Lord;
    everything growing from the
    earth, bless the Lord.

12. Seas and rivers,
    bless the Lord; fountains, bless
    the Lord.

13. Whales and all that move in the
    waters, bless the Lord;
    all you fowls of the air,
    bless the Lord.

14. All you beasts and cattle bless
    the Lord;
    sons of men,
    bless the Lord.

15. Israel bless the Lord;
    praise and exalt him
    above all forever.

16. Priests of the Lord,
    bless the Lord;
    servants of the Lord,
    bless the Lord.

17. Spirits and souls of the just,
    bless the Lord;
    holy men of humble heart,
    bless the Lord.

18. Ananias, Azarias and Mizael,
    bless the Lord;
    praise and exalt him
    above all for ever.

9. Benedicite,
   lux et tenebræ, Domino,*
   benedicite,
   fulgura et nubes, Domino.

10. Benedicat terra Dominum,*
    laudet et superexaltet
    eum in sæcula.

11. Benedicite,
    montes et colles, Domino,*
    benedicite, universa
    germinantia in terra, Domino.

12. Benedicite,
    maria et flumina, Domino,*
    benedicite, fontes, Domino.

13. Benedicite, cete et omnia quæ
    moventur in aquis, Domino,*
    benedicite, omnes volucres
    cæli, Domino.

14. Benedicite, omnes bestiæ
    et pecora, Domino,*
    benedicite,
    filii hominum, Domino.

15. Benedic, Israel, Domino,*
    laudate et superexaltate
    eum in sæcula.

16. Benedicite,
    sacerdotes Domini, Domino,*
    benedicite, servi Domini,
    Domino.

17. Benedicite, spiritus et animæ
    iustorum, Domino,*
    benedicite,
    sancti et humiles corde, Domino.

18. Benedicite,
    Anania, Azaria, Misaël, Domino,*
    laudate et superexaltate
    eum in sæcula.

19. Let us bless the Father and the
    Son, with the Holy Spirit;
    let us praise and exalt him
    above all forever.

20. Blessed are you, Lord,
    in the firmament of heaven;
    and worthy of praise,
    and glorious above all forever.

Psalm 150

1. Praise the Lord in his holy place,
   praise him in his mighty heavens.

2. Praise him for his powerful deeds,
   praise his surpassing greatness.

3. O praise him with sound
       of trumpet,
   praise him with lute and harp.
4. Praise him with timbrel
       and dance,
   praise him with strings and pipes.

5. O praise him with
       resounding cymbals,
   praise him with clashing
       of cymbals.
   Let everything that lives and
       that breathes
   give praise to the Lord.
Glory be to the Father . . .

Ant. Let us sing the hymn of the
three children,* which these
holy ones sang of old in the fiery
furnace, giving praise to the Lord.
(E.T. Alleluia).

---

19. Benedicamus Patrem et Filium
    cum Sancto Spiritu;*
    laudemus et superexaltemus
    eum in sæcula.

20. Benedictus es
    in firmamento cæli*
    et laudabilis
    et gloriosus in sæcula.

Psalmus 150

1. Laudate Dominum
       in sanctuario eius,*
   laudate eum in firmamento
       virtutis eius.
2. Laudate eum in magnalibus eius,*
   laudate eum secundum
       multitudinem magnitudinis
       eius.
3. Laudate eum in sono tubæ,*
   laudate eum in psalterio
       et cithara.
4. Laudate eum in tympano
       et choro,*
   laudate eum in chordis
       et organo.
5. Laudate eum in cymbalis
       benesonantibus,*
   laudate eum in cymbalis
       iubilationis:*
   omne quod spirat,
       laudet Dominum.
Gloria Patri . . .

Ant. Trium puerorum*cantemus
hymnum, quem cantabant sancti in
camino ignis,
    benedicentes Dominum.
(T.P. Alleluia).

Lord, have mercy. Christ, have mercy.
  Lord, have mercy.
Our Father ...

V. And lead us not into temptation.
R. But deliver us from evil.
V. Let all your works praise you, Lord.
R. And let your Saints bless you.
V. Your saints shall rejoice in glory.
R. They shall rejoice in their
  resting place.
V. Not unto us, Lord, not unto us.
R. But unto your name give glory.
V. O Lord, hear my prayer.
R. And let my cry come unto you.

Priests add:
V. The Lord be with you.
R. And with your spirit. Let us pray.

God, who did allay the flames of
fire for three children, grant in your
mercy that the flame of vice may
not consume us your servants.

Direct, we beseech you, Lord, our
actions by your inspirations, and
further them by your assistance:
that every word and work of ours
may begin always from you and by
you be likewise ended.

Quench in us, we beseech you,
Lord, the flame of vice even as
you did enable blessed Lawrence
to overcome his fire of sufferings.
Through Christ our Lord.
R. Amen.

Kyrie, eleison. Christe, eleison.
  Kyrie, eleison.
Pater noster ...

V. Et ne nos inducas in tentationem.
R. Sed libera nos a malo.
V. Confiteantur tibi, Domine,
  omnia opera tua.
R. Et Sancti tui benedicant tibi.
V. Exsultabunt sancti in gloria.
R. Lætabuntur in cubilibus suis.
V. Non nobis, Domine, non nobis.
R. Sed nomini tuo da gloriam.
V. Domine exaudi orationem meam.
R. Et clamor meus ad te veniat.

V. Dominus vobiscum.
R. Et cum spiritu tuo. Oremus.

Deus, qui tribus pueris mitigasti
flammas ignium: concede
propitius; ut nos famulos tuos non
exurat flamma vitiorum.

Actiones nostras, quæsumus, Domine,
aspirando præveni et adiuvando
prosequere: ut cuncta nostra oratio
et operatio a te semper incipiat, et
per te cœpta finiatur.

Da nobis, quæsumus, Domine,
vitiorum nostrorum flammas
extinguere: qui beato Laurentio
tribuisti tormentorum suorum
incendia superare.
Per Christum, Dominum nostrum.
R. Amen.

Psalm 2	Psalmus 2

Ant. His kingdom is a kingdom of all ages, and all kings shall serve and obey him. (E.T. Alleluia).

Ant. Regnum eius* regnum sempiternum est, et omnes reges servient ei et obœdient. (T.P. Alleluia).

1. Why this tumult among nations, among peoples this useless murmuring?

2. They arise, the kings of the earth, princes plot against the Lord and his anointed.

3. "Come, let us break their fetters, come let us cast off their yoke."

4. He who sits in the heavens laughs; the Lord is laughing them to scorn.

5. Then he will speak in his anger, his rage will strike them with terror.

6. "It is I who have set up my king on Zion, my holy mountain."

7. I will announce the decree of the Lord: The Lord said to me: "You are my Son. It is I who have begotten you this day.

8. Ask and I shall bequeath you the nations, put the ends of the earth in your possession.

9. With a rod of iron you will break them, shatter them like a potter's jar."

1. Quare fremuerunt gentes, * et populi meditati sunt inania?

2. Astiterunt reges terræ, et principes convenerunt in unum* adversus Dominum et adversus Christum eius:

3. "Dirumpamus vincula eorum* et proiciamus a nobis iugum ipsorum!"

4. Qui habitat in cælis irridebit eos,* Dominus subsannabit eos.

5. Tunc loquetur ad eos in ira sua* et in furore suo conturbabit eos:

6. "Ego autem constitui regem meum* super Sion, montem sanctum meum!"

7. Prædicabo decretum eius: Dominus dixit ad me: "Filius meus es tu;* ego hodie genui te.

8. Postula a me, et dabo tibi gentes hereditatem tuam* et possessionem tuam terminos terræ.

9. Reges eos in virga ferrea* et tamquam vas figuli confringes eos."

10. Now, O kings, understand,
     take warning, rulers of the earth;
11. Serve the Lord with awe
     and trembling,
12. Pay him your homage,
     lest he be angry and you perish,
     for suddenly his anger will blaze.

     Blessed are they
         who put their trust in God.
13. Glory be to the Father . . .
14. As it was in the beginning . . .

Ant. His kingdom is a kingdom of
     all ages, and all kings shall serve
     and obey him. (E.T. Alleluia).

V. O Lord, hear my prayer.
R. And let my cry come unto you.

Priests add:
V. The Lord be with you.
R. And with your spirit. Let us pray.

Almighty and eternal God,
you have renewed all creation in
your beloved Son,
the King of the whole universe.
May all the people of the earth,
now torn apart by the wound of sin,
become subject to the gentle rule
of your only-begotten Son.
Who lives and reigns with you
and the Holy Spirit,
one God,
for ever and ever.
R. Amen.

10. Et nunc reges intellegite,*
     erudimini, qui iudicatis terram.
11. Servite Domino in timore*
     et exsultate ei cum tremore.
12. Apprehendite disciplinam,
     ne quando irascatur,
     et pereatis de via,*
     cum exarserit in brevi ira eius.
     Beati omnes,*
     qui confidunt in eo.
13. Gloria Patri . . .
14. Sicut erat in principio . . .

Ant. Regnum eius*regnum
     sempiternum est, et omnes
     reges servient ei et obœdient.
     (T.P. Alleluia).

V. Domine, exaudi orationem meam.
R. Et clamor meus ad te veniat.

V. Dominus vobiscum.
R. Et cum spiritu tuo. Oremus.

Omnipotens sempiterne Deus,
qui in dilecto Filio tuo,
universorum Rege,
omnia instaurare voluisti,
concede propitius,
ut cunctæ familiæ gentium,
peccati vulnere disgregatæ,
eius suavissimo
subdantur imperio.
Qui tecum vivit et regnat in unitate
Spiritus Sancti Deus:
per omnia sæcula sæculorum.
R. Amen.

Adoro Te Devote

O Godhead hid,
 devoutly I adore Thee,
Who truly art within the forms
 before me;
To Thee my heart I bow with
 bended knee,
As failing quite in
 contemplating Thee.

Sight, touch, and taste in Thee are
 each deceived;
The ear alone most safely is believed:
I believe all the Son of God
 has spoken,
Than Truth's own word there is
 no truer token.

God only on the Cross lay hid
 from view;
But here lies hid at once
 the Manhood too;
And I, in both professing my belief,
 Make the same prayer as the
 repentant thief.

Thy wounds, as Thomas saw,
 I do not see;
Yet Thee confess my Lord and
 God to be:
Make me believe Thee
 ever more and more;
In Thee my hope,
 in Thee my love to store.

O thou Memorial of our Lord's
 own dying!
O Bread that living art and vivifying!
Make ever Thou my soul on
 Thee to live;
Ever a taste of Heavenly sweetness give.

Adoro te devote, latens Deitas,
Quæ sub his figuris vere latitas:
Tibi se cor meum totum subiicit,
Quia te contemplans totum deficit.

Visus, tactus, gustus in te fallitur,
Sed auditu solo tuto creditur.
Credo quidquid dixit Dei Filius:
Nil hoc verbo Veritatis verius.

In cruce latebat sola Deitas,
At hic latet simul et humanitas;
Ambo tamen credens
 atque confitens,
Peto quod petivit latro pænitens.

Plagas, sicut Thomas,
 non intueor;
Deum tamen meum te confiteor.
Fac me tibi semper magis credere,
In te spem habere,
 te diligere.

O memoriale mortis Domini!
Panis vivus,
vitam præstans homini!
Præsta meæ menti de te vivere.
Et te illi semper dulce sapere.

O loving Pelican! O Jesu, Lord!
Unclean I am,
    but cleanse me in Thy Blood;
Of which a single drop,
    for sinners spilt,
Is ransom for a world's entire guilt.

Jesu! Whom for the present
    veil'd I see,
What I so thirst for,
    O vouchsafe to me:
That I may see Thy
    countenance unfolding,
And may be blest Thy glory
    in beholding. Amen.

Translated by E. Caswall

Pie pellicane, Iesu Domine,
Me immundum munda
    tuo sanguine.
Cuius una stilla salvum facere
Totum mundum quit ab
    omni scelere.

Iesu, quem velatum nunc aspicio,
Oro fiat illud quod tam sitio;
Ut te revelata cernens facie,
Visu sim beatus tuæ gloriæ.

Amen.

Prayer to Saint Michael

Holy Michael Archangel,
defend us in the day of battle;
be our safeguard
against the wickedness and snares
    of the devil.
May God rebuke him,
we humbly pray
and do thou,
prince of the heavenly host,
by the power of God thrust
down to hell Satan
and all wicked spirits,
who wander through the world
for the ruin of souls.
Amen.

Oratio ad S. Michael

Sancte Michael Archangele,
defende nos in prœlio,
contra nequitiam
et insidias diaboli esto præsidium.
Imperet illi Deus,
supplices deprecamur:
tuque,
Princeps militiæ cælestis,
Satanam aliosque
    spiritus malignos,
qui ad perditionem animarum
pervagantur in mundo,
divina virtute,
in infernum detrude.
Amen.

The Te Deum

We praise you, O God:
we acclaim you as the Lord.
Everlasting Father,
all the world bows down
    before you.
All the angels sing your praise,
the hosts of heaven and all the
    angelic powers,
all the cherubim and seraphim
call out to you in unending song:
Holy, Holy, Holy,
Is the Lord God of angel hosts!
The heavens and the earth are filled
with your majesty and glory.
The glorious band of apostles,
the noble company of prophets,
the white-robed army who shed
    their blood for Christ,
all sing your praise.
	Te Deum laudamus:
	te Dominum confitemur.
	Te æternum Patrem,
	omnis terra veneratur.
	Tibi omnes angeli,
	tibi cæli
	    et universæ potestates:
	tibi cherubim et seraphim
	incessabili voce proclamant:

We praise you, O God:
we acclaim you as the Lord.
Everlasting Father,
all the world bows down
   before you.
All the angels sing your praise,
the hosts of heaven and all the
   angelic powers,
all the cherubim and seraphim
call out to you in unending song:
Holy, Holy, Holy,
Is the Lord God of angel hosts!
The heavens and the earth are filled
with your majesty and glory.
The glorious band of apostles,
the noble company of prophets,
the white-robed army who shed
   their blood for Christ,
all sing your praise.

And to the ends of the earth
your holy Church proclaims her
   faith in you:
Father, whose majesty is boundless,
your true and only Son, who is to
   be adored,
the Holy Spirit sent to be
   our Advocate.
You, Christ, are the king of glory,
Son of the eternal Father.
When you took our nature
   to save mankind
you did not shrink from birth
   in the Virgin's womb.
You overcame the power of death,
opening the Father's kingdom to
   all who believe in you.

Te Deum laudamus:
te Dominum confitemur.
Te æternum Patrem,
omnis terra veneratur.
Tibi omnes angeli,
tibi cæli
   et universæ potestates:
tibi cherubim et seraphim
incessabili voce proclamant:

Sanctus, Sanctus, Sanctus,
Dominus Deus Sabaoth.
Pleni sunt cæli et terra
maiestatis gloriæ tuæ.
Te gloriosus
apostolorum chorus,
te prophetarum
laudabilis numerus,
te martyrum candidatus
laudat exercitus.
Te per orbem terrarum
sancta confitetur Ecclesia,
Patrem immensæ maiestatis;
venerandum tuum verum
et unicum Filium;
Sanctum quoque
Paraclitum Spiritum.
Tu rex gloriæ, Christe.
Tu Patris
sempiternus es Filius.
Tu, ad liberandum
   suscepturus hominem,
non horruisti Virginis uterum.
Tu, devicto mortis aculeo,
aperuisti credentibus
regna cælorum.

Enthroned at God's right hand in
   the glory of the Father,
you will come in judgment
   according to your promise.
You redeemed your people by your
   precious blood.
Come, we implore you, to our aid.
Grant us with the saints
a place in eternal glory.
Lord, save your people
and bless your inheritance.
Rule them and uphold them
for ever and ever.
Day by day we praise you:
we acclaim you now and
   to all eternity.
In your goodness, Lord,
   keep us free from sin.
Have mercy on us, Lord,
   have mercy.
May your mercy always be with us,
   Lord,
for we have hoped in you.
In you, Lord, we put our trust:
we shall not be put to shame.

Tu ad dexteram Dei sedes,
in gloria Patris.
Iudex crederis
esse venturus.
Te ergo, quæsumus,
tuis famulis subveni,
quos pretioso sanguine redemisti.
Æterna fac cum sanctis tuis
in gloria numerari.
Salvum fac populum tuum, Domine,
et benedic hereditati tuæ.
Et rege eos, et extolle illos
   usque in æternum.
Per singulos dies benedicimus te;
et laudamus nomen tuum
   in sæculum,
et in sæculum sæculi.
Dignare, Domine, die isto
   sine peccato nos custodire.
Miserere nostri, Domine,
   miserere nostri.
Fiat misericordia tua,
   Domine, super nos,
quemadmodum speravimus in te.
In te, Domine, speravi:
non confundar in æternum.

SUNDAYS IN ORDINARY TIME

First Sunday in Ordinary Time

THE BAPTISM OF THE LORD

Feast

See p.128.

SECOND SUNDAY IN ORDINARY TIME (YEAR A)

Entrance Antiphon Ps 65:4	**Ant. ad introitum**
ALL the earth shall bow down before you, O God, and shall sing to you, shall sing to your name, O Most High!	OMNIS terra adoret te, Deus, et psallat tibi; psalmum dicat nomini tuo, Altissime.
Collect	**Collecta**
Almighty ever-living God, who govern all things, both in heaven and on earth, mercifully hear the pleading of your people and bestow your peace on our times. Through our Lord Jesus Christ, your Son, who lives and reigns with you in the unity of the Holy Spirit, one God, for ever and ever.	Omnipotens sempiterne Deus, qui cælestia simul et terrena moderaris, supplicationes populi tui clementer exaudi, et pacem tuam nostris concede temporibus. Per Dominum nostrum Iesum Christum Filium tuum, qui tecum vivit et regnat in unitate Spiritus Sancti, Deus, per omnia sæcula sæculorum.

FIRST READING

A reading from the prophet Isaiah   49:3,5-6

I will make you the light of the nations so that my salvation may reach to the ends of the earth.

The Lord said to me, 'You are my servant, Israel,
in whom I shall be glorified';
I was honoured in the eyes of the Lord,
my God was my strength.
And now the Lord has spoken,
he who formed me in the womb to be his servant,
to bring Jacob back to him,
to gather Israel to him:

'It is not enough for you to be my servant,
to restore the tribes of Jacob and bring back the survivors of Israel;
I will make you the light of the nations
so that my salvation may reach to the ends of the earth.'
The word of the Lord.

Responsorial Psalm   Ps 39:2,4,7-10. R. vv.8,9

R. **Here I am, Lord!**
   I come to do your will.

I waited, I waited for the Lord
and he stooped down to me;
he heard my cry.
He put a new song into my mouth,
praise of our God. R.

You do not ask for sacrifice and offerings,
but an open ear.
You do not ask for holocaust and victim.
Instead, here am I. R.

In the scroll of the book it stands written
that I should do your will.
My God, I delight in your law
in the depth of my heart. R.

Your justice I have proclaimed
in the great assembly.
My lips I have not sealed;
you know it, O Lord. R.

SECOND READING

A reading from the first letter of St Paul to the Corinthians   1:1-3

May God our Father and the Lord Jesus Christ send you grace and peace.

I Paul, appointed by God to be an apostle, together with brother Sosthenes,
send greetings to the church of God in Corinth, to the holy people of Jesus
Christ, who are called to take their place among all the saints everywhere
who pray to our Lord Jesus Christ; for he is their Lord no less than ours.
May God our Father and the Lord Jesus Christ send you grace and peace.
The word of the Lord.

Gospel Acclamation

R. **Alleluia, alleluia!**
Blessings on the King who comes,
in the name of the Lord!
Peace in heaven
and glory in the highest heavens!
R. **Alleluia!**

Or: Jn 1:14,12

R. **Alleluia, alleluia!**
The Word was made flesh and lived among us;
to all who did accept him
he gave power to become children of God.
R. **Alleluia!**

GOSPEL

A reading from the holy Gospel according to John   1:29-34
Look, there is the lamb of God that takes away the sin of the world.

Seeing Jesus coming towards him, John said, 'Look, there is the lamb of God that takes away the sin of the world. This is the one I spoke of when I said: A man is coming after me who ranks before me because he existed before me. I did not know him myself, and yet it was to reveal him to Israel that I came baptising with water.' John also declared, 'I saw the Spirit coming down on him from heaven like a dove and resting on him. I did not know him myself, but he who sent me to baptise with water had said to me, "The man on whom you see the Spirit come down and rest is the one who is going to baptise with the Holy Spirit." Yes, I have seen and I am the witness that he is the Chosen One of God.'

The Gospel of the Lord.

Prayer over the Offerings	Super oblata
Grant us, O Lord, we pray, that we may participate worthily in these mysteries, for whenever the memorial of this sacrifice is celebrated the work of our redemption is accomplished. Through Christ our Lord.	Concede nobis, quæsumus, Domine, hæc digne frequentare mysteria, quia, quoties huius hostiæ commemoratio celebratur, opus nostræ redemptionis exercetur. Per Christum Dominum nostrum.

Preface of Sundays in Ordinary Time I-VIII, pp.566-573.

Communion Antiphon Cf. Ps 22:5
You have prepared a table before me,
and how precious is the chalice
　　that quenches my thirst.

Ant. ad communionem
Parasti in conspectu meo mensam,
et calix meus inebrians quam
　　præclarus est!

Or:　　　　　　　　　1 Jn 4:16
We have come to know
　　and to believe
in the love that God has for us.

Vel:
Nos cognovimus
　　et credidimus caritati,
quam Deus habet in nobis.

Prayer after Communion
Pour on us, O Lord,
　　the Spirit of your love,
and in your kindness
make those you have nourished
by this one heavenly Bread
one in mind and heart.
Through Christ our Lord.

Post communionem
Spiritum nobis, Domine,
　　tuæ caritatis infunde,
ut, quos uno cælesti pane satiasti,
una facias pietate concordes.
Per Christum Dominum nostrum.

THIRD SUNDAY IN ORDINARY TIME (YEAR A)

Entrance Antiphon　　　Cf. Ps 95:1,6
O SING a new song to the Lord;
　　sing to the Lord, all the earth.
In his presence are majesty
　　and splendour,
strength and honour
　　in his holy place.

Ant. ad introitum
CANTATE Domino
　　canticum novum,
cantate Domino, omnis terra.
Confessio et pulchritudo
　　in conspectu eius,
sanctitas et magnificentia
　　in sanctificatione eius.

Collect
Almighty ever-living God,
direct our actions according
　　to your good pleasure,
that in the name of your beloved Son
we may abound in good works.
Through our Lord Jesus Christ,
　　your Son,
who lives and reigns with you
　　in the unity of the Holy Spirit,
one God, for ever and ever.

Collecta
Omnipotens sempiterne Deus,
dirige actus nostros
　　in beneplacito tuo,
ut in nomine dilecti Filii tui
mereamur bonis operibus abundare.
Per Dominum nostrum Iesum
　　Christum Filium tuum,
qui tecum vivit et regnat
　　in unitate Spiritus Sancti,
Deus, per omnia sæcula sæculorum.

FIRST READING

A reading from the prophet Isaiah   8:23-9:3

In Galilee of the nations the people has seen a great light.

In days past the Lord humbled the land of Zebulun and the land of
Naphtali, but in days to come he will confer glory on the Way of the Sea
on the far side of Jordan, province of the nations.

The people that walked in darkness
has seen a great light;
on those who live in a land of deep shadow
a light has shone.
You have made their gladness greater,
you have made their joy increase;
they rejoice in your presence
as men rejoice at harvest time,
as men are happy when they are dividing the spoils.

For the yoke that was weighing on him,
the bar across his shoulders,
the rod of his oppressor,
these you break as on the day of Midian.

    The word of the Lord.

Responsional Psalm   Ps 26:1,4,13-14. R. v.1

R. **The Lord is my light and my help.**

The Lord is my light and my help;
whom shall I fear?
The Lord is the stronghold of my life;
before whom shall I shrink? R.

There is one thing I ask of the Lord,
for this I long,
to live in the house of the Lord,
all the days of my life,
to savour the sweetness of the Lord,
to behold his temple. R.

I am sure I shall see the Lord's goodness
in the land of the living.
Hope in him, hold firm and take heart.
Hope in the Lord! R.

SECOND READING

A reading from the first letter of St Paul to the Corinthians   1:10-13,17

Make up the differences between you instead of disagreeing among yourselves.

I appeal to you, brothers, for the sake of our Lord Jesus Christ, to make up the differences between you, and instead of disagreeing among yourselves, to be united again in your belief and practice. From what Chloe's people have been telling me, my dear brothers, it is clear that there are serious differences among you. What I mean are all these slogans that you have, like: 'I am for Paul,' 'I am for Apollos,' 'I am for Cephas,' 'I am for Christ.' Has Christ been parcelled out? Was it Paul that was crucified for you? Were you baptised in the name of Paul?

For Christ did not send me to baptise, but to preach the Good News, and not to preach that in the terms of philosophy in which the crucifixion of Christ cannot be expressed.

The word of the Lord.

Gospel Acclamation   Cf. Mt 4:23

R. **Alleluia, alleluia!**
Jesus proclaimed the Good News of the kingdom,
and cured all kinds of sickness among the people.
R. **Alleluia!**

GOSPEL

A reading from the holy Gospel according to Matthew   4:12-23

He went and settled in Capernaum: in this way the prophecy of Isaiah was to be fulfilled.

[Hearing that John had been arrested Jesus went back to Galilee, and leaving Nazareth he went and settled in Capernaum, a lakeside town on the borders of Zebulun and Naphtali. In this way the prophecy of Isaiah was to be fulfilled:

Land of Zebulun! Land of Naphtali!
Way of the sea on the far side of Jordan,
Galilee of the nations!
The people that lived in darkness
has seen a great light;
on those who dwell in the land and shadow of death
a light has dawned.

From that moment Jesus began his preaching with the message, 'Repent, for the kingdom of heaven is close at hand.]

As he was walking by the Sea of Galilee he saw two brothers, Simon, who was called Peter, and his brother Andrew; they were making a cast in the lake with their net, for they were fishermen. And he said to them, 'Follow me and I will make you fishers of men.' And they left their nets at once and followed him.

Going on from there he saw another pair of brothers, James son of Zebedee and his brother John; they were in their boat with their father Zebedee, mending their nets, and he called them. At once, leaving the boat and their father, they followed him.

He went round the whole of Galilee teaching in their synagogues, proclaiming the Good News of the kingdom and curing all kinds of diseases and sickness among the people.

[The Gospel of the Lord.]

Shorter Form, verses 12-17. Read between [ ]

Prayer over the Offerings	Super oblata
Accept our offerings, O Lord, we pray, and in sanctifying them grant that they may profit us for salvation. Through Christ our Lord.	Munera nostra, Domine, suscipe placatus, quæ sanctificando nobis, quæsumus, salutaria fore concede. Per Christum Dominum nostrum.

Preface of Sundays in Ordinary Time I-VIII, pp.566-573.

Communion Antiphon Cf. Ps 33:6	Ant. ad communionem
Look toward the Lord and be radiant; let your faces not be abashed.	Accedite ad Dominum et illuminamini, et facies vestræ non confundentur.

Or: Jn 8:12	Vel:
I am the light of the world, says the Lord; whoever follows me will not walk in darkness, but will have the light of life.	Ego sum lux mundi, dicit Dominus: qui sequitur me non ambulat in tenebris, sed habebit lumen vitæ.

Prayer after Communion

Grant, we pray, almighty God,
that, receiving the grace
by which you bring us to new life,
we may always glory in your gift.
Through Christ our Lord.

Post communionem

Præsta nobis, quæsumus,
    omnipotens Deus,
ut, vivificationis tuæ
    gratiam consequentes,
in tuo semper munere gloriemur.
Per Christum Dominum nostrum.

FOURTH SUNDAY IN ORDINARY TIME (YEAR A)

Entrance Antiphon   Ps 105:47

SAVE us, O Lord our God!
And gather us from the nations,
to give thanks to your holy name,
and make it our glory to praise you.

Ant. ad introitum

SALVOS nos fac,
Domine Deus noster,
et congrega nos de nationibus,
ut confiteamur nomini sancto tuo,
et gloriemur in laude tua.

Collect

Grant us, Lord our God,
that we may honour you
    with all our mind,
and love everyone in truth of heart.
Through our Lord Jesus Christ,
    your Son,
who lives and reigns with you
    in the unity of the Holy Spirit,
one God, for ever and ever.

Collecta

Concede nobis,
    Domine Deus noster,
ut te tota mente veneremur,
et omnes homines rationabili
    diligamus affectu.
Per Dominum nostrum Iesum
    Christum Filium tuum,
qui tecum vivit et regnat
    in unitate Spiritus Sancti,
Deus, per omnia sæcula sæculorum.

FIRST READING

A reading from the prophet Zephaniah   2:3; 3:12-13
In your midst I will leave a humble and lowly people.

Seek the Lord
all you, the humble of the earth,
who obey his commands.
Seek integrity,
seek humility:
you may perhaps find shelter
on the day of the anger of the Lord.

In your midst I will leave
a humble and lowly people,
and those who are left in Israel will seek refuge in the name of the Lord.
They will do no wrong,
will tell no lies;
and the perjured tongue will no longer
be found in their mouths.
But they will be able to graze and rest
with no one to disturb them.

    The word of the Lord.

Responsorial Psalm   Ps 145:7-10. R. Mt 5:3

R. **How happy are the poor in spirit;**
    theirs is the kingdom of heaven.
    Or: **Alleluia!**

    It is the Lord who keeps faith for ever,
    who is just to those who are oppressed.
    It is he who gives bread to the hungry,
    the Lord, who sets prisoners free. R.

    It is the Lord who gives sight to the blind,
    who raises up those who are bowed down,
    the Lord, who protects the stranger
    and upholds the widow and orphan. R.

    It is the Lord who loves the just
    but thwarts the path of the wicked.
    The Lord will reign for ever,
    Zion's God, from age to age. R.

SECOND READING

A reading from the first letter of St Paul to the Corinthians   1:26-31

God chose what is foolish by human reckoning.

Take yourselves, brothers, at the time when you were called: how many of
you were wise in the ordinary sense of the word, how many were influential
people, or came from noble families? No, it was to shame the wise that
God chose what is foolish by human reckoning, and to shame what is
strong that he chose what is weak by human reckoning; those whom the
world thinks common and contemptible are the ones that God has chosen

– those who are nothing at all to show up those who are everything. The human race has nothing to boast about to God. but you, God has made members of Christ Jesus and by God's doing he has become our wisdom, and our virtue, and our holiness, and our freedom. As scripture says: if anyone wants to boast, let him boast about the Lord.

The word of the Lord.

Gospel Acclamation   Mt 11:25

R. **Alleluia, alleluia!**
Blessed are you, Father,
Lord of heaven and earth,
for revealing the mysteries of the kingdom
to mere children.
R. **Alleluia!**

Or: Mt 5:12

R. **Alleluia, alleluia!**
Rejoice and be glad:
your reward will be great in heaven.
R. **Alleluia!**

GOSPEL

A reading from the holy Gospel according to Matthew   5:1-12
How happy are the poor in spirit.

Seeing the crowds, Jesus went up the hill. There he sat down and was joined by his disciples. Then he began to speak. This is what he taught them:

'How happy are the poor in spirit:
theirs is the kingdom of heaven.
Happy the gentle:
they shall have the earth for their heritage.
Happy those who mourn:
they shall be comforted.
Happy those who hunger and thirst for what is right:
they shall be satisfied.
Happy the merciful:
they shall have mercy shown them.
Happy the pure in heart:
they shall see God.
Happy the peacemakers:
they shall be called sons of God.

Happy those who are persecuted in the cause of right:
theirs is the kingdom of heaven.

'Happy are you when people abuse you and persecute you and speak all kinds of calumny against you on my account. Rejoice and be glad, for your reward will be great in heaven.'

The Gospel of the Lord.

Prayer over the Offerings	Super oblata
O Lord, we bring to your altar these offerings of our service: be pleased to receive them, we pray, and transform them into the Sacrament of our redemption. Through Christ our Lord.	Altaribus tuis, Domine, munera nostræ servitutis inferimus, quæ, placatus assumens, sacramentum nostræ redemptionis efficias. Per Christum Dominum nostrum.

Preface of Sundays in Ordinary Time I-VIII, pp.566-573.

Communion Antiphon Cf. Ps 30:17-18	Ant. ad communionem
Let your face shine on your servant. Save me in your merciful love. O Lord, let me never be put to shame, for I call on you.	Illumina faciem tuam super servum tuum, et salvum me fac in tua misericordia. Domine, non confundar, quoniam invocavi te.

Or: Mt 5:3-4	Vel:
Blessed are the poor in spirit, for theirs is the Kingdom of Heaven. Blessed are the meek, for they shall possess the land.	Beati pauperes spiritu, quoniam ipsorum est regnum cælorum. Beati mites, quoniam ipsi possidebunt terram.

Prayer after Communion	Post communionem
Nourished by these redeeming gifts, we pray, O Lord, that through this help to eternal salvation true faith may ever increase. Through Christ our Lord.	Redemptionis nostræ munere vegetati, quæsumus, Domine, ut hoc perpetuæ salutis auxilio fides semper vera proficiat. Per Christum Dominum nostrum.

FIFTH SUNDAY IN ORDINARY TIME (YEAR A)

Entrance Antiphon　　　Ps 94:6-7	Ant. ad introitum
O COME, let us worship God and bow low before the God who made us, for he is the Lord our God.	VENITE, adoremus Deum, et procidamus ante Dominum, qui fecit nos; quia ipse est Dominus Deus noster.
Collect	Collecta
Keep your family safe, O Lord, with unfailing care, that, relying solely on the hope of heavenly grace, they may be defended always by your protection. Through our Lord Jesus Christ, your Son, who lives and reigns with you in the unity of the Holy Spirit, one God, for ever and ever.	Familiam tuam, quæsumus, Domine, continua pietate custodi, ut, quæ in sola spe gratiæ cælestis innititur, tua semper protectione muniatur. Per Dominum nostrum Iesum Christum Filium tuum, qui tecum vivit et regnat in unitate Spiritus Sancti, Deus, per omnia sæcula sæculorum.

FIRST READING

A reading from the prophet Isaiah　　　　　　　　　58:7-10

Then will your light shine like the dawn.

Thus says the Lord:

> Share your bread with the hungry,
> and shelter the homeless poor,
>
> clothe the man you see to be naked
> and turn not from your own kin.
> Then will your light shine like the dawn
> and your wound be quickly healed over.
>
> Your integrity will go before you
> and the glory of the Lord behind you.
> Cry, and the Lord will answer;
> call, and he will say, 'I am here.'
>
> If you do away with the yoke,
> the clenched fist, the wicked word,

if you give your bread to the hungry,
and relief to the oppressed,
your light will rise in the darkness,
and your shadows become like noon.

The word of the Lord.

Responsial Psalm   Ps 111:4-9. R. v.4

R. **The good man is a light in the darkness for the upright.**
Or: **Alleluia!**

He is a light in the darkness for the upright:
he is generous, merciful and just.
The good man takes pity and lends,
he conducts his affairs with honour. R.

The just man will never waver:
he will be remembered for ever.
He has no fear of evil news;
with a firm heart he trusts in the Lord. R.

With a steadfast heart he will not fear;
open-handed, he gives to the poor;
his justice stands firm for ever.
His head will be raised in glory. R.

SECOND READING

A reading from the first letter of St Paul to the Corinthians   2:1-5

During my stay with you, the only knowledge I claimed to have was about Jesus as the crucified Christ.

When I came to you, brothers, it was not with any show of oratory or philosophy, but simply to tell you what God had guaranteed. During my stay with you, the only knowledge I claimed to have was about Jesus, and only about him as the crucified Christ. Far from relying on any power of my own, I came among you in great 'fear and trembling' and in my speeches and the sermons that I gave, there were none of the arguments that belong to philosophy; only a demonstration of the power of the Spirit. And I did this so that your faith should not depend on human philosophy but on the power of God.

The word of the Lord.

Gospel Acclamation   Jn 8:12

R. **Alleluia, alleluia!**
I am the light of the world, says the Lord,
anyone who follows me
will have the light of life.
R. **Alleluia!**

GOSPEL

A reading from the holy Gospel according to Matthew   5:13-16

You are the light of the world.

Jesus said to his disciples: 'You are the salt of the earth. But if salt becomes tasteless, what can make it salty again? It is good for nothing, and can only be thrown out to be trampled underfoot by men.

'You are the light of the world. A city built on a hill-top cannot be hidden. No one lights a lamp to put it under a tub; they put it on the lamp-stand where it shines for everyone in the house. In the same way your light must shine in the sight of men, so that, seeing your good works, they may give the praise to your Father in heaven.'

The Gospel of the Lord.

Prayer over the Offerings	Super oblata
O Lord our God,	Domine Deus noster,
who once established these created things	qui has potius creaturas
to sustain us in our frailty,	ad fragilitatis nostræ subsidium condidisti,
grant, we pray,	tribue, quæsumus,
that they may become for us now the Sacrament of eternal life.	ut etiam æternitatis nobis fiant sacramentum.
Through Christ our Lord.	Per Christum Dominum nostrum.

Preface of Sundays in Ordinary Time I-VIII, pp.566-573.

Communion Antiphon Cf. Ps 106:8-9	Ant. ad communionem
Let them thank the Lord for his mercy,	Confiteantur Domino misericordiæ eius,
his wonders for the children of men	et mirabilia eius filiis hominum,
for he satisfies the thirsty soul,	quia satiavit animam inanem,
and the hungry he fills with good things.	et animam esurientem satiavit bonis.

Or: Mt 5:5-6

Blessed are those who mourn,
    for they shall be consoled.
Blessed are those who hunger
    and thirst for righteousness,
for they shall have their fill.

Prayer after Communion

O God, who have willed
    that we be partakers
in the one Bread and the one Chalice,
grant us, we pray, so to live that,
    made one in Christ,
we may joyfully bear fruit
for the salvation of the world.
Through Christ our Lord.

Vel:

Beati qui lugent,
    quoniam ipsi consolabuntur.
Beati qui esuriunt
    et sitiunt iustitiam,
quoniam ipsi saturabuntur.

Post communionem

Deus, qui nos de uno pane
    et de uno calice
participes esse voluisti,
da nobis, quæsumus, ita vivere, ut,
    unum in Christo effecti,
fructum afferamus pro mundi
    salute gaudentes.
Per Christum Dominum nostrum.

SIXTH SUNDAY IN ORDINARY TIME

(YEAR A)

Entrance Antiphon   Cf. Ps 30:3-4

BE my protector, O God,
a mighty stronghold to save me.
For you are my rock, my stronghold!
Lead me, guide me,
    for the sake of your name.

Ant. ad introitum

ESTO mihi
in Deum protectorem,
et in locum refugii,
    ut salvum me facias.
Quoniam firmamentum meum
    et refugium meum es tu,
et propter nomen tuum dux
    mihi eris, et enutries me.

Collect	Collecta

O God, who teach us that you abide
in hearts that are just and true,
grant that we may be so fashioned
    by your grace
as to become a dwelling pleasing
    to you.
Through our Lord Jesus Christ,
    your Son,
who lives and reigns with you
    in the unity of the Holy Spirit,
one God, for ever and ever.
	Deus, qui te in rectis et sinceris
	    manere pectoribus asseris,
	da nobis tua gratia tales exsistere,
	in quibus habitare digneris.
	Per Dominum nostrum Iesum
	    Christum Filium tuum,
	qui tecum vivit et regnat
	    in unitate Spiritus Sancti,
	Deus, per omnia sæcula sæculorum.

FIRST READING

A reading from the book of Ecclesiasticus   15:16-20

He never commanded anyone to be godless.

If you wish, you can keep the commandments,
to behave faithfully is within your power.
He has set fire and water before you;
put out your hand to whichever you prefer.
Man has life and death before him;
whichever a man likes better will be given him.
For vast is the wisdom of the Lord;
he is almighty and all-seeing.
His eyes are on those who fear him,
he notes every action of man.
He never commanded anyone to be godless,
he has given no one permission to sin.

   The word of the Lord.

Responsorial Psalm   Ps 118:1-2,4-5,17-18,33-34. R. v.1

R. **They are happy who follow God's law!**

   They are happy whose life is blameless,
   who follow God's law!
   They are happy those who do his will,
   seeking him with all their hearts. R.

   You have laid down your precepts
   to be obeyed with care.
   May my footsteps be firm
   to obey your statutes. R.

Bless your servant and I shall live
and obey your word.
Open my eyes that I may consider
the wonders of your law. R.

Teach me the demands of your statutes
and I will keep them to the end.
Train me to observe your law,
to keep it with my heart. R.

SECOND READING

A reading from the first letter of St Paul to the Corinthians   2:6-10

God predestined wisdom to be for our glory before the ages began.

We have a wisdom to offer those who have reached maturity: not a philosophy of our age, it is true, still less of the masters of our age, which are coming to their end. The hidden wisdom of God which we teach in our mysteries is the wisdom that God predestined to be for our glory before the ages began. It is a wisdom that none of the masters of this age have ever known, or they would not have crucified the Lord of Glory; we teach what scripture calls: the things that no eye has seen and no ear has heard, things beyond the mind of man, all that God has prepared for those who love him.

These are the very things that God has revealed to us through the Spirit, for the Spirit reaches the depths of everything, even the depths of God.

The word of the Lord.

Gospel Acclamation   1 S 3:9; Jn 6:68

R. **Alleluia, alleluia!**
Speak, Lord, your servant is listening:
you have the message of eternal life.
R. **Alleluia!**

Or: Cf. Mt 11:25

R. **Alleluia, alleluia!**
Blessed are you, Father,
Lord of heaven and earth,
for revealing the mysteries of the kingdom.
to mere children.
R. **Alleluia!**

GOSPEL

A reading from the holy Gospel according to Matthew   5:17-37
You have learnt how it was said to our ancestors; but I say this to you.

[Jesus said to his disciples:] 'Do not imagine that I have come to abolish the Law or the Prophets. I have come not to abolish them but to complete them. I tell you solemnly, till heaven and earth disappear, not one dot, one little stroke, shall disappear from the Law until its purpose is achieved. Therefore, the man who infringes even one of the least of these commandments and teaches others to do the same will be considered the least in the kingdom of heaven; but the man who keeps them and teaches them will be considered great in the kingdom of heaven.

['For I tell you, if your virtue goes no deeper than that of the scribes and Pharisees, you will never get into the kingdom of heaven.

'You have learnt how it was said to our ancestors: You must not kill; and if anyone does kill he must answer for it before the court. But I say this to you: anyone who is angry with his brother will answer for it before the court;] if a man calls his brother "Fool" he will answer for it before the Sanhedrin; and if a man calls him "Renegade" he will answer for it in hell fire. So then, if you are bringing your offering to the altar and there remember that your brother has something against you, leave your offering there before the altar, go and be reconciled with your brother first, and then come back and present your offering. Come to terms with your opponent in good time while you are still on the way to the court with him, or he may hand you over to the judge and the judge to the officer, and you will be thrown into prison. I tell you solemnly, you will not get out till you have paid the last penny.

[You have learnt how it was said: You must not commit adultery. But I say this to you: if a man looks at a woman lustfully, he has already committed adultery with her in his heart.] If your right eye should cause you to sin, tear it out and throw it away; for it will do you less harm to lose one part of you than to have your whole body thrown into hell. And if your right hand should cause you to sin, cut it off and throw it away; for it will do you less harm to lose one part of you than to have your whole body go to hell.

'It has also been said: Anyone who divorces his wife must give her a writ of dismissal. But I say this to you: everyone who divorces his wife, except for the case of fornication, makes her an adulteress; and anyone who marries a divorced woman commits adultery.

['Again, you have learnt how it was said to our ancestors: You must not break your oath, but must fulfil your oaths to the Lord. But I say this to you: do not swear at all,] either by heaven, since that is God's throne; or by the earth, since that is his footstool; or by Jerusalem, since that is the city of the great king. Do not swear by your own head either, since you cannot turn a single hair white or black. [All you need say is "Yes" if you mean yes, "No" if you mean no; anything more than this comes from the evil one.'

The Gospel of the Lord.]

Shorter Form, verses 20-22,27-28,33-34,37. Read between [ ]

Prayer over the Offerings	Super oblata
May this oblation, O Lord, we pray, cleanse and renew us and may it become for those who do your will the source of eternal reward. Through Christ our Lord.	Hæc nos oblatio, quæsumus, Domine, mundet et renovet, atque tuam exsequentibus voluntatem fiat causa remunerationis æternæ. Per Christum Dominum nostrum.

Preface of Sundays in Ordinary Time I-VIII, pp.566-573.

Communion Antiphon Cf. Ps 77:29-30	Ant. ad communionem
They ate and had their fill, and what they craved the Lord gave them; they were not disappointed in what they craved.	Manducaverunt, et saturati sunt nimis, et desiderium eorum attulit eis Dominus; non sunt fraudati a desiderio suo.

Or: Jn 3:16	Vel:
God so loved the world that he gave his Only Begotten Son, so that all who believe in him may not perish, but may have eternal life.	Sic Deus dilexit mundum, ut Filium suum Unigenitum daret, ut omnis qui credit in eum non pereat, sed habeat vitam æternam.

Prayer after Communion	Post communionem
Having fed upon these heavenly delights, we pray, O Lord, that we may always long for that food by which we truly live. Through Christ our Lord.	Cælestibus, Domine, pasti deliciis, quæsumus, ut semper eadem, per quæ veraciter vivimus, appetamus. Per Christum Dominum nostrum.

SEVENTH SUNDAY IN ORDINARY TIME (YEAR A)

Entrance Antiphon   Ps 12:6

O LORD, I trust in your
   merciful love.
My heart will rejoice
   in your salvation.
I will sing to the Lord
   who has been bountiful with me.

Ant. ad introitum

D OMINE, in tua
   misericordia speravi.
Exsultavit cor meum in salutari tuo,
cantabo Domino,
   qui bona tribuit mihi.

Collect

Grant, we pray, almighty God,
that, always pondering
   spiritual things,
we may carry out in both
   word and deed
that which is pleasing to you.
Through our Lord Jesus Christ,
   your Son,
who lives and reigns with you
   in the unity of the Holy Spirit,
one God, for ever and ever.

Collecta

Præsta, quæsumus,
   omnipotens Deus,
ut, semper rationabilia meditantes,
quæ tibi sunt placita,
   et dictis exsequamur et factis.
Per Dominum nostrum Iesum
   Christum Filium tuum,
qui tecum vivit et regnat
   in unitate Spiritus Sancti,
Deus, per omnia sæcula sæculorum.

FIRST READING

A reading from the book of Leviticus   19:1-2,17-18
You must love your neighbour as yourself.

The Lord spoke to Moses; he said: 'Speak to the whole community of the
sons of Israel and say to them: "Be holy, for I, the Lord your God, am holy.

   "You must not bear hatred for your brother in your heart. You must
openly tell him, your neighbour, of his offence; this way you will not take
a sin upon yourself. You must not exact vengeance, nor must you bear a
grudge against the children of your people. You must love your neighbour
as yourself. I am the Lord."'

   The word of the Lord.

Responsorial Psalm   Ps 102:1-4,8,10,12-13. R. v.8

R. **The Lord is compassion and love.**

   My soul, give thanks to the Lord,
   all my being, bless his holy name.
   My soul, give thanks to the Lord
   and never forget all his blessings. R.

It is he who forgives all your guilt,
who heals every one of your ills,
who redeems your life from the grave,
who crowns you with love and compassion. R.

The Lord is compassion and love,
slow to anger and rich in mercy.
He does not treat us according to our sins
nor repay us according to our faults. R.

As far as the east is from the west
so far does he remove our sins.
As a father has compassion on his sons,
the Lord has pity on those who fear him. R.

SECOND READING

A reading from the first letter of St Paul to the Corinthians   3:16-23
All are your servants, but you belong to Christ and Christ belongs to God.

Didn't you realise that you were God's temple and that the Spirit of God was living among you? If anybody should destroy the temple of God, God will destroy him, because the temple of God is sacred; and you are that temple.

Make no mistake about it: if any one of you thinks of himself as wise, in the ordinary sense of the word, then he must learn to be a fool before he really can be wise. Why? Because the wisdom of this world is foolishness to God. As scripture says: The Lord knows wise men's thoughts: he knows how useless they are, or again: God is not convinced by the arguments of the wise. So there is nothing to boast about in anything human: Paul, Apollos, Cephas, the world, life and death, the present and the future, are all your servants; but you belong to Christ and Christ belongs to God.

The word of the Lord.

Gospel Acclamation   Jn 14:23

R. **Alleluia, alleluia!**
If anyone loves me he will keep my word,
and my Father will love him,
and we shall come to him.
R. **Alleluia!**

Or: 1 Jn 2:5
R. **Alleluia, alleluia!**
When anyone obeys what Christ has said,
God's love comes to perfection in him.
R. **Alleluia!**

GOSPEL

A reading from the holy Gospel according to Matthew   5:38-48
Love your enemies.

Jesus said to his disciples: 'You have learnt how it was said: Eye for eye and
tooth for tooth. But I say this to you: offer the wicked man no resistance. On
the contrary, if anyone hits you on the right cheek, offer him the other as
well; if a man takes you to law and would have your tunic, let him have your
cloak as well. And if anyone orders you to go one mile, go two miles with him.
Give to anyone who asks, and if anyone wants to borrow, do not turn away.

'You have learnt how it was said: You must love your neighbour and
hate your enemy. But I say this to you: love your enemies and pray for
those who persecute you; in this way you will be sons of your Father in
heaven, for he causes his sun to rise on bad men as well as good, and his
rain to fall on honest and dishonest men alike. For if you love those who
love you, what right have you to claim any credit? Even the tax collectors
do as much, do they not? And if you save your greetings for your brothers,
are you doing anything exceptional? Even the pagans do as much, do they
not? You must therefore be perfect just as your heavenly Father is perfect.'

The Gospel of the Lord.

Prayer over the Offerings	Super oblata
As we celebrate your mysteries, O Lord, with the observance that is your due, we humbly ask you, that what we offer to the honour of your majesty may profit us for salvation. Through Christ our Lord.	Mysteria tua, Domine, debitis servitiis exsequentes, supplices te rogamus, ut, quod ad honorem tuæ maiestatis offerimus, nobis proficiat ad salutem. Per Christum Dominum nostrum.

Preface of Sundays in Ordinary Time I-VIII, pp.566-573.

Communion Antiphon   Ps 9:2-3

I will recount all your wonders,
I will rejoice in you and be glad,
and sing psalms to your name,
     O Most High.

Or: Jn 11:27

Lord, I have come to believe
     that you are the Christ,
the Son of the living God,
     who is coming into this world.

Prayer after Communion

Grant, we pray, almighty God,
that we may experience the effects
     of the salvation
which is pledged to us
     by these mysteries.
Through Christ our Lord.

Ant. ad communionem

Narrabo omnia mirabilia tua.
Lætabor et exsultabo in te,
psallam nomini tuo, Altissime.

Vel:

Domine, ego credidi quia
     tu es Christus Filius Dei vivi,
qui in hunc mundum venisti.

Post communionem

Præsta, quæsumus,
     omnipotens Deus,
ut illius salutis capiamus effectum,
cuius per hæc mysteria
     pignus accepimus.
Per Christum Dominum nostrum.

EIGHTH SUNDAY IN ORDINARY TIME (YEAR A)

Entrance Antiphon Cf. Ps 17:19-20

THE Lord became my protector.
He brought me out to a place
     of freedom;
he saved me because he delighted
     in me.

Collect

Grant us, O Lord, we pray,
that the course of our world
may be directed by your peaceful rule
and that your Church may rejoice,
untroubled in her devotion.
Through our Lord Jesus Christ,
     your Son,
who lives and reigns with you
     in the unity of the Holy Spirit,
one God, for ever and ever.

Ant. ad introitum

FACTUS est Dominus
protector meus,
et eduxit me in latitudinem,
salvum me fecit,
     quoniam voluit me.

Collecta

Da nobis, quæsumus, Domine,
ut et mundi cursus pacifico nobis
     tuo ordine dirigatur,
et Ecclesia tua tranquilla
     devotione lætetur.
Per Dominum nostrum Iesum
     Christum Filium tuum,
qui tecum vivit et regnat
     in unitate Spiritus Sancti,
Deus, per omnia sæcula sæculorum.

FIRST READING

A reading from the prophet Isaiah   49:14-15

I will never forget you.

Zion was saying, 'The Lord has abandoned me,
the Lord has forgotten me.'
Does a woman forget her baby at the breast,
or fail to cherish the son of her womb?
Yet even if these forget,
I will never forget you.

   The word of the Lord.

Responsorial Psalm   Ps 61:2-3,6-9. R. v.6

R. **In God alone is my soul at rest.**

   In God alone is my soul at rest;
   my help comes from him.
   He alone is my rock, my stronghold,
   my fortress: I stand firm. R.

   In God alone be at rest, my soul;
   for my hope comes from him.
   He alone is my rock, my stronghold,
   my fortress: I stand firm. R.

   In God is my safety and glory,
   the rock of my strength.
   Take refuge in God all you people.
   Trust him at all times.
   Pour out your hearts before him. R.

SECOND READING

A reading from the first letter of St Paul to the Corinthians   4:1-5

The Lord will reveal the secret intentions of men's hearts.

People must think of us as Christ's servants, stewards entrusted with the
mysteries of God. What is expected of stewards is that each one should
be found worthy of his trust. Not that it makes the slightest difference
to me whether you, or indeed any human tribunal, find me worthy or
not. I will not even pass judgement on myself. True, my conscience does
not reproach me at all, but that does not prove that I am acquitted: the
Lord alone is my judge. There must be no passing of premature judgement.
Leave that until the Lord comes: he will light up all that is hidden in the

dark and reveal the secret intentions of men's hearts. Then will be the time for each one to have whatever praise he deserves, from God.

The word of the Lord.

Gospel Acclamation   Jn 17:17

R. **Alleluia, alleluia!**
Your word is truth, O Lord,
consecrate us in the truth.
R. **Alleluia!**
Or: Heb 4:12

R. **Alleluia, alleluia!**
The word of God is something alive and active;
it can judge secret emotions and thoughts.
R. **Alleluia!**

GOSPEL

A reading from the holy Gospel according to Matthew   6:24-34
Do not worry about tomorrow.

Jesus said to his disciples: 'No one can be the slave of two masters: he will either hate the first and love the second, or treat the first with respect and the second with scorn. You cannot be the slave both of God and of money.

'That is why I am telling you not to worry about your life and what you are to eat, nor about your body and how you are to clothe it. Surely life means more than food, and the body more than clothing! Look at the birds in the sky. They do not sow or reap or gather into barns; yet your heavenly Father feeds them. Are you not worth much more than they are? Can any of you, for all his worrying, add one single cubit to his span of life? And why worry about clothing? Think of the flowers growing in the fields; they never have to work or spin; yet I assure you that not even Solomon in all his regalia was robed like one of these. Now if that is how God clothes the grass in the field which is there today and thrown into the furnace tomorrow, will he not much more look after you, you men of little faith? So do not worry; do not say, "What are we to eat? What are we to drink? How are we to be clothed?" It is the pagans who set their hearts on all these things. Your heavenly Father knows you need them all. Set your hearts on his kingdom first, and on his righteousness, and all these other things will be given you as well. So do not worry about tomorrow; tomorrow will take care of itself. Each day has enough trouble of its own.'

The Gospel of the Lord.

Prayer over the Offerings

O God, who provide gifts
to be offered to your name
and count our oblations as signs
of our desire to serve you
with devotion,
we ask of your mercy
that what you grant as the source
of merit
may also help us to attain
merit's reward.
Through Christ our Lord.

Super oblata

Deus, qui offerenda tuo
nomini tribuis,
et oblata devotioni nostræ
servitutis ascribis,
quæsumus clementiam tuam,
ut, quod præstas unde sit meritum,
proficere nobis largiaris
ad præmium.
Per Christum Dominum nostrum.

Preface of Sundays in Ordinary Time I-VIII, pp.566-573.

Communion Antiphon Cf. Ps 12:6

I will sing to the Lord who has been
bountiful with me,
sing psalms to the name
of the Lord Most High.

Or: Mt 28:20

Behold, I am with you always,
even to the end of the age,
says the Lord.

Ant. ad communionem

Cantabo Domino,
qui bona tribuit mihi,
et psallam nomini
Domini Altissimi.

Vel:

Ecce ego vobiscum sum
omnibus diebus,
usque ad consummationem sæculi,
dicit Dominus.

Prayer after Communion

Nourished by your saving gifts,
we beseech your mercy, Lord,
that by this same Sacrament
with which you feed us
in the present age,
you may make us partakers
of life eternal.
Through Christ our Lord.

Post communionem

Satiati munere salutari,
tuam, Domine,
misericordiam deprecamur,
ut, hoc eodem quo nos
temporaliter vegetas sacramento,
perpetuæ vitæ participes
benignus efficias.
Per Christum Dominum nostrum.

NINTH SUNDAY IN ORDINARY TIME (YEAR A)

Entrance Antiphon   Cf. Ps 24:16,18

Turn to me and have mercy
on me, O Lord,
for I am alone and poor.
See my lowliness and suffering
and take away all my sins, my God.

Ant. ad introitum

Respice in me,
et miserere mei, Domine,
quoniam unicus et pauper sum ego.
Vide humilitatem meam
    et laborem meum,
et dimitte omnia peccata mea,
    Deus meus.

Collect

O God, whose providence never
    fails in its design,
keep from us, we humbly
    beseech you,
all that might harm us
and grant all that works for our good.
Through our Lord Jesus Christ,
    your Son,
who lives and reigns with you
    in the unity of the Holy Spirit,
one God, for ever and ever.

Collecta

Deus, cuius providentia in sui
    dispositione non fallitur,
te supplices exoramus,
ut noxia cuncta submoveas,
et omnia nobis profutura concedas.
Per Dominum nostrum Iesum
    Christum Filium tuum,
qui tecum vivit et regnat
    in unitate Spiritus Sancti,
Deus, per omnia sæcula sæculorum.

FIRST READING

A reading from the book of Deuteronomy   11:18,26-28,32

See, I set before you today a blessing and a curse.

Moses said to the people: 'Let these words of mine remain in your heart
and in your soul; fasten them on your hand as a sign and on your forehead
as a circlet.

'See, I set before you today a blessing and a curse: a blessing, if you
obey the commandments of the Lord our God that I enjoin on you today;
a curse, if you disobey the commandments of the Lord your God and leave
the way I have marked out for you today, by going after other gods you
have not known. You must keep and observe all the laws and customs that
I set before you today.'

The word of the Lord.

Responsorial Psalm   Ps 30:2-4,17,25. R. v.3

R. **Be a rock of refuge for me, O Lord.**

In you, O Lord, I take refuge.
Let me never be put to shame.
In your justice, set me free,
hear me and speedily rescue me. R.

Be a rock of refuge for me,
a mighty stronghold to save me,
for you are my rock, my stronghold.
For your name's sake, lead me and guide me. R.

Let your face shine on your servant.
Save me in your love.
Be strong, let your heart take courage,
all who hope in the Lord. R.

SECOND READING

A reading from the letter of St Paul to the Romans   3:21-25,28

A man is justified by faith and not by doing something the Law tells him to do.

God's justice that was made known through the Law and the Prophets
has now been revealed outside the Law, since it is the same justice of God
that comes through faith to everyone, Jew and pagan alike, who believes
in Jesus Christ. Both Jew and pagan sinned and forfeited God's glory, and
both are justified through the free gift of his grace by being redeemed in
Christ Jesus who was appointed by God to sacrifice his life so as to win
reconciliation through faith since, as we see it, a man is justified by faith
and not by doing something the Law tells him to do.

The word of the Lord.

Gospel Acclamation   Jn 14:23

R. **Alleluia, alleluia!**
If anyone loves me he will keep my word,
and my Father will love him,
and we shall come to him.
R. **Alleluia!**

Or: Jn 15:5

R. **Alleluia, alleluia!**
I am the vine, you are the branches,
says the Lord.
Whoever remains in me, with me in him,
bears fruit in plenty.
R. **Alleluia!**

FIRST READING

A reading from the prophet Hosea   6:3-6

What I want is love, not sacrifice.

Let us set ourselves to know the Lord;
that he will come is as certain as the dawn
his judgement will rise like the light,
he will come to us as showers come,
like spring rains watering the earth.

What am I to do with you, Ephraim?
What am I to do with you, Judah?
This love of yours is like a morning cloud,
like the dew that quickly disappears.
This is why I have torn them to pieces by the prophets,
why I slaughtered them with the words from my mouth,
since what I want is love, not sacrifice;
knowledge of God, not holocausts.

   The word of the Lord.

Responsorial Psalm   Ps 49:1,8,12-15. R. v.23

R. **I will show God's salvation to the upright.**

   The God of gods, the Lord,
   has spoken and summoned the earth,
   from the rising of the sun to its setting.
   'I find no fault with your sacrifices,
   your offerings are always before me. R.

   'Were I hungry, I would not tell you,
   for I own the world and all it holds.
   Do you think I eat the flesh of bulls,
   or drink the blood of goats? R.

   'Pay your sacrifice of thanksgiving to God
   and render him your votive offerings.
   Call on me in the day of distress.
   I will free you and you shall honour me.' R.

SECOND READING

A reading from the letter of St Paul to the Romans   4:18-25

Abraham drew strength from faith and gave glory to God.

Though it seemed Abraham's hope could not be fulfilled, he hoped and he believed, and through doing so he did become the father of many nations exactly as he had been promised: Your descendants will be as many as the stars. Even the thought that his body was past fatherhood – he was about a hundred years old – and Sarah too old to become a mother, did not shake his belief. Since God had promised it, Abraham refused either to deny it or even to doubt it, but drew strength from faith and gave glory to God, convinced that God had power to do what he had promised. This is the faith that was 'considered as justifying him'. Scripture however does not refer only to him but to us as well when it says that his faith was thus 'considered'; our faith too will be 'considered' if we believe in him who raised Jesus our Lord from the dead, Jesus who was put to death for our sins and raised to life to justify us.

The word of the Lord.

Gospel Acclamation   Cf. Ac 16:14

R. **Alleluia, alleluia!**
Open our heart, O Lord,
to accept the words of your Son.
R. **Alleluia!**

Or: Lk 4:18

R. **Alleluia, alleluia!**
The Lord has sent me to bring the good news to the poor,
to proclaim liberty to captives.
R. **Alleluia!**

GOSPEL

A reading from the holy Gospel according to Matthew   9:9-13

I did not come to call the virtuous, but sinners.

As Jesus was walking on he saw a man named Matthew sitting by the customs house, and he said to him, 'Follow me.' And he got up and followed him.

While he was at dinner in the house it happened that a number of tax collectors and sinners came to sit at the table with Jesus and his disciples. When the Pharisees saw this, they said to his disciples, 'Why does your master eat with tax collectors and sinners?' When he heard this he replied, 'It is not the healthy who need the doctor, but the sick. Go and learn the meaning of the words: What I want is mercy, not sacrifice. And indeed I did not come to call the virtuous, but sinners.'

The Gospel of the Lord.

Prayer over the Offerings

Look kindly upon our service,
   O Lord, we pray,
that what we offer
may be an acceptable oblation to you
and lead us to grow in charity.
Through Christ our Lord.

Super oblata

Respice, Domine, quæsumus,
   nostram propitius servitutem,
ut quod offerimus sit tibi
   munus acceptum,
et nostræ caritatis augmentum.
Per Christum Dominum nostrum.

Preface of Sundays in Ordinary Time I-VIII, pp.566-573.

Communion Antiphon   Ps 17:3

The Lord is my rock, my fortress,
   and my deliverer;
my God is my saving strength.

Ant. ad communionem

Dominus firmamentum meum,
et refugium meum, et liberator meus.
Deus meus adiutor meus.

Or: 1 Jn 4:16

God is love, and whoever abides
   in love
abides in God, and God in him.

Vel:

Deus caritas est,
   et qui manet in caritate
in Deo manet et Deus in eo.

Prayer after Communion

May your healing work, O Lord,
free us, we pray, from doing evil
and lead us to what is right.
Through Christ our Lord.

Post communionem

Tua nos, Domine,
   medicinalis operatio,
et a nostris perversitatibus
   clementer expediat,
et ad ea quæ sunt recta perducat.
Per Christum Dominum nostrum.

ELEVENTH SUNDAY IN ORDINARY TIME
(YEAR A)

Entrance Antiphon   Cf. Ps 26:7,9

O LORD, hear my voice,
   for I have called to you;
   be my help.
Do not abandon or forsake me,
   O God, my Saviour!

Ant. ad introitum

E XAUDI, Domine, vocem meam,
   qua clamavi ad te.
Adiutor meus esto,
   ne derelinquas me,
neque despicias me,
   Deus salutaris meus.

Collect	Collecta
O God, strength of those who hope in you, graciously hear our pleas, and, since without you mortal frailty can do nothing, grant us always the help of your grace, that in following your commands we may please you by our resolve and our deeds. Through our Lord Jesus Christ, your Son, who lives and reigns with you in the unity of the Holy Spirit, one God, for ever and ever.	Deus, in te sperantium fortitudo, invocationibus nostris adesto propitius, et, quia sine te nihil potest mortalis infirmitas, gratiæ tuæ præsta semper auxilium, ut, in exsequendis mandatis tuis, et voluntate tibi et actione placeamus. Per Dominum nostrum Iesum Christum Filium tuum, qui tecum vivit et regnat in unitate Spiritus Sancti, Deus, per omnia sæcula sæculorum.

FIRST READING

A reading from the book of Exodus   19:2-6

I will count you a kingdom of priests, a consecrated nation.

From Rephidim the Israelites set out again; and when they reached the wilderness of Sinai, there in the wilderness they pitched their camp; there facing the mountain Israel pitched camp.

Moses then went up to God, and the Lord called to him from the mountain, saying, 'Say this to the House of Jacob, declare this to the sons of Israel, "You yourselves have seen what I did with the Egyptians, how I carried you on eagle's wings and brought you to myself. From this you know that now, if you obey my voice and hold fast to my covenant, you of all the nations shall be my very own, for all the earth is mine. I will count you a kingdom of priests, a consecrated nation."'

The word of the Lord.

Responsorial Psalm   Ps 99:1-3,5. R. v.3

R. **We are his people:
the sheep of his flock.**

Cry out with joy to the Lord, all the earth.
Serve the Lord with gladness.
Come before him, singing for joy. R.

Know that he, the Lord, is God.
He made us, we belong to him,
we are his people, the sheep of his flock. R.

Indeed, how good is the Lord,
eternal his merciful love.
He is faithful from age to age. R.

SECOND READING

A reading from the letter of St Paul to the Romans   5:6-11

Now that we have been reconciled by the death of his Son, surely we may count on being saved by the life of his Son.

We were still helpless when at his appointed moment Christ died for sinful men. It is not easy to die even for a good man – though of course for someone really worthy, a man mighty be prepared to die – but what proves that God loves us is that Christ died for us while we were still sinners. Having died to make us righteous, is it likely that he would now fail to save us from God's anger? When we were reconciled to God by the death of his Son, we were still enemies; now that we have been reconciled, surely we may count on being saved by the life of his Son? Not merely because we have been reconciled but because we are filled with joyful trust in God through our Lord Jesus Christ, through whom we have already gained our reconciliation.

The word of the Lord.

Gospel Acclamation   Jn 10:27

R. **Alleluia, alleluia!**
The sheep that belong to me listen to my voice,
says the Lord,
I know them and they follow me.
R. **Alleluia!**

Or: Mk 1:15

R. **Alleluia, alleluia!**
The kingdom of God is close at hand.
Repent, and believe the Good News.
R. **Alleluia!**

GOSPEL

A reading from the holy Gospel according to Matthew   9:36-10:8

He summoned his twelve disciples and sent them out.

When Jesus saw the crowds he felt sorry for them because they were harassed and dejected, like sheep without a shepherd. Then he said to his disciples, 'The harvest is rich but the labourers are few, so ask the Lord of the harvest to send labourers to his harvest.'

He summoned his twelve disciples, and gave them authority over unclean spirits with power to cast them out and to cure all kinds of diseases and sickness.

These are the names of the twelve apostles: first, Simon who is called Peter, and his brother Andrew; James the son of Zebedee, and his brother John; Philip and Bartholomew; Thomas, and Matthew the tax collector; James the son of Alphaeus, and Thaddaeus; Simon the Zealot and Judas Iscariot, the one who was to betray him. These twelve Jesus sent out, instructing them as follows:

'Do not turn your steps to pagan territory, and do not enter any Samaritan town; go rather to the lost sheep of the House of Israel. And as you go, proclaim that the kingdom of heaven is close at hand. Cure the sick, raise the dead, cleanse the lepers, cast out devils. You received without charge, give without charge.'

The Gospel of the Lord.

Prayer over the Offerings	Super oblata
O God, who in the offerings presented here	Deus, qui humani generis utramque substantiam
provide for the twofold needs of human nature,	præsentium munerum et alimento vegetas
nourishing us with food and renewing us with your Sacrament,	et renovas sacramento, tribue, quæsumus, ut eorum
grant, we pray, that the sustenance they provide may not fail us in body or in spirit.	et corporibus nostris subsidium non desit et mentibus.
Through Christ our Lord.	Per Christum Dominum nostrum.

Preface of Sundays in Ordinary Time I-VIII, pp.566-573.

Communion Antiphon Ps 26:4	Ant. ad communionem
There is one thing I ask of the Lord, only this do I seek:	Unum petii a Domino, hoc requiram,
to live in the house of the Lord all the days of my life.	ut inhabitem in domo Domini omnibus diebus vitæ meæ.

Or: Jn 17:11

Holy Father, keep in your name
    those you have given me,
that they may be one as we are one,
    says the Lord.

Prayer after Communion

As this reception of your
    Holy Communion, O Lord,
foreshadows the union
    of the faithful in you,
so may it bring about unity
    in your Church.
Through Christ our Lord.

Vel:

Pater sancte,
    serva eos in nomine tuo,
quos dedisti mihi, ut sint unum
    sicut et nos, dicit Dominus.

Post communionem

Hæc tua, Domine,
    sumpta sacra communio,
sicut fidelium in te
    unionem præsignat,
sic in Ecclesia tua unitatis
    operetur effectum.
Per Christum Dominum nostrum.

TWELFTH SUNDAY IN ORDINARY TIME
(YEAR A)

Entrance Antiphon   Cf. Ps 27:8-9

THE Lord is the strength
    of his people,
a saving refuge for the one
    he has anointed.
Save your people, Lord,
    and bless your heritage,
and govern them for ever.

Ant. ad introitum

DOMINUS fortitudo plebis suæ,
    et protector salutarium Christi
    sui est.
Salvum fac populum
    tuum, Domine,
et benedic hereditati tuæ,
et rege eos usque in sæculum.

Collect

Grant, O Lord,
that we may always revere and love
    your holy name,
for you never deprive
    of your guidance
those you set firm
    on the foundation of your love.
Through our Lord Jesus Christ,
    your Son,
who lives and reigns with you
    in the unity of the Holy Spirit,
one God, for ever and ever.

Collecta

Sancti nominis tui, Domine,
timorem pariter et amorem fac nos
    habere perpetuum,
quia numquam tua
    gubernatione destituis,
quos in soliditate tuæ
    dilectionis instituis.
Per Dominum nostrum Iesum
    Christum Filium tuum,
qui tecum vivit et regnat
    in unitate Spiritus Sancti,
Deus, per omnia sæcula sæculorum.

FIRST READING

A reading from the prophet Jeremiah   20:10-13

He has delivered the soul of the needy from the hands of evil men.

Jeremiah said:

    I hear so many disparaging me,
    '"Terror from every side!"
    Denounce him! Let us denounce him!'
    All those who used to be my friends
    watched for my downfall,
    'Perhaps he will be seduced into error.
    Then we will master him
    and take our revenge!'
    But the Lord is at my side, a mighty hero;
    my opponents will stumble, mastered,
    confounded by their failure;
    everlasting, unforgettable disgrace will be theirs.
    But you, Lord of Hosts, you who probe with justice,
    who scrutinise the loins and heart,
    let me see the vengeance you will take on them,
    for I have committed my cause to you.
    Sing to the Lord,
    praise the Lord,
    for he has delivered the soul of the needy
    from the hands of evil men.

The word of the Lord.

Responsorial Psalm   Ps 68:8-10,14,17,33-35. R. v.14

R. **In your great love, answer me, O God.**

    It is for you that I suffer taunts,
    that shame covers my face,
    that I have become a stranger to my brothers,
    an alien to my own mother's sons.
    I burn with zeal for your house
    and taunts against you fall on me. R.

    This is my prayer to you,
    my prayer for your favour.
    In your great love, answer me, O God,
    with your help that never fails:
    Lord, answer, for your love is kind;
    in your compassion, turn towards me. R.

The poor when they see it will be glad
and God-seeking hearts will revive;
for the Lord listens to the needy
and does not spurn his servants in their chains.
Let the heavens and the earth give him praise,
the sea and all its living creatures. R.

SECOND READING

A reading from the letter of St Paul to the Romans   5:12-15
The gift considerably outweighed the fall.

Sin entered the world through one man, and through sin death, and thus death has spread through the whole human race because everyone has sinned. Sin existed in the world long before the Law was given. There was no law and so no one could be accused of the sin of 'law-breaking', yet death reigned over all from Adam to Moses, even though their sin, unlike that of Adam, was not a matter of breaking a law.

   Adam prefigured the One to come, but the gift itself considerably outweighed the fall. If it is certain that through one man's fall so many died, it is even more certain that divine grace, coming through the one man, Jesus Christ, came to so many as an abundant free gift.

   The word of the Lord.

Gospel Acclamation   Jn 1:14,12

R. **Alleluia, alleluia!**
The Word was made flesh and lived among us;
to all who did accept him
he gave power to become children of God.
R. **Alleluia!**

Or: Jn 15:26,27

R. **Alleluia, alleluia!**
The Spirit of truth will be my witness;
and you too will be my witnesses.
R. **Alleluia!**

GOSPEL

A reading from the holy Gospel according to Matthew   10:26-33
Do not be afraid of those who kill the body.

Jesus instructed the Twelve as follows: 'Do not be afraid. For everything that is now covered will be uncovered, and everything now hidden will be made clear. What I say to you in the dark, tell in the daylight; what you hear in whispers, proclaim from the house-tops.

'Do not be afraid of those who kill the body but cannot kill the soul; fear him rather who can destroy both body and soul in hell. Can you not buy two sparrows for a penny? And yet not one falls to the ground without your Father knowing. Why, every hair on your head has been counted. So there is no need to be afraid; you are worth more than hundreds of sparrows.

'So if anyone declares himself for me in the presence of men, I will declare myself for him in the presence of my Father in heaven. But the one who disowns me in the presence of men, I will disown in the presence of my Father in heaven.'

The Gospel of the Lord.

Prayer over the Offerings	Super oblata
Receive, O Lord, the sacrifice of conciliation and praise and grant that, cleansed by its action, we may make offering of a heart pleasing to you. Through Christ our Lord.	Suscipe, Domine, sacrificium placationis et laudis, et præsta, ut, huius operatione mundati, beneplacitum tibi nostræ mentis offeramus affectum. Per Christum Dominum nostrum.

Preface of Sundays in Ordinary Time I-VIII, pp.566-573.

Communion Antiphon Ps 144:15	Ant. ad communionem
The eyes of all look to you, Lord, and you give them their food in due season.	Oculi omnium in te sperant, Domine, et tu das illis escam in tempore opportuno.
Or: Jn 10:11,15	Vel:
I am the Good Shepherd, and I lay down my life for my sheep, says the Lord.	Ego sum pastor bonus, et animam meam pono pro ovibus meis, dicit Dominus.
Prayer after Communion	Post communionem
Renewed and nourished by the Sacred Body and Precious Blood of your Son, we ask of your mercy, O Lord, that what we celebrate with constant devotion may be our sure pledge of redemption. Through Christ our Lord.	Sacri Corporis et Sanguinis pretiosi alimonia renovati, quæsumus, Domine, clementiam tuam, ut, quod gerimus devotione frequenti, certa redemptione capiamus. Per Christum Dominum nostrum.

THIRTEENTH SUNDAY IN ORDINARY TIME
(YEAR A)

Entrance Antiphon Ps 46:2	Ant. ad introitum

ALL peoples, clap your hands.
Cry to God with shouts of joy!

OMNES gentes,
plaudite manibus,
iubilate Deo in voce exsultationis.

Collect	Collecta

O God, who through the grace
   of adoption
chose us to be children of light,
grant, we pray,
that we may not be wrapped
   in the darkness of error
but always be seen to stand
   in the bright light of truth.
Through our Lord Jesus Christ,
   your Son,
who lives and reigns with you
   in the unity of the Holy Spirit,
one God, for ever and ever.

Deus, qui, per adoptionem gratiæ,
lucis nos esse filios voluisti,
præsta, quæsumus, ut errorum
   non involvamur tenebris,
sed in splendore veritatis semper
   maneamus conspicui.
Per Dominum nostrum Iesum
   Christum Filium tuum,
qui tecum vivit et regnat
   in unitate Spiritus Sancti,
Deus, per omnia sæcula sæculorum.

FIRST READING

A reading from the second book of the Kings   4:8-11,14-16
This is a holy man of God, let him rest there.

One day as Elisha was on his way to Shunem, a woman of rank who lived there pressed him to stay and eat there. After this he always broke his journey for a meal when he passed that way. She said to her husband, 'Look, I am sure the man who is constantly passing our way must be a holy man of God. Let us build him a small room on the roof, and put him a bed in it, and a table and chair and lamp; whenever he comes to us he can rest there.'

One day when he came, he retired to the upper room and lay down. 'What can be done for her?' he asked. Gehazi, his servant, answered, 'Well, she has no son and her husband is old.' Elisha said, 'Call her.' The servant called her and she stood at the door. 'This time next year,' Elisha said 'you will hold a son in your arms.'

The word of the Lord.

Responsorial Psalm   Ps 88:2-3,16-19. R. v.2

R. **I will sing for ever of your love, O Lord.**

I will sing for ever of your love, O Lord;
through all ages my mouth will proclaim your truth.
Of this I am sure, that your love lasts for ever,
that your truth is firmly established as the heavens. R.

Happy the people who acclaim such a king,
who walk, O Lord, in the light of your face,
who find their joy every day in your name,
who make your justice the source of their bliss. R.

For it is you, O Lord, who are the glory of their strength;
it is by your favour that our might is exalted:
for our ruler is in the keeping of the Lord;
our king in the keeping of the Holy One of Israel. R.

SECOND READING

A reading from the letter of St Paul to the Romans   6:3-4,8-11

When we were baptised we went into the tomb with Christ, so that we too might live a new life.

When we were baptised in Christ Jesus we were baptised in his death; in other words, when we were baptised we went into the tomb with him and joined him in death, so that as Christ was raised from the dead by the Father's glory, we too might live a new life.

But we believe that having died with Christ we shall return to life with him: Christ, as we know, having been raised from the dead will never die again. Death has no power over him any more. When he died, he died, once for all, to sin, so his life now is life with God; and in that way, you too must consider yourselves to be dead to sin but alive for God in Christ Jesus.

The word of the Lord.

Gospel Acclamation   Cf. Ac 16:14

R. **Alleluia, alleluia!**
Open our heart, O Lord,
to accept the words of your Son.
R. **Alleluia!**

Or: 1 P 2:9

R. **Alleluia, alleluia!**
You are a chosen race, a royal priesthood, a people set apart
to sing the praises of God
who called you out of darkness into his wonderful light.
R. **Alleluia!**

GOSPEL

A reading from the holy Gospel according to Matthew   10:37-42
Anyone who does not take his cross is not worthy of me. Anyone who welcomes you welcomes me.

Jesus instructed the Twelve as follows: 'Anyone who prefers father or mother to me is not worthy of me. Anyone who prefers son or daughter to me is not worthy of me. Anyone who does not take his cross and follow in my footsteps is not worthy of me. Anyone who finds his life will lose it; anyone who loses his life for my sake will find it.

'Anyone who welcomes you welcomes me; and those who welcome me welcome the one who sent me.

'Anyone who welcomes a prophet because he is a prophet will have a prophet's reward; and anyone who welcomes a holy man because he is a holy man will have a holy man's reward.

'If anyone gives so much as a cup of cold water to one of these little ones because he is a disciple, then I tell you solemnly, he will most certainly not lose his reward.'

The Gospel of the Lord.

Prayer over the Offerings	Super oblata
O God, who graciously accomplish the effects of your mysteries, grant, we pray, that the deeds by which we serve you may be worthy of these sacred gifts. Through Christ our Lord.	Deus, qui mysteriorum tuorum dignanter operaris effectus, præsta, quæsumus, ut sacris apta muneribus fiant nostra servitia. Per Christum Dominum nostrum.

Preface of Sundays in Ordinary Time I-VIII, pp.566-573.

Communion Antiphon Cf. Ps 102:1	Ant. ad communionem
Bless the Lord, O my soul, and all within me, his holy name.	Benedic, anima mea, Domino, et ea quæ intra me sunt nomini sancto eius.

Or: Jn 17:20-21
O Father, I pray for them,
    that they may be one in us,
that the world may believe that you
    have sent me, says the Lord.

Prayer after Communion
May this divine sacrifice
    we have offered and received
fill us with life, O Lord, we pray,
so that, bound to you
    in lasting charity,
we may bear fruit that lasts for ever.
Through Christ our Lord.

Vel:
Pater, pro eis rogo,
    ut ipsi in nobis unum sint,
ut credat mundus quia tu me
    misisti, dicit Dominus.

Post communionem
Vivificet nos, quæsumus, Domine,
divina quam obtulimus et
    sumpsimus hostia,
ut, perpetua tibi caritate coniuncti,
fructum qui semper
    maneat afferamus.
Per Christum Dominum nostrum.

FOURTEENTH SUNDAY IN ORDINARY TIME
(YEAR A)

Entrance Antiphon Cf. Ps 47:10-11

YOUR merciful love, O God,
    we have received in the midst
    of your temple.
Your praise, O God, like your name,
reaches the ends of the earth;
your right hand is filled
    with saving justice.

Ant. ad introitum

SUSCEPIMUS, Deus,
    misericordiam tuam
in medio templi tui.
Secundum nomen tuum, Deus,
ita et laus tua in fines terræ;
iustitia plena est dextera tua.

Collect
O God, who in the abasement
    of your Son
have raised up a fallen world,
fill your faithful with holy joy,
for on those you have rescued
    from slavery to sin
you bestow eternal gladness.
Through our Lord Jesus Christ,
    your Son,
who lives and reigns with you
    in the unity of the Holy Spirit,
one God, for ever and ever.

Collecta
Deus, qui in Filii tui humilitate
iacentem mundum erexisti,
fidelibus tuis sanctam
    concede lætitiam,
ut, quos eripuisti
    a servitute peccati,
gaudiis facias perfrui sempiternis.
Per Dominum nostrum Iesum
    Christum Filium tuum,
qui tecum vivit et regnat
    in unitate Spiritus Sancti,
Deus, per omnia sæcula sæculorum.

FIRST READING

A reading from the prophet Zechariah   9:9-10

See now, your king comes humbly to you.

The Lord says this:

> 'Rejoice heart and soul, daughter of Zion!
> Shout with gladness, daughter of Jerusalem!
> See now, your king comes to you;
> he is victorious, he is triumphant,
> humble and riding on a donkey,
> on a colt, the foal of a donkey.
> He will banish chariots from Ephraim
> and horses from Jerusalem;
> the bow of war will be banished.
> He will proclaim peace for the nations.
> His empire shall stretch from sea to sea,
> from the River to the ends of the earth.'

The word of the Lord.

Responsorial Psalm   Ps 144:1-2,8-11,13-14. R. v.1

R. **I will bless your name for ever,**
   O God my King.
   Or: **Alleluia!**

I will give you glory, O God my King,
I will bless your name for ever.
I will bless you day after day
and praise your name for ever. R.

The Lord is kind and full of compassion,
slow to anger, abounding in love.
How good is the Lord to all,
compassionate to all his creatures. R.

All your creatures shall thank you, O Lord,
and your friends shall repeat their blessing.
They shall speak of the glory of your reign
and declare your might, O God. R.

The Lord is faithful in all his words
and loving in all his deeds.
The Lord supports all who fall
and raises all who are bowed down. R.

SECOND READING

A reading from the letter of St Paul to the Romans   8:9,11-13

If by the Spirit you put an end to the misdeeds of the body you will live.

Your interests are not in the unspiritual, but in the spiritual, since the Spirit of God has made his home in you. In fact, unless you possessed the Spirit of Christ you would not belong to him, and if the Spirit of him who raised Jesus from the dead is living in you, then he who raised Jesus from the dead will give life to your own mortal bodies through his Spirit living in you.

So then, my brothers, there is no necessity for us to obey our unspiritual selves or to live unspiritual lives. If you do live in that way, you are doomed to die, but if by the Spirit you put an end to the misdeeds of the body you will live.

The word of the Lord.

Gospel Acclamation   Cf. Mt 11:25

R. **Alleluia, alleluia!**
Blessed are you, Father,
Lord of heaven and earth;
for revealing the mysteries of the kingdom.
to mere children.
R. **Alleluia!**

GOSPEL

A reading from the holy Gospel according to Matthew   11:25-30

I am gentle and humble in heart.

Jesus exclaimed, 'I bless you, Father, Lord of heaven and of earth, for hiding these things from the learned and the clever and revealing them to mere children. Yes, Father, for that is what it pleased you to do. Everything has been entrusted to me by my Father; and no one knows the Son except the Father, just as no one knows the Father except the Son and those to whom the Son chooses to reveal him.

'Come to me, all you who labour and are overburdened, and I will give you rest. Shoulder my yoke and learn from me, for I am gentle and humble in heart, and you will find rest for your souls. Yes, my yoke is easy and my burden light.'

The Gospel of the Lord.

Prayer over the Offerings

May this oblation dedicated
   to your name
purify us, O Lord,
and day by day bring our conduct
closer to the life of heaven.
Through Christ our Lord.

Super oblata

Oblatio nos, Domine,
   tuo nomini dicata purificet,
et de die in diem ad cælestis vitæ
   transferat actionem.
Per Christum Dominum nostrum.

Preface of Sundays in Ordinary Time I-VIII, pp.566-573.

Communion Antiphon   Ps 33:9

Taste and see that the Lord is good;
blessed the man who seeks refuge
   in him.

Ant. ad communionem

Gustate et videte, quoniam suavis
   est Dominus;
beatus vir, qui sperat in eo.

Or: Mt 11:28

Come to me, all who labour
   and are burdened,
and I will refresh you,
   says the Lord.

Vel:

Venite ad me, omnes qui laboratis
   et onerati estis,
et ego reficiam vos, dicit Dominus.

Prayer after Communion

Grant, we pray, O Lord,
that, having been replenished
   by such great gifts,
we may gain the prize of salvation
and never cease to praise you.
Through Christ our Lord.

Post communionem

Tantis, Domine, repleti muneribus,
præsta, quæsumus, ut et salutaria
   dona capiamus,
et a tua numquam laude cessemus.
Per Christum Dominum nostrum.

FIFTEENTH SUNDAY IN ORDINARY TIME
(YEAR A)

Entrance Antiphon   Cf. Ps 16:15

AS for me, in justice I shall
   behold your face;
I shall be filled with the vision
   of your glory.

Ant. ad introitum

EGO autem cum iustitia
   apparebo in conspectu tuo;
satiabor dum manifestabitur
   gloria tua.

Collect

O God, who show the light
   of your truth
to those who go astray,
so that they may return
   to the right path,
give all who for the faith they profess
are accounted Christians
the grace to reject whatever
   is contrary to the name of Christ
and to strive after all that does
   it honour.
Through our Lord Jesus Christ,
   your Son,
who lives and reigns with you
   in the unity of the Holy Spirit,
one God, for ever and ever.

Collecta

Deus, qui errantibus,
   ut in viam possint redire,
veritatis tuæ lumen ostendis,
da cunctis qui christiana
   professione censentur,
et illa respuere, quæ huic inimica
   sunt nomini,
et ea quæ sunt apta sectari.
Per Dominum nostrum Iesum
   Christum Filium tuum,
qui tecum vivit et regnat
   in unitate Spiritus Sancti,
Deus, per omnia sæcula sæculorum.

FIRST READING

A reading from the prophet Isaiah   55:10-11
The rain makes the earth give growth.

Thus says the Lord: 'As the rain and the snow come down from the heavens and do not return without watering the earth, making it yield and giving growth to provide seed for the sower and bread for the eating, so the word that goes from my mouth does not return to me empty, without carrying out my will and succeeding in what it was sent to do.'

   The word of the Lord.

Responsorial Psalm   Ps 64:10-14. R. Lk 8:8

R. **Some seed fell into rich soil**
   and produced its crop.

   You care for the earth, give it water,
   you fill it with riches.
   Your river in heaven brims over
   to provide its grain. R.

   And thus you provide for the earth;
   you drench its furrows,
   you level it, soften it with showers,
   you bless its growth. R.

You crown the year with your goodness.
Abundance flows in your steps,
in the pastures of the wilderness it flows. R.

The hills are girded with joy,
the meadows covered with flocks,
the valleys are decked with wheat.
They shout for joy, yes, they sing. R.

SECOND READING

A reading from the letter of St Paul to the Romans   8:18-23

The whole creation is eagerly waiting for God to reveal his sons.

I think that what we suffer in this life can never be compared to the glory, as yet unrevealed, which is waiting for us. The whole creation is eagerly waiting for God to reveal his sons. It was not for any fault on the part of creation that it was made unable to attain its purpose, it was made so by God; but creation still retains the hope of being freed, like us, from its slavery to decadence, to enjoy the same freedom and glory as the children of God. From the beginning till now the entire creation, as we know, has been groaning in one great act of giving birth; and not only creation, but all of us who possess the first-fruits of the Spirit, we too groan inwardly as we wait for our bodies to be set free.

The word of the Lord.

Gospel Acclamation   1 S 3:9; Jn 6:68

R. **Alleluia, alleluia!**
Speak, Lord, your servant is listening:
you have the message of eternal life.
R. **Alleluia!**

Or:

R. **Alleluia, alleluia!**
The seed is the word of God, Christ the sower;
whoever finds this seed will remain for ever.
R. **Alleluia!**

GOSPEL

A reading from the holy Gospel according to Matthew   13:1-23

A sower went out to sow.

[Jesus left the house and sat by the lakeside, but such crowds gathered round him that he got into a boat and sat there. The people all stood on the beach, and he told them many things in parables.

He said, 'Imagine a sower going out to sow. As he sowed, some seeds fell on the edge of the path, and the birds came and ate them up. Others fell on patches of rock where they found little soil and sprang up straight away, because there was no depth of earth; but as soon as the sun came up they were scorched and, not having any roots, they withered away. Others fell among thorns, and the thorns grew up and choked them. Others fell on rich soil and produced their crop, some a hundredfold, some sixty, some thirty. Listen, anyone who has ears!']

Then the disciples went up to him and asked, 'Why do you talk to them in parables?' 'Because' he replied 'the mysteries of the kingdom of heaven are revealed to you, but they are not revealed to them. For anyone who has will be given more, and he will have more than enough; but from anyone who has not, even what he has will be taken away. The reason I talk to them in parables is that they look without seeing and listen without hearing or understanding. So in their case this prophecy of Isaiah is being fulfilled:

You will listen and listen again, but not understand,
see and see again, but not perceive.
For the heart of this nation has grown coarse,
their ears are dull of hearing, and they have shut their eyes,
for fear they should see with their eyes,
hear with their ears,
understand with their heart,
and be converted
and be healed by me.

'But happy are your eyes because they see, your ears because they hear! I tell you solemnly, many prophets and holy men longed to see what you see, and never saw it; to hear what you hear, and never heard it.

'You, therefore, are to hear the parable of the sower. When anyone hears the word of the kingdom without understanding, the evil one comes and carries off what was sown in his heart: this is the man who received the seed on the edge of the path. The one who received it on patches of rock is the man who hears the word and welcomes it at once with joy. But he has no root in him, he does not last; let some trial come, or some persecution on account of the word, and he falls away at once. The one who received the seed in thorns is the man who hears the word but the worries of this world and the lure of riches choke the word and so he produces nothing. And the one who received the seed in rich soil is the man who hears the word and understands it; he is the one who yields a harvest and produces now a hundredfold, now sixty, now thirty.'

| [The Gospel of the Lord.]

Shorter Form, verses 1-9. Read between [ ]

Prayer over the Offerings

Look upon the offerings
    of the Church, O Lord,
as she makes her prayer to you,
and grant that, when consumed
    by those who believe,
they may bring ever
    greater holiness.
Through Christ our Lord.

Super oblata

Respice, Domine, munera
    supplicantis Ecclesiæ,
et pro credentium
    sanctificationis incremento
sumenda concede.
Per Christum Dominum nostrum.

Preface of Sundays in Ordinary Time I-VIII, pp.566-573.

Communion Antiphon Cf. Ps 83:4-5

The sparrow finds a home,
and the swallow a nest for her young:
by your altars, O Lord of hosts,
    my King and my God.
Blessed are they who dwell
    in your house,
for ever singing your praise.

Ant. ad communionem

Passer invenit sibi domum,
et turtur nidum,
    ubi reponat pullos suos.
Altaria tua, Domine virtutum,
    Rex meus, et Deus meus!
Beati qui habitant in domo tua,
in sæculum sæculi laudabunt te.

Or: Jn 6:57

Whoever eats my flesh
    and drinks my blood
remains in me and I in him,
    says the Lord.

Vel:

Qui manducat meam carnem
    et bibit meum sanguinem,
in me manet et ego in eo,
    dicit Dominus.

Prayer after Communion

Having consumed these gifts,
    we pray, O Lord,
that, by our participation
    in this mystery,
its saving effects upon us may grow.
Through Christ our Lord.

Post communionem

Sumptis muneribus,
    quæsumus, Domine,
ut, cum frequentatione mysterii,
crescat nostræ salutis effectus.
Per Christum Dominum nostrum.

SIXTEENTH SUNDAY IN ORDINARY TIME
(YEAR A)

Entrance Antiphon   Ps 53:6,8

SEE, I have God for my help.
The Lord sustains my soul.
I will sacrifice to you
    with willing heart,
and praise your name, O Lord,
    for it is good.

Collect

Show favour, O Lord, to your servants
and mercifully increase the gifts
    of your grace,
that, made fervent in hope,
    faith and charity,
they may be ever watchful
    in keeping your commands.
Through our Lord Jesus Christ,
    your Son,
who lives and reigns with you
    in the unity of the Holy Spirit,
one God, for ever and ever.

Ant. ad introitum

ECCE Deus adiuvat me,
et Dominus susceptor est
    animæ meæ.
Voluntarie sacrificabo tibi,
et confitebor nomini tuo, Domine,
    quoniam bonum est.

Collecta

Propitiare, Domine, famulis tuis,
et clementer gratiæ tuæ super eos
    dona multiplica,
ut, spe, fide et caritate ferventes,
semper in mandatis tuis vigili
    custodia perseverent.
Per Dominum nostrum Iesum
    Christum Filium tuum,
qui tecum vivit et regnat
    in unitate Spiritus Sancti,
Deus, per omnia sæcula sæculorum.

FIRST READING

A reading from the book of Wisdom   12:13,16-19

After sin you will grant repentance.

There is no god, other than you, who cares for everything,
to whom you might have to prove that you never judged unjustly.
Your justice has its source in strength,
your sovereignty over all makes you lenient to all.
You show your strength when your sovereign power is questioned
and you expose the insolence of those who know it;
but, disposing of such strength, you are mild in judgement,
you govern us with great lenience,
for you have only to will, and your power is there.
By acting thus you have taught a lesson to your people
how the virtuous man must be kindly to his fellow men,
and you have given your sons the good hope
that after sin you will grant repentance.

    The word of the Lord.

Responsorial Psalm   Ps 85:5-6,9-10,15-16. R. v.5

R. **O Lord, you are good and forgiving**.

O Lord, you are good and forgiving,
full of love to all who call.
Give heed, O Lord, to my prayer
and attend to the sound of my voice. R.

All the nations shall come to adore you
and glorify your name, O Lord:
for you are great and do marvellous deeds,
you who alone are God. R.

But you, God of mercy and compassion,
slow to anger, O Lord,
abounding in love and truth,
turn and take pity on me. R.

SECOND READING

A reading from the letter of St Paul to the Romans   8:26-27

The Spirit expresses our plea in a way that could never be put into words.

The Spirit comes to help us in our weakness. For when we cannot choose words in order to pray properly, the Spirit himself expresses our plea in a way that could never be put into words, and God who knows everything in our hearts knows perfectly well what he means, and that the pleas of the saints expressed by the Spirit are according to the mind of God.

The word of the Lord.

Gospel Acclamation   Cf. Ep 1:17,18

R. **Alleluia, alleluia!**
May the Father of our Lord Jesus Christ
enlighten the eyes of our mind,
so that we can see what hope his call holds for us.
R. **Alleluia!**

Or: Cf. Mt 11:25

R. **Alleluia, alleluia!**
Blessed are you, Father,
Lord of heaven and earth,
for revealing the mysteries of the kingdom
to mere children.
R. **Alleluia!**

GOSPEL

A reading from the holy Gospel according to Matthew   13:24-43

Let them both grow till the harvest.

[Jesus put another parable before the crowds: 'The kingdom of heaven may be compared to a man who sowed good seed in his field. While everybody was asleep his enemy came, sowed darnel all among the wheat, and made off. When the new wheat sprouted and ripened, the darnel appeared as well. The owner's servants went to him and said, "Sir, was it not good seed that you sowed in your field? If so, where does the darnel come from?" "Some enemy has done this" he answered. And the servants said, "Do you want us to go and weed it out?" But he said, "No, because when you weed out the darnel you might pull up the wheat with it. Let them both grow till the harvest; and at harvest time I shall say to the reapers: First collect the darnel and tie it in bundles to be burnt, then gather the wheat into my barn."']

He put another parable before them, 'The kingdom of heaven is like a mustard seed which a man took and sowed in his field. It is the smallest of all the seeds, but when it has grown it is the biggest shrub of all and becomes a tree so that the birds of the air come and shelter in its branches.'

He told them another parable, 'The kingdom of heaven is like the yeast a woman took and mixed in with three measures of flour till it was leavened all through.'

In all this Jesus spoke to the crowds in parables; indeed, he would never speak to them except in parables. This was to fulfill the prophecy:

I will speak to you in parables
and expound things hidden since the foundation of the world.

Then, leaving the crowds, he went to the house; and his disciples came to him and said, 'Explain the parable about the darnel in the field to us.' He said in reply, 'The sower of the good seed is the Son of Man. The field is the world; the good seed is the subjects of the kingdom; the darnel, the subjects of the evil one; the enemy who sowed them, the devil; the harvest is the end of the world, the reapers are the angels. Well then, just as the darnel is gathered up and burnt in the fire, so it will be at the end of time. The Son of Man will send his angels and they will gather out of his kingdom all things that provoke offences and all who do evil, and throw them into the blazing furnace, where there will be weeping and grinding of teeth. Then the virtuous will shine like the sun in the kingdom of their Father. Listen, anyone who has ears!'

[The Gospel of the Lord.]

Shorter Form, verses 24-30. Read between [ ]

Prayer over the Offerings

O God, who in the one
   perfect sacrifice
brought to completion varied
   offerings of the law,
accept, we pray, this sacrifice
   from your faithful servants
and make it holy, as you blessed
   the gifts of Abel,
so that what each has offered
   to the honour of your majesty
may benefit the salvation of all.
Through Christ our Lord.

Super oblata

Deus, qui legalium
   differentiam hostiarum
unius sacrificii perfectione sanxisti,
accipe sacrificium a devotis
   tibi famulis,
et pari benedictione,
   sicut munera Abel, sanctifica,
ut, quod singuli obtulerunt
   ad maiestatis tuæ honorem,
cunctis proficiat ad salutem.
Per Christum Dominum nostrum.

Preface of Sundays in Ordinary Time I-VIII, pp.566-573.

Communion Antiphon Ps 110:4-5

The Lord, the gracious, the merciful,
has made a memorial of his wonders;
he gives food to those who fear him.

Ant. ad communionem

Memoriam fecit mirabilium suorum
misericors et miserator Dominus;
escam dedit timentibus se.

Or: Rv 3:20

Behold, I stand at the door
   and knock, says the Lord.
If anyone hears my voice
   and opens the door to me,
I will enter his house and dine
   with him, and he with me.

Vel:

Ecce sto ad ostium et pulso,
   dicit Dominus:
si quis audierit vocem meam,
   et aperuerit mihi ianuam,
intrabo ad illum, et cenabo
   cum illo, et ipse mecum.

Prayer after Communion

Graciously be present to your people,
   we pray, O Lord,
and lead those you have imbued
   with heavenly mysteries
to pass from former ways
   to newness of life.
Through Christ our Lord.

Post communionem

Populo tuo, quæsumus, Domine,
   adesto propitius,
et, quem mysteriis
   cælestibus imbuisti,
fac ad novitatem vitæ
   de vetustate transire.
Per Christum Dominum nostrum.

SEVENTEENTH SUNDAY IN ORDINARY TIME
(YEAR A)

Entrance Antiphon Cf. Ps 67:6-7,36	Ant. ad introitum
GOD is in his holy place, God who unites those who dwell in his house; he himself gives might and strength to his people.	DEUS in loco sancto suo; Deus qui inhabitare facit unanimes in domo, ipse dabit virtutem et fortitudinem plebi suæ.
Collect	Collecta
O God, protector of those who hope in you, without whom nothing has firm foundation, nothing is holy, bestow in abundance your mercy upon us and grant that, with you as our ruler and guide, we may use the good things that pass in such a way as to hold fast even now to those that ever endure. Through our Lord Jesus Christ, your Son, who lives and reigns with you in the unity of the Holy Spirit, one God, for ever and ever.	Protector in te sperantium, Deus, sine quo nihil est validum, nihil sanctum, multiplica super nos misericordiam tuam ut, te rectore, te duce, sic bonis transeuntibus nunc utamur, ut iam possimus inhærere mansuris. Per Dominum nostrum Iesum Christum Filium tuum, qui tecum vivit et regnat in unitate Spiritus Sancti, Deus, per omnia sæcula sæculorum.

FIRST READING

A reading from the first book of the Kings   3:5,7-12

You have asked for a discerning judgement for yourself.

The Lord appeared to Solomon in a dream and said, 'Ask what you would like me to give you.' Solomon replied, 'Lord, my God, you have made your servant king in succession to David my father. But I am a very young man, unskilled in leadership. Your servant finds himself in the midst of this people of yours that you have chosen, a people so many its numbers cannot be counted or reckoned. Give your servant a heart to understand how to discern between good and evil, for who could govern this people of yours that is so great?' It pleased the Lord that Solomon should have asked for this. 'Since you have asked for this' the Lord said 'and not asked for long life for yourself or riches or the lives of your enemies, but have asked for a discerning judgement for yourself, here and now I do what you ask. I give you a heart wise and shrewd as none before you has had and none will have after you.'

The word of the Lord.

Responsional Psalm   Ps 118:57,72,76-77,127-130. R. v.97

R. **Lord how I love your law!**

My part, I have resolved, O Lord,
is to obey your word.
The law from your mouth means more to me
than silver and gold. R.

Let your love be ready to console me
by your promise to your servant.
Let your love come to me and I shall live
for your law is my delight. R.

That is why I love your commands
more than finest gold,
That is why I rule my life by your precepts:
I hate false ways. R.

Your will is wonderful indeed;
therefore I obey it.
The unfolding of your word gives light
and teaches the simple. R.

SECOND READING

A reading from the letter of St Paul to the Romans   8:28-30

God intended us to become true images of his Son.

We know that by turning everything to their good God co-operates with all those who love him, with all those that he has called according to his purpose. They are the ones he chose specially long ago and intended to become true images of his Son, so that his Son might be the eldest of many brothers. He called those he intended for this; those he called he justified, and with those he justified he shared his glory.

The word of the Lord.

Gospel Acclamation   Jn 15:15

R. **Alleluia, alleluia!**
I call you friends, says the Lord,
because I have made known to you
everything I have learnt from my Father.
R. **Alleluia!**

Or: Cf. Mt 11:25

R. **Alleluia, alleluia!**
Blessed are you, Father,
Lord of heaven and earth,
for revealing the mysteries of the kingdom
to mere children.
R. **Alleluia!**

GOSPEL

A reading from the holy Gospel according to Matthew   13:44-52

He sells everything he owns and buys the field.

[Jesus said to the crowds: 'The kingdom of heaven is like treasure hidden
in a field which someone has found; he hides it again, goes off happy, sells
everything he owns and buys the field.

'Again, the kingdom of heaven is like a merchant looking for fine
pearls; when he finds one of great value he goes and sells everything he
owns and buys it.]

'Again, the kingdom of heaven is like a dragnet cast into the sea that
brings in a haul of all kinds. When it is full, the fishermen haul it ashore;
then, sitting down, they collect the good ones in a basket and throw away
those that are no use. This is how it will be at the end of time: the angels
will appear and separate the wicked from the just to throw them into the
blazing furnace where there will be weeping and grinding of teeth.

'Have you understood all this?' They said, 'Yes.' And he said to them,
'Well then, every scribe who becomes a disciple of the kingdom of heaven
is like a householder who brings out from his storeroom things both new
and old.'

[The Gospel of the Lord.]

Shorter Form, verses 44-46. Read between [ ]

Prayer over the Offerings

Accept, O Lord, we pray, the offerings
which we bring from the abundance
　　of your gifts,
that through the powerful working
　　of your grace
these most sacred mysteries may
　　sanctify our present way of life
and lead us to eternal gladness.
Through Christ our Lord.

Preface of Sundays in Ordinary Time I-VIII, pp.566-573.

Communion Antiphon　Ps 102:2

Bless the Lord, O my soul,
and never forget all his benefits.

Or:　　　　　　　　　　Mt 5:7-8

Blessed are the merciful,
　　for they shall receive mercy.
Blessed are the clean of heart,
　　for they shall see God.

Prayer after Communion

We have consumed, O Lord,
　　this divine Sacrament,
the perpetual memorial
　　of the Passion of your Son;
grant, we pray, that this gift,
which he himself gave us with love
　　beyond all telling,
may profit us for salvation.
Through Christ our Lord.

Super oblata

Suscipe, quæsumus,
　　Domine, munera,
quæ tibi de tua largitate deferimus,
ut hæc sacrosancta mysteria,
　　gratiæ tuæ operante virtute,
et præsentis vitæ nos
　　conversatione sanctificent,
et ad gaudia sempiterna perducant.
Per Christum Dominum nostrum.

Ant. ad communionem

Benedic, anima mea, Domino,
et noli oblivisci omnes
　　retributiones eius.

Vel:

Beati misericordes,
quoniam ipsi
　　misericordiam consequentur.
Beati mundo corde,
quoniam ipsi Deum videbunt.

Post communionem

Sumpsimus, Domine,
　　divinum sacramentum,
passionis Filii tui
　　memoriale perpetuum;
tribue, quæsumus,
ut ad nostram salutem hoc
　　munus proficiat,
quod ineffabili nobis caritate
　　ipse donavit.
Qui vivit et regnat
　　in sæcula sæculorum.

EIGHTEENTH SUNDAY IN ORDINARY TIME
(YEAR A)

Entrance Antiphon   Ps 69:2,6

O GOD, come to my assistance;
  O Lord, make haste to help me!
You are my rescuer, my help;
O Lord, do not delay.

Ant. ad introitum

D EUS, in adiutorium
  meum intende;
Domine, ad adiuvandum me festina.
Adiutor meus et liberator meus es tu;
Domine, ne moreris.

Collect

Draw near to your servants, O Lord,
and answer their prayers
  with unceasing kindness,
that, for those who glory in you
  as their Creator and guide,
you may restore what you
  have created
and keep safe what you have restored.
Through our Lord Jesus Christ,
  your Son,
who lives and reigns with you
  in the unity of the Holy Spirit,
one God, for ever and ever.

Collecta

Adesto, Domine, famulis tuis,
et perpetuam benignitatem
  largire poscentibus,
ut his, qui te auctorem et
  gubernatorem gloriantur habere,
et creata restaures,
  et restaurata conserves.
Per Dominum nostrum Iesum
  Christum Filium tuum,
qui tecum vivit et regnat
  in unitate Spiritus Sancti,
Deus, per omnia sæcula sæculorum.

FIRST READING

A reading from the prophet Isaiah   55:1-3

Come and eat.

Thus says the Lord:
  Oh, come to the water all you who are thirsty;
  though you have no money, come!
  Buy corn without money, and eat,
  and, at no cost, wine and milk.
  Why spend money on what is not bread,
  your wages on what fails to satisfy?
  Listen, listen to me and you will have good things to eat
  and rich food to enjoy.
  Pay attention, come to me;
  listen, and your soul will live.
  With you I will make an everlasting covenant
  out of the favours promised to David.
  The word of the Lord.

Responsial Psalm   Ps 144:8-9,15-18. R. v.16

R. **You open wide your hand, O Lord,
you grant our desires.**

The Lord is kind and full of compassion,
slow to anger, abounding in love.
How good is the Lord to all,
compassionate to all his creatures. R.

The eyes of all creatures look to you
and you give them their food in due time.
You open wide your hand,
grant the desires of all who live. R.

The Lord is just in all his ways
and loving in all his deeds.
He is close to all who call him,
call on him from their hearts. R.

SECOND READING

A reading from the letter of St Paul to the Romans   8:35,37-39

No created thing can ever come between us and the love of God made visible in Christ.

Nothing can come between us and the love of Christ, even if we are
troubled or worried, or being persecuted, or lacking food or clothes, or
being threatened or even attacked. These are the trials through which we
triumph, by the power of him who loved us.

For I am certain of this: neither death nor life, no angel, no prince,
nothing that exists, nothing still to come, not any power, or height or
depth, nor any created thing, can ever come between us and the love of
God made visible in Christ Jesus our Lord.

The word of the Lord.

Gospel Acclamation   Lk 19:38

R. **Alleluia, alleluia!**
Blessings on the King who comes,
in the name of the Lord!
Peace in heaven
and glory in the highest heavens!
R. **Alleluia!**

Or: Mt 4:4

R. **Alleluia, alleluia!**
Man does not live on bread alone,
but on every word that comes from the mouth of God.
R. **Alleluia!**

GOSPEL

A reading from the holy Gospel according to Matthew   14:13-21

They all ate as much as they wanted.

When Jesus received the news of John the Baptist's death he withdrew by boat to a lonely place where they could be by themselves. But the people heard of this and, leaving the towns, went after him on foot. So as he stepped ashore he saw a large crowd; and he took pity on them and healed their sick.

When evening came, the disciples went to him and said, 'This is a lonely place, and the time has slipped by; so send the people away, and they can go to the villages to buy themselves some food.' Jesus replied, 'There is no need for them to go: give them something to eat yourselves.' But they answered, 'All we have with us is five loaves and two fish.' 'Bring them here to me,' he said. He gave orders that the people were to sit down on the grass; then he took the five loaves and the two fish, raised his eyes to heaven and said the blessing. And breaking the loaves he handed them to his disciples who gave them to the crowds. They all ate as much as they wanted, and they collected the scraps remaining, twelve baskets full. Those who ate numbered about five thousand men, to say nothing of women and children.

The Gospel of the Lord.

Prayer over the Offerings	Super oblata

Graciously sanctify these gifts,
   O Lord, we pray,
and, accepting the oblation
   of this spiritual sacrifice,
make of us an eternal offering to you.
Through Christ our Lord.
	Propitius, Domine, quæsumus,
	   hæc dona sanctifica,
	et, hostiæ spiritalis
	   oblatione suscepta,
	nosmetipsos tibi perfice
	   munus æternum.
	Per Christum Dominum nostrum.

Preface of Sundays in Ordinary Time I-VIII, pp.566-573.

Communion Antiphon Ws 16:20	Ant. ad communionem

You have given us, O Lord,
   bread from heaven,
endowed with all delights
   and sweetness in every taste.
	Panem de cælo dedisti
	   nobis, Domine,
	habentem omne delectamentum,
	et omnem saporem suavitatis.

Or: Jn 6:35	Vel:

I am the bread of life, says the Lord;
whoever comes to me will not hunger
and whoever believes in me will
   not thirst.
	Ego sum panis vitæ, dicit Dominus.
	Qui venit ad me non esuriet,
	   et qui credit in me non sitiet.

Prayer after Communion

Accompany with constant
    protection, O Lord,
those you renew with these
    heavenly gifts
and, in your never-failing care
    for them,
make them worthy
    of eternal redemption.
Through Christ our Lord.

Post communionem

Quos cælesti recreas munere,
perpetuo, Domine,
    comitare præsidio,
et, quos fovere non desinis,
dignos fieri sempiterna
    redemptione concede.
Per Christum Dominum nostrum.

NINETEENTH SUNDAY IN ORDINARY TIME
(YEAR A)

Entrance Antiphon Cf. Ps 73:20,19,22,23

LOOK to your covenant, O Lord,
and forget not the life of your
    poor ones for ever.
Arise, O God, and defend your cause,
and forget not the cries of those
    who seek you.

Ant. ad introitum

RESPICE, Domine,
in testamentum tuum,
et animas pauperum tuorum
    ne derelinquas in finem.
Exsurge, Domine,
    et iudica causam tuam,
et ne obliviscaris voces
    quærentium te.

Collect

Almighty ever-living God,
whom, taught by the Holy Spirit,
we dare to call our Father,
bring, we pray, to perfection
    in our hearts
the spirit of adoption as your sons
    and daughters,
that we may merit
    to enter into the inheritance
which you have promised.
Through our Lord Jesus Christ,
    your Son,
who lives and reigns with you
    in the unity of the Holy Spirit,
one God, for ever and ever.

Collecta

Omnipotens sempiterne Deus,
quem, docente Spiritu Sancto,
paterno nomine
    invocare præsumimus,
perfice in cordibus nostris spiritum
    adoptionis filiorum,
ut promissam hereditatem
    ingredi mereamur.
Per Dominum nostrum Iesum
    Christum Filium tuum,
qui tecum vivit et regnat
    in unitate Spiritus Sancti,
Deus, per omnia sæcula sæculorum.

FIRST READING

A reading from the first book of the Kings   19:9,11-13

Stand on the mountain before the Lord.

When Elijah reached Horeb, the mountain of God, he went into the cave and spent the night in it. Then he was told, 'Go out and stand on the mountain before the Lord.' Then the Lord himself went by. There came a mighty wind, so strong it tore the mountains and shattered the rocks before the Lord. But the Lord was not in the wind. After the wind came an earthquake. But the Lord was not in the earthquake. After the earthquake came a fire. But the Lord was not in the fire. And after the fire there came the sound of a gentle breeze. And when Elijah heard this, he covered his face with his cloak and went out and stood at the entrance of the cave.

The word of the Lord.

Responsorial Psalm   Ps 84:9-14. R. v.8

R. **Let us see, O Lord your mercy**
    and give us your saving help.

I will hear what the Lord God has to say,
a voice that speaks of peace.
His help is near for those who fear him
and his glory will dwell in our land. R.

Mercy and faithfulness have met;
justice and peace have embraced.
Faithfulness shall spring from the earth
and justice look down from heaven. R.

The Lord will make us prosper
and our earth shall yield its fruit.
Justice shall march before him
and peace shall follow his steps. R.

SECOND READING

A reading from the letter of St Paul to the Romans   9:1-5

I would willingly be condemned if it could help my brothers.

What I want to say is no pretence; I say it in union with Christ – it is the truth – my conscience in union with the Holy Spirit assures me of it too. What I want to say is this: my sorrow is so great, my mental anguish so endless, I would willingly be condemned and be cut off from Christ if it could help my brothers of Israel, my own flesh and blood. They were adopted as sons, they were given the glory and the covenants; the Law and the ritual were drawn up for them, and the promises were made to them. They are descended from the patriarchs and from their flesh and blood came Christ who is above all, God for ever blessed! Amen.

The word of the Lord.

Gospel Acclamation   Lk 19:38

R. **Alleluia, alleluia!**
Blessings on the King who comes, in the name of the Lord!
Peace in heaven and glory in the highest heavens!
R. **Alleluia**

Or: Ps 129:5

R. **Alleluia, alleluia!**
My soul is waiting for the Lord,
I count on his word.
R. **Alleluia**

GOSPEL

A reading from the holy Gospel according to Matthew   14:22-33
Tell me to come to you across the water.

Jesus made the disciples get into the boat and go on ahead to the other side while he would send the crowds away. After sending the crowds away he went up into the hills by himself to pray. When evening came, he was there alone, while the boat, by now far out on the lake, was battling with a heavy sea, for there was a headwind. In the fourth watch of the night he went towards them, walking on the lake, and when the disciples saw him walking on the lake they were terrified. 'It is a ghost' they said, and cried out in fear. But at once Jesus called out to them, saying, 'Courage! It is I! Do not be afraid.' It was Peter who answered. 'Lord,' he said 'if it is you, tell me to come to you across the water.' 'Come' said Jesus. Then Peter got out of the boat and started walking towards Jesus across the water, but as soon as he felt the force of the wind, he took fright and began to sink. 'Lord! Save me!' he cried. Jesus put out his hand at once and held him. 'Man of little faith,' he said 'why did you doubt?' And as they got into the boat the wind dropped. The men in the boat bowed down before him and said, 'Truly, you are the Son of God.'

The Gospel of the Lord.

Prayer over the Offerings

Be pleased, O Lord, to accept
   the offerings of your Church,
for in your mercy you have given
   them to be offered
and by your power
   you transform them
into the mystery of our salvation.
Through Christ our Lord.

Super oblata

Ecclesiæ tuæ, Domine, munera
   placatus assume,
quæ et misericors
   offerenda tribuisti,
et in nostræ salutis potenter efficis
   transire mysterium.
Per Christum Dominum nostrum.

Preface of Sundays in Ordinary Time I-VIII, pp.566-573.

Communion Antiphon Ps 147:12,14

O Jerusalem, glorify the Lord,
who gives you your fill
   of finest wheat.

Or: Cf. Jn 6:51

The bread that I will give,
   says the Lord,
is my flesh for the life of the world.

Ant. ad communionem

Lauda, Ierusalem, Dominum,
qui adipe frumenti satiat te.

Vel:

Panis, quem ego dedero,
caro mea est pro sæculi vita,
dicit Dominus.

Prayer after Communion

May the communion
   in your Sacrament
that we have consumed, save us,
   O Lord,
and confirm us in the light
   of your truth.
Through Christ our Lord.

Post communionem

Sacramentorum tuorum, Domine,
communio sumpta nos salvet,
et in tuæ veritatis luce confirmet.
Per Christum Dominum nostrum.

TWENTIETH SUNDAY IN ORDINARY TIME
(YEAR A)

Entrance Antiphon   Ps 83:10-11

TURN your eyes, O God,
   our shield;
and look on the face
   of your anointed one;
one day within your courts
is better than a thousand elsewhere.

Ant. ad introitum

PROTECTOR noster,
   aspice, Deus,
et respice in faciem Christi tui,
quia melior est dies una in atriis
   tuis super millia.

Collect

O God, who have prepared
for those who love you
good things which no eye can see,
fill our hearts, we pray,
with the warmth of your love,
so that, loving you in all things
and above all things,
we may attain your promises,
which surpass every human desire.
Through our Lord Jesus Christ,
your Son,
who lives and reigns with you
in the unity of the Holy Spirit,
one God, for ever and ever.

Collecta

Deus, qui diligentibus te bona
invisibilia præparasti,
infunde cordibus nostris
tui amoris affectum,
ut, te in omnibus et super
omnia diligentes,
promissiones tuas, quæ omne
desiderium superant,
consequamur.
Per Dominum nostrum Iesum
Christum Filium tuum,
qui tecum vivit et regnat
in unitate Spiritus Sancti,
Deus, per omnia sæcula sæculorum.

FIRST READING

A reading from the prophet Isaiah   56:1,6-7

I will bring foreigners to my holy mountain.

Thus says the Lord: Have a care for justice, act with integrity, for soon my salvation will come and my integrity be manifest.

Foreigners who have attached themselves to the Lord to serve him and to love his name and be his servants – all who observe the sabbath, not profaning it, and cling to my covenant – these I will bring to my holy mountain. I will make them joyful in my house of prayer. Their holocausts and their sacrifices will be accepted on my altar, for my house will be called a house of prayer for all the peoples.

The word of the Lord.

Responsorial Psalm   Ps 66:2-3,5-6,8. R. v.4

R. **Let the peoples praise you, O God;**
let all the peoples praise you.

O God, be gracious and bless us
and let your face shed its light upon us.
So will your ways be known upon earth
and all nations learn your saving help. R.

Let the nations be glad and exult
for you rule the world with justice.
With fairness you rule the peoples,
you guide the nations on earth. R.

Let the peoples praise you, O God;
> let all the peoples praise you.
> May God still give us his blessing
> till the ends of the earth revere him. R.

R. **Let the peoples praise you, O God;**
> **let all the peoples praise you.**

SECOND READING

A reading from the letter of St Paul to the Romans   11:13-15,29-32

With Israel, God never takes back his gifts or revokes his choice.

Let me tell you pagans this: I have been sent to the pagans as their apostle,
and I am proud of being sent, but the purpose of it is to make my own
people envious of you, and in this way save some of them. Since their
rejection meant the reconciliation of the world, do you know what their
admission will mean? Nothing less than a resurrection from the dead!
God never takes back his gifts or revokes his choice.

Just as you changed from being disobedient to God, and now enjoy
mercy because of their disobedience, so those who are disobedient now
– and only because of the mercy shown to you – will also enjoy mercy
eventually. God has imprisoned all men in their own disobedience only to
show mercy to all mankind.

The word of the Lord.

Gospel Acclamation   Cf. Jn 10:27

R. **Alleluia, alleluia!**
The sheep that belong to me listen to my voice,
says the Lord,
I know them and they follow me.
R. **Alleluia!**

Or: Cf. Mt 4:23

R. **Alleluia, alleluia!**
Jesus proclaimed the Good News of the kingdom,
and cured all kinds of sicknesses among the people.
R. **Alleluia!**

GOSPEL

A reading from the holy Gospel according to Matthew   15:21-28

Woman, you have great faith.

Jesus left Gennesaret and withdrew to the region of Tyre and Sidon. Then
out came a Canaanite woman from that district and started shouting, 'Sir,
Son of David, take pity on me. My daughter is tormented by a devil.' But

he answered her not a word. And his disciples went and pleaded with him. 'Give her what she wants,' they said 'because she is shouting after us.' He said in reply, 'I was sent only to the lost sheep of the House of Israel.' But the woman had come up and was kneeling at his feet. 'Lord,' she said 'help me.' He replied, 'It is not fair to take the children's food and throw it to the house-dogs.' She retorted, 'Ah yes, sir; but even house-dogs can eat the scraps that fall from their master's table.' Then Jesus answered her, 'Woman, you have great faith. Let your wish be granted.' And from that moment her daughter was well again.

The Gospel of the Lord.

Prayer over the Offerings	Super oblata
Receive our oblation, O Lord, by which is brought about a glorious exchange, that, by offering what you have given, we may merit to receive your very self. Through Christ our Lord.	Suscipe, Domine, munera nostra, quibus exercentur commercia gloriosa, ut, offerentes quæ dedisti, teipsum mereamur accipere. Per Christum Dominum nostrum.

Preface of Sundays in Ordinary Time I-VIII, pp.566-573.

Communion Antiphon Ps 129:7	Ant. ad communionem
With the Lord there is mercy; in him is plentiful redemption.	Apud Dominum misericordia, et copiosa apud eum redemptio.
Or: Jn 6:51-52	Vel:
I am the living bread that came down from heaven, says the Lord. Whoever eats of this bread will live for ever.	Ego sum panis vivus, qui de cælo descendi, dicit Dominus: si quis manducaverit ex hoc pane, vivet in æternum.

Prayer after Communion	Post communionem
Made partakers of Christ through these Sacraments, we humbly implore your mercy, Lord, that, conformed to his image on earth, we may merit also to be his coheirs in heaven. Who lives and reigns for ever and ever.	Per hæc sacramenta, Domine, Christi participes effecti, clementiam tuam humiliter imploramus, ut, eius imaginis conformes in terris, et eius consortes in cælis fieri mereamur. Qui vivit et regnat in sæcula sæculorum.

TWENTY-FIRST SUNDAY IN ORDINARY TIME
(YEAR A)

Entrance Antiphon   Cf. Ps 85:1-3

TURN your ear, O Lord,
and answer me;
save the servant who trusts in you,
    my God.
Have mercy on me, O Lord,
    for I cry to you all the day long.

Collect

O God, who cause the minds
    of the faithful
to unite in a single purpose,
grant your people to love
    what you command
and to desire what you promise,
that, amid the uncertainties
    of this world,
our hearts may be fixed on that place
where true gladness is found.
Through our Lord Jesus Christ,
    your Son,
who lives and reigns with you
    in the unity of the Holy Spirit,
one God, for ever and ever.

Ant. ad introitum

INCLINA, Domine, aurem tuam
ad me, et exaudi me.
Salvum fac servum tuum,
    Deus meus, sperantem in te.
Miserere mihi, Domine,
    quoniam ad te clamavi tota die.

Collecta

Deus, qui fidelium mentes unius
    efficis voluntatis,
da populis tuis id amare
    quod præcipis,
id desiderare quod promittis,
ut, inter mundanas varietates,
ibi nostra fixa sint corda,
    ubi vera sunt gaudia.
Per Dominum nostrum Iesum
    Christum Filium tuum,
qui tecum vivit et regnat
    in unitate Spiritus Sancti,
Deus, per omnia sæcula sæculorum.

FIRST READING

A reading from the prophet Isaiah   22:19-23

I place the key of the House of David upon his shoulder.

Thus says the Lord of hosts to Shebna, the master of the palace:
    I dismiss you from your office,
    I remove you from your post,
    and the same day I call on my servant
    Eliakim son of Hilkiah.
    I invest him with your robe,
    gird him with your sash,
    entrust him with your authority,
    and he shall be a father

to the inhabitants of Jerusalem
and to the House of Judah.
I place the key of the House of David
on his shoulder;
should he open, no one shall close,
should he close, no one shall open.
I drive him like a peg
into a firm place;
he will become a throne of glory
for his father's house.

The word of the Lord.

Responsorial Psalm   Ps 137:1-3,6,8. R. v.8

R. **Your love, O Lord, is eternal,
discard not the work of your hands.**

I thank you, Lord, with all my heart,
you have heard the words of my mouth.
Before the angels I will bless you.
I will adore before your holy temple. R.

I thank you for your faithfulness and love
which excel all we ever knew of you.
On the day I called, you answered;
you increased the strength of my soul. R.

The Lord is high yet he looks on the lowly
and the haughty he knows from afar.
Your love, O Lord, is eternal,
discard not the work of your hands. R.

SECOND READING

A reading from the letter of St Paul to the Romans   11:33-36
All that exists comes from him; all is by him and from him.

How rich are the depths of God – how deep his wisdom and knowledge –
and how impossible to penetrate his motives or understand his methods!
Who could ever know the mind of the Lord? Who could ever be his
counsellor? Who could ever give him anything or lend him anything? All
that exists comes from him; all is by him and for him. To him be glory for
ever! Amen.

The word of the Lord.

Gospel Acclamation   2 Co 5:19

R. **Alleluia, alleluia!**
God in Christ was reconciling the world to himself,
and he has entrusted to us the news that they are reconciled.
R. **Alleluia!**

Or: Mt 16:18

R. **Alleluia, alleluia!**
You are Peter,
and on this rock I will build my Church.
And the gates of the underworld can never hold out against it.
R. **Alleluia!**

GOSPEL

A reading from the holy Gospel according to Matthew   16:13-20
You are Peter, and I will give you the keys of the kingdom of heaven.

When Jesus came to the region of Caesarea Philippi he put this question
to his disciples, 'Who do people say the Son of Man is?' And they said,
'Some say he is John the Baptist, some Elijah, and others Jeremiah or one
of the prophets.' 'But you,' he said, 'who do you say I am?' Then Simon
Peter spoke up, 'You are the Christ,' he said 'the Son of the living God.'
Jesus replied, 'Simon son of Jonah, you are a happy man! Because it was
not flesh and blood that revealed this to you but my Father in heaven. So
I now say to you: You are Peter and on this rock I will build my Church.
And the gates of the underworld can never hold out against it. I will give
you the keys of the kingdom of heaven: whatever you bind on earth shall
be considered bound in heaven; whatever you loose on earth shall be
considered loosed in heaven.' Then he gave the disciples strict orders not
to tell anyone that he was the Christ.

The Gospel of the Lord.

Prayer over the Offerings | Super oblata

O Lord, who gained for yourself
    a people by adoption
through the one sacrifice offered
    once for all,
bestow graciously on us, we pray,
the gifts of unity and peace
    in your Church.
Through Christ our Lord.

Qui una semel hostia, Domine,
adoptionis tibi populum acquisisti,
unitatis et pacis in Ecclesia tua
propitius nobis dona concedas.
Per Christum Dominum nostrum.

Preface of Sundays in Ordinary Time I-VIII, pp.566-573.

Communion Antiphon Cf. Ps 103:13-15	Ant. ad communionem

The earth is replete with the fruits
    of your work, O Lord;
you bring forth bread from the earth
and wine to cheer the heart.
	De fructu operum tuorum,
	    Domine, satiabitur terra,
	ut educas panem de terra,
	    et vinum lætificet cor hominis.

Or: Cf. Jn 6:54	Vel:

Whoever eats my flesh
    and drinks my blood
has eternal life, says the Lord,
and I will raise him up
    on the last day.
	Qui manducat meam carnem
	    et bibit meum sanguinem,
	habet vitam æternam,
	    dicit Dominus;
	et ego resuscitabo eum
	    in novissimo die.

Prayer after Communion	Post communionem

Complete within us, O Lord,
    we pray,
the healing work of your mercy
and graciously perfect
    and sustain us,
so that in all things we may
    please you.
Through Christ our Lord.
	Plenum, quæsumus, Domine,
	in nobis remedium tuæ
	    miserationis operare
	ac tales nos esse perfice propitius
	    et sic foveri,
	ut tibi in omnibus
	    placere valeamus.
	Per Christum Dominum nostrum.

TWENTY-SECOND SUNDAY IN ORDINARY TIME
(YEAR A)

Entrance Antiphon Cf. Ps 85:3,5	Ant. ad introitum

HAVE mercy on me, O Lord,
for I cry to you all the day long.
O Lord, you are good and forgiving,
full of mercy to all who call to you.
	MISERERE mihi, Domine,
	quoniam ad te clamavi
	    tota die:
	quia tu, Domine, suavis ac mitis es,
	et copiosus in misericordia
	    omnibus invocantibus te.

Collect

God of might, giver of every
    good gift,
put into our hearts the love
    of your name,
so that, by deepening our sense
    of reverence,
you may nurture in us what is good
and, by your watchful care,
keep safe what you have nurtured.
Through our Lord Jesus Christ,
    your Son,
who lives and reigns with you
    in the unity of the Holy Spirit,
one God, for ever and ever.

Collecta

Deus virtutum, cuius est totum
    quod est optimum,
insere pectoribus nostris tui
    nominis amorem,
et præsta, ut in nobis,
religionis augmento,
    quæ sunt bona nutrias,
ac, vigilanti studio,
    quæ sunt nutrita custodias.
Per Dominum nostrum Iesum
    Christum Filium tuum,
qui tecum vivit et regnat
    in unitate Spiritus Sancti,
Deus, per omnia sæcula sæculorum.

FIRST READING

A reading from the prophet Jeremiah   20:7-9

The word of the Lord has meant insult for me.

You have seduced me, Lord, and I have let myself be seduced;
you have overpowered me: you were the stronger.
I am a daily laughing-stock,
everybody's butt.
Each time I speak the word, I have to howl
and proclaim: 'Violence and ruin!'
The word of the Lord has meant for me
insult, derision, all day long.
I used to say, 'I will not think about him,
I will not speak in his name anymore.'
Then there seemed to be a fire burning in my heart,
imprisoned in my bones.
The effort to restrain it wearied me,
I could not bear it.

    The word of the Lord.

Responsorial Psalm   Ps 62:2-6,8-9. R. v.2

R. **For you my soul is thirsting, O Lord my God.**

> O God, you are my God, for you I long;
> for you my soul is thirsting.
> My body pines for you
> like a dry, weary land without water. R.

> So I gaze on you in the sanctuary
> to see your strength and your glory.
> For your love is better than life,
> my lips will speak your praise. R.

> So I will bless you all my life,
> in your name I will lift up my hands.
> My soul shall be filled as with a banquet,
> my mouth shall praise you with joy. R.

> For you have been my help;
> in the shadow of your wings I rejoice.
> My soul clings to you;
> your right hand holds me fast. R.

SECOND READING

A reading from the letter of St Paul to the Romans   12:1-2

Offer your bodies as a living sacrifice.

Think of God's mercy, my brothers, and worship him, I beg you, in a way
that is worthy of thinking beings, by offering your living bodies as a holy
sacrifice, truly pleasing to God. Do not model yourselves on the behaviour
of the world around you, but let your behaviour change, modelled by your
new mind. This is the only way to discover the will of God and know what
is good, what it is that God wants, what is the perfect thing to do.

The word of the Lord.

Gospel Acclamation   Cf. Ep 1:17-18

R. **Alleluia, alleluia!**
May the Father of our Lord Jesus Christ
enlighten the eyes of our mind,
so that we can see
what hope his call holds for us.
R. **Alleluia!**

GOSPEL

A reading from the holy Gospel according Matthew   16:21-27

If anyone wants to be a follower of mine, let him renounce himself.

Jesus began to make it clear to his disciples that he was destined to go to Jerusalem and suffer grievously at the hands of the elders and chief priests and scribes, to be put to death and to be raised up on the third day. Then, taking him aside, Peter started to remonstrate with him. 'Heaven preserve you, Lord,' he said. 'This must not happen to you.' But he turned and said to Peter, 'Get behind me, Satan! You are an obstacle in my path, because the way you think is not God's way but man's.'

Then Jesus said to his disciples, 'If anyone wants to be a follower of mine, let him renounce himself and take up his cross and follow me. For anyone who wants to save his life will lose it; but anyone who loses his life for my sake will find it. What, then, will a man gain if he wins the whole world and ruins his life? Or what has a man to offer in exchange for his life?

'For the Son of Man is going to come in the glory of his Father with his angels, and, when he does, he will reward each one according to his behaviour.'

The Gospel of the Lord.

Prayer over the Offerings	Super oblata
May this sacred offering, O Lord, confer on us always the blessing of salvation, that what it celebrates in mystery it may accomplish in power. Through Christ our Lord.	Benedictionem nobis, Domine, conferat salutarem sacra semper oblatio, ut, quod agit mysterio, virtute perficiat. Per Christum Dominum nostrum.

Preface of Sundays in Ordinary Time I-VIII, pp.566-573.

Communion Antiphon Ps 30:20	Ant. ad communionem
How great is the goodness, Lord, that you keep for those who fear you.	Quam magna multitudo dulcedinis tuæ, Domine, quam abscondisti timentibus te.
Or: Mt 5:9-10	Vel:
Blessed are the peacemakers, for they shall be called children of God. Blessed are they who are persecuted for the sake of righteousness, for theirs is the Kingdom of Heaven.	Beati pacifici, quoniam filii Dei vocabuntur. Beati qui persecutionem patiuntur propter iustitiam, quoniam ipsorum est regnum cælorum.

Prayer after Communion
Renewed by this bread
    from the heavenly table,
we beseech you, Lord,
that, being the food of charity,
it may confirm our hearts
and stir us to serve you
    in our neighbour.
Through Christ our Lord.

Post communionem
Pane mensæ cælestis refecti, te,
    Domine, deprecamur,
ut hoc nutrimentum caritatis corda
    nostra confirmet,
quatenus ad tibi ministrandum
    in fratribus excitemur.
Per Christum Dominum nostrum.

TWENTY-THIRD SUNDAY IN ORDINARY TIME
(YEAR A)

Entrance Antiphon Ps 118:137,124

YOU are just, O Lord,
    and your judgement is right;
treat your servant in accord
    with your merciful love.

Ant. ad introitum

IUSTUS es, Domine,
    et rectum iudicium tuum;
fac cum servo tuo secundum
    misericordiam tuam.

Collect
O God, by whom we are redeemed
    and receive adoption,
look graciously upon your beloved
    sons and daughters,
that those who believe in Christ
may receive true freedom
and an everlasting inheritance.
Through our Lord Jesus Christ,
    your Son,
who lives and reigns with you
    in the unity of the Holy Spirit,
one God, for ever and ever.

Collecta
Deus, per quem nobis
et redemptio venit
    et præstatur adoptio,
filios dilectionis tuæ
    benignus intende,
ut in Christo credentibus
et vera tribuatur libertas,
    et hereditas æterna.
Per Dominum nostrum Iesum
    Christum Filium tuum,
qui tecum vivit et regnat
    in unitate Spiritus Sancti,
Deus, per omnia sæcula sæculorum.

FIRST READING
A reading from the prophet Ezekiel   33:7-9
If you do not speak to the wicked man, I will hold you responsible for his death.

The word of the Lord was addressed to me as follows, 'Son of man, I have appointed you as sentry to the House of Israel. When you hear a word from my mouth, warn them in my name. If I say to a wicked man:

Wicked wretch, you are to die, and you do not speak to warn the wicked man to renounce his ways, then he shall die for his sin, but I will hold you responsible for his death. If, however, you do warn a wicked man to renounce his ways and repent, and he does not repent, then he shall die for his sin but you yourself will have saved your life.'

The word of the Lord.

Responsial Psalm   Ps 94:1-2,6-9. R. v.8

R. **O that today you would listen to his voice!**
Harden not your hearts.

Come, ring out our joy to the Lord;
hail the rock who saves us.
Let us come before him, giving thanks,
with songs let us hail the Lord. R.

Come in; let us bow and bend low;
let us kneel before the God who made us
for he is our God and we
the people who belong to his pasture,
the flock that is led by his hand. R.

O that today you would listen to his voice!
'Harden not your hearts as at Meribah,
as on that day at Massah in the desert
when your fathers put me to the test;
when they tried me, though they saw my work.' R.

SECOND READING

A reading from the letter of St Paul to the Romans   13:8-10

Love is the answer to every one of the commandments.

Avoid getting into debt, except the debt of mutual love. If you love your fellow men you have carried out your obligations. All the commandments: You shall not commit adultery, you shall not kill, you shall not steal, you shall not covet, and so on, are summed up in this single command: You must love your neighbour as yourself. Love is the one thing that cannot hurt your neighbour; that is why it is the answer to every one of the commandments.

The word of the Lord.

Gospel Acclamation   Jn 17:17

R. **Alleluia, alleluia!**
Your word is truth, O Lord,
consecrate us in the truth.
R. **Alleluia!**

Or: 2 Co 5:19

R. **Alleluia, alleluia!**
God in Christ was reconciling the world to himself,
and he has entrusted to us the news that they are reconciled.
R. **Alleluia!**

GOSPEL

A reading from the holy Gospel according to Matthew   18:15-20

If he listens to you, you have won back your brother.

Jesus said to his disciples: 'If your brother does something wrong, go and
have it out with him alone, between your two selves. If he listens to you,
you have won back your brother. If he does not listen, take one or two
others along with you: the evidence of two or three witnesses is required
to sustain any charge. But if he refuses to listen to these, report it to the
community; and if he refuses to listen to the community, treat him like a
pagan or a tax collector.

'I tell you solemnly, whatever you bind on earth shall be considered
bound in heaven; whatever you loose on earth shall be considered loosed
in heaven.

'I tell you solemnly once again, if two of you on earth agree to ask
anything at all, it will be granted to you by my Father in heaven. For where
two or three meet in my name, I shall be there with them.'

The Gospel of the Lord.

Prayer over the Offerings	Super oblata

O God, who give us the gift
    of true prayer and of peace,
graciously grant that,
    through this offering,
we may do fitting homage to your
    divine majesty
and, by partaking
    of the sacred mystery,
we may be faithfully united
    in mind and heart.
Through Christ our Lord.
	Deus, auctor sinceræ
	    devotionis et pacis,
	da, quæsumus,
	    ut et maiestatem tuam
	convenienter hoc
	    munere veneremur,
	et sacri participatione mysterii
	    fideliter sensibus uniamur.
	Per Christum Dominum nostrum.

Preface of Sundays in Ordinary Time I-VIII, pp.566-573.

Communion Antiphon Cf. Ps 41:2-3	Ant. ad communionem

Like the deer that yearns
   for running streams,
so my soul is yearning for you,
   my God;
my soul is thirsting for God,
   the living God.
	Quemadmodum desiderat cervus
	   ad fontes aquarum,
	ita desiderat anima mea
	   ad te, Deus:
	sitivit anima mea ad Deum
	   fortem vivum.

Or: Jn 8:12	Vel:

I am the light of the world,
   says the Lord;
whoever follows me will not walk
   in darkness,
but will have the light of life.
	Ego sum lux mundi,
	   dicit Dominus:
	qui sequitur me non ambulat
	   in tenebris,
	sed habebit lumen vitæ.

Prayer after Communion	Post communionem

Grant that your faithful, O Lord,
whom you nourish and endow
   with life
through the food of your Word
   and heavenly Sacrament,
may so benefit from your beloved
   Son's great gifts
that we may merit an eternal share
   in his life.
Who lives and reigns
   for ever and ever.
	Da fidelibus tuis, Domine,
	quos et verbi tui et cælestis
	   sacramenti pabulo
	nutris et vivificas,
	ita dilecti Filii tui tantis
	   muneribus proficere,
	ut eius vitæ semper consortes
	   effici mereamur.
	Qui vivit et regnat
	   in sæcula sæculorum.

TWENTY-FOURTH SUNDAY IN ORDINARY TIME
(YEAR A)

Entrance Antiphon Cf. Sir 36:18	Ant. ad introitum

GIVE peace, O Lord,
   to those who wait for you,
that your prophets be found true.
Hear the prayers of your servant,
and of your people Israel.
	DA pacem, Domine,
	   sustinentibus te,
	ut prophetæ tui fideles inveniantur;
	exaudi preces servi tui,
	   et plebis tuæ Israel.

Collect

Look upon us, O God,
Creator and ruler of all things,
and, that we may feel the working
   of your mercy,
grant that we may serve you
   with all our heart.
Through our Lord Jesus Christ,
   your Son,
who lives and reigns with you
   in the unity of the Holy Spirit,
one God, for ever and ever.

Collecta

Respice nos, rerum omnium Deus
   creator et rector,
et, ut tuæ propitiationis
   sentiamus effectum,
toto nos tribue tibi corde servire.
Per Dominum nostrum Iesum
   Christum Filium tuum,
qui tecum vivit et regnat
   in unitate Spiritus Sancti,
Deus, per omnia sæcula sæculorum.

FIRST READING

A reading from the book of Ecclesiasticus   27:30-28:7

Forgive your neighbour the hurt he does you, and when you pray, your sins will be forgiven.

Resentment and anger, these are foul things,
and both are found with the sinner.
He who exacts vengeance will experience the vengeance of the Lord,
who keeps strict account of sin.
Forgive your neighbour the hurt he does you,
and when you pray, your sins will be forgiven.
If a man nurses anger against another,
can he then demand compassion from the Lord?
Showing no pity for a man like himself,
can he then plead for his own sins?
Mere creature of flesh, he cherishes resentment;
who will forgive him his sins?
Remember the last things, and stop hating,
remember dissolution and death, and live by the commandments.
Remember the commandments, and do not bear your neighbour ill-will;
remember the covenant of the Most High, and overlook the offence.

   The word of the Lord.

Responsorial Psalm   Ps 102:1-4,9-12. R. v.8

R. **The Lord is compassion and love,**
   slow to anger and rich in mercy.

   My soul, give the thanks to the Lord,
   all my being, bless his holy name.
   My soul, give thanks to the Lord
   and never forget all his blessings. R.

It is he who forgives all your guilt,
who heals every one of your ills,
who redeems your life from the grave,
who crowns you with love and compassion. R.

His wrath will come to an end;
he will not be angry for ever.
He does not treat us according to our sins
nor repay us according to our faults. R.

For as the heavens are high above the earth
so strong is his love for those who fear him.
As far as the east is from the west
so far does he remove our sins. R.

R. **The Lord is compassion and love,
slow to anger and rich in mercy.**

SECOND READING

A reading from the letter of St Paul to the Romans   14:7-9

Alive or dead we belong to the Lord.

The life and death of each of us has its influence on others; if we live, we live for the Lord; and if we die, we die for the Lord, so that alive or dead we belong to the Lord. This explains why Christ both died and came to life, it was so that he might be Lord both of the dead and of the living.

The word of the Lord.

Gospel Acclamation   1 S 3:9; Jn 6:68

R. **Alleluia, alleluia!**
Speak, Lord, your servant is listening:
you have the message of eternal life.
R. **Alleluia!**

Or: Jn 13:34

R. **Alleluia, alleluia!**
I give you a new commandment:
love one another, just as I have loved you,
says the Lord.
R. **Alleluia!**

GOSPEL

A reading from the holy Gospel according to Matthew   18:21-35

I do not tell you to forgive seven times, but seventy-seven times.

Peter went up to Jesus and said, 'Lord, how often must I forgive my brother if he wrongs me? As often as seven times?' Jesus answered, 'Not seven, I tell you, but seventy-seven times.

'And so the kingdom of heaven may be compared to a king who decided to settle his accounts with his servants. When the reckoning began, they brought him a man who owed ten thousand talents; but he had no means of paying, so his master gave orders that he should be sold, together with his wife and children and all his possessions, to meet the debt. At this, the servant threw himself down at his master's feet. "Give me time," he said "and I will pay the whole sum." And the servant's master felt so sorry for him that he let him go and cancelled the debt. Now as this servant went out, he happened to meet a fellow servant who owed him one hundred denarii; and he seized him by the throat and began to throttle him. "Pay what you owe me," he said. His fellow servant fell at his feet and implored him, saying, "Give me time and I will pay you." But the other would not agree; on the contrary, he had him thrown into prison till he should pay the debt. His fellow servants were deeply distressed when they saw what had happened, and they went to their master and reported the whole affair to him. Then the master sent for him. "You wicked servant," he said "I cancelled all that debt of yours when you appealed to me. Were you not bound, then, to have pity on your fellow servant just as I had pity on you?" And in his anger the master handed him over to the torturers till he should pay all his debt. And that is how my heavenly Father will deal with you unless you each forgive your brother from your heart.'

The Gospel of the Lord.

Prayer over the Offerings	Super oblata
Look with favour on our supplications, O Lord, and in your kindness accept these, your servants' offerings, that what each has offered to the honour of your name may serve the salvation of all. Through Christ our Lord.	Propitiare, Domine, supplicationibus nostris, et has oblationes famulorum tuorum benignus assume, ut, quod singuli ad honorem tui nominis obtulerunt, cunctis proficiat ad salutem. Per Christum Dominum nostrum.

Preface of Sundays in Ordinary Time I-VIII, pp.566-573.

Communion Antiphon Cf. Ps 35:8	Ant. ad communionem
How precious is your mercy, O God! The children of men seek shelter in the shadow of your wings.	Quam pretiosa est misericordia tua, Deus! Filii hominum sub umbra alarum tuarum confugient.

Or: Cf. 1 Co 10:16
The chalice of blessing that we bless
is a communion in the Blood
     of Christ;
and the bread that we break
is a sharing in the Body of the Lord.

Prayer after Communion

May the working of this heavenly
     gift, O Lord, we pray,
take possession of our minds
     and bodies,
so that its effects,
     and not our own desires,
may always prevail in us.
Through Christ our Lord.

Vel:

Calix benedictionis,
     cui benedicimus,
communicatio Sanguinis Christi est;
et panis, quem frangimus,
participatio Corporis Domini est.

Post communionem

Mentes nostras et corpora possideat,
quæsumus, Domine,
     doni cælestis operatio,
ut non noster sensus in nobis,
sed eius præveniat semper effectus.
Per Christum Dominum nostrum.

TWENTY-FIFTH SUNDAY IN ORDINARY TIME
(YEAR A)

Entrance Antiphon

I AM the salvation of the people,
     says the Lord.
Should they cry to me in any distress,
I will hear them, and I will be their
     Lord for ever.

Collect

O God, who founded all the
     commands of your sacred Law
upon love of you
     and of our neighbour,
grant that, by keeping your precepts,
we may merit to attain eternal life.
Through our Lord Jesus Christ,
     your Son,
who lives and reigns with you
     in the unity of the Holy Spirit,
one God, for ever and ever.

Ant. ad introitum

S ALUS populi ego sum,
     dicit Dominus.
De quacumque tribulatione
     clamaverint ad me,
exaudiam eos, et ero illorum
     Dominus in perpetuum.

Collecta

Deus, qui sacræ legis
     omnia constituta
in tua et proximi dilectione posuisti,
da nobis, ut,
     tua præcepta servantes,
ad vitam mereamur
     pervenire perpetuam.
Per Dominum nostrum Iesum
     Christum Filium tuum,
qui tecum vivit et regnat
     in unitate Spiritus Sancti,
Deus, per omnia sæcula sæculorum.

FIRST READING

A reading from the prophet Isaiah   55:6-9
My thoughts are not your thoughts.

Seek the Lord while he is still to be found,
call to him while he is still near.
Let the wicked man abandon his way,
the evil man his thoughts.
Let him turn back to the Lord who will take pity on him,
to our God who is rich in forgiving;
for my thoughts are not your thoughts,
my ways not your ways – it is the Lord who speaks.
Yes, the heavens are as high above earth
as my ways are above your ways,
my thoughts above your thoughts.

The word of the Lord.

Responsorial Psalm   Ps 144:2-3,8-9,17-18. R. v.18

R. **The Lord is close to all who call him.**

I will bless you day after day
and praise your name for ever.
The Lord is great, highly to be praised,
his greatness cannot be measured. R.

The Lord is kind and full of compassion,
slow to anger, abounding in love.
How good is the Lord to all,
compassionate to all his creatures. R.

The Lord is just in all his ways
and loving in all his deeds.
He is close to all who call him,
who call on him from their hearts. R.

SECOND READING

A reading from the letter of St Paul to the Philippians   1:20-24,27
Life to me is Christ

Christ will be glorified in my body, whether by my life or by my death.
Life to me, of course, is Christ, but then death would bring me something
more; but then again, if living in this body means doing work which is
having good results – I do not know what I should choose. I am caught in
this dilemma: I want to be gone and be with Christ, which would be very

much the better, but for me to stay alive in this body is a more urgent need for your sake.

Avoid anything in your everyday lives that would be unworthy of the gospel of Christ.

The word of the Lord.

Gospel Acclamation   Lk 19:38

R. **Alleluia, alleluia!**
Blessings on the King who comes,
in the name of the Lord!
Peace in heaven
and glory in the highest heavens!
R. **Alleluia!**

Or: Cf. Ac 16:14

R. **Alleluia, alleluia!**
Open our hearts, O Lord,
to accept the words of your Son.
R. **Alleluia!**

GOSPEL

A reading from the holy Gospel according to Matthew   20:1-16

Why be envious because I am generous?

Jesus told this parable to his disciples: 'The kingdom of heaven is like a landowner going out at daybreak to hire workers for his vineyard. He made an agreement with the workers for one denarius a day, and sent them to his vineyard. Going out at about the third hour he saw others standing idle in the market place and said to them, "You go to my vineyard too and I will give you a fair wage." So they went. At about the sixth hour and again at about the ninth hour, he went out and did the same. Then at about the eleventh hour he went out and found more men standing round, and he said to them, "Why have you been standing here idle all day?" "Because no one has hired us" they answered. He said to them, "You go into my vineyard too." In the evening, the owner of the vineyard said to his bailiff, "Call the workers and pay them their wages, starting with the last arrivals and ending with the first." So those who were hired at about the eleventh hour came forward and received one denarius each. When the first came, they expected to get more, but they too received one denarius each. They took it, but grumbled at the landowner. "The men who came last" they said "have done only one hour, and you have treated them the same as us, though we have done a heavy day's work in all the heat." He answered one of them and said, "My friend, I am not being unjust to you; did we not agree on one denarius? Take your earnings and go. I choose to pay the last-comer as much as I pay you. Have I no right to do what I like with my own? Why be envious because I am generous?" Thus the last will be first, and the first, last.'

The Gospel of the Lord.

Prayer over the Offerings	Super oblata
Receive with favour, O Lord, we pray, the offerings of your people, that what they profess with devotion and faith may be theirs through these heavenly mysteries. Through Christ our Lord.	Munera, quæsumus, Domine, tuæ plebis propitiatus assume, ut, quæ fidei pietate profitentur, sacramentis cælestibus apprehendant. Per Christum Dominum nostrum.

Preface of Sundays in Ordinary Time I-VIII, pp.566-573.

Communion Antiphon Ps 118:4-5	Ant. ad communionem
You have laid down your precepts to be carefully kept; may my ways be firm in keeping your statutes.	Tu mandasti mandata tua custodiri nimis; utinam dirigantur viæ meæ ad custodiendas iustificationes tuas.

Or: Jn 10:14	Vel:
I am the Good Shepherd, says the Lord; I know my sheep, and mine know me.	Ego sum pastor bonus, dicit Dominus; et cognosco oves meas, et cognoscunt me meæ.

Prayer after Communion	Post communionem
Graciously raise up, O Lord, those you renew with this Sacrament, that we may come to possess your redemption both in mystery and in the manner of our life. Through Christ our Lord.	Quos tuis, Domine, reficis sacramentis, continuis attolle benignus auxiliis, ut redemptionis effectum et mysteriis capiamus et moribus. Per Christum Dominum nostrum.

TWENTY-SIXTH SUNDAY IN ORDINARY TIME
(YEAR A)

Entrance Antiphon Dn 3:31,29,30,43,42

Aᴸᴸ that you have done to us,
O Lord,
 you have done with true judgement,
for we have sinned against you
and not obeyed
    your commandments.
But give glory to your name
and deal with us according
    to the bounty of your mercy.

Ant. ad introitum

Oᴹᴺᴵᴬ, quæ fecisti nobis,
Domine,
in vero iudicio fecisti, quia
    peccavimus tibi,
et mandatis tuis non obœdivimus;
sed da gloriam nomini tuo,
et fac nobiscum secundum
    multitudinem misericordiæ tuæ.

Collect

O God, who manifest
    your almighty power
above all by pardoning
    and showing mercy,
bestow, we pray, your grace
    abundantly upon us
and make those hastening to attain
    your promises
heirs to the treasures of heaven.
Through our Lord Jesus Christ,
    your Son,
who lives and reigns with you
    in the unity of the Holy Spirit,
one God, for ever and ever.

Collecta

Deus, qui omnipotentiam tuam
parcendo maxime
    et miserando manifestas,
multiplica super nos gratiam tuam,
ut, ad tua promissa currentes,
cælestium bonorum facias
    esse consortes.
Per Dominum nostrum Iesum
    Christum Filium tuum,
qui tecum vivit et regnat
    in unitate Spiritus Sancti,
Deus, per omnia sæcula sæculorum.

FIRST READING

A reading from the prophet Ezekiel   18:25-28

When the sinner renounces sin, he shall certainly live.

The word of the Lord was addressed to me as follows: 'You object, "What the Lord does is unjust." Listen, you House of Israel: is what I do unjust? Is it not what you do that is unjust? When the upright man renounces his integrity to commit sin and dies because of this, he dies because of the evil that he himself has committed. When the sinner renounces sin to become law-abiding and honest, he deserves to live. He has chosen to renounce all his previous sins; he shall certainly live; he shall not die.'

The word of the Lord.

Responsorial Psalm   Ps 24:4-9. R. v.6

R. **Remember your mercy, Lord.**

Lord, make me know your ways.
Lord, teach me your paths.
Make me walk in your truth, and teach me:
for you are God my saviour. R.

Remember your mercy, Lord,
and the love you have shown from of old.
Do not remember the sins of my youth.
In your love remember me,
because of your goodness, O Lord. R.

The Lord is good and upright.
He shows the path to those who stray,
he guides the humble in the right path;
he teaches his way to the poor. R.

SECOND READING

A reading from the letter of St Paul to the Philippians   2:1-11

In your minds you must be the same as Christ Jesus.

[If our life in Christ means anything to you, if love can persuade at all, or the Spirit that we have in common, or any tenderness and sympathy, then be united in your convictions and united in your love, with a common purpose and a common mind. That is the one thing which would make me completely happy. There must be no competition among you, no conceit; but everybody is to be self-effacing. Always consider the other person to be better than your self, so that nobody thinks of his own interests first but everybody thinks of other people's interests instead. In your minds you must be the same as Christ Jesus:]

His state was divine,
yet he did not cling
to his equality with God
but emptied himself
to assume the condition of a slave,
and became as men are;
and being as all men are,

he was humbler yet,
even to accepting death,
death on a cross.
But God raised him high
and gave him the name
which is above all other names
so that all beings
in the heavens, on earth and in the underworld,
should bend the knee at the name of Jesus
and that every tongue should acclaim
Jesus Christ as Lord,
to the glory of God the Father.

| [The word of the Lord.]

Shorter Form, verses 1-5. Read between [ ]

Gospel Acclamation   Jn 14:23
R. **Alleluia, alleluia!**
If anyone loves me he will keep my word.
and my Father will love him,
and we shall come to him.
R. **Alleluia!**

Or: Jn 10:27
R. **Alleluia, alleluia!**
The sheep that belong to me listen to my voice,
says the Lord,
I know them and they follow me.
R. **Alleluia!**

GOSPEL
A reading from the holy Gospel according to Matthew   21:28-32

He thought better of it and went. Tax collectors and prostitutes are making their way into the kingdom of God before you.

Jesus said to the chief priests and the elders of the people, 'What is your opinion? A man had two sons. He went and said to the first, "My boy, you go and work in the vineyard today." He answered, "I will not go", but afterwards thought better of it and went. The man then went and said the same thing to the second who answered, "Certainly, sir", but did not go. Which of the two did the father's will?' 'The first' they said. Jesus said to them, 'I tell you solemnly, tax collectors and prostitutes are making their way into the kingdom of God before you. For John came to you, a pattern of true righteousness, but you did not believe him, and yet the tax collectors and prostitutes did. Even after seeing that, you refused to think better of it and believe in him.'

The Gospel of the Lord.

Prayer over the Offerings	Super oblata

Grant us, O merciful God,
that this our offering may find
  acceptance with you
and that through it the wellspring
  of all blessing
may be laid open before us.
Through Christ our Lord.
	Concede nobis, misericors Deus,
	ut hæc nostra oblatio tibi
	  sit accepta,
	et per eam nobis fons omnis
	  benedictionis aperiatur.
	Per Christum Dominum nostrum.

Preface of Sundays in Ordinary Time I-VIII, pp.566-573.

Communion Antiphon Cf. Ps 118:49-50	Ant. ad communionem

Remember your word to your servant,
  O Lord,
by which you have given me hope.
This is my comfort when I am
  brought low.
	Memento verbi tui
	  servo tuo, Domine,
	in quo mihi spem dedisti;
	hæc me consolata est
	  in humilitate mea.

Or: 1 Jn 3:16	Vel:

By this we came to know
  the love of God:
that Christ laid down his life for us;
so we ought to lay down our lives
  for one another.
	In hoc cognovimus caritatem Dei:
	quoniam ille animam suam
	  pro nobis posuit;
	et nos debemus pro fratribus
	  animas ponere.

Prayer after Communion	Post communionem

May this heavenly mystery, O Lord,
restore us in mind and body,
that we may be coheirs in glory
  with Christ,
to whose suffering we are united
whenever we proclaim his Death.
Who lives and reigns
  for ever and ever.
	Sit nobis, Domine,
	  reparatio mentis et corporis
	cæleste mysterium, ut simus eius
	  in gloria coheredes,
	cui, mortem ipsius
	  annuntiando, compatimur.
	Qui vivit et regnat
	  in sæcula sæculorum.

TWENTY-SEVENTH SUNDAY IN ORDINARY TIME
(YEAR A)

Entrance Antiphon Cf. Est 4:17	**Ant. ad introitum**
WITHIN your will, O Lord, all things are established,	IN voluntate tua, Domine, universa sunt posita,
and there is none that can resist your will.	et non est qui possit resistere voluntati tuæ.
For you have made all things, the heaven and the earth,	Tu enim fecisti omnia, cælum et terram,
and all that is held within the circle of heaven;	et universa quæ cæli ambitu continentur;
you are the Lord of all.	Dominus universorum tu es.
Collect	**Collecta**
Almighty ever-living God,	Omnipotens sempiterne Deus,
who in the abundance of your kindness	qui abundantia pietatis tuæ
surpass the merits and the desires of those who entreat you,	et merita supplicum excedis et vota, effunde super nos
pour out your mercy upon us	misericordiam tuam,
to pardon what conscience dreads	ut dimittas quæ conscientia metuit,
and to give what prayer does not dare to ask.	et adicias quod oratio non præsumit.
Through our Lord Jesus Christ, your Son,	Per Dominum nostrum Iesum Christum Filium tuum,
who lives and reigns with you	qui tecum vivit et regnat
in the unity of the Holy Spirit,	in unitate Spiritus Sancti,
one God, for ever and ever.	Deus, per omnia sæcula sæculorum.

FIRST READING

A reading from the prophet Isaiah   5:1-7

The vineyard of the Lord of hosts is the House of Israel.

Let me sing to my friend
the song of his love for his vineyard.
My friend had a vineyard
on a fertile hillside.
He dug the soil, cleared it of stones,
and planted choice vines in it.

In the middle he built a tower,
he dug a press there too.
He expected it to yield grapes,
but sour grapes were all that it gave.

And now, inhabitants of Jerusalem
and men of Judah,
I ask you to judge
between my vineyard and me.
What could I have done for my vineyard
that I have not done?
I expected it to yield grapes.
Why did it yield sour grapes instead?

Very well, I will tell you
what I am going to do to my vineyard:
I will take away its hedge for it to be grazed on,
and knock down its wall for it to be trampled on.
I will lay it waste, unpruned, undug;
overgrown by the briar and the thorn.
I will command the clouds
to rain no rain on it.
Yes, the vineyard of the Lord of hosts
is the House of Israel,
and the men of Judah
that chosen plant.
He expected justice, but found bloodshed,
integrity, but only a cry of distress.

The word of the Lord.

Responsorial Psalm   Ps 79:9,12-16,19-20. R. Is 5:7

R. **The vineyard of the Lord is the House of Israel.**

You brought a vine out of Egypt;
to plant it you drove out the nations.
It stretched out its branches to the sea,
to the Great River it stretched out its shoots. R.

Then why have you broken down its walls?
It is plucked by all who pass by.
It is ravaged by the boar of the forest,
devoured by the beasts of the field. R.

God of hosts, turn again, we implore,
look down from heaven and see.
Visit this vine and protect it,
the vine your right hand has planted. R.

And we shall never forsake you again:
give us life that we may call upon your name.
God of hosts, bring us back;
let your face shine on us and we shall be saved. R.

R. **The vineyard of the Lord is the House of Israel.**

SECOND READING

A reading from the letter of St Paul to the Philippians   4:6-9

The God of peace will be with you.

There is no need to worry; but if there is anything you need, pray for it, asking God for it with prayer and thanksgiving, and that peace of God, which is so much greater than we can understand, will guard your hearts and your thoughts, in Christ Jesus. Finally, brothers, fill your minds with everything that is true, everything that is noble, everything that is good and pure, everything that we love and honour, and everything that can be thought virtuous or worthy of praise. Keep doing all the things that you learnt from me and have been taught by me and have heard or seen that I do. Then the God of peace will be with you.

The word of the Lord.

Gospel Acclamation   Jn 15:15

R. **Alleluia, alleluia!**
I call you friends, says the Lord,
because I have made known to you
everything I have learnt from my Father.
R. **Alleluia!**

Or: Cf. Jn 15:16

R. **Alleluia, alleluia!**
I chose you from the world
to go out and bear fruit,
fruit that will last,
says the Lord.
R. **Alleluia!**

GOSPEL

A reading from the holy Gospel according to Matthew   21:33-43

He will lease the vineyard to other tenants.

Jesus said to the chief priests and the elders of the people, 'Listen to another parable. There was a man, a landowner, who planted a vineyard; he fenced it round, dug a winepress in it and built a tower; then he leased it to tenants and went abroad. When vintage time drew near he sent his servants to the tenants to collect his produce. But the tenants seized his servants, thrashed one, killed another and stoned a third. Next he sent some more servants, this time a larger number, and they dealt with them in the same way. Finally he sent his son to them. "They will respect my son" he said. But when the tenants saw the son, they said to each other, "This is the heir. Come on, let us kill him and take over his inheritance." So they seized him and threw him out of the vineyard and killed him. Now when the owner of the vineyard comes, what will he do to those tenants?' They answered, 'He will bring those wretches to a wretched end and lease the vineyard to other tenants who will deliver the produce to him when the season arrives.' Jesus said to them, 'Have you never read in the scriptures:

It was the stone rejected by the builders
that became the keystone.
This was the Lord's doing
and it is wonderful to see?

'I tell you, then, that the kingdom of God will be taken from you and given to a people who will produce its fruit.'

The Gospel of the Lord.

Prayer over the Offerings	Super oblata
Accept, O Lord, we pray, the sacrifices instituted by your commands and, through the sacred mysteries, which we celebrate with dutiful service, graciously complete the sanctifying work by which you are pleased to redeem us. Through Christ our Lord.	Suscipe, quæsumus, Domine, sacrificia tuis instituta præceptis, et sacris mysteriis, quæ debitæ servitutis celebramus officio, sanctificationem tuæ nobis redemptionis dignanter adimple. Per Christum Dominum nostrum.

Preface of Sundays in Ordinary Time I-VIII, pp.566-573.

Communion Antiphon Lm 3:25	Ant. ad communionem

Communion Antiphon Lm 3:25

The Lord is good to those
   who hope in him,
to the soul that seeks him.

Or: Cf. 1 Co 10:17

Though many, we are one bread,
   one body,
for we all partake of the one Bread
   and one Chalice.

Ant. ad communionem

Bonus est Dominus
   sperantibus in eum,
animæ quærenti illum.

Vel:

Unus panis et unum corpus
   multi sumus,
omnes qui de uno pane et de uno
   calice participamus.

Prayer after Communion

Grant us, almighty God,
that we may be refreshed
   and nourished
by the Sacrament which
   we have received,
so as to be transformed
   into what we consume.
Through Christ our Lord.

Post communionem

Concede nobis, omnipotens Deus,
ut de perceptis sacramentis
   inebriemur atque pascamur,
quatenus in id quod
   sumimus transeamus.
Per Christum Dominum nostrum.

TWENTY-EIGHTH SUNDAY IN ORDINARY TIME

(YEAR A)

Entrance Antiphon Ps 129:3-4

IF you, O Lord,
   should mark iniquities,
Lord, who could stand?
But with you is found forgiveness,
O God of Israel.

Ant. ad introitum

SI iniquitates observaveris,
   Domine,
Domine, quis sustinebit?
Quia apud te propitiatio est,
   Deus Israel.

Collect

May your grace, O Lord, we pray,
at all times go before us
   and follow after
and make us always determined
to carry out good works.
Through our Lord Jesus Christ,
   your Son,
who lives and reigns with you
   in the unity of the Holy Spirit,
one God, for ever and ever.

Collecta

Tua nos, quæsumus,
   Domine, gratia
semper et præveniat et sequatur,
ac bonis operibus iugiter præstet
   esse intentos.
Per Dominum nostrum Iesum
   Christum Filium tuum,
qui tecum vivit et regnat
   in unitate Spiritus Sancti,
Deus, per omnia sæcula sæculorum.

FIRST READING

A reading from the prophet Isaiah   25:6-10

The Lord will prepare a banquet, and will wipe away tears from every cheek.

On this mountain,
the Lord of hosts will prepare for all people
a banquet of rich food, a banquet of fine wines,
of food rich and juicy, of fine strained wines.
On this mountain he will remove
the mourning veil covering all peoples,
and the shroud enwrapping all nations,
he will destroy Death for ever.
The Lord will wipe away
the tears from every cheek;
he will take away his people's shame
everywhere on earth,
for the Lord has said so.
That day, it will be said: See, this is our God
in whom we hoped for salvation;
the Lord is the one in whom we hoped.
We exult and we rejoice
that he has saved us;
for the hand of the Lord
rests on this mountain.

The word of the Lord.

Responsorial Psalm   Ps 22. R. v.6

R. **In the Lord's own house shall I dwell
for ever and ever.**

The Lord is my shepherd;
there is nothing I shall want.
Fresh and green are the pastures
where he gives me repose.
Near restful waters he leads me,
to revive my drooping spirit. R.

He guides me along the right path;
he is true to his name.
If I should walk in the valley of darkness
no evil would I fear.
You are there with your crook and your staff;
with these you give me comfort. R.

You have prepared a banquet for me
in the sight of my foes.
My head you have anointed with oil;
my cup is overflowing. R.

Surely goodness and kindness shall follow me
all the days of my life.
In the Lord's own house shall I dwell
for ever and ever. R.

R. **In the Lord's own house shall I dwell
for ever and ever.**

SECOND READING

A reading from the letter of St Paul to the Philippians   4:12-14,19-20
There is nothing I cannot master with the help of the One who gives me strength.

I know how to be poor and I know how to be rich too. I have been through my initiation and now I am ready for anything anywhere: full stomach or empty stomach, poverty or plenty. There is nothing I cannot master with the help of the One who gives me strength. All the same, it was good of you to share with me in my hardships. In return my God will fulfil all your needs, in Christ Jesus, as lavishly as only God can. Glory to God, our Father, for ever and ever. Amen.

The word of the Lord.

Gospel Acclamation   Jn 1:12,14
R. **Alleluia, alleluia!**
The Word has made flesh and lived among us;
to all who did accept him
he gave power to become children of God.
R. **Alleluia!**
Or: Cf. Ep 1:17-18

R. **Alleluia, alleluia!**
May the Father of our Lord Jesus Christ
enlighten the eyes of our mind,
so that we can see what hope his call holds for us.
R. **Alleluia!**

GOSPEL

A reading from holy Gospel according to Matthew   22:1-14
Invite everyone you can find to the wedding.

[Jesus said to the chief priests and elders of the people: 'The kingdom of heaven may be compared to a king who gave a feast for his son's wedding.

He sent his servants to call those who had been invited, but they would not come. Next he sent some more servants. "Tell those who have been invited" he said "that I have my banquet all prepared, my oxen and fattened cattle have been slaughtered, everything is ready. Come to the wedding." But they were not interested: one went off to his farm, another to his business, and the rest seized his servants, maltreated them and killed them. The king was furious. He despatched his troops, destroyed those murderers and burnt their town. Then he said to his servants, "The wedding is ready; but as those who were invited proved to be unworthy, go to the crossroads in the town and invite everyone you can find to the wedding." So these servants went out on to the roads and collected together everyone they could find, bad and good alike; and the wedding hall was filled with guests.]When the king came in to look at the guests he noticed one man who was not wearing a wedding garment, and said to him, "How did you get in here, my friend, without a wedding garment?" And the man was silent. Then the king said to the attendants, "Bind him hand and foot and throw him out into the dark, where there will be weeping and grinding of teeth." For many are called, but few are chosen.'

[The Gospel of the Lord.]

Shorter Form, verses 1-10. Read between [ ]

Prayer over the Offerings	**Super oblata**
Accept, O Lord,	Suscipe, Domine,
the prayers of your faithful	fidelium preces cum
with the sacrificial offerings,	oblationibus hostiarum,
that, through these acts	ut, per hæc piæ devotionis officia,
of devotedness,	ad cælestem gloriam transeamus.
we may pass over to the glory	Per Christum Dominum nostrum.
of heaven.	
Through Christ our Lord.	

Preface of Sundays in Ordinary Time I-VIII, pp.566-573.

Communion Antiphon Cf. Ps 33:11	**Ant. ad communionem**
The rich suffer want and go hungry,	Divites eguerunt et esurierunt;
but those who seek the Lord lack	quærentes autem Dominum non
no blessing.	minuentur omni bono.
Or: 1 Jn 3:2	Vel:
When the Lord appears,	Cum apparuerit Dominus,
we shall be like him,	similes ei erimus,
for we shall see him as he is.	quoniam videbimus eum sicuti est.

Prayer after Communion

We entreat your majesty most
   humbly, O Lord,
that, as you feed us
   with the nourishment
which comes from the most holy
   Body and Blood of your Son,
so you may make us sharers
   of his divine nature.
Who lives and reigns
   for ever and ever.

Post communionem

Maiestatem tuam, Domine,
   suppliciter deprecamur,
ut, sicut nos Corporis
   et Sanguinis sacrosancti
pascis alimento,
ita divinæ naturæ facias
   esse consortes.
Per Christum Dominum nostrum.

TWENTY-NINTH SUNDAY IN ORDINARY TIME
(YEAR A)

Entrance Antiphon   Cf. Ps 16:6.8

To you I call; for you will surely
   heed me, O God;
turn your ear to me; hear my words.
Guard me as the apple of your eye;
in the shadow of your wings
   protect me.

Ant. ad introitum

EGO clamavi,
   quoniam exaudisti me, Deus;
inclina aurem tuam,
   et exaudi verba mea.
Custodi me, Domine,
   ut pupillam oculi;
sub umbra alarum tuarum
   protege me.

Collect

Almighty ever-living God,
grant that we may always conform
   our will to yours
and serve your majesty in sincerity
   of heart.
Through our Lord Jesus Christ,
   your Son,
who lives and reigns with you
   in the unity of the Holy Spirit,
one God, for ever and ever.

Collecta

Omnipotens sempiterne Deus,
fac nos tibi semper et devotam
   gerere voluntatem,
et maiestati tuæ sincero
   corde servire.
Per Dominum nostrum Iesum
   Christum Filium tuum,
qui tecum vivit et regnat
   in unitate Spiritus Sancti,
Deus, per omnia sæcula sæculorum.

FIRST READING

A reading from the prophet Isaiah   45:1.4-6

I have taken Cyrus by his right hand to subdue nations before him.

Thus says the Lord to his anointed, to Cyrus,
whom he has taken by his right hand
to subdue nations before him
and strip the loins of kings,
to force gateways before him
that their gates be closed no more:

> It is for the sake of my servant Jacob,
> of Israel my chosen one,
> that I have called you by your name,
> conferring a title though you do not know me.
> I am the Lord, unrivalled;
> there is no other God besides me.
> Though you do not know me, I arm you
> that men may know from the rising to the setting of the sun
> that, apart from me, all is nothing.

The word of the Lord.

Responsorial Psalm   Ps 95:1,3-5,7-10. R. v.7

R. **Give the Lord glory and power.**

> O sing a new song to the Lord,
> sing to the Lord all the earth.
> Tell among the nations his glory
> and his wonders among all the peoples. R.

> The Lord is great and worthy of praise,
> to be feared above all gods;
> the gods of the heathens are naught.
> It was the Lord who made the heavens. R.

> Give the Lord, you families of peoples,
> give the Lord glory and power,
> give the Lord the glory of his name.
> Bring an offering and enter his courts. R.

> Worship the Lord in his temple.
> O earth, tremble before him.
> Proclaim to the nations: 'God is king.'
> He will judge the peoples in fairness. R.

SECOND READING

A reading from the first letter of St Paul to the Thessalonians   1:1-5

We constantly remember your faith, your love and your hope.

From Paul, Silvanus and Timothy, to the Church in Thessalonika which is in God the Father and the Lord Jesus Christ; wishing you grace and peace from God the Father and the Lord Jesus Christ.

We always mention you in our prayers and thank God for you all, and constantly remember before God our Father how you have shown your faith in action, worked for love and persevered through hope, in our Lord Jesus Christ.

We know, brothers, that God loves you and that you have been chosen, because when we brought the Good News to you, it came to you not only as words, but as power and as the Holy Spirit and as utter conviction.

The word of the Lord.

Gospel Acclamation   Jn 17:17

R. **Alleluia, alleluia!**
Your word is truth, O Lord,
consecrate us in the truth.
R. **Alleluia!**

Or: Ph 2:15-16

R. **Alleluia, alleluia!**
You will shine on the world like bright stars
because you are offering it the word of life.
R. **Alleluia!**

GOSPEL

A reading from the holy Gospel according to Matthew   22:15-21

Give back to Caesar what belongs to Caesar – and to God what belongs to God.

The Pharisees went away to work out between them how to trap Jesus in what he said. And they sent their disciples to him, together with the Herodians, to say, 'Master, we know that you are an honest man and teach the way of God in an honest way, and that you are not afraid of anyone, because a man's rank means nothing to you. Tell us your opinion, then. Is it permissible to pay taxes to Caesar or not?' But Jesus was aware of their malice and replied, 'You hypocrites! Why do you set this trap for me? Let me see the money you pay the tax with.' They handed him a denarius, and he said, 'Whose head is this? Whose name?' 'Caesar's' they replied. He then said to them, 'Very well, give back to Caesar what belongs to Caesar – and to God what belongs to God.'

The Gospel of the Lord.

Prayer over the Offerings	Super oblata
Grant us, Lord, we pray, a sincere respect for your gifts, that, through the purifying action of your grace, we may be cleansed by the very mysteries we serve. Through Christ our Lord.	Tribue nos, Domine, quæsumus, donis tuis libera mente servire, ut, tua purificante nos gratia, iisdem quibus famulamur mysteriis emundemur. Per Christum Dominum nostrum.

Preface of Sundays in Ordinary Time I-VIII, pp.566-573.

Communion Antiphon Cf. Ps 32:18-19	Ant. ad communionem
Behold, the eyes of the Lord are on those who fear him, who hope in his merciful love, to rescue their souls from death, to keep them alive in famine.	Ecce oculi Domini super timentes eum, et in eis qui sperant super misericordia eius; ut eruat a morte animas eorum, et alat eos in fame.

Or: Mk 10:45	Vel:
The Son of Man has come to give his life as a ransom for many.	Filius hominis venit, ut daret animam suam redemptionem pro multis.

Prayer after Communion	Post communionem
Grant, O Lord, we pray, that, benefiting from participation in heavenly things, we may be helped by what you give in this present age and prepared for the gifts that are eternal. Through Christ our Lord.	Fac nos, quæsumus, Domine, cælestium rerum frequentatione proficere, ut et temporalibus beneficiis adiuvemur, et erudiamur æternis. Per Christum Dominum nostrum.

THIRTIETH SUNDAY IN ORDINARY TIME
(YEAR A)

Entrance Antiphon Cf. Ps 104:3-4

LET the hearts that seek
the Lord rejoice;
turn to the Lord and his strength;
constantly seek his face.

Ant. ad introitum

LÆTETUR cor
quærentium Dominum.
Quærite Dominum et confirmamini,
quærite faciem eius semper.

Collect

Almighty ever-living God,
increase our faith, hope and charity,
and make us love
 what you command,
so that we may merit
 what you promise.
Through our Lord Jesus Christ,
 your Son,
who lives and reigns with you
 in the unity of the Holy Spirit,
one God, for ever and ever.

Collecta

Omnipotens sempiterne Deus,
da nobis fidei,
 spei et caritatis augmentum,
et, ut mereamur assequi
 quod promittis,
fac nos amare quod præcipis.
Per Dominum nostrum Iesum
 Christum Filium tuum,
qui tecum vivit et regnat
 in unitate Spiritus Sancti,
Deus, per omnia sæcula sæculorum.

FIRST READING

A reading from the book of Exodus   22:20-26

If you are harsh with the widow, the orphan, my anger will flare against you.

The Lord said to Moses, 'Tell the sons of Israel this, "You must not molest the stranger or oppress him, for you lived as strangers in the land of Egypt. You must not be harsh with the widow, or with the orphan; if you are harsh with them, they will surely cry out to me, and be sure I shall hear their cry; my anger will flare and I shall kill you with the sword, your own wives will be widows, your own children orphans.

"If you lend money to any of my people, to any poor man among you, you must not play the usurer with him: you must not demand interest from him.

"If you take another's cloak as a pledge, you must give it back to him before sunset. It is all the covering he has; it is the cloak he wraps his body in; what else would he sleep in? If he cries to me, I will listen, for I am full of pity."'

The word of the Lord.

Responsorial Psalm   Ps 17:2-4,47,51. R. v.2

R. **I love you, Lord, my strength.**

I love you, Lord, my strength,
my rock, my fortress, my saviour.
My God is the rock where I take refuge;
my shield, my mighty help, my stronghold.
The Lord is worthy of all praise:
when I call I am saved from my foes. R.

Long life to the Lord, my rock!
Praised be the God who saves me.
He has given great victories to his king
and shown his love for his anointed. R.

SECOND READING

A reading from the first letter of St Paul to the Thessalonians   1:5-10

You broke with idolatry and became servants of God; you are now waiting for his Son.

You observed the sort of life we lived when we were with you, which was for your instruction, and you were led to become imitators of us, and of the Lord; and it was with the joy of the Holy Spirit that you took to the gospel, in spite of the great opposition all round you. This has made you the great example to all believers in Macedonia and Achaia since it was from you that the word of the Lord started to spread – and not only throughout Macedonia and Achaia, for the news of your faith in God has spread everywhere. We do not need to tell other people about it: other people tell us how we started the work among you, how you broke with idolatry when you were converted to God and became servants of the real, living God; and how you are now waiting for Jesus, his Son, whom he raised from the dead, to come from heaven to save us from the retribution which is coming.

The word of the Lord.

Gospel Acclamation   Cf. Ac 16:14

R. **Alleluia, alleluia!**
Open our heart, O Lord,
to accept the words of your Son.
R. **Alleluia!**

Or: Jn 14:23

R. **Alleluia, alleluia!**
If anyone loves me he will keep my word,
and my Father will love him,
and we shall come to him.
R. **Alleluia!**

GOSPEL

A reading from the holy Gospel according to Matthew   22:34-40
You must love the Lord your God and your neighbour as yourself.
When the Pharisees heard that Jesus had silenced the Sadducees they got
together and, to disconcert him, one of them put a question, 'Master,
which is the greatest commandment of the Law?' Jesus said, 'You must
love the Lord your God with all your heart, with all your soul, and with all
your mind. This is the greatest and the first commandment. The second
resembles it: you must love your neighbour as yourself. On these two commandments hang the whole Law, and the Prophets also.'

     The Gospel of the Lord.

Prayer over the Offerings	Super oblata
Look, we pray, O Lord, on the offerings we make to your majesty, that whatever is done by us in your service may be directed above all to your glory. Through Christ our Lord.	Respice, quæsumus, Domine, munera quæ tuæ offerimus maiestati, ut, quod nostro servitio geritur, ad tuam gloriam potius dirigatur. Per Christum Dominum nostrum.

Preface of Sundays in Ordinary Time I-VIII, pp.566-573.

Communion Antiphon Cf. Ps 19:6	Ant. ad communionem
We will ring out our joy at your saving help and exult in the name of our God.	Lætabimur in salutari tuo, et in nomine Dei nostri magnificabimur.
Or: Ep 5:2	Vel:
Christ loved us and gave himself up for us, as a fragrant offering to God.	Christus dilexit nos, et tradidit semetipsum pro nobis, oblationem Deo in odorem suavitatis.

Prayer after Communion

May your Sacraments, O Lord,
    we pray,
perfect in us what lies within them,
that what we now celebrate in signs
we may one day possess in truth.
Through Christ our Lord.

Post communionem

Perficiant in nobis,
    Domine, quæsumus,
tua sacramenta quod continent,
ut, quæ nunc specie gerimus,
rerum veritate capiamus.
Per Christum Dominum nostrum.

THIRTY-FIRST SUNDAY IN ORDINARY TIME
(YEAR A)

Entrance Antiphon Cf. Ps 37:22-23

FORSAKE me not, O Lord,
    my God;
be not far from me!
Make haste and come to my help,
O Lord, my strong salvation!

Ant. ad introitum

NE derelinquas me,
    Domine Deus meus,
ne discedas a me;
    intende in adiutorium meum,
Domine, virtus salutis meæ.

Collect

Almighty and merciful God,
by whose gift your faithful offer you
right and praiseworthy service,
grant, we pray,
that we may hasten
    without stumbling
to receive the things you
    have promised.
Through our Lord Jesus Christ,
    your Son,
who lives and reigns with you
    in the unity of the Holy Spirit,
one God, for ever and ever.

Collecta

Omnipotens et misericors Deus,
    de cuius munere venit,
ut tibi a fidelibus tuis digne
    et laudabiliter serviatur,
tribue, quæsumus, nobis,
ut ad promissiones tuas
    sine offensione curramus.
Per Dominum nostrum Iesum
    Christum Filium tuum,
qui tecum vivit et regnat
    in unitate Spiritus Sancti,
Deus, per omnia sæcula sæculorum.

FIRST READING

A reading from the prophet Malachi   1:14-2:2,8-10

You have strayed from the way; you have caused many to stumble by your teaching.

I am a great king, says the Lord of hosts, and my name is feared throughout the nations. And now, priests, this warning is for you. If you do not listen, if you do not find it in your heart to glorify my name, says the Lord of hosts, I will send the curse on you and curse your very blessing. You have strayed from the way; you have caused many to stumble by your teaching. You have destroyed the covenant of Levi, says the Lord of hosts. And so I in my turn have made you contemptible and vile in the eyes of the whole people in repayment for the way you have not kept to my paths but have shown partiality in your administration.

Have we not all one Father? Did not one God create us? Why, then, do we break faith with one another, profaning the covenant of our ancestors?

The word of the Lord.

Responsial Psalm   Ps 130

R. **Keep my soul in peace before you, O Lord.**

O Lord, my heart is not proud
nor haughty my eyes.
I have not gone after things too great
nor marvels beyond me. R.

Truly I have set my soul
in silence and peace.
A weaned child on its mother's breast,
even so is my soul. R.

O Israel, hope in the Lord
both now and for ever. R.

SECOND READING

A reading from the first letter of St Paul to the Thessalonians   2:7-9,13

We were eager to hand over to you not only the Good News but our whole lives as well.

Like a mother feeding and looking after her own children, we felt so devoted and protective towards you, and had come to love you so much, that we were eager to hand over to you not only the Good News but our whole lives as well. Let me remind you, brothers, how hard we used to work, slaving night and day so as not to be a burden on any one of you while we were proclaiming God's Good News to you.

Another reason why we constantly thank God for you is that as soon as you heard the message that we brought you as God's message, you accepted it for what it really is, God's message and not some human thinking; and it is still a living power among you who believe it.

The word of the Lord.

Gospel Acclamation   1 S 3:9; Jn 6:68
R. **Alleluia, alleluia!**
Speak, Lord, your servant is listening:
you have the message of eternal life.
R. **Alleluia!**

Or: Mt 23:9,10

R. **Alleluia, alleluia!**
You have only one Father, and he is in heaven;
 you have only one Teacher, the Christ!
R. **Alleluia!**

GOSPEL

A reading from the holy Gospel according to Matthew   23:1-12
They do not practise what they preach.

Addressing the people and his disciples Jesus said, 'The scribes and the
Pharisees occupy the chair of Moses. You must therefore do what they tell
you and listen to what they say; but do not be guided by what they do:
since they do not practise what they preach. They tie up heavy burdens
and lay them on men's shoulders, but will they lift a finger to move them?
Not they! Everything they do is done to attract attention, like wearing
broader phylacteries and longer tassels, like wanting to take the place of
honour at banquets and the front seats in the synagogues, being greeted
obsequiously in the market squares and having people call them Rabbi.

   'You, however, must not allow yourselves to be called Rabbi, since you
have only one Master, and you are all brothers. You must call no one on earth
your father, since you have only one Father, and he is in heaven. Nor must
you allow yourselves to be called teachers, for you have only one Teacher,
the Christ. The greatest among you must be your servant. Anyone who exalts
himself will be humbled, and anyone who humbles himself will be exalted.'

   The Gospel of the Lord.

Prayer over the Offerings	Super oblata
May these sacrificial offerings, O Lord,	Fiat hoc sacrificium, Domine, oblatio tibi munda,
become for you a pure oblation, and for us a holy outpouring of your mercy.	et nobis misericordiæ tuæ sancta largitio.
Through Christ our Lord.	Per Christum Dominum nostrum.

Preface of Sundays in Ordinary Time I-VIII, pp.566-573.

Communion Antiphon Cf. Ps 15:11	Ant. ad communionem
You will show me the path of life, the fullness of joy in your presence, O Lord.	Notas mihi fecisti vias vitæ, adimplebis me lætitia cum vultu tuo, Domine.

Or: Jn 6:58	Vel:
Just as the living Father sent me and I have life because of the Father, so whoever feeds on me shall have life because of me, says the Lord.	Sicut misit me vivens Pater, et ego vivo propter Patrem, et qui manducat me, et ipse vivet propter me, dicit Dominus.

Prayer after Communion	Post communionem
May the working of your power, O Lord, increase in us, we pray, so that, renewed by these heavenly Sacraments, we may be prepared by your gift for receiving what they promise. Through Christ our Lord.	Augeatur in nobis, quæsumus, Domine, tuæ virtutis operatio, ut, refecti cælestibus sacramentis, ad eorum promissa capienda tuo munere præparemur. Per Christum Dominum nostrum.

THIRTY-SECOND SUNDAY IN ORDINARY TIME
(YEAR A)

Entrance Antiphon Cf. Ps 87:3	Ant. ad introitum
LET my prayer come into your presence. Incline your ear to my cry for help, O Lord.	INTRET oratio mea in conspectu tuo; inclina aurem tuam ad precem meam, Domine.

Collect

Almighty and merciful God,
graciously keep from us all adversity,
so that, unhindered in mind
    and body alike,
we may pursue in freedom of heart
the things that are yours.
Through our Lord Jesus Christ,
    your Son,
who lives and reigns with you
    in the unity of the Holy Spirit,
one God, for ever and ever.

Collecta

Omnipotens et misericors Deus,
universa nobis adversantia
    propitiatus exclude,
ut, mente et corpore pariter expediti,
quæ tua sunt liberis
    mentibus exsequamur.
Per Dominum nostrum Iesum
    Christum Filium tuum,
qui tecum vivit et regnat
    in unitate Spiritus Sancti,
Deus, per omnia sæcula sæculorum.

FIRST READING

A reading from the book of Wisdom   6:12-16

Wisdom is found by those who look for her.

Wisdom is bright, and does not grow dim.
By those who love her she is readily seen,
and found by those who look for her.
Quick to anticipate those who desire her, she makes herself known to them.
Watch for her early and you will have no trouble;
you will find her sitting at your gates.
Even to think about her is understanding fully grown;
be on the alert for her and anxiety will quickly leave you.
She herself walks about looking for those who are worthy of her
and graciously shows herself to them as they go,
in every thought of theirs coming to meet them.

The word of the Lord.

Responsial Psalm   Ps 62:2-8. R. v.2

R. **For you my soul is thirsting, O God, my God.**

O God, you are my God, for you I long;
for you my soul is thirsting.
My body pines for you
like a dry, weary land without water. R.

So I gaze on you in the sanctuary
to see your strength and your glory.

For your love is better than life,
my lips will speak your praise. R.

So I will bless you all my life,
in your name I will lift up my hands.
My soul shall be filled as with a banquet,
my mouth shall praise you with joy. R.

On my bed I remember you.
On you I muse through the night
for you have been my help;
in the shadow of your wings I rejoice. R.

R. **For you my soul is thirsting, O God, my God.**

SECOND READING

A reading from the first letter of St Paul to the Thessalonians   4:13-18

God will bring with him those who have died in Jesus.

[We want you to be quite certain, brothers, about those who have died, to make sure that you do not grieve about them, like the other people who have no hope. We believe that Jesus died and rose again, and that it will be the same for those who have died in Jesus: God will bring them with him.] We can tell you this from the Lord's own teaching, that any of us who are left alive until the Lord's coming will not have any advantage over those who have died. At the trumpet of God, the voice of the archangel will call out the command and the Lord himself will come down from heaven; those who have died in Christ will be the first to rise, and then those of us who are still alive will be taken up in the clouds, together with them, to meet the Lord in the air. So we shall stay with the Lord for ever. With such thoughts as these you should comfort one another.

[The word of the Lord.]

Shorter Form, verses 13-14. Read between [ ]

Gospel Acclamation   Mt 24:42,44

R. **Alleluia, alleluia!**
Stay awake and stand ready,
because you do not know the hour
when the Son of Man is coming.
R. **Alleluia!**

GOSPEL

A reading from the holy Gospel according to Matthew   25:1-13

The bridegroom is here! Go out and meet him.

Jesus told this parable to his disciples: 'The kingdom of heaven will be like this: Ten bridesmaids took their lamps and went to meet the bridegroom. Five of them were foolish and five were sensible: the foolish ones did take their lamps, but they brought no oil, whereas the sensible ones took flasks of oil as well as their lamps. The bridegroom was late, and they all grew drowsy and fell asleep. But at midnight there was a cry, "The bridegroom is here! Go out and meet him." At this, all those bridesmaids woke up and trimmed their lamps, and the foolish ones said to the sensible ones, "Give us some of your oil: our lamps are going out." But they replied, "There may not be enough for us and for you; you had better go to those who sell it and buy some for yourselves." They had gone off to buy it when the bridegroom arrived. Those who were ready went in with him to the wedding hall and the door was closed. The other bridesmaids arrived later. "Lord, Lord," they said "open the door for us." But he replied, "I tell you solemnly, I do not know you." So stay awake, because you do not know either the day or the hour.'

The Gospel of the Lord.

Prayer over the Offerings	Super oblata
Look with favour, we pray, O Lord, upon the sacrificial gifts offered here, that, celebrating in mystery the Passion of your Son, we may honour it with loving devotion. Through Christ our Lord.	Sacrificiis præsentibus, Domine, quæsumus, intende placatus, ut, quod passionis Filii tui mysterio gerimus, pio consequamur affectu. Per Christum Dominum nostrum.

Preface of Sundays in Ordinary Time I-VIII, pp.566-573.

Communion Antiphon Cf. Ps 22:1-2	Ant. ad communionem
The Lord is my shepherd; there is nothing I shall want. Fresh and green are the pastures where he gives me repose, near restful waters he leads me.	Dominus regit me, et nihil mihi deerit; in loco pascuæ ibi me collocavit, super aquam refectionis educavit me.

Or: Cf. Lk 24:35

The disciples recognised the Lord
    Jesus in the breaking of bread.

Prayer after Communion

Nourished by this sacred gift,
    O Lord,
we give you thanks and beseech
    your mercy,
that, by the pouring forth
    of your Spirit,
the grace of integrity may endure
in those your heavenly power
    has entered.
Through Christ our Lord.

Vel:

Cognoverunt discipuli Dominum
    Iesum in fractione panis.

Post communionem

Gratias tibi, Domine, referimus
    sacro munere vegetati,
tuam clementiam implorantes,
ut, per infusionem Spiritus tui,
in quibus cælestis virtus introivit,
sinceritatis gratia perseveret.
Per Christum Dominum nostrum.

THIRTY-THIRD SUNDAY IN ORDINARY TIME
(YEAR A)

Entrance Antiphon   Jr 29:11,12,14

THE Lord said: I think thoughts
   of peace and not of affliction.
You will call upon me,
    and I will answer you,
and I will lead back your captives
    from every place.

Ant. ad introitum

DICIT Dominus:
   Ego cogito cogitationes pacis
   et non afflictionis;
invocabitis me, et ego exaudiam vos,
et reducam captivitatem vestram
    de cunctis locis.

Collect

Grant us, we pray, O Lord our God,
the constant gladness of being
    devoted to you,
for it is full and lasting happiness
to serve with constancy
the author of all that is good.
Through our Lord Jesus Christ,
    your Son,
who lives and reigns with you
    in the unity of the Holy Spirit,
one God, for ever and ever.

Collecta

Da nobis, quæsumus,
    Domine Deus noster,
in tua semper devotione gaudere,
quia perpetua est et plena felicitas,
si bonorum omnium iugiter
    serviamus auctori.
Per Dominum nostrum Iesum
    Christum Filium tuum,
qui tecum vivit et regnat
    in unitate Spiritus Sancti,
Deus, per omnia sæcula sæculorum.

FIRST READING

A reading from the book of Proverbs 31:10-13,19-20,30-31

A perfect wife - who can find her?

A perfect wife – who can find her?
She is far beyond the price of pearls.
Her husband's heart has confidence in her,
from her he will derive no little profit.
Advantage and not hurt she brings him
all the days of her life.
She is always busy with wool and with flax,
she does her work with eager hands.
She sets her hands to the distaff,
her fingers grasp the spindle.
She holds out her hands to the poor,
she opens her arms to the needy.
Charm is deceitful, and beauty empty;
the woman who is wise is the one to praise.
Give her a share in what her hands have worked for,
and let her works tell her praises at the city gates.

The word of the Lord.

Responsorial Psalm Ps 127:1-5. R. v.1

R. **O blessed are those who fear the Lord.**

O blessed are those who fear the Lord
and walk in his ways!
By the labour of your hands you shall eat.
You will be happy and prosper. R.

Your wife like a fruitful vine
in the heart of your house;
your children like shoots of the olive,
around your table. R.

Indeed thus shall be blessed
the man who fears the Lord.
May the Lord bless you from Zion
in a happy Jerusalem
all the days of your life. R.

SECOND READING

A reading from the first letter of St Paul to the Thessalonians 5:1-6

Let not the Day of the Lord overtake you like a thief.

You will not be expecting us to write anything to you, brothers, about 'times and seasons', since you know very well that the Day of the Lord is going to come like a thief in the night. It is when people are saying, 'How quiet and peaceful it is' that the worst suddenly happens, as suddenly as labour pains come on a pregnant woman; and there will be no way for anybody to evade it.

But it is not as if you live in the dark, my brothers, for that Day to overtake you like a thief. No, you are all sons of light and sons of the day: we do not belong to the night or to darkness, so we should not go on sleeping, as everyone else does, but stay wide awake and sober.

The word of the Lord.

Gospel Acclamation   Rv 2:10

R. **Alleluia, alleluia!**
Even if you have to die, says the Lord,
keep faithful, and I will give you
the crown of life.
R. **Alleluia!**

Or: Jn 15:4,5

R. **Alleluia, alleluia!**
Make your home in me, as I make mine in you,
says the Lord.
Whoever remains in me bears fruit in plenty.
R. **Alleluia!**

GOSPEL

A reading from the holy Gospel according to Matthew   25:14-30

You have been faithful in small things; come and join in your master's happiness.

[Jesus spoke this parable to his disciples: 'The kingdom of heaven is like a man on his way abroad who summoned his servants and entrusted his property to them. To one he gave five talents, to another two, to a third one; each in proportion to his ability. Then he set out.] The man who had received the five talents promptly went and traded with them and made five more. The man who had received two made two more in the same way. But the man who had received one went off and dug a hole in the ground and hid his master's money. [Now a long time after, the master of those servants came back and went through his accounts with them. The man who had received the five talents came forward bringing five more. "Sir," he said "you entrusted me with five talents; here are five more that I have made."] His master said to him, "Well done, good and faithful servant; you have shown you can be faithful in small things, I will trust you with greater; come and join in your master's happiness." Next the man with the two talents came forward. "Sir," he said "you entrusted me with two talents; here are two more that I have made." His master said to him, "Well done, good and faithful servant; you have shown you can be faithful in small things, I will trust you with greater; come and join in your master's happiness." Last came forward the man who had the one talent. "Sir," said he "I had heard you were a hard man, reaping where you have not sown and gathering where you have not scattered; so I was afraid, and I went off and hid your talent in the ground. Here it is; it was yours, you have it back." But his master answered him, "You wicked and lazy servant! So you knew that I reap where I have not sown and gather where I have not scattered? Well then, you should have deposited my money with the bankers, and on my return I would have recovered my capital with interest. So now, take the talent from him and give it to the man who has the five talents. For to everyone who has will be given more, and he will have more than enough; but from the man who has not, even what he has will be taken away. As for this good-for-nothing servant, throw him out into the dark, where there will be weeping and grinding of teeth.'"

[The Gospel of the Lord.]

Shorter Form, verses 14-15, 19-20. Read between [ ]

Prayer over the Offerings	Super oblata
Grant, O Lord, we pray,	Concede, quæsumus, Domine,
that what we offer in the sight	ut oculis tuæ maiestatis
of your majesty	munus oblatum
may obtain for us the grace	et gratiam nobis
of being devoted to you	devotionis obtineat,
and gain us the prize	et effectum beatæ
of everlasting happiness.	perennitatis acquirat.
Through Christ our Lord.	Per Christum Dominum nostrum.

Preface of Sundays in Ordinary Time I-VIII, pp.566-573.

Communion Antiphon   Ps 72:28
To be near God is my happiness,
to place my hope in God the Lord.

Or: Mk 11:23-24
Amen, I say to you:
   Whatever you ask in prayer,
believe that you will receive,
and it shall be given to you,
   says the Lord.

Prayer after Communion

We have partaken of the gifts
   of this sacred mystery,
humbly imploring, O Lord,
that what your Son commanded
   us to do
in memory of him
may bring us growth in charity.
Through Christ our Lord.

Ant. ad communionem
Mihi autem adhærere Deo
   bonum est,
ponere in Domino Deo spem meam.

Vel:
Amen dico vobis,
   quidquid orantes petitis,
credite quia accipietis, et fiet vobis,
   dicit Dominus.

Post communionem
Sumpsimus, Domine,
   sacri dona mysterii,
humiliter deprecantes,
ut, quæ in sui commemorationem
nos Filius tuus facere præcepit,
in nostræ proficiant
   caritatis augmentum.
Per Christum Dominum nostrum.

Last Sunday in Ordinary Time

OUR LORD JESUS CHRIST, KING OF THE UNIVERSE (YEAR A)

Solemnity

Entrance Antiphon   Rv 5:12; 1:6

HOW worthy is the Lamb
who was slain,
to receive power and divinity,
and wisdom and strength
 and honour.
To him belong glory and power
 for ever and ever.

Ant. ad introitum

DIGNUS est Agnus,
qui occisus est,
accipere virtutem et divinitatem
et sapientiam et fortitudinem
 et honorem.
Ipsi gloria et imperium
 in sæcula sæculorum.

The Gloria in excelsis (Glory to God in the highest) is said.

Collect

Almighty ever-living God,
whose will is to restore all things
in your beloved Son,
 the King of the universe,
grant, we pray,
that the whole creation,
 set free from slavery,
may render your majesty service
and ceaselessly proclaim
 your praise.
Through our Lord Jesus Christ,
 your Son,
who lives and reigns with you
 in the unity of the Holy Spirit,
one God, for ever and ever.

The Creed is said.

Collecta

Omnipotens sempiterne Deus,
qui in dilecto Filio tuo,
 universorum Rege,
omnia instaurare voluisti,
concede propitius,
ut tota creatura,
 a servitute liberata,
tuæ maiestati deserviat ac te sine
 fine collaudet.
Per Dominum nostrum Iesum
 Christum Filium tuum,
qui tecum vivit et regnat in unitate
 Spiritus Sancti,
Deus, per omnia sæcula sæculorum.

FIRST READING

A reading from the prophet Ezekiel   34:11-12,15-17

As for you, my sheep, I will judge between sheep and sheep.

The Lord says this: I am going to look after my flock myself and keep all of it in view. As a shepherd keeps all his flock in view when he stands up in the middle of his scattered sheep, so shall I keep my sheep in view. I shall rescue them from wherever they have been scattered during the mist and darkness. I myself will pasture my sheep, I myself will show them where to rest – it is the Lord who speaks. I shall look for the lost one, bring back the stray, bandage the wounded and make the weak strong. I shall watch over the fat and healthy. I shall be a true shepherd to them.

    As for you, my sheep, the Lord says this: I will judge between sheep and sheep, between rams and he-goats.

    The word of the Lord.

Responsorial Psalm   cf. Ps 22:1-3,5-6. R. v.1

R. **The Lord is my shepherd;**
   there is nothing I shall want.

   The Lord is my shepherd;
   there is nothing I shall want.
   Fresh and green are the pastures
   where he gives me repose. R.

   Near restful waters he leads me,
   to revive my drooping spirit.
   He guides me along the right path;
   he is true to his name. R.

   You have prepared a banquet for me
   in the sight of my foes.
   My head you have anointed with oil;
   my cup is overflowing. R.

   Surely goodness and kindness shall follow
   me all the days of my life.
   In the Lord's own house shall I dwell
   for ever and ever. R.

SECOND READING

A reading from the first letter of St Paul to the Corinthians   15:20-26,28

He will hand over the kingdom to God the Father; so that God may be all in all.

Christ has been raised from the dead, the first-fruits of all who have fallen asleep. Death came through one man and in the same way the resurrection of the dead has come through one man. Just as all men die in Adam, so all men will be brought to life in Christ; but all of them in their proper order: Christ as the first-fruits and then, after the coming of Christ, those who belong to him. After that will come the end, when he hands over the kingdom to God the Father, having done away with every sovereignty, authority and power. For he must be king until he has put all his enemies under his feet and the last of the enemies to be destroyed is death. And when everything is subjected to him, then the Son himself will be subject in his turn to the One who subjected all things to him, so that God may be all in all.

The word of the Lord.

Gospel Acclamation   Mk 11:10

R. **Alleluia, alleluia!**

Blessings on him who comes in the name of the Lord!
Blessings on the coming kingdom of our father David!

R. **Alleluia!**

GOSPEL

A reading from the holy Gospel according to Matthew   25:31-46

He will take his seat on his throne of glory, and he will separate men one from another.

Jesus said to his disciples: 'When the Son of Man comes in his glory, escorted by all the angels, then he will take his seat on his throne of glory. All the nations will be assembled before him and he will separate men one from another as the shepherd separates sheep from goats. He will place the sheep on his right hand and the goats on his left. Then the King will say to those on his right hand, "Come, you whom my Father has blessed, take for your heritage the kingdom prepared for you since the foundation of the world. For I was hungry and you gave me food; I was thirsty and you gave me drink; I was a stranger and you made me welcome; naked and you clothed me, sick and you visited me, in prison and you came to see me." Then the virtuous will say to him in reply, "Lord, when did we see you hungry and feed you; or thirsty and give you drink? When did we see you a stranger and make you welcome; naked and clothe you; sick or in prison and go to see you?" And the King will answer, "I tell you solemnly, in so far as you did this to one of the least of these brothers of mine, you did it to me." Next he will say to those on his left hand, "Go away from me, with your curse upon you, to the eternal fire prepared for the devil and his angels. For I was hungry and you never gave me food; I was thirsty and you never gave me anything to drink; I was a stranger and you never made me welcome, naked and you never clothed me, sick and in prison and you never visited me." Then it will be their turn to ask, "Lord, when did we see you hungry or thirsty, a stranger or naked, sick or in prison, and did not come to your help?" Then he will answer, "I tell you solemnly, in so far as you neglected to do this to one of the least of these, you neglected to do it to me." And they will go away to eternal punishment, and the virtuous to eternal life.'

The Gospel of the Lord.

Prayer over the Offerings

As we offer you, O Lord,
   the sacrifice
by which the human race
   is reconciled to you,
we humbly pray
that your Son himself may bestow
   on all nations
the gifts of unity and peace.
Through Christ our Lord.

Super oblata

Hostiam tibi, Domine,
humanæ reconciliationis
   offerentes, suppliciter deprecamur,
ut ipse Filius tuus cunctis gentibus
unitatis et pacis dona concedat.
Qui vivit et regnat
   in sæcula sæculorum.

Preface: Christ, King of the Universe.

It is truly right and just,
   our duty and our salvation,
always and everywhere
   to give you thanks,
Lord, holy Father,
   almighty and eternal God.

For you anointed your Only
   Begotten Son,
our Lord Jesus Christ,
   with the oil of gladness
as eternal Priest and King
   of all creation,

Præfatio: De Christo universorum Rege.

Vere dignum et iustum est,
   æquum et salutare,
nos tibi semper
   et ubique gratias agere:
Domine, sancte Pater,
   omnipotens æterne Deus:

Qui Unigenitum Filium tuum,
Dominum nostrum
   Iesum Christum,
Sacerdotem æternum
   et universorum Regem,
oleo exsultationis unxisti:

so that, by offering himself
    on the altar of the Cross
as a spotless sacrifice
    to bring us peace,
he might accomplish the mysteries
    of human redemption
and, making all created things
    subject to his rule,
he might present to the immensity
    of your majesty
an eternal and universal kingdom,
a kingdom of truth and life,
a kingdom of holiness and grace,
a kingdom of justice, love and peace.

And so, with Angels and Archangels,
with Thrones and Dominions,
and with all the hosts and Powers
    of heaven,
we sing the hymn of your glory,
as without end we acclaim:

Holy, Holy, Holy Lord God of hosts...

ut, seipsum in ara crucis
hostiam immaculatam
    et pacificam offerens,
redemptionis humanæ
    sacramenta perageret:
et, suo subiectis imperio
    omnibus creaturis,
æternum et universale regnum
immensæ tuæ traderet maiestati:
regnum veritatis et vitæ;
regnum sanctitatis et gratiæ;
regnum iustitiæ,
    amoris et pacis.

Et ideo cum Angelis et Archangelis,
cum Thronis et Dominationibus,
cumque omni
    militia cælestis exercitus,
hymnum gloriæ tuæ canimus,
sine fine dicentes:

Sanctus, Sanctus, Sanctus . . .

Communion Antiphon Ps 28:10-11

The Lord sits as King for ever.
The Lord will bless his people
    with peace.

Ant. ad communionem

Sedebit Dominus Rex in æternum;
Dominus benedicet populo suo
    in pace.

Prayer after Communion

Having received the food
    of immortality,
we ask, O Lord,
that, glorying in obedience
to the commands of Christ,
    the King of the universe,
we may live with him eternally
    in his heavenly Kingdom.
Who lives and reigns
    for ever and ever.

Post communionem

Immortalitatis alimoniam consecuti,
quæsumus, Domine,
ut, qui Christi Regis universorum
gloriamur obœdire mandatis,
cum ipso in cælesti regno sine fine
    vivere valeamus.
Qui vivit et regnat
    in sæcula sæculorum.

SOLEMNITIES OF THE LORD IN ORDINARY TIME

Sunday after Pentecost

THE MOST HOLY TRINITY (YEAR A)

On this Solemnity, the liturgy invites us to praise God not merely for the wonders that he has worked, but for who he is; for the beauty and goodness of his being from which his action stems. We are invited to contemplate, so to speak, the Heart of God, his deepest reality which is his being One in the Trinity, a supreme and profound communion of love and life. The whole of Sacred Scripture speaks to us of him. Indeed, it is he who speaks to us of himself in the Scriptures and reveals himself as Creator of the universe and Lord of history. Today we heard a passage from the Book of Exodus in which – something quite exceptional – God proclaims his own Name! He does so in the presence of Moses with whom he spoke face to face, as with a friend. And what is God's Name? It never fails to move us: "The Lord, the Lord, a God merciful and gracious, slow to anger, and abounding in steadfast love and faithfulness".

(Pope Benedict XVI)

Solemnity

Entrance Antiphon	Ant. ad introitum
BLEST be God the Father, and the Only Begotten Son of God, and also the Holy Spirit, for he has shown us his merciful love.	BENEDICTUS sit Deus Pater, Unigenitusque Dei Filius, Sanctus quoque Spiritus, quia fecit nobiscum misericordiam suam.

The Gloria in excelsis (Glory to God in the highest) is said.

Collect

God our Father, who by sending
   into the world
the Word of truth and the Spirit
   of sanctification
made known to the human race
   your wondrous mystery,
grant us, we pray, that in professing
   the true faith,
we may acknowledge the Trinity
   of eternal glory
and adore your Unity,
   powerful in majesty.
Through our Lord Jesus Christ,
   your Son,
who lives and reigns with you
   in the unity of the Holy Spirit,
one God, for ever and ever.

Collecta

Deus Pater, qui Verbum veritatis
et Spiritum sanctificationis mittens
   in mundum,
admirabile mysterium tuum
   hominibus declarasti,
da nobis, in confessione veræ fidei,
æternæ gloriam Trinitatis agnoscere,
et Unitatem adorare
   in potentia maiestatis.
Per Dominum nostrum Iesum
   Christum Filium tuum,
qui tecum vivit et regnat
   in unitate Spiritus Sancti,
Deus, per omnia sæcula sæculorum.

FIRST READING

A reading from the book of Exodus   34:4-6,8-9

Lord, Lord, a God of tenderness and compassion.

With the two tablets of stone in his hands, Moses went up the mountain of Sinai in the early morning as the Lord had commanded him. And the Lord descended in the form of a cloud, and Moses stood with him there.

He called on the name of the Lord. The Lord passed before him and proclaimed, 'Lord, Lord, a God of tenderness and compassion, slow to anger, rich in kindness and faithfulness.' And Moses bowed down to the ground at once and worshipped. 'If I have indeed won your favour, Lord,' he said 'let my Lord come with us, I beg. True, they are a headstrong people, but forgive us our faults and our sins, and adopt us as your heritage.'

The word of the Lord.

Responsorial Psalm   Dn 3:52-56. R. v.52

You are blest, Lord God of our fathers.
R. **To you glory and praise for evermore.**

Blest your glorious holy name.
R. **To you glory and praise for evermore.**

You are blest in the temple of your glory.
R. **To you glory and praise for evermore.**

You are blest on the throne of your kingdom.
R. **To you glory and praise for evermore.**

You are blest who gaze into the depths.
R. **To you glory and praise for evermore.**

You are blest in the firmament of heaven.
R. **To you glory and praise for evermore.**

SECOND READING

A reading from the second letter of St Paul to the Corinthians   13:11-13
The grace of Jesus Christ, the love of God, and the fellowship of the Holy Spirit.

Brothers, we wish you happiness; try to grow perfect; help one another.
Be united; live in peace, and the God of love and peace will be with you.

Greet one another with the holy kiss. All the saints send you greetings.

The grace of the Lord Jesus Christ, the love of God and the fellowship
of the Holy Spirit be with you all.

The word of the Lord.

Gospel Acclamation   Cf. Rv 1:8

R. **Alleluia, alleluia!**
Glory be to the Father, and to the Son, and to the Holy Spirit,
the God who is, who was, and who is to come.
R. **Alleluia!**

GOSPEL

A reading from the holy Gospel according to John   3:16-18
God sent his Son so that through him the world might be saved.

Jesus said to Nicodemus:

'God loved the world so much
that he gave his only Son,
so that everyone who believes in him may not be lost

but may have eternal life.
For God sent his Son into the world
not to condemn the world,
but so that through him the world might be saved.
No one who believes in him will be condemned;
but whoever refuses to believe is condemned already,
because he has refused to believe
in the name of God's only Son.

The Gospel of the Lord.

The Creed is said.

Prayer over the Offerings	Super oblata
Sanctify by the invocation	Sanctifica, quæsumus,
of your name,	Domine Deus noster,
we pray, O Lord our God,	per tui nominis invocationem,
this oblation of our service,	hæc munera nostræ servitutis,
and by it make of us an eternal	et per ea nosmetipsos tibi perfice
offering to you.	munus æternum.
Through Christ our Lord.	Per Christum Dominum nostrum.

Preface: The Mystery of the Most Holy Trinity.	Præfatio: De mysterio Sanctissimæ Trinitatis.
It is truly right and just,	Vere dignum et iustum est,
our duty and our salvation,	æquum et salutare,
always and everywhere	nos tibi semper et ubique
to give you thanks,	gratias agere:
Lord, holy Father,	Domine, sancte Pater,
almighty and eternal God.	omnipotens æterne Deus:
For with your Only Begotten Son	Qui cum Unigenito Filio tuo
and the Holy Spirit	et Spiritu Sancto
you are one God, one Lord:	unus es Deus, unus es Dominus:
not in the unity of a single person,	non in unius singularitate personæ,
but in a Trinity of one substance.	sed in unius Trinitate substantiæ.
For what you have revealed to us	Quod enim de tua gloria,
of your glory	revelante te, credimus,
we believe equally of your Son	hoc de Filio tuo,
and of the Holy Spirit,	hoc de Spiritu Sancto,
so that, in the confessing of the true	sine discretione sentimus.
and eternal Godhead,	

you might be adored in what
    is proper to each Person,
their unity in substance,
and their equality in majesty.

For this is praised by Angels
    and Archangels,
Cherubim, too, and Seraphim,
who never cease to cry out each day,
as with one voice they acclaim:

Holy, Holy, Holy Lord God of hosts...

Ut in confessione veræ
    sempiternæque Deitatis,
et in personis proprietas,
et in essentia unitas,
et in maiestate adoretur æqualitas.

Quem laudant Angeli
    atque Archangeli,
Cherubim quoque ac Seraphim,
qui non cessant clamare cotidie,
    una voce dicentes:

Sanctus, Sanctus, Sanctus . . .

Communion Antiphon   Ga 4:6

Since you are children of God,
God has sent into your hearts
    the Spirit of his Son,
the Spirit who cries out:
    Abba, Father.

Ant. ad communionem

Quoniam autem estis filii,
misit Deus Spiritum Filii sui
    in corda vestra
clamantem: Abba, Pater.

Prayer after Communion

May receiving this Sacrament,
    O Lord our God,
bring us health of body and soul,
as we confess your eternal holy
    Trinity and undivided Unity.
Through Christ our Lord.

Post communionem

Proficiat nobis ad salutem
    corporis et animæ,
Domine Deus noster,
    huius sacramenti susceptio,
et sempiternæ sanctæ Trinitatis
eiusdemque individuæ
    Unitatis confessio.
Per Christum Dominum nostrum.

THE MOST HOLY BODY AND BLOOD OF CHRIST (CORPUS CHRISTI) (YEAR A)

Everything begins, one might say, from the heart of Christ who, at the Last Supper, on the eve of his passion, thanked and praised God and by so doing, with the power of his love, transformed the meaning of death which he was on his way to encounter. The fact that the Sacrament of the Altar acquired the name "Eucharist" – "thanksgiving" – expresses precisely this: that changing the substance of the bread and wine into the Body and Blood of Christ is the fruit of the gift that Christ made of himself, the gift of a Love stronger than death, divine Love which raised him from the dead. This is why the Eucharist is the food of eternal life, the Bread of Life.

(Pope Benedict XVI)

Solemnity

Where the Solemnity of the Most Holy Body and Blood of Christ is not a Holyday of Obligation, it is assigned to the Sunday after the Most Holy Trinity as its proper day.

Entrance Antiphon Cf. Ps 80:17	Ant. ad introitum
HE fed them with the finest wheat and satisfied them with honey from the rock.	CIBAVIT eos ex adipe frumenti, et de petra melle saturavit eos.

The Gloria in excelsis (Glory to God in the highest) is said.

Collect	Collecta
O God, who in this wonderful Sacrament have left us a memorial of your Passion, grant us, we pray, so to revere the sacred mysteries of your Body and Blood that we may always experience in ourselves the fruits of your redemption. Who live and reign with God the Father in the unity of the Holy Spirit, one God, for ever and ever.	Deus, qui nobis sub sacramento mirabili passionis tuæ memoriam reliquisti, tribue, quæsumus, ita nos Corporis et Sanguinis tui sacra mysteria venerari, ut redemptionis tuæ fructum in nobis iugiter sentiamus. Qui vivis et regnas cum Deo Patre in unitate Spiritus Sancti, Deus, per omnia sæcula sæculorum.

FIRST READING

A reading from the book of Deuteronomy   8:2-3,14-16

He fed you with manna which neither you nor your fathers had known.

Moses said to the people: 'Remember how the Lord your God led you for forty years in the wilderness, to humble you, to test you and know your inmost heart – whether you would keep his commandments or not. He humbled you, he made you feel hunger, he fed you with manna which neither you nor your fathers had known, to make you understand that man does not live on bread alone but that man lives on everything that comes from the mouth of the Lord.

'Do not then forget the Lord your God who brought you out of the land of Egypt, out of the house of slavery: who guided you through this vast and dreadful wilderness, a land of fiery serpents, scorpions, thirst; who in this waterless place brought you water from the hardest rock; who in this wilderness fed you with manna that your fathers had not known.'

The word of the Lord.

Responsorial Psalm   Ps 147:12-15,19-20. R. v.12

R. **O praise the Lord, Jerusalem!**
  Or: **Alleluia!**

O praise the Lord, Jerusalem!
Zion, praise your God!
He has strengthened the bars of your gates,
he has blessed the children within you. R.

He established peace on your borders,
he feeds you with finest wheat.
He sends out his word to the earth
and swiftly runs his command. R.

He makes his word known to Jacob,
to Israel his laws and decrees.
He has not dealt thus with other nations;
He has not taught them his decrees. R.

SECOND READING

A reading from the first letter of St Paul to the Corinthians   10:16-17

That there is only one loaf means that, though there are many of us, we form a single body.

The blessing-cup that we bless is a communion with the blood of Christ, and the bread that we break is a communion with the body of Christ. The fact that there is only one loaf means that, though there are many of us, we form a single body because we all have a share in this one loaf.

The word of the Lord.

SEQUENCE

The Sequence may be said or sung in full, or using the shorter form indicated by the asterisked verses.

Sing forth, O Zion, sweetly sing
The praises of thy Shepherd-King,
    In hymns and canticles divine;
Dare all thou canst, thou hast no song
Worthy his praises to prolong,
    So far surpassing powers like thine.
	Lauda Sion Salvatorem
	Lauda ducem et pastorem
	    In hymnis et canticis.
	Quantum potes, tantum aude:
	Quia major omni laude,
	    Nec laudare sufficis.

Today no theme of common praise
Forms the sweet burden of thy lays –
    The living, life-dispensing food –
That food which at the sacred board
Unto the brethren twelve our Lord
    His parting legacy bestowed.
	Laudis thema specialis,
	Panis vivus et vitalis,
	    Hodie proponitur.
	Quem in sacræ mensa cenæ,
	Turbæ fratrum duodenæ
	    Datum non ambigitur.

Then be the anthem clear and strong,
Thy fullest note, thy sweetest song,
    The very music of thy breast:
For now shines forth the day sublime
That brings remembrance of the time
    When Jesus first his table blessed.
	Sit laus plena, sit sonora,
	Sit iucunda, sit decora
	    Mentis iubilatio.
	Dies enim solemnis agitur,
	In qua mensæ prima recolitur
	    Huius institutio.

Within our new King's banquet-hall
They meet to keep the festival
    That closed the ancient paschal rite:
The old is by the new replaced;
The substance hath
        the shadows chased;
        And rising day dispels the night.
	In hac mensa novi Regis,
	Novum Pascha novæ legis,
	    Phase vetus terminat.
	Vetustatem novitas,
	Umbram fugat veritas,
	    Noctem lux eliminat.

Christ willed what He Himself
   had done
Should be renewed while time
   should run,
     in memory of His parting hour:
Thus, tutored in His school divine,
We consecrate the bread and wine;
   And lo – a Host of saving power.

This faith to Christian men is given –
Bread is made flesh by words
   from heaven:
     Into his Blood the wine is turned:
What though it baffles
   nature's powers
Of sense and sight? This faith of ours
   Proves more than nature
   e'er discerned.

Concealed beneath the two-fold sign
Meet symbols of the gifts divine,
   There lie the mysteries adored:
The living body is our food;
Our drink the ever precious blood;
   In each, one undivided Lord.

Not he that eateth it divides
The sacred food, which whole abides
   Unbroken still, nor knows decay;
Be one, or be a thousand fed,
They eat alike the Living Bread
   Which, still received,
   ne'er wastes away.

The good, the guilty share therein,
With sure increase of grace or sin,
   The ghostly life, or ghostly death:
Death to the guilty; to the good
Immortal life. See how one food
   Man's joy or woe accomplisheth.

Quod in cœna Christus gessit,
Faciendum hoc expressit
   In sui memoriam.
Docti sacris institutis,
Panem, vinum, in salutis
   Consecramus hostiam.

Dogma datur Christianis,
Quod in carnem transit panis,
   Et vinum in sanguinem.
Quod non capis, quod non vides,
Animosa firmat fides,
   Præter rerum ordinem.

Sub diversis speciebus,
Signis tantum, et non rebus,
   Latent res eximiæ.
Caro cibus, sanguis potus:
Manet tamen Christus totus,
   Sub utraque specie.

A sumente non concisus,
Non confractus, non divisus:
   Integer accipitur.
Sumit unus, sumunt mille:
Quantum isti, tantum ille:
   Nec sumptus consumitur.

Sumunt boni, sumunt mali:
Sorte tamen inæquali,
   Vitæ vel interitus.
Mors est malis, vita bonis:
Vide paris sumptionis
   Quam sit dispar exitus.

We break the Sacrament; but bold
And firm thy faith shall keep its hold;
Deem not the whole doth
     more enfold
     Than in the fractured part resides:
Deem not that Christ doth broken lie;
'Tis but the sign that meets the eye;
The hidden deep reality
     In all its fulness still abides.

Fracto demum Sacramento,
Ne vacilles, sed memento,
Tantum esse sub fragmento,
     Quantum toto tegitur.
Nulla rei fit scissura:
Signi tantum fit fractura:
Qua nec status nec statura
     Signati minuitur.

*Behold the bread of angels, sent
For pilgrims in their banishment,
The bread for God's true
     children meant,
     That may not unto dogs be given:
Oft in the olden types foreshadowed;
In Isaac on the altar bowed,
And in the ancient paschal food,
     And in the manna sent
     from heaven.

*Ecce panis Angelorum,
Factus cibus viatorum:
Vere panis filiorum,
     Non mittendus canibus.
In figuris præsignatur,
Cum Isaac immolatur:
Agnus paschæ deputatur
     Datur manna patribus.

*Come then, good shepherd,
     bread divine,
Still show to us Thy mercy sign;
Oh, feed us still, still keep us Thine;
So may we see Thy glories shine
     In fields of immortality;

*Bone pastor, panis vere,
Iesu, nostri miserere:
Tu nos pasce, nos tuere:
Tu nos bona fac videre
     In terra viventium.

*O Thou, the wisest, mightiest, best,
Our present food, our future rest,
Come, make us each Thy
     chosen guest,
Coheirs of Thine, and comrades blest
     With saints whose dwelling
     is with Thee.
Amen. Alleluia.

*Tu, qui cuncta scis et vales:
Qui nos pascis hic mortales:
Tuos ibi commensales,
Cohæredes et sodales,
     Fac sanctorum civium.
Amen. Alleluia.

Gospel Acclamation   Jn 6:51

R. **Alleluia, alleluia!**
I am the living bread which has come down from heaven, says the Lord.
Anyone who eats this bread will live for ever.
R. **Alleluia**

GOSPEL

A reading from the holy Gospel according to John   6:51-58

My flesh is real food and my blood is real drink.

Jesus said to the Jews:

'I am the living bread which has come down from heaven.
Anyone who eats this bread will live for ever;
and the bread that I shall give
is my flesh, for the life of the world.'

Then the Jews started arguing with one another: 'How can this man give us his flesh to eat?' they said. Jesus replied:

'I tell you most solemnly,
if you do not eat the flesh of the Son of Man
and drink his blood,
you will not have life in you.
Anyone who does eat my flesh and drink my blood
has eternal life,
and I shall raise him up on the last day.
For my flesh is real food
and my blood is real drink.
He who eats my flesh and drinks my blood
lives in me
and I live in him.
As I, who am sent by the living Father,
myself draw life from the Father,
so whoever eats me will draw life from me.
This is the bread come down from heaven,
not like the bread our ancestors ate:
they are dead,
but anyone who eats this bread will live for ever.'

The Gospel of the Lord.

The Creed is said.

Prayer over the Offerings	Super oblata

Grant your Church, O Lord,
    we pray,
the gifts of unity and peace,
whose signs are to be seen in mystery
in the offerings we here present.
Through Christ our Lord.
	Ecclesiæ tuæ, quæsumus, Domine,
	unitatis et pacis propitius
	    dona concede,
	quæ sub oblatis muneribus
	    mystice designantur.
	Per Christum Dominum nostrum.

Preface of the Holy Eucharist I or II, pp.574-575.

Communion Antiphon Jn 6:57	Ant. ad communionem

Whoever eats my flesh
    and drinks my blood
remains in me and I in him,
    says the Lord.
	Qui manducat meam carnem
	    et bibit meum sanguinem,
	in me manet et ego in eo,
	    dicit Dominus.

Prayer after Communion	Post communionem

Grant, O Lord, we pray,
that we may delight for all eternity
in that share in your divine life,
which is foreshadowed
    in the present age
by our reception of your precious
    Body and Blood.
Who live and reign for ever and ever.
	Fac nos, quæsumus, Domine,
	divinitatis tuæ sempiterna
	    fruitione repleri,
	quam pretiosi Corporis
	    et Sanguinis tui
	temporalis perceptio præfigurat.
	Qui vivis et regnas
	    in sæcula sæculorum.

It is desirable that a procession take place after the Mass in which the Host to be carried in the procession is consecrated. However, nothing prohibits a procession from taking place even after a public and lengthy period of adoration following the Mass. If a procession takes place after Mass, when the Communion of the faithful is over, the monstrance in which the consecrated host has been placed is set on the altar. When the Prayer after Communion has been said, the Concluding Rites are omitted and the procession forms.

THE MOST SACRED HEART OF JESUS (YEAR A)

To celebrate the Heart of Christ means to go to the inner centre of the Person of the Saviour, the centre which the Bible identifies as his Heart, the seat of the love that has redeemed the world. If the human heart is really an unfathomable mystery known only to God, how much more sublime is the Heart of Jesus in whom the very life of the Word is pulsating. Echoing the Scriptures, as the beautiful Litany of the Sacred Heart suggests that we find in the Heart of Jesus all the treasures of wisdom and knowledge and the whole fullness of divinity. To save man, the victim of his own disobedience, God wanted to give him a "new heart" that would be faithful to his loving will. This heart is the Heart of Jesus, the Holy Spirit's masterpiece, which began to beat in Mary's virginal womb and was pierced by the spear as Jesus hung on the Cross, becoming for all an inexhaustible source of eternal life. That Heart is now a pledge of hope for every man and woman.

(Blessed Pope John Paul II)

Solemnity

Entrance Antiphon   Ps 32:11,19

THE designs of his Heart
are from age to age,
to rescue their souls from death,
and to keep them alive in famine.

Ant. ad introitum

COGITATIONES Cordis eius in
generatione et generationem,
ut eruat a morte animas eorum
et alat eos in fame.

The Gloria in excelsis (Glory to God in the highest) is said.

Collect

Grant, we pray, almighty God,
that we, who glory in the Heart
    of your beloved Son
and recall the wonders of his
    love for us,
may be made worthy to receive
an overflowing measure of grace
from that fount of heavenly gifts.
Through our Lord Jesus Christ,
    your Son,
who lives and reigns with you in the
    unity of the Holy Spirit,
one God, for ever and ever.

Collecta

Concede, quæsumus,
    omnipotens Deus,
ut qui, dilecti Filii tui
    Corde gloriantes,
eius præcipua in nos beneficia
    recolimus caritatis,
de illo donorum fonte cælesti
supereffluentem gratiam
    mereamur accipere.
Per Dominum nostrum Iesum
    Christum Filium tuum,
qui tecum vivit et regnat in unitate
    Spiritus Sancti, Deus,
per omnia sæcula sæculorum.

Or:

O God, who in the Heart of your Son, wounded by our sins, bestow on us in mercy the boundless treasures of your love, grant, we pray, that, in paying him the homage of our devotion we may also offer worthy reparation. Through our Lord Jesus Christ, your Son, who lives and reigns with you in the unity of the Holy Spirit, one God, for ever and ever.	Vel:

Vel:

Deus, qui nobis in Corde Filii tui,
nostris vulnerato peccatis,
infinitos dilectionis thesauros
misericorditer largiri dignaris,
concede, quæsumus,
ut, illi devotum pietatis nostræ
   præstantes obsequium,
dignæ quoque satisfactionis
   exhibeamus officium.
Per Dominum nostrum Iesum
   Christum Filium tuum,
qui tecum vivit et regnat
   in unitate Spiritus Sancti,
Deus, per omnia sæcula sæculorum.

FIRST READING

A reading from the book of Deuteronomy   7:6-11

The Lord set his heart on you and chose you.

Moses said to the people: 'You are a people consecrated to the Lord your God; it is you that the Lord our God has chosen to be his very own people out of all the peoples on the earth.

'If the Lord set his heart on you and chose you, it was not because you outnumbered other peoples: you were the least of all peoples. It was for love of you and to keep the oath he swore to your fathers that the Lord brought you out with his mighty hand and redeemed you from the house of slavery, from the power of Pharaoh king of Egypt. Know then that the Lord your God is God indeed, the faithful God who is true to his covenant and his graciousness for a thousand generations towards those who love him and keep his commandments, but who punishes in their own persons those that hate him; he makes him work out his punishment in person. You are therefore to keep and observe the commandments and statutes and ordinances that I lay down for you today.'

The word of the Lord.

Responsorial Psalm   Ps 102:1-4,6-8,10. R. v.17

R. **The love of the Lord is everlasting**
   upon those who hold him in fear.

My soul, give thanks to the Lord,
all my being, bless his holy name.
My soul, give thanks to the Lord
and never forget all his blessings. R.

It is he who forgives all your guilt,
who heals every one of your ills,
who redeems your life from the grave,
who crowns you with love and compassion. R.

The Lord does deeds of justice,
gives judgment for all who are oppressed.
He made known his ways to Moses
and his deeds to Israel's sons. R.

The Lord is compassion and love,
slow to anger and rich in mercy.
He does not treat us according to our sins
nor repay us according to our faults. R.

SECOND READING

A reading from the first letter of St John   4:7-16

Love comes from God.

My dear people,
let us love one another
since love comes from God
and everyone who loves is begotten by God and knows God.
Anyone who fails to love can never have known God,
because God is love.
God's love for us was revealed
when God sent into the world his only Son
so that we could have life through him;
this is the love I mean:
not our love for God,
but God's love for us when he sent his Son
to be the sacrifice that takes our sins away.
My dear people,
since God has loved us so much,
we too should love one another.

No one has ever seen God;
but as long as we love one another
God will live in us
and his love will be complete in us.
We can know that we are living in him
and he is living in us
because he lets us share his Spirit.
We ourselves saw and we testify
that the Father sent his Son
as saviour of the world.
If anyone acknowledges that Jesus is the Son of God,
God lives in him, and he in God.
We ourselves have known and put our faith in
God's love towards ourselves.
God is love
and anyone who lives in love lives in God,
and God lives in him.

The word of the Lord.

Gospel Acclamation   Mt 11:29
R. **Alleluia, alleluia!**
Shoulder my yoke and learn from me,
for I am gentle and humble in heart.
R. **Alleluia!**

GOSPEL
A reading from the holy Gospel according to Matthew   11:25-30
I am gentle and humble in heart.

Jesus exclaimed, 'I bless you, Father, Lord of heaven and of earth, for hiding these things from the learned and the clever and revealing them to mere children. Yes, Father, for that is what it pleased you to do. Everything has been entrusted to me by my Father; and no one knows the Son except the Father, just as no one knows the Father except the Son and those to whom the Son chooses to reveal him.

'Come to me, all you who labour and are overburdened, and I will give you rest. Shoulder my yoke and learn from me, for I am gentle and humble in heart, and you will find rest for your souls. Yes, my yoke is easy and my burden light.'

The Gospel of the Lord.

The Creed is said.

Prayer over the Offerings

Look, O Lord, we pray,
   on the surpassing charity
in the Heart of your beloved Son,
that what we offer may be a gift
   acceptable to you
and an expiation of our offences.
Through Christ our Lord.

Preface: The boundless charity of Christ

It is truly right and just,
   our duty and our salvation,
always and everywhere
   to give you thanks,
Lord, holy Father,
   almighty and eternal God,
through Christ our Lord.

For raised up high on the Cross,
he gave himself up for us
   with a wonderful love
and poured out blood and water
   from his pierced side,
the wellspring of the Church's
   Sacraments,
so that, won over to the open heart
   of the Saviour,
all might draw water joyfully
   from the springs of salvation.

And so, with all the Angels
   and Saints,
we praise you, as without end
   we acclaim:

Holy, Holy, Holy Lord God of hosts...

Super oblata

Respice, quæsumus, Domine,
ad ineffabilem Cordis dilecti Filii
   tui caritatem,
ut quod offerimus sit tibi
   munus acceptum
et nostrorum expiatio delictorum.
Per Christum Dominum nostrum.

Præfatio: De immense caritate Christi

Vere dignum et iustum est,
   æquum et salutare,
nos tibi semper et ubique
   gratias agere:
Domine, sancte Pater,
   omnipotens æterne Deus:
per Christum Dominum nostrum:

Qui, mira caritate, exaltatus in cruce,
pro nobis tradidit semetipsum,
atque de transfixo latere sanguinem
   fudit et aquam,
ex quo manarent Ecclesiæ
   sacramenta,
ut omnes, ad Cor apertum
   Salvatoris attracti,
iugiter haurirent e fontibus salutis
   in gaudio.

Et ideo, cum Sanctis
   et Angelis universis,
te collaudamus, sine fine dicentes:
Sanctus, Sanctus, Sanctus . . .

Communion Antiphon Cf. Jn 7:37-38 | Ant. ad communionem

Thus says the Lord: | Dicit Dominus:
Let whoever is thirsty come to me | Si quis sitit, veniat ad me et bibat.
and drink. | Qui credit in me, flumina de ventre
Streams of living water will flow | eius fluent aquæ vivæ.
from within the one who believes
in me.

Or: Jn 19:34 | Vel:

One of the soldiers opened his side | Unus militum lancea
with a lance, | latus eius aperuit,
and at once there came forth blood | et continuo exivit sanguis et aqua.
and water.

Prayer after Communion | Post communionem

May this sacrament of charity, | Sacramentum caritatis, Domine,
O Lord, | sancta nos faciat dilectione fervere,
make us fervent with the fire | qua, ad Filium tuum
of holy love, | semper attracti,
so that, drawn always to your Son, | ipsum in fratribus
we may learn to see him in | agnoscere discamus.
our neighbour. | Qui vivit et regnat
Through Christ our Lord. | in sæcula sæculorum.

First Sunday in Ordinary Time

THE BAPTISM OF THE LORD

Feast

See p.133.

SECOND SUNDAY IN ORDINARY TIME (YEAR B)

Entrance Antiphon Ps 65:4	Ant. ad introitum
ALL the earth shall bow down before you, O God, and shall sing to you, shall sing to your name, O Most High!	OMNIS terra adoret te, Deus, et psallat tibi; psalmum dicat nomini tuo, Altissime.
Collect	**Collecta**
Almighty ever-living God, who govern all things, both in heaven and on earth, mercifully hear the pleading of your people and bestow your peace on our times. Through our Lord Jesus Christ, your Son, who lives and reigns with you in the unity of the Holy Spirit, one God, for ever and ever.	Omnipotens sempiterne Deus, qui cælestia simul et terrena moderaris, supplicationes populi tui clementer exaudi, et pacem tuam nostris concede temporibus. Per Dominum nostrum Iesum Christum Filium tuum, qui tecum vivit et regnat in unitate Spiritus Sancti, Deus, per omnia sæcula sæculorum.

FIRST READING

A reading from the first book of Samuel   3:3-10,19

Speak, Lord, your servant is listening.

Samuel was lying in the sanctuary of the Lord where the ark of God was, when the Lord called, 'Samuel! Samuel!' He answered, 'Here I am.' Then he ran to Eli and said, 'Here I am, since you called me.' Eli said, 'I did not call. Go back and lie down.' So he went and lay down. Once again the Lord called, 'Samuel! Samuel!' Samuel got up and went to Eli and said, 'Here I am, since you called me.' He replied, 'I did not call you, my son; go back and lie down.' Samuel had as yet no knowledge of the Lord and the word of the Lord had not yet been revealed to him. Once again the Lord called, the third time. He got up and went to Eli and said, 'Here I am, since you called me.' Eli then understood that it was the Lord who was calling the boy, and he said to Samuel, 'Go and lie down, and if someone calls say, "Speak, Lord, your servant is listening."' So Samuel went and lay down in his place.

The Lord then came and stood by, calling as he had done before, 'Samuel! Samuel!' Samuel answered, 'Speak, Lord, your servant is listening.'

Samuel grew up and the Lord was with him and let no word of his fall to the ground.

The word of the Lord.

Responsorial Psalm   Ps 39:2,4,7-10 R. vv.8,9

R. **Here I am, Lord!**
   I come to do your will.

   I waited, I waited for the Lord
   and he stooped down to me.
   He heard my cry
   He put a new song into my mouth,
   praise of our God. R.

   You do not ask for sacrifice and offerings,
   but an open ear.
   You do not ask for holocaust and victim.
   Instead, here am I. R.

   In the scroll of the book it stands written
   that I should do your will.
   My God, I delight in your law
   in the depth of my heart. R.

   Your justice I have proclaimed
   in the great assembly.
   My lips I have not sealed;
   you know it, O Lord. R.

SECOND READING

A reading from the first letter of St Paul to the Corinthians   6:13-15,17-20
Your bodies are members making up the body of Christ.

The body is not meant for fornication; it is for the Lord, and the Lord for the body. God who raised the Lord from the dead, will by his power raise us up too.

You know, surely, that your bodies are members making up the body of Christ; anyone who is joined to the Lord is one spirit with him.

Keep away from fornication. All the other sins are committed outside the body; but to fornicate is to sin against your own body. Your body, you know, is the temple of the Holy Spirit, who is in you since you received him from God. You are not your own property; you have been bought and paid for. That is why you should use your body for the glory of God.

The word of the Lord.

Gospel Acclamation   1 S 3:9; Jn 6:68
R. **Alleluia, alleluia!**
Speak, Lord, your servant is listening:
you have the message of eternal life.
R. **Alleluia!**

Or: Jn 1:14,17

R. **Alleluia, alleluia!**
We have found the Messiah - which means the Christ -
grace and truth have come through him.
R. **Alleluia!**

GOSPEL

A reading from holy Gospel according to John   Jn 1:35-42
They saw where he lived, and stayed with him.

As John stood with two of his disciples, Jesus passed, and John stared hard at him and said, 'Look, there is the lamb of God.' Hearing this, the two disciples followed Jesus. Jesus turned round, saw them following and said, 'What do you want?' They answered, 'Rabbi,' – which means Teacher – 'where do you live?' 'Come and see' he replied; so they went and saw where he lived and stayed with him the rest of that day. It was about the tenth hour.

One of these two who became followers of Jesus after hearing what John had said was Andrew, the brother of Simon Peter. Early next morning, Andrew met his brother and said to him 'We have found the Messiah' – which means the Christ – and he took Simon to Jesus. Jesus looked hard at him and said, 'You are Simon son of John; you are to be called Cephas' – meaning Rock.

The Gospel of the Lord.

Prayer over the Offerings	Super oblata
Grant us, O Lord, we pray,	Concede nobis,
that we may participate worthily	quæsumus, Domine,
in these mysteries,	hæc digne frequentare mysteria,
for whenever the memorial	quia, quoties huius hostiæ
of this sacrifice is celebrated	commemoratio celebratur,
the work of our redemption	opus nostræ
is accomplished.	redemptionis exercetur.
Through Christ our Lord.	Per Christum Dominum nostrum.

Preface of Sundays in Ordinary Time I-VIII, pp.566-573.

Communion Antiphon Cf. Ps 22:5	Ant. ad communionem
You have prepared a table before me, and how precious is the chalice that quenches my thirst.	Parasti in conspectu meo mensam, et calix meus inebrians quam præclarus est!
Or: 1 Jn 4:16	Vel:
We have come to know and to believe in the love that God has for us.	Nos cognovimus et credidimus caritati, quam Deus habet in nobis.

Prayer after Communion

Pour on us, O Lord,
   the Spirit of your love,
and in your kindness
make those you have nourished
by this one heavenly Bread
one in mind and heart.
Through Christ our Lord.

Post communionem

Spiritum nobis, Domine,
   tuæ caritatis infunde,
ut, quos uno cælesti pane satiasti,
una facias pietate concordes.
Per Christum Dominum nostrum.

THIRD SUNDAY IN ORDINARY TIME (YEAR B)

Entrance Antiphon   Cf. Ps 95:1,6

O SING a new song to the Lord;
  sing to the Lord, all the earth.
In his presence are majesty
   and splendour,
strength and honour
   in his holy place.

Ant. ad introitum

CANTATE Domino
  canticum novum,
cantate Domino, omnis terra.
Confessio et pulchritudo
   in conspectu eius,
sanctitas et magnificentia
   in sanctificatione eius.

Collect

Almighty ever-living God,
direct our actions according
   to your good pleasure,
that in the name of your beloved Son
we may abound in good works.
Through our Lord Jesus Christ,
   your Son,
who lives and reigns with you
   in the unity of the Holy Spirit,
one God, for ever and ever.

Collecta

Omnipotens sempiterne Deus,
dirige actus nostros
   in beneplacito tuo,
ut in nomine dilecti Filii tui
mereamur bonis operibus abundare.
Per Dominum nostrum Iesum
   Christum Filium tuum,
qui tecum vivit et regnat
   in unitate Spiritus Sancti,
Deus, per omnia sæcula sæculorum.

FIRST READING

A reading from the prophet Jonah   3:1-5,10

The people of Nineveh renounce their evil behaviour.

The word of the Lord was addressed to Jonah: 'Up!' he said 'Go to Nineveh, the great city, and preach to them as I told you to.' Jonah set out and went to Nineveh in obedience to the word of the Lord. Now Nineveh was a city great beyond compare: it took three days to cross it. Jonah went on into the city, making a day's journey. He preached in these words, 'Only forty days more and Nineveh is going to be destroyed.' And the people of Nineveh believed in God; they proclaimed a fast and put on sackcloth, from the greatest to the least.

God saw their efforts to renounce their evil behaviour. And God relented: he did not inflict on them the disaster which he had threatened.

The word of the Lord.

Responsorial Psalm   Ps 24:4-9. R. v.4

R. **Lord, make me know your ways.**

Lord, make me know your ways.
Lord, teach me your paths.
Make me walk in your truth, and teach me:
for you are God my saviour. R.

Remember your mercy, Lord,
and the love you have shown from of old.
In your love remember me,
because of your goodness, O Lord. R.

The Lord is good and upright.
He shows the path to those who stray,
he guides the humble in the right path;
he teaches his way to the poor. R.

SECOND READING

A reading from the first letter of St Paul to the Corinthians   7:29-31

The world as we know it is passing away.

Brothers: our time is growing short. Those who have wives should live as though they had none, and those who mourn should live as though they had nothing to mourn for; those who are enjoying life should live as though there were nothing to laugh about; those whose life is buying things should live as though they had nothing of their own; and those who have to deal with the world should not become engrossed in it. I say this because the world as we know it is passing away.

The word of the Lord.

Gospel Acclamation   Mk 1:15

R. **Alleluia, alleluia!**
The kingdom of God is close at hand;
believe the Good News.
R. **Alleluia!**

GOSPEL

A reading from the holy Gospel according to Mark   1:14-20
Repent, and believe the Good News.

After John had been arrested, Jesus went into Galilee. There he proclaimed the Good News from God. 'The time has come' he said 'and the kingdom of God is close at hand. Repent, and believe the Good News.'

As he was walking along by the Sea of Galilee he saw Simon and his brother Andrew casting a net in the lake – for they were fishermen. And Jesus said to them, 'Follow me and I will make you into fishers of men.' And at once they left their nets and followed him.

Going on a little further, he saw James son of Zebedee and his brother John; they too were in their boat, mending their nets. He called them at once and, leaving their father Zebedee in the boat with the men he employed, they went after him.

The Gospel of the Lord.

Prayer over the Offerings	Super oblata
Accept our offerings, O Lord, we pray, and in sanctifying them grant that they may profit us for salvation. Through Christ our Lord.	Munera nostra, Domine, suscipe placatus, quæ sanctificando nobis, quæsumus, salutaria fore concede. Per Christum Dominum nostrum.

Preface of Sundays in Ordinary Time I-VIII, pp.566-573.

Communion Antiphon Cf. Ps 33:6	Ant. ad communionem
Look toward the Lord and be radiant; let your faces not be abashed.	Accedite ad Dominum et illuminamini, et facies vestræ non confundentur.

Or: Jn 8:12

I am the light of the world,
   says the Lord;
whoever follows me will not walk
   in darkness,
but will have the light of life.

Vel:

Ego sum lux mundi, dicit Dominus:
qui sequitur me non ambulat
   in tenebris,
sed habebit lumen vitæ.

Prayer after Communion

Grant, we pray, almighty God,
that, receiving the grace
by which you bring us to new life,
we may always glory in your gift.
Through Christ our Lord.

Post communionem

Præsta nobis, quæsumus,
   omnipotens Deus,
ut, vivificationis tuæ
   gratiam consequentes,
in tuo semper munere gloriemur.
Per Christum Dominum nostrum.

FOURTH SUNDAY IN ORDINARY TIME (YEAR B)

Entrance Antiphon   Ps 105:47

S AVE us, O Lord our God!
  And gather us from the nations,
to give thanks to your holy name,
and make it our glory to praise you.

Ant. ad introitum

S ALVOS nos fac,
  Domine Deus noster,
et congrega nos de nationibus,
ut confiteamur nomini sancto tuo,
et gloriemur in laude tua.

Collect

Grant us, Lord our God,
that we may honour you
   with all our mind,
and love everyone in truth of heart.
Through our Lord Jesus Christ,
   your Son,
who lives and reigns with you
   in the unity of the Holy Spirit,
one God, for ever and ever.

Collecta

Concede nobis,
   Domine Deus noster,
ut te tota mente veneremur,
et omnes homines rationabili
   diligamus affectu.
Per Dominum nostrum Iesum
   Christum Filium tuum,
qui tecum vivit et regnat
   in unitate Spiritus Sancti,
Deus, per omnia sæcula sæculorum.

FIRST READING

A reading from the book of Deuteronomy   18:15-20

I will raise up a prophet and I will put my words into his mouth.

Moses said to the people: 'Your God will raise up for you a prophet like myself, from among yourselves, from your own brothers; to him you must listen. This is what you yourselves asked of the Lord your God at Horeb on the day of the Assembly. "Do not let me hear again" you said, "the voice of the Lord my God, nor look any longer on this great fire, or I shall die"; and the Lord said to me, "All they have spoken is well said. I will raise up a prophet like yourself for them from their own brothers; I will put my words into his mouth and he shall tell them all I command him. The man who does not listen to my words that he speaks in my name, shall be held answerable to me for it. But the prophet who presumes to say in my name a thing I have not commanded him to say, or who speaks in the name of other gods, that prophet shall die."'

The word of the Lord.

Responsorial Psalm   Ps 94:1-2,6-9. R. v.9

R. **O that today you would listen to his voice!**
   Harden not your hearts.

   Come, ring out our joy to the Lord,
   hail the rock who saves us.
   Let us come before him, giving thanks,
   with songs let us hail the Lord. R.

   Come in; let us kneel and bend low;
   let us kneel before the God who made us
   for he is our God and we
   the people who belong to his pasture,
   the flock that is led by his hand. R.

   O that today you would listen to his voice!
   'Harden not your hearts as at Meribah,
   as on that day at Massah in the desert
   when your fathers put me to the test;
   when they tried me, though they saw my work.' R.

SECOND READING

A reading from the first letter of St Paul to the Corinthians   7:32-35

An unmarried woman can devote herself to the Lord's affairs; all she need worry about is being holy.

I would like to see you free from all worry. An unmarried man can devote himself to the Lord's affairs, all he need worry about is pleasing the Lord; but a married man has to bother about the world's affairs and devote himself to pleasing his wife: he is torn two ways. In the same way an unmarried woman, like a young girl, can devote herself to the Lord's affairs; all she need worry about is being holy in body and spirit. The married woman, on the other hand, has to worry about the world's affairs and devote herself to pleasing her husband. I say this only to help you, not to put a halter round your necks, but simply to make sure that everything is as it should be, and that you give your undivided attention to the Lord.

The word of the Lord.

Gospel Acclamation   Mt 11:25

R. **Alleluia, alleluia!**
Blessed are you, Father,
Lord of heaven and earth,
for revealing the mysteries of the kingdom
to mere children.
R. **Alleluia!**
Or: Mt 4:16
R. **Alleluia, alleluia!**
The people that lived in darkness
has seen a great light;
on those who dwell in the land and shadow of death
a light has dawned.
R. **Alleluia!**

GOSPEL

A reading from the holy Gospel according to Mark   1:21-28
He taught them with authority.

Jesus and his followers went as far as Capernaum, and as soon as the Sabbath came Jesus went to the synagogue and began to teach. And his teaching made a deep impression on them because, unlike the scribes, he taught them with authority.

In their synagogue just then there was a man possessed by an unclean spirit, and it shouted, 'What do you want with us, Jesus of Nazareth? Have you come to destroy us? I know who you are: the Holy One of God.' But Jesus said sharply, 'Be quiet! Come out of him!' And the unclean spirit threw the man into convulsions and with a loud cry went out of him. The people were so astonished that they started asking each other what it all meant. 'Here is a teaching that is new' they said 'and with authority behind it: he gives orders even to unclean spirits and they obey him.' And his reputation rapidly spread everywhere, through all the surrounding Galilean countryside.

The Gospel of the Lord.

Prayer over the Offerings	Super oblata
O Lord, we bring to your altar these offerings of our service: be pleased to receive them, we pray, and transform them into the Sacrament of our redemption. Through Christ our Lord.	Altaribus tuis, Domine, munera nostræ servitutis inferimus, quæ, placatus assumens, sacramentum nostræ redemptionis efficias. Per Christum Dominum nostrum.

Preface of Sundays in Ordinary Time I-VIII, pp.566-573.

Communion Antiphon Cf. Ps 30:17-18	Ant. ad communionem
Let your face shine on your servant. Save me in your merciful love. O Lord, let me never be put to shame, for I call on you.	Illumina faciem tuam super servum tuum, et salvum me fac in tua misericordia. Domine, non confundar, quoniam invocavi te.

Or: Mt 5:3-4	Vel:
Blessed are the poor in spirit, for theirs is the Kingdom of Heaven. Blessed are the meek, for they shall possess the land.	Beati pauperes spiritu, quoniam ipsorum est regnum cælorum. Beati mites, quoniam ipsi possidebunt terram.

Prayer after Communion	Post communionem
Nourished by these redeeming gifts, we pray, O Lord, that through this help to eternal salvation true faith may ever increase. Through Christ our Lord.	Redemptionis nostræ munere vegetati, quæsumus, Domine, ut hoc perpetuæ salutis auxilio fides semper vera proficiat. Per Christum Dominum nostrum.

FIFTH SUNDAY IN ORDINARY TIME (YEAR B)

Entrance Antiphon   Ps 94:6-7

O COME, let us worship God
and bow low before the God
who made us,
for he is the Lord our God.

Ant. ad introitum

VENITE, adoremus Deum,
et procidamus ante Dominum,
qui fecit nos;
quia ipse est Dominus Deus noster.

Collect

Keep your family safe, O Lord,
    with unfailing care,
that, relying solely on the hope
    of heavenly grace,
they may be defended always
    by your protection.
Through our Lord Jesus Christ,
    your Son,
who lives and reigns with you
    in the unity of the Holy Spirit,
one God, for ever and ever.

Collecta

Familiam tuam,
    quæsumus, Domine,
continua pietate custodi,
ut, quæ in sola spe gratiæ
    cælestis innititur,
tua semper protectione muniatur.
Per Dominum nostrum Iesum
    Christum Filium tuum,
qui tecum vivit et regnat
    in unitate Spiritus Sancti,
Deus, per omnia sæcula sæculorum.

FIRST READING

A reading from the book of Job   7:1-4,6-7

Restlessly I fret till twilight falls.

Job began to speak:

Is not man's life on earth nothing more than pressed service,
his time no better than hired drudgery?
Like the slave, sighing for the shade,
or the workman with no thought but his wages,
months of delusion I have assigned to me,
nothing for my own but nights of grief.
Lying in bed I wonder, 'When will it be day?'
Risen I think, 'How slowly evening comes!'
Restlessly I fret till twilight falls.
Swifter than a weaver's shuttle my days have passed,
and vanished, leaving no hope behind.
Remember that my life is but a breath,
and that my eyes will never again see joy.

The word of the Lord.

Responsorial Psalm   Ps 146:1-6. R. v.3

R. **Praise the Lord who heals the broken-hearted.**
    Or: **Alleluia!**
    Praise the Lord for he is good;
    sing to our God for he is loving:
    to him our praise is due. R.

    The Lord builds up Jerusalem
    and brings back Israel's exiles,
    He heals the broken-hearted,
    he binds up all their wounds.
    He fixes the number of the stars;
    he calls each one by its name. R.

    Our Lord is great and almighty;
    his wisdom can never be measured.
    The Lord raises the lowly;
    he humbles the wicked to the dust. R.

SECOND READING

A reading from the first letter of St Paul to the Corinthians   9:16-19,22-23
I should be punished if I did not preach the Gospel.

I do not boast of preaching the gospel, since it is a duty which has been laid on me; I should be punished if I did not preach it! If I had chosen this work myself, I might have been paid for it, but as I have not, it is a responsibility which has been put into my hands. Do you know what my reward is? It is this: in my preaching, to be able to offer the Good News free, and not insist on the rights which the gospel gives me.

So though I am not a slave of any man I have made myself the slave of everyone so as to win as many as I could. For the weak I made myself weak. I made myself all things to all men in order to save some at any cost; and I still do this, for the sake of the gospel, to have a share in its blessing.

The word of the Lord.

Gospel Acclamation   Jn 8:12
R. **Alleluia, alleluia!**
I am the light of the world, says the Lord,
anyone who follows me
will have the light of life.
R. **Alleluia!**

Or: Mt 8:17

R. **Alleluia, alleluia!**
He took our sicknesses away,
and carried our diseases for us.
R. **Alleluia!**

GOSPEL

A reading from the holy Gospel according to Mark   1:29-39

He cured many who were suffering from diseases of one kind or another.

On leaving the synagogue, Jesus went with James and John straight to the house of Simon and Andrew. Now Simon's mother-in-law had gone to bed with fever, and they told him about her straightaway. He went to her, took her by the hand and helped her up. And the fever left her and she began to wait on them.

That evening, after sunset, they brought to him all who were sick and those who were possessed by devils. The whole town came crowding round the door, and he cured many who were suffering from diseases of one kind or another; he also cast out many devils, but he would not allow them to speak, because they knew who he was.

In the morning, long before dawn, he got up and left the house, and went off to a lonely place and prayed there. Simon and his companions set out in search of him; and when they found him they said, 'Everybody is looking for you.' He answered, 'Let us go elsewhere, to the neighbouring country towns, so that I can preach there too, because that is why I came.' And he went all through Galilee, preaching in their synagogues and casting out devils.

The Gospel of the Lord.

Prayer over the Offerings	Super oblata
O Lord our God,	Domine Deus noster,
who once established these created things	qui has potius creaturas
to sustain us in our frailty,	ad fragilitatis nostræ subsidium condidisti,
grant, we pray,	tribue, quæsumus,
that they may become for us now the Sacrament of eternal life.	ut etiam æternitatis nobis fiant sacramentum.
Through Christ our Lord.	Per Christum Dominum nostrum.

Preface of Sundays in Ordinary Time I-VIII, pp.566-573.

Communion Antiphon Cf. Ps 106:8-9	Ant. ad communionem

Let them thank the Lord
    for his mercy,
his wonders for the children of men
for he satisfies the thirsty soul,
and the hungry he fills
    with good things.
	Confiteantur Domino
	    misericordiæ eius,
	et mirabilia eius filiis hominum,
	quia satiavit animam inanem,
	et animam esurientem
	    satiavit bonis.

Or: Mt 5:5-6	Vel:

Blessed are those who mourn,
    for they shall be consoled.
Blessed are those who hunger
    and thirst for righteousness,
for they shall have their fill.
	Beati qui lugent,
	    quoniam ipsi consolabuntur.
	Beati qui esuriunt
	    et sitiunt iustitiam,
	quoniam ipsi saturabuntur.

Prayer after Communion	Post communionem

O God, who have willed
    that we be partakers
in the one Bread and the one Chalice,
grant us, we pray, so to live that,
    made one in Christ,
we may joyfully bear fruit
for the salvation of the world.
Through Christ our Lord.
	Deus, qui nos de uno pane
	    et de uno calice
	participes esse voluisti,
	da nobis, quæsumus, ita vivere, ut,
	    unum in Christo effecti,
	fructum afferamus pro mundi
	    salute gaudentes.
	Per Christum Dominum nostrum.

SIXTH SUNDAY IN ORDINARY TIME (YEAR B)

Entrance Antiphon Cf. Ps 30:3-4	Ant. ad introitum

BE my protector, O God,
    a mighty stronghold to save me.
For you are my rock, my stronghold!
Lead me, guide me,
    for the sake of your name.
	ESTO mihi
	    in Deum protectorem,
	et in locum refugii,
	    ut salvum me facias.
	Quoniam firmamentum meum
	    et refugium meum es tu,
	et propter nomen tuum dux
	    mihi eris, et enutries me.

Collect

O God, who teach us that you abide
in hearts that are just and true,
grant that we may be so fashioned
   by your grace
as to become a dwelling pleasing
   to you.
Through our Lord Jesus Christ,
   your Son,
who lives and reigns with you
   in the unity of the Holy Spirit,
one God, for ever and ever.

Collecta

Deus, qui te in rectis et sinceris
   manere pectoribus asseris,
da nobis tua gratia tales exsistere,
in quibus habitare digneris.
Per Dominum nostrum Iesum
   Christum Filium tuum,
qui tecum vivit et regnat
   in unitate Spiritus Sancti,
Deus, per omnia sæcula sæculorum.

FIRST READING

A reading from the book of Leviticus   13:1-2,44-46

The leper must live apart: he must live outside the camp.

The Lord said to Moses and Aaron, 'If a swelling or scab or shiny spot appears
on a man's skin, a case of leprosy of the skin is to be suspected. The man
must be taken to Aaron, the priest, or to one of the priests who are his sons.

   'The man is leprous: he is unclean. The priest must declare him unclean;
he is suffering from leprosy of the head. A man infected with leprosy must
wear his clothing torn and his hair disordered; he must shield his upper
lip and cry, "Unclean, unclean." As long as the disease lasts he must be
unclean; and therefore he must live apart; he must live outside the camp.'

   The word of the Lord.

Responsorial Psalm   Ps 31:1-2,5,11. R. v.7

R. **You are my refuge, O Lord;**
   you fill me with the joy of salvation.

   Happy the man whose offence is forgiven,
   whose sin is remitted.
   O happy the man to whom the Lord
   imputes no guilt,
   in whose spirit is no guile. R.

   But now I have acknowledged my sins;
   my guilt I did not hide.
   I said: 'I will confess
   my offence to the Lord.'

And you, Lord, have forgiven
the guilt of my sin. R.

Rejoice, rejoice in the Lord,
exult, you just!
O come, ring out your joy,
all you upright of heart. R.

R. **You are my refuge, O Lord;**
you fill me with the joy of salvation.

SECOND READING

A reading from the first letter of St Paul to the Corinthians   10:31-11:1
Take me for your model, as I take Christ.

Whatever you eat, whatever you drink, whatever you do at all, do it for the
glory of God. Never do anything offensive to anyone – to Jews or Greeks or
to the Church of God; just as I try to be helpful to everyone at all times, not
anxious for my own advantage but for the advantage of everybody else, so
that they may be saved.

  Take me for your model, as I take Christ.

  The word of the Lord.

Gospel Acclamation   Cf. Ep 1:17,18
R. **Alleluia, alleluia!**
May the Father of our Lord Jesus Christ
enlighten the eyes of our mind,
so that we can see what hope his call holds for us.
R. **Alleluia!**
Or: Lk 7:16
R. **Alleluia, alleluia!**
A great prophet has appeared among us;
God has visited his people.
R. **Alleluia!**

GOSPEL

A reading from the holy Gospel according to Mark   1:40-45
The leprosy left him at once and he was cured.

A leper came to Jesus and pleaded on his knees: 'If you want to' he said
'you can cure me.' Feeling sorry for him, Jesus stretched out his hand and
touched him. 'Of course I want to!' he said. 'Be cured!' And the leprosy

left him at once and he was cured. Jesus immediately sent him away and sternly ordered him, 'Mind you say nothing to anyone, but go and show yourself to the priest, and make the offering for your healing prescribed by Moses as evidence of your recovery.' The man went away, but then started talking about it freely and telling the story everywhere, so that Jesus could no longer go openly into any town, but had to stay outside in places where nobody lived. Even so, people from all around would come to him.

The Gospel of the Lord.

Prayer over the Offerings	Super oblata
May this oblation, O Lord, we pray, cleanse and renew us and may it become for those who do your will the source of eternal reward. Through Christ our Lord.	Hæc nos oblatio, quæsumus, Domine, mundet et renovet, atque tuam exsequentibus voluntatem fiat causa remunerationis æternæ. Per Christum Dominum nostrum.

Preface of Sundays in Ordinary Time I-VIII, pp.566-573.

Communion Antiphon Cf. Ps 77:29-30	Ant. ad communionem
They ate and had their fill, and what they craved the Lord gave them; they were not disappointed in what they craved.	Manducaverunt, et saturati sunt nimis, et desiderium eorum attulit eis Dominus; non sunt fraudati a desiderio suo.

Or: Jn 3:16	Vel:
God so loved the world that he gave his Only Begotten Son, so that all who believe in him may not perish, but may have eternal life.	Sic Deus dilexit mundum, ut Filium suum Unigenitum daret, ut omnis qui credit in eum non pereat, sed habeat vitam æternam.

Prayer after Communion	Post communionem
Having fed upon these heavenly delights, we pray, O Lord, that we may always long for that food by which we truly live. Through Christ our Lord.	Cælestibus, Domine, pasti deliciis, quæsumus, ut semper eadem, per quæ veraciter vivimus, appetamus. Per Christum Dominum nostrum.

SEVENTH SUNDAY IN ORDINARY TIME (YEAR B)

Entrance Antiphon   Ps 12:6

O LORD, I trust in your
merciful love.
My heart will rejoice
   in your salvation.
I will sing to the Lord
   who has been bountiful with me.

Ant. ad introitum

D OMINE, in tua
misericordia speravi.
Exsultavit cor meum in salutari tuo,
cantabo Domino,
   qui bona tribuit mihi.

Collect

Grant, we pray, almighty God,
that, always pondering
   spiritual things,
we may carry out in both
   word and deed
that which is pleasing to you.
Through our Lord Jesus Christ,
   your Son,
who lives and reigns with you
   in the unity of the Holy Spirit,
one God, for ever and ever.

Collecta

Præsta, quæsumus,
   omnipotens Deus,
ut, semper rationabilia meditantes,
quæ tibi sunt placita,
   et dictis exsequamur et factis.
Per Dominum nostrum Iesum
   Christum Filium tuum,
qui tecum vivit et regnat
   in unitate Spiritus Sancti,
Deus, per omnia sæcula sæculorum.

FIRST READING

A reading from the prophet Isaiah   43:18-19,21-22,24-25

I it is who must blot out everything.

Thus says the Lord:
   No need to recall the past,
   no need to think about what was done before.
   See, I am doing a new deed,
   even now it comes to light; can you not see it?
   Yes, I am making a road in the wilderness,
   paths in the wilds.
   The people I have formed for myself
   will sing my praises.
   Jacob, you have not invoked me,
   you have not troubled yourself, Israel, on my behalf.
   Instead you have burdened me with your sins,
   troubled me with your iniquities.
   I it is, I it is who must blot out everything
   and not remember your sins.
   The word of the Lord.

Responsorial Psalm   Ps 40:2-5,13-14. R. v.5

R. **Heal my soul for I have sinned against you.**

> Happy the man who considers the poor and the weak.
> The Lord will save him in the day of evil,
> will guard him, give him life, make him happy in the land
> and will not give him up to the will of his foes. R.

> The Lord will help him on his bed of pain,
> he will bring him back from sickness to health.
> As for me, I said: 'Lord, have mercy on me,
> heal my soul for I have sinned against you.' R.

> If you uphold me I shall be unharmed
> and set in your presence for evermore.
> Blessed be the Lord, the God of Israel
> from age to age. Amen. Amen. R.

SECOND READING

A reading from the second letter of St Paul to the Corinthians   1:18-22

Jesus was never Yes and No: with him it was always Yes.

I swear by God's truth, there is no Yes and No about what we say to you. The Son of God, the Christ Jesus that we proclaimed among you – I mean Silvanus and Timothy and I – was never Yes and No: with him it was always Yes, and however many the promises God made, the Yes to them all is in him. That is why it is 'through him' that we answer Amen to the praise of God. Remember it is God himself who assures us all, and you, of our standing in Christ, and has anointed us, marking us with his seal and giving us the pledge, the Spirit, that we carry in our hearts.

The word of the Lord.

Gospel Acclamation   Jn 1:14,12

R. **Alleluia, alleluia!**
The Word was made flesh and lived among us;
to all who did accept him
he gave power to become children of God.
R. **Alleluia!**

Or: Lk 4:18

R. **Alleluia, alleluia!**
The Lord has sent me to bring the good news to the poor,
to proclaim liberty to captives.
R. **Alleluia!**

GOSPEL

A reading from the holy Gospel according to Mark   2:1-12

The Son of Man has authority on earth to forgive sins.

When Jesus returned to Capernaum some time later, word went round that he was back; and so many people collected that there was no room left, even in front of the door. He was preaching the word to them when some people came bringing him a paralytic carried by four men, but as the crowds made it impossible to get the man to him, they stripped the roof over the place where Jesus was; and when they had made an opening, they lowered the stretcher on which the paralytic lay. Seeing their faith, Jesus said to the paralytic, 'My child, your sins are forgiven.' Now some scribes were sitting there, and they thought to themselves, 'How can this man talk like that? He is blaspheming. Who can forgive sins but God?' Jesus, inwardly aware that this was what they were thinking, said to them, 'Why do you have these thoughts in your hearts? Which of these is easier: to say to the paralytic, "Your sins are forgiven" or to say, "Get up, pick up your stretcher and walk?" But to prove to you that the Son of Man has authority on earth to forgive sins,' – he said to the paralytic – 'I order you: get up, pick up your stretcher, and go off home.' And the man got up, picked up his stretcher at once and walked out in front of everyone, so that they were all astounded and praised God saying, 'We have never seen anything like this.'

The Gospel of the Lord.

Prayer over the Offerings	Super oblata

As we celebrate your mysteries,
   O Lord,
with the observance that is your due,
we humbly ask you,
that what we offer to the honour
   of your majesty
may profit us for salvation.
Through Christ our Lord.
	Mysteria tua, Domine,
	   debitis servitiis exsequentes,
	supplices te rogamus,
	ut, quod ad honorem tuæ
	   maiestatis offerimus,
	nobis proficiat ad salutem.
	Per Christum Dominum nostrum.

Preface of Sundays in Ordinary Time I-VIII, pp.566-573.

Communion Antiphon Ps 9:2-3	Ant. ad communionem
I will recount all your wonders, I will rejoice in you and be glad, and sing psalms to your name, O Most High.	Narrabo omnia mirabilia tua. Lætabor et exsultabo in te, psallam nomini tuo, Altissime.

Or: Jn 11:27

Lord, I have come to believe
   that you are the Christ,
the Son of the living God,
   who is coming into this world.

Vel:

Domine, ego credidi quia
   tu es Christus Filius Dei vivi,
qui in hunc mundum venisti.

Prayer after Communion

Grant, we pray, almighty God,
that we may experience the effects
   of the salvation
which is pledged to us
   by these mysteries.
Through Christ our Lord.

Post communionem

Præsta, quæsumus,
   omnipotens Deus,
ut illius salutis capiamus effectum,
cuius per hæc mysteria
   pignus accepimus.
Per Christum Dominum nostrum.

EIGHTH SUNDAY IN ORDINARY TIME (YEAR B)

Entrance Antiphon Cf. Ps 17:19-20

THE Lord became my protector.
  He brought me out to a place
   of freedom;
he saved me because he delighted
   in me.

Ant. ad introitum

FACTUS est Dominus
  protector meus,
et eduxit me in latitudinem,
salvum me fecit, quoniam
   voluit me.

Collect

Grant us, O Lord, we pray,
that the course of our world
may be directed by your peaceful rule
and that your Church may rejoice,
untroubled in her devotion.
Through our Lord Jesus Christ,
   your Son,
who lives and reigns with you
   in the unity of the Holy Spirit,
one God, for ever and ever.

Collecta

Da nobis, quæsumus, Domine,
ut et mundi cursus pacifico nobis
   tuo ordine dirigatur,
et Ecclesia tua tranquilla
   devotione lætetur.
Per Dominum nostrum Iesum
   Christum Filium tuum,
qui tecum vivit et regnat
   in unitate Spiritus Sancti,
Deus, per omnia sæcula sæculorum.

FIRST READING

A reading from the prophet Hosea   2:16,17,21-22

I will betroth you to myself for ever.

Thus says the Lord:

> I am going to lure her
> and lead her out into the wilderness
> and speak to her heart.
> There she will respond to me as she did when she was young,
> as she did when she came out of the land of Egypt.
> I will betroth you to myself for ever,
> betroth you with integrity and justice,
> with tenderness and love;
> I will betroth you to myself with faithfulness,
> and you will come to know the Lord.

The word of the Lord.

Responsional Psalm   Ps 102:1-4,8,10,12-13. R. v.8

R. **The Lord is compassion and love.**

> My soul, give thanks to the Lord,
> all my being, bless his holy name.
> My soul, give thanks to the Lord
> and never forget all his blessings. R.

> It is he who forgives all your guilt,
> who heals every one of your ills,
> who redeems your life from the grave,
> who crowns you with love and compassion. R.

> The Lord is compassion and love,
> slow to anger and rich in mercy.
> He does not treat us according to our sins
> nor repay us according to our faults. R.

> So far as the east is from the west
> so far does he remove our sins.
> As a father has compassion on his sons,
> the Lord has pity on those who fear him. R.

SECOND READING

A reading from the second letter of St Paul to the Corinthians   3:1-6

You are a letter from Christ drawn up by us.

Unlike other people, we need no letters of recommendation either to you
or from you, because you are yourselves our letter, written in our hearts,

that anybody can see and read, and it is plain that you are a letter from Christ, drawn up by us, and written not with ink but with the Spirit of the living God, not on stone tablets but on the tablets of your living hearts.

Before God, we are confident of this through Christ: not that we are qualified in ourselves to claim anything as our own work: all our qualifications come from God. He is the one who has given us the qualifications to be the administrators of this new covenant, which is not a covenant of written letters but of the Spirit: the written letters bring death, but the Spirit gives life.

The word of the Lord.

Gospel Acclamation   Jn 10:27
R. **Alleluia, alleluia!**
The sheep that belong to me listen to my voice,
says the Lord,
I know them and they follow me.
R. **Alleluia!**
Or: Jm 1:18
R. **Alleluia, alleluia!**
By his own choice the Father made us his children
by the message of the truth,
so that we should be a sort of first-fruits
of all that he created.
R. **Alleluia!**

GOSPEL

A reading from the holy Gospel according to Mark   2:18-22
The bridegroom is with them.

One day when John's disciples and the Pharisees were fasting, some people came and said to Jesus, 'Why is it that John's disciples and the disciples of the Pharisees fast, but your disciples do not?' Jesus replied, 'Surely the bridegroom's attendants would never think of fasting while the bridegroom is still with them? As long as they have the bridegroom with them, they could not think of fasting. But the time will come for the bridegroom to be taken away from them, and then, on that day, they will fast. No one sews a piece of unshrunken cloth on an old cloak; if he does, the patch pulls away from it, the new from the old, and the tear gets worse. And nobody puts new wine into old wineskins; if he does, the wine will burst the skins, and the wine is lost and the skins too. No! New wine, fresh skins!'

The Gospel of the Lord.

Prayer over the Offerings

O God, who provide gifts
  to be offered to your name
and count our oblations as signs
of our desire to serve you
  with devotion,
we ask of your mercy
that what you grant as the source
  of merit
may also help us to attain
  merit's reward.
Through Christ our Lord.

Super oblata

Deus, qui offerenda tuo
  nomini tribuis,
et oblata devotioni nostræ
  servitutis ascribis,
quæsumus clementiam tuam,
ut, quod præstas unde sit meritum,
proficere nobis largiaris
  ad præmium.
Per Christum Dominum nostrum.

Preface of Sundays in Ordinary Time I-VIII, pp.566-573.

Communion Antiphon Cf. Ps 12:6

I will sing to the Lord who has been
  bountiful with me,
sing psalms to the name
  of the Lord Most High.

Or: Mt 28:20

Behold, I am with you always,
even to the end of the age,
  says the Lord.

Ant. ad communionem

Cantabo Domino,
  qui bona tribuit mihi,
et psallam nomini
  Domini Altissimi.

Vel:

Ecce ego vobiscum sum
  omnibus diebus,
usque ad consummationem sæculi,
  dicit Dominus.

Prayer after Communion

Nourished by your saving gifts,
we beseech your mercy, Lord,
that by this same Sacrament
with which you feed us
  in the present age,
you may make us partakers
  of life eternal.
Through Christ our Lord.

Post communionem

Satiati munere salutari,
tuam, Domine,
  misericordiam deprecamur,
ut, hoc eodem quo nos
  temporaliter vegetas sacramento,
perpetuæ vitæ participes
  benignus efficias.
Per Christum Dominum nostrum.

NINTH SUNDAY IN ORDINARY TIME (YEAR B)

Entrance Antiphon Cf. Ps 24:16,18 | Ant. ad introitum

TURN to me and have mercy
on me, O Lord,
for I am alone and poor.
See my lowliness and suffering
and take away all my sins, my God.

RESPICE in me,
et miserere mei, Domine,
quoniam unicus et pauper sum ego.
Vide humilitatem meam
    et laborem meum,
et dimitte omnia peccata mea,
    Deus meus.

Collect | Collecta

O God, whose providence never
    fails in its design,
keep from us, we humbly
    beseech you,
all that might harm us
and grant all that works for our good.
Through our Lord Jesus Christ,
    your Son,
who lives and reigns with you
    in the unity of the Holy Spirit,
one God, for ever and ever.

Deus, cuius providentia in sui
    dispositione non fallitur,
te supplices exoramus,
ut noxia cuncta submoveas,
et omnia nobis profutura concedas.
Per Dominum nostrum Iesum
    Christum Filium tuum,
qui tecum vivit et regnat
    in unitate Spiritus Sancti,
Deus, per omnia sæcula sæculorum.

FIRST READING

A reading from the book of Deuteronomy   5:12-15

Remember that you were a servant in the land of Egypt.

The Lord says this: 'Observe the sabbath day and keep it holy, as the Lord
your God has commanded you. For six days you shall labour and do all
your work, but the seventh day is a sabbath for the Lord your God. You
shall do no work that day, neither you nor your son nor your daughter
nor your servants, men or women, nor your ox nor your donkey nor any
of your animals, nor the stranger who lives with you. Thus your servant,
man or woman, shall rest as you do. Remember that you were a servant in
the land of Egypt, and that the Lord your God brought you out from there
with mighty hand and outstretched arm; because of this, the Lord your
God has commanded you to keep the sabbath day.'

    The word of the Lord.

Responsorial Psalm   Ps 80:3-8,10-11. R. v.2

R. **Ring out your joy to God our strength.**

Raise a song and sound the timbrel,
the sweet-sounding harp and the lute,
blow the trumpet at the new moon,
when the moon is full, on our feast. R.

For this is Israel's law,
a command of the God of Jacob.
He imposed it as a rule on Joseph,
when he went out against the land of Egypt. R.

A voice I did not know said to me:
'I freed your shoulder from the burden;
your hands were freed from the load.
You called in distress and l saved you. R.

'Let there be no foreign god among you,
no worship of an alien god.
I am the Lord your God,
who brought you from the land of Egypt.' R.

SECOND READING

A reading from the second letter of St Paul to the Corinthians   4:6-11

In our mortal flesh the life of Jesus is openly shown.

It is the same God that said, 'Let there be light shining out of darkness,' who has shone in our minds to radiate the light of the knowledge of God's glory, the glory on the face of Christ.

We are only the earthenware jars that hold this treasure, to make it clear that such an overwhelming power comes from God and not from us. We are in difficulties on all sides, but never cornered; we see no answer to our problems, but never despair; we have been persecuted, but never deserted; knocked down, but never killed; always, wherever we may be, we carry with us in our body the death of Jesus, so that the life of Jesus, too, may always be seen in our body. Indeed, while we are still alive, we are consigned to our death every day, for the sake of Jesus, so that in our mortal flesh the life of Jesus, too, may be openly shown.

The word of the Lord.

Gospel Acclamation   Cf. Jn 6:63,68

R. **Alleluia, alleluia!**
Your words are spirit, Lord,
and they are life:
you have the message of eternal life.
R. **Alleluia!**

Or: Jn 17:17

R. **Alleluia, alleluia!**
Your word is truth, O Lord,
consecrate us in the truth.
R. **Alleluia!**

GOSPEL

A reading from the holy Gospel according to Mark   2:23-3:6

The Son of Man is master even of the Sabbath.

[One sabbath day, Jesus happened to be taking a walk through the cornfields, and his disciples began to pick ears of corn as they went along. And the Pharisees said to him, 'Look, why are they doing something on the sabbath day that is forbidden?' And he replied, 'Have you never read what David did in his time of need when he and his followers were hungry – how he went into the house of God when Abiathar was high priest, and ate the loaves of offering which only the priests are allowed to eat, and how he also gave some to the men with him?'

And he said to them, 'The sabbath was made for man, not man for the sabbath; so the Son of Man is master even of the sabbath.']

He went again into a synagogue, and there was a man there who had a withered hand. And they were watching him to see if he would cure him on the sabbath day, hoping for something to use against him. He said to the man with the withered hand, 'Stand up out in the middle!' Then he said to them, 'Is it against the law on the sabbath day to do good, or to do evil; to save life, or to kill?' But they said nothing. Then, grieved to find them so obstinate, he looked angrily round at them, and said to the man, 'Stretch out your hand.' He stretched it out and his hand was better. The Pharisees went out and at once began to plot with the Herodians against him, discussing how to destroy him.

[The Gospel of the Lord.]

Shorter Form, verses 23-28, read between[ ]

Prayer over the Offerings

Trusting in your compassion,
O Lord,
we come eagerly with our offerings
to your sacred altar,
that, through the purifying action
of your grace,
we may be cleansed by the very
mysteries we serve.
Through Christ our Lord.

Super oblata

In tua pietate confidentes, Domine,
cum muneribus ad altaria
veneranda concurrimus,
ut, tua purificante nos gratia,
iisdem quibus famulamur
mysteriis emundemur.
Per Christum Dominum nostrum.

Preface of Sundays in Ordinary Time I-VIII, pp.566-573.

Communion Antiphon Cf. Ps 16:6

To you I call, for you will surely
heed me, O God;
turn your ear to me;
hear my words.

Ant. ad communionem

Ego clamavi, quoniam
exaudisti me, Deus:
inclina aurem tuam,
et exaudi verba mea.

Or: Mk 11:23,24

Amen, I say to you:
Whatever you ask for in prayer,
believe you will receive it,
and it will be yours, says the Lord.

Vel:

Amen dico vobis,
quidquid orantes petitis,
credite quia accipietis, et fiet vobis,
dicit Dominus.

Prayer after Communion

Govern by your Spirit, we pray,
O Lord,
those you feed with the Body
and Blood of your Son,
that, professing you not just
in word or in speech,
but also in works and in truth,
we may merit to enter
the Kingdom of Heaven.
Through Christ our Lord.

Post communionem

Rege nos Spiritu tuo,
quæsumus, Domine,
quos pascis Filii tui Corpore
et Sanguine,
ut te, non solum verbo
neque lingua,
sed opere et veritate confitentes,
intrare mereamur
in regnum cælorum.
Per Christum Dominum nostrum.

TENTH SUNDAY IN ORDINARY TIME (YEAR B)

Entrance Antiphon   Cf. Ps 26:1-2

THE Lord is my light and my
salvation; whom shall I fear?
The Lord is the stronghold
  of my life; whom should I dread?
When those who do evil draw near,
  they stumble and fall.

Ant. ad introitum

DOMINUS illuminatio mea,
et salus mea, quem timebo?
Dominus defensor vitæ meæ,
  a quo trepidabo?
Qui tribulant me inimici mei,
  ipsi infirmati sunt.

Collect

O God, from whom all good
  things come,
grant that we, who call on you
  in our need,
may at your prompting discern
  what is right,
and by your guidance do it.
Through our Lord Jesus Christ,
  your Son,
who lives and reigns with you
  in the unity of the Holy Spirit,
one God, for ever and ever.

Collecta

Deus, a quo bona
  cuncta procedunt,
tuis largire supplicibus,
ut cogitemus, te inspirante,
  quæ recta sunt,
et, te gubernante, eadem faciamus.
Per Dominum nostrum Iesum
  Christum Filium tuum,
qui tecum vivit et regnat
  in unitate Spiritus Sancti,
Deus, per omnia sæcula sæculorum.

FIRST READING

A reading from the book of Genesis   3:9-15

*I will make you enemies of each other: you and the woman, your offspring and
her offspring.*

The Lord God called to the man. 'Where are you?' he asked. 'I heard the
sound of you in the garden,' he replied 'I was afraid because I was naked,
so I hid.' 'Who told you that you were naked?' he asked. 'Have you been
eating of the tree I forbade you to eat?' The man replied, 'It was the woman
you put with me; she gave me the fruit, and I ate it.' Then the Lord God
asked the woman, 'What is this you have done?' The woman replied, 'The
serpent tempted me and I ate.'

   Then the Lord God said to the serpent, 'Because you have done this,
   'Be accursed beyond all cattle,
   all wild beasts.

You shall crawl on your belly and eat dust
every day of your life.
I will make you enemies of each other:
you and the woman,
your offspring and her offspring.
It will crush your head
and you will strike its heel.'

The word of the Lord.

Responsive Psalm   Ps 129. R. v.7

R. **With the Lord there is mercy
and fullness of redemption.**

Out of the depths I cry to you, O Lord,
Lord, hear my voice!
O let your ears be attentive
to the voice of my pleading. R.

If you, O Lord, should mark our guilt,
Lord, who would survive?
But with you is found forgiveness:
for this we revere you. R.

My soul is waiting for the Lord,
I count on his word.
My soul is longing for the Lord
more than watchman for daybreak. R.

Because with the Lord there is mercy
and fullness of redemption,
Israel indeed he will redeem
from all its iniquity. R.

SECOND READING

A reading from the second letter of St Paul to the Corinthians   4:13-5:1
We believe and therefore we also speak.

As we have the same spirit of faith that is mentioned in scripture – I
believed, and therefore I spoke – we too believe and therefore we too
speak, knowing that he who raised the Lord Jesus to life will raise us with
Jesus in our turn, and put us by his side and you with us. You see, all this
is for your benefit, so that the more grace is multiplied among people, the
more thanksgiving there will be, to the glory of God.

That is why there is no weakening on our part, and instead, though
this outer man of ours may be falling into decay, the inner man is renewed

day by day. Yes, the troubles which are soon over, though they weigh little, train us for the carrying of a weight of eternal glory which is out of all proportion to them. And so we have no eyes for things that are visible, but only for things that are invisible; for visible things last only for a time, and the invisible things are eternal.

For we know that when the tent that we live in on earth is folded up, there is a house built by God for us, an everlasting home not made by human hands, in the heavens.

The word of the Lord.

Gospel Acclamation   Jn 14:23

R. **Alleluia, alleluia!**
If anyone loves me he will keep my word,
and my Father will love him,
and we shall come to him.
R. **Alleluia!**

Or: Jn 12:31-32

R. **Alleluia, alleluia!**
Now the prince of this world is to be overthrown,
says the Lord.
And when I am lifted up from the earth,
I shall draw all men to myself.
R. **Alleluia!**

GOSPEL

A reading from the holy Gospel according to Mark   3:20-35
It is the end of Satan.

Jesus went home with his disciples, and such a crowd collected that they could not even have a meal. When his relatives heard of this, they set out to take charge of him, convinced he was out of his mind.

The scribes who had come down from Jerusalem were saying, 'Beelzebul is in him,' and, 'It is through the prince of devils that he casts devils out.' So he called them to him and spoke to them in parables, 'How can Satan cast out Satan? If a kingdom is divided against itself, that kingdom cannot last. And if a household is divided against itself, that household can never stand. Now if Satan has rebelled against himself and is divided, he cannot stand either – it is the end of him. But no one can make his way into a strong man's house and burgle his property unless he has tied up the strong man first. Only then can he burgle his house.

'I tell you solemnly, all men's sins will be forgiven, and all their blasphemies; but let anyone blaspheme against the Holy Spirit and he will never have forgiveness: he is guilty of an eternal sin.' This was because they were saying, 'An unclean spirit is in him.'

His mother and brothers now arrived and, standing outside, sent in a message asking for him. A crowd was sitting round him at the time the message was passed to him, 'Your mother and brothers and sisters are outside asking for you.' He replied, 'Who are my mother and my brothers? And looking round at those sitting in a circle about him, he said, 'Here are my mother and my brothers. Anyone who does the will of God, that person is my brother and sister and mother.'

The Gospel of the Lord.

Prayer over the Offerings

Look kindly upon our service,
   O Lord, we pray,
that what we offer
may be an acceptable oblation to you
and lead us to grow in charity.
Through Christ our Lord.

Super oblata

Respice, Domine, quæsumus,
   nostram propitius servitutem,
ut quod offerimus sit tibi
   munus acceptum,
et nostræ caritatis augmentum.
Per Christum Dominum nostrum.

Preface of Sundays in Ordinary Time I-VIII, pp.566-573.

Communion Antiphon   Ps 17:3

The Lord is my rock, my fortress,
   and my deliverer;
my God is my saving strength.

Or: 1 Jn 4:16

God is love, and whoever abides
   in love
abides in God, and God in him.

Ant. ad communionem

Dominus firmamentum meum,
et refugium meum, et liberator meus.
Deus meus adiutor meus.

Vel:

Deus caritas est,
   et qui manet in caritate
in Deo manet et Deus in eo.

Prayer after Communion

May your healing work, O Lord,
free us, we pray, from doing evil
and lead us to what is right.
Through Christ our Lord.

Post communionem

Tua nos, Domine,
   medicinalis operatio,
et a nostris perversitatibus
   clementer expediat,
et ad ea quæ sunt recta perducat.
Per Christum Dominum nostrum.

ELEVENTH SUNDAY IN ORDINARY TIME
(YEAR B)

Entrance Antiphon   Cf. Ps 26:7,9

O LORD, hear my voice,
for I have called to you;
be my help.
Do not abandon or forsake me,
O God, my Saviour!

Ant. ad introitum

EXAUDI, Domine, vocem meam,
qua clamavi ad te.
Adiutor meus esto,
ne derelinquas me,
neque despicias me,
Deus salutaris meus.

Collect

O God, strength of those
who hope in you,
graciously hear our pleas,
and, since without you mortal
frailty can do nothing,
grant us always the help
of your grace,
that in following your commands
we may please you by our resolve
and our deeds.
Through our Lord Jesus Christ,
your Son,
who lives and reigns with you
in the unity of the Holy Spirit,
one God, for ever and ever.

Collecta

Deus, in te sperantium fortitudo,
invocationibus nostris
adesto propitius,
et, quia sine te nihil potest
mortalis infirmitas,
gratiæ tuæ præsta semper auxilium,
ut, in exsequendis mandatis tuis,
et voluntate tibi
et actione placeamus.
Per Dominum nostrum Iesum
Christum Filium tuum,
qui tecum vivit et regnat
in unitate Spiritus Sancti,
Deus, per omnia sæcula sæculorum.

FIRST READING

A reading from the prophet Ezekiel   17:22-24

I make low trees grow.

The Lord says this:

'From the top of the cedar,
from the highest branch I will take a shoot
and plant it myself on a very high mountain.
I will plant it on the high mountain of Israel.
It will sprout branches and bear fruit,
and become a noble cedar.
Every kind of bird will live beneath it,

every winged creature rest in the shade of its branches.
And every tree of the field will learn that I, the Lord, am the one
who stunts tall trees and makes the low ones grow,
who withers green trees and makes the withered green.
I, the Lord, have spoken, and I will do it.'

The word of the Lord.

Responsorial Psalm   Ps 91:2-3,13-16. R. Cf.v.2

R. **It is good to give you thanks, O Lord.**

It is good to give thanks to the Lord
to make music to your name, O Most High,
to proclaim your love in the morning
and your truth in the watches of the night. R.

The just will flourish like the palm-tree
and grow like a Lebanon cedar. R.

Planted in the house of the Lord
they will flourish in the courts of our God,
still bearing fruit when they are old,
still full of sap, still green,
to proclaim that the Lord is just.
In him, my rock, there is no wrong. R.

SECOND READING

A reading from the second letter of St Paul to the Corinthians   5:6-10

Whether we are living in the body or exiled from it, we are intent on pleasing the Lord.

We are always full of confidence when we remember that to live in the body means to be exiled from the Lord, going as we do by faith and not by sight – we are full of confidence, I say, and actually want to be exiled from the body and make our home with the Lord. Whether we are living in the body or exiled from it, we are intent on pleasing him. For all the truth about us will be brought out in the law court of Christ, and each of us will get what he deserves for the things he did in the body, good or bad.

The word of the Lord.

Gospel Acclamation   Jn 15:15

R. **Alleluia, alleluia!**
I call you friends, says the Lord,
because I have made known to you
everything I have learnt from my Father.
R. **Alleluia!**

Or:

R. **Alleluia, alleluia!**
The seed is the word of God, Christ the sower;
whoever finds the seed will remain for ever.
R. **Alleluia!**

GOSPEL

A reading from the holy Gospel according to Mark   4:26-34
It is the smallest of all the seeds; yet it grows into the biggest shrub of them all.

Jesus said to the crowds: 'This is what the kingdom of God is like. A man throws seed on the land. Night and day, while he sleeps, when he is awake, the seed is sprouting and growing; how, he does not know. Of its own accord the land produces first the shoot, then the ear, then the full grain in the ear. And when the crop is ready, he loses no time: he starts to reap because the harvest has come.'

He also said, 'What can we say the kingdom of God is like? What parable can we find for it? It is like a mustard seed which at the time of its sowing in the soil is the smallest of all the seeds on earth; yet once it is sown it grows into the biggest shrub of them all and puts out big branches so that the birds of the air can shelter in its shade.'

Using many parables like these, he spoke the word to them, so far as they were capable of understanding it. He would not speak to them except in parables, but he explained everything to his disciples when they were alone.

The Gospel of the Lord.

Prayer over the Offerings	Super oblata
O God, who in the offerings presented here provide for the twofold needs of human nature, nourishing us with food and renewing us with your Sacrament, grant, we pray, that the sustenance they provide may not fail us in body or in spirit. Through Christ our Lord.	Deus, qui humani generis utramque substantiam præsentium munerum et alimento vegetas et renovas sacramento, tribue, quæsumus, ut eorum et corporibus nostris subsidium non desit et mentibus. Per Christum Dominum nostrum.

Preface of Sundays in Ordinary Time I-VIII, pp.566-573.

Communion Antiphon Ps 26:4	Ant. ad communionem

There is one thing I ask of the Lord,
  only this do I seek:
to live in the house of the Lord
  all the days of my life.

Unum petii a Domino,
  hoc requiram,
ut inhabitem in domo Domini
omnibus diebus vitæ meæ.

Or: Jn 17:11

Vel:

Holy Father, keep in your name
  those you have given me,
that they may be one as we are one,
  says the Lord.

Pater sancte,
  serva eos in nomine tuo,
quos dedisti mihi, ut sint unum
  sicut et nos, dicit Dominus.

Prayer after Communion

Post communionem

As this reception of your
  Holy Communion, O Lord,
foreshadows the union
  of the faithful in you,
so may it bring about unity
  in your Church.
Through Christ our Lord.

Hæc tua, Domine,
  sumpta sacra communio,
sicut fidelium in te
  unionem præsignat,
sic in Ecclesia tua unitatis
  operetur effectum.
Per Christum Dominum nostrum.

TWELFTH SUNDAY IN ORDINARY TIME
(YEAR B)

Entrance Antiphon Cf. Ps 27:8-9	Ant. ad introitum

THE Lord is the strength
  of his people,
a saving refuge for the one
  he has anointed.
Save your people, Lord,
  and bless your heritage,
and govern them for ever.

DOMINUS fortitudo plebis suæ,
  et protector salutarium Christi
sui est.
Salvum fac populum
  tuum, Domine,
et benedic hereditati tuæ,
et rege eos usque in sæculum.

Collect	Collecta
Grant, O Lord,	Sancti nominis tui, Domine,
that we may always revere and love your holy name,	timorem pariter et amorem fac nos habere perpetuum,
for you never deprive of your guidance those you set firm on the foundation of your love.	quia numquam tua gubernatione destituis, quos in soliditate tuæ dilectionis instituis.
Through our Lord Jesus Christ, your Son,	Per Dominum nostrum Iesum Christum Filium tuum,
who lives and reigns with you in the unity of the Holy Spirit,	qui tecum vivit et regnat in unitate Spiritus Sancti,
one God, for ever and ever.	Deus, per omnia sæcula sæculorum.

FIRST READING

A reading from the book of Job   38:1,8-11

Here your proud waves shall break.

From the heart of tempest the Lord gave Job his answer. He said:

> Who pent up the sea behind closed doors
> when it leapt tumultuous out of the womb,
> when I wrapped it in a robe of mist
> and made black clouds its swaddling bands;
> when I marked the bounds it was not to cross
> and made it fast with a bolted gate?
> Come thus far, I said, and no farther:
> here your proud waves shall break.

The word of the Lord.

Responsorial Psalm   Ps 106:23-26,28-31. R. v.1

R. **O give thanks to the Lord,
   for his love endures for ever.**
   Or: **Alleluia!**

> Some sailed to the sea in ships
> to trade on the mighty waters.
> These men have seen the Lord's deeds,
> the wonders he does in the deep. R.

> For he spoke; he summoned the gale,
> tossing the waves of the sea

up to heaven and back into the deep;
their soul melted away in their distress. R.

Then they cried to the Lord in their need
and he rescued them from their distress.
He stilled the storm to a whisper:
all the waves of the sea were hushed. R.

They rejoiced because of the calm
and he led them to the haven they desired.
Let them thank the Lord for his love,
the wonders he does for men. R.

R. **O give thanks to the Lord,**
   for his love endures for ever.
   Or: **Alleluia!**

SECOND READING

A reading from the second letter of St Paul to the Corinthians   5:14-17
Now the new creation is here.

The love of Christ overwhelms us when we reflect that if one man has died
for all, then all men should be dead; and the reason he died for all was so
that living men should live no longer for themselves, but for him who
died and was raised to life for them.

From now onwards, therefore, we do not judge anyone by the standards
of the flesh. Even if we did once know Christ in the flesh, that is not how
we know him now. And for anyone who is in Christ, there is a new creation;
the old creation has gone, and now the new one is here.

The word of the Lord.

Gospel Acclamation   Cf. Ep 1:17,18

R. **Alleluia, alleluia!**
May the Father of our Lord Jesus Christ
enlighten the eyes of our mind
so that we can see what hope his call holds for us.
R. **Alleluia!**

Or: Lk 7:16

R. **Alleluia, alleluia!**
A great prophet has appeared among us;
God has visited his people.
R. **Alleluia!**

GOSPEL

A reading from the holy Gospel according to Mark   4:35-41

Who can this be? Even the wind and the sea obey him.

With the coming of evening, Jesus said to his disciples, 'Let us cross over to the other side.' And leaving the crowd behind they took him, just as he was, in the boat; and there were other boats with him. Then it began to blow a gale and the waves were breaking into the boat so that it was almost swamped. But he was in the stern, his head on the cushion, asleep. They woke him and said to him, 'Master, do you not care? We are going down!' And he woke up and rebuked the wind and said to the sea, 'Quiet now! Be calm!' And the wind dropped, and all was calm again. Then he said to them, 'Why are you so frightened? How is it that you have no faith?' They were filled with awe and said to one another, 'Who can this be? Even the wind and the sea obey him.'

The Gospel of the Lord.

Prayer over the Offerings	Super oblata
Receive, O Lord, the sacrifice of conciliation and praise and grant that, cleansed by its action, we may make offering of a heart pleasing to you. Through Christ our Lord.	Suscipe, Domine, sacrificium placationis et laudis, et præsta, ut, huius operatione mundati, beneplacitum tibi nostræ mentis offeramus affectum. Per Christum Dominum nostrum.

Preface of Sundays in Ordinary Time I-VIII, pp.566-573.

Communion Antiphon Ps 144:15	Ant. ad communionem
The eyes of all look to you, Lord, and you give them their food in due season.	Oculi omnium in te sperant, Domine, et tu das illis escam in tempore opportuno.

Or: Jn 10:11,15	Vel:
I am the Good Shepherd, and I lay down my life for my sheep, says the Lord.	Ego sum pastor bonus, et animam meam pono pro ovibus meis, dicit Dominus.

Prayer after Communion

Renewed and nourished
by the Sacred Body and Precious
   Blood of your Son,
we ask of your mercy, O Lord,
that what we celebrate
   with constant devotion
may be our sure pledge
   of redemption.
Through Christ our Lord.

Post communionem

Sacri Corporis et Sanguinis pretiosi
   alimonia renovati,
quæsumus, Domine,
   clementiam tuam,
ut, quod gerimus
   devotione frequenti,
certa redemptione capiamus.
Per Christum Dominum nostrum.

THIRTEENTH SUNDAY IN ORDINARY TIME
(YEAR B)

Entrance Antiphon   Ps 46:2
ALL peoples, clap your hands.
Cry to God with shouts of joy!

Ant. ad introitum
OMNES gentes,
plaudite manibus,
iubilate Deo in voce exsultationis.

Collect

O God, who through the grace
   of adoption
chose us to be children of light,
grant, we pray,
that we may not be wrapped
   in the darkness of error
but always be seen to stand
   in the bright light of truth.
Through our Lord Jesus Christ,
   your Son,
who lives and reigns with you
   in the unity of the Holy Spirit,
one God, for ever and ever.

Collecta

Deus, qui, per adoptionem gratiæ,
lucis nos esse filios voluisti,
præsta, quæsumus, ut errorum
   non involvamur tenebris,
sed in splendore veritatis semper
   maneamus conspicui.
Per Dominum nostrum Iesum
   Christum Filium tuum,
qui tecum vivit et regnat
   in unitate Spiritus Sancti,
Deus, per omnia sæcula sæculorum.

FIRST READING

A reading from the book of Wisdom   1:13-15; 2:23-24
It was the devil's envy that brought death into the world.

Death was not God's doing,
he takes no pleasure in the extinction of the living.
To be – for this he created all;
the world's created things have health in them,

in them no fatal poison can be found,
and Hades holds no power on earth;
for virtue is undying.
Yet God did make man imperishable,
he made him in the image of his own nature;
it was the devil's envy that brought death into the world,
as those who are his partners will discover.

   The word of the Lord.

Responsorial Psalm   Ps 29:2,4-6,11-13. R. v.2

R. **I will praise you, Lord, you have rescued me.**

   I will praise you, Lord, you have rescued me
   and have not let my enemies rejoice over me.
   O Lord, you have raised my soul from the dead,
   restored me to life from those who sink into the grave. R.

   Sing psalms to the Lord, you who love him,
   give thanks to his holy name.
   His anger lasts but a moment; his favour through life.
   At night there are tears, but joy comes with dawn. R.

   The Lord listened and had pity.
   The Lord came to my help.
   For me you have changed my mourning into dancing,
   O Lord my God, I will thank you for ever. R.

SECOND READING

A reading from the second letter of St Paul to the Corinthians   8:7,9,13-15

In giving relief to others, balance what happens to be your surplus now against their present need.

You always have the most of everything – of faith, of eloquence, of understanding, of keenness for any cause, and the biggest share of our affection – so we expect you to put the most into this work of mercy too. Remember how generous the Lord Jesus was: he was rich, but he became poor for your sake, to make you rich out of his poverty. This does not mean that to give relief to others you ought to make things difficult for yourselves: it is a question of balancing what happens to be your surplus now against their present need, and one day they may have something to spare that will supply your own need. That is how we strike a balance: as scripture says: The man who gathered much had none too much, the man who gathered little did not go short.

   The word of the Lord.

Gospel Acclamation   Cf. Jn 6:63,68
R. **Alleluia, alleluia!**
Your words are spirit, Lord,
and they are life:
you have the message of eternal life.
R. **Alleluia!**

Or: Cf. 2 Tm 1:10

R. **Alleluia, alleluia!**
Our Saviour Christ Jesus abolished death,
and he has proclaimed life through the Good News.
R. **Alleluia!**

GOSPEL

A reading from the holy Gospel according to Mark   5:21-43
Little girl, I tell you to get up.

[When Jesus had crossed in the boat to the other side, a large crowd gathered round him and he stayed by the lakeside. Then one of the synagogue officials came up, Jairus by name, and seeing him, fell at his feet and pleaded with him earnestly, saying, 'My little daughter is desperately sick. Do come and lay your hands on her to make her better and save her life.' Jesus went with him and a large crowd followed him; they were pressing all round him.]

Now there was a woman who had suffered from a haemorrhage for twelve years; after long and painful treatment under various doctors, she had spent all she had without being any the better for it, in fact, she was getting worse. She had heard about Jesus, and she came up behind him through the crowd and touched his cloak. 'If I can touch even his clothes,' she had told herself 'I shall be well again.' And the source of the bleeding dried up instantly, and she felt in herself that she was cured of her complaint. Immediately aware that power had gone out from him Jesus turned round in the crowd and said, 'Who touched my clothes?' His disciples said to him, 'You see how the crowd is pressing round you and yet you say, "Who touched me?"' But he continued to look all round to see who had done it. Then the woman came forward, frightened and trembling because she knew what had happened to her, and she fell at his feet and told him the whole truth. 'My daughter,' he said 'your faith has restored you to health; go in peace and be free from your complaint.'

[While he was still speaking some people arrived from the house of the synagogue official to say, 'Your daughter is dead: why put the Master to any further trouble?' But Jesus had overheard this remark of theirs and he said to the official, 'Do not be afraid; only have faith.' And he allowed no one to go with him except Peter and James and John the brother of James. So they came to the official's house and Jesus noticed all the commotion, with people weeping and wailing unrestrainedly. He went in and said to them, 'Why all this commotion and crying? The child is not dead, but asleep.' But they laughed at him. So he turned them all out and, taking with him the child's father and mother and his own companions, he went into the place where the child lay. And taking the child by the hand he said to her, 'Talitha, kum!' which means, 'Little girl, I tell you to get up.' The little girl got up at once and began to walk about, for she was twelve years old. At this they were overcome with astonishment, and he ordered them strictly not to let anyone know about it, and told them to give her something to eat.

The Gospel of the Lord.]

Shorter Form, verses 21-24, 35-43. Read between [ ]

Prayer over the Offerings	Super oblata
O God, who graciously accomplish the effects of your mysteries, grant, we pray, that the deeds by which we serve you may be worthy of these sacred gifts. Through Christ our Lord.	Deus, qui mysteriorum tuorum dignanter operaris effectus, præsta, quæsumus, ut sacris apta muneribus fiant nostra servitia. Per Christum Dominum nostrum.

Preface of Sundays in Ordinary Time I-VIII, pp.566-573.

Communion Antiphon Cf. Ps 102:1	Ant. ad communionem
Bless the Lord, O my soul, and all within me, his holy name.	Benedic, anima mea, Domino, et ea quæ intra me sunt nomini sancto eius.

Or: Jn 17:20-21	Vel:
O Father, I pray for them, that they may be one in us, that the world may believe that you have sent me, says the Lord.	Pater, pro eis rogo, ut ipsi in nobis unum sint, ut credat mundus quia tu me misisti, dicit Dominus.

Prayer after Communion

May this divine sacrifice
    we have offered and received
fill us with life, O Lord, we pray,
so that, bound to you
    in lasting charity,
we may bear fruit that lasts for ever.
Through Christ our Lord.

Post communionem

Vivificet nos, quæsumus, Domine,
divina quam obtulimus
    et sumpsimus hostia,
ut, perpetua tibi caritate coniuncti,
fructum qui semper
    maneat afferamus.
Per Christum Dominum nostrum.

FOURTEENTH SUNDAY IN ORDINARY TIME
(YEAR B)

Entrance Antiphon Cf. Ps 47:10-11

YOUR merciful love, O God,
    we have received in the midst
    of your temple.
Your praise, O God, like your name,
reaches the ends of the earth;
your right hand is filled
    with saving justice.

Ant. ad introitum

SUSCEPIMUS, Deus,
    misericordiam tuam
in medio templi tui.
Secundum nomen tuum, Deus,
ita et laus tua in fines terræ;
iustitia plena est dextera tua.

Collect

O God, who in the abasement
    of your Son
have raised up a fallen world,
fill your faithful with holy joy,
for on those you have rescued
    from slavery to sin
you bestow eternal gladness.
Through our Lord Jesus Christ,
    your Son,
who lives and reigns with you
    in the unity of the Holy Spirit,
one God, for ever and ever.

Collecta

Deus, qui in Filii tui humilitate
iacentem mundum erexisti,
fidelibus tuis sanctam
    concede lætitiam,
ut, quos eripuisti
    a servitute peccati,
gaudiis facias perfrui sempiternis.
Per Dominum nostrum Iesum
    Christum Filium tuum,
qui tecum vivit et regnat
    in unitate Spiritus Sancti,
Deus, per omnia sæcula sæculorum.

FIRST READING

A reading from the prophet Ezekiel   2:2-5

The sons are defiant and obstinate and they shall know that there is a prophet among them.

The spirit came into me and made me stand up, and I heard the Lord speaking to me. He said, 'Son of man, I am sending you to the Israelites, to the rebels who have turned against me. Till now they and their ancestors have been in revolt against me. The sons are defiant and obstinate; I am sending you to them, to say, "The Lord says this." Whether they listen or not, this set of rebels shall know there is a prophet among them.'

The word of the Lord.

Responsible Psalm   Ps 122: R. v.2

R. **Our eyes are on the Lord**
till he shows us his mercy.

To you have I lifted up my eyes,
you who dwell in the heavens:
my eyes, like the eyes of slaves
on the hand of their lords. R.

Like the eyes of a servant
on the hand of her mistress,
so our eyes are on the Lord our God
till he show us his mercy. R.

Have mercy on us, Lord, have mercy.
We are filled with contempt.
Indeed all too full is our soul
with the scorn of the rich,
with the proud man's disdain. R.

SECOND READING

A reading from the second letter of St Paul to the Corinthians   12:7-10

I shall be very happy to make my weaknesses my special boast so that the power of Christ may stay over me.

In view of the extraordinary nature of these revelations, to stop me from getting too proud I was given a thorn in the flesh, an angel of Satan to beat me and stop me from getting too proud! About this thing, I have pleaded with the Lord three times for it to leave me, but he has said, 'My grace is enough for you: my power is at its best in weakness.' So I shall be very happy to make my weaknesses my special boast so that the power of Christ may stay over me, and that is why I am quite content with my weaknesses, and with insults, hardships, persecutions, and the agonies I go through for Christ's sake. For it is when I am weak that I am strong.

The word of the Lord.

Gospel Acclamation   Jn 1:14,12

R. **Alleluia, alleluia!**
The Word was made flesh and lived among us;
to all who did accept him
he gave power to become children of God.
R. **Alleluia!**

Or: Cf. Lk 4:18

R. **Alleluia, alleluia!**
The Lord has sent me to bring the good news to
     the poor,
to proclaim liberty to captives.
R. **Alleluia!**

GOSPEL

A reading from the holy Gospel according to Mark   6:1-6
A prophet is despised only in his own country.

Jesus went to his home town and his disciples accompanied him. With the coming of the sabbath he began teaching in the synagogue and most of them were astonished when they heard him. They said, 'Where did the man get all this? What is this wisdom that has been granted him, and these miracles that are worked through him? This is the carpenter, surely, the son of Mary, the brother of James and Joset and Jude and Simon? His sisters, too are they not here with us?' And they would not accept him. And Jesus said to them, 'A prophet is only despised in his own country among his own relations and in his own house'; and he could work no miracle there, though he cured a few sick people by laying his hands on them. He was amazed at their lack of faith.

     The Gospel of the Lord.

Prayer over the Offerings	Super oblata
May this oblation dedicated to your name purify us, O Lord, and day by day bring our conduct closer to the life of heaven. Through Christ our Lord.	Oblatio nos, Domine, tuo nomini dicata purificet, et de die in diem ad cælestis vitæ transferat actionem. Per Christum Dominum nostrum.

Preface of Sundays in Ordinary Time I-VIII, pp.566-573.

Communion Antiphon Ps 33:9	Ant. ad communionem
Taste and see that the Lord is good; blessed the man who seeks refuge in him.	Gustate et videte, quoniam suavis est Dominus; beatus vir, qui sperat in eo.

Or: Mt 11:28

Come to me, all who labour
    and are burdened,
and I will refresh you, says the Lord.

Vel:

Venite ad me, omnes qui laboratis
    et onerati estis,
et ego reficiam vos, dicit Dominus.

Prayer after Communion

Grant, we pray, O Lord,
that, having been replenished
    by such great gifts,
we may gain the prize of salvation
and never cease to praise you.
Through Christ our Lord.

Post communionem

Tantis, Domine, repleti muneribus,
præsta, quæsumus, ut et salutaria
    dona capiamus,
et a tua numquam laude cessemus.
Per Christum Dominum nostrum.

FIFTEENTH SUNDAY IN ORDINARY TIME
(YEAR B)

Entrance Antiphon   Cf. Ps 16:15

AS for me, in justice I shall
    behold your face;
I shall be filled with the vision
    of your glory.

Ant. ad introitum

EGO autem cum iustitia
    apparebo in conspectu tuo;
satiabor dum manifestabitur
    gloria tua.

Collect

O God, who show the light
    of your truth
to those who go astray,
so that they may return
    to the right path,
give all who for the faith they profess
are accounted Christians
the grace to reject whatever
    is contrary to the name of Christ
and to strive after all that does
    it honour.
Through our Lord Jesus Christ,
    your Son,
who lives and reigns with you
    in the unity of the Holy Spirit,
one God, for ever and ever.

Collecta

Deus, qui errantibus,
    ut in viam possint redire,
veritatis tuæ lumen ostendis,
da cunctis qui christiana
    professione censentur,
et illa respuere, quæ huic inimica
    sunt nomini,
et ea quæ sunt apta sectari.
Per Dominum nostrum Iesum
    Christum Filium tuum,
qui tecum vivit et regnat
    in unitate Spiritus Sancti,
Deus, per omnia sæcula sæculorum.

FIRST READING

A reading from the prophet Amos   7:12-15

Go, prophesy to my people.

Amaziah, the priest of Bethel, said to Amos, 'Go away, seer; get back to the land of Judah; earn your bread there, do your prophesying there. We want no more prophesying in Bethel; this is the royal sanctuary, the national temple.' 'I was no prophet, neither did I belong to any of the brotherhoods of prophets,' Amos replied to Amaziah. 'I was a shepherd, and looked after sycamores: but it was the Lord who took me from herding the flock, and the Lord who said, "Go, prophesy to my people Israel."'

The word of the Lord.

Responsorial Psalm   Ps 84:9-14. R. v.8

R. **Let us see, O Lord, your mercy
and give us your saving help.**

I will hear what the Lord God has to say,
a voice that speaks of peace,
peace for his people.
His help is near for those who fear him
and his glory will dwell in our land. R.

Mercy and faithfulness have met;
justice and peace have embraced.
Faithfulness shall spring from the earth
and justice look down from heaven. R.

The Lord will make us prosper
and our earth shall yield its fruit.
Justice shall march before him
and peace shall follow his steps. R.

SECOND READING

A reading from the letter of St Paul to the Ephesians   1:3-14

Before the world was made, God chose us.

[Blessed be God the Father of our Lord Jesus Christ,
who has blessed us with all the spiritual blessings of heaven in Christ.
Before the world was made, he chose us, chose us in Christ,
to be holy and spotless, and to live through love in his presence,
determining that we should become his adopted sons, through Jesus Christ
for his own kind purposes,
to make us praise the glory of his grace,

his free gift to us in the Beloved
in whom, through his blood, we gain our freedom, the forgiveness of our sins.
Such is the richness of the grace
which he has showered on us
in all wisdom and insight.
He has let us know the mystery of his purpose,
the hidden plan he so kindly made in Christ from the beginning
to act upon when the times had run their course to the end:
that he would bring everything together under Christ, as head
everything in the heavens and everything on earth.]

And it is in him that we were claimed as God's own,
chosen from the beginning,
under the predetermined plan of the one who guides all things
as he decides by his own will;
chosen to be,
for his greater glory,
the people who would put their hopes in Christ before he came.
Now you too, in him,
have heard the message of the truth and the good news of your salvation,
and have believed it:
and you too have been stamped with the seal of the Holy Spirit of the Promise,
the pledge of our inheritance
which brings freedom for those whom God has taken for his own,
to make his glory praised.

[The word of the Lord.]

Shorter Form, verses 3-10. Read between [ ]

Gospel Acclamation   Cf. Jn 6:63,68

R. **Alleluia, alleluia!**
Your words are spirit, Lord,
and they are life:
you have the message of eternal life.
R. **Alleluia!**

Or: Cf. Ep 1:17,18

R. **Alleluia, alleluia!**
May the Father of our Lord Jesus Christ
enlighten the eyes of our mind
so that we can see what hope his call holds for us.
R. **Alleluia!**

GOSPEL

A reading from the holy Gospel according to Mark 6:7-13

He began to send them out.

Jesus summoned the Twelve and began to send them out in pairs giving them authority over the unclean spirits. And he instructed them to take nothing for the journey except a staff – no bread, no haversack, no coppers for their purses. They were to wear sandals but, he added, 'Do not take a spare tunic.' And he said to them, 'If you enter a house anywhere, stay there until you leave the district. And if any place does not welcome you and people refuse to listen to you, as you walk away shake off the dust from under your feet as a sign to them.' So they set off to preach repentance; and they cast out many devils, and anointed many sick people with oil and cured them.

The Gospel of the Lord.

Prayer over the Offerings	Super oblata
Look upon the offerings of the Church, O Lord, as she makes her prayer to you, and grant that, when consumed by those who believe, they may bring ever greater holiness. Through Christ our Lord.	Respice, Domine, munera supplicantis Ecclesiæ, et pro credentium sanctificationis incremento sumenda concede. Per Christum Dominum nostrum.

Preface of Sundays in Ordinary Time I-VIII, pp.566-573.

Communion Antiphon Cf. Ps 83:4-5	Ant. ad communionem
The sparrow finds a home, and the swallow a nest for her young: by your altars, O Lord of hosts, my King and my God. Blessed are they who dwell in your house, for ever singing your praise.	Passer invenit sibi domum, et turtur nidum, ubi reponat pullos suos. Altaria tua, Domine virtutum, Rex meus, et Deus meus! Beati qui habitant in domo tua, in sæculum sæculi laudabunt te.
Or: Jn 6:57	Vel:
Whoever eats my flesh and drinks my blood remains in me and I in him, says the Lord.	Qui manducat meam carnem et bibit meum sanguinem, in me manet et ego in eo, dicit Dominus.

Prayer after Communion

Having consumed these gifts,
    we pray, O Lord,
that, by our participation
    in this mystery,
its saving effects upon us may grow.
Through Christ our Lord.

Post communionem

Sumptis muneribus,
    quæsumus, Domine,
ut, cum frequentatione mysterii,
crescat nostræ salutis effectus.
Per Christum Dominum nostrum.

SIXTEENTH SUNDAY IN ORDINARY TIME

(YEAR B)

Entrance Antiphon   Ps 53:6,8

SEE, I have God for my help.
    The Lord sustains my soul.
I will sacrifice to you
    with willing heart,
and praise your name, O Lord,
    for it is good.

Ant. ad introitum

ECCE Deus adiuvat me,
    et Dominus susceptor
    est animæ meæ.
Voluntarie sacrificabo tibi,
et confitebor nomini tuo, Domine,
    quoniam bonum est.

Collect

Show favour, O Lord, to your servants
and mercifully increase the gifts
    of your grace,
that, made fervent in hope,
    faith and charity,
they may be ever watchful
    in keeping your commands.
Through our Lord Jesus Christ,
    your Son,
who lives and reigns with you
    in the unity of the Holy Spirit,
one God, for ever and ever.

Collecta

Propitiare, Domine, famulis tuis,
et clementer gratiæ tuæ super eos
    dona multiplica,
ut, spe, fide et caritate ferventes,
semper in mandatis tuis vigili
    custodia perseverent.
Per Dominum nostrum Iesum
    Christum Filium tuum,
qui tecum vivit et regnat
    in unitate Spiritus Sancti,
Deus, per omnia sæcula sæculorum.

FIRST READING

A reading from the prophet Jeremiah   23:1-6

The remnant of my flock I will gather and I will raise up shepherds to look after them.

'Doom for the shepherds who allow the flock of my pasture to be destroyed
and scattered – it is the Lord who speaks! This, therefore, is what the Lord,

the God of Israel, says about the shepherds in charge of my people: You have let my flock be scattered and go wandering and have not taken care of them. Right, I will take care of you for your misdeeds – it is the Lord who speaks! But the remnant of my flock I myself will gather from all the countries where I have dispersed them, and will bring them back to their pastures: they shall be fruitful and increase in numbers. I will raise up shepherds to look after them and pasture them; no fear, no terror for them anymore; not one shall be lost – it is the Lord who speaks!

'See, the days are coming – it is the Lord who speaks –
when I will raise a virtuous Branch for David,
who will reign as true king and be wise,
practising honesty and integrity in the land.
In his days Judah will be saved
and Israel dwell in confidence.
And this is the name he will be called:
The Lord-our-integrity.'

The word of the Lord.

Responsorial Psalm   Ps 22. R. v.1

R. **The Lord is my shepherd;
there is nothing I shall want.**

The Lord is my shepherd;
there is nothing I shall want.
Fresh and green are the pastures
where he gives me repose.
Near restful waters he leads me,
to revive my drooping spirit. R.

He guides me along the right path;
he is true to his name.
If I should walk in the valley of darkness
no evil would I fear.
You are there with your crook and your staff;
with these you give me comfort. R.

You have prepared a banquet for me
in the sight of my foes.
My head you have anointed with oil;
my cup is overflowing. R.

Surely goodness and kindness shall follow me
all the days of my life.
In the Lord's own house shall I dwell
for ever and ever. R.

SECOND READING

A reading from the letter of St Paul to the Ephesians   2:13-18

Christ Jesus is the peace between us, and has made the two into one.

In Christ Jesus, you that used to be so far apart from us have been brought very close, by the blood of Christ. For he is the peace between us, and has made the two into one and broken down the barrier which used to keep them apart, actually destroying in his own person the hostility caused by the rules and decrees of the Law. This was to create one single New Man in himself out of the two of them and by restoring peace through the cross, to unite them both in a single Body and reconcile them with God. In his own person he killed the hostility. Later he came to bring the good news of peace, peace to you who were far away and peace to those who were near at hand. Through him, both of us have in the one Spirit our way to come to the Father.

The word of the Lord.

Gospel Acclamation   Jn 10:27

R. **Alleluia, alleluia!**
The sheep that belong to me listen to my voice,
says the Lord,
I know them and they follow me.
R. **Alleluia!**

GOSPEL

A reading from the holy Gospel according to Mark   6:30-34

They were like sheep without a shepherd.

The apostles rejoined Jesus and told him all they had done and taught. Then he said to them, 'You must come away to some lonely place all by yourselves and rest for a while'; for there were so many coming and going that the apostles had no time even to eat. So they went off in a boat to a lonely place where they could be by themselves. But people saw them going, and many could guess where; and from every town they all hurried to the place on foot and reached it before them. So as he stepped ashore he saw a large crowd; and he took pity on them because they were like sheep without a shepherd, and he set himself to teach them at some length.

The Gospel of the Lord.

Prayer over the Offerings

O God, who in the one
    perfect sacrifice
brought to completion varied
    offerings of the law,
accept, we pray, this sacrifice
    from your faithful servants
and make it holy, as you blessed
    the gifts of Abel,
so that what each has offered
    to the honour of your majesty
may benefit the salvation of all.
Through Christ our Lord.

Super oblata

Deus, qui legalium
    differentiam hostiarum
unius sacrificii perfectione sanxisti,
accipe sacrificium a devotis
    tibi famulis,
et pari benedictione,
    sicut munera Abel, sanctifica,
ut, quod singuli obtulerunt
    ad maiestatis tuæ honorem,
cunctis proficiat ad salutem.
Per Christum Dominum nostrum.

Preface of Sundays in Ordinary Time I-VIII, pp.566-573.

Communion Antiphon Ps 110:4-5

The Lord, the gracious, the merciful,
has made a memorial of his wonders;
he gives food to those who fear him.

Ant. ad communionem

Memoriam fecit mirabilium suorum
misericors et miserator Dominus;
escam dedit timentibus se.

Or: Rv 3:20

Behold, I stand at the door
    and knock, says the Lord.
If anyone hears my voice
    and opens the door to me,
I will enter his house and dine
    with him, and he with me.

Vel:

Ecce sto ad ostium et pulso,
    dicit Dominus:
si quis audierit vocem meam,
    et aperuerit mihi ianuam,
intrabo ad illum, et cenabo
    cum illo, et ipse mecum.

Prayer after Communion

Graciously be present to your people,
    we pray, O Lord,
and lead those you have imbued
    with heavenly mysteries
to pass from former ways
    to newness of life.
Through Christ our Lord.

Post communionem

Populo tuo, quæsumus, Domine,
    adesto propitius,
et, quem mysteriis
    cælestibus imbuisti,
fac ad novitatem vitæ
    de vetustate transire.
Per Christum Dominum nostrum.

SEVENTEENTH SUNDAY IN ORDINARY TIME
(YEAR B)

Entrance Antiphon Cf. Ps 67:6-7,36

GOD is in his holy place,
God who unites those
who dwell in his house;
he himself gives might and strength
to his people.

Ant. ad introitum

DEUS in loco sancto suo;
Deus qui inhabitare facit
unanimes in domo,
ipse dabit virtutem et fortitudinem
plebi suæ.

Collect

O God, protector of those
who hope in you,
without whom nothing has firm
foundation, nothing is holy,
bestow in abundance your mercy
upon us
and grant that, with you as our ruler
and guide,
we may use the good things that pass
in such a way as to hold fast even now
to those that ever endure.
Through our Lord Jesus Christ,
your Son,
who lives and reigns with you
in the unity of the Holy Spirit,
one God, for ever and ever.

Collecta

Protector in te sperantium, Deus,
sine quo nihil est validum,
nihil sanctum,
multiplica super nos
misericordiam tuam
ut, te rectore, te duce, sic bonis
transeuntibus nunc utamur,
ut iam possimus
inhærere mansuris.
Per Dominum nostrum Iesum
Christum Filium tuum,
qui tecum vivit et regnat
in unitate Spiritus Sancti,
Deus, per omnia sæcula sæculorum.

FIRST READING

A reading from the second book of the Kings　　　4:42-44

They will eat and have some left over.

A man came from Baal-shalishah, bringing Elisha, the man of God, bread from the first-fruits, twenty barley loaves and fresh grain in the ear. 'Give it to the people to eat,' Elisha said. But his servant replied, 'How can l serve this to a hundred men?' 'Give it to the people to eat' he insisted 'for the Lord says this, "They will eat and have some left over."' He served them; they ate and had some over, as the Lord had said.

The word of the Lord.

Responsorial Psalm   Ps 144:10-11,15-18. R. v.16

R. **You open wide your hand, O Lord,**
   you grant our desires.

All your creatures shall thank you, O Lord
and your friends shall repeat their blessing.
They shall speak of the glory of your reign
and declare your might, O God. R.

The eyes of all creatures look to you
and you give them their food in due time.
You open wide your hand,
grant the desires of all who live. R.

The Lord is just in all his ways
and loving in all his deeds.
He is close to all who call him,
who call on him from their hearts. R.

SECOND READING

A reading from the letter of St Paul to the Ephesians   4:1-6
One Body, one Lord, one faith, one baptism.

I, the prisoner in the Lord, implore you to lead a life worthy of your
vocation. Bear with one another charitably, in complete selflessness,
gentleness and patience. Do all you can to preserve the unity of the Spirit
by the peace that binds you together. There is one Body, one Spirit, just
as you were all called into one and the same hope when you were called.
There is one Lord, one faith, one baptism, and one God who is Father of
all, through all and within all.

The word of the Lord.

Gospel Acclamation   Cf. Jn 6:63,68

R. **Alleluia, alleluia!**
Your words are spirit, Lord,
and they are life:
you have the message of eternal life.
R. **Alleluia!**

Or: Lk 7:16

R. **Alleluia, alleluia!**
A great prophet has appeared among us;
God has visited his people.
R. **Alleluia!**

GOSPEL

A reading from the holy Gospel according to John   6:1-15

Jesus gave out as much as was wanted to all who were sitting ready.

Jesus went off to the other side of the Sea of Galilee – or of Tiberias – and a large crowd followed him, impressed by the signs he gave by curing the sick. Jesus climbed the hillside, and sat down there with his disciples. It was shortly before the Jewish feast of Passover.

Looking up, Jesus saw the crowds approaching and said to Philip, 'Where can we buy some bread for these people to eat?' He only said this to test Philip; he himself knew exactly what he was going to do. Philip answered, 'Two hundred denarii would only buy enough to give them a small piece each.' One of his disciples, Andrew, Simon Peter's brother, said, 'There is a small boy here with five barley loaves and two fish; but what is that between so many?' Jesus said to them, 'Make the people sit down.' There was plenty of grass there, and as many as five thousand men sat down. Then Jesus took the loaves, gave thanks, and gave them out to all who were sitting ready; he then did the same with the fish, giving out as much as was wanted. When they had eaten enough he said to the disciples, 'Pick up the pieces left over, so that nothing gets wasted.' So they picked them up, and filled twelve hampers with scraps left over from the meal of five barley loaves. The people, seeing this sign that he had given, said, 'This really is the prophet who is to come into the world.' Jesus, who could see they were about to come and take him by force and make him king, escaped back to the hills by himself.

The Gospel of the Lord.

Prayer over the Offerings	Super oblata
Accept, O Lord, we pray, the offerings which we bring from the abundance of your gifts, that through the powerful working of your grace these most sacred mysteries may sanctify our present way of life and lead us to eternal gladness. Through Christ our Lord.	Suscipe, quæsumus, Domine, munera, quæ tibi de tua largitate deferimus, ut hæc sacrosancta mysteria, gratiæ tuæ operante virtute, et præsentis vitæ nos conversatione sanctificent, et ad gaudia sempiterna perducant. Per Christum Dominum nostrum.

Preface of Sundays in Ordinary Time I-VIII, pp.566-573.

Communion Antiphon   Ps 102:2

Bless the Lord, O my soul,
and never forget all his benefits.

Or: Mt 5:7-8

Blessed are the merciful,
    for they shall receive mercy.
Blessed are the clean of heart,
    for they shall see God.

Prayer after Communion

We have consumed, O Lord,
    this divine Sacrament,
the perpetual memorial
    of the Passion of your Son;
grant, we pray, that this gift,
which he himself gave us with love
    beyond all telling,
may profit us for salvation.
Through Christ our Lord.

Ant. ad communionem

Benedic, anima mea, Domino,
et noli oblivisci omnes
        retributiones eius.

Vel:

Beati misericordes,
quoniam ipsi
    misericordiam consequentur.
Beati mundo corde,
quoniam ipsi Deum videbunt.

Post communionem

Sumpsimus, Domine,
    divinum sacramentum,
passionis Filii tui
    memoriale perpetuum;
tribue, quæsumus,
ut ad nostram salutem hoc
    munus proficiat,
quod ineffabili nobis caritate
    ipse donavit.
Qui vivit et regnat
    in sæcula sæculorum.

EIGHTEENTH SUNDAY IN ORDINARY TIME
(YEAR B)

Entrance Antiphon   Ps 69:2,6

O GOD, come to my assistance;
    O Lord, make haste to help me!
You are my rescuer, my help;
O Lord, do not delay.

Ant. ad introitum

DEUS, in adiutorium
    meum intende;
Domine, ad adiuvandum me festina.
Adiutor meus et liberator meus es tu;
Domine, ne moreris.

Collect

Draw near to your servants, O Lord,
and answer their prayers
   with unceasing kindness,
that, for those who glory in you
   as their Creator and guide,
you may restore what you
   have created
and keep safe what you have restored.
Through our Lord Jesus Christ,
   your Son,
who lives and reigns with you
   in the unity of the Holy Spirit,
one God, for ever and ever.

Collecta

Adesto, Domine, famulis tuis,
et perpetuam benignitatem
   largire poscentibus,
ut his, qui te auctorem et
   gubernatorem gloriantur habere,
et creata restaures,
   et restaurata conserves.
Per Dominum nostrum Iesum
   Christum Filium tuum,
qui tecum vivit et regnat
   in unitate Spiritus Sancti,
Deus, per omnia sæcula sæculorum.

FIRST READING

A reading from the book of Exodus   16:2-4,12-15

I will rain down bread for you from the heavens.

The whole community of the sons of Israel began to complain against Moses and Aaron in the wilderness and said to them, 'Why did we not die at the Lord's hand in the land of Egypt, when we were able to sit down to pans of meat and could eat bread to our heart's content! As it is, you have brought us to this wilderness to starve this whole company to death!'

Then the Lord said to Moses, 'Now I will rain down bread for you from the heavens. Each day the people are to go out and gather the day's portion; I proposed to test them in this way to see whether they will follow my law or not.'

'I have heard the complaints of the sons of Israel. Say this to them, "Between the two evenings you shall eat meat, and in the morning you shall have bread to your heart's content. Then you will learn that I, the Lord, am your God."' And so it came about: quails flew up in the evening, and they covered the camp; in the morning there was a coating of dew all round the camp. When the coating of dew lifted, there on the surface of the desert was a thing delicate, powdery, as fine as hoarfrost on the ground. When they saw this, the sons of Israel said to one another, 'What is that?' not knowing what it was. 'That' said Moses to them 'is the bread the Lord gives you to eat.'

The word of the Lord.

Responsorial Psalm   Ps 77:3-4,23-25,54. R. v.24

R. **The Lord gave them bread from heaven.**

The things we have heard and understood,
the things our fathers have told us,
we will tell to the next generation:
the glories of the Lord and his might. R.

He commanded the clouds above
and opened the gates of heaven.
He rained down manna for their food,
and gave them bread from heaven. R.

Mere men ate the bread of angels.
He sent them abundance of food.
He brought them to his holy land,
to the mountain which his right hand had won. R.

SECOND READING

A reading from the letter of St Paul to the Ephesians   4:17,20-24
Put on the new self that has been created in God's way.

I want to urge you in the name of the Lord, not to go on living the aimless
kind of life that pagans live. Now that is hardly the way you have learnt
from Christ, unless you failed to hear him properly when you were taught
what the truth is in Jesus. You must give up your old way of life; you must
put aside your old self, which gets corrupted by following illusory desires.
Your mind must be renewed by a spiritual revolution so that you can put
on the new self that has been created in God's way, in the goodness and
holiness of the truth.

The word of the Lord.

Gospel Acclamation   Jn 14:5

R. **Alleluia, alleluia!**
I am the Way, the Truth and the Life, says the Lord;
no one can come to the Father except through me.
R. **Alleluia!**

Or: Mt 4:4

R. **Alleluia, alleluia!**
Man does not live on bread alone,
but on every word that comes from the mouth of God.
R. **Alleluia!**

GOSPEL

A reading from the holy Gospel according to John   6:24-35

He who comes to me will never be hungry; he who believes in me will never thirst.

When the people saw that neither Jesus nor his disciples were there, they got into boats and crossed to Capernaum to look for Jesus. When they found him on the other side, they said to him, 'Rabbi, when did you come here?' Jesus answered:

> 'I tell you most solemnly,
> you are not looking for me
> because you have seen the signs
> but because you had all the bread you wanted to eat.
> Do not work for food that cannot last,
> but work for food that endures to eternal life,
> the kind of food the Son of Man is offering you,
> for on him the Father, God himself, has set his seal.'

Then they said to him, 'What must we do if we are to do the works that God wants?' Jesus gave them this answer, 'This is working for God: you must believe in the one he has sent.' So they said, 'What sign will you give to show us that we should believe in you? What work will you do? Our fathers had manna to eat in the desert; as scripture says: He gave them bread from heaven to eat.'

Jesus answered:

> 'I tell you most solemnly,
> it was not Moses who gave you bread from heaven,
> it is my Father who gives you the bread from heaven,
> the true bread;
> for the bread of God
> is that which comes down from heaven
> and gives life to the world.'

'Sir,' they said 'give us that bread always.' Jesus answered:

> 'I am the bread of life.
> He who comes to me will never be hungry;
> he who believes in me will never thirst.'

The Gospel of the Lord.

Prayer over the Offerings

Graciously sanctify these gifts,
    O Lord, we pray,
and, accepting the oblation
    of this spiritual sacrifice,
make of us an eternal offering to you.
Through Christ our Lord.

Super oblata

Propitius, Domine, quæsumus,
    hæc dona sanctifica,
et, hostiæ spiritalis
    oblatione suscepta,
nosmetipsos tibi perfice
    munus æternum.
Per Christum Dominum nostrum.

Preface of Sundays in Ordinary Time I-VIII, pp.566-573.

Communion Antiphon Wis 16:20

You have given us, O Lord,
    bread from heaven,
endowed with all delights
    and sweetness in every taste.

Ant. ad communionem

Panem de cælo dedisti
    nobis, Domine,
habentem omne delectamentum,
et omnem saporem suavitatis.

Or: Jn 6:35

I am the bread of life, says the Lord;
whoever comes to me will not hunger
and whoever believes in me
    will not thirst.

Vel:

Ego sum panis vitæ, dicit Dominus.
Qui venit ad me non esuriet,
    et qui credit in me non sitiet.

Prayer after Communion

Accompany with constant
    protection, O Lord,
those you renew with these
    heavenly gifts
and, in your never-failing care
    for them,
make them worthy
    of eternal redemption.
Through Christ our Lord.

Post communionem

Quos cælesti recreas munere,
perpetuo, Domine,
    comitare præsidio,
et, quos fovere non desinis,
dignos fieri sempiterna
    redemptione concede.
Per Christum Dominum nostrum.

NINETEENTH SUNDAY IN ORDINARY TIME
(YEAR B)

Entrance Antiphon Cf. Ps 73:20,19,22,23	Ant. ad introitum

LOOK to your covenant, O Lord, and forget not the life of your poor ones for ever.
Arise, O God, and defend your cause, and forget not the cries of those who seek you.

RESPICE, Domine, in testamentum tuum, et animas pauperum tuorum ne derelinquas in finem.
Exsurge, Domine, et iudica causam tuam, et ne obliviscaris voces quærentium te.

Collect	Collecta

Almighty ever-living God,
whom, taught by the Holy Spirit,
we dare to call our Father,
bring, we pray, to perfection
    in our hearts
the spirit of adoption as your sons
    and daughters,
that we may merit to enter
    into the inheritance
which you have promised.
Through our Lord Jesus Christ,
    your Son,
who lives and reigns with you
    in the unity of the Holy Spirit,
one God, for ever and ever.

Omnipotens sempiterne Deus,
quem, docente Spiritu Sancto,
paterno nomine
    invocare præsumimus,
perfice in cordibus nostris spiritum
    adoptionis filiorum,
ut promissam hereditatem
    ingredi mereamur.
Per Dominum nostrum Iesum
    Christum Filium tuum,
qui tecum vivit et regnat
    in unitate Spiritus Sancti,
Deus, per omnia sæcula sæculorum.

FIRST READING

A reading from the first book of the Kings   19:4-8

Strengthened by the food he walked until he reached the mountain of God.

Elijah went into the wilderness, a day's journey, and sitting under a furze bush wished he were dead. 'Lord,' he said 'I have had enough. Take my life; I am no better than my ancestors.' Then he lay down and went to sleep. But an angel touched him and said, 'Get up and eat.' He looked round, and there at his head was a scone baked on hot stones, and a jar of water. He ate and drank and then lay down again. But the angel of the Lord came back a second time and touched him and said, 'Get up and eat, or the journey will be too long for you.' So he got up and ate and drank, and strengthened by that food he walked for forty days and forty nights until he reached Horeb, the mountain of God.

The word of the Lord.

Responsorial Psalm   Ps 33:2-9. R. v.9

R. **Taste and see that the Lord is good.**

I will bless the Lord at all times,
his praise always on my lips;
in the Lord my soul shall make its boast.
The humble shall hear and be glad. R.

Glorify the Lord with me.
Together let us praise his name.
I sought the Lord and he answered me;
from all my terrors he set me free. R.

Look towards him and be radiant;
let your faces not be abashed.
This poor man called; the Lord heard him
and rescued him from all his distress. R.

The angel of the Lord is encamped
around those who revere him, to rescue them.
Taste and see that the Lord is good.
He is happy who seeks refuge in him. R.

SECOND READING

A reading from the letter of St Paul to the Ephesians   4:30-5:2

Follow Christ by loving as he loved you.

Do not grieve the Holy Spirit of God who has marked you with his seal for you to be set free when the day comes. Never have grudges against others, or lose your temper, or raise your voice to anybody, or call each other names, or allow any sort of spitefulness. Be friends with one another, and kind, forgiving each other as readily as God forgave you in Christ.

Try, then, to imitate God, as children of his that he loves, and follow Christ by loving as he loved you, giving himself up in our place as a fragrant offering and a sacrifice to God.

The word of the Lord.

Gospel Acclamation   Jn 14:23
R. **Alleluia, alleluia!**
If anyone loves me he will keep my word,
and my Father will love him,
and we shall come to him.
R. **Alleluia!**

Or: Jn 6:51

R. **Alleluia, alleluia!**
I am the living bread which has come down from heaven,
says the Lord.
Anyone who eats this bread will live for ever.
R. **Alleluia!**

GOSPEL

A reading from the holy Gospel according to John   6:41-51
I am the living bread which has come down from heaven.

The Jews were complaining to each other about Jesus, because he had said,
'I am the bread that came down from heaven.' 'Surely this is Jesus son of
Joseph' they said. 'We know his father and mother. How can he now say,
"I have come down from heaven"?' Jesus said in reply, 'Stop complaining
to each other.

'No one can come to me
unless he is drawn by the Father who sent me,
and I will raise him up at the last day.
It is written in the prophets:
They will all be taught by God,
and to hear the teaching of the Father,
and learn from it,
is to come to me.
Not that anybody has seen the Father,
except the one who comes from God:
he has seen the Father.
I tell you most solemnly,
everybody who believes has eternal life.
I am the bread of life.
Your fathers ate the manna in the desert
and they are dead;
but this is the bread that comes down from heaven,
so that a man may eat it and not die.
I am the living bread which has come down from heaven.

NINETEENTH SUNDAY IN ORDINARY TIME (YEAR B)

Anyone who eats this bread will live for ever;
and the bread that I shall give
is my flesh, for the life of the world.'
The Gospel of the Lord.

Prayer over the Offerings

Be pleased, O Lord, to accept
the offerings of your Church,
for in your mercy you have given
them to be offered
and by your power
you transform them
into the mystery of our salvation.
Through Christ our Lord.

Super oblata

Ecclesiæ tuæ, Domine,
munera placatus assume,
quæ et misericors
offerenda tribuisti,
et in nostræ salutis potenter efficis
transire mysterium.
Per Christum Dominum nostrum.

Communion Antiphon Ps 147:12,14

O Jerusalem, glorify the Lord,
who gives you your fill
of finest wheat.

Ant. ad communionem

Lauda, Ierusalem, Dominum,
qui adipe frumenti satiat te.

Or: Cf. Jn 6:51

The bread that I will give,
says the Lord,
is my flesh for the life of the world.

Vel:

Panis, quem ego dedero,
caro mea est pro sæculi vita,
dicit Dominus.

Prayer after Communion

May the communion
in your Sacrament
that we have consumed, save us,
O Lord,
and confirm us in the light
of your truth.
Through Christ our Lord.

Post communionem

Sacramentorum tuorum, Domine,
communio sumpta nos salvet,
et in tuæ veritatis luce confirmet.
Per Christum Dominum nostrum.

TWENTIETH SUNDAY IN ORDINARY TIME
(YEAR B)

Entrance Antiphon Ps 83:10-11	Ant. ad introitum

TURN your eyes, O God,
　our shield;
and look on the face
　of your anointed one;
one day within your courts
is better than a thousand elsewhere.

PROTECTOR noster,
　aspice, Deus,
et respice in faciem Christi tui,
quia melior est dies una in atriis
　tuis super millia.

Collect	Collecta

O God, who have prepared
　for those who love you
good things which no eye can see,
fill our hearts, we pray,
　with the warmth of your love,
so that, loving you in all things
　and above all things,
we may attain your promises,
which surpass every human desire.
Through our Lord Jesus Christ,
　your Son,
who lives and reigns with you
　in the unity of the Holy Spirit,
one God, for ever and ever.

Deus, qui diligentibus te bona
　invisibilia præparasti,
infunde cordibus nostris
　tui amoris affectum,
ut, te in omnibus et super
　omnia diligentes,
promissiones tuas, quæ omne
　desiderium superant,
consequamur.
Per Dominum nostrum Iesum
　Christum Filium tuum,
qui tecum vivit et regnat
　in unitate Spiritus Sancti,
Deus, per omnia sæcula sæculorum.

FIRST READING

A reading from the book of Proverbs   9:1-6

Eat my bread, drink the wine I have prepared for you.

Wisdom has built herself a house,
she has erected her seven pillars,
she has slaughtered her beasts, prepared her wine,
she has laid her table.
She has despatched her maidservants
and proclaimed from the city's heights:
'Who is ignorant? Let him step this way.'
To the fool she says,
'Come and eat my bread,

drink the wine I have prepared!
Leave your folly and you will live,
walk in the ways of perception.'

The word of the Lord.

Responsorial Psalm   Ps 33:2-3,10-15. R. v.9

R. **Taste and see the Lord is good.**

I will bless the Lord at all times,
his praise always on my lips;
in the Lord my soul shall make its boast.
The humble shall hear and be glad. R.

Revere the Lord, you his saints.
They lack nothing, those who revere him.
Strong lions suffer want and go hungry
but those who seek the Lord lack no blessing. R.

Come, children, and hear me
that I may teach you the fear of the Lord.
Who is he who longs for life
and many days, to enjoy his prosperity? R.

Then keep your tongue from evil
and your lips from speaking deceit.
Turn aside from evil and do good;
seek and strive after peace. R.

SECOND READING

A reading from the letter of St Paul to the Ephesians   5:15-20
Recognise what is the will of God.

Be very careful about the sort of lives you lead, like intelligent and not like
senseless people. This may be a wicked age, but your lives should redeem
it. And do not be thoughtless but recognise what is the will of the Lord.
Do not drug yourselves with wine, this is simply dissipation; be filled with
the Spirit. Sing the words and tunes of the psalms and hymns when you
are together, and go on singing and chanting to the Lord in your hearts, so
that always and everywhere you are giving thanks to God who is our Father
in the name of our Lord Jesus Christ.

The word of the Lord.

Gospel Acclamation   Jn 1:14,12

R. **Alleluia, alleluia!**
The Word was made flesh and lived among us;
to all who did accept him
he gave power to become children of God.
R. **Alleluia!**

Or: Jn 6:56

R. **Alleluia, alleluia!**
He who eats my flesh and drinks my blood
lives in me, and I live in him,
says the Lord.
R. **Alleluia!**

GOSPEL

A reading from the holy Gospel according to John   6:51-58
My flesh is real food and my blood is real drink.

Jesus said to the crowd:

'I am the living bread which has come down from heaven.
Anyone who eats this bread will live for ever;
and the bread that I shall give
is my flesh, for the life of the world.'

Then the Jews started arguing with one another: 'How can this man give
us his flesh to eat?' they said. Jesus replied:

'I tell you most solemnly,
if you do not eat the flesh of the Son of Man
and drink his blood,
you will not have life in you.
Anyone who does eat my flesh and drink my blood
has eternal life,
and I shall raise him up on the last day.
For my flesh is real food
and my blood is real drink.
He who eats my flesh and drinks my blood
lives in me
and I live in him.
As I, who am sent by the living Father,
myself draw life from the Father,
so whoever eats me will draw life from me.

This the bread come down from heaven;
not like the bread our ancestors ate:
they are dead,
but anyone who eats this bread will live for ever.'

The Gospel of the Lord.

Prayer over the Offerings | Super oblata

Receive our oblation, O Lord,
by which is brought about
   a glorious exchange,
that, by offering what you have given,
we may merit to receive
   your very self.
Through Christ our Lord.

Suscipe, Domine, munera nostra,
quibus exercentur
   commercia gloriosa,
ut, offerentes quæ dedisti,
teipsum mereamur accipere.
Per Christum Dominum nostrum.

Preface of Sundays in Ordinary Time I-VIII, pp.566-573.

Communion Antiphon   Ps 129:7 | Ant. ad communionem

With the Lord there is mercy;
in him is plentiful redemption.

Apud Dominum misericordia,
et copiosa apud eum redemptio.

Or: Jn 6:51 | Vel:

I am the living bread that came
   down from heaven, says the Lord.
Whoever eats of this bread
   will live for ever.

Ego sum panis vivus, qui de cælo
   descendi, dicit Dominus:
si quis manducaverit ex hoc pane,
   vivet in æternum.

Prayer after Communion | Post communionem

Made partakers of Christ through
   these Sacraments,
we humbly implore your
   mercy, Lord,
that, conformed to his image
   on earth,
we may merit also to be his coheirs
   in heaven.
Who lives and reigns
   for ever and ever.

Per hæc sacramenta, Domine,
   Christi participes effecti,
clementiam tuam
   humiliter imploramus,
ut, eius imaginis conformes
   in terris,
et eius consortes in cælis
   fieri mereamur.
Qui vivit et regnat
   in sæcula sæculorum.

TWENTY-FIRST SUNDAY IN ORDINARY TIME
(YEAR B)

Entrance Antiphon   Cf. Ps 85:1-3

TURN your ear, O Lord,
 and answer me;
save the servant who trusts in you,
   my God.
Have mercy on me, O Lord,
   for I cry to you all the day long.

Ant. ad introitum

INCLINA, Domine, aurem tuam
 ad me, et exaudi me.
Salvum fac servum tuum,
   Deus meus, sperantem in te.
Miserere mihi, Domine,
   quoniam ad te clamavi tota die.

Collect

O God, who cause the minds
   of the faithful
to unite in a single purpose,
grant your people to love
   what you command
and to desire what you promise,
that, amid the uncertainties
   of this world,
our hearts may be fixed on that place
where true gladness is found.
Through our Lord Jesus Christ,
   your Son,
who lives and reigns with you
   in the unity of the Holy Spirit,
one God, for ever and ever.

Collecta

Deus, qui fidelium mentes unius
   efficis voluntatis,
da populis tuis id amare
   quod præcipis,
id desiderare quod promittis,
ut, inter mundanas varietates,
ibi nostra fixa sint corda,
   ubi vera sunt gaudia.
Per Dominum nostrum Iesum
   Christum Filium tuum,
qui tecum vivit et regnat
   in unitate Spiritus Sancti,
Deus, per omnia sæcula sæculorum.

FIRST READING

A reading from the book of Joshua   24:1-2,15-17,18

We will serve the Lord, for he is our God.

Joshua gathered all the tribes of Israel together at Shechem; then he called
the elders, leaders, judges and scribes of Israel, and they presented themselves
before God. Then Joshua said to all the people: 'If you will not serve the Lord,
choose today whom you wish to serve, whether the gods that your ancestors
served beyond the River, or the gods of the Amorites in whose land you are
now living. As for me and my House, we will serve the Lord.'

The people answered, 'We have no intention of deserting the Lord our
God and serving other gods! Was it not the Lord our God who brought

us and our ancestors out of the land of Egypt, the house of slavery, who worked those great wonders before our eyes and preserved us all along the way we travelled and among all the peoples through whom we journeyed? We too will serve the Lord, for he is our God.'

The word of the Lord.

Responsorial Psalm   Ps 33:2-3,16-23. R. v.9

R. **Taste and see that the Lord is good.**

I will bless the Lord at all times,
his praise always on my lips;
in the Lord my soul shall make its boast.
The humble shall hear and be glad. R.

The Lord turns his face against the wicked
to destroy their remembrance from the earth.
The Lord turns his eyes to the just
and his ears to their appeal. R.

They call and the Lord hears
and rescues them in all their distress.
The Lord is close to the broken-hearted;
those whose spirit is crushed he will save. R.

Many are the trials of the just man
but from them all the Lord will rescue him.
He will keep guard over all his bones,
not one of his bones shall be broken. R.

Evil brings death to the wicked;
those who hate the good are doomed.
The Lord ransoms the souls of his servants.
Those who hide in him shall not be condemned. R.

SECOND READING

A reading from the letter of St Paul to the Ephesians   5:21-32

This mystery has many implications for Christ and his Church.

Give way to one another in obedience to Christ. Wives should regard their husbands as they regard the Lord, since as Christ is head of the Church and saves the whole body, so is a husband the head of his wife; and as the Church submits to Christ, so should wives to their husbands, in everything. Husbands should love their wives just as Christ loved the Church and sacrificed himself for her to make her holy. He made her clean by washing her in water with a form of words, so that when he took her to himself she would be glorious, with no speck or wrinkle or anything like that, but holy and faultless. In the same way, husbands must love their wives as they love their own bodies; for a man to love his wife is for him to love himself. A man never hates his own body, but he feeds it and looks after it; and that is the way Christ treats the Church, because it is his body – and we are its living parts. For this reason, a man must leave his father and mother and be joined to his wife, and the two will become one body. This mystery has many implications; but I am saying it applies to Christ and the Church.

The word of the Lord.

Gospel Acclamation   Cf. Jn 6:63,68

R. **Alleluia, alleluia!**
Your words are spirit, Lord,
and they are life:
you have the message of eternal life.
R. **Alleluia!**

GOSPEL

A reading from the holy Gospel according to John   6:60-69
Who shall we go to? You have the message of eternal life.

After hearing his doctrine many of the followers of Jesus said, 'This is intolerable language. How could anyone accept it?' Jesus was aware that his followers were complaining about it and said, 'Does this upset you? What if you should see the Son of Man ascend to where he was before?

'It is the spirit that gives life,
the flesh has nothing to offer.
The words I have spoken to you are spirit
and they are life.

'But there are some of you who do not believe.' For Jesus knew from the outset those who did not believe, and who it was that would betray him. He went on, 'This is why I told you that no one could come to me unless the Father allows him.' After this, many of his disciples left him and stopped going with him.

Then Jesus said to the Twelve, 'What about you, do you want to go away too?' Simon Peter answered, 'Lord, who shall we go to? You have the message of eternal life, and we believe; we know that you are the Holy One of God.'

The Gospel of the Lord.

Prayer over the Offerings

O Lord, who gained for yourself
    a people by adoption
through the one sacrifice offered
    once for all,
bestow graciously on us, we pray,
the gifts of unity and peace
    in your Church.
Through Christ our Lord.

Super oblata

Qui una semel hostia, Domine,
adoptionis tibi populum acquisisti,
unitatis et pacis in Ecclesia tua
propitius nobis dona concedas.
Per Christum Dominum nostrum.

Preface of Sundays in Ordinary Time I-VIII, pp.566-573.

Communion Antiphon Cf. Ps 103:13-15

The earth is replete with the fruits
    of your work, O Lord;
you bring forth bread from the earth
and wine to cheer the heart.

Ant. ad communionem

De fructu operum tuorum,
    Domine, satiabitur terra,
ut educas panem de terra,
    et vinum lætificet cor hominis.

Or: Cf. Jn 6:54

Whoever eats my flesh
    and drinks my blood
has eternal life, says the Lord,
and I will raise him up
    on the last day.

Vel:

Qui manducat meam carnem
    et bibit meum sanguinem,
habet vitam æternam,
    dicit Dominus;
et ego resuscitabo eum
    in novissimo die.

Prayer after Communion

Complete within us, O Lord,
    we pray,
the healing work of your mercy
and graciously perfect
    and sustain us,
so that in all things we may
    please you.
Through Christ our Lord.

Post communionem

Plenum, quæsumus, Domine,
in nobis remedium tuæ
    miserationis operare
ac tales nos esse perfice propitius
    et sic foveri,
ut tibi in omnibus
    placere valeamus.
Per Christum Dominum nostrum.

TWENTY-SECOND SUNDAY IN ORDINARY TIME
(YEAR B)

Entrance Antiphon   Cf. Ps 85:3,5

HAVE mercy on me, O Lord,
for I cry to you all the day long.
O Lord, you are good and forgiving,
full of mercy to all who call to you.

Ant. ad introitum

MISERERE mihi, Domine,
quoniam ad te clamavi
    tota die:
quia tu, Domine, suavis ac mitis es,
et copiosus in misericordia
    omnibus invocantibus te.

Collect

God of might, giver of every
    good gift,
put into our hearts the love
    of your name,
so that, by deepening our sense
    of reverence,
you may nurture in us what is good
and, by your watchful care,
keep safe what you have nurtured.
Through our Lord Jesus Christ,
    your Son,
who lives and reigns with you
    in the unity of the Holy Spirit,
one God, for ever and ever.

Collecta

Deus virtutum, cuius est totum
    quod est optimum,
insere pectoribus nostris
    tui nominis amorem,
et præsta, ut in nobis,
religionis augmento,
    quæ sunt bona nutrias,
ac, vigilanti studio,
    quæ sunt nutrita custodias.
Per Dominum nostrum Iesum
    Christum Filium tuum,
qui tecum vivit et regnat
    in unitate Spiritus Sancti,
Deus, per omnia sæcula sæculorum.

FIRST READING

A reading from the book of Deuteronomy   4:1-2,6-8

Add nothing to what I command you, keep the commandments of the Lord.

Moses said to the people: 'Now, Israel, take notice of the laws and customs that I teach you today, and observe them, that you may have life and may enter and take possession of the land that the Lord the God of your fathers is giving you. You must add nothing to what I command you, and take nothing from it, but keep the commandments of the Lord your God just as I lay them down for you. Keep them, observe them, and they will demonstrate to the peoples your wisdom and understanding. When they come to know of all these laws they will exclaim, "No other people is as wise and prudent as this great nation." And indeed, what great nation is there that has its gods so near as the Lord our God is to us whenever we call to him? And what great nation is there that has laws and customs to match this whole Law that I put before you today?'

The word of the Lord.

Responsorial Psalm   Ps 14:2-5. R. v.1

R. **The just will live in the presence of the Lord.**

Lord, who shall dwell on your holy mountain?
He who walks without fault,
he who acts with justice
and speaks the truth from his heart. R.

He who does no wrong to his brother,
who casts no slur on his neighbour,
who holds the godless in disdain,
but honours those who fear the Lord. R.

He who keeps his pledge, come what may;
who takes no interest on a loan
and accepts no bribes against the innocent.
Such a man will stand firm for ever. R.

SECOND READING

A reading from the letter of St James   1:17-18,21-22,27
You must do what the word tells you.

It is all that is good, everything that is perfect, which is given us from above; it comes down from the Father of all light; with him there is no such thing as alteration, no shadow of a change. By his own choice he made us his children by the message of the truth so that we should be a sort of first-fruits of all that he had created.

Accept and submit to the word which has been planted in you and can save your souls. But you must do what the word tells you, and not just listen to it and deceive yourselves.

Pure unspoilt religion, in the eyes of God our Father is this: coming to the help of orphans and widows when they need it, and keeping oneself uncontaminated by the world.

The word of the Lord.

Gospel Acclamation   Cf. Jn 6:63,68
R. **Alleluia, alleluia!**
Your words are spirit, Lord,
and they are life:
you have the message of eternal life.
R. **Alleluia!**

Or: Jm 1:18

R. **Alleluia, alleluia!**
By his own choice the Father made us his children
by the message of the truth,
so that we should be a sort of first-fruits
of all that he created.
R. **Alleluia!**

GOSPEL

A reading from the holy Gospel according to Mark   7:1-8,14-15,21-23
You put aside the commandment of God to cling to human traditions.

The Pharisees and some of the scribes who had come from Jerusalem
gathered round Jesus, and they noticed that some of his disciples were eating
with unclean hands, that is, without washing them. For the Pharisees, and
the Jews in general, follow the tradition of the elders and never eat without
washing their arms as far as the elbow; and on returning from the market
place they never eat without first sprinkling themselves. There are also many
other observances which have been handed down to them concerning the
washing of cups and pots and bronze dishes. So these Pharisees and scribes
asked him, 'Why do your disciples not respect the tradition of the elders but
eat their food with unclean hands?' He answered, 'It was of you hypocrites
that Isaiah so rightly prophesied in this passage of scripture:

This people honours me only with lip-service,
while their hearts are far from me.
The worship they offer me is worthless,
the doctrines they teach are only human regulations.

You put aside the commandment of God to cling to human traditions.'

He called the people to him again and said, 'Listen to me, all of you,
and understand. Nothing that goes into a man from outside can make him
unclean; it is the things that come out of a man that make him unclean. For
it is from within, from men's hearts, that evil intentions emerge: fornication,
theft, murder, adultery, avarice, malice, deceit, indecency, envy, slander,
pride, folly. All these evil things come from within and make a man unclean.'

The Gospel of the Lord.

Prayer over the Offerings
May this sacred offering, O Lord,
confer on us always the blessing
   of salvation,
that what it celebrates in mystery
it may accomplish in power.
Through Christ our Lord.

Super oblata
Benedictionem nobis, Domine,
   conferat salutarem
sacra semper oblatio,
ut, quod agit mysterio,
   virtute perficiat.
Per Christum Dominum nostrum.

Preface of Sundays in Ordinary Time I-VIII, pp.566-573.

Communion Antiphon   Ps 30:20
How great is the goodness, Lord,
that you keep for those who fear you.

Ant. ad communionem
Quam magna multitudo
   dulcedinis tuæ, Domine,
quam abscondisti timentibus te.

Or: Mt 5:9-10
Blessed are the peacemakers,
for they shall be called
   children of God.
Blessed are they who are persecuted
   for the sake of righteousness,
for theirs is the Kingdom of Heaven.

Vel:
Beati pacifici, quoniam filii
   Dei vocabuntur.
Beati qui persecutionem patiuntur
   propter iustitiam,
quoniam ipsorum
   est regnum cælorum.

Prayer after Communion
Renewed by this bread
   from the heavenly table,
we beseech you, Lord,
that, being the food of charity,
it may confirm our hearts
and stir us to serve you
   in our neighbour.
Through Christ our Lord.

Post communionem
Pane mensæ cælestis refecti, te,
   Domine, deprecamur,
ut hoc nutrimentum caritatis corda
   nostra confirmet,
quatenus ad tibi ministrandum
   in fratribus excitemur.
Per Christum Dominum nostrum.

TWENTY-THIRD SUNDAY IN ORDINARY TIME
(YEAR B)

Entrance Antiphon Ps 118:137,124
YOU are just, O Lord,
   and your judgement is right;
treat your servant in accord
   with your merciful love.

Ant. ad introitum
IUSTUS es, Domine,
   et rectum iudicium tuum;
fac cum servo tuo secundum
   misericordiam tuam.

Collect	Collecta
O God, by whom we are redeemed and receive adoption,	Deus, per quem nobis et redemptio venit et præstatur adoptio,
look graciously upon your beloved sons and daughters,	filios dilectionis tuæ benignus intende,
that those who believe in Christ	ut in Christo credentibus
may receive true freedom	et vera tribuatur libertas,
and an everlasting inheritance.	et hereditas æterna.
Through our Lord Jesus Christ, your Son,	Per Dominum nostrum Iesum Christum Filium tuum,
who lives and reigns with you in the unity of the Holy Spirit,	qui tecum vivit et regnat in unitate Spiritus Sancti,
one God, for ever and ever.	Deus, per omnia sæcula sæculorum.

FIRST READING

A reading from the prophet Isaiah   35:4-7

The ears of the deaf shall be unsealed and the tongues of the dumb shall be loosed.

Say to all faint hearts,
'Courage! Do not be afraid.

'Look, your God is coming,
vengeance is coming,
the retribution of God;
he is coming to save you.'

Then the eyes of the blind shall be opened,
the ears of the deaf unsealed,
then the lame shall leap like a deer
and the tongues of the dumb sing for joy;

for water gushes in the desert,
streams in the wasteland,
the scorched earth becomes a lake,
the parched land springs of water.

This word of the Lord.

Responsorial Psalm   Ps 145:7-10. R. v.1

R. **My soul, give praise to the Lord.**
   Or: **Alleluia!**

   It is the Lord who keeps faith for ever,
   who is just to those who are oppressed.
   It is he who gives bread to the hungry,
   the Lord, who sets prisoners free. R.

It is the Lord who gives sight to the blind,
who raises up those who are bowed down,
the Lord who loves the just,
the Lord, who protects the stranger. R.

The Lord upholds the widow and orphan,
but thwarts the path of the wicked.
The Lord will reign for ever,
Zion's God, from age to age. R.

R. **My soul, give praise to the Lord.**
Or: **Alleluia!**

SECOND READING

A reading from the letter of St James   2:1-5
God chose the poor to be the heirs to the kingdom.

My brothers, do not try to combine faith in Jesus Christ, our glorified Lord,
with the making of distinctions between classes of people. Now suppose a
man comes into your synagogue, beautifully dressed and with a gold ring
on, and at the same time a poor man comes in, in shabby clothes, and you
take notice of the well-dressed man, and say, 'Come this way to the best
seats'; then you tell the poor man, 'Stand over there' or 'You can sit on
the floor by my foot-rest.' Can't you see that you have used two different
standards in your mind, and turned yourselves into judges, and corrupt
judges at that?

Listen, my dear brothers: it was those who are poor according to the
world that God chose, to be rich in faith and to be the heirs to the kingdom
which he promised to those who love him.

The word of the Lord.

Gospel Acclamation   1 S 3:9; Jn 6:68

R. **Alleluia, alleluia!**
Speak, Lord, your servant is listening:
you have the message of eternal life.
R. **Alleluia!**

Or: Cf. Mt 4:23

R. **Alleluia, alleluia!**
Jesus proclaimed the Good News of the kingdom,
and cured all kinds of sickness among the people.
R. **Alleluia!**

GOSPEL

A reading from the holy Gospel according to Mark 7:31-37

He makes the deaf hear and the dumb speak.

Returning from the district of Tyre, Jesus went by way of Sidon towards the Sea of Galilee, right through the Decapolis region. And they brought him a deaf man who had an impediment in his speech; and they asked him to lay his hand on him. He took him aside in private, away from the crowd, put his fingers into the man's ears and touched his tongue with spittle. Then looking up to heaven he sighed; and he said to him, 'Ephphatha,' that is, 'Be opened.' And his ears were opened, and the ligament of his tongue was loosened and he spoke clearly. And Jesus ordered them to tell no one about it, but the more he insisted, the more widely they published it. Their admiration was unbounded. 'He has done all things well,' they said 'he makes the deaf hear and the dumb speak.'

The Gospel of the Lord.

Prayer over the Offerings	Super oblata
O God, who give us the gift of true prayer and of peace, graciously grant that, through this offering, we may do fitting homage to your divine majesty and, by partaking of the sacred mystery, we may be faithfully united in mind and heart. Through Christ our Lord.	Deus, auctor sinceræ devotionis et pacis, da, quæsumus, ut et maiestatem tuam convenienter hoc munere veneremur, et sacri participatione mysterii fideliter sensibus uniamur. Per Christum Dominum nostrum.

Preface of Sundays in Ordinary Time I-VIII, pp.566-573.

Communion Antiphon Cf. Ps 41:2-3	Ant. ad communionem
Like the deer that yearns for running streams, so my soul is yearning for you, my God; my soul is thirsting for God, the living God.	Quemadmodum desiderat cervus ad fontes aquarum, ita desiderat anima mea ad te, Deus: sitivit anima mea ad Deum fortem vivum.

Or: Jn 8:12

I am the light of the world,
    says the Lord;
whoever follows me will not walk
    in darkness,
but will have the light of life.

Vel:

Ego sum lux mundi,
    dicit Dominus:
qui sequitur me non ambulat
    in tenebris,
sed habebit lumen vitæ.

Prayer after Communion

Grant that your faithful, O Lord,
whom you nourish and endow
    with life
through the food of your Word
    and heavenly Sacrament,
may so benefit from your beloved
    Son's great gifts
that we may merit an eternal share
    in his life.
Who lives and reigns
    for ever and ever.

Post communionem

Da fidelibus tuis, Domine,
quos et verbi tui et cælestis
    sacramenti pabulo
nutris et vivificas,
ita dilecti Filii tui tantis
    muneribus proficere,
ut eius vitæ semper consortes
    effici mereamur.
Qui vivit et regnat
    in sæcula sæculorum.

TWENTY-FOURTH SUNDAY IN ORDINARY TIME

(YEAR B)

Entrance Antiphon   Cf. Si 36:18

G IVE peace, O Lord,
   to those who wait for you,
that your prophets be found true.
Hear the prayers of your servant,
and of your people Israel.

Ant. ad introitum

D A pacem, Domine,
   sustinentibus te,
ut prophetæ tui fideles inveniantur;
exaudi preces servi tui,
    et plebis tuæ Israel.

Collect

Look upon us, O God,
Creator and ruler of all things,
and, that we may feel the working
    of your mercy,
grant that we may serve you
    with all our heart.
Through our Lord Jesus Christ,
    your Son,
who lives and reigns with you
    in the unity of the Holy Spirit,
one God, for ever and ever.

Collecta

Respice nos, rerum omnium Deus
    creator et rector,
et, ut tuæ propitiationis
    sentiamus effectum,
toto nos tribue tibi corde servire.
Per Dominum nostrum Iesum
    Christum Filium tuum,
qui tecum vivit et regnat
    in unitate Spiritus Sancti,
Deus, per omnia sæcula sæculorum.

FIRST READING

A reading from the prophet Isaiah   50:5-9

I offered my back to those who struck me.

The Lord has opened my ear.

For my part, I made no resistance,
neither did I turn away.
I offered my back to those who struck me,
my cheeks to those who tore at my beard;
I did not cover my face
against insult and spittle.

The Lord comes to my help,
so that I am untouched by the insults.
So, too, I set my face like flint;
I know I shall not be shamed.

My vindicator is here at hand. Does anyone start proceedings against me?
Then let us go to court together.
Who thinks he has a case against me?
Let him approach me.
The Lord is coming to my help,
who dare condemn me?

The word of the Lord.

Responsorial Psalm   Ps 114:1-6,8-9. R. v.9

R. **I will walk in the presence of the Lord,
    in the land of the living.**
    Or: **Alleluia!**

I love the Lord for he has heard
the cry of my appeal;
for he turned his ear to me
in the day when I called him. R.

They surrounded me, the snares of death,
with the anguish of the tomb;
they caught me, sorrow and distress.
I called on the Lord's name.
O Lord my God, deliver me! R.

How gracious is the Lord, and just;
our God has compassion.
The Lord protects the simple hearts;
I was helpless so he saved me. R.

He has kept my soul from death,
my eyes from tears
and my feet from stumbling.
I will walk in the presence of the Lord
in the land of the living. R.

R. **I will walk in the presence of the Lord,**
　　in the land of the living.
　　Or:**Alleluia!**

SECOND READING

A reading from the letter of St James　　　　　　　　2:14-18

If good works do not go with faith, it is quite dead.

Take the case, my brothers, of someone who has never done a single good act
but claims that he has faith. Will that faith save him? If one of the brothers
or one of the sisters is in need of clothes and has not enough food to live on,
and one of you says to them, 'I wish you well; keep yourself warm and eat
plenty,' without giving them these bare necessities of life, then what good is
that? Faith is like that: if good works do not go with it, it is quite dead.

　　This is the way to talk to people of that kind: 'You say you have faith and I
have good deeds; I will prove to you that I have faith by showing my good deeds
– now you prove to me that you have faith without any good deeds to show.'

　　The word of the Lord.

Gospel Acclamation　　　　　　　　　　　　　　　　　Jn 14:5

R.**Alleluia, alleluia!**
I am the Way, the Truth and the Life, says the Lord;
no one can come to the Father except through me.
R.**Alleluia!**

Or:　　　　　　　　　　　　　　　　　　　　　　　　Ga 6:14

R.**Alleluia, alleluia!**
The only thing I can boast about is the cross
　　of our Lord,
through whom the world is crucified to me, and I to the world.
R.**Alleluia!**

GOSPEL

A reading from the holy Gospel according to Mark　　　8:27-35

You are the Christ. The Son of Man is destined to suffer grievously.

Jesus and his disciples left for the villages round Caesarea Philippi. On the
way he put this question to his disciples, 'Who do people say I am?' And
they told him. 'John the Baptist,' they said 'others Elijah; others again, one

of the prophets.' 'But you,' he asked 'who do you say I am?' Peter spoke up and said to him, 'You are the Christ.' And he gave them strict orders not to tell anyone about him.

And he began to teach them that the Son of Man was destined to suffer grievously, to be rejected by the elders and the chief priests and the scribes, and to be put to death, and after three days to rise again; and he said all this quite openly. Then, taking him aside, Peter started to remonstrate with him. But, turning and seeing his disciples, he rebuked Peter and said to him, 'Get behind me, Satan! Because the way you think is not God's way but man's.'

He called the people and his disciples to him and said, 'If anyone wants to be a follower of mine, let him renounce himself and take up his cross and follow me. For anyone who wants to save his life will lose it; but anyone who loses his life for my sake, and for the sake of the gospel, will save it.'

The Gospel of the Lord.

Prayer over the Offerings

Look with favour on our
    supplications, O Lord,
and in your kindness accept these,
    your servants' offerings,
that what each has offered
    to the honour of your name
may serve the salvation of all.
Through Christ our Lord.

Super oblata

Propitiare, Domine,
    supplicationibus nostris,
et has oblationes famulorum
    tuorum benignus assume,
ut, quod singuli ad honorem
    tui nominis obtulerunt,
cunctis proficiat ad salutem.
Per Christum Dominum nostrum.

Preface of Sundays in Ordinary Time I-VIII, pp.566-573.

Communion Antiphon Cf. Ps 35:8

How precious is your mercy, O God!
The children of men seek shelter
    in the shadow of your wings.

Or: Cf. 1 Co 10:16
The chalice of blessing that we bless
is a communion in the Blood
    of Christ;
and the bread that we break
is a sharing in the Body of the Lord.

Ant. ad communionem

Quam pretiosa
    est misericordia tua, Deus!
Filii hominum sub umbra alarum
    tuarum confugient.

Vel:
Calix benedictionis,
    cui benedicimus,
communicatio Sanguinis Christi est;
et panis, quem frangimus,
participatio Corporis Domini est.

Prayer after Communion

May the working of this heavenly
     gift, O Lord, we pray,
take possession of our minds
     and bodies,
so that its effects,
     and not our own desires,
may always prevail in us.
Through Christ our Lord.

Post communionem

Mentes nostras et corpora possideat,
quæsumus, Domine,
     doni cælestis operatio,
ut non noster sensus in nobis,
sed eius præveniat semper effectus.
Per Christum Dominum nostrum.

TWENTY-FIFTH SUNDAY IN ORDINARY TIME
(YEAR B)

Entrance Antiphon

I AM the salvation of the people,
     says the Lord.
Should they cry to me in any distress,
I will hear them, and I will be
     their Lord for ever.

Ant. ad introitum

S ALUS populi ego sum,
     dicit Dominus.
De quacumque tribulatione
     clamaverint ad me,
exaudiam eos, et ero illorum
     Dominus in perpetuum.

Collect

O God, who founded all the
     commands of your sacred Law
upon love of you
     and of our neighbour,
grant that, by keeping your precepts,
we may merit to attain eternal life.
Through our Lord Jesus Christ,
     your Son,
who lives and reigns with you
     in the unity of the Holy Spirit,
one God, for ever and ever.

Collecta

Deus, qui sacræ legis
     omnia constituta
in tua et proximi dilectione posuisti,
da nobis, ut, tua præcepta servantes,
ad vitam mereamur
     pervenire perpetuam.
Per Dominum nostrum Iesum
     Christum Filium tuum,
qui tecum vivit et regnat
     in unitate Spiritus Sancti,
Deus, per omnia sæcula sæculorum.

FIRST READING

A reading from the book of Wisdom   2:12,17-20
Let us condemn him to a shameful death.

The godless say to themselves,
'Let us lie in wait for the virtuous man, since he annoys us
  and opposes our way of life,
  reproaches us for our breaches of the law
  and accuses us of playing false to our upbringing.
Let us see if what he says is true,
  let us observe what kind of end he himself will have.
If the virtuous man is God's son, God will take his part
  and rescue him from the clutches of his enemies.
Let us test him with cruelty and with torture,
  and thus explore this gentleness of his
  and put his endurance to the proof.
Let us condemn him to a shameful death
  since he will be looked after – we have his word for it.'

   The word of the Lord.

Responsorial Psalm   Ps 53:3-6,8. R. v.6

R. **The Lord upholds my life.**

   O God, save me by your name;
   by your power, uphold my cause.
   O God, hear my prayer;
   listen to the words of my mouth. R.

   For proud men have risen against me,
   ruthless men seek my life.
   They have no regard for God. R.

   But I have God for my help.
   The Lord upholds my life.
   I will sacrifice to you with willing heart
   and praise your name for it is good. R.

SECOND READING

A reading from the letter of St James   3:16-4:3
Peacemakers, when they work for peace, sow the seeds which will bear fruit in holiness.

Wherever you find jealousy and ambition, you find disharmony, and
wicked things of every kind being done; whereas the wisdom that comes
down from above is essentially something pure; it also makes for peace, and

is kindly and considerate, it is full of compassion and shows itself by doing good; nor is there any trace of partiality or hypocrisy in it. Peacemakers, when they work for peace, sow the seeds which will bear fruit in holiness.

Where do these wars and battles between yourselves first start? Isn't it precisely in the desires fighting inside your own selves? You want something and you haven't got it; so you are prepared to kill. You have an ambition that you cannot satisfy; so you fight to get your way by force. Why you don't have what you want is because you don't pray for it; when you do pray and don't get it, it is because you have not prayed properly, you have prayed for something to indulge your own desires.

The word of the Lord.

Gospel Acclamation   Jn 8:12

R. **Alleluia, alleluia!**
I am the light of the world, says the Lord,
anyone who follows me
will have the light of life.
R. **Alleluia!**

Or: Cf. 2 Th 2:14

R. **Alleluia, alleluia!**
Through the Good News God called us
to share the glory of our Lord Jesus Christ.
R. **Alleluia!**

GOSPEL

A reading from the holy Gospel according to Mark   9:30-37

The Son of Man will be delivered. If anyone wants to be first, he must make himself servant of all.

After leaving the mountain Jesus and his disciples made their way through Galilee; and he did not want anyone to know because he was instructing his disciples; he was telling them, 'The Son of Man will be delivered into the hands of men; they will put him to death; and three days after he has been put to death he will rise again.' But they did not understand what he said and were afraid to ask him.

They came to Capernaum, and when he was in the house he asked them, 'What were you arguing about on the road?' They said nothing because they had been arguing which of them was the greatest. So he sat down, called the

Twelve to him and said, 'If anyone wants to be first, he must make himself last of all and servant of all.' He then took a little child, set him in front of them put his arms round him, and said to them, 'Anyone who welcomes one of these little children in my name, welcomes me; and anyone who welcomes me welcomes not me but the one who sent me.'

The Gospel of the Lord.

Prayer over the Offerings

Receive with favour, O Lord, we pray,
the offerings of your people,
that what they profess
　　with devotion and faith
may be theirs through
　　these heavenly mysteries.
Through Christ our Lord.

Super oblata

Munera, quæsumus, Domine,
　　tuæ plebis propitiatus assume,
ut, quæ fidei pietate profitentur,
sacramentis cælestibus
　　apprehendant.
Per Christum Dominum nostrum.

Preface of Sundays in Ordinary Time I-VIII, pp.566-573.

Communion Antiphon Ps 118:4-5

You have laid down your precepts
　　to be carefully kept;
may my ways be firm in keeping
　　your statutes.

Ant. ad communionem

Tu mandasti mandata tua
　　custodiri nimis;
utinam dirigantur viæ meæ
ad custodiendas iustificationes tuas.

Or:　　　　　　　　　　Jn 10:14

I am the Good Shepherd,
　　says the Lord;
I know my sheep,
　　and mine know me.

Vel:

Ego sum pastor bonus,
　　dicit Dominus;
et cognosco oves meas,
　　et cognoscunt me meæ.

Prayer after Communion

Graciously raise up, O Lord,
those you renew
　　with this Sacrament,
that we may come to possess
　　your redemption
both in mystery and in the manner
　　of our life.
Through Christ our Lord.

Post communionem

Quos tuis, Domine,
　　reficis sacramentis,
continuis attolle benignus auxiliis,
ut redemptionis effectum
et mysteriis capiamus et moribus.
Per Christum Dominum nostrum.

TWENTY-SIXTH SUNDAY IN ORDINARY TIME
(YEAR B)

Entrance Antiphon Dn 3:31,29,30,43,42

ALL that you have done to us,
O Lord,
you have done with true judgement,
for we have sinned against you
and not obeyed
    your commandments.
But give glory to your name
and deal with us according
    to the bounty of your mercy.

Ant. ad introitum

OMNIA, quæ fecisti nobis,
Domine,
in vero iudicio fecisti,
    quia peccavimus tibi,
et mandatis tuis non obœdivimus;
sed da gloriam nomini tuo,
et fac nobiscum secundum
    multitudinem misericordiæ tuæ.

Collect

O God, who manifest
    your almighty power
above all by pardoning
    and showing mercy,
bestow, we pray, your grace
    abundantly upon us
and make those hastening to attain
    your promises
heirs to the treasures of heaven.
Through our Lord Jesus Christ,
    your Son,
who lives and reigns with you
    in the unity of the Holy Spirit,
one God, for ever and ever.

Collecta

Deus, qui omnipotentiam tuam
parcendo maxime
    et miserando manifestas,
multiplica super nos gratiam tuam,
ut, ad tua promissa currentes,
cælestium bonorum facias
    esse consortes.
Per Dominum nostrum Iesum
    Christum Filium tuum,
qui tecum vivit et regnat
    in unitate Spiritus Sancti,
Deus, per omnia sæcula sæculorum.

FIRST READING

A reading from the book of Numbers   11:25-29

Are you jealous on my account? If only the whole people of the Lord were prophets!

The Lord came down in the Cloud. He spoke with Moses, but took some of
the spirit that was on him and put it on the seventy elders. When the spirit
came on them they prophesied, but not again.

Two men had stayed back in the camp; one was called Eldad and the
other Medad. The spirit came down on them; though they had not gone to

the Tent, their names were enrolled among the rest. These began to prophesy in the camp. The young man ran to tell this to Moses, 'Look,' he said 'Eldad and Medad are prophesying in the camp.' Then said Joshua the son of Nun, who had served Moses from his youth, 'My Lord Moses, stop them!' Moses answered him, 'Are you jealous on my account? If only the whole people of the Lord were prophets, and the Lord gave his Spirit to them all!'

The word of the Lord.

Responsorial Psalm   Ps 18:8,10,12-14. R. v.9

R. **The precepts of the Lord gladden the heart.**

The law of the Lord is perfect,
it revives the soul.
The rule of the Lord is to be trusted,
it gives wisdom to the simple. R.

The fear of the Lord is holy,
abiding for ever.
The decrees of the Lord are truth
and all of them just. R.

So in them your servant finds instruction;
great reward is in their keeping.
But who can detect all his errors?
From hidden faults acquit me. R.

From presumption restrain your servant
and let it not rule me.
Then shall I be blameless,
clean from grave sin. R.

SECOND READING

A reading from the letter of St James   5:1-6

Your wealth is rotting.

An answer for the rich. Start crying, weep for the miseries that are coming to you. Your wealth is all rotting, your clothes are all eaten up by moths. All your gold and your silver are corroding away, and the same corrosion will be your own sentence, and eat into your body. It was a burning fire that you stored up as your treasure for the last days. Labourers mowed your fields, and you cheated them – listen to the wages that you kept back, calling out; realise that the cries of the reapers have reached the ears of the Lord of hosts. On earth you have had a life of comfort and luxury; in the time of slaughter you went on eating to your heart's content. It was you who condemned the innocent and killed them; they offered you no resistance.

The word of the Lord.

Gospel Acclamation   Cf. Jn 17:17

R. **Alleluia, alleluia!**

Your word is truth, O Lord,

consecrate us in the truth.

R. **Alleluia!**

GOSPEL

A reading from the holy Gospel according to Mark   9:38-43,45,47-48

Anyone who is not against us is for us. If your hand should cause you to sin, cut it off.

John said to Jesus, 'Master, we saw a man who is not one of us casting out devils in your name; and because he was not one of us we tried to stop him.' But Jesus said, 'You must not stop him: no one who works a miracle in my name is likely to speak evil of me. Anyone who is not against us is for us.

'If anyone gives you a cup of water to drink just because you belong to Christ, then I tell you solemnly, he will most certainly not lose his reward.

'But anyone who is an obstacle to bring down one of these little ones who have faith, would be better thrown into the sea with a great millstone round his neck. And if your hand should cause you to sin, cut it off; it is better for you to enter into life crippled, than to have two hands and go to hell, into the fire that cannot be put out. And if your foot should cause you to sin, cut it off; it is better for you to enter into life lame, than to have two feet and be thrown into hell. And if your eye should cause you to sin, tear it out; it is better for you to enter into the kingdom of God with one eye, than to have two eyes and be thrown into hell where their worm does not die nor their fire go out.'

The Gospel of the Lord.

Prayer over the Offerings	Super oblata
Grant us, O merciful God, that this our offering may find acceptance with you and that through it the wellspring of all blessing may be laid open before us. Through Christ our Lord.	Concede nobis, misericors Deus, ut hæc nostra oblatio tibi sit accepta, et per eam nobis fons omnis benedictionis aperiatur. Per Christum Dominum nostrum.

Preface of Sundays in Ordinary Time I-VIII, pp.566-573.

Communion Antiphon Cf.Ps118:49-50

Remember your word to your servant,
    O Lord,
by which you have given me hope.
This is my comfort when I am
    brought low.

Or: 1 Jn 3:16

By this we came to know
    the love of God:
that Christ laid down his life for us;
so we ought to lay down our lives
    for one another.

Ant. ad communionem

Memento verbi tui
    servo tuo, Domine,
in quo mihi spem dedisti;
hæc me consolata
    est in humilitate mea.

Vel:

In hoc cognovimus caritatem Dei:
quoniam ille animam suam
    pro nobis posuit;
et nos debemus pro fratribus
    animas ponere.

Prayer after Communion

May this heavenly mystery, O Lord,
restore us in mind and body,
that we may be coheirs in glory
    with Christ,
to whose suffering we are united
whenever we proclaim his Death.
Who lives and reigns
    for ever and ever.

Post communionem

Sit nobis, Domine,
    reparatio mentis et corporis
cæleste mysterium, ut simus eius
    in gloria coheredes,
cui, mortem ipsius
    annuntiando, compatimur.
Qui vivit et regnat
    in sæcula sæculorum.

TWENTY-SEVENTH SUNDAY IN ORDINARY TIME
(YEAR B)

Entrance Antiphon   Cf. Est 4:17

WITHIN your will, O Lord,
    all things are established,
and there is none that can resist
    your will.
For you have made all things,
    the heaven and the earth,
and all that is held within the circle
    of heaven;
you are the Lord of all.

Ant. ad introitum

IN voluntate tua, Domine,
    universa sunt posita,
et non est qui possit resistere
    voluntati tuæ.
Tu enim fecisti omnia,
    cælum et terram,
et universa quæ cæli
    ambitu continentur;
Dominus universorum tu es.

Collect

Almighty ever-living God,
who in the abundance
   of your kindness
surpass the merits and the desires
   of those who entreat you,
pour out your mercy upon us
to pardon what conscience dreads
and to give what prayer does
   not dare to ask.
Through our Lord Jesus Christ,
   your Son,
who lives and reigns with you
   in the unity of the Holy Spirit,
one God, for ever and ever.

Collecta

Omnipotens sempiterne Deus,
   qui abundantia pietatis tuæ
et merita supplicum excedis et vota,
effunde super nos
   misericordiam tuam,
ut dimittas quæ conscientia metuit,
et adicias quod oratio non præsumit.
Per Dominum nostrum
   Iesum Christum Filium tuum,
qui tecum vivit et regnat
   in unitate Spiritus Sancti,
Deus, per omnia sæcula sæculorum.

FIRST READING

A reading from the book of Genesis   2:18-24

They become one body.

The Lord God said, 'It is not good that the man should be alone. I will make him a helpmate.' So from the soil the Lord God fashioned all the wild beasts and all the birds of heaven. These he brought to the man to see what he would call them; each one was to bear the name the man would give it. The man gave names to all the cattle, all the birds of heaven and all the wild beasts. But no helpmate suitable for man was found for him. So the Lord God made the man fall into a deep sleep. And while he slept, he took one of his ribs and enclosed it in flesh. The Lord God built the rib he had taken from the man into a woman, and brought her to the man. The man exclaimed:

   'This at last is bone from my bones
   and flesh from my flesh!
   This is to be called woman,
   for this was taken from man.'

   This is why a man leaves his father and mother and joins himself to his wife, and they become one body.

   The word of the Lord.

Responsorial Psalm   Ps 127. R. v.5

R. **May the Lord bless us
   all the days of our lives.**

   O blessed are those who fear the Lord
   and walk in his ways!

By the labour of your hands you shall eat.
You will be happy and prosper. R.

Your wife will be like a fruitful vine
in the heart of your house;
your children like shoots of the olive,
around your table. R.

Indeed thus shall be blessed
the man who fears the Lord.
May the Lord bless you from Zion
in a happy Jerusalem
all the days of your life!
May you see your children's children.
On Israel, peace! R.

SECOND READING

A reading from the letter to the Hebrews   2:9-11

The one who sanctifies, and the ones who are sanctified, are of the same stock.

We see in Jesus one who was for a short while made lower than the angels and is now crowned with glory and splendour because he submitted to death; by God's grace he had to experience death for all mankind.

As it was his purpose to bring a great many of his sons into glory, it was appropriate that God, for whom everything exists and through whom everything exists, should make perfect, through suffering, the leader who would take them to their salvation. For the one who sanctifies, and the ones who are sanctified, are of the same stock; that is why he openly calls them brothers.

The word of the Lord.

Gospel Acclamation   Cf. Jn 17:17

R. **Alleluia, alleluia!**
Your word is truth, O Lord,
consecrate us in the truth.
R. **Alleluia!**

Or: 1 Jn 4:12

R. **Alleluia, alleluia!**
As long as we love one another
God will live in us
and his love will be complete in us.
R. **Alleluia!**

GOSPEL

A reading from the holy Gospel according to Mark   10:2-16

What God has united, man must not divide.

[Some Pharisees approached Jesus and asked, 'Is it against the law for a man to divorce his wife?' They were testing him. He answered them, 'What did Moses command you?' 'Moses allowed us' they said 'to draw up a writ of dismissal and so to divorce.' Then Jesus said to them, 'It was because you were so unteachable that he wrote this commandment for you. But from the beginning of creation God made them male and female. This is why a man must leave father and mother, and the two become one body. They are no longer two, therefore, but one body. So then, what God has united, man must not divide.' Back in the house the disciples questioned him again about this, and he said to them, 'The man who divorces his wife and marries another is guilty of adultery against her. And if a woman divorces her husband and marries another she is guilty of adultery too.']

People were bringing little children to him, for him to touch them. The disciples turned them away, but when Jesus saw this he was indignant and said to them, 'Let the little children come to me; do not stop them; for it is to such as these that the kingdom of God belongs. I tell you solemnly, anyone who does not welcome the kingdom of God like a little child will never enter it.' Then he put his arms round them, laid his hands on them and gave them his blessing.

[The Gospel of the Lord.]

Shorter Form, verses 2-12. Read between [ ]

Prayer over the Offerings	Super oblata
Accept, O Lord, we pray, the sacrifices instituted by your commands and, through the sacred mysteries, which we celebrate with dutiful service, graciously complete the sanctifying work by which you are pleased to redeem us. Through Christ our Lord.	Suscipe, quæsumus, Domine, sacrificia tuis instituta præceptis, et sacris mysteriis, quæ debitæ servitutis celebramus officio, sanctificationem tuæ nobis redemptionis dignanter adimple. Per Christum Dominum nostrum.

Preface of Sundays in Ordinary Time I-VIII, pp.566-573.

Communion Antiphon Lm 3:25	Ant. ad communionem

The Lord is good to those
    who hope in him,
to the soul that seeks him.
	Bonus est Dominus
	    sperantibus in eum,
	animæ quærenti illum.

Or: Cf. 1 Co 10:17	Vel:

Though many, we are one bread,
    one body,
for we all partake of the one Bread
    and one Chalice.
	Unus panis et unum corpus
	    multi sumus,
	omnes qui de uno pane et de uno
	    calice participamus.

Prayer after Communion	Post communionem

Grant us, almighty God,
that we may be refreshed
    and nourished
by the Sacrament which
    we have received,
so as to be transformed
    into what we consume.
Through Christ our Lord.
	Concede nobis, omnipotens Deus,
	ut de perceptis sacramentis
	    inebriemur atque pascamur,
	quatenus in id quod
	    sumimus transeamus.
	Per Christum Dominum nostrum.

TWENTY-EIGHTH SUNDAY IN ORDINARY TIME
(YEAR B)

Entrance Antiphon Ps 129:3-4	Ant. ad introitum

IF you, O Lord,
  should mark iniquities,
Lord, who could stand?
But with you is found forgiveness,
O God of Israel.
	SI iniquitates observaveris,
	  Domine,
	Domine, quis sustinebit?
	Quia apud te propitiatio est,
	    Deus Israel.

Collect	Collecta

May your grace, O Lord, we pray,
at all times go before us
    and follow after
and make us always determined
to carry out good works.
Through our Lord Jesus Christ,
    your Son,
who lives and reigns with you
    in the unity of the Holy Spirit,
one God, for ever and ever.
	Tua nos, quæsumus,
	    Domine, gratia
	semper et præveniat et sequatur,
	ac bonis operibus iugiter præstet
	    esse intentos.
	Per Dominum nostrum Iesum
	    Christum Filium tuum,
	qui tecum vivit et regnat
	    in unitate Spiritus Sancti,
	Deus, per omnia sæcula sæculorum.

FIRST READING

A reading from the book of Wisdom   7:7-11

Compared with wisdom, I held riches as nothing.

I prayed, and understanding was given me;
I entreated, and the spirit of Wisdom came to me.
I esteemed her more than sceptres and thrones;
compared with her, I held riches as nothing.
I reckoned no priceless stone to be her peer,
for compared with her, all gold is a pinch of sand,
and beside her silver ranks as mud.
I loved her more than health or beauty,
preferred her to the light,
since her radiance never sleeps.
In her company all good things came to me,
at her hands riches not to be numbered.

  The word of the Lord.

Responsorial Psalm   Ps 89:12-17. R. v.14

R. **Fill us with your love that we may rejoice.**

  Make us know the shortness of our life
  that we may gain wisdom of heart.
  Lord, relent! Is your anger for ever?
  Show pity to your servants. R.

  In the morning, fill us with your love;
  we shall exult and rejoice all our days.
  Give us joy to balance our affliction
  for the years when we knew misfortune. R.

  Show forth your work to your servants;
  let your glory shine on their children.
  Let the favour of the Lord be upon us:
  give success to the work of our hands. R.

SECOND READING

A reading from the letter to the Hebrews   4:12-13

The word of God can judge secret emotions and thoughts.

The word of God is something alive and active: it cuts like any double-edged sword but more finely: it can slip through the place where the soul is divided from the spirit, or joints from the marrow; it can judge the secret emotions and thoughts. No created thing can hide from him; everything is uncovered and open to the eyes of the one to whom we must give account of ourselves.

The word of the Lord.

Gospel Acclamation   Cf. Mt 11:25
R. **Alleluia, alleluia!**
Blessed are you, Father,
Lord of heaven and earth,
for revealing the mysteries of the kingdom
to mere children.
R. **Alleluia!**

Or: Mt 5:3

R. **Alleluia, alleluia!**
How happy the poor in spirit;
theirs is the kingdom of heaven.
R. **Alleluia!**

GOSPEL

A reading from the holy Gospel according to Mark   10:17-30
Go and sell everything you own and follow me.

[Jesus was setting out on a journey when a man ran up, knelt before him and put this question to him, 'Good master, what must I do to inherit eternal life?' Jesus said to him, 'Why do you call me good? No one is good but God alone. You know the commandments: You must not kill; You must not commit adultery, You must not steal; You must not bring false witness; You must not defraud; Honour your father and mother.' And he said to him, 'Master, I have kept all these from my earliest days.' Jesus looked steadily at him and loved him, and he said, 'There is one thing you lack. Go and sell everything you own and give the money to the poor, and you will have treasure in heaven; then come, follow me.' But his face fell at these words and he went away sad, for he was a man of great wealth.

Jesus looked round and said to his disciples, 'How hard it is for those who have riches to enter the kingdom of God!' The disciples were astounded by these words, but Jesus insisted, 'My children,' he said to them, 'how hard it is to enter the kingdom of God! It is easier for a camel to pass through the eye of a needle than for a rich man to enter the kingdom of God.' They were more astonished than ever. 'In that case' they said to one another 'who can be saved?' Jesus gazed at them. 'For men' he said 'it is impossible, but not for God: because everything is possible for God.']

Peter took this up. 'What about us?' he asked him. 'We have left everything and followed you.' Jesus said, 'I tell you solemnly, there is no one who has left house, brothers, sisters, father, children or land for my sake and for the sake of the gospel who will not be repaid a hundred times over, houses, brothers, sisters, mothers, children and land – not without persecutions – now in this present time and, in the world to come, eternal life.'

[The Gospel of the Lord.]

Shorter Form, verses 17-27. Read between [ ]

Prayer over the Offerings

Accept, O Lord, the prayers
    of your faithful
with the sacrificial offerings,
that, through these acts
    of devotedness,
we may pass over to the glory
    of heaven.
Through Christ our Lord.

Super oblata

Suscipe, Domine,
fidelium preces cum
    oblationibus hostiarum,
ut, per hæc piæ devotionis officia,
ad cælestem gloriam transeamus.
Per Christum Dominum nostrum.

Preface of Sundays in Ordinary Time I-VIII, pp.566-573.

Communion Antiphon Cf. Ps 33:11

The rich suffer want and go hungry,
but those who seek the Lord
    lack no blessing.
Or: 1 Jn 3:2
When the Lord appears,
    we shall be like him,
for we shall see him as he is.

Ant. ad communionem

Divites eguerunt et esurierunt;
quærentes autem Dominum
    non minuentur omni bono.
Vel:
Cum apparuerit Dominus,
    similes ei erimus,
quoniam videbimus eum sicuti est.

Prayer after Communion

We entreat your majesty most
    humbly, O Lord,
that, as you feed us
    with the nourishment
which comes from the most holy
    Body and Blood of your Son,
so you may make us sharers
    of his divine nature.
Who lives and reigns
    for ever and ever.

Post communionem

Maiestatem tuam, Domine,
    suppliciter deprecamur,
ut, sicut nos Corporis
    et Sanguinis sacrosancti
pascis alimento,
ita divinæ naturæ facias
    esse consortes.
Per Christum Dominum nostrum.

TWENTY-NINTH SUNDAY IN ORDINARY TIME
(YEAR B)

Entrance Antiphon   Cf. Ps 16:6,8

TO you I call; for you will surely heed me, O God;
turn your ear to me; hear my words.
Guard me as the apple of your eye;
in the shadow of your wings
    protect me.

Ant. ad introitum

EGO clamavi,
  quoniam exaudisti me, Deus;
inclina aurem tuam,
    et exaudi verba mea.
Custodi me, Domine,
    ut pupillam oculi;
sub umbra alarum tuarum
    protege me.

Collect

Almighty ever-living God,
grant that we may always conform
    our will to yours
and serve your majesty in sincerity
    of heart.
Through our Lord Jesus Christ,
    your Son,
who lives and reigns with you
    in the unity of the Holy Spirit,
one God, for ever and ever.

Collecta

Omnipotens sempiterne Deus,
fac nos tibi semper et devotam
    gerere voluntatem,
et maiestati tuæ sincero
    corde servire.
Per Dominum nostrum Iesum
    Christum Filium tuum,
qui tecum vivit et regnat
    in unitate Spiritus Sancti,
Deus, per omnia sæcula sæculorum.

FIRST READING

A reading from the prophet Isaiah   53:10-11

If he offers his life in atonement, he shall see his heirs, he shall have a long life.

The Lord has been pleased to crush his servant with suffering.
If he offers his life in atonement,
he shall see his heirs, he shall have a long life
and through him what the Lord wishes will be done.

His soul's anguish over
he shall see the light and be content.
By his sufferings shall my servant justify many, taking
their faults on himself.

    The word of the Lord.

Responsorial Psalm   Ps 32:4-5,18-20,22. R. v.2

R. **May your love be upon us, O Lord,**
   as we place all our hope in you.

The word of the Lord is faithful
and all his works to be trusted.
The Lord loves justice and right
and fills the earth with his love. R.

The Lord looks on those who revere him,
on those who hope in his love,
to rescue their souls from death,
to keep them alive in famine. R.

Our soul is waiting for the Lord.
The Lord is our help and our shield.
May your love be upon us, O Lord,
as we place all our hope in you. R.

SECOND READING

A reading from the letter to the Hebrews   4:14-16
Let us be confident in approaching the throne of grace.

Since in Jesus, the Son of God, we have the supreme high priest who has
gone through to the highest heaven, we must never let go of the faith that
we have professed. For it is not as if we had a high priest who was incapable
of feeling our weaknesses with us; but we have one who has been tempted
in every way that we are, though he is without sin. Let us be confident,
then, in approaching the throne of grace, that we shall have mercy from
him and find grace when we are in need of help.

    The word of the Lord.

Gospel Acclamation   Jn 14:6

R. **Alleluia, alleluia!**
I am the Way, the Truth and the Life, says the Lord;
no one can come to the Father except through me.
R. **Alleluia!**

Or: Mk 10:45

R. **Alleluia, alleluia!**
The Son of Man came to save
and to give his life as a ransom for many.
R. **Alleluia!**

GOSPEL

A reading from the holy Gospel according to Mark   10:35-45

The Son of Man came to give his life as a ransom for many.

James and John, the sons of Zebedee, approached Jesus. 'Master,' they said to him 'we want you to do us a favour.' He said to them, 'What is it you want me to do for you?' They said to him, 'Allow us to sit one at your right hand and the other at your left in your glory.' 'You do not know what you are asking' Jesus said to them. 'Can you drink the cup that I must drink, or be baptised with the baptism with which I must be baptised?' They replied, 'We can.' Jesus said to them, 'The cup that I must drink you shall drink, and with the baptism with which I must be baptised you shall be baptised, but as for seats at my right hand or my left, these are not mine to grant; they belong to those to whom they have been allotted.'

When the other ten heard this they began to feel indignant with James and John, so [Jesus called them to him and said to them, 'You know that among the pagans their so-called rulers lord it over them, and their great men make their authority felt. This is not to happen among you. No; anyone who wants to become great among you must be your servant, and anyone who wants to be first among you must be slave to all. For the Son of Man himself did not come to be served but to serve, and to give his life as a ransom for many.'

The Gospel of the Lord.]

Shorter Form, verses 42-45. Read between [ ]

Prayer over the Offerings	Super oblata
Grant us, Lord, we pray,	Tribue nos, Domine, quæsumus,
a sincere respect for your gifts,	donis tuis libera mente servire,
that, through the purifying action of your grace,	ut, tua purificante nos gratia, iisdem quibus famulamur
we may be cleansed by the very mysteries we serve.	mysteriis emundemur.
Through Christ our Lord.	Per Christum Dominum nostrum.

Preface of Sundays in Ordinary Time I-VIII, pp.566-573.

Communion Antiphon Cf. Ps 32:18-19	Ant. ad communionem
Behold, the eyes of the Lord	Ecce oculi Domini super timentes eum,
are on those who fear him,	et in eis qui sperant super
who hope in his merciful love,	misericordia eius;
to rescue their souls from death,	ut eruat a morte animas eorum,
to keep them alive in famine.	et alat eos in fame.

Or: Mk 10:45

The Son of Man has come
to give his life as a ransom for many.

Prayer after Communion

Grant, O Lord, we pray,
that, benefiting from participation
    in heavenly things,
we may be helped by what you give
    in this present age
and prepared for the gifts
    that are eternal.
Through Christ our Lord.

Vel:

Filius hominis venit,
ut daret animam suam
    redemptionem pro multis.

Post communionem

Fac nos, quæsumus, Domine,
cælestium rerum
    frequentatione proficere,
ut et temporalibus
    beneficiis adiuvemur,
et erudiamur æternis.
Per Christum Dominum nostrum.

THIRTIETH SUNDAY IN ORDINARY TIME
(YEAR B)

Entrance Antiphon   Cf. Ps 104:3-4

LET the hearts that seek
the Lord rejoice;
turn to the Lord and his strength;
constantly seek his face.

Collect

Almighty ever-living God,
increase our faith, hope and charity,
and make us love
    what you command,
so that we may merit
    what you promise.
Through our Lord Jesus Christ,
    your Son,
who lives and reigns with you
    in the unity of the Holy Spirit,
one God, for ever and ever.

Ant. ad introitum

LÆTETUR cor
quærentium Dominum.
Quærite Dominum et confirmamini,
quærite faciem eius semper.

Collecta

Omnipotens sempiterne Deus,
da nobis fidei,
    spei et caritatis augmentum,
et, ut mereamur assequi
    quod promittis,
fac nos amare quod præcipis.
Per Dominum nostrum Iesum
    Christum Filium tuum,
qui tecum vivit et regnat
    in unitate Spiritus Sancti,
Deus, per omnia sæcula sæculorum.

FIRST READING

A reading from the prophet Jeremiah   31:7-9

I will comfort the blind and the lame as I lead them back.

The Lord says this:

Shout with joy for Jacob!
Hail the chief of nations!
Proclaim! Praise! Shout:
'The Lord has saved his people,
the remnant of Israel!'
See, I will bring them back
from the land of the North
and gather them from the far ends of earth;
all of them: the blind and the lame,
women with child, women in labour:
a great company returning here.
They had left in tears,
I will comfort them as I lead them back;
I will guide them to streams of water,
by a smooth path where they will not stumble.
For I am a father to Israel,
and Ephraim is my first-born son.

The word of the Lord.

Responsorial Psalm   Ps 125. R. v.3

R. **What marvels the Lord worked for us!**
   Indeed we were glad.

When the Lord delivered Zion from bondage,
it seemed like a dream.
Then was our mouth filled with laughter,
on our lips there were songs. R.

The heathens themselves said: 'What marvels
the Lord worked for them!'
What marvels the Lord worked for us!
Indeed we were glad. R.

Deliver us, O Lord, from our bondage
as streams in dry land.
Those who are sowing in tears
will sing when they reap. R.

They go out, they go out, full of tears,
carrying seed for the sowing:
they come back, they come back, full of song,
carrying their sheaves. R.

SECOND READING

A reading from the letter to the Hebrews   5:1-6

You are a priest of the order of Melchizedek, and for ever.

Every high priest has been taken out of mankind and is appointed to act for men in their relations with God, to offer gifts and sacrifices for sins; and so he can sympathise with those who are ignorant or uncertain because he too lives in the limitations of weakness. That is why he has to make sin offerings for himself as well as for the people. No one takes this honour on himself, but each one is called by God, as Aaron was. Nor did Christ give himself the glory of becoming high priest, but he had it from the one who said to him: You are my son, today I have become your father, and in another text: You are a priest of the order of Melchizedek, and for ever.

The word of the Lord.

Gospel Acclamation   Jn 8:12

R. **Alleluia, alleluia!**
I am the light of the world, says the Lord,
anyone who follows me
will have the light of life.
R. **Alleluia!**

Or: Cf. 2 Tm 1:10

R. **Alleluia, alleluia!**
Our Saviour Christ Jesus abolished death,
and he has proclaimed life through the Good News.
R. **Alleluia!**

GOSPEL

A reading from the holy Gospel according to Mark   10:46-52

Master, let me see again.

As Jesus left Jericho with his disciples and a large crowd, Bartimaeus (that is, the son of Timaeus), a blind beggar, was sitting at the side of the road. When he heard that it was Jesus of Nazareth, he began to shout and to say, 'Son of David, Jesus, have pity on me.' And many of them scolded him and told him to keep quiet, but he only shouted all the louder, 'Son of David, have pity on me.' Jesus stopped and said, 'Call him here.' So they called the blind man. 'Courage,' they said 'get up; he is calling you.' So throwing off his cloak, he jumped up and went to Jesus. Then Jesus spoke, 'What do you want me to do for you?' 'Rabbuni,' the blind man said to him 'Master, let me see again.' Jesus said to him, 'Go; your faith has saved you.' And immediately his sight returned and he followed him along the road.

The Gospel of the Lord.

Prayer over the Offerings
Look, we pray, O Lord,
on the offerings we make
   to your majesty,
that whatever is done by us
   in your service
may be directed above all
   to your glory.
Through Christ our Lord.

Super oblata
Respice, quæsumus, Domine,
munera quæ tuæ
   offerimus maiestati,
ut, quod nostro servitio geritur,
ad tuam gloriam potius dirigatur.
Per Christum Dominum nostrum.

Preface of Sundays in Ordinary Time I-VIII, pp.566-573.

Communion Antiphon Cf. Ps 19:6
We will ring out our joy at your
   saving help
and exult in the name of our God.

Ant. ad communionem
Lætabimur in salutari tuo,
et in nomine Dei
   nostri magnificabimur.

Or: Ep 5:2
Christ loved us and gave himself up
   for us,
as a fragrant offering to God.

Vel:
Christus dilexit nos, et tradidit
   semetipsum pro nobis,
oblationem Deo
   in odorem suavitatis.

Prayer after Communion
May your Sacraments, O Lord,
   we pray,
perfect in us what lies within them,
that what we now celebrate in signs
we may one day possess in truth.
Through Christ our Lord.

Post communionem
Perficiant in nobis,
   Domine, quæsumus,
tua sacramenta quod continent,
ut, quæ nunc specie gerimus,
rerum veritate capiamus.
Per Christum Dominum nostrum.

THIRTY-FIRST SUNDAY IN ORDINARY TIME
(YEAR B)

Entrance Antiphon Cf. Ps 37:22-23
FORSAKE me not, O Lord,
   my God;
be not far from me!
Make haste and come to my help,
O Lord, my strong salvation!

Ant. ad introitum
NE derelinquas me,
   Domine Deus meus,
ne discedas a me;
   intende in adiutorium meum,
Domine, virtus salutis meæ.

Collect	Collecta
Almighty and merciful God,	Omnipotens et misericors Deus,
by whose gift your faithful offer you	de cuius munere venit,
right and praiseworthy service,	ut tibi a fidelibus tuis digne
grant, we pray,	et laudabiliter serviatur,
that we may hasten	tribue, quæsumus, nobis,
without stumbling	ut ad promissiones tuas sine
to receive the things you	offensione curramus.
have promised.	Per Dominum nostrum Iesum
Through our Lord Jesus Christ,	Christum Filium tuum,
your Son,	qui tecum vivit et regnat
who lives and reigns with you	in unitate Spiritus Sancti,
in the unity of the Holy Spirit,	Deus, per omnia sæcula sæculorum.
one God, for ever and ever.	

FIRST READING

A reading from the book of Deuteronomy   6:2-6

Listen, Israel: You shall love the Lord Your God with all your heart.

Moses said to the people: 'If you fear the Lord your God all the days of your life and if you keep all his laws and commandments which I lay on you, you will have a long life, you and your son and your grandson. Listen then, Israel, keep and observe what will make you prosper and give you great increase, as the Lord God of your fathers has promised you, giving you a land where milk and honey flow.

'Listen, Israel: The Lord our God is the one Lord. You shall love the Lord your God with all your heart, with all your soul, with all your strength. Let these words I urge on you today be written on your heart.'

The word of the Lord.

Responsorial Psalm   Ps 17:2-4,47,51. R. v.2

R. **I love you, Lord, my strength**.

I love you, Lord, my strength,
my rock, my fortress, my saviour.
My God is the rock where I take refuge;
my shield, my mighty help, my stronghold.
The Lord is worthy of all praise:
when I call I am saved from my foes. R.

Long life to the Lord, my rock!
Praised be the God who saves me.
He has given great victories to his king
and shown his love for his anointed. R.

SECOND READING

A reading from the letter to the Hebrews   7:23-28

Because he remains for ever, Christ can never lose his priesthood.

There used to be a great number of priests under the former covenant, because death put an end to each one of them; but this one, Christ, because he remains for ever, can never lose his priesthood. It follows, then, that his power to save is utterly certain, since he is living for ever to intercede for all who come to God through him.

To suit us, the ideal high priest would have to be holy, innocent and uncontaminated, beyond the influence of sinners, and raised up above the heavens; one who would not need to offer sacrifices every day, as the other high priests do for their own sins and then for those of the people, because he has done this once and for all by offering himself. The Law appoints high priests who are men subject to weakness; but the promise on oath, which came after the Law, appointed the Son who is made perfect for ever.

The word of the Lord.

Gospel Acclamation   Cf. Jn 6:63,68

R. **Alleluia, alleluia!**
Your words are spirit, Lord,
and they are life:
you have the message of eternal life.
R. **Alleluia!**

Or: Jn 14:23

R. **Alleluia, alleluia!**
If anyone loves me he will keep my word,
and my Father will love him,
and we shall come to him.
R. **Alleluia!**

GOSPEL

A reading from the holy Gospel according to Mark   12:28-34

This is the first commandment. The second is like it.

One of the scribes came up to Jesus and put a question to him, 'Which is the first of all the commandments?' Jesus replied, 'This is the first: Listen, Israel, the Lord our God is the one Lord, and you must love the Lord your God with all your heart, with all your soul, with all your mind and with all your strength. The second is this: You must love your neighbour as yourself. There is no commandment greater than these.' The scribe said to him, 'Well spoken, Master; what you have said is true: that he is one and there is no other. To love with all your heart, with all your understanding and strength, and to love your neighbour as yourself, this is far more important than any holocaust or sacrifice.' Jesus, seeing how wisely he had spoken said, 'You are not far from the kingdom of God.' And after that no one dared to question him any more.

The Gospel of the Lord.

Prayer over the Offerings	Super oblata
May these sacrificial offerings, O Lord, become for you a pure oblation, and for us a holy outpouring of your mercy. Through Christ our Lord.	Fiat hoc sacrificium, Domine, oblatio tibi munda, et nobis misericordiæ tuæ sancta largitio. Per Christum Dominum nostrum.

Preface of Sundays in Ordinary Time I-VIII, pp.566-573.

Communion Antiphon Cf. Ps 15:11	Ant. ad communionem
You will show me the path of life, the fullness of joy in your presence, O Lord.	Notas mihi fecisti vias vitæ, adimplebis me lætitia cum vultu tuo, Domine.

Or: Jn 6:58	Vel:
Just as the living Father sent me and I have life because of the Father, so whoever feeds on me shall have life because of me, says the Lord.	Sicut misit me vivens Pater, et ego vivo propter Patrem, et qui manducat me, et ipse vivet propter me, dicit Dominus.

Prayer after Communion	Post communionem
May the working of your power, O Lord, increase in us, we pray, so that, renewed by these heavenly Sacraments, we may be prepared by your gift for receiving what they promise. Through Christ our Lord.	Augeatur in nobis, quæsumus, Domine, tuæ virtutis operatio, ut, refecti cælestibus sacramentis, ad eorum promissa capienda tuo munere præparemur. Per Christum Dominum nostrum.

THIRTY-SECOND SUNDAY IN ORDINARY TIME
(YEAR B)

Entrance Antiphon   Ps 87:3

LET my prayer come
into your presence.
Incline your ear
   to my cry for help, O Lord.

Ant. ad introitum

INTRET oratio mea
in conspectu tuo;
inclina aurem tuam
   ad precem meam, Domine.

Collect

Almighty and merciful God,
graciously keep from us all adversity,
so that, unhindered in mind
   and body alike,
we may pursue in freedom of heart
the things that are yours.
Through our Lord Jesus Christ,
   your Son,
who lives and reigns with you
   in the unity of the Holy Spirit,
one God, for ever and ever.

Collecta

Omnipotens et misericors Deus,
universa nobis adversantia
   propitiatus exclude,
ut, mente et corpore pariter expediti,
quæ tua sunt liberis
   mentibus exsequamur.
Per Dominum nostrum Iesum
   Christum Filium tuum,
qui tecum vivit et regnat
   in unitate Spiritus Sancti,
Deus, per omnia sæcula sæculorum.

FIRST READING

A reading from the first book of the Kings   17:10-16

The widow made a little scone from her meal and brought it to Elijah.

Elijah the Prophet went off to Sidon. And when he reached the city gate, there was a widow gathering sticks; addressing her he said, 'Please bring a little water in a vessel for me to drink.' She was setting off to bring it when he called after her. 'Please' he said 'bring me a scrap of bread in your hand.' 'As the Lord your God lives,' she replied 'I have no baked bread, but only a handful of meal in a jar and a little oil in a jug; I am just gathering a stick or two to go and prepare this for myself and my son to eat, and then we shall die.' But Elijah said to her, 'Do not be afraid, go and do as you have said; but first make a little scone of it for me and bring it to me, and then make some for yourself and for your son. For thus the Lord speaks, the God of Israel:

"Jar of meal shall not be spent,
jug of oil shall not be emptied,
before the day when the Lord sends
rain on the face of the earth."'

The woman went and did as Elijah told her and they ate the food, she, himself and her son. The jar of meal was not spent nor the jug of oil emptied, just as the Lord had foretold through Elijah.

The word of the Lord.

Responsial Psalm   Ps 145:7-10. R. v.2

R. **My soul, give praise to the Lord.**
   Or: **Alleluia!**

It is the Lord who keeps faith for ever,
who is just to those who are oppressed.
It is he who gives bread to the hungry,
the Lord, who sets prisoners free. R.

It is the Lord who gives sight to the blind,
who raises up those who are bowed down.
It is the Lord who loves the just,
the Lord, who protects the stranger. R.

The Lord upholds the widow and orphan
but thwarts the path of the wicked.
The Lord will reign for ever,
Zion's God, from age to age. R.

SECOND READING

A reading from the letter to the Hebrews   9:24-28

Christ offers himself only once to take the faults of many on himself.

It is not as though Christ had entered a man-made sanctuary which was only modelled on the real one; but it was heaven itself, so that he could appear in the actual presence of God on our behalf. And he does not have to offer himself again and again, like the high priest going into the sanctuary year after year with the blood that is not his own, or else he would have had to suffer over and over again since the world began. Instead of that, he has made his appearance once and for all, now at the end of the last age, to do away with sin by sacrificing himself. Since men only die once, and after that comes judgement, so Christ, too, offers himself only once to take the faults of many on himself, and when he appears a second time, it will not be to deal with sin but to reward with salvation those who are waiting for him.

The word of the Lord.

Gospel Acclamation   Rv 2:10

R. **Alleluia, alleluia!**
Even if you have to die, says the Lord,
keep faithful, and I will give you
the crown of life.
R. **Alleluia!**

Or: Mt 5:3

R. **Alleluia, alleluia!**
How happy are the poor in spirit;
theirs is the kingdom of heaven.
R. **Alleluia!**

GOSPEL

A reading from the holy Gospel according to Mark   12:38-44
This poor widow has put in more than all.

In his teaching Jesus said, 'Beware of the scribes who like to walk about in long robes, to be greeted obsequiously in the market squares, to take the front seats in the synagogues and the places of honour at banquets; these are the men who swallow the property of widows, while making a show of lengthy prayers. The more severe will be the sentence they receive.'

[He sat down opposite the treasury and watched the people putting money into the treasury, and many of the rich put in a great deal. A poor widow came and put in two small coins, the equivalent of a penny. Then he called his disciples and said to them, 'I tell you solemnly, this poor widow has put in more than all who have contributed to the treasury; for they have all put in money they had over, but she from the little she had has put in everything she possessed, all she had to live on.'

The Gospel of the Lord.]

Shorter Form, verses 41-44. Read between [ ]

Prayer over the Offerings	Super oblata
Look with favour, we pray, O Lord, upon the sacrificial gifts offered here, that, celebrating in mystery the Passion of your Son, we may honour it with loving devotion. Through Christ our Lord.	Sacrificiis præsentibus, Domine, quæsumus, intende placatus, ut, quod passionis Filii tui mysterio gerimus, pio consequamur affectu. Per Christum Dominum nostrum.

Preface of Sundays in Ordinary Time I-VIII, pp.566-573.

Communion Antiphon Ps 22:1-2	Ant. ad communionem

The Lord is my shepherd;
   there is nothing I shall want.
Fresh and green are the pastures
   where he gives me repose,
near restful waters he leads me.
	Dominus regit me,
	   et nihil mihi deerit;
	in loco pascuæ ibi me collocavit,
	super aquam refectionis
	   educavit me.

Or: Lk 24:35	Vel:

The disciples recognised the Lord
   Jesus in the breaking of bread.
	Cognoverunt discipuli Dominum
	   Iesum in fractione panis.

Prayer after Communion	Post communionem

Nourished by this sacred gift,
   O Lord,
we give you thanks and beseech
   your mercy,
that, by the pouring forth
   of your Spirit,
the grace of integrity may endure
in those your heavenly power
   has entered.
Through Christ our Lord.
	Gratias tibi, Domine, referimus
	   sacro munere vegetati,
	tuam clementiam implorantes,
	ut, per infusionem Spiritus tui,
	in quibus cælestis virtus introivit,
	sinceritatis gratia perseveret.
	Per Christum Dominum nostrum.

THIRTY-THIRD SUNDAY IN ORDINARY TIME
(YEAR B)

Entrance Antiphon Jer 29:11,12,14	Ant. ad introitum

THE Lord said: I think thoughts
of peace and not of affliction.
You will call upon me,
   and I will answer you,
and I will lead back your captives
   from every place.
	DICIT Dominus:
	Ego cogito cogitationes pacis
	   et non afflictionis;
	invocabitis me, et ego exaudiam vos,
	et reducam captivitatem vestram
	   de cunctis locis.

Collect

Grant us, we pray, O Lord our God,
the constant gladness of being
    devoted to you,
for it is full and lasting happiness
to serve with constancy
the author of all that is good.
Through our Lord Jesus Christ,
    your Son,
who lives and reigns with you
    in the unity of the Holy Spirit,
one God, for ever and ever.

Collecta

Da nobis, quæsumus,
    Domine Deus noster,
in tua semper devotione gaudere,
quia perpetua est et plena felicitas,
si bonorum omnium iugiter
    serviamus auctori.
Per Dominum nostrum Iesum
    Christum Filium tuum,
qui tecum vivit et regnat
    in unitate Spiritus Sancti,
Deus, per omnia sæcula sæculorum.

FIRST READING

A reading from the prophet Daniel   12:1-3

When that time comes, your own people will be spared.

'At that time Michael will stand up, the great prince who mounts guard over your people. There is going to be a time of great distress, unparalleled since nations first came into existence. When that time comes, your own people will be spared, all those whose names are found written in the Book. Of those who lie sleeping in the dust of the earth many will awake, some to everlasting life, some to shame and everlasting disgrace. The learned will shine as brightly as the vault of heaven, and those who have instructed many in virtue, as bright as stars for all eternity.'

The word of the Lord.

Responsorial Psalm   Ps 15:5,8-11. R. v.1

R. **Preserve me, God, I take refuge in you.**

O Lord, it is you who are my portion and cup;
it is you yourself who are my prize.
I keep the Lord ever in my sight:
since he is at my right hand, I shall stand firm. R.

And so my heart rejoices, my soul is glad;
even my body shall rest in safety.
For you will not leave my soul among the dead,
nor let your beloved know decay. R.

You will show me the path of life,
the fullness of joy in your presence,
at your right hand happiness for ever. R.

SECOND READING

A reading from the letter to the Hebrews   10:11-14,18

By virtue of one single offering, he has achieved the eternal perfection of all whom he is sanctifying.

All the priests stand at their duties every day, offering over and over again the same sacrifices which are quite incapable of taking sins away. Christ, on the other hand, has offered one single sacrifice for sins, and then taken his place for ever, at the right hand of God, where he is now waiting until his enemies are made into a footstool for him. By virtue of that one single offering, he has achieved the eternal perfection of all whom he is sanctifying. When all sins have been forgiven, there can be no more sin offerings.

The word of the Lord.

Gospel Acclamation   Mt 24:42,44

R. **Alleluia, alleluia!**
Stay awake and stand ready,
because you do not know the hour
when the Son of Man is coming.
R. **Alleluia!**

Or: Lk 21:36

R. **Alleluia, alleluia!**
Stay awake, praying at all times
for the strength to stand with confidence
before the Son of Man.
R. **Alleluia!**

GOSPEL

A reading from the holy Gospel according to Mark   13:24-32

He will gather his chosen from the four winds.

Jesus said to his disciples: 'In those days, after the time of distress, the sun will be darkened, the moon will lose its brightness, the stars will come falling from heaven and the powers in the heavens will be shaken. And then they will see the Son of Man coming in the clouds with great power and glory; then too he will send the angels to gather his chosen from the four winds, from the ends of the world to the ends of heaven.

'Take the fig tree as a parable: as soon as its twigs grow supple and its leaves come out, you know that summer is near. So with you when you see these things happening: know that he is near, at the very gates. I tell you solemnly, before this generation has passed away all these things will have taken place. Heaven and earth will pass away, but my words will not pass away.

'But as for that day or hour, nobody knows it, neither the angels of heaven, nor the Son; no one but the Father.'

The Gospel of the Lord.

Prayer over the Offerings	Super oblata

Grant, O Lord, we pray,
that what we offer in the sight
   of your majesty
may obtain for us the grace
   of being devoted to you
and gain us the prize
   of everlasting happiness.
Through Christ our Lord.
	Concede, quæsumus, Domine,
	ut oculis tuæ maiestatis
	   munus oblatum
	et gratiam nobis
	   devotionis obtineat,
	et effectum beatæ
	   perennitatis acquirat.
	Per Christum Dominum nostrum.

Preface of Sundays in Ordinary Time I-VIII, pp.566-573.

Communion Antiphon Ps 72:28	Ant. ad communionem
To be near God is my happiness, to place my hope in God the Lord.	Mihi autem adhærere Deo bonum est, ponere in Domino Deo spem meam.

Or: Mk 11:23-24	Vel:

Amen, I say to you:
   Whatever you ask in prayer,
believe that you will receive,
and it shall be given to you,
   says the Lord.
	Amen dico vobis,
	   quidquid orantes petitis,
	credite quia accipietis, et fiet vobis,
	   dicit Dominus.

Prayer after Communion	Post communionem

We have partaken of the gifts
   of this sacred mystery,
humbly imploring, O Lord,
that what your Son commanded
   us to do
in memory of him
may bring us growth in charity.
Through Christ our Lord.
	Sumpsimus, Domine,
	   sacri dona mysterii,
	humiliter deprecantes,
	ut, quæ in sui commemorationem
	nos Filius tuus facere præcepit,
	in nostræ proficiant
	   caritatis augmentum.
	Per Christum Dominum nostrum.

OUR LORD JESUS CHRIST, KING OF THE UNIVERSE (YEAR B)

Solemnity

Entrance Antiphon   Rv 5:12; 1:6

HOW worthy is the Lamb
who was slain,
to receive power and divinity,
and wisdom and strength
   and honour.
To him belong glory and power
   for ever and ever.

Ant. ad introitum

DIGNUS est Agnus,
qui occisus est,
accipere virtutem et divinitatem
et sapientiam et fortitudinem
   et honorem.
Ipsi gloria et imperium
   in sæcula sæculorum.

The Gloria in excelsis (Glory to God in the highest) is said.

Collect

Almighty ever-living God,
whose will is to restore all things
in your beloved Son,
   the King of the universe,
grant, we pray,
that the whole creation,
   set free from slavery,
may render your majesty service
and ceaselessly proclaim your praise.
Through our Lord Jesus Christ,
   your Son,
who lives and reigns with you
   in the unity of the Holy Spirit,
one God, for ever and ever.

Collecta

Omnipotens sempiterne Deus,
qui in dilecto Filio tuo,
   universorum Rege,
omnia instaurare voluisti,
concede propitius,
ut tota creatura, a servitute liberata,
tuæ maiestati deserviat ac te sine
   fine collaudet.
Per Dominum nostrum Iesum
   Christum Filium tuum,
qui tecum vivit et regnat
   in unitate Spiritus Sancti,
Deus, per omnia sæcula sæculorum.

FIRST READING

A reading from the prophet Daniel   7:13-14

His sovereignty is an eternal sovereignty.

I gazed into the visions of the night.
And I saw, coming on the clouds of heaven,
one like a son of man.

He came to the one of great age
and was led into his presence.
On him was conferred sovereignty,
glory and kingship,
and men of all peoples, nations and languages became his servants.
His sovereignty is an eternal sovereignty
which shall never pass away,
nor will his empire ever be destroyed.

The word of the Lord.

Responsorial Psalm   Ps 92:1-2,5. R. v.1

R. **The Lord is king, with majesty enrobed.**

The Lord is king, with majesty enrobed;
the Lord has robed himself with might,
he has girded himself with power. R.

The world you made firm, not to be moved;
your throne has stood firm from of old.
From all eternity, O Lord, you are. R.

Truly your decrees are to be trusted.
Holiness is fitting to your house,
O Lord, until the end of time. R.

SECOND READING

A reading from the book of the Apocalypse   1:5-8
Ruler of the kings of the earth. . . he made us a line of kings, priests to serve his God.

Jesus Christ is the faithful witness, the First-born from the dead, the Ruler
of the kings of the earth. He loves us and has washed away our sins with
his blood, and made us a line of kings, priests to serve his God and Father;
to him, then, be glory and power for ever and ever. Amen. It is he who
is coming on the clouds; everyone will see him, even those who pierced
him, and all the races of the earth will mourn over him. This is the truth.
Amen. 'I am the Alpha and the Omega' says the Lord God, who is, who
was, and who is to come, the Almighty.

The word of the Lord.

Gospel Acclamation   Mk 11:9,10

R. **Alleluia, alleluia!**
Blessings on him who comes in the name of the Lord!
Blessings on the coming kingdom of our father David!
R. **Alleluia!**

GOSPEL

A reading from the holy Gospel according to John   18:33-37

It is you who say that I am a king.

'Are you the king of the Jews?' Pilate asked. Jesus replied, 'Do you ask this of your own accord, or have others spoken to you about me?' Pilate answered, 'Am I a Jew? It is your own people and the chief priests who have handed you over to me: what have you done?' Jesus replied, 'Mine is not a kingdom of this world; if my kingdom were of this world, my men would have fought to prevent my being surrendered to the Jews. But my kingdom is not of this kind.' 'So you are a king then?' said Pilate. 'It is you who say it' answered Jesus. 'Yes, I am a king. I was born for this, I came into the world for this: to bear witness to the truth; and all who are on the side of truth listen to my voice.'

The Gospel of the Lord.

The Creed is said.

Prayer over the Offerings	Super oblata

As we offer you, O Lord,
     the sacrifice
by which the human race
     is reconciled to you,
we humbly pray
that your Son himself may bestow
     on all nations
the gifts of unity and peace.
Through Christ our Lord.
	Hostiam tibi, Domine,
	humanæ reconciliationis
	     offerentes,
	suppliciter deprecamur,
	ut ipse Filius tuus cunctis gentibus
	unitatis et pacis dona concedat.
	Qui vivit et regnat
	     in sæcula sæculorum.

Preface: Christ, King of the Universe, see pp.814-815.

Communion Antiphon Ps 28:10-11	Ant. ad communionem

The Lord sits as King for ever.
The Lord will bless his people
     with peace.
	Sedebit Dominus Rex in æternum;
	Dominus benedicet populo suo
	     in pace.

Prayer after Communion

Having received the food
    of immortality,
we ask, O Lord,
that, glorying in obedience
to the commands of Christ,
    the King of the universe,
we may live with him eternally
    in his heavenly Kingdom.
Who lives and reigns
    for ever and ever.

Post communionem

Immortalitatis alimoniam consecuti,
quæsumus, Domine,
ut, qui Christi Regis universorum
gloriamur obœdire mandatis,
cum ipso in cælesti regno sine fine
    vivere valeamus.
Qui vivit et regnat
    in sæcula sæculorum.

SOLEMNITIES OF THE LORD IN ORDINARY TIME

Sunday after Pentecost

THE MOST HOLY TRINITY (YEAR B)

Today we contemplate the Most Holy Trinity as Jesus introduced us to it. He revealed to us that God is love "not in the oneness of a single Person, but in the Trinity of one substance" (Preface). He is the Creator and merciful Father; he is the Only-Begotten Son, eternal Wisdom incarnate, who died and rose for us; he is the Holy Spirit who moves all things, cosmos and history, toward their final, full recapitulation. Three Persons who are one God because the Father is love, the Son is love, the Spirit is love. God is wholly and only love, the purest, infinite and eternal love. He does not live in splendid solitude but rather is an inexhaustible source of life that is ceaselessly given and communicated. To a certain extent we can perceive this by observing both the macro-universe: our earth, the planets, the stars, the galaxies; and the micro-universe: cells, atoms, elementary particles. The "name" of the Blessed Trinity is, in a certain sense, imprinted upon all things because all that exists, down to the last particle, is in relation; in this way we catch a glimpse of God as relationship and ultimately, Creator Love.

(Pope Benedict XVI)

Solemnity

Entrance Antiphon

BLEST be God the Father,
and the Only Begotten Son
of God,
and also the Holy Spirit,
for he has shown us his
merciful love.

Ant. ad introitum

BENEDICTUS sit Deus Pater,
Unigenitusque Dei Filius,
Sanctus quoque Spiritus,
quia fecit nobiscum
misericordiam suam.

The Gloria in excelsis (Glory to God in the highest) is said.

Collect

God our Father, who by sending
into the world
the Word of truth and the Spirit
of sanctification
made known to the human race
your wondrous mystery,
grant us, we pray, that in professing
the true faith,

Collecta

Deus Pater, qui Verbum veritatis
et Spiritum sanctificationis
mittens in mundum,
admirabile mysterium tuum
hominibus declarasti,
da nobis, in confessione veræ fidei,
æternæ gloriam

we may acknowledge the Trinity
of eternal glory
and adore your Unity,
powerful in majesty.
Through our Lord Jesus Christ,
your Son,
who lives and reigns with you
in the unity of the Holy Spirit,
one God, for ever and ever.

Trinitatis agnoscere,
et Unitatem adorare
in potentia maiestatis.
Per Dominum nostrum Iesum
Christum Filium tuum,
qui tecum vivit et regnat
in unitate Spiritus Sancti,
Deus, per omnia sæcula sæculorum.

FIRST READING

A reading from the book of Deuteronomy   4:32-34,39-40

The Lord is God indeed, in heaven above as on earth beneath, he and no other.

Moses said to the people: 'Put this question to the ages that are past, that went before you, from the time God created man on earth: Was there ever a word so majestic, from one end of heaven to the other? Was anything ever heard? Did ever a people hear the voice of the living God speaking from the heart of the fire, as you heard it, and remain alive? Has any god ventured to take to himself one nation from the midst of another by ordeals, signs, wonders, war with mighty hand and outstretched arm, by fearsome terrors – all this that the Lord your God did for you before your eyes in Egypt?

'Understand this today, therefore, and take it to heart: the Lord is God indeed, in heaven above as on earth beneath, he and no other. Keep his laws and commandments as I give them to you today, so that you and your children may prosper and live long in the land that the Lord your God gives you for ever.'

The word of the Lord.

Responsional Psalm   Ps 32:4-6,9,18-20. R. v.12

R. **Happy the people the Lord has chosen as his own.**

The word of the Lord is faithful
and all his works to be trusted.
The Lord loves justice and right
and fills the earth with his love. R.

By his word the heavens were made,
by the breath of his mouth all the stars.

He spoke; and they came to be.
He commanded; they sprang into being. R.

The Lord looks on those who revere him,
on those who hope in his love,
to rescue their souls from death,
to keep them alive in famine. R.

Our soul is waiting for the Lord.
The Lord is our help and our shield.
May your love be upon us, O Lord,
as we place all our hope in you. R.

R. **Happy the people the Lord has chosen as his own.**

SECOND READING

A reading from the letter of St Paul to the Romans   8:14-17
You received the spirit of sons, and it makes us cry out, 'Abba, Father!'

Everyone moved by the Spirit is a son of God. The spirit you received is
not the spirit of slaves bringing fear into your lives again; it is the spirit
of sons, and it makes us cry out, 'Abba Father!' The Spirit himself and
our spirit bear united witness that we are children of God. And if we are
children we are heirs as well: heirs of God and coheirs with Christ, sharing
his sufferings so as to share his glory.

   The word of the Lord.

Gospel Acclamation   Cf. Rv 1:8

R. **Alleluia, alleluia!**
Glory be to the Father, and to the Son, and to the Holy Spirit,
the God who is, who was, and who is to come.
R. **Alleluia!**

GOSPEL

A reading from the holy Gospel according to Matthew   28:16-20
Baptise them in the name of the Father and of the Son and of the Holy Spirit.

The eleven disciples set out for Galilee, to the mountain where Jesus had
arranged to meet them. When they saw him they fell down before him,
though some hesitated. Jesus came up and spoke to them. He said, 'All
authority in heaven and on earth has been given to me. Go, therefore,
make disciples of all the nations; baptise them in the name of the Father

and of the Son and of the Holy Spirit, and teach them to observe all the commands I gave you. And know that I am with you always; yes, to the end of time.'

The Gospel of the Lord.

The Creed is said.

Prayer over the Offerings	Super oblata
Sanctify by the invocation of your name, we pray, O Lord our God, this oblation of our service, and by it make of us an eternal offering to you. Through Christ our Lord.	Sanctifica, quæsumus, Domine Deus noster, per tui nominis invocationem, hæc munera nostræ servitutis, et per ea nosmetipsos tibi perfice munus æternum. Per Christum Dominum nostrum.

Preface: The Mystery of the Most Holy Trinity, pp.819-820.

Communion Antiphon Ga 4:6	Ant. ad communionem
Since you are children of God, God has sent into your hearts the Spirit of his Son, the Spirit who cries out: Abba, Father.	Quoniam autem estis filii, misit Deus Spiritum Filii sui in corda vestra clamantem: Abba, Pater.

Prayer after Communion	Post communionem
May receiving this Sacrament, O Lord our God, bring us health of body and soul, as we confess your eternal holy Trinity and undivided Unity. Through Christ our Lord.	Proficiat nobis ad salutem corporis et animæ, Domine Deus noster, huius sacramenti susceptio, et sempiternæ sanctæ Trinitatis eiusdemque individuæ Unitatis confessio. Per Christum Dominum nostrum.

THE MOST HOLY
BODY AND BLOOD OF CHRIST
(CORPUS CHRISTI) (YEAR B)

We begin to understand why the Lord chooses this piece of bread to represent him. Creation, with all of its gifts, aspires above and beyond itself to something even greater. Over and above the synthesis of its own forces, above and beyond the synthesis also of nature and of spirit that, in some way, we detect in the piece of bread, creation is projected towards divinization, toward the holy wedding feast, toward unification with the Creator himself. And still, we have not yet explained in depth the message of this sign of bread. The Lord mentioned its deepest mystery on Palm Sunday, when some Greeks asked to see him. In his answer to this question is the phrase: "Truly, truly, I say to you, unless a grain of wheat falls into the earth and dies, it remains alone; but if it dies, it bears much fruit" (Jn 12: 24). The mystery of the Passion is hidden in the bread made of ground grain. Flour, the ground wheat, presuppose the death and resurrection of the grain. In being ground and baked, it carries in itself once again the same mystery of the Passion. Only through death does resurrection arrive, as does the fruit and new life.

(Pope Benedict XVI)

Solemnity

Where the Solemnity of the Most Holy Body and Blood of Christ is not a Holyday of Obligation, it is assigned to the Sunday after the Most Holy Trinity as its proper day.

Entrance Antiphon Cf. Ps 80:17	Ant. ad introitum
HE fed them with the finest wheat and satisfied them with honey from the rock.	CIBAVIT eos ex adipe frumenti, et de petra melle saturavit eos.

The Gloria in excelsis (Glory to God in the highest) is said.

Collect

O God, who in this
    wonderful Sacrament
have left us a memorial
    of your Passion,
grant us, we pray,
so to revere the sacred mysteries
    of your Body and Blood
that we may always experience
    in ourselves
the fruits of your redemption.
Who live and reign with God
    the Father
in the unity of the Holy Spirit,
    one God, for ever and ever.

Collecta

Deus, qui nobis sub
    sacramento mirabili
passionis tuæ memoriam reliquisti,
tribue, quæsumus,
ita nos Corporis et Sanguinis tui
    sacra mysteria venerari,
ut redemptionis tuæ fructum
    in nobis iugiter sentiamus.
Qui vivis et regnas cum Deo Patre
in unitate Spiritus Sancti,
    Deus, per omnia sæcula
    sæculorum.

FIRST READING

A reading from the book of Exodus   24:3-8

This is the blood of the Covenant that the Lord has made with you.

Moses went and told the people all the commands of the Lord and all the
ordinances. In answer, all the people said with one voice, 'We will observe
all the commands that the Lord has decreed.' Moses put all the commands
of the Lord into writing, and early next morning he built an altar at the
foot of the mountain, with twelve standing-stones for the twelve tribes of
Israel. Then he directed certain young Israelites to offer holocausts and to
immolate bullocks to the Lord as communion sacrifices. Half of the blood
Moses took up and put into basins, the other half he cast on the altar. And
taking the Book of the Covenant he read it to the listening people, and
they said, 'We will observe all that the Lord has decreed; we will obey.'
Then Moses took the blood and cast it towards the people. 'This' he said
'is the blood of the Covenant that the Lord has made with you, containing
all these rules.'

    The word of the Lord.

Responsorial Psalm   Ps 115:12-13,15-18. R. v.13

R. **The cup of salvation I will raise;**
   I will call on the Lord's name.
   Or: **Alleluia!**

How can I repay the Lord
for his goodness to me?
The cup of salvation I will raise;
I will call on the Lord's name. R.

O precious in the eyes of the Lord
is the death of his faithful.
Your servant, Lord, your servant am I;
you have loosened my bonds. R.

A thanksgiving sacrifice I make:
I will call on the Lord's name.
My vows to the Lord I will fulfil
before all his people. R.

SECOND READING

A reading from the letter to the Hebrews   9:11-15

The blood of Christ can purify our inner self from dead actions.

Now Christ has come, as the high priest of all the blessings which were to come. He has passed through the greater, the more perfect tent, which is better than one made by men's hands because it is not of this created order; and he has entered the sanctuary once and for all, taking with him not the blood of goats and bull calves, but his own blood, having won an eternal redemption for us. The blood of goats and bulls and the ashes of a heifer are sprinkled on those who have incurred defilement and they restore the holiness of their outward lives; how much more effectively the blood of Christ, who offered himself as the perfect sacrifice to God through the eternal Spirit, can purify our inner self from dead actions so that we do our service to the living God.

He brings a new covenant, as the mediator, only so that the people who were called to an eternal inheritance may actually receive what was promised: his death took place to cancel the sins that infringed the earlier covenant.

The word of the Lord.

The Sequence, *Lauda Sion*, may be said or sung in its longer or shorter form. p.823ff.

Gospel Acclamation   Jn 6:51

R. **Alleluia, alleluia!**
I am the living bread which has come down from heaven,
says the Lord;
Anyone who eats this bread will live for ever.
R. **Alleluia!**

GOSPEL

A reading from the holy Gospel according to Mark   14:12-16,22-26

This is my body. This is my blood.

On the first day of Unleavened Bread, when the Passover lamb was
sacrificed, his disciples said to Jesus, 'Where do you want us to go and
make the preparations for you to eat the Passover?' So he sent two of
his disciples, saying to them, 'Go into the city and you will meet a man
carrying a pitcher of water. Follow him, and say to the owner of the house
which he enters, "The Master says: Where is my dining room in which I
can eat the Passover with my disciples?" He will show you a large upper
room furnished with couches, all prepared. Make the preparations for us
there.' The disciples set out and went to the city and found everything as
he had told them, and prepared the Passover.

And as they were eating he took some bread, and when he had said the
blessing he broke it and gave it to them. 'Take it,' he said 'this is my body.'
Then he took a cup, and when he had returned thanks he gave it to them,
and all drank from it, and he said to them, 'This is my blood, the blood
of the covenant, which is to be poured out for many. I tell you solemnly,
I shall not drink any more wine until the day I drink the new wine in the
kingdom of God.'

After psalms had been sung they left for the Mount of Olives.

The Gospel of the Lord.

The Creed is said.

Prayer over the Offerings

Grant your Church, O Lord,
    we pray,
the gifts of unity and peace,
whose signs are to be seen in mystery
in the offerings we here present.
Through Christ our Lord.

Super oblata

Ecclesiæ tuæ, quæsumus, Domine,
unitatis et pacis propitius
    dona concede,
quæ sub oblatis muneribus
    mystice designantur.
Per Christum Dominum nostrum.

Preface of the Most Holy Eucharist I or II, pp.574-575.

Communion Antiphon   Jn 6:57

Whoever eats my flesh
    and drinks my blood
remains in me and I in him,
    says the Lord.

Ant. ad communionem

Qui manducat meam carnem
    et bibit meum sanguinem,
in me manet et ego in eo,
    dicit Dominus.

Prayer after Communion

Grant, O Lord, we pray,
that we may delight for all eternity
in that share in your divine life,
which is foreshadowed
    in the present age
by our reception of your precious
    Body and Blood.
Who live and reign
    for ever and ever.

Post communionem

Fac nos, quæsumus, Domine,
divinitatis tuæ sempiterna
    fruitione repleri,
quam pretiosi Corporis
    et Sanguinis tui
temporalis perceptio præfigurat.
Qui vivis et regnas
    in sæcula sæculorum.

It is desirable that a procession take place after the Mass in which the Host to be carried in the procession is consecrated. However, nothing prohibits a procession from taking place even after a public and lengthy period of adoration following the Mass. If a procession takes place after Mass, when the Communion of the faithful is over, the monstrance in which the consecrated host has been placed is set on the altar. When the Prayer after Communion has been said, the Concluding Rites are omitted and the procession forms.

THE MOST SACRED HEART OF JESUS (YEAR B)

On today's solemnity of the Sacred Heart of Jesus the Church presents us this mystery for our contemplation: the mystery of the heart of a God who feels compassion and who bestows all his love upon humanity. A mysterious love, which in the texts of the New Testament is revealed to us as God's boundless and passionate love for mankind. God does not lose heart in the face of ingratitude or rejection by the people he has chosen; rather, with infinite mercy he sends his only-begotten Son into the world to take upon himself the fate of a shattered love, so that by defeating the power of evil and death he could restore to human beings enslaved by sin their dignity as sons and daughters.

(Pope Benedict XVI)

Solemnity

Entrance Antiphon Ps 32:11,19	Ant. ad introitum
THE designs of his Heart are from age to age, to rescue their souls from death, and to keep them alive in famine.	COGITATIONES Cordis eius in generatione et generationem, ut eruat a morte animas eorum et alat eos in fame.

The Gloria in excelsis (Glory to God in the highest) is said.

Collect	Collecta
Grant, we pray, almighty God, that we, who glory in the Heart of your beloved Son and recall the wonders of his love for us, may be made worthy to receive an overflowing measure of grace from that fount of heavenly gifts. Through our Lord Jesus Christ, your Son, who lives and reigns with you in the unity of the Holy Spirit, one God, for ever and ever.	Concede, quæsumus, omnipotens Deus, ut qui, dilecti Filii tui Corde gloriantes, eius præcipua in nos beneficia recolimus caritatis, de illo donorum fonte cælesti supereffluentem gratiam mereamur accipere. Per Dominum nostrum Iesum Christum Filium tuum, qui tecum vivit et regnat in unitate Spiritus Sancti, Deus, per omnia sæcula sæculorum.

966	THE MOST SACRED HEART OF JESUS (YEAR B)

Or:

O God, who in the Heart of your Son,
wounded by our sins,
bestow on us in mercy
the boundless treasures of your love,
grant, we pray,
that, in paying him the homage
    of our devotion
we may also offer
    worthy reparation.
Through our Lord Jesus Christ,
    your Son,
who lives and reigns with you
    in the unity of the Holy Spirit,
one God, for ever and ever.

Vel:

Deus, qui nobis in Corde Filii tui,
nostris vulnerato peccatis,
infinitos dilectionis thesauros
misericorditer largiri dignaris,
concede, quæsumus,
ut, illi devotum pietatis nostræ
    præstantes obsequium,
dignæ quoque satisfactionis
    exhibeamus officium.
Per Dominum nostrum Iesum
    Christum Filium tuum,
qui tecum vivit et regnat
    in unitate Spiritus Sancti,
Deus, per omnia sæcula sæculorum.

FIRST READING

A reading from the prophet Hosea   11:1,3-4,8-9

My heart recoils from it.

Listen to the word of the Lord:

When Israel was a child I loved him,
and I called my son out of Egypt.
I myself taught Ephraim to walk,
I took them in my arms;
yet they have not understood that I was the one looking after them.
I led them with reins of kindness,
with leading-strings of love.
I was like someone who lifts an infant close against his cheek;
stooping down to him I gave him his food.
How could I treat you like Admah,
or deal with you like Zeboiim?
My heart recoils from it,
my whole being
trembles at the thought.
I will not give rein to my fierce anger,
I will not destroy Ephraim again,
for I am God, not man:
I am the Holy One in your midst
and have no wish to destroy.

The word of the Lord.

Responsorial Psalm   Is 12:2-6. R. v.3

R. **With joy you will draw water**
   from the wells of the Saviour.

Truly God is my salvation,
I trust, I shall not fear.
For the Lord is my strength, my song,
he became my saviour.
With joy you will draw water
from the wells of Salvation. R.

Give thanks to the Lord, give praise to his name!
Make his mighty deeds known to the peoples!
Declare the greatness of his name. R.

Sing a psalm to the Lord
for he has done glorious deeds;
make them known to all the earth!
People of Zion, sing and shout for joy
for great in your midst is the Holy One of Israel. R.

SECOND READING

A reading from the letter of St Paul to the Ephesians   3:8-12,14-19
The love of Christ is beyond all knowledge.

I, Paul, who am less than the least of all the saints, have been entrusted
with this special grace, not only of proclaiming to the pagans the
infinite treasure of Christ but also of explaining how the mystery is to be
dispensed. Through all the ages, this has been kept hidden in God, the
creator of everything. Why? So that the Sovereignties and Powers should
learn only now, through the Church, how comprehensive God's wisdom
really is, exactly according to the plan which he had had from all eternity
in Christ Jesus our Lord. This is why we are bold enough to approach God
in complete confidence, through our faith in him.

   This, then, is what I pray, kneeling before the Father, from whom every
family, whether spiritual or natural, takes its name.

   Out of his infinite glory, may he give you the power through his
Spirit for your hidden self to grow strong, so that Christ may live in your
hearts through faith, and then, planted in love and built on love, you
will with all the saints have strength to grasp the breadth and the length,
the height and the depth; until, knowing the love of Christ, which is
beyond all knowledge, you are filled with the utter fullness of God.

   The word of the Lord.

Gospel Acclamation   Mt 11:29

R. **Alleluia, alleluia!**
Shoulder my yoke and learn from me,
for I am gentle and humble in heart.
R. **Alleluia!**
Or: 1 Jn 4:10
R. **Alleluia, alleluia!**
This is the love I mean:
God's love for us when he sent his Son
to be the sacrifice that takes our sins away.
R. **Alleluia!**

GOSPEL

A reading from the holy Gospel according to John   19:31-37
One of the soldiers pierced his side and there came out blood and water.

It was Preparation Day, and to prevent the bodies remaining on the cross
during the sabbath – since that sabbath was a day of special solemnity –
the Jews asked Pilate to have the legs broken and the bodies taken away.
Consequently the soldiers came and broke the legs of the first man who
had been crucified with him and then of the other. When they came
to Jesus, they found he was already dead, and so instead of breaking his
legs one of the soldiers pierced his side with a lance; and immediately
there came out blood and water. This is the evidence of one who saw it
– trustworthy evidence, and he knows he speaks the truth – and he gives
it so that you may believe as well. Because all this happened to fulfil the
words of scripture:

Not one bone of his will be broken;
and again, in another place scripture says:

They will look on the one whom they have pierced.

The Gospel of the Lord.

The Creed is said.

Prayer over the Offerings	Super oblata
Look, O Lord, we pray,	Respice, quæsumus, Domine,
on the surpassing charity	ad ineffabilem Cordis dilecti Filii
in the Heart of your beloved Son,	tui caritatem,
that what we offer may be a gift	ut quod offerimus sit tibi
acceptable to you	munus acceptum
and an expiation of our offences.	et nostrorum expiatio delictorum.
Through Christ our Lord.	Per Christum Dominum nostrum.

Preface: The boundless charity of Christ, see p.832.

Communion Antiphon Cf. Jn 7:37-38	Ant. ad communionem
Thus says the Lord:	Dicit Dominus:
Let whoever is thirsty come to me and drink.	Si quis sitit, veniat ad me et bibat.
Streams of living water will flow from within the one who believes in me.	Qui credit in me, flumina de ventre eius fluent aquæ vivæ.

Or: Jn 19:34	Vel:
One of the soldiers opened his side with a lance, and at once there came forth blood and water.	Unus militum lancea latus eius aperuit, et continuo exivit sanguis et aqua.

Prayer after Communion	Post communionem
May this sacrament of charity, O Lord, make us fervent with the fire of holy love, so that, drawn always to your Son, we may learn to see him in our neighbour. Through Christ our Lord.	Sacramentum caritatis, Domine, sancta nos faciat dilectione fervere, qua, ad Filium tuum semper attracti, ipsum in fratribus agnoscere discamus. Qui vivit et regnat in sæcula sæculorum.

First Sunday in Ordinary Time

THE BAPTISM OF THE LORD

Feast

See p.138.

SECOND SUNDAY IN ORDINARY TIME (YEAR C)

Entrance Antiphon Ps 65:4	**Ant. ad introitum**
ALL the earth shall bow down before you, O God, and shall sing to you, shall sing to your name, O Most High!	OMNIS terra adoret te, Deus, et psallat tibi; psalmum dicat nomini tuo, Altissime.
Collect	**Collecta**
Almighty ever-living God, who govern all things, both in heaven and on earth, mercifully hear the pleading of your people and bestow your peace on our times. Through our Lord Jesus Christ, your Son, who lives and reigns with you in the unity of the Holy Spirit, one God, for ever and ever.	Omnipotens sempiterne Deus, qui cælestia simul et terrena moderaris, supplicationes populi tui clementer exaudi, et pacem tuam nostris concede temporibus. Per Dominum nostrum Iesum Christum Filium tuum, qui tecum vivit et regnat in unitate Spiritus Sancti, Deus, per omnia sæcula sæculorum.

FIRST READING

A reading from the prophet Isaiah   62:1-5

The bridegroom rejoices in his bride.

About Zion I will not be silent,
about Jerusalem I will not grow weary,
until her integrity shines out like the dawn
and her salvation flames like a torch.
The nations then will see your integrity,
all the kings your glory,

and you will be called by a new name,
one which the mouth of the Lord will confer.
You are to be a crown of splendour in the hand of the Lord,
a princely diadem in the hand of your God;
no longer are you to be named 'Forsaken',
nor your land 'Abandoned',
but you shall be called 'My Delight'
and your land 'The Wedded';
for the Lord takes delight in you
and your land will have its wedding.
Like a young man marrying a virgin,
so will the one who built you wed you,
and as the bridegroom rejoices in his bride,
so will your God rejoice in you.

   The word of the Lord.

Responsorial Psalm   Ps 95:1-3,7-10. R. v.3

R. **Proclaim the wonders of the Lord
   among all the peoples.**

   O sing a new song to the Lord,
   sing to the Lord all the earth.
   O sing to the Lord, bless his name. R.

   Proclaim his help day by day,
   tell among the nations his glory
   and his wonders among all the peoples. R.

   Give the Lord, you families of peoples,
   give the Lord glory and power,
   give the Lord the glory of his name. R.

   Worship the Lord in his temple.
   O earth, tremble before him.
   Proclaim to the nations: 'God is king.'
   He will judge the peoples in fairness. R.

SECOND READING

A reading from the first letter of St Paul to the Corinthians   12:4-11
One and the same Spirit, who distributes gifts to different people just as he chooses.

There is a variety of gifts but always the same Spirit; there are all sorts of
service to be done, but always to the same Lord; working in all sorts of
different ways in different people, it is the same God who is working in all

of them. The particular way in which the Spirit is given to each person is for a good purpose. One may have the gift of preaching with wisdom given him by the Spirit; another may have the gift of preaching instruction given him by the same Spirit; and another the gift of faith given by the same Spirit; another again the gift of healing, through this one Spirit; one, the power of miracles; another, prophecy; another the gift of recognising spirits, another the gift of tongues and another the ability to interpret them. All these are the work of one and the same Spirit, who distributes different gifts to different people just as he chooses.

The word of the Lord.

Gospel Acclamation   Cf. Jn 6:63,68

R. **Alleluia, alleluia!**
Your words are spirit, Lord,
and they are life:
you have the message of eternal life.
R. **Alleluia!**

Or: Cf. 2 Th 2:14

R. **Alleluia, alleluia!**
Through the Good News God called us
to share the glory of our Lord Jesus Christ.
R. **Alleluia!**

GOSPEL

A reading from the holy Gospel according to John   2:1-11

This was the first of the signs given by Jesus: it was given at Cana in Galilee.

There was a wedding at Cana in Galilee. The mother of Jesus was there, and Jesus and his disciples had also been invited. When they ran out of wine, since the wine provided for the wedding was all finished, the mother of Jesus said to him, 'They have no wine.' Jesus said, 'Woman why turn to me? My hour has not come yet.' His mother said to the servants, 'Do whatever he tells you.' There were six stone water jars standing there, meant for the ablutions that are customary among the Jews; each could hold twenty or thirty gallons. Jesus said to the servants, 'Fill the jars with water,' and they filled them to the brim. 'Draw some out now' he told them 'and take it to the steward.' They did this; the steward tasted the water, and it had turned into wine. Having no idea where it came from – only the servants who had drawn the water knew – the steward called the bridegroom and said, 'People generally serve the best wine first, and keep the cheaper sort till the guests have plenty to drink; but you have kept the best wine till now.'

This was the first of the signs given by Jesus: it was given at Cana in Galilee. He let his glory be seen, and his disciples believed in him.

The Gospel of the Lord.

Prayer over the Offerings	Super oblata

Grant us, O Lord, we pray,
that we may participate worthily
   in these mysteries,
for whenever the memorial
   of this sacrifice is celebrated
the work of our redemption
   is accomplished.
Through Christ our Lord.
	Concede nobis,
	   quæsumus, Domine,
	hæc digne frequentare mysteria,
	quia, quoties huius hostiæ
	   commemoratio celebratur,
	opus nostræ redemptionis exercetur.
	Per Christum Dominum nostrum.

Preface of Sundays in Ordinary Time I-VIII, pp.566-573.

Communion Antiphon Cf. Ps 22:5	Ant. ad communionem

You have prepared a table before me,
and how precious is the chalice
   that quenches my thirst.
	Parasti in conspectu meo mensam,
	et calix meus inebrians quam
	   præclarus est!

Or: 1 Jn 4:16	Vel:

We have come to know
   and to believe
in the love that God has for us.
	Nos cognovimus
	   et credidimus caritati,
	quam Deus habet in nobis.

Prayer after Communion	Post communionem

Pour on us, O Lord,
   the Spirit of your love,
and in your kindness
make those you have nourished
by this one heavenly Bread
one in mind and heart.
Through Christ our Lord.
	Spiritum nobis, Domine,
	   tuæ caritatis infunde,
	ut, quos uno cælesti pane satiasti,
	una facias pietate concordes.
	Per Christum Dominum nostrum.

THIRD SUNDAY IN ORDINARY TIME (YEAR C)

Entrance Antiphon   Cf. Ps 95:1,6

O SING a new song to the Lord;
sing to the Lord, all the earth.
In his presence are majesty
    and splendour,
strength and honour
    in his holy place.

Ant. ad introitum

C ANTATE Domino
canticum novum,
cantate Domino, omnis terra.
Confessio et pulchritudo
    in conspectu eius,
sanctitas et magnificentia
    in sanctificatione eius.

Collect

Almighty ever-living God,
direct our actions according
    to your good pleasure,
that in the name of your beloved Son
we may abound in good works.
Through our Lord Jesus Christ,
    your Son,
who lives and reigns with you
    in the unity of the Holy Spirit,
one God, for ever and ever.

Collecta

Omnipotens sempiterne Deus,
dirige actus nostros
    in beneplacito tuo,
ut in nomine dilecti Filii tui
mereamur bonis operibus abundare.
Per Dominum nostrum Iesum
    Christum Filium tuum,
qui tecum vivit et regnat
    in unitate Spiritus Sancti,
Deus, per omnia sæcula sæculorum.

FIRST READING

A reading from the book of Nehemiah   8:2-6,8-10

Ezra read from the law of God and the people understood what was read.

Ezra the priest brought the Law before the assembly, consisting of men, women, and children old enough to understand. This was the first day of the seventh month. On the square before the Water Gate, in the presence of the men and women, and children old enough to understand, he read from the book from early morning till noon; all the people listened attentively to the Book of the Law.

Ezra the scribe stood on a wooden dais erected for the purpose. In full view of all the people – since he stood higher than all the people – Ezra opened the book; and when he opened it all the people stood up. Then Ezra blessed the Lord, the great God, and all the people raised their hands and answered, 'Amen! Amen!'; then they bowed down and, face to the ground, prostrated themselves before the Lord. And Ezra read from the Law of God, translating and giving the sense, so that the people understood what was read.

Then Nehemiah – His Excellency – and Ezra, priest and scribe (and the Levites who were instructing the people) said to all the people, 'This day is sacred to the Lord your God. Do not be mournful, do not weep.' For the people were all in tears as they listened to the words of the Law.

He then said, 'Go, eat the fat, drink the sweet wine, and send a portion to the man who has nothing prepared ready. For this day is sacred to our Lord. Do not be sad: the joy of the Lord is your stronghold.'

The word of the Lord.

Responsorial Psalm   Ps 18:8-10,15. R. Jn 6:63

R. **Your words are spirit, Lord,**
and they are life.

The law of the Lord is perfect,
it revives the soul.
The rule of the Lord is to be trusted,
it gives wisdom to the simple. R.

The precepts of the Lord are right,
they gladden the heart.
The command of the Lord is clear,
it gives light to the eyes. R.

The fear of the Lord is holy,
abiding for ever.
The decrees of the Lord are truth
and all of them just. R.

May the spoken words of my mouth,
the thoughts of my heart,
win favour in your sight, O Lord,
my rescuer, my rock! R.

SECOND READING

A reading from the first letter of St Paul to the Corinthians   12:12-30
You together are Christ's body; but each of you is a different part of it.

[Just as a human body, though it is made up of many parts is a single unit because all these parts, though many, make one body, so it is with Christ. In the one Spirit we were all baptised, Jews as well as Greeks, slaves as well as citizens, and one Spirit was given to us all to drink.

Nor is the body to be identified with any one of its many parts.] If the foot were to say, 'I am not a hand and so I do not belong to the body,' would that mean that it stopped being part of the body? If the ear were to say, 'I am not an eye, and so I do not belong to the body,' would that mean that it is not a part of the body? If your whole body was just one eye, how would you hear anything? If it was just one ear, how would you smell anything?

Instead of that, God put all the separate parts into the body on purpose. If all the parts were the same, how could it be a body? As it is, the parts are many but the body is one. The eye cannot say to the hand, 'I do not need you,' nor can the head say to the feet, 'I do not need you.'

What is more, it is precisely the parts of the body that seem to be the weakest which are the indispensable ones; and it is the least honourable parts of the body that we clothe with the greatest care. So our more improper parts get decorated in a way that our more proper parts do not need. God has arranged the body so that more dignity is given to the parts which are without it, and so that there may not be disagreements inside the body, but that each part may be equally concerned for all the others. If one part is hurt, all parts are hurt with it. If one part is given special honour, all parts enjoy it.

[Now you together are Christ's body; but each of you is a different part of it.] In the Church, God has given the first place to apostles, the second to prophets, the third to teachers; after them, miracles, and after them the gift of healing; helpers, good leaders, those with many languages. Are all of them apostles, or all of them prophets, or all of them teachers? Do they all have the gift of miracles, or all have the gift of healing? Do all speak strange languages, and all interpret them?

[The word of the Lord.]

Shorter Form, verses 12-14,17. Read between [ ]

Gospel Acclamation   Lk 4:18

R. **Alleluia, alleluia!**
The Lord has sent me to bring the good news to the poor,
to proclaim liberty to captives.
R. **Alleluia!**

GOSPEL

A reading from the holy Gospel according to Luke   1:1-4,4:14-21
The text is being fulfilled today.

Seeing that many others have undertaken to draw up accounts of the events that have taken place among us, exactly as these were handed down to us by those who from the outset were eyewitnesses and ministers of the word, I in my turn, after carefully going over the whole story from the beginning, have decided to write an ordered account for you, Theophilus, so that your Excellency may learn how well founded the teaching is that you have received.

Jesus, with the power of the Spirit in him, returned to Galilee; and his reputation spread throughout the countryside. He taught in their synagogues and everyone praised him.

He came to Nazara, where he had been brought up, and went into the synagogue on the sabbath day as he usually did. He stood up to read, and they handed him the scroll of the prophet Isaiah. Unrolling the scroll he found the place where it is written:

The spirit of the Lord has been given to me, for he has anointed me.
He has sent me to bring the good news to the poor,
to proclaim liberty to captives
and to the blind new sight,
to set the downtrodden free,
to proclaim the Lord's year of favour.

He then rolled up the scroll, gave it back to the assistant and sat down. And all eyes in the synagogue were fixed on him. Then he began to speak to them, 'This text is being fulfilled today even as you listen.'

The Gospel of the Lord.

Prayer over the Offerings	Super oblata
Accept our offerings, O Lord, we pray, and in sanctifying them grant that they may profit us for salvation. Through Christ our Lord.	Munera nostra, Domine, suscipe placatus, quæ sanctificando nobis, quæsumus, salutaria fore concede. Per Christum Dominum nostrum.

Preface of Sundays in Ordinary Time I-VIII, pp.566-573.

Communion Antiphon Cf. Ps 33:6	Ant. ad communionem
Look toward the Lord and be radiant; let your faces not be abashed.	Accedite ad Dominum et illuminamini, et facies vestræ non confundentur.
Or: Jn 8:12	Vel:
I am the light of the world, says the Lord; whoever follows me will not walk in darkness, but will have the light of life.	Ego sum lux mundi, dicit Dominus: qui sequitur me non ambulat in tenebris, sed habebit lumen vitæ.

Prayer after Communion

Grant, we pray, almighty God,
that, receiving the grace
by which you bring us to new life,
we may always glory in your gift.
Through Christ our Lord.

Post communionem

Præsta nobis, quæsumus,
    omnipotens Deus,
ut, vivificationis tuæ
    gratiam consequentes,
in tuo semper munere gloriemur.
Per Christum Dominum nostrum.

FOURTH SUNDAY IN ORDINARY TIME (YEAR C)

Entrance Antiphon   Ps 105:47

SAVE us, O Lord our God!
And gather us from the nations,
to give thanks to your holy name,
and make it our glory to praise you.

Ant. ad introitum

SALVOS nos fac,
Domine Deus noster,
et congrega nos de nationibus,
ut confiteamur nomini sancto tuo,
et gloriemur in laude tua.

Collect

Grant us, Lord our God,
that we may honour you
    with all our mind,
and love everyone in truth of heart.
Through our Lord Jesus Christ,
    your Son,
who lives and reigns with you
    in the unity of the Holy Spirit,
one God, for ever and ever.

Collecta

Concede nobis,
    Domine Deus noster,
ut te tota mente veneremur,
et omnes homines rationabili
    diligamus affectu.
Per Dominum nostrum Iesum
    Christum Filium tuum,
qui tecum vivit et regnat
    in unitate Spiritus Sancti,
Deus, per omnia sæcula sæculorum.

FIRST READING

A reading from the prophet Jeremiah   1:4-5,17-19

I have appointed you as prophet to the nations.

In the days of Josiah, the word of the Lord was addressed to me, saying,

'Before I formed you in the womb I knew you;
before you came to birth I consecrated you;
I have appointed you as prophet to the nations.
So now brace yourself for action.
Stand up and tell them
all I command you.
Do not be dismayed at their presence,

or in their presence I will make you dismayed.
I, for my part, today will make you
into a fortified city,
a pillar of iron,
and a wall of bronze
to confront all this land:
the kings of Judah, its princes,
its priests and the country people.
They will fight against you
but shall not overcome you,
for I am with you to deliver you –
it is the Lord who speaks.'

The word of the Lord.

Responsorial Psalm   Ps 70:1-6,15,17. R. v.15

R. **My lips will tell of your help.**

In you, O Lord, I take refuge;
let me never be put to shame.
In your justice rescue me, free me:
pay heed to me and save me. R.

Be a rock where I can take refuge,
a mighty stronghold to save me;
for you are my rock, my stronghold.
Free me from the hand of the wicked. R.

It is you, O Lord, who are my hope,
my trust, O Lord, since my youth.
On you I have leaned from my birth,
from my mother's womb you have been my help. R.

My lips will tell of your justice
and day by day of your help.
O God, you have taught me from my youth
and I proclaim your wonders still. R.

SECOND READING

A reading from the first letter of St Paul to the Corinthians   12:31-13:13
There are three things that last: faith, hope and love; and the greatest of these is love.

Be ambitious for the higher gifts. And I am going to show you a way that
is better than any of them.

If I have all the eloquence of men or of angels, but speak without love, I am simply a gong booming or a cymbal clashing. If I have the gift of prophecy, understanding all the mysteries there are, and knowing everything, and if I have faith in all its fulness, to move mountains, but without love, then I am nothing at all. If I give away all that I possess, piece by piece, and if I even let them take my body to burn it, but am without love, it will do me no good whatever.

[Love is always patient and kind; it is never jealous; love is never boastful or conceited; it is never rude or selfish; it does not take offence, and is not resentful. Love takes no pleasure in other people's sins but delights in the truth; it is always ready to excuse, to trust, to hope, and to endure whatever comes.

Love does not come to an end. But if there are gifts of prophecy, the time will come when they must fail; or the gift of languages, it will not continue for ever; and knowledge – for this, too, the time will come when it must fail. For our knowledge is imperfect and our prophesying is imperfect; but once perfection comes, all imperfect things will disappear. When I was a child, I used to talk like a child, and think like a child, and argue like a child, but now I am a man, all childish ways are put behind me. Now we are seeing a dim reflection in a mirror; but then we shall be seeing face to face. The knowledge that I have now is imperfect; but then I shall know as fully as I am known.

In short, there are three things that last: faith, hope and love; and the greatest of these is love.

The word of the Lord.]

Shorter Form, verses 4-13. Read between [ ]

Gospel Acclamation   Jn 14:5

R. **Alleluia, alleluia!**
I am the Way, the Truth and the Life, says the Lord;
no one can come to the Father except through me.
R. **Alleluia!**

Or: Lk 4:18

R. **Alleluia, alleluia!**
The Lord sent me to bring the good news to the poor,
to proclaim liberty to captives.
R. **Alleluia!**

GOSPEL

A reading from the holy Gospel according to Luke 4:21-30

Like Elijah and Elisha, Jesus is not sent to the Jews only.

Jesus began to speak in the synagogue, 'This text is being fulfilled today even as you listen.' And he won the approval of all, and they were astonished by the gracious words that came from his lips.

They said, 'This is Joseph's son, surely?' But he replied, 'No doubt you will quote me the saying, "Physician, heal yourself" and tell me, "We have heard all that happened in Capernaum, do the same here in your own countryside."' And he went on, 'I tell you solemnly, no prophet is ever accepted in his own country.

'There were many widows in Israel, I can assure you, in Elijah's day, when heaven remained shut for three years and six months and a great famine raged throughout the land, but Elijah was not sent to any one of these: he was sent to a widow at Zarephath, a Sidonian town. And in the prophet Elisha's time there were many lepers in Israel, but none of these was cured, except the Syrian, Naaman.'

When they heard this everyone in the synagogue was enraged. They sprang to their feet and hustled him out of the town; and they took him up to the brow of the hill their town was built on, intending to throw him down the cliff, but he slipped through the crowd and walked away.

The Gospel of the Lord.

Prayer over the Offerings	Super oblata
O Lord, we bring to your altar	Altaribus tuis, Domine,
these offerings of our service:	munera nostræ
be pleased to receive them, we pray,	servitutis inferimus,
and transform them	quæ, placatus assumens,
into the Sacrament	sacramentum nostræ
of our redemption.	redemptionis efficias.
Through Christ our Lord.	Per Christum Dominum nostrum.

Preface of Sundays in Ordinary Time I-VIII, pp.566-573.

Communion Antiphon Cf. Ps 30:17-18	Ant. ad communionem
Let your face shine on your servant.	Illumina faciem tuam super
Save me in your merciful love.	servum tuum,
O Lord, let me never be put to shame,	et salvum me fac in tua misericordia.
for I call on you.	Domine, non confundar,
	quoniam invocavi te.

Or: Mt 5:3-4 | Vel:

Blessed are the poor in spirit, | Beati pauperes spiritu,
for theirs is the Kingdom of Heaven. | quoniam ipsorum
Blessed are the meek, | est regnum cælorum.
   for they shall possess the land. | Beati mites,
 | quoniam ipsi possidebunt terram.

Prayer after Communion | Post communionem

Nourished by these redeeming gifts, | Redemptionis nostræ munere
we pray, O Lord, | vegetati, quæsumus, Domine,
that through this help | ut hoc perpetuæ salutis auxilio
   to eternal salvation | fides semper vera proficiat.
true faith may ever increase. | Per Christum Dominum nostrum.
Through Christ our Lord. |

FIFTH SUNDAY IN ORDINARY TIME (YEAR C)

Entrance Antiphon   Ps 94:6-7 | Ant. ad introitum

O COME, let us worship God
and bow low before the God
  who made us,
for he is the Lord our God.

VENITE, adoremus Deum,
  et procidamus ante Dominum,
  qui fecit nos;
quia ipse est Dominus Deus noster.

Collect | Collecta

Keep your family safe, O Lord, | Familiam tuam,
  with unfailing care, | quæsumus, Domine,
that, relying solely on the hope | continua pietate custodi,
  of heavenly grace, | ut, quæ in sola spe gratiæ
they may be defended always | cælestis innititur,
  by your protection. | tua semper protectione muniatur.
Through our Lord Jesus Christ, | Per Dominum nostrum Iesum
  your Son, | Christum Filium tuum,
who lives and reigns with you | qui tecum vivit et regnat
  in the unity of the Holy Spirit, | in unitate Spiritus Sancti,
one God, for ever and ever. | Deus, per omnia sæcula sæculorum.

FIRST READING

A reading from the prophet Isaiah   6:1-8

Here I am, send me.

In the year of King Uzziah's death I saw the Lord seated on a high throne; his train filled the sanctuary; above him stood seraphs, each one with six wings.

>   And they cried out one to another in this way,
>   'Holy, holy, holy is the Lord of hosts.
>   His glory fills the whole earth.'

The foundations of the threshold shook with the voice of the one who cried out, and the Temple was filled with smoke. I said:

>   'What a wretched state I am in! I am lost,
>   for I am a man of unclean lips
>   and I live among a people of unclean lips,
>   and my eyes have looked at the King, the Lord of hosts.'

Then one of the seraphs flew to me, holding in his hand a live coal which he had taken from the altar with a pair of tongs. With this he touched my mouth and said:

>   'See now, this has touched your lips,
>   your sin is taken away,
>   your iniquity is purged.'

Then I heard the voice of the Lord saying:

>   'Whom shall I send? Who will be our messenger?'

I answered, 'Here I am, send me.'

>   The word of the Lord.

Responsorial Psalm   Ps 137:1-5,7-8. R. v.1

R. **Before the angels I will bless you, O Lord.**

>   I thank you, Lord, with all my heart,
>   you have heard the words of my mouth.
>   Before the angels I will bless you.
>   I will adore before your holy temple. R.

>   I thank you for your faithfulness and love
>   which excel all we ever knew of you.
>   On the day I called, you answered;
>   you increased the strength of my soul. R.

>   All earth's kings shall thank you
>   when they hear the words of your mouth.

They shall sing of the Lord's ways:
'How great is the glory of the Lord!' R.

You stretch out your right hand and save me.
Your hand will do all things for me.
Your love, O Lord, is eternal,
discard not the work of your hand. R.

SECOND READING

A reading from the first letter of St Paul to the Corinthians   15:1-11

I preach what they preach, and this is what you all believed.

Brothers, I want to remind you of the gospel I preached to you, the gospel
that you received and in which you are firmly established; because the
gospel will save you only if you keep believing exactly what I preached to
you – believing anything else will not lead to anything.

   Well then, [in the first place, I taught you what I had been taught myself,
namely that Christ died for our sins, in accordance with the scriptures; that
he was buried; and that he was raised to life on the third day, in accordance
with the scriptures; that he appeared first to Cephas and secondly to the
Twelve. Next he appeared to more than five hundred of the brothers at the
same time, most of whom are still alive, though some have died; then he
appeared to James, and then to all the apostles; and last of all he appeared
to me too; it was as though I was born when no one expected it.]

   I am the least of the apostles; in fact, since I persecuted the Church of
God, I hardly deserve the name apostle; but by God's grace that is what I
am, and the grace that he gave me has not been fruitless. On the contrary,
I, or rather the grace of God that is with me, have worked harder than any
of the others; [but what matters is that I preach what they preach, and this
is what you all believed.

   The word of the Lord.]

Shorter Form, verses 3-8,11. Read between [ ]

Gospel Acclamation   Jn 15:15

R. **Alleluia, alleluia!**
I call you friends, says the Lord,
because I have made known to you
everything I have learnt from my Father.
R. **Alleluia!**

Or: Mt 4:19

R. **Alleluia, alleluia!**
Follow me, says the Lord,
and I will make you fishers of men.
R. **Alleluia!**

GOSPEL

A reading from the holy Gospel according to Luke   5:1-11
They left everything and followed him.

Jesus was standing one day by the lake of Gennesaret, with the crowd
pressing round him listening to the word of God, when he caught sight of
two boats close to the bank. The fishermen had gone out of them and were
washing their nets. He got into one of the boats – it was Simon's – and
asked him to put out a little from the shore. Then he sat down and taught
the crowds from the boat.

When he had finished speaking he said to Simon, 'Put out into deep
water and pay out your nets for a catch.' 'Master,' Simon replied 'we worked
hard all night long and caught nothing, but if you say so, I will pay out the
nets.' And when they had done this they netted such a huge number of
fish that their nets began to tear, so they signalled to their companions in
the other boats to come and help them; when these came, they filled the
two boats to sinking point.

When Simon Peter saw this he fell at the knees of Jesus saying 'Leave me,
Lord; I am a sinful man.' For he and all his companions were completely
overcome by the catch they had made; so also were James and John, sons
of Zebedee, who were Simon's partners. But Jesus said to Simon, 'Do not
be afraid; from now on it is men you will catch.' Then, bringing their boats
back to land, they left everything and followed him.

The Gospel of the Lord.

Prayer over the Offerings	Super oblata
O Lord our God,	Domine Deus noster,
who once established these	qui has potius creaturas
created things	ad fragilitatis nostræ
to sustain us in our frailty,	subsidium condidisti,
grant, we pray,	tribue, quæsumus,
that they may become for us now	ut etiam æternitatis nobis
the Sacrament of eternal life.	fiant sacramentum.
Through Christ our Lord.	Per Christum Dominum nostrum.

Preface of Sundays in Ordinary Time I-VIII, pp.566-573.

Communion Antiphon Cf. Ps106:8-9	Ant. ad communionem
Let them thank the Lord 　　for his mercy, his wonders for the children of men for he satisfies the thirsty soul, and the hungry he fills 　　with good things.	Confiteantur Domino 　　misericordiæ eius, et mirabilia eius filiis hominum, quia satiavit animam inanem, et animam esurientem 　　satiavit bonis.
Or:　　　　　　　　　　　Mt 5:5-6	Vel:
Blessed are those who mourn, 　　for they shall be consoled. Blessed are those who hunger 　　and thirst for righteousness, for they shall have their fill.	Beati qui lugent, 　　quoniam ipsi consolabuntur. Beati qui esuriunt 　　et sitiunt iustitiam, quoniam ipsi saturabuntur.
Prayer after Communion	Post communionem
O God, who have willed 　　that we be partakers in the one Bread and the one Chalice, grant us, we pray, so to live that, 　　made one in Christ, we may joyfully bear fruit for the salvation of the world. Through Christ our Lord.	Deus, qui nos de uno pane 　　et de uno calice participes esse voluisti, da nobis, quæsumus, ita vivere, ut, 　　unum in Christo effecti, fructum afferamus pro mundi 　　salute gaudentes. Per Christum Dominum nostrum.

SIXTH SUNDAY IN ORDINARY TIME (YEAR C)

Entrance Antiphon　　Cf. Ps 30:3-4	Ant. ad introitum
BE my protector, O God, 　a mighty stronghold to save me. For you are my rock, my stronghold! Lead me, guide me, 　　for the sake of your name.	ESTO mihi 　in Deum protectorem, et in locum refugii, 　　ut salvum me facias. Quoniam firmamentum meum 　　et refugium meum es tu, et propter nomen tuum dux 　　mihi eris, et enutries me.

Collect	Collecta
O God, who teach us that you abide in hearts that are just and true,	Deus, qui te in rectis et sinceris manere pectoribus asseris,
grant that we may be so fashioned by your grace	da nobis tua gratia tales exsistere,
as to become a dwelling pleasing to you.	in quibus habitare digneris.
Through our Lord Jesus Christ, your Son,	Per Dominum nostrum Iesum Christum Filium tuum,
who lives and reigns with you in the unity of the Holy Spirit,	qui tecum vivit et regnat in unitate Spiritus Sancti,
one God, for ever and ever.	Deus, per omnia sæcula sæculorum.

FIRST READING

A reading from the prophet Jeremiah   17:5-8

A curse on the man who puts his trust in man, a blessing on the man who puts his trust in the Lord.

The Lord says this:

'A curse on the man who puts his trust in man,
who relies on things of flesh,
whose heart turns from the Lord.
He is like dry scrub in the wastelands:
if good comes, he has no eyes for it,
he settles in the parched places of the wilderness,
a salt land, uninhabited.

'A blessing on the man who puts his trust in the Lord,
with the Lord for his hope.
He is like a tree by the waterside
that thrusts its roots to the stream:
when the heat comes it feels no alarm,
its foliage stays green;
it has no worries in a year of drought,
and never ceases to bear fruit.'

The word of the Lord.

Responsorial Psalm   Ps 1:1-4,6. R. Ps 39:5

R. **Happy the man who has placed his trust in the Lord.**

Happy indeed is the man
who follows not the counsel of the wicked;
nor lingers in the way of sinners

nor sits in the company of scorners,
but whose delight is the law of the Lord
and who ponders his law day and night. R.

He is like a tree that is planted
beside the flowing waters,
that yields its fruit in due season
and whose leaves shall never fade;
and all that he does shall prosper. R.

Not so are the wicked, not so!
For they like winnowed chaff
shall be driven away by the wind.
For the Lord guards the way of the just
but the way of the wicked leads to doom. R.

SECOND READING

A reading from the first letter of St Paul to the Corinthians   15:12,16-20

If Christ has not been raised, your believing is useless.

If Christ raised from the dead is what has been preached, how can some of
you be saying that there is no resurrection of the dead? For if the dead are
not raised, Christ has not been raised, and if Christ has not been raised,
you are still in your sins. And what is more serious, all who have died in
Christ have perished. If our hope in Christ has been for this life only, we
are the most unfortunate of all people.

But Christ has in fact been raised from the dead, the first-fruits of all
who have fallen asleep.

The word of the Lord.

Gospel Acclamation   Cf. Mt 11:25

R. **Alleluia, alleluia!**
Blessed are you, Father,
Lord of heaven and earth;
for revealing the mysteries of the kingdom.
to mere children.
R. **Alleluia!**

Or: Lk 6:23

R. **Alleluia, alleluia!**
Rejoice and be glad;
your reward will be great in heaven.
R. **Alleluia!**

GOSPEL

A reading from the holy Gospel according to Luke   6:17,20-26

How happy are you who are poor. Alas for you who are rich.

Jesus came down with the Twelve and stopped at a piece of level ground where there was a large gathering of his disciples with a great crowd of people from all parts of Judaea and from Jerusalem and from the coastal region of Tyre and Sidon who had come to hear him and to be cured of their diseases.

Then fixing his eyes on his disciples he said:

'How happy are you who are poor: yours is the kingdom of God.
Happy you who are hungry now: you shall be satisfied.
Happy you who weep now: you shall laugh.

'Happy are you when people hate you, drive you out, abuse you, denounce your name as criminal, on account of the Son of Man. Rejoice when that day comes and dance for joy, for then your reward will be great in heaven. This was the way their ancestors treated the prophets.

'But alas for you who are rich: you are having your consolation now.
Alas for you who have your fill now: you shall go hungry.
Alas for you who laugh now: you shall mourn and weep.

'Alas for you when the world speaks well of you! This was the way their ancestors treated the false prophets.'

The Gospel of the Lord.

Prayer over the Offerings	Super oblata
May this oblation, O Lord, we pray, cleanse and renew us and may it become for those who do your will the source of eternal reward. Through Christ our Lord.	Hæc nos oblatio, quæsumus, Domine, mundet et renovet, atque tuam exsequentibus voluntatem fiat causa remunerationis æternæ. Per Christum Dominum nostrum.

Preface of Sundays in Ordinary Time I-VIII, pp.566-573.

Communion Antiphon Cf. Ps 77:29-30	Ant. ad communionem
They ate and had their fill, and what they craved the Lord gave them; they were not disappointed in what they craved.	Manducaverunt, et saturati sunt nimis, et desiderium eorum attulit eis Dominus; non sunt fraudati a desiderio suo.

Or: Jn 3:16 | Vel:

God so loved the world | Sic Deus dilexit mundum,
that he gave his Only Begotten Son, | ut Filium suum Unigenitum daret,
so that all who believe in him | ut omnis qui credit in eum
    may not perish, | non pereat,
but may have eternal life. | sed habeat vitam æternam.

Prayer after Communion | Post communionem

Having fed upon these | Cælestibus, Domine, pasti deliciis,
    heavenly delights, | quæsumus, ut semper eadem,
we pray, O Lord, | per quæ veraciter
that we may always long | vivimus, appetamus.
for that food by which we truly live. | Per Christum Dominum nostrum.
Through Christ our Lord. |

SEVENTH SUNDAY IN ORDINARY TIME (YEAR C)

Entrance Antiphon   Ps 12:6 | Ant. ad introitum

O LORD, I trust in your
  merciful love. | D OMINE, in tua
  misericordia speravi.
My heart will rejoice | Exsultavit cor meum in salutari tuo,
  in your salvation. | cantabo Domino,
I will sing to the Lord | qui bona tribuit mihi.
  who has been bountiful with me. |

Collect | Collecta

Grant, we pray, almighty God, | Præsta, quæsumus,
that, always pondering | omnipotens Deus,
  spiritual things, | ut, semper rationabilia meditantes,
we may carry out in both | quæ tibi sunt placita,
  word and deed | et dictis exsequamur et factis.
that which is pleasing to you. | Per Dominum nostrum Iesum
Through our Lord Jesus Christ, | Christum Filium tuum,
  your Son, | qui tecum vivit et regnat
who lives and reigns with you | in unitate Spiritus Sancti,
  in the unity of the Holy Spirit, | Deus, per omnia sæcula sæculorum.
one God, for ever and ever. |

FIRST READING

A reading from the first book of Samuel   26:2,7-9,12-13,22-23

The Lord put you in my power, but I would not raise my hand.

Saul set off and went down to the wilderness of Ziph, accompanied by three thousand men chosen from Israel to search for David in the wilderness of Ziph.

So in the dark David and Abishai made their way towards the force, where they found Saul lying asleep inside the camp, his spear stuck in the ground beside his head, with Abner and the troops lying round him.

Then Abishai said to David, 'Today God has put your enemy in your power; so now let me pin him to the ground with his own spear. Just one stroke! I will not need to strike him twice.' David answered Abishai, 'Do not kill him, for who can lift his hand against the Lord's anointed and be without guilt?' David took the spear and the pitcher of water from beside Saul's head, and they made off. No one saw, no one knew, no one woke up; they were all asleep, for a deep sleep from the Lord had fallen on them.

David crossed to the other side and halted on the top of the mountain a long way off; there was a wide space between them. David then called out, 'Here is the king's spear. Let one of the soldiers come across and take it. The Lord repays everyone for his uprightness and loyalty. Today the Lord put you in my power, but I would not raise my hand against the Lord's anointed.'

The word of the Lord.

Responsorial Psalm   Ps 102:1-4,8,10,12-13. R. v.8

R. **The Lord is compassion and love.**

My soul, give thanks to the Lord,
all my being, bless his holy name.
My soul, give thanks to the Lord
and never forget all his blessings. R.

It is he who forgives all your guilt,
who heals every one of your ills,
who redeems your life from the grave,
who crowns you with love and compassion. R.

The Lord is compassion and love,
slow to anger and rich in mercy.
He does not treat us according to our sins
nor repay us according to our faults. R.

As far as the east is from the west
so far does he remove our sins.
As a father has compassion on his sons,
the Lord has pity on those who fear him. R.

SECOND READING

A reading from the first letter of St Paul to the Corinthians   15:45-49

We who have been modelled on the earthly man will be modelled on the heavenly man.

The first man, Adam, as scripture says, became a living soul; but the last Adam has become a life-giving spirit. That is, first the one with the soul, not the spirit, and after that, the one with the spirit. The first man, being from the earth, is earthly by nature; the second man is from heaven. As this earthly man was, so are we on earth; and as the heavenly man is, so are we in heaven. And we, who have been modelled on the earthly man, will be modelled on the heavenly man.

The word of the Lord.

Gospel Acclamation   Cf. Ac 16:14

R. **Alleluia, alleluia!**
Open our heart, O Lord,
to accept the words of your Son.
R. **Alleluia!**

Or: Jn 13:34

R. **Alleluia, alleluia!**
I give you a new commandment:
love one another,
just as I have loved you,
says the Lord.
R. **Alleluia!**

GOSPEL

A reading from the holy Gospel according to Luke   6:27-38

Be compassionate as your Father is compassionate.

Jesus said to his disciples: 'I say this to you who are listening: Love your enemies, do good to those who hate you, bless those who curse you, pray for those who treat you badly. To the man who slaps you on one cheek, present the other cheek too; to the man who takes your cloak from you, do not refuse your tunic. Give to everyone who asks you, and do not ask for your property back from the man who robs you. Treat others as you would like them to treat you. If you love those who love you, what thanks can you expect? Even sinners love those who love them. And if you do good to those who do good to you, what thanks can you expect? For even sinners do that much. And if you lend to those from whom you hope to receive, what thanks can you expect? Even sinners lend to sinners to get back the same amount. Instead, love your enemies and do good, and lend without any hope of return. You will have a great reward, and you will be sons of the Most High, for he himself is kind to the ungrateful and the wicked.

'Be compassionate as your Father is compassionate. Do not judge, and you will not be judged yourselves; do not condemn, and you will not be condemned yourselves; grant pardon, and you will be pardoned. Give, and there will be gifts for you: a full measure, pressed down, shaken together, and running over, will be poured into your lap; because the amount you measure out is the amount you will be given back.'

The Gospel of the Lord.

Prayer over the Offerings	Super oblata

As we celebrate your mysteries,
   O Lord,
with the observance that is your due,
we humbly ask you,
that what we offer to the honour
   of your majesty
may profit us for salvation.
Through Christ our Lord.
	Mysteria tua, Domine,
	   debitis servitiis exsequentes,
	supplices te rogamus,
	ut, quod ad honorem tuæ
	   maiestatis offerimus,
	nobis proficiat ad salutem.
	Per Christum Dominum nostrum.

Preface of Sundays in Ordinary Time I-VIII, pp.566-573.

Communion Antiphon Ps 9:2-3	Ant. ad communionem
I will recount all your wonders, I will rejoice in you and be glad, and sing psalms to your name, O Most High.	Narrabo omnia mirabilia tua. Lætabor et exsultabo in te, psallam nomini tuo, Altissime.
Or: Jn 11:27	Vel:

Lord, I have come to believe
   that you are the Christ,
the Son of the living God,
   who is coming into this world.
	Domine, ego credidi quia
	   tu es Christus Filius Dei vivi,
	qui in hunc mundum venisti.

Prayer after Communion	Post communionem
Grant, we pray, almighty God, that we may experience the effects of the salvation which is pledged to us by these mysteries. Through Christ our Lord.	Præsta, quæsumus, omnipotens Deus, ut illius salutis capiamus effectum, cuius per hæc mysteria pignus accepimus. Per Christum Dominum nostrum.

EIGHTH SUNDAY IN ORDINARY TIME (YEAR C)

Entrance Antiphon Cf. Ps 17:19-20	Ant. ad introitum
THE Lord became my protector. He brought me out to a place of freedom; he saved me because he delighted in me.	FACTUS est Dominus protector meus, et eduxit me in latitudinem, salvum me fecit, quoniam voluit me.
Collect	Collecta
Grant us, O Lord, we pray, that the course of our world may be directed by your peaceful rule and that your Church may rejoice, untroubled in her devotion. Through our Lord Jesus Christ, your Son, who lives and reigns with you in the unity of the Holy Spirit, one God, for ever and ever.	Da nobis, quæsumus, Domine, ut et mundi cursus pacifico nobis tuo ordine dirigatur, et Ecclesia tua tranquilla devotione lætetur. Per Dominum nostrum Iesum Christum Filium tuum, qui tecum vivit et regnat in unitate Spiritus Sancti, Deus, per omnia sæcula sæculorum.

FIRST READING

A reading from the book of Ecclesiasticus   27:4-7

Do not praise a man before he has spoken.

In a shaken sieve the rubbish is left behind,
so too the defects of a man appear in his talk.
The kiln tests the work of the potter,
the test of a man is in his conversation.
The orchard where the tree grows is judged on the quality of its fruit,
similarly a man's words betray what he feels.
Do not praise a man before he has spoken,
since this is the test of men.

   The word of the Lord.

Responsional Psalm   Ps 91:2-3,13-16. R. Cf. v.2

R. **It is good to give you thanks, O Lord.**

It is good to give thanks to the Lord
to make music to your name, O Most High,
to proclaim your love in the morning
and your truth in the watches of the night. R.

The just will flourish like the palm-tree
and grow like a Lebanon cedar. R.

Planted in the house of the Lord
they will flourish in the courts of our God,
still bearing fruit when they are old,
still full of sap, still green,
to proclaim that the Lord is just.
In him, my rock, there is no wrong. R.

SECOND READING

A reading from first letter of St Paul to the Corinthians   15:54-58
He has given us the victory through our Lord Jesus Christ.

When this perishable nature has put on imperishability, and when this
mortal nature has put on immortality, then the words of scripture will
come true: Death is swallowed up in victory. Death, where is your victory?
Death, where is your sting? Now the sting of death is sin, and sin gets its
power from the Law. So let us thank God for giving us the victory through
our Lord Jesus Christ.

Never give in then, my dear brothers, never admit defeat; keep on
working at the Lord's work always, knowing that, in the Lord, you cannot
be labouring in vain.

The word of the Lord.

Gospel Acclamation   Cf. Ac 16:14

R. **Alleluia, alleluia!**
Open our heart, O Lord,
to accept the words of your Son.
R. **Alleluia!**

Or: Ph 2:15-16

R. **Alleluia, alleluia!**
You will shine in the world like bright stars
because you are offering it the word of life.
R. **Alleluia!**

GOSPEL

A reading from the holy Gospel according to Luke   6:39-45

A man's words flow out of what fills his heart.

Jesus told a parable to his disciples. 'Can one blind man guide another? Surely both will fall into a pit? The disciple is not superior to his teacher; the fully trained disciple will always be like his teacher. Why do you observe the splinter in your brother's eye and never notice the plank in your own? How can you say to your brother, "Brother, let me take out the splinter that is in your eye," when you cannot see the plank in your own? Hypocrite! Take the plank out of your own eye first, and then you will see clearly enough to take out the splinter that is in your brother's eye.

'There is no sound tree that produces rotten fruit, nor again a rotten tree that produces sound fruit. For every tree can be told by its own fruit; people do not pick figs from thorns, nor gather grapes from brambles. A good man draws what is good from the store of goodness in his heart; a bad man draws what is bad from the store of badness. For a man's words flow out of what fills his heart.'

The Gospel of the Lord.

Prayer over the Offerings	Super oblata
O God, who provide gifts to be offered to your name and count our oblations as signs of our desire to serve you with devotion, we ask of your mercy that what you grant as the source of merit may also help us to attain merit's reward. Through Christ our Lord.	Deus, qui offerenda tuo nomini tribuis, et oblata devotioni nostræ servitutis ascribis, quæsumus clementiam tuam, ut, quod præstas unde sit meritum, proficere nobis largiaris ad præmium. Per Christum Dominum nostrum.

Preface of Sundays in Ordinary Time I-VIII, pp.566-573.

Communion Antiphon Cf. Ps 12:6	Ant. ad communionem
I will sing to the Lord who has been bountiful with me, sing psalms to the name of the Lord Most High.	Cantabo Domino, qui bona tribuit mihi, et psallam nomini Domini Altissimi.

Or: Mt 28:20 | Vel:

Behold, I am with you always,
even to the end of the age,
    says the Lord.

Ecce ego vobiscum sum
    omnibus diebus,
usque ad consummationem sæculi,
    dicit Dominus.

Prayer after Communion | Post communionem

Nourished by your saving gifts,
we beseech your mercy, Lord,
that by this same Sacrament
with which you feed us
    in the present age,
you may make us partakers
    of life eternal.
Through Christ our Lord.

Satiati munere salutari,
tuam, Domine,
    misericordiam deprecamur,
ut, hoc eodem quo nos
    temporaliter vegetas sacramento,
perpetuæ vitæ participes
    benignus efficias.
Per Christum Dominum nostrum.

NINTH SUNDAY IN ORDINARY TIME (YEAR C)

Entrance Antiphon Cf. Ps 24:16,18 | Ant. ad introitum

TURN to me and have mercy
    on me, O Lord,
for I am alone and poor.
See my lowliness and suffering
and take away all my sins, my God.

RESPICE in me,
    et miserere mei, Domine,
quoniam unicus et pauper sum ego.
Vide humilitatem meam
    et laborem meum,
et dimitte omnia peccata mea,
    Deus meus.

Collect | Collecta

O God, whose providence never
    fails in its design,
keep from us, we humbly
    beseech you,
all that might harm us
and grant all that works for our good.
Through our Lord Jesus Christ,
    your Son,
who lives and reigns with you
    in the unity of the Holy Spirit,
one God, for ever and ever.

Deus, cuius providentia in sui
    dispositione non fallitur,
te supplices exoramus,
ut noxia cuncta submoveas,
et omnia nobis profutura concedas.
Per Dominum nostrum Iesum
    Christum Filium tuum,
qui tecum vivit et regnat
    in unitate Spiritus Sancti,
Deus, per omnia sæcula sæculorum.

FIRST READING

A reading from the first book of the Kings   8:41-43

If a foreigner comes, grant all he asks.

Solomon stood before the altar of the Lord and, stretching out his hands towards heaven, said:

'If a foreigner, not belonging to your people Israel, comes from a distant country for the sake of your name – for men will hear of your name, of your mighty hand and outstretched arm – if he comes and prays in this Temple, hear from heaven where your home is, and grant all the foreigner asks, so that all the peoples of the earth may come to know your name and, like your people Israel, revere you, and know that your name is given to the Temple I have built.'

The word of the Lord.

Responsorial Psalm   Ps 116:1-2, R. Mk 16:15

R. **Go out to the whole world
and proclaim the Good News.**
Or: **Alleluia!**

O praise the Lord, all you nations,
acclaim him all you peoples! R.

Strong is his love for us;
he is faithful for ever. R.

SECOND READING

A reading from the letter of St Paul to the Galatians   1:1-2,6-10

If I still wanted man's approval, I should not be a servant of Christ.

From Paul to the churches of Galatia, and from all the brothers who are here with me, an apostle who does not owe his authority to men or his appointment to any human being but who has been appointed by Jesus Christ and by God the Father who raised Jesus from the dead.

I am astonished at the promptness with which you have turned away from the one who called you and have decided to follow a different version of the Good News. Not that there can be more than one Good News; it is merely that some troublemakers among you want to change the Good News of Christ; and let me warn you that if anyone preaches a version of the Good News different from the one we have already preached to you, whether it be ourselves or an angel from heaven, he is to be condemned. I am only repeating what we told you before: if anyone preaches a version of the Good News different from the one you have already heard, he is to be condemned. So now whom am I trying to please – man, or God? Would you say it is men's approval I am looking for? If I still wanted that, I should not be what I am – a servant of Christ.

The word of the Lord.

Gospel Acclamation   Jn 1:14,12

R. **Alleluia, alleluia!**
The Word was made flesh and lived among us;
to all who did accept him
he gave power to become children of God.
R. **Alleluia!**

Or: Jn 3:16

R. **Alleluia, alleluia!**
God loved the world so much
that he gave us his only Son
so that everyone who believes in him
may have eternal life.
R. **Alleluia!**

GOSPEL

A reading from the holy Gospel according to Luke   7:1-10
Not even in Israel have I found faith like this.

When Jesus had come to the end of all he wanted the people to hear, he went into Capernaum. A centurion there had a servant, a favourite of his, who was sick and near death. Having heard about Jesus he sent some Jewish elders to him to ask him to come and heal his servant. When they came to Jesus they pleaded earnestly with him. 'He deserves this of you,' they said 'because he is friendly towards our people; in fact, he is the one who built the synagogue.' So Jesus went with them, and was not very far from the house when the centurion sent word to him by some friends: 'Sir,' he said 'do not put yourself to trouble; because I am not worthy to have you under my roof; and for this same reason I did not presume to come to you myself; but give the word and let my servant be cured. For I am under authority myself, and have soldiers under me; and I say to one man: Go, and he goes; to another: Come here, and he comes; to my servant: Do this, and he does it.' When Jesus heard these words he was astonished at him and, turning round, said to the crowd following him, 'I tell you, not even in Israel have I found faith like this.' And when the messengers got back to the house they found the servant in perfect health.

The Gospel of the Lord.

NINTH SUNDAY IN ORDINARY TIME (YEAR C) 1001

Prayer over the Offerings

Trusting in your compassion,
O Lord,
we come eagerly with our offerings
to your sacred altar,
that, through the purifying action
of your grace,
we may be cleansed by the very
mysteries we serve.
Through Christ our Lord.

Super oblata

In tua pietate confidentes, Domine,
cum muneribus ad altaria
veneranda concurrimus,
ut, tua purificante nos gratia,
iisdem quibus famulamur
mysteriis emundemur.
Per Christum Dominum nostrum.

Preface of Sundays in Ordinary Time I-VIII, pp.566-573.

Communion Antiphon Cf. Ps 16:6

To you I call, for you will surely
heed me, O God;
turn your ear to me;
hear my words.

Ant. ad communionem

Ego clamavi, quoniam
exaudisti me, Deus:
inclina aurem tuam,
et exaudi verba mea.

Or: Mk 11:23,24

Amen, I say to you:
Whatever you ask for in prayer,
believe you will receive it,
and it will be yours, says the Lord.

Vel:

Amen dico vobis,
quidquid orantes petitis,
credite quia accipietis, et fiet vobis,
dicit Dominus.

Prayer after Communion

Govern by your Spirit, we pray,
O Lord,
those you feed with the Body
and Blood of your Son,
that, professing you not just
in word or in speech,
but also in works and in truth,
we may merit to enter
the Kingdom of Heaven.
Through Christ our Lord.

Post communionem

Rege nos Spiritu tuo,
quæsumus, Domine,
quos pascis Filii tui Corpore
et Sanguine,
ut te, non solum verbo
neque lingua,
sed opere et veritate confitentes,
intrare mereamur
in regnum cælorum.
Per Christum Dominum nostrum.

TENTH SUNDAY IN ORDINARY TIME (YEAR C)

Entrance Antiphon   Cf. Ps 26:1-2

THE Lord is my light and my
salvation; whom shall I fear?
The Lord is the stronghold
of my life; whom should I dread?
When those who do evil draw near,
they stumble and fall.

Ant. ad introitum

DOMINUS illuminatio mea,
et salus mea, quem timebo?
Dominus defensor vitæ meæ,
a quo trepidabo?
Qui tribulant me inimici mei,
ipsi infirmati sunt.

Collect

O God, from whom all good
things come,
grant that we, who call on you
in our need,
may at your prompting discern
what is right,
and by your guidance do it.
Through our Lord Jesus Christ,
your Son,
who lives and reigns with you
in the unity of the Holy Spirit,
one God, for ever and ever.

Collecta

Deus, a quo bona
cuncta procedunt,
tuis largire supplicibus,
ut cogitemus, te inspirante,
quæ recta sunt,
et, te gubernante, eadem faciamus.
Per Dominum nostrum Iesum
Christum Filium tuum,
qui tecum vivit et regnat
in unitate Spiritus Sancti,
Deus, per omnia sæcula sæculorum.

FIRST READING

A reading from the first book of the Kings   17:17-24

Look, your son is alive.

The son of the mistress of the house fell sick; his illness was so severe that in the end he had no breath left in him. And the woman said to Elijah, 'What quarrel have you with me, man of God? Have you come here to bring my sins home to me and to kill my son?' 'Give me your son,' he said, and taking him from her lap, carried him to the upper room where he was staying and laid him on his own bed. He cried out to the Lord, 'Lord my God, do you mean to bring grief to the widow who is looking after me by killing her son?' He stretched himself on the child three times and cried out to the Lord, 'Lord my God, may the soul of this child, I beg you, come into him again!' The Lord heard the prayer of Elijah and the soul of the child returned to him again and he revived. Elijah took the child, brought him down from the upper room into the house, and gave him to his mother. 'Look,' Elijah said 'your son is alive.' And the woman replied,

'Now I know you are a man of God and the word of the Lord in your mouth is truth itself.'

The word of the Lord.

Responsial Psalm   Ps 29:2,4-6,11-13. R. v.2

R. **I will praise you, Lord,**
   you have rescued me.

I will praise you, Lord, you have rescued me
and have not let my enemies rejoice over me.
O Lord, you have raised my soul from the dead,
restored me to life from those who sink into the grave. R.

Sing psalms to the Lord, you who love him,
give thanks to his holy name.
His anger lasts a moment; his favour through life.
At night there are tears, but joy comes with dawn. R.

The Lord listened and had pity.
The Lord came to my help.
For me you have changed my mourning into dancing;
O Lord my God, I will thank you for ever. R.

SECOND READING

A reading from the letter of St Paul to the Galatians   1:11-19

God revealed his Son to me, so that I might preach the Good News about him to the pagans.

The Good News I preached is not a human message that I was given by men, it is something I learnt only through a revelation of Jesus Christ. You must have heard of my career as a practising Jew, how merciless I was in persecuting the Church of God, how much damage I did to it, how I stood out among other Jews of my generation, and how enthusiastic I was for the traditions of my ancestors.

Then God, who had specially chosen me while I was still in my mother's womb, called me through his grace and chose to reveal his Son in me, so that I might preach the Good News about him to the pagans. I did not stop to discuss this with any human being, nor did I go up to Jerusalem to see those who were already apostles before me, but I went off to Arabia at once and later went straight back from there to Damascus. Even when after three years I went up to Jerusalem to visit Cephas and stayed with him for fifteen days, I did not see any of the other apostles; I only saw James, the brother of the Lord.

The word of the Lord.

Gospel Acclamation   Cf. Ep 1:17,18

R. **Alleluia, alleluia!**
May the Father of our Lord Jesus Christ
enlighten the eyes of our mind
so that we can see what hope his call holds for us.
R. **Alleluia!**

Or: Lk 7:16

R. **Alleluia, alleluia!**
A great prophet has appeared among us;
God has visited his people.
R. **Alleluia!**

GOSPEL

A reading from the holy Gospel according to Luke   7:11-17

Young man, I tell you to get up.

Jesus went to a town called Nain, accompanied by his disciples and a great number of people. When he was near the gate of the town it happened that a dead man was being carried out for burial, the only son of his mother, and she was a widow. And a considerable number of the townspeople were with her. When the Lord saw her he felt sorry for her. 'Do not cry' he said. Then he went up and put his hand on the bier and the bearers stood still, and he said, 'Young man, I tell you to get up.' And the dead man sat up and began to talk, and Jesus gave him to his mother. Everyone was filled with awe and praised God saying, 'A great prophet has appeared among us; God has visited his people.' And this opinion of him spread throughout Judaea and all over the countryside.

The Gospel of the Lord.

Prayer over the Offerings	Super oblata

Look kindly upon our service,
   O Lord, we pray,
that what we offer
may be an acceptable oblation to you
and lead us to grow in charity.
Through Christ our Lord.
	Respice, Domine, quæsumus,
	   nostram propitius servitutem,
	ut quod offerimus sit tibi
	   munus acceptum,
	et nostræ caritatis augmentum.
	Per Christum Dominum nostrum.

Preface of Sundays in Ordinary Time I-VIII, pp.566-573.

Communion Antiphon Ps 17:3	Ant. ad communionem

Communion Antiphon   Ps 17:3

The Lord is my rock, my fortress,
    and my deliverer;
my God is my saving strength.

Or: 1 Jn 4:16

God is love, and whoever
    abides in love
abides in God, and God in him.

Prayer after Communion

May your healing work, O Lord,
free us, we pray, from doing evil
and lead us to what is right.
Through Christ our Lord.

Ant. ad communionem

Dominus firmamentum meum,
et refugium meum, et liberator meus.
Deus meus adiutor meus.

Vel:

Deus caritas est,
    et qui manet in caritate
in Deo manet et Deus in eo.

Post communionem

Tua nos, Domine,
    medicinalis operatio,
et a nostris perversitatibus
    clementer expediat,
et ad ea quæ sunt recta perducat.
Per Christum Dominum nostrum.

ELEVENTH SUNDAY IN ORDINARY TIME (YEAR C)

Entrance Antiphon   Cf. Ps 26:7,9

O LORD, hear my voice,
    for I have called to you;
    be my help.
Do not abandon or forsake me,
    O God, my Saviour!

Collect

O God, strength of those
    who hope in you,
graciously hear our pleas,
and, since without you mortal
    frailty can do nothing,
grant us always the help
    of your grace,
that in following your commands
we may please you by our resolve

Ant. ad introitum

EXAUDI, Domine, vocem meam,
    qua clamavi ad te.
Adiutor meus esto,
    ne derelinquas me,
neque despicias me,
    Deus salutaris meus.

Collecta

Deus, in te sperantium fortitudo,
invocationibus nostris
    adesto propitius,
et, quia sine te nihil potest
    mortalis infirmitas,
gratiæ tuæ præsta semper auxilium,
ut, in exsequendis mandatis tuis,
et voluntate tibi
    et actione placeamus.

and our deeds.
Through our Lord Jesus Christ,
   your Son,
who lives and reigns with you
   in the unity of the Holy Spirit,
one God, for ever and ever.

Per Dominum nostrum Iesum
   Christum Filium tuum,
qui tecum vivit et regnat
   in unitate Spiritus Sancti,
Deus, per omnia sæcula sæculorum.

FIRST READING

A reading from the second book of Samuel   12:7-10,13

The Lord forgives your sin; you are not to die.

Nathan said to David, 'The Lord the God of Israel says this, "I anointed you king over Israel; I delivered you from the hands of Saul; I gave your master's house to you, his wives into your arms; I gave you the House of Israel and of Judah; and if this were not enough, I would add as much again for you. Why have you shown contempt for the Lord, doing what displeases him? You have struck down Uriah the Hittite with the sword, taken his wife for your own, and killed him with the sword of the Ammonites. So now the sword will never be far from your House, since you have shown contempt for me and taken the wife of Uriah the Hittite to be your wife."'

David said to Nathan, 'I have sinned against the Lord.' Then Nathan said to David, 'The Lord, for his part, forgives your sin; you are not to die.'

The word of the Lord.

Responsorial Psalm   Ps 31:1-2,5,7,11. R. Cf. v.5

R. **Forgive, Lord, the guilt of my sin.**

   Happy the man whose offence is forgiven
   whose sin is remitted.
   O happy the man to whom the Lord
   imputes no guilt,
   in whose spirit is no guile. R.

   But now I have acknowledged my sins:
   my guilt I did not hide.
   I said: 'I will confess
   my offence to the Lord.'
   And you, Lord, have forgiven
   the guilt of my sin. R.

   You are my hiding place, O Lord;
   you save me from distress.
   You surround me with cries of deliverance. R.

Rejoice, rejoice in the Lord,
exult, you just!
O come, ring out your joy,
all you upright of heart. R.

SECOND READING

A reading from the letter of St Paul to the Galatians   2:16,19-21

I live now not with my own life but with the life of Christ who lives in me.

We acknowledge that what makes a man righteous is not obedience to the Law, but faith in Jesus Christ. We had to become believers in Christ Jesus no less than you had, and now we hold that faith in Christ rather than fidelity to the Law is what justifies us, and that no one can be justified by keeping the Law. In other words, through the Law I am dead to the Law, so that now I can live for God. I have been crucified with Christ, and I live now not with my own life but with the life of Christ who lives in me. The life I now live in this body I live in faith: faith in the Son of God who loved me and who sacrificed himself for my sake. I cannot bring myself to give up God's gift: if the Law can justify us, there is no point in the death of Christ.

The word of the Lord.

Gospel Acclamation   Jn 14:6

R. **Alleluia, alleluia!**
I am the Way, the Truth and the Life, says the Lord;
no one can come to the Father except through me.
R. **Alleluia!**

Or: 1 Jn 4:10

R. **Alleluia, alleluia!**
God so loved us when he sent his Son
to be the sacrifice that takes our sins away.
R. **Alleluia!**

GOSPEL

A reading from the holy Gospel according to Luke   7:36-8:3

Her many sins have been forgiven, or she would not have shown such great love.

[One of the Pharisees invited Jesus to a meal. When he arrived at the Pharisee's house and took his place at table, a woman came in, who had a bad name in the town. She had heard he was dining with the Pharisee and had brought with her an alabaster jar of ointment. She waited behind him at his feet, weeping, and her tears fell on his feet, and she wiped them away with her hair; then she covered his feet with kisses and anointed them with the ointment.

When the Pharisee who had invited him saw this, he said to himself, 'If this man were a prophet, he would know who this woman is that is touching him and what a bad name she has.' Then Jesus took him up and said, 'Simon, I have something to say to you.' 'Speak, Master' was the reply. 'There was once a creditor who had two men in his debt; one owed him five hundred denarii, the other fifty. They were unable to pay, so he pardoned them both. Which of them will love him more?' 'The one who was pardoned more, I suppose' answered Simon. Jesus said, 'You are right.'

Then he turned to the woman. 'Simon,' he said 'you see this woman? I came into your house, and you poured no water over my feet, but she has poured out her tears over my feet and wiped them away with her hair. You gave me no kiss, but she has been covering my feet with kisses ever since I came in. You did not anoint my head with oil, but she has anointed my feet with ointment. For this reason I tell you that her sins, her many sins, must have been forgiven her, or she would not have shown such great love. It is the man who is forgiven little who shows little love.' Then he said to her, 'Your sins are forgiven.' Those who were with him at table began to say to themselves, 'Who is this man, that he even forgives sins?' But he said to the woman, 'Your faith has saved you; go in peace.']

Now after this he made his way through towns and villages, preaching, and proclaiming the Good News of the kingdom of God. With him went the Twelve, as well as certain women who had been cured of evil spirits and ailments: Mary surnamed the Magdalene, from whom seven demons had gone out, Joanna the wife of Herod's steward Chuza, Susanna, and several others who provided for them out of their own resources.

[The Gospel of the Lord.]

Shorter Form, verses 36-50. Read between [ ]

Prayer over the Offerings	Super oblata
O God, who in the offerings presented here provide for the twofold needs of human nature, nourishing us with food and renewing us with your Sacrament, grant, we pray, that the sustenance they provide may not fail us in body or in spirit. Through Christ our Lord.	Deus, qui humani generis utramque substantiam præsentium munerum et alimento vegetas et renovas sacramento, tribue, quæsumus, ut eorum et corporibus nostris subsidium non desit et mentibus. Per Christum Dominum nostrum.

Preface of Sundays in Ordinary Time I-VIII, pp.566-573.

Communion Antiphon Ps 26:4	Ant. ad communionem

Communion Antiphon   Ps 26:4

There is one thing I ask of the Lord,
   only this do I seek:
to live in the house of the Lord
   all the days of my life.

Or: Jn 17:11

Holy Father, keep in your name
   those you have given me,
that they may be one as we are one,
   says the Lord.

Ant. ad communionem

Unum petii a Domino,
   hoc requiram,
ut inhabitem in domo Domini
omnibus diebus vitæ meæ.

Vel:

Pater sancte,
   serva eos in nomine tuo,
quos dedisti mihi, ut sint unum
   sicut et nos, dicit Dominus.

Prayer after Communion

As this reception of your
   Holy Communion, O Lord,
foreshadows the union
   of the faithful in you,
so may it bring about unity
   in your Church.
Through Christ our Lord.

Post communionem

Hæc tua, Domine,
   sumpta sacra communio,
sicut fidelium in te
   unionem præsignat,
sic in Ecclesia tua unitatis
   operetur effectum.
Per Christum Dominum nostrum.

TWELFTH SUNDAY IN ORDINARY TIME
(YEAR C)

Entrance Antiphon   Cf. Ps 27:8-9

THE Lord is the strength
of his people,
a saving refuge for the one
   he has anointed.
Save your people, Lord,
   and bless your heritage,
and govern them for ever.

Ant. ad introitum

DOMINUS fortitudo plebis suæ,
et protector salutarium Christi
sui est.
Salvum fac populum
   tuum, Domine,
et benedic hereditati tuæ,
et rege eos usque in sæculum.

Collect

Grant, O Lord,
that we may always revere and love
   your holy name,
for you never deprive
   of your guidance

Collecta

Sancti nominis tui, Domine,
timorem pariter et amorem fac nos
   habere perpetuum,
quia numquam tua
   gubernatione destituis,

those you set firm
   on the foundation of your love.
Through our Lord Jesus Christ,
   your Son,
who lives and reigns with you
   in the unity of the Holy Spirit,
one God, for ever and ever.
	quos in soliditate tuæ
	   dilectionis instituis.
	Per Dominum nostrum Iesum
	   Christum Filium tuum,
	qui tecum vivit et regnat
	   in unitate Spiritus Sancti,
	Deus, per omnia sæcula sæculorum.

FIRST READING

A reading from the prophet Zechariah   12:10-11; 13:1

They will look on the one whom they have pierced.

It is the Lord who speaks: 'Over the House of David and the citizens of Jerusalem I will pour out a spirit of kindness and prayer. They will look on the one whom they have pierced; they will mourn for him as for an only son, and weep for him as people weep for a first-born child. When that day comes, there will be great mourning in Judah, like the mourning of Hadadrimmon in the plain of Megiddo. When that day comes, a fountain will be opened for the House of David and the citizens of Jerusalem, for sin and impurity.'

   The word of the Lord.

Responsorial Psalm   Ps 62:2-6,8-9, R. v. 2

R. **For you my soul is thirsting,**
   O God, my God.

O God, you are my God, for you I long;
for you my soul is thirsting.
My body pines for you
like a dry, weary land without water. R.

So I gaze on you in the sanctuary
to see your strength and your glory.
For your love is better than life,
my lips will speak your praise. R.

So I will bless you all my life,
in your name I will lift up my hands.
My soul shall be filled as with a banquet,
my mouth shall praise you with joy. R.

For you have been my help;
in the shadow of your wings I rejoice.
My soul clings to you;
your right hand holds me fast. R.

SECOND READING

A reading from the letter of St Paul to the Galatians   3:26-29
All baptised in Christ, you have all clothed yourselves in Christ.

You are, all of you, sons of God through faith in Christ Jesus. All baptised in Christ, you have all clothed yourselves in Christ, and there are no more distinctions between Jew and Greek, slave and free, male and female, but all of you are one in Christ Jesus. Merely by belonging to Christ you are the posterity of Abraham, the heirs he was promised.

The word of the Lord.

Gospel Acclamation   Jn 8:12

R. **Alleluia, alleluia!**
I am the light of the world, says the Lord;
anyone who follows me
will have the light of life.
R. **Alleluia!**

Or: Jn 10:27

R. **Alleluia, alleluia!**
The sheep that belong to me listen to my voice,
says the Lord,
I know them and they follow me.
R. **Alleluia!**

GOSPEL

A reading from the holy Gospel according to Luke   9:18-24
You are the Christ of God. The Son of Man is destined to suffer grievously.

One day when Jesus was praying alone in the presence of his disciples he put this question to them, 'Who do the crowds say I am?' And they answered, 'John the Baptist; others Elijah; and others say one of the ancient prophets come back to life.' 'But you,' he said 'who do you say I am?' It was Peter who spoke up. 'The Christ of God' he said. But he gave them strict orders not to tell anyone anything about this.

'The Son of Man' he said 'is destined to suffer grievously, to be rejected by the elders and chief priests and scribes and to be put to death, and to be raised up on the third day.'

Then to all he said, 'If anyone wants to be a follower of mine, let him renounce himself and take up his cross every day and follow me. For anyone who wants to save his life will lose it; but anyone who loses his life for my sake, that man will save it.'

The Gospel of the Lord.

Prayer over the Offerings	Super oblata

Receive, O Lord, the sacrifice
    of conciliation and praise
and grant that,
    cleansed by its action,
we may make offering of a heart
    pleasing to you.
Through Christ our Lord.
	Suscipe, Domine,
	    sacrificium placationis et laudis,
	et præsta, ut,
	    huius operatione mundati,
	beneplacitum tibi nostræ mentis
	    offeramus affectum.
	Per Christum Dominum nostrum.

Preface of Sundays in Ordinary Time I-VIII, pp.566-573.

Communion Antiphon Ps 144:15	Ant. ad communionem

The eyes of all look to you, Lord,
and you give them their food
    in due season.
	Oculi omnium in te sperant,
	    Domine,
	et tu das illis escam
	    in tempore opportuno.

Or: Jn 10:11,15	Vel:

I am the Good Shepherd,
and I lay down my life for my sheep,
    says the Lord.
	Ego sum pastor bonus,
	et animam meam pono pro ovibus
	    meis, dicit Dominus.

Prayer after Communion	Post communionem

Renewed and nourished
by the Sacred Body and Precious
    Blood of your Son,
we ask of your mercy, O Lord,
that what we celebrate
    with constant devotion
may be our sure pledge
    of redemption.
Through Christ our Lord.
	Sacri Corporis et Sanguinis pretiosi
	    alimonia renovati,
	quæsumus, Domine,
	    clementiam tuam,
	ut, quod gerimus
	    devotione frequenti,
	certa redemptione capiamus.
	Per Christum Dominum nostrum.

THIRTEENTH SUNDAY IN ORDINARY TIME
(YEAR C)

Entrance Antiphon Ps 46:2	Ant. ad introitum

A LL peoples, clap your hands.
Cry to God with shouts of joy!

O MNES gentes,
plaudite manibus,
iubilate Deo in voce exsultationis.

Collect

Collecta

O God, who through the grace
of adoption
chose us to be children of light,
grant, we pray,
that we may not be wrapped
in the darkness of error
but always be seen to stand
in the bright light of truth.
Through our Lord Jesus Christ,
your Son,
who lives and reigns with you
in the unity of the Holy Spirit,
one God, for ever and ever.

Deus, qui, per adoptionem gratiæ,
lucis nos esse filios voluisti,
præsta, quæsumus, ut errorum
non involvamur tenebris,
sed in splendore veritatis semper
maneamus conspicui.
Per Dominum nostrum Iesum
Christum Filium tuum,
qui tecum vivit et regnat
in unitate Spiritus Sancti,
Deus, per omnia sæcula sæculorum.

FIRST READING

A reading from the first book of the Kings   19:16,19-21
Elisha rose and followed Elijah.

The Lord said to Elijah: 'Go, you are to anoint Elisha son of Shaphat, of
Abel Meholah, as prophet to succeed you.'

Leaving there, Elijah came on Elisha son of Shaphat as he was
ploughing behind twelve yoke of oxen, he himself being with the twelfth.
Elijah passed near to him and threw his cloak over him. Elisha left his oxen
and ran after Elijah. 'Let me kiss my father and mother, then I will follow
you' he said. Elijah answered, 'Go, go back, for have I done anything to
you?' Elisha turned away, took the pair of oxen and slaughtered them. He
used the plough for cooking the oxen, then gave to his men, who ate. He
then rose, and followed Elijah and became his servant.

The word of the Lord.

Responsorial Psalm   Ps 15:1-2,5,7-11. R. Cf. v.5

R. **O Lord, it is you who are my portion.**

Preserve me, God, I take refuge in you.
I say to the Lord: 'You are my God.'
O Lord, it is you who are my portion and cup;
it is you yourself who are my prize. R.

I will bless the Lord who gives me counsel,
who even at night directs my heart.
I keep the Lord ever in my sight:
since he is at my right hand, I shall stand firm. R.

And so my heart rejoices, my soul is glad;
even my body shall rest in safety.
For you will not leave my soul among the dead,
nor let your beloved know decay. R.

You will show me the path of life,
the fullness of joy in your presence
at your right hand happiness for ever. R.

SECOND READING

A reading from the letter of St Paul to the Galatians   5:1,13-18

You were called to liberty.

When Christ freed us, he meant us to remain free. Stand firm, therefore, and do not submit again to the yoke of slavery.

My brothers, you were called, as you know, to liberty; but be careful, or this liberty will provide an opening for self-indulgence. Serve one another, rather, in works of love, since the whole of the Law is summarised in a single command: Love your neighbour as yourself. If you go snapping at each other and tearing each other to pieces, you had better watch or you will destroy the whole community.

Let me put it like this: if you are guided by the Spirit you will be in no danger of yielding to self-indulgence, since self-indulgence is the opposite of the Spirit, the Spirit is totally against such a thing, and it is precisely because the two are so opposed that you do not always carry out your good intentions. If you are led by the Spirit, no law can touch you.

The word of the Lord.

Gospel Acclamation   1 S 3:9; Jn 6:68

R. **Alleluia, alleluia!**

Speak, Lord, your servant is listening:
you have the message of eternal life.

R. **Alleluia!**

GOSPEL

A reading from the holy Gospel according to Luke   9:51-62

Jesus resolutely took the road for Jerusalem. I will follow you wherever you go.

As the time drew near for him to be taken up to heaven, Jesus resolutely
took the road for Jerusalem and sent messengers ahead of him. These
set out, and they went into a Samaritan village to make preparations for
him, but the people would not receive him because he was making for
Jerusalem. Seeing this, the disciples James and John said, 'Lord, do you
want us to call down fire from heaven to burn them up?' But he turned
and rebuked them, and they went off to another village.

As they travelled along they met a man on the road who said to him, 'I
will follow you wherever you go.' Jesus answered, 'Foxes have holes and the
birds of the air have nests, but the Son of Man has nowhere to lay his head.'

Another to whom he said, 'Follow me,' replied, 'Let me go and bury my
father first.' But he answered, 'Leave the dead to bury their dead; your duty
is to go and spread the news of the kingdom of God.'

Another said, 'I will follow you, sir, but first let me go and say good-bye
to my people at home.' Jesus said to him, 'Once the hand is laid on the
plough, no one who looks back is fit for the kingdom of God.'

The Gospel of the Lord.

Prayer over the Offerings	Super oblata
O God, who graciously accomplish the effects of your mysteries, grant, we pray, that the deeds by which we serve you may be worthy of these sacred gifts. Through Christ our Lord.	Deus, qui mysteriorum tuorum dignanter operaris effectus, præsta, quæsumus, ut sacris apta muneribus fiant nostra servitia. Per Christum Dominum nostrum.

Preface of Sundays in Ordinary Time I-VIII, pp.566-573.

Communion Antiphon Cf. Ps 102:1

Bless the Lord, O my soul,
and all within me, his holy name.

Or: Jn 17:20-21

O Father, I pray for them,
    that they may be one in us,
that the world may believe that you
    have sent me, says the Lord.

Prayer after Communion

May this divine sacrifice
    we have offered and received
fill us with life, O Lord, we pray,
so that, bound to you
    in lasting charity,
we may bear fruit that lasts for ever.
Through Christ our Lord.

Ant. ad communionem

Benedic, anima mea, Domino,
et ea quæ intra me sunt nomini
    sancto eius.

Vel:

Pater, pro eis rogo,
    ut ipsi in nobis unum sint,
ut credat mundus quia tu me
    misisti, dicit Dominus.

Post communionem

Vivificet nos, quæsumus, Domine,
divina quam obtulimus
    et sumpsimus hostia,
ut, perpetua tibi caritate coniuncti,
fructum qui semper
    maneat afferamus.
Per Christum Dominum nostrum.

FOURTEENTH SUNDAY IN ORDINARY TIME
(YEAR C)

Entrance Antiphon Cf. Ps 47:10-11

YOUR merciful love, O God,
    we have received in the midst
of your temple.
Your praise, O God, like your name,
reaches the ends of the earth;
your right hand is filled
    with saving justice.

Collect

O God, who in the abasement
    of your Son
have raised up a fallen world,
fill your faithful with holy joy,
for on those you have rescued
    from slavery to sin

Ant. ad introitum

SUSCEPIMUS, Deus,
misericordiam tuam
in medio templi tui.
Secundum nomen tuum, Deus,
ita et laus tua in fines terræ;
iustitia plena est dextera tua.

Collecta

Deus, qui in Filii tui humilitate
iacentem mundum erexisti,
fidelibus tuis sanctam
    concede lætitiam,
ut, quos eripuisti a
    servitute peccati,

you bestow eternal gladness.
Through our Lord Jesus Christ,
    your Son,
who lives and reigns with you
    in the unity of the Holy Spirit,
one God, for ever and ever.

gaudiis facias perfrui sempiternis.
Per Dominum nostrum
    Iesum Christum Filium tuum,
qui tecum vivit et regnat
    in unitate Spiritus Sancti,
Deus, per omnia sæcula sæculorum.

FIRST READING

A reading from the prophet Isaiah   66:10-14

Towards her I send flowing peace, like a river.

Rejoice, Jerusalem,
be glad for her, all you who love her!
Rejoice, rejoice for her,
all you who mourned her!

That you may be suckled, filled,
from her consoling breast,
that you may savour with delight
her glorious breasts.

For thus says the Lord:
Now towards her I send flowing
peace, like a river,
and like a stream in spate
the glory of the nations.

At her breast will her nurslings be carried
and fondled in her lap.
Like a son comforted by his mother
will I comfort you.
And by Jerusalem you will be comforted.

At the sight your heart will rejoice,
and your bones flourish like the grass.
To his servants the Lord will reveal his hand.

    The word of the Lord.

Responsorial Psalm   Ps 65:1-7,16,20. R. v.1

R. **Cry out with joy to God all the earth.**

    Cry out with joy to God all the earth,
    O sing to the glory of his name.
    O render him glorious praise.
    Say to God: 'How tremendous your deeds! R.

'Before you all the earth shall bow;
shall sing to you, sing to your name!'
Come and see the works of God,
tremendous his deeds among men. R.

He turned the sea into dry land,
they passed through the river dry-shod.
Let our joy then be in him;
he rules for ever by his might. R.

Come and hear, all who fear God.
I will tell what he did for my soul.
Blessed be God who did not reject my prayer
nor withhold his love from me. R.

R. **Cry out with joy to God all the earth.**

SECOND READING

A reading from the letter of St Paul to the Galatians   6:14-18
The marks on my body are those of the Lord Jesus.

The only thing I can boast about is the cross of our Lord Jesus Christ, through whom the world is crucified to me, and I to the world. It does not matter if a person is circumcised or not; what matters is for him to become an altogether new creature. Peace and mercy to all who follow this rule, who form the Israel of God. I want no more trouble from anybody after this; the marks on my body are those of Jesus. The grace of our Lord Jesus Christ be with your spirit, my brothers. Amen.

The word of the Lord.

Gospel Acclamation   Jn 15:15

R. **Alleluia, alleluia!**
I call you friends, says the Lord,
because I have made known to you
everything I have learnt from my Father.
R. **Alleluia!**

Or: Col 3:15,16

R. **Alleluia, alleluia!**
May the peace of Christ
reign in your hearts,
because it is for this that you were called together
as part of one body.
R. **Alleluia!**

GOSPEL

A reading from the holy Gospel according to Luke   10:1-12,17-20

Your peace will rest on that man.

[The Lord appointed seventy-two others and sent them out ahead of him, in pairs, to all the towns and places he himself was to visit. He said to them, 'The harvest is rich but the labourers are few, so ask the Lord of the harvest to send labourers to his harvest. Start off now, but remember, I am sending you out like lambs among wolves. Carry no purse, no haversack, no sandals. Salute no one on the road. Whatever house you go into, let your first words be, "Peace to this house!" And if a man of peace lives there, your peace will go and rest on him; if not, it will come back to you. Stay in the same house, taking what food and drink they have to offer, for the labourer deserves his wages; do not move from house to house. Whenever you go into a town where they make you welcome, eat what is set before you. Cure those in it who are sick, and say, "The kingdom of God is very near to you."] But whenever you enter a town and they do not make you welcome, go out into its streets and say, "We wipe off the very dust of your town that clings to our feet, and leave it with you. Yet be sure of this: the kingdom of God is very near." I tell you, that on that day it will not go as hard with Sodom as with that town.'

The seventy-two came back rejoicing. 'Lord,' they said 'even the devils submit to us when we use your name.' He said to them, 'I watched Satan fall like lightning from heaven. Yes, I have given you power to tread underfoot serpents and scorpions and the whole strength of the enemy; nothing shall ever hurt you. Yet do not rejoice that the spirits submit to you; rejoice rather that your names are written in heaven.'

[The Gospel of the Lord.]

Shorter Form, verses 1-9. Read between [ ]

Prayer over the Offerings	Super oblata
May this oblation dedicated to your name purify us, O Lord, and day by day bring our conduct closer to the life of heaven. Through Christ our Lord.	Oblatio nos, Domine, tuo nomini dicata purificet, et de die in diem ad cælestis vitæ transferat actionem. Per Christum Dominum nostrum.

Preface of Sundays in Ordinary Time I-VIII, pp.566-573.

Communion Antiphon Ps 33:9	Ant. ad communionem
Taste and see that the Lord is good; blessed the man who seeks refuge in him.	Gustate et videte, quoniam suavis est Dominus; beatus vir, qui sperat in eo.
Or: Mt 11:28	Vel:
Come to me, all who labour and are burdened, and I will refresh you, says the Lord.	Venite ad me, omnes qui laboratis et onerati estis, et ego reficiam vos, dicit Dominus.
Prayer after Communion	Post communionem
Grant, we pray, O Lord, that, having been replenished by such great gifts, we may gain the prize of salvation and never cease to praise you. Through Christ our Lord.	Tantis, Domine, repleti muneribus, præsta, quæsumus, ut et salutaria dona capiamus, et a tua numquam laude cessemus. Per Christum Dominum nostrum.

FIFTEENTH SUNDAY IN ORDINARY TIME
(YEAR C)

Entrance Antiphon Cf. Ps 16:15	Ant. ad introitum
AS for me, in justice I shall behold your face; I shall be filled with the vision of your glory.	EGO autem cum iustitia apparebo in conspectu tuo; satiabor dum manifestabitur gloria tua.
Collect	Collecta
O God, who show the light of your truth to those who go astray, so that they may return to the right path, give all who for the faith they profess are accounted Christians the grace to reject whatever is contrary to the name of Christ	Deus, qui errantibus, ut in viam possint redire, veritatis tuæ lumen ostendis, da cunctis qui christiana professione censentur, et illa respuere, quæ huic inimica sunt nomini, et ea quæ sunt apta sectari.

and to strive after all that does
   it honour.
Through our Lord Jesus Christ,
   your Son,
who lives and reigns with you
   in the unity of the Holy Spirit,
one God, for ever and ever.

Per Dominum nostrum Iesum
   Christum Filium tuum,
qui tecum vivit et regnat
   in unitate Spiritus Sancti,
Deus, per omnia sæcula sæculorum.

FIRST READING

A reading from the book of Deuteronomy   30:10-14

The Word is very near to you for your observance.

Moses said to the people: 'Obey the voice of the Lord your God, keeping those commandments and laws of his that are written in the Book of this Law, and you shall return to the Lord your God with all your heart and soul.

   'For this Law that I enjoin on you today is not beyond your strength or beyond your reach. It is not in heaven, so that you need to wonder, "Who will go up to heaven for us and bring it down to us, so that we may hear it and keep it?" Nor is it beyond the seas, so that you need to wonder, "Who will cross the seas for us and bring it back to us, so that we may hear it and keep it?" No, the Word is very near to you, it is in your mouth and in your heart for your observance.'

   The word of the Lord.

Responsorial Psalm   Ps 68:14,17,30-31,33-34,36-37. R. Cf. v.33

R. **Seek the Lord, you who are poor,**
   and your hearts will revive.

   This is my prayer to you,
   my prayer for your favour.
   In your great love, answer me, O God,
   with your help that never fails:
   Lord, answer, for your love is kind;
   in your compassion, turn towards me. R.

   As for me in my poverty and pain
   let your help, O God, lift me up.
   I will praise God's name with a song;
   I will glorify him with thanksgiving. R.

   The poor when they see it will be glad
   and God-seeking hearts will revive;

for the Lord listens to the needy
and does not spurn his servants in their chains. R.

For God will bring help to Zion
and rebuild the cities of Judah.
The sons of his servants shall inherit it;
those who love his name shall dwell there. R.

R. **Seek the Lord, you who are poor,
and your hearts will revive.**

Alternative Responsorial Psalm   Ps 18:8-11. R. v.9

R. **The precepts of the Lord
gladden the heart.**

The law of the Lord is perfect,
it revives the soul.
The rule of the Lord is to be trusted,
it gives wisdom to the simple. R.

The precepts of the Lord are right,
they gladden the heart.
The command of the Lord is clear,
it gives light to the eyes. R.

The fear of the Lord is holy,
abiding for ever.
The decrees of the Lord are truth
and all of them just. R.

They are more to be desired than gold
than the purest of gold
and sweeter are they than honey,
than honey from the comb. R.

SECOND READING

A reading from the letter of St Paul to the Colossians   1:15-20

All things were created through Christ and for him.

Christ Jesus is the image of the unseen God
and the first-born of all creation,
for in him were created
all things in heaven and on earth:
everything visible and everything invisible,
Thrones, Dominations, Sovereignties, Powers –
all things were created through him and for him.

Before anything was created, he existed,
and he holds all things in unity.
Now the Church is his body,
he is its head.
As he is the Beginning,
he was first to be born from the dead,
so that he should be first in every way;
because God wanted all perfection
to be found in him
and all things to be reconciled through him and for him,
everything in heaven and everything on earth,
when he made peace
by his death on the cross.

    The word of the Lord.

Gospel Acclamation   Jn 10:27
R. **Alleluia, alleluia!**
The sheep that belong to me listen to my voice,
says the Lord,
I know them and they follow me.
R. **Alleluia!**

Or: Cf. Jn 6:63,68
R. **Alleluia, alleluia!**
Your words are spirit, Lord,
and they are life:
you have the message of eternal life.
R. **Alleluia!**

GOSPEL
A reading from the holy Gospel according to Luke   10:25-37
Who is my neighbour?

There was a lawyer who, to disconcert Jesus, stood up and said to him,
'Master, what must I do to inherit eternal life?' He said to him, 'What is
written in the law? What do you read there?' He replied, 'You must love
the Lord your God with all your heart, with all your soul, with all your
strength, and with all your mind, and your neighbour as yourself.' 'You
have answered right,' said Jesus 'do this and life is yours.'

    But the man was anxious to justify himself and said to Jesus, 'And who
is my neighbour?' Jesus replied, 'A man was once on his way down from

Jerusalem to Jericho and fell into the hands of brigands; they took all he had, beat him and then made off, leaving him half dead. Now a priest happened to be travelling down the same road, but when he saw the man, he passed by on the other side. In the same way a Levite who came to the place saw him, and passed by on the other side. But a Samaritan traveller who came upon him was moved with compassion when he saw him. He went up and bandaged his wounds, pouring oil and wine on them. He then lifted him on to his own mount, carried him to the inn and looked after him. Next day, he took out two denarii and handed them to the innkeeper. "Look after him," he said "and on my way back I will make good any extra expense you have." Which of these three, do you think, proved himself a neighbour to the man who fell into the brigands' hands?' 'The one who took pity on him' he replied. Jesus said to him, 'Go, and do the same yourself.'

The Gospel of the Lord.

Prayer over the Offerings

Look upon the offerings
    of the Church, O Lord,
as she makes her prayer to you,
and grant that, when consumed
    by those who believe,
they may bring ever greater holiness.
Through Christ our Lord.

Super oblata

Respice, Domine, munera
    supplicantis Ecclesiæ,
et pro credentium
    sanctificationis incremento
sumenda concede.
Per Christum Dominum nostrum.

Preface of Sundays in Ordinary Time I-VIII, pp.566-573.

Communion Antiphon Cf. Ps 83:4-5

The sparrow finds a home,
and the swallow a nest for her young:
by your altars, O Lord of hosts,
    my King and my God.
Blessed are they who dwell
    in your house,
for ever singing your praise.

Ant. ad communionem

Passer invenit sibi domum,
et turtur nidum,
    ubi reponat pullos suos.
Altaria tua, Domine virtutum,
    Rex meus, et Deus meus!
Beati qui habitant in domo tua,
in sæculum sæculi laudabunt te.

Or: Jn 6:57

Whoever eats my flesh
    and drinks my blood
remains in me and I in him,
    says the Lord.

Vel:

Qui manducat meam carnem
    et bibit meum sanguinem,
in me manet et ego in eo,
    dicit Dominus.

Prayer after Communion	Post communionem

Having consumed these gifts,
    we pray, O Lord,
that, by our participation
    in this mystery,
its saving effects upon us may grow.
Through Christ our Lord.
	Sumptis muneribus,
	    quæsumus, Domine,
	ut, cum frequentatione mysterii,
	crescat nostræ salutis effectus.
	Per Christum Dominum nostrum.

SIXTEENTH SUNDAY IN ORDINARY TIME
(YEAR C)

Entrance Antiphon Ps 53:6,8	Ant. ad introitum

SEE, I have God for my help.
The Lord sustains my soul.
I will sacrifice to you
    with willing heart,
and praise your name, O Lord,
    for it is good.
	ECCE Deus adiuvat me,
	et Dominus susceptor
	    est animæ meæ.
	Voluntarie sacrificabo tibi,
	et confitebor nomini tuo, Domine,
	    quoniam bonum est.

Collect	Collecta

Show favour, O Lord, to your servants
and mercifully increase the gifts
    of your grace,
that, made fervent in hope,
    faith and charity,
they may be ever watchful
    in keeping your commands.
Through our Lord Jesus Christ,
    your Son,
who lives and reigns with you
    in the unity of the Holy Spirit,
one God, for ever and ever.
	Propitiare, Domine, famulis tuis,
	et clementer gratiæ tuæ super eos
	    dona multiplica,
	ut, spe, fide et caritate ferventes,
	semper in mandatis tuis vigili
	    custodia perseverent.
	Per Dominum nostrum Iesum
	    Christum Filium tuum,
	qui tecum vivit et regnat
	    in unitate Spiritus Sancti,
	Deus, per omnia sæcula sæculorum.

FIRST READING

A reading from the book of Genesis   18:1-10

Lord, do not pass your servant by.

The Lord appeared to Abraham at the Oak of Mamre while he was sitting by the entrance of the tent during the hottest part of the day. He looked up, and there he saw three men standing near him. As soon as he saw them he ran from the entrance of the tent to meet them, and bowed to the ground. 'My Lord,' he said 'I beg you, if I find favour with you, kindly do not pass your servant by. A little water shall be brought; you shall wash your feet and lie down under the tree. Let me fetch a little bread and you shall refresh yourselves before going further. That is why you have come in your servant's direction.' They replied, 'Do as you say.'

Abraham hastened to the tent to find Sarah. 'Hurry,' he said 'knead three bushels of flour and make loaves.' Then running to the cattle Abraham took a fine and tender calf and gave it to the servant, who hurried to prepare it. Then taking cream, milk and the calf he had prepared, he laid all before them, and they ate while he remained standing near them under the tree.

'Where is your wife Sarah?' they asked him. 'She is in the tent' he replied. Then his guest said, 'I shall visit you again next year without fail and your wife will then have a son.'

The word of the Lord.

Responsorial Psalm   Ps 14:2-5. R. v.1

R. **The just will live in the presence of the Lord.**

Lord, who shall dwell on your holy mountain?
He who walks without fault;
he who acts with justice
and speaks the truth from his heart;
he who does not slander with his tongue. R.

He who does no wrong to his brother,
who casts no slur on his neighbour,
who holds the godless in disdain,
but honours those who fear the Lord. R.

He who keeps his pledge, come what may;
who takes no interest on a loan
and accepts no bribes against the innocent.
Such a man will stand firm for ever. R.

SECOND READING

A reading from the letter of St Paul to the Colossians   1:24-28

A mystery hidden for centuries has now been revealed to God's saints.

It makes me happy to suffer for you, as I am suffering now, and in my own body to do what I can to make up all that has still to be undergone by Christ for the sake of his body, the Church. I became the servant of the Church when God made me responsible for delivering God's message to you, the message which was a mystery hidden for generations and centuries and has now been revealed to his saints. It was God's purpose to reveal it to them and to show all the rich glory of this mystery to pagans. The mystery is Christ among you, your hope of glory: this is the Christ we proclaim, this is the wisdom in which we thoroughly train everyone and instruct everyone, to make them all perfect in Christ.

The word of the Lord.

Gospel Acclamation   Cf. Ac 16:14

R. **Alleluia, alleluia!**
Open our heart, O Lord,
to accept the words of your Son.
R. **Alleluia!**

Or: Cf. Lk 8:15

R. **Alleluia, alleluia!**
Blessed are those who,
with a noble and generous heart,
take the word of God to themselves
and yield a harvest through their perseverance.
R. **Alleluia!**

GOSPEL

A reading from the holy Gospel according to Luke   10:38-42
Martha welcomed Jesus into her house. Mary has chosen the better part.

Jesus came to a village, and a woman named Martha welcomed him into her house. She had a sister called Mary, who sat down at the Lord's feet and listened to him speaking. Now Martha who was distracted with all the serving said, 'Lord, do you not care that my sister is leaving me to do the serving all by myself? Please tell her to help me.' But the Lord answered 'Martha, Martha,' he said 'you worry and fret about so many things, and yet few are needed, indeed only one. It is Mary who has chosen the better part; it is not to be taken from her.'

The Gospel of the Lord.

Prayer over the Offerings

O God, who in the one
    perfect sacrifice
brought to completion varied
    offerings of the law,
accept, we pray, this sacrifice
    from your faithful servants
and make it holy, as you blessed
    the gifts of Abel,
so that what each has offered
    to the honour of your majesty
may benefit the salvation of all.
Through Christ our Lord.

Super oblata

Deus, qui legalium
    differentiam hostiarum
unius sacrificii perfectione sanxisti,
accipe sacrificium a devotis
    tibi famulis,
et pari benedictione,
    sicut munera Abel, sanctifica,
ut, quod singuli obtulerunt
    ad maiestatis tuæ honorem,
cunctis proficiat ad salutem.
Per Christum Dominum nostrum.

Preface of Sundays in Ordinary Time I-VIII, pp.566-573.

Communion Antiphon Ps 110:4-5

The Lord, the gracious, the merciful,
has made a memorial of his wonders;
he gives food to those who fear him.

Ant. ad communionem

Memoriam fecit mirabilium suorum
misericors et miserator Dominus;
escam dedit timentibus se.

Or: Rv 3:20

Behold, I stand at the door
    and knock, says the Lord.
If anyone hears my voice
    and opens the door to me,
I will enter his house and dine
    with him, and he with me.

Vel:

Ecce sto ad ostium et pulso,
    dicit Dominus:
si quis audierit vocem meam,
    et aperuerit mihi ianuam,
intrabo ad illum, et cenabo
    cum illo, et ipse mecum.

Prayer after Communion

Graciously be present to your people,
    we pray, O Lord,
and lead those you have imbued
    with heavenly mysteries
to pass from former ways
    to newness of life.
Through Christ our Lord.

Post communionem

Populo tuo, quæsumus, Domine,
    adesto propitius,
et, quem mysteriis
    cælestibus imbuisti,
fac ad novitatem vitæ
    de vetustate transire.
Per Christum Dominum nostrum.

SEVENTEENTH SUNDAY IN ORDINARY TIME
(YEAR C)

Entrance Antiphon Cf. Ps 67:6-7,36

GOD is in his holy place,
God who unites those
who dwell in his house;
he himself gives might and strength
to his people.

Ant. ad introitum

DEUS in loco sancto suo;
Deus qui inhabitare facit
unanimes in domo,
ipse dabit virtutem et fortitudinem
plebi suæ.

Collect

O God, protector of those
who hope in you,
without whom nothing has firm
foundation, nothing is holy,
bestow in abundance your mercy
upon us
and grant that, with you as our ruler
and guide,
we may use the good things that pass
in such a way as to hold fast even now
to those that ever endure.
Through our Lord Jesus Christ,
your Son,
who lives and reigns with you
in the unity of the Holy Spirit,
one God, for ever and ever.

Collecta

Protector in te sperantium, Deus,
sine quo nihil est validum,
nihil sanctum,
multiplica super nos
misericordiam tuam
ut, te rectore, te duce, sic bonis
transeuntibus nunc utamur,
ut iam possimus
inhærere mansuris.

Per Dominum nostrum Iesum
Christum Filium tuum,
qui tecum vivit et regnat
in unitate Spiritus Sancti,
Deus, per omnia sæcula sæculorum.

FIRST READING

A reading from the book of Genesis   18:20-32

I trust my Lord will not be angry, but give me leave to speak.

The Lord said, 'How great an outcry there is against Sodom and Gomorrah!
How grievous is their sin! I propose to go down and see whether or not
they have done all that is alleged in the outcry against them that has come
up to me. I am determined to know.'

The men left there and went to Sodom while Abraham remained
standing before the Lord. Approaching him he said, 'Are you really going
to destroy the just man with the sinner? Perhaps there are fifty just men
in the town. Will you really overwhelm them, will you not spare the place

for the fifty just men in it? Do not think of doing such a thing: to kill the just man with the sinner, treating just and sinner alike! Do not think of it! Will the judge of the whole earth not administer justice?' The Lord replied, 'If at Sodom I find fifty just men in the town, I will spare the whole place because of them.'

Abraham replied, 'I am bold indeed to speak like this to my Lord, I who am dust and ashes. But perhaps the fifty just men lack five: will you destroy the whole city for five?' 'No,' he replied, 'I will not destroy it if I find forty-five just men there.' Again Abraham said to him, 'Perhaps there will only be forty there.' 'I will not do it' he replied 'for the sake of the forty.'

Abraham said, 'I trust my Lord will not be angry, but give me leave to speak: perhaps there will only be thirty there.' 'I will not do it' he replied 'if I find thirty there.' He said, 'I am bold indeed to speak like this, but perhaps there will only be twenty there.' 'I will not destroy it' he replied 'for the sake of the twenty.' He said, 'I trust my Lord will not be angry if I speak once more: perhaps there will only be ten.' 'I will not destroy it' he replied 'for the sake of the ten.'

The word of the Lord.

Responsorial Psalm   Ps 137:1-3,6-8. R. v.3

R. **On the day I called,**
   you answered me, O Lord.

I thank you, Lord, with all my heart,
you have heard the words of my mouth.
In the presence of the angels I will bless you.
I will adore before your holy temple. R.

I thank you for your faithfulness and love
which excel all we ever knew of you.
On the day I called, you answered;
you increased the strength of my soul. R.

The Lord is high yet he looks on the lowly
and the haughty he knows from afar.
Though I walk in the midst of affliction
you give me life and frustrate my foes. R.

You stretch out your hand and save me,
your hand will do all things for me.
Your love, O Lord, is eternal,
discard not the work of your hands. R.

SECOND READING

A reading from the letter of St Paul to the Colossians   2:12-14

He has brought you to life with him, he has forgiven us all our sins.

You have been buried with Christ, when you were baptised; and by baptism, too, you have been raised up with him through your belief in the power of God who raised him from the dead. You were dead, because you were sinners and had not been circumcised: he has brought you to life with him, he has forgiven us all our sins.

He has overridden the Law, and cancelled every record of the debt that we had to pay; he has done away with it by nailing it to the cross.

The word of the Lord.

Gospel Acclamation   Jn 1:14,12

R. **Alleluia, alleluia!**

The Word was made flesh and lived among us;
to all who did accept him
he gave power to become children of God.

R. **Alleluia!**

Or: Rm 8:15

R. **Alleluia, alleluia!**

The spirit you received is the spirit of sons,
and it makes us cry out, 'Abba Father!'

R. **Alleluia!**

GOSPEL

A reading from the holy Gospel according to Luke   11:1-13

Ask, and it will be given to you.

Once Jesus was in a certain place praying, and when he had finished, one of his disciples said, 'Lord, teach us to pray, just as John taught his disciples.' He said to them, 'Say this when you pray:

"Father, may your name be held holy,
your kingdom come;
give us each day our daily bread,
and forgive us our sins,
for we ourselves forgive each one who is in debt to us.
And do not put us to the test."'

He also said to them, 'Suppose one of you has a friend and goes to him in the middle of the night to say, "My friend, lend me three loaves, because a friend of mine on his travels has just arrived at my house and I have nothing to offer him"; and the man answers from inside the house, "Do not bother me. The door is bolted now, and my children and I are in bed; I cannot get up to give it to you." I tell you, if the man does not get up and give it him for friendship's sake, persistence will be enough to make him get up and give his friend all he wants.

'So I say to you: Ask, and it will be given to you; search, and you will find; knock, and the door will be opened to you. For the one who asks always receives; the one who searches always finds; the one who knocks will always have the door opened to him. What father among you would hand his son a stone when he asked for bread? Or hand him a snake instead of a fish? Or hand him a scorpion if he asked for an egg? If you then, who are evil, know how to give your children what is good, how much more will the heavenly Father give the Holy Spirit to those who ask him!'

The Gospel of the Lord.

Prayer over the Offerings	Super oblata
Accept, O Lord, we pray, the offerings which we bring from the abundance of your gifts, that through the powerful working of your grace these most sacred mysteries may sanctify our present way of life and lead us to eternal gladness. Through Christ our Lord.	Suscipe, quæsumus, Domine, munera, quæ tibi de tua largitate deferimus, ut hæc sacrosancta mysteria, gratiæ tuæ operante virtute, et præsentis vitæ nos conversatione sanctificent, et ad gaudia sempiterna perducant. Per Christum Dominum nostrum.

Preface of Sundays in Ordinary Time I-VIII, pp.566-573.

Communion Antiphon Ps 102:2	Ant. ad communionem
Bless the Lord, O my soul, and never forget all his benefits.	Benedic, anima mea, Domino, et noli oblivisci omnes retributiones eius.

Or: Mt 5:7-8	Vel:
Blessed are the merciful, for they shall receive mercy. Blessed are the clean of heart, for they shall see God.	Beati misericordes, quoniam ipsi misericordiam consequentur. Beati mundo corde, quoniam ipsi Deum videbunt.

Prayer after Communion

We have consumed, O Lord,
    this divine Sacrament,
the perpetual memorial
    of the Passion of your Son;
grant, we pray, that this gift,
which he himself gave us with love
    beyond all telling,
may profit us for salvation.
Through Christ our Lord.

Post communionem

Sumpsimus, Domine,
    divinum sacramentum,
passionis Filii tui
    memoriale perpetuum;
tribue, quæsumus,
ut ad nostram salutem hoc
    munus proficiat,
quod ineffabili nobis caritate
    ipse donavit.
Qui vivit et regnat
    in sæcula sæculorum.

EIGHTEENTH SUNDAY IN ORDINARY TIME
(YEAR C)

Entrance Antiphon   Ps 69:2,6

O GOD, come to my assistance;
    O Lord, make haste to help me!
You are my rescuer, my help;
O Lord, do not delay.

Ant. ad introitum

DEUS, in adiutorium
    meum intende;
Domine, ad adiuvandum me festina.
Adiutor meus et liberator meus es tu;
Domine, ne moreris.

Collect

Draw near to your servants, O Lord,
and answer their prayers
    with unceasing kindness,
that, for those who glory in you
    as their Creator and guide,
you may restore what you
    have created
and keep safe what you have restored.
Through our Lord Jesus Christ,
    your Son,
who lives and reigns with you
    in the unity of the Holy Spirit,
one God, for ever and ever.

Collecta

Adesto, Domine, famulis tuis,
et perpetuam benignitatem
    largire poscentibus,
ut his, qui te auctorem et
    gubernatorem gloriantur habere,
et creata restaures,
    et restaurata conserves.
Per Dominum nostrum Iesum
    Christum Filium tuum,
qui tecum vivit et regnat
    in unitate Spiritus Sancti,
Deus, per omnia sæcula sæculorum.

FIRST READING

A reading from the book of Ecclesiastes 1:2; 2:21-23

What does man gain for all his toil?

Vanity of vanities, the Preacher says. Vanity of vanities. All is vanity!

For so it is that a man who has laboured wisely, skilfully and successfully must leave what is his own to someone who has not toiled for it at all. This, too, is vanity and great injustice; for what does he gain for all the toil and strain that he has undergone under the sun? What of all his laborious days, his cares of office, his restless nights? This, too, is vanity.

The word of the Lord.

Responsorial Psalm Ps 89:3-6,12-14,17. R. v.1

R. **O Lord, you have been our refuge**
   from one generation to the next.

   You turn men back into dust
   and say: 'Go back, sons of men.'
   To your eyes a thousand years
   are like yesterday, come and gone,
   no more than a watch in the night. R.

   You sweep men away like a dream,
   like grass which springs up in the morning.
   In the morning it springs up and flowers:
   by evening it withers and fades. R.

   Make us know the shortness of our life
   that we may gain wisdom of heart.
   Lord, relent! Is your anger for ever?
   Show pity to your servants. R.

   In the morning, fill us with your love;
   we shall exult and rejoice all our days.
   Let the favour of the Lord be upon us:
   give success to the work of our hands. R.

Alternative Responsorial Psalm Ps 94:1-2,6-9. R. vv. 7-8

R. **O that today you would listen to his voice!**
   Harden not your hearts.

   Come, ring out our joy to the Lord;
   hail the rock who saves us.

Let us come before him, giving thanks,
with songs let us hail the Lord. R.

Come in; let us bow and bend low;
let us kneel before the God who made us
for he is our God and we
the people who belong to his pasture,
the flock that is led by his hand. R.

O that today you would listen to his voice!
'Harden not your hearts as at Meribah,
as on that day at Massah in the desert
when your fathers put me to the test;
when they tried me, though they saw my work.' R.

SECOND READING

A reading from the letter of St Paul to the Colossians   3:1-5,9-11

You must look for the things that are in heaven, where Christ is.

Since you have been brought back to true life with Christ, you must look for the things that are in heaven, where Christ is, sitting at God's right hand. Let your thoughts be on heavenly things, not on the things that are on the earth, because you have died, and now the life you have is hidden with Christ in God. But when Christ is revealed – and he is your life – you too will be revealed in all your glory with him.

That is why you must kill everything in you that belongs only to earthly life: fornication, impurity, guilty passion, evil desires and especially greed, which is the same thing as worshipping a false god; and never tell each other lies. You have stripped off your old behaviour with your old self, and you have put on a new self which will progress towards true knowledge the more it is renewed in the image of its creator; and in that image there is no room for distinction between Greek and Jew, between the circumcised or the uncircumcised, or between barbarian and Scythians, slave and free man. There is only Christ: he is everything and he is in everything.

The word of the Lord.

Gospel Acclamation   Cf. Jn 17:17

R. **Alleluia, alleluia!**
Your word is truth, O Lord,
consecrate us in the truth.
R. **Alleluia!**

Or: Mt 5:3

R. **Alleluia, alleluia!**
How happy are the poor in spirit;
theirs is the kingdom of heaven.
R. **Alleluia!**

GOSPEL

A reading from the holy Gospel according to Luke   12:13-21

This hoard of yours, whose will it be?

A man in the crowd said to Jesus, 'Master, tell my brother to give me a share of our inheritance.' 'My friend,' he replied, 'who appointed me your judge, or the arbitrator of your claims?' Then he said to them, 'Watch, and be on your guard against avarice of any kind, for a man's life is not made secure by what he owns, even when he has more than he needs.'

Then he told them a parable: 'There was once a rich man who, having had a good harvest from his land, thought to himself, "What am I to do? I have not enough room to store my crops." Then he said, "This is what I will do: I will pull down my barns and build bigger ones, and store all my grain and my goods in them, and I will say to my soul: My soul, you have plenty of good things laid by for many years to come; take things easy, eat, drink, have a good time." But God said to him, "Fool! This very night the demand will be made for your soul; and this hoard of yours, whose will it be then?" So it is when a man stores up treasure for himself in place of making himself rich in the sight of God.'

The Gospel of the Lord.

Prayer over the Offerings	Super oblata

Graciously sanctify these gifts,
   O Lord, we pray,
and, accepting the oblation
   of this spiritual sacrifice,
make of us an eternal offering to you.
Through Christ our Lord.
	Propitius, Domine, quæsumus,
	   hæc dona sanctifica,
	et, hostiæ spiritalis
	   oblatione suscepta,
	nosmetipsos tibi perfice
	   munus æternum.
	Per Christum Dominum nostrum.

Preface of Sundays in Ordinary Time I-VIII, pp.566-573.

Communion Antiphon Ws 16:20	Ant. ad communionem

You have given us, O Lord,
   bread from heaven,
endowed with all delights
   and sweetness in every taste.
	Panem de cælo dedisti
	   nobis, Domine,
	habentem omne delectamentum,
	et omnem saporem suavitatis.

Or: Jn 6:35
I am the bread of life, says the Lord;
whoever comes to me will not hunger
and whoever believes in me
    will not thirst.

Vel:
Ego sum panis vitæ, dicit Dominus.
Qui venit ad me non esuriet,
    et qui credit in me non sitiet.

Prayer after Communion
Accompany with constant
    protection, O Lord,
those you renew with these
    heavenly gifts
and, in your never-failing care
    for them,
make them worthy
    of eternal redemption.
Through Christ our Lord.

Post communionem
Quos cælesti recreas munere,
perpetuo, Domine,
    comitare præsidio,
et, quos fovere non desinis,
dignos fieri sempiterna
    redemptione concede.
Per Christum Dominum nostrum.

NINETEENTH SUNDAY IN ORDINARY TIME
(YEAR C)

Entrance Antiphon Cf. Ps 73:20,19,22,23
LOOK to your covenant, O Lord,
    and forget not the life
    of your poor ones for ever.
Arise, O God, and defend your cause,
and forget not the cries of those
    who seek you.

Ant. ad introitum
RESPICE, Domine,
    in testamentum tuum,
et animas pauperum tuorum
    ne derelinquas in finem.
Exsurge, Domine,
    et iudica causam tuam,
et ne obliviscaris
    voces quærentium te.

Collect
Almighty ever-living God,
whom, taught by the Holy Spirit,
we dare to call our Father,
bring, we pray, to perfection
    in our hearts
the spirit of adoption as your sons
    and daughters,
that we may merit to enter

Collecta
Omnipotens sempiterne Deus,
quem, docente Spiritu Sancto,
paterno nomine invocare
    præsumimus,
perfice in cordibus nostris spiritum
    adoptionis filiorum,
ut promissam hereditatem
    ingredi mereamur.

into the inheritance	Per Dominum nostrum Iesum

into the inheritance
which you have promised.
Through our Lord Jesus Christ,
   your Son,
who lives and reigns with you
   in the unity of the Holy Spirit,
one God, for ever and ever.

Per Dominum nostrum Iesum
   Christum Filium tuum,
qui tecum vivit et regnat
   in unitate Spiritus Sancti,
Deus, per omnia sæcula sæculorum.

FIRST READING

A reading from the book of Wisdom   18:6-9

By the same act with which you took vengeance on ours foes you made us glorious by calling us to you.

That night had been foretold to our ancestors, so that,
once they saw what kind of oaths they had put their trust in
they would joyfully take courage.
This was the expectation of your people,
the saving of the virtuous and the ruin of their enemies;
for by the same act with which you took vengeance on our foes
you made us glorious by calling us to you.
The devout children of worthy men offered sacrifice in secret
and this divine pact they struck with one accord:
that the saints would share the same blessings and dangers alike;
and forthwith they had begun to chant the hymns of the fathers.

   The word of the Lord.

Responsorial Psalm   Ps 32:1,12,18-20,22. R. v.12

R. **Happy the people the Lord has chosen as his own.**

Ring out your joy to the Lord, O you just;
for praise is fitting for loyal hearts.
They are happy, whose God is the Lord,
the people he has chosen as his own. R.

The Lord looks on those who revere him,
on those who hope in his love,
to rescue their souls from death,
to keep them alive in famine. R.

Our soul is waiting for the Lord.
The Lord is our help and our shield.
May your love be upon us, O Lord,
as we place all our hope in you. R.

SECOND READING

A reading from the letter to the Hebrews   11:1-2,8-19

Abraham looked forward to a city founded, designed and built by God.

[Only faith can guarantee the blessings that we hope for, or prove the existence of the realities that at present remain unseen. It was for faith that our ancestors were commended.

It was by faith that Abraham obeyed the call to set out for a country that was the inheritance given to him and his descendants, and that he set out without knowing where he was going. By faith he arrived, as a foreigner, in the Promised Land, and lived there as if in a strange country, with Isaac and Jacob, who were heirs with him of the same promise. They lived there in tents while he looked forward to a city founded, designed and built by God.

It was equally by faith that Sarah, in spite of being past the age, was made able to conceive, because she believed that he who had made the promise would be faithful to it. Because of this, there came from one man, and one who was already as good as dead himself, more descendants than could be counted, as many as the stars of heaven or the grains of sand on the seashore.]

All these died in faith, before receiving any of the things that had been promised, but they saw them in the far distance and welcomed them, recognising that they were only strangers and nomads on earth. People who use such terms about themselves make it quite plain that they are in search of their real homeland. They can hardly have meant the country they came from, since they had the opportunity to go back to it; but in fact they were longing for a better homeland, their heavenly homeland. That is why God is not ashamed to be called their God, since he has founded the city for them.

It was by faith that Abraham, when put to the test, offered up Isaac. He offered to sacrifice his only son even though the promises had been made to him and he had been told: It is through Isaac that your name will be carried on. He was confident that God had the power even to raise the dead; and so, figuratively speaking, he was given back Isaac from the dead.

[The word of the Lord.]

Shorter Form, verses 1-2,8-12. Read between [ ]

Gospel Acclamation   Cf. Mt 11:25
R. **Alleluia, alleluia!**
Blessed are you, Father,
Lord of heaven and earth,
for revealing the mysteries of the kingdom
to mere children.
R. **Alleluia!**

Or: Mt 24:42,44
R. **Alleluia, alleluia!**
Stay awake and stand ready,
because you do not know the hour
when the Son of Man is coming.
R. **Alleluia!**

GOSPEL

A reading from the holy Gospel according to Luke   12:32-48
You too must stand ready.

| [Jesus said to his disciples:] 'There is no need to be afraid, little flock, for it has pleased your Father to give you the kingdom.

'Sell your possessions and give alms. Get yourselves purses that do not wear out, treasure that will not fail you, in heaven where no thief can reach it and no moth destroy it. For where your treasure is, there will your heart be also.

['See that you are dressed for action and have your lamps lit. Be like men waiting for their master to return from the wedding feast, ready to open the door as soon as he comes and knocks. Happy those servants whom the master finds awake when he comes. I tell you solemnly, he will put on an apron, sit them down at table and wait on them. It may be in the second watch he comes, or in the third, but happy those servants if he finds them ready. You may be quite sure of this, that if the householder had known at what hour the burglar would come, he would not have let anyone break through the wall of his house. You too must stand ready, because the Son of Man is coming at an hour you do not expect.']

Peter said, 'Lord, do you mean this parable for us, or for everyone?' The Lord replied, 'What sort of steward, then, is faithful and wise enough for the master to place him over his household to give them their allowance of food at the proper time? Happy that servant if his master's arrival finds him at this employment. I tell you truly, he will place him over everything he owns. But as for the servant who says to himself, "My master is taking his time coming", and sets about beating the menservants and the maids, and eating and drinking and getting drunk, his master will come on a day he does not expect and at an hour he does not know. The master will cut him off and send him to the same fate as the unfaithful.

   'The servant who knows what his master wants, but has not even started to carry out those wishes, will receive very many strokes of the lash. The one who did not know, but deserves to be beaten for what he has done, will receive fewer strokes. When a man has had a great deal given him, a great deal will be demanded of him, when a man has had a great deal given him on trust, even more will be expected of him.'

| [The Gospel of the Lord.]

Shorter Form, verses 35-40. Read between [ ]

Prayer over the Offerings
Be pleased, O Lord, to accept
   the offerings of your Church,
for in your mercy you have given
   them to be offered
and by your power you
   transform them
into the mystery of our salvation.
Through Christ our Lord.

Super oblata
Ecclesiæ tuæ, Domine,
   munera placatus assume,
quæ et misericors
   offerenda tribuisti,
et in nostræ salutis potenter efficis
   transire mysterium.
Per Christum Dominum nostrum.

Preface of Sundays in Ordinary Time I-VIII, pp.566-573.

Communion Antiphon Ps 147:12,14
O Jerusalem, glorify the Lord,
who gives you your fill
   of finest wheat.
Or: Cf. Jn 6:51
The bread that I will give,
   says the Lord,
is my flesh for the life of the world.

Ant. ad communionem
Lauda, Ierusalem, Dominum,
qui adipe frumenti satiat te.

Vel:
Panis, quem ego dedero,
caro mea est pro sæculi vita,
dicit Dominus.

Prayer after Communion
May the communion
   in your Sacrament
that we have consumed, save us,
   O Lord,
and confirm us in the light
   of your truth.
Through Christ our Lord.

Post communionem
Sacramentorum tuorum, Domine,
communio sumpta nos salvet,
et in tuæ veritatis luce confirmet.
Per Christum Dominum nostrum.

TWENTIETH SUNDAY IN ORDINARY TIME
(YEAR C)

Entrance Antiphon   Ps 83:10-11

TURN your eyes, O God,
  our shield;
and look on the face
  of your anointed one;
one day within your courts
is better than a thousand elsewhere.

Ant. ad introitum

PROTECTOR noster,
  aspice, Deus,
et respice in faciem Christi tui,
quia melior est dies una in atriis
  tuis super millia.

Collect

O God, who have prepared
  for those who love you
good things which no eye can see,
fill our hearts, we pray,
  with the warmth of your love,
so that, loving you in all things
  and above all things,
we may attain your promises,
which surpass every human desire.
Through our Lord Jesus Christ,
  your Son,
who lives and reigns with you
  in the unity of the Holy Spirit,
one God, for ever and ever.

Collecta

Deus, qui diligentibus te bona
  invisibilia præparasti,
infunde cordibus nostris
  tui amoris affectum,
ut, te in omnibus et super
  omnia diligentes,
promissiones tuas, quæ omne
  desiderium superant,
consequamur.
Per Dominum nostrum Iesum
  Christum Filium tuum,
qui tecum vivit et regnat
  in unitate Spiritus Sancti,
Deus, per omnia sæcula sæculorum.

FIRST READING

A reading from the prophet Jeremiah   38:4-6,8-10

You have borne me to be a man of dissension for all the land.

The king's leading men spoke to the king. 'Let Jeremiah be put to death: he is unquestionably disheartening the remaining soldiers in the city, and all the people too, by talking like this. The fellow does not have the welfare of this people at heart so much as its ruin.' 'He is in your hands, as you know,' King Zedekiah answered 'for the king is powerless against you.' So they took Jeremiah and threw him into the well of Prince Malchiah in the Court of the Guard, letting him down with ropes. There was no water in the well, only mud, and into the mud Jeremiah sank.

Ebed-melech came out from the palace and spoke to the king. 'My lord king,' he said 'these men have done a wicked thing by treating the prophet Jeremiah like this: they have thrown him into the well where he will die.' At this the king gave Ebed-melech the Cushite the following order: 'Take three men with you from here and pull the prophet Jeremiah out of the well before he dies.'

The word of the Lord.

Responsorial Psalm   Ps 39:2-4,18. R. v.14

R. **Lord, come to my aid!**

I waited, I waited for the Lord
and he stooped down to me;
he heard my cry. R.

He drew me from the deadly pit,
from the miry clay.
He set my feet upon a rock
and made my footsteps firm. R.

He put a new song into my mouth,
praise of our God.
Many shall see and fear
and shall trust in the Lord. R.

As for me, wretched and poor,
the Lord thinks of me.
You are my rescuer, my help,
O God, do not delay. R.

SECOND READING

A reading from the letter to the Hebrews   12:1-4

We shall keep running steadily in the race we have started.

With so many witnesses in a great cloud on every side of us, we too, then, should throw off everything that hinders us, especially the sin that clings so easily, and keep running steadily in the race we have started. Let us not lose sight of Jesus, who leads us in our faith and brings it to perfection: for the sake of the joy which was still in the future, he endured the cross, disregarding the shamefulness of it, and from now on has taken his place at the right of God's throne. Think of the way he stood such opposition from sinners and then you will not give up for want of courage. In the fight against sin, you have not yet had to keep fighting to the point of death.

The word of the Lord.

Gospel Acclamation Cf. Ac 16:14
R. **Alleluia, alleluia!**
Open our heart, O Lord,
to accept the words of your Son.
R. **Alleluia!**

Or: Jn 10:27

R. **Alleluia, alleluia!**
The sheep that belong to me listen to my voice,
says the Lord,
I know them and they follow me.
R. **Alleluia!**

GOSPEL

A reading from the holy Gospel according to Luke 12:49-53
I am not here to bring peace, but rather division.

Jesus said to his disciples: 'I have come to bring fire to the earth, and how I wish it were blazing already! There is a baptism I must still receive, and how great is my distress till it is over!

'Do you suppose that I am here to bring peace on earth? No, I tell you, but rather division. For from now on a household of five will be divided: three against two and two against three; the father divided against the son, son against father, mother against daughter, daughter against mother, mother-in-law against daughter-in-law, daughter-in-law against mother-in-law.'

The Gospel of the Lord.

Prayer over the Offerings | Super oblata

Receive our oblation, O Lord,
by which is brought about
a glorious exchange,
that, by offering what you have given,
we may merit to receive
your very self.
Through Christ our Lord.

Suscipe, Domine, munera nostra,
quibus exercentur
commercia gloriosa,
ut, offerentes quæ dedisti,
teipsum mereamur accipere.
Per Christum Dominum nostrum.

Preface of Sundays in Ordinary Time I-VIII, pp.566-573.

Communion Antiphon Ps 129:7 | Ant. ad communionem

With the Lord there is mercy;
in him is plentiful redemption.

Apud Dominum misericordia,
et copiosa apud eum redemptio.

Or: Jn 6:51-52

I am the living bread that came
    down from heaven, says the Lord.
Whoever eats of this bread
    will live for ever.

Prayer after Communion

Made partakers of Christ through
    these Sacraments,
we humbly implore your
    mercy, Lord,
that, conformed to his image
    on earth,
we may merit also to be his coheirs
    in heaven.
Who lives and reigns
    for ever and ever.

Vel:

Ego sum panis vivus, qui de cælo
    descendi, dicit Dominus:
si quis manducaverit ex hoc pane,
    vivet in æternum.

Post communionem

Per hæc sacramenta, Domine,
    Christi participes effecti,
clementiam tuam
    humiliter imploramus,
ut, eius imaginis conformes
    in terris,
et eius consortes in cælis
    fieri mereamur.
Qui vivit et regnat
    in sæcula sæculorum.

TWENTY-FIRST SUNDAY IN ORDINARY TIME
(YEAR C)

Entrance Antiphon   Cf. Ps 85:1-3

TURN your ear, O Lord,
    and answer me;
save the servant who trusts in you,
    my God.
Have mercy on me, O Lord,
    for I cry to you all the day long.

Collect

O God, who cause the minds
    of the faithful
to unite in a single purpose,
grant your people to love
    what you command
and to desire what you promise,
that, amid the uncertainties
    of this world,
our hearts may be fixed on that place
where true gladness is found.

Ant. ad introitum

INCLINA, Domine, aurem tuam
    ad me, et exaudi me.
Salvum fac servum tuum,
    Deus meus, sperantem in te.
Miserere mihi, Domine,
    quoniam ad te clamavi tota die.

Collecta

Deus, qui fidelium mentes unius
    efficis voluntatis,
da populis tuis id amare
    quod præcipis,
id desiderare quod promittis,
ut, inter mundanas varietates,
ibi nostra fixa sint corda,
    ubi vera sunt gaudia.
Per Dominum nostrum Iesum
    Christum Filium tuum,

Through our Lord Jesus Christ,
    your Son,
who lives and reigns with you
    in the unity of the Holy Spirit,
one God, for ever and ever.
	qui tecum vivit et regnat
	    in unitate Spiritus Sancti,
	Deus, per omnia sæcula sæculorum.

FIRST READING

A reading from the prophet Isaiah   66:18-21

They will bring all your brothers from all the nations.

The Lord says this: I am coming to gather the nations of every language. They shall come to witness my glory. I will give them a sign and send some of their survivors to the nations: to Tarshish, Put, Lud, Moshech, Rosh, Tubal, and Javan, to the distant islands that have never heard of me or seen my glory. They will proclaim my glory to the nations. As an offering to the Lord they will bring all your brothers, in horses, in chariots, in litters, on mules, on dromedaries, from all the nations to my holy mountain in Jerusalem, says the Lord, like Israelites bringing oblations in clean vessels to the Temple of the Lord. And of some of them I will make priests and Levites, says the Lord.

The word of the Lord.

Responsorial Psalm   Ps 116. R. Mk 16:15

R. **Go out to the whole world;
proclaim the Good News.**

Or: **Alleluia!**

O praise the Lord, all you nations,
acclaim him all you peoples! R.

Strong is his love for us;
he is faithful for ever. R.

SECOND READING

A reading from the letter to the Hebrews   12:5-7,11-13

The Lord trains the one that he loves.

Have you forgotten that encouraging text in which you are addressed as sons? My son, when the Lord corrects you, do not treat it lightly; but do not get discouraged when he reprimands you. For the Lord trains the ones that he loves and he punishes all those that he acknowledges as his sons. Suffering is part of your training; God is treating you as his sons. Has there ever been any son whose father did not train him? Of course, any punishment is most painful at the time, and far from pleasant; but later, in those on whom it has been used, it bears fruit in peace and goodness. So hold up your limp arms and steady your trembling knees and smooth out the path you tread; there the injured limb will not be wrenched, it will grow strong again.

The word of the Lord.

Gospel Acclamation   Jn 14:23

R. **Alleluia, alleluia!**
If anyone loves me he will keep my word,
and my Father will love him,
and we shall come to him.
R. **Alleluia!**

Or: Jn 14:6

R. **Alleluia, alleluia!**
I am the Way, the Truth and the Life, says the Lord;
no one can come to the Father except through me.
R. **Alleluia!**

GOSPEL

A reading from the holy Gospel according to Luke   13:22-30
Men from east and west will come to take their places at the feast in the kingdom of God.

Through towns and villages Jesus went teaching, making his way to Jerusalem. Someone said to him, 'Sir, will there be only a few saved?' He said to them, 'Try your best to enter by the narrow door, because, I tell you, many will try to enter and will not succeed.

'Once the master of the house has got up and locked the door, you may find yourself knocking on the door, saying, "Lord, open to us" but he will answer, "I do not know where you come from." Then you will find yourself saying, "We once ate and drank in your company; you taught in our streets" but he will reply, "I do not know where you come from. Away from me, all you wicked men!"

'Then there will be weeping and grinding of teeth, when you see Abraham and Isaac and Jacob and all the prophets in the kingdom of God, and yourselves turned outside. And men from east and west, from north and south, will come to take their places at the feast in the kingdom of God.

'Yes, there are those now last who will be first, and those now first who will be last.'

The Gospel of the Lord.

Prayer over the Offerings

O Lord, who gained for yourself
    a people by adoption
through the one sacrifice offered
    once for all,
bestow graciously on us, we pray,
the gifts of unity and peace
    in your Church.
Through Christ our Lord.

Super oblata

Qui una semel hostia, Domine,
adoptionis tibi populum acquisisti,
unitatis et pacis in Ecclesia tua
propitius nobis dona concedas.
Per Christum Dominum nostrum.

Preface of Sundays in Ordinary Time I-VIII, pp.566-573.

Communion Antiphon Cf. Ps 103:13-15

The earth is replete with the fruits
    of your work, O Lord;
you bring forth bread from the earth
and wine to cheer the heart.

Or: Cf. Jn 6:54

Whoever eats my flesh
    and drinks my blood
has eternal life, says the Lord,
and I will raise him up on the last day.

Ant. ad communionem

De fructu operum tuorum,
    Domine, satiabitur terra,
ut educas panem de terra,
    et vinum lætificet cor hominis.

Vel:

Qui manducat meam carnem
    et bibit meum sanguinem,
habet vitam æternam,
    dicit Dominus;
et ego resuscitabo eum
    in novissimo die.

Prayer after Communion

Complete within us, O Lord,
    we pray,
the healing work of your mercy
and graciously perfect
    and sustain us,
so that in all things we may
    please you.
Through Christ our Lord.

Post communionem

Plenum, quæsumus, Domine,
in nobis remedium tuæ
    miserationis operare
ac tales nos esse perfice propitius
    et sic foveri,
ut tibi in omnibus
    placere valeamus.
Per Christum Dominum nostrum.

TWENTY-SECOND SUNDAY IN ORDINARY TIME
(YEAR C)

Entrance Antiphon   Cf. Ps 85:3,5

HAVE mercy on me, O Lord,
for I cry to you all the day long.
O Lord, you are good and forgiving,
full of mercy to all who call to you.

Ant. ad introitum

MISERERE mihi, Domine,
quoniam ad te clamavi
tota die:
quia tu, Domine, suavis ac mitis es,
et copiosus in misericordia
omnibus invocantibus te.

Collect

God of might, giver of every
good gift,
put into our hearts the love
of your name,
so that, by deepening our sense
of reverence,
you may nurture in us what is good
and, by your watchful care,
keep safe what you have nurtured.
Through our Lord Jesus Christ,
your Son,
who lives and reigns with you
in the unity of the Holy Spirit,
one God, for ever and ever.

Collecta

Deus virtutum, cuius est totum
quod est optimum,
insere pectoribus nostris tui
nominis amorem,
et præsta, ut in nobis,
religionis augmento,
quæ sunt bona nutrias,
ac, vigilanti studio,
quæ sunt nutrita custodias.
Per Dominum nostrum Iesum
Christum Filium tuum,
qui tecum vivit et regnat
in unitate Spiritus Sancti,
Deus, per omnia sæcula sæculorum.

FIRST READING

A reading from the book of Ecclesiasticus   3:19-21,30-31

Behave humbly, and then you will find favour with the Lord.

My son, be gentle in carrying out your business,
and you will be better loved than a lavish giver.
The greater you are, the more you should behave humbly,
and then you will find favour with the Lord;
for great though the power of the Lord is,
he accepts the homage of the humble.
There is no cure for the proud man's malady,
since an evil growth has taken root in him.
The heart of a sensible man will reflect on parables,
an attentive ear is the sage's dream.

The word of the Lord.

Responsorial Psalm   Ps 67:4-7,10-11. R. Cf. v.11

R. **In your goodness, O God, you prepared a home for the poor.**

The just shall rejoice at the presence of God,
they shall exult and dance for joy.
O sing to the Lord, make music to his name;
rejoice in the Lord, exult at his presence. R.

Father of the orphan, defender of the widow,
such is God in his holy place.
God gives the lonely a home to live in;
he leads the prisoners forth into freedom. R.

You poured down, O God, a generous rain:
when your people were starved you gave them new life.
It was there that your people found a home,
prepared in your goodness, O God, for the poor. R.

SECOND READING

A reading from the letter to the Hebrews   12:18-19,22-24

You have to come to Mount Zion and to the city of the living God.

What you have come to is nothing known to the senses: not a blazing fire, or
a gloom turning to total darkness, or a storm; or trumpeting thunder or the
great voice speaking which made everyone that heard it beg that no more
should be said to them. But what you have come to is Mount Zion and the
city of the living God, the heavenly Jerusalem where the millions of angels
have gathered for the festival, with the whole Church in which everyone is
a 'first-born son' and a citizen of heaven. You have come to God himself,
the supreme Judge, and been placed with spirits of the saints who have been
made perfect; and to Jesus, the mediator who brings a new covenant.

The word of the Lord.

Gospel Acclamation   Jn 14:23

R. **Alleluia, alleluia!**
If anyone loves me he will keep my word,
and my Father will love him,
and we shall come to him.
R. **Alleluia!**

Or: Mt 11:29

R. **Alleluia, alleluia!**
Shoulder my yoke and learn from me,
for I am gentle and humble in heart.
R. **Alleluia!**

GOSPEL

A reading from the holy Gospel according to Luke   14:1,7-14

Everyone who exalts himself will be humbled, and the man who humbles himself will be exalted.

On a sabbath day Jesus had gone for a meal to the house of one of the leading Pharisees; and they watched him closely. He then told the guests a parable, because he had noticed how they picked the places of honour. He said this, 'When someone invites you to a wedding feast, do not take your seat in the place of honour. A more distinguished person than you may have been invited, and the person who invited you both may come and say, "Give up your place to this man." And then, to your embarrassment, you would have to go and take the lowest place. No; when you are a guest, make your way to the lowest place and sit there, so that, when your host comes, he may say, "My friend, move up higher." In that way, everyone with you at the table will see you honoured. For everyone who exalts himself will be humbled, and the man who humbles himself will be exalted.'

Then he said to his host, 'When you give a lunch or a dinner, do not ask your friends, brothers, relations or rich neighbours, for fear they repay your courtesy by inviting you in return. No; when you have a party, invite the poor, the crippled, the lame, the blind; that they cannot pay you back means that you are fortunate, because repayment will be made to you when the virtuous rise again.'

The Gospel of the Lord.

Prayer over the Offerings	Super oblata
May this sacred offering, O Lord, confer on us always the blessing of salvation, that what it celebrates in mystery it may accomplish in power. Through Christ our Lord.	Benedictionem nobis, Domine, conferat salutarem sacra semper oblatio, ut, quod agit mysterio, virtute perficiat. Per Christum Dominum nostrum.

Preface of Sundays in Ordinary Time I-VIII, pp.566-573.

Communion Antiphon Ps 30:20	Ant. ad communionem
How great is the goodness, Lord, that you keep for those who fear you.	Quam magna multitudo dulcedinis tuæ, Domine, quam abscondisti timentibus te.

Or: Mt 5:9-10

Blessed are the peacemakers,
for they shall be called
   children of God.
Blessed are they who are persecuted
   for the sake of righteousness,
for theirs is the Kingdom of Heaven.

Vel:

Beati pacifici,
   quoniam filii Dei vocabuntur.
Beati qui persecutionem patiuntur
   propter iustitiam,
quoniam ipsorum
   est regnum cælorum.

Prayer after Communion

Renewed by this bread
   from the heavenly table,
we beseech you, Lord,
that, being the food of charity,
it may confirm our hearts
and stir us to serve you
   in our neighbour.
Through Christ our Lord.

Post communionem

Pane mensæ cælestis refecti, te,
   Domine, deprecamur,
ut hoc nutrimentum caritatis corda
   nostra confirmet,
quatenus ad tibi ministrandum
   in fratribus excitemur.
Per Christum Dominum nostrum.

TWENTY-THIRD SUNDAY IN ORDINARY TIME
(YEAR C)

Entrance Antiphon Ps 118:137,124

YOU are just, O Lord,
  and your judgement is right;
treat your servant in accord
   with your merciful love.

Ant. ad introitum

IUSTUS es, Domine,
  et rectum iudicium tuum;
fac cum servo tuo secundum
   misericordiam tuam.

Collect

O God, by whom we are redeemed
   and receive adoption,
look graciously upon your beloved
   sons and daughters,
that those who believe in Christ
may receive true freedom
and an everlasting inheritance.
Through our Lord Jesus Christ,
   your Son,
who lives and reigns with you
   in the unity of the Holy Spirit,
one God, for ever and ever.

Collecta

Deus, per quem nobis
et redemptio venit
   et præstatur adoptio,
filios dilectionis tuæ
   benignus intende,
ut in Christo credentibus
et vera tribuatur libertas,
   et hereditas æterna.
Per Dominum nostrum Iesum
   Christum Filium tuum,
qui tecum vivit et regnat
   in unitate Spiritus Sancti,
Deus, per omnia sæcula sæculorum.

FIRST READING

A reading from the book of Wisdom   9:13-18

Who can divine the will of God?

What man can know the intentions of God?
Who can divine the will of the Lord?
The reasonings of mortals are unsure
and our intentions unstable;
for a perishable body presses down the soul,
and this tent of clay weighs down the teeming mind.
It is hard enough for us to work out what is on earth,
laborious to know what lies within our reach;
who, then, can discover what is in the heavens?
As for your intention, who could have learnt it, had you not granted Wisdom
and sent your holy spirit from above?
Thus have the paths of those on earth been straightened
and men been taught what pleases you,
and saved, by Wisdom.

    The word of the Lord.

Responsorial Psalm   Ps 89:3-6,12-14,17. R. v.1

R. **O Lord, you have been our refuge**
   from one generation to the next.

   You turn men back into dust
   and say 'Go back, sons of men.'
   To your eyes a thousand years
   are like yesterday, come and gone,
   no more than a watch in the night. R.

   You sweep men away like a dream,
   like grass which springs up in the morning.
   In the morning it springs up and flowers:
   by evening it withers and fades. R.

   Make us know the shortness of our life
   that we may gain wisdom of heart.
   Lord, relent! Is your anger for ever?
   Show pity to your servants. R.

   In the morning, fill us with your love;
   we shall exult and rejoice all our days.
   Let the favour of the Lord be upon us:
   give success to the work of our hands. R.

SECOND READING

A reading from the letter of St Paul to Philemon   9-10,12-17

Have him back, not as a slave any more, but as a dear brother.

This is Paul writing, an old man now and, what is more, still a prisoner of Christ Jesus. I am appealing to you for a child of mine, whose father I became while wearing these chains: I mean Onesimus. I am sending him back to you, and with him – I could say – a part of my own self. I should have liked to keep him with me; he could have been a substitute for you, to help me while I am in the chains that the Good News has brought me. However, I did not want to do anything without your consent; it would have been forcing your act of kindness, which should be spontaneous. I know you have been deprived of Onesimus for a time, but it was only so that you could have him back for ever, not as a slave any more, but something much better than a slave, a dear brother; especially dear to me, but how much more to you, as a blood-brother as well as a brother in the Lord. So if all that we have in common means anything to you, welcome him as you would me.

    The word of the Lord.

Gospel Acclamation   Jn 15:15

R. **Alleluia, alleluia!**
I call you friends, says the Lord,
because I have made known to you
everything I have learnt from my Father.
R. **Alleluia!**

Or: Ps 118:135

R. **Alleluia, alleluia!**
Let your face shine on your servant,
and teach me your decrees.
R. **Alleluia!**

GOSPEL

A reading from the holy Gospel according to Luke   14:25-33

None of you can be my disciple unless he gives up all his possessions.

Great crowds accompanied Jesus on his way and he turned and spoke to them. 'If any man comes to me without hating his father, mother, wife, children, brothers, sisters, yes and his own life too, he cannot be my disciple. Anyone who does not carry his cross and come after me cannot be my disciple.

    'And indeed, which of you here, intending to build a tower, would not first sit down and work out the cost to see if he had enough to complete

TWENTY-THIRD SUNDAY IN ORDINARY TIME (YEAR C)

it? Otherwise, if he laid the foundation and then found himself unable to finish the work, the onlookers would all start making fun of him and saying, "Here is a man who started to build and was unable to finish." Or again, what king marching to war against another king would not first sit down and consider whether with ten thousand men he could stand up to the other who advanced against him with twenty thousand? If not, then while the other king was still a long way off, he would send envoys to sue for peace. So in the same way, none of you can be my disciple unless he gives up all his possessions.'

The Gospel of the Lord.

Prayer over the Offerings	Super oblata

O God, who give us the gift
    of true prayer and of peace,
graciously grant that,
    through this offering,
we may do fitting homage to your
    divine majesty
and, by partaking
    of the sacred mystery,
we may be faithfully united
    in mind and heart.
Through Christ our Lord.
	Deus, auctor sinceræ
	    devotionis et pacis,
	da, quæsumus,
	    ut et maiestatem tuam
	convenienter hoc
	    munere veneremur,
	et sacri participatione mysterii
	    fideliter sensibus uniamur.
	Per Christum Dominum nostrum.

Preface of Sundays in Ordinary Time I-VIII, pp.566-573.

Communion Antiphon Cf. Ps 41:2-3	Ant. ad communionem

Like the deer that yearns
    for running streams,
so my soul is yearning for you,
    my God;
my soul is thirsting for God,
    the living God.
	Quemadmodum desiderat cervus
	    ad fontes aquarum,
	ita desiderat anima mea
	    ad te, Deus:
	sitivit anima mea ad Deum
	    fortem vivum.

Or: Jn 8:12	Vel:

I am the light of the world,
    says the Lord;
whoever follows me will not walk
    in darkness,
but will have the light of life.
	Ego sum lux mundi,
	    dicit Dominus:
	qui sequitur me non ambulat
	    in tenebris,
	sed habebit lumen vitæ.

Prayer after Communion

Grant that your faithful, O Lord,
whom you nourish and endow
   with life
through the food of your Word
   and heavenly Sacrament,
may so benefit from your beloved
   Son's great gifts
that we may merit an eternal share
   in his life.
Who lives and reigns
   for ever and ever.

Post communionem

Da fidelibus tuis, Domine,
quos et verbi tui et cælestis
   sacramenti pabulo
nutris et vivificas,
ita dilecti Filii tui tantis
   muneribus proficere,
ut eius vitæ semper consortes
   effici mereamur.
Qui vivit et regnat
   in sæcula sæculorum.

TWENTY-FOURTH SUNDAY IN ORDINARY TIME
(YEAR C)

Entrance Antiphon   Cf. Si 36:18

GIVE peace, O Lord,
   to those who wait for you,
that your prophets be found true.
Hear the prayers of your servant,
and of your people Israel.

Ant. ad introitum

DA pacem, Domine,
   sustinentibus te,
ut prophetæ tui fideles inveniantur;
exaudi preces servi tui,
   et plebis tuæ Israel.

Collect

Look upon us, O God,
Creator and ruler of all things,
and, that we may feel the working
   of your mercy,
grant that we may serve you
   with all our heart.
Through our Lord Jesus Christ,
   your Son,
who lives and reigns with you
   in the unity of the Holy Spirit,
one God, for ever and ever.

Collecta

Respice nos, rerum omnium Deus
   creator et rector,
et, ut tuæ propitiationis
   sentiamus effectum,
toto nos tribue tibi corde servire.
Per Dominum nostrum Iesum
   Christum Filium tuum,
qui tecum vivit et regnat
   in unitate Spiritus Sancti,
Deus, per omnia sæcula sæculorum.

FIRST READING

A reading from the book of Exodus   32:7-11,13-14

The Lord relented and did not bring on his people the disaster he had threatened.

The Lord spoke to Moses, 'Go down now, because your people whom you brought out of Egypt have apostasised. They have been quick to leave the way I marked out for them; they have made themselves a calf of molten metal and have worshipped it and offered it sacrifice. "Here is your God, Israel," they have cried "who brought you up from the land of Egypt!"' The Lord then said to Moses, 'I can see how headstrong these people are! Leave me, now, my wrath shall blaze out against them and devour them; of you, however, I will make a great nation.'

But Moses pleaded with the Lord his God. 'Lord,' he said, 'why should your wrath blaze out against this people of yours whom you brought out of the land of Egypt with arm outstretched and mighty hand? Remember Abraham, Isaac and Jacob, your servants to whom by your own self you swore and made this promise: I will make your offspring as many as the stars of heaven, and all this land which I promised I will give to your descendants, and it shall be their heritage for ever.' So the Lord relented and did not bring on his people the disaster he had threatened.

The word of the Lord.

Responsorial Psalm   Ps 50:3-4,12-13,17,19. R. Lk 15:18

R. **I will leave this place and go to my father.**

Have mercy on me, God, in your kindness.
In your compassion blot out my offence.
O wash me more and more from my guilt
and cleanse me from my sin. R.

A pure heart create for me, O God,
put a steadfast spirit within me.
Do not cast me away from your presence,
nor deprive me of your holy spirit. R.

O Lord, open my lips
and my mouth shall declare your praise.
My sacrifice is a contrite spirit;
a humbled, contrite heart you will not spurn. R.

SECOND READING

A reading from the first letter of St Paul to Timothy 1:12-17

Christ Jesus came into the world to save sinners.

I thank Christ Jesus our Lord, who has given me strength, and who judged me faithful enough to call me into his service even though I used to be a blasphemer and did all I could to injure and discredit the faith. Mercy, however, was shown me, because until I became a believer I had been acting in ignorance; and the grace of our Lord filled me with faith and with the love that is in Christ Jesus. Here is a saying that you can rely on and nobody should doubt: that Christ Jesus came into the world to save sinners. I myself am the greatest of them; and if mercy has been shown to me, it is because Jesus Christ meant to make me the greatest evidence of his inexhaustible patience for all the other people who would later have to trust in him to come to eternal life. To the eternal King, the undying, invisible and only God, be honour and glory for ever and ever. Amen.

The word of the Lord.

Gospel Acclamation   Cf. Ep 1:17,18

R. **Alleluia, alleluia!**
May the Father of our Lord Jesus Christ
enlighten the eyes of our mind,
so that we can see what hope his call holds for us.
R. **Alleluia!**

Or: 2 Co 5:19

R. **Alleluia, alleluia!**
God in Christ was reconciling the world to himself,
and he has entrusted to us the news that they are reconciled.
R. **Alleluia!**

GOSPEL

A reading from the holy Gospel according to Luke 15:1-32

There will be rejoicing in heaven over one repentant sinner.

[The tax collectors and the sinners were all seeking the company of Jesus to hear what he had to say, and the Pharisees and the scribes complained. 'This man' they said 'welcomes sinners and eats with them.' So he spoke this parable to them:

'What man among you with a hundred sheep, losing one, would not leave the ninety-nine in the wilderness and go after the missing one till he found it? And when he found it, would he not joyfully take it on his shoulders and then, when he got home, call together his friends, and neighbours? "Rejoice with me," he would say "I have found my sheep that was lost." In the same way, I tell you, there will be more rejoicing in heaven over one repentant sinner than over ninety-nine virtuous men who have no need of repentance.

'Or again, what woman with ten drachmas would not, if she lost one, light a lamp and sweep out the house and search thoroughly till she found it? And then, when she had found it, call together her friends and neighbours? "Rejoice with me," she would say "I have found the drachma I lost." In the same way, I tell you, there is rejoicing among the angels of God over one repentant sinner.']

He also said, 'A man had two sons. The younger said to his father, "Father, let me have the share of the estate that would come to me." So the father divided the property between them. A few days later, the younger son got together everything he had and left for a distant country where he squandered his money on a life of debauchery.

'When he had spent it all, that country experienced a severe famine, and now he began to feel the pinch, so he hired himself out to one of the local inhabitants who put him on his farm to feed the pigs. And he would willingly have filled his belly with the husks the pigs were eating but no one offered him anything. Then he came to his senses and said, "How many of my father's paid servants have more food than they want, and here am I dying of hunger! I will leave this place and go to my father and say: Father, I have sinned against heaven and against you; I no longer deserve to be called your son; treat me as one of your paid servants." So he left the place and went back to his father.

'While he was still a long way off, his father saw him and was moved with pity. He ran to the boy, clasped him in his arms and kissed him tenderly. Then his son said, "Father, I have sinned against heaven and against you. I no longer deserve to be called your son." But the father said to his servants, "Quick! Bring out the best robe and put it on him; put a ring on his finger and sandals on his feet. Bring the calf we have been fattening, and kill it; we are going to have a feast, a celebration, because this son of mine was dead and has come back to life; he was lost and is found." And they began to celebrate.

'Now the elder son was out in the fields, and on his way back, as he drew near the house, he could hear music and dancing. Calling one of the servants he asked what it was all about. "Your brother has come" replied the servant "and your father has killed the calf we had fattened because he has got him back safe and sound." He was angry then and refused to go in, and his father came out to plead with him; but he answered his father, "Look, all these years I have slaved for you and never once disobeyed your orders, yet you never offered me so much as a kid for me to celebrate with my friends. But, for this son of yours, when he comes back after swallowing up your property – he and his women – you kill the calf we had been fattening."

'The father said, "My son, you are with me always and all I have is yours. But it was only right we should celebrate and rejoice, because your brother here was dead and has come to life; he was lost and is found."'

[The Gospel of the Lord.]

Shorter Form, verses 1-10. Read between [ ]

Prayer over the Offerings	Super oblata
Look with favour on our supplications, O Lord, and in your kindness accept these, your servants' offerings, that what each has offered to the honour of your name may serve the salvation of all. Through Christ our Lord.	Propitiare, Domine, supplicationibus nostris, et has oblationes famulorum tuorum benignus assume, ut, quod singuli ad honorem tui nominis obtulerunt, cunctis proficiat ad salutem. Per Christum Dominum nostrum.

Preface of Sundays in Ordinary Time I-VIII, pp.566-573.

Communion Antiphon Cf. Ps 35:8	Ant. ad communionem
How precious is your mercy, O God! The children of men seek shelter in the shadow of your wings.	Quam pretiosa est misericordia tua, Deus! Filii hominum sub umbra alarum tuarum confugient.

Or: Cf. 1 Co 10:16	Vel:
The chalice of blessing that we bless is a communion in the Blood of Christ; and the bread that we break is a sharing in the Body of the Lord.	Calix benedictionis, cui benedicimus, communicatio Sanguinis Christi est; et panis, quem frangimus, participatio Corporis Domini est.

Prayer after Communion	Post communionem
May the working of this heavenly gift, O Lord, we pray, take possession of our minds and bodies, so that its effects, and not our own desires, may always prevail in us. Through Christ our Lord.	Mentes nostras et corpora possideat, quæsumus, Domine, doni cælestis operatio, ut non noster sensus in nobis, sed eius præveniat semper effectus. Per Christum Dominum nostrum.

TWENTY-FIFTH SUNDAY IN ORDINARY TIME
(YEAR C)

Entrance Antiphon

I AM the salvation of the people,
says the Lord.
Should they cry to me in any distress,
I will hear them, and I will be their
    Lord for ever.

Ant. ad introitum

SALUS populi ego sum,
dicit Dominus.
De quacumque tribulatione
    clamaverint ad me,
exaudiam eos, et ero illorum
    Dominus in perpetuum.

Collect

O God, who founded all the
    commands of your sacred Law
upon love of you
    and of our neighbour,
grant that, by keeping your precepts,
we may merit to attain eternal life.
Through our Lord Jesus Christ,
    your Son,
who lives and reigns with you
    in the unity of the Holy Spirit,
one God, for ever and ever.

Collecta

Deus, qui sacræ legis
    omnia constituta
in tua et proximi dilectione posuisti,
da nobis, ut, tua præcepta servantes,
ad vitam mereamur
    pervenire perpetuam.
Per Dominum nostrum Iesum
    Christum Filium tuum,
qui tecum vivit et regnat
    in unitate Spiritus Sancti,
Deus, per omnia sæcula sæculorum.

FIRST READING

A reading from the prophet Amos   8:4-7

Against those who 'buy up the poor for money'.

Listen to this, you who trample on the needy
and try to suppress the poor people of the country,
you who say, 'When will the New Moon be over
so that we can sell our corn,
and sabbath, so that we can market our wheat?
Then by lowering the bushel, raising the shekel,
by swindling and tampering with the scales,
we can buy up the poor for money,
and the needy for a pair of sandals,
and get a price even for the sweepings of the wheat.'
The Lord swears it by the pride of Jacob,
'Never will I forget a single thing you have done.'

   The word of the Lord.

Responsorial Psalm   Ps 112:1-2,4-8. R. Cf. vv. 1,7

R. **Praise the Lord, who raises the poor.**
   Or: **Alleluia!**

Praise, O servants of the Lord,
praise the name of the Lord!
May the name of the Lord be blessed
both now and for evermore! R.

High above all nations is the Lord,
above the heavens his glory.
Who is like the Lord, our God,
who has risen on high to his throne
yet stoops from the heights to look down,
to look down upon heaven and earth? R.

From the dust he lifts up the lowly,
from the dungheap he raises the poor
to set him in the company of princes,
yes, with the princes of his people. R.

SECOND READING

A reading from the first letter of St Paul to Timothy   2:1-8

There should be prayers offered for everyone to God, who wants everyone to be saved.

My advice is that, first of all, there should be prayers offered for everyone – petitions, intercessions and thanksgiving – and especially for kings and others in authority, so that we may be able to live religious and reverent lives in peace and quiet. To do this is right, and will please God our saviour: he wants everyone to be saved and reach full knowledge of the truth. For there is only one God, and there is only one mediator between God and mankind, himself a man, Christ Jesus, who sacrificed himself as a ransom for them all. He is the evidence of this, sent at the appointed time, and I have been named a herald and apostle of it and – I am telling the truth and no lie – a teacher of the faith and the truth to the pagans.

In every place, then, I want the men to lift their hands up reverently in prayer, with no anger or argument.

The word of the Lord.

Gospel Acclamation   Cf. Ac 16:14

R. **Alleluia, alleluia!**
Open our heart, O Lord,
to accept the words of your Son.
R. **Alleluia!**

Or: 2 Co 8:9

R. **Alleluia, alleluia!**
Jesus Christ was rich,
but he became poor for your sake,
to make you rich out of his poverty.
R. **Alleluia!**

GOSPEL

A reading from the holy Gospel according to Luke   16:1-13
You cannot be the slave of both God and money.

[Jesus said to his disciples:] 'There was a rich man and he had a steward who was denounced to him for being wasteful with his property. He called for the man and said, "What is this I hear about you? Draw me up an account of your stewardship because you are not to be my steward any longer." Then the steward said to himself, "Now that my master is taking the stewardship from me, what am I to do? Dig? I am not strong enough. Go begging? I should be too ashamed. Ah, I know what I will do to make sure that when I am dismissed from office there will be some to welcome me into their homes."

'Then he called his master's debtors one by one. To the first he said, "How much do you owe my master?" "One hundred measures of oil" was the reply. The steward said, "Here, take your bond; sit down straight away and write fifty." To another he said, "And you, sir, how much do you owe?" "One hundred measures of wheat" was the reply. The steward said, "Here, take your bond and write eighty."

'The master praised the dishonest steward for his astuteness. For the children of this world are more astute in dealing with their own kind than are the children of light.

'And so I tell you this: use money, tainted as it is, to win you friends, and thus make sure that when it fails you, they will welcome you into the tents of eternity. [The man who can be trusted in little things can be trusted in great; the man who is dishonest in little things will be dishonest in great. If then you cannot be trusted with money, that tainted thing, who will trust you with genuine riches? And if you cannot be trusted with what is not yours, who will give you what is your very own?

'No servant can be the slave of two masters: he will either hate the first and love the second, or treat the first with respect and the second with scorn. You cannot be the slave both of God and of money.'

The Gospel of the Lord.]

Shorter Form, verses 10-13. Read between [ ]

Prayer over the Offerings

Receive with favour, O Lord, we pray,
the offerings of your people,
that what they profess
    with devotion and faith
may be theirs through
    these heavenly mysteries.
Through Christ our Lord.

Super oblata

Munera, quæsumus, Domine,
    tuæ plebis propitiatus assume,
ut, quæ fidei pietate profitentur,
sacramentis cælestibus
    apprehendant.
Per Christum Dominum nostrum.

Preface of Sundays in Ordinary Time I-VIII, pp.566-573.

Communion Antiphon Ps 118:4-5

You have laid down your precepts
    to be carefully kept;
may my ways be firm in keeping
    your statutes.

Ant. ad communionem

Tu mandasti mandata tua
    custodiri nimis;
utinam dirigantur viæ meæ
ad custodiendas iustificationes tuas.

Or: Jn 10:14

I am the Good Shepherd,
    says the Lord;
I know my sheep,
    and mine know me.

Vel:

Ego sum pastor bonus,
    dicit Dominus;
et cognosco oves meas,
    et cognoscunt me meæ.

Prayer after Communion

Graciously raise up, O Lord,
those you renew
    with this Sacrament,
that we may come to possess
    your redemption
both in mystery and in the manner
    of our life.
Through Christ our Lord.

Post communionem

Quos tuis, Domine,
    reficis sacramentis,
continuis attolle benignus auxiliis,
ut redemptionis effectum
et mysteriis capiamus et moribus.
Per Christum Dominum nostrum.

TWENTY-SIXTH SUNDAY IN ORDINARY TIME
(YEAR C)

ALL that you have done to us,
O Lord,
you have done with true judgement,
for we have sinned against you
and not obeyed
  your commandments.
But give glory to your name
and deal with us according
  to the bounty of your mercy.

Ant. ad introitum

OMNIA, quæ fecisti nobis,
Domine,
in vero iudicio fecisti,
  quia peccavimus tibi,
et mandatis tuis non obœdivimus;
sed da gloriam nomini tuo,
et fac nobiscum secundum
  multitudinem misericordiæ tuæ.

Collect

O God, who manifest
  your almighty power
above all by pardoning
  and showing mercy,
bestow, we pray, your grace
  abundantly upon us
and make those hastening to attain
  your promises
heirs to the treasures of heaven.
Through our Lord Jesus Christ,
  your Son,
who lives and reigns with you
  in the unity of the Holy Spirit,
one God, for ever and ever.

Collecta

Deus, qui omnipotentiam tuam
parcendo maxime
  et miserando manifestas,
multiplica super nos gratiam tuam,
ut, ad tua promissa currentes,
cælestium bonorum facias
  esse consortes.
Per Dominum nostrum Iesum
  Christum Filium tuum,
qui tecum vivit et regnat
  in unitate Spiritus Sancti,
Deus, per omnia sæcula sæculorum.

FIRST READING

A reading from the prophet Amos   6:1,4-7

Those who sprawl and those who bawl will be exiled.

The almighty Lord says this:

> Woe to those ensconced so snugly in Zion
> and to those who feel so safe on the mountain of Samaria.
> Lying on ivory beds
> and sprawling on their divans,
> they dine on lambs from the flock,
> and stall-fattened veal;

they bawl to the sound of the harp,
they invent new instruments of music like David,
they drink wine by the bowlful,
and use the finest oil for anointing themselves,
but about the ruin of Joseph they do not care at all.
That is why they will be the first to be exiled;
the sprawlers' revelry is over.

The word of the Lord.

Responsorial Psalm   Ps 145:6-10. R. v.2

R. **My soul, give praise to the Lord.**
   Or: **Alleluia!**

It is the Lord who keeps faith for ever,
who is just to those who are oppressed.
It is he who gives bread to the hungry,
the Lord, who sets prisoners free. R.

It is the Lord who gives sight to the blind,
who raises up those who are bowed down.
It is the Lord who loves the just,
the Lord, who protects the stranger. R.

He upholds the widow and orphan
but thwarts the path of the wicked.
The Lord will reign for ever,
Zion's God, from age to age. R.

SECOND READING

A reading from the first letter of St Paul to Timothy   6:11-16

Do all that you have been told until the Appearing of the Lord.

As a man dedicated to God, you must aim to be saintly and religious, filled
with faith and love, patient and gentle. Fight the good fight of the faith and
win for yourself the eternal life to which you were called when you made
your profession and spoke up for the truth in front of many witnesses.
Now, before God the source of all life and before Jesus Christ, who spoke
up as a witness for the truth in front of Pontius Pilate, I put to you the duty
of doing all that you have been told, with no faults or failures, until the
Appearing of our Lord Jesus Christ,

who at the due time will be revealed
by God, the blessed and only Ruler of all,
the King of kings and the Lord of lords,
who alone is immortal,

whose home is in inaccessible light,
whom no man has seen and no man is able to see:
to him be honour and everlasting power. Amen.

The word of the Lord.

Gospel Acclamation   Jn 10:27
R. **Alleluia, alleluia!**
The sheep that belong to me listen to my voice,
says the Lord,
I know them and they follow me.
R. **Alleluia!**

Or: 2 Co 8:9

R. **Alleluia, alleluia!**
Jesus Christ was rich,
but he became poor for your sake,
to make you rich out of his poverty.
R. **Alleluia!**

GOSPEL

A reading from the holy Gospel according to Luke   16:19-31
*Good things came your way, just as bad things came the way of Lazarus. Now he is
being comforted here while you are in agony.*

Jesus said to the Pharisees: 'There was a rich man who used to dress in
purple and fine linen and feast magnificently everyday. And at his gate
there lay a poor man called Lazarus, covered with sores, who longed to fill
himself with the scraps that fell from the rich man's table. Dogs even came
and licked his sores. Now the poor man died and was carried away by the
angels to the bosom of Abraham. The rich man also died and was buried.

'In his torment in Hades he looked up and saw Abraham a long way off
with Lazarus in his bosom. So he cried out, "Father Abraham, pity me and
send Lazarus to dip the tip of his finger in water and cool my tongue, for I
am in agony in these flames." "My son," Abraham replied "remember that
during your life good things came your way, just as bad things came the
way of Lazarus. Now he is being comforted here while you are in agony.
But that is not all: between us and you a great gulf has been fixed, to stop
anyone, if he wanted to, crossing from our side to yours, and to stop any
crossing from your side to ours."

'The rich man replied, "Father, I beg you then to send Lazarus to my
father's house, since I have five brothers, to give them warning so that
they do not come to this place of torment too." "They have Moses and

the prophets," said Abraham "let them listen to them." "Ah no, father Abraham," said the rich man "but if someone comes to them from the dead, they will repent." Then Abraham said to him, "If they will not listen either to Moses or to the prophets, they will not be convinced even if someone should rise from the dead."'

The Gospel of the Lord.

Prayer over the Offerings	**Super oblata**
Grant us, O merciful God,	Concede nobis, misericors Deus,
that this our offering may find acceptance with you	ut hæc nostra oblatio tibi sit accepta,
and that through it the wellspring of all blessing	et per eam nobis fons omnis benedictionis aperiatur.
may be laid open before us.	Per Christum Dominum nostrum.
Through Christ our Lord.	

Preface of Sundays in Ordinary Time I-VIII, pp.566-573.

Communion Antiphon Cf.Ps 118:49-50	**Ant. ad communionem**
Remember your word to your servant, O Lord,	Memento verbi tui servo tuo, Domine,
by which you have given me hope.	in quo mihi spem dedisti;
This is my comfort when I am brought low.	hæc me consolata est in humilitate mea.
Or: 1 Jn 3:16	Vel:
By this we came to know the love of God:	In hoc cognovimus caritatem Dei:
that Christ laid down his life for us;	quoniam ille animam suam pro nobis posuit;
so we ought to lay down our lives for one another.	et nos debemus pro fratribus animas ponere.

Prayer after Communion	**Post communionem**
May this heavenly mystery, O Lord, restore us in mind and body,	Sit nobis, Domine, reparatio mentis et corporis
that we may be coheirs in glory with Christ,	cæleste mysterium, ut simus eius in gloria coheredes,
to whose suffering we are united whenever we proclaim his Death.	cui, mortem ipsius annuntiando, compatimur.
Who lives and reigns for ever and ever.	Qui vivit et regnat in sæcula sæculorum.

TWENTY-SEVENTH SUNDAY IN ORDINARY TIME
(YEAR C)

Entrance Antiphon   Cf. Est 4:17

WITHIN your will, O Lord,
   all things are established,
and there is none that can resist
   your will.
For you have made all things,
   the heaven and the earth,
and all that is held within the circle
   of heaven;
you are the Lord of all.

Ant. ad introitum

IN voluntate tua, Domine,
   universa sunt posita,
et non est qui possit resistere
   voluntati tuæ.
Tu enim fecisti omnia,
   cælum et terram,
et universa quæ cæli
   ambitu continentur;
Dominus universorum tu es.

Collect

Almighty ever-living God,
who in the abundance
   of your kindness
surpass the merits and the desires
   of those who entreat you,
pour out your mercy upon us
to pardon what conscience dreads
and to give what prayer does
   not dare to ask.
Through our Lord Jesus Christ,
   your Son,
who lives and reigns with you
   in the unity of the Holy Spirit,
one God, for ever and ever.

Collecta

Omnipotens sempiterne Deus,
   qui abundantia pietatis tuæ
et merita supplicum excedis et vota,
effunde super nos
   misericordiam tuam,
ut dimittas quæ conscientia metuit,
et adicias quod oratio non præsumit.
Per Dominum nostrum Iesum
   Christum Filium tuum,
qui tecum vivit et regnat
   in unitate Spiritus Sancti,
Deus, per omnia sæcula sæculorum.

FIRST READING

A reading from the prophet Habakkuk   1:2-3; 2:2-4
The upright man will live by his faithfulness.

How long, Lord, am I to cry for help
while you will not listen;
to cry 'Oppression!' in your ear
and you will not save?
Why do you set injustice before me,
why do you look on where there is tyranny?

Outrage and violence, this is all I see,
all is contention, and discord flourishes.
Then the Lord answered and said,

'Write the vision down,
inscribe it on tablets
to be easily read,
since this vision is for its own time only:
eager for its own fulfillment, it does not deceive;
if it comes slowly, wait,
for come it will, without fail.
See how he flags, he whose soul is not at rights,
but the upright man will live by his faithfulness.'

The word of the Lord.

Responsorial Psalm   Ps 94:1-2,6-9. R. v.8

R. **O that today you would listen to his voice!
Harden not your hearts.**

Come, ring out our joy to the Lord;
hail the rock who saves us.
Let us come before him, giving thanks,
with songs let us hail the Lord. R.

Come in; let us bow and bend low;
let us kneel before the God who made us
for he is our God and we
the people who belong to his pasture,
the flock that is led by his hand. R.

O that today you would listen to his voice!
'Harden not your hearts as at Meribah,
as on that day at Massah in the desert
when your fathers put me to the test;.
when they tried me, though they saw my work.' R.

SECOND READING

A reading from the second letter of St Paul to Timothy   1:6-8,13-14
Never be ashamed of witnessing to our Lord.

I am reminding you to fan into a flame the gift that God gave you when I laid
my hands on you. God's gift was not a spirit of timidity, but the Spirit of power,
and love, and self-control. So you are never to be ashamed of witnessing to
the Lord, or ashamed of me for being his prisoner; but with me, bear the
hardships for the sake of the Good News, relying on the power of God.

Keep as your pattern the sound teaching you have heard from me, in the faith and love that are in Christ Jesus. You have been trusted to look after something precious; guard it with the help of the Holy Spirit who lives in us.

The word of the Lord.

Gospel Acclamation   1 S 3:9; Jn 6:68

R. **Alleluia, alleluia!**
Speak, Lord, your servant is listening:
you have the message of eternal life.
R. **Alleluia!**

Or: 1 P 1:25

R. **Alleluia, alleluia!**
The word of the Lord remains for ever:
What is this word?
It is the Good News that has been brought to you.
R. **Alleluia!**

GOSPEL

A reading from the holy Gospel according to Luke   17:5-10
If only you had faith!

The apostles said to the Lord, 'Increase our faith.' The Lord replied, 'Were your faith the size of a mustard seed you could say to this mulberry tree, "Be uprooted and planted in the sea," and it would obey you.

'Which of you, with a servant ploughing or minding sheep, would say to him when he returned from the fields, "Come and have your meal immediately"? Would he not be more likely to say, "Get my supper laid; make yourself tidy and wait on me while I eat and drink. You can eat and drink yourself afterwards"? Must he be grateful to the servant for doing what he was told? So with you: when you have done all you have been told to do, say, "We are merely servants: we have done no more than our duty."'

The Gospel of the Lord.

Prayer over the Offerings	Super oblata
Accept, O Lord, we pray,	Suscipe, quæsumus, Domine,
the sacrifices instituted	sacrificia tuis instituta præceptis,
by your commands	et sacris mysteriis,
and, through the sacred mysteries,	quæ debitæ servitutis
which we celebrate	celebramus officio,
with dutiful service,	

graciously complete
the sanctifying work
by which you are pleased
to redeem us.
Through Christ our Lord.

sanctificationem tuæ nobis
redemptionis dignanter adimple.
Per Christum Dominum nostrum.

Preface of Sundays in Ordinary Time I-VIII, pp.566-573.

Communion Antiphon   Lm 3:25

The Lord is good to those
who hope in him,
to the soul that seeks him.

Ant. ad communionem

Bonus est Dominus
sperantibus in eum,
animæ quærenti illum.

Or: Cf. 1 Co 10:17

Though many, we are one bread,
one body,
for we all partake of the one Bread
and one Chalice.

Vel:

Unus panis et unum corpus
multi sumus,
omnes qui de uno pane et de uno
calice participamus.

Prayer after Communion

Grant us, almighty God,
that we may be refreshed
and nourished
by the Sacrament which
we have received,
so as to be transformed
into what we consume.
Through Christ our Lord.

Post communionem

Concede nobis, omnipotens Deus,
ut de perceptis sacramentis
inebriemur atque pascamur,
quatenus in id quod
sumimus transeamus.
Per Christum Dominum nostrum.

TWENTY-EIGHTH SUNDAY IN ORDINARY TIME
(YEAR C)

Entrance Antiphon   Ps 129:3-4

IF you, O Lord,
should mark iniquities,
Lord, who could stand?
But with you is found forgiveness,
O God of Israel.

Ant. ad introitum

SI iniquitates observaveris,
Domine,
Domine, quis sustinebit?
Quia apud te propitiatio est,
Deus Israel.

Collect

May your grace, O Lord, we pray,
at all times go before us
   and follow after
and make us always determined
to carry out good works.
Through our Lord Jesus Christ,
   your Son,
who lives and reigns with you
   in the unity of the Holy Spirit,
one God, for ever and ever.

Collecta

Tua nos, quæsumus,
   Domine, gratia
semper et præveniat et sequatur,
ac bonis operibus iugiter præstet
   esse intentos.
Per Dominum nostrum Iesum
   Christum Filium tuum,
qui tecum vivit et regnat
   in unitate Spiritus Sancti,
Deus, per omnia sæcula sæculorum.

FIRST READING

A reading from the second book of the Kings   5:14-17

Naaman returned to Elisha and acknowledged the Lord.

Naaman the leper went down and immersed himself seven times in the Jordan, as Elisha had told him to do. And his flesh became clean once more like the flesh of a little child.

Returning to Elisha with his whole escort, he went in and stood before him. 'Now I know' he said 'that there is no God in all the earth except in Israel. Now, please, accept a present from your servant.' But Elisha replied, 'As the Lord lives, whom I serve, I will accept nothing.' Naaman pressed him to accept, but he refused. Then Naaman said, 'Since your answer is "No," allow your servant to be given as much earth as two mules may carry, because your servant will no longer offer holocaust or sacrifice to any god except the Lord.'

The word of the Lord.

Responsorial Psalm   Ps 97:1-4. R. Cf. v.2

R. **The Lord has shown his salvation to the nations.**

Sing a new song to the Lord
for he has worked wonders.
His right hand and his holy arm
have brought salvation. R.

The Lord has made known his salvation;
has shown his justice to the nations.
He has remembered his truth and love
for the house of Israel. R.

All the ends of the earth have seen
the salvation of our God.
Shout to the Lord all the earth,
ring out your joy. R.

SECOND READING

A reading from the second letter of St Paul to Timothy   2:8-13
If we hold firm, then we shall reign with Christ.

Remember the Good News that I carry, 'Jesus Christ risen from the dead, sprung from the race of David'; it is on account of this that I have my own hardships to bear, even to being chained like a criminal – but they cannot chain up God's news. So I bear it all for the sake of those who are chosen, so that in the end they may have the salvation that is in Christ Jesus and the eternal glory that comes with it.

Here is a saying that you can rely on:

If we have died with him, then we shall live with him.
If we hold firm, then we shall reign with him.
If we disown him, then he will disown us.
We may be unfaithful, but he is always faithful,
for he cannot disown his own self.

The word of the Lord.

Gospel Acclamation   Cf. Jn 6:63,68

R. **Alleluia, alleluia!**
Your words are spirit, Lord,
and they are life:
you have the message of eternal life.
R. **Alleluia!**

Or: 1 Th 5:18

R. **Alleluia, alleluia!**

For all things give thanks,
because this is what God expects you to do in Jesus Christ.

R. **Alleluia!**

GOSPEL

A reading from the holy Gospel according to Luke   17:11-19
No one can come back to give praise to God, except this foreigner.

On the way to Jerusalem Jesus travelled along the border between Samaria and Galilee. As he entered one of the villages, ten lepers came to meet him. They stood some way off and called to him, 'Jesus! Master! Take pity on us.' When he saw them he said, 'Go and show yourselves to the priests.' Now as they were going away they were cleansed. Finding himself cured, one of them turned back praising God at the top of his voice and threw himself at the feet of Jesus and thanked him. The man was a Samaritan. This made Jesus say, 'Were not all ten made clean? The other nine, where are they? It seems that no one has come back to give praise to God, except this foreigner.' And he said to the man, 'Stand up and go on your way. Your faith has saved you.'

The Gospel of the Lord.

Prayer over the Offerings

Accept, O Lord, the prayers
　　of your faithful
with the sacrificial offerings,
that, through these acts
　　of devotedness,
we may pass over to the glory
　　of heaven.
Through Christ our Lord.

Super oblata

Suscipe, Domine,
fidelium preces cum
　　oblationibus hostiarum,
ut, per hæc piæ devotionis officia,
ad cælestem gloriam transeamus.
Per Christum Dominum nostrum.

Preface of Sundays in Ordinary Time I-VIII, pp.566-573.

Communion Antiphon Cf. Ps 33:11

The rich suffer want and go hungry,
but those who seek the Lord
　　lack no blessing.
Or:　　　　　　　　　　　　1 Jn 3:2
When the Lord appears,
　　we shall be like him,
for we shall see him as he is.

Ant. ad communionem

Divites eguerunt et esurierunt;
quærentes autem Dominum
　　non minuentur omni bono.
Vel:

Cum apparuerit Dominus,
　　similes ei erimus,
quoniam videbimus eum sicuti est.

Prayer after Communion

We entreat your majesty most
　　humbly, O Lord,
that, as you feed us
　　with the nourishment
which comes from the most holy
　　Body and Blood of your Son,
so you may make us sharers
　　of his divine nature.
Who lives and reigns
　　for ever and ever.

Post communionem

Maiestatem tuam, Domine,
　　suppliciter deprecamur,
ut, sicut nos Corporis
　　et Sanguinis sacrosancti
pascis alimento,
ita divinæ naturæ facias
　　esse consortes.
Per Christum Dominum nostrum.

TWENTY-NINTH SUNDAY IN ORDINARY TIME
(YEAR C)

Entrance Antiphon   Cf. Ps 16:6,8

To you I call; for you will surely
  heed me, O God;
turn your ear to me; hear my words.
Guard me as the apple of your eye;
in the shadow of your wings
    protect me.

Ant. ad introitum

EGO clamavi,
  quoniam exaudisti
  me, Deus;
inclina aurem tuam,
  et exaudi verba mea.
Custodi me, Domine,
  ut pupillam oculi;
sub umbra alarum tuarum
  protege me.

Collect

Almighty ever-living God,
grant that we may always conform
  our will to yours
and serve your majesty in sincerity
  of heart.
Through our Lord Jesus Christ,
  your Son,
who lives and reigns with you
  in the unity of the Holy Spirit,
one God, for ever and ever.

Collecta

Omnipotens sempiterne Deus,
fac nos tibi semper et devotam
  gerere voluntatem,
et maiestati tuæ sincero
  corde servire.
Per Dominum nostrum Iesum
  Christum Filium tuum,
qui tecum vivit et regnat
  in unitate Spiritus Sancti,
Deus, per omnia sæcula sæculorum.

FIRST READING

A reading from the book of Exodus   17:8-13

As long as Moses kept his arms raised, Israel had the advantage.

The Amalekites came and attacked Israel at Rephidim. Moses said to Joshua, 'Pick out men for yourself, and tomorrow morning march out to engage Amalek. I, meanwhile, will stand on the hilltop, the staff of God in my hand.' Joshua did as Moses told him and marched out to engage Amalek, while Moses and Aaron and Hur went up to the top of the hill. As long as Moses kept his arms raised, Israel had the advantage; when he let his arms fall, the advantage went to Amalek. But Moses's arms grew heavy, so they took a stone and put it under him and on this he sat, Aaron and Hur supporting his arms, one on one side, one on the other; and his arms remained firm till sunset. With the edge of the sword Joshua cut down Amalek and his people.

    The word of the Lord.

Responsorial Psalm   Ps 120. R. Cf. v.2

R. **Our help is in the name of the Lord**
   who made heaven and earth.

I lift up my eyes to the mountains:
from where shall come my help?
My help shall come from the Lord
who made heaven and earth. R.

May he never allow you to stumble!
Let him sleep not, your guard.
No, he sleeps not nor slumbers,
Israel's guard. R.

The Lord is your guard and your shade;
at your right side he stands.
By day the sun shall not smite you
nor the moon in the night. R.

The Lord will guard you from evil,
he will guard your soul.
The Lord will guard your going and coming
both now and for ever. R.

SECOND READING

A reading from the second letter of St Paul to Timothy   3:14-4:2

The man who is dedicated to God becomes fully equipped and ready for any good work.

You must keep to what you have been taught and know to be true; remember who your teachers were, and how, ever since you were a child, you have known the holy scriptures – from these you can learn the wisdom that leads to salvation through faith in Christ Jesus. All scripture is inspired by God and can profitably be used for teaching, for refuting error, for guiding people's lives and teaching them to be holy. This is how the man who is dedicated to God becomes fully equipped and ready for any good work.

Before God and before Christ Jesus who is to be judge of the living and dead, I put this duty to you, in the name of his Appearing and of his kingdom: proclaim the message and, welcome or unwelcome, insist on it. Refute falsehood, correct error, call to obedience – but do all with patience and with the intention of teaching.

The word of the Lord.

Gospel Acclamation   Cf. Ep 1:17,18

R. **Alleluia, alleluia!**
May the Father of our Lord Jesus Christ
enlighten the eyes of our mind,
so that we can see what hope his call holds for us.
R. **Alleluia!**

Or: Heb 4:12

R. **Alleluia, alleluia!**
The word of God is something alive and active;
it can judge secret emotions and thoughts.
R. **Alleluia!**

GOSPEL

A reading from the holy Gospel according to Luke   18:1-8
God will see justice done to his chosen who cry to him.

Jesus told his disciples a parable about the need to pray continually and
never lose heart. 'There was a judge in a certain town' he said 'who had
neither fear of God nor respect for man. In the same town there was a
widow who kept on coming to him and saying, "I want justice from you
against my enemy!" For a long time he refused, but at last he said to
himself, "Maybe I have neither fear of God nor respect for man, but since
she keeps pestering me I must give this widow her just rights, or she will
persist in coming and worry me to death."'

And the Lord said, 'You notice what the unjust judge has to say? Now
will not God see justice done to his chosen who cry to him day and night
even when he delays to help them? I promise you, he will see justice done
to them, and done speedily. But when the Son of Man comes, will he find
any faith on earth?'

The Gospel of the Lord.

Prayer over the Offerings | Super oblata

Grant us, Lord, we pray, | Tribue nos, Domine, quæsumus,
a sincere respect for your gifts, | donis tuis libera mente servire,
that, through the purifying action | ut, tua purificante nos gratia,
   of your grace, | iisdem quibus famulamur
we may be cleansed by the very | mysteriis emundemur.
   mysteries we serve. | Per Christum Dominum nostrum.
Through Christ our Lord. |

Preface of Sundays in Ordinary Time I-VIII, pp.566-573.

Communion Antiphon Cf.Ps 32:18-19	Ant. ad communionem

Behold, the eyes of the Lord
are on those who fear him,
who hope in his merciful love,
to rescue their souls from death,
to keep them alive in famine.
	Ecce oculi Domini super
	    timentes eum,
	et in eis qui sperant super
	    misericordia eius;
	ut eruat a morte animas eorum,
	    et alat eos in fame.

Or: Mk 10:45	Vel:
The Son of Man has come to give his life as a ransom for many.	Filius hominis venit, ut daret animam suam redemptionem pro multis.
Prayer after Communion	Post communionem

Grant, O Lord, we pray,
that, benefiting from participation
    in heavenly things,
we may be helped by what you give
    in this present age
and prepared for the gifts
    that are eternal.
Through Christ our Lord.
	Fac nos, quæsumus, Domine,
	cælestium rerum
	    frequentatione proficere,
	ut et temporalibus
	    beneficiis adiuvemur,
	et erudiamur æternis.
	Per Christum Dominum nostrum.

THIRTIETH SUNDAY IN ORDINARY TIME
(YEAR C)

Entrance Antiphon Cf. Ps 104:3-4	Ant. ad introitum
L ET the hearts that seek the Lord rejoice; turn to the Lord and his strength; constantly seek his face.	LÆTETUR cor quærentium Dominum. Quærite Dominum et confirmamini, quærite faciem eius semper.

Collect	Collecta
Almighty ever-living God,	Omnipotens sempiterne Deus,
increase our faith, hope and charity,	da nobis fidei,
and make us love	spei et caritatis augmentum,
what you command,	et, ut mereamur assequi
so that we may merit	quod promittis,
what you promise.	fac nos amare quod præcipis.
Through our Lord Jesus Christ,	Per Dominum nostrum Iesum
your Son,	Christum Filium tuum,
who lives and reigns with you	qui tecum vivit et regnat
in the unity of the Holy Spirit,	in unitate Spiritus Sancti,
one God, for ever and ever.	Deus, per omnia sæcula sæculorum.

FIRST READING

A reading from the book of Ecclesiasticus   35:12-14,16-19

The humble man's prayer pierces the clouds.

The Lord is a judge
who is no respecter of personages.
He shows no respect of personages to the detriment of a poor man,
he listens to the plea of the injured party.
He does not ignore the orphan's supplication,
nor the widow's as she pours out her story.

The man who with his whole heart serves God will be accepted,
his petitions will carry to the clouds.
The humble man's prayer pierces the clouds,
until it arrives he is inconsolable,
nor will he desist until the Most High takes notice of him,
acquits the virtuous and delivers judgement.
And the Lord will not be slow,
nor will he be dilatory on their behalf.

    The word of the Lord.

Responsorial Psalm   Ps 32:2-3,17-19,23. R. v.7

R. **This poor man called; the Lord heard him**.

    I will bless the Lord at all times,
    his praise always on my lips;
    in the Lord my soul shall make its boast.
    The humble shall hear and be glad. R.

The Lord turns his face against the wicked
to destroy their remembrance from the earth.
The just call and the Lord hears
and rescues them in all their distress. R.

The Lord is close to the broken-hearted;
those whose spirit is crushed he will save.
The Lord ransoms the souls of his servants.
Those who hide in him shall not be condemned. R.

SECOND READING

A reading from the second letter of St Paul to Timothy   4:6-8,16-18

All there is to come now is the crown of righteousness reserved for me.

My life is already being poured away as a libation, and the time has come
for me to be gone. I have fought the good fight to the end; I have run
the race to the finish; I have kept the faith; all there is to come now is
the crown of righteousness reserved for me, which the Lord, the righteous
judge, will give to me on that Day; and not only to me but to all those who
have longed for his Appearing.

The first time I had to present my defence, there was not a single
witness to support me. Every one of them deserted me – may they not
be held accountable for it. But the Lord stood by me and gave me power,
so that through me the whole message might be proclaimed for all the
pagans to hear; and so I was rescued from the lion's mouth. The Lord
will rescue me from all evil attempts on me, and bring me safely to his
heavenly kingdom. To him be glory for ever and ever. Amen.

The word of the Lord.

Gospel Acclamation   Cf. Mt 11:25

R. **Alleluia, alleluia!**
Blessed are you, Father,
Lord of heaven and earth,
for revealing the mysteries of the kingdom
to mere children.
R. **Alleluia!**

Or: 2 Co 5:19

R. **Alleluia, alleluia!**
God was in Christ was reconciling the world to himself,
and he has entrusted to us the news that they are reconciled.
R. **Alleluia!**

GOSPEL

A reading from the holy Gospel according to Luke   18:9-14

The publican went home at rights with God; the Pharisee did not.

Jesus spoke the following parable to some people who prided themselves on being virtuous and despised everyone else: 'Two men went up to the Temple to pray, one a Pharisee, the other a tax collector. The Pharisee stood there and said this prayer to himself, "I thank you, God, that I am not grasping, unjust, adulterous like the rest of mankind, and particularly that I am not like this tax collector here. I fast twice a week; I pay tithes on all I get." The tax collector stood some distance away, not daring even to raise his eyes to heaven; but he beat his breast and said, "God, be merciful to me, a sinner." This man, I tell you, went home again at rights with God; the other did not. For everyone who exalts himself will be humbled, but the man who humbles himself will be exalted.'

The Gospel of the Lord.

Prayer over the Offerings	Super oblata

Look, we pray, O Lord,
on the offerings we make
    to your majesty,
that whatever is done by us
    in your service
may be directed above all
    to your glory.
Through Christ our Lord.
	Respice, quæsumus, Domine,
	munera quæ tuæ
	    offerimus maiestati,
	ut, quod nostro servitio geritur,
	ad tuam gloriam potius dirigatur.
	Per Christum Dominum nostrum.

Preface of Sundays in Ordinary Time I-VIII, pp.566-573.

Communion Antiphon Cf. Ps 19:6	Ant. ad communionem

We will ring out our joy at your
    saving help
and exult in the name of our God.
	Lætabimur in salutari tuo,
	et in nomine Dei
	    nostri magnificabimur.

Or: Ep 5:2	Vel:

Christ loved us and gave himself up
    for us,
as a fragrant offering to God.
	Christus dilexit nos, et tradidit
	    semetipsum pro nobis,
	oblationem Deo
	    in odorem suavitatis.

Prayer after Communion

May your Sacraments, O Lord,
    we pray,
perfect in us what lies within them,
that what we now celebrate in signs
we may one day possess in truth.
Through Christ our Lord.

Post communionem

Perficiant in nobis,
    Domine, quæsumus,
tua sacramenta quod continent,
ut, quæ nunc specie gerimus,
rerum veritate capiamus.
Per Christum Dominum nostrum.

THIRTY-FIRST SUNDAY IN ORDINARY TIME
(YEAR C)

Entrance Antiphon Cf. Ps 37:22-23

FORSAKE me not, O Lord,
    my God;
be not far from me!
Make haste and come to my help,
O Lord, my strong salvation!

Ant. ad introitum

NE derelinquas me,
    Domine Deus meus,
ne discedas a me;
intende in adiutorium meum,
Domine, virtus salutis meæ.

Collect

Almighty and merciful God,
by whose gift your faithful offer you
right and praiseworthy service,
grant, we pray,
that we may hasten
    without stumbling
to receive the things you
    have promised.
Through our Lord Jesus Christ,
    your Son,
who lives and reigns with you
    in the unity of the Holy Spirit,
one God, for ever and ever.

Collecta

Omnipotens et misericors Deus,
    de cuius munere venit,
ut tibi a fidelibus tuis digne
    et laudabiliter serviatur,
tribue, quæsumus, nobis,
ut ad promissiones tuas sine
    offensione curramus.
Per Dominum nostrum Iesum
    Christum Filium tuum,
qui tecum vivit et regnat
    in unitate Spiritus Sancti,
Deus, per omnia sæcula sæculorum.

FIRST READING

A reading from the book of Wisdom   11:22-12:2

You are merciful to all because you love all that exists.

In your sight, Lord the whole world is like a grain of dust that tips the scales,
like a drop of morning dew falling on the ground.
Yet you are merciful to all, because you can do all things
and overlook men's sins so that they can repent.
Yes, you love all that exists, you hold nothing of what you have made
  in abhorrence,
for had you hated anything, you would not have formed it.
And how, had you not willed it, could a thing persist,
how be conserved if not called forth by you?
You spare all things because all things are yours, Lord, lover of life,
you whose imperishable spirit is in all.
Little by little, therefore, you correct those who offend,
you admonish and remind them of how they have sinned,
so that they may abstain from evil and trust in you, Lord.

  The word of the Lord.

Responsorial Psalm   Ps 144:1-2,8-11,13-14. R. Cf. v.1

R. **I will bless your name for ever,**
  O God my King.

  I will give you glory, O God my King,
  I will bless your name for ever.
  I will bless you day after day
  and praise your name for ever. R.

  The Lord is kind and full of compassion,
  slow to anger, abounding in love.
  How good is the Lord to all,
  compassionate to all his creatures. R.

  All your creatures shall thank you, O Lord,
  and your friends shall repeat their blessing.
  They shall speak of the glory of your reign
  and declare your might, O God. R.

  The Lord is faithful in all his words
  and loving in all his deeds.
  The Lord supports all who fall
  and raises all who are bowed down. R.

SECOND READING

A reading from the second letter of St Paul to the Thessalonians　1:11-2:2

The name of Christ will be glorified in you and you in him.

We pray continually that our God will make you worthy of his call, and by his power fulfil all your desires for goodness and complete all that you have been doing through faith; because in this way the name of our Lord Jesus Christ will be glorified in you and you in him, by the grace of our God and the Lord Jesus Christ.

To turn now, brothers, to the coming of our Lord Jesus Christ and how we shall all be gathered round him: please do not get excited too soon or alarmed by any prediction or rumour or any letter claiming to come from us, implying that the Day of the Lord has already arrived.

The word of the Lord.

Gospel Acclamation　　　　　　　　　　　　　　　　　　Lk 19:38; 2:14

R. **Alleluia, alleluia!**
Blessings on the King who comes,
in the name of the Lord!
Peace in heaven
and glory in the highest heavens!
R. **Alleluia!**

Or:　　　　　　　　　　　　　　　　　　　　　　　　　　Jn 3:16

R. **Alleluia, alleluia!**
God loved the world so much
that he gave his only Son,
so that everyone who believes in him
may have eternal life.
R. **Alleluia!**

GOSPEL

A reading from holy Gospel according to Luke　　　　　　　19:1-10

The Son of Man has come to seek out and save what was lost.

Jesus entered Jericho and was going through the town when a man whose name was Zacchaeus made his appearance; he was one of the senior tax collectors and a wealthy man. He was anxious to see what kind of man Jesus was, but he was too short and could not see him for the crowd; so he ran ahead and climbed a sycamore tree to catch a glimpse of Jesus who was to pass that way. When Jesus reached the spot he looked up and spoke to him: 'Zacchaeus, come down. Hurry, because I must stay at your house today.'

And he hurried down and welcomed him joyfully. They all complained when they saw what was happening. 'He has gone to stay at a sinner's house' they said. But Zacchaeus stood his ground and said to the Lord, 'Look, sir, I am going to give half my property to the poor, and if I have cheated anybody I will pay him back four times the amount.' And Jesus said to him, 'Today salvation has come to this house, because this man too is a son of Abraham; for the Son of Man has come to seek out and save what was lost.'

The Gospel of the Lord.

Prayer over the Offerings

May these sacrificial offerings,
    O Lord,
become for you a pure oblation,
and for us a holy outpouring
    of your mercy.
Through Christ our Lord.

Super oblata

Fiat hoc sacrificium, Domine,
    oblatio tibi munda,
et nobis misericordiæ tuæ
    sancta largitio.
Per Christum Dominum nostrum.

Preface of Sundays in Ordinary Time I-VIII, pp.566-573.

Communion Antiphon Cf. Ps 15:11

You will show me the path of life,
the fullness of joy in your presence,
    O Lord.

Ant. ad communionem

Notas mihi fecisti vias vitæ,
adimplebis me lætitia
    cum vultu tuo, Domine.

Or: Jn 6:58

Just as the living Father sent me
and I have life because of the Father,
so whoever feeds on me
shall have life because of me,
    says the Lord.

Vel:

Sicut misit me vivens Pater,
    et ego vivo propter Patrem,
et qui manducat me,
    et ipse vivet propter me,
dicit Dominus.

Prayer after Communion

May the working of your power,
    O Lord,
increase in us, we pray,
so that, renewed by these
    heavenly Sacraments,
we may be prepared by your gift
for receiving what they promise.
Through Christ our Lord.

Post communionem

Augeatur in nobis,
    quæsumus, Domine,
tuæ virtutis operatio,
ut, refecti cælestibus sacramentis,
ad eorum promissa capienda tuo
    munere præparemur.
Per Christum Dominum nostrum.

THIRTY-SECOND SUNDAY IN ORDINARY TIME
(YEAR C)

Entrance Antiphon   Ps 87:3

LET my prayer come
into your presence.
Incline your ear
    to my cry for help, O Lord.

Ant. ad introitum

INTRET oratio mea
in conspectu tuo;
inclina aurem tuam
    ad precem meam, Domine.

Collect

Almighty and merciful God,
graciously keep from us all adversity,
so that, unhindered in mind
    and body alike,
we may pursue in freedom of heart
the things that are yours.
Through our Lord Jesus Christ,
    your Son,
who lives and reigns with you
    in the unity of the Holy Spirit,
one God, for ever and ever.

Collecta

Omnipotens et misericors Deus,
universa nobis adversantia
    propitiatus exclude,
ut, mente et corpore pariter expediti,
quæ tua sunt liberis
    mentibus exsequamur.
Per Dominum nostrum Iesum
    Christum Filium tuum,
qui tecum vivit et regnat
    in unitate Spiritus Sancti,
Deus, per omnia sæcula sæculorum.

FIRST READING

A reading from the second book of Maccabees   7:1-2,9-14

The King of the world will raise us up to live for ever.

There were seven brothers who were arrested with their mother. The king tried to force them to taste pig's flesh, which the Law forbids, by torturing them with whips and scourges. One of them, acting as spokesman for the others, said, 'What are you trying to find out from us? We are prepared to die rather then break the Law of our ancestors.'

    With his last breath the second brother exclaimed, 'Inhuman fiend, you may discharge us from this present life, but the King of the world will raise us up, since it is for his laws that we die, to live again for ever.'

    After him, they amused themselves with the third, who on being asked for his tongue promptly thrust it out and boldly held out his hands, with these honourable words, 'It was heaven that gave me these limbs; for the sake of his laws I disdain them; from him I hope to receive them again.'

The king and his attendants were astounded at the young man's courage and his utter indifference to suffering.

When this one was dead they subjected the fourth to the same savage torture. When he neared his end he cried, 'Ours is the better choice, to meet death at men's hands, yet relying on God's promise that we shall be raised up by him; whereas for you there can be no resurrection, no new life.'

The word of the Lord.

Responsorial Psalm   Ps 16:1,5-6,8,15. R. v.15

R. **I shall be filled, when I awake,**
   with the sight of your glory, O Lord.

Lord, hear a cause that is just,
pay heed to my cry
Turn your ear to my prayer:
no deceit is on my lips. R.

I kept my feet firmly in your paths;
there was no faltering in my steps.
I am here and I call, you will hear me, O God.
Turn your ear to me; hear my words. R.

Guard me as the apple of your eye.
Hide me in the shadow of your wings.
As for me, in my justice I shall see your face
and be filled, when I awake, with the sight of your glory. R.

SECOND READING

A reading from the second letter of St Paul to the Thessalonians   2:16-3:5

May the Lord strengthen you in everything good that you do or say.

May our Lord Jesus Christ himself, and God our Father who has given us his love and, through his grace, such inexhaustible comfort and such sure hope, comfort you and strengthen you in everything good that you do or say.

Finally, brothers, pray for us; pray that the Lord's message may spread quickly, and be received with honour as it was among you; and pray that we may be preserved from the interference of bigoted and evil people, for faith is not given to everyone. But the Lord is faithful, and he will give you strength and guard you from the evil one, and we, in the Lord, have every confidence that you are doing and will go on doing all that we tell you. May the Lord turn your hearts towards the love of God and the fortitude of Christ.

The word of the Lord.

Gospel Acclamation   Lk 21:36

R. **Alleluia, alleluia!**
Stay awake praying at all times
for the strength to stand with confidence
before the Son of Man.
R. **Alleluia!**

Or: Rv 1:5,6

R. **Alleluia, alleluia!**
Jesus Christ is the First-born from the dead;
to him be glory and power for ever and ever.
R. **Alleluia!**

GOSPEL

A reading from the holy Gospel according to Luke   20:27-38
He is of God, not of the dead, but of the living.

[Some Sadducees – those who say that there is no resurrection – approached Jesus and they put this question to him,] 'Master, we have it from Moses in writing, that if a man's married brother dies childless, the man must marry the widow to raise up children for his brother. Well, then, there were seven brothers. The first, having married a wife, died childless. The second and then the third married the widow. And the same with all seven, they died leaving no children. Finally the woman herself died. Now, at the resurrection, to which of them will she be wife since she had been married to all seven?'

[Jesus replied, 'The children of this world take wives and husbands, but those who are judged worthy of a place in the other world and in the resurrection from the dead do not marry because they can no longer die, for they are the same as the angels, and being children of the resurrection they are sons of God. And Moses himself implies that the dead rise again, in the passage about the bush where he calls the Lord the God of Abraham, the God of Isaac and the God of Jacob. Now he is God, not of the dead, but of the living; for to him all men are in fact alive.'

The Gospel of the Lord.]

Shorter Form, verses 27,34-38. Read between [ ]

Prayer over the Offerings

Look with favour, we pray, O Lord,
upon the sacrificial gifts offered here,
that, celebrating in mystery
   the Passion of your Son,
we may honour it
   with loving devotion.
Through Christ our Lord.

Super oblata

Sacrificiis præsentibus, Domine,
quæsumus, intende placatus,
ut, quod passionis Filii tui
   mysterio gerimus,
pio consequamur affectu.
Per Christum Dominum nostrum.

Preface of Sundays in Ordinary Time I-VIII, pp.566-573.

Communion Antiphon   Ps 22:1-2

The Lord is my shepherd;
   there is nothing I shall want.
Fresh and green are the pastures
   where he gives me repose,
near restful waters he leads me.

Ant. ad communionem

Dominus regit me,
   et nihil mihi deerit;
in loco pascuæ ibi me collocavit,
super aquam refectionis
   educavit me.

Or: Lk 24:35

The disciples recognised the Lord
   Jesus in the breaking of bread.

Vel:

Cognoverunt discipuli Dominum
   Iesum in fractione panis.

Prayer after Communion

Nourished by this sacred gift,
   O Lord,
we give you thanks and beseech
   your mercy,
that, by the pouring forth
   of your Spirit,
the grace of integrity may endure
in those your heavenly power
   has entered.
Through Christ our Lord.

Post communionem

Gratias tibi, Domine, referimus
   sacro munere vegetati,
tuam clementiam implorantes,
ut, per infusionem Spiritus tui,
in quibus cælestis virtus introivit,
sinceritatis gratia perseveret.
Per Christum Dominum nostrum.

THIRTY-THIRD SUNDAY IN ORDINARY TIME
(YEAR C)

Entrance Antiphon Jr 29:11,12,14

THE Lord said: I think thoughts of peace and not of affliction.
You will call upon me,
and I will answer you,
and I will lead back your captives
from every place.

Ant. ad introitum

DICIT Dominus:
Ego cogito cogitationes pacis
et non afflictionis;
invocabitis me, et ego exaudiam vos,
et reducam captivitatem vestram
de cunctis locis.

Collect

Grant us, we pray, O Lord our God,
the constant gladness of being
devoted to you,
for it is full and lasting happiness
to serve with constancy
the author of all that is good.
Through our Lord Jesus Christ,
your Son,
who lives and reigns with you
in the unity of the Holy Spirit,
one God, for ever and ever.

Collecta

Da nobis, quæsumus,
Domine Deus noster,
in tua semper devotione gaudere,
quia perpetua est et plena felicitas,
si bonorum omnium iugiter
serviamus auctori.
Per Dominum nostrum Iesum
Christum Filium tuum,
qui tecum vivit et regnat
in unitate Spiritus Sancti,
Deus, per omnia sæcula sæculorum.

FIRST READING

A reading from the prophet Malachi   3:19-20

For you the sun of righteousness will shine out.

The day is coming now, burning like a furnace, and all the arrogant and the evil-doers will be like stubble. The day that is coming is going to burn them up, says the Lord of hosts, leaving them neither root nor stalk. But for you who fear my name, the sun of righteousness will shine out with healing in its rays.

The word of the Lord.

Responsorial Psalm   Ps 97:5-9. R. Cf. v.9

R. **The Lord comes to rule the peoples with fairness.**

Sing psalms to the Lord with the harp,
with the sound of music.
With trumpets and the sound of the horn
acclaim the King, the Lord. R.

Let the sea and all within it, thunder
the world, and all its peoples.
Let the rivers clap their hands
and the hills ring out their joy
at the presence of the Lord. R.

For the Lord comes,
he comes to rule the earth.
He will rule the world with justice
and the peoples with fairness. R.

R. **The Lord comes to rule the peoples with fairness.**

SECOND READING

A reading from the second letter of St Paul to the Thessalonians   3:7-12

Do not let anyone have food if he refuses to work.

You know how you are supposed to imitate us: now we were not idle when
we were with you, nor did we ever have our meals at anyone's table without
paying for them; no, we worked night and day, slaving and straining, so as
not to be a burden on any of you. This was not because we had no right to
be, but in order make ourselves an example for you to follow.

   We gave you a rule when we were with you: not to let anyone have any
food if he refused to do any work. Now we hear that there are some of you
who are living in idleness, doing no work themselves but interfering with
everyone else's. In the Lord Jesus Christ, we order and call on people of
this kind to go on quietly working and earning the food that they eat.

   The word of the Lord.

Gospel Acclamation   Lk 21:36
R. **Alleluia, alleluia!**
Stay awake, praying at all times
for the strength to stand with confidence
before the Son of Man.
R. **Alleluia!**

Or: Lk 21:28
R. **Alleluia, alleluia!**
Stand erect, hold your heads high,
because your liberation is near at hand.
R. **Alleluia!**

GOSPEL

A reading from the holy Gospel according to Luke   21:5-19

Your endurance will win you your lives.

When some were talking about the Temple, remarking how it was adorned with fine stonework and votive offerings, Jesus said, 'All these things you are staring at now – the time will come when not a single stone will be left on another: everything will be destroyed.' And they put to him this question: 'Master,' they said 'when will this happen, then, and what sign will there be that this is about to take place?'

'Take care not to be deceived,' he said 'because many will come using my name and saying, "I am he" and, "The time is near at hand." Refuse to join them. And when you hear of wars and revolutions, do not be frightened, for this is something that must happen but the end is not so soon.' Then he said to them, 'Nation will fight against nation, and kingdom against kingdom. There will be great earthquakes and plagues and famines here and there; there will be fearful sights and great signs from heaven.

'But before all this happens, men will seize you and persecute you; they will hand you over to the synagogues and to imprisonment, and bring you before kings and governors because of my name – and that will be your opportunity to bear witness. Keep this carefully in mind: you are not to prepare your defence, because I myself shall give you an eloquence and a wisdom that none of your opponents will be able to resist or contradict. You will be betrayed even by parents and brothers, relations and friends; and some of you will be put to death. You will be hated by all men on account of my name, but not a hair of your head will be lost. Your endurance will win you your lives.'

The Gospel of the Lord.

Prayer over the Offerings	Super oblata
Grant, O Lord, we pray,	Concede, quæsumus, Domine,
that what we offer in the sight	ut oculis tuæ maiestatis
of your majesty	munus oblatum
may obtain for us the grace	et gratiam nobis
of being devoted to you	devotionis obtineat,
and gain us the prize	et effectum beatæ
of everlasting happiness.	perennitatis acquirat.
Through Christ our Lord.	Per Christum Dominum nostrum.

Preface of Sundays in Ordinary Time I-VIII, pp.566-573.

Communion Antiphon   Ps 72:28

To be near God is my happiness,
to place my hope in God the Lord.

Or: Mk 11:23-24

Amen, I say to you:
   Whatever you ask in prayer,
believe that you will receive,
and it shall be given to you,
   says the Lord.

Prayer after Communion

We have partaken of the gifts
   of this sacred mystery,
humbly imploring, O Lord,
that what your Son commanded
   us to do
in memory of him
may bring us growth in charity.
Through Christ our Lord.

Ant. ad communionem

Mihi autem adhærere Deo
   bonum est,
ponere in Domino Deo spem meam.

Vel:

Amen dico vobis,
   quidquid orantes petitis,
credite quia accipietis, et fiet vobis,
   dicit Dominus.

Post communionem

Sumpsimus, Domine,
   sacri dona mysterii,
humiliter deprecantes,
ut, quæ in sui commemorationem
nos Filius tuus facere præcepit,
in nostræ proficiant
   caritatis augmentum.
Per Christum Dominum nostrum.

OUR LORD JESUS CHRIST, KING OF THE UNIVERSE (YEAR C)

Solemnity

Entrance Antiphon Rv 5:12; 1:6	Ant. ad introitum
HOW worthy is the Lamb who was slain, to receive power and divinity, and wisdom and strength and honour. To him belong glory and power for ever and ever.	DIGNUS est Agnus, qui occisus est, accipere virtutem et divinitatem et sapientiam et fortitudinem et honorem. Ipsi gloria et imperium in sæcula sæculorum.

The Gloria in excelsis (Glory to God in the highest) is said.

Collect	Collecta
Almighty ever-living God, whose will is to restore all things in your beloved Son, the King of the universe, grant, we pray, that the whole creation, set free from slavery, may render your majesty service and ceaselessly proclaim your praise. Through our Lord Jesus Christ, your Son, who lives and reigns with you in the unity of the Holy Spirit, one God, for ever and ever.	Omnipotens sempiterne Deus, qui in dilecto Filio tuo, universorum Rege, omnia instaurare voluisti, concede propitius, ut tota creatura, a servitute liberata, tuæ maiestati deserviat ac te sine fine collaudet. Per Dominum nostrum Iesum Christum Filium tuum, qui tecum vivit et regnat in unitate Spiritus Sancti, Deus, per omnia sæcula sæculorum.

FIRST READING

A reading from the second book of Samuel   5:1-3

They anointed David king of Israel.

All the tribes of Israel came to David at Hebron. 'Look' they said 'we are your own flesh and blood. In days past when Saul was our king, it was you who led Israel in all their exploits; and the Lord said to you, "You are the

man who shall be shepherd of my people Israel, you shall be the leader of
Israel.'" So all the elders of Israel came to the king at Hebron, and King
David made a pact with them at Hebron in the presence of the Lord, and
they anointed David king of Israel.

The word of the Lord.

Responsial Psalm   Ps 121:1-5. R. Cf. v.2

R. **I rejoiced when I heard them say:**
   'Let us go to God's house.'

I rejoiced when I heard them say:
'Let us go to God's house.'
And now our feet are standing
within your gates, O Jerusalem. R.

Jerusalem is built as a city
strongly compact.
It is there that the tribes go up,
the tribes of the Lord. R.

For Israel's law it is,
there to praise the Lord's name.
There were set the thrones of judgement
of the house of David. R.

SECOND READING

A reading from the letter of St Paul to the Colossians   1:12-20
He has created a place for us in the kingdom of the Son that he loves.

We give thanks to the Father who has made it possible for you to join the
saints and with them to inherit the light.

Because that is what he has done: he has taken us out of the power
of darkness and created a place for us in the kingdom of the Son that he
loves, and in him, we gain our freedom, the forgiveness of our sins.

He is the image of the unseen God
and the first-born of all creation,
for in him were created
all things in heaven and on earth:
everything visible and everything invisible,
Thrones, Dominations, Sovereignties, Powers –
all things were created through him and for him.

Before anything was created, he existed,
and he holds all things in unity.
Now the Church is his body,
he is its head.
As he is the Beginning,
he was first to be born from the dead,
so that he should be first in every way;
because God wanted all perfection
to be found in him
and all things to be reconciled through him and for him,
everything in heaven and everything on earth,
when he made peace
by his death on the cross.

The word of the Lord.

Gospel Acclamation   Mk 11:9.10

R. **Alleluia, alleluia!**
Blessings on him who comes in the name of the Lord!
Blessings on the coming kingdom of our father David!
R. **Alleluia!**

GOSPEL

A reading from the holy Gospel according to Luke   23:35-43
Lord, remember me when you come into your kingdom.

The people stayed there before the cross watching Jesus. As for the leaders, they jeered at him. 'He saved others,' they said 'let him save himself if he is the Christ of God, the Chosen One.' The soldiers mocked him too, and when they approached to offer him vinegar they said, 'If you are the king of the Jews, save yourself.' Above him there was an inscription: 'This is the King of the Jews.'

One of the criminals hanging there abused him. 'Are you not the Christ?' he said. 'Save yourself and us as well.' But the other spoke up and rebuked him. 'Have you no fear of God at all?' he said. 'You got the same sentence as he did, but in our case we deserved it: we are paying for what we did. But this man has done nothing wrong. Jesus,' he said 'remember me when you come into your kingdom.' 'Indeed, I promise you,' he replied 'today you will be with me in paradise.'

The Gospel of the Lord.

The Creed is said.

Prayer over the Offerings

As we offer you, O Lord,
  the sacrifice
by which the human race
  is reconciled to you,
we humbly pray
that your Son himself may bestow
  on all nations
the gifts of unity and peace.
Through Christ our Lord.

Preface: Christ, King of the Universe, see pp.814-815.

Super oblata

Hostiam tibi, Domine,
humanæ reconciliationis
  offerentes,
suppliciter deprecamur,
ut ipse Filius tuus cunctis gentibus
unitatis et pacis dona concedat.
Qui vivit et regnat
  in sæcula sæculorum.

Communion Antiphon Ps 28:10-11

The Lord sits as King for ever.
The Lord will bless his people
  with peace.

Ant. ad communionem

Sedebit Dominus Rex in æternum;
Dominus benedicet populo suo
  in pace.

Prayer after Communion

Having received the food
  of immortality,
we ask, O Lord,
that, glorying in obedience
to the commands of Christ,
  the King of the universe,
we may live with him eternally
  in his heavenly Kingdom.
Who lives and reigns
  for ever and ever.

Post communionem

Immortalitatis alimoniam consecuti,
quæsumus, Domine,
ut, qui Christi Regis universorum
gloriamur obœdire mandatis,
cum ipso in cælesti regno sine fine
  vivere valeamus.
Qui vivit et regnat
  in sæcula sæculorum.

SOLEMNITIES OF THE LORD IN ORDINARY TIME

THE MOST HOLY TRINITY (YEAR C)

After the Easter Season that ended last Sunday with Pentecost, the Liturgy has returned to "Ordinary Time". This does not mean, however, that Christians must be less any committed: indeed, having entered divine life through the sacraments, we are called daily to be open to the action of divine Grace, to progress in love of God and of neighbour. This Sunday of the Most Holy Trinity, in a certain sense sums up God's revelation which was brought about through the Paschal Mysteries: Christ's death and Resurrection, his Ascension to the right hand of the Father and the outpouring of the Holy Spirit. The human mind and language are inadequate to explain the relationship that exists between the Father, the Son and the Holy Spirit; yet the Fathers of the Church sought to illustrate the mystery of the Triune God by living it with deep faith in their own lives.

(Pope Benedict XVI)

Solemnity

Entrance Antiphon	Ant. ad introitum
BLEST be God the Father, and the Only Begotten Son of God, and also the Holy Spirit, for he has shown us his merciful love.	**B**ENEDICTUS sit Deus Pater, Unigenitusque Dei Filius, Sanctus quoque Spiritus, quia fecit nobiscum misericordiam suam.

The Gloria in excelsis (Glory to God in the highest) is said.

Collect

God our Father, who by sending
   into the world
the Word of truth and the Spirit
   of sanctification
made known to the human race
   your wondrous mystery,
grant us, we pray, that in professing
   the true faith,
we may acknowledge the Trinity
   of eternal glory
and adore your Unity,
   powerful in majesty.
Through our Lord Jesus Christ,
   your Son,
who lives and reigns with you
   in the unity of the Holy Spirit,
one God, for ever and ever.

Collecta

Deus Pater, qui Verbum veritatis
et Spiritum sanctificationis
   mittens in mundum,
admirabile mysterium tuum
   hominibus declarasti,
da nobis, in confessione veræ fidei,
æternæ gloriam
   Trinitatis agnoscere,
et Unitatem adorare
   in potentia maiestatis.
Per Dominum nostrum Iesum
   Christum Filium tuum,
qui tecum vivit et regnat
   in unitate Spiritus Sancti,
Deus, per omnia sæcula sæculorum.

FIRST READING

A reading from the book of Proverbs   8:22-31

Before the earth came into being, Wisdom was born.

The Wisdom of God cries aloud:

   The Lord created me when his purpose first unfolded,
   before the oldest of his works.
   From everlasting I was firmly set,
   from the beginning, before earth came into being.
   The deep was not, when I was born,
   there were no Springs to gush with water.
   Before the mountains were settled,
   before the hills, I came to birth;
   before he made the earth, the countryside,
   or the first grains of the world's dust.
   When he fixed the heavens firm, I was there,
   when he drew ring on the surface of the deep,
   when he thickened the cloud above,
   when he fixed fast the springs of the deep,
   when he assigned the sea its boundaries
   − and the waters will not invade the shore −
   when he laid down the foundations of the earth,

I was by his side, a master craftsman,
delighting in him day after day,
ever at play in his presence,
at play everywhere in the world,
delighting to be with the sons of men.

The word of the Lord.

Responsorial Psalm   Ps 8:4-9. R. v.2

R. **How great is your name, O Lord our God,
through all the earth!**

When I see the heavens, the work of your hands,
the moon and the stars which you arranged,
what is man that you should keep him in mind,
mortal man that you care for him? R.

Yet you have made him little less than a god;
with glory and honour you crowned him,
gave him power over the works of your hand,
put all things under his feet. R.

All of them, sheep and cattle,
yes, even the savage beasts,
birds of the air, and fish
that make their way through the waters. R.

SECOND READING

A reading from the letter of St Paul to the Romans   5:1-5

To God, through Christ, in the love poured out by the Spirit.

Through our Lord Jesus Christ, by faith we are judged righteous and
at peace with God, since it is by faith and through Jesus that we have
entered this state of grace in which we can boast about looking forward
to God's glory. But that is not all we can boast about; we can boast about
our sufferings. These sufferings bring patience, as we know, and patience
brings perseverance, and perseverance brings hope, and this hope is not
deceptive, because the love of God has been poured into our hearts by the
Holy Spirit which has been given us.

The word of the Lord.

Gospel Acclamation   Cf. Rv 1:8

R. **Alleluia, alleluia!**
Glory be to the Father, and to the Son,
     and to the Holy Spirit,
the God who is, who was, and who is to come.
R. **Alleluia!**

GOSPEL

A reading from the holy Gospel according to John   16:12-15
Everything the Father has is mine; all the Spirit tells you will be taken from what is mine.

Jesus said to his disciples:

   'I still have many things to say to you
   but they would be too much for you now.
   But when the Spirit of truth comes
   he will lead you to the complete truth,
   since he will not be speaking as from himself
   but will say only what he has learnt;
   and he will tell you of the things to come.
   He will glorify me,
   since all he tells you
   will be taken from what is mine.
   Everything the Father has is mine;
   that is why I said:
   All he tells you
   will be taken from what is mine.'

   The Gospel of the Lord.

The Creed is said.

Prayer over the Offerings	Super oblata
Sanctify by the invocation of your name,	Sanctifica, quæsumus, Domine Deus noster,
we pray, O Lord our God,	per tui nominis invocationem,
this oblation of our service,	hæc munera nostræ servitutis,
and by it make of us an eternal offering to you.	et per ea nosmetipsos tibi perfice munus æternum.
Through Christ our Lord.	Per Christum Dominum nostrum.

Preface: The Mystery of the Most Holy Trinity, pp.819-820.

Communion Antiphon　　Ga 4:6	Ant. ad communionem

Since you are children of God,
God has sent into your hearts
　　the Spirit of his Son,
the Spirit who cries out:
　　Abba, Father.

Quoniam autem estis filii,
misit Deus Spiritum Filii sui
　　in corda vestra
clamantem: Abba, Pater.

Prayer after Communion	Post communionem

May receiving this Sacrament,
　　O Lord our God,
bring us health of body and soul,
as we confess your eternal holy
　　Trinity and undivided Unity.
Through Christ our Lord.

Proficiat nobis ad salutem
　　corporis et animæ,
Domine Deus noster,
　　huius sacramenti susceptio,
et sempiternæ sanctæ Trinitatis
eiusdemque individuæ
　　Unitatis confessio.
Per Christum Dominum nostrum.

Thursday after Trinity Sunday

THE MOST HOLY
BODY AND BLOOD OF CHRIST (YEAR C)
(CORPUS CHRISTI)

The Eucharist is the food reserved for those who in Baptism were delivered from slavery and have become sons; it is the food that sustained them on the long journey of the exodus through the desert of human existence. Like the manna for the people of Israel, for every Christian generation the Eucharist is the indispensable nourishment that sustains them as they cross the desert of this world, parched by the ideological and economic systems that do not promote life but rather humiliate it. It is a world where the logic of power and possessions prevails rather than that of service and love; a world where the culture of violence and death is frequently triumphant. Yet Jesus comes to meet us and imbues us with certainty: he himself is "the Bread of life". He repeated this to us in the words of the Gospel Acclamation: "I am the living bread from Heaven, if any one eats of this bread, he will live for ever".

(Pope Benedict XVI)

Solemnity

Where the Solemnity of the Most Holy Body and Blood of Christ is not a Holyday of Obligation, it is assigned to the Sunday after the Most Holy Trinity as its proper day.

Entrance Antiphon   Cf. Ps 80:17 | Ant. ad introitum

HE fed them with the finest wheat and satisfied them with honey from the rock. | CIBAVIT eos ex adipe frumenti, et de petra melle saturavit eos.

The Gloria in excelsis (Glory to God in the highest) is said.

Collect	Collecta
O God, who in this 　wonderful Sacrament have left us a memorial 　of your Passion, grant us, we pray, so to revere the sacred mysteries 　of your Body and Blood that we may always experience 　in ourselves the fruits of your redemption. Who live and reign with God 　the Father in the unity of the Holy Spirit, 　one God, for ever and ever.	Deus, qui nobis sub 　sacramento mirabili passionis tuæ memoriam reliquisti, tribue, quæsumus, ita nos Corporis et Sanguinis tui 　sacra mysteria venerari, ut redemptionis tuæ fructum 　in nobis iugiter sentiamus. Qui vivis et regnas cum Deo Patre in unitate Spiritus Sancti, Deus, per omnia sæcula sæculorum.

FIRST READING

A reading from the book of Genesis　　　　　　　　14:18-20

He brought bread and wine.

Melchizedek king of Salem brought bread and wine; he was a priest of God Most High. He pronounced this blessing:

> 'Blessed be Abraham by God Most High, creator of heaven and earth,
> and blessed be God Most High for handing over your enemies to you.'

And Abraham gave him a tithe of everything.

　The word of the Lord.

Responsorial Psalm　　　　　　　　　　　　　　Ps 109:1-4. R. v.4

R. **You are a priest for ever,**
　a priest like Melchizedek of old.

　The Lord's revelation to my Master:
　'Sit on my right:
　I will put your foes beneath your feet.' R.

　The Lord will send from Zion
　your sceptre of power:
　rule in the midst of all your foes. R.

　A prince from the day of your birth
　on the holy mountains;
　from the womb before the dawn I begot you. R.

The Lord has sworn an oath he will not change.
'You are a priest for ever,
a priest like Melchizedek of old.' R.

R. **You are a priest for ever,
a priest like Melchizedek of old.**

SECOND READING

A reading from the first letter of St Paul to the Corinthians   11:23-26
Every time you eat this bread and drink this cup, you are proclaiming the Lord's death.

This is what I received from the Lord, and in turn passed on to you: that on the same night that he was betrayed, the Lord Jesus took some bread, and thanked God for it and broke it, and he said, 'This is my body, which is for you; do this as a memorial of me.' In the same way he took the cup after supper, and said, 'This cup is the new covenant in my blood. Whenever you drink it, do this as a memorial of me.' Until the Lord comes, therefore, every time you eat this bread and drink this cup, you are proclaiming his death.

The word of the Lord.

The Sequence, *Lauda Sion,* may be said or sung in its longer or shorter form. p.823ff.

Gospel Acclamation   Jn 6:51

R. **Alleluia, alleluia!**
I am the living bread which has come down from heaven,
says the Lord;
Anyone who eats this bread will live for ever.
R. **Alleluia!**

GOSPEL

A reading from the holy Gospel according to Luke   9:11-17
They all ate as much as they wanted.

Jesus made the crowds welcome and talked to them about the kingdom of God; and he cured those who were in need of healing.

It was late afternoon when the Twelve came to him and said, 'Send the people away, and they can go to the villages and farms round about to find lodging and food; for we are in a lonely place here.' He replied, 'Give them something to eat yourselves.' But they said, 'We have no more than five loaves and two fish, unless we are to go ourselves and buy food for all these people.' For there were about five thousand men. But he said to his disciples, 'Get them to sit down in parties of about fifty.' They did so and made them all sit down. Then he took the five loaves and the two fish, raised his eyes to heaven, and said the blessing over them; then he broke them and handed them to his disciples to distribute among the crowd. They all ate as much as they wanted, and when the scraps remaining were collected they filled twelve baskets.

The Gospel of the Lord.

The Creed is said.

Prayer over the Offerings	Super oblata
Grant your Church, O Lord, we pray, the gifts of unity and peace, whose signs are to be seen in mystery in the offerings we here present. Through Christ our Lord.	Ecclesiæ tuæ, quæsumus, Domine, unitatis et pacis propitius dona concede, quæ sub oblatis muneribus mystice designantur. Per Christum Dominum nostrum.

Preface of the Most Holy Eucharist I or II, pp.574-575.

Communion Antiphon Jn 6:57	Ant. ad communionem
Whoever eats my flesh and drinks my blood remains in me and I in him, says the Lord.	Qui manducat meam carnem et bibit meum sanguinem, in me manet et ego in eo, dicit Dominus.

Prayer after Communion	Post communionem
Grant, O Lord, we pray, that we may delight for all eternity in that share in your divine life, which is foreshadowed in the present age by our reception of your precious Body and Blood. Who live and reign for ever and ever.	Fac nos, quæsumus, Domine, divinitatis tuæ sempiterna fruitione repleri, quam pretiosi Corporis et Sanguinis tui temporalis perceptio præfigurat. Qui vivis et regnas in sæcula sæculorum.

It is desirable that a procession take place after the Mass in which the Host to be carried in the procession is consecrated. However, nothing prohibits a procession from taking place even after a public and lengthy period of adoration following the Mass. If a procession takes place after Mass, when the Communion of the faithful is over, the monstrance in which the consecrated host has been placed is set on the altar. When the Prayer after Communion has been said, the Concluding Rites are omitted and the procession forms.

THE MOST SACRED HEART OF JESUS
(YEAR C)

We are celebrating the feast of the Sacred Heart of Jesus, and in the liturgy we peer, as it were, into the heart of Jesus opened in death by the spear of the Roman soldier. Jesus's heart was indeed opened for us and before us – and thus God's own heart was opened. The liturgy interprets for us the language of Jesus's heart, which tells us above all that God is the shepherd of mankind, and so it reveals to us Jesus's priesthood, which is rooted deep within his heart; so too it shows us the perennial foundation and the effective criterion of all priestly ministry, which must always be anchored in the heart of Jesus and lived out from that starting-point.

(Pope Benedict XVI)

Entrance Antiphon Ps 32:11,19	Ant. ad introitum
THE designs of his Heart are from age to age, to rescue their souls from death, and to keep them alive in famine.	COGITATIONES Cordis eius in generatione et generationem, ut eruat a morte animas eorum et alat eos in fame.

The Gloria in excelsis (Glory to God in the highest) is said.

Collect	Collecta
Grant, we pray, almighty God, that we, who glory in the Heart of your beloved Son and recall the wonders of his love for us, may be made worthy to receive an overflowing measure of grace from that fount of heavenly gifts. Through our Lord Jesus Christ, your Son, who lives and reigns with you in the unity of the Holy Spirit, one God, for ever and ever.	Concede, quæsumus, omnipotens Deus, ut qui, dilecti Filii tui Corde gloriantes, eius præcipua in nos beneficia recolimus caritatis, de illo donorum fonte cælesti supereffluentem gratiam mereamur accipere. Per Dominum nostrum Iesum Christum Filium tuum, qui tecum vivit et regnat in unitate Spiritus Sancti, Deus, per omnia sæcula sæculorum.

Or:

| Vel: |

O God, who in the Heart of your Son,
wounded by our sins,
bestow on us in mercy
the boundless treasures of your love,
grant, we pray,
that, in paying him the homage
   of our devotion
we may also offer worthy reparation.
Through our Lord Jesus Christ,
   your Son,
who lives and reigns with you
   in the unity of the Holy Spirit,
one God, for ever and ever.

Deus, qui nobis in Corde Filii tui,
nostris vulnerato peccatis,
infinitos dilectionis thesauros
misericorditer largiri dignaris,
concede, quæsumus,
ut, illi devotum pietatis nostræ
   præstantes obsequium,
dignæ quoque satisfactionis
   exhibeamus officium.
Per Dominum nostrum Iesum
   Christum Filium tuum,
qui tecum vivit et regnat
   in unitate Spiritus Sancti,
Deus, per omnia sæcula sæculorum.

FIRST READING

A reading from the prophet Ezekiel   34:11-16

I myself will pasture my sheep, I myself will show them where to rest.

The Lord God says this: I am going to look after my flock myself and keep all of it in view. As a shepherd keeps all his flock in view when he stands up in the middle of his scattered sheep, so shall I keep my sheep in view. I shall rescue them from wherever they have been scattered during the mist and darkness. I shall bring them out of the countries where they are; I shall gather them together from foreign countries and bring them back to their own land. I shall pasture them on the mountains of Israel, in the ravines and in every inhabited place in the land. I shall feed them in good pasturage; the high mountains of Israel will be their grazing ground. There they will rest in good grazing ground; they will browse in rich pastures on the mountains of Israel. I myself will pasture my sheep, I myself will show them where to rest – it is the Lord who speaks. I shall look for the lost one, bring back the stray, bandage the wounded and make the weak strong. I shall watch over the fat and healthy. I shall be a true shepherd to them.

The word of the Lord.

R. **The Lord is my shepherd;**
there is nothing I shall want.

The Lord is my shepherd;
there is nothing I shall want.
Fresh and green are the pastures
where he gives me repose.
Near restful waters he leads me,
to revive my drooping spirit. R.

He guides me along the right path;
he is true to his name.
If I should walk in the valley of darkness
no evil would I fear.
You are there with your crook and your staff;
with these you give me comfort. R.

You have prepared a banquet for me
in the sight of my foes.
My head you have anointed with oil;
my cup is overflowing. R.

Surely goodness and kindness shall follow me
all the days of my life.
In the Lord's own house shall I dwell
for ever and ever. R.

SECOND READING

A reading from the letter of St Paul to the Romans   5:5-11

What proves that God loves us is that Christ died for us.

The love of God has been poured into our hearts by the Holy Spirit which
has been given us. We were still helpless when at his appointed moment
Christ died for sinful men. It is not easy to die even for a good man –
though of course for someone really worthy, a man might be prepared
to die – but what proves that God loves us is that Christ died for us while
we were still sinners. Having died to make us righteous, is it likely that he
would now fail to save us from God's anger? When we were reconciled to
God by the death of his Son, we were still enemies; now that we have been
reconciled, surely we may count on being saved by the life of his Son? Not

merely because we have been reconciled but because we are filled with joyful trust in God, through our Lord Jesus Christ, through whom we have already gained our reconciliation.

The word of the Lord.

Gospel Acclamation   Mt 11:29

R. **Alleluia, alleluia!**
Shoulder my yoke and learn from me,
for I am gentle and humble in heart.
R. **Alleluia!**

Alternative Gospel Acclamation   Jn 10:14

R. **Alleluia, alleluia!**
I am the good shepherd, says the Lord;
I know my own sheep and my own know me.
R. **Alleluia!**

GOSPEL

A reading from the holy Gospel according to Luke   15:3-7

Rejoice with me, I have found my sheep that was lost.

Jesus spoke this parable to the scribes and Pharisees:

'What man among you with a hundred sheep, losing one, would not leave the ninety-nine in the wilderness and go after the missing one till he found it? And when he found it, would he not joyfully take it on his shoulders and then, when he got home, call together his friends and neighbours? "Rejoice with me," he would say "I have found my sheep that was lost." In the same way, I tell you, there will be more rejoicing in heaven over one repentant sinner than over ninety-nine virtuous men who have no need of repentance.'

The Gospel of the Lord.

The Creed is said.

Prayer over the Offerings

Look, O Lord, we pray,
　　on the surpassing charity
in the Heart of your beloved Son,
that what we offer may be a gift
　　acceptable to you
and an expiation of our offences.
Through Christ our Lord.

Preface: The boundless charity of Christ, see p.832.

Communion Antiphon Cf. Jn 7:37-38

Thus says the Lord:
Let whoever is thirsty
　　come to me and drink.
Streams of living water will flow
from within the one
　　who believes in me.

Or: Jn 19:34

One of the soldiers opened his side
　　with a lance,
and at once there came forth blood
　　and water.

Prayer after Communion

May this sacrament of charity,
　　O Lord,
make us fervent with the fire
　　of holy love,
so that, drawn always to your Son,
we may learn to see him
　　in our neighbour.
Through Christ our Lord.

Super oblata

Respice, quæsumus, Domine,
ad ineffabilem Cordis dilecti Filii
　　tui caritatem,
ut quod offerimus sit tibi
　　munus acceptum
et nostrorum expiatio delictorum.
Per Christum Dominum nostrum.

Ant. ad communionem

Dicit Dominus:
Si quis sitit,
　　veniat ad me et bibat.
Qui credit in me,
　　flumina de ventre eius
　　fluent aquæ vivæ.

Vel:

Unus militum lancea
　　latus eius aperuit,
et continuo exivit sanguis et aqua.

Post communionem

Sacramentum caritatis, Domine,
sancta nos faciat dilectione fervere,
qua, ad Filium tuum semper attracti,
ipsum in fratribus
　　agnoscere discamus.
Qui vivit et regnat
　　in sæcula sæculorum.

HOLY DAYS,
FEASTS OF THE LORD
AND SOLEMNITIES

THE PRESENTATION OF THE LORD

On today's Feast we contemplate the Lord Jesus, whom Mary and Joseph bring to the Temple "to present him to the Lord". Simeon identifies him as "a light for revelation to the Gentiles" and announces with prophetic words his supreme offering to God and his final victory (Cf. Lk 2:32-35). This is the meeting point of the two Testaments, Old and New. Jesus enters the ancient temple, he who is the new Temple of God: he comes to visit his people, thus bringing to fulfilment obedience to the Law and ushering in the last times of salvation. It is interesting to take a close look at this entrance of the Child Jesus into the solemnity of the temple, in the great comings and goings of many people, busy with their work: priests and Levites taking turns to be on duty, the numerous devout people and pilgrims anxious to encounter the Holy God of Israel. Yet none of them noticed anything. Jesus was a child like the others, a first-born son of very simple parents. Even the priests proved incapable of recognizing the signs of the new and special presence of the Messiah and Saviour. Alone two elderly people, Simeon and Anna, discover this great newness. Led by the Holy Spirit, in this Child they find the fulfilment of their long waiting and watchfulness. Their prophetic attitude contains the entire Old Covenant which expresses the joy of the encounter with the Redeemer.

(Pope Benedict XVI)

Feast

THE BLESSING OF CANDLES AND THE PROCESSION

First Form: The Procession

1. At an appropriate hour, a gathering takes place at a smaller church or other suitable place other than inside the church to which the procession will go. The faithful hold in their hands unlighted candles.

2. The Priest, wearing white vestments as for Mass, approaches with the ministers. Instead of the chasuble, the Priest may wear a cope, which he leaves aside after the procession is over.

3. While the candles are being lit, the following antiphon or another appropriate chant is sung.

Behold, our Lord will come
    with power,
to enlighten the eyes
    of his servants, alleluia.
	Ecce Dominus noster
	    cum virtute veniet,
	ut illuminet oculos servorum
	    suorum, alleluia.

4. When the chant is concluded, the Priest, facing the people, says: In the name of the Father, and of the Son, and of the Holy Spirit. Then the Priest greets the people in the usual way, and next he gives an introductory address, encouraging the faithful to celebrate the rite of this feast day actively and consciously. He may use these or similar words:

Dear brethren
    (brothers and sisters),
forty days have passed since
    we celebrated the joyful feast
of the Nativity of the Lord.
Today is the blessed day
when Jesus was presented in
    the Temple by Mary and Joseph.
Outwardly he was fulfilling the Law,
but in reality he was coming
    to meet his believing people.
Prompted by the Holy Spirit,
Simeon and Anna came
    to the Temple.
Enlightened by the same Spirit,
they recognised the Lord
and confessed him with exultation.
So let us also, gathered together
    by the Holy Spirit,
proceed to the house of God
    to encounter Christ.
There we shall find him
and recognise him in the breaking
    of the bread,
until he comes again,
    revealed in glory.
	Fratres carissimi:
	Ante dies quadraginta celebravimus
	    cum gaudio festum
	    Nativitatis Domini.
	Hodie vero occurrit dies ille beatus,
	    quo Iesus a Maria et Ioseph
	    præsentatus est in templo,
	exterius quidem legem implens,
	rerum veritate autem occurrens
	    populo suo credenti.
	
	Spiritu Sancto impulsi, in templum
	    venerunt beati illi senes
	    et cognoverunt Dominum
	    eodem Spiritu illuminati,
	et confessi sunt eum
	    in exsultatione.
	Ita et nos, congregati in unum
	    per Spiritum Sanctum,
	procedamus ad domum
	    Dei obviam Christo.
	Inveniemus eum et cognoscemus
	    in fractione panis,
	donec veniat manifestus in gloria.

5. After the address the Priest blesses the candles, saying, with hands extended:

Let us pray.

O God, source and origin
    of all light,
who on this day showed
    to the just man Simeon
the Light for revelation
    to the Gentiles,
we humbly ask that,
in answer to your people's prayers,
you may be pleased to sanctify
    with your blessing ✠ these candles,
which we are eager to carry
    in praise of your name,
so that, treading the path of virtue,
we may reach that light
    which never fails.
Through Christ our Lord.
R. Amen.

Oremus

Deus, omnis luminis fons et origo,
qui iusto Simeoni Lumen
    ad revelationem gentium
hodie demonstrasti,
te supplices deprecamur,
ut hos cereos sanctificare tua ✠
    benedictione digneris,
tuæ plebis vota suscipiens,
quæ ad tui nominis laudem eos
    gestatura concurrit,
quatenus per virtutum semitam
ad lucem indeficientem
    pervenire mereatur.
Per Christum Dominum nostrum.
R. Amen.

Or:

O God, true light,
    who create light eternal,
spreading it far and wide,
pour, we pray, into the hearts
    of the faithful
the brilliance of perpetual light,
so that all who are brightened
    in your holy temple
by the splendour of these candles
may happily reach the light
    of your glory.
Through Christ our Lord.
R. Amen.

Vel:

Deus, lumen verum, æternæ lucis
    propagator et auctor,
cordibus infunde fidelium perpetui
    luminis claritatem,
ut, quicumque in templo
    sancto tuo
splendore præsentium
    luminum adornantur,
ad lumen gloriæ tuæ feliciter
    valeant pervenire
Per Christum Dominum nostrum.
R. Amen.

He sprinkles the candles with holy water without saying anything, and puts incense into the thurible for the procession.

6. Then the Priest receives from the Deacon or a minister the lighted candle prepared for him and the procession begins, with the Deacon announcing (or, if there is no Deacon, the Priest himself):

Let us go in peace to meet the Lord.	Procedamus in pace ad occurrendum Domino.
Or:	Vel:
Let us go in peace.	Procedamus in pace.
In this case, all respond:	
In the name of Christ. Amen.	In nomine Christi. Amen.

7. All carry lighted candles. As the procession moves forward, one or other of the antiphons that follow is sung, namely the antiphon A light for revelation with the canticle (Lk 2:29-32), or the antiphon Sion, adorn your bridal chamber or another appropriate chant.

I

Antiphon Lk 2:29-32	Antiphona
Ant. A light for revelation to the Gentiles and the glory of your people Israel. Lord, now you let your servant go in peace, in accordance with your word. Ant. For my eyes have seen your salvation. Ant. Which you have prepared in the sight of all peoples. Ant.	Ant. Lumen ad revelationem gentium, et gloriam plebis tuæ Israel. Nunc dimittis servum tuum, Domine, secundum verbum tuum in pace. Ant. Quia viderunt oculi mei salutare tuum. Ant. Quod parasti ante faciem omnium populorum. Ant.

II

Ant. Sion, adorn your bridal chamber and welcome Christ the King; take Mary in your arms, who is the gate of heaven, for she herself is carrying the King of glory and new light. A Virgin she remains, though bringing in her hands the Son before the morning star begotten, whom Simeon, taking in his arms announced to the peoples as Lord of life and death and Saviour of the world.	Ant. Adorna thalamum tuum, Sion, et suscipe Regem Christum: amplectere Mariam, quæ est cælestis porta: ipsa enim portat Regem gloriæ novi luminis: subsistit Virgo, adducens manibus Filium ante luciferum genitum: quem accipiens Simeon in ulnas suas, prædicavit populis, Dominum eum esse vitæ et mortis, et Salvatorem mundi.

8. As the procession enters the church, the Entrance Antiphon of the Mass is sung. When the Priest has arrived at the altar, he venerates it and, if appropriate, incenses it. Then he goes to the chair, where he takes off the cope, if he used it in the procession, and puts on a chasuble. After the singing of the hymn Gloria in excelsis (Glory to God in the highest), he says the Collect as usual. The Mass continues in the usual manner.

Second Form: The Solemn Entrance

9. Whenever a procession cannot take place, the faithful gather in church, holding candles in their hands. The Priest, wearing white sacred vestments as for Mass, together with the ministers and a representative group of the faithful, goes to a suitable place, either in front of the church door or inside the church itself, where at least a large part of the faithful can conveniently participate in the rite.

10. When the Priest reaches the place appointed for the blessing of the candles, candles are lit while the antiphon Behold, our Lord (no. 3) or another appropriate chant is sung.

11. Then, after the greeting and address, the Priest blesses the candles, as above nos. 4-5; and then the procession to the altar takes place, with singing (nos. 6-7). For Mass, what is indicated in no. 8 above is observed.

At the Mass

Entrance Antiphon Cf. Ps 47:10-11

YOUR merciful love, O God, we have received in the midst of your temple.
Your praise, O God, like your name, reaches the ends of the earth;
your right hand is filled with saving justice.

Ant. ad introitum

SUSCEPIMUS, Deus, misericordiam tuam in medio templi tui.
Secundum nomen tuum, Deus, ita et laus tua in fines terræ;
iustitia plena est dextera tua.

The Gloria in excelsis (Glory to God in the highest) is said.

Collect	Collecta
Almighty ever-living God,	Omnipotens sempiterne Deus,
we humbly implore your majesty	maiestatem tuam
that, just as your Only Begotten Son	supplices exoramus,
was presented on this day	ut, sicut Unigenitus Filius tuus
in the Temple	hodierna die cum nostræ
in the substance of our flesh,	carnis substantia
so, by your grace,	in templo est præsentatus,
we may be presented to you	ita nos facias purificatis tibi
with minds made pure.	mentibus præsentari.
Through our Lord Jesus Christ,	Per Dominum nostrum Iesum
your Son,	Christum Filium tuum,
who lives and reigns with you	qui tecum vivit et regnat
in the unity of the Holy Spirit,	in unitate Spiritus Sancti,
one God, for ever and ever.	Deus, per omnia sæcula sæculorum.

When this Feast does not fall on a Sunday then there is usually only one reading before the Gospel.

FIRST READING

A reading from the prophet Malachi   3:1-4

The Lord you are seeking will suddenly enter his Temple.

The Lord God says this: Look, I am going to send my messenger to prepare a way before me. And the Lord you are seeking will suddenly enter his Temple; and the angel of the covenant whom you are longing for, yes, he is coming, says the Lord of hosts.

Who will be able to resist the day of his coming? Who will remain standing when he appears? For he is like the refiner's fire and the fuller's alkali. He will take his seat as refiner and purifier; he will purify the sons of Levi and refine them like gold and silver, and then they will make the offering to the Lord as it should be made. The offering of Judah and Jerusalem will then be welcomed by the Lord as in former days, as in the years of old.

The word of the Lord.

Responsorial Psalm   Ps 23:7-10. R. v.8

R. **Who is the king of glory?**
   It is the Lord.

   O gates, lift up your heads;
   grow higher, ancient doors.
   get him enter, the king of glory! R.

Who is the king of glory?
The Lord, the mighty, the valiant,
the Lord, the valiant in war. R.

O gates, lift high your heads;
grow higher, ancient doors.
Let him enter, the king of glory! R.

Who is he, the king of glory?
He, the Lord of armies,
he is the king of glory. R.

R. **Who is the king of glory?
It is the Lord.**

SECOND READING

A reading from the letter to the Hebrews   2:14-18

It was essential that he should in this way become completely like his brothers.

Since all the children share the same blood and flesh, Jesus too shared equally in it, so that by his death he could take away all the power of the devil, who had power over death, and set free all those who had been held in slavery all their lives by the fear of death. For it was not the angels that he took to himself; he took to himself descent from Abraham. It was essential that he should in this way become completely like his brothers so that he could be a compassionate and trustworthy high priest of God's religion, able to atone for human sins. That is, because he has himself been through temptation he is able to help others who are tempted.

The word of the Lord.

Gospel Acclamation   Lk 2:32

R. **Alleluia, alleluia!**
The light to enlighten the Gentiles
and give glory to Israel, your people.
R. **Alleluia!**

GOSPEL

A reading from the holy Gospel according to Luke   2:22-40

My eyes have seen your salvation.

[When the day came for them to be purified as laid down by the Law of Moses, the parents of Jesus took him up to Jerusalem to present him to the Lord – observing what stands written in the Law of the Lord: Every first-born male must be consecrated to the Lord – and also to offer in sacrifice, in accordance with what is said in the Law of the Lord, a pair of turtledoves or two young pigeons. Now in Jerusalem there was a man named Simeon. He was an upright and devout man; he looked forward to Israel's comforting and the Holy Spirit rested on him. It had been revealed to him by the Holy Spirit that he would not see death until he had set eyes on the Christ of the Lord. Prompted by the Spirit he came to the Temple; and when the parents brought in the child Jesus to do for him what the Law required, he took him into his arms and blessed God; and he said:

'Now, Master, you can let your servant go in peace,
just as you promised;
because my eyes have seen the salvation
which you have prepared for all the nations to see,
a light to enlighten the pagans
and the glory of your people Israel.']

As the child's father and mother stood there wondering at the things that were being said about him, Simeon blessed them and said to Mary his mother, 'You see this child: he is destined for the fall and for the rising of many in Israel, destined to be a sign that is rejected – and a sword will pierce your own soul too so that the secret thoughts of many may be laid bare.'

There was a prophetess also, Anna the daughter of Phanuel, of the tribe of Asher. She was well on in years. Her days of girlhood over, she had been married for seven years before becoming a widow. She was now eighty-four years old and never left the Temple, serving God night and day with fasting and prayer. She came by just at that moment and began to praise God; and she spoke of the child to all who looked forward to the deliverance of Jerusalem.

When they had done everything the Law of the Lord required, they went back to Galilee, to their own town of Nazareth. Meanwhile the child grew to maturity, and he was filled with wisdom; and God's favour was with him.

[The Gospel of the Lord.]

Shorter Form, verses 2:22-32. Read between [ ]

When this Feast falls on a Sunday, the Creed is said.

Prayer over the Offerings

May the offering made
    with exultation by your Church
be pleasing to you, O Lord, we pray,
for you willed that your
    Only Begotten Son
be offered to you for the life
    of the world
as the Lamb without blemish.
Who lives and reigns
    for ever and ever.

Super oblata

Gratum tibi sit,
    Domine, quæsumus,
exsultantis Ecclesiæ
    munus oblatum,
qui Unigenitum Filium
    tuum voluisti
Agnum immaculatum tibi
    offerri pro sæculi vita.
Qui vivit et regnat
    in sæcula sæculorum.

Preface: The Mystery of the Presentation of the Lord

It is truly right and just,
    our duty and our salvation,
always and everywhere
    to give you thanks,
Lord, holy Father,
    almighty and eternal God.

For your co-eternal Son was presented
    on this day in the Temple
and revealed by the Spirit
as the glory of Israel
    and Light of the nations.

And so, we, too, go forth, rejoicing
    to encounter your Salvation,
and with the Angels and Saints
praise you, as without end
    we acclaim:

Holy, Holy, Holy Lord God of hosts...

Præfatio: De mysterio Præsentationis Domini.

Vere dignum et iustum est,
    æquum et salutare,
nos tibi semper et ubique
    gratias agere:
Domine, sancte Pater,
    omnipotens æterne Deus:

Quia coæternus hodie in templo
    tuus Filius præsentatus
gloria Israel et lumen gentium
    a Spiritu declaratur.

Unde et nos, Salutari tuo
    in gaudiis occurrentes,
cum Angelis et Sanctis te laudamus,
    sine fine dicentes:

Sanctus, Sanctus, Sanctus. . .

Communion Antiphon Lk 2:30-31

My eyes have seen your salvation,
which you prepared in the sight
    of all the peoples.

Ant. ad communionem

Viderunt oculi mei salutare tuum,
quod parasti ante faciem
    omnium populorum.

Prayer after Communion	Post communionem
By these holy gifts which we have received, O Lord, bring your grace to perfection within us, and, as you fulfilled Simeon's expectation that he would not see death until he had been privileged to welcome the Christ, so may we, going forth to meet the Lord, obtain the gift of eternal life. Through Christ our Lord.	Per hæc sancta quæ sumpsimus, Domine, perfice in nobis gratiam tuam, qui exspectationem Simeonis implesti, ut, sicut ille mortem non vidit nisi prius Christum suscipere mereretur, ita et nos, in occursum Domini procedentes, vitam obtineamus æternam. Per Christum Dominum nostrum.

In Wales

1 March

SAINT DAVID, BISHOP, PATRON OF WALES

Saint David was one of the great saints of the sixth century, that golden age of saints and missionaries in these isles, and he was thus a founder of the Christian culture which lies at the root of modern Europe. David's preaching was simple yet profound: his dying words to his monks were, "Be joyful, keep the faith, and do the little things". It is the little things that reveal our love for the one who loved us first (Cf. 1 Jn 4:19) and that bind people into a community of faith, love and service. May Saint David's message, in all its simplicity and richness, continue to resound today, drawing the hearts of people to renewed love for Christ and his Church.

(Pope Benedict XVI)

Solemnity

Entrance Antiphon   Is 52:7

H OW beautiful upon the mountains are the feet of him who brings glad tidings of peace, bearing good news, announcing salvation!

The Gloria in excelsis (Glory to God in the highest) is said.

Collect

O God, who graciously bestowed on your Bishop Saint David of Wales
the virtue of wisdom and the gift of eloquence
and made him an example of prayer and pastoral zeal,
grant that, through his intercession
your Church may ever prosper and render you joyful praise.
Through our Lord Jesus Christ, your Son,
who lives and reigns with you in the unity of the Holy Spirit,
one God, for ever and ever.

Alternative readings may be taken from the Common of Pastors, or from the
Common of Holy Men and Women.

FIRST READING

A reading from the letter of St Paul to the Philippians   3:8-14

*I am racing for the finish, for the prize to which God calls us upward to receive in
Christ Jesus.*

I believe nothing can happen that will outweigh the supreme advantage
of knowing Christ Jesus my Lord. For him I have accepted the loss of
everything, and I look on everything as so much rubbish if only I can have
Christ and be given a place in him. I am no longer trying for perfection
by my own efforts, the perfection that comes from the Law, but I want
only the perfection that comes through faith in Christ, and is from God
and based on faith. All I want is to know Christ and the power of his
resurrection and to share his sufferings by reproducing the pattern of his
death. That is the way I can hope to take my place in the resurrection of the
dead. Not that I have become perfect yet. I have not yet won, but I am still
running, trying to capture the prize for which Christ Jesus captured me.
I can assure you my brothers, I am far from thinking that I have already
won. All I can say is that I forget the past and I strain ahead for what is still
to come; I am racing for the finish, for the prize to which God calls us
upwards to receive in Christ Jesus.

The word of the Lord.

Responsorial Psalm   Ps 1:14,6. R. Ps 39:5

R. **Happy the man who has placed
his trust in the Lord.**

Happy indeed is the man
who follows not the counsel of the wicked;
nor lingers in the way of sinners
nor sits in the company of scorners,

but whose delight is the law of the Lord
and who ponders his law day and night. R.

He is like a tree that is planted
beside the flowing waters,
that yields its fruit in due season
and whose leaves shall never fade;
and all that he does shall prosper. R.

Not so are the wicked, not so!
For they like winnowed chaff
shall be driven away by the wind.
For the Lord guards the way of the just
but the way of the wicked leads to doom. R.

A second reading may be chosen from the options given above.

Gospel Acclamation   Mt 23:9-10
                          Outside Lent

R. **Alleluia, alleluia!**
If you make my word your home
you will indeed be my disciples,
and you will learn the truth, says the Lord.
R. **Alleluia!**

                            In Lent

R. **Glory to you, O Christ, you are the Word of God.**
If you make my word your home
you will indeed be my disciples,
and you will learn the truth, says the Lord.
R. **Glory to you, O Christ, you are the Word of God.**

GOSPEL
A reading from the holy Gospel according to Matthew   5:13-19
You are the light of the world.
Jesus said to his disciples: 'You are the salt of the earth. But if salt becomes
tasteless, what can make it salty again? It is good for nothing, and can only
be thrown out to be trampled underfoot by men.

  'You are the light of the world. A city built on a hill-top can not be
hidden. No one lights a lamp to put it under a tub; they put it on the lamp-
stand where it shines for everyone in the house. In the same way your light
must shine in the sight of men, so that, seeing your good works, they may
give the praise to your Father in heaven.'

  The Gospel of the Lord.

Prayer over the Offerings

Look with favour, O Lord, we pray,
on the offerings we set upon this sacred altar
on the feast day of the Bishop Saint David,
that, bestowing on us your pardon,
our oblations may give honour to your name.
Through Christ our Lord.

Communion Antiphon   Cf. 1 Co 1:23-24

We proclaim Christ crucified,
Christ, the power of God, and the wisdom of God.

Prayer after Communion

We pray, almighty God,
that we, who are fortified by the power of this Sacrament,
may learn through the example of your Bishop Saint David
to seek you always above all things
and to bear in this world the likeness of the New Man.
Who lives and reigns for ever and ever.

In Ireland

17 March

SAINT PATRICK, BISHOP, PATRON OF IRELAND

Solemnity

Entrance Antiphon   Gn 12:1-2

GO from your country and your kindred and your father's house to
the land that I will show you.
I will make of you a great nation, and I will bless you,
and make your name great, so that you will be a blessing.

The Gloria in excelsis (Glory to God in the highest) is said.

Collect

Lord, through the work of Saint Patrick in Ireland
we have come to acknowledge the mystery of the one true God
and give thanks for our salvation in Christ;
grant by his prayers

that we who celebrate this festival
may keep alive the fire of faith he kindled.
Through our Lord Jesus Christ, your Son,
who lives and reigns with you in the unity of the Holy Spirit,
one God, for ever and ever.

FIRST READING

A reading from the prophet Jeremiah   1:1,4-9

Go now to those to whom I send you.

The word of the Lord was addressed to me, saying,
    'Before I formed you in the womb I knew you;
    before you came to birth I consecrated you;
    I have appointed you as prophet to the nations.'
    I said, 'Ah, Lord, look, I do not know how to speak: I am a child!'
But the Lord replied,
    'Do not say, "I am a child."
    Go now to those to whom I send you
    and say whatever I command you.
    Do not be afraid of them,
    for I am with you to protect you
    – it is the Lord who speaks!'
    Then the Lord put out his hand and touched my mouth and said to me:
    'There! I am putting my words into your mouth.'
    The word of the Lord.

Responsorial Psalm   Ps 116. R. Mk 16:15

R. **Go out to all the world,**
    and tell the Good News.

    Or: (outside Lent only) **Alleluia!**

    O praise the Lord, all you nations,
    acclaim him all you peoples! R.

    Strong is his love for us;
    he is faithful for ever. R.

SECOND READING

A reading from the Acts of the Apostles   13:46-49

We must turn to the pagans.

Paul and Barnabas spoke out boldly to the Jews, 'We had to proclaim the word of God to you first, but since you have rejected it, since you do not think yourselves worthy of eternal life, we must turn to the pagans. For this is what the Lord commanded us to do when he said:

"I have made you a light for the nations,
so that my salvation may reach the ends of the earth."'

It made the pagans very happy to hear this and they thanked the Lord for his message; all who were destined for eternal life became believers. Thus the word of the Lord spread through the whole countryside.

The word of the Lord.

Gospel Acclamation   Mt 23:9-10

Outside Lent

R. **Alleluia, alleluia!**
The Lord sent me to bring Good News to the poor,
and freedom to prisoners.
R. **Alleluia!**

In Lent

R. **Praise and honour to you, Lord Jesus!**
The Lord sent me to bring Good News to the poor,
and freedom to prisoners.
R. **Praise and honour to you, Lord Jesus!**

GOSPEL

A reading from the holy Gospel according to Luke   10:1-12,17-20

Your peace will rest on that man.

The Lord appointed seventy-two others and sent them out ahead of him, in pairs, to all the towns and places he himself was to visit. He said to them, 'The harvest is rich but the labourers are few, so ask the Lord of the harvest to send labourers to his harvest. Start off now, but remember, I am sending you out like lambs among wolves. Carry no purse, no haversack, no sandals. Salute no one on the road. Whatever house you go into, let your first words be, "Peace to this house!" And if a man of peace lives there, your peace will go and rest on him; if not, it will come back to you.

Stay in the same house, taking what food and drink they have to offer, for the labourer deserves his wages; do not move from house to house. Whenever you go into a town where they make you welcome, eat what is set before you. Cure those in it who are sick, and say, "The kingdom of God is very near to you." But whenever you enter a town and they do not make you welcome, go out into its streets and say, "We wipe off the very dust of your town that clings to our feet, and leave it with you. Yet be sure of this: the kingdom of God is very near." I tell you, that on that day it will not go as hard with Sodom as with that town.'

The seventy-two came back rejoicing. 'Lord,' they said 'even the devils submit to us when we use your name.' He said to them, 'I watched Satan fall like lightning from heaven. Yes, I have given you power to tread underfoot serpents and scorpions and the whole strength of the enemy; nothing shall ever hurt you. Yet do not rejoice that the spirits submit to you; rejoice rather that your names are written in heaven.'

The Gospel of the Lord.

The Creed is said.

Prayer over the Offerings

Lord, accept this pure sacrifice
which, through the labours of Saint Patrick,
your grateful people make
to the glory of your name.
Through Christ our Lord.

Preface

It is truly right and just, our duty and our salvation,
always and everywhere to give you thanks,
Lord, holy Father, almighty and eternal God,
and to proclaim your greatness with due praise
as we honour Saint Patrick.

For you drew him through daily prayer
in captivity and hardship
to know you as a loving Father.

You chose him out of all the world
to return to the land of his captors,
that they might acknowledge Jesus Christ, their Redeemer.

In the power of your Spirit you directed his paths
to win the sons and daughters of the Irish
to the service of the Triune God.

And so, with the Angels and Archangels,
and with the great multitude of the Saints,
we sing the hymn of your praise, as without end we acclaim:

Holy, Holy, Holy Lord God of hosts ...

Communion Antiphon   Cf. Mt 8:11

Many will come from east and west
and sit down with Abraham, Isaac and Jacob
at the feast in the Kingdom of Heaven, says the Lord.

Prayer after Communion

Strengthen us, O Lord, by this sacrament
so that we may profess the faith taught by Saint Patrick
and to proclaim it in our way of living.
Through Christ our Lord.

Solemn Blessing

May God the Father, who called us together
to celebrate this feast of Saint Patrick,
bless you, protect you and keep you faithful.
R. Amen.

May Christ the Lord, the High King of Heaven,
be near you at all times and shield you from evil.
R. Amen.

May the Holy Spirit, who is the source of all holiness,
make you rich in the love of God's people.
R. Amen.

And may the blessing of almighty God,
the Father, and the Son, ✠ and the Holy Spirit,
come down on you and remain with you for ever.
R. Amen.

19 March

SAINT JOSEPH,
SPOUSE OF THE BLESSED VIRGIN MARY

The figure of this great Saint, even though remaining somewhat hidden, is of fundamental importance in the history of salvation. Above all, as part of the tribe of Judah, he united Jesus to the Davidic lineage so that, fulfilling the promises regarding the Messiah, the Son of the Virgin Mary may truly be called the "son of David". The Gospel of Matthew highlights in a special way the Messianic prophecies which reached fulfilment through the role that Joseph played: the birth of Jesus in Bethlehem; his journey through Egypt, where the Holy Family took refuge; the nickname, the "Nazarene". In all of this he showed himself, like his spouse Mary, an authentic heir of Abraham's faith: faith in God who guides the events of history according to his mysterious salvific plan. His greatness, like Mary's, stands out even more because his mission was carried out in the humility and hiddenness of the house of Nazareth. Moreover, God himself, in the person of his Incarnate Son, chose this way and style of life – humility and hiddenness – in his earthly existence. From the example of Saint Joseph we all receive a strong invitation to carry out with fidelity, simplicity and modesty the task that Providence has entrusted to us.

(Pope Benedict XVI)

Solemnity

Entrance Antiphon Cf. Lk 12:42	Ant. ad introitum

BEHOLD, a faithful and prudent steward, whom the Lord set over his household.

ECCE fidelis servus et prudens, quem constituit Dominus super familiam suam.

The Gloria in excelsis (Glory to God in the highest) is said.

Collect

Grant, we pray, almighty God,
that by Saint Joseph's intercession
your Church may constantly
   watch over
the unfolding of the mysteries
   of human salvation,
whose beginnings you entrusted
   to his faithful care.

Collecta

Præsta, quæsumus,
   omnipotens Deus,
ut humanæ salutis mysteria,
cuius primordia beati Ioseph fideli
   custodiæ commisisti,
Ecclesia tua, ipso intercedente,
   iugiter servet implenda.

Through our Lord Jesus Christ,
    your Son,
who lives and reigns with you
    in the unity of the Holy Spirit,
one God, for ever and ever.
	Per Dominum nostrum Iesum
	    Christum Filium tuum,
	qui tecum vivit et regnat
	    in unitate Spiritus Sancti,
	Deus, per omnia sæcula sæculorum.

FIRST READING

A reading from the second book of Samuel   7:4-5,12-14,16

The Lord will give him the throne of his ancestor David.

The word of the Lord came to Nathan:

    'Go and tell my servant David, "Thus the Lord speaks: When your days are ended and you are laid to rest with your ancestors, I will preserve the offspring of your body after you and make his sovereignty secure. (It is he who shall build a house for my name and I will make his royal throne secure for ever.) I will be a father to him and he a son to me. Your House and your sovereignty will always stand secure before me and your throne be established for ever."'

    The word of the Lord.

Responsorial Psalm   Ps 88:2-5,27,29. R. v.37

R. **His dynasty shall last for ever.**

    I will sing for ever of your love, O Lord;
    through all ages my mouth will proclaim your truth.
    Of this I am sure, that your love lasts for ever,
    that your truth is firmly established as the heavens. R.

    'I have made a covenant with my chosen one;
    I have sworn to David my servant:
    I will establish your dynasty for ever
    and set up your throne through all ages.' R.

    He will say to me: 'You are my father,
    my God, the rock who saves me.'
    I will keep my love for him always;
    for him my covenant shall endure. R.

SECOND READING

A reading from the letter of St Paul to the Romans   4:13,16-18,22

Though it seemed Abraham's hope could not be fulfilled, he hoped and he believed.

The promise of inheriting the world was not made to Abraham and his descendants on account of any law but on account of the righteousness which consists in faith. That is why what fulfils the promise depends on faith, so that it may be a free gift and be available to all of Abraham's descendants, not only those who belong to the Law but also to those who belong to the faith of Abraham who is the father of all of us. As scripture says: I have made you the ancestor of many nations – Abraham is our father in the eyes of God, in whom he put his faith, and who brings the dead to life and calls into being what does not exist.

Though it seemed Abraham's hope could not be fulfilled, he hoped and he believed, and through doing so he did become the father of many nations exactly as he had been promised: Your descendants will be as many as the stars. This is the faith that was 'considered as justifying him'.

The word of the Lord.

Gospel Acclamation   Ps 83:5

R. **Glory and praise to you, O Christ.**

They are happy who dwell in your house, O Lord,
for ever singing your praise.

R. **Glory and praise to you, O Christ.**

GOSPEL

A reading from the holy Gospel according to Matthew   1:16,18-21,24

Joseph did what the angel of the Lord had told him to do.

Jacob was the father of Joseph the husband of Mary; of her was born Jesus who is called Christ.

This is how Jesus Christ came to be born. His mother Mary was betrothed to Joseph; but before they came to live together she was found to be with child through the Holy Spirit. Her husband Joseph, being a man of honour and wanting to spare her publicity, decided to divorce her informally. He had made up his mind to do this when the angel of the Lord appeared to him in a dream and said, 'Joseph son of David, do not be afraid to take Mary home as your wife, because she has conceived what is in her by the Holy Spirit. She will give birth to a son and you must name him Jesus, because he is the one who is to save his people from their sins.' When Joseph woke up he did what the angel of the Lord had told him to do.

The Gospel of the Lord.

ALTERNATIVE GOSPEL

A reading from the holy Gospel according to Luke   2:41-51

See how worried your father and I have been, looking for you.

Every year the parents of Jesus used to go to Jerusalem for the feast of the Passover. When he was twelve years old, they went up for the feast as usual. When they were on their way home after the feast, the boy Jesus stayed behind in Jerusalem without his parents knowing it. They assumed he was with the caravan, and it was only after a day's journey that they went to look for him among their relations and acquaintances. When they failed to find him they went back to Jerusalem looking for him everywhere.

Three days later, they found him in the Temple, sitting among the doctors, listening to them, and asking them questions; and all those who heard him were astounded at his intelligence and his replies. They were overcome when they saw him and his mother said to him, 'My child, why have you done this to us? See how worried your father and I have been, looking for you.' 'Why were you looking for me?' he replied. 'Did you not know that I must be busy with my Father's affairs?' But they did not understand what he meant.

He then went down with them and came to Nazareth and lived under their authority.

The Gospel of the Lord.

The Creed is said.

Prayer over the Offerings	Super oblata
We pray, O Lord,	Quæsumus, Domine, ut,
that, just as Saint Joseph	sicut beatus Ioseph
served with loving care	Unigenito tuo,
your Only Begotten Son,	nato de Maria Virgine,
born of the Virgin Mary,	pia devotione deserviit,
so we may be worthy to minister	ita et nos mundo corde
with a pure heart at your altar.	tuis altaribus mereamur ministrare.
Through Christ our Lord.	Per Christum Dominum nostrum.

Preface: The mission of Saint Joseph.

It is truly right and just,
our duty and our salvation,
always and everywhere
to give you thanks,
Lord, holy Father,
almighty and eternal God,
and on the Solemnity of Saint Joseph
to give you fitting praise,
to glorify you and bless you.

For this just man was given by you
as spouse to the Virgin Mother of God
and set as a wise and faithful servant
in charge of your household
to watch like a father over your
Only Begotten Son,
who was conceived by the
overshadowing of the Holy Spirit,
our Lord Jesus Christ.

Through him the Angels praise
your majesty,
Dominions adore and Powers
tremble before you.
Heaven and the Virtues of heaven
and the blessed Seraphim
worship together with exultation.

May our voices, we pray,
join with theirs
in humble praise, as we acclaim:

Holy, Holy, Holy Lord God of hosts...

Communion Antiphon   Mt 25:21

Well done, good and faithful servant.
Come, share your master's joy.

Præfatio: De missione sancti Ioseph.

Vere dignum et iustum est,
æquum et salutare,
nos tibi semper et ubique
gratias agere:
Domine, sancte Pater,
omnipotens æterne Deus:

Et te in sollemnitate beati Ioseph
debitis magnificare præconiis,
benedicere et prædicare.
Qui et vir iustus, a te Deiparæ
Virgini Sponsus est datus,
et fidelis servus ac prudens,
super Familiam tuam est constitutus,
ut Unigenitum tuum,
Sancti Spiritus obumbratione
conceptum,
paterna vice custodiret,
Iesum Christum Dominum nostrum.

Per quem maiestatem tuam
laudant Angeli,
adorant Dominationes,
tremunt Potestates.
Cæli cælorumque Virtutes,
ac beata Seraphim,
socia exsultatione concelebrant.

Cum quibus et nostras voces ut
admitti iubeas, deprecamur,
supplici confessione dicentes:

Sanctus, Sanctus, Sanctus. . .

Ant. ad communionem

Euge, serve bone et fidelis:
intra in gaudium Domini tui.

Prayer after Communion	Post communionem
Defend with unfailing protection, O Lord, we pray, the family you have nourished with food from this altar, as they rejoice at the Solemnity of Saint Joseph, and graciously keep safe your gifts among them. Through Christ our Lord.	Familiam tuam, quæsumus, Domine, quam de beati Ioseph sollemnitate lætantem ex huius altaris alimonia satiasti, perpetua protectione defende, et tua in ea propitiatus dona custodi. Per Christum Dominum nostrum.

25 March

THE ANNUNCIATION OF THE LORD

The Annunciation, recounted at the beginning of Saint Luke's Gospel, is a humble, hidden event – no one saw it, no one except Mary knew of it –, but at the same time it was crucial to the history of humanity. When the Virgin said her "yes" to the Angel's announcement, Jesus was conceived and with him began the new era of history that was to be ratified in Easter as the "new and eternal Covenant". In fact, Mary's "yes" perfectly mirrors that of Christ himself when he entered the world, as the Letter to the Hebrews says, interpreting Psalm 40[39]: "As is written of me in the book, I have come to do your will, O God" (Heb 10:7). The Son's obedience was reflected in that of the Mother and thus, through the encounter of these two "yeses", God was able to take on a human face. This is why the Annunciation is a Christological feast as well, because it celebrates a central mystery of Christ: the Incarnation.

(Pope Benedict XVI)

Solemnity

Whenever this Solemnity occurs during Holy Week, it is transferred to the Monday after the Second Sunday of Easter.

Entrance Antiphon Heb 10:5,7	Ant. ad introitum
THE Lord said, as he entered the world: Behold, I come to do your will, O God.	DOMINUS ingrediens mundum dixit: Ecce venio ut faciam, Deus, voluntatem tuam.

The Gloria in excelsis (Glory to God in the highest) is said.

Collect

O God, who willed that your Word
should take on the reality
    of human flesh
in the womb of the Virgin Mary,
grant, we pray,
that we, who confess our Redeemer
    to be God and man,
may merit to become partakers
    even in his divine nature.
Who lives and reigns with you
    in the unity of the Holy Spirit,
one God, for ever and ever.

Collecta

Deus, qui Verbum tuum in utero
    Virginis Mariæ
veritatem carnis humanæ
    suscipere voluisti,
concede, quæsumus,
ut, qui Redemptorem nostrum
Deum et hominem confitemur,
ipsius etiam divinæ naturæ
    mereamur esse consortes.
Per Dominum nostrum Iesum
    Christum Filium tuum,
qui tecum vivit et regnat
    in unitate Spiritus Sancti,
Deus, per omnia sæcula sæculorum.

FIRST READING

A reading from the prophet Isaiah   7:10-14; 8: 10

The maiden is with child.

The Lord spoke to Ahaz and said, 'Ask the Lord your God for a sign for yourself coming either from the depths of Sheol or from the heights above.' 'No,' Ahaz answered, 'I will not put the Lord to the test.'

Then Isaiah said:

Listen now, House of David:
are you not satisfied with trying the patience of men
without trying the patience of my God, too?
The Lord himself, therefore,
will give you a sign.
It is this: the maiden is with child
and will soon give birth to a son
whom she will call Emmanuel,
a name which means 'God-with-us'.

The word of the Lord.

Responsorial Psalm   Ps 39:7-11. R. vv.8,9

R. **Here I am, Lord!**
   I come to do your will.

   You do not ask for sacrifice and offerings,
   but an open ear.
   You do not ask for holocaust and victim.
   Instead, here am I. R.

In the scroll of the book it stands written
that I should do your will.
My God, I delight in your law
in the depth of my heart. R.

Your justice I have proclaimed
in the great assembly.
My lips I have not sealed;
you know it, O Lord. R.

I have not hidden your justice in my heart
but declared your faithful help.
I have not hidden your love and your truth
from the great assembly. R.

R. **Here I am, Lord!**
I come to do your will.

SECOND READING

A reading from the letter to the Hebrews   10:4-10

I was commanded in the scroll of the book, 'God, here I am! I am coming to obey your will.'

Bulls' blood and goats' blood are useless for taking away sins, and this is what Christ said, on coming into the world:

You who wanted no sacrifice or oblation,
prepared a body for me.
you took no pleasure in holocausts or sacrifices for sin;
then I said,
just as I was commanded in the scroll of the book,
'God, here I am! I am coming to obey your will.'

Notice that he says first: You did not want what the Law lays down as the things to be offered, that is: the sacrifices, the oblations, the holocausts and the sacrifices for sin, and you took no pleasure in them; and then he says: Here I am! I am coming to obey your will. He is abolishing the first sort to replace it with the second. And this will was for us to be made holy by the offering of his body made once and for all by Jesus Christ.

The word of the Lord.

Gospel Acclamation   Jn 1:14,12

R. **Praise to you, O Christ, king of eternal glory!**
The Word was made flesh,
he lived among us,
and we saw his glory.
R. **Praise to you, O Christ, king of eternal glory!**

GOSPEL

A reading from the Gospel according to Luke   1:26-38

Listen! You are to conceive and bear a son.

The angel Gabriel was sent by God to a town in Galilee called Nazareth, to a virgin betrothed to a man named Joseph, of the house of David; and the virgin's name was Mary. He went in and said to her, "Rejoice, so highly favoured! The Lord is with you.' She was deeply disturbed by these words and asked herself what this greeting could mean, but the angel said to her, 'Mary, do not be afraid; you have won God's favour. Listen! You are to conceive and bear a son, and you must name him Jesus. He will be great and will be called Son of the Most High. The Lord God will give him the throne of his ancestor David; he will rule over the House of Jacob for ever and his reign will have no end.' Mary said to the angel, 'But how can this come about, since I am a virgin?' 'The Holy Spirit will come upon you, the angel answered, 'and the power of the Most High will cover you with its shadow. And so the child will be holy and will be called Son of God. Know this too: your kinswoman Elizabeth also, in her old age, herself conceived a son, and she whom people called barren is now in her sixth month, for nothing is impossible to God.' 'I am the handmaid of the Lord,' said Mary, 'let what you have said be done to me.' And the angel left her.

The Gospel of the Lord.

The Creed is said. At the words and was incarnate all genuflect.

Prayer over the Offerings

Be pleased, almighty God,
to accept your Church's offering,
so that she,
   who is aware that her beginnings
lie in the Incarnation of your Only
   Begotten Son,
may rejoice to celebrate his
   mysteries on this Solemnity.
Who lives and reigns
   for ever and ever.

Super oblata

Ecclesiæ tuæ munus, omnipotens
   Deus, dignare suscipere,
ut, quæ in Unigeniti
   tui incarnatione
primordia sua constare cognoscit,
ipsius gaudeat hac sollemnitate
   celebrare mysteria.
Per Christum Dominum nostrum.

Preface: The Mystery of
the Incarnation.

Præfatio: De mysterio Incarnationis

It is truly right and just,
    our duty and our salvation,
always and everywhere
    to give you thanks,
Lord, holy Father,
    almighty and eternal God,
through Christ our Lord.

Vere dignum et iustum est,
    æquum et salutare,
nos tibi semper et ubique
    gratias agere:
Domine, sancte Pater,
    omnipotens æterne Deus:
per Christum Dominum nostrum.

For the Virgin Mary heard with faith
that the Christ was to be born
    among men and for men's sake
by the overshadowing power
    of the Holy Spirit.
Lovingly she bore him in her
    immaculate womb,
that the promises to the children
    of Israel might come about
and the hope of nations be
    accomplished beyond all telling.

Quem inter homines et propter
    homines nasciturum,
Spiritus Sancti obumbrante virtute,
a cælesti nuntio Virgo
    fidenter audivit
et immaculatis visceribus
    amanter portavit,
ut et promissiones filiis Israel
    perficeret veritas,
et gentium exspectatio pateret
    ineffabiliter adimplenda.

Through him the host of Angels
    adores your majesty
and rejoices in your presence for ever.

Per quem maiestatem tuam adorat
    exercitus Angelorum,
ante conspectum tuum
    in æternitate lætantium.

May our voices, we pray,
    join with theirs
in one chorus of exultant praise,
    as we acclaim:

Cum quibus et nostras voces
    ut admitti iubeas, deprecamur,
socia exsultatione dicentes:

Holy, Holy, Holy Lord God of hosts...

Sanctus, Sanctus, Sanctus. . .

Communion Antiphon   Is 7:14

Ant. ad communionem

Behold, a Virgin shall conceive
    and bear a son;
and his name will be called
    Emmanuel.

Ecce Virgo concipiet,
    et pariet Filium;
et vocabitur nomen
    eius Emmanuel.

Prayer after Communion	Post communionem
Confirm in our minds the mysteries of the true faith, we pray, O Lord, so that, confessing that he who was conceived of the Virgin Mary is true God and true man, we may, through the saving power of his Resurrection, merit to attain eternal joy. Through Christ our Lord.	In mentibus nostris, quæsumus, Domine, veræ fidei sacramenta confirma, ut, qui conceptum de Virgine Deum verum et hominem confitemur, per eius salutiferæ resurrectionis potentiam, ad æternam mereamur pervenire lætitiam. Per Christum Dominum nostrum.

In England

23 April

SAINT GEORGE, MARTYR, PATRON OF ENGLAND

The Church's action is credible and effective only to the extent to which those who belong to her are prepared to pay in person for their fidelity to Christ in every circumstance. When this readiness is lacking, the crucial argument of truth on which the Church herself depends is also absent. Dear brothers and sisters, as in early times, today too Christ needs apostles ready to sacrifice themselves. He needs witnesses and martyrs.

(Pope Benedict XVI)

Solemnity

Entrance Antiphon   Cf. Mt 25:34

REJOICE, you Saints, in the presence of the Lamb;
a kingdom has been prepared for you
from the foundation of the world, alleluia.

Or: Ps 90:13

On the asp and the viper you will tread,
and trample the young lion and the dragon, alleluia.

The Gloria in excelsis (Glory to God in the highest) is said.

Collect

God of hosts,
who so kindled the fire of charity
in the heart of Saint George your martyr
that he bore witness to the risen Lord
both by his life and by his death,
grant us through his intercession, we pray,
the same faith and power of love,
that we who rejoice in his triumph
may be led to share with him
in the fullness of the resurrection.
Through our Lord Jesus Christ, your Son,
who lives and reigns with you in the unity of the Holy Spirit,
one God, for ever and ever.

Alternative readings may be taken from the Common of Martyrs, or from the Common of Holy Men and Women.

FIRST READING

A reading from the book of the Apocalypse   12:10-12

In the face of death they would not cling to life.

I, John, heard a voice shout from heaven, 'Victory and power and empire for ever have been won by our God, and all authority for his Christ, now that the persecutor, who accused our brothers day and night before our God, has been brought down. They have triumphed over him by the blood of the Lamb and by the witness of their martyrdom, because even in the face of death they would not cling to life. Let the heavens rejoice and all who live there.'

The word of the Lord.

Responsorial Psalm   Ps 30

R. **Those who are sowing in tears**
   will sing when they reap.

When the Lord delivered Zion from bondage,
it seemed like a dream.
Then was our mouth filled with laughter,
on our lips there were songs. R.

The heathens themselves said: 'What marvels
the Lord worked for them!'

What marvels the Lord worked for us!
Indeed we were glad. R.

Deliver us, O Lord, from our bondage
as streams in dry land.
Those who are sowing in tears
will sing when they reap. R.

They go out, they go out, full of tears,
carrying seed for the sowing;
they come back, they come back, full of song,
carrying their sheaves. R.

A second reading may be chosen from the options given above.

Gospel Acclamation   Mt 23:9-10

R. **Alleluia, alleluia!**
Happy the man who stands firm,
for he has proved himself,
and will win the crown of life.
R. **Alleluia!**

GOSPEL

A reading from the holy Gospel according to John   15:18-21
If they persecuted me, they will persecute you.

Jesus said to his disciples:
  'If the world hates you,
  remember that it hated me before you.
  If you belonged to the world,
  the world would love you as its own;
  but because you do not belong to the world,
  because my choice withdrew you from the world,
  therefore the world hates you.
  Remember the words I said to you:
  A servant is not greater than his master.
  If they persecuted me,
  they will persecute you too;
  if they kept my word,
  they will keep yours as well.
  But it will be on my account that they will do all this,
  because they do not know the one who sent me.'

  The Gospel of the Lord.

ALTERNATIVE GOSPEL

A reading from the holy Gospel according to John   15:1-8

Whoever remains in me, with me in him, bears fruit in plenty.

Jesus said to his disciples:

'I am the true vine,
and my Father is the vinedresser.
Every branch in me that bears no fruit
he cuts away,
and every branch that does bear fruit he prunes
to make it bear even more.
You are pruned already,
by means of the word that I have spoken to you.
Make your home in me, as I make mine in you.
As a branch cannot bear fruit all by itself,
but must remain part of the vine,
neither can you unless you remain in me.
I am the vine,
you are the branches.
Whoever remains in me, with me in him,
bears fruit in plenty;
for cut off from me you can do nothing.
Anyone who does not remain in me
is like a branch that has been thrown away
– he withers;
these branches are collected and thrown on the fire,
and they are burnt.
If you remain in me
and my words remain in you,
you may ask what you will
and you shall get it.
It is to the glory of my Father that you should bear much fruit,
and then you will be my disciples.'

The Gospel of the Lord.

The creed is said.

Prayer over the Offerings

Receive, we pray, O Lord,
the sacrifice of conciliation and praise,
which we offer to your majesty
in commemoration of the blessed Martyr Saint George,

that it may lead us to forgiveness
and confirm us in constant thanksgiving.
Through Christ our Lord.

Preface I or II of Holy Martyrs, pp.580-581.

Communion Antiphon   Cf. 2 Tm 2:11-12

If we have died with Christ, we shall also live with him;
if we persevere, we shall also reign with him, alleluia.

Prayer after Communion

Rejoicing on this festival day, O Lord,
we have received your heavenly gifts;
grant, we pray,
that we who in this divine banquet
proclaim the death of your Son
may merit with Saint George to be partakers
in his resurrection and glory.
Through Christ our Lord.

---

24 June

THE NATIVITY OF SAINT JOHN THE BAPTIST

Today, the liturgy invites us to celebrate the Solemnity of the Birth of Saint John the Baptist, whose life was totally directed to Christ, as was that of Mary, Christ's Mother. John the Baptist was the forerunner, the "voice" sent to proclaim the Incarnate Word. Thus, commemorating his birth actually means celebrating Christ, the fulfilment of the promises of all the prophets, among whom the greatest was the Baptist, called to "prepare the way" for the Messiah. All the Gospels introduce the narrative of Jesus' public life with the account of his baptism by John in the River Jordan. When Jesus, after receiving baptism, emerged from the water, John saw the Spirit descending upon him in the form of a dove. It was then that he "knew" the full reality of Jesus of Nazareth and began to make him "known to Israel", pointing him out as the Son of God and Redeemer of man: "Behold, the Lamb of God, who takes away the sin of the world!".

(Pope Benedict XVI)

Solemnity

At the Vigil Mass

This Mass is used on the evening of 23 June, either before or after First Vespers (Evening Prayer I) of the Solemnity.

Entrance Antiphon Lk 1:15-14	Ant. ad introitum

HE will be great in the sight of the Lord
and will be filled with the
    Holy Spirit,
even from his mother's womb;
and many will rejoice at his birth.

HIC erit magnus
coram Domino,
et Spiritu Sancto replebitur adhuc
    ex utero matris suæ,
et multi in nativitate
    eius gaudebunt.

The Gloria in excelsis (Glory to God in the highest) is said.

Collect	Collecta

Grant, we pray, almighty God,
that your family may walk in the
    way of salvation
and, attentive to what Saint John
    the Precursor urged,
may come safely to the One
    he foretold,
our Lord Jesus Christ.
Who lives and reigns with you
    in the unity of the Holy Spirit,
one God, for ever and ever.

Præsta, quæsumus,
    omnipotens Deus,
ut familia tua per viam
    salutis incedat,
et, beati Ioannis Præcursoris
    hortamenta sectando,
ad eum quem prædixit,
    secura perveniat,
Dominum nostrum
    Iesum Christum.
Qui tecum vivit et regnat
    in unitate Spiritus Sancti,
Deus, per omnia sæcula sæculorum.

FIRST READING

A reading from the prophet Jeremiah   1:4-10

Before I formed you in the womb, I knew you.

In the days of Josiah, the word of the Lord was addressed to me, saying,

    'Before I formed you in the womb I knew you;
    before you came to birth I consecrated you;
    I have appointed you as prophet to the nations.'

I said, 'Ah, Lord, look, I do not know how to speak: I am a child!'

But the Lord replied,

'Do not say, "I am a child."
Go now to those to whom I send you
and say whatever I command you.
Do not be afraid of them,
for I am with you to protect you –
it is the Lord who speaks!'

Then the Lord put out his hand and touched my mouth and said to me:

'There! I am putting my words into your mouth.
Look, today I am setting you
over nations and over kingdoms,
to tear up and to knock down,
to destroy and to overthrow,
to build and to plant.'

The word of the Lord.

Responsorial Psalm   Ps 70:1-6,15,17. R. v.6

R. **From my mother's womb you have been my help.**

In you, O Lord, I take refuge;
let me never be put to shame.
In your justice rescue me, free me:
pay heed to me and save me. R.

Be a rock where I can take refuge,
a mighty stronghold to save me;
for you are my rock, my stronghold.
Free me from the hand of the wicked. R.

It is you, O Lord, who are my hope,
my trust, O Lord, since my youth.
On you I have leaned from my birth,
from my mother's womb you have been my help. R.

My lips will tell of your justice
and day by day of your help.
O God, you have taught me from my youth
and I proclaim your wonders still. R.

SECOND READING

A reading from the first letter of St Peter   1:8-12

It was this salvation that the prophets were looking and searching so hard for.

You did not see Jesus Christ, yet you love him; and still without seeing him, you are already filled with joy so glorious that it cannot be described, because you believe; and you are sure of the end to which your faith looks forward, that is, the salvation of your souls.

It was this salvation that the prophets were looking and searching so hard for; their prophecies were about the grace which was to come to you. The Spirit of Christ which was in them foretold the sufferings of Christ and the glories that would come after them, and they tried to find out at what time and in what circumstances all this was to be expected. It was revealed to them that the news they brought of all the things which have now been announced to you, by those who preached to you the Good News through the Holy Spirit sent from heaven, was for you and not for themselves. Even the angels long to catch a glimpse of these things.

The word of the Lord.

Gospel Acclamation   Cf. Jn 1:7; Lk 1:17

R. **Alleluia, alleluia!**
He came as a witness,
as a witness to speak for the light,
preparing for the Lord a people fit for him.
R. **Alleluia!**

GOSPEL

A reading from the holy Gospel according to Luke   1:5-17

She is to bear you a son and you must name him John.

In the days of King Herod of Judaea there lived a priest called Zechariah who belonged to the Abijah section of the priesthood, and he had a wife, Elizabeth by name, who was a descendant of Aaron. Both were worthy in the sight of God, and scrupulously observed all the commandments and observances of the Lord. But they were childless: Elizabeth was barren and they were both getting on in years.

Now it was the turn of Zechariah's section to serve, and he was exercising his priestly office before God when it fell to him by lot, as the ritual custom was, to enter the Lord's sanctuary and burn incense there. And at the hour of incense the whole congregation was outside, praying.

Then there appeared to him the angel of the Lord, standing on the right of the altar of incense. The sight disturbed Zechariah and he was overcome with fear. But the angel said to him, 'Zechariah, do not be afraid, your prayer has been heard. Your wife Elizabeth is to bear you a son and you must name him John. He will be your joy and delight and many will rejoice at his birth, for he will be great in the sight of the Lord; he must drink no wine, no strong drink. Even from his mother's womb he will be filled with the Holy Spirit, and he will bring back many of the sons of Israel to the Lord their God. With the spirit and power of Elijah, he will go before him to turn the hearts of fathers towards their children and the disobedient back to the wisdom that the virtuous have, preparing for the Lord a people fit for him.'

The Gospel of the Lord.

The Creed is said.

Prayer over the Offerings

Look with favour, O Lord,
upon the offerings made
   by your people
on the Solemnity of
   Saint John the Baptist,
and grant that what we celebrate in
   mystery
we may follow with deeds
   of devoted service.
Through Christ our Lord.

Super oblata

Munera populi tui, Domine,
   propitius intende,
in beati Ioannis Baptistæ
   sollemnitate delata,
et præsta, ut,
   quæ mysterio gerimus,
debitæ servitutis actione sectemur.
Per Christum Dominum nostrum.

Proper Preface, as in the following Mass, pp. 1153-1154.

Communion Antiphon   Lk 1:68

Blessed be the Lord,
   the God of Israel!
He has visited his people
   and redeemed them.

Ant. ad communionem

Benedictus Dominus Deus Israel,
quia visitavit et fecit redemptionem
   plebi suæ.

Prayer after Communion

May the marvellous prayer of Saint
   John the Baptist
accompany us who have
   eaten our fill

Post communionem

Sacris dapibus satiatos,
beati Ioannis Baptistæ nos,
   Domine,
præclara comitetur oratio,

at this sacrificial feast, O Lord,
and, since Saint John
    proclaimed your Son
to be the Lamb who would
    take away our sins,
may he implore now for us
    your favour.
Through Christ our Lord.

et, quem Agnum nostra ablaturum
    crimina nuntiavit,
ipsum Filium tuum poscat nobis
    fore placatum.
Qui vivit et regnat
    in sæcula sæculorum.

At the Mass during the Day

Entrance Antiphon Jn 1:6-7; Lk 1:17

A MAN was sent from God,
    whose name was John.
He came to testify to the light,
to prepare a people fit for the Lord.

Ant. ad introitum

F UIT homo missus a Deo,
    cui nomen erat Ioannes.
Hic venit, ut testimonium
    perhiberet de lumine,
parare Domino plebem perfectam.

The Gloria in excelsis (Glory to God in the highest) is said.

Collect

O God, who raised up
    Saint John the Baptist
to make ready a nation fit for
    Christ the Lord,
give your people, we pray,
the grace of spiritual joys
and direct the hearts
    of all the faithful
into the way of salvation and peace.
Through our Lord Jesus Christ,
    your Son,
who lives and reigns with you
    in the unity of the Holy Spirit,
one God, for ever and ever.

Collecta

Deus, qui beatum Ioannem
    Baptistam suscitasti,
ut perfectam plebem
    Christo Domino præpararet,
da populis tuis spiritalium
    gratiam gaudiorum,
et omnium fidelium mentes
    dirige in viam salutis et pacis.
Per Dominum nostrum
    Iesum Christum Filium tuum,
qui tecum vivit et regnat
    in unitate Spiritus Sancti,
Deus, per omnia sæcula sæculorum.

FIRST READING

A reading from the prophet Isaiah   49:1-6

I will make you the light of the nations.

Islands, listen to me,
pay attention, remotest peoples.
The Lord called me before I was born,
from my mother's womb he pronounced my name.

He made my mouth a sharp sword,
and hid me in the shadow of his hand.
He made me into a sharpened arrow,
and concealed me in his quiver.

He said to me, 'You are my servant (Israel)
in whom I shall be glorified';
while I was thinking, 'I have toiled in vain,
I have exhausted myself for nothing';
and all the while my cause was with the Lord,
my reward with my God.
I was honoured in the eyes of the Lord,
my God was my strength.

And now the Lord has spoken,
he who formed me in the womb to be his servant,
to bring Jacob back to him,
to gather Israel to him:
'It is not enough for you to be my servant,
to restore the tribes of Jacob and bring back the survivors of Israel;
I will make you the light of the nations
so that my salvation may reach to the ends of the earth.'

The word of the Lord.

Responsorial Psalm   Ps 138:1-3,13-15. R. v.14

R. **I thank you for the wonder of my being.**

O Lord, you search me and you know me,
you know my resting and my rising,
you discern my purpose from afar.
You mark when I walk or lie down,
all my ways lie open to you. R.

For it was you who created my being,
knit me together in my mother's womb.

I thank you for the wonder of my being,
for the wonders of all your creation. R.

Already you knew my soul,
my body held no secret from you
when I was being fashioned in secret
and moulded in the depths of the earth. R.

R. **I thank you for the wonder of my being.**

SECOND READING

A reading from the Acts of the Apostles   13:22-26

Jesus, whose coming was heralded by John.

Paul said: 'God made David the king of our ancestors, of whom he approved in these words, "I have elected David son of Jesse, a man after my own heart, who will carry out my whole purpose." To keep his promise, God has raised up for Israel one of David's descendants, Jesus, as Saviour, whose coming was heralded by John when he proclaimed a baptism of repentance for the whole people of Israel. Before John ended his career he said, "I am not the one you imagine me to be; that one is coming after me and I am not fit to undo his sandal."

'My brothers, sons of Abraham's race, and all you who fear God, this message of salvation is meant for you.'

The word of the Lord.

Gospel Acclamation   Cf. Lk 1:76

R. **Alleluia, alleluia!**
As for you, little child, you shall be called
a prophet of God, the Most High.
You shall go ahead of the Lord
to prepare his ways before him.
R. **Alleluia!**

GOSPEL

A reading from the holy Gospel according to Luke   1:57-66,80

His name is John.

The time came for Elizabeth to have her child, and she gave birth to a son; and when her neighbours and relations heard that the Lord had shown her so great a kindness, they shared her joy.

Now on the eighth day they came to circumcise the child; they were going to call him Zechariah after his father, but his mother spoke up. 'No,' she said 'he is to be called John.' They said to her, 'But no one in your family has that name', and made signs to his father to find out what he wanted him called. The father asked for a writing-tablet and wrote, 'His name is John.' And they were all astonished. At that instant his power of speech returned and he spoke and praised God. All their neighbours were filled with awe and the whole affair was talked about throughout the hill country of Judaea. All those who heard of it treasured it in their hearts. 'What will this child turn out to be?' they wondered. And indeed the hand of the Lord was with him. Meanwhile, the child grew up and his spirit matured. And he lived out in the wilderness until the day he appeared openly to Israel.

The Gospel of the Lord.

The Creed is said.

Prayer over the Offerings

We place these offerings on your
    altar, O Lord,
to celebrate with fitting honour
    the nativity of him
who both foretold the coming
    of the world's Saviour
and pointed him out
    when he came.
Who lives and reigns
    for ever and ever.

Super oblata

Tua, Domine, muneribus
    altaria cumulamus,
illius nativitatem honore
    debito celebrantes,
qui Salvatorem mundi
    et cecinit affuturum,
et adesse monstravit.
Qui vivit et regnat
    in sæcula sæculorum.

Preface: The mission of the Precursor

It is truly right and just,
    our duty and our salvation,
always and everywhere
    to give you thanks,
Lord, holy Father,
    almighty and eternal God,
through Christ our Lord.

In his Precursor, Saint John
    the Baptist,
we praise your great glory,
for you consecrated him
    for a singular honour
among those born of women.

Præfatio: De missione Præcursoris

Vere dignum et iustum est,
    æquum et salutare,
nos tibi semper et ubique
    gratias agere:
Domine, sancte Pater,
    omnipotens æterne Deus:
per Christum Dominum nostrum.

In cuius Præcursore beato Ioanne
tuam magnificentiam collaudamus,
quem inter natos mulierum honore
    præcipuo consecrasti.

His birth brought great rejoicing;
even in the womb he leapt for joy
at the coming of human salvation.
He alone of all the prophets
pointed out the Lamb of redemption.

And to make holy the flowing waters,
he baptised the very author
   of Baptism
and was privileged to bear him
   supreme witness
by the shedding of his blood.

And so, with the Powers of heaven,
we worship you constantly on earth,
and before your majesty
without end we acclaim:

Holy, Holy, Holy Lord God of hosts...

Qui cum nascendo multa gaudia
   præstitisset,
et nondum editus exsultasset
   ad humanæ salutis adventum,
ipse solus omnium prophetarum
Agnum redemptionis ostendit.

Sed et sanctificandis etiam
   aquæ fluentis
ipsum baptismatis lavit auctorem,
et meruit fuso sanguine supremum
illi testimonium exhibere.

Et ideo, cum cælorum virtutibus,
in terris te iugiter prædicamus,
maiestati tuæ sine fine clamantes:

Sanctus, Sanctus, Sanctus. . .

Communion Antiphon Cf. Lk 1:78

Through the tender mercy
   of our God,
the Dawn from on high will visit us.

Ant. ad communionem

Per viscera misericordiæ Dei nostri,
visitavit nos Oriens ex alto.

Prayer after Communion

Having feasted at the banquet
   of the heavenly Lamb,
we pray, O Lord,
that, finding joy in the nativity
   of Saint John the Baptist,
your Church may know as
   the author of her rebirth
the Christ whose coming
   John foretold.
Who lives and reigns
   for ever and ever.

Post communionem

Cælestis Agni convivio refecti,
quæsumus, Domine,
   ut Ecclesia tua,
sumens de beati Ioannis Baptistæ
   generatione lætitiam,
quem ille prænuntiavit venturum,
suæ regenerationis
   cognoscat auctorem.
Qui vivit et regnat
   in sæcula sæculorum.

29 June

SAINTS PETER AND PAUL, APOSTLES

In their great wealth, the biblical texts of this Eucharistic Liturgy on the Solemnity of the Holy Apostles Peter and Paul highlight a theme that could be summed up in these words: God is close to his faithful servants and delivers them from all evil and delivers the Church from negative powers. It is the theme of the Church's freedom, that presents an historical aspect and another that is more profoundly spiritual. We see that Jesus' promise "the powers of death shall not prevail against" the Church does indeed include the historical experiences of persecution that Peter and Paul and other Gospel witnesses suffered, but goes beyond them, with the intention of assuring protection, especially from threats of a spiritual kind. Therefore a guarantee exists of the freedom that God assures the Church, freedom both from material ties that seek to prevent or to coerce her mission and from spiritual and moral evils that can tarnish her authenticity and credibility.

(Pope Benedict XVI)

Solemnity

At the Vigil Mass

This Mass is used on the evening of 28 June, either before or after First Vespers (Evening Prayer I) of the Solemnity.

Entrance Antiphon	Ant. ad introitum
PETER the Apostle, and Paul the teacher of the Gentiles, these have taught us your law, O Lord.	PETRUS apostolus et Paulus doctor gentium, ipsi nos docuerunt legem tuam, Domine.

The Gloria in excelsis (Glory to God in the highest) is said.

Collect	Collecta
Grant, we pray, O Lord our God, that we may be sustained by the intercession of the blessed Apostles Peter and Paul, that, as through them you gave your Church the foundations of her heavenly office,	Da nobis, quæsumus, Domine Deus noster, beatorum apostolorum Petri et Pauli intercessionibus sublevari, ut, per quos Ecclesiæ tuæ superni muneris rudimenta donasti,

so through them you may help her to eternal salvation.	per eos subsidia perpetuæ salutis impendas.
Through our Lord Jesus Christ, your Son,	Per Dominum nostrum Iesum Christum Filium tuum,
who lives and reigns with you in the unity of the Holy Spirit,	qui tecum vivit et regnat in unitate Spiritus Sancti,
one God, for ever and ever.	Deus, per omnia sæcula sæculorum.

FIRST READING

A reading from the Acts of the Apostles   3:1-10

I will give you what I have: in the name of Jesus, walk!

Once, when Peter and John were going up to the Temple for the prayers at the ninth hour, it happened that there was a man being carried past. He was a cripple from birth; and they used to put him down every day near the Temple entrance called the Beautiful Gate so that he could beg from the people going in. When this man saw Peter and John on their way into the Temple he begged from them. Both Peter and John looked straight at him and said, 'Look at us.' He turned to them expectantly, hoping to get something from them, but Peter said, 'I have neither silver nor gold, but I will give you what I have: in the name of Jesus Christ the Nazarene, walk!' Peter then took him by the hand and helped him to stand up. Instantly his feet and ankles became firm, he jumped up, stood, and began to walk, and he went with them into the Temple, walking and jumping and praising God. Everyone could see him walking and praising God, and they recognised him as the man who used to sit begging at the Beautiful Gate of the Temple. They were all astonished and unable to explain what had happened to him.

The word of the Lord.

Responsorial Psalm   Ps 18:2-5. R. v.5

R. **Their word goes forth through all the earth.**

The heavens proclaim the glory of God
and the firmament shows forth the work of his hands.
Day unto day takes up the story
and night unto night makes known the message. R.

No speech, no word, no voice is heard
yet their span extends through all the earth,
their words to the utmost bounds of the world. R.

SECOND READING

A reading from the letter of St Paul to the Galatians   1:11-20

God specially chose me while I was still in my mother's womb.

The Good News I preached is not a human message that I was given by men, it is something I learnt only through a revelation of Jesus Christ. You must have heard of my career as a practising Jew, how merciless I was in persecuting the Church of God, how much damage I did to it, how I stood out among other Jews of my generation, and how enthusiastic I was for the traditions of my ancestors.

Then God, who had specially chosen me while I was still in my mother's womb, called me through his grace and chose to reveal his Son in me, so that I might preach the Good News about him to the pagans. I did not stop to discuss this with any human being, nor did I go up to Jerusalem to see those who were already apostles before me, but I went off to Arabia at once and later went straight back from there to Damascus. Even when after three years I went up to Jerusalem to visit Cephas and stayed with him for fifteen days, I did not see any of the other apostles; I only saw James, the brother of the Lord, and I swear before God that what I have just written is the literal truth.

The word of the Lord.

Gospel Acclamation   Jn 21:17

R. **Alleluia, alleluia!**
Lord, you know everything;
you know I love you.
R. **Alleluia!**

GOSPEL

A reading from the holy Gospel according to John   21:15-19

Feed my lambs, feed my sheep.

After Jesus had shown himself to his disciples and eaten with them, he said to Simon Peter, 'Simon son of John, do you love me more than these others do?' He answered, 'Yes Lord, you know I love you.' Jesus said to him, 'Feed my lambs.' A second time he said to him, 'Simon son of John, do you love me?' He replied, 'Yes, Lord, you know I love you.' Jesus said to him, 'Look after my sheep.' Then he said to him a third time, 'Simon son of John, do you love me?' Peter was upset that he asked him the third time, 'Do you love me?' and said, 'Lord, you know everything; you know I love you.' Jesus said to him, 'Feed my sheep.

'I tell you most solemnly,
when you were young

you put on your own belt
and walked where you liked;
but when you grow old
you will stretch out your hands,
and somebody else will put a belt round you
and take you where you would rather not go.'

In these words he indicated the kind of death by which Peter would give
glory to God. After this he said, 'Follow me.'

The Gospel of the Lord.

The Creed is said.

Prayer over the Offerings	Super oblata
We bring offerings to your altar, O Lord,	Munera, Domine, tuis altaribus adhibemus,
as we glory in the solemn feast of the blessed Apostles Peter and Paul,	de beatorum apostolorum Petri et Pauli sollemnitatibus gloriantes,
so that the more we doubt our own merits,	ut quantum sumus de nostro merito formidantes,
the more we may rejoice that we are to be saved	tantum de tua benignitate gloriemur salvandi.
by your loving kindness.	Per Christum Dominum nostrum.
Through Christ our Lord.	

Proper Preface, as in the following Mass, pp.1162-1163.

Communion Antiphon Cf. Jn 21:15,17	Ant. ad communionem
Simon, Son of John, do you love me more than these?	Simon Ioannis, diligis me plus his? Domine, tu omnia nosti;
Lord, you know everything; you know that I love you.	tu scis, Domine, quia amo te.

Prayer after Communion	Post communionem
By this heavenly Sacrament, O Lord, we pray,	Cælestibus sacramentis, quæsumus, Domine,
strengthen your faithful,	fideles tuos corrobora,
whom you have enlightened with the teaching of the Apostles.	quos Apostolorum doctrina illuminasti.
Through Christ our Lord.	Per Christum Dominum nostrum.

A formula of Solemn Blessing, pp.654-657, may be used.

At the Mass during the Day

Entrance Antiphon | Ant. ad introitum

THESE are the ones who,
living in the flesh,
planted the Church with their blood;
they drank the chalice of the Lord
and became the friends of God.

ISTI sunt qui, viventes in carne,
plantaverunt Ecclesiam
sanguine suo:
calicem Domini biberunt,
et amici Dei facti sunt.

The Gloria in excelsis (Glory to God in the highest) is said.

Collect | Collecta

O God, who on the Solemnity
of the Apostles Peter and Paul
give us the noble and holy joy
of this day,
grant, we pray, that your Church
may in all things follow the teaching
of those through whom she received
the beginnings of right religion.
Through our Lord Jesus Christ,
your Son,
who lives and reigns with you
in the unity of the Holy Spirit,
one God, for ever and ever.

Deus, qui huius diei venerandam
sanctamque lætitiam
in apostolorum Petri et Pauli
sollemnitate tribuisti,
da Ecclesiæ tuæ eorum in omnibus
sequi præceptum,
per quos religionis sumpsit exordium.
Per Dominum nostrum Iesum
Christum Filium tuum,
qui tecum vivit et regnat
in unitate Spiritus Sancti,
Deus, per omnia sæcula sæculorum.

FIRST READING

A reading from the Acts of the Apostles 12:1-11

Now I know the Lord really did save me from Herod.

King Herod started persecuting certain members of the Church. He beheaded James the brother of John, and when he saw that this pleased the Jews he decided to arrest Peter as well. This was during the days of Unleavened Bread, and he put Peter in prison, assigning four squads of four soldiers each to guard him in turns. Herod meant to try Peter in public after the end of Passover week. All the time Peter was under guard the Church prayed to God for him unremittingly.

On the night before Herod was to try him, Peter was sleeping between two soldiers, fastened with double chains, while guards kept watch at the main entrance to the prison. Then suddenly the angel of the Lord stood there, and the cell was filled with light. He tapped Peter on the side and woke him. 'Get up!' he said 'Hurry!' – and the chains fell from his hands. The angel then said, 'Put on your belt and sandals.' After he had done this, the angel next said, 'Wrap your cloak round you and follow me.' Peter followed him, but had no idea that what the angel did was all happening in reality; he thought he was seeing a vision. They passed through two guard posts one after the other, and reached the iron gate leading to the city. This opened of its own accord; they went through it and had walked the whole length of one street when suddenly the angel left him. It was only then that Peter came to himself. 'Now I know it is all true,' he said. 'The Lord really did send his angel and has saved me from Herod and from all that the Jewish people were so certain would happen to me.'

The word of the Lord.

Responsorial Psalm   Ps 33:2-9. R. v.5. Alt. R. v.8

R. **From all my terrors the Lord set me free.**
    Or: **The angel of the Lord rescues those who revere him.**

I will bless the Lord at all times
his praise always on my lips;
in the Lord my soul shall make its boast.
The humble shall hear and be glad. R.

Glorify the Lord with me.
Together let us praise his name.
I sought the Lord and he answered me;
from all my terrors he set me free. R.

Look towards him and be radiant;
let your faces not be abashed.
This poor man called; the Lord heard him
and rescued him from all his distress. R.

The angel of the Lord is encamped
around those who revere him, to rescue them.
Taste and see that the Lord is good.
He is happy who seeks refuge in him. R.

SECOND READING

A reading from the second letter of St Paul to Timothy   4:6-8,17-18

All there is to come now is the crown of righteousness reserved for me.

My life is already being poured away as a libation, and the time has come for me to be gone. I have fought the good fight to the end; I have run the race to the finish; I have kept the faith; all there is to come now is the crown of righteousness reserved for me, which the Lord, the righteous judge, will give to me on that Day; and not only to me but to all those who have longed for his Appearing.

The Lord stood by me and gave me power, so that through me the whole message might be proclaimed for all the pagans to hear; and so I was rescued from the lion's mouth. The Lord will rescue me from all evil attempts on me, and bring me safely to his heavenly kingdom. To him be glory for ever and ever. Amen.

The word of the Lord.

Gospel Acclamation   Mt 16:18

R. **Alleluia, alleluia!**
You are Peter and on this rock I will build my Church.
And the gates of the underworld can never hold out against it.
R. **Alleluia!**

GOSPEL

A reading from the holy Gospel according to Matthew   16:13-19

You are Peter, and I will give you the keys of the kingdom of heaven.

When Jesus came to the region of Caesarea Philippi he put this question to his disciples, 'Who do people say the Son of Man is?' And they said, 'Some say he is John the Baptist, some Elijah, and others Jeremiah or one of the prophets.' 'But you,' he said 'who do you say I am?' Then Simon Peter spoke up, 'You are the Christ,' he said 'the Son of the living God.' Jesus replied, 'Simon son of Jonah, you are a happy man! Because it was not flesh and blood that revealed this to you but my Father in heaven. So I now say to you: You are Peter and on this rock I will build my Church. And the gates of the underworld can never hold out against it. I will give you the keys of the kingdom of heaven: whatever you bind on earth shall be considered bound in heaven; whatever you loose on earth shall be considered loosed in heaven.'

The Gospel of the Lord.

The Creed is said.

Prayer over the Offerings	Super oblata

May the prayer of the Apostles,
   O Lord,
accompany the sacrificial gift
that we present to your name
   for consecration,
and may their intercession make us
   devoted to you
in celebration of the sacrifice.
Through Christ our Lord.

Hostiam, Domine, quam nomini
   tuo exhibemus sacrandam,
apostolica prosequatur oratio,
nosque tibi reddat in sacrificio
   celebrando devotos.
Per Christum Dominum nostrum.

Preface: The twofold mission of
Peter and Paul in the Church.

Præfatio: De duplici missione Petri
et Pauli in Ecclesia.

It is truly right and just,
   our duty and our salvation,
always and everywhere to give
   you thanks,
Lord, holy Father,
   almighty and eternal God.

Vere dignum et iustum est,
   æquum et salutare,
nos tibi semper et ubique
   gratias agere:
Domine, sancte Pater,
   omnipotens æterne Deus.

For by your providence
the blessed Apostles Peter and Paul
   bring us joy:
Peter, foremost in confessing
   the faith,
Paul, its outstanding preacher,
Peter, who established the early
   Church from the remnant
   of Israel,
Paul, master and teacher
   of the Gentiles that you call.

Quia nos beati apostoli
   Petrus et Paulus
tua dispositione lætificant:
hic princeps fidei confitendæ,
ille intellegendæ clarus assertor;
hic reliquiis Israel instituens
   Ecclesiam primitivam,
ille magister et doctor
   gentium vocandarum.

And so, each in a different way
gathered together the one family
   of Christ;
and revered together throughout
   the world,
they share one Martyr's crown.

Sic diverso consilio unam Christi
   familiam congregantes,
par mundo venerabile,
   una corona sociavit.

And therefore, with all the Angels
  and Saints,
we praise you, as without end
  we acclaim:

Holy, Holy, Holy Lord God of hosts...

Et ideo, cum Sanctis
  et Angelis universis
te collaudamus, sine fine dicentes:

Sanctus, Sanctus, Sanctus. . .

Communion Antiphon Cf. Mt 16:16,18

Ant. ad communionem

Peter said to Jesus:
  You are the Christ,
  the Son of the living God.
And Jesus replied: You are Peter,
and upon this rock I will build
  my Church.

Dixit Petrus ad Iesum:
  Tu es Christus, Filius Dei vivi.
Respondit Iesus: Tu es Petrus,
et super hanc petram ædificabo
  Ecclesiam meam.

Prayer after Communion

Post communionem

Grant us, O Lord,
who have been renewed
  by this Sacrament,
so to live in the Church,
that, persevering in the breaking
  of the Bread
and in the teaching of the Apostles,
we may be one heart and one soul,
made steadfast in your love.
Through Christ our Lord.

Da nobis, Domine,
  hoc sacramento refectis,
ita in Ecclesia conversari,
ut, perseverantes in fractione panis
Apostolorumque doctrina,
cor unum simus et anima una,
  tua caritate firmati.
Per Christum Dominum nostrum.

A formula of Solemn Blessing, pp.654-657, may be used.

6 August

THE TRANSFIGURATION OF THE LORD

Today, the liturgy invites us to focus our gaze on this mystery of light. On the transfigured face of Jesus a ray of light which he held within shines forth. This same light was to shine on Christ's face on the day of the Resurrection. In this sense, the Transfiguration appears as a foretaste of the Paschal Mystery. The Transfiguration invites us to open the eyes of our hearts to the mystery of God's light, present throughout salvation history. At the beginning of creation, the Almighty had already said: "Fiat lux – let there be light!" (Gn 1:2), and the light was separated from the darkness. Like the other created things, light is a sign that reveals something of God: it is, as it were, a reflection of his glory which accompanies its manifestations. Light, it is said in the Psalms, is the mantle with which God covers himself. In the Book of Wisdom, the symbolism of light is used to describe the very essence of God: wisdom, an outpouring of his glory, is "a reflection of eternal light" superior to any created light. In the New Testament, it is Christ who constitutes the full manifestation of God's light. His Resurrection defeated the power of the darkness of evil forever. With the Risen Christ, truth and love triumph over deceit and sin. In him, God's light henceforth illumines definitively human life and the course of history: "I am the light of the world", he says in the Gospel, "he who follows me will not walk in darkness, but will have the light of life" (Jn 8:12).

(Pope Benedict XVI)

Feast

Entrance Antiphon   Cf. Mt 17:5

IN a resplendent cloud the Holy Spirit appeared.
The Father's voice was heard:
   This is my beloved Son,
with whom I am well pleased.
   Listen to him.

Ant. ad introitum

IN splendenti nube Spiritus Sanctus visus est,
paterna vox audita est:
   Hic est Filius meus dilectus,
in quo mihi bene complacui:
   ipsum audite.

The Gloria in excelsis (Glory to God in the highest) is said.

Collect

O God, who in the glorious
    Transfiguration
of your Only Begotten Son
confirmed the mysteries of faith
    by the witness of the Fathers
and wonderfully prefigured our full
    adoption to sonship,
grant, we pray, to your servants,
that, listening to the voice
    of your beloved Son,
we may merit to become coheirs
    with him.
Who lives and reigns with you
    in the unity of the Holy Spirit,
one God, for ever and ever.

Collecta

Deus, qui fidei sacramenta
in Unigeniti tui gloriosa
    Transfiguratione
patrum testimonio roborasti,
et adoptionem filiorum perfectam
    mirabiliter præsignasti,
concede nobis famulis tuis,
ut, ipsius dilecti Filii
    tui vocem audientes,
eiusdem coheredes effici mereamur.
Qui tecum vivit et regnat
    in unitate Spiritus Sancti,
Deus, per omnia sæcula sæculorum.

When this Feast is not celebrated on a Sunday there may only be one reading before the Gospel.

FIRST READING

A reading from the prophet Daniel   7:9-10,13-14

His robe was white as snow.

As I watched:
Thrones were set in place
and one of great age took his seat.
His robe was white as snow,
the hair of his head as pure as wool.
His throne was a blaze of flames,
its wheels were a burning fire.
A stream of fire poured out,
issuing from his presence.
A thousand thousand waited on him,
ten thousand times ten thousand stood before him.
A court was held and the books were opened.
I gazed into the visions of the night.
And I saw, coming on the clouds of heaven,
one like a son of man.
He came to the one of great age
and was led into his presence.

On him was conferred sovereignty,
glory and kingship,
and men of all peoples, nations and languages became his servants.
His sovereignty is an eternal sovereignty
which shall never pass away,
nor will his empire ever be destroyed.

The word of the Lord.

Responsorial Psalm   Ps 96:1-2,5-6,9. R. vv.1,9

R. **The Lord is king,**
   most high above all the earth.

The Lord is king, let earth rejoice,
let all the coastlands be glad.
Cloud and darkness are his raiment;
his throne, justice and right. R.

The mountains melt like wax
before the Lord of all the earth.
The skies proclaim his justice;
all peoples see his glory. R.

For you indeed are the Lord
most high above all the earth
exalted far above all spirits. R.

SECOND READING

A reading from the second letter of St Peter   1:16-19

We heard this ourselves, spoken from heaven.

It was not any cleverly invented myths that we were repeating when we
brought you the knowledge of the power and the coming of our Lord Jesus
Christ; we had seen his majesty for ourselves. He was honoured and glorified
by God the Father, when the Sublime Glory itself spoke to him and said,
'This is my Son, the Beloved; he enjoys my favour.' We heard this ourselves,
spoken from heaven, when we were with him on the holy mountain.

So we have confirmation of what was said in prophecies; and you will be
right to depend on prophecy and take it as a lamp for lighting a way through
the dark until the dawn comes and the morning star rises in your minds.

The word of the Lord.

Gospel Acclamation   Mt 17:5

R. **Alleluia, alleluia!**
This is my Son, the Beloved,
he enjoys my favour;
listen to him.
R. **Alleluia!**

GOSPEL

YEAR A

A reading from the holy Gospel according to Matthew   17:1-9
His face shone like the sun.

Jesus took with him Peter and James and his brother John and led them up a high mountain where they could be alone. There in their presence he was transfigured: his face shone like the sun and his clothes became as white as the light. Suddenly Moses and Elijah appeared to them; they were talking with him. Then Peter spoke to Jesus. 'Lord,' he said 'it is wonderful for us to be here; if you wish, I will make three tents here, one for you, one for Moses and one for Elijah.' He was still speaking when suddenly a bright cloud covered them with shadow, and from the cloud there came a voice which said, 'This is my Son, the Beloved; he enjoys my favour. Listen to him.' When they heard this, the disciples fell on their faces, overcome with fear. But Jesus came up and touched them. 'Stand up,' he said 'do not be afraid.' And when they raised their eyes they saw no one but only Jesus.

As they came down from the mountain Jesus gave them this order, 'Tell no one about the vision until the Son of Man has risen from the dead.'

The Gospel of the Lord.

YEAR B

A reading from the holy Gospel according to Mark   9:2-10
This is my Son the Beloved.

Jesus took with him Peter and James and John and led them up a high mountain where they could be alone by themselves. There in their presence he was transfigured: his clothes became dazzlingly white, whiter than any earthly bleacher could make them. Elijah appeared to them with Moses; and they were talking with Jesus. Then Peter spoke to Jesus: 'Rabbi,' he said 'it is wonderful for us to be here; so let us make three tents, one for you, one for Moses and one for Elijah.' He did not know what to say; they were so frightened. And a cloud came, covering them in shadow; and there came a voice from the cloud, 'This is my Son, the Beloved. Listen to him.' Then suddenly, when they looked round, they saw no one with them any more but only Jesus.

As they came down the mountain he warned them to tell no one what they had seen, until after the Son of Man had risen from the dead. They observed the warning faithfully, though among themselves they discussed what 'rising from the dead' could mean.

The Gospel of the Lord.

YEAR C

A reading from the holy Gospel according to Luke   9:28-36

Moses and Elijah were talking about his death.

Jesus took with him Peter and John and James and went up the mountain to pray. As he prayed, the aspect of his face was changed and his clothing became brilliant as lightning. Suddenly there were two men there talking to him; they were Moses and Elijah appearing in glory, and they were speaking of his passing which he was to accomplish in Jerusalem. Peter and his companions were heavy with sleep, but they kept awake and saw his glory and the two men standing with him. As these were leaving him, Peter said to Jesus, 'Master, it is wonderful for us to be here; so let us make three tents, one for you, one for Moses and one for Elijah.' – He did not know what he was saying. As he spoke, a cloud came and covered them with shadow; and when they went into the cloud the disciples were afraid. And a voice came from the cloud, saying, 'This is my Son, the Chosen One. Listen to him.' And after the voice had spoken, Jesus was found alone. The disciples kept silence and, at that time, told no one what they had seen.

The Gospel of the Lord.

When this Feast falls on a Sunday, the Creed is said.

Prayer over the Offerings	Super oblata
Sanctify, O Lord, we pray, these offerings here made to celebrate the glorious Transfiguration of your Only Begotten Son, and by his radiant splendour cleanse us from the stains of sin. Through Christ our Lord.	Oblata munera, quæsumus, Domine, gloriosa Unigeniti tui Transfiguratione sanctifica, nosque a peccatorum maculis, splendoribus ipsius illustrationis, emunda. Per Christum Dominum nostrum.

Preface: The Mystery of
the Transfiguration.

| Praefatio: De mysterio |
| Transfigurationis. |

It is truly right and just, our duty
    and our salvation,
always and everywhere to give
    you thanks,
Lord, holy Father, almighty
    and eternal God,
through Christ our Lord.

Vere dignum et iustum est,
    æquum et salutare,
nos tibi semper et ubique
    gratias agere:
Domine, sancte Pater,
    omnipotens æterne Deus:
per Christum Dominum nostrum.

For he revealed his glory in
    the presence of chosen witnesses
and filled with the greatest
    splendour that bodily form
which he shares with all humanity,
that the scandal of the Cross
might be removed from the hearts
    of his disciples
and that he might show
how in the Body of the whole
    Church is to be fulfilled
what so wonderfully shone forth
    first in its Head.

Qui coram electis testibus suam
    gloriam revelavit,
et communem illam cum ceteris
    corporis formam
maximo splendore perfudit,

ut de cordibus discipulorum crucis
    scandalum tolleretur,
et in totius Ecclesiæ corpore
    declararet implendum
quod eius mirabiliter præfulsit
    in capite.

And so, with the Powers of heaven,
we worship you constantly
    on earth,
and before your majesty
without end we acclaim:

Et ideo cum cælorum Virtutibus
in terris te iugiter celebramus,
maiestati tuæ sine fine clamantes:

Holy, Holy, Holy Lord God of hosts...   **Sanctus, Sanctus, Sanctus. . .**

Communion Antiphon Cf. 1 Jn 3:2   Ant. ad communionem

When Christ appears, we shall
    be like him,
for we shall see him as he is.

Cum Christus apparuerit,
similes ei erimus,
quoniam videbimus eum sicuti est.

Prayer after Communion	Post communionem
May the heavenly nourishment we have received, O Lord, we pray, transform us into the likeness of your Son, whose radiant splendour you willed to make manifest in his glorious Transfiguration. Who lives and reigns for ever and ever.	Cælestia, quæsumus, Domine, alimenta quæ sumpsimus in eius nos transforment imaginem, cuius claritatem gloriosa Transfiguratione manifestare voluisti. Qui vivit et regnat in sæcula sæculorum.

15 August

THE ASSUMPTION OF THE BLESSED VIRGIN MARY

The Assumption reminds us that Mary's life, like that of every Christian, is a journey of following, following Jesus, a journey that has a very precise destination, a future already marked out: the definitive victory over sin and death and full communion with God, because as Paul says in his Letter to the Ephesians the Father "raised us up with him, and made us sit with him in the heavenly places in Christ Jesus" (Eph 2:6). This means that with Baptism we have already fundamentally been raised and are seated in the heavenly places in Christ Jesus, but we must physically attain what was previously begun and brought about in Baptism. In us, union with Christ resurrection is incomplete, but for the Virgin Mary it is complete, despite the journey that Our Lady also had to make. She has entered into the fullness of union with God, with her Son, she draws us onwards and accompanies us on our journey.

(Pope Benedict XVI)

Solemnity

At the Vigil Mass

This Mass is used on the evening of 14 August, either before or after First Vespers (Evening Prayer I) of the Solemnity.

Entrance Antiphon

GLORIOUS things are spoken
of you, O Mary,
who today were exalted above
the choirs of Angels
into eternal triumph with Christ.

Ant. ad introitum

GLORIOSA dicta sunt de te,
Maria,
quæ hodie exaltata es super
choros Angelorum,
et in æternum cum
Christo triumphas.

The Gloria in excelsis (Glory to God in the highest) is said.

Collect

O God, who, looking on the lowliness
of the Blessed Virgin Mary,
raised her to this grace,
that your Only Begotten Son was
born of her according to the flesh
and that she was crowned this day
with surpassing glory,
grant through her prayers,
that, saved by the mystery
of your redemption,
we may merit to be exalted by you
on high.
Through our Lord Jesus Christ,
your Son,
who lives and reigns with you
in the unity of the Holy Spirit,
one God, for ever and ever.

Collecta

Deus, qui beatam
Virginem Mariam,
eius humilitatem respiciens,
ad hanc gratiam evexisti,
ut Unigenitus tuus ex ipsa
secundum carnem nasceretur,
et hodierna die superexcellenti
gloria coronasti,
eius nobis precibus concede,
ut, redemptionis tuæ
mysterio salvati,
a te exaltari mereamur.
Per Dominum nostrum Iesum
Christum Filium tuum,
qui tecum vivit et regnat
in unitate Spiritus Sancti,
Deus, per omnia sæcula sæculorum.

Alternative readings may be taken from the Common of Martyrs, or from the Common of Holy Men and Women.

FIRST READING

A reading from the first book of Chronicles   15:3-4,15-16; 16:1-2

They brought in the ark of God and set it inside the tent which David had pitched for it.

David gathered all Israel together in Jerusalem to bring the ark of God up to the place he had prepared for it. David called together the sons of Aaron and the sons of Levi. And the Levites carried the ark of God with the shafts on their shoulders, as Moses had ordered in accordance with the word of the Lord.

David then told the heads of the Levites to assign duties for their kinsmen as cantors, with their various instruments of music, harps and lyres and cymbals, to play joyful tunes. They brought the ark of God in and put it inside the tent that David had pitched for it; and they offered holocausts before God, and communion sacrifices. And when David had finished offering holocausts and communion sacrifices, he blessed the people in the name of the Lord.

The word of the Lord.

Responsorial Psalm   Ps 131:6-7,9-10,13-14. R. v.8

R. **Go up, Lord, to the place of your rest,**
    you and the ark of your strength.

At Ephrata we heard of the ark;
we found it in the plains of Yearim.
'Let us go to the place of his dwelling;
let us go to kneel at his footstool.' R.

Your priests shall be clothed with holiness:
your faithful shall ring out their joy.
For the sake of David your servant
do not reject your anointed. R.

For the Lord has chosen Zion;
he has desired it for his dwelling:
'This is my resting-place for ever,
here have I chosen to live.' R.

SECOND READING

A reading from the first letter of St Paul to the Corinthians   15:54-57

He gave us victory through our Lord Jesus Christ.

When this perishable nature has put on imperishability, and when this mortal nature has put on immortality, then the words of scripture will come true: Death is swallowed up in victory. Death, where is your victory? Death, where is your sting? Now the sting of death is sin, and sin gets its power from the Law. So let us thank God for giving us the victory through our Lord Jesus Christ.

The word of the Lord.

Gospel Acclamation   Lk 11:28

R. **Alleluia, alleluia!**
Happy are those
who hear the word of God,
and keep it.
R. **Alleluia!**

GOSPEL

A reading from the holy Gospel according to Luke   11:27-28

Happy the womb that bore you!

As Jesus was speaking, a woman in the crowd raised her voice and said, 'Happy the womb that bore you and the breasts you sucked!' But he replied, 'Still happier those who hear the word of God and keep it!'

The Gospel of the Lord.

The Creed is said.

Prayer over the Offerings	Super oblata
Receive, we pray, O Lord, the sacrifice of conciliation and praise, which we celebrate on the Assumption of the holy Mother of God, that it may lead us to your pardon and confirm us in perpetual thanksgiving. Through Christ our Lord.	Suscipe, quæsumus, Domine, sacrificium placationis et laudis, quod in sanctæ Dei Genetricis Assumptione celebramus, ut ad veniam nos obtinendam perducat, et in perpetua gratiarum constituat actione. Per Christum Dominum nostrum.

Proper Preface, as in the following Mass, p.1178.

Communion Antiphon Cf. Lk 11:27	Ant. ad communionem

Blessed is the womb
    of the Virgin Mary,
which bore the Son
    of the eternal Father.
	Beata viscera Mariæ Virginis,
	quæ portaverunt æterni
	    Patris Filium.

Prayer after Communion	Post communionem

Having partaken of this
    heavenly table,
we beseech your mercy,
    Lord our God,
that we, who honour
    the Assumption of the Mother
    of God,
may be freed from every threat
    of harm.
Through Christ our Lord.
	Mensæ cælestis participes effecti,
	imploramus clementiam tuam,
	    Domine Deus noster,
	ut, qui Assumptionem Dei
	    Genetricis colimus,
	a cunctis malis
	    imminentibus liberemur.
	Per Christum Dominum nostrum.

A formula of Solemn Blessing, pp.654-655, may be used.

At the Mass during the Day

Entrance Antiphon Cf. Rv 12:1	Ant. ad introitum

A GREAT sign appeared
in heaven:
a woman clothed with the sun,
    and the moon beneath her feet,
and on her head a crown
    of twelve stars.
	SIGNUM magnum apparuit
	in cælo:
	mulier amicta sole, et luna sub
	    pedibus eius,
	et in capite eius corona
	    stellarum duodecim.

Or:	Vel:

Let us all rejoice in the Lord,
as we celebrate the feast day
    in honour of the Virgin Mary,
at whose Assumption
    the Angels rejoice
and praise the Son of God.
	Gaudeamus omnes in Domino,
	diem festum celebrantes sub
	    honore Mariæ Virginis,
	de cuius Assumptione
	    gaudent Angeli,
	et collaudant Filium Dei.

The Gloria in excelsis (Glory to God in the highest) is said.

Collect	Collecta
Almighty ever-living God,	Omnipotens sempiterne Deus,
who assumed the Immaculate Virgin Mary, the Mother of your Son,	qui immaculatam Virginem Mariam, Filii tui Genetricem,
body and soul into heavenly glory,	corpore et anima ad cælestem gloriam assumpsisti,
grant, we pray,	
that, always attentive to the things that are above,	concede, quæsumus, ut, ad superna semper intenti,
we may merit to be sharers of her glory.	ipsius gloriæ mereamur esse consortes.
Through our Lord Jesus Christ, your Son,	Per Dominum nostrum Iesum Christum Filium tuum,
who lives and reigns with you in the unity of the Holy Spirit,	qui tecum vivit et regnat in unitate Spiritus Sancti,
one God, for ever and ever.	Deus, per omnia sæcula sæculorum.

FIRST READING

A reading from the book of the Apocalypse   11:19; 12:1-6,10

A woman adorned with the sun standing on the moon.

The sanctuary of God in heaven opened, and the ark of the covenant could be seen inside it.

Now a great sign appeared in heaven: a woman, adorned with the sun, standing on the moon, and with the twelve stars on her head for a crown. She was pregnant, and in labour, crying aloud in the pangs of childbirth. Then a second sign appeared in the sky, a huge red dragon which had seven heads and ten horns, and each of the seven heads crowned with a coronet. Its tail dragged a third of the stars from the sky and dropped them to the earth, and the dragon stopped in front of the woman as she was having the child, so that he could eat it as soon as it was born from its mother. The woman brought a male child into the world, the son who was to rule all nations with an iron sceptre, and the child was taken straight up to God and to his throne, while the woman escaped into the desert, where God had made a place of safety ready. Then I heard a voice shout from heaven, 'Victory and power and empire for ever have been won by our God, and all authority for his Christ.'

The word of the Lord.

Responsorial Psalm   Ps 44:10-12,16. R. v.10

R. **On your right stands the queen,**
    in garments of gold.

The daughters of kings are among your loved ones.
On your right stands the queen in gold of Ophir.
Listen, O daughter, give ear to my words:
forget your own people and your father's house. R.

So will the king desire your beauty:
He is your lord, pay homage to him.
They are escorted amid gladness and joy;
they pass within the palace of the king. R.

SECOND READING

A reading from the first letter of St Paul to the Corinthians   15:20-26
Christ as the first-fruits and then, those who belong to him.

Christ has been raised from the dead, the first-fruits of all who have fallen asleep. Death came through one man and in the same way the resurrection of the dead has come through one man. Just as all men die in Adam, so all men will be brought to life in Christ; but all of them in their proper order: Christ as the first-fruits and then, after the coming of Christ, those who belong to him. After that will come the end, when he hands over the kingdom to God the Father, having done away with every sovereignty, authority and power. For he must be king until he has put all his enemies under his feet and the last of the enemies to be destroyed is death, for everything is to be put under his feet.

The word of the Lord.

Gospel Acclamation

R. **Alleluia, alleluia!**
Mary has been taken up into heaven;
all the choirs of angels are rejoicing.
R. **Alleluia!**

GOSPEL

A reading from the holy Gospel according to Luke   1:39-56
The Almighty has done great things for me, he has exalted up the lowly.

Mary set out and went as quickly as she could to a town in the hill country of Judah. She went into Zechariah's house and greeted Elizabeth. Now as soon as Elizabeth heard Mary's greeting, the child leapt in her womb and Elizabeth was filled with the Holy Spirit. She gave a loud cry and said, 'Of all women you are the most blessed, and blessed is the fruit of your womb. Why should I be honoured with a visit from the mother of my Lord? For the moment your greeting reached my ears, the child in my womb leapt for joy. Yes, blessed is she who believed that the promise made her by the Lord would be fulfilled.'

And Mary said:

> 'My soul proclaims the greatness of the Lord
> and my spirit exults in God my saviour;
> because he has looked upon his lowly handmaid.
> Yes, from this day forward all generations will call me blessed,
> for the Almighty has done great things for me.
> Holy is his name,
> and his mercy reaches from age to age for those who fear him.
> He has shown the power of his arm,
> he has routed the proud of heart.
> He has pulled down princes from their thrones and exalted the lowly.
> The hungry he has filled with good things, the rich sent empty away.
> He has come to the help of Israel his servant, mindful of his mercy
> – according to the promise he made to our ancestors –
> of his mercy to Abraham and to his descendants for ever.'

Mary stayed with Elizabeth about three months and then went back home.

The Gospel of the Lord.

The Creed is said.

Prayer over the Offerings
May this oblation, our tribute
    of homage,
rise up to you, O Lord,
and, through the intercession
    of the most Blessed Virgin Mary,
whom you assumed into heaven,
may our hearts,
    aflame with the fire of love,
constantly long for you.
Through Christ our Lord.

Super oblata
Ascendat ad te, Domine, nostræ
    devotionis oblatio,
et, beatissima Virgine Maria
in cælum assumpta intercedente,
corda nostra, caritatis igne succensa,
ad te iugiter aspirent.
Per Christum Dominum nostrum.

Preface: The Glory of Mary assumed into heaven.

Præfatio: De Gloria Mariæ Assumptæ.

It is truly right and just, our duty
and our salvation,
always and everywhere to give
you thanks,
Lord, holy Father, almighty
and eternal God,
through Christ our Lord.

*Vere dignum et iustum est,
æquum et salutare,
nos tibi semper et ubique
gratias agere:
Domine, sancte Pater,
omnipotens æterne Deus:
per Christum Dominum nostrum.*

For today the Virgin Mother of God
was assumed into heaven
as the beginning and image
of your Church's coming
to perfection
and a sign of sure hope and comfort
to your pilgrim people;
rightly you would not allow her
to see the corruption of the tomb,
since from her own body she
marvellously brought forth
your incarnate Son,
the Author of all life.

*Quoniam hodie Virgo Deipara
in cælos assumpta est,
Ecclesiæ tuæ consummandæ
initium et imago,
ac populo peregrinanti certæ spei
et solacii documentum;
corruptionem enim sepulcri
eam videre merito noluisti,
quæ Filium tuum,
vitæ omnis auctorem,
ineffabiliter de se
genuit incarnatum.*

And so, in company with the choirs
of Angels,
we praise you, and with joy
we proclaim:

*Et ideo, choris angelicis sociati,
te laudamus, in gaudio confitentes:*

Holy, Holy, Holy Lord God of hosts...

Sanctus, Sanctus, Sanctus. . .

Communion Antiphon Lk 1:48-49

Ant. ad communionem

All generations will call me blessed,
for he who is mighty has done
great things for me.

*Beatam me dicent
omnes generationes,
quia fecit mihi magna
qui potens est.*

Prayer after Communion	Post communionem

Having received the Sacrament
of salvation,
we ask you to grant, O Lord,
that, through the intercession
of the Blessed Virgin Mary,
whom you assumed into heaven,
we may be brought to the glory
of the resurrection.
Through Christ our Lord.

Sumptis, Domine,
salutaribus sacramentis,
da, quæsumus,
ut, intercessione beatæ Mariæ
Virginis in cælum assumptæ,
ad resurrectionis
gloriam perducamur.
Per Christum Dominum nostrum.

A formula of Solemn Blessing, p.654-655, may be used.

14 September

THE EXALTATION OF THE HOLY CROSS

"What a great thing it is to possess the Cross! He who possesses it possesses a treasure" (Saint Andrew of Crete). On this day, the Gospel reminds us of the meaning of this great mystery: God so loved the world that he gave his only Son, so that men might be saved. The Son of God became vulnerable, assuming the condition of a slave, obedient even to death, death on a cross. By his Cross we are saved. The instrument of torture which, on Good Friday, manifested God's judgement on the world, has become a source of life, pardon, mercy, a sign of reconciliation and peace. By raising our eyes towards the Crucified one, we adore him who came to take upon himself the sin of the world and to give us eternal life. And the Church invites us proudly to lift up this glorious Cross so that the world can see the full extent of the love of the Crucified one for mankind, for every man and woman. She invites us to give thanks to God because from a tree which brought death, life has burst out anew. In our midst is he who loved us even to giving his life for us, he who invites every human being to draw near to him with trust.

(Pope Benedict XVI)

Feast

Entrance Antiphon Cf. Ga 6:14	Ant. ad introitum
We should glory in the Cross of our Lord Jesus Christ,	Nos autem gloriari oportet in cruce Domini nostri Iesu Christi,
in whom is our salvation, life and resurrection,	in quo est salus, vita et resurrectio nostra,
through whom we are saved and delivered.	per quem salvati et liberati sumus.

The Gloria in excelsis (Glory to God in the highest) is said.

Collect	Collecta
O God, who willed that your Only Begotten Son	Deus, qui Unigenitum tuum crucem subire voluisti,
should undergo the Cross to save the human race,	ut salvum faceret genus humanum,
grant, we pray,	præsta, quæsumus,
that we, who have known his mystery on earth,	ut, cuius mysterium in terra cognovimus,
may merit the grace of his redemption in heaven.	eius redemptionis præmia in cælo consequi mereamur.
Through our Lord Jesus Christ, your Son,	Per Dominum nostrum Iesum Christum Filium tuum,
who lives and reigns with you in the unity of the Holy Spirit,	qui tecum vivit et regnat in unitate Spiritus Sancti,
one God, for ever and ever.	Deus, per omnia sæcula sæculorum.

When this Feast does not fall on a Sunday there may only be one reading before the Gospel.

FIRST READING

A reading from the book of Numbers   21:4-9

If anyone was bitten by a serpent, he looked at the bronze serpent and lived.

On the way through the wilderness, the Israelites lost patience. They spoke against God and against Moses, 'Why did you bring us out of Egypt to die in this wilderness? For there is neither bread nor water here: we are sick of this unsatisfying food.'

    At this God sent fiery serpents among the people; their bite brought death to many in Israel. The people came and said to Moses, 'We have sinned by speaking against the Lord and against you. Intercede for us with the Lord to save us from these serpents.' Moses interceded for the people, and the Lord answered him, 'Make a fiery serpent and put it on a standard. If anyone is bitten and looks at it, he shall live.' So Moses fashioned a bronze serpent which he put on a standard, and if anyone was bitten by a serpent, he looked at the bronze serpent and lived.

The word of the Lord.

Responsorial Psalm   Ps 77:1-2,34-38. R. v.7

R. **Never forget the deeds of the Lord.**

Give heed, my people, to my teaching;
turn your ear to the words of my mouth.
I will open my mouth in a parable
and reveal hidden lessons of the past. R.

When he slew them then they would seek him,
return and seek him in earnest.
They would remember that God was their rock,
God the Most High their redeemer. R.

But the words they spoke were mere flattery;
they lied to him with their lips.
For their hearts were not truly with him;
they were not faithful to his covenant. R.

Yet he who is full of compassion
forgave their sin and spared them.
So often he held back his anger
when he might have stirred up his rage. R.

SECOND READING

A reading from the letter of St Paul to the Philippians   2:6-11
He humbled himself, therefore God raised him high.

The state of Jesus Christ was divine,
yet he did not cling
to his equality with God
but emptied himself
to assume the condition of a slave,
and became as men are;
and being as all men are,
he was humbler yet,
even to accepting death,

death on a cross.
But God raised him high
and gave him the name
which is above all other names
so that all beings
in the heavens, on earth and in the underworld,
should bend the knee at the name of Jesus
and that every tongue should acclaim
Jesus Christ as Lord,
to the glory of God the Father.

   The word of the Lord.

Gospel Acclamation

R. **Alleluia, alleluia!**
We adore you, O Christ,
and we bless you;
because by your cross
you have redeemed the world.
R. **Alleluia!**

GOSPEL

A reading from the holy Gospel according to John   3:13-17
The Son of Man must be lifted up.

Jesus said to Nicodemus:

   'No one has gone up to heaven
   except the one who came down from heaven,
   the Son of Man who is in heaven;
   and the Son of Man must be lifted up
   as Moses lifted up the serpent in the desert,
   so that everyone who believes may have eternal life in him.
   Yes, God loved the world so much
   that he gave his only Son,
   so that everyone who believes in him may not be lost
   but may have eternal life.
   For God sent his Son into the world
   not to condemn the world,
   but so that through him the world might be saved.'

   The Gospel of the Lord.

When this Feast falls on a Sunday, the Creed is said.

Prayer over the Offerings

May this oblation, O Lord,
which on the altar of the Cross
cancelled the offence
   of the whole world,
cleanse us, we pray, of all our sins.
Through Christ our Lord.

Super oblata

Hæc oblatio, Domine, quæsumus,
ab omnibus nos purget offensis,
quæ in ara crucis totius mundi
   tulit offensam.
Per Christum Dominum nostrum.

Preface: The victory of the glorious Cross.

It is truly right and just, our duty
   and our salvation,
always and everywhere to give
   you thanks,
Lord, holy Father, almighty
   and eternal God.

For you placed the salvation
   of the human race
on the wood of the Cross,
so that, where death arose,
life might again spring forth
and the evil one,
   who conquered on a tree,
might likewise on a tree
   be conquered,
through Christ our Lord.

Through him the Angels praise
   your majesty,
Dominions adore and Powers
   tremble before you.
Heaven and the Virtues of heaven
   and the blessed Seraphim
worship together with exultation.
May our voices, we pray,
   join with theirs
in humble praise, as we acclaim:

Holy, Holy, Holy Lord God of hosts...

Præfatio: De victoria crucis gloriosæ.

Vere dignum et iustum est,
   æquum et salutare,
nos tibi semper et ubique
   gratias agere:
Domine, sancte Pater, omnipotens
   æterne Deus:

Qui salutem humani generis
   in ligno crucis constituisti,
ut unde mors oriebatur,
   inde vita resurgeret;
et, qui in ligno vincebat, in ligno
   quoque vinceretur:
per Christum Dominum nostrum.

Per quem maiestatem tuam
   laudant Angeli,
adorant Dominationes,
   tremunt Potestates.
Cæli cælorumque Virtutes,
   ac beata Seraphim,
socia exsultatione concelebrant.

Cum quibus et nostras voces ut
   admitti iubeas, deprecamur,
supplici confessione dicentes:

Sanctus, Sanctus, Sanctus. . .

Preface I of the Passion of the Lord, pp.558-559, may also be used.

Communion Antiphon Jn 12:32	Ant. ad communionem
When I am lifted up from the earth, I will draw everyone to myself, says the Lord.	Ego si exaltatus fuero a terra, omnes traham ad meipsum, dicit Dominus.

Prayer after Communion	Post communionem
Having been nourished by your holy banquet, we beseech you, Lord Jesus Christ, to bring those you have redeemed by the wood of your life-giving Cross to the glory of the resurrection. Who live and reign for ever and ever.	Refectione tua sancta enutriti, Domine Iesu Christe, supplices deprecamur, ut, quos per lignum crucis vivificæ redemisti, ad resurrectionis gloriam perducas. Qui vivis et regnas in sæcula sæculorum.

1 November

ALL SAINTS

The Solemnity of All Saints, which we celebrate today, invites us to raise our gaze to Heaven and to meditate on the fullness of the divine life which awaits us. "We are God's children now; it does not yet appear what we shall be" (1 Jn 3:2): with these words the Apostle John assures us of the reality of our profound relation to God, as too, of the certainty of our destiny. Like beloved children, therefore, we also receive the grace to support the trials of this earthly existence – the hunger and the thirst for justice, the misunderstandings, the persecutions (Cf. Mt 5:3-11) – and, at the same time, we inherit what is promised in the Gospel Beatitudes. The holiness, imprinted in us by Christ himself, is the goal of Christian life. And we have a foretaste of the gift and the beauty of sanctity every time that we participate in the Eucharistic Liturgy, the communion with the "great multitude" of holy souls, which in Heaven eternally acclaim the salvation of God and of the Lamb (Cf. Rv 7:9-10).

(Pope Benedict XVI)

Solemnity

Entrance Antiphon	Ant. ad introitum
LET us all rejoice in the Lord, as we celebrate the feast day in honour of all the Saints, at whose festival the Angels rejoice and praise the Son of God.	GAUDEAMUS omnes in Domino, diem festum celebrantes sub honore Sanctorum omnium, de quorum sollemnitate gaudent Angeli, et collaudant Filium Dei.

The Gloria in excelsis (Glory to God in the highest) is said.

Collect	Collecta
Almighty ever-living God, by whose gift we venerate in one celebration the merits of all the Saints, bestow on us, we pray, through the prayers of so many intercessors, an abundance of the reconciliation with you for which we earnestly long. Through our Lord Jesus Christ, your Son, who lives and reigns with you in the unity of the Holy Spirit, one God, for ever and ever.	Omnipotens sempiterne Deus, qui nos omnium Sanctorum tuorum merita sub una tribuisti celebritate venerari, quæsumus, ut desideratam nobis tuæ propitiationis abundantiam, multiplicatis intercessoribus, largiaris. Per Dominum nostrum Iesum Christum Filium tuum, qui tecum vivit et regnat in unitate Spiritus Sancti, Deus, per omnia sæcula sæculorum.

FIRST READING

A reading from the book of the Apocalypse   7:2-4,9-14

I saw a huge number, impossible to count, of people from every nation, race, tribe and language.

I, John, saw another angel rising where the sun rises, carrying the seal of the living God; he called in a powerful voice to the four angels whose duty was to devastate land and sea, 'Wait before you do any damage on land or at sea or to the trees, until we have put the seal on the foreheads of the servants of our God.' Then I heard how many were sealed: a hundred and forty-four thousand, out of all the tribes of Israel.

After that I saw a huge number, impossible to count, of people from every nation, race, tribe and language; they were standing in front of the throne and in front of the Lamb, dressed in white robes and holding palms in their hands. They shouted aloud, 'Victory to our God, who sits on the throne, and to the Lamb!' And all the angels who were standing in a circle round the throne, surrounding the elders and the four animals, prostrated themselves before the throne, and touched the ground with their foreheads, worshipping God with these words: 'Amen. Praise and glory and wisdom and thanksgiving and honour and power and strength to our God for ever and ever. Amen.'

One of the elders then spoke, and asked me, 'Do you know who these people are, dressed in white robes, and where they have come from?' I answered him, 'You can tell me, my Lord.' Then he said, 'These are the people who have been through the great persecution, and they have washed their robes white again in the blood of the Lamb.'

The word of the Lord.

Responsorial Psalm   Ps 23:1-6. R. Cf. v.6

R. **Such are the men who seek your face, O Lord.**

The Lord's is the earth and its fullness,
the world and all its peoples.
It is he who set it on the seas;
on the waters he made it firm. R.

Who shall climb the mountain of the Lord?
Who shall stand in his holy place?
The man with clean hands and pure heart,
who desires not worthless things. R.

He shall receive blessings from the Lord
and reward from the God who saves him.
Such are the men who seek him,
seek the face of the God of Jacob. R.

SECOND READING

A reading from the first letter of St John   3:1-3
We shall see God as he really is.

Think of the love that the Father has lavished on us,
by letting us be called God's children;
and that is what we are.

Because the world refused to acknowledge him,
therefore it does not acknowledge us.
My dear people, we are already the children of God
but what we are to be in the future has not yet been revealed,
all we know is, that when it is revealed
we shall be like him
because we shall see him as he really is.
Surely everyone who entertains this hope
must purify himself, must try to be as pure as Christ.

The word of the Lord.

Gospel Acclamation   Mt 11:28

R. **Alleluia, alleluia!**
Come to me, all of you who labour
    and are overburdened,
and I will give you rest, says the Lord.
R. **Alleluia!**

GOSPEL

A reading from the holy Gospel according to Matthew   5:1-12
Rejoice and be glad, for your reward will be great in heaven.

Seeing the crowds, Jesus went up the hill. There he sat down and was joined
by his disciples. Then he began to speak. This is what he taught them:

    'How happy are the poor in spirit;
    theirs is the kingdom of heaven.
    Happy the gentle:
    they shall have the earth for their heritage.
    Happy those who mourn:
    they shall be comforted.
    Happy those who hunger and thirst for what is right:
    they shall be satisfied.
    Happy the merciful:
    they shall have mercy shown them.
    Happy the pure in heart:
    they shall see God.
    Happy the peacemakers:
    they shall be called sons of God.
    Happy those who are persecuted in the cause of right:
    theirs is the kingdom of heaven.

'Happy are you when people abuse you and persecute you and speak all kinds of calumny against you on my account. Rejoice and be glad, for your reward will be great in heaven.'

The Gospel of the Lord.

The Creed is said.

Prayer over the Offerings

May these offerings we bring
  in honour of all the Saints
be pleasing to you, O Lord,
and grant that, just as we believe
  the Saints
to be already assured of immortality,
so we may experience their concern
  for our salvation.
Through Christ our Lord.

Preface: The glory of Jerusalem, our mother.

It is truly right and just,
  our duty and our salvation,
always and everywhere
  to give you thanks,
Lord, holy Father,
  almighty and eternal God.

For today by your gift we celebrate
  the festival of your city,
the heavenly Jerusalem,
  our mother,
where the great array
  of our brothers and sisters
already gives you eternal praise.

Towards her, we eagerly hasten
  as pilgrims advancing by faith,
rejoicing in the glory bestowed
  upon those exalted members
  of the Church

Super oblata

Grata tibi sint, Domine, munera,
quæ pro cunctorum offerimus
  honore Sanctorum,
et concede,
ut, quos iam credimus de sua
  immortalitate securos,
sentiamus de nostra salute
  sollicitos.
Per Christum Dominum nostrum.

Præfatio: De gloria matris nostræ Ierusalem

Vere dignum et iustum est,
  æquum et salutare,
nos tibi semper et ubique
  gratias agere:
Domine, sancte Pater,
  omnipotens æterne Deus:

Nobis enim hodie civitatem tuam
  tribuis celebrare,
quæ mater nostra est,
  cælestique Ierusalem,
ubi iam te in æternum fratrum
  nostrorum corona collaudat.

Ad quam peregrini,
  per fidem accedentes,
alacriter festinamus,
  congaudentes de Ecclesiæ
sublimium glorificatione
  membrorum,

through whom you give us,
in our frailty, both strength
and good example.

And so, we glorify you with the
multitude of Saints and Angels,
as with one voice of praise
we acclaim:

Holy, Holy, Holy Lord God of hosts...

qua simul fragilitati nostræ
adiumenta et exempla concedis.

Et ideo, cum ipsorum
Angelorumque frequentia,
una te magnificamus,
laudis voce clamantes:

Sanctus, Sanctus, Sanctus. . .

Communion Antiphon Mt 5:8-10

Blessed are the clean of heart,
for they shall see God.
Blessed are the peacemakers,
for they shall be called
children of God.
Blessed are they who are persecuted
for the sake of righteousness,
for theirs is the Kingdom of Heaven.

Ant. ad communionem

Beati mundo corde, quoniam ipsi
Deum videbunt;
beati pacifici, quoniam filii
Dei vocabuntur;
beati qui persecutionem patiuntur
propter iustitiam,
quoniam ipsorum
est regnum cælorum.

Prayer after Communion

As we adore you, O God, who alone
are holy
and wonderful in all your Saints,
we implore your grace,
so that, coming to perfect holiness
in the fullness of your love,
we may pass from this pilgrim table
to the banquet
of our heavenly homeland.
Through Christ our Lord.

Post communionem

Mirabilem te, Deus,
et unum Sanctum in omnibus
Sanctis tuis adorantes,
tuam gratiam imploramus,
qua, sanctificationem
in tui amoris plenitudine
consummantes,
ex hac mensa peregrinantium
ad cælestis patriæ convivium
transeamus.
Per Christum Dominum nostrum.

A formula of Solemn Blessing, pp.656-659, may be used.

2 November

THE COMMEMORATION
OF ALL THE FAITHFUL DEPARTED
(ALL SOULS' DAY)

Today we renew the hope in eternal life, truly founded on Christ's death and Resurrection. "I am risen and I am with you always", the Lord tells us, and my hand supports you. Wherever you may fall, you will fall into my hands and I will be there even to the gates of death. Where no one can accompany you any longer and where you can take nothing with you, there I will wait for you to transform for you the darkness into light. Christian hope, however, is not solely individual, it is also always a hope for others. Our lives are profoundly linked, one to the other, and the good and the bad that each of us does always affects others too. Hence, the prayer of a pilgrim soul in the world can help another soul that is being purified after death. This is why the Church invites us today to pray for our beloved deceased and to pause at their tombs in the cemeteries.

(Pope Benedict XVI)

The Masses that follow may be used at the discretion of the celebrant.

Even when 2 November falls on a Sunday, the Mass celebrated is that of the Commemoration of All the Faithful Departed. (In England & Wales, when 2 November is a Sunday the Solemnity of All Saints is celebrated).

1

Entrance Antiphon Cf. 1 Th 4:14; 1 Co 15:22	Ant. ad introitum
Just as Jesus died and has risen again, so through Jesus God will bring with him those who have fallen asleep; and as in Adam all die, so also in Christ will all be brought to life.	Sicut Iesus mortuus est et resurrexit, ita et Deus eos qui dormierunt per Iesum adducet cum eo. Et sicut in Adam omnes moriuntur, ita et in Christo omnes vivificabuntur.
Collect	Collecta
Listen kindly to our prayers, O Lord, and, as our faith in your Son, raised from the dead, is deepened,	Preces nostras, quæsumus, Domine, benignus exaudi, ut, dum attollitur nostra fides

so may our hope of resurrection
for your departed servants
also find new strength.
Through our Lord Jesus Christ,
your Son,
who lives and reigns with you
in the unity of the Holy Spirit,
one God, for ever and ever.

in Filio tuo a mortuis suscitato,
in famulorum tuorum
præstolanda resurrectione
spes quoque nostra firmetur.
Per Dominum nostrum Iesum
Christum Filium tuum,
qui tecum vivit et regnat
in unitate Spiritus Sancti,
Deus, per omnia sæcula sæculorum.

Prayer over the Offerings

Look favourably on our offerings,
O Lord,
so that your departed servants
may be taken up into glory
with your Son,
in whose great mystery of love
we are all united.
Who lives and reigns
for ever and ever.

Preface for the Dead, pp.584-589.

Super oblata

Nostris, Domine,
propitiare muneribus,
ut famuli tui defuncti assumantur
in gloriam cum Filio tuo,
cuius magno pietatis
iungimur sacramento.
Qui vivit et regnat
in sæcula sæculorum.

Communion Antiphon Cf. Jn 11:25-26

I am the Resurrection and the Life,
says the Lord.
Whoever believes in me, even
though he dies, will live,
and everyone who lives and believes
in me will not die for ever.

Ant. ad communionem

Ego sum resurrectio et vita, dicit
Dominus.
Qui credit in me, etiam si mortuus
fuerit, vivet;
et omnis, qui vivit et credit in me,
non morietur in æternum.

Prayer after Communion

Grant we pray, O Lord, that your
departed servants,
for whom we have celebrated this
paschal Sacrament,
may pass over to a dwelling place of
light and peace.
Through Christ our Lord.

Post communionem

Præsta, quæsumus, Domine,
ut famuli tui defuncti
in mansionem lucis transeant
et pacis,
pro quibus paschale celebravimus
sacramentum.
Per Christum Dominum nostrum.

A formula of Solemn Blessing, pp.658-661, may be used.

2

Entrance Antiphon Cf. 4 Esdr 2:34-35

Eternal rest grant unto them, O Lord,
and let perpetual light shine
    upon them.

Ant. ad introitum

Requiem æternam dona eis, Domine,
et lux perpetua luceat eis.

Collect

O God, glory of the faithful and
    life of the just,
by the Death and Resurrection
    of whose Son
we have been redeemed,
look mercifully on your departed
    servants,
that, just as they professed the
    mystery of our resurrection,
so they may merit to receive the
    joys of eternal happiness.
Through our Lord Jesus Christ,
    your Son,
who lives and reigns with you
    in the unity of the Holy Spirit,
one God, for ever and ever.

Collecta

Deus, gloria fidelium
    et vita iustorum,
cuius Filii morte et resurrectione
    redempti sumus,
propitiare famulis tuis defunctis,
ut, qui resurrectionis nostræ
    mysterium agnoverunt,
æternæ beatitudinis gaudia
    percipere mereantur.
Per Dominum nostrum Iesum
    Christum Filium tuum,
qui tecum vivit et regnat
    in unitate Spiritus Sancti,
Deus, per omnia sæcula sæculorum.

Prayer over the Offerings

Almighty and merciful God,
by means of these
    sacrificial offerings
wash away, we pray,
    in the Blood of Christ,
the sins of your departed servants,
for you purify unceasingly by your
    merciful forgiveness
those you once cleansed in the
    waters of Baptism.
Through Christ our Lord.

Preface for the Dead, pp.584-589.

Super oblata

Omnipotens et misericors Deus,
his sacrificiis ablue, quæsumus,
    famulos tuos defunctos
a peccatis eorum
    in sanguine Christi,
ut, quos mundasti
    aqua baptismatis,
indesinenter purifices
    indulgentia pietatis.
Per Christum Dominum nostrum.

Communion Antiphon Cf. 4 Esdr 2:35,34

Let perpetual light shine upon
   them, O Lord,
with your Saints for ever,
   for you are merciful.

Ant. ad communionem

Lux æterna luceat eis, Domine,
cum Sanctis tuis in æternum,
   quia pius es.

Prayer after Communion

Having received the Sacrament of
   your Only Begotten Son,
who was sacrificed for us
   and rose in glory,
we humbly implore you, O Lord,
for your departed servants,
that, cleansed by
   the paschal mysteries,
they may glory in the gift of the
   resurrection to come.
Through Christ our Lord.

Post communionem

Sumpto sacramento Unigeniti tui,
qui pro nobis immolatus
   resurrexit in gloria,
te, Domine, suppliciter exoramus
   pro famulis tuis defunctis,
ut, paschalibus mysteriis mundati,
futuræ resurrectionis
   munere glorientur.
Per Christum Dominum nostrum.

A formula of Solemn Blessing, pp.658-661, may be used.

3

Entrance Antiphon   Cf. Rm 8:11

God, who raised Jesus from the dead,
will give life also to your
   mortal bodies,
through his Spirit that dwells in you.

Ant. ad introitum

Deus, qui suscitavit Iesum a mortuis,
vivificabit et mortalia
   corpora nostra,
propter inhabitantem Spiritum
   eius in nobis.

Collect

O God, who willed that your Only
   Begotten Son,
having conquered death,
should pass over into the realm
   of heaven,
grant, we pray,
   to your departed servants
that, with the mortality
   of this life overcome,
they may gaze eternally on you,
their Creator and Redeemer.

Collecta

Deus, qui Unigenitum tuum,
   devicta morte,
ad cælestia transire fecisti,
concede famulis tuis defunctis,
ut, huius vitæ mortalitate devicta,
te conditorem et redemptorem
possint perpetuo contemplari.

Through our Lord Jesus Christ,
    your Son,
who lives and reigns with you in
    the unity of the Holy Spirit,
one God, for ever and ever.

Per Dominum nostrum Iesum
    Christum Filium tuum,
qui tecum vivit et regnat
    in unitate Spiritus Sancti,
Deus, per omnia sæcula sæculorum.

Prayer over the Offerings

Super oblata

Receive, Lord, in your kindness,
the sacrificial offering we make
for all your servants who sleep
    in Christ,
that, set free from the bonds
    of death
by this singular sacrifice,
they may merit eternal life.
Through Christ our Lord.

Pro omnibus famulis tuis in Christo
    dormientibus
hostiam, Domine, suscipe
    benignus oblatam,
ut, per hoc sacrificium singulare
    vinculis mortis exuti,
vitam mereantur æternam.
Per Christum Dominum nostrum.

Preface for the Dead, pp.584-589.

Communion Antiphon Cf. Ph 3:20-21

Ant. ad communionem

We await a saviour,
    the Lord Jesus Christ,
who will change our mortal bodies,
to conform with his glorified body.

Salvatorem exspectamus
    Dominum Iesum Christum,
qui reformabit corpus
    humilitatis nostræ,
configuratum corpori claritatis suæ.

Prayer after Communion

Post communionem

Through these sacrificial gifts
which we have received, O Lord,
bestow on your departed servants
    your great mercy
and, to those you have endowed
    with the grace of Baptism,
grant also the fullness of
    eternal joy.
Through Christ our Lord.

Multiplica, Domine,
    his sacrificiis susceptis,
super famulos tuos defunctos
    misericordiam tuam,
et, quibus donasti
    baptismi gratiam,
da eis æternorum
    plenitudinem gaudiorum.
Per Christum Dominum nostrum.

A formula of Solemn Blessing, pp.658-661, may be used.

FIRST READING

A reading from the prophet Isaiah   25:6-9

The Lord will destroy Death for ever.

On this mountain,
the Lord of hosts will prepare for all peoples
a banquet of rich food.
On this mountain he will remove
the mourning veil covering all peoples,
and the shroud enwrapping all nations,
he will destroy Death for ever.
The Lord will wipe away
the tears from every cheek;
he will take away his people's shame
everywhere on earth,
for the Lord has said so.
That day, it will be said: See, this is our God
in whom we hoped for salvation;
the Lord is the one in whom we hoped.
We exult and we rejoice
that he has saved us.

   The word of the Lord.

Responsorial Psalm   Ps 26:1,4,7-9,13-14. R. v.1. Alt. R. v.13

R. **The Lord is my light and my help.**

   Or: **I am sure I shall see the Lord's goodness
   in the land of the living.**

   The Lord is my light and my help;
   whom shall I fear?
   The Lord is the stronghold of my life;
   before whom shall I shrink? R.

   There is one thing I ask of the Lord,
   for this I long,
   to live in the house of the Lord,
   all the days of my life,
   to savour the sweetness of the Lord,
   to behold his temple. R.

   O Lord, hear my voice when I call;
   have mercy and answer.
   It is your face, O Lord, that I seek;
   hide not your face. R.

I am sure I shall see the Lord's goodness
in the land of the living.
Hope in him, hold firm and take heart.
Hope in the Lord! R.

R. **The Lord is my light and my help.**

Or: **I am sure I shall see the Lord's goodness
in the land of the living.**

SECOND READING

A reading from the letter of St Paul to the Romans   5:5-11

Having died to make us righteous, is it likely that he would now fail to save us from God's anger?

Hope is not deceptive, because the love of God has been poured into our hearts by the Holy Spirit which has been given us. We were still helpless when at his appointed moment Christ died for sinful men. It is not easy to die even for a good man – though of course for someone really worthy, a man might be prepared to die – but what proves that God loves us is that Christ died for us while we were still sinners. Having died to make us righteous, is it likely that he would now fail to save us from God's anger? When we were reconciled to God by the death of his Son, we were still enemies; now that we have been reconciled, surely we may count on being saved by the life of his Son? Not merely because we have been reconciled but because we are filled with joyful trust in God, through our Lord Jesus Christ, through whom we have already gained our reconciliation.

The word of the Lord.

Gospel Acclamation   Jn 6:39

R. **Alleluia, alleluia!**
It is my Father's will, says the Lord,
that I should lose nothing
of all that he has given to me,
and that I should raise it up on the last day.
R. **Alleluia!**

GOSPEL

YEAR A

A reading from the holy Gospel according to Matthew   11:25-30

You have hidden these things from the learned and have revealed them to mere children.

Jesus exclaimed, 'I bless you, Father, Lord of heaven and of earth, for hiding these things from the learned and the clever and revealing them to mere children. Yes, Father, for that is what it pleased you to do. Everything has been entrusted to me by my Father; and no one knows the Son except the Father, just as no one knows the Father except the Son and those to whom the Son chooses to reveal him.

'Come to me, all you who labour and are over burdened, and I will give you rest. Shoulder my yoke and learn from me, for I am gentle and humble in heart, and you will find rest for your souls. Yes, my yoke is easy and my burden light.'

The Gospel of the Lord.

YEAR B

A reading from the holy Gospel according to Mark   15:33-39; 16:1-6

Jesus gave a loud cry and breathed his last.

When the sixth hour came there was darkness over the whole land until the ninth hour. And at the ninth hour Jesus cried out in a loud voice, 'Eloi, Eloi, lama sabachthani?' which means, 'My God, my God, why have you deserted me?' When some of those who stood by heard this, they said, 'Listen, he is calling on Elijah'. Someone ran and soaked a sponge in vinegar and, putting it on a reed, gave it to him to drink saying, 'Wait and see if Elijah will come to take him down'. But Jesus gave a loud cry and breathed his last. And the veil of the Temple was torn in two from top to bottom. The centurion, who was standing in front of him, had seen how he had died, and he said, 'In truth this man was a son of God'.

When the sabbath was over, Mary of Magdala, Mary the mother of James, and Salome, bought spices with which to go and anoint him. And very early in the morning on the first day of the week they went to the tomb, just as the sun was rising.

They had been saying to one another, 'Who will roll away the stone for us from the entrance to the tomb?' But when they looked they could see that the stone – which was very big – had already been rolled back. On entering the tomb they saw a young man in a white robe seated on the right-hand side, and they were struck with amazement. But he said to them, 'There is no need for alarm. You are looking for Jesus of Nazareth, who was crucified: he has risen, he is not here. See, here is the place where they laid him.'

The Gospel of the Lord.

YEAR C

A reading from the holy Gospel according to Luke   7:11-17
Young man, I tell you to get up.

Jesus went to a town called Nain, accompanied by his disciples and a great
number of people. When he was near the gate of the town it happened that
a dead man was being carried out for burial, the only son of his mother,
and she was a widow. And a considerable number of the townspeople were
with her. When the Lord saw her he felt sorry for her. 'Do not cry,' he said.
Then he went up and put his hand on the bier and the bearers stood still,
and he said, 'Young man, I tell you to get up'. And the dead man sat up and
began to talk, and Jesus gave him to his mother. Everyone was filled with
awe and praised God saying, 'A great prophet has appeared among us; God
has visited his people'. And this opinion of him spread throughout Judaea
and all over the countryside.

   The Gospel of the Lord.

9 November

THE DEDICATION OF THE LATERAN BASILICA

Feast

In the basilica itself, the Mass of the Common of the Dedication of a Church is
used, pp.1212ff.

Entrance Antiphon Cf. Rv 21:2	Ant. ad introitum
I saw the holy city, a new Jerusalem, coming down out of heaven from God, prepared like a bride adorned for her husband.	Vidi civitatem sanctam, Ierusalem novam, descendentem de cælo a Deo, paratam sicut sponsam ornatam viro suo.
Or: Cf. Rv 21:3	Vel:
Behold God's dwelling with the human race. He will dwell with them and they will be his people, and God himself with them will be their God.	Ecce tabernaculum Dei cum hominibus! Et habitabit cum eis, et ipsi populus eius erunt, et ipse Deus cum eis erit eorum Deus.

The Gloria in excelsis (Glory to God in the highest) is said.

Collect

O God, who from living and
   chosen stones
prepare an eternal dwelling
   for your majesty,
increase in your Church the spirit
   of grace you have bestowed,
so that by new growth your
   faithful people
may build up the
   heavenly Jerusalem.
Through our Lord Jesus Christ,
   your Son,
who lives and reigns with you in
   the unity of the Holy Spirit,
one God, for ever and ever.

Or:

O God, who were pleased to call
   your Church the Bride,
grant that the people that
   serves your name
may revere you, love you and
   follow you,
and may be led by you
to attain your promises in heaven.
Through our Lord Jesus Christ,
   your Son,
who lives and reigns with you
   in the unity of the Holy Spirit,
one God, for ever and ever.

Collecta

Deus, qui de vivis et
   electis lapidibus
æternum habitaculum tuæ
   præparas maiestati,
multiplica in Ecclesia tua
   spiritum gratiæ, quem dedisti,
ut fidelis tibi populus
in cælestis ædificationem
   Ierusalem semper accrescat.
Per Dominum nostrum
   Iesum Christum Filium tuum,
qui tecum vivit et regnat
   in unitate Spiritus Sancti,
Deus, per omnia sæcula sæculorum.

Vel:

Deus, qui Ecclesiam tuam sponsam
   vocare dignatus es,
da, ut plebs nomine tuo inserviens
te timeat, te diligat, te sequatur
et ad cælestia promissa,
   te ducente, perveniat.
Per Dominum nostrum
   Iesum Christum Filium tuum,
qui tecum vivit et regnat
   in unitate Spiritus Sancti,
Deus, per omnia sæcula sæculorum.

When this Feast does not fall on a Sunday there may only be one reading before
the Gospel.

FIRST READING

A reading from the prophet Ezekiel   47:1-2,8-9,12

I saw a stream of water coming from the Temple, bringing life to all wherever it flowed.

The angel brought me to the entrance of the Temple, where a stream
came out from under the Temple threshold and flowed eastwards, since
the Temple faced east. The water flowed from under the right side of the
Temple, south of the altar. He took me out by the north gate and led me
right round outside as far as the outer east gate where the water flowed out
on the right-hand side. He said, 'This water flows east down to the Arabah

and to the sea; and flowing into the sea it makes its waters wholesome. Wherever the river flows, all living creatures teeming in it will live. Fish will be very plentiful, for wherever the water goes it brings health, and life teems wherever the river flows. Along the river, on either bank, will grow every kind of fruit tree with leaves that never wither and fruit that never fails; they will bear new fruit every month, because this water comes from the sanctuary. And their fruit will be good to eat and the leaves medicinal.'

The word of the Lord.

Responsorial Psalm   Ps 45:2-3,5-6,8-9. R. v.5

R. **The waters of a river give joy to God's city,**
   the holy place where the Most High dwells.

God is for us a refuge and strength,
a helper close at hand, in time of distress:
so we shall not fear though the earth should rock,
though the mountains fall into the depths of the sea. R.

The waters of a river give joy to God's city,
the holy place where the Most High dwells.
God is within, it cannot be shaken;
God will help it at the dawning of the day. R.

The Lord of hosts is with us:
the God of Jacob is our stronghold.
Come, consider the works of the Lord
the redoubtable deeds he has done on the earth. R.

SECOND READING

A reading from the first letter of St Paul to the Corinthians   3:9-11,16-17

You are the temple of God.

You are God's building. By the grace God gave me, I succeeded as an architect and laid the foundations, on which someone else is doing the building. Everyone doing the building must work carefully. For the foundation, nobody can lay any other than the one which has already been laid, that is Jesus Christ.

Didn't you realise that you were God's temple and that the Spirit of God was living among you? If anybody should destroy the temple of God, God will destroy him, because the temple of God is sacred; and you are that temple.

The word of the Lord.

Gospel Acclamation   2 Ch 7:16

R. **Alleluia, alleluia!**
I have chosen and consecrated this house, says the Lord,
for my name to be there for ever.
R. **Alleluia!**

GOSPEL

A reading from the holy Gospel according to John   2:13-22
He was speaking of the sanctuary that was his body.

Just before the Jewish Passover Jesus went up to Jerusalem, and in the Temple
he found people selling cattle and sheep and pigeons, and the money
changers sitting at their counters there. Making a whip out of some chord,
he drove them all out of the Temple, cattle and sheep as well, scattered the
money changers' coins, knocked their tables over and said to the pigeon-
sellers, 'Take all this out of here and stop turning my Father's house into
a market.' Then his disciples remembered the words of scripture: Zeal for
your house will devour me. The Jews intervened and said, 'What sign can
you show us to justify what you have done?' Jesus answered, 'Destroy this
sanctuary and in three days I will raise it up.' The Jews replied, 'It has taken
forty-six years to build this sanctuary: are you going to raise it up in three
days?' But he was speaking of the sanctuary that was his body, and when
Jesus rose from the dead, his disciples remembered that he had said this,
and they believed the scripture and the words he had said.

The Gospel of the Lord.

When this Feast falls on a Sunday, the Creed is said.

Prayer over the Offerings	Super oblata
Accept, we pray, O Lord,	Suscipe, quæsumus, Domine,
the offering made here	munus oblatum,
and grant that by it those who	et poscentibus concede,
seek your favour	ut hic sacramentorum virtus et
may receive in this place	votorum obtineatur effectus.
the power of the Sacraments	Per Christum Dominum nostrum.
and the answer to their prayers.	
Through Christ our Lord.	

Preface: The Mystery of the Church, the Bride of Christ and the Temple of the Spirit.

It is truly right and just,
   our duty and our salvation,
always and everywhere
   to give you thanks,
Lord, holy Father,
   almighty and eternal God.

For in your benevolence you
   are pleased
to dwell in this house of prayer
in order to perfect us as the temple
   of the Holy Spirit,
supported by the perpetual help
   of your grace
and resplendent with the glory
   of a life acceptable to you.

Year by year you sanctify
   the Church, the Bride of Christ,
foreshadowed in visible buildings,
so that, rejoicing as the mother
   of countless children,
she may be given her place in your
   heavenly glory.

And so, with all the Angels and Saints,
we praise you, as without end
   we acclaim:

Holy, Holy, Holy Lord God of hosts...

Communion Antiphon Cf. 1 P 2:5

Be built up like living stones,
into a spiritual house,
   a holy priesthood.

Prayer after Communion

O God, who chose to
   foreshadow for us
the heavenly Jerusalem
through the sign of your

Præfatio: De mysterio Ecclesiæ, quæ est sponsa Christi templumque Spiritus

Vere dignum et iustum est,
   æquum et salutare,
nos tibi semper et ubique
   gratias agere:
Domine, sancte Pater,
   omnipotens æterne Deus:

Qui domum orationis munificus
   inhabitare dignaris,
ut, gratia tua perpetuis
   fovente subsidiis,
templum Spiritus Sancti ipse
   nos perficias,
acceptabilis vitæ
   splendore coruscans.

Sed et visibilibus
   ædificiis adumbratam,
Christi sponsam Ecclesiam perenni
   operatione sanctificas,
ut, innumerabili prole
   mater exsultans,
in gloriam tuam collocetur in cælis.

Et ideo, cum Sanctis
   et Angelis universis,
te collaudamus, sine fine dicentes:

Sanctus, Sanctus, Sanctus. . .

Ant. ad communionem

Tamquam lapides
   vivi superædificamini,
domus spiritalis,
   sacerdotium sanctum.

Post communionem

Deus, qui nobis
   supernam Ierusalem
per temporale Ecclesiæ tuæ
   signum adumbrare voluisti,

<table>
<tr><td>

Church on earth,
grant, we pray,
that, by our partaking of
   this Sacrament,
we may be made the temple of
   your grace
and may enter the dwelling
   place of your glory.
Through Christ our Lord.

</td><td>

da, quæsumus, ut, huius
   participatione sacramenti,
nos tuæ gratiæ templum efficias,
et habitationem gloriæ tuæ
   ingredi concedas.
Per Christum Dominum nostrum.

</td></tr>
</table>

A formula of Solemn Blessing, pp.658-659, may be used.

---

30 November

In Scotland

SAINT ANDREW, APOSTLE AND MARTYR, PATRON OF SCOTLAND

The lesson of the grain of wheat that dies in order to bear fruit also has a parallel in the life of Saint Andrew. Tradition tells us that he followed the fate of his Lord and Master, ending his days in Patras, Greece. Like Peter, he endured martyrdom on a cross, the diagonal cross that we venerate today as the cross of Saint Andrew. From his example we learn that the path of each single Christian, like that of the Church as a whole, leads to new life, to eternal life, through the imitation of Christ and the experience of his cross.

(Pope Benedict XVI)

Solemnity

Entrance Antiphon Cf. Mt 4:18-19	Ant. ad introitum
BESIDE the Sea of Galilee, the Lord saw two brothers, Peter and Andrew, and he said to them: Come after me and I will make you fishers of men.	DOMINUS secus mare Galilææ vidit duos fratres, Petrum et Andream, et vocavit eos: Venite post me, faciam vos fieri piscatores hominum.

The Gloria in excelsis (Glory to God in the highest) is said.

Collect

We humbly implore your majesty,
   O Lord,
that, just as the blessed
   Apostle Andrew
was for your Church a preacher
   and pastor,
so he may be for us a constant
   intercessor before you.
Through our Lord Jesus Christ,
   your Son,
who lives and reigns with you
   in the unity of the Holy Spirit,
one God, for ever and ever.

Collecta

Maiestatem tuam, Domine,
   suppliciter exoramus,
ut, sicut Ecclesiæ tuæ beatus
   Andreas apostolus
exstitit prædicator et rector,
ita apud te sit pro nobis
   perpetuus intercessor.
Per Dominum nostrum Iesum
   Christum Filium tuum,
qui tecum vivit et regnat
   in unitate Spiritus Sancti,
Deus, per omnia sæcula sæculorum.

FIRST READING

A reading from the book of Wisdom   3:1-9

He accepted them as a holocaust.

The souls of the virtuous are in the hands of God,
no torment shall ever touch them.
In the eyes of the unwise, they did appear to die,
their going looked like a disaster,
their leaving us, like annihilation;
but they are in peace.
If they experienced punishment as men see it,
their hope was rich with immortality;
slight was their affliction, great will their blessings be.
God has put them to the test
and proved them worthy to be with him;
he has tested them like gold in a furnace,
and accepted them as a holocaust.
When the time comes for his visitation they will shine out;
as sparks run through the stubble, so will they.
They shall judge nations, rule over peoples,
and the Lord will be their king for ever.
They who trust in him will understand the truth,
those who are faithful will live with him in love;
for grace and mercy await those he has chosen.

   The word of the Lord.

Responsorial Psalm   Ps 30:3-4,6,8,17,21. R. v.6

R. **Into your hands, O Lord,**
   I commend my spirit.

Be a rock of refuge for me,
a mighty stronghold to save me,
for you are my rock, my stronghold.
For your name's sake, lead me and guide me. R.

Into your hands I commend my spirit.
It is you who will redeem me, Lord.
As for me, I trust in the Lord:
let me be glad and rejoice in your love. R.

Let your face shine on your servant.
Save me in your love.
You hide them in the shelter of your presence
from the plotting of men. R.

SECOND READING

A reading from the letter of St Paul to the Romans   10:9-18

Faith comes from what is preached, and what is preached comes from the word of Christ.

If your lips confess that Jesus is Lord and if you believe in your heart that God raised him from the dead, then you will be saved. By believing from the heart you are made righteous; by confessing with your lips you are saved. When scripture says: those who believe in him will have no cause for shame, it makes no distinction between Jew and Greek: all belong to the same Lord who is rich enough, however many ask his help, for everyone who calls on the name of the Lord will be saved.

But they will not ask his help unless they believe in him, and they will not believe in him unless they have heard him, and they will not hear him unless they get a preacher, and they will never have a preacher unless one is sent, but as scripture says: The footsteps of those who bring good news are a welcome sound. Not everyone, of course, listens to the Good News. As Isaiah says: Lord, how many believe what we proclaimed? So faith comes from what is preached, and what is preached comes from the word of Christ.

Let me put the question: is it possible that they did not hear? Indeed they did; in the words of the psalm, their voice has gone out through all the earth, and their message to the ends of the world.

The word of the Lord.

Gospel Acclamation   2 Ch 7:16

R. **Alleluia, alleluia!**
Follow me, says the Lord,
and I will make you fishers of men.
R. **Alleluia!**

GOSPEL

A reading from the holy Gospel according to Matthew   4:18-22

And they left their nets at once and followed him.

As Jesus was walking by the Sea of Galilee he saw two brothers, Simon,
who was called Peter, and his brother Andrew; they were making a cast
in the lake with their net, for they were fishermen. And he said to them,
'Follow me and I will make you fishers of men.' And they left their nets at
once and followed him.

Going on from there he saw another pair of brothers, James son of Zebedee
and his brother John; they were in their boat with their father Zebedee,
mending their nets, and he called them. At once, leaving the boat and
their father, they followed him.

The Gospel of the Lord.

Prayer over the Offerings	Super oblata
Grant us, almighty God, that through these offerings, which we bring on the feast day of Saint Andrew, we may please you by what we have brought and be given life by what you have accepted. Through Christ our Lord.	Concede nobis, omnipotens Deus, ut his muneribus, quæ in beati Andreæ festivitate deferimus, et tibi placeamus exhibitis, et vivificemur acceptis. Per Christum Dominum nostrum.

Preface of the Apostles, pp.576-577.

Communion Antiphon Cf. Jn 1:41-42	Ant. ad communionem
Andrew told his brother Simon: We have found the Messiah, the Christ, and he brought him to Jesus.	Dixit Andreas Simoni fratri suo: Invenimus Messiam, qui dicitur Christus. Et adduxit eum ad Iesum.

Prayer after Communion	Post communionem
May communion in your Sacrament strengthen us, O Lord, so that by the example of the blessed Apostle Andrew	Roboret nos, Domine, sacramenti tui communio, ut, exemplo beati Andreæ apostoli, Christi mortificationem ferentes,

we, who carry in our body
    the Death of Christ,
may merit to live with him in glory.
Who lives and reigns
    for ever and ever.
	cum ipso vivere mereamur
	    in gloria.
	Qui vivit et regnat
	    in sæcula sæculorum.

A formula of Solemn Blessing, pp.656-657, may be used.

---

8 December

THE IMMACULATE CONCEPTION
OF THE BLESSED VIRGIN MARY

On the path of Advent shines the star of Mary Immaculate, "a sign of certain hope and comfort" (Lumen Gentium, n. 68). To reach Jesus, the true light, the sun that dispels all the darkness of history, we need light near us, human people who reflect Christ's light and thus illuminate the path to take. And what person is more luminous than Mary? Who can be a better star of hope for us than she, the dawn that announced the day of salvation? For this reason, the liturgy has us celebrate today, as Christmas approaches, the Solemn Feast of the Immaculate Conception of Mary: the mystery of God's grace that enfolded her from the first instant of her existence as the creature destined to be Mother of the Redeemer, preserving her from the stain of original sin. Looking at her, we recognise the loftiness and beauty of God's plan for everyone: to become holy and immaculate in love, in the image of our Creator.

(Pope Benedict XVI)

Solemnity

Entrance Antiphon Is 61:10	Ant. ad introitum

I REJOICE heartily in the Lord,
    in my God is the joy of my soul;
for he has clothed me with a robe
    of salvation,
and wrapped me in a mantle
    of justice,
like a bride adorned with her jewels.
	GAUDENS gaudebo in Domino,
	    et exsultabit anima mea
	    in Deo meo;
	quia induit me vestimentis salutis,
	et indumento iustitiæ
	    circumdedit me,
	quasi sponsam ornatam
	    monilibus suis.

The Gloria in excelsis (Glory to God in the highest) is said.

Collect

O God, who by the Immaculate
   Conception of the Blessed Virgin
prepared a worthy dwelling
   for your Son,
grant, we pray,
that, as you preserved her
   from every stain
by virtue of the Death of your Son,
   which you foresaw,
so, through her intercession,
we, too, may be cleansed
   and admitted to your presence.
Through our Lord Jesus Christ,
   your Son,
who lives and reigns with you
   in the unity of the Holy Spirit,
one God, for ever and ever.

Collecta

Deus, qui per immaculatam
   Virginis Conceptionem
dignum Filio tuo
   habitaculum præparasti,
quæsumus, ut, qui ex morte
   eiusdem Filii tui prævisa,
eam ab omni labe præservasti,
nos quoque mundos,
   eius intercessione,
ad te pervenire concedas.
Per Dominum nostrum Iesum
   Christum Filium tuum,
qui tecum vivit et regnat
   in unitate Spiritus Sancti,
Deus, per omnia sæcula sæculorum.

FIRST READING

A reading from the book of Genesis   3:9-15,20

I will make you enemies of each other; your offspring and her offspring.

After Adam had eaten of the tree, the Lord God called to him, 'Where are you?' he asked. 'I heard the sound of you in the garden,' he replied. 'I was afraid because I was naked, so I hid.' 'Who told you that you were naked?' he asked. 'Have you been eating of the tree I forbade you to eat?' The man replied, 'It was the woman you put with me; she gave me the fruit, and I ate it.' Then the Lord God asked the woman, 'What is this you have done?' The woman replied, 'The serpent tempted me and I ate.'

Then the Lord God said to the serpent, 'Because you have done this,
'Be accursed beyond all cattle,
all wild beasts.
You shall crawl on your belly and eat dust
every day of your life.
I will make you enemies of each other:
you and the woman,
your offspring and her offspring.
It will crush your head
and you will strike its heel.'

The man named his wife 'Eve' because she was the mother of all those who live.

The word of the Lord.

Responsorial Psalm   Ps 97:1-4. R. v.1

R. **Sing a new song to the Lord
for he has worked wonders.**

Sing a new song to the Lord
for he has worked wonders.
His right hand and his holy arm
have brought salvation. R.

The Lord has made known his salvation;
has shown his justice to the nations.
He has remembered his truth and love
for the house of Israel. R.

All the ends of the earth have seen
the salvation of our God.
Shout to the Lord all the earth,
ring out your joy. R.

SECOND READING

A reading from the letter of St Paul to the Ephesians   1:3-6,11-12

Before the world was made, God chose us in Christ.

Blessed be God the Father of our Lord Jesus Christ,
who has blessed us with all the spiritual blessings of heaven in Christ.
Before the world was made, he chose us, chose us in Christ,
to be holy and spotless, and to live through love in his presence,
determining that we should become his adopted sons,
     through Jesus Christ
for his own kind purposes,
to make us praise the glory of his grace,
his free gift to us in the Beloved.
And it is in him that we were claimed as God's own,
chosen from the beginning,
under the predetermined plan of the one who guides all things
as he decides by his own will;
chosen to be,
for his greater glory,
the people who would put their hopes in Christ before he came.

The word of the Lord.

Gospel Acclamation   Cf. Lk 1:28

R. **Alleluia, alleluia!**
Hail, Mary, full of grace; the Lord is with thee!
Blessed art thou among women.
R. **Alleluia!**

GOSPEL

A reading from the holy Gospel according to Luke   1:26-38
Rejoice, so highly favoured! The Lord is with you.

The angel Gabriel was sent by God to a town in Galilee called Nazareth, to a virgin betrothed to a man named Joseph, of the house of David; and the virgin's name was Mary. He went in and said to her, 'Rejoice, so highly favoured! The Lord is with you.' She was deeply disturbed by these words and asked herself what this greeting could mean, but the angel said to her, 'Mary, do not be afraid; you have won God's favour. Listen! You are to conceive and bear a son, and you must name him Jesus. He will be great and will be called Son of the Most High. The Lord God will give him the throne of his ancestor David; he will rule over the House of Jacob for ever and his reign will have no end.' Mary said to the angel, 'But how can this come about, since I am a virgin?' 'The Holy Spirit will come upon you' the angel answered, 'and the power of the Most High will cover you with its shadow. And so the child will be holy and will be called Son of God. Know this too: your kinswoman Elizabeth has, in her old age, herself conceived a son, and she whom people called barren is now in her sixth month, for nothing is impossible to God.' 'I am the handmaid of the Lord,' said Mary, 'let what you have said be done to me.' And the angel left her.

The Gospel of the Lord.

The Creed is said.

Prayer over the Offerings

Graciously accept the saving sacrifice which we offer you, O Lord, on the Solemnity of the Immaculate Conception of the Blessed Virgin Mary, and grant that, as we profess her, on account of your prevenient grace, to be untouched by any stain of sin, so, through her intercession, we may be delivered from all our faults.
Through Christ our Lord.

Super oblata

Salutarem hostiam, quam in sollemnitate immaculatæ Conceptionis beatæ Virginis Mariæ tibi, Domine, offerimus, suscipe dignanter, et præsta, ut, sicut illam tua gratia præveniente ab omni labe profitemur immunem, ita, eius intercessione, a culpis omnibus liberemur.
Per Christum Dominum nostrum.

Preface: The Mystery of Mary and the Church.

It is truly right and just,
   our duty and our salvation,
always and everywhere
   to give you thanks,
Lord, holy Father,
   almighty and eternal God.

For you preserved the most Blessed
   Virgin Mary
from all stain of original sin,
so that in her, endowed with
   the rich fullness of your grace,
you might prepare a worthy
   Mother for your Son
and signify the beginning
   of the Church,
his beautiful Bride without spot
   or wrinkle.

She, the most pure Virgin,
   was to bring forth a Son,
the innocent Lamb who would
   wipe away our offences;
you placed her above all others
to be for your people an advocate
   of grace
and a model of holiness.

And so, in company with the choirs
   of Angels,
we praise you, and with joy
   we proclaim:

Holy, Holy, Holy Lord God of hosts...

Communion Antiphon

Glorious things are spoken of you,
   O Mary,
for from you arose the sun of justice,
Christ our God.

Præfatio: De mysterio Mariæ et Ecclesiæ.

Vere dignum et iustum est,
   æquum et salutare,
nos tibi semper et ubique
   gratias agere:
Domine, sancte Pater,
   omnipotens æterne Deus:

Qui beatissimam Virginem Mariam
ab omni originalis culpæ
   labe præservasti,
ut in ea,
   gratiæ tuæ plenitudine ditata,
dignam Filio tuo
   Genetricem præparares
et Sponsæ eius Ecclesiæ,
sine ruga vel macula formosæ,
   signares exordium.

Filium enim erat purissima
   Virgo datura,
qui crimina nostra Agnus
   innocens aboleret;
et ipsam præ omnibus tuo
   populo disponebas
advocatam gratiæ
   et sanctitatis exemplar.

Et ideo, choris angelicis sociati,
te laudamus in gaudio confitentes:

Sanctus, Sanctus, Sanctus. . .

Ant. ad communionem

Gloriosa dicta sunt de te, Maria,
quia ex te ortus est sol iustitiæ,
Christus Deus noster.

Prayer after Communion	Post communionem
May the Sacrament we have received, O Lord our God, heal in us the wounds of that fault from which in a singular way you preserved Blessed Mary in her Immaculate Conception. Through Christ our Lord.	Sacramenta quæ sumpsimus, Domine Deus noster, illius in nobis culpæ vulnera reparent, a qua immaculatam beatæ Mariæ Conceptionem singulariter præservasti. Per Christum Dominum nostrum.

A formula of Solemn Blessing, pp.654-655, may be used.

ANNIVERSARY OF THE DEDICATION OF A CHURCH

This Mass is for use in the Dedicated Church. For Mass outside the Dedicated Church, the prayers and antiphons given for the Dedication of the Lateran Basilica, pp.1198ff above, are used, with readings as below, or as in the full Lectionary.

In the Church that was Dedicated

Entrance Antiphon Ps 67:36	Ant. ad introitum
WONDERFUL are you, O God in your holy place. The God of Israel himself gives his people strength and courage. Blessed be God! (E.T. alleluia).	MIRABILIS, Deus, de sanctuario tuo! Deus Israel ipse tribuet virtutem et fortitudinem plebi suæ. Benedictus Deus! (T.P. alleluia).

The Gloria in excelsis (Glory to God in the highest) is said.

Collect	Collecta
O God, who year by year renew for us the day when this your holy temple was consecrated, hear the prayers of your people and grant that in this place for you there may always be pure worship and for us, fullness of redemption. Through our Lord Jesus Christ, your Son,	Deus, qui nobis per singulos annos huius sancti templi tui consecrationis reparas diem, exaudi preces populi tui, et præsta, ut fiat hic tibi semper purum servitium et nobis plena redemptio. Per Dominum nostrum Iesum Christum Filium tuum, qui tecum vivit et regnat

who lives and reigns with you
  in the unity of the Holy Spirit,
one God, for ever and ever.

in unitate Spiritus Sancti,
Deus, per omnia sæcula sæculorum.

FIRST READING

A reading from the second book of Chronicles   5:6-11,13-6:2

I have built you a dwelling, a place for you to live in for ever.

King Solomon, and all the community of Israel gathering with him in front of the ark, sacrificed sheep and oxen, countless, innumerable. The priests brought the ark of the covenant of the Lord to its place, in the Debir of the Temple, that is, in the Holy of Holies, under the cherubs' wings. For there where the ark was placed the cherubs spread out their wings and sheltered the ark and its shafts. These were long enough for their ends to be seen from the Holy Place in front of the Debir, but not from outside. There was nothing in the ark except the two tablets that Moses had placed in it at Horeb, where the Lord had made a covenant with the Israelites when they came out of Egypt.

Now when the priests came out of the sanctuary, a cloud filled the sanctuary, the Temple of the Lord.

All those who played the trumpet, or who sang, united in giving praise and glory to the Lord. Lifting their voices to the sound of the trumpet and cymbal and instruments of music, they gave praise to the Lord, 'for he is good, for his love is everlasting'.

Because of the cloud the priests could no longer perform their duties; the glory of the Lord filled the Temple of God.

Then Solomon said:

'The Lord has chosen to dwell in the thick cloud.
Yes, I have built you a dwelling,
a place for you to live for ever.'

The word of the Lord.

In the Easter Season

A reading from the Acts of the Apostles   7:44-50

The Most High does not live in a house that human hands have built.

Stephen said to the people, the elders and scribes, 'While they were in the desert our ancestors possessed the Tent of Testimony that had been constructed according to the instructions God gave Moses, telling him to make an exact copy of the pattern he had been shown. It was handed down from one ancestor of ours to another until Joshua brought it into the country we had conquered from the nations which were driven out by God as we advanced. Here it stayed until the time of David. He won God's favour and asked permission to have a temple built for the House of Jacob, though it was Solomon who actually built God's house for him. Even so the Most High does not live in a house that human hands have built: for as the prophet says:

'With heaven my throne
and earth my footstool,
what house could you build for me,
what place could you make for my rest?
Was not all this made by my hand?''

The word of the Lord.

Responsorial Psalm   Ps 83:3-5,10-11. R. v.2. Alt. R. Rv 21:3

R. **How lovely is your dwelling place,**
   Lord, God of hosts.

   Or: **Here God lives among men.**

   My soul is longing and yearning,
   is yearning for the courts of the Lord.
   My heart and my soul ring out their joy
   to God, the living God. R.

   The sparrow herself finds a home
   and the swallow a nest for her brood;
   she lays her young by your altars,
   Lord of hosts, my king and my God. R.

   They are happy, who dwell in your house
   for ever singing your praise.
   Turn your eyes, O God, our shield,
   look on the face of your anointed. R.

   One day within your courts
   is better than a thousand elsewhere.
   The threshold of the house of God
   I prefer to the dwelling of the wicked. R.

SECOND READING

A reading from the first letter of St Paul to the Corinthians   3:9-11,16-17

You are the temple of God.

You are God's building. By the grace God gave me, I succeeded as an architect and laid the foundations, on which someone else is doing the building. Everyone doing the building must work carefully. For the foundation, nobody can lay any other than the one which has already been laid, that is Jesus Christ.

Didn't you realise that you were God's temple and that the Spirit of God was living among you? If anybody should destroy the temple of God, God will destroy him, beause the temple of God is sacred; and you are the temple.

The word of the Lord.

Gospel Acclamation   Ez 37:27

R. **Alleluia, alleluia!**
I shall make my home among them, says the Lord;
I will be their God,
they shall be my people.
R. **Alleluia!**

GOSPEL

A reading from the holy Gospel according to John   4:19-24

A true worshippers will worship the Father in Spirit and truth.

The Samaritan woman said to Jesus, 'I see you are a prophet, sir. Our fathers worshipped on this mountain, while you say that Jerusalem is the place where one ought to worship.' Jesus said:

'Believe me, woman, the hour is coming
when you will worship the Father
neither on this mountain nor in Jerusalem.
You worship what you do not know;
we worship what we do know;
for salvation comes from the Jews.
But the hour will come – in fact is is here already –
when true worshippers will worship the Father in spirit and truth:
that is the kind of worshipper
the Father wants.
God is spirit,

and those who worship
    must worship in spirit and truth.'

The Gospel of the Lord.

The creed is said.

Prayer over the Offerings

Recalling the day when you
    were pleased
to fill your house with glory
    and holiness, O Lord,
we pray that you may make of us
a sacrificial offering always
    acceptable to you.
Through Christ our Lord.

Super oblata

Memores diei quo domum tuam,
    Domine,
gloria dignatus es ac
    sanctitate replere,
nosmetipsos, quæsumus,
fac hostias tibi semper acceptas.
Per Christum Dominum nostrum.

Preface: The mystery of the Temple
of God, which is the Church.

It is truly right and just,
    our duty and our salvation,
always and everywhere
    to give you thanks,
Lord, holy Father,
    almighty and eternal God,
through Christ our Lord.
For in this visible house that
    you have let us build
and where you never cease to
    show favour
to the family on pilgrimage
    to you in this place,
you wonderfully manifest
    and accomplish
the mystery of your
    communion with us.
Here you build up for yourself
    the temple that we are
and cause your Church,
    spread throughout the world,

De mysterio templi Dei,
quod est Ecclesia

Vere dignum et iustum est,
    æquum et salutare,
nos tibi semper
    et ubique gratias agere:
Domine, sancte Pater,
    omnipotens æterne Deus:
per Christum Dominum nostrum.
Quia in domo visibili quam nobis
    exstruere concessisti,
ubi familiæ in hoc loco
    ad te peregrinanti
favere non desinis,
mysterium tuæ
    nobiscum communionis
mire figuras et operaris:

hic enim tibi templum illud quod
    nos sumus ædificas,
et Ecclesiam per orbem diffusam

to grow ever more and more as the
　　Lord's own Body,
till she reaches her fullness in the
　　vision of peace,
the heavenly city of Jerusalem.
And so, with the countless ranks of
　　the blessed,
in the temple of your glory we
　　praise you,
we bless you, and proclaim your
　　greatness, as we acclaim:
Holy, Holy, Holy Lord God of hosts...

in dominici compagem corporis
　　facis augeri,
in pacis visione complendam, cælesti
　　civitate Ierusalem.

Et ideo, cum multitudine ordinum
　　beatorum,
in templo gloriæ tuæ,
　　te collaudamus,
benedicimus et magnificamus,
　　dicentes:
Sanctus, Sanctus, Sanctus. . .

Communion Antiphon Cf. 1 Co 3:16-17
You are the temple of God, and the
　　Spirit of God dwells in you.
The temple of God, which you are,
　　is holy (E.T. alleluia).

Ant. ad communionem
Templum Dei estis, et Spiritus Dei
　　habitat in vobis.
Templum Dei sanctum est, quod
　　estis vos (T.P. alleluia).

Prayer after Communion
May the people consecrated to you,
　　O Lord, we pray,
receive the fruits and joy
　　of your blessing,
that the festive homage
they have offered you today
　　in the body
may redound upon them
　　as a spiritual gift.
Through Christ our Lord.

Post communionem
Benedictionis tuæ, quæsumus,
　　Domine,
plebs tibi sacra fructus reportet
　　et gaudium,
ut, quod in huius festivitatis die
corporali servitio exhibuit,
spiritaliter se rettulisse cognoscat.
Per Christum Dominum nostrum.

MASSES FOR THE DEAD

Although for the sake of convenience, complete Masses with their own antiphons and prayers are given here, all the texts may be exchanged one for another, especially the prayers. In these latter, however, changes should be made, according to circumstances, in gender and number.

Similarly, if the prayers given here for funerals and anniversaries are used in other circumstances, the phrasing that appears less suited should be omitted.

In Easter Time, the Alleluia at the end of the antiphons may, if appropriate, be omitted.

FOR THE FUNERAL

The Funeral Mass may be celebrated on any day, except on Solemnities that are Holydays of Obligation, on Thursday of Holy Week, during the Paschal Triduum, and on the Sundays of Advent, Lent and Easter Time.

Outside Easter Time

Entrance Antiphon Cf. 4 Esdr 2:34-35	Ant. ad introitum
Eternal rest grant unto them, O Lord, and let perpetual light shine upon them.	Requiem æternam dona eis, Domine, et lux perpetua luceat eis.
Collect	Collecta
O God, almighty Father, our faith professes that your Son died and rose again; mercifully grant, that through this mystery your servant N., who has fallen asleep in Christ, may rejoice to rise again through him. Who lives and reigns with you in the unity of the Holy Spirit, one God, for ever and ever.	Deus, Pater omnipotens, cuius Filium mortuum fuisse et resurrexisse fides nostra fatetur, concede propitius, ut hoc mysterio famulus tuus N., qui in illo dormivit, per illum resurgere lætetur. Qui tecum vivit et regnat in unitate Spiritus Sancti, Deus, per omnia sæcula sæculorum.

Or:

O God, whose nature
is always to forgive and
    to show mercy,
we humbly implore you
    for your servant N.,
whom you have called (this day)
    to journey to you,
and, since he (she) hoped and
    believed in you,
grant that he (she) may be
    led to our true homeland
to delight in its everlasting joys.
Through our Lord Jesus Christ,
    your Son,
who lives and reigns with you
    in the unity of the Holy Spirit,
one God, for ever and ever.

Vel:

Deus, cui proprium est misereri
    semper et parcere,
te supplices exoramus pro
    famulo tuo N.,
quem (hodie) ad te migrare iussisti,
ut, quia in te speravit et credidit,
concedas eum ad veram
    patriam perduci,
et gaudiis perfrui sempiternis.
Per Dominum nostrum
    Iesum Christum Filium tuum,
qui tecum vivit et regnat
    in unitate Spiritus Sancti,
Deus, per omnia sæcula sæculorum.

Prayer over the Offerings

As we humbly present to you
these sacrificial offerings, O Lord,
for the salvation of your servant N.,
we beseech your mercy,
that he (she),
    who did not doubt your Son
to be a loving Saviour,
may find in him a merciful Judge.
Who lives and reigns
    for ever and ever.

Preface for the Dead, pp.584-589.

Super oblata

Pro famuli tui N. salute
hostias tibi, Domine,
    suppliciter offerimus
tuam clementiam deprecantes,
ut, qui Filium tuum pium
    Salvatorem esse non dubitavit,
misericordem Iudicem inveniat.
Qui vivit et regnat
    in sæcula sæculorum.

Communion Antiphon Cf. 4 Esdr 2:34-35	Ant. ad communionem

Let perpetual light shine
    upon them,
with your Saints for ever,
    for you are merciful.
Eternal rest grant unto them, O Lord,
and let perpetual light shine
    upon them,
with your Saints for ever,
    for you are merciful.

Lux æterna luceat eis, Domine,
cum Sanctis tuis in æternum,
    quia pius es.
Requiem æternam dona eis,
    Domine,
et lux perpetua luceat eis,
cum Sanctis tuis in æternum,
    quia pius es.

Prayer after Communion — **Post communionem**

Lord God, whose Son left us,
in the Sacrament of his Body,
food for the journey,
mercifully grant that,
    strengthened by it,
our brother (sister) N. may come
to the eternal table of Christ.
Who lives and reigns
    for ever and ever.

Domine Deus, cuius Filius
    in sacramento Corporis sui
viaticum nobis reliquit,
concede propitius, ut per hoc frater
    noster N.
ad ipsam Christi perveniat
    mensam æternam.
Qui vivit et regnat
    in sæcula sæculorum.

During Easter Time

Entrance Antiphon 1 Th 4:14; 1 Co 15:22	Ant. ad introitum

Just as Jesus died and rose again,
so, through Jesus, God will bring
    with him
those who have fallen asleep;
and as in Adam all die,
so also in Christ will all be brought
    to life, alleluia.

Sicut Iesus mortuus
    est et resurrexit,
ita et Deus eos qui dormierunt
per Iesum adducet cum eo.
Et sicut in Adam omnes moriuntur,
ita et in Christo omnes
    vivificabuntur, alleluia.

Collect

Listen kindly to our prayers,
O Lord:
as our faith in your Son,
raised from the dead, is deepened,
may our hope of resurrection
for your departed servant N.
also find new strength.
Through our Lord Jesus Christ,
your Son,
who lives and reigns with you
in the unity of the Holy Spirit,
one God, for ever and ever.

Or:

O God, who through the ending
of present things
open up the beginning of things
to come,
grant, we pray, that the soul
of your servant N.
may be led by you
to attain the inheritance
of eternal redemption.
Through our Lord Jesus Christ,
your Son,
who lives and reigns with you
in the unity of the Holy Spirit,
one God, for ever and ever.

Prayer over the Offerings

Look favourably on our offerings,
O Lord,
so that your departed servant N.
may be taken up into glory
with your Son,
in whose great mystery of love
we are all united.
Through Christ our Lord.

Collecta

Preces nostras, quæsumus,
Domine, benignus exaudi,
ut, dum extollitur nostra fides
in Filio tuo a mortuis suscitato,
in famuli tui N.
præstolanda resurrectione
spes quoque nostra firmetur.
Per Dominum nostrum
Iesum Christum Filium tuum,
qui tecum vivit et regnat
in unitate Spiritus Sancti,
Deus, per omnia sæcula sæculorum.

Vel:

Deus, qui per finem præsentium
principia pandis futurorum,
præsta, quæsumus,
ut anima famuli tui N.
ad redemptionis æternæ
perveniat, te ducente,
consortium.
Per Dominum nostrum Iesum
Christum Filium tuum,
qui tecum vivit et regnat
in unitate Spiritus Sancti,
Deus, per omnia sæcula sæculorum.

Super oblata

Nostris, Domine,
propitiare muneribus,
ut famulus tuus N. assumatur
in gloriam cum Filio tuo,
cuius magno pietatis
iungimur sacramento.
Qui vivit et regnat
in sæcula sæculorum.

Preface for the Dead, pp.584-589.

Communion Antiphon Jn 11:25-26	Ant. ad communionem

I am the Resurrection and the Life,
   says the Lord.
Whoever believes in me,
   even though he dies, will live,
and everyone who lives
   and believes in me
will not die for ever, alleluia.

Ego sum resurrectio et vita,
   dicit Dominus.
Qui credit in me,
   etiam si mortuus fuerit, vivet;
et omnis, qui vivit et credit in me,
non morietur in æternum, alleluia.

Prayer after Communion	Post communionem

Grant, we pray, O Lord,
   that your servant N.,
for whom we have celebrated
   this paschal Sacrament,
may pass over to a dwelling place
   of light and peace.
Through Christ our Lord.

Præsta, quæsumus, Domine,
ut famulus tuus N. in mansionem
   lucis transeat et pacis,
pro quo paschale
   celebravimus sacramentum.
Per Christum Dominum nostrum.

ON THE ANNIVERSARY

This Mass may be celebrated on the first anniversary even on days within the Octave
of the Nativity of the Lord, and on days when an Obligatory Memorial occurs and on
weekdays, with the exception of Ash Wednesday and weekdays during Holy Week.

On other anniversaries, this Mass may be celebrated on weekdays in Ordinary Time
even when an Optional Memorial occurs.

Outside Easter Time

Entrance Antiphon Rv 21:4	Ant. ad introitum

God will wipe every tear
   from their eyes,
and there shall be no more death
or mourning, crying or pain,
for former things have passed away.

Absterget Deus omnem lacrimam
   ab oculis eorum,
et mors ultra non erit,
neque luctus, neque clamor,
   neque dolor erit ultra,
quia prima transierunt.

Collect

O God, glory of the faithful
  and life of the just,
by the Death and Resurrection
  of whose Son
we have been redeemed,
look mercifully on
  your departed servant N.,
that, just as he (she) professed
the mystery of our resurrection,
so he (she) may merit to receive
the joys of eternal happiness.
Through our Lord Jesus Christ,
  your Son,
who lives and reigns with you
  in the unity of the Holy Spirit,
one God, for ever and ever.

Collecta

Deus, gloria fidelium
  et vita iustorum,
cuius Filii morte
  et resurrectione redempti sumus,

propitiare famulo tuo N.,
ut, qui resurrectionis nostræ
  mysterium agnovit,
æternæ beatitudinis gaudia
  percipere mereatur.

Per Dominum nostrum
  Iesum Christum Filium tuum,
qui tecum vivit et regnat
  in unitate Spiritus Sancti, Deus,
per omnia sæcula sæculorum.

Prayer over the Offerings

Look with favour, we pray, O Lord,
on the offerings we make for the
  soul of your servant N.,
that, being cleansed
  by heavenly remedies,
his (her) soul may be ever alive
and blessed in your glory.
Through Christ our Lord.

Preface for the Dead, pp.584-589.

Super oblata

Munera, quæsumus, Domine,
quæ tibi pro anima famuli
  tui N. offerimus,
placatus intende, ut,
  remediis purgata cælestibus,
in tua gloria semper viva sit
  et beata.
Per Christum Dominum nostrum.

Communion Antiphon Jn 11:25; 3:36; 5:24

I am the Resurrection and the Life,
  says the Lord.
Whoever believes in me
  has eternal life
and does not come to condemnation,
but has passed from death to life.

Ant. ad communionem

Ego sum resurrectio et vita,
  dicit Dominus.
Qui credit in me,
  habet vitam æternam,
et in iudicium non venit, sed
  transiit de morte ad vitam.

Prayer after Communion	Post communionem
Restored by these sacred mysteries, we humbly beseech you, O Lord, that your servant N. may be cleansed from all offences and merit for all eternity the precious gift of the resurrection. Through Christ our Lord.	Sacris reparati mysteriis, te, Domine, suppliciter exoramus, ut famulus tuus N., a delictis omnibus emundatus, æterno resurrectionis munere ditari mereatur. Per Christum Dominum nostrum.

During Easter Time

Entrance Antiphon Cf. Rm 8:11	Ant. ad introitum
God, who raised Jesus from the dead, will give life also to your mortal bodies, through his Spirit that dwells in you, alleluia.	Deus, qui suscitavit Iesum a mortuis, vivificabit et mortalia corpora nostra, propter inhabitantem Spiritum eius in nobis, alleluia.

Collect	Collecta
Almighty and merciful God, whose Son, for our sake, willingly underwent death in the flesh, grant mercifully, we pray, that your servant N. may have part in the wondrous victory of Christ's Resurrection. Who lives and reigns with you in the unity of the Holy Spirit, one God, for ever and ever.	Omnipotens et misericors Deus, cuius Filius voluntarie pro nobis carnis subiit mortem, concede propitius famulo tuo N. admirabili eius resurrectionis victoriæ sociari. Qui tecum vivit et regnat in unitate Spiritus Sancti, Deus, per omnia sæcula sæculorum.

Prayer over the Offerings

Almighty and merciful God,
by means of these
    sacrificial offerings,
wash away, we pray,
    in the Blood of Christ,
the sins of your departed servant N.,
for you purify unceasingly
    by your merciful forgiveness
those you once cleansed
    in the waters of Baptism.
Through Christ our Lord.

Preface for the Dead, pp.584-589.

Super oblata

Omnipotens et misericors Deus,
his sacrificiis ablue, quæsumus,
    animam famuli tui N.
a peccatis suis in sanguine Christi,
ut, quem aqua
    baptismatis mundasti,
indesinenter purifices
    indulgentia pietatis.
Per Christum Dominum nostrum.

Communion Antiphon Jn 6:51-52

I am the living bread, that came
    down from heaven,
    says the Lord.
Whoever eats of this bread
    will live for ever,
and the bread that I will give
is my flesh for the life of the world,
    alleluia.

Ant. ad communionem

Ego sum panis vivus, qui de cælo
    descendi, dicit Dominus.
Si quis manducaverit ex hoc pane,
    vivet in æternum;
et panis, quem ego dabo,
caro mea est pro mundi vita,
    alleluia.

Prayer after Communion

Having received the Sacrament
    of your Only Begotten Son,
who was sacrificed for us
    and rose in glory,
we humbly implore you, O Lord,
for your departed servant N.,
that, cleansed by
    the paschal mysteries,
he (she) may glory in the gift
    of the resurrection to come.
Through Christ our Lord.

Post communionem

Sumpto sacramento Unigeniti tui,
qui pro nobis immolatus resurrexit
    in gloria,
te, Domine, suppliciter exoramus
pro famulo tuo N.,
ut, paschalibus
    mysteriis emundatus,
futuræ resurrectionis
    munere glorietur.
Per Christum Dominum nostrum.

PRAYERS AND DEVOTIONS

RITE OF EUCHARISTIC EXPOSITION AND BENEDICTION

The service of Benediction developed during the Middle Ages during the Corpus Christi processions in which the Blessed Sacrament was held up for veneration. The service was subsequently used at other times throughout the year as an opportunity to give thanks for the Mass and adore Christ present under the form of bread.

Today, the Church encourages this rite to be celebrated in the context of a longer period of reading, prayer and reflection.

Exposition

First of all, the minister exposes the Blessed Sacrament while a hymn is sung, during which he incenses the Sacrament. The following or another hymn may be chosen.

O saving Victim, opening wide,	O salutaris hostia,
The gate of heav'n to man below	Quæ cæli pandis ostium;
Our foes press on from every side;	Bella premunt hostilia,
Thine aid supply,	Da robur, fer auxilium.
thy strength bestow.	
To thy great name be endless praise,	Uni Trinoque Domino
Immortal Godhead, One in Three;	Sit sempiterna gloria,
O grant us endless length of days	Qui vitam sine termino
In our true native land with thee.	Nobis donet in patria.
Amen.	Amen.

Adoration

A time for silent prayer, readings from Scripture, litanies or other prayers and hymns may be used. On some occasions, the Prayer of the Church might be said or sung.

Of the Glorious Body Telling	Pange Lingua
Of the glorious Body telling,	Pange lingua gloriosi
O my tongue, its mysteries sing,	Corporis mysterium,
And the Blood, all price excelling,	Sanguinisque pretiosi,
Which the world's eternal King,	Quem in mundi pretium
In a noble womb once dwelling	Fructus ventris generosi,
Shed for the world's ransoming.	Rex effudit gentium.

Given for us, for us descending,
Of a Virgin to proceed,
Man with man in
   converse blending,
Scattered he the Gospel seed,
Till his sojourn drew to ending,
Which he closed in wondrous deed.

At the last great Supper lying
Circled by his brethren's band,
Meekly with the law complying,
First he finished its command
Then, immortal Food supplying,
Gave himself with his own hand.

Word made Flesh,
   by word he maketh
Very bread his Flesh to be;
Man in wine Christ's Blood
   partaketh,
And if senses fail to see,
Faith alone the true heart waketh
To behold the mystery.

Nobis datus, nobis natus
Ex intacta Virgine,
Et in mundo conversatus,
Sparso verbi semine,
Sui moras incolatus
Miro clausit ordine.

In supremae nocte cœnæ
Recumbens cum fratribus,
Observata lege plene
Cibis in legalibus,
Cibum turbæ duodenæ
Se dat suis manibus

Verbum caro, panem verum
Verbo carnem efficit,
Fitque sanguis Christi merum,
Et, si sensus deficit,
Ad firmandum cor sincerum
Sola fides sufficit.

Sweet Sacrament Divine

Sweet Sacrament divine,
Hid in thine earthly home;
Lo! round thy lowly shrine,
With suppliant hearts we come;
Jesus, to thee our voice we raise
In songs of love and heartfelt praise
Sweet Sacrament divine. (repeat)

Sweet Sacrament of peace,
Dear home of every heart,
Where restless yearnings cease,
And sorrows all depart.
There in thine ear, all trustfully,
We tell our tale of misery,
Sweet Sacrament of peace. (repeat)

Sweet Sacrament of rest,
Ark from the ocean's roar,
Within thy shelter blest
Soon may we reach the shore;
Save us, for still the tempest raves,
Save, lest we sink beneath the waves:
Sweet Sacrament of rest. (repeat)

Sweet Sacrament divine,
Earth's light and jubilee,
In thy far depths doth shine
The Godhead's majesty;
Sweet light, so shine on us, we pray
That earthly joys may fade away:
Sweet Sacrament divine. (repeat)

(Francis Stanfield)

Benediction

Towards the end of the exposition, the priest or deacon goes to the altar, genuflects and kneels. Then this hymn or a suitable alternative is sung, during which the minister incenses the sacrament.

Therefore we, before him bending This great Sacrament revere Types and shadows have their ending for the newer rite is here Faith, our outward sense befriending Makes the inward vision clear.	Tantum ergo Sacramentum Veneremur cernui, Et antiquum documentum Novo cedat ritui; Præstet fides supplementum Sensuum defectui.
Glory let us give, and blessing To the Father and the Son Honour, might, and praise addressing While eternal ages run Ever too his love confessing Who, from both, with both is one. Amen.	Genitori, Genitoque Laus et iubilatio. Salus, honor, virtus quoque Sit et benedictio; Procedenti ab utroque Compar sit laudatio. Amen.

The minister then says the following prayer (or a suitable alternative)

Let us pray.
Lord Jesus Christ,
you gave us the eucharist
as the memorial of your suffering
    and death.
May our worship of this sacrament
    of your body and blood
Help us to experience the salvation
    you won for us
and the peace of the kingdom
where you live with the Father
    and the Holy Spirit,
one God, for ever and ever.
R. Amen.
	Oremus.
	Deus, qui nobis sub
	    sacramento mirabili
	passionis tuæ memoriam reliquisti:
	tribue, quæsumus,
	ita nos Corporis et Sanguinis
	    tui sacra mysteria venerari,
	ut redemptionis tuæ
	    fructum in nobis
	    iugiter sentiamus.
	Qui vivis et regnas
	    in sæcula sæculorum.
	R. Amen.

The Priest or Deacon now puts on the humeral veil and blesses the congregation with the Blessed Sacrament.

The Divine Praises formerly said at this point may more properly be included within the period of adoration.

The Divine Praises

Blessed be God.
Blessed be his holy Name.
Blessed be Jesus Christ, true God and true Man.
Blessed be the name of Jesus.
Blessed be his most Sacred Heart.
Blessed be his most Precious Blood.
Blessed be Jesus in the most holy Sacrament of the Altar.
Blessed be the Holy Spirit, the Paraclete.
Blessed be the great Mother of God, Mary, most holy.
Blessed be her holy and Immaculate Conception.
Blessed be her glorious Assumption.
Blessed be the name of Mary, Virgin and Mother.
Blessed be St Joseph, her spouse most chaste.
Blessed be God in his Angels and in his Saints.

Reposition

Immediately after the Blessed Sacrament is reposed in the tabernacle, the following may be sung:

Ant. Let us adore for ever
the most holy Sacrament.

Ps. O praise the Lord,
all you nations
Acclaim him, all you peoples
For his mercy is confirmed upon us
and the truth of the Lord
remains for ever.

Glory be to the Father,
and to the Son
and to the Holy Spirit
As it was in the beginning, is now
and ever shall be,
world without end. Amen.

Ant. Let us adore for ever the most
holy Sacrament.

Ant. Adoremus in æternum
sanctissimum Sacramentum.

Ps. Laudate Dominum,
omnes gentes;
laudate eum omnes populi.
Quoniam confirmata est super
nos misericordia eius;
et veritas Domini manet
in æternum.

Gloria Patri, et Filio,
et Spiritui Sancto.
Sicut erat in principio,
et nunc, et semper,
et in sæcula sæculorum. Amen.

Ant. Adoremus in æternum
sanctissimum Sacramentum.

An alternative acclamation:
O Sacrament most holy,
O Sacrament divine!
All praise, and all thanksgiving,
Be every moment thine!

STATIONS OF THE CROSS

Meditations by Blessed John Henry Cardinal Newman

Begin with an Act of Contrition

O my God, because you are so good, I am very sorry that I have sinned against you and by the help of your grace I will not sin again.

The First Station

Jesus is condemned to Death

V. We adore you, O Christ,
    and we bless you.
	V. Adoramus te, Christe,
	    et benedicimus tibi.

R. Because by your holy Cross
    you have redeemed the world.
	R. Quia per sanctam crucem tuam
	    redemisti mundum.

Leaving the house of Caiaphas, and dragged before Pilate and Herod, mocked, beaten, and spat upon, His back torn with scourges, His head crowned with thorns, Jesus, who on the last day will judge the world, is Himself condemned by unjust judges to a death of ignominy and torture.

Jesus is condemned to death. His death-warrant is signed, and who signed it but I, when I committed my first mortal sins? My first mortal sins, when I fell away from the state of grace into which Thou didst place me by baptism; these it was that were Thy death-warrant, O Lord. The innocent suffered for the guilty. Those sins of mine were the voices which cried out, 'Let Him be crucified.' That willingness and delight of heart with which I committed them was the consent which Pilate gave to this clamorous multitude. And the hardness of heart which followed upon them, my disgust, my despair, my proud impatience, my obstinate resolve to sin on, the love of sin which took possession of me – what were these contrary and impetuous feelings but the blows and the blasphemies with which the fierce soldiers and the populace received Thee, thus carrying out the sentence which Pilate had pronounced?

Our Father, Hail Mary, Glory be to the Father.

V. Have mercy on us, O Lord.	V. Miserere nostri, Domine.
R. Have mercy on us.	R. Miserere nostri.

At the Cross her station keeping, Stood the mournful Mother weeping, Close to Jesus to the last.	Stabat Mater dolorosa, Iuxta crucem lacrimosa, Dum pendebat Filius.

The Second Station

Jesus receives His Cross

V. We adore you, O Christ,
and we bless you.
R. Because by your holy Cross
you have redeemed the world.

V. Adoramus te, Christe,
et benedicimus tibi.
R. Quia per sanctam crucem tuam
redemisti mundum.

A strong, and therefore heavy, Cross, for it is strong enough to bear Him on it when He arrives at Calvary, is placed upon His torn shoulders. He receives it gently and meekly, nay, with gladness of heart, for it is to be the salvation of mankind.

True; but recollect, that heavy Cross is the weight of our sins. As it fell upon His neck and shoulders, it came down with a shock. Alas! what a sudden, heavy weight have I laid upon Thee, O Jesus! And though in the calm and clear foresight of Thy mind – for Thou seest all things – Thou wast fully prepared for it, yet Thy feeble frame tottered under it when it dropped down upon Thee. Ah! how great a misery is it that I have lifted up my hand against my God! How could I ever fancy He would forgive me unless He had Himself told us that He underwent His bitter Passion in order that he might forgive us. I acknowledge, O Jesus, in the anguish and agony of my heart, that my sins it was that struck Thee on the face, that bruised Thy sacred arms, that tore Thy flesh with iron rods, that nailed Thee to the Cross, and let Thee slowly die upon it.

Our Father, Hail Mary, Glory be to the Father.

V. Have mercy on us, O Lord.
R. Have mercy on us.

V. Miserere nostri, Domine.
R. Miserere nostri.

Through her heart His
sorrow sharing,
All His bitter anguish bearing,
Now at length the sword has passed.

Cuius animam gementem,
Contristatam et dolentem,
Pertransivit gladius.

The Third Station

Jesus falls the first time beneath the Cross

V. We adore you, O Christ,
and we bless you.
R. Because by your holy Cross
you have redeemed the world.

V. Adoramus te, Christe,
et benedicimus tibi.
R. Quia per sanctam crucem tuam
redemisti mundum.

Jesus, bowed down under the weight and the length of the unwieldy Cross, which trailed after Him, slowly sets forth on His way, amid the mockeries and insults of the crowd. His agony in the Garden itself was sufficient to exhaust Him; but it was only the first of a multitude of sufferings. He sets off with His whole heart, but His limbs fail Him, and He falls. Yes, it is as I feared. Jesus, the strong and mighty Lord, has found for the moment our sins stronger than Himself. He falls, yet He bore the load for a while; He tottered, but He bore up and walked onwards. What, then, made Him give way? I say, I repeat, it is an intimation and a memory to thee, O my soul, of thy falling back into mortal sin. I repented of the sins of my youth, and went on well for a time; but at length a new temptation came, when I was off my guard, and I suddenly fell away. Then all my good habits seemed to go at once; they were like a garment which is stripped off, so quickly and utterly did grace depart from me. And at that moment I looked at my Lord, and lo! He had fallen down, and I covered my face with my hands, and remained in a state of great confusion.

Our Father, Hail Mary, Glory be to the Father.

V. Have mercy on us, O Lord.	V. Miserere nostri, Domine.
R. Have mercy on us.	R. Miserere nostri.

Oh, how sad and sore distressed	O quam tristis et afflicta
Was that Mother highly blessed	Fuit illa benedicta
Of the sole-begotten One!	Mater Unigeniti!

The Fourth Station

Jesus meets His Mother

V. We adore you, O Christ, and we bless you.	V. Adoramus te, Christe, et benedicimus tibi.
R. Because by your holy Cross you have redeemed the world.	R. Quia per sanctam crucem tuam redemisti mundum.

Jesus rises; though wounded by His fall, He journeys on, with His Cross still on His shoulders. He is bent down; but at one place, looking up, He sees His Mother. For an instant they just see each other, and He goes forward.

Mary would rather have had all His sufferings herself, could that have been, than not have known what they were by ceasing to be near Him. He, too, gained a refreshment, as from some soothing and grateful breath of air, to see her sad smile amid the sights and the noises which were about

Him. She had known Him beautiful and glorious, with the freshness of divine innocence and peace upon His countenance; now she saw Him so changed and deformed that she could scarce have recognised Him, save for the piercing, thrilling peace-inspiring look He gave her. Still, He was now carrying the load of the world's sins, and, all-holy though He was, He carried the image of them on His very face. He looked like some outcast or outlaw who had frightful guilt upon Him. He had been made sin for us, who knew no sin; not a feature, not a limb, but spoke of guilt, of a curse, of punishment, of agony. Oh, what a meeting of Son and Mother! Yet there was a mutual comfort, for there was a mutual sympathy. Jesus and Mary – do they forget that Passiontide through all eternity?

Our Father, Hail Mary, Glory be to the Father.

V. Have mercy on us, O Lord.	V. Miserere nostri, Domine.
R. Have mercy on us.	R. Miserere nostri.
Christ above in torments hangs;	Quae mærebat, et dolebat,
She beneath beholds the pangs	Pia mater, dum videbat
Of her dying glorious Son.	Nati pœnas inclyti.

The Fifth Station

Simon of Cyrene helps Jesus to carry the Cross

V. We adore You, O Christ, and we bless You.	V. Adoramus te, Christe, et benedicimus tibi.
R. Because by Your holy Cross you have redeemed the world.	R. Quia per sanctam crucem tuam redemisti mundum.

At length His strength fails utterly, and He is unable to proceed. The executioners stand perplexed. What are they to do? How is He to get to Calvary? Soon they see a stranger who seems strong and active – Simon of Cyrene. They seize on him, and compel him to carry the Cross with Jesus. The sight of the Sufferer pierces the man's heart. Oh, what a privilege! O happy soul, elect of God! He takes the part assigned to him with joy.

This came of Mary's intercession. He prayed not for Himself, except that He might drink the full chalice of suffering and do His Father's will; but she showed herself a mother by following Him with her prayers, since she could help Him in no other way. She then sent this stranger to help Him. It was she who led the soldiers to see that they might not be too fierce with Him. Sweet Mother, even do the like to us. Pray for us ever, Holy

Mother of God, pray for us, whatever be our cross, as we pass along on our way. Pray for us, and we shall rise again though we have fallen. Pray for us when sorrow, anxiety, or sickness comes upon us. Pray for us when we are prostrate under the power of temptation, and send some faithful servant of thine to succour us. And in the world to come, if found worthy to expiate our sins in the fiery prison, send some good angel to give us a season of refreshment. Pray for us, Holy Mother of God.

Our Father, Hail Mary, Glory be to the Father.

V. Have mercy on us, O Lord.	V. Miserere nostri, Domine.
R. Have mercy on us.	R. Miserere nostri.

Is there one who would not weep,	Quis est homo qui non fleret,
Whelmed in miseries so deep,	Matrem Christi si videret
Christ's dear Mother to behold?	In tanto supplicio?

The Sixth Station

Jesus and Veronica

V. We adore You, O Christ, and we bless You.	V. Adoramus te, Christe, et benedicimus tibi.
R. Because by Your holy Cross you have redeemed the world.	R. Quia per sanctam crucem tuam redemisti mundum.

As Jesus toils along up the hill, covered with the sweat of death, a woman makes her way through the crowd, and wipes His face with a napkin. In reward of her piety the cloth retains the impression of the Sacred Countenance upon it.

The relief which a mother's tenderness secured is not yet all she did. Her prayers sent Veronica as well as Simon – Simon to do a man's work, Veronica to do the part of a woman. The devout servant of Jesus did what she could. As Magdalen had poured the ointment at the feast, so Veronica now offered Him this napkin in His passion. 'Ah,' she said, 'would I could do more! Why have I not the strength of Simon, to take part in the burden of the Cross? But men only can serve the Great High Priest, now that He is celebrating the solemn act of sacrifice.' O Jesus! let us one and all minister to Thee according to our places and powers. And as Thou didst accept from Thy followers refreshment in Thy hour of trial, so give to us the support of Thy grace when we are hard pressed by our foe. I feel I cannot bear up against temptation, weariness, despondency, and sin. I say to myself, what is the good of being religious? I shall fall, O my dear Saviour, I shall certainly fall, unless Thou dost renew for me my vigour like the eagle's, and breathe life into me by the soothing application and the touch of the holy Sacraments which Thou hast appointed.

Our Father, Hail Mary, Glory be to the Father.

| V. Have mercy on us, O Lord. | V. Miserere nostri, Domine. |
| R. Have mercy on us. | R. Miserere nostri. |

Bruised, derided, cursed, defiled,	Pro peccatis suæ gentis,
She beheld her tender Child,	Vidit Iesum in tormentis,
All with bloody scourges rent.	Et flagellis subditum.

The Seventh Station

Jesus falls a second time

| V. We adore you, O Christ, and we bless you. | V. Adoramus te, Christe, et benedicimus tibi. |
| R. Because by your holy Cross you have redeemed the world. | R. Quia per sanctam crucem tuam redemisti mundum. |

The pain of His wounds and the loss of blood increasing at every step of His way, again His limbs fail Him, and He falls on the ground.

What has He done to deserve all this? This is the reward received by the long-expected Messiah from the Chosen People, the Children of Israel. I know what to answer. He falls because I have fallen. I have fallen again. I know well that without Thy grace, O Lord, I could not stand; and I fancied that I had kept closely to Thy Sacraments; yet in spite of my going to Mass and to my duties, I am out of grace again. Why is it but because I have lost my devotional spirit, and have come to Thy holy ordinances in a cold, formal way, without inward affection. I became lukewarm, tepid. I thought the battle of life was over, and became secure. I had no lively faith, no sight of spiritual things. I came to church from habit, and because I thought others would observe it. I ought to be a new creature, I ought to live by faith, hope, and charity; but I thought more of this world than the world to come – and at last I forgot that I was a servant of God, and followed the broad way that leadeth to destruction, not the narrow way which leadeth to life. And thus I fell from Thee.

Our Father, Hail Mary, Glory be to the Father.

| V. Have mercy on us, O Lord. | V. Miserere nostri, Domine. |
| R. Have mercy on us. | R. Miserere nostri. |

Can the human heart refrain,	Quis non posset contristari,
From partaking in her pain,	Christi Matrem contemplari,
In that Mother's pain untold?	Dolentem cum Filio?

The Eighth Station

Jesus comforts the Women of Jerusalem

V. We adore you, O Christ,	V. Adoramus te, Christe,
and we bless you.	et benedicimus tibi.
R. Because by your holy Cross	R. Quia per sanctam crucem tuam
you have redeemed the world.	redemisti mundum.

At the sight of the sufferings of Jesus the holy women are so pierced with grief that they cry out and bewail Him, careless what happens to them by so doing. Jesus, turning to them, said, 'Daughters of Jerusalem, weep not over Me, but weep for yourselves and for your children.'

Ah! can it be, O Lord, that I shall prove one of those sinful children for whom Thou biddest their mothers to weep? Weep not for Me,' He said, 'for I am the Lamb of God, and am making atonement at My own will for the sins of the world. I am suffering now, but I shall triumph; and, when I triumph, those souls for whom I am dying, will either be my dearest friends or my deadliest enemies.' Is it possible? O my Lord, can I grasp the terrible thought that Thou really didst weep for me – weep for me, as Thou didst weep over Jerusalem? Is it possible that I am one of the reprobate? Possible that I shall lose by Thy passion and death, not gain by it? Oh, withdraw not from me. I am in a very bad way. I have so much evil in me. I have so little of an earnest, brave spirit to set against that evil. O Lord, what will become of me? It is so difficult for me to drive away the Evil Spirit from my heart. Thou alone canst effectually cast him out.

Our Father, Hail Mary, Glory be to the Father.

| V. Have mercy on us, O Lord. | V. Miserere nostri, Domine. |
| R. Have mercy on us. | R. Miserere nostri. |

Let me share with You His pain,	Tui nati vulnerati,
Who for all my sins was slain,	Tam dignati pro me pati,
Who for me in torments died.	Pœnas mecum divide.

The Ninth Station

Again, a third time, Jesus falls

V. We adore you, O Christ, and we bless you.	V. Adoramus te, Christe, et benedicimus tibi.
R. Because by your holy Cross you have redeemed the world.	R. Quia per sanctam crucem tuam redemisti mundum.

Jesus had now reached almost to the top of Calvary; but, before He had gained the very spot where He was to be crucified, again He fell, and was again dragged up and goaded onwards by the brutal soldiery.

We are told in Holy Scripture of three falls of Satan, the Evil Spirit. The first was in the beginning; the second, when the Gospel and the Kingdom of Heaven were preached to the world; the third will be at the end of all things. The first is told us by St John the Evangelist. He says: 'There was a great battle in heaven. Michael and his angels fought with the dragon, and the dragon fought, and his angels. And they prevailed not, neither was their place found any more in heaven. And that great dragon was cast out, the old serpent, who is called the devil and Satan.' The second fall, at the time of the Gospel, is spoken of by our Lord when He says, 'I saw Satan, like lightning, falling from heaven.' And the third by the same St John: 'There came down fire from God out of heaven,. . . and the devil . . . was cast into the pool of fire and brimstone.' These three falls – the past, the present, and the future – the Evil Spirit had in mind when he moved Judas to betray our Lord. This was just his hour. Our Lord, when He was seized, said to His enemies, 'This is your hour and the power of darkness.' Satan knew his time was short, and thought he might use it to good effect. But – little dreaming that he would be acting in behalf of the world's redemption, which our Lord's passion and death were to work out – in revenge, and, as he thought, in triumph, he smote Him once, he smote Him twice, he smote Him thrice, each successive time a heavier blow. The weight of the Cross, the barbarity of the soldiers and the crowd, were but his instruments. O Jesus, the only-begotten Son of God, the Word Incarnate, we praise, adore, and love Thee for Thy ineffable condescension, even to allow Thyself thus for a time to fall into the hands and under the power of the Enemy of God and man, in order thereby to save us from being his servants and companions for eternity.

Or this:

This is the worst fall of the three. His strength has for a while utterly failed Him, and it is some time before the barbarous soldiers can bring Him to. Ah! it was His anticipation of what was to happen to me. I get worse and worse. He sees the end from the beginning. He was thinking of me all the time He dragged Himself along, up the hill of Calvary. He saw that I should fall again in spite of all former warnings and former assistance. He saw that I should become secure and self-confident, and that my enemy would then assail me with some new temptation, to which I never thought I should be exposed. I thought my weakness lay all on one particular side which I knew. I had not a dream that I was not strong on the other. And so Satan came down on my unguarded side, and got the better of me from my self-trust and self-satisfaction. I was wanting in humility. I thought no harm would come on me; I thought I had outlived the danger of sinning; I thought it was an easy thing to get to heaven, and I was not watchful. It was my pride, and so I fell a third time.

Our Father, Hail Mary, Glory be to the Father.

V. Have mercy on us, O Lord.	V. Miserere nostri, Domine.
R. Have mercy on us.	R. Miserere nostri.

O thou Mother! fount of love!	Eia, Mater, fons amoris!
Touch my spirit from above.	Me sentire vim doloris
Make my heart with yours accord.	Fac, ut tecum lugeam.

The Tenth Station

Jesus is stripped, and drenched with gall

V. We adore you, O Christ, and we bless you.	V. Adoramus te, Christe, et benedicimus tibi.
R. Because by your holy Cross you have redeemed the world.	R. Quia per sanctam crucem tuam redemisti mundum.

At length He has arrived at the place of sacrifice, and they begin to prepare Him for the Cross. His garments are torn from His bleeding body, and He, the Holy of Holies, stands exposed to the gaze of the coarse and scoffing multitude.

O Thou who in Thy Passion wast stripped of all Thy clothes, and held up to the curiosity and mockery of the rabble, strip me of myself here and now, that in the Last Day I come not to shame before men and angels. Thou didst endure the shame on Calvary, that I might be spared the shame at the Judgement. Thou hadst nothing to be ashamed of personally, and the shame which Thou didst feel was because Thou hadst taken on Thee man's nature. When they took from Thee Thy garments, those innocent limbs of Thine were but objects of humble and loving adoration to the highest Seraphim. They stood around in speechless awe, wondering at Thy beauty, and they trembled at Thy infinite self-abasement. But I, O Lord, how shall I appear if Thou shalt hold me up hereafter to be gazed upon, stripped of that robe of grace which is Thine, and seen in my own personal life and nature? O how hideous I am in myself, even in my best estate. Even when I am cleansed from my mortal sins, what disease and corruption is seen even in my venial sins. How shall I be fit for the society of angels, how for Thy presence, until Thou burnest this foul leprosy away in the fire of Purgatory?

Our Father, Hail Mary, Glory be to the Father.

V. Have mercy on us, O Lord.
R. Have mercy on us.

Make me feel as You have felt;
Make my soul to glow and melt,
With the love of Christ my Lord.

V. Miserere nostri, Domine.
R. Miserere nostri.

Fac ut ardeat cor meum
In amando Christum Deum,
Ut sibi complaceam.

The Eleventh Station

Jesus is nailed to the Cross

V. We adore you, O Christ,
and we bless you.
R. Because by your holy Cross
you have redeemed the world.

V. Adoramus te, Christe,
et benedicimus tibi.
R. Quia per sanctam crucem tuam
redemisti mundum.

The Cross is laid on the ground, and Jesus stretched upon it, and then, swaying heavily to and fro, it is, after much exertion, jerked into the hole ready to receive it. Or, as others think, it is set upright, and Jesus is raised up and fastened to it. As the savage executioners drive in the huge nails, He offers Himself to the Eternal Father as a ransom for the world. The blows are struck – the blood gushes forth.

Yes, they set up the Cross on high, and they placed a ladder against it, and, having stripped Him of His garments, made Him mount. With His hands feebly grasping its sides and cross-woods, and His feet slowly, uncertainly, with much effort, with many slips, mounting up, the soldiers propped Him on each side or He would have fallen. When He reached the projection where His sacred feet were to be, He turned round with sweet modesty and gentleness towards the fierce rabble, stretching out His arms, as if He would embrace them. Then He lovingly placed the backs of His hands close against the transverse beam, waiting for the executioners to come with their sharp nails and heavy hammers to dig into the palms of His hands, and to fasten them securely to the wood. There He hung, a perplexity to the multitude, a terror to evil spirits, the wonder, the awe, yet the joy, the adoration, of the holy angels.

Our Father, Hail Mary, Glory be to the Father.

V. Have mercy on us, O Lord.	V. Miserere nostri, Domine.
R. Have mercy on us.	R. Miserere nostri.

Holy Mother, pierce me through,	Sancta Mater, istud agas,
In my heart each wound renew,	Crucifixi fige plagas
Of my Saviour crucified.	Cordi meo valide.

The Twelfth Station

Jesus dies upon the Cross

V. We adore you, O Christ, and we bless you.	V. Adoramus te, Christe, et benedicimus tibi.
R. Because by your holy Cross you have redeemed the world.	R. Quia per sanctam crucem tuam redemisti mundum.

Jesus hung for three hours. During this time He prayed for His murderers, promised Paradise to the penitent robber, and committed His Blessed Mother to the guardianship of St John. Then all was finished, and He bowed His head and gave up His Spirit.

Here pause and kneel.

The worst is over. The Holiest is dead and departed. The most tender, the most affectionate, the holiest of the sons of men is gone. Jesus is dead, and with His death my sin shall die. I protest once for all, before men and angels, that sin shall no more have dominion over me. This Lent I make myself God's own for ever. The salvation of my soul shall be my first concern. With the aid of His grace I will create in me a deep hatred and sorrow for my past sins. I will try hard to detest sin, as much as I have ever loved it. Into God's hands I put myself, not by halves, but unreservedly. I promise Thee, O Lord, with the help of Thy grace to keep out of the way of temptation, to avoid all occasions of sin, to turn at once from the voice of the Evil One, to be regular in my prayers, so to die to sin that Thou mayest not have died for me on the Cross in vain.

Our Father, Hail Mary, Glory be to the Father.

V. Have mercy on us, O Lord.	V. Miserere nostri, Domine.
R. Have mercy on us.	R. Miserere nostri.

Let me mingle tears with You,	Fac me vere tecum flere,
Mourning Him who mourned for me,	Crucifixo condolore,
All the days that I may live.	Donec ego vixero.

The Thirteenth Station

Jesus is taken from the Cross, and laid in Mary's bosom

V. We adore you, O Christ, and we bless you.	V. Adoramus te, Christe, et benedicimus tibi.
R. Because by your holy Cross you have redeemed the world.	R. Quia per sanctam crucem tuam redemisti mundum.

The multitude have gone home; Calvary is left solitary and still, except that St John and the holy women are there. Then come Joseph of Arimathea and Nicodemus, and take down from the Cross the body of Jesus, and place it in the arms of Mary.

O Mary, at last thou hast possession of thy Son. Now, when His enemies can do no more, they leave Him in contempt to thee. As His unexpected friends perform their difficult work, thou lookest on with unspeakable thoughts. Thy heart is pierced with the sword of which Simeon spoke. O Mother most sorrowful; yet in thy sorrow there is a still greater joy. The joy in prospect nerved thee to stand by Him as He hung upon the Cross; much more now, without swooning, without trembling, thou dost receive Him to thy arms and on thy lap. Now thou art supremely happy as having Him, though He comes to thee not as He went from thee. He went from thy home, O Mother of God, in the strength and beauty of His manhood, and He comes back to thee dislocated, torn to pieces, mangled, dead. Yet, O Blessed Mary, thou art happier in the hour of woe than on the day of the marriage feast, for then He was leaving thee, and now in the future, as a risen Saviour, He will be separated from thee no more.

Our Father, Hail Mary, Glory be to the Father.

V. Have mercy on us, O Lord.	V. Miserere nostri, Domine.
R. Have mercy on us.	R. Miserere nostri.

For the sins of His own nation,	Vidit suum dulcem natum
Saw Him hang in desolation,	Morientum, desolatum,
Till His spirit forth He sent.	Dum emisit spiritum.

The Fourteenth Station

Jesus is laid in the Tomb

V. We adore you, O Christ, and we bless you.	V. Adoramus te, Christe, et benedicimus tibi.
R. Because by your holy Cross you have redeemed the world.	R. Quia per sanctam crucem tuam redemisti mundum.

But for a short three days, for a day and a half – Mary then must give Him up. He is not yet risen. His friends and servants take Him from her, and place Him in an honourable tomb. They close it safely, till the hour comes for His resurrection.

Lie down and sleep in peace in the calm grave for a little while, dear Lord, and then wake up for an everlasting reign. We, like the faithful women, will watch around Thee, for all our treasure, all our life, is lodged with Thee. And, when our turn comes to die, grant, sweet Lord, that we may sleep calmly too, the sleep of the just. Let us sleep peacefully for the brief interval between death and the general resurrection. Guard us from the enemy, save us from the pit. Let our friends remember us and pray for us, O dear Lord. Let Masses be said for us, so that the pains of Purgatory, so much deserved by us and therefore so truly welcomed by us, may be over with little delay. Give us seasons of refreshment there; wrap us round with holy dreams and soothing contemplations, while we gather strength to ascend the heavens. And then let our faithful guardian angels help us up the glorious ladder, reaching from earth to heaven, which Jacob saw in vision. And when we reach the everlasting gates, let them open upon us with the music of angels; and let St Peter receive us, and our Lady, the glorious Queen of Saints, embrace us, and bring us to Thee, and to Thy Eternal Father, and to Thy Co-equal Spirit, Three Persons, One God, to reign with Them for ever and ever.

Our Father, Hail Mary, Glory be to the Father

| V. Have mercy on us, O Lord. | V. Miserere nostri, Domine. |
| R. Have mercy on us. | R. Miserere nostri. |

While my body here decays,	Quando corpus morietur,
May my soul thy goodness praise,	Fac ut animæ donetur
Safe in paradise with thee. Amen.	Paradisi gloria. Amen.

Let us pray:

God who by the Precious Blood of Thy only-begotten Son didst sanctify the Standard of the Cross, grant, we beseech Thee, that we who rejoice in the glory of the same holy Cross may at all times and places rejoice in Thy protection through the same Christ our Lord.

End with one Our Father, Hail Mary, and Glory be for the intention of the Holy Father.

THE ROSARY

Rosary Meditations before The Blessed Sacrament

Contemplate the beauty of Christ with Mary

With Mary, we will understand better the transforming power of the Eucharist. By listening to her, we will find in the Eucharistic mystery the courage and energy to follow Christ, the Good Shepherd, and to serve him in the brethren.

The Rosary, while Marian in character, is a prayer with Christ at its centre. It contains all the depth of the Gospel message in its entirety. With the rosary we sit at the school of Mary and are led to contemplate the beauty of Christ and experience the depth of his love. To recite the Rosary is nothing other than to contemplate with Mary the face of Christ. Our faith tells us that Christ is as really present today as he was to his mother and his disciples. What better way to pray the Rosary than when gazing on Christ, veiled in the form of Bread.

The Mysteries of the Rosary

Traditionally, different Mysteries of the Rosary are said on different days of the week.

The Joyful Mysteries	Mondays, Saturdays
The Luminous Mysteries	Thursdays
The Sorrowful Mysteries	Tuesdays, Fridays
The Glorious Mysteries	Wednesdays, Sundays

The Prayers of the Rosary

Apostles' Creed

I believe in God,	Credo in Deum,
the Father almighty,	Patrem omnipotentem,
Creator of heaven and earth,	Creatorem cæli et terræ,
and in Jesus Christ, his only Son,	et in Iesum Christum,
our Lord,	Filium eius unicum,
who was conceived by the	Dominum nostrum,
Holy Spirit,	qui conceptus est de Spiritu Sancto,
born of the Virgin Mary,	natus ex Maria Virgine,
suffered under Pontius Pilate,	passus sub Pontio Pilato,
was crucified, died and was buried;	crucifixus, mortuus, et sepultus,
he descended into hell;	descendit ad inferos,
on the third day he rose again from	tertia die resurrexit a mortuis,
the dead;	ascendit ad cælos,
he ascended into heaven,	
and is seated at the right hand of	sedet ad dexteram
God the Father almighty;	Dei Patris omnipotentis,
from there he will come to judge	inde venturus est iudicare vivos
the living and the dead.	et mortuos.
I believe in the Holy Spirit,	Credo in Spiritum Sanctum,
the holy catholic Church,	sanctam Ecclesiam Catholicam,
the communion of saints,	sanctorum communionem,
the forgiveness of sins,	remissionem peccatorum,
the resurrection of the body,	carnis resurrectionem,
and life everlasting. Amen.	vitam æternam. Amen.

Our Father

Our Father, who art in heaven,	Pater noster, qui es in cælis:
hallowed be thy name.	sanctificetur nomen tuum;
Thy Kingdom come.	adveniat regnum tuum;
Thy will be done	fiat voluntas tua,
on earth as it is in heaven.	sicut in cælo, et in terra.
Give us this day our daily bread,	Panem nostrum cotidianum da
and forgive us our trespasses,	nobis hodie;
as we forgive those who trespass	et dimitte nobis debita nostra,
against us,	sicut et nos dimittimus
and lead us not into temptation,	debitoribus nostris;
but deliver us from evil. Amen.	et ne nos inducas in tentationem;
	sed libera nos a malo. Amen.

Hail Mary

Hail, Mary, full of grace,	Ave Maria, gratia plena,
the Lord is with thee:	Dominus tecum;
blessed art thou among women,	benedicta tu in mulieribus,
and blessed is the fruit of thy	et benedictus fructus
womb, Jesus.	ventris tui, Iesus.
Holy Mary, Mother of God,	Sancta Maria, Mater Dei,
pray for us sinners, now,	ora pro nobis peccatoribus,
and at the hour of our death.	nunc et in hora mortis nostræ.
Amen.	Amen.

Glory be

Glory be to the Father,	Gloria Patri,
and to the Son,	et Filio,
and to the Holy Spirit.	et Spiritui Sancto.
As it was in the beginning, is now,	Sicut erat in principio,
and ever shall be,	et nunc et semper,
world without end. Amen.	et in sæcula sæculorum. Amen.

At the end of the Rosary we say:

Hail, holy Queen,	Salve, Regina,
mother of mercy;	mater misericordiæ;
hail, our life, our sweetness,	vita, dulcedo et spes nostra, salve.
and our hope!	Ad te clamamus,
To thee do we cry,	exsules filii Evæ.
poor banished children of Eve;	Ad te suspiramus, gementes
to thee do we send up our sighs,	et flentes in hac
mourning and weeping in this vale	lacrimarum valle.
of tears.	Eia ergo, advocata nostra,
Turn then, most gracious advocate,	illos tuos misericordes oculos
thine eyes of mercy towards us;	ad nos converte.
and after this our exile,	Et Iesum, benedictum fructum
show to us the blessed fruit	ventris tui,
of thy womb, Jesus.	nobis post hoc exsilium ostende.
O clement, O loving,	O clemens, o pia,
O sweet Virgin Mary.	o dulcis Virgo Maria!

| V. Pray for us, O holy Mother of God. | V. Ora pro nobis sancta Dei Genitrix. |
| R. That we may be made worthy of the promises of Christ. | R. Ut digni efficiamur promissionibus Christi. |

Let us pray.

O God, whose only-begotten Son, by his life, death and resurrection, has purchased for us the rewards of eternal life; grant, we beseech you, that meditating on these Mysteries of the most holy Rosary of the Blessed Virgin Mary, we may both imitate what they contain, and obtain what they promise, through the same Christ our Lord. Amen.

THE JOYFUL MYSTERIES

The First Joyful Mystery

The Annunciation and the Holy Eucharist

Behold the handmaid of the Lord: let it be done to me according to your word. (Luke 1:38)

The Holy Eucharist is the extension of the Mystery of the Incarnation. When Mary said "let it be done to me according to your word", then the Incarnation took place. When the priest says in Mass "this is my Body" and "this is my Blood", Jesus himself is made present in the Eucharistic elements.

In the Incarnation God unites himself to human nature. In Holy Communion, God unites himself mystically to the person of each communicant.

The Incarnation is the humility of God, "who emptied himself, taking the form of a slave." (Ph 2:7) and of Mary, who through complete obedience to the Word, was chosen to be the Mother of God.

Intention: That we may always make a worthy communion.

Lord Jesus,
May we receive the Holy Sacrament as Mary
Received your Word,
And like her, be always ready to
Do your will. Amen.

The Second Joyful Mystery

The Visitation and the Holy Eucharist

Mary arose and went with haste into the hill country. (Luke 1:39)

Mary carries Jesus secretly in her womb along a hurried journey, a journey of corporal and spiritual mercy. She utters her greeting to Elizabeth; the babe in her womb leaps for joy, and Elizabeth herself is filled with the Holy Spirit.

The Blessed Sacrament is carried by priests and ministers of the Eucharist on journeys of corporal and spiritual mercy. The sick restored to health and the dying strengthened and comforted and the good news of salvation is proclaimed.

Intention: We remember those who cannot get to Mass.

Lord Jesus,
Transformed by your grace,
Help us to make known your presence
When we are with those whom
We know and love. Amen.

The Third Joyful Mystery

The Nativity and the Holy Eucharist

She wrapped him in swaddling clothes and laid him in a manger because there was no room for them at the inn. (Luke 2:7)

Jesus is born in poverty and cold, in a stable on a winter's night. The richest and grandest altar is as unworthy of his eucharistic birth as the stable was unworthy of his human birth.

Jesus comes to us at Mass in poverty. The scoffing of unbelievers, the indifference of the lukewarm and those who receive communion unworthily is surely more painful to him than the cold of the stable at Bethlehem.

As in the stable, so in the Blessed Sacrament, the angels, the shepherds and the poor adore him while to the world he remains unknown.

Intention: That we may set our hearts on Christ and not on this world.

Lord Jesus,
Keep our heart set upon the things of heaven
And not of earth.
For where our heart is, so will be our true home. Amen.

The Fourth Joyful Mystery

The Presentation and the Holy Eucharist

My eyes have seen the salvation which you have prepared before the face of all peoples. (Luke 2:30)

At the Presentation in the Temple, Simeon, who had looked forward to the consolation of Israel, at last received Jesus as his Viaticum. In the Blessed Sacrament, Jesus is the Viaticum of dying Catholics.

In the Temple, Simeon made his irrevocable act of poverty and obedience, his detachment from the world and joyful conformity to God's will and his promise of salvation. "Now Lord you give leave to your servant to go in peace."

How many faithful Christians on the threshold of eternity are embracing Jesus for the last time on earth, with hearts overflowing with gratitude, breathing their own "Nunc dimittis!"

Intention: That we may have a holy death.

Lord Jesus,
In the Blessed Sacrament,
Our eyes have truly seen your salvation.
Be with us on our earthly journey,
And bring us at last to your heavenly home. Amen.

The Fifth Joyful Mystery

The Finding of the young Jesus in the Temple and the Holy Eucharist

Did you not know that I must be about my Father's business? (Luke 2:49)

After losing Jesus for three days – a time of spiritual darkness and heart-breaking sorrow – Mary and Joseph find him in the Temple, listening and asking questions. What rapture of joy to find him again!

How many of us, after losing Jesus by sin or in the desolation of spiritual darkness find him again when we celebrate the Eucharist? He finds us and makes his dwelling with us, in the Temple that is our own mortal body.

Intention: That we may constantly seek the Lord.

Lord Jesus,
Too often do we depart from you
Through weakness and hardness of heart.
Give us a heart of flesh;
Transform our mortal frame into a tabernacle,
Where you dwell for ever. Amen.

THE LUMINOUS MYSTERIES

The First Luminous Mystery

Christ's Baptism and the Holy Eucharist

He saw the heavens open and the Spirit descending upon him like a dove. (Mark 1:10)

The sacraments of the Church are effective signs and means of our salvation, the ordinary is transformed into the extraordinary through the action of the Holy Spirit. At Mass, the priest invokes the Holy Spirit: "Make holy, therefore, these gifts, we pray, by sending down your Spirit upon them like the dewfall, so that they may become for us the Body and Blood of our Lord Jesus Christ."

Whether the Mass is celebrated in the grandeur of a gothic cathedral or in a humble chapel or prison cell, the Mass is the moment when the heavens truly do open.

Intention: That we may have greater awareness of the Holy Spirit.

Lord Jesus, beloved of the Father,
Give us eyes to see and ears to hear,
That we may recognise your Holy Spirit
At work in the Church and in our daily lives. Amen.

The Second Luminous Mystery

Christ's self-revelation at the wedding of Cana and the Holy Eucharist

His mother said to the servants "Do whatever he tells you. (John 2:5)

The wedding at Cana in Galilee marks the opening of Jesus' public ministry and was the "first of his signs." Christ reveals his glory by changing the water into wine, after which his disciples believed in him. Mary must have already believed, for she said to the servants "do whatever he tells you."

Doubtless the rest of the wedding party were too busy enjoying their own festivities to notice the glorious presence among them.

Likewise in the Eucharist, Christ's glory is hidden in the form of bread and wine. In countless churches and chapels, Christ's Eucharistic glory is adored by those who see with faith, while the world outside carries on much as before.

Intention: That we may have a faith like Mary's.

Lord Jesus,
Give us a firm and lively faith.
May we learn to see your glory revealed
In the sights, sounds and symbols of our faith. Amen.

The Third Luminous Mystery

Christ's proclamation of the Kingdom of God and the Holy Eucharist

The time is fulfilled and the kingdom of God is at hand. Repent and believe in the good news (Mark 1:15)

Jesus's proclamation of the kingdom of God is made real not just by words but by his actions. His very words bring about the reality they signify.

Early in his public ministry a paralytic is brought to Jesus by lowering him through the roof, so anxious were the crowds to hear Jesus speak. And when Jesus pronounces forgiveness of the man's sins, some of the scribes cannot believe and murmur among themselves: "who can forgive sins but God alone." But Jesus responds "so that you may know that the Son of man has authority on earth to forgive sins," he says to the sick man "arise, take up your stretcher and go home."

At Mass, the very words of consecration bring about the transformation of bread and wine. As Christ's Eucharistic presence is real and efficacious, so is his forgiveness.

Intention: We pray to have hearts that listen to the voice of the Lord.

Lord Jesus,
We believe in your promise of salvation.
Grant us a spirit of true repentance,
That we may experience its fruits. Amen.

The Fourth Luminous Mystery

The Transfiguration and the Holy Eucharist

They lifted up their eyes, and saw no one but Jesus. (Matthew 17:8)

Jesus takes with him Peter, James and John up a high mountain, where "his face shone like the sun and his garments became white as light." Moses and Elijah appear with Jesus, representing the Law and the prophets. Yet these two withdraw from view, for when the disciples look up, they see only Jesus.

The Eucharist is a fulfilment of the promises of the old covenant. The Law commanded Israel to celebrate the Passover as an everlasting reminder of God's victory over Pharaoh and their liberation from slavery. When we celebrate the Eucharist, we commemorate Christ's paschal victory and the liberation from sin he won for us. We join Christ who, like Moses, crossed the Red Sea of death. Truly the table of the Lord is the holy mountain!

Intention: We pray for greater attention at Mass.

Lord Jesus,
Remove the veil from our face which is the
Cares and distractions of the world,
That we may worship you with heart and mind. Amen.

The Fifth Luminous Mystery

The Institution of the Holy Eucharist

I tell you I shall not drink again of the fruit of the vine until that day when I drink it anew with you in my Father's kingdom. (Matthew 26:29)

Isaiah looked forward to that day when God would "prepare a rich feast of food for all nations, ...the best of meats and the finest of wines."

The Eucharist is but a foretaste of the heavenly banquet which Christ has prepared for those who love him, when all the tribes will be gathered up, when every tear will be wiped away. We look back with remembrance to the upper room, we look forward in hope to the Father's house.

Let us invite Christ into our lives at Holy Communion, in joyful hope, let us trust his pledge of future glory. "Behold I stand at the door and knock; if anyone hears my voice and opens the door, I will come to him and eat with him, and he with me."

Intention: That we may long for the food which lasts.

Lord Jesus,
May we always reverence these sacred mysteries,
And so experience the redemption you won for us. Amen.

THE SORROWFUL MYSTERIES

The First Sorrowful Mystery

The Agony in the Garden and the Holy Eucharist

His sweat became like great drops of blood. (Luke 22:44)

Imagine the sanctuary of a church as the garden of the Christian soul. Jesus calls his disciples to be with him, to watch and pray.

Though the spirit is willing, the flesh is weak. Some fall asleep. Some even come into his presence and betray him with a kiss, and deliver him into the hands of sinners.

In the garden of the sanctuary, the blood of Christ is always pleading. Great drops, greater in value than the wealth of this world are offered by Christ in the sacrifice of the Mass.

Intention: That we may have a humble heart and a contrite spirit.

Lord Jesus,
Give us a spirit of true contrition;
And wash away our sins by your Precious Blood. Amen.

The Second Sorrowful Mystery

The Scourging at the Pillar and the Holy Eucharist

Pilate took Jesus and had him scourged. (John 19:1)

In the mystery of the Eucharist, Jesus has bound himself to the consecrated species of bread and wine, as it were to a pillar, to be scourged by the ingratitude of men and women, not for one day only, but till the end of time.

The forgetfulness of believers, the sneers of unbelievers and sceptics, the innumerable communions taken without thought, are a never ceasing flagellation to the incomprehensible love of Jesus in the Blessed Sacrament.

Intention: May we be ever conscious of our sins and their consequences.

Lord Jesus,
May we always be grateful
For how much you suffered for our sins. Amen.

The Third Sorrowful Mystery

The Crowning with thorns and the Holy Eucharist

Kneeling before him they mocked him. (Matthew 27:29)

In the Blessed Sacrament we place Jesus on a throne and ask for his blessing. We bend the knee and adore him. But how do the royal honours we pay him appear in the sight of angels who veil their faces in his presence and cry: Holy! Holy! Holy!? Almost a mockery.

It is too often mere formality. And when we receive communion without gratitude for Jesus's immense love, is not our indifference worse than the sneers, blows and spittle of brutal soldiers.

Intention: That we may have great reverence for the Blessed Sacrament.

Lord Jesus,
We believe; help us in our unbelief.
May we worship you in sincerity and truth. Amen.

The Fourth Sorrowful Mystery

The Carrying of the Cross and the Holy Eucharist

Carrying his own cross he went out to the Place of the Skull. (John 19:18)

In the Blessed Sacrament Jesus makes each one's cross his own. Nothing raises the soul above the sorrows, disappointments and sufferings of life like Holy Communion. Jesus, who carried the weight of the cross to Calvary assures us that "my yoke is easy and my burden light."

An ancient tradition relates how he imprinted his sorrow-worn features on the veil of Veronica. The Blessed Sacrament is an even more real memorial to the sufferings of Jesus than the veil. To the eyes of faith, there is not the mere likeness but the real face itself.

Intention: That we may be patient in tribulation.

Lord Jesus,
We lay our burdens at your feet,
Knowing that you have already paid the price
For our human weakness.
May we help our brothers and sisters
When they too are in need. Amen.

The Fifth Sorrowful Mystery

The Crucifixion and the Holy Eucharist

Father, into your hands I commend my spirit. (Luke 23:46)

The very same sacrifice which took place on the cross is mystically and sacramentally made present at the celebration of the Eucharist. As Mary and John, standing at the foot of the cross, were drawn together by Christ's death and his command, so are members brought into ever closer communion by the mystery they celebrate.

Our communion with Christ is the consummation of his sacrifice for us. As in the sacrifices of the old Law, the victim was partly eaten, partly consumed by fire. At holy communion, the Saving Victim is consumed by being materially eaten, and spiritually consumed by the fire of love.

"As often as you eat this bread and drink this cup, you proclaim the Lord's death until he comes in glory." (1 Co 11:26)

Intention: That we may love God above all else and our neighbour as ourself.

Lord Jesus,
May the mystery we celebrate in the Holy Eucharist
Bring us into ever closer communion with you,
And with one another. Amen.

THE GLORIOUS MYSTERIES
The First Glorious Mystery

The Resurrection and the Holy Eucharist

He is going before you to Galilee, there you will see him. (Mark 16:7)

Holy Communion is the pledge of the Resurrection to everlasting life. "The one who eats my flesh and drinks my blood has eternal life, and I will raise him up on the last day." (Jn 6:54)

The life of Jesus in the Blessed Sacrament is a kind of continuation of the forty days after the Resurrection. His human nature – now glorified – is immortal; hidden yet intimately present.

The same Risen Lord who walked beside his disciples on the road to Emmaus is continually revealing himself in the sacramental life; affirming the faith of the doubtful; encouraging the slow of heart; above all, making himself known in the breaking of bread.

Intention: We pray for joy in Christ's sacramental presence.

Lord Jesus,
May our hearts burn within us
When you reveal yourself in the scriptures
And in the breaking of bread. Amen.

The Second Glorious Mystery

The Ascension and the Holy Eucharist

He was taken up to heaven and sat down at the right hand of God. (Mark 16:19)

That same Jesus whom we adore in the Blessed Sacrament has been on the throne of God since the Ascension, pronouncing judgement. "Before him will be gathered all the nations, and he will separate them one from another as a shepherd separates the sheep from the goats." (Mt 25:32)

The glorified humanity, which at the Ascension became the joy of the Angels and crown of the saints, is with us here in the Blessed Sacrament.

And as he ascended in order to prepare a place for each one of us in heaven, so in Holy Communion, he prepares a place for each one us in his divine life. As an ancient collect puts it: "Grant that, as he came to share in our humanity, so we may share the life of his divinity."

Intention: We pray for confidence in the love of God for us.

Lord Jesus,
Your life and redeeming work
Wonderfully restores our true humanity.
Grant that we may share in your divine life
At the Eucharist and in the world to come. Amen.

The Third Glorious Mystery

The Descent of the Holy Spirit and the Holy Eucharist

They were all filled with the Holy Spirit and began to speak in other tongues. (Acts 2:4)

The Holy Spirit who conceived Jesus in the womb of the Virgin Mary today conceives him in the hearts of those who believe. That same Spirit prepares every soul to receive Christ at Holy Communion.

It is the Spirit who inspires the contrition, the faith, hope and love that makes the poor sinner worthy to receive Jesus. He also inspires the aspirations, petitions and resolutions we make for ourselves and those who are dear to us after Communion.

The light, joy, peace, comfort and wisdom that may be experienced in Holy Communion is the presence of the Holy Spirit – the best gift of Jesus to each soul he espouses.

Intention: We pray for zeal to spread the Gospel.

Lord Jesus,
Strengthened by the bread of heaven
And the indwelling of the Holy Spirit
May we proclaim without ceasing
The good news of your kingdom. Amen.

The Fourth Glorious Mystery

The Assumption of our Lady and the Holy Eucharist

If I go and prepare a place for you, I will come back and take you with me so that you also may be where I am. (John 14:3)

The Assumption was the completion of Mary's life-long communion with Jesus. She had always given hospitality to Jesus in her soul. Mary dwelt in Jesus and he in her. That is what Holy Communion is. By her Assumption into heaven, the earthly union of Jesus and his mother matured, was consummated and sealed for eternity in glory.

"Those who have died in Christ will be the first to rise, then those of us who are still alive will be taken up into the clouds, together with them; to meet the Lord in the air. So we shall stay with the Lord for ever. With such thoughts as these you should comfort one another." (1 Th 4:13-18)

Intention: We remember all those who have died.

Lord Jesus,
Bring those who have died to share eternal life
with Mary and all the saints. Amen.

The Fifth Glorious Mystery

The Crowning of our Lady and the Holy Eucharist

A great sign appeared in heaven: a woman, adorned with the sun, standing on the moon, and with the twelve stars on her head for a crown. (Revelations 12:1)

When crowned by her Divine Son, Mary is made Queen of the mystical Body of Christ – the Church. She is Mother of the Body and Blood, the principal bond which unites its members to each other and to Christ.

This is a glorious fulfilment of the words which seemed so sad when uttered in the darkest hour of the Passion: "Woman, behold your son." Now in the eternal glory of heaven she does indeed behold her Son, her sons both real and mystical – both Jesus and John. They are united as one son to her, thanks to the Holy Eucharist.

Intention: That our longing for heaven and eternal life may always increase.

Lord Jesus,
May the Sacrament of your Body and Blood
Strengthen and fortify us on our earthly journey,
And be a foretaste of the heavenly banquet. Amen.